SOUTH AMERICA

7th Edition

**Where to Stay and Eat
for All Budgets**

**Must-See Sights
and Local Secrets**

Ratings You Can Trust

Fodor's Travel Publications   New York, Toronto, London, Sydney, Auckland
www.fodors.com

FODOR'S SOUTH AMERICA
Editor: Felice Aarons

Editorial Production: Tom Holton
Editorial Contributors: Emmanuelle Alspaugh, Eddy Ancinas, Diego Bigongiari, Carissa Bluestone, Brian Byrnes, Joyce Dalton, Michael de Zayas, Rhan Flatin, Sarah Gold, Robin Goldstein, Dominic Hamilton, Margaret Kelly, Shannon Kelly, Laura Kidder, Brian Kluepfel, Victoria Patience, Mark Sullivan, Jeffrey Van Fleet
Maps: David Lindroth, *cartographer*; Rebecca Baer and Bob Blake, *map editors*
Design: Fabrizio La Rocca, *creative director*; Guido Caroti, *art director*; Moon Sun Kim, *cover designer*; Melanie Marin, *senior picture editor*
Production/Manufacturing: Robert B. Shields
Cover Photo (Chimborazo, near Guamote, Ecuador): Paul Harris/Stone/Getty Images

Seventh Edition

ISBN-10: 1–4000–1648–7

ISBN-13: 978–1–4000–1648–8

ISSN: 0362–0220

SPECIAL SALES
This book is available at special discounts for bulk purchases for sales promotions or premiums. Special editions, including personalized covers, excerpts of existing books, and corporate imprints, can be created in large quantities for special needs. For more information, write to Special Markets/Premium Sales, 1745 Broadway, MD 6-2, New York, New York 10019, or e-mail specialmarkets@randomhouse.com.

AN IMPORTANT TIP & AN INVITATION
Although all prices, opening times, and other details in this book are based on information supplied to us at press time, changes occur all the time in the travel world, and Fodor's cannot accept responsibility for facts that become outdated or for inadvertent errors or omissions. So **always confirm information when it matters,** especially if you're making a detour to visit a specific place. Your experiences—positive and negative—matter to us. If we have missed or misstated something, **please write to us.** We follow up on all suggestions. Contact the South America editor at editors@fodors.com or c/o Fodor's at 1745 Broadway, New York, NY 10019.

PRINTED IN THE UNITED STATES OF AMERICA

10 9 8 7 6 5 4 3 2

OCT 0 8

Be a Fodor's Correspondent

Your opinion matters. It matters to us. It matters to your fellow Fodor's travelers, too. And we'd like to hear it. In fact, we *need* to hear it.

When you share your experiences and opinions, you become an active member of the Fodor's community. That means we'll not only use your feedback to make our books better, but we'll publish your names and comments whenever possible. Throughout our guides, look for "Word of Mouth," excerpts of your unvarnished feedback.

Here's how you can help improve Fodor's for all of us.

Tell us when we're right. We rely on local writers to give you an insider's perspective. But our writers and staff editors—who are the best in the business—depend on you. Your positive feedback is a vote to renew our recommendations for the next edition.

Tell us when we're wrong. We're proud that we update most of our guides every year. But we're not perfect. Things change. Hotels cut services. Museums change hours. Charming cafés lose charm. If our writer didn't quite capture the essence of a place, tell us how you'd do it differently. If any of our descriptions are inaccurate or inadequate, we'll incorporate your changes in the next edition and will correct factual errors at fodors.com *immediately.*

Tell us what to include. You probably have had fantastic travel experiences that aren't yet in Fodor's. Why not share them with a community of like-minded travelers? Maybe you chanced upon a great museum or restaurant or B&B that you don't want to keep to yourself. Tell us why we should include it. And share your discoveries and experiences with everyone directly at fodors.com. Your input may lead us to add a new listing or highlight a place we cover with a "Highly Recommended" star or with our highest rating, "Fodor's Choice."

Give us your opinion instantly at our feedback center at www.fodors.com/feedback. You may also e-mail editors@fodors.com with the subject line "South America Editor." Or send your nominations, comments, and complaints by mail to South America Editor, Fodor's, 1745 Broadway, New York, NY 10019.

You and travelers like you are the heart of the Fodor's community. Make our community richer by sharing your experiences. Be a Fodor's correspondent.

Happy traveling!

Tim Jarrell, Publisher

CONTENTS

CONTENTS

ABOUT THIS BOOK

Our Ratings

Sometimes you find terrific travel experiences and sometimes they just find you. But usually the burden is on you to select the right combination of experiences. That's where our ratings come in.

As travelers we've all discovered a place so wonderful that its worthiness is obvious. And sometimes that place is so unique that superlatives don't do it justice: you just have to be there to know. These sights, properties, and experiences get our highest rating, **Fodor's Choice**, indicated by orange stars throughout this book.

Black stars highlight sights and properties we deem **Highly Recommended**, places that our writers, editors, and readers praise again and again for consistency and excellence.

By default, there's another category: any place we include in this book is by definition worth your time, unless we say otherwise. And we will.

Disagree with any of our choices? Care to nominate a place or suggest that we rate one more highly? Visit our feedback center at www.fodors.com/feedback.

Budget Well

Hotel and restaurant price categories from ¢ to $$$$ are defined in the opening pages of each chapter. For attractions, we always give standard adult admission fees; reductions are usually available for children, students, and senior citizens. Want to pay with plastic? **AE, D, DC, MC, V** following restaurant and hotel listings indicate whether American Express, Discover, Diner's Club, MasterCard, and Visa are accepted.

Restaurants

Unless we state otherwise, restaurants are open for lunch and dinner daily. We mention dress only when there's a specific requirement and reservations only when they're essential or not accepted—it's always best to book ahead.

Hotels

Hotels have private bath, phone, TV, and air-conditioning and operate on the European Plan (aka EP, meaning without meals), unless we specify that they use the Continental Plan (CP, with a Continental breakfast), Breakfast Plan (BP, with a full breakfast), or Modified American Plan (MAP, with breakfast and dinner) or are all-inclusive (AI, including all meals and most activities). We always

list facilities but not whether you'll be charged an extra fee to use them, so when pricing accommodations, find out what's included.

Many Listings
- ★ Fodor's Choice
- ★ Highly recommended
- ⊠ Physical address
- ✛ Directions
- 🕮 Mailing address
- ☏ Telephone
- 🖷 Fax
- ⊕ On the Web
- ✉ E-mail
- 🕾 Admission fee
- ☉ Open/closed times
- ▶ Start of walk/itinerary
- Ⓜ Metro stations
- ▭ Credit cards

Hotels & Restaurants
- 🏨 Hotel
- ⇙ Number of rooms
- ♿ Facilities
- ⑩ Meal plans
- ✕ Restaurant
- ⌲ Reservations
- 🏛 Dress code
- ⚐ Smoking
- ⑭ BYOB
- ✕🏨 Hotel with restaurant that warrants a visit

Outdoors
- ⚑ Golf
- ⛺ Camping

Other
- ☺ Family-friendly
- 🔢 Contact information
- ⇨ See also
- ⊠ Branch address
- ☞ Take note

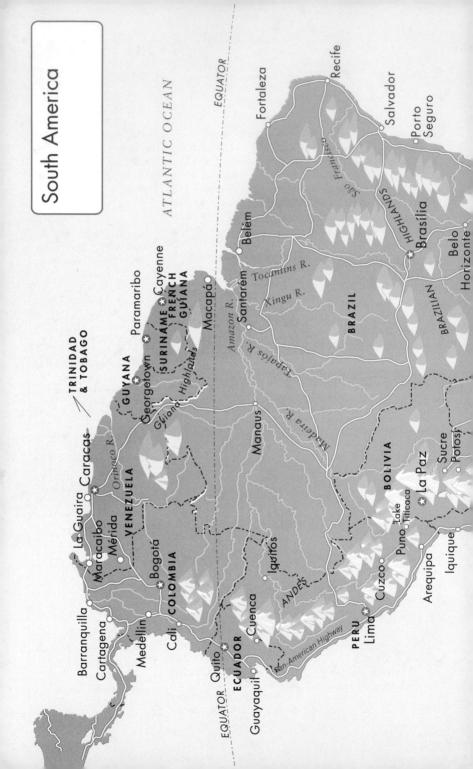

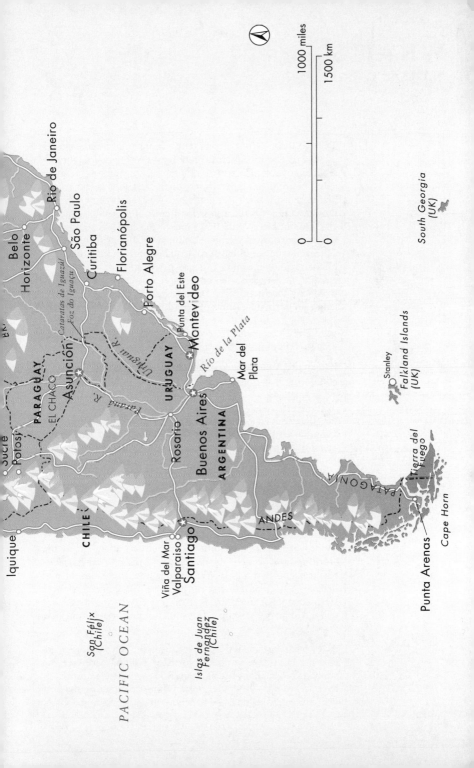

WHAT'S WHERE

The profusion of fascinating destinations might make choosing just one South American country—or even two or three—seem impossible. The truth is that the jagged spine of the Andes splits the continent into two very distinct regions, which makes planning trips much less daunting. West of this monumental mountain range is the thin strip of land running along the Pacific Ocean. Here you'll find some of the continent's most intriguing port towns, from the colonial splendor of Colombia's Cartagena to the jumble of colorful houses tumbling down the hills surrounding Chile's Valparaíso, and some of the most fascinating archaeological discoveries, from Ingapirca in Ecuador to Machu Picchu in Peru. The topography is remarkably varied, from the high plateaus of Ecuador, Peru, and Bolivia to the sprawling deserts of Chile. Many head to the western side of the continent en route to see the unique creatures of the Galápagos or the stoic stone heads of Easter Island.

East of the Andes, the marvels are no less alluring. The Amazon Basin—extending across parts of nine countries and covering more than 10 million square km (4 million square mi)—eclipses all other natural wonders. But there are many other sights well worth seeing, from the endless plains of the Pantanal in Brazil to the steely blue glaciers of Patagonia. Some of the world's largest and most exciting cities—Rio de Janeiro, São Paulo, Montevideo, and Buenos Aires—are settled along the Atlantic coast.

ARGENTINA

Romantic notions of gauchos riding the ranges and tango dancers gliding across the floor have given Argentina a mystique, but these images tell only half the story. Duck into the upscale boutiques of Buenos Aires's Recoleta district, drop by for tea at an elegant *confitería,* or attend an opera at the world-famous Teatro Colón, and you'll realize that *porteños* (the residents of this port city) are educated, sophisticated, and urbane. Like a certain city to the north, Buenos Aires never sleeps: dinner is often taken at midnight, and the streets are still full of people when you leave the restaurant sometime past 2 AM.

Away from the capital the pace is slower, the people more open, and the landscape striking. North of Buenos Aires are the stunning Iguazú Falls—in all, some 300 separate waterfalls that thunder over a 4-km-wide (2½-mi-wide) precipice on the border of Brazil, Argentina, and Paraguay. In Patagonia to the south,

	you'll find the ski resort of Bariloche; the icy monoliths of Parque Nacional los Glaciares; and the famous Parque Nacional Tierra del Fuego at the very tip of the country.
BOLIVIA	Visitors are often giddy upon arrival in La Paz, perhaps with relief at having landed safely in the world's highest capital city. More likely it's *soroche,* a wooziness caused by the lack of oxygen at high altitudes. But even after you've sipped the local remedy called *mate de coca* you may find that Bolivia still leaves you breathless. Although it lacks a coastline (that was lost to Chile more than a century ago), Bolivia has a bit of everything else, from lofty Andean peaks to lush Amazon rain forests.

Not far from La Paz, the ruins of Tiwanaku are set in the strangely beautiful altiplano, the barren plateau that lies between two branches of the Andes. Here you'll find La Puerta del Sol (Gate of the Sun), an imposing stone fixture believed to be a solar calendar built by a civilization that surfaced around 600 BC and mysteriously disappeared around AD 1200. Another Bolivian sight on everyone's agenda is Lake Titicaca—the highest navigable lake in the world and the legendary birthplace of the Inca empire. Hydrofoils and hovercrafts ply the waters, passing traditional gondola-shape boats made of reeds. |
| **BRAZIL** | Portuguese-speaking Brazil is the fifth-largest country in the world and has an oversized vitality to match. Its high-energy attitude can be seen everywhere—in highways, dams, industrial complexes, and even in the capital city of Brasília, which was constructed from scratch in the wilderness in an effort to promote development of the nation's vast interior.

To most visitors, Brazil is Rio de Janeiro, famous for its spectacular bay-side setting, fabulous beaches, skimpy string bikinis, and riotous Carnaval. But Brazil goes far beyond Rio's beaches and hedonistic pleasures. Skyscrapers, stock markets, and agribusiness set the pace in the megalopolis of São Paulo. Far to the southwest is the mighty Foz de Iguaçu (Iguaçu Falls). The massive Pantanal—an untamable mosaic of swamp and forest teeming with wildlife—is the dominant feature of Brazil's far west both in geography and in tourist appeal. A unique Afro-Brazilian culture thrives in tropical Salvador, capital of Bahia State. And then there's the Amazon, a gargantuan waterway flowing for more than 4,000 mi, so wide in |

WHAT'S
WHERE

	places you can't see the shore from a riverboat's deck, and banked by a rainforest that houses the greatest variety of life on earth.
CHILE	You're never far from the ocean in this 4,267-km-long (2,650-mi-long) country, as it averages only 177 km (110 mi) in width. Chile is justly famous for its twin resort cities of Valparaíso and Viña del Mar, known for their wide swaths of sand and nonstop nightlife. But this ribbon of country isn't just a string of beautiful beaches—it has everything from desolate salt flats to awe-inspiring glaciers. In the north you'll find the Atacama Desert, so dry that in some areas no rain has ever been recorded. Next come the copper mines that brought great wealth to the country, followed by the fertile Central Valley region that's home to the sprawling capital of Santiago. The green and aquamarine waters of the Lake District are to the south, offering outstanding fishing and water sports. Finally, in the extreme south lies the forbidding landscape of windswept Tierra del Fuego.
	Lauded for its award-winning wines and world-renowned seafood, Chile draws raves for its succulent *centolla* (king crab) and *congrio* (conger eel). Patagonia is known for its tender and moist *cordero asado* (grilled lamb). You'll work up quite an appetite with all the country's outdoor activities, from hiking up smoldering volcanoes to rafting down raging rivers. Jet-set skiers from all over the world prefer the championship slopes at Valle Nevado, not far from Santiago, where they can schuss during summer months when snows melt in the Northern Hemisphere.
COLOMBIA	Colombia is the continent's only country to touch both the Pacific and the Atlantic. The Andes begin here, which means the topography ranges from chilly mountain peaks to sultry coastal lowlands. The country's major cities sit at different altitudes, and with each comes a different attitude. Bogotá, the sprawling capital, sits at 8,700 ft and has a formal air that recalls its colonial past. The atmosphere grows more relaxed and informal, however, if you descend 2,000 ft to Medellín, a small but vibrant city whose mild climate has earned it the name "city of eternal spring."
	Sadly, much of the country is embroiled in bitter battles between the government and factions on the left and right. But

some parts of Colombia are far removed from the fighting. The historical port of Cartagena, for example, is a destination for many tourists. It is one of the best-preserved colonial cities in the Americas; it's also a lively, exuberant town with strong Afro-Caribbean influence.

ECUADOR

A patchwork of highland and jungle, this tiny nation claims some of the hemisphere's most impressive landscapes. A living quilt of terraced green plots covers the lower slopes of cloud-capped volcanoes, where corn grows twice as tall as the sturdy peasant farmers. Quito, the capital, lies at the foot of Volcán Pichincha, a mighty volcano that sometimes sputters to life. The city has two distinct faces, the Old City, with its carefully preserved colonial buildings and the New City, where luxury hotels are sprouting as fast as flowers after a spring rain. Just 24 km (15 mi) outside the city you can have your picture taken as you straddle the equator at a monument indicating the dividing line between the Northern and Southern hemispheres. In Ecuador, if you are patient, you can eventually see all the stars in our universe.

Cuenca, a beautifully preserved colonial city, offers both architectural charm and an outstanding market. No rainbow could possibly compete with the flaming colors worn by the highland women, who adorn their necks with strands of golden beads. The coastal region is home to the bustling metropolis of Guayaquil, a once seedy port city slowly recovering its status. Guayaquil also serves as a departure point for planes and ships to the enchanting Galápagos Islands, home of the remarkable wildlife that sparked naturalist Charles Darwin's theories of evolution.

PARAGUAY

In this unspoiled land, time and tradition have stood still for generations. Paraguay may be short on trendy eateries and luxurious accommodations, but it's long on charm. Asunción is a provincial capital whose pleasures are simple: a stroll through the botanical gardens; a leisurely lunch at an outdoor café; or an afternoon of shopping for *ñandutí,* the country's unique, intricate, spiderweb lace. In the countryside, motorcycles and pop music compete with oxcarts and traditional *polca* music in the hearts and minds of the rural people. The country's original inhabitants were the Guaraní, and the ruins of missions near Encarnación are an impressive reminder of their fascinating legacy. Here Jesuit missionaries converted the native pop-

WHAT'S
WHERE

ulation and organized a unique communal society. Several of the lovely colonial-era buildings, abandoned when the Jesuits were expelled from the region in 1767, are currently being restored.

PERU

Peru contains a wealth of history within its borders. Cusco, once the capital of the Inca empire, is one of the hemisphere's most beautiful cities. Although the Spaniards who conquered the region in the 16th century tried to superimpose their culture on the indigenous people, they never really succeeded. When a 1953 earthquake struck the city, it felled much of the convent of Santo Domingo, which had been built over the ruins of the sacred Temple of the Sun. Hidden for so long beneath the facade built by the Spanish, the Inca walls beneath withstood the disaster.

On a hilltop outside of Cusco is the massive fortress of Sacsayhuaman, whose zigzag shape is visible only from the air. It's a great introduction to Inca culture before you head to the unforgettable Machu Picchu. Thought by many archaeologists to have been the last refuge of the Incas, Machu Picchu was never discovered by the Spaniards. The maze of temples, houses, terraces, and stairways lay abandoned in lofty solitude until explorer Hiram Bingham stumbled upon the city in 1911. The three-hour train trip from Cusco to Machu Picchu is exhilarating, passing by dozens of smaller ruins before finally reaching the famed "lost city."

If the gems of Peru's Inca past are locked away on the altiplano, then its capital, Lima, is the safekeeper of colonial treasures. Perhaps no other city in the Americas enjoyed such power and prestige during the height of the colonial era. For an entirely different side of Peru, visit the rain forest near Puerto Maldonado, where the sounds of the Amazon jungle are ever present.

URUGUAY

Gently rolling hills and grasslands are the hallmarks of Uruguay, one of South America's smallest countries. Ninety percent of the land is used for grazing, and Uruguayans are justifiably proud of their fine beef cattle. A visit to an *estancia* (ranch) is an excellent way to experience both the scenery and the people—well educated yet unpretentious, industrious yet relaxed, they're the most remarkable aspect of Uruguay. Another culture altogether exists along the coast. The country's beaches are among the best on the continent; without even leaving Montevideo, Uruguay's gracious capital, you can sample more than half a dozen of them. The most fashionable beach, however, is 137 km (85 mi) to the east at Punta del Este, a haven for well-heeled foreign visitors. Often called the South American Riviera, this resort is also a popular site for international conferences and movie festivals.

VENEZUELA

Just a few hours from the eastern United States, Venezuela is perhaps the continent's most accessible destination for North American travelers. Caracas, the crowded capital, is a futuristic blend of glass office towers and concrete apartment buildings built on the heels of the oil boom. You can find a bit of colonial charm around tree-lined Plaza Bolívar, but Caracas is better known for its selection of world-class restaurants, interesting art galleries, and stylish nightspots.

Venezuela enjoys South America's longest Caribbean coast, with stretches of pristine white sand lapped by warm turquoise waters. Isla Margarita has long been a destination popular with sun-seeking Europeans, and North Americans have been, increasingly, discovering its charms. In the Andean city of Mérida, the world's longest and highest cable car carries you to the foot of glacier-topped Pico Bolívar. In the southeast, huge table-top mountains called *tepuis* tower over the grasslands of Parque Nacional Canaima, a national park the size of Belgium. Here the spectacular Angel Falls plummet more than 2,647 ft into a bizarre landscape of black lagoons, pink-sand beaches, and unique plant life.

WHEN TO GO

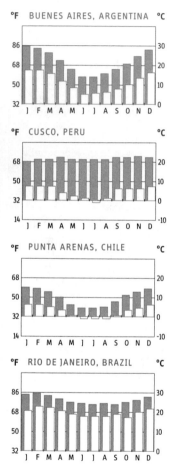

Seasons below the Equator are the reverse of those in the north—summer in Argentina, Bolivia, Chile, Paraguay, Peru, and Uruguay, and portions of Brazil and Ecuador, runs from December to March and winter from June to September. Prices in beach resorts invariably are higher during the summer months. If you're looking for a bargain, stick to the off-season.

Climate

Because of the great variety of latitudes, altitudes, and climatic zones on the continent, you'll encounter many different kinds of weather in any given month. The highland areas of the Andes—which run north to south down the west coast of South America from Colombia through Ecuador, Peru, Bolivia, Chile, and Argentina—are at their most accessible and most comfortable in the dry season, May–October. July–September is ski season in Chile and Argentina.

An entirely different climate reigns in the Amazon basin, whose tropical and subtropical rain forests spread from Ecuador and Peru across the northern third of Brazil. The dry season runs from May to September—which means it's simply less rainy than at any other time. Contrary to what you may have heard, the rainy season is a great time for an Amazon River trip; the waters are higher then and boats can venture farther upriver into the tributaries.

Certain ocean regions—the Atlantic coast from Brazil all the way down to the famous resort of Punta del Este in Uruguay, as well as the Caribbean shore of Venezuela—are at their hottest and most crowded when it's North America's winter. The sea moderates temperatures in most South American cities year-round, even as far south as Buenos Aires. The Pacific coast is bordered mainly by a strip of desert, where the climate is always hospitable. Argentine and Chilean Patagonia hold countless fjords, perfect for cruising from November to March.

Weather wise, May and June are probably the best months to visit South America, as you can expect both good weather and off-season prices. These months, as well as September and October, are also relatively uncrowded.

🗺 Forecasts **Weather Channel Connection** ☎ 900/932-8437 95¢ per minute from a Touch-Tone phone ⊕ www.weather.com.

Argentina

"Isn't it great how you can live like a king in Argentina for very little money?"

—msteacher

"My friend and I fell in love with Argentina. Most of our trip was spent in Buenos Aires—an amazing city. We also spent three days in Iguazú—a must (the falls are really something else). I simply want to express how happily surprised I was with this country. Lots of history and passion there. I'll definitely go back to visit other parts."

—rozelle

"I am hoping for a trip to Argentina—after waiting for about three years. Maybe this year it will happen finally."

—Brahmama

www.fodors.com/forums

MOST TRAVELERS THINK THEY'VE STUMBLED ON a long-lost European country when they get to Argentina. Most Argentines, too, are convinced they're more European than South American. A quick look at the people walking down the avenues of any Argentine city confirms the impression. There are more Italian surnames than Spanish, and the largest colony of Yugoslavs outside of their fractured homeland. There are tens of thousands of descendants of Jewish immigrants from Eastern Europe, and communities of British, French, and German families enjoy cultural and financial clout far beyond their insignificant numbers.

But in spite of the symbiosis with Europe, the country has had a chaotic past, politically and economically. The pitfalls of Argentine politics weren't inappropriately characterized in the musical *Evita*: "Truth is stranger than fiction" is a maxim confirmed by the musical-chairs–like process that has placed both soldiers and civilians in the country's presidency. Further, Argentina is a me-first society that considers government a thorn in its side, and whose citizens avoid paying taxes with the finesse of bullfighters. As a community, it's totally chaotic, but as individuals, Argentines are generous and delightful, full of life, and eager to explain the intricacies of their complex society. They're also philosophers, anxious to justify their often enviable existence. Friendship is a time-consuming priority, and family connections are strong. Argentines work longer hours than New Yorkers—just not so efficiently—and rival Madrileños at dining until dawn.

Argentina's vast territory stretches more than 5,000 km (3,000 mi) from north to south and encompasses everything from snow-covered mountains to subtropical jungle. In the north, in the sultry province of Misiones, nature is raucous and rampant; here the spectacular Iguazú Falls flow amid foliage that is rain-forest thick. In the pampas, or plains, of central Argentina, the countryside recalls the American West: Gauchos herd the cattle that provide Argentina with the beef it consumes in massive quantities. In the west, the Andean backbone Argentina shares with Chile attracts climbers to Mt. Aconcagua, the Southern Hemisphere's highest peak, and draws skiers to Bariloche and other resorts. Patagonia, in the south, is like no other place on earth. Monumental glaciers tumble into mountain lakes, depositing icebergs like meringue on a floating island. Penguins troop along beaches like invading forces, whales hang out with several yards of their tails emerging from the sea, and at the tip of Patagonia, South America slips into Beagle Channel in Tierra del Fuego.

Exploring Argentina

Buenos Aires is the political, economic, and cultural capital of Argentina and the gateway to the rest of the country. The pampas—vast plains of cattle ranches and home of the gauchos—extend south from the capital. The Iguazú Falls lie roughly 1,300 km (800 mi) to the city's northeast on the border with Paraguay and Brazil. Nestled in the shadow of the soaring Andes, Mendoza was once a desert before irrigation transformed it into the fourth-largest wine-producing region in the

Top Reasons to Go

The Beef. Argentina is cow country. The beef is so good, most Argentines see little reason to eat anything else, though pork, lamb, and chicken are tasty alternatives, and *civito* (kid), when in season, is outstanding. *Carne asado* (roasted meat) usually means grilled *a la parrilla* (on a grill over hot coals), but it can also be baked in an oven or slowly roasted at an outdoor barbecue (*asado*).

Futbol. Nothing unites and divides Argentines as much as their passion for soccer. Local teams are the subject of fiery dispute and serious rivalry; the national team brings the country together for displays of unrivaled passion and suicidal despair, especially during the World Cup. Argentina's blue-and-white striped jerseys have flashed across TV screens since it won the 1978 and 1986 World Cups, and nothing can lift—or crush—the spirits of the nation like the result of a soccer match.

The Outdoors. Fishing in Patagonia's northern Lake District (especially around Bariloche) is legendary. Hiking and mountain biking in national and provincial parks—over mountain trails, and through forests to lakes, villages, and campgrounds—provide unique memories of an abundant and vast wilderness. The Club Andinos (Andean Mountaineering Clubs) in Bariloche, Mendoza, Ushuaia, and other towns organizes national and international excursions. Since Argentina's seasons are the opposite of North America's, you can ski or snowboard from June to September.

Tango. From its beginnings in portside brothels at the turn of the 19th century, tango has marked and reflected the character of Buenos Aires and its inhabitants. Although visitors associate tango with dance, for locals it's more about the music and the lyrics, and you can't help but cross paths with both forms. You may hear strains of tango on the radio while sipping coffee in a boulevard café or see high-kicking sequined dancers in a glitzy dinner show or listen to musicians in a cabaret. Regardless, you'll experience the best of this broody, melancholic, but impassioned, art form.

Vino. Given the high consumption of beef rather than fish, Argentines understandably drink a lot of *vino tinto* (red wine); Malbec and Cabernet are the most popular. If you prefer *vino blanco* (white wine), try a sauvignon blanc or chardonnay from Mendoza, or lesser-known wineries from farther north, such as La Rioja and Salta, where the Torrontés grape thrives. This varietal produces a dry white with a lovely floral bouquet.

world. Patagonia is the rough and largely uninhabited territory that extends south to Tierra del Fuego and consumes a third of Argentina. It's divided into two regions: the Atlantic, with an incomparable variety of marine life, including whales, sea elephants, and penguins, and the Andes, with frozen lakes, glaciers, and thousand-year-old forests.

Restaurants & Cuisine

Dining in Argentina is an art, a passion, and a pastime. Whether eaten at home or in a restaurant, meals are events. *Sobremesa* (chatting at the table after the meal) is just as important as the dining ritual itself, and people linger over wine or coffee long after the dishes have been cleared away. Breakfast is usually served until 11 AM; lunch runs from 12:30 to 3:30; dinner is from 8 to around midnight. Several restaurants in Buenos Aires and other large cities stay open all night, or at least well into the morning, catering to the after-theater and nightclub crowd.

WHAT IT COSTS In Argentine Pesos				
	$$$$	$$$	$$	$	¢
AT DINNER	over 32	25–32	17–24	9–16	under 9

Prices are for one main course at dinner.

About the Hotels

Buenos Aires has an array of hotels, inns, *apart-hotels* (short-term rental apartments), and hostels. Mendoza has many good, small to medium-size hotels. Idyllic lake-view lodges, cozy *cabañas* (cabins), vast *estancias* (ranches), and inexpensive *hospedajes* or *residenciales* (bed-and-breakfasts) are found in towns and in the countryside throughout Patagonia. High season in Argentina includes the summer months of mid-December through February, and the winter holidays that fall in July.

WHAT IT COSTS In Argentine Pesos				
	$$$$	$$$	$$	$	¢
BUENOS AIRES	over 550	401–550	251–400	100–250	under 100
ELSEWHERE	over 300	220–300	140–220	80–140	under 80

Prices are for two people in a standard double room in high season.

When to Go

CLIMATE Because of Argentina's great variety of latitudes, altitudes, and zones, you can encounter many different climates in any given month. The most important thing to remember is the most obvious—when it's summer in the northern hemisphere, it's winter in Argentina. Winter in Argentina stretches from July through October, and summer settles in from December through March.

If you can handle the heat, Buenos Aires is wonderful January through February. Spring and fall are temperate: it's usually warm enough for just a light jacket, and it's right before or after the peak (and expensive) season. The best time for trips to Iguazú Falls is August–October, when temperatures are lower, the falls are fuller, and the spring coloring is at its brightest.

1

Ski resorts such as Bariloche are obviously packed in winter. If you're heading to the Lake District or Patagonia, visit during the shoulder seasons of December and March. The Patagonia coast is on the infamous latitude that sailors call the "Roaring Forties," with southern seas that batter the region year-round. Thirty-mile-per-hour winds are common, and 100-mile-per-hour gales aren't unusual. In Tierra del Fuego fragments of glaciers cave into lakes with a rumble throughout the thaw from October to the end of April—the best time to enjoy the show.

⛏ Forecasts **Servicio Meteorológico Nacional** (National Weather Service for Argentina) ☎ 11/4514-4248 automated information ⊕ www.meteofa.mil.ar has information in Spanish.

BUENOS AIRES	**Jan.**	85F	29C	**May**	64F	18C	**Sept.**	64F	18C
		63	17		47	8		46	8
	Feb.	83F	28C	**June**	57F	14C	**Oct.**	69F	21C
		63	17		41	5		50	10
	Mar.	79F	26C	**July**	57F	14C	**Nov.**	76F	24C
		60	16		42	6		56	13
	Apr.	72F	22C	**Aug.**	60F	16C	**Dec.**	82F	28C
		53	12		43	6		61	16
BARILOCHE	**Jan.**	70F	21C	**May**	50F	10C	**Sept.**	50F	10C
		46	6		36	2		34	1
	Feb.	70F	21C	**June**	45F	7C	**Oct.**	52F	11C
		46	8		34	1		37	3
	Mar.	64F	18C	**July**	43F	6C	**Nov.**	61F	16C
		43	6		32	0		41	5
	Apr.	57F	14C	**Aug.**	46F	8C	**Dec.**	64F	18C
		39	4		32	0		45	7

HOLIDAYS January through March is summer holiday season for Argentines, and the second and third weeks of July are winter school holidays.

New Year's Day; Day of the Epiphany (January 6); Veteran's Day (April 2); Labor Day (May 1); Anniversary of the 1810 Revolution (May 25); Semana Santa (Holy Week; 4 days in April leading up to Easter Sunday); National Sovereignty Day (June 10); Flag Day (June 20); Independence Day (July 9); Anniversary of San Martín's Death (August 17); Día de la Raza (Race Recognition Day) (October 12); Day of the Immaculate Conception (December 8); and Christmas. Some holidays that fall on weekdays may be moved to Monday to create a three-day weekend. Note that all banks and most commercial and entertainment centers are closed on these days.

FESTIVALS **Summer:** Scores of performances, concerts, and classes mark the **Festival Buenos Aires Tango,** the world's biggest tango festival, which culminates in a massive outdoor *milonga* along Avenida Corrientes. **Carnaval** comes in many guises in Argentina throughout February. Andean rituals prevail in Jujuy, while in Buenos Aires urban dance and drumming

Argentina

BOLIVIA

Tartagal

PARAGUAY

JUJUY
San
Salvador
de Jujuy

Rivadavia

Pilcomayo

Asunción

EL REY
NATIONAL
PARK

Bermejo

FORMOSA

Salta

Formosa

PARQUE
NACIONAL
IGUAZÚ

SALTA

CHACO

San Miguel
de Tucumán

TUCUMAN

Santiago
del Estero

Resistencia

Corrientes

MISIONES

Posadas

CATAMARCA

SANTIAGO
DEL ESTERO

CORRIENTES

SANTA
FE

S. Fdo. del Valle
de Catamarca

Salinas
Ambargasta

Monte
Caseros

BRAZIL

LA RIOJA

Salinas
Grandes

Laguna
Chiquita

SAN JUAN

Córdoba

Santa Fe

ENTRE
RÍOS

San Juan

Dolores

Paraná

URUGUAY

Mendoza

Río Cuarto

Rosario

San Luis

CORDOBA

Santiago

Mercedes

Rufino

Buenos
Aires

Montevídeo

CHILE

MENDOZA

SAN
LUIS

General
Pico

La Plata

San Rafael

BUENOS
AIRES

Bahía
Samborombón

Las Leñas

Santa
Rosa

Dolores

Cabo
San Antonio

Malargüe

Azul

LA PAMPA

Puelches

Tandil

NEUQUÉN

Bahía
Blanca

Mar del Plata

Neuquén

Cipolletti

Punta Alta

Necochea

NAHUEL
HUAPI
NATIONAL
PARK

Negro

RÍO NEGRO

Bahía San Blas

Ingeniero
Jacobacci

Golfo
San Matías

Viedma

Bariloche

Puerto
Madryn

Península
Valdés

Trelew

Las Plumas

Rawson

CHUBUT

Cabo Raso

Malaspina

Punta Tombo

ATLANTIC
OCEAN

Comodoro
Rivadavia

Golfo
San Jorge

Deseado

Cabo Blanco

PETRIFIED
FOREST
NATIONAL
PARK

Las Horquetas

SANTA
CRUZ

Puerto
Santa Cruz

Lago Argentino

El Calafate

Bahía
Grande

FALKLAND ISLANDS
(ISLAS MALVINAS)

Perito
Moreno
Glacier

Río Gallegos

Stanley
(Puerto Argentino)

Strait of
Magellan

TIERRA DEL FUEGO

PARQUE
NACIONAL
TIERRA
DEL FUEGO

Río Grande

ISLA GRANDE DE
TIERRA DEL FUEGO

Ushuaia

Isla de los
Estados

Cape Horn

PACIFIC OCEAN

PATAGONIA

0   200 miles

0   200 kilometers

troupes known as *murgas* take to the streets on weekends throughout the month.

Fall: In March, Mendoza celebrates the **Festival de La Vendimia,** the grape-harvest festival, during the first week of March. Parades, folk dancing, and fireworks take place, and the crowning of a queen marks the grand finale. In April, independent, arty flicks are the order of the day at **Festival Internacional de Cine Independiente de Buenos Aires,** which attracts a handful of top international actors and directors.

Winter: The **Fiesta Nacional de la Nieve** (National Snow Festival) is a month-long winter carnival that takes place in August all over Bariloche and at the Catedral ski area.

In the last two weeks of July all the country action is in Buenos Aires, at **La Rural.** Argentina's biggest agricultural show includes displays of gaucho riding skills and even horses trained to dance the tango.

Spring: During Bariloche's **Semana Musical Llao Llao** (Llao Llao Musical Week) in September, international soloists and orchestras perform classical, jazz, and tango music at the Llao Llao Hotel & Resort. In November, some of the world's best polo players and the snooty jet set gather every year for chukkas and sundowners at the **Abierto Argentino de Polo,** played out on the hallowed turfs of the Argentine Polo fields in Buenos Aires.

Language

Argentines speak *Castellano,* Castilian Spanish, which differs slightly from the Spanish of most other Latin American countries. For example, the informal *vos* (you) is used instead of *tu,* in conjunction with the verb *sos* (are) instead of *eres.* The double "L" found in words like *pollo* phonetically translates to the ZH-sound, rather than a Y-sound. English is considered the second most widely used language. Services geared toward tourism generally employ an English-speaking staff. It's also common to find English-speaking staff at commercial and entertainment centers.

BUENOS AIRES

This city is really hot. Incredible food, fresh young designers, and a cultural scenethat's thriving despite tough economic times—all these Buenos Aires has. Yet less tangible things are at the heart of the city's sizzle—namely the spirit of its often divided but never indifferent inhabitants. Here a flirtatious glance can be as passionate as a tango; a heated sports discussion as important as a world-class soccer match. It's this zest for life that's making Buenos Aires Latin America's hottest destination.

The world's ninth-largest city rises from the Río de la Plata and stretches more than 200 square km (75 square mi) to the surrounding pampas, Argentina's fertile plains. With more than one-third of the country's 39 million inhabitants living in or around the city, it's clearly the country's hub as well as it's main gateway.

Buenos Aires locals refer to themselves as *porteños* because many of them originally arrived by boat from Europe and settled in the port area. Known as thinkers, Porteños delve into philosophical discussions and psychoanalysis (as proven by the large number of psychoanalysts per capita—in fact, the most of any city in the world). With 85% of the Argentine population of European origin, there's a blurred sense of national identity in Buenos Aires—South American or European?—and residents are often concerned with how outsiders perceive them. People here look at one another closely, whether it be a casual, appreciative glance or a curious stare, making many of them deeply image-conscious.

Exploring Buenos Aires

By Victoria
Patience

Buenos Aires's identity lies in its 48 *barrios* (neighborhoods)—each with its own character and history. Several generations of many families have lived in the same barrio, and traditionally people feel more of an affinity to their neighborhood than to the city as a whole.

Try to take things one neighborhood at a time, exploring on foot and by *colectivo* (bus), *subte* (subway), and/or relatively inexpensive taxis. Streets are basically laid out in a grid, though a few cut across the grid diagonally; these are helpfully called *diagonales*. *Avenidas* are broader, often two-way, streets, while regular streets (officially *calles* but actually referred to just by their name) are generally one-way. Streets and avenues running north–south change names at Avenida Rivadavía. Each city block is 100 meters (328 feet) long, and addresses are based on the building's measured position from the corner (for instance, 180 Calle Florida is 80 meters from the corner, and 100 meters, or one block, from 80 Calle Florida).

El Centro

The term *el centro* is confusing: although people tend to say *"Voy al centro"* or *"Trabajo en el centro"* (without the capitals), meaning "I'm going downtown" or "I work downtown," they're using the term generally. The official barrio names of the downtown area are San Nicolás and Monserrat, though few people use these either. Suffice to say that "el centro" is really an umbrella term to cover several action-packed districts at the city's heart. In it are theaters, bars, cafés, bookstores, and the crowded streets you'd expect to find in any major city center.

The Microcentro is the unofficial name for the barrio of San Nicolás: the area north of Avenida Rivadavia, west of Avenida 9 de Julio, and south of Avenida Santa Fe. This is effectively Buenos Aires's central business district, and the action focuses on the pedestrian-only street Florida. The next district west is Tribunales, meaning law courts, so called be-

WORD OF MOUTH
"Amazing city. We discovered it by *barrio* (neighborhood). Our favorites were San Telmo (loved the Sunday market) and Palermo Viejo. Some drawbacks though: lots of noise and pollution. And the taxi drivers are crazy. Aside from that, we loved every minute of it." —rozelle

cause of the supreme court and other civic buildings that are here; it's also where you'll find the world-famous Colón Theater.

Plaza de Mayo was where Buenos Aires started: the square once sat right on the river and, in keeping the traditions of Spanish colonies, was home to the city's central institutions, both governmental and religious. The Plaza de Mayo is not technically a district, but few people use the area's official handle, Monserrat. Regardless, the square has enough worthy offerings for you to treat it as a neighborhood for the purpose of sight-seeing. West along Avenida de Mayo is Congreso, a part-residential, part-commercial barrio named for the nation's congress, which is at its heart.

TIMING & PRECAUTIONS Half a day in the Microcentro and Tribunales is enough to take in the sights and have your fill of risky street-crossing, though you could spend a lot more time caught up in shops or seeing shows. A leisurely walk through the Plaza de Mayo area should take two or three hours, but allow up to a day if you plan to visit all the sights here.

Walking along Florida, with its countless salesmen and money changers, can feel like running the gauntlet, but a purposeful look and *"No, gracias"* gets you past them. Many stores close in the evening and on weekends, leaving things deserted; wander with care at these times. Although Lavalle is a commercial hub, it is also peppered with adult entertainment; again, use caution here. Corrientes is usually packed with theatergoers; keep an eye out for purse snatchers.

The Plaza de Mayo area can be very busy on weekdays, but given that weekend opening hours are erratic—indeed, most of the government-owned sights are closed on Saturday—it's best to brave the chaos and visit the area midweek and see it as most porteños do. The area is very quiet at night, as there isn't much to do here; visit during the day.

Always use ATMs within bank hours (weekdays 10–3), as they're common target areas for thieves. Hail taxis far from banks and ATMs in this part of town. Robbers have been known to pose as taxi drivers and search for potential victims—that is visitors who have just withdrawn money. In general, looking aware is enough to make someone else a better target than you. In the unlikely event that you are held up, comply with the perpetrator's requests quickly and quietly.

WHAT TO SEE **Calle Florida.** When porteños talk about Florida (pronounced flo-*ree*-da, they aren't referring to a vacation but rather a pedestrian street that crosses the Microcenter's heart. This downtown axis is a riot of office workers, fast-food chains, boutiques, and vendors selling (and haggling over) leather goods. The commercial institutions that line the street are battered and paint-splattered—unhappy customers have been taking out their anger at these *corralitos* (banks retaining their savings) since the economic crisis of 2001–02. You'll also find souvenir shops, grocers, and bookstores. The closer you get to Plaza San Martín, the better the offerings.

Milan's Galleria Vittorio Emanuele served as the architectural model for **Galerías Pacífico** (Pacific Gallery), designed during Buenos Aires's turn-of-the-20th-century golden age. Once the headquarters of the Buenos Aires–Pacific Railway, it's now a posh mall. Head to the central stairwell to see the allegorical murals painted by local greats Juan Carlos Castagnino, Antonio Berni, Cirilo Colmenio, Lino Spilimbergo, and Demetrio Urruchúa. The Centro Cultural Borges, which hosts small international exhibitions and musical events, is on the mezzanine level. ⊠ *Florida 753, Microcentro* ☎ *11/5555–5100* ⊕ *www.galeriaspacifico. com.ar; www.ccborges.org.ar* Ⓜ *B to Florida.*

If all the activity of Florida becomes too much, just steps away is **Plaza San Martín** (San Martín Square), a great place to put down your shopping bags and rest your feet. French landscape architect Charles Thays designed the square in the 1800s, juxtaposing local and exotic trees. An imposing bronze equestrian monument to General José de San Martín watches over lunching office workers. The Monumento a los Caídos en las Malvinas is a more somber presence. Guarded by a grenadier, the monument's 25 black marble slabs are engraved with the names of those who died in the 1982 Falkland Islands War. ⊠ *Av. Libertador and Calle Florida, Microcentro* Ⓜ *C to San Martín.*

❶ **Catedral Metropolitana.** The Metropolitan Cathedral's columned neoclassical facade makes it seem more like a temple than a church, and its history follows the pattern of many structures in the Plaza de Mayo area. The first of six buildings on this site was a 16th-century adobe ranch house; the current structure dates from 1822, but has been added to several times. The embalmed remains of General José de San Martín, known as the Liberator of Argentina for his role in the War of Independence, rest here in a marble mausoleum lit by an eternal flame. Soldiers of the Grenadier Regiment, an elite troop created and trained by San Martín in 1811, permanently guard the tomb. Group tours in English are available, but you need to call ahead. ⊠ *Rivadavía and San Martín, Plaza de Mayo* ☎ *11/4331–2845* 🖭 *Free* ☉ *Weekdays 8–7, weekends 9–7:30* Ⓜ *A to Plaza de Mayo, D to Catedral, E to Bolívar.*

❸ **La Manzana de Las Luces** (The Block of Illumination). Constructed by the Jesuits in the early 1800s, prior to their expulsion, La Manzana de Las Luces, a cluster of buildings southwest of Plaza de Mayo, was an enclave meant for higher learning. The metaphorical *luces* (lights) of its name refer to the "illuminated" scholars who lived within. This was the colonial administrative headquarters for the Jesuits' vast land holdings in northeastern Argentina and Paraguay. In 1780 the city's first school of medicine was established here, and it became home to the University of Buenos Aires early in the 19th century. Among the historic buildings still standing are the Parroquia de San Ignacio de Loyola and the neoclassic Colegio Nacional, a top-notch public school and a hotbed of political activism.

You can tour parts of the historic tunnels, still undergoing archaeological excavation, which linked several churches in the area to the Cabildo and the port. The original purpose of these tunnels is a source of speculation—were they used for defense or smuggling? ⊠ *Perú 272, at Av. Julio A. Roca (known as Diagonal Sur), Plaza de Mayo* ☎ *11/4342–6973* 🖭 *Free* ☉ *Weekdays 10–7, weekends 3–7* Ⓜ *A to Plaza de Mayo, D to Catedral, E to Bolívar.*

★ ❷ **Plaza de Mayo.** Dating from 1580, the Plaza de Mayo itself has been the stage for many important events throughout the nation's history, including the uprising against Spanish colonial rule on May 25, 1810—hence its name. The square was once divided in two by a *recova* (gallery), but this reminder of colonial times was demolished in 1883 and the square's central monument, the Pirámide de Mayo, was later moved to its place. The pyramid you see is actually a 1911 extension of the original, erected in 1811 on the anniversary of the Revolution of May, which is hidden inside. The 1873 bronze equestrian statue of General Manuel Belgrano, designer of Argentina's flag, at the plaza's east end.

The plaza remains the traditional site for ceremonies as well as mass protests, including the bloody clashes in December 2001, as testified by ongoing police presence and crowd-control barriers. The white headscarves painted round the Pirámide de Mayo represent the Madres de la Plaza de Mayo (Mothers of May Square), who have marched here every Thursday at 3:30 for more than two decades. Housewives and mothers turned activists, they demand justice for *los desaparecidos,* the people who were "disappeared" during the military government's reign from 1976 to 1983. Here, too, you can witness the changing of the Grenadier Regiment guards weekdays every two hours from 9 until 7, Saturday at 9 and 11, and Sunday at 9, 11, and 1.

The eclectic Casa de Gobierno, better known as the **Casa Rosada** (✉ Hipólito Yrigoyen 219, Plaza de Mayo ☎ 11/4344–3802 or 11/4344–3600 ⊕ www.museo.gov.ar) or Pink House, is at the plaza's eastern end, with its back to the river. The building houses the government's executive branch—the president works here but lives elsewhere—and was built in the late 19th century over the foundations of an earlier customhouse and fortress. Swedish, Italian, and French architects have since modified the structure, which accounts for the odd mix of styles.

The balcony facing Plaza de Mayo has served as a presidential podium. From this lofty stage Evita rallied the *descamisados* (the shirtless—meaning the working class), Maradona sang along with soccer fans after winning one World Cup and coming second in another, and Madonna sang her filmed rendition of "Don't Cry for Me Argentina." Check for a small banner hoisted alongside the nation's flag, indicating "the president is in." Behind the structure, you can find the brick-wall remains of the 1845 Taylor Customs House, discovered after being buried for almost a century. Enter the Casa Rosada through the basement level of the Museo de la Casa Rosada, the only area open to the public, which exhibits presidential memorabilia along with objects from the original customhouse and fortress. Admission to

WHY PINK?

The curious hue dates from the presidency of Domingo Sarmiento, who ordered it painted pink as a symbol of unification between two warring political factions, the *federales* (whose color was red) and the *unitarios* (represented by white). Local legend has it that the original paint was made by mixing whitewash with bull's blood.

the museum is free. It's open weekdays 10–6 and Sunday 2–6. Call ahead to arrange an English-language tour. To reach the Plaza de Mayo and the Casa Rosada, take Línea A to Plaza de Mayo, D to Catedral, or E to Bolívar.

⑪ **Teatro Colón.** Its magnitude, magnificent acoustics, and opulence (grander
Fodor'sChoice than Milan's La Scala) position the Colón Theater among the world's
★ top five opera. An ever-changing stream of imported talent bolsters the well-regarded local lyric and ballet companies. After an eventful 18-year building process involving the death of one architect and the murder of another, the ornate Italianate structure was finally inaugurated in 1908 with Verdi's *Aïda*. It has hosted the likes of Maria Callas, Richard Strauss, Arturo Toscanini, Igor Stravinsky, Enrico Caruso, and Luciano Pavarotti, who has said that the Colón has only one flaw: the acoustics are so good, every mistake can be heard.

The theater's sumptuous building materials—three kinds of Italian marble, French stained glass, and Venetian mosaics—were imported from Europe to create large-scale lavishness. The seven-tier main theater is breathtaking in size, and has a grand central chandelier with 700 lights to illuminate the 3,000 mere mortals in its red-velvet seats.

The opera and ballet seasons run from April through December, but many seats are reserved for season-ticket holders. Throughout the year you can buy tickets for any performance from the box office in Pasaje Toscanini. If seats are sold out—or beyond your pocketbook—you can buy standing-room tickets on the day of the performance for a fraction of the cost. These are for the lofty upper-tier *paraíso,* from which you can both see and hear perfectly, although three-hour-long operas are hard on the feet. Shorter options in the main theater include symphonic cycles by the stable orchestra, as well as international orchestral visits.

You can see the splendor up close and get in on all the behind-the-scenes action with the theater's extremely popular guided tours. The whirlwind visits take you up and down innumerable staircases to rehearsal rooms and to the costume, shoe, and scenery workshops, before letting you gaze at the stage from a sought-after box. Arrive at least a half hour before the tour starts as places fill up very quickly. ⊠ *Main entrance: Libertad between Tucumán and Viamonte; Box office: Pasaje Toscanini 1180, Microcentro* ☎ *11/4378–7100 tickets, 11/4378–7132 tours* ⊕ *www. teatrocolon.org.ar* ☉ *Tours in English: weekdays 11, 12, 1, and 3; Sat. 9, 11, 1, and 3; Sun. 11, 1, and 3* Ⓜ *D to Tribunales.*

San Telmo

Highlights of bohemian San Telmo include Sunday strolls, antiques shopping at Feria de San Pedro and surrounding stores, and the tango halls that come to life nightly. Cobblestone streets teem with 19th-century buildings, once inhabited by affluent Spaniards. Thanks to preservation efforts, the area is now a cradle of history and culture, and all its landmarks have been declared national monuments.

TIMING &   San Telmo thrives on Sunday, thanks to the art and antiques market in
PRECAUTIONS   Plaza Dorrego. Crowds can get so thick that only judicious elbowing

gets you close to the stalls on the squares; explore this neighborhood during the week for more relaxed strolling. A few hours will give you time to see the sights, though you could easily spend a full day wandering. San Telmo is one of the city's seediest districts, and you should exercise caution when walking here—especially at night. Violent crime is rare, but unemployment in the area, combined with the knowledge that it's popular with tourists, has led to instances of petty crime.

WHAT TO SEE
❺ **Museo Histórico Nacional.** Enormous magnolia, palm, cedar, and elm trees shade the sloping hillside of Parque Lezama, site of the National History Museum. Bronze statues of Greek heroes, stone urns, and an imposing fountain shipped from Paris are part of the landscaping. Patchy grass, cracked paths, and unpainted benches suggest that San Telmo's wave of renovation hasn't made it south yet.

Entrepreneur and horticulturalist Gregorio Lezama purchased the large tract of land and the chestnut-and-white Italianate mansion on it in 1858. The building was subsequently used as a refuge from both the cholera and yellow-fever epidemics. It was extensively remodeled prior to opening as this museum in 1897. The mansion houses artifacts and paintings spanning the 16th through 20th centuries. Although most items have inventively translated English labels, there are no explanations of their significance, so unless you have a detailed knowledge of Argentine history many exhibits will be meaningless. Nonetheless, an hour perusing maps, clothing, and personal effects is enough to get an idea of what life in Buenos Aires used to be like. Scuffed walls, lighting in need of replacement, and dry displays are partly made up for by endearingly enthusiastic staff. ☒ *Calle Defensa 1600, San Telmo* ☏ *11/4307–4457* ☐ *2 pesos* ☉ *Feb.–Dec., Tues.–Fri and Sun. 11–5.*

★ ❹ **Plaza Dorrego.** Stately trees shade outdoor tables in the city's second-oldest square. The surrounding architecture provides an overview of the influences—Spanish colonial, French classical, and ornate Italian masonry—that shaped the city in the 19th and 20th centuries. On Sunday from 10 to 5 the square comes alive with the Feria de San Pedro Telmo (San Pedro Telmo Fair) and its vendors and tango dancers. Shop for tango memorabilia, leather goods, antique silver, brass, jewelry, crystal, and turn-of-the-20th-century Argentine and European curios. Prices are high at stalls on the square and astronomical in the shops surrounding it, and don't expect to bargain.

La Boca

The vibrant working-class neighborhood of La Boca, just south of San Telmo, served as the first port of Buenos Aires. Many who settled here were immigrants from Genoa, Italy, and the district retains much of its Italian heritage, although time as a tourist center is taking its toll on La Boca's authenticity. You can still enjoy inexpensive Italian fare in a cantina along Avenida Patricios.

TIMING &
PRECAUTIONS
A couple of hours should give you enough time to explore La Boca. Expect crowds on weekends, when the market is in full swing. Although the nightlife here is singular, it's best not to wander about after dark. Stay in the area of the Caminito and avoid straying into surrounding

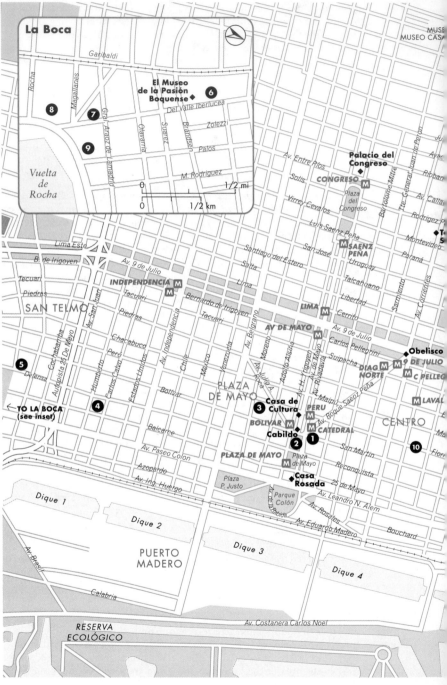

La Boca

Garibaldi

Rocha
Magallanes

El Museo
de la Pasión
Boquense ◆ **6**

8

Gral. Araoz de Lamadrid

7

Del Valle Iberlucea

Olavarria
Suarez
Brandsen
Zofezzi

9

Palos

*Vuelta
de
Rocha*

M. Rodriguez

0 ———— 1/2 mi
0 ———— 1/2 km

MUSE
MUSEO CAS

Av. Entre Ríos

**Palacio del
Congreso** ◆

Ayac

Solis

CONGRESO Ⓜ

Tte. General Juan Don Perón

Rioban

Av. Calla

Virrey Cevallos

Plaza
del
Congreso

Bartolome Mitre

Rodriguez P

Luis Saenz Peña

Montevideo

Santiago del Estero

San José

Ⓜ**SAENZ
PEÑA**

Paraná

Lima Este

Av. 9 de Julio

Salta

Uruguay

B. de Irigoyen

Tacuari
Piedres

SAN TELMO

Tacuari

Piedras

Bernardo de Irigoyen

Lima

Tacuari

Libertad

Tatcahuano

INDEPENDENCIA Ⓜ
Ⓜ

Av. San Juan

Chacabuco

Av. Independencia

Av. Belgrano

LIMA Ⓜ

Cerrito

Sarmiento

Av. Corrientes

Chile

Moreno

AV DE MAYO

Av. 9 de Julio

Ⓜ

Carlos Pellegrini

Suipacha

Obelisco
◆ DE JULIO

Cochabamba
Autopista 25 de Mayo

Humberto

Peru
Carlos Calvo

Estados Unidos

Mexico
Venezuela

Adolfo Alsina
Av. Julio A.

H. Irigoyen
Av. de Mayo
Av. Rivadavia

9
**DIAG
NORTE** Ⓜ

Ⓜ
C PELLEG

5

Defensa

4

Bolivar

**PLAZA
DE MAYO**

3 **Casa de
Cultura** ◆
BOLIVAR Ⓜ

Mainú
Av. Roque Saenz Peña

PERU
Ⓜ

Ⓜ **LAVAL**

CENTRO

← **TO LA BOCA
(see inset)**

Balcarce

Cabildo

2 **1**

CATEDRAL

San Martin

10

Flora

Av. Paseo Colon

Azopardo

Av. Ing. Huergo

PLAZA DE MAYO

Plaza
de Mayo Ⓜ

Reconquista

25 de Mayo

Dique 1

Plaza
P. Justo

**Casa
Rosada** ◆

Av. Leandro N. Alem

Av. Brasil

Dique 2

Parque
Colón

Dique 3

Av. Rosales

Av. Eduardo Madero

Bouchard

Calabria

**PUERTO
MADERO**

Dique 4

**RESERVA
ECOLÓGICO**

Av. Costanera Carlos Noel

Exploring Buenos Aires

Get Your Kicks

FOR MOST PORTEÑOS, *fútbol* (soccer) is a fervent passion. The national team is one of the top five of 203 teams in the FIFA–Coca-Cola World Ranking. The World Cup can bring the country to a standstill. Matches are held year-round, and are as exciting as they are dangerous. You're safest in the *platea* (preferred seating area), which cost around 20–60 pesos, rather than in the chaotic 10 pesos *popular* (standing-room) section. Passions run especially high when the Boca Juniors take on their arch rivals, the River Plate in the match known as the *supercláisco. Hinchas* (fans) paint their faces accordingly: blue and yellow for Boca Juniors or red and white for the River Plate.

Argentina's international soccer matches take place at the River Plate stadium, **Estadio Antonio Vespucio Liberti** (⊠ Av. Pte. Figueroa Alcorta 7597, Núñez ☎ 11/4788-1200 ⊕ www.cariverplate.com.ar), better known as the Monumental, for its size. The stadium is far out in the northwest of the city; you can get there by suburban train from Retiro (get off at Nuñez station) or by Línea D to Congreso de Tucumán and then taking a taxi.

areas. Note that the subte does not go to La Boca, and the surrounding neighborhoods are rough; taxi travel is a good bet.

WHAT TO SEE
❼ Calle Museo Caminito (Little Path Museum Street). Since 1959 the pedestrian-only Caminito has been an open-air art museum and market, flanked by colorful, haphazardly constructed dwellings. The two-block walk along the street takes you past local artists, many of whom create their work on-site against a backdrop of tango music and dancers. You may find the perfect souvenir here. ⊠ *Caminito, between Av. Pedro de Mendoza (La Vuelta de Rocha promenade) and Olivarría, La Boca* ⊠ *Free* ☉ *Daily 10–6.*

★ ❻ **Estadio Boca Juniors** (Boca Juniors Stadium). The Boca Juniors, one of Argentina's most popular soccer teams, are the proud owners of this distinctive stadium, with vibrant murals by artists Pérez Celis and Romulo Macció. Should you chance a game, be prepared for throngs, pandemonium, and street revelry—and never wear red and white, the colors of the rival River Plate team. The bordering street shops sell Boca paraphernalia. Inside the stadium is **El Museo de la Pasión Boquense** (The Museum of Boca Passion), a large-scale celebration of the club. Pricey admission and slick displays are testament to the club's affluence under the guidance of dollar-savvy businessman and wannabe-politician Mauricio Macri. The modern, two-floor space chronicles Boca's rise from neighborhood club in 1905 to a world-class team. ⊠ *Brandsen 805, at del Valle Iberlucea, La Boca* ☎ *11/4309–4700 stadium, 11/4362–1100 museum* ⊕ *www.bocasistemas.com.ar, www.musoboquense.com* ⊠ *Museum: 7.90 pesos. Stadium: 7.90 pesos. Museum and stadium: 12.90 pesos* ☉ *Museum daily 10–6 except when Boca plays at home; stadium tours hourly 11–5 (English usually available, call ahead to check).*

8 Fundación Proa (Prow Foundation). This thoroughly modern art museum is a refreshing addition to the traditional neighborhood—the building fuses classic Italianate architecture with modern elements to represent the prow of a ship. Choice international exhibits, concerts, and events take place year-round. After you're done looking at the artwork, you can watch the sun set over the river from the terrace. English versions of all exhibition information are available. ⊠ *Av. Pedro de Mendoza 1929, La Boca* ☎ *11/4303–0909* ⊕ *www.proa.org* ☜ *3 pesos* ⊘ *Tues.–Sun. 11–7.*

9 Museo de Bellas Artes de La Boca de Artistas Argentinos (La Boca Fine Arts Museum of Argentine Artists). Artist and philanthropist Benito Quinquela Martín donated this building to the state to create a cultural center in 1933. Then he personally set out to fill it from top to bottom with an extensive collection of works by Argentine artists. You'll also find some 800 works by Martín, who was known for his vibrant depictions of the port area. The view from the terrace alone makes the museum worth a visit. Signs about the history of the museum are translated into English, but nothing else is. ⊠ *Av. Pedro de Mendoza 1835, La Boca* ☎ *11/4301–1080* ☜ *3 pesos* ⊘ *Tues.–Fri. 10–5, weekends 11–5.*

La Recoleta

This neighborhood to the east of El Centro has seen it all. It was settled in the 1700s by the Franciscan Recoleto friars. The needs of the spirit eventually gave way to those of the flesh, and the neighborhood became home to brothels and tango halls. In the late 1800s the elite swarmed here to escape yellow fever, and the district remains upscale and European in style. People-watching at sidewalk bars and cafés here is an art.

TIMING &
PRECAUTIONS
You can explore La Recoleta in half a day, though you could easily spend a full morning or afternoon in the cemetery or museums alone. This area is relatively safe day and night; still, be aware of your surroundings.

WHAT TO SEE   **Basílica de Nuestra Señora del Pilar.**
13 This basilica beside the famous Cementerio de la Recoleta on Junín is where Buenos Aires's elite families hold weddings and other ceremonies. It was built by the Franciscan Recoleto friars in 1732, and is considered a national treasure for its six German baroque-style altars, the central one overlaid with Peruvian engraved silver, and relics sent by Spain's King Carlos III. In the church cloisters,

> ### FUN TIMES
>
> On weekends the entire area around the basilica and cemetery teems with artisans and street performers in one of the city's largest artisan fairs, known as **La Feria de Plaza Francia.**

which date from 1716, is the **Museo de los Claustros del Pilar,** a small museum of religious artifacts as well as pictures and photographs documenting the Recoleta area's evolution. There are excellent views of the cemetery from the small upstairs windows. More of the church's former cloisters and internal patios of the Franciscan monks have been converted into **Centro Cultural La Recoleta** (⊠ Junín1930 ☎ 11/4803–1040 ⊕ www.centroculturalrecoleta.org ⊘ Tues.–Fri. 2–9, Weekends 10–9), a dynamic cultural center with exhibits, performances, and workshops. Kids love the minimuseum inside it, whose name, Prohibido No Tocar (Not Touching Is Forbidden), says it all. At the end of a *veredita* (little sidewalk), you'll find the Paseo del Pilar lined with expensive places to eat and the Buenos Aires Design Center.

⑫ **Cementerio de La Recoleta** (La Recoleta Cemetery). The ominous gates,
Fodor'sChoice Doric-columned portico, and labyrinthine pathways of the oldest ceme-
★ tery in Buenos Aires (1822) lend a sense of foreboding to this virtual city of the dead. The cemetery covers 13½ acres and has more than 6,400 elaborate vaulted tombs and majestic mausoleums, 70 of which have been declared historic monuments. The mausoleums resemble chapels, Greek temples, pyramids, and miniature mansions. This is the final resting place for the nation's most illustrious figures. The administrative offices at the entrance provide a free map, and caretakers can help you locate the more intriguing tombs, such as the embalmed remains of Eva Perón and her family; Napoléon Bonaparte's granddaughter; the brutal *caudillo* (dictator) Facundo Quiroga, buried standing, at his request; and prominent landowner Dorrego Ortiz Basualdo, in the most monumental sepulchre, complete with chandelier. ⊠ *Junín 1760, La Recoleta* ☎ *11/4803–1594* ⊠ *Free* ☉ *Daily 8–5:30.*

★ ⑭ **Museo Nacional de Bellas Artes** (National Museum of Fine Arts). Some 11,000 works of art—from drawings and paintings to statues and tapestries—are displayed in a building that used to be the city's waterworks. The museum's exhibits of significant international and local masters range from medieval times to the postmodern era, and the collection of 19th- and 20th-century Argentine art is its crowning achievement. You'll also find a gift shop, library, and cafeteria here. Multitasking security staff in the entrance hall are too rushed to deal with questions, and although the themed guided tours are excellent, they're only offered in Spanish. If you only speak English, check out the MP3 audio guides (15 pesos) in the scant gift shop at the bottom of the stairs. ⊠ *Av. del Libertador 1473, La Recoleta* ☎ *11/4803–0802 tours (in Spanish)* ⊕ *www.mnba. org.ar* ⊠ *Free* ☉ *Tues.–Fri. 12:30–7:30, weekends 9:30–7:30.*

⑮ **Museo Nacional de Arte Decorativo** (National Museum of Decorative Art). This dignified, harmonious French neoclassical landmark houses a fascinating collection of period furnishings, silver, and objets d'art— but it's worth the price of admission just to enter this breathtaking structure. The museum also contains Asian art as well as the Zubov Collection of miniatures from Imperial Russia. Stop in for tea or lunch at the elegant museum café, Errázuriz. ⊠ *Av. del Libertador 1902, La Recoleta* ☎ *11/4801–8248* ⊕ *www.mnad.org* ⊠ *2 pesos, free Tues.* ☉ *Tues.–Sun. 2–7; free guided tours in English Sun. at 5:30.*

Palermo

With nearly 350 acres of parks, wooded areas, and lakes, Palermo provides a peaceful escape from the rush of downtown. Families flock here on weekends to picnic, suntan, bicycle, in-line skate, and jog. The polo field and hippodrome make this the city's nerve center for equestrian activities. One of the largest barrios, Palermo is also one of the most

Horsing Around

IT'S SAID THAT THE MIGHTY Argentine Thoroughbreds contributed greatly to the British victory in the South African Boer War. Argentines import select stock for breeding swift horses, prized throughout the world. Although the past 40 years of economic instability have handicapped the industry, Argentine horses still win their share of races worldwide. Catch the Thoroughbreds in action at the **Hipódromo Argentino de Palermo** (⊠ Av. del Libertador 4101, Palermo ☎ 11/4777-9009). In Argentina's golden days the 100,000-capacity grandstand was always full, and even now major races pull a crowd. The 1878 belle-époque architecture and gardens give an elegant touch to the sport. Check the *Buenos Aires Herald* for schedules.

Major polo tournaments take place at the **Campo Argentino de Polo**

(Argentine Polo Field; ⊠ Av. del Libertador 4000 at Dorrego, Palermo). The stunning athletic showmanship displayed at these events is a source of national pride—indeed, the top-ranked polo players in the world are all Argentine. Admission to autumn (March–May) and spring (September–December) matches is free. The much-heralded Campeonato Argentino Abierto (Argentine Open Championship) takes place in November; admission runs 15 to 200 pesos. You can by tickets in advance by phone through **Ticketek** (☎ 11/4323-7200) or at the polo field on the day of the event. For polo match information contact the **Asociación Argentina de Polo** (☎ 11/4331-4646 ⊕ www.aapolo.com).

---

dynamic, with several distinct sub-neighborhoods: Palermo Viejo has classic Spanish-style architecture; Las Cañitas, Palermo Hollywood, and SoHo have trendy shopping, nightlife, and dining. Some of the most exclusive and expensive real estate in Buenos Aires can be found here, in opulent Palermo Chico, an elegant residential area, and in the prime properties lining the Avenida del Libertador and overlooking the parks.

TIMING An even-pace ramble through Palermo should take no more than two hours, though you could easily spend an entire afternoon at the zoo, Japanese Garden, and the Botanical Garden. If you're up for shopping, visit the Alto Palermo shopping center (at the Bulnes stop on Line D) or the entire length of shops and boutiques along Avenida Santa Fe.

WHAT TO SEE **Jardín Botánico Carlos Thays.** With 18 acres of gardens and 5,500 vari-
20 eties of exotic and local flora, the Charles Thays Botanical Garden is an unexpected green haven wedged between three busy Palermo streets. Different sections re-create the environments of Asia, Africa, Oceania, Europe, and the Americas. Among the treasures is the Chinese "tree of gold," purportedly the only one of its kind. Winding paths lead to hidden statues, a brook, and past the resident cats and dragonflies. The central area contains a beautiful greenhouse brought from France in 1900 and the exposed-brick botanical school and library. ⊠ *Av. Santa Fe 3951,*

Palermo ☎ *11/4832–1552* ✉ *Free* ⊙ *Sept.–Mar., daily 8–8; Apr.–Aug., daily 9–6.*

🐾 ⓳ **Jardín Zoológico.** You enter through the quasi-Roman triumphal arch into the architecturally eclectic, 45-acre city zoo. The pens, mews, statuary, and fountains themselves—many dating from the zoo's opening in 1874—are well worth a look. Jorge Luis Borges said the recurring presence of tigers in his work was inspired by time spent here. Among the expected zoo community are a few surprises: a rare albino tiger; indigenous monkeys, known to perform lewd acts for their audiences; and llamas (watch out—they spit). Smaller animals roam freely, and there are play areas for children, a petting farm, and a seal show. *Mateos* (horse-drawn carriages) stand poised at the entrance to whisk you around. ✉ *Avs. General Las Heras and Sarmiento, Palermo* ☎ *11/4806–7412* ⊕ *www. zoobuenosaires.com.ar* ✉ *8 pesos* ⊙ *Tues.–Sun. 10–5:30.*

★ ⓲ **Museo Evita.** Eva Duarte de Perón, known universally as Evita, was the wife of populist president Juan Domingo Perón and one of the most important and controversial figures of recent Argentine history. She unfailingly caused extreme reactions and was both revered as a saint by her working-class followers and despised by the anglophile oligarchy of the time. The excellent Museo Evita tries to get away from images of Madonna belting out "Don't Cry For Me Argentina" and convey as many facts about Evita's life and works as possible.

The main entrance leads into a columned medieval-style hall watched over by portraits of Evita and General Perón. To the right, a darkened room screening intense footage of thousands of mourners queuing to see Evita's body begins the well-labeled route through the collection. Evita's humble origins and life as a B-list actress before meeting Perón are documented on the ground floor.

Upstairs, shining parquet, heavy wood doors, and ornamental stone molding surround videos and artifacts that tell the tale of Evita's political career, particularly the social aid programs she instituted and her key role in getting women the vote. Evita's reputation as national fashion plate is reflected in the many designer outfits on display. The final rooms follow Evita's withdrawal from political life and her death from cancer at age 33. Laminated cards with English translations of the exhibits are available in each room and at the ticket booth. Knowledgeable, friendly staffers answer questions enthusiastically. Excellent guided visits are available in Spanish or English but must be arranged by phone in advance. Don't pass up a creamy slice of *torta de ricotta* (ricotta cheesecake) and a *café con leche* (coffee with frothy milk) at one of the museum café's outside tables, shaded by classy black umbrellas. ✉ *Lafinur 2988, 1 block north of Av. Las Heras, Palermo* ☎ *11/4807–9433* ⊕ *www.museoevita. org* ✉ *5 pesos* ⊙ *Tues.–Sun. 1–7* Ⓜ *D to Plaza Italia.*

⓰ **Museo MALBA** (Museo de Arte de Latinoamericano de Buenos Aires). This
Fodor's Choice fabulous museum has more than 220 works from the private collection
★ of businessman and founder Eduardo Constantini. The sleek, modern structure is home to one of the largest collections of Latin American art

in the world, including original works by Frida Kahlo, Fernando Botero, and a slew of Argentine artists. The museum also features seasonal exhibitions, lectures, movies, and live music. The café is a fashionable place to rest with a cup of coffee and some cake. ⊠ *Av. Presidente Figueroa Alcorta 3415, Palermo* ☎ *11/4808–6500* ⊕ *www.malba.org.ar* ☞ *7 pesos, free on Wed.* ⊙ *Thurs.—Mon. noon–8, Wed. noon–9.*

★ ☺ ⑰ **Parque Tres de Febrero** has nearly 200 acres of lawns, copses, lakes, and trails, but is really a crazy-quilt of smaller parks known locally as Los Bosques de Palermo. Rich grass and shady trees make this an urban oasis, although the busy roads and horn-honking drivers that crisscross the park never quite let you forget what city you're in. South of Avenida Figueroa Alcorta you can take part in organized tai chi and exercise classes or impromptu soccer matches; you can also jog, bike, in-line skate, or take a boat out on the small lake.

If you're looking for a sedate activity, try the **Museo de Artes Plásticas Eduardo Sívori** (Eduardo Sívori Art Museum; ⊠ Av. Infanta Isabel 555, Palermo ☎ 11/4774–9452 ⊕ www.museosivori.org ☞ 3 pesos, Wed. free ⊙ Tues.–Fri. noon–6, weekends 10–6), exhibiting 19th- and 20th-century Argentine art. Close to the Museo de Artes Plásticas Eduardo Sívori is the **Paseo del Rosedal** (Rose Garden; ⊠ Avs. Infanta Isabel and Iraola), where approximately 15,000 rosebushes, representing more than 1,000 different species, bloom seasonally.

The sci-fi exterior of the landmark **Planetario Galileo Galilei** (Galileo Galilei Planetarium; ⊠ Avs. Sarmiento and Belisario Roldán ☎ 11/4771–6629 ☞ Free ⊙ Weekdays 9–5, weekends 3–8) holds more appeal than its flimsy content. A highlight is the authentic asteroid at the entrance; the pond with swans, geese, and ducks is a favorite with children.

Arched wooden bridges and walkways traverse still waters in the **Jardín Japonés** (Japanese Garden) (⊠ Avs. Casares and Adolfo Berro ☎ 11/4804–4922 ⊕ www.jardinjapones.com.ar ☞ 3 pesos ⊙ Daily 10–6). A variety of shrubs and flowers frame the ponds, which brim with koi carp. The traditional teahouse, where you can enjoy adzuki-bean sweets and tea, overlooks a zen garden.

On sunny weekends Los Bosques de Palermo get crowded and garbage-strewn, as this is where families come for strolls or picnics. Street vendors sell refreshments and *choripan* (chorizo sausage in a bread roll) within the park, and there are also many posh cafés lining the Paseo de la Infanta (running from Libertador toward Sarmiento in the park). ⊠ *Bounded by Avs. del Libertador, Sarmiento, Leopoldo Lugones, and Dorrego, Palermo.*

Where to Eat

By Robin Goldstein

Although international cuisine can be found throughout Buenos Aires, it's the traditional *parrilla*—a restaurant serving grilled meat—that Argentines (and most visitors) flock to. These restaurants vary from upscale eateries to local spots. The meal often starts off with *chorizo* (a large, spicy sausage), *morcilla* (blood sausage), and *chinchulines* (tripe), before moving on to the myriad cuts of beef that make Argentina famous. Don't pass up the rich *provoleta* (grilled provolone cheese sprinkled with olive oil and oregano) and garlic-soaked grilled red peppers as garnish.

Cafés are a big part of Buenos Aires culture: open long hours, they constantly brim with locals knocking back a quick *cafecito* (espresso) or taking their time over a *café con leche* (coffee with milk) served with *medialunas* (croissants) or *facturas* (small pastries). Many places have bilingual menus or someone on hand who is eager to practice his or her English.

El Centro

Restaurants here specialize more in lunch than dinner; you can expect crowds of office workers at midday. You can also expect much more traditional Argentine fare than the modern fusion cuisine that characterizes hipper neighborhoods.

CAFÉS ✕ **Confitería La Ideal.** Part of the charm of this spacious 1918 coffeeshop-
¢–$ milonga is its sense of nostalgia: think fleur-de-lis motifs, time-worn European furnishings, and stained glass. No wonder they chose to film the 1998 movie *The Tango Lesson* here. La Ideal is famous for its *palmeritas* (glazed cookies) and tea service. Tango lessons are offered Monday through Thursday from noon to 3, with a full-blown tango ball Wednesday and Saturday from 3 to 8. The waitstaff seem to be caught up in their own dreams—service is listless. ⊠ *Suipacha 384, at Av. Corrientes, El Centro* ☎ *11/4326–0521* ▤ *No credit cards* ☉ *No breakfast weekends* Ⓜ *C to C. Pellegrini, D to 9 de Julio.*

★ ¢–$ ✕ **Gran Café Tortoni.** In the city's first confitería (confectionery), established in 1858, art nouveau decor and high ceilings transport you back in time. Carlos Gardel, one of Argentina's most famous tango stars; writer Jorge Luis Borges; local and visiting dignitaries; and intellectuals have all eaten and sipped coffee here. Don't miss the *chocolate con churros* (thick hot chocolate with baton-shaped donuts for dipping). You must reserve ahead of time for the nightly tango shows, for which you'll pay a 20-peso cover. ⊠ *Av. de Mayo 825, Plaza de Mayo* ☎ *11/4342–4328* ⊕ *www.cafetortoni.com.ar* ▤ *AE, MC, V* Ⓜ *A to Perú.*

ITALIAN ✕ **La Parolaccia.** A polite waitstaff serves decent Italian food in a warm,
$–$$ relaxing environment. Lasagna and other pasta dishes are well executed. The real reason to go, though, is for the amazing-value three-course set lunch—including a free lemon digestif—which will set you back 12 whole pesos or so. It's enough to make you wonder why you live in such an overpriced country—wherever that might be. ⊠ *Riobamba 146, El Centro* ☎ *11/4812–1053* ▤ *AE, MC, V* Ⓜ *C to Congreso, B to Callao.*

NEW ARGENTINE ✕ **Restó.** Reserve at least a week in advance. Seriously. After training with
$$$$ two of the world's most renowned chefs—Spain's Ferran Adriá and
Fodor's Choice France's Michel Bras—chef-owner María Barrutia came back to Buenos
★ Aires and made a very big splash in this very small space, hidden deep inside the Society of Architects. Three set-price menus pair exotic ingredients like *codorniz* (quail) with Argentina's more traditional foods

like *zapallo* (squash). They're all honored with classic European treatments, including expertly reduced sauces. The molten chocolate cake, adapted from Bras, is unforgettable. ⊠ *Montevideo 938, El Centro* ☎ *11/4816–6711* ▭ *No credit cards* Ⓜ *D to Callao* ☉ *Closed Sat.–Sun. No dinner Mon.–Wed.* ⚜ *Reservations essential.*

★ **$$$$** ✕ **Tomo I.** The famed Concaro sisters have made this restaurant, on the mezzanine of the Hotel Panamericano, a household name. The French-inspired menu has excellent fried, breaded calf brains, and a chocolate tart that oozes warm, dark ganache. White linen–covered tables are set far apart in the romantic red room, making quiet conversation easy. Service is arguably tops in the city. ⊠ *Carlos Pellegrini 521, El Centro* ☎ *11/ 4326–6698* ⚜ *Reservations recommended* ▭ *AE, DC, MC, V* ☉ *Closed Sun. No lunch Sat.* Ⓜ *B to Carlos Pellegrini, D to 9 de Julio.*

PIZZA ✕ **Las Cuartetas.** The huge, flavor-packed deep-dish pizzas are a chal-
⟲ **¢–$** lenge to finish. If you want, you can walk up to the bar and order just a slice; the simplest version—*muzzarella*—is usually the freshest. They also do a good *fugazza* (onions, but no tomatoes). Las Cuartetas is a good place for a quick solo lunch—among the mobs at the Formica-top tables you'll see not just older men but also women eating alone, a rarity in Buenos Aires. ⊠ *Corrientes 838, El Centro* ☎ *11/4326–0171* ▭ *No credit cards* ☉ *No lunch Sun.* Ⓜ *B to C. Pellegrini, C to Diagonal Norte, D to Estación 9 de Julio.*

SPANISH ✕ **El Imparcial.** Founded in 1860, the oldest restaurant in town owes its
$–$$ name (meaning impartial) to its neutrality in the face of the warring political factions of Buenos Aires's Spanish immigrants. Hand-painted tiles, heavy wooden furniture, and paintings of Spain are all strong reminders of the restaurant's origins, as are the polite, elderly waiters, many of whom are from the old country. Talking politics is no longer banned within, good news for today's Argentines, who keep coming to El Imparcial for the renowned *puchero* as well as seafood specialties like paella. ⊠ *Hipólito Yrigoyen 1201, Plaza de Mayo* ☎ *11/4383–2919* ▭ *AE, DC, MC, V* Ⓜ *C to Av. de Mayo, A to Lima.*

TRADITIONAL ✕ **Sabot.** You might consider Sabot a find if you're a tourist—but this
ARGENTINE dignified, timeless lunch room is part of daily life to scores of down-
★ **$–$$$$** town businesspeople. For more than three decades they've been doing the same things, day after (week)day. This means impeccable service, fresh centolla, and a *puchero* that gets at the very essence of what boiled meat is all about. ⊠ *25 de Mayo 756, between Cordoba and Viamonte, El Centro* ☎ *11/4313–6587* ▭ *AE, DC, MC, V* Ⓜ *B to L. N. Alem* ☉ *Closed Sat.–Sun. No dinner* ⚜ *Reservations essential.*

¢–$$ ✕ **El Palacio de la Papa Frita.** This longtime standby is popular for its fanciful old-world atmosphere and hearty traditional meals—succulent steaks, homemade pastas, and fresh salads. The *papas soufflé* (inflated french fries) reign supreme; try them *a la provençal* (sprinkled with garlic and parsley) along with the classic *bife a medio caballo* (steak topped with a fried egg). ⊠ *Lavalle 735, El Centro* ☎ *11/4393–5849* Ⓜ *C to Lavalle* ⊠ *Av. Corrientes 1612, El Centro* ☎ *11/4374–8063* Ⓜ *B to Callao* ▭ *AE, DC, MC, V.*

San Telmo

CAFÉ
★ ¢–$

✗ **Bar Dorrego.** It probably hasn't changed much for the last 100 years or so. Dark wood and politely aloof waiters set the stage; good coffee, *tragos* (alcoholic drinks), sangria, and snacks complete the scene. On nice days you can sit out on Plaza Dorrego and take in one of San Telmo's most classic hubs of activity, most lively during the Sunday festival. ⊠ *Defensa 1098 and Humberto I, on Plaza Dorrego, San Telmo* ☎ *11/4361–0141* ▭ *No credit cards* Ⓜ *C or E to Independencia.*

NEW ARGENTINE
$–$$

✗ **La Farmacia.** Mismatched tables and chairs, comfy leather sofas, and poptastic colors fill this cute, century-old corner house that used to be a traditional pharmacy. Generous breakfasts and afternoon teas are served on the cozy ground floor, lunch and dinner are in the first-floor dining room, and you can have late-night drinks on the bright-yellow roof terrace. Arts and dance workshops are run upstairs, and the building has two boutiques selling local designers' work. The modern Argentine dishes are simple but well done. ⊠ *Bolívar 898, San Telmo* ☎ *11/4300–6151* ▭ *No credit cards* ⊙ *Closed Mon.* Ⓜ *C or E to Independencia.*

PARRILLA
$–$$$
Fodor'sChoice
★

✗ **La Brigada.** You'd be hard-pressed to do better for Argentine steaks, anytime, anyplace. Amid elaborate decor, including scores of soccer mementos, a courtly staff will treat you to unimpeachable *mollejas* (sweetbreads) and *chinchulines de chivito* (kid intestines), plus a brilliant array of grilled steaks. The baby beef is tender enough to cut with a spoon. Skip the sister restaurant in Barrio Norte, which isn't up to the same standard. ⊠ *Estados Unidos 465, between Bolívar and Defensa, San Telmo* ☎ *11/4361–5557* ⬧ *Reservations recommended* ▭ *AE, DC, MC, V* ⊙ *Closed Mon.* Ⓜ *C or E to Independencia.*

La Boca

PARRILLA
$–$$$

✗ **El Obrero.** When the rock band U2 played Buenos Aires and asked to be taken to a traditional Argentine restaurant, they were brought to this legendary hole-in-the-wall. For 50 years El Obrero has served juicy grilled steaks, sweetbreads, sausages, and chicken. The extensive blackboard menu includes *rabas* (fried calamari) and puchero. Try the *budín de pan* (Argentine version of bread pudding). This spot is popular, so expect a short wait. La Boca is sketchy at night, so lunch is preferable; in any case, take a taxi. ⊠ *Augustín R. Caffarena 64, La Boca* ☎ *11/4363–9912* ▭ *No credit cards* ⊙ *Closed Sun.*

La Recoleta

CAFÉ
¢–$$

✗ **La Biela.** Porteños linger at this quintessential sidewalk café opposite the Recoleta Cemetery, sipping espressos, discussing politics, and people-watching—all of which are best done at a table beneath the shade of an ancient rubber tree. ⊠ *Quintana 600, at Junín, La Recoleta* ☎ *11/4804–0449* ▭ *V.*

FRENCH
★ $$$$

✗ **La Bourgogne.** White tablecloths and fresh roses emphasize the restaurant's innate elegance. A sophisticated waitstaff brings you complimentary hors d'oeuvres as you choose from chef Jean-Paul Bondoux's creations, which include foie gras, rabbit, escargots, chateaubriand, *côte de veau* (veal steak), and wild boar cooked in cassis. The fixed-price

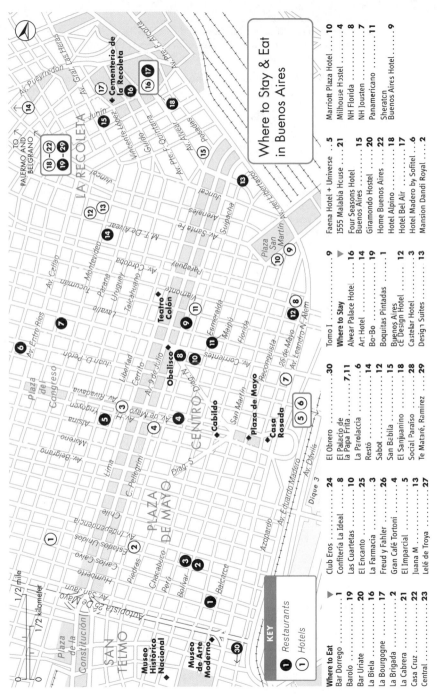

Where to Stay & Eat in Buenos Aires

KEY

▶ Restaurants
① Hotels

Where to Eat

Bar Dorrego	1
Barolo	19
Bar Uriate	20
La Biela	16
La Bourgogne	17
La Brigada	2
La Cabrera	21
Casa Cruz	22
Central	23
Club Eros	24
Confitería La Ideal	8
Las Cuartetas	10
El Encanto	25
La Farmacia	3
Freud y Fahler	26
Gran Café Tortoni	4
El Imparcial	5
Juana M	13
Lelé de Troya	27
El Obrero	30
El Palacio de la Papa Frita	7,11
La Parolaccia	6
Restó	14
Sabot	12
San Babila	15
El Sanjuanino	18
Social Paraíso	28
Te Mataré, Ramírez	29
Tomo I	9

Where to Stay

Alvear Palace Hotel	16
Art Hotel	14
Bo-Bo	19
Boquitas Pintadas	1
Buenos Aires cE Design Hotel	12
Castelar Hotel	3
Design Suites	13
Faena Hotel + Universe	5
1555 Malabia House	21
Four Seasons Hotel Buenos Aires	15
Giramondo Hostel	20
Home Buenos Aires	22
Hotel Alpino	18
Hotel Bel Air	17
Hotel Madero by Sofitel	6
Mansion Dandi Royal	2
Marriott Plaza Hotel	10
Milhouse Hostel	4
NH Florida	8
NH Jousten	7
Panamericano	11
Sheraton Buenos Aires Hotel	9

menu is more affordable than à la carte selections. ✉ *Alvear Palace Hotel, Ayacucho 2027, La Recoleta* ☎ *11/4805–3857 or 11/4808–2100* ⌨ *Reservations essential* 🏠 *Jacket and tie* ▭ *AE, DC, MC, V* ⊘ *Closed Sun. No lunch Sat.*

ITALIAN
$$$–$$$$ ✗ **San Babila.** This trattoria is known for its excellent handmade pastas and classic Italian dishes created from the century-old recipes of the chef's grandmother. *Cappelletti di formaggio* (cheese-filled round pasta) and *risotto alla milanese* are good bets. Prices are high, but there are fixed-price menus to choose from and a friendly English-speaking staff. The outdoor terrace is a treat. ✉ *R. M. Ortíz 1815, La Recoleta* ☎ *11/4804–1214* ▭ *AE, DC, MC, V* ⊘ *No lunch Mon.*

PARRILLA
$ ✗ **Juana M.** The minimalist chic decor of this basement restaurant stands in stark contrast to the menu: down-to-earth parrilla fare at good prices. Catch a glimpse of meats sizzling on the grill behind the salmon-color bar—the only swath of color—then head to your table to devour your steak and *chorizo* (fat, spicy sausage). The homemade pastas aren't bad, either. The staff is young and friendly. ✉ *Carlos Pellegrini 1535, La Recoleta* ☎ *11/4326–0462* ⊘ *No lunch Sat.* Ⓜ *C to San Martín.*

TRADITIONAL
ARGENTINE
¢–$$ ✗ **El Sanjuanino.** Northern Argentine fare is served at this long-established, if touristy, spot. El Sanjuanino is known city-wide for its tamales, *humitas* (steamed corn cakes wrapped in husks), and especially its empanadas, for which crowds of people line up to take out for a picnic in the park (they're 20% cheaper to go). But they also make good *locro, pollo a la piedra* (chicken pressed flat by stones), venison, and antelope stew; skip the boring, hamlike *lomito de cerdo* (pork steak). The decor in the cozy space borders on cheesy, with hanging hams and a stuffed deer head, but the feeling is still fun. ✉ *Posadas 1515 at Callao, La Recoleta* ☎ *11/4805–2683* ▭ *AE, MC, V.*

Palermo

ECLECTIC
$$–$$$ ✗ **Te Mataré, Ramírez.** Te Mataré, Ramírez, which translates as "I Will Kill You, Ramirez," is as unusual as it sounds. This self-styled "erotic restaurant" seduces with such dishes as "With Two Women" (caramelized chicken in a sherry, ginger, and grapefruit sauce) and desserts such as "Premature Palpitations of Pleasure" (warm white-chocolate cake). Thursday the temperature rises with a tastefully done "erotic theater" show and Wednesday night brings live jazz. Sip cocktails at the red-velvet bar as you peruse the illustrated menu or gaze at the erotic art collection. ✉ *Paraguay 4062, Palermo Soho* ☎ *11/4831–9156* Ⓜ *D to Scalabrini Ortíz* ✉ *Primera Junta 702, San Isidro* ☎ *11/4747–8618* ▭ *AE, DC, MC, V* ⊘ *Closed Mon. No lunch.*

$–$$ ✗ **Lelé de Troya.** Each room of this converted old house is drenched in a different color—from the walls to the chairs and plates—and the food is just as bold. The kitchen is on view from the vine-covered lemon-yellow patio, and you can watch as loaf after loaf of the restaurant's homemade bread is drawn from the clay oven. Follow dishes like salmon ravioli or mollejas in cognac with one of Lelé's many Middle Eastern and Italian desserts. The restaurant holds tango classes on Monday nights and has a changing art space. ✉ *Costa Rica 4901, Palermo Soho* ☎ *11/4832–2726* ▭ *AE, MC, V.*

NEW ARGENTINE **✕ Casa Cruz.** Trendsetters come and go, but there are few whose food
$$$$ is truly sublime. Casa Cruz impresses with its unmarked entrance, dim
FodorśChoice lighting, expanses of mahogany, and cozy banquettes. Chef Germán Mar-
★ titegui works rabbit medallions into a state of melting tenderness and
pairs crisped *morcilla* (blood sausage) with jammy fruit. Is this the single best restaurant in Buenos Aires? Believe the hype. ☒ *Uriarte 1656,
Palermo Soho* ☏ *11/4833–1112* ⊟ *AE, DC, MC, V* ☺ *Closed Sun. No
lunch* ⌖ *Reservations essential.*

★ **$$–$$$$** **✕ Bar Uriarte.** There is perhaps no place that better represents Palermo
Viejo's dining revolution than the bustling kitchen of Bar Uriarte, which
is enticingly set in the front of the restaurant, exposed to the street. In-
side lies a sophisticated bar with two intimate dining spaces. You can
even take your meal while lounging on a sofa. Chef Paula de Felipe's
dishes are as sleek as the surroundings. Best are the pizzas and other
dishes that come out of the prominent wood-fired mud oven. For lunch,
there's a ridiculously cheap prix-fixe. ☒ *Uriarte 1572, Palermo Soho*
☏ *11/4834–6004* ⊟ *AE, DC, MC, V.*

$$–$$$ **✕ Barolo.** Its opening in 1998 helped to spark Palermo Hollywood's emer-
gence as a dining mecca. It's on a quiet street in an old town house done
up in bright green and mauve. Don't miss the Patagonian lamb or the
risotto with cognac-sautéed sweetbreads, spinach, Gruyère cheese, and
Chardonnay. Wines of the month are chalked up on a blackboard over
the bar. ☒ *Bonpland 1612, Palermo Hollywood* ☏ *11/4772–0841*
⊟ *AE, V* ☺ *Closed Sun. No lunch Sat.*

$$ **✕ Central.** This candlelit space wins you over with its looks; so do the
servers, who are uniformly sexy, whether male or female. You can chill
out at the bar or eat side-by-side on low-slung couches. Don't expect
fireworks from the menu, but the cocktails are well thought out and they
do an unusually good job with *rollos de pollo* (chicken rolled with ham
and cheese). In keeping with the spirit of the neighborhood, there are
also plenty of lighter and vegetarian options (how else would everyone
here be so thin?). ☒ *Costa Rica 5644, Palermo Hollywood* ☏ *11/
4776–7370* ⊟ *AE, DC, MC, V.*

$–$$ **✕ Social Paraíso.** Simple, airy, friendly, elegant—this Med-Argentine
bistro has just the vibe for a lunch or dinner stop after a cheery round
of shopping. Pastas such as ravioli are best; vegetarians will also be happy
here, with inventive entrées that feature meaty vegetables like eggplant.
Social Paraíso has also refreshingly kept its prices low even as its fame
has grown, and the two-course lunch for (at last check) 12 pesos is a
gift. ☒ *Honduras 5182, Palermo Soho* ☏ *4831–4556* ⊟ *AE, MC, V*
☺ *Closed Mon. No dinner Sun.*

¢–$$ **✕ Freud y Fahler.** Red walls, screens of colored glass, and vintage chan-
deliers give warmth to this glassed-in corner restaurant along a peace-
ful cobblestoned street. The menu is short but imaginative; try the
braised lamb, if available, perhaps followed by spiced white-chocolate
cake with plum ice cream and orange sauce. The young, well-informed
staff gives friendly advice on food and wine. The lunch menus, which
are more vegetable-oriented, are an excellent value. ☒ *Gurruchaga
1750, Palermo Soho* ☏ *11/4833–2153* ⊟ *AE, V* ☺ *Closed Sun.*

PARRILLA ★ ✕ **La Cabrera.** Palermo's best parrilla is on the quiet corner of Cabrera and Thames. Fun ancient paraphernalia hangs everywhere, giving the feel of an old grocery store. La Cabrera is particularly known for its excellent *provoleta de queso de cabra* (grilled goat cheese) and its *chinchulines de cordero* (small intestines of lamb). Try also the *cuadril vuelta y vuelta* (rare rump steak) and the mollejas. ⊠ *Cabrera 5099, Palermo Hollywood* ☎ *11/4831–7002* ☾ *No lunch Mon.*

★ ¢–$ ✕ **El Encanto.** The hardest thing about eating in this soccer-memorabilia-packed space is getting a seat. Come early or come late; otherwise, it will be packed. Don't expect tip-top service; do expect perfectly good grilled meat and a certain chaos that makes for a fun evening—if you're in the mood for chaos, that is. ⊠ *Bonpland 1690, Palermo Hollywood* ☎ *No phone* ▤ *No credit cards.*

TRADITIONAL ✕ **Club Eros.** A basic dining room attached to an old soccer club, Club
ARGENTINE Eros has developed a cult following for its downscale charm. The ex-
¢–$ cellent renditions of classic *criolla* fare at rock-bottom prices have begun to draw young Palermo trendies as well as older customers. There's no menu, but you can confidently order a crispy milanesa, or, if available, a bife de chorizo and fries. Pasta sauces fall flat, but the flan con dulce de leche is one of the best (and biggest) in town. ⊠ *Uriarte 1609, Palermo Soho* ☎ *11/4832–1313* ▤ *No credit cards.*

Where to Stay

By Brian
Byrnes

Buenos Aires is experiencing a tourism boom unlike any in its history. The cheap peso has made it one of the planet's most affordable cities, and dollar- and euro-wielding visitors are arriving in record numbers. How is this good news in terms of where to stay? Well, lots of new hotels have been built, and many existing ones have been renovated, so you have more (and better) choices than ever, regardless of preferences and price limits.

Smaller hotels have a family-run feel, with all the charming quirks that entails. Rooms in medium-price hotels may be smaller than expected, but the facilities and service are usually of high quality. Posh properties obviously provide world-class comforts. In general, hotels have bidets (a nod to the Continent) and Internet and/or e-mail access (a nod to going global) but not, say, ice makers or vending machines (a nod to the fact that South Americans have different ideas about creature comforts than their neighbors to the north). As a rule, check-in is after 3 PM, checkout before noon; smaller hotels tend to be more flexible.

El Centro

$$$$ ⊞ **Marriott Plaza Hotel.** Built in 1909 and renovated in 2003, this land-
FodorśChoice mark hotel sits at the top of pedestrian-only Florida Street and over-
★ looks the leafy Plaza San Martín. The elegant lobby, crystal chandeliers, and swanky cigar bar evoke Argentina's opulent, if distant, past. Rooms are comfortable and clean, if not particularly spacious. The hotel is next to both the Kavanagh Building, a 1930's art deco masterpiece that was once South America's tallest, and the Basilica Santísimo Sacramento, where renowned Argentines of all stripes, like Diego Maradona, have tied the

knot. Exploring the myriad nooks and crannies of this grand old hotel is part of its timeless appeal. ☒ *Florida 1005, El Centro, 1005* ☏ *11/4318–3000, 800/228–9290 in U.S.* ⊕ *www.marriott.com* ☎ *313 rooms, 12 suites* ⌂ *2 restaurants, coffee shop, room service, IDD phones, in-room safes, minibars, cable TV with movies, in-room data ports, pool, gym, health club, hair salon, hot tub, sauna, bar, laundry service, concierge, DSL Internet, Wi-Fi in lobby, business services, meeting rooms* ☰ *AE, DC, MC, V* ⦿ *BP* Ⓜ *C to San Martín.*

★ **$$$** ⌂ **Buenos Aires cE Design Hotel.** It drips with coolness. The lobby's glass floor looks down to a small pool, just one example of the transparency theme that runs throughout. Floor-to-ceiling windows afford amazing views, and mirrors are placed for maximum effect. Rooms feel like pimped-out Tribeca lofts, with rotating flat-screen TVs—watch from bed or a leather recliner. Mattresses are high and mighty and covered in shades of brown and orange. Kudos to architect, Ernesto Goransky, who also did the Design Suites next door. ☒ *Marcelo T. Alvear 1695, El Centro, 1060* ☏ *11/5237–3100* ⊕ *www.designce.com* ☎ *28 rooms* ⌂ *In-room safes, hot tub, kitchenettes, cable TV, in-room data ports, pool, gym, bar, laundry service, DSL Internet, Wi-Fi in lobby, meeting room, travel services* ☰ *AE, DC, MC, V* Ⓜ *D to Callao.*

$$$ ⌂ **Panamericano.** The popular, upscale Panamericano is near the famed Teatro Colón and the landmark Obelisco. The lobby's checked-marble floors lead to large salons, a snazzy café, and an Irish pub. Rooms are spacious and elegant, with dark wooden headboards and smart furnishings. Don't miss a chance to dine in the outstanding Tomo I restaurant or at what must be the nation's highest sushi bar, Kasuga, on the 23rd floor. The top-floor pool and spa afford amazing views. Visit in the late afternoon to watch the soft pastels of a smoggy sunset give way to the neon glow on the world's widest avenue, Av. 9 de Julio. ☒ *Carlos Pellegrini 551, 1009* ☏ *11/4348–5000* ⊕ *www.panamericanobuenosaires.com* ☎ *345 rooms* ⌂ *3 restaurants, coffee shop, room service, IDD phones, in-room safes, mini-bars, cable TV, pool, gym, health club, sauna, bar, laundry service, concierge, DSL Internet, Wi-Fi in rooms, business services, meeting rooms, parking (fee)* ☰ *AE, DC, MC, V* Ⓜ *B to C. Pellegrini.*

$$$ ⌂ **Sheraton Buenos Aires Hotel.** What it lacks in charm, it makes up for in practicality, professionalism, and energy. There's always something happening here: a visiting dignitary, an international conference. Rooms are standard, clean, and well equipped, all of which explain the hotel's popularity among American businesspeople. The luxurious Park Tower Hotel, next door, has large, lavish rooms with round-the-clock butler service. When Latin heartthrobs like Luis Miguel or Ricky Martin are in town, they stay in the penthouse suite; scores of ecstatic Argentine females hold vigils outside. ☒ *San Martín 1225, El Centro, 1104* ☏ *11/4318–9000, 800/325–3535 in U.S.* ⊕ *www.sheraton.com* ☎ *713 rooms, 29 suites* ⌂ *2 restaurants, coffee shop, room service, IDD phones, in-room fax, in-room safes, minibars, cable TV with movies, in-room data ports, 2 tennis courts, 2 pools, fitness classes, gym, health club, hair salon, massage, sauna, bar, lobby lounge, babysitting, laundry service, concierge, DSL Internet, Wi-Fi in lobby, business services, convention center, meet-*

ing rooms, car rental, travel services, parking (fee), no-smoking rooms ⊟ *AE, DC, MC, V* ⏐◎⏐ *BP* Ⓜ *C to Retiro.*

$$ ⊞ **Design Suites.** It can be hard to find a well-located, modern, minimalist hotel that's also reasonably priced. This is it. The futuristic lobby cranks chill house music and has a slim little swimming pool that's often used for photo shoots with equally slim models. Sleek rooms have wooden floors, chrome furniture, and kitchenettes with espresso machines. You're close to excellent shopping on Avenida Santa Fe and in the stately Palacio Pizzurno. ⊠ *M. T. de Alvear 1683, El Centro, 1060* ☏ *11/4814–8700* ⊕ *www.designsuites.com* ⇅ *40 rooms* ⟐ *Restaurant, room service, in-room safes, some in-room hot tubs, some kitchenettes, cable TV, in-room data ports, pool, gym, bar, laundry service, DSL Internet, meeting room* ⊟ *AE, DC, MC, V* Ⓜ *D to Callao.*

$$ ⊞ **NH Florida.** Shiny parquet wood floors, extra fluffy pillows, and smiling young staffers are among the reasons to stay. The hotel sits in the shadow of the massive Harrod's Building; the famed British department store was once *the* place for porteños to shop, but it has been sitting dark and abandoned on Florida Street for years. A few blocks away, the NH Latino has similar decor and services. ⊠ *San Martín 839, El Centro, 1004* ☏ *11/4321–9850* ⊕ *www.nh-hoteles.com* ⇅ *148 rooms* ⟐ *Restaurant, IDD phones, in-room safes, minibars, cable TV, in-room data ports, bar, laundry service, DSL Internet, business services, free parking* ⊟ *AE, DC, MC, V* ⏐◎⏐ *BP* Ⓜ *C to San Martín.*

$$ ⊞ **NH Jousten.** The historic Jousten Building on crazy Avenida Corrientes has some of the most luxurious rooms in the NH chain, and has hosted the likes of Evita Perón over the years. Rooms have big, bouncy beds and handsome wood desks; the small bathrooms disappoint, though. The lobby café sits a half-story above the sidewalk and offers grand views of the chaos below. Suites have private terraces overlooking the city and the River Plate. ⊠ *Corrientes 280, El Centro, 1043* ☏ *11/ 4321–6750* ⊕ *www.nh-hoteles.com* ⇅ *80 rooms, 5 suites* ⟐ *Restaurant, room service, IDD phones, in-room safes, minibars, cable TV, in-room data ports, lobby lounge, babysitting, dry cleaning, laundry service, concierge, DSL Internet, Wi-Fi in lobby, business services, travel services* ⊟ *AE, DC, MC, V* ⏐◎⏐ *BP* Ⓜ *B to L. N. Alem.*

$ ⊞ **Castelar Hotel.** This 1929 hotel is a European potpourri: Spanish architecture, French interior design, Italian marble. Revolving doors lead to the impressive lobby bar–restaurant, whose shiny floor and bold bronze ornamentation are throwbacks to the days when Buenos Aires earned its reputation as the so-called Paris of Latin America. The charm stops there, though: tired rooms have sparse old furnishings. ⊠ *Av. de Mayo 1152, El Centro, 1085* ☏ *11/4383–5000* ⊕ *www.castelarhotel.com.ar* ⇅ *153 rooms, 7 suites* ⟐ *Restaurant, coffee shop, room service, IDD phones, in-room safes, minibars, health club, hair salon, massage, sauna, spa, Turkish bath, laundry service, Internet, business services, meeting room, parking (fee)* ⊟ *AE, MC, V* ⏐◎⏐ *BP* Ⓜ *A to Lima.*

¢ ⊞ **Milhouse Hostel.** This lovely and lively hostel goes the extra mile to make backpackers feel welcome. The house, which dates from the late 1800s, has been tricked out with funky artwork and accessories. Its three

floors overlook a beautiful tiled patio and all lead out to a sunny terrace. Morning yoga classes here may well be followed by rowdy beer-
swilling *asados* (barbecues). The dorm rooms are clean and big, and most
have private bathrooms. ⊠ *Hipólito Irigoyen 959, El Centro, 1086* ☎ *11/
4345–9604 or 11/4343–5038* ⊕ *www.milhousehostel.com* ⤳ *13 private rooms, 150 beds total* ⌂ *Restaurant, fans, Ping-Pong, bar, library,
laundry facilities, DSL Internet, travel services, parking (fee); no a/c, no
room phones, no room TVs* ⊟ *No credit cards* ⑩ *CP* Ⓜ *A to Piedras,
C to Av. de Mayo.*

San Telmo

$$$$
Fodor'sChoice
★

Ⓗ **Mansion Dandi Royal.** For a glimpse into early-20th-century high society, look no farther than this hotel. Owner and tango legend Hector
Villalba painstakingly transformed this 100-year-old mansion into both
a hotel and a tango academy. The 15 exquisite rooms are decorated with
classic wood furnishings and period murals. A stunning chandelier, a
sweeping staircase, and original artwork lend still more authenticity. Tango
lessons take place daily in the gorgeous dance hall, and every evening
the staff accompanies dancers to milongas, all-night tango parties that
take place all over town. ⊠ *Piedras 922, San Telmo, 1070* ☎ *11/
4307–7623* ⊕ *www.mansiondandiroyal.com* ⤳ *15 rooms* ⌂ *Room
service, IDD phones, in-room safes, pool, gym, spa, hair salon, cable
TV, bar, library, laundry service, DSL Internet, meeting room, airport
shuttle, parking (fee)* ⊟ *AE, DC, MC, V* Ⓜ *C to San Juan.*

$

Ⓗ **Boquitas Pintadas.** The whimsically named "Little Painted Mouths"
(a tribute to Manuel Puig's novel of the same name) is a self-proclaimed
"pop hotel," and the German owner, Heike Thelen, goes out of her way
to keep things weird and wild. World-famous "nude" photographer,
Spencer Tunick, staged a shoot here in 2002 and ended up spending the
night. Local artists redecorate the six rooms every two months. The restaurant serves dishes not found often in the city, including goulash. DJs spin
tunes until dawn. The hotel is in the Constitución neighborhood, west
of San Telmo, across Avenida 9 de Julio. Use caution at night; the surrounding area is dodgy. ⊠ *Estados Unidos 1393, Constitución, 1101*
☎ *11/4381–6064* ⊕ *www.boquitas-pintadas.com.ar* ⤳ *5 rooms, 1
suite* ⌂ *Restaurant, room service, cable TV, bar, library, nightclub, dry
cleaning, laundry service, Wi-Fi Internet, business services, travel services* ⊟ *No credit cards* Ⓜ *E to San José.*

Puerto Madero

The newest barrio has a view of the sprouting skyline on one side and
the exclusive yacht club on the other. Once an abandoned port area, its
multimillion dollar facelift imitated that of London's Docklands. Its main
draw is a chic riverside promenade, which has become *the* place to go
for a casual stroll, elegant dining, and nightlife.

$$$$
Fodor'sChoice
★

Ⓗ **Faena Hotel + Universe.** Lenny Kravitz and his entourage stayed here,
and actor Owen Wilson said it was, "one of the coolest hotels I've ever
been to in my life." If a rock god and the Butterscotch Stallion can dig
this creation of Argentine fashion impresario Alan Faena and famed
French architect Philippe Starck, then chances are you can, too. Rooms

are feng-shui perfect with rich reds and crisp whites. Velvet curtains and Venetian blinds open electronically to river and city views; marble floors fill expansive baths; velvet couches, leather armchairs, flat-screen TVs, and surround-sound stereos lend still more luxury. The so-called Experience Managers are basically personal assistants, making reservations and tending to every whim. Other highlights are two excellent restaurants, an elaborate spa with a Turkish bath, and a swanky, sexy cabaret. ⊠ *Martha Salotti 445, Puerto Madero, 1107* ☎ *11/4010–9000* ⊕ *www. faenahotelanduniverse.com* ➳ *105 rooms* ⚬ *2 restaurants, room service, 24-hour butler service, flexible check-in, IDD phones, in-room safes, minibars, cable TV, DVD player, in-room data ports, pool, gym, health club, massage, sauna, Turkish baths, 2 bars, lounge, babysitting, laundry service, DSL Internet, Wi-Fi in all rooms, concierge, business services, meeting rooms, parking (fee), no-smoking rooms* ≡ *AE, DC, MC, V.*

$$ 🏨 **Hotel Madero by Sofitel.** This slick, affordable hotel is within walking distance of downtown as well as the riverside ecological reserve. The big, bright, modern rooms have wood accents and white color schemes. Many rooms also have fantastic views of the docks and city skyline. The restaurant, Red, serves great Argentine–French fusion cuisine in an intimate setting. The breakfast buffet features tons of exotic fresh fruits and Argentine baked goods. ⊠ *Rosario Vera Penaloza 360, Dique 2, Puerto Madero, 1007* ☎ *11/5776–7777* ⊕ *www.hotelmadero.com* ➳ *165 rooms, 28 suites* ⚬ *Restaurant, bar, 24-hour room service, in-room safes, cable TV, in-room data ports, pool, gym, bar, laundry service, DSL Internet, meeting room* ≡ *AE, DC, MC, V.*

La Recoleta

★ **$$$$** 🏨 **Alvear Palace Hotel.** If James Bond were in town, this is where he'd hang his hat. In fact, Sean Connery *has* stayed here, because when it comes to sophistication, the Alvear Palace is the best bet in Buenos Aires. It's hosted scores of dignitaries since opening its doors in 1932, and although new and more affordable hotels are making it something of a gray ghost, the Alvear is still stately and swanky. It's all about world-class service and thoughtful touches: butler service, fresh flowers, feather-beds with Egyptian-cotton linens. The lunch buffet is out of this world, and the super-chic French restaurant, La Bourgogne, is one of the city's best. ⊠ *Av. Alvear 1891, La Recoleta, 1129* ☎ *11/4808–2100, 11/ 4804–7777, 800/448–8355 in U.S.* ⊕ *www.alvearpalace.com* ➳ *100 rooms, 100 suites* ⚬ *2 restaurants, coffee shop, room service, IDD phones, in-room safes, some in-room hot tubs, minibars, in-room data ports, indoor pool, gym, health club, sauna, bar, laundry service, concierge, DSL Internet, Wi-Fi in all rooms, business services, meeting room, no-smoking rooms* ≡ *AE, DC, MC, V* ⦿ *BP.*

★ **$$$$** 🏨 **Four Seasons Hotel Buenos Aires.** This exquisite hotel envelops you in a pampering atmosphere that screams turn-of-the-19th-century Paris. In fact, the gorgeous French embassy is just up the block. The hotel's 13-floor marble tower has an impressive art collection and large, luxurious rooms. The neighboring hotel mansion draws famous folks: Madonna (who stayed while filming *Evita*), the Rolling Stones, Jennifer Lopez, and Robbie Williams, to name a few. ⊠ *Posadas 1086, La Recoleta, 1011* ☎ *11/4321–1200* ⊕ *www.fourseasons.com/buenosaires*

🛏 *138 rooms, 27 suites* ♿ *Restaurant, room service, IDD phones, in-room fax, in-room safes, minibars, cable TV, in-room data ports, pool, fitness classes, gym, health club, massage, sauna, bar, lobby lounge, babysitting, dry cleaning, laundry service, concierge, DSL Internet, Wi-Fi in all rooms, business services, meeting rooms, airport shuttle, travel services, parking (fee), no-smoking rooms* ⊟ *AE, DC, MC, V* 🍴| *BP.*

★ **$$** 🏨 **Hotel Bel Air.** Given the fancy French-style facade, you could mistake the Bel Air for a neighborhood hotel somewhere in Paris. Inside, a more modern feel takes over, with a round wood-paneled lobby bar and a snazzy café that looks onto exclusive Arenales Street. Rooms have handsome wooden floors and simple but stylish desks and couches. ⊠ *Arenales 1462, La Recoleta, 1062* ☎ *11/4021–4000* ⊕ *www.hotelbelair.com.ar* 🛏 *77 rooms* ♿ *Restaurant, café, room service, IDD phones, in-room safes, minibars, cable TV, in-room data ports, gym, bar, dry cleaning, laundry service, Internet, business services, meeting rooms, airport shuttle, travel services, no-smoking rooms* ⊟ *AE, DC, MC, V* 🍴| *BP.*

$ 🏨 **Art Hotel.** The aptly named Art Hotel has an impressive ground-floor gallery where exhibits of paintings, photographs, and sculptures by acclaimed Argentine artists change monthly. You might even run into some fabulous art aficionados sipping Chardonnay and admiring the creations. Rooms are classified as "small and cozy," "queen," or "king" and many have wrought-iron bed frames with white canopies. The building's 100-year-old elevator will take you to the rooftop patio, where there's a hot tub. ⊠ *Azcuenaga 1268, 1115* ☎ *11/4821–4744* ⊕ *www.arthotel.com.ar* 🛏 *36 rooms* ♿ *Café, IDD phones, in-room safes, mini-bar, cable TV, bar, laundry service, DSL Internet, travel services* ⊟ *AE, MC, V* Ⓜ *D to Pueyrredón.*

Palermo

$$ 🏨 **1555 Malabia House.** Behind the unassuming white facade of this 100-year-old Palermo Soho town house is what the proprietors have dubbed Argentina's "first designer B&B." Common areas have bold, colorful paintings and fanciful sculptures. Rooms, only some of which have en-suite baths, are all about pale-wood floors and furnishings and simple white bedding and curtains. Both sides of the narrow hallways are lined with rooms, eliminating any sense of privacy, but the bustling Palermo location is hard to beat. The young staff can steer you toward the neighborhood's newest restaurants and nightspots. ⊠ *Malabia 1555, Palermo Soho, 1414* ☎ *11/4832–3345 or 11/4833–2410* ⊕ *www.malabiahouse.com.ar* 🛏 *11 rooms, 4 suites* ♿ *Room service, IDD phones, fans, in-room safes, minibars, cable TV, bar, library, laundry service, concierge, DSL Internet, meeting room, airport shuttle, parking (fee)* ⊟ *AE, DC, MC, V* 🍴| *CP* Ⓜ *D to Scalabrini Ortiz.*

★ **$$** 🏨 **Home Buenos Aires.** It's run by Argentine Patricia O'Shea and her British husband, Tom Rixton, a well-known music producer, and it oozes coolness and class. Each distinct room is decorated with vintage French wallpaper and has a stereo, a laptop-friendly safe, and either a bathtub or a wet room. On-site there's a vast garden; a barbecue area; an infinity pool; a holistic spa; and a funky lounge bar where you can sip a cocktail and listen to mood music created especially for the hotel by famed record producer Flood (U2, Smashing Pumpkins, Nine Inch Nails), one of the hotel's investors. ⊠ *Honduras 5860, Palermo Hollywood, 1414* ☎ *11/4778–1008* ⊕ *www.homebuenosaires.com* ⇨ *14 rooms, 4 suites* ⌂ *Restaurant, room service, bar, IDD phones, in-room safes, minibars, cable TV, stereo, spa, pool, library, DSL Internet, Wi-Fi in all rooms, travel services* ═ *AE, MC, V* Ⓜ *D to Ministro Carranza.*

$$ ▦ **Bo-Bo.** Quaint, quirky Bo-Bo shrewdly combines the bourgeois with the bohemian. In fact, the hotel's name is a play on David Brooks' 2000 book, *Bobos in Paradise,* which you can find in the lobby library. Each room has a different motif—art deco, minimalist, techno. The largest and most luxurious, the Argentina Suite, is decorated in bright colors and has a small outdoor patio and hot tub. All rooms have such creature comforts as soft robes and such technological comforts as Wi-Fi access and DVD players. The downstairs restaurant-café is a nice place to relax after pounding Palermo's pavement all day. ⊠ *Guatemala 4882, Palermo Soho, 1425* ☎ *11/4774–0505* ⊕ *www.bobohotel.com* ⇨ *7 rooms* ⌂ *Restaurant, room service, IDD phones, in-room safes, cable TV, bar, library, laundry service, DSL Internet, Wi-Fi in rooms, parking (fee)* ═ *AE, MC, V* Ⓜ *D to Plaza Italia.*

$ ▦ **Hotel Alpino.** This simple neighborhood hotel is decorated in dark browns and has wood paneling. Rooms are clean and comfortable, although they could definitely use a touching up. The location is good, though: close to the Parque Zoológico and the Jardín Botánico as well as the nightlife and restaurants in Palermo Soho. ⊠ *Cabello 3318, Palermo, 1425* ☎ *11/4802–5151* ⊕ *www.geocities.com/alpinohotel* ⇨ *35 rooms* ⌂ *Room service, IDD phones, in-room safes, minibars, cable TV, in-room data ports, DSL Internet, laundry service, meeting rooms, parking (fee)* ═ *AE, DC, MC, V* ⓘ⦿ *CP* Ⓜ *D to Plaza Italia.*

¢–$ ▦ **Giramondo Hostel.** The funky Giramondo has all that a hostel needs: plenty of beds and bathrooms, a kitchen, a TV and computer lounge, and a patio, where backpackers from around the world grill up slabs of Argentine beef. The dark, dank underground bar serves up cheap drinks; it also has a small wine cellar. Giramondo is two blocks from buses and the subte on Avenida Santa Fe—an ideal locale for taking part in Palermo's pulsing nightlife while also being close to downtown. ⊠ *Guemes 4802, Palermo Soho, 1425* ☎ *11/4772–6740* ⊕ *www.hostelgiramondo. com.ar* ⌂ *Kitchen, fans, bar, library, TV/DVD room, safety boxes, laundry facilities, DSL Internet, travel services; no a/c, no room phones, no room TVs* ═ *No credit cards* Ⓜ *D to Palermo.*

Nightlife

By Brian Byrnes

Porteños *love* to party. Many don't think twice about dancing until 6 AM and heading to work at 8 AM. And alcohol doesn't play a vital role in whether people enjoy themselves or not; porteños could have fun at an insurance convention, provided the conversation and music were good and everyone looked marvelous. Indeed, for many, it's better to *look* good than to *feel* good.

Being stylish is just one factor for a successful night on the town. Another is knowing that when we say this is a late-night town, we mean it. Clubs, which generally attract crowds in the 18–35 age range, don't begin to fill up until 2 or 3 AM. Theater performances start at 9 PM or 9:30 PM, and the last movie begins after midnight. That said, the subte closes at 10 PM, so going out late means taking a taxi home or waiting until 5 AM for trains to resume running.

> **WORD OF MOUTH**
>
> "Buenos Aires is one of the most vibrant big cities on the planet. . . ."
>
> —drdawgqy

The Palermo and La Recoleta areas have the most diverse nightlife, and places are fairly close to one another. El Centro and San Telmo have equally good options, but things are more spread out; for your well-being and that of your feet, take a taxi.

El Centro

BARS **La Cigale.** Sip cocktails at a large turquoise bar while smooth sounds and heavy cigarette smoke spin around you. Tuesday is French Soirée Night, and things get lively with techno and trance music mixed with sounds straight from Gay Paree. ⊠ *25 de Mayo 722, El Centro* ☎ *11/4312–8275* Ⓜ *C to San Martín.*

The Kilkenny. It serves surprisingly good Irish food and has Guinness on draft. Celtic or rock bands play every night, entertaining the after-work crowd from nearby government and commercial buildings. ⊠ *Marcelo T. De Alvear 399, El Centro* ☎ *11/4312–7291* Ⓜ *C to San Martín.*

★ **Milión.** At this beautiful mansion you can enjoy a cold Cosmopolitan or a nice Malbec at the upstairs bar while sophisticates chat around you. Be sure to explore all the hidden corners, including the back garden salon, which is lit with candles and soft colored lights. ⊠ *Paraná 1048, El Centro* ☎ *11/4815–9925* Ⓜ *D to Callao.*

DANCE CLUBS **Bahrein.** Chic (some might say "sheik") and super-stylish, this party palace
Fodor'sChoice is in a 100-year-old former bank. Upstairs is a fantastic restaurant,
★ Crizia. In the main floor's Funky Room, young women in tight denim and even tighter halter tops groove to pop, rock, and funk. The downstairs Excess Room has a heady mix of electronic beats and dizzying wall visuals. Five-hundred pesos gets you locked inside the steel vault, where you can guzzle champagne all night with other beautiful (and bewildered) people—an entirely new kind of VIP experience. ⊠ *Lavalle 345, El Centro* ☎ *11/4315–2403* Ⓜ *B to Alem.*

Cocoliche. Cocoliche enjoys cult-like status in both the straight and gay communities for its diverse artistic and musical offerings. Upstairs it's all about culture, with a gallery of art by young locals. Downstairs it's all about anonymous anarchy, with house music motivating the masses to move on one of the city's darkest dance floors. ⊠ *Rivadavía 878, El Centro* ☎ *11/4331–6413* Ⓜ *A to Piedras.*

GAY & LESBIAN **Angels.** Angels has several dance floors that play electronica, pop, and
CLUBS Latin music. It attracts a primarily gay male and transvestite clientele, but heterosexuals are welcome, too. ⊠ *Viamonte 2168, El Centro* ☎ *No phone* Ⓜ *D to Facultad de Medicina.*

Contramano. It's been around since 1984, when it was the city's most popular and pioneering gay disco, but today it operates more as a laid-

Tango 1: The Dances

TANGO IS MUCH MORE than just a spectator sport, and if you want to take to the floor yourself there are plenty of neighborhood *milongas* (dance halls) to choose from. It's a complex cultural scene and not for the fainthearted. Dancers of all ages sit at tables that edge the floor, and men invite women to dance through subtle eye contact and head-nodding, known as *cabeceo*—a hard art to master. Women sitting with male partners won't be asked to the floor by other men, so couples wanting variety should sit apart.

Dances come in sets of three, four, or five, broken by an obvious divider of non-tango music, and it's common to stay with the same partner for a set. Being discarded in the middle is a sign that you're not up to scratch. Staying for more than two sets with the same partner could be interpreted as a come-on. Although clement dancing kings and queens may take pity on left-footed beginners, getting a partner can be hard at first. Many milongas start with chaotic group classes and practice sessions, but if you want to be taken seriously, take some private lessons. Good teachers will also give you clued-in advice for making the most of the milonga.

Behind the unmarked doors of **La Catedral** (✉ Sarmiento 4006, Almagro ☎ No phone) is a hip club

where the tango is very rock, somehow—the milonga is casual, and it's a cool night out even if you're not planning to dance. Watch locals in action in the open air at **Glorieta Barrancas de Belgrano** (✉ 11 de Septiembre at Echeverría, Belgrano), which takes place in a park every Sunday evening. On Monday afternoon, golden oldies cut a rug on the first floor of **La Ideal** (✉ Suipacha 384, Plaza de Mayo ☎ 11/4601–8234), an old-world tearoom, and a great place to learn from their experience.

The gay milonga of the week is held on Wednesday at **La Marshall** (✉ Yatay 961, Almagro ☎ 11/4912–9043). The Wednesday-night milonga at **El Nacional** (✉ Alsina 1465, Congreso ☎ 11/4307–0146) is a mid-week favorite with locals. Belle-époque-style **El Niño Bien** (✉ Humberto I 1462, Constitución ☎ 11/4147–8687) is the place to go late on Thursday night. On Monday and Friday nights head for **Salón Canning** (✉ Av. Scalabrini Ortíz 1331, Palermo ☎ 11/4832–6753), a serious milonga where the action goes on into the small hours. A young crowd gathers on weekends at chaotic club **La Viruta-La Estrella** (✉ Armenia 1366, Palermo ☎ 11/4774–6357), which mixes tango with rock, salsa, and cumbia.

—Victoria Patience

back bar with an older, male-only clientele. Occasionally there's live music and male strippers. ✉ *Rodríguez Peña 1082, El Centro* ☎ *No phone* Ⓜ *D to Callao.*

Palacio. This massive downtown club attracts a mixed-age crowd of gays and lesbians on Friday and Sunday nights for electronic music and pop tunes. On Saturday the club goes straight and changes its name to Big

One for a night of hard-core techno. ✉ *Alsina 940, El Centro* ☎ *11/4331–1277* Ⓜ *A to Piedras.*

San Telmo

DANCE CLUBS **Club Museum.** It's an enormous, multilevel love den that packs in college kids looking to party like its 1995. From the second- and third-floor balconies overlooking the gigantic dance floor, some flirtatious souls have tried (unsuccessfully) to introduce Mardi Gras–like behavior to the mix. But flashing is entirely unnecessary; this place gets wild enough on its own. ✉ *Perú 535, San Telmo* ☎ *11/4654–1774* Ⓜ *C to San Juan.*

Rey Castro. Just because this Cuban restaurant-bar gets jumping and jiving on weekends, doesn't mean things get out of hand: the bad-ass bouncers look like they could play in the NBA. This place is popular for birthday parties and serves great mojitos. After the nightly live dance show, DJs crank up the Cuban rhythms. You'll definitely learn some sexy new dance moves here. ✉ *Perú 342, San Telmo* ☎ *11/4342–9998* Ⓜ *C to San Juan.*

La Recoleta

BARS **Buller Brew Pub.** The city's only brewpub has six tasty homemade choices on tap, including Honey Beer and India Pale Ale. Locals and tourists mingle here over pints, peanuts, and pop music. ✉ *R. M. Ortíz 1827, La Recoleta* ☎ *11/4808–9061.*

Deep Blue. It draws a steady stream of foreign students and the Argentines who are anxious to woo them. The billiards tables attract some serious pool sharks. The coolest thing about this place is that each plush blue booth has its own self-service beer tap, which doesn't seem to excite the alcohol-apathetic Argentines but can prove devastatingly dangerous for American and European visitors. ✉ *Ayacucho 1240, La Recoleta* ☎ *11/4827–4415* Ⓜ *D to Pueyrredón.*

DANCE CLUB **Shamrock.** This rowdy place is owned by a couple of Irish guys and is one of the city's most popular expat hangouts. You can drink a Guinness and yap away in English, easily forgetting that you're in South America. Follow the techno beats to the smoky downstairs dance club, where the enormous disco ball reminds you (1) that you're in Buenos Aires and (2) why you came in the first place. ✉ *Rodríguez Peña 1220, La Recoleta* ☎ *11/4812–3584* Ⓜ *D to Callao.*

GAY & LESBIAN CLUB **Glam.** Young, hip, and buff men come for smooth cruising in a classy setting: a fashionably restored home. Lesbians and straight women come for the festive atmosphere and raucous music. ✉ *Cabrera 3046, La Recoleta* ☎ *11/4963–2521* Ⓜ *D to Pueyrredón.*

WINE BAR **Gran Bar Danzon.** If Carrie, Samantha, Charlotte, and Miranda lived in Buenos Aires, they'd probably frequent this first-floor hot spot where local business sharks and chic internationals sip wine and eat sushi by candlelight. It's extremely popular for happy hour, but people stick around for dinner and the occasional live jazz shows, too. The wine list and the appetizers are superb. ✉ *Libertad 1161* ☎ *11/4811–1108* Ⓜ *C to Retiro.*

Tango 2: The Shows

FOR MANY the tango experience begins and ends with the flashy *cena-shows* in expensive clubs. These usually include drinks and a three-course dinner. Expect sequined costumes, gelled hairdos, and high-kicking moves, known as *tango de fantasía*. The shows might not be so fancy, but the dancing at more traditional, lower-key venues is just as skilled.

Musicians and dancers perform at **Bar Sur** (✉ Estados Unidos 299, San Telmo ☎ 11/4362–6086 ⊕ www.bar-sur.com.ar), a traditional bar. **La Esquina de Homero Manzi** (✉ San Juan 3601, Boedo ☎ 11/4957–8488 ⊕ www.esquinahomeromanzi.com.ar) has reasonably priced shows in an opulent café. An evening at **Madero Tango** (✉ Alicia Moreau de Justo at Brasil, Puerto Madero ☎ 11/4314–6688 ⊕ www.maderotango.

com) may break the bank, but the chef is a local legend, and the dancing is fantastic.

Consistently well-attended performances are held at the classic café **El Querandí** (✉ Perú 302, at Moreno, San Telmo ☎ 11/4342–1760 ⊕ www.querandi.com.ar). The daily shows at glitzy **Señor Tango** (✉ Vieytes 1655, Barracas ☎ 11/4303–0231 ⊕ www.senortango.com.ar) are aimed at tourists. The fancy show at **Taconeando** (✉ Balcarce 725, San Telmo ☎ 11/4307–6696 ⊕ www.taconeando.com) is popular with foreigners. A traditional show takes place at **Viejo Almacén** (✉ Balcarce 786, at Independencia, San Telmo ☎ 11/4307–6689 ⊕ www.viejo-almacen.com.ar).

–Victoria Patience

Palermo

BARS ★ **Congo.** A fashionable post-dinner, pre-club crowd—in faded fitted jeans, hipster sneakers, and leather jackets—frequents this hangout. The back garden can get lively enough on warm nights to cause many would-be clubgoers to stick around for another gin and tonic. ✉ *Honduras 5329, Palermo Soho* ☎ *11/4833—5857.*

Mundo Bizarro. It has one of the city's most extensive cocktails lists, including such concoctions as MintSake (mint, lime, apple juice, ginger, and sake) and The Sinner (Jack Daniels, peach schnapps, pastis, and orange juice). Day-glow artwork, random B-movie images, and red lighting lend an underground and (sometimes) uneasy feel. ✉ *Guatemala 4802, Palermo Soho* ☎ *11/4773–1967.*

Spell Café. All three levels of this massive place offer something different: dining downstairs, drinks at mid-level, and DJs upstairs. Another location in Puerto Madero offers a more American speakeasy atmosphere with beer and burger options. ✉ *Malabia 1738, Palermo Soho* ☎ *11/4832–3389.*

DANCE CLUBS **Club Aráoz.** It may be intimate, but it attracts a serious party crowd. Thursday night is hip-hop night; Friday and Saturday see DJs from Asia, Europe, or the Middle East. ✉ *Aráoz 2424, Palermo* ☎ *11/4833–7775.*

Niceto. Although its ever-changing lineup of artists represents the whole spectrum of local music, Niceto is best known for Club 69, a raucous Thursday night party that combines cocktails and campy bravado. The main room has a balcony with the best views of the dance floor. A chillout room in the back always has great projected visuals on the walls. ⊠ *Cnel. Niceto Vega 5510, Palermo Hollywood* ☎ *11/4779–9396.*

Podestá Super Club de Copas. It's like the 1969 Altamont Raceway concert in this place, except the Hells Angels and hippies get along a lot better. The dark ground-floor room plays rock and serves stiff drinks. Upstairs, dance-friendly music is pumped into a psychedelic setting. ⊠ *Armenia 1742, Palermo Soho* ☎ *11/4832–2776.*

The Roxy. The cream of the Argentine rock-and-roll scene hangs out at this large club, so black-leather jackets and long locks are the norm most nights. It hosts a '70s disco party and other events, often with scantily clad dancers. Order a Quilmes beer and take in the scene. ⊠ *Arcos del Sol, between Casares and Sarmiento, Palermo* ☎ *11/4899–0313.*

GAY CLUB **Kim y Novak Bar.** On the edge of Palermo Soho, Kim y Novak is a kitschy cocktail bar that attracts both gay and straight lounge lizards. Upstairs you can enjoy a mixed drink seated on vintage couches or in booths. Downstairs it's about predominantly gay men dancing to heavy electronic beats. ⊠ *Guemes 4900, Palermo Soho* ☎ *11/4773–7521.*

Shopping

By Victoria Patience

Porteños are known for their obsession with fashion. As a result, Buenos Aires has a wide range of options for buying clothing and footwear, from shopping malls and commercial strips to cobbled streets with designer boutiques. Open-air markets are a great source for souvenir handicrafts.

Many shops in traditional tourist areas (such as Calle Florida) are taking advantage of the confusion caused by currency devaluation, and may try to charge tourists in dollars for what they charge Argentines for in pesos, so always confirm which currency you're dealing with up front.

When shopping in Buenos Aires, keep your receipts: the 21% VAT tax, included in the sales price, is entirely refundable for purchases exceeding $200 at stores displaying a duty-free sign. When you depart, allow plenty of time to visit the return desk at the airport to obtain your refund.

El Centro

CRAFTS **Platería Parodi.** This über-traditional store is chock-a-block with everything a gaucho about town needs to accessorize with, all in top-quality silver. There are belt buckles and knives for the boys, and the no-nonsense pampa-style women's jewelry would go great with Gap and Ralph

Tango 3: The Music

THE AVERAGE PORTEÑO is much more likely to go to see tango musicians than tango dancers. Offerings range from orchestras churning out tunes as was done in Gardel's day to sexy, bluesy vocals from divas like Adriana Varela to pared-down revisitings of the tango underworld by young groups like 34 Puñaladas. If you want tango that packs a punch, look out for the electronic fusion of groups like Gotan Project and Bajofondo Tango Club.

Young musicians perform hip sets at **Centro Cultural Torcuato Tasso** (⊠ Defensa 1575, San Telmo ☏ 11/ 4307–6506), which also holds milongas at weekends. Celebrated old-guard tango musicians Salgán and De Lío frequently perform in the intimate surroundings of the **Club del Vino** (⊠ Cabrera 4737, Palermo ☏ 11/ 4833–0050). The classic **Gran Café Tortoni** (⊠ Av. de Mayo 829, Plaza de Mayo ☏ 11/4342–4328) is one of the best places to listen to tango music. Small, recycled theater **ND Ateneo** (⊠ Paraguay 918, Microcentro ☏ 11/ 4328–2888) has become a showcase for live music performances.

–Victoria Patience

Lauren alike. ⊠ *Av. de Mayo 720, Plaza de Mayo* ☏ *11/4342–2207* Ⓜ *A to Piedras.*

Fodor'sChoice ★ **Tierra Adentro.** Beautiful indigenous crafts come with a clean conscience at Tierra Adentro, which insists on trading fairly with the native Argentine craftsmen whose work they stock. Fine weavings are the shop's hallmark, but wide silver bracelets and gobstopper-size turquoise beads are other tempting offers. Mapuche earrings, cut entirely out of a sheet of silver hammered flat, are a bold accessory. ⊠ *Arroyo 946* ☏ *11/ 4393–8552* ⊕ *www.tierraadentro.info* Ⓜ *C to San Martín.*

JEWELRY **Cousiño.** Veined pinky-red rhodochrosite, Argentina's national stone, comes both in classic settings and as diminutive sculptures at this shop specializing in the unusual stone. Cousiño's sculptures of birds in flight are also exhibited in the National Museum of Decorative Arts. ⊠ *Sheraton Buenos Aires Hotel, San Martín 1225, El Centro* ☏ *11/4318–9000* ⊕ *www.cousinojewels.com* Ⓜ *C to Retiro.*

Fodor'sChoice ★ **Plata Nativa.** This tiny shop tucked away in an arcade is filled with delights for both boho chicks and collectors of singular ethnic jewelry. Complex, chunky necklaces with turquoise, amber, and malachite—all based on original Araucanian (ethnic Argentine) pieces—and Mapuche-style silver earrings and brooches are some of the offerings. Sharon Stone and Liv Ullman have fallen for Florencia Bernales's knitted silver necklaces; other happy customers include Pedro Almodóvar and the Textile Museum in Washington, D.C. Weavings and wooden religious statues complete the finds. ⊠ *Unit 4, Galería del Sol, Florida 860* ☏ *11/4312–1398* ⊕ *www.platanativa.com* Ⓜ *C to San Martín.*

LEATHER **Arandú.** For sheepskin jackets, head to Arandú, which also sells fur-lined saddles, boots, and other leather goods for that Marlboro-man look,

Argentine-style. If you find the supple canvas and leather sports bags too conventional, check out such novelties as leather rifle-cases. ⊠ *Paraguay 1259, El Centro* ☎ *11/4816–6191* ⊕ *www.tal-arandu.com* Ⓜ *D to Tribunales.*

Carpincho. This shop specializes in the stippled leather of the carpincho (cabybara—the world's largest rodent, native to Argentina), which has super-soft skin. The real draw, though, are the gloves, which come in both carpincho and kidskin and in many colors, from classic chocolate brown to tangerine and lime. ⊠ *Esmeralda 775* ☎ *11/4322–9919* ⊕ *www.carpinchonet.com.ar* Ⓜ *C to Lavalle.*

MALLS **Abasto.** The soaring art deco architecture of what was once the city's central market is as much a reason to come as the three levels of shops. Although Abasto has many top local chains, it's not as exclusive as other malls, so you can find bargains. Take a break in the fourth-floor food court beneath the glass panes and steel supports of the building's original roof. ⊠ *Av. Corrientes 3247, Almagro* ☎ *11/4959–3400* ⊕ *www.abasto-shopping.com.ar* Ⓜ *B to Carlos Gardel.*

Galerías Pacífico. Upscale shops line the three levels of this building, designed during the city's turn-of-the-20th-century golden age. The mall is particularly strong on leather clothing. It also has a basement food court, a cinema, and the Centro Cultural Borges, whose art exhibitions have featured Andy Warhol, Salvador Dalí, and Henri Cartier-Bresson. ⊠ *Calle Florida 753, at Av. Córdoba, Microcentro* ☎ *11/4319–5100* ⊕ *www.galeriaspacificos.com.ar* Ⓜ *B to Florida.*

WINE **Ligier.** Ligier has a string of shops across town and lots of experience guiding bewildered shoppers through their impressive selection. Although they stock some boutique-vineyard wines, they truly specialize in the big names like Rutini and Luigi Bosca. Their leather wine carrying cases make a great picnic accessory. ⊠ *Av. Santa Fe 800* ☎ *11/4515–0126* ⊕ *www.ligier.com.ar* Ⓜ *C to San Martín.*

San Telmo

ART & ANTIQUES **Arte y Diseño de la Pampa.** An artist-and-architect duo is behind these original works, which are inspired by native Argentine art. They use an unusual papier-mâché technique to create boxes, frames, wall-hangings, and freestanding sculptures. The primitive-looking pieces, a vision of rich rusts and earthy browns, make highly original gifts. ⊠ *Defensa 917, San Telmo* ☎ *11/4362–6406* ⊕ *www.artepampa.com.*

Churrinche. Hidden in the dusty chaos are old train sets and nests of silver-topped walking sticks. Glasses are another forte: there are 20-piece sets—many in two-tone cut glass—in the appropriate shapes for wine, water, brandy, sherry, and just about anything else. If you need to fix a chandelier, a rack of replacement glass baubles fills the window—mounted on wire hooks, they'd also make innovative earrings. ⊠ *Defensa 1031, San Telmo* ☎ *11/4362–7612* ⊕ *www.churrinche.com.ar.*

★ **Juan Carlos Pallarols Orfebre.** Argentina's legendary silversmith has made pieces for a mile-long list of celebrities that includes Frank Sinatra, Sharon Stone, Jacqueline Bisset, Bill Clinton, Nelson Mandela, the king and queen of Spain, and Princess Máxima Zorrequieta—Argentina's export to the Dutch royal family. He's designed everything from tableware and trays to papal chalices; a set of his ornate silver-handled steak knives is the perfect way to celebrate cow country, though you'll part with a few grand for the pleasure. The less pragmatic can make like Antonio Banderas and Maradona: commission a silver rose (thorns and all) for their true love. ⊠ *Defensa 1039, San Telmo* ☎ *11/4362–0641* ⊕ *www.pallarols.com.ar.*

★ **Silvia Petroccia.** Despite being crammed with furniture, this corner store manages to look extravagant rather than chaotic. It's probably due to the alluring collectibles, which range from Louis XV–style chairs reupholstered in buttercup-yellow silk to packable gilt-wood church candles. Gold-framed mirrors and a host of chandeliers round out the luxuries. ⊠ *Defensa 1002, San Telmo* ☎ *11/4362–0156.*

CLOTHING **La Pescadería.** This small store wears its nostalgic heart on its sleeve—all its products are tongue-in-cheek celebrations of what Argentine childhood used to be about. For wistful sports fans there are cotton piqué football shirts that imitate club jerseys of the 1950s and replica old-style leather football shoes—studs 'n' all. Cool kids wear includes little tees with the faces of Gardel and Che Guevara—revolutionary gifts. ⊠ *Carlos Calvo 467, San Telmo* ☎ *11/4361–6287.*

Un Lugar En El Mundo. The barrio's hippest shop showcases young designers, whose men's and women's clothing is both wearable and affordable. Un Lugar en el Mundo is also one of the few places in town to get a bag by Bolsas de Viaje, whose vinyl and canvas creations evoke the golden age of air travel. Mir's satchels and totes in heavily stitched chestnut leather make you want to go back to school, and Paz Portnoi's cowhide heels are perfect for dressing up. ⊠ *Defensa 891, San Telmo* ☎ *11/4362–3836.*

MARKET **Feria de San Pedro Telmo.** The town's busiest market packs a small San Telmo square every Sunday. Elbow your way through the crowds to pick through antiques and curios of varying vintages as well as tango memorabilia, or watch dolled-up professional tango dancers perform on the surrounding cobbled streets. As it gets dark, the square turns into a *milonga,* where locals show you how it's done. ⊠ *Plaza Dorrego, Humberto I y Defensa, San Telmo* ☎ *11/4331–9855* ⊕ *www.feriadesantelmo. com* ☉ *Sun. 10–5* Ⓜ *E to Independencia (then walk 9 blocks east along Independencia to Defensa). Alternatively, A to Plaza de Mayo, D to Catedral, E to Bolívar (then walk 8 blocks south on Bolívar).*

La Recoleta

CLOTHING
FodorsChoice
★
Cat Ballou. As the name suggests, golden-age Hollywood glamour is the order of the day at Cat Ballou. Everything in this tiny corner boutique breathes delicacy, from bias-cut satin dresses with whispery tulle details to llama-wool felt jackets with berry-colored belts. The shop's housewares, including pink-velvet loveseats and antique chandeliers, are the icing on this slice of urban luxury. ⊠ *Av. Alvear 1702, La Recoleta* ☎ *11/ 4811–9792.*

★ **La Dolfina Polo Lifestyle.** Being the world's best polo player wasn't enough for Adolfo Cambiaso—he founded his own team in 1995, and then started a clothing line for which he does the modeling. And if you think polo is all about knee-high boots and preppy chinos think again: Cambiaso sells some of the best urban menswear in town. The Italian-cotton shirts, sharp leather jackets, and to-die-for totes from the After Polo collection are perfect for after just about anything. ⊠ *Av. Alvear 1315, La Recoleta* ☎ *11/4815–2698* ⊕ *www.ladolfina.com.*

Locos X El Fútbol. The merchandising section of Locos X El Fútbol has everything a serious football fan needs to dress like the best. You can get jerseys for local, national, and international teams. ⊠ *Inside Village Recoleta complex, Vicente López at Uriburú, La Recoleta* ☎ *11/ 4807–3777* ⊕ *www.codigofutbol.com.ar.*

★ **Pablo Ramírez.** The simple but spacey dresses of porteño fashion god Pablo Ramirez were once only available by hard-won appointment, but the opening of this Recoleta store means even non-celebrities can have a masterpiece. Pablo's couture doesn't come cheap, but given the peso prices, his dressy numbers are a (relative) bargain. Black is the color he favors both for women's wear and slick gent's suits, though a few other shades are beginning to creep in. ⊠ *Callao 1315, La Recoleta* ☎ *11/4815–5147* ⊕ *www.pabloramirez.com.ar.*

Fodor'sChoice **Tramando, Martín Churba.** Martín Churba, the undisputed leader of local
★ textile design, is one of Argentina's few designers to have gone international with boutiques in New York and Tokyo. Unique evening tops made of layers of sheer fabric adorned with geometric slashes and perfectly circular beads look like something an urban mermaid would wear. Sheer microfiber bustiers and screen-printed tees are some of the other woven wonders in the town house store. ⊠ *Rodríguez Peña 1973, La Recoleta* ☎ *11/4811–0465* ⊕ *www.tramando.com.*

CRAFTS **Aire del Sur.** Alpaca, carved deer bone, onyx, and leather are some of the
★ materials that might be combined into perfectly crafted trays, candelabras, or photo frames at Aire del Sur. The winning mix of these traditional materials with contemporary designs has won the hearts of stores like Barneys in New York and Paul Smith in London. You can cut out all those middle men, though, on a visit to this Recoleta showroom. ⊠ *Arenales 1618, 9th floor, La Recoleta* ☎ *11/5811–3640* ⊕ *www.airedelsur.com.*

LEATHER **Cardon.** Pine floors, pine walls, and pine cabinets—it's all very country down at Cardon. The estancia crowd comes here for reasonably priced, no-nonsense sheepskin jackets, cashmere sweaters, and riding boots. Items from the line of *talabartería* (traditional gaucho-style leather items), including cowboy hats, make great gifts. ⊠ *Av. Alvear 1847, La Recoleta* ☎ *11/4804–8424* ⊕ *www.cardon.com.ar.*

Mayorano. If Katharine Hepburn had dressed in leather, Mayorano would have been just up her alley. The selection is small, but the ultrasimple tan suits and trench coats in flawless calfskin are more than enough to justify a visit. ⊠ *Av. Alvear 1824, La Recoleta* ☎ *11/4804–2398.*

Rossi y Caruso. Top-quality workmanship and classic cuts are what bring distinguished customers like King Juan Carlos of Spain to Rossi y Caruso. The shop specializes in riding gear (think Marlborough foxhunt rather than Marlboro man) but also sells conservative handbags, leather jackets, and shoes. And should you need a saddle during your trip, those sold here are the best in town. ⊠ *Posadas 1387, La Recoleta* ☎ *11/4811–1538* ⊕ *www.rossicaruso.com.*

MALLS **Buenos Aires Design.** This fledgling mall alongside the Recoleta Cemetery mainly sells housewares—most of them imported and no less expensive than stuff back home. There are, however, a few shops with noteworthy suitcase-size bits and pieces. Two-level Morph does all manner of quirky colorful household items (think Philippe Starck on a budget). The must-see, though, is one-stop **Puro Diseño Argentino** (☎ 11/5777–6104 ⊕ www.purodiseno.com.ar), where Argentine designers show their wares. ✉ *Pueyrredón 2501, La Recoleta* ☎ *11/5777–6000* ⊕ *www.purodiseno.com.ar.*

Patio Bullrich. The city's most upscale mall was once the headquarters for the Bullrich family's meat-auction house. Inside, stone cow heads mounted on pillars still watch over the clientele. Top local stores that usually occupy prime mall space are relegated to the lowest level, making way for the likes of Lacroix, Cacharel, and Maxmara. Urban leatherware brand Uma has a shop here, as does Palermo fashion princess Jessica Trosman, whose spare women's clothes are decorated with unusual heavy beadwork. ✉ *Enter at Posadas 1245 or Av. del Libertador 750, La Recoleta* ☎ *11/4815–3501* ⊕ *www.shoppingbullrich.com.ar* Ⓜ *C to Retiro (walk 7 blocks up Av. del Libertador).*

MARKET **Feria Artesanal de la Recoleta.** The largest crafts market in town winds its way through several linked squares outside the Recoleta Cemetery. Artisans sell handmade clothes, jewelry, and housewares as well as more traditional crafts here. ✉ *Avs. Libertador and Pueyrredón, La Recoleta* ☎ *11/4343–0309* ⊙ *Weekends 10–6.*

SHOES **Guido.** In Argentina, loafers means Guido, whose retro-looking logo has been the hallmark of quality footwear since 1952. The old-world mahogany interior is the perfect place to try on timeless handmade Oxfords and brogues. There are also fun items (e.g., raspberry cow-skin handbags) on offer. ✉ *Av. Quintana 333, La Recoleta* ☎ *11/4811–4567* ⊕ *www.guidomocasines.com.ar.*

Lonte. There's something naughty-but-oh-so-nice about Lonte's shoes. Chunky gold peep-toe heels are a retro-queen's dream, and the outré animal-print numbers are a favorite of local diva Susana Giménez. For more discreet feet there are tweed boots or classic heels in straightforward colors. ✉ *Av. Alvear 1814, La Recoleta* ☎ *11/4804–9270* ⊕ *www.lonteweb.com.*

Zapatos de María. María Conorti was one of the first young designers to set up shop in the area, and she's going strong. Wedge heels, satin ankle-ties, and abundant use of patent leather are the trademark touches of her quirky designs. Knee-high suede pirate boots come in colors like ochre and lavender. ✉ *Libertad 1661, La Recoleta* ☎ *11/4815–5001* ⊕ *www.zapatosdemaria.com.ar.*

WINE **Grand Cru.** Don't let the small shop-front put you off: as with all the
Fodor's Choice best wine shops, the action is underground. Grand Cru's peerless selec-
★ tion includes wines from Patagonian vineyard Noemia, one of the country's best and exclusive to the shop. The Pulenta Gran Corte 2003, from Mendoza, is highly recommended. Incredibly savvy staffers will guide you, and should you buy more than your suitcase can hold, they can FedEx up to 12 bottles anywhere in the world. ✉ *Av. Alvear 1718, La Recoleta* ☎ *11/4816–3975* ⊕ *www.grandcru.com.ar.*

Palermo

CLOTHING: MEN'S **Bolivia.** Porteño dandies know that Bolivia is *the* place for metrosexual fashion relief. Floral prints feature big: expect them on shirts, leather belts, and Filofaxes. Aged denim, top-quality silk-screen T-shirts, vintage military jackets, and even hand-knit slippers fill this converted Palermo townhouse almost to bursting. ⊠ *Gurruchaga 1581 Palermo Viejo* ☎ *11/4832–6284* ⊕ *www.boliviaonline.com.ar.*

★ **Félix.** Waxed floorboards covered with worn rugs, exposed brick, and aging cabinets are the backdrop to the shop's very cool clothes. Beat-up denim, crisp shirts, and knits that look like a loving granny whipped them up are among the metrosexual delights. ⊠ *Gurruchaga 1670, Palermo Viejo* ☎ *11/4832–2994* ⊕ *www.felixba.com.ar.*

Hermanos Estebecorena. The approach to design at this trendy street-wear store is 100% practical. All the flat-front shirts, pants, and rain jackets have pockets, seams, and buttons positioned for maximum utility. Everything looks good, too, and the range of products, which includes footwear and underwear, makes this a one-stop guy shop. ⊠ *El Salvador 5960, Palermo Viejo* ☎ *11/4772–2145* ⊕ *www.hermanosestebecorena.com.*

Kristobelga. Lovers of Carhartt-style utility wear will find plenty of heavy-duty clothing at Kristobelga. As well as standard khakis and grays, the store also has carpenter trousers, tees in more upbeat colors, and hard-wearing canvas anoraks. ⊠ *Gurruchaga 1677, Palermo Viejo* ☎ *11/4831–6677* ⊕ *www.kristobelga.com.*

CLOTHING: WOMEN'S **Adorhada Guillermina.** Local cinema and graphic-design students love Adorhada Guillermina's '80s-feel clothes. Box-pleated denim skirts are edgy but practical. More unusual materials such as metallic plush are also on hand. Dress things up or down with one of a hundred tops in fine, bias-cut T-shirt fabric. ⊠ *El Salvador 4723, Palermo Viejo* ☎ *11/4831–2553* ⊕ *www.adorhadaguillermina.com.ar.*

La Aurora. At La Aurora it's clear that work clothes don't have to be drab. Details like geometric embroidery or satin trims spice up the clean lines and natural fabrics of Birkin's shirts and skirts. Even the most basic of trench coats stands out here in emerald green. Glass-topped cabinets display Mariana Arbusti's beautiful cotton underwear with contrasting lace trims. ⊠ *Honduras 4838, Palermo Viejo* ☎ *11/4833–4965.*

Cora Groppo. One of the queens of porteño haute couture, Cora Groppo made her name designing flirty cocktail dresses with lots of cleavage and swooping skirts. Her small prêt-à-porter Palermo store sells lower-key clothing, though the whisper-thin cotton jersey most things are made of doesn't do much for those without catwalk figures. ⊠ *El Salvador 4696, Palermo Viejo* ☎ *11/4832–5877* ⊕ *www.coragroppo.com.*

Fortunata Alegría. The sparse, all-white interior of this Palermo stalwart makes it easy to appreciate the fresh colors of the clothes it sells. Many of the A-line skirts and deep-V tops are adorned with simple geometric line-and-ball designs. Winter sees bright knits come with huge buttons and collars ideal for snuggling down into. ⊠ *Gurruchaga 1739, Palermo Viejo* ☎ *11/4831–8197* ⊕ *www.fortunataalegria.com.ar.*

Marcelo Senra. Irregular natural linen, heavy hand-knit sweaters, cow-hair boots around—it's all about texture at Marcelo Senra. At the front of an old town house, beige walls and a fountain set the tone for the clean, low-profile but elegant designs. Natural leather accessories complement the clothes' earthy palette. ⊠ *Gurruchaga 1519, Palermo Viejo* ☏ *11/4833–6230* ⊕ *www.marcelosenra.com.*

María Alló. Trashy but nice is the best way to describe María Alló's full-on designs. Although the black-gingham skirt suit with blood-red lace trim might be hard to wear to work, less outré possibilities include pearl-leather cowboy boots, ideal for glamming up your jeans. ⊠ *Armenia 1637, Palermo Viejo* ☏ *11/4831–3733.*

María Cher. Let the yards of racks draw you into this lanky shop, where simple cuts and natural fabrics make urban working clothes feel just a tad Jedi-like. The earthy, deconstructed look of the linen cache-coeurs and printed canvas skirts is also due to details like unfinished hems or exposed seams. ⊠ *El Salvador 4714, Palermo Viejo* ☏ *11/4833–4736* ⊕ *www.maria-cher.com.ar.*

María Marta Facchinelli. The designs of this Palermo goddess are feminine but not girly. Shirts and jackets are close-fitting but not vampish and come in pastels. Evening dresses follow the same lines: those done in fabrics like heavily-draped rose satin are glamorous but not flashy. ⊠ *El Salvador 4741, Palermo Viejo* ☏ *11/4831–8424* ⊕ *www.facchinelli.com.*

Objeto. Creative use of fabrics and quirky crafting make the everyday clothes Objeto sells something special. Their feminine T-shirts are textile collages combining silk screening and appliqué techniques; their skirts and jackets often mix new materials with original '60s offcuts. If you like to make a splash on rainy days, check out the waterproof jackets cut from gingham-print tablecloths complete with photos of food. ⊠ *Gurruchaga 1649, Palermo Viejo* ☏ *11/4834–6866.*

Pesqueira. Big girls and little girls can thrill together at the quirky but feminine silk-screen T-shirts that are Pesqueira's signature garments. Most have beautifully transferred photos of objects like an old Pentax that looks like it's hung round your neck. Simple casual clothes in pastels— a blush-colored denim sailor jacket, for instance—are here to combine with the tees. ⊠ *Armenia 1493, Palermo Viejo* ☏ *11/4833–7218.*

Salsipuedes. Carrie Bradshaw would have loved the cocktail dresses of Aida Sirinian, one of several designers showcased in this party-frock boutique. Geometrically embroidered turquoise satin with tulle underskirts and 1930s-style bias-cut velvet are worth organizing a ball for. Salsipuedes also sells hard-to-find Manto Abrigo woolen coats—one-off, hand-made designs from the north of Argentina. ⊠ *Honduras 4814, Palermo Viejo* ☏ *11/4831–8467.*

Tienda Tres. Three designers, three styles; hence the *tres* of this shop's name. What the chic clothes of Verónica Alfie, María Lombardi, and Flavia Martini have in common, though, are excellent cuts and a feminine feel. Dress up any of their outfits with satin-beribboned fur clutches that are strokeable enough to become your new pet. ⊠ *Armenia 1655, Palermo Viejo* ☏ *11/4831–4193.*

★ **Trosman.** Highly unusual beadwork is the only adornment on designer Jessica Trosman's simple clothes. There's nothing small and sparkling at hand, though: her beads are smooth, inch-wide acrylic orbs, that, when grouped together, look futuristic but organic at the same time. A toned-down palette, soft natural fabrics, and draped necklines are taking Trosman international: look for stores in Paris and Tokyo. ⊠ *Armenia 1998, Palermo Viejo* ☎ *11/4833–3085* ⊕ *www.trosman.com.*

LEATHER **Devacas.** "From the cows" is roughly how this corner store's name translates. It's apt: everything is made from Argentine cow skin and leather. In addition to your straightforward attaché cases, the store sells beautifully crafted chocolate-color mate carrying cases and novel cow skin–covered cocktail shakers. ⊠ *Gurruchaga 1660, Palermo Viejo* ☎ *11/4831–6570.*

Fodor'sChoice **Humawaca.** After years of operating from a showroom for a privileged
★ few, the city's trendiest leather brand finally has its own shop. Mere mortals can now delight in the signature circular leather handbags, cowhide clogs, and butterfly-shaped backpacks. Price tags may make you gulp. ⊠ *El Salvador 4692, Palermo Viejo* ☎ *11/4832–2662* ⊕ *www. humawaca.com.*

★ **Uma.** Light, butter-soft leather takes very modern forms here, with geometric stitching the only adornment on jackets and asymmetric bags that might come in rich violet in winter and aqua-blue in summer. The top-quality footwear includes teetering heels and ultra-simple boots and sandals with, mercifully, next to no elevation. ⊠ *Honduras 5225, Palermo Viejo* ☎ *11/4832–2122* ⊕ *www.umacuero.com.*

MALL **Alto Palermo.** A prime Palermo location, choice shops, and a pushy mar-
★ keting campaign have made Alto Palermo popular. Giggly teenage hordes are seduced by its long, winding layout. Ladies who lunch sip espresso in the cafés of its top-level food hall. The 154 shops are particularly strong on local street-wear brands like Bensimon and Bowen for the boys and Akiabara, Ona Saez, and Rapsodia for the girls. International names include the ubiquitous Levi's as well as Spanish megabrand Zara. ⊠ *Av. Santa Fe 3251, at Av. Colonel Díaz, Palermo* ☎ *11/5777–8000* ⊕ *www.altopalermo.com.ar* Ⓜ *D to Bulnes.*

SHOES **Josefina Ferroni.** Points that taper out way beyond the norm and thickly wedged heels are some of the trademarks. For stepping out in a crowd try the high heels in metallic leather with a contrasting trim or the slick black boots with a detail down the back that looks like leather tickertape. ⊠ *Armenia 1471, Palermo Viejo* ☎ *11/4831–4033* ⊕ *www. josefinaferroni.com.ar.*

Mandarine. High-heeled spats and brightly colored cowboy boots are some of the fun shoes here. Sturdy, top-quality leather, careful crafting, and reasonable prices ensure good value for the money. If your size is out of stock, ask whether the branch around the corner on Gurruchaga has it. ⊠ *Honduras 4940, Palermo Viejo* ☎ *11/4833–0094.*

Mariano Toledo. There's something very Vivienne Westwood about the arching high-heel brogues at Mariano Toledo, only a good few inches lower. Draping is his other forte: affordable party dresses hang in semi-sheer, toga-like folds; colors like aubergine and lime are arresting. ⊠ *Armenia 1564, Palermo Viejo* ☎ *11/4831–4861* ⊕ *www.marianotoledo. com.ar.*

Mishka. At this long-time Palermo favorite your feet can be sexy in high-heel lace-ups or brash in metallic pirate boots. The footwear comes in leather as well as in fabrics like brocade. Most styles are very narrow—truly flattering to some, merely painful to others. ⊠ *El Salvador 4673, Palermo Viejo* ☎ *11/4833–6566.*

Mourelos. The only adornments at this hole-in-the-wall boutique are elegant, understated leather shoes. Men can dress up with mildly gleaming chestnut city shoes or play it cool in camper-ish sneakers. Although many of the women's shoes have extremely pointed toes, there's nothing punishing about the heels. ⊠ *Armenia 1693, Palermo Viejo* ☎ *11/4833–6222* ⊕ *www.mourelos.com.ar.*

WINE **La Finca.** Great-value finds, including unusual wines from boutique vine★ yards are the specialty. Like their stock, the staff hails from Mendoza, capital of Argentine oenology, and they're a friendly, knowledgeable crew. Past the rustic shelving piled high with bottles are a few tables where you can sample the produce of vineyards like Carmelo Patti or Bramare, accompanied by a light *picada* (snack) of goat cheese and black olives, also from Mendoza. ⊠ *Honduras 5147, Palermo Viejo* ☎ *11/4832–3004.*

Terroir. A wine-lovers heaven is tucked away in this white stone town house. Expert staffers are on hand to help you make sense of the massive selection of Argentine wine, which includes collector's gems like the 1999 Angélica Zapata Cabernet Sauvignon. Terroir ships all over the world. ⊠ *Buschiazzo 3040, Palermo* ☎ *11/4778–3443* ⊕ *www.terroir. com.ar.*

Buenos Aires Essentials

Transportation

By Brian
Byrnes

BY AIR

International flights arrive at and depart from Aeropuerto Internacional Ministro Pistarini de Ezeiza, known simply as Ezeiza (EZE), 47 km (29 mi) west of downtown Buenos Aires. Ezeiza is served by foreign carriers as well as domestic lines with international routes. Upon leaving the country you must pay an $18 departure tax inside the airport after checking in for your flight; cash (pesos, dollars, or euros) and major credit or debit cards are accepted.

Flights within Argentina generally depart from Aeroparque Jorge Newbery (AEP), known as Aeroparque, about 15 minutes north of downtown.

🛪 **Aeroparque Jorge Newbery (AEP)** ☎ 11/5480-6111 ⊕ www.aa2000.com.ar. **Aeropuerto Internacional Ministro Pistarini de Ezeiza (EZE)** ☎ 11/5480-6111 ⊕ www. aa2000.com.ar.

AIRPORT Information counters within the airports can help you choose among
TRANSFERS the various licensed transport services that run between the airports and into town. Generally, *colectivos* (city buses) are cheapest, but you're only allowed two bags. You can catch the buses outside Terminal B at Ezeiza (2 pesos; two hours to downtown) and directly outside Aeroparque's main entrance (80¢; 15 minutes to downtown)

Private bus or van service costs about 25 pesos per person to downtown from Ezeiza and about 10 pesos from Aeroparque to downtown. Manuel Tienda Leon provides comfortable, reliable bus service from Ezeiza every 30 minutes to various spots downtown. *Remises* (unmarked cars with drivers that work with prearranged fixed prices) run around 60 pesos from Ezeiza and 15 pesos from Aeroparque; they're limited to four passengers. Metered taxis, available at the sidewalk outside the terminals, can be steeper depending on traffic.

The main highway connecting Ezeiza with the city is the Autopista Ricchieri, which you can reach by taking Autopista 25 de Mayo out of the city or the Avenida General Paz, which circles the entire city. The trip from downtown to Ezeiza takes around 45 minutes. Note that most flights to the United States depart from Buenos Aires in the evening, so plan to offset afternoon traffic snarls with at least an hour of travel time to Ezeiza.

There are several routes to Aeroparque from downtown—about a 15-minute trip. The easiest way is to take Avenida Libertador north to Avenida Sarmiento, and then take a right and follow it until Costanera Rafael Obligado. The airport will be on your left. Traffic isn't usually an issue. A private car will cost around 20 pesos, van service about 10 pesos.

Allow 45 minutes for travel between the two airports. Aeroparque is near Avenida General Paz, which circles the entire city and can connect you with the Autopista Ricchieri toward Ezeiza. A private car will cost around 50 pesos; a van will cost roughtly 25 pesos.

🚌 Bus Info **Manuel Tienda León** ☎ 11/4383-4454 or 0810/888-5366 ⊕ www.tiendaleon. com.ar.

🚌 Remises **Annie Millet Transfers** ☎ 11/6777-7777. **Remises Full-Time** ☎ 11/4775-9596 or 11/4775-1011. **Remises REB** ☎ 11/4863-1226 or 11/4862-6271. **Remises Rioja** ☎ 11/ 4794-4677. **Remises Universal** ☎ 11/4315-6555.

BY BUS

Most long-distance and international buses use the Estación Terminal de Omnibus in Retiro. The terminal houses more than 60 companies, arranged by destinations served, not by name. Rates vary according to distance, services, and season; compare prices before purchasing.

Colectivos connect the city's barrios and greater Buenos Aires. You're assured a seat on a *diferencial* bus (indicated by a sign on the front); they run less frequently than colectivos and are more expensive. Stops are every other block (200 meters [656 feet] apart) and are marked by small, easy-to-miss metal signs citing the number of the bus line. Buses, which are generally safe, run 24 hours a day; service is less frequent at night.

Hail your bus and let the driver know your destination; then insert your coins in the machine (exact change isn't necessary, but coins are), which will print your ticket. Fares are 80¢ within the city, 1.25 to 1.65 pesos outside the city; diferencials cost 2 pesos. There are no daily or weekly discount passes. Once on board, head for the back, which is where you exit. A small bell on the grab bar lets you signal for a stop. Don't depend on drivers for much assistance; they're busy navigating traffic. You can purchase a *Guia T,* an essential guide to the routes, at any news kiosk, or visit the Spanish-language colectivo Web site for info.

🚌 **Colectivo** ⊕ www.loscolectivos.com.ar. **Estación Terminal de Omnibus** ✉ Av. Ramos Mejía 1680, Retiro ☎ 11/4310-0700.

BY CAR

Avenida General Paz completely encircles Buenos Aires. If you're driving into the city, you'll know you're in Buenos Aires proper once you cross this road. If you're entering from the north, chances are you will be on the Ruta Panamericana, which has wide lanes and good lighting. The quickest way from downtown to Ezeiza Airport is Autopista 25 de Mayo to Autopista Ricchieri.

Porteños drive with verve and a disdain for the rules. Having a car is really more hassle than it's worth; there are ample taxis and public transportation options. If you're are up to the challenge, however, drive defensively. And be cautious when approaching or exiting overpasses; there have been incidences of *ladrillazo* (brick throwing) for the purpose of theft. Daily rental rates range from around 75 pesos to 200 pesos, depending on the type of car and the distance you plan to travel.

A more convenient option than driving yourself is to have your travel agent or hotel arrange for a *remis* (car and driver), especially for a day's tour of the suburbs or nearby pampas. This service costs about 30–40 pesos per hour, sometimes with a three-hour minimum and an additional charge per kilometer (½ mi) if you drive outside the city limits. Remises usually end up being cheaper than cabs, especially during peak hours. If your driver is helpful and friendly, a 10% tip is appropriate.

PARKING   Parking can be a problem in the city, though there are several underground municipal parking garages and numerous private ones. Look for a blue sign with an E (for *estacionamiento* [parking]). The cost is about 3–4 pesos for the first hour and 1–1.50 pesos for each additional half hour. Most malls have garages, which are usually free or give you a reduced rate with a purchase.

BY SUBTE

The *subte* (subway) is generally safe and pleasant. During morning and evening commuter hours, cars do get crowded, though. The stations are well patrolled by police and many are decorated with artworks, including murals by Argentine artists. You'll likely hear musicians and see actors performing on trains and in the stations. Single-ride tickets cost 70¢ to anywhere in the city; you can buy passes in stations for 1, 2, 5, or 10 trips or a rechargeable card. The subte shuts down around 11 PM and reopens at 5 AM.

🚇 **Metrovías** ⊕ www.metrovias.com.ar.

BY TAXI

All taxis in Buenos Aires city are black and have yellow tops. An unoccupied one will have a small, red LIBRE sign on the left-hand side of its windshield. When hailing a taxi on the street, make sure it says RADIO TAXI and that you see a CB antenna attached to the hood. Radio taxis are part of licensed fleets and are in constant contact with dispatchers; nonlicensed cabs are occasionally driven by unscrupulous men looking to rip off tourists; avoid them. If you call for a taxi, you'll have to wait a few minutes, but you can be sure of its origin and safety. All taxis are supposed to have working seatbelts, but this isn't always the case.

Meters start at 1.98 pesos and charge 22¢ per ¼ km (⅛ mi); you'll also end up paying for standing time spent at a light or in a traffic jam. From the central downtown area, it will cost you around 6 pesos to Recoleta, 5 pesos to San Telmo, 9 pesos to Palermo, and 11 pesos to Belgrano. Drivers don't expect tips; if you round up to the next peso and pay that fare, most drivers will be thrilled.

🔄 **Taxi Companies Blue Way Taxi** ☎ 11/4/77-8888. **Cirtax Taxi** ☎ 11/4504-8440. **City Taxi** ☎ 11/4585-5544. **Su Taxi** ☎ 11/4635-2500.

Contacts & Resources

BANKS & EXCHANGE SERVICES

In the Ezeiza airport you can exchange money at Casa Piano and Banco Nación in Terminal A on the ground level. Staffers at exchange houses will require a passport to conduct transactions. You can also hit the ATM in Terminal A, extracting pesos at a decent exchange rate. If you're taking licensed transportation into town, you can pay in dollars or euros at the stands next to the arrival gates. You can find ATMs throughout the city. Those that are part of the Banelco network are the most prevalent. They're identified by a burgundy sign, and you'll find them in banks, service stations, and malls. Of course, while conducting any financial transaction, be aware of your surroundings and don't flash cash.

🔄 **American Express** ✉ Arenales 707, El Centro ☎ 11/4310-3000. **Banco Piano** ✉ San Martín 345, El Centro ☎ 11/4394-2463. **BankBoston** ✉ Florida 99, El Centro ☎ 11/4820-2000. **Cambio America** ✉ Sarmiento 501, El Centro ☎ 11/4393-0054. **Citibank** ✉ Florida 199, El Centro ☎ 11/4329-1000. **Forex Cambio** ✉ M. T. de Alvear 540, El Centro ☎ 11/4010-2000. **HSBC Republic** ✉ Florida 201, El Centro ☎ 11/4320-2800. **Western Union** ✉ J. L. Borges 2472, Palermo ☎ 11/4777-1940.

VISITOR INFORMATION

You can get information over the phone weekdays from 9 to 5, from the city tourism office: the Dirección de Turismo del Gobierno de la Ciudad de Buenos Aires. Its excellent Web site has printable walking tours. The Secretaría de Turismo de la Nación (National Secretary of Tourism) has a 24-hour hotline that's toll-free from any point in Argentina.

🔄 **Dirección de Turismo del Gobierno de la Ciudad de Buenos Aires** ☎ 11/4313-0187 ⊕ www.buenosaires.gov.ar. The **Secretaría de Turismo de la Nación** ✉ Av. Santa Fe 883, Microcentro ☎ 11/4312-2232 or 0800/555-0016 ⊕ www.turismo.gov.ar.

IGUAZÚ FALLS

Revised by Victoria Patience

Iguazú, 1,357 km (841 mi) northeast of Buenos Aires, consists of some 275 separate waterfalls—in the rainy season there are as many as 350—that send their white cascades plunging more than 200 feet onto the rocks below. Dense, lush jungle surrounds the falls: here the tropical sun and the omnipresent moisture make the jungle grow at a pace that produces a towering pine tree in two decades instead of the seven it takes in, say, Scandinavia. By the falls and along the roadside, rainbows and butterflies are set off against vast walls of red earth, which is so ubiquitous that eventually even peso bills in the area turn red from exposure to the stuff.

Puerto Iguazú, a town of 25,000 people 17 km (11 mi) west of the falls, is the best base. The town originated as a port for shipping wood from the region. It was in the early 20th century that Victoria Aguirre, a high-society porteña, funded the building of a road that extends to Cataratas del Iguazú to make it easier for people to visit the falls. You may find Puerto Iguazú preferable to its livelier Brazilian counterpart, Foz do Iguaçu—it's considerably more tranquil and safer (when you go to the Brazilian side, leave your valuables in the hotel and be on the alert; crime is more frequent there).

> ### WORD OF MOUTH
>
> In Iguazú we took a 20-minute ride in a 4x4 on a jungle trail to the river's edge, where we entered a speedboat. It flew downriver to the first set of falls, allowing us to take photos before moving forward into the spray, which drenched us head to toe.
>
> –Nicci

Border Crossing

Border procedure for crossing into Brazil at Iguazú is inconsistent. In theory, Brazil operates a reciprocal visa policy, which means that it requires visas of citizens of countries who require them of Brazilians, usually at the same price. So, technically speaking, Canadian and American citizens crossing into Brazil to visit the falls need a visa, while British visitors don't. In practice, however, authorities rarely stamp visitors in and out, especially if you are with an organized tour, but sometimes just note down your name and passport number. Opinions are divided on whether it's worth the hassle (and cost) of getting a visa when you probably won't be asked for one. If you want to be on the safe side, allow a couple of days for processing. In Puerto Iguazú, the Brazilian consulate is open weekdays 8–12:30, and in Buenos Aires from 10–1 PM.

🚩 **Brazilian Consulates In Puerto Iguazú** ✉ Av. Córdoba 264 Puerto Iguazú ☎ 3757/421-348. **In Buenos Aires** ✉ Carlos Pellegrini 1363, 5th fl., Buenos Aires ☎ 11/4515-6500 ⊕ www.conbrasil.org.ar.

Exploring the Falls

The best way to immerse yourself in the falls is to wander the many access paths, which are a combination of bridges, ramps, stone staircases, and metal catwalks set in a forest of ferns, begonias, orchids, and tropical trees. The catwalks over the water put you right in the middle of the action, so be ready to get doused by the rising spray. (Be sure to bring rain gear.)

The Brazilians are blessed with the best panoramic view, an awesome vantage point that suffers only from the sound of the gnatlike helicopters that erupt out of the lawn of the Hotel das Cataratas right in front of the falls. (Unfortunately, most indigenous macaws and toucans have abandoned the area to escape the whine of the helicopters' engines.) The Argentine side offers the better close-up experience of the falls, with excellent hiking paths, catwalks that approach the falls, a sandy beach to relax on, and places to bathe in the froth of the Río Iguazú.

The falls on the Argentine side are in the **Parque Nacional Iguazú** (Iguazú National Park), which was founded in 1934, declared a World Heritage Site in 1984, and refurbished by a private concession in 2001. There's

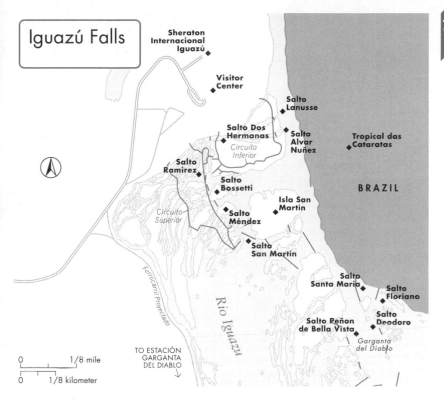

Iguazú Falls

Sheraton
Internacional
Iguazú

Visitor
Center

Salto
Lanusse

Salto Dos
Hermanas

Salto
Alvar
Nuñez

*Circuito
Inferior*

Tropical das
Cataratas

Salto
Ramírez

BRAZIL

Salto
Bossetti

Isla San
Martín

*Circuito
Superior*

Salto
Méndez

Salto
San Martín

Ferrocarril Proyectado

Salto
Santa María

Salto
Floriano

Salto Peñon
de Bella Vista

Salto
Deodoro

Río Iguazú

*Garganta
del Diablo*

0   1/8 mile

0   1/8 kilometer

TO ESTACIÓN
GARGANTA
DEL DIABLO
↓

a Visitor Center, called Yvyra Reta ("country of the trees" in Guaraní) with excellent facilities, including a good explanation of the region's ecology and human history. From here you can catch the gas-propelled Tren de la Selva (Jungle Train), which departs every 20 minutes. It makes a stop at Estación Cataratas and then proceeds to Estación Garganta del Diablo (Devil's Throat Station), where a wheelchair-accessible, metal catwalk leads to a platform beside one of the world's most dizzying spots. Here the Iguazú River plummets, with an awesome roar, more than 230 feet into a horseshoe-shape gorge, amid a cloud of mist. Be sure to take a plastic bag to stash your camera in.

If a more relaxed stroll is preferred, take the well-marked, ½-km (.3-mi) **Sendero Verde** (Green Path) past Estación Cataratas and connect with the **Circuito Superior** (Upper Circuit), which stretches along the top of the falls for 1 km (½ mi). With six sightseeing balconies, this easy walk of about an hour and a half provides great upper views of the falls Dos Hermanas, Ramírez, Bossetti, Méndez, and the most impressive, named after the Libertador (Liberator) San Martín. Near the falls look for *vencejos*, swallows that nest behind the curtains of water. Note that the paths beyond the San Martín have more than a few stairways and, therefore, are not wheelchair-accessible.

The **Circuito Inferior** (Lower Circuit) starts by a water-and-watch tower and is a 1.7-km-long (1.1-mi-long) loop that consists of a metal catwalk, lots of stairways, and protected promontories at the best spots. At the beginning of this walk you'll pass the small Alvar Núñez Cabeza de Vaca Falls, named after the Spanish

conquistador who stumbled onto the spectacle in the 16th century; the Peñón de Bella Vista (Rock of the Beautiful View); and the Salto Lanusse (Lanusse Falls). These are just preliminaries to get you warmed up for the main event. Halfway along this circuit you get a panoramic peek at what's to come—through the foliage you can see the gigantic curtain of water in the distance. The trail leads along the lower side of Brazo San Martín, a branch of the Iguazú river that makes a wide loop to the south before following the same vertical fate as the main branch, along a mile-long series of falls. The last part of the trail offers the most exciting views of the main falls, including Garganta del Diablo in the background. Allow about an hour and a half to walk this circuit. There's no way to get lost on the catwalk, but English-speaking guides, found at the visitor center, can be hired to provide detailed explanations of the falls.

From the Circuito Inferior you can reach the pier where a free boat service crosses the river to **Isla San Martín** (San Martín Island). This service operates all day, except when the river is too high. On the island, after a steep climb up a rustic stairway, a circular trail opening presents three spectacular panoramas of Salto San Martín, Garganta del Diablo, and Salto Ventana (Window Falls). Few people make the effort to cross the river to Isla San Martín and do this climb, so you can often enjoy the show in solitude.

The **Sendero Macuco** (Macuco Trail) extends 4 km (2½ mi) into the jungle, ending at the Salto Arrechea (Arrechea Falls) farther downriver from the main falls. The trail is very carefully marked, and descriptive signs in Spanish explain the jungle's flora and fauna. The closest you'll get to a wild animal is likely to be a paw print in the dirt, though you may be lucky enough to glimpse a monkey. The foliage is dense, so the most common surprises are the jungle sounds that seem to emerge out of nowhere. You can turn back at any point, or continue on to the refreshing view of the river and Salto Arrechea, where there is a swimming spot. The best time to hear animal calls and to avoid the heat is either early in the morning or just before sunset. The battalions of butterflies, also best seen in the early morning or late afternoon, can be marvelous, and the intricate glistening cobwebs crisscrossing the trail are a treat in the dawn light. Plan on spending about three hours for the whole trip. The **Centro de Investigaciones Ecológicas Subtropicales** (Center for Subtropical Ecological Investigation; ☎ 3757/421–222) maintains the trail.

On the Brazilian side, the falls, known in Portuguese as the Foz do Iguaçu, can be seen from the **Parque Nacional Foz do Iguaçu**, Brazil's national park. The park runs for 25 km (16 mi) along a paved highway south-west of downtown Foz do Iguaçu, the nearest town. Note that from No-vember through February Brazil is one hour ahead of Argentina. The **park entrance** (✉ Km 17, Rodovia das Cataratas ☎ 005545/529–8383) is the best place to get information; it's open daily 8–5, and the entrance fee is roughly 20 reales. Much of the park's 457,000 acres is protected rain forest—off-limits to visitors and home to the last viable popula-tions of panthers as well as rare flora such as bromeliads and orchids. The falls are 11 km (7 mi) from the park entrance. The luxurious, his-toric Hotel das Cataratas sits near the trailhead. Public parking is al-lowed on the highway shoulder and in a small lot near the hotel. The path to the falls is 2 km (1 mi) long, and its walkways, bridges, and stone staircases lead through the rain forest to concrete and wooden catwalks that take you to the falls. Highlights of the Brazilian side of the falls in-clude first the Salto Santa Maria, from which catwalks branch off to the Salto Deodoro and Salto Floriano, where you'll be doused by the spray. The end of the catwalk puts you right in the heart of the specta-cle at Garganta do Diablo ("Devil's Throat" in Portuguese), for a per-spective different from the Argentine side. On the last section of the main trail is a building with facilities, including a panoramic elevator; it's open daily 8:30–6, and there's a small fee.

Where to Stay & Eat

Neither Puerto Iguazú nor Foz do Iguaçu is known for its restaurant scene. While eateries in both places are generally cheap, quality is rarely anything to write home about, and you may well be the only diner in the place. Most hotels and even hostels have their own restaurants, which are the best—and most convenient—options.

$ ✗ **Jardín Iguazú.** At lunch and at odd hours, when everything else is closed, this restaurant serves a good fixed-price meal—for about $5 you get an empanada, a salad, a main dish with pasta and meat, and a beverage. The place is rather shiny, with highly polished stones on the floor and a stage (used for live music in the evenings) speckled with silver chips. Jardín Iguazú is close to the bus terminal and stays open until 2 AM. ✉ *Avs. Misiones and Córdoba, Puerto Iguazú, Argentina* ☎ *3757/423–200.*

¢–$ ✗ **El Charo.** This restaurant is in a shabby old house that looks like it could be blown down with a huff and a puff: the paintings are tilted, the roof is sinking, and the cowhide seats are faded. Nevertheless, this is one of town's most popular restaurants because of its consistently de-licious and inexpensive *parrilladas* (grilled meats), as well as its pasta and grilled fish. Note that napkins come only by request. ✉ *Av. Cór-doba 106, Puerto Iguazú, Argentina* ☎ *3757/421–529* ▭ *No credit cards.*

★ $$$$ ✗🔲 **Hotel Cataratas.** Though this redbrick hotel with green windowsills and white awnings isn't especially attractive from the outside, inside is a different story: the classy lobby and ample guest rooms are tastefully decorated with the finest materials and furnishings. Ask for a master double, which is the same price as the standard double but slightly nicer. The hotel also has beautiful grounds and excellent facilities, including an enormous pool with landscaped waterfalls. The high-quality restaurant, serving international cuisine, has an à la carte menu and a fixed-price buffet (dinner only). ✉ *R12, Km 4, Argentina 3370* ☎ *3757/421–100* 🛏 *112 rooms, 4 suites* ⚬ *Restaurant, room service, in-room safes, minibars, tennis court, pool, gym, massage, sauna, volleyball, bar, business services, meeting room, travel services* ▤ *AE, DC, MC, V.*

★ **$$$$** ✕▦ **Sheraton International Iguazú.** The building may be an eyesore, but it's just a short walk from the falls. Half the rooms have direct views of them—be sure to reserve one of these well in advance (note that they're about 30% more expensive). Floor-to-ceiling windows reveal the inspiring scene to the lobby, restaurants, bars, and even the pool. The Garganta del Diablo ($$–$$$) restaurant is one of the area's finest; the trout in pastry and the surubí in banana leaves are exquisite. The restaurant is only open for dinner, which starts after the last bus to Puerto Iguazú leaves; if you're not a Sheraton guest, plan on laying out over 50 pesos for the taxi ride back to your hotel. ✉ *Parque Nacional Iguazú, Argentina 3370* ☎ *3757/41800* ⊕ *www.sheraton.com* 🛏 *176 rooms, 4 suites* ⚬ *2 restaurants, room service, IDD phones, in-room safes, minibars, cable TV, 3 tennis courts, pool, gym, sauna, bicycles, bars, lobby lounge, babysitting, laundry service, Internet, business services, convention center, airport shuttle, car rental, travel services, free parking, no-smoking rooms* ▤ *AE, DC, MC, V.*

★ **$$$$** ✕▦ **Tropical das Cataratas.** Not only is this stately hotel within the national park on the Brazilian side just a stone's throw from the falls, but it provides many comforts—large rooms, terraces, even hammocks. Galleries and gardens surround this pink building, and its main section has been declared a Brazilian national heritage site. The restaurant serves traditional Brazilian food. ✉ *Km 25, Rodovia das Cataratas, Brazil 85850-970* ☎ *5545/521–7000* ⊕ *www.tropicalhotel.com.br* 🛏 *200 rooms* ⚬ *2 restaurants, coffee shop, 2 tennis courts, pool, bar, shops, business services, meeting room* ▤ *AE, DC, MC, V.*

¢ ✕▦ **Los Helechos.** This hotel is such a great bargain it doesn't have to discount its rooms during the off-season to draw travelers. It's also convenient to the center of town and two blocks from the bus terminal. Rooms are simple but clean and comfortable; half have air-conditioning and television (these cost 10 pesos more). Be sure to get up in time for the buffet breakfast, which includes platters of tropical fruit. ✉ *Paulino Amarante 76, Puerto Iguazú, Argentina 3370* ☎☎ *3757/420–338* 🛏 *25 rooms* ⚬ *Restaurant, pool, bar; no a/c in some rooms* ▤ *AE, DC, MC, V.*

★ ¢ ✕▦ **Hostel-Inn Iguazú.** Don't be put off by the "hostel" in the name: as well as great-value dorm accommodations there are double rooms with private bathrooms. All rooms are spacious, with huge windows and lots of light. The Hostel-Inn is on the road halfway between Puerto Iguazú and the falls, which makes getting to the park early much easier; the friendly staff can sort out excursions. At night the restaurant does simple fare like stuffed pork. A lovely outdoor pool, a bar, and a lounge area are three more reasons not to have to make the trek to town. ✉ *Ruta 12, Km. 5, 3370* ☎ *3757/421823* ⊕ *www.hostel-inn.com* 🛏 *36 rooms (206 beds)* ⚬ *Restaurant, pool, bar, Ping-Pong, laundry services, travel services.* ▤ *No credit cards* ◉ *CP.*

Iguazú Essentials

Transportation

BY AIR

Aerolíneas Argentinas flies three times daily between Buenos Aires and the Argentine airport near Iguazú; the trip takes an hour and three quarters. LAN does the same trip twice daily. Southern Winds also flies daily to and from Buenos Aires and can be cheaper, especially if you book in advance. Normal rates are about 200 pesos each way, but promotional rates, called *bandas negativas,* are sometimes available if you reserve ahead. The Brazilian airline Varig has offices in Foz do Iguaçu and offers connecting flights all over Brazil.

Argentina and Brazil each have an airport at Iguazú. The Argentine airport is 20 km (12 mi) southeast of Puerto Iguazú, Argentina; the Brazilian airport is 11 km (7 mi) from Foz do Iguaçu and 17 km (11 mi) from the national park. The Colectivo Aeropuerto shuttle has service to hotels in Puerto Iguazú for 3 pesos. To get from the hotel to the airport, call two hours before your departure, and the shuttle will pick you up. Taxis to Puerto Iguazú cost 25 pesos.

🛪 Airlines **Aerolíneas Argentinas** ☎ 11/4320-2000 in Buenos Aires, 223/496-0101 in Mar del Plata, 3757/420-849 or 3757/420-168 in Puerto Iguazú ⊕ www.aerolineas.com. ar. **LAN** ☎ 1174378-2200 ⊕ www.lan.com. **Varig** ☎ 5545/523-2111 in Foz do Iguaçu, 11/4329-9211 in Buenos Aires.

🛪 Airports **Aeropuerto Internacional de Puerto Iguazú** ✉ Ruta Provincial 101, Puerto Iguazú ☎ 3757/421-996. **Foz do Iguaçu Cataratas International Airport** ✉ BR 469, Km. 16, Foz do Iguaçu, Brazil ☎ 5545/574-1744.

BY BUS

Organized tours to Puerto Iguazú and the Cataratas del Iguazú can be arranged through most Buenos Aires travel agencies, though they're often not that much less expensive than traveling by plane. Via Bariloche has the quickest and most comfortable service between Puerto Iguazú and Buenos Aires; be sure to ask for the *coche cama* (sleeper) service. The trip takes 16 hours, costs about 90 pesos, and includes meals. Expreso Singer takes 18 hours and costs 82 pesos. The Puerto Iguazú Terminal de Ómnibus is in the center of town.

From Puerto Iguazú to the falls, take El Práctico from the terminal; buses leave every 45 minutes 7–7 and cost 6 pesos round-trip.

🚍 Bus Depots **Puerto Iguazú Terminal de Ómnibus** ✉ Avs. Córdoba and Misiones, Puerto Iguazú ☎ 3757/422-730. **Terminal de Ómnibus Retiro** ✉ Av. Antártida Argentina and Av. Ramos Mejía, Buenos Aires ☎ 11/4310-0700 ⊕ www.tebasa.com.ar.

🚍 Bus Lines **Agencia de Pasajes Noelia** ☎ 3757/422-722 in Puerto Iguazú. **Chevallier** ☎ 11/4311-0033 ⊕ www.nuevachevallier.com. **El Cóndor** ☎ 11/4313-3762. **El Práctico** ☎ 3757/422-722 in Puerto Iguazú. **Expreso Singer** ☎ 11/4313-3927. **Flechabus** ☎ 11/4315-2781 ⊕ www.flechabus.com.ar. **Pullman General Belgrano** ☎ 11/4315-6522 ⊕ www.gralbelgrano.com.ar. **Via Bariloche** ☎ 11/4315-3122 in Buenos Aires, 3757/420-854 in Puerto Iguazú ⊕ www.viabariloche.com.ar.

Contacts & Resources

BANKS & EXCHANGE SERVICES

Local banks in all towns have 24-hour ATMs, recognizable by the LINK or BANELCO signs. As a rule, banks are open from 10 AM to 3 PM, though those specializing in currency exchange may stay open longer. Dollars and pesos are used interchangeably in Puerto Iguazú; to exchange other currencies, but not traveler's checks, go to Argecam. For other banking needs in Puerto Iguazú, try Banco Macro, which has ATMs. You will need Brazilian currency on the Brazilian side: there are small exchange booths in the bus stations at Puerto Iguazú and Foz do Iguaçu, and the Banco do Brasil also changes currency.

Brazil's unit of currency is the real (R$; plural: *reais,* though it's sometimes seen as *reales*). One real is 100 centavos (cents). There are notes worth 1, 5, 10, 20, 50, and 100 reais, together with coins worth 1, 5, 10, 25, and 50 centavos and 1 real.

🖪 **Argecam** ✉ Av. Victoria Aguirre 562, Puerto Iguazú 🕾 3757/420-273 ⊙ Weekdays 8-7. **Banco do Brasil** ✉ Av. Brasil 1377, Foz do Iguaçu, Brazil 🕾 55/45/3521-2525 ⊕ www. bb.com.br. **Banco Macro** ✉ Av. Victoria Aguirre 330, Puerto Iguazú 🕾 3757/420-212 ⊙ Weekdays 8-1.

TOURS

Many travel agencies offer packages from Buenos Aires that include flights, transfers, accommodation, and visits to the falls (and surrounding areas, depending on the length of your stay). Local travel agencies and tour operators also offer trips that will take you to both sides. Be sure to book a deal that includes a boat trip, an unmissable—though drenching—experience which gets you almost under the falls. Operators that cover both sides of the falls will help with border formalities, though those that only work on the Argentine side have a reputation for complicating the issue to get you to do all your tourism on their side of the falls. If you want to set your own pace, you can tour the Argentine side and then take a taxi or one of the regularly scheduled buses across the International Bridge, officially called the Ponte Presidente Tancredo Neves, to Brazil.

Three of the most reliable agencies are Aguas Grandes, Sol Iguazú, and the popular Iguazú Jungle Explorer, which has four trips to the jungle and falls. The best of these is the Gran Aventura trip, which includes a truck ride through the forest and a boat ride to San Martín, Bossetti, and the Salto Tres Mosqueteros (be ready to get soaked). Another tour takes you to Garganta del Diablo. Park ranger Daniel Somay organizes personalized Jeep tours with an ecological focus through his Explorador Expediciones in Puerto Iguazú. Bring binoculars to see the birds.

Helisul operates short helicopter rides over the falls, which leave opposite the Tropical das Cataratas hotel, on the Brazilian side. Though they offer a fabulous view, they have a detrimental effect on local wildlife, hence Argentina's ban on their side.

🖪 **Tour Companies Aguas Grandes** 🕾 3757/421-140 ⊕ www.aguasgrandes.com. **Explorador Expediciones** 🕾 3757/421-632 ⊕ www.hotelguia.com/turismo/explorador-expediciones. **Helisul** 🕾 5545/529-7474 in Brazil ⊕ www.helisul.com. **Iguazú Jungle**

Explorer ☎ 3757/421-600 ⊕ www.iguazujungleexporer.com. **Sol Iguazú Turismo** ☎ 3757/421-008 ⊕ www.soliguazu.com.ar.

VISITOR INFORMATION

🛈 **Tourist Offices Cataratas del Iguazú** ✉ Visitor center at park entrance ☎ 3757/420-180. **Foz do Iguaçu** ✉ Av. Jorge Schimmelpfeng and Rua Benjamin Constant, Foz do Iguaçu, Brazil ☎ 5545/574-2196 ⊕ www.fozdoiguacu.pr.gov.br. **Puerto Iguazú** ✉ Av. Victoria Aguirre 311, Puerto Iguazú ☎ 3757/420-800.

MENDOZA PROVINCE

By Eddy Ancinas

Mendoza is one of the world's wine capitals, and although this is certainly a major reason to visit, it's not the only one. You can also go rafting, soak in thermal baths, ski at Penitentes, go horseback riding, and hike on Aconcagua—the western hemisphere's highest mountain. The Andean communities of Potrerillos and Uspallata, the Atuel Canyon near San Rafael, and Malargüe in the south are filled with wild rivers and majestic mountains.

The province has a population of 1,579,651 people, with 110,477 living in the city. The urban area known as Gran Mendoza (greater Mendoza) includes the city of Mendoza and the departments of Godoy Cruz, Guaymallén, Maipú, Junín, Luján de Cuyo, and Las Heras. These departments have grand shopping centers along the main highway, and small hotels, restaurants, wineries, and vineyards tucked back along country roads. Other wine-growing departments in Mendoza Province are the Valle de Uco and San Rafael.

The Wineries

Located 1,040 km (600 mi) northwest of Buenos Aires, Mendoza is the main city in the Wine Regions. A cool canopy of poplars, elms, and sycamores shades its sidewalks, plazas, and low-rises. Water runs along the streets in *acéquias* (canals), disappears at intersections, then bursts from fountains in the city's 74 parks and squares. Many acéquias were built by the Huarpe Indians and improved upon by the Incas long before the city was founded in 1561 by Pedro del Castillo.

In 1861 an earthquake destroyed the city, killing 11,000 people. Mendoza was reconstructed on a grid, making it easy to explore on foot. Four smaller squares (Chile, San Martín, Italia, and España) radiate from the four corners of Plaza Independencia, the main square. Their Spanish tiles, exuberant fountains, shaded walkways, and myriad trees and flowers lend peace and beauty. Avenida San Martín, the town's major thoroughfare, runs north–south out into the southern departments and wine districts. Calle Sarmiento intersects San Martín at the tourist office and becomes a *peatonal* (pedestrian mall) bustling with outdoor cafés, shops, offices, and bars. It crosses the Plaza Independencia, stops in front of the Hyatt Plaza, then continues on the other side of the hotel. In winter, a Bus Turístico departs every two hours on a guided tour, letting you on and off at designated stops. Be sure to pick up the walking-tour map "*Circuitos Peatonales*" in your hotel or at the city tourist office.

Wine Glossary

ARGENTINA WAS ONCE the world's fourth-largest wine-consuming nation (behind France, Italy, and Spain) Unremarkable reds were either downed by beef-eating Argentines or exported in tankers to Europe. But in the 1980s Dr. Nicolás Catena recognized his country's potential to compete in the world market by producing lower-yield, higher-quality grapes, and Argentine vintners began planting single varietals in ideal locations. They also improved irrigation and invested in new technology. Today you can find world-class Argentine wine in the U.S., Canada, Asia, and Europe.

Principal Wines produced in Argentina:

Whites:

Chardonnay: Rootstock from the U.S; golden to amber; fruit aromas of apple, pear, bananas.

Chenin Blanc: Ideal grape for hot areas; good acidity and flavor; compatible for blending. Argentina's grape of the future.

Torrontés: Argentine grape born in Spain of the muscat grape. Pale gold; aromatic; citrusy with tropical fruits. Refreshing when very cold; similar to a dry Gerwürztraminer.

Sauvignon Blanc: Recent arrival from France. Pale yellow; aromas of eucalyptus, grass, mango, apples.

Sémillon: Long history in Argentina; pale gold to straw; light citrus with aromas of peach, apricot.

Spumante: Argentina's sparkling wine. In the last few years, Argentine vintners and foreign investors have been making bubbles with a variety of grapes.

Viognier: French grape; new in Argentina and gaining popularity. Light gold; aromatic; melon, peaches, and slight white pepper.

Reds:

Bonarda: Intense red with violet hues; strong tannins; black fruit and plums; ages well.

Cabernet Sauvignon: Adapts well to all Argentine regions. Complex aromas of tobacco, black pepper, red fruits. Full-bodied and structured through aging.

Malbec: Argentina's signature grape; originally a blending grape from Cahors, France. Thrives in Argentina's loose, sandy soil, sun, and cold nights. Deep red color; plums, cherries, and red fruits; sweet tannins; aging potential.

Merlot: French variety; has adapted to cooler climates of Valle de Uco, Río Negro, and Neuquén provinces. Robust tannins; low yield; highest potential in cool zones.

Pinot Noir: French lineage; blended with chardonnay for champagne (spumante in Argentina). Best potential in colder zones of Río Negro and Valle de Uco provinces; generous tannins; with aging, develops notes of coffee and tobacco.

Syrah: Originally from Persia (Shiraz in Iran); adapted well to warmer climates of San Juan and La Rioja provinces. Intense red; sweet, soft tannins; spicy flavors of ripe red fruit.

Tempranillo: From Spain; thrives in warm climates. Strong tannins; elegant red fruit; slightly dry.

The department of Maipú, south and slightly east of Mendoza City, has some 12 wineries in the districts of General Gutierrez, Coquimbito, and Cruz de Piedra. To the south, the department of Luján de Cuyo borders both sides of the Mendoza River and has 27 wineries in the districts of Agrelo, Carodilla, Chacras de Coria, Drummond, Perdriel, Ugarteche, and Vistalba. Aceso Sur (RN40), the main highway south, is the fastest way to get to the area.

> **WORD OF MOUTH**
>
> "If you can, do lunch at one of the wineries. My wife and I ate a wonderful three-course meal outdoors with a spectacular view of the Andes, and the winemaker gave us an impromptu wine appreciation course. It doesn't get any better than this!"
>
> –Jason01

Godoy Cruz

❶ Bodega Escorihuela. Founded in 1884 by Spaniard Miguel Escorihuela Gascón, this large winery features a 63,000-liter French barrel—the largest in the province. In 1993 a group of investors led by pioneer vintner Nicolás Catena bought the interests in the Bodega Escorihuela. Experimentation and innovation continue here with art exhibits and Francis Mallmanns' renowned restaurant, 1884. ⊠ *Belgrano 1188, Godoy Cruz* ☎ *261/499–7044* ⊕ *www.escorihuela.com.ar* ☉ *Weekdays 9:30–12:30 and 2:30–3:30; guided tours on the hour.*

Maipú

❸ Bodega la Rural. In 1855, Felipe Rutini left the hills of Italy to found a winery in the raw land of Coquimbito, Argentina. His descendants planted the first grapes (chardonnay and merlot) in the now-popular Tupungato District of the Valle de Uco. Today Bodega la Rural is still family-owned and -operated. The winery's well-known San Felipe label was created by Alejandro Sirio, a famous Spanish artist. Inside the original adobe barns the Museo del Vino (Wine Museum) has a fascinating collection of machinery, vintage carriages, and tools. ⊠ *11 km (6.8 mi) from Mendoza, Montecaseros 2625, Coquimbito, Maipú* ☎ *261/497–2013* ⊕ *www.bodegalarural.com.ar* ☉ *Tours every 30 min Mon.–Sat. 9–1 and 2–5; Sun. and holidays 10–1 with reservation.*

❹ Bodegas y Viñedos López. Wines up to 60 years old are stored in the main cellar of this traditional family winery, established in 1898. After a tour of the winery, tastings take place in the cave, where lunches can be arranged with a two-day notice. ⊠ *Ozamis 375, Maipú, Mendoza, 13km/8mi/20 min from Mendoza* ☎ *261/497–2406* ⊕ *www.bodegaslopez.com.ar/* ☉ *Mon.–Fri. hourly tours 9–5; Sat. and holidays hourly tours 9:30–10:30, and 12:30; Sun. by appt.*

❷ Familia Zuccardi. In 1950 Don Alberto Zuccardi, a civil engineer, developed a more modern system of irrigation for his vineyards in Maipú, and later in Santa Rosa. He and his team of 450 workers continue to discover new approaches to viniculture and wine tourism; their newest innovation, the "Cava de Turísmo," is an air-conditioned cave where you can join tours of the bodega, often led by family members or an oenologist. A soft, soothing light glows on cobblestone floors, cement walls, and warm woodwork in the tasting room and gift shop. Outside, you

Fodor'sChoice
★

can walk shoulder-to-shoulder with the neatly labeled vines to the garden restaurant for a wine-tasting lunch or tea. ⊠ *35 km (21.7 mi) from Mendoza, RP33, Km 7.5, Maipú, Mendoza* ☎ *261/441–0000* ⊕ *www.familiazuccardi.com* ☉ *Mon.–Sat. 9–5:30; Sun. and holidays 10–5.*

⑫ Finca Flichman. In 1873 Don Sami Flichman, a Jewish immigrant, planted the first vines in the stony soil of a former riverbed in the *barrancas* (ravines) next to the Mendoza River. His son Isaac acquired the property during the 1930s Depression and had the foresight to produce only high-quality grapes. In 1983 the Wertheim family bought the winery, introduced new technology, and added another winery. Underground cellars—some ancient, some new—stainless-steel tanks, and computerized temperature controls make this one of Argentina's most modern wineries. ⊠ *40 km (25 mi) from Mendoza, Munives 800, Barrancas/Maipú, Mendoza* ☎ *261/497–2039* ⊕ *www.flichman.com.ar* ☉ *Wed.–Sun. 10–5.*

Luján de Cuyo

㉑ Bodega Catena Zapata. A faux Maya pyramid rising from the vineyards fronts the towering snow-clad Andes at this landmark winery, where the architecture rivals the wine. Visitors descend from a crystal cupola through concentric spaces to the tasting room, which is surrounded by 400 oak barrels. Columbia University economics professor Nicolás Catena planted his vineyards at varying altitudes, then blended varietals from these different microclimates to create complex, distinctive wines. ⊠ *45 km (28 mi) from Mendoza, Calle J. Cobos s/n, Agrelo, Luján de Cuyo* ☎ *261/490–0214* ⊕ *www.catenawines.com.*

⑩ Bodega Lagarde. Founded in 1897, Lagarde is one of the oldest and most traditional wineries in Mendoza. The third generation of the Pescarmona family remains committed to excellence in cultivating their grapes and producing limited quantities of quality wine, searching for ways to improve while avoiding fashionable trends. ⊠ *30 km (18 mi) from Mendoza, San Martín 1745, Mayor Drummond, Luján de Cuyo* ☎ *261/498–0011* ⊕ *www.lagarde.com.ar* ☉ *Mon.–Fri. 10–5.*

⑯ Bodega Norton. In 1895 English engineer Sir Edmund Norton built the first winery in the valley south of the Mendoza River. Part of the old adobe house and a wing of the winery demonstrate the traditional construction of beamed ceilings with bamboo reeds under a zinc roof. In 1989 an Austrian businessman purchased the company, and his son continues to modernize and expand the 100-year-old vineyards. ⊠ *RP 15, Km 23.5, Perdriel, Luján de Cuyo, Mendoza* ☎ *261/490–9700* ⊕ *www.norton.com.ar* ☉ *Hourly tours daily 9–12, 2–5.*

⑧ Bodegas Nieto y Senetiner S.A. White adobe walls, tile roofs, colorful flowerbeds lining the walkways, and huge shade trees welcome you to this bodega, where groups can harvest grapes right alongside the experts from March 10 to mid-April. From mid-August until the end of September, pruning (*podar*) takes place, and you can join the experts in cutting, tying, and modifying vines. All activities include lunch at the bodega, tasting, and a tour, and all require reservations. ⊠ *Guaradia Viaje, between Ruta Panamericana and Rosque Sáenz Peña s/n, Vistalba, Luján de Cuyo, Mendoza* ☎ *261/498–0315* ⊕ *www.nietosenetiner.com.*

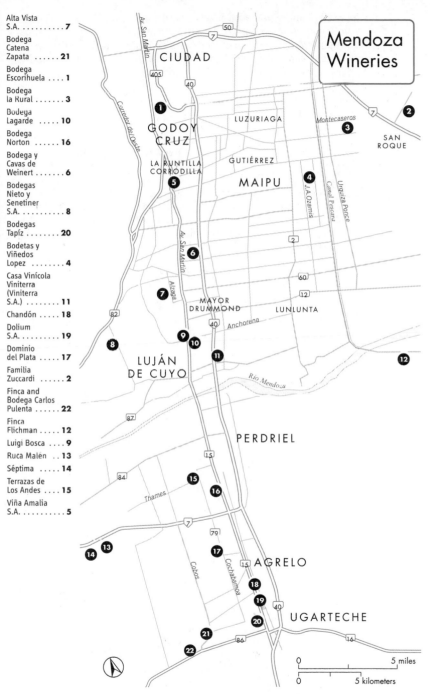

Mendoza
Wineries

com/ ⊙ *Summer: tours Mon.–Fri. at 10, 11, 12:30, and 4; Other seasons: tours Mon.–Fri. at 10, 11, 12:30, and 3.*

㉒ Bodegas Tapíz. When Kendall Jackson sold this modern bodega to the Ortiz family in 2003, CEO Patricia Ortiz, a medical doctor and mother of five, embarked on a slightly different approach to winemaking. Oenologist Fabián Valenzuela wants to make "happier wines" that are easier to drink and more food-friendly. Inside the bodega, walls of loose river rocks held in place by wire mesh contrast with slick granite walls and long corridors. Club Tapiz, a seven room inn with a spa, restaurant, and bicycles, is only 20 minutes away. ⊠ *RP 15, Km 32, Agrelo, Luján de Cuyo* ☎ *261/490–0202* ⊕ *www.tapiz.com* ⊙ *Mon.–Fri. 9–5.*

⑱ Chandón. The president of Moët & Chandon was so impressed by the terroir and climate in Agrelo that he decided to build the first foreign branch of his family's company there. Today, the busy winery is producing wine and *vino spumante* (sparkling wine) in great quantities. In a one-hour class for groups of 2–15, an oenologist will guide you through the process of blending wine. ⊠ *40 km (25 mi) from Mendoza, Ruta 40, Km 29, Agrelo, Luján de Cuyo* ☎ *261/490–9968* ⊕ *www. chandon.com.ar* ⊙ *Hourly tours Mon.–Fri. 10–1, 2–5; winter and holidays 11:30, 2, 3:30, and 5. Sat. with reservation.*

⑲ Dolium S.A. "Dolium" is the Latin for the type of amphora used by the Romans to store wine underground. Modern, innovative, and simple, the whole winemaking process occurs in what appears to be a small gray box set in the middle of a vineyard. Everything happens underground, but you can taste the wines upstairs in a glass-and-steel reception area that looks down into the wine works. ⊠ *32 km (20 mi) from Mendoza, Ruta Provincial 15, Km 30, Agrelo, Luján de Cuyo* ☎ *261/490–0200* ⊕ *www.dolium.com* ⊙ *Weekdays 9–5, weekends by appointment.*

⑰ Dominio del Plata. Since 2001 Susana Balbo and her husband, viticulturalist Pedro Marchevsky, have combined their skills with the newest technology and a passion for their land. Balbo, Argentina's first licensed female oenologist and an internationally known winemaking consultant, can look out her living-room window across a sea of vineyards to the sparkling Cordón de Plata mountain range. ⊠ *30 km (18.6 mi) from Mendoza, Cochebamba 7801, Agrelo, Luján de Cuyo* ☎ *261/498– 6572* ⊙ *Mon.–Fri. 9–1, 3–5* ⌲ *Reservations essential.*

㉒ Finca and Bodega Carlos Pulenta. Carlos Pulenta has been referred to as
Fodor'sChoice "the Robert Mondavi of Argentina." During his seven years as presi-
★ dent of Salentein, a Dutch company with three bodegas, he increased the number of European varietals, installed the latest technology, and put Salentein wine on the tables of the world. In 2004 he returned to his family's land in Vistalba, where he built his own bodega in the middle of the vineyard. The light stone and polished concrete complex houses an ultramodern 12-room inn, perhaps the best restaurant in the region (La Bourgogne), and a conference center. Inside the bodega, glass walls expose the tumbled rocks and

WORD OF MOUTH

"If you are planning to visit wineries on your own rather than taking an organized tour, try to make an appointment before you leave."
–lovesprada

dirt that malbec thrives in. Pulenta and his team have created three blends using malbec, cabernet, merlot, and bonarda, plus a delicate sauvignon blanc. ⊠ *Roque Saenz Peña 3531, Vistalba, Luján de Cuyo* ☎ *261/498–9400* ⊕ *www.carlospulentawines.com.*

⑨ Luigi Bosca. Albereto, Raul, and Roberto Arizú—descendents of Leoncio Arizú, who brought the original vines from Spain in 1890—believe that a winemaker's job is to preserve what nature has delivered. Here nature is on their side. Distinctive environments (*terroir*) produced by a variety of soils, climates, and vineyard locations have much to do with the unique character of Luigi Bosca's wine. This bodega has carved reliefs depicting the history of wine in Argentina, tile floors, inlaid wood ceilings, and painted arches. ⊠ *San Martín 2044, Drummond, Luján de Cuyo, Mendoza* ☎ *261/498–0437* ⊕ *www.luigibosca.com.ar* ☉ *Daily tours at 10, 11, 12:30, and 4 (3 in winter).*

⑬ Ruca Malén. Jon Pierre Thibaud brings 10 years of experience as president of neighboring Chandon vineyards to this modern, compact boutique winery. Thibaud and his French partner, Jacques Louis de Montalembert, have dedicated their collective skill and passion to selecting the finest grapes for quality wines. Wine tours are led by an oenologist. With one day's notice a gourmet lunch and wine tasting is available for 55 pesos per person. ⊠ *RN7, Km 1059, Agrelo, Luján de Cuyo, Mendoza* ☎ *261/410–6214* ⊕ *bodegarucamalen.com* ☉ *Mon.–Fri. 10–5, Sat. 10–1* ⚑ *Reservations essential.*

⑭ Séptima. When the Spanish wine group Codorniú decided that Argentina would be their seventh great wine investment, they constructed their winery in the "pirca" style, in which natural stones are piled one atop the other. The Huarpe natives used this technique to build walls, dwellings, and sacred places. Inside the massive walls is a state-of-the-art winery with sleek wood and glass corridors. You climb over hoses and machinery, following the grapes from vineyard to bottle in a natural working atmosphere. A rosé blend of malbec and pinot noir is an interesting invention. ⊠ *RN 7, Km 6.5, Agrelo, Luján de Cuyo, Mendoza* ☎ *261/498–5164* ⊕ *www.bodegaseptima.com.ar* ☉ *Mon.–Fri. 10–5* ⚑ *Reservations required.*

⑮ Terrazas de Los Andes. Four vineyards at different heights (terraces)—Syrah at 800 meters (2,600 feet), cabernet sauvignon at 980 meters (3,200 feet), malbec slightly higher, and chardonnay at 1,200 meters (3,993 feet)—take advantage of different microclimates. Bare brick walls, high ceilings, and a labyrinth of soaring arches store premium wines in stainless-steel tanks and oak barrels. Everything in the tasting room—from the bar to the tables to the leather chairs—is made with recycled barrels. There's a six-room guest house and a dining room. ⊠ *32 km (20mi) from Mendoza, Thames and Cochebamba, Perdriel, Luján de Cuyo, Mendoza* ☎ *261/448–0058* ⊕ *www.terrazasdelosandes.com* ☉ *Mon.–Fri. 10–12* ⚑ *required one day in advance by phone or e-mail.*

Other Wineries

⑦ Alta Vista S.A. ⊠ *Álzaga 3972, Chacras de Coria, Luján de Cuyo, Mendoza* ☎ *261/496–4684* ⊕ *www.altavistawines.com* ☉ *Tues.–Sat. tours at 9:30, 11, 12:30, 3, and 4:30.*

⑥ Bodega y Cavas de Weinert. ✉ *San Martín 5923 Chacras de Coria, Luján de Cuyo, Mendoza* ☎ *261/496–0409* ⊕ *www.bodegaweinert.com* ⊙ *Mon.–Fri. tours 9–1, 2–5; Sat. tours 9:30–4:30.*

⑪ Casa Vinícola Viniterra (Viniterra S.A.). ✉ *Av. Acceso Sur, Km 17.5, Luján de Cuyo, Mendoza* ☎ *261/498–5888 or 261/498–0073* ⊕ *www.viniterra. com.ar* ⊙ *Mon.–Fri. 9–5 hourly, Sat. 9–12, with reservations.*

⑤ Viña Amalia S.A. ✉ *San Martin 7440, Carrodilla, Luján de Cuyo, Mendoza* ☎ *261/436–0677* ⊕ *www.vinamalia.com.ar.*

Other Sights & Activities

In Mendoza

Museo del Area Fundacional. On the site of the original *cabildo* (town hall), the Foundation Museum explains the region's social and historical development. Of note is the display of a mummified child found on Aconcagua, with photos of his burial treasures—presumably an Inca or pre-Inca sacrifice. Underground excavations, made visible by a glass-covered viewing area, reveal layers of pre-Hispanic and Spanish remains. ✉ *Beltrán and Videla Castillo* ☎ *261/425–6927* 🎫 *$1.50* ⊙ *Tues.–Sat. 8 AM–10 PM, Sun. 3 PM–8 PM.*

Museo Histórico de San Martín. The San Martín Historical Museum has a decent library and a token collection of artifacts from campaigns of the Great Liberator. ✉ *Av. San Martín 1843* ☎ *261/425–7947* 🎫 *$1* ⊙ *Weekdays 8:30–1:30.*

Museo del Pasado Cuyano. Twice-governor and senator Emilio Civit's 26-bedroom 1873 mansion was the gathering place of the belle époque elite. Today it's the Museum of the Cuyo's Past, a gallery and archive with paintings, antiques, manuscripts, and newspapers. ✉ *Montevideo 544* ☎ *261/423–6031* 🎫 *Donation* ⊙ *Weekdays 9–12:30.*

Parque General San Martín. This grand public space has more than 50,000 trees from all over the world. Fifteen km (9 mi) of paths and walkways meander through the park, and the rose garden has about 500 varieties. You can observe nautical competitions from the rowing club's balcony restaurant, visit the zoo, or play tennis or golf. Scenes of the 1817 Andes crossing by José de San Martín and his army during the campaign to liberate Argentina are depicted on a monument on top of Cerro de la Gloria (Glory Hill) in the park's center. The soccer stadium and Greek theater (capacity 22,500) attract thousands during vendimia, the annual wine harvest festival.

Plaza Independencia. In Mendoza's main square you can sit on a bench in the shade of a sycamore tree and watch children playing in the fountains, browse the stands at a weekend fair, visit the Museo de Arte Moderno, or take a stroll after lunch at the historic Plaza Hotel (now a Hyatt) on your way to the shops and outdoor cafés on the pedestrian-only Calle Sarmiento, which bisects the square.

NIGHTLIFE **Avenida Arístedes Villanueva** is a hot spot of inexpensive bars and cafés. The area wakes up around 6 PM, when the bars, boutiques, wine shops, and sidewalk cafés open their doors. As the evening progresses, crowds get bigger, and the music—rock, tango, salsa—gets louder. The action peaks between 10 and midnight.

Inexpensive, casual **El Bar del José** (✉ Arístedes Villanueva 740 ☎ No phone) was the first gathering place in the trendy Villanueva neighborhood. **Por Acá** (✉ Arístedes Villanueva 557) attracts a cosmopolitan crowd of locals and European travelers. Live rock music begins after 10 PM. The **Regency Casino** (✉ 25 de Mayo and Sarmiento ☎ 261/441–2844) at the Park Hyatt Mendoza has blackjack, stud poker, roulette tables, slot machines, and an exclusive bar.

SHOPPING   Pick up leather goods, shoes, and clothing along the pedestrian part of Sarmiento, on Avenida Heras, and on side streets between. *Talabarterías* sell fine leather goods and everything equestrian, from saddles and hand-made tack to hats, vests, and other gaucho-inspired gift items. The 1884 **Mercado Central** (✉ Av. Heras and Patricias Mendocinas) is the oldest market in Mendoza. Ponchos, Indian weavings, olive oil, fruit, and handcrafts are sold daily from 9 to 1:30 and from 4:30 to 9. South of Mendoza, **Palmares Shopping Mall** (✉ Panamericano 2650) has 10 movie theaters and many good shops and restaurants.

Azafrán is a wine bar, café, wine shop, and delicatessen with regional olive oil, jams, meats, and cheeses (✉ Sarmiento 765 and Av. Villanueva 287 ☎ 261/429–4200). On the Peatonal, **Cardón** (✉ Sarmiento 224) carries gaucho clothing and accessories: bombachas (baggy, pleated pants), leather jackets and vests, boots, belts, scarves, ponchos, and silver knives. You'll find a huge selection of wine at **La Casa del Vino** (✉ Villanueva 160 ☎ 261/423–5862). Before your picnic, grab a bottle of Malbec at **Juan Cedrón** (✉ Peatonal Sarmiento 278). Mendocinos shop at **La Matera** (✉ Villanueva 314 ☎ 261/425–3332) for boots, vests, belts, scarves, and riding equipment. **Pura Cepa** (✉ Peatonal Sarmiento 664) conducts in-store wine tastings.

Elsewhere in the Region

Uspallata. This small town in the Uspallata River valley roughly 125 km (77 mi) west of Mendoza, between the foothills and the front range of the Andes, is ideally located at the crossroads of three important routes: R7 from Mendoza across the Andes to Chile, R57 from Mendoza via Villavicencio, and R39 from San Juan via Barreal in the Calingasta Valley. More than an overnight stopover, Uspallata is a good base for excursions into the mountains by 4x4 or on horseback to abandoned mines, a desert ghost town, and spectacular mountain scenery where the 1997 movie *Seven Years in Tibet* was filmed. Metals have been forged at **Las Bóvedas,** the pointed adobe cupolas a few miles north of town, since pre-Columbian time. Arms and cannons for San Martín's army were made there.

★   **Camino del Año (Road of the Year).** From Mendoza traveling north on RP52, passing through Canota, you arrive at Villavicencio (47 km [29 mi]), the source of mineral water sold throughout Argentina. The nearby **Hostaria Villavicencio** serves lunch and dinner. Farther up the road, the Camino del Año begins its serpentine ascent around 365 turns to **El Balcón** on the top of the pass at **Cruz de Paramillo** (2,999 meters [9,840 feet]). Get out and look for the ruins of a Jesuit mine, the **Arucarias de Darwin** (petrified trees found by Darwin in 1835), and 1,000-year-old petroglyphs on **Tunderqueral Hill.** From the top of the pass you can see three of the highest mountains outside of Asia, all over 6,000 meters (20,000 feet): Aconcagua to the west, Tupungato south, and Mercederio north. At 67 km (41 mi), the road straightens out and descends into Uspallata, where you can continue west on RN7 to Chile or north on RN39 to **Barreal** in San Juan Province (108 km [67 mi]). The road to Barreal crosses a high desert valley, where the only sign of life is an occasional estancia partially hidden in a grove of alamos. At **Los Tambillos,** about 40 km (25 mi) from Uspallata, the Inca road that ran from Cusco, Peru, through Bolivia and into northern Argentina crosses the road. The site is surrounded by a fence that protects traces of the original road and remains of an Inca *tambo* (resting place). A map shows the route of the Incas. The mountains to the west, including Mercedario (6,768 meters [22,205 feet]), get higher and more spectacular as you approach Barreal. At the San Juan Province border, the road becomes R412 and is paved the remaining 50 km (31 mi) to Barreal.

Potrerillos. This little town in the Potrerillos Valley, 53 km (33 mi) west of Mendoza, is protected from the elements by the surrounding mountains. Its agreeable microclimate and the rushing Río Mendoza have made Potrerillos an ideal adventure-sports center, and summer homes attract vacationing Mendocinos to the area. Rafting companies, mountain-bike rental shops, stables, and hiking and camping guides are headquartered here.

Fodor'sChoice **Parque Provincial Aconcagua.** This provincial park extends for 66,773
★ hectares (165,000 acres) over wild, high country with few trails other than those used by expeditions climbing the impressive Cerro Aconcagua (Aconcagua Mountain), the park's main attraction. At 6,957 meters (22,825 feet), it's the highest mountain in the Americas, and it towers over the Andes, its five gigantic glaciers gleaming in the sun. Although it seems amazingly accessible from the roadside, Aconcagua has claimed 37 climbers from the more than 400 expeditions that have attempted the summit. Nevertheless, every year hundreds of mountaineers try to conquer the "giant of America." A trail into the park begins at the ranger's cabin, follows the Río Horcones past a lagoon, and continues upward to the Plaza de Mulas base camp at 4,325 meters (14,190 feet), where there's a refugio (basic mountain cabin with bunk beds; ☎ 261/423–1571 in Mendoza for reservations).

Organized tours on horse or foot can be arranged in Mendoza. The drive up the Uspallata Pass to the Parque Provincial Aconcagua is as spectacular as the mountain itself. Renting a car is worthwhile; there are many sights to stop and photograph along the way. You can make the 195-km (121-mi) trip from Mendoza in one long, all-day drive. Note that roads become icy in winter, and the altitude jumps from 762 meters (2,500 feet) in Mendoza to 3,184 meters (10,446 feet) at the top.

To reach the park, take the Camino del Año, or leave Mendoza heading south on Avenida San Martín to the Panamerican Highway (R7) and turn right. Vineyards soon give way to barren hills and scrub brush as you follow the river for 30 km (19 mi) past the Termas Cacheuta. If you're still engulfed in fog and drizzle, don't despair: you'll likely find brilliant sunshine when you reach the Potrerillos Valley at 39 km (24 mi).

Beyond Uspallata, the last town before the Chilean frontier, the road goes through rolling hills into brooding black mountains. The ríos Blanco and Tambillos rush down from the mountains into the Río Mendoza, and remnants of Inca tambos remind you that this was once an Inca route from Chile. At Punta de Vacas, corrals that once held herds of cattle on their way to Chile lie abandoned alongside now-defunct railway tracks. Two kilometers (1 mi) beyond the army barracks and customs office, three wide valleys converge. Looking south, the second-highest mountain in the region, Cerro Tupungato (6,798 meters [22,304 feet]), a white-capped volcano, reigns supreme above the Valle de Uco.

After passing the ski area at Los Penitentes (named for the rock formations on the southern horizon that resemble penitent monks), you arrive at Puente del Inca (2,700 meters [9,000 feet]), a natural bridge of red rocks encrusted with yellow sulphur that spans the river. The hot springs below are slippery to walk on but fine for soaking tired feet. A few miles farther west, after you pass the Chilean customs check, is the entrance to the park and the park ranger's cabin. About 15 km (9 mi) beyond the park entrance, the highway passes Las Cuevas, a settlement where the road forks right to Chile or left to the statue of Cristo Redentor (Christ the Redeemer) on the Chilean border (4,206 meters [13,800 feet]), commemorating the 1902 peace pact between the two countries.

OUTDOOR ACTIVITIES

November through March is the best time to take day-hikes or week-long treks along rivers and an Inca trail, through canyons and indigenous forests, or to the highest mountain peaks in the Andes. *Cabalgatas* (horseback riding) is another enjoyable way to explore the area; excursions vary in duration. Many adventure-tour companies also organize rafting or kayaking trips on the Río Mendoza. They can be combined with horseback treks. Cycling Mendoza's back roads can take you through the suburbs and vineyards into the Andean foothills and upward to mountain villages—or all the way to Chile. Every February, La Vuelta Ciclista de Mendoza, a bicycle race around Mendoza Province, attracts cycling enthusiasts.

Mendoza offers challenging mountaineering adventures on Cordón de Plata, Tupungato, and Aconcagua. Permits for climbing Aconcagua can be obtained personally in Mendoza at **Centro de Visitantes** (⌧ Av. de Los Robles and Rotondo de Rosedal), in Parque San Martín near the entrance. The center is open weekdays 8–6 and weekends 9–1.

Los Penitentes, which has 20 ski runs and cross-country skiing, is 153 km (95 mi) northwest of Mendoza on the Panamerican Highway. Despite the elevation (3,194 meters [10,479 feet]), the snow here is often thin, and the danger of avalanches can sometimes be severe. At the base of the ski area are hotels, restaurants, ski rentals, day care, a first-aid clinic, and a disco. In the hills rising up to the Cordón de Plata range, **Vallecitos,** only 80 km (49 mi) from Mendoza in Luján de Cuyo, attracts families with nearby vacation homes, as well as summer hikers and mountaineers who come to train for an assault on Aconcagua. For information, contact any of the tour agencies in Mendoza.

Argentine Rafting Expeditions (⊠ Ruta Nacionál 7, Km 53, Potrerillos ☏ 262/482–037 ⊕ www.argentinarafting.com) offers rafting and kayak classes and day trips. **Aymará Turismo** (⊠ 9 de Julio 1023, Mendoza ☎☎ 261/420–2064 ⊕ www.aymara.com.ar) organizes hikes, horseback trips, mountain climbing (including a 19-day guided ascent of Aconcagua), white-water rafting, skiing, and mountain bike tours.

Betancourt Rafting (⊠ Lavalle 36, Galería Independencia, Loc. No. 8, Mendoza ☎☎ 261/429–9665 ⊕ www.betancourt.com.ar) has three small cabins and a lodge 25 km (15 mi) from Mendoza (transportation is included) at the Cacheuta Hot Springs. Their standard two-day trip, with medium to difficult rapids, includes an *asado* (traditional outdoor barbecue) and accommodations.

Cordon del Plata (⊠ Av. Las Heras 341 ☏ 264/48303 ⊕ www. cordondelplata.com.ar) offers horseback rides from a day to a week and combination horse/trek/rafting trips. They also arrange mountain biking trips. **Fernando Grajales** (⊠ 25 de Mayo 2985, Guaymallén ☎☎ 261/429–3830) is a veteran of many Aconcagua summits. **Fortuna Viajes** (⊠ Mariano Moreno s/n, Barreal ☏ 264/844–1004 ⊕ www.fortunaviajes. com.ar) has 20 years experience in outdoor adventure tourism. They offer a variety of horseback trips, hiking, mountaineering, rafting, fishing, sandsurfing, and 4x4 excursions. **Hotel Club de la Nieve** (⊠ San Martín 793, 14A, Buenos Aires ☎☎ 11/4315–2067 ⊕ www.clubdelanieve.com) can handle ski-related reservations.

Huentata (⊠ Av. Las Heras 663, Mendoza ☎☎ 261/425–3108 ⊕ www. huentata.com.ar) does trekking, mountain biking, and horseback riding out of Potrerillos in the pre-cordillera. **Inka Expeditions** (⊠ Av. Juan B. Justo 345, Mendoza ☏ 261/425–0871 ⊕ www.inka.com.ar) has 10 years of experience leading tours to base camp at Aconcagua; they specialize in trekking and mountaineering.

Limité Zero (☏ 261/429–9165 in Mendoza, 11/5032–9932 in Buenos Aires ⊕ www.aventurarse.com) expertly handles guided horseback rides, trekking, mountain climbing, and ice climbing. **Travesía** (⊠ Montecaseros 699, Godoy Cruz ☏ 261/448–0289) conducts biking tours and provides maps for the suburbs and foothills outside of Mendoza.

Where to Stay & Eat

Mendoza

$$$$ ✕ **La Bourgogne.** "Cooking comes from regional traditions. My cuisine is tied to the land," says Jean Paul Bondoux, Argentina's only Relais Gourmand. He applies his French culinary skills to the best local produce, and every bite is fantastic in this casually elegant restaurant at Carlos Pulenta's winery. Lunch and cocktails are served on a porch overlooking the vineyards, Andean peaks looming in the distance. Guests are invited to cooking classes in the open kitchen. ⊠ *Roque Sáenz*

Peña 3531, Vistalba, Luján de Cuyo ☎ *261/498–9400* ☺ *No dinner Sun. Closed Mon.* ⊕ *www.carlospulentawines.com* ⌂ *Reservations essential* ☰ *AE, MC, V.*

$$$ ✕**Terruño.** Light from a whimsical chandelier high in the timbered ceiling highlights the malbec-colored walls and worn floors of this 1890 vintner's residence. Appetizers, such as Andean trout with mushrooms or a corn, tomato, and onion tart, are as good as the entrées. An experienced staff can pair local wine with each course, including a unique dessert tasting course. ⊠ *Club Tapiz, Pedro Molina (RP60) s/n, Maipú* ☎ *261/496–4815* ⌂ *Reservations essential* ⊕ *www.tapiz.com.*

★ **$$–$$$** ✕**1884 Restaurante Francis Mallman.** The soft glow of candles on the patio under the prune trees at the 100-year-old Bodega Escorihuela sets the tone for Francis Mallman, who put Argentina on the map of international *alta cocina* (haute cuisine), to present his version of Patagonian cuisine. Empanadas are baked in mud ovens, a custom derived from the Incas. Students from his culinary school tend to guests with discreet enthusiasm, and the 36-page wine list has detailed information on grapes and bodegas. ⊠ *Belgrano 1188* ☎ *261/424–2698* ☰ *AE, DC, MC, V.*

$–$$ ✕**La Florencia.** Sidewalk tables invite strollers to stop and peruse the menu: grilled, baked, and broiled meats and fish; pastas; pizzas; game; and a variety of salads, along with a lengthy wine list. Step inside and admire the eclectic displays of antique weapons, telephones, and gaucho artifacts. The upstairs dining room has a breezy street view. ⊠ *Sarmiento and Perú* ☎ *261/429–1564* ☰ *AE, DC, MC, V.*

$–$$ ✕**La Tasca de Plaza España.** If the bright red walls with strange faces painted above the entrance and the eclectic array of art inside don't get your attention, the excellent tapas and Mediterranean dishes will. Seafood tapas, veal and artichoke stew, and a casserole of zucchini, onions, and peppers in a cheese sauce are a few of the tempting dishes served in this venerable—but irreverent—old house. ⊠ *Montevideo 117* ☎ *261/423–3466* ☰ *AE, MC, V.*

$ ✕**La Marchigiana.** Homemade pasta has been served under the thatched roof and whirring fans of this cheerful Italo-Argentine eatery since 1950. Concoct your own salad and try a pitcher of sangria or clérico. ⊠ *Patricias Mendocinas 1550* ☎ *261/423–071* ⊠ *Palmares Shopping Mall, Godoy Cruz* ☎ *261/439–1961* ☰ *AE, DC, MC, V.*

$ ✕**El Meson Español.** Stained-glass windows, bullfight posters, reproductions of works by famous Spanish artists, and a worn tile floor transport you to Spain as you enter this old colonial house. Start with a cup of garlic soup, followed by paella or tapas, as Lucho, the blind pianist, plays blues, tango, swing, and Sinatra. ⊠ *Montevideo 244* ☎ *261/429–6175* ☰ *AE, DC, MC, V* ☺ *No lunch.*

★ **¢–$** ✕**Azafrán.** Whether you view it as a gourmet grocery, wine shop, or restaurant, Azafrán (which means saffron) is a pleasant diversion. In the wine bar an old wine press has been converted into a tasting table. Farther inside this 19th-century brick building, diners seated at small café tables enjoy cheeses, pâtés, and hot and cold tapas served on wooden platters. Shelves are stocked with Mendoza's finest: olive oils, smoked meats, dried herbs, mushrooms, olives, jams, and breads. ⊠ *Sarmiento 765* ☎ *261/429–4200* ⊠ *Villanueva 287* ☰ *MC, V* ☺ *Closed Sun.*

$$$$ ⊞ **Park Hyatt Mendoza.** Hyatt has preserved the landmark Plaza Hotel's 19th-century Spanish colonial facade: a grand pillared entrance and a wide veranda that extends the width of the building. Lunch, afternoon tea, and dinner are served to views of Mendoza's main square. A two-story wine wall separates the restaurant from the lobby. Minimalist bedrooms are softened by plump white pillows and duvets covering ebony beds. Bathrooms have plenty of mirrors to complement chrome and marble accents. ⊠ *Calle Chile 1124, 5500* ☎ *261/441–1234* ⊕ *mendoza. park.hyatt.com* ⊃ *171 rooms, 15 suites* ⟠ *Restaurant, café, dining room, pool, health club, spa, bar, casino, business services, meeting rooms, free parking* ⊟ *AE, DC, MC, V* ⟦ *CP.*

★ **$$$** ×⊞ **Chacras de Coria Lodge.** This casually elegant lodge, located in an upscale residential area 15 minutes from Mendoza, is ideal for visits to wineries in Maipú and Luján de Cuyo. Guests enjoy custom tours with oenologists and the intimate atmosphere of evening wine tastings, outdoor cooking classes, an outdoor asado, and candlelit dinners on the veranda. The manager can arrange privately catered meals as well as tours, golf, tennis, horseback riding, mountain biking—even tango lessons. ⊠ *Viamonte 4762, Chacras de Coria, Luján de Cuyo, M5528CCC* ☎ *261/496–1888* ⊕ *www.postalesdelplata.com* ⊃ *6 rooms, 1 apt. with 2 rooms* ⟠ *Restaurant, bar, outdoor dining, swimming pool, Jacuzzi, Internet access, wine tours, outdoor activities arranged, wine tastings, cooking classes* ⊟ *AE, MC, V* ⟦ *CP.*

$$$$ ×⊞ **La Posada Carlos Pulenta.** The enormous rooms on the second floor
Fodor'sChoice of this two story Tuscan terra-cotta building face east, where the sun rises
★ over the vineyards, or west, where it sets over the majestic Andes. Cream-colored tile floors, dark wicker furniture, and taupe and café-au-lait-covered furnishings are luxurious, but comfortable. Sumptuous chairs await you on the veranda for lunch, wine tasting, or daydreaming. Breakfast and lunch or dinner are complementary, and meals can be served in your room. Equally appealing is the restaurant, La Borgogne, which has an open kitchen where guests can join a cooking class. Wine tours are also available. ⊠ *Roque Sáenz Peña 3531, Vitalba, Luján de Cuyo* ☎ *261/498–9400* ⊕ *www.carlospulentawines.com* ⊃ *2 rooms* ⟠ *Restaurant, Wi-Fi, bar, lounge, business services, meeting rooms,* ⊟ *AE, MC, V* ⟦ *MA.*

★ **$$$** ×⊞ **Club Tapiz.** This 1890 governor's mansion will feel like your own private villa. Stroll through the old winery, lounge on the enclosed patio, or gaze at the Andes from the outdoor pool or indoor Jacuzzi. Evening wine tastings in the reading room will whet your appetite for dinner in Terruña (Terroir). ⊠ *Pedro Molina (RP60) s/n, Maipú* ☎ *261/ 496–4815* ⊕ *www.tapiz.com* ⊃ *7 rooms* ⟠ *Restaurant, bicycles, private rooftop dining room, bar, business center, library, spa, winery, winery tours* ⊟ *AE, MC, V.*

$$ ⊞ **Hotel Aconcagua.** You'll appreciate the service at this modern hotel on a quiet street near shops and restaurants. Serene tones of mauve and blue create a soothing atmosphere throughout the lobby and in meeting and guest rooms. Los Parrales, the restaurant, uses a mud oven and wood-fired grill to create typical Mendocino meals. ⊠ *San Lorenzo 545, M5500GFK* ☎ *261/520–0500* ⊕ *www.hotelaconcagua.com.ar* ⊃ *159 rooms, 9 suites* ⟠ *Restaurant, pool, massage, sauna, business center, meeting rooms, travel services, free parking* ⊟ *AE, DC, MC, V* ⟦ *CP.*

$ 🏨 **Hotel Cervantes.** The simple rooms in this small, downtown owner-operated hotel are cheerfully decorated in floral prints. The front desk is knowledgeable, and a big-screen TV in the living room makes you feel at home. Sancho, the hotel's excellent restaurant and bar, is a popular lunch spot. ⊠ *Amigorena 65, 5500* ☎ *261/520–0400 or 261/520–0446* ⊕ *www.hotelcervantesmza.com.ar* ⌁ *60 rooms, 5 suites* ♿ *Restaurant, bar, business services, meeting rooms, travel services, free parking* ▭ *AE, DC, MC, V* ⅋⦿⅋ *CP.*

$ 🏨 **Hotel Crillón.** The loyal clientele of this small hotel returns for the tranquil neighborhood—within walking distance of plazas, restaurants, museums, and shops. Small suites have separate work stations, and the helpful staff can plan excursions. ⊠ *Perú 1065, 5500* ☎ *261/429–8494* ⊕ *www.hcrillon.com.ar* ⌁ *70 rooms, 6 suites* ♿ *Café, pool, bar, meeting room* ▭ *AE, DC, MC, V* ⅋⦿⅋ *CP.*

¢ 🏨 **Damajuana.** The only property in Mendoza resembling a hostel has rooms for two, four, or six people, with lockers and shared baths. Guests feel at home inside or out: a bar, restaurant, fireplace, and TV are in the living room, and the backyard has a grill and hammocks. The neighborhood—steps from bars, boutiques, and cafés—is popular with young Mendocinos. ⊠ *Aristedes Villanueva 282, 5500* ☎ *261/425–5858* ⊕ *www.damajuanahostel.com.ar* ⌁ *8 rooms* ♿ *Restaurant, outdoor grill and firewood, pool, bar, Internet; no a/c.*

Uspallata

¢–$ ✕ **Lo de Pato.** This casual roadside grill and café serves cafeteria-style lunches and grilled meat and pasta dinners; get yourself a cold drink from the refrigerator. The souvenir shop sells candy bars, postcards, T-shirts, and other mementos. ⊠ *R7* ☎ *264/420–249* ▭ *AE, MC, V.*

$ 🏨 **Hotel Uspallata.** Cavernous hallways, minimal decor, barren walls, and dim lighting are legacies of the Perón era, when the government built grand hotels for its employees and cronies. A facelift in 2004 improved the overall appearance somewhat, and the surrounding scenery compensates for the rather dull interior. The grounds and gardens are impressive, the dining room is grand, and the large rooms have closets for a month's stay. ⊠ *R7, Km 1149, 5500* ☎ *2624/420–066, Mendoza 261/420–4820* ⊕ *www.atahoteleria.com.ar* ⌁ *73 rooms* ♿ *Restaurant, café, pool, bar, bowling and Ping-Pong in the recreation room, travel services* ▭ *No credit cards* ⅋⦿⅋ *CP.*

$ 🏨 **Hotel Valle Andino.** As you drive along R7, this brick building with a pitched tile roof and wood trim looks inviting. Inside you'll find an open, airy living room with places to sit around a woodstove. Outside, a large glass-enclosed swimming pool is surrounded by a lawn big enough for a soccer game. Rooms are modern; some have bunk beds, and all have brick walls and minimalist furniture. ⊠ *R7, 5500* ☎ *2624/420–033* ⊕ *www.hotelguia.com/hoteles/valleandino* ⌁ *26 rooms* ♿ *Restaurant, pool, bar, recreation room* ▭ *AE, MC, V* ⅋⦿⅋ *CP.*

Potrerillos

$–$$ 🏨 **Hotel Potrerillos.** This Spanish-style, stucco- and tile-roofed building overlooks the foothills and is surrounded by lawns, gardens, and sports facilities. It was originally built by the government, and the public spaces were made to accommodate large groups, but tasteful wooden furnishings and woven rugs give it a more personal appeal. ☒ *R7, Km 50 (from Mendoza), 5549* ☎ *2624/482–010* ⚹ *Restaurant, café, tea shop, bar, pool, tennis, volleyball, meeting room.*

\$\$ ✕☒ **Hotel Termas Cacheuta.** Stop at this mountain spa for a sauna in a natural grotto, a volcanic mud bath, a hydromassage, and a soak in the large swimming pool filled with water from hot springs. Rooms overlook the lawn and swimming pool. The restaurant's healthy, natural cuisine features vegetables grown on site. Rates include three meals, two thermal baths, and one massage per day; hiking, river rafting, and mountain biking can be arranged. ☒ *R7, Km 38, Cacheuta, 5500* ☎ *2624/482–082* ☒ *Reservations: Rodríguez Peña 1412, Godoy Cruz, 5501* ☎ *261/431–6085* ⟿ *16 rooms* ⚹ *Restaurant, massage, sauna* ▬ *No credit cards* ⊙│ *FAP.*

Parque Provincial Aconcagua

¢ ☒ **Hostería Puente del Inca.** Vintage photos in the dining room document this hostel's history as a mountaineering outpost. Climbers still gear up here before attempting Aconcagua and afterward to relate their adventures. Guides and mules can be arranged. ☒ *R7, Km 175, Puente del Inca* ☒ *Turismo Aymara SRL, 9 de Julio 1023, Mendoza, 5500* ☎ *261/ 420–2064* ✉ *info@aymara.com.ar* ⟿ *82 beds in doubles, 4- to 6-person dorms* ⚹ *Dining room* ▬ *MC.*

Mendoza Essentials

Transportation

BY AIR
Mendoza's Aeropuerto Internacional Francisco Gabrielli is 6 km (4 mi) from town on R40. Aerolíneas Argentinas flies from Buenos Aires.

▯ **Airlines Aerolíneas Argentinas** ☎ 261/420-4101.
▯ **Airports Aeropuerto Internacional de Mendoza (Francisco Gabrielli)** ☒ Route 40, 6 km (4 mi) from Mendoza City ☎ 261/448-2603.

BY BUS
Mendoza's busy Terminal del Sol is in Guaymallén, a suburb east of downtown. From here buses travel to every major Argentine city. Transport companies include: Chevallier, with daily service to Buenos Aires; El Rápido, with daily buses to Buenos Aires and Santiago, Chile, and three trips weekly to Lima, Peru; and T.A.C., with service to Bariloche, Buenos Aires, and Córdoba.

Mendoza has local buses, and if you can express where you want to go and understand the reply, you can travel cheaply (but slowly). A number in brackets on the bus indicates the route. Almost every tour agency runs minivans to local sights.

▯ **Chevallier** ☎ 261/431-0235. **La Cumbre** ☎ 261/431-9252. **El Rápido** ☎ 261/431-4094. **T.A.C** ☎ 261/431-1039, 2627/422-209 in San Rafael. **Terminal de Ómnibus** ☒ Av. Gobernador Videla and Av. Acceso Oeste, Mendoza ☎ 261/448-0057.

BY CAR
You can rent cars and 4x4s in all major cities, but it's a good idea to make reservations in advance during peak season. Avis has a large fleet

at the Mendoza airport. The trip from Buenos Aires to Mendoza is 1,060 km (664 mi) along lonely, paved R7.

Finding wineries on your own requires a good map and some knowledge of Spanish. Driving to the high Andean villages and the border with Chile is a remarkable experience, worth the expense of a rental car. If you fear getting lost or breaking down in remote areas, hire a *remis* (a car with a driver). Pay attention to weather and road information. During winter, snow and avalanches close some roads. Torrential rainstorms can cause flash floods and obliterate seldom-used dirt roads. Good maps can be found in bookstores and at Automóvil Club Argentino.

🚗 **Auto Club Contacts** **Automóvil Club Argentino (ACA)** ☎ 11/4808-4460 in Buenos Aires, 261/431-4100in Mendoza. **Roadside Assistance** ☎ 0800/888-9888.

BY TAXI

Metered taxis are inexpensive and plentiful. There's usually a taxi stand near the central plaza, and hotels and restaurants will call one for you. To tip, round the fare up. Drivers are generally honest, but for long trips it's a good idea to agree upon the fare before you go. Though more expensive, remises are good value for groups. They don't mind stopping for photos, meals, or shopping, and they're often good guides. Arrangements can be made through your hotel or at the airport or bus station.

🚗 **Class Remise** ☎ 261/431-8238 local guided tours, 261/431-8244 airport transfers. **Imperio Remises** ☎ 261/432-2222 or 0800/433-368. **La Veloz del Este** ☎ 261/423-9090.

Contacts & Resources

BANKS & EXCHANGE SERVICES

Banks in the region are generally open weekdays 10–4. ATMs are available everywhere (Banelco and LINK have ATMs in most cities). Hotels and some travel agencies will exchange dollars. Traveler's checks are inconvenient; you must go to a bank and pay a fee.

🚗 **Banelco** ✉ Av. San Martín 831 ✉ Sarmiento 29. **Banco de la Nación** ✉ Av. San Martín and Gutiérrez ☎ 261/423-4500 ✉ At bus terminal. **Citibank** ✉ Av. San Martín 1098 ☎ 261/420-4113. **Exprinter** ✉ Espejo 74 ☎ 261/429-1200.

Tours

You can arrange tours to vineyards and other activities through your hotel or the tourist office in Mendoza before you arrive; this is particularly a good idea if you're traveling with a group and/or during the harvest. You can also hire a *remis* (hired car with driver) for an hour or a day and plan your own itinerary. Renting a car and hitting the road may end in frustration and wasted time, as signs outside of Mendoza are often misleading or invisible. Road construction, detours, and muddy roads during spring can add to the frustration or the spirit of adventure, depending on your temperament. If time isn't an issue and you have the patience, exploring on your own—stopping for photos, chatting with locals, and discovering new territory—has its rewards.

Most wineries don't charge for tours or tastings but do request reservations; if you're visiting independently, call first. Don't be put off by such security precautions as a locked gate or a uniformed guard—the guards are friendly and will call the winery to announce your arrival.

Andesmar is a large company with offices all over Argentina. They own the bus company of the same name and offer country-wide tours, outdoor excursions, and seven wine tours that visit three wineries per day in Mendoza. Aventura and Wine (Bacchus Tours) creates custom wine tours that allow you to tour the winery with the owner or winemaker. The company can also arrange anything from cooking classes to golf. Top hotels call on Aventura's multilingual staff as consultants for visiting VIPs. Aymará Turismo offers 4- to 11-day wine tours with an oenologist; longer tours cross the Andes to Chilean wineries. The vineyard tour on horseback is an original option. Mendoza Viajes is a full-service travel agency with city tours and day trips.

🚌 **Andesmar** ☎ 261/405-0800 ⊕ www.andesmar.com. **Aventura and Wine (Bacchus Tours)** ☎ 261/429-3014 ⊕ www.aventurawine.com. **Aymará Turismo** ☎🖨 261/420-2064 ⊕ www.aymara.com.ar. **Mendoza Viajes** ☎🖨 261/461-0210 ⊕ www.mdzviajes.com.ar.

VISITOR INFORMATION
🚌 **Mendoza Provincial Tourist Office** ✉ San Martín 1143 and Garibaldi ☎ 261/420-1333 ⊕ www.turismo.mendoza.gov.ar.

PATAGONIA

By Robin Goldstein

Patagonia, that fabled land of endless, empty, open space at the end of the world, has humbled the most fearless explorers. Many have described it as a cruel and lonely windswept place unfit for humans. Darwin called Patagonia "wretched and useless," yet he was deeply moved by its desolation and forever attracted to it. Today the 800,000 square km (309,000 square mi) that make up Argentine Patagonia continue to challenge and fascinate explorers, mountaineers, nature lovers, sports enthusiasts, and curious visitors from around the world. Because the population in Patagonia is small relative to its land mass, a staggering variety of plants and wildlife exists in pristine habitats.

A new airport in Calafate, with direct flights from Buenos Aires and Bariloche has made the far reaches of Patagonia much more accessible to tourists. Covering the great distances between Bariloche, in the north; Ushuaia, in the south; and El Calafate, Río Gallegos, and Trelew, in the middle, requires careful planning—air travel is essential. Tours to popular sights along the Atlantic coast, to the glaciers, or in and around Bariloche, can be arranged in Buenos Aires or in each destination. If you want to see it all, packaged tours can make the whole trip easier.

Bariloche & the Parque Nacional Nahuel Huapi

1,615 km (1,001 mi) southwest of Buenos Aires (2 hrs by plane), 432 km (268 mi) south of Neuquén on R237, 1,639 km (1,016 mi) north of Río Gallegos, 876 km (543 mi) northwest of Trelew, 357 km (221 mi) east of Puerto Montt, Chile, via lake crossing.

Modern Bariloche is the gateway to all the recreational and scenic splendors of the northern Lake District. However, as it's also the most popular vacation destination in Patagonia, with the region's busiest airport and one of the liveliest ski scenes in South America—particularly popular among the high-school party crowd—Bariloche has lost some of its luster. Although development in the area has maintained a sense of architectural restraint, it can be hard here, especially within the city itself, to experience the communion with nature that characterizes so much of Patagonia. Accordingly, many people choose to base themselves outside the city—on Avenida Bustillo along the Circuito Chico, around the Península Llao Llao, and in the nearby retreats of Villa La Angostura and San Martín de los Andes. But all is not lost in Bariloche: although planes, buses, trains, boats, and tour groups arrive daily, you can escape into the stunning wilderness of clear blue lakes, misty lagoons, rivers, waterfalls, mountain glaciers, forests, and flower-filled meadows on foot, mountain bike, or horseback, or by boat. You can also fish peacefully in one of the 40 nearby lakes and countless streams. It's best to get around on your own with the help of a rental car, although myriad planned excursions are available with local tour companies.

The rustic gray-green stone-and-log buildings of the Centro Cívico (Civic Center) were designed by Alejandro Bustillo, the architect who also designed the Llao Llao Hotel and the National Park office in San Martín de los Andes. His Andean-Swiss style is recognizable in lodges and buildings throughout the Lake District. The spacious square in front of the Civic Center, with an equestrian statue of General Roca (1843–1914) and a wide-angle view of the lake, is a good place to begin exploring Bariloche. Note that the Civic Center is Km 0 for measuring points from Bariloche.

The **Museo de la Patagonia** (Patagonia Museum) tells the social and geological history of northern Patagonia through displays of Indian and gaucho artifacts and exhibits on regional flora and fauna. The history of the Mapuche and the Conquista del Desierto (Conquest of the Desert) is also explained in detail. ⊠ *Centro Cívico, next to arch over Bartolomé Mitre* ☎ *2944/422–330* ✉ *2.50 pesos* ☉ *Mon. and Sat. 10–1, Tues.–Fri. 10–12:30 and 2–7.*

The National Park

The **Parque Nacional Nahuel Huapi,** created in 1943, is Argentina's oldest national park, and Lago Nahuel Huapi is the sapphire in its crown. The park extends over 2 million acres along the eastern side of the Andes in the provinces of Neuquén and Río Negro, on the frontier with Chile. It contains the highest concentration of lakes in Argentina. The biggest is Lago Nahuel Huapi, a 897-square-km (346-square-mi) body of water, whose seven long arms (the longest is 96 km [60 mi] long, 12 km [7 mi] wide) reach deep into forests of *coihué* (a native beech tree), *cyprés* (cypress), and *lenga* (deciduous beech) trees. Intensely blue across its vast expanse and aqua green in its shallow bays, the lake meanders into distant lagoons and misty inlets where the mountains, covered with vegetation at their base, rise straight up out of the water. Every water sport invented and tours to islands and other extraordinarily beautiful spots can be arranged through local travel agencies, tour offices, and through hotels. Information offices throughout the park offer help in exploring the miles of mountain and woodland trails, lakes, rivers, and streams. 🖾 *Park entry 12 pesos.*

For information on mountain climbing, trails, *refugios* (mountain cabins), and campgrounds, visit the **Intendencia del Parque Nacional Nahuel Huapi** (🖾 Av. San Martín 24 ☏ 2944/423–111 ⊕ www.parquesnacionales. gov.ar) at the Civic Center. Another source of information on local activities, excursions, lodging, and private and public campgrounds is the **Oficina Municipal de Turismo** (🖾 Centro Cívico, across from clock tower ☏ 2944/429–850), open daily 8:30 AM–9 PM.

The most popular excursion on Lago Nahuel Huapi is the 30-minute boat ride to **Isla Victoria** (Victoria Island), the largest island in the lake. A grove of redwoods transplanted from California thrives in the middle of the island. After a walk on trails that lead to enchanting views of emerald bays and still lagoons, the boat crosses to the tip of the Península Quetrihué for a visit to the **Parque Nacional los Arrayanes,** a unique forest of cinnamon-color myrtle trees. Like most boat trips on the lake, tours to Isla Victoria and Arrayanes begin at Puerto Pañuelo, on the Península Llao Llao. They run twice daily (more in high season), at 10 AM and 2 PM, by **Cau Cau** (🖾 Mitre 139, Bariloche ☏ 2944/431– 372 ⊕ www.islavictoriayarrayanes.com) and **Turisur** (🖾 Mitre 219, Bariloche ☏ 2944/426–109 ⊕ www.bariloche.com/turisur).

The renowned ski area at **Cerro Catedral** (Mt. Cathedral) is 46 km (28½ mi) west of town on Avenida Ezequiel Bustillo (R237); turn left at Km 8.5 just past Playa Bonita. The mountain was named for the Gothic-looking spires that crown its peaks. Though skiing is the main activity here, the view from the top of the chairlift at 6,600 feet is spectacular any time of year. To the southwest, Monte Tronadór, a 12,000-foot extinct volcano, straddles the border with Chile, towering above lesser peaks that surround Lago Nahuel Huapi as it meanders around islands and disappears into invisible bays beneath mountains and volcanoes miles away. Lanín Volcano is visible on the horizon.

You can reach the summit of **Cerro Otto** (Mt. Otto; 4,608 feet), a small ski area, by hiking, mountain biking, or driving 8 km (5 mi) up a gravel road from Bariloche. Hiking to the top of the mountain takes you through a forest of lenga trees to Argentina's first ski area, at Piedras Blancas. Here Herbert Tutzauer, Bariloche's first ski instructor, won the first ski race by climbing the mountain, then skiing down it through the forest in 1½ hours. You can also take the **Teleférico Cerro Otto** (🖾 Av. de Los Pioneros 🖾 30 pesos ⊗ Daily 10–5), 5 km (3 mi) west of town; a free shuttle bus leaves from the corner of Mitre and Villegas, and Perito Moreno and Independencia. The ride up takes about 12 minutes. At the top, a revolving cafeteria with a 360-degree panorama takes in Monte Tronadór, lakes in every direction, and Bariloche. In winter, skis and sleds are available for rent at the cafeteria. In summer, hiking and mountain biking are the main activities. Or try soaring in a paraplane over the lake with the condors. Call for **information** (☏ 2944/441–035) on schedules and sled or ski rentals.

A visit to **Monte Tronadór** (Thunder Mountain) requires an all-day outing of 170 km (105 mi) round-trip from Bariloche. The 12,000-foot extinct volcano, the highest mountain in the northern Lake District, sits astride the frontier with Chile, with one peak on either side. Take R258 south along the shore of Lago Gutiérrez and Lago Mascardi. Between the two lakes the road crosses from the Atlantic to the Pacific watershed. At Km 35, turn off onto a road marked TRONADÓR and PAMPA LINDA and continue along the shore of Lago Mascardi, passing a village of the same name. Just beyond the village, the road forks and you continue on a gravel road, R254. Near the bridge the road branches left to Lago Hess and Cascada Los Alerces—a detour to consider on your way out.

As you bear right after crossing Los Rápidos Bridge, the road narrows to one direction only: it's important to remember this when you set out in the morning, as you can only go up the road before 2 PM and down it after 4 PM. The lake ends in a narrow arm (Brazo Tronadór) at the Hotel Tronadór, which has a dock for tours arriving by boat. The road then follows the Río Manso (Manso River) to **Pampa Linda,** which has a lodge, restaurant, park ranger's office, campsites, and the trailhead for the climb up to the Refugio Otto Meiling at the snow line. Guided horseback rides are organized at the lodge. The road ends 7 km (4½ mi) beyond Pampa Linda in a parking lot that was once at the tip of the now receding **Glaciar Negro** (Black Glacier). As the glacier flows down from the mountain, the dirt and black sediment of its lateral moraines are ground up and cover the ice. At first glance, it's hard to imagine the tons of ice that lie beneath its black cap.

The detour to **Cascada Los Alerces** (Los Alerces Falls), 17 km (10 mi) from the turnoff at the bridge near Mascardi, follows the wild Río Manso, where it branches off to yet another lake, Lago Hess. At this junction are a campground, refugio, restaurant, and trailhead for the 1,000-foot climb to the falls. The path through dense vegetation over wooden bridges crosses a rushing river as it spills over steep, rocky cliffs in a grand finale to a day of viewing nature at its most powerful and beautiful.

Scenic Routes

A possible excursion from Bariloche is the **Circuito Chico** (Small Circuit), a half-day, 70-km (43½-mi) scenic trip along the west shore of Lago Nahuel Huapi. You can do it by car, tour bus (trips cost 20 pesos–30 pesos), or mountain bike. First, head west on Avenida Bustillo (R237) toward Península Llao Llao. At Km 20 you can take a brief side trip on an 11-km-long (7-mi-long) dirt road to the **Península San Pedro,** then follow the shore road that passes some fine homes set back in the woods. Back on R237, continue west to **Puerto Pañuelo** (Km 25½) in a little bay on the right, on the Península Llao Llao; it's the embarkation point for lake excursions and for the boat crossing to Chile.

Across from the port, a long driveway leads up a knoll to the Hotel Llao Llao, which you'll only be able to admire from afar if you're not a guest.

The Circuito Chico then follows R77 to Bahía Lopez, winding along the lake's edge through a forest of ghostly, leafless lenga trees. After crossing the bridge that links Lago Moreno and Lago Nahuel Huapi at Bahía Lopez, the road crosses the Arroyo Lopez (Lopez Creek). Here you can stop for a hike up to a waterfall and then climb above Lago Moreno to Punto Panoramico, a scenic overlook well worth a photo stop. Just before you cross Lago Moreno, an unmarked dirt road off to the right leads to the rustic village of **Colonia Suiza,** a good spot to stop for tea or lunch. After passing Laguna El Trebol (a small lake on your left), R77 joins R237 from Bariloche.

The **Circuito Grande** (Large Circuit), a more ambitious excursion than the Circuito Chico that's particularly lovely in spring or fall, covers 250 km (155 mi). Along the way there are plenty of spots to stop and enjoy the view, have a picnic lunch, or even stay overnight. Tour buses do it as an all-day trip costing 30 pesos–40 pesos. Leaving Bariloche on R237 heading east, follow the Río Limay into the Valle Encantado (Enchanted Valley), with its magical red-rock formations. Before crossing the bridge at Confluéncia (where the Río Traful joins the Limay), turn left onto R65 to Lago Traful. Five kilometers (3 mi) beyond the turnoff, on a dirt road heading toward Cuyín Manzano, are some astounding sandstone rock formations. As you follow the shore of Lago Traful, a sign indicates a *mirador* (lookout) on a high rock promontory, which you can climb up to on wooden stairs. The road from Villa Traful dives into a dense forest until it comes to the intersection with the Seven Lakes Circuit (R237). Turn right if you want to add the Seven Lakes Circuit. Otherwise, turn left and follow the shore of Lago Correntoso to the paved road down to the bay at Villa La Angostura.

The **Circuito de los Siete Lagos** (Seven Lakes Circuit) is an all-day trip of 360 km (223½ mi) round-trip, which could be extended to include an overnight in San Martín de los Andes or Villa La Angostura. Drive north on R237 for 21 km (13 mi), and turn left on R231 to Villa La Angostura, 65 km (40 mi) from Bariloche. About 11 km (7 mi) farther along the same road is the Seven Lakes Road (R234), which branches right and along the way passes Lago Correntoso, Lago Espejo, Lago Villarino, Lago Falkner, and Lago Hermoso. After lunch or tea or an overnight in San Martín de los Andes, head south to Bariloche on the dirt road over Paso Córdoba, passing Lago Meliquina on the way. At Confluéncia the road joins R237, following the Río Limay through Valle Encantado to Bariloche.

FodorśChoice   The **Cruce a Chile por Los Lagos** (Chile Lake Crossing) is a unique excur-
★   sion by land and lakes that began in the 1930s, when oxcarts used to haul people. These days you can do the tour in one or two days. Most people choose to do the crossing through an organized tour company, which generally stops for lunch in Puerto Blest and then continues on to Puerto Fríos on Laguna Frías. After docking at Puerto Fríos and clearing Argentine customs, you'll get on another bus that climbs through lush rain forest over a pass, then descends to Peulla, where Chilean customs is cleared (bring your passport). A little farther on is a comfortable lodge by Lago Todos los Santos. Early the next morning a catamaran

sets out across the lake, providing views of the volcanoes Putiagudo (which lost its *punto* [peak] in an earthquake) and Osorno. The boat trip ends at the port of Petrohué. Another (and final) bus skirts Lago Llanqui-hue, stopping for a visit at the rockbound Petrohué waterfalls, passing through the town of Puerto Varas (famous for its roses), and arriving, at last, at the Chilean port town of Puerto Montt. Catedral Turismo specializes in this trip, which costs 140 pesos; you'll spend an additional 125 pesos–140 pesos for a night's stay at Blest and/or Peulla.

Where to Stay & Eat

$$$$ ✕ **Kandahar.** A rustic wood building with a woodstove and cozy window seats in alcoves around the bar is the perfect setting for a pisco sour, smoked meats, and guacamole. Start with unusual appetizers such as *tarteleta de hongos* (mushroom tart), followed by wild game and profiteroles with hot chocolate sauce. ⊠ *20 de Febrero 698* ☎ *2944/424–702* ⊟ *AE, MC, V.*

$$$–$$$$ ✕ **Il Gabbiano.** "We don't serve lunch," the folks at this cozy, candlelit house out along the Circuito Chico boast, "because preparing dinner takes all day long." It's hard to argue with that philosophy after you sample the exquisite pastas, which change daily. Look for *tortelli* stuffed with wild boar, or pumpkin ravioli; they also have a way with fresh trout. With stucco, tile, and a beautiful wine cellar that's open to guests, the restaurant conjures up an easy feeling of rustic elegance. Bring a wad of cash, because in spite of the high prices, your plastic is no good here. ⊠ *Av. Bustillo, Km 24.3* ☎ *2944/448–346* ⊟ *No credit cards* ⚑ *Reservations essential* ☾ *Closed Tues. No lunch.*

$$–$$$ ✕ **El Patacón.** Constructed of local stone and wood, with large picture windows looking out over the lake, this restaurant is going for the log-cabin look. It's less than 10 minutes west of downtown toward the Llao Llao Peninsula, and you'll find all manner of gaucho tools, local art, and weavings on its wooden walls. Leather and sheepskin furniture add to the country atmosphere. An organic garden with fresh herbs, berries, and vegetables enhances the menu of meats, game, and fish. Trout in leek sauce with risotto is a standout, homemade pastas are delicious, and the brownie with ice cream and red fruit sauce is extraordinary. Don't bother with the game carpaccio. ⊠ *Av. Bustillo, Km 7* ☎ *2944/442–800* ⊟ *AE, DC, V.*

$–$$$ ✕ **Berlina.** One of Bariloche's newest entries into the Patagonia microbrew craze, this modern brewpub always has at least six of their own beers on tap to complement the beer-themed cuisine, such as *trucha Berlina* (whole trout cooked with stout and chocolate malt), beef Wellington marinated in beer and orange juice, or a simple, well-executed grilled pizza. Best is the complex Belgian strong dark ale, whose notes of caramel are cut by an intense bitterness. They're serious about coffee, too, and the angular, two-floor interior is flooded with light and views of the surrounding mountains. ⊠ *Av. Bustillo, Km 11.7* ☎ *2944/523–336* ⊕ *www.cervezaberlina.com* ⊟ *AE, MC, V.*

$–$$$ ✕ **Don Molina.** There is always lamb *a la cruz* ("crucified," meaning vertically spit-roasted over an open fire) in the window at this immensely, and deservedly, popular eatery on the west end of Bariloche's main drag.

This is a great opportunity to try this Patagonian specialty, but the products of the *parrilla* are also great. The owners and staff simply couldn't be any nicer. ⊠ *Av. San Martín 607* ☎ *2944/436–616* ▤ *AE, DC, MC, V.*

$–$$ ✕ **Cerveceria Blest.** This warm, lively spot boasts that it was the first brewpub in Argentina. It's certainly one of the most atmospheric, too, with a relaxed bustle that hits the spot after a day on the slopes. Don't miss the excellent bock beer, with a toasty coffee flavor, or if you prefer hard cider, the Fruto Prohibido. You can come in just for an après-ski beer sampler, or stay for dinner, which might include *costillitas de cerdo ahumadas con chucrut* (smoked pork chops with sauerkraut—is there a more classic beer food than that?). ⊠ *Av. Bustillo, Km 11.6* ☎ *2944/461–026* ▤ *AE, MC, V.*

$–$$ ✕ **Confitería La Alpina.** When a place is crowded all day long, there's usually something to it. At this restaurant on a busy corner of the main street, the reasons are at least threefold. First, there's a roaring fireplace right in the middle of the restaurant, illuminating and warming the dark wood tables, even the ones that are in cozy, private nooks. Second, there are the late hours; the place is essentially open all night. And finally, there's the food, which includes fondue—that ski-town classic—along with very competent preparations of local specialties, like Patagonian lamb *al ajillo* (with a savory, tomato-based garlic sauce). ⊠ *Moreno 98* ☎ *2944/ 425–693* ▤ *AE, DC, MC, V.*

$ ✕ **El Boliche de Alberto.** This local classic is always brightly lit, and always full. Just point at a slab of beef, chicken, lamb, or sausages, and have it grilled to your liking. It'll arrive sizzling on a wooden platter, accompanied by empanadas, salad, fried potatoes, and chimichurri sauce (slather it on the bread). ⊠ *Villegas 347* ☎ *2944/431–433* ⊠ *Bustillo 8800* ☎ *2944/462–285* ⊕ *www.elbolichedealberto.com* ▤ *AE, DC, MC, V.*

¢–$$ ✕ **La Esquina.** This immensely popular *confitería* on the corner of Urquiza and Moreno serves all the standards—lamb, pastas, personal-sized pizzas, and such. Still, it's more notable as a place to sit and sip, or hang out by the bar, than to eat; their hot chocolate is delicious, and the wooden interior, full of knick-knacks and cheery music, has a pleasant bustle. ⊠ *Moreno 10* ☎ *2944/428–900* ▤ *AE, DC, MC, V.*

★ $$$$ ✕▨ **Hotel Edelweiss.** Fresh flowers from the owner's nursery are arranged throughout this excellent medium-size hotel, which is within walking distance of just about everything. The modern, spacious rooms and suites have lake views from their bay windows. Both lunch and dinner consist of good salads, grilled fish, fowl, game, and beef prepared with fresh vegetables and tasty sauces. Most ski and tour buses, whether arranged through the hotel or other travel agencies, pick up passengers at this hotel. ⊠ *Av. San Martín 202, 8400* ☎ *2944/445–500* ⊕ *www.edelweiss.com. ar* ➲ *94 rooms, 6 suites* ⚐ *Restaurant, in-room safes, indoor pool, gym, hair salon, massage, sauna, bar, meeting room, travel services, free parking* ▤ *AE, DC, MC, V* ⦿ *CP.*

$$$$ ▨ **La Cascada.** Named for its lovely waterfall plunging into an idyllic pool a few steps from the entrance, this lake-view hotel 6 km (4 mi) from Bariloche on the road to Llao Llao brings the outdoors inside through its floor-to-ceiling windows in the living room, dining room, and bar. Views through the trees of blue Nahuel Huapi Lake and distant peaks are often enhanced by bay windows. ✉ *Av. E. Bustillo, Km 6, CC 279, 8400* ☎ *2944/441–088* ⊕ *www.lacascada.com* ➦ *25 rooms* ♿ *Restaurant, indoor pool, gym, sauna, bar* ▤ *DC, MC, V* ⦿| *CP.*

$$$$ ⊞ **Llao Llao Hotel & Resort.** This masterpiece by architect Alejandro Bustillo sits on a grassy knoll surrounded by three lakes with a backdrop of rock cliffs and snow-covered mountains. Local wood—alerce, cypress, and hemlock—has been used for the walls along the 100-yard hallway, where paintings by local artists are displayed between fine boutiques. Service is formal, sometimes stuffy (other times rude), and prices are through the roof, but every room has a view, as does the restaurant. ✉ *Av. Ezequiel Bustillo, Km 25, 25 km (15½ mi) west of Bariloche, 8400* ☎ *2944/448–530* ⊕ *www.llaollao.com* ➦ *153 rooms, 12 suites, 1 cabin* ♿ *2 restaurants, in-room safes, minibars, 18-hole golf course, tennis court, pool, fitness classes, gym, hair salon, hot tub, massage, sauna, spa, yoga, dock, windsurfing, boating, mountain bikes, archery, paddle tennis, piano bar, recreation room, babysitting, children's programs (ages 2–12), business services, convention center, meeting rooms, travel services, no-smoking rooms* ▤ *AE, DC, MC, V* ⦿| *CP.*

★ $$$$ ⊞ **Villa Huinid.** This peaceful complex of cabins is lorded over by a grand hotel, opened in 2005, which has immaculate rooms featuring such modern amenities as 21-inch flat-panel TVs, as well as an impressive lakeview spa. Scattered on the lawns below the hotel is an older network of two-story log and stucco cottages (one, two, or three bedrooms). With their stone chimneys and wooden decks, the cabins look like private homes with well-tended gardens. Cypress plank floors with radiant heat, carved wooden counters, slate floors in the bathroom, and cozy plaids and prints in the bedrooms add to the total comfort—all this and a view of Nahuel Huapi Lake. ✉ *Av. Bustillo, Km 2.6, 8402* ☎☎ *2944/523–523* ⊕ *www. villahuinid.com.ar* ➦ *46 rooms, 17 cabins* ♿ *Restaurant, bar, gym, indoor pool, hot tub, sauna, steam room, massage, IDD phones, kitchens, cable TV, library, playground* ▤ *AE, MC, V.*

$$$–$$$$ ⊞ **Club Hotel Catedral.** Popular with Argentine and Brazilian skiers (so book well in advance), this venerable stone-and-wood apart-hotel sits on a hill just beyond the tram building across the road from the Cerro Catedral ski area, 16 km (10 mi) from Bariloche. The gracious former dining room, with its large windows framing a perfect postcard view of the lake and surrounding mountains, has been reinvented as a living room. Apartments sleep up to four people. ✉ *Base Cerro Catedral, 8400* ☎ *2944/460–006* ⊕ *www.clubhotel.com.ar* ✉ *Av. Córdoba 1345, fl. 7, Buenos Aires, 1055* ☎ *11/4816–4811* ➦ *60 apartments* ♿ *3 restaurants, kitchenettes, 2 tennis courts, pool, sauna, bar, travel services, Internet* ▤ *AE, DC, MC, V* ⊗ *Closed Apr.–May and Oct.–Nov.* ⦿| *BP.*

$$ ⊞ **Aconcagua Hotel.** A tidy stucco building close to the Civic Center, this four-story hotel has weekly rates for its simple basic rooms, some of which have lake views. It's neither luxurious nor particularly attractive, but it provides reasonable comfort for little money. ✉ *Av. San Martín 289, 8400* ☎ *2944/424–718* ⊕ *www.aconcaguahotel.com.ar* ➦ *32 rooms* ♿ *Snack bar, free parking* ▤ *AE, MC, V* ⦿| *CP.*

$ ☒ **Casita Suiza.** Swiss-owned and -operated since 1961, this charming downtown chalet exudes old-world hospitality. The owners have lovingly painted flowers on the walls. Rooms are well maintained, and rates include a hearty breakfast with homemade wheat bread, jams, and juices. In summer and spring the street-side terrace explodes with blossoming pansies and violets. ☒ *Quaglia 342, 8400* 🕿 *2944/426–111* ⊕ *www.casitasuiza.com* ⇲ *13 rooms* ⌂ *Restaurant, cable TV, bar, laundry service* ≡ *AE, DC, MC, V* ☉ *Closed July 10–23* ⦿⎸ *CP.*

Nightlife & the Arts

The **Map Room** (☒ Urquiza 248 🕿 2944/456–856 ⊕ www.themaproom. com.ar) is a delightfully dim haunt, lined with maps from the world travels of the friendly Canadian-Argentine couple that owns the place. The twenty-to-thirtysomething crowd comes for good local beer on tap and meals—including English breakfast—served in the restaurant.

Three of the town's most popular *discotecas* (discos) are all on the same street, Avenida J. M. de Rosas. Whole families—from children to grandparents—go to discos, though on Saturday night only people 25 years and older are admitted. The clubs are especially busy during school holidays and ski season. You can dance the night away at **Cerebro** (☒ 405 Av. J. M. de Rosas 🕿 2944/424–948). Bariloche's oldest disco is **El Grisú** (☒ 574 Av. J. M. de Rosas 🕿 2944/424–483). **Roket** (☒ 424 Av. J. M. de Rosas 🕿 2944/431–940 ⊕ www.roket.com) has a cutting-edge sound system.

Patagonia has a thriving culture of microbrewed beer, and Bariloche is a natural center of the industry. The **Bariloche Microbrew Tour** (☒ Information at The Map Room bar, Urquiza 248 🕿 Randy at 2994/1551–7677 or 2944/525–237, The Map Room 2944/456–856 ⊕ www.brewtour. com.ar ☒ 80 pesos ⌂ Reservations required) is a lively tour of four brewpubs around Bariloche, given in English and Spanish, that leaves at 7 PM each Wednesday and goes until midnight.

Outdoor Activities

FISHING Fishing season runs November 15–May 1. In some areas, catch-and-release is allowed year-around; in some places it's compulsory, and in some, catches may be kept. Guides are available by the day or the week. Nahuel Huapi, Gutiérrez, Mascardi, Correntoso, and Traful are just a few of the many lakes in the northern Lake District that attract fishing fanatics from all over the world. If you're seeking the perfect pool or secret stream for fly-fishing, you may have to do some hiking, particularly along the banks of the Chimehuín, Limay, Traful, and Correntoso rivers. Near Junín de los Andes, the Río Malleo (Malleo River) and the Currihué, Huechulafquen, Paimún, and Lácar lakes are also good fishing grounds.

Fishing licenses allowing you to catch brown, rainbow, and brook trout as well as perch and *salar sebago* (landlocked salmon) are available in Bariloche at the **Direcciones Provinciales de Pesca** (☒ Elfleín 10 🕿 2944/425–160). You can also get licenses at the Nahuel Huapi National Park office and at most tackle shops. Boats can be rented at **Charlie Lake Rent-A-Boat** (☒ Av. Ezequiel Bustillo, Km 16.6 🕿 2944/448–562).

Oscar Baruzzi at **Baruzzi Deportes** (✉ Urquiza 250 ☎ 2944/424–922) is a good local fishing guide. **Martín Pescador** (✉ Rolando 257 ☎ 2944/422–275) has a shop with fishing and hunting equipment. Ricardo Almeijeiras, also a guide, owns the **Patagonia Fly Shop** (✉ Quinchahuala 200, Av. Bustillo, Km 6.7 🖶 2944/441–944).

HIKING Nahuel Huapi National Park has trails that lead to hidden lakes, tumbling streams, waterfalls, glaciers, and mountaintop vistas. For maps and information in English on trails, distances, and degree of difficulty, visit the **Parques Nacionales** (✉ Av. San Martín 24 ☎ 2944/423–111) office at the Civic Center. For ambitious treks, mountaineering, or use of mountain huts and climbing permits, contact **Club Andino Bariloche** (✉ 20 de Febrero 30 ☎ 2944/422–266 ⊕ www.clubandino.com).

HORSEBACK RIDING *Cabalgatas* (horseback outings) can be arranged by the day or the week. Argentine horses are sturdy and well trained, much like American quarter horses. *Tábanas* (horseflies) attack humans and animals in summer months, so bring repellent. **El Manso** (☎ 2944/523–641 or 2944/441–378) combines riding and rafting over the border to Chile. Tom Wesley at the **Club Hípico Bariloche** (✉ Av. Bustillo, Km 15.5 🖶 2944/448–193 ⊕ www.bariloche.org/twesley.html) does rides lasting from one hour to a week.

MOUNTAIN BIKING The entire Nahuel Huapi National Park is ripe for mountain biking. Whether you're a beginner or an expert, you can find a trail to suit your ability. Popular rides are from the parking lot at the Cerro Catedral ski area to Lago Gutiérrez and down from Cerro Otto.

Adventure World (✉ Base of Cerro Catedral ☎ 2944/460–164 or 2944/422–637) rents bikes at the ski area. From there you can ride off on your own or follow a guide down to Lago Guitérrez. **Dirty Bikes** (✉ Vice Almirante O'Connor 681 ☎ 2944/425–616 ⊕ www.dirtybikes.com.ar) rents, repairs, and sells bikes and arranges local tours. **La Bolsa del Deporte** (✉ Diagonal Capraro 1081 ☎ 944/433–111) rents and sells new and used bikes.

PARAGLIDING & ZIPLINE TOURS *Parapente* (paragliding) gives you the opportunity to soar with the condors through mountains and out over lakes, lagoons, and valleys. Cerro Otto and Cerro Catedral (both accessible by ski lifts) are popular launch sites. For equipment and guide information, contact **Parapente Bariloche** (☎ 2944/462–234, 2944/1555–2403 cell). **Canopy** (☎ 2944/1560–7191 ⊕ www.canopybariloche.com) allows you to zipline through (or, rather, above) the forest of Colonia Suiza.

SKIING **Cerro Catedral** is the largest and oldest ski area in South America, with 29 lifts, mostly intermediate terrain, and a comfortable altitude of 6,725 feet. The runs are long, varied, and very scenic. Two ski areas share 4,500 acres of skiable terrain. Avoid Catedral during the first three weeks of July, when the slopes are absolutely packed with youngsters. **Lado Bueno** (The Good Side) has a vertical drop of 3,000 feet, mostly in the fall line. **Robles** goes about 300 feet higher, offering open bowls and better snow for beginners and intermediates at higher elevation. From the top of the second Robles chair, a Poma Lift transports skiers to a weather station at 7,385 feet, where a small restaurant, Refugio Lynch, is tucked into a wind-sculpted snow pocket on the edge of an abyss with a stupendous 360-degree view of Nahuel Huapi Lake, Monte Tronadór, and the Andes. **Villa Catedral,** at the base of the mountain, has ski retail and rental shops, information and ticket sales, ski school offices, restaurants, private ski clubs, an ice rink, and even a disco. Frequent buses transport skiers from Bariloche to the ski area. Adult lift tickets run 95 pesos in high season. For more information, contact **Catedral Alta Patagonia** (☎ 2944/423–776, 11/4780–3300 in Buenos Aires ⊕ www. catedralaltapatagonia.com).

For information and trail maps, contact **La Secretaría de Turismo de Río Negro** (✉ 12 de Octubre 605 ☎ 2944/423–188). **Club Andino Bariloche** (✉ 20 de Febrero 30 ☎ 2944/422–266) also has information and trail maps.

WHITE-WATER
RAFTING

With all the interconnected lakes and rivers in the national park, there's something for everyone—from your basic family float down the swift-flowing, scenic Río Limay to a wild and exciting ride down Río Manso (Class II), which takes you 16 km (10 mi) in three hours. If you're really adventurous, you can take the Manso all the way to Chile (Class IV) through spectacular scenery. Some tour companies organize a trip down the Manso with return by horseback and a cookout at a ranch. **Adventure World** (✉ At the Base of Cerro Catedral ☎ 2944/460–164) does one-day and three-day raft trips on the Río Manso, with a combination horseback trip to the Chilean border available. **Alunco** (✉ Moreno 187 ☎ 2944/422–283 ⊕ www.alcunoturismo.com.ar) arranges rafting trips throughout the area. **Bariloche Rafting** (✉ Mitre 86, Room 5 ☎ 2944/435–708) offers trips along the Limay.

Puerto Madryn

67 km (41½ mi) north of Trelew, 450 km (279 mi) north of Comodoro Rivadavía, 104 km (64 mi) west of Puerto Pirámides, 1,380 km (856 mi) south of Buenos Aires.

Puerto Madryn, on the Atlantic coast in the province of Chubut, is the gateway to the Península Valdés and its unending show of marine life. The Welsh people, who came to Patagonia to seek refuge from religious persecution in Great Britain, landed first in Puerto Madryn in 1865 (and the anniversary of their arrival is celebrated every July 28 here and in other Chubut towns). You can still find many of their descendants today, but there isn't much evidence of the indigenous people who helped the Welsh survive and become the first foreigners to unveil the secrets of Patagonia's interior.

> **WORD OF MOUTH**
>
> "Ushuaia is very special as the world's southernmost city, but its nature-related sites aren't as beautiful as in El Calafate. You can see the animals much closer near Puerto Madryn, which is definitely a 'happy' city. We talked to the locals, and they truly enjoy living there. Peninsula Valdés is an amazing place where we got very close to the penguins and seals."
>
> –dudi

1

Puerto Madryn's main hotels and residences are on or near the 3½-km-long (2-mi-long) Rambla, the pedestrian stretch that hugs Golfo Nuevo; it's also a favorite place for joggers and strollers. As recently as 1980 you could reliably see scores of southern right whales—the creatures for which Atlantic Patagonia is most famous—from the city streets and dock, but migration patterns have changed, and now the whale-watching has largely moved to sleepy Puerto Pirámides out on the peninsula. Still, many people choose to base themselves in livelier Madryn, with its myriad restaurants and nightlife, and see the whales on day-trips. In high whale-watching season—from September through December—the city's nearly 5,000 hotel rooms and its campgrounds usually fill up.

The **Museo Oceanográfico y Ciencias Naturales** (Oceanographic and Natural Science Museum) is worth a visit if you have the time. Housed in a lovely 1917 colonial building once owned by the Pujol family (original settlers), the museum focuses on marine life. You can see a giant squid preserved in formaldehyde and learn how fish breathe. ⊠ *Domecq García and Menéndez* ☎ *2965/451–139* 🖃 *Free* ☉ *Weekdays 9–7, weekends 2:30–7.*

Furthering Puerto Madryn's reputation as the eco-conscious center of Patagonia is the spectacular **EcoCentro,** a modern hands-on museum and research center that strives to promote the protection of the sea and its inhabitants through education. Exhibits provide background on local marine life, and the invertebrates "touch pool" allows visitors to get a real feel for the fish. The center is on a cliff at the north end of the city's beach. ⊠ *Julio Verne 3784* 🖃 *2965/457–470* ⊕ *www.ecocentro.org. ar* 🖃 *15 pesos* ☉ *Wed.–Mon. 10–6.*

Where to Stay & Eat

$–$$$$ ✕ **La Barra Bar y Comidas.** Usually it's not a good sign when a restaurant tries to do everything at once: *parrilla,* pizza, and elaborate meat and seafood dishes. However, La Barra does it all well, and the never-ending crowds at this restaurant, just steps from the shore, attest to the quality found here. Skip the mediocre fried calamari, however. ⊠ *Blvd. Brown and Lugones* ☎ *2965/455–550 or 2965/454–279* 🖃 *AE, DC, MC, V.*

$$ ✕ **La Gaviota Cocinera.** The secret of this restaurant from husband-and-wife team Pablo and Flavia Tolosa is the combination of cozy rooms and reliable food at extraordinarily reasonable prices. The three-course set-price meals might feature tenderloin with leek and mustard sauce, or grilled chicken stuffed with olives and dried tomatoes. ⊠ *Galles 32* ☎ *2965/456–033* 🖃 *AE, MC, V.*

$–$$ ✕ **Ambigú.** This stylish place to eat and drink is across the street from the beach. The menu has 60 pizzas to choose from, as well as entrées like sirloin medallion (*medallón de lomo*) with pumpkin puree. A clean, contemporary style complemented by well-mounted photographs documenting the history of the building (note the art deco detailing, including original iron cresting, on the exterior) lends the restaurant both authenticity and sophistication. ⊠ *Av. Roca at Av. Saénz Peña* ☎ *2965/ 452–541* 🖃 *AE, MC, V.*

$–$$ ✕ **Cantina El Náutico.** Don't let the corny, yellow-neon sign outside dissuade you; this local favorite run by three generations of a French Basque family serves fantastic homemade pasta and fresh seafood. Even the "butter" that accompanies the bread is a cut above—a mixture of mayonnaise with garlic, parsley, and pepper. For dessert, try the outstanding *macedonia* (fruit salad with ice cream). ☒ *Av. Roca 790* ☎ *2965/471–404* ⊕ *www.elnauticocantina.com.ar* ☰ *AE, DC, MC, V.*

$–$$ ✕ **Mr. Jones.** This brewpub is the closest thing to an Irish pub in Atlantic Patagonia, and it's packed every night. Although the beer is good, the food is not just an afterthought; offerings include potpies, sausages with kraut, pizzas, and other brew-happy food. ☒ *9 de Julio 116 at 25 de Mayo* ☎ *2965/475–368* ☰ *AE, MC, V.*

$–$$ ✕ **Restaurant Estela.** Run lovingly by Estela Guevara, who could easily pass for anybody's favorite aunt, this restaurant is a real pleasure. There are menus in English, German, French, and Italian; the postcards from all over the world sent by dinner guests and displayed on the walls attest to the owner's popularity. Ms. Guevara, who is of Ukrainian descent and speaks perfect English, tends to all her guests personally and will even offer travel advice. The restaurant serves hearty meals of beef, chicken, and fish at reasonable prices. ☒ *R. S. Peña 27* ☎ *2965/451–573* ☰ *AE, MC, V* ☉ *Closed Mon.*

$$$ ✕⌖ **Estancia San Guillermo.** If you want to experience a Chubut farm filled with snorting pigs, overfriendly guanacos, and strutting roosters, head for Estancia San Guillermo. Just a few miles outside Puerto Madryn, owners Alfredo and Cristina Casado make you feel at home with their 1,200 sheep, which roam their 7,400-acre fossil-filled farm. Watch Alfredo shear a sheep or his helpers prepare the parrilla. Stay in roomy, comfortable villas with kitchens and bathrooms; rates include all meals. The estancia has a dining room, too, if you're just coming for the day. ☒ *Contact info in Puerto Madryn: Av. 28 de Julio 90, 9120* ☎ *2965/452–150* ⊕ *www.san-guillermo.com* ⚷ *Dining room, horseback riding* ☰ *No credit cards* ☉ *Closed mid-May–mid-June* ⧆ *FAP.*

$$$ ⌖ **Hotel Peninsula Valdés.** With nondescript white block architecture, this waterfront hotel may look bland from the outside, but it's simple, spotless, well-appointed rooms look out over the bay, and there's an elaborate spa hidden within. Ask for a room with a view on an upper floor for the best experience. ☒ *Av. Roca 155, 9120* ☎ *2965/471–292* ⊕ *www.hotel-peninsula-valdes.com* ⤳ *76 rooms* ⚷ *Restaurant, bar, breakfast room, gym, sauna, health club, Internet, laundry service* ☰ *AE, DC, MC, V* ⧆ *BP.*

$ ⌖ **Bahía Nueva Hotel.** This hotel on the bay has clean and spacious rooms and a great location. Only stay here if you can get a room facing the bay, however; the dark back rooms are not worth the price. The English-speaking staff are eager to please, and the eco-conscious literature and decor make guests aware of their awesome natural surroundings. The warm brick lobby area features a library, communal wired computers, comfortable armchairs, and a fireplace. ☒ *Av. Julio A. Roca 67, 9120* ☎ *2965/450–045 or 2965/450–145* ⊕ *www.bahianueva.com.ar* ⤳ *40 rooms* ⚷ *Cable TV, bar, library, laundry service, Internet, business services* ☰ *AE, DC, MC, V* ⧆ *CP.*

$ 🏨 **Hotel Aguas Mansas.** This hotel is one block from the beach in a pretty residential neighborhood and a few blocks from the center of town. It's nothing fancy—just clean, quiet rooms and good, personable service. It's one of the few lodgings with a pool, especially in this price range. ✉ *José Hernandez 51, 9120* 📞 *2965/473–103* ⊕ *www.aguamansas.com* 🛏 *20 rooms* ⚒ *Cable TV, pool, bar, laundry service* ═ *MC, V* ❢❢ *CP.*

Outdoor Activities

There are all sorts of sports in and around Puerto Madryn, ranging from bicycling and fishing to sand-boarding (basically, surfing on the sand). Puerto Madryn is also Argentina's scuba-diving capital. In an effort to further boost interest in scuba diving—by giving divers something else to explore—town officials sank the *Albatros,* a large fishing vessel, off the coast in Golfo Nuevo. Several scuba shops rent equipment and can arrange dives for you. Most of them are found on Boulevard Brown, which runs along the beach; almost all of them have small restaurants and bars complete with tiki huts, reclining chairs, and music. **Ocean Divers** (✉ Blvd. Brown 700 📞 2965/472–569 or 2965/1566–0865) is a reliable place to find scuba equipment. **Scuba Duba** (✉ Blvd. Brown 893 📞 2965/452–699) is an established dive shop.

Several companies rent bicycles for about 20 pesos a day, including **XT Mountain Bike** (✉ Av. Roca 742 📞 2965/472–232). **Costas Patagonicas** (📞 2965/451–131) organizes fishing trips. **Jorge Schmid** (📞 2965/451–511), a respected guide in the area, offers fishing trips, as well as whale-watching and dolphin-viewing trips.

Península Valdés

Fodor'sChoice ★   *Puerto Pirámides is 104 km (64 mi) northeast of Puerto Madryn.*

The Península Valdés is one of Argentina's most important wildlife reserves. Its biggest attractions are the *ballenas francas* (southern right whales) that feed, mate, give birth, and nurse their offspring here. Each year, a few hundred whales come in to mate, rotating through from among a total population of about 2,000 (once 100,000-strong, the worldwide population of these giant mammals has declined drastically, a result of being hunted for their blubber). Each whale comes to the peninsula once every three or four years. One unique characteristic of these whales is that they have two external blowholes on top of their heads, and when they emerge from the water, they blow a *V*-shape water blast that can be seen for miles away. The protected mammals attract some 120,000 visitors every year from June, when they first arrive, through December. Especially during the peak season of September and October, people crowd into boats small and large to observe at close range as the 30- to 35-ton whales leap out of the water and blow water from their spouts.

Off-season the peninsula is still worth visiting: sea lions, elephant seals, Magellanic penguins, egrets, and cormorants as well as land mammals like guanacos, gray fox, and Patagonian *mara,* a harelike animal, all make their home here. Discovered by Spanish explorer Hernando de Magallanes in 1520 and named after Don Antonio Valdés, minister of the Spanish navy in the late 18th century, Península Valdés is a protected zone.

The peninsula's animal population is so valued, it earned the area a UN-ESCO World Heritage site designation. It's also the lowest point on the South American continent, at 132 feet below sea level.

To get to the peninsula, you must drive along lonely roads surrounded by vast estancias dotted with sheep and a handful of cows. At the park gates you must pass through the **Information Center and Museum** (☎ 2965/1556–5222 ☉ Daily 8–8), where you'll pay an entrance fee of 35 pesos. There you can also get a map of the peninsula and check out a small but interesting display of peninsula lore.

Puerto Pirámides, the only village on Península Valdés, is a more tranquil, isolated base than Puerto Madryn from which to explore the area's natural attractions. For ecological reasons, only 350 people are allowed to live here, but there are a handful of campsites, hotels, and restaurants. Bring plenty of cash to the town with you, because there are often no working ATM machines. Aside from whale-watching and lounging around with a beer in hand and looking out on the pyramid-shape cliffs of Valdés Bay, the only activities in town are scuba diving and surfing. Whale-watching excursions leave from the little harbor, generally at 8:30 AM or 9 AM—check with your hotel to reserve with one of the local outfits. Smaller boats are preferable to big ones, as they tend to get closer to the whales.

Although full-day tours from Puerto Madryn are available, the peninsula is really best seen by renting a car in Madryn and staying for a couple of nights in Pirámides. Plan on at least two days and nights to see the sights of the peninsula, which should include at the least a one-hour boat trip from the harbor of Pirámides to see the whales (in season). For starters, the Lobería Puerto Pirámides is a sea lion colony 4 km (2½ mi) from the town (on the way to Punta Delgada). It's walkable if you don't have wheels. From June through November, whales can often be seen, just 30 meters offshore or so, from the Observatorio de la Fundación Patagonia Natural at Playa Faro, 12 km (7½ mi) from Pirámides toward Punta Flecha.

The most rewarding sights, however, come from driving all the way around the peninsula. Beginning in Pirámides, you can take an easy circuit route along the peninsula's desolate, unpaved roads (keep your speed below 60 kph at all times—the roads are notoriously slippery).

Begin by heading southeast (with a full tank of gas) along RP 2 for about 70 km (43 mi) to get to the elephant seals and sea lion colonies at **Punta Delgada,** on the southeastern tip of the peninsula. The elephant seals' breeding season starts in August when the males compete for beach space, after which females arrive, form harems, and give birth. The seals all head out to sea in November. Here there's a starkly beautiful old lighthouse, which you can climb to the top of and appreciate the open-sea views, and guard's quarters that have been turned into an upmarket hotel and restaurant. You have to walk down a set of stairs and paths to get to the animal observation area, which is only open 9:30 AM–4:30 PM. From there, head up the eastern coast of the island (RP 47, though it's unmarked), another 70 km (43 mi) or so, toward Caleta Valdés, near which you can stop at Parador La Elvira), a complex with a restaurant, gift shop, and cliffside walkway to another impressive elephant-seal beach, whose activity peaks in September. Head north to the northeastern corner of the peninsula and Punta Norte, the most remote and largest sea-lion settlement of all; here orcas cruise through town from time to time, and Magellanic penguins roam the land from October through March. From Punta Norte, RP 3 is an inland shortcut that heads straight back southwest to Pirámides to complete this substantial, but eminently worthwhile, day trip.

Where to Stay & Eat

$–$$$ ✕ **Posada Pirámides.** This impossibly cute little restaurant, which feels like a living room, is across the street from the Hotel Paradise. Its kitchen and delightful staff proffer creative Argentine cuisine, with a spotlight on seafood—this is probably the best place to eat in town. Perhaps because the place doubles as a hostel (with very basic accommodation for youths or families), there's a young, informal attitude, but the preparations are serious; don't miss the signature *vieyras gratinados* (baked scallops with melted cheese) or a heavy but good preparation of *lenguado con salsa de camarones* (sole in shrimp sauce) with potatoes noisette. ✉ *Avda. de las Ballenas s/n* ☎ *2965/4950* ⊕ *www.posadapiramides. com* ⊟ *AE* ✇ *Closed Apr.–May.*

$–$$ ✕ **Parador La Elvira.** This stop along the unpaved RP 47 might at first seem like a mirage: out of nowhere arises a complex with tour buses, gift shops, and a grand, picture-windowed restaurant that looks down the gentle arc of the peninsula's coastline. But the food is for real, in spite of the cafeteria-style self-service system. The crowning achievement is delectable *cordero al asador* (that classic Patagonian specialty of lamb spit-roasted "on the cross," which is hacked to pieces and served directly from the *asador*). The hearty soups and salad bar are a bit disappointing, however. ✉ *Near Caleta Valdés, along RP 47 on the Peninsula Valdés* ⊟ *No credit cards.*

¢–$ ✕ **La Estación Pub.** The coolest bar in Pirámides is also a simple but good restaurant. Specialties include delicious *milanesas* and vegetable-heavy pasta dishes. This is where all the town's twentysomethings congregate after hours; not surprisingly, the restaurant is lively and funky with bizarre rock posters decorating the walls. ✉ *Av. de las Ballenas s/n* ☎ *2965/ 495–047* ⊟ *No credit cards.*

★ $$$ ✕⊡ **Punta Delgada.** This former lighthouse (along with a navy station, a post office, and a little school for the guards' families) is a sea-lion-colony observation station and elegant hotel. The Punta Delgada's luxuries are simple and aristocratically old-fashioned: comfortable beds, a tennis court, a pleasant pub with pool and darts, starry night skies, board games, and utter tranquillity. Excursions are organized by the staff. There are no telephones or even cell service, never mind television; there's no electricity 9–noon and 3–7. Nor are there water views from the rooms, unfortunately; the hotel sits too far inland on the knoll for that. Still, it's one of the most impressively isolated hotels in Patagonia. Dinner is served for hotel guests only, but nonguests who are day-tripping can lunch at the restaurant ($–$$$$), which features chicken curry, king crab, and *cordero al asador* at midday. Tour groups tend to stop here for lunch. ✉ *Punta Delgada, Peninsula Valdés* ☎ *2965/458–444* ⊕ *www.*

puntadelgada.com ⊅ *27 rooms* ⚹ *Restaurant, bar, tennis court, horseback riding; no TV, no phone* ▤ *AE, MC, V* ⊘ *Closed Apr.–July.*

$$ ✕⊡ **The Paradise.** This hotel and restaurant is overpriced, but if you're seeking reliability, look no further. Rooms are clean and spare. Those on the second floor have a few more amenities like cable TV. The restaurant ($$–$$$) is one of the better ones in town, decorated with postcards and photographs left behind by visitors, and a fireplace in the back. Two bars create atmosphere enough to distract you from seafood dishes that lack flair. The hotel can organize scuba-diving tours and activities like sand surfing. ⊠ *Av. Julio A. Roca, 9121* ☎ *2965/495–030 or 2965/ 495–003* ⊕ *www.puerto-piramides.com.ar* ⊅ *12 rooms* ⚹ *Restaurant, some in-room hot tubs, fishing, bar, laundry service; no TV in some rooms* ▤ *AE, MC, V* ⎨◯⎬ *CP.*

★ $$$ ⊡ **Las Restingas.** This is the most luxurious hotel in town; it's also the only place in town where you can view the whales from your hotel. Rooms boast crisp linens and huge picture windows from which you can watch the creatures bob in and out of the water on a good day. The harbor from which whale-watching trips leave is right at the property's border. ⊠ *Primera Bajada al Mar and Ribera Marítima* ☎ *2965/495–006 or 2965/495–101* ⊕ *www.lasrestingas.com* ⊅ *12 rooms* ⚹ *Restaurant, bar, laundry service, solarium, Internet, private beach* ▤ *AE, MC, V.*

$ ⊡ **Cabañas en el Mar.** Families would do well to stay in one of these wooden cabañas that have small private balconies looking seaward. They come with small kitchens and can accommodate up to six people. Since the food options in town are limited, the cabañas are also popular with biologists on extended stays. ⊠ *Av. de las Ballenas s/n, 9121* ☎ *2965/ 495–049* ⊕ *www.piramides.net/cabanas* ⊅ *6 cabañas* ⚹ *Cafeteria, laundry service; no room TVs* ▤ *No credit cards.*

Outdoor Activities

For whale-watching, **Jorge Schmid** (☎ 2965/295–012 or 2965/295– 112) is a reliable operator, operating from the little harbor of Pirámides. They also rent scuba equipment. **Mar Patag** (☎ 5411/5031–0756 ⊕ www. crucerosmarpatag.com) offers multiday luxury boat tours of Valdés Bay and the Atlantic Ocean. Its brand-new ship has seven well-equipped rooms and can accommodate up to 50 people. The all-inclusive cruises run two to three days and cost about $150 per person per day.

El Calafate & the Parque Nacional los Glaciares

320 km (225 mi) north of Río Gallegos via R5, 253 km (157 mi) east of Río Turbio on Chilean border via R40, 213 km (123 mi) south of El Chaltén via R40.

Founded in 1927 as a frontier town, El Calafate is the base for excursions to the Parque Nacional los Glaciares (Glaciers National Park), which was created in 1937 as a showcase for one of South America's most spectacular sights, the Perito Moreno Glacier. Because of its location on the southern shore of Lago Argentino, the town enjoys a microclimate much milder than the rest of southern Patagonia. During the long summer days between December and February (when the sun sets around 10 PM), and during Easter vacation, thousands of visitors come to see the glaciers and fill the hotels and restaurants. This is the area's high season, so be sure to make reservations well in advance. October, November, March, and April are less crowded and less expensive periods to visit. March through May can be rainy and cool, but also less windy and often quite pleasant. The only bad time to visit is winter, particularly June, July, and August.

To call El Calafate a boomtown would be to put it mildly. Between 2001 and 2005, the town's population exploded from 4,000 to 15,000, and it shows no signs of slowing down; at every turn you'll see new construction. Unsurprisingly, the downtown has a very new feel to it, although most buildings are constructed of wood, with a rustic aesthetic that seems to respect the majestic natural environment. As the paving of the road between El Calafate and the Perito Moreno Glacier nears completion, the visitors continue to flock in—whether luxury-package tourists bound for the legendary Hostería Los Notros, backpackers over from Chile's Parque Nacional Torres del Paine, or *porteños* in town for a long weekend.

Daily flights from Buenos Aires, Ushuaia, and Río Gallegos, as well as direct flights from Bariloche, transport tourists in a few hours to El Calafate's 21st-century glass and steel airport—an island of modernity surrounded by the lonely expanse of Patagonia—with the promise of adventure and discovery in distant mountains and unseen glaciers. El Calafate is so popular that the flights are selling out weeks in advance, so don't plan on booking at the last minute.

Driving from Río Gallegos takes about four hours across desolate plains, enlivened occasionally by the sight of a gaucho, his dogs, and a herd of sheep, as well as *ñandú* (rheas), shy llamalike guanacos, silver-gray foxes, and fleet-footed hares the size of small deer. **Esperanza** is the only gas, food, and bathroom stop halfway between the two towns.

Avenida del Libertador San Martín (known as Libertador or San Martín) is the main street, with tour offices, restaurants, and shops selling regional specialities, sportswear, camping and fishing equipment, souvenirs, and food. A staircase in the middle of San Martín ascends to Avenida Julio Roca, where you'll find the bus terminal and a very busy **Oficina de Turismo** (⊠ Av. Julio Roca 1004 🕾🕾 2902/491–090 ⊕ www.elcalafate. gov.ar) with a board listing available accommodations and campgrounds; you can also get brochures and maps, and there's a multilingual staff to help plan excursions. It's open daily 7 AM–10 PM. The **Parques Nacionales** (⊠ Av. Libertador 1302 🕾 2902/491–005), open weekdays 7–2, has information on the entire park, the glaciers, area history, hiking trails, and flora and fauna.

The Hielo Continental (Continental Ice Cap) spreads its icy mantle from the Pacific Ocean across Chile and the Andes into Argentina, covering an area of 21,700 square km (8,400 square mi). Approximately 1.5 million acres of it are contained within the **Parque Nacional los Glaciares,** a UNESCO World Heritage site. Extending along the Chilean border for 350 km (217 mi), the park is 40% covered with ice fields that branch off into 47 major glaciers that feed two lakes—the 15,000-year-old **Lago Argentino** (Argentine Lake, the largest body of water in Argentina and the third-largest in South America) in the southern end of the park, where you'll see the occasional group of flamingos, and **Lago Viedma** (Lake Viedma) at the northern end near **Cerro Fitz Roy**, which rises 11,138 feet. Plan on a minimum of two to three days to see the glaciers and enjoy the town—more if you plan to visit El Chaltén or any of the other lakes. Entrance to the park costs 30 pesos.

Fodor'sChoice ★ The **Glaciar Perito Moreno** lies 80 km (50 mi) away on R11, which is paved from El Calafate to the national park entrance. From there, a road that's partly paved (it's scheduled to be entirely paved by the end of 2006) winds through hills and forests of lengas and ñires, until suddenly, the startling sight of the glacier comes into full view. Descending like a long white tongue through distant mountains, it ends abruptly in a translucent blue wall 3 km (2 mi) wide and 165 feet high at the edge of frosty green Lago Argentino.

Although it's possible to rent a car and go on your own, virtually everyone visits the park on day-trip tours that are booked through one of the many travel agents in El Calafate (unless, that is, you're staying in Los Notros, the only hotel inside the park itself; they arrange all the treks and such themselves). The most basic of these tours just take you to see the glacier up close from a viewing area composed of a series of platforms that are wrapped around the point of the Península de Magallanes. The viewing area, which might ultimately be the most impressive view of the glacier, allows you to wander back and forth, looking across the Canal de los Tempanos (Iceberg Channel). Here you listen and wait for nature's number one ice show—first a cracking sound, followed by tons of ice breaking away and falling with a thunderous crash into the lake. Sometimes the icy water splashes onlookers across the channel! As the glacier creeps across this narrow channel and meets the land on the other side, an ice dam sometimes builds up between the inlet of Brazo Rico on the left and the rest of the lake on the right. As the pressure on the dam increases, everyone waits for the day it will rupture again. The last time was in March 2004, when the whole thing collapsed in a series of explosions that lasted hours and could be heard in El Calafate. You can look at photos of the event at the top of the "platforms."

Glaciar Upsala, the largest glacier in South America, is 60 km (37 mi) long and 10 km (6 mi) wide, and accessible only by boat. Daily cruises depart from Puerto Banderas (40 km [25 mi] west of El Calafate via R11) for the 2½-hour trip. While dodging floating icebergs (*tempanos*), some as large as a small island, the boats maneuver as close as they dare to the wall of ice rising from the aqua-green water of Lago Argentino. The seven glaciers that feed the lake deposit their debris into the runoff, causing the water to cloud with minerals ground to fine powder by the glacier's moraine (the accumulation of earth and stones left by the glacier). Con-

1

dors and black-chested buzzard eagles build their nests in the rocky cliffs above the lake. When the boat stops for lunch at Onelli Bay, don't miss the walk behind the restaurant into a wild landscape of small glaciers and milky rivers carrying chunks of ice from four glaciers into Lago Onelli.

Where to Stay & Eat

$$$–$$$$ ✕ **Toma Wine Bar y Restó.** This hip restaurant represents the new, yuppie face of El Calafate, with creative preparations like *ojo de bife con calabazas confitadas* (ribeye with pumpkin confit) and *papas Toma* (french fries with melted cheese, smoked bacon, spring onion, and cream). Wine pairings are suggested with each main course, and to finish, there's good ol' apple pie à la mode, perhaps washed down by the port-style Malamado, made from Malbec grapes. The atmosphere is cool, dark, and trendy, and the service deferential. ✉ *Av. del Libertador 1359* ☎ *2902/492–993* ▭ *AE, MC, V* ☺ *No lunch. Closed Sun.*

★ $$ ✕ **Pura Vida.** Modernity merges with tradition at this hippieish, veggie-friendly restaurant a few blocks out of the center of El Calafate. It's a real treat to find such creative fare, funky decor, cool candles, and modern art in such a frontier town. The beef stew served inside a *calabaza* (pumpkin) has an irresistible flair to it and is excellently seasoned, although the beef isn't particularly tender. Even if, technically speaking, the cooking isn't quite top-flight, Pura Vida is more than the sum of its parts, drawing in backpackers and older folks alike with an almost mystical allure. ✉ *Libertador 1876* ☎ *2902/493–356* ▭ *AE, MC, V.*

$$ ✕ **Rick's Café.** It's *tenedor libre* (all you can eat) for 22 pesos at this immensely popular *parrilla* in a big yellow building on El Calafate's main street. In part because of the value proposition, the place is packed full of locals and tourists day and night. The room is big and bustling, if not particularly interesting, and the spread includes lamb and *vacío* (flank steak). ✉ *Libertador 1091* ☎ *2902/492–148* ▭ *MC, V.*

$–$$$ ✕ **Casimiro Biguá.** This restaurant and wine bar is another one with a hipper-than-thou interior and an inventive menu serving such delectable delights as Patagonian lamb with *calafate* sauce (calafate is actually a local wild berry). The *cordero al asador* (spit-roasted lamb) displayed in the window, though, is the one throwback the place allows. There's an outdoor garden in the back, and a great wine list. ✉ *Libertador 963* ☎ *2902/492–590* ⊕ *www.interpatagonia.com/casimiro* ▭ *AE, DC, MC, V* ☺ *No lunch. Closed Sun.*

$–$$ ✕ **La Lechuza.** This cozy, bustling local place is known for having some of the best pizza in town. The brick oven and thin crust make for a more Italian-style taste and texture than at most spots. ✉ *Libertador and 1 de Mayo* ☎ *2902/491–610* ▭ *No credit cards* ☺ *No lunch Sun.*

$–$$ ✕ **La Tablita.** It's a couple of extra blocks away from downtown, across
Fodor'sChoice   a little white bridge, but this bustling parrilla is where all the locals go
★   for a special night out. You can watch your food as it's prepared: Patagonian lamb and beef ribs cook gaucho-style on an asador, or meat sizzling on the grill, including steaks, chorizos, and excellent *morcilla* (blood sausage). The enormous *parrillada* for two is an excellent way to sample it all, and the wine list is well priced and well chosen. ✉ *Coronel Rosales 28* ☎ *2902/491–065* ⊕ *www.interpatagonia.com/latablita* ▭ *AE, DC, MC, V* ☺ *No lunch Mon.–Thurs. June–July.*

$$$$ ✕⊞ **Hostería los Notros.** Weathered wood buildings cling to the moun-
Fodor'sChoice tainside that overlooks the Perito Moreno Glacier as it descends into
★ Lago Argentino. This inn, seemingly at the end of the world, is 73 km
(45 mi) west of El Calafate. The glacier is framed in the windows of every
room. A path through the garden and over a bridge spanning a canyon
connects rooms to the main lodge. Appetizers and wine are served in
full view of sunset (or moonrise) over the glacier, followed by an absolutely spectacular menu that spotlights game, including delicious venison and creative preparations of Argentine classics. Note that a two-night
minimum stay is required. This property is extremely expensive (up to
US$674 per night); prices include all meals, cocktails, park entry, and
a glacier excursion. If you don't feel like spending that much, come just
for a meal. ✉ *Reservations in Buenos Aires: Arenales 1457, fl. 7, 1961*
☎ *11/4814–3934 in Buenos Aires, 2902/499–510 in El Calafate* ⊕ *www.
losnotros.com* ⇆ *32 rooms* ⚘ *Restaurant, fishing, hiking, horseback
riding, bar, recreation room, playground, Internet, airport shuttle, travel
services; no room phones; no room TVs* ▤ *AE, DC, MC, V* ۞ *Closed
June–mid-Sept.* ⍾ *FAP.*

$$$ ✕⊞ **Hotel Kau-Yatun.** Books, games, and magazines clutter the tables in
the large living room of this former ranch house; guests congregate at
the bar or in front of the fireplace. Rooms vary in size, shape, and decor,
all following a casual ranch theme. Country cuisine (meat, pasta, and
vegetables) is served in the dining room, and wild game dishes are avail-
able at La Brida restaurant. On weekends, steaks and chorizos sizzle on
a large open grill in the *quincho* (combination kitchen, grill, and din-
ing room), while lamb or beef cooks gaucho style on an asador. ✉ *25
de Mayo, 9405* ☎ *2902/491–059* ⊘ *kauyatun@cotecal.com.ar* ⇆ *45
rooms* ⚘ *Restaurant, horseback riding, bar, Internet, airport shuttle* ▤*AE,
MC, V* ۞ *Closed May–Sept.* ⍾ *CP.*

$$$$ ⊞ **El Quijote.** Sun shines through picture windows onto polished slate
floors and high beams in this modern hotel next to Sancho restaurant
a few blocks from the main street. Rooms are carpeted and have plain
white walls (which some readers have reported are paper-thin) and
wood furniture. ✉ *Gregores 1155, 9405* ☎ *2902/491–017*
⊘ *elquijote@cotecal.com.ar* ⇆ *80 rooms* ⚘ *Café, bar, travel services*
▤ *AE, DC, MC, V* ۞ *Closed June–July* ⍾ *CP.*

$$$ ⊞ **Posada los Alamos.** Surrounded by tall, leafy alamo trees and constructed
of brick and dark *quebracho* (ironwood), this attractive country manor
house uses rich woods, leather, and handwoven fabrics to produce con-
versation-friendly furniture groupings in the large lobby. Plush comforters
and fresh flowers in the rooms and a staff ready with helpful suggestions make this a top-notch hotel. Lovingly tended gardens surround
the building and line a walkway through the woods to the restaurant
and the shore of Lago Argentino. ✉ *Moyano 1355 at Bustillo, 9405*
☎ *2902/491–144* ⊕ *www.posadalosalamos.com* ⇆ *140 rooms, 4
suites* ⚘ *Restaurant, 3-hole golf course, tennis court, 2 bars, travel
services* ▤ *AE, MC, V* ⍾ *CP.*

$$ ⊞ **El Mirador del Lago.** The best thing about this hotel is neither the zigzag
brick facade offering all the front rooms a corner view of Lago Argentino,
nor the cozy bar and sitting room, nor the collection of games, books,

videos, and magazines to enjoy on stormy days. The best thing is the unfailingly friendly staff. They're all related and take great pride in helping their guests enjoy everything the region has to offer. They know the roads, the restaurants, and the best way to get to all the attractions. ⊠ *Av. Libertador 2047, 9405* ☎ *2902/493–213* ⊕ *www.miradordellago.com. ar* ⇨ *20 rooms* ⌂ *Dining room, sauna, bar, recreation room, travel services* ⊟ *AE, DC, MC, V* ⊙ *Closed June* ⍢⌶ *CP.*

$ 🏨 **Calafate Hostel.** This hostel caters to every demographic, with dorm-style accommodations for backpackers in one building and well-kept private rooms with private baths—and, believe it or not, Internet-connected desktop computers—in a separate structure next door. Both buildings share the bar-lounge and breakfast room. The bar is something of a hangout; this might not be the most upscale accommodation in town, but it's very comfortable, and it's right downtown. ⊠ *Gobernador Moyano 1226, 9405* ☎ *2902/492–450* ⊕ *www.calafatehostels. com* ⌂ *Internet, kitchen facilities, travel services* ⊟ *AE, MC, V.*

¢–$ 🏨 **América del Sur.** The only downside to this new hostel, which caters largely to younger backpackers, is its location (a 10-minute uphill walk from downtown), but there are beautiful views of the lake and mountains, and a free shuttle service to compensate for the distance. Otherwise, the place is simple but spectacular—sparklingly clean and legendarily friendly. There are rooms with 2 beds and 4 beds. It's a particularly cheap deal for groups of 4. ⊠ *Calle Pto. Deseado, 9405* ☎ *2902/493–525* ⊕ *www.americahostel.com.ar* ⌂ *Restaurant, bar, Internet, travel services; no TV* ⊟ *No credit cards.*

Outdoor Activities

BOAT TOURS The two most popular scenic boat rides in the Parque Nacional los Glaciares are the hour-long **Safari Náutico,** in which your boat cruises just a few meters away from the face of the Glaciar Perito Moreno, and the full-day **Upsala Glacier Tour,** in which you navigate through a more extensive selection of glaciers, including Upsala and Onelli, as well as several lakes within the park that are inaccessible by land. The Safari Náutico costs 60 pesos and includes transportation from El Calafate. The full-day Upsala trip, including lunch, costs around 175 pesos. **Upsala Explorer** (⊠ 9 de Julio 69, El Calafate ☎ 2902/491–034 ⊕ www. upsalaexplorer.com.ar) is the most popular operator of the boat tours. **René Fernández Campbell** (⊠ Avenida del Libertador 867, El Calafate ☎ 2902/491–155) is another local tour operator that runs boat tours around the glaciers.

HIKING You can hike anywhere in the Parque Nacional los Glaciares. Close to El Calafate are trails along the shore of Lago Argentino and in the hills south and west of town. El Chaltén is usually a better base than El Calafate for hikes up mountain peaks like Cerro Torre.

HORSEBACK RIDING Anything from a short day ride along Lago Argentino to a weeklong camping excursion on and around the glaciers can be arranged in El Calafate by **Gustavo Holzmann** (⊠ Av. Libertador 3600 ☎ 2902/493–203, 2966/1562–0935 cell) or through the tourist office. *Estancias Turísticas* (tourist ranches) are ideal for a combination of horseback riding, ranch activities, and local excursions. Information on **Estancias de Santa Cruz** is available in Buenos Aires at the **Provincial tourist office** (✉ Suipacha 1120 ☎ 11/4325–3098 ⊕ www.estanciasdesantacruz. com). **Estancia El Galpón del Glaciar** (✉ Ruta 11, Km 22 ☎☎ 2902/492–509 or 11/4774–1069 ⊕ www.estanciaalice.com.ar) welcomes guests overnight or for the day—for a horseback ride, bird-watching, or an afternoon program that includes a demonstration of sheep dogs working, a walk to the lake with a naturalist, sheep-shearing, and dinner in the former sheep-shearing barn, served right off the grill and the asador by knife-wielding gauchos. **Estancia Maria Elisa** (☎☎ 2902/492–583 or 11/4774–1069) is an upscale choice among estancias. Other estancias close to Calafate are **Nibepo Aike** (✉ 50 km/31 mi from Calafate ☎ 2966/492–797 ⊕ www.nibepoaike.com.ar), **Alta Vista** (✉ 33 km/20 mi from Calafate ☎ 2966/491–247), and **Huyliche** (✉ 3 km/2 mi from Calafate ☎ 2902/491–025).

ICE TREKKING
★
A two-hour minitrek on the Perito Moreno Glacier involves transfer from El Calafate to Brazo Rico by bus and a short lake crossing to a dock and refugio, where you set off with a guide, put crampons over your shoes, and literally walk right across a stable portion of the glacier, scaling ridges of ice and ducking through bright blue ice tunnels. It is one of the most unique experiences in Argentina. The entire outing lasts about five hours. Hotels generally arrange minitreks through **Hielo y Aventura** (✉ Av. Libertador 935 ☎ 2902/492–205 ⊕ www.hieloyaventura.com), which also organizes much longer, more difficult trips of eight hours to a week to other glaciers; you can also arrange the trek directly through their office in downtown El Calafate. Minitrekking runs about 250 pesos for the day.

MOUNTAIN
BIKING
Mountain biking is popular along the dirt roads and mountain paths that lead to the lakes, glaciers, and ranches. Rent bikes and get information at **Alquiler de Bicicletas** (✉ Av. Libertador 689 and Comandante Espora ☎ 2902/491–398).

Ushuaia & the Tierra del Fuego

914 km (567 mi) south of El Calafate, 3,580 km (2,212 mi) south of Buenos Aires.

At 55 degrees south latitude, Ushuaia (pronounced oo-swy-ah; the Argentines don't pronounce the "h") is closer to the South Pole (2,480 mi) than to Argentina's northern border with Bolivia (2,540 mi). It is the capital and tourism base for Tierra del Fuego, an island at the southernmost tip of Argentina.Although its stark physical beauty is striking, Tierra del Fuego's historical allure is based more on its mythical past than on reality. The island was inhabited for 6,000 years by Yámana, Haush, Selk'nam, and Alakaluf Indians. But in 1902 Argentina, eager to populate Patagonia to bolster its territorial claims, moved to initiate an Ushuaian penal colony, establishing the permanent settlement of its most southern territories and, by implication, everything in between.

When the prison closed in 1947, Ushuaia had a population of about 3,000, made up mainly of former inmates and prison staff. Today, the Indians

1

of Darwin's "missing link" theory are long gone—wiped out by disease and indifference brought by settlers—and the 50,000 residents of Ushuaia are hitching their star to tourism. The city rightly (if perhaps too loudly) promotes itself as the southernmost city in the world (Puerto Williams, a few miles south on the Chilean side of the Beagle Channel, is but a tiny town). Ushuaia feels a bit like a frontier boomtown, with the heart of a rugged, weather-beaten fishing village and the frayed edges of a city that quadrupled in size in the '70s and '80s. Unpaved portions of R3, the last stretch of the Panamerican Highway, which connects Alaska to Tierra del Fuego, are finally, albeit slowly, being paved. The summer months—December through March—draw 120,000 visitors, and the city is trying to extend those visits with events like March's Marathon at the End of the World.

Tierra del Fuego could be called picturesque, at a stretch. A chaotic and contradictory urban landscape includes a handful of luxury hotels amid the concrete of public housing projects. Scores of "sled houses" (wooden shacks) sit precariously on upright piers, ready for speedy displacement to a different site. Many of the newer homes are built in a Swiss-chalet style, reinforcing the idea that this is a town into which tourism has breathed new life. At the same time, the weather-worn pastel colors that dominate the town's landscape remind you that Ushuaia was once just a tiny fishing village, populated by criminals, snuggled at the end of the Earth.

As you stand on the banks of the Canal Beagle (Beagle Channel) near Ushuaia, as Captain Robert Fitz Roy—the captain who was sent by the English government in 1832 to survey Patagonia, including Tierra del Fuego—must have done, the spirit of the farthest corner of the world takes hold. What stands out is the light: at sundown the landscape is cast in a subdued, sensual tone; everything feels closer, softer, more human in dimension despite the vastness of the setting. The snowcapped mountains of Chile reflect the setting sun back onto a stream rolling into the channel, as nearby peaks echo their image—on a windless day—in the still waters.

Above the city, the last mountains of the Andean Cordillera rise, and just south and west of Ushuaia they finally vanish into the often stormy sea. Snow whitens the peaks well into summer. Nature is the principal attraction here, with trekking, fishing, horseback riding, and sailing among the most rewarding activities, especially in the Parque Nacional Tierra del Fuego (Tierra del Fuego National Park).

As Ushuaia converts to a tourism-based economy, the city seeks ways to utilize its 3,000 hotel rooms in the lonely winter season. Though most international tourists stay home to enjoy their own summer, the adventurous have the place to themselves for snowmobiling, dogsledding, and skiing at Cerro Castor. The **tourist office** (⊠ Av. San Martín 674 ☎ 2901/432–000 or 0800/333–1476 ⊕ www.e-ushuaia.com) is a great resource for information on the town's and Tierra del Fuego's attractions. It's open weekdays 8 AM–10 PM, weekends 9–8. Several people on the cheerful staff speak English.

The **Antigua Casa Beben** (Old Beben House) is one of Ushuaia's original houses, and long served as the city's social center. Built between 1911 and 1913, the house is said to have been ordered through a Swiss catalog. In the 1980s the Beben family donated the house to the city to avoid demolition. It was moved to its current location along the coast and restored, and is now a cultural center with art exhibits. ⊠ *Maipú and Pluschow* ☎ *No phone* ☒ *Free* ⊙ *Tues.–Fri. 10–8, weekends 4–8.*

Rainy days are a reality in Ushuaia, but two museums give you an avenue for urban exploration and a glimpse into Tierra del Fuego's fascinating past. Part of the original penal colony, the Presidio building was built to hold political prisoners, street orphans, and a variety of other social undesirables from the north. Today it holds the **Museo Marítimo** (Maritime Museum), within Ushuaia's naval base, which has exhibits on the town's extinct indigenous population, Tierra del Fuego's navigational past, Antarctic explorations, and life and times in an Argentine penitentiary. You can enter cell blocks and read the stories of the prisoners who lived in them while gazing upon their eerie effigies. Well-presented tours (in Spanish only) are conducted at 3:30 daily. ⊠ *Gobernador Paz and Yaganes* ☎ *2901/437–481* ☒ *15 pesos* ⊙ *Daily 10–8.*

Fodor's Choice
★

At the **Museo del Fin del Mundo** (End of the World Museum), you can see a large stuffed condor, as well as other native birds, indigenous artifacts, maritime instruments, and such seafaring-related objects as an impressive mermaid figurehead taken from the bowsprit of a galleon. There are also photographs and histories of El Presidio's original inmates, such as Simon Radowitzky, a Russian immigrant anarchist who received a life sentence for killing an Argentine police colonel. The museum is in the 1905 residence of a Fuegonian governor. The home was later converted into a bank, and some of the exhibits are showcased in the former vault. ⊠ *Maipú 173 and Rivadavia* ☎ *2901/421–863* ☒ *5 pesos* ⊙ *Oct.–Mar., daily 10–8; Apr.–Sept., daily noon–7.*

Tierra del Fuego was the last land mass in the world to be inhabited—it was not until 9,000 BC that the ancestors of those native coastal inhabitants, the Yámana, arrived. The **Museo Yámana** chronicles their lifestyle and history. The group was decimated in the late 19th century, mostly by European disease. (There is said to be, at this writing, one remaining Yámana descendant, who lives a few miles away in Puerto Williams.) Photographs and good English placards depict the unusual, hunched posture of the Yámana; their unusual, wobbly walk; and their hunting of cormorants, which were killed with a bite through the neck. ⊠ *Rivadavia 56* ☎ *2901/422–874* ⊕ *www.tierradelfuego.org.ar/mundoyamana* ☒ *5 pesos* ⊙ *Daily 10–8.*

The **Tren del Fin del Mundo** (End of the World Train) takes you to Estación Ande, inside the Parque Nacional Tierra del Fuego, 12 km (7½ mi) away. The train ride, which lasts about an hour each way, is a simulation of the trip on which El Presidio prisoners were taken into the forest to chop wood; but unlike them, you'll also get a good presentation of Ushuaia's history (in Spanish and English). The train departs daily at 9:30 AM, noon, and

3 PM in summer, and just once a day, at 10 AM, in winter, from a stop near the national park entrance. If you have a rental car, you'll want to do the round trip, but if not, one common way to do the trip is to hire a *remis* (car service) that will drop you at the station for a one-way train ride, pick you up at the other end, and then drive you around the Parque Nacional for two or three hours of sightseeing (which is more scenic than the train ride itself). ✉ *Ruta 3, Km 3042* ☎ *2901/431–600* ⊕ *www. trendelfindelmundo.com.ar* ✐ *95 pesos first-class ticket, 50 pesos tourist-class ticket, 20 pesos national park entrance fee (no park fee in winter).*

Tour operators run trips along the **Canal Beagle,** on which you can get a startling close-up view of all kinds of sea mammals and birds on Isla de los Lobos, Isla de los Pájaros, and near Les Eclaireurs Lighthouse. There are catamarans that make three-hour trips, generally leaving from the Tourist Pier at 3 PM, and motorboats and sailboats that leave twice a day, once at 9:30 AM and once at 3 PM (all of these weather allowing; few trips go in winter). Prices range 60 pesos–140 pesos; some include hikes on the islands. Check with the tourist office for the latest details; you can also book through any of the local travel agencies.

One good excursion in the area is to **Lago Escondido** (Hidden Lake) and **Lago Fagnano** (Fagnano Lake). The Panamerican Highway out of Ushuaia goes through deciduous beechwood forest and past beavers' dams, peat bogs, and glaciers. The lakes have campsites and fishing and are good spots for a picnic or a hike. This can be done on your own or as a seven-hour trip, including lunch, booked through the local travel agencies (75 pesos without lunch, 95 pesos with lunch). One recommended operator, offering a comfortable bus, a bilingual guide, and lunch at Las Cotorras, is **All Patagonia** (✉ Juana Fadul 26 ☎ 2901/433–622 or 2901/ 430–725).

A rougher, more unconventional tour of the lake area goes to **Monte Olivia** (Mt. Olivia), the tallest mountain along the Canal Beagle, rising 4,455 feet above sea level. You also pass the **Five Brothers Mountains** and go through the **Garibaldi Pass,** which begins at the Rancho Hambre, climbs into the mountain range, and ends with a spectacular view of Lago Escondido. From here you continue on to Lago Fagnano through the countryside past sawmills and lumberyards. To do this tour in a four-wheel-drive truck with an excellent bilingual guide, contact **Canal Fun** (✉ Rivadavía 82 ☎ 2901/437–395); you'll drive *through* Lago Fagnano (about 3 feet of water at this point) to a secluded cabin on the shore and have a delicious *asado,* complete with wine and dessert.

Estancia Harberton (Harberton Ranch; ☎ 2901/422–742) consists of 50,000 acres of coastal marshland and wooded hillsides. The property was a late-19th-century gift from the Argentine government to Reverend Thomas Bridges, officially considered the Father of Tierra del Fuego. Today the ranch is managed by Bridges's great-grandson, Thomas Goodall, and his American wife, Natalie, a scientist and author who has cooperated with the National Geographic Society on conservation projects. Most people visit as part of organized tours, but you'll be welcome if you arrive alone. They serve up a solid and tasty tea in their home, the oldest building on the island. For safety reasons, exploration of the ranch can only be done with a guide. Lodging is not available, but you can arrange to dine at the ranch by calling ahead for a reservation. Most tours reach the estancia by boat, offering a rare opportunity to explore the **Isla Martillo** penguin colony, in addition to a sea lion refuge on **Isla de los Lobos** (Island of the Wolves) along the way.

If you've never butted heads with a glacier, and especially if you won't be covering El Calafate on your trip, then you should check out **Glaciar Martial,** in the mountain range just above Ushuaia. Named after Frenchman Luís F. Martial, a 19th-century scientist who wandered this way aboard the warship *Romanche* to observe the passing of the planet Venus, the glacier is reached via a panoramic *aerosilla* (ski lift). Take the Camino al Glaciar (Glacier Road) 7 km (4 mi) out of town until it ends (this route is also served by the local tour companies). Even if you don't plan to hike to see the glacier, it's a great pleasure to ride the 15-minute lift, which is open daily 10–5, weather permitting (it's often closed from mid-May until August), and costs 10 pesos round-trip. If you're afraid of heights, you can instead enjoy a small nature trail here, and a teahouse. You can return on the lift, or continue on to the beginning of a 1-km (½-mi) trail that winds its way over lichen and shale straight up the mountain. After a strenuous 90-minute hike, you can cool your heels in one of the many gurgling, icy rivulets that cascade down water-worn shale shoots or enjoy a picnic while you wait for sunset (you can walk all the way down if you want to wait until after the *aerosilla* closes). When the sun drops behind the glacier's jagged crown of peaks, brilliant rays beam over the mountain's crest, spilling a halo of gold-flecked light on the glacier, valley, and channel below. Moments like these are why this land is so magical. Note that temperatures drop dramatically after sunset, so come prepared with warm clothing.

Parque Nacional Tierra del Fuego

★ The pristine park, 21 km (13 mi) west of Ushuaia, offers a chance to wander through peat bogs; stumble upon hidden lakes; trek through native *canelo,* lenga, and wild cherry forests; and experience the wonders of wind-whipped Tierra del Fuego's rich flora and fauna. Everywhere, lichens line the trunks of the ubiquitous *lenga* trees, and "chinese lantern" parasites hang from the branches.

Everywhere, too, you'll see *castoreros* (beaver dams) and lodges. 50 beaver couples were first brought in from Canada in 1948 so that they would breed and create a fur industry. In the years since, however, the beaver population has grown to more than 50,000, and now represents a major threat to the forests, as the dams flood the roots of the trees; you can see their effects on the gnawed-down trees everywhere. Believe it or not, the government now pays hunters a bounty of 30 pesos for each beaver they kill (they need to show a tail and head as proof).

Visits to the park, which is tucked up against the Chilean border, are commonly arranged through tour companies. Trips range from bus tours to horseback riding to more adventurous excursions, such as canoe trips across Lapataia Bay. Another way to get to the park is to take the Tren del Fin del Mundo (⇨ *above*). **Transportes Kaupen** (☏ 2901/ 434–015), one of several private bus companies, has buses that travel through the park, making several stops within it; you can get off the bus, explore the park, and then wait for the next bus to come by or trek to the next stop (the service only operates in summer). Yet one more option is to drive to the park on R3 (take it until it ends and you see the famous sign indicating the end of the Pan-American Highway, which starts 17,848 km (11,065 mi) away in Alaska, and ends here). If you don't have a car, you can also hire a private *remis* to spend a few hours driving you through the park, including the Pan-American terminus, and perhaps also combining the excursion with the Tren del Fin del Mundo. Trail and camping information is available at the park-entrance ranger station or at the Ushuaia tourist office. At the entrance to the park is a gleaming new restaurant and teahouse set amidst the hills, **Patagonia Mia** (✉ Ruta 3, Entrada Parque Nacional ☏ 2901/1560–2757 ⊕ www. patagoniamia.com); it's a great place to stop for tea or coffee, or a full meal of roast lamb or Fuegian seafood.

A nice excursion in the park is by boat from lovely **Bahía Ensenada** to **Isla Redonda**, a wildlife refuge where you can follow a footpath to the western side and see a wonderful view of the Canal Beagle. This is included on some of the day tours; it's harder to arrange on your own, but you can contact the tourist office to try. While on Isla Redonda you can send a postcard and get your passport stamped at the world's southernmost post office. You can also see the Ensenada bay and island (from afar) from a point on the shore that is reachable by car.

Other highlights of the park include the spectacular mountain-ringed lake, **Lago Roca**, as well as **Laguna Verde**, a lagoon whose green color comes from algae at its bottom. Much of the park is closed from roughly June through September, when the descent to Bahía Ensenada is blocked by up to 6 feet of snow. Even in May and October, chains for your car are a good idea. There are no hotels within the park—the only one burned down in the 1980s, and you can see its carcass driving by—but there are three simple camping areas around Lago Roca. Tours to the park are run by **All Patagonia** (✉ Juana Fadul 26 ☏ 2901/433–622 or 2901/430–725).

Where to Stay & Eat

Dotting the perimeter of the park are five free campgrounds, none of which has much more than a spot to pitch a tent and a fire pit. Call the **park office** (☏ 2901/421–315) or consult the ranger station at the park entrance for more information. **Camping Lago Roca** (✉ South on R3 for 20 km [12 mi] ☏ No phone), within the park, charges 8 pesos per person per day and has bathrooms, hot showers, and a small market. Of all the campgrounds, **La Pista del Andino** (✉ Av. Alem 2873 ☏ 2901/435–890) is the only one within the city limits. Outside of town, **Camping Río Pipo** (☏ 2901/435–796) is the closest to Ushuaia (it's 18 km [11 mi] away).

Choosing a place to stay depends in part on whether you want to spend the night in town or 3 mi uphill. Las Hayas Resort, Hotel Glaciar, Cumbres de Martial, and Los Yámanas have stunning views, but require a taxi ride to reach Ushuaia.

$$–$$$$
Fodor'sChoice
★
✕ **Chez Manu.** *Herbes de provence* in the greeting room tip French owner-chef Manu Herbin's hand: he uses local seafood with a French touch to create some of Ushuaia's most memorable meals. Perched a couple of miles above town, across the street from the Hotel Glaciar, this expensive restaurant has grand views of the Beagle Channel. The good wine list includes Patagonian selections. Don't miss the *trucha fueguina* (local trout) in white wine sauce, served with buttery rice cooked in fish stock or the *centolla* (king crab) au gratin. ✉ *Camino Luís Martial 2135* ☎ *2901/432–253* ▤ *AE, MC, V* ✆ *Closed Mon.*

$–$$$$
✕ **La Estancia.** This restaurant in the center of town, set in a pleasant wooden A-frame room, is one of the classiest of the good-value "tenedor libre" (all-you-can-eat) parrillas on the main strip—nobody here orders à la carte. Skip the Italian buffet and fill up instead on the mouth-watering spit-roasted Patagonian lamb, grilled meats, and delicious *morcilla*. It's all you can eat for 21 pesos. Sit by the glass wall to see the *parrillero* artfully coordinate the flames and spits. ✉ *Av. San Martín 257* ☎ *2901/1556–8587* ▤ *AE, DC, MC, V.*

$–$$$$
✕ **Tía Elvira.** On the street that runs right along the Beagle Channel, this is an excellent place to sample the local catch. Garlicky shellfish appetizers and *centolla* (king crab) are delicious, and even more memorable is the dreamy, tender *merluza negra* (black sea bass). The room is decked out with nautical knick-knacks that are perhaps a bit tacky for such a pricey place. The service is friendly and familial. ✉ *Maipú 349* ☎ *2901/424–725* ▤ *AE, DC, MC, V* ✆ *Closed July.*

★ $–$$$$
✕ **Volver.** A giant plastic king crab sign beckons you into this red tin restaurant, which provides some major relief from Avenida San Martin's row of all-you-can-eat parrillas. The name means "return" and it's the kind of place that calls for repeat visits. Newspapers from the 1930s line the walls in this century-old home; informal table settings have placemats depicting old London landmarks; and fishing nets hang from the ceiling, along with hams, a disco ball, tricycles, and antique lamps. The culinary highlight is, of course, king crab (*centolla*), which comes served with a choice of five different sauces. ✉ *Maipú 37* ☎ *2901/423–977* ▤ *AE, DC, MC, V* ✆ *No lunch May–Aug.*

$$$$
🏨 **Hotel del Glaciar.** Just above the Hayas hotel in the Martial Mountains, this hotel has the best views of Ushuaia and the Beagle Channel. The rooms are bright, clean, and very comfortable. After a long day in the woods, you can curl up on the large sofa next to the fire pit or make your way over to the cozy wood-paneled bar for a drink. Hourly shuttle buses take you to the town center. ✉ *2355 Camino Glaciar Martial, Km 3.5, 9410* ☎ *2901/430–640* ☞ *73 rooms, 4 suites* ⚒ *Restaurant, café, minibars, cable TV, bar, laundry service, Internet, convention center, airport shuttle, travel services* ▤ *AE, DC, MC* ⏐○⏐ *CP.*

$$$$
Fodor'sChoice
★
🏨 **Hotel y Resort Las Hayas.** Las Hayas is in the wooded foothills of the Andes, overlooking the town and channel below. Ask for a *canal* view. Rooms are all decorated differently, but all feature Portuguese linen, solid oak furnishings, and fabric-padded walls. A suspended glass bridge connects the hotel to a spectacular health spa, which includes a heated pool and even a squash court. The wonderful restaurant prepares an excellent version of *mollejas de cordero* (lamb sweetbreads) with scal-

lops. Frequent shuttle buses take you into town. ⊠ *1650 Camino Luís Martial, Km 3, 9410* ☎ *2901/430710, 11/4393–4750 in Buenos Aires* ⊕ *www.lashayashotel.com* ⥲ *85 rooms, 7 suites* ⅏ *Restaurant, coffee shop, in-room safes, golf privileges, indoor pool, health club, hot tub, massage, sauna, spa treatments, squash, bar, laundry service, convention center, meeting rooms, airport shuttle, travel services* ☰ *AE, DC, MC, V* ⦿ *CP.*

$$$ ▦ **Hotel Los Yámanas.** This cozy new hotel 4 km (2½ mi) from the center of town is named after the local tribe and blends a rustic mountain aesthetic with impeccable elegance. Some rooms have stunning views over the Beagle Channel, and all have wrought-iron bed frames and are furnished with simple good taste. The expansive lobby and the second-floor restaurant are just as welcoming. ⊠ *Los Ñires 1850, Km 3, 9410* ☎ *2901/445–960* ⊕ *hotelyamanas.com.ar* ⥲ *18 rooms* ⅏ *Restaurant, bar, in-room safes, minibars, gym, Internet, laundry service, gift shop, game room* ☰ *AE, DC, MC, V* ⦿ *CP.*

$$ ▦ **Hotel Cabo de Hornos.** Cabo de Hornos is a cut above other downtown hotels in the same price category. The rooms are clean and simple, and all have cable TV and telephones. The lobby-lounge is tacky and tasteful at the same time, decorated with currency and postcards from all over the world. Its old ski-lodge feel makes it a nice place to relax and watch *fútbol* with a cup of coffee or a beer. ⊠ *San Martín and Rosas, 9410* ☎ *2901/430–677* ⥲ *30 rooms* ⅏ *Restaurant, bar* ☰ *AE, MC, V* ⦿ *CP.*

Nightlife & the Arts

Ushuaia has a lively nightlife scene in summer, with its casino, discos, and cozy cafés all within close proximity of each other. The biggest and most popular restaurant-pub is **El Náutico** (⊠ Maipú 1210 ☎ 2901/430-415), which plays all kinds of music, from Latin to techno. It's pumping Thursday through Saturday nights from midnight to 6 AM.

A popular nightspot is **Lenon Pub** (⊠ Maipú 263 ☎ 2901/435-255), which serves drinks and food to those 21 and older. It's open 11 AM–6 AM. For more traditional Argentine entertainment, **Hotel del Glaciar** (⊠ 2355 Camino Glaciar Martial, Km 3.5 ☎ 2901/430–640) has tango shows Saturday at 11 PM. **Bar Ideal** (⊠ San Martín 393) is a cozy and historic bar and café. **Tante Sara** (⊠ San Martín 701 ☎ 2901/433–710 ⊕ cafebartantesara.com.ar) is a popular café-bar in the very heart of town, where locals kick back with a book or a beer (they pour Beagle, the local artisanal brew).

Outdoor Activities

FISHING The rivers of Tierra del Fuego are home to trophy-size freshwater trout—including browns, rainbows, and brooks. Both fly- and spin-casting are available. The fishing season runs November–March; fees range from 10 pesos a day to 40 pesos for a month. Fishing expeditions are organized by the following companies. Founded in 1959, the **Asociación de Caza y Pesca** (⊠ Av. Maipú 822 ☎ 2901/423–168) is the principal hunting and fishing organization in the city. **Rumbo Sur** (⊠ Av. San Martín 350 ☎ 2901/421–139 ⊕ www.rumbosur.com.ar) is the city's oldest travel agency and can assist in setting up fishing trips. **Wind Fly** (✉ Av. 25 de Mayo 143 ☎ 2901/431–713 or 2901/1544–9116 ⊕ www. windflyushuaia.com.ar) is dedicated exclusively to fishing, and offers classes, arranges trips, and rents equipment.

FLIGHT-SEEING The gorgeous scenery and island topography are readily appreciated on a Cessna tour of the area. A half-hour flight (US$70 per passenger, US$100 for one passenger alone) with a local pilot takes you over Ushuaia and the Beagle Channel with views of area glaciers and snow-capped islands south to Cape Horn. A 60-minute flight crosses the Andes to the Escondida and Fagnano lakes. **Aero Club Ushuaia** (✉ Antiguo Aerpuerto ☎ 2901/421–717 ⊕ www.aeroclubushuaia.org.ar) offers half-hour and hour-long trips.

MOUNTAIN BIKING A mountain bike is an excellent mode of transport in Ushuaia, giving you the freedom to roam without the rental-car price tag. Good mountain bikes normally cost about 5 pesos an hour or 15 pesos–20 pesos for a full day. Bikes can be rented at the base of the glacier, at the **Refugio de Montaña** (✉ Base Glaciar Martial ☎ 2901/1556–8587), or at **D. T. T. Cycles** (✉ Av. San Martín 903 ☎ 2901/434–939). Guided bicycle tours (including rides through the national park), for about 50 pesos a day, are organized by **All Patagonia** (✉ Fadul 26 ☎ 2901/430–725). **Rumbo Sur** (✉ San Martín 350 ☎ 2901/421–139 ⊕ www.rumbosur.com.ar) is the city's biggest travel agency and can arrange trips. **Tolkeyén Patagonia** (✉ San Martín 1267 ☎ 2901/437–073) rents bikes and arranges trips.

SKIING Ushuaia is the cross-country skiing (*esqui de fondo* in Spanish) center of South America, thanks to enthusiastic **Club Andino** (☎ 2901/422–335) members who took to the sport in the 1980s and made the forested hills of a high valley about 20 minutes from town a favorite destination for skiers. **Glaciar Martial Ski Lodge** (☎ 2901/243–3712), open year-round, Tuesday–Sunday 10–7, functions as a cross-country ski center from June through October. Skis can also be rented in town, as can snowmobiles.

For downhill (or *alpino*) skiers, Club Andino has bulldozed a couple of short, flat runs directly above Ushuaia. The area's newest downhill ski area, **Cerro Castor** (☎ 2901/422–244 ⊕ www.cerrocastor.com), is 26 km (17 mi) northeast of Ushuaia on R3, and has 19 trails and four high-speed ski lifts. More than half the trails are at the beginner level, six are intermediate, and three are expert trails, but none of this terrain is very challenging for an experienced skier. You can rent skis and snowboards and take ski lessons. **Transportes Kaupen** (☎ 2901/434–015) and other local bus companies run service back and forth from town.

Patagonia Essentials

Transportation

BY AIR

Aerolíneas Argentinas flies (along with its subsidiary Austral) from Buenos Aires to Bariloche, El Calafate, Trelew, and Ushuaia. Southern Winds flies to Bariloche from Buenos Aires. Lan, formerly LanChile, competes with Aerolíneas on the Buenos Aires–Bariloche route.

1

Trelew and Comodoro Rivadavía have Atlantic Patagonia's largest airports; the proximity of Trelew to Madryn and the Peninsula Valdés makes it the best option, generally speaking, although there's also a smaller, less well-connected airport in Puerto Madryn.

For intra-Patagonia air travel, LADE (Líneas Aéreas del Estado) flies small planes, some jets and some propellers, from Bariloche across to Puerto Madryn in Atlantic Patagonia, and south to El Calafate and Río Gallegos.

🔲 **Aerolíneas Argentinas** ☎ 0810/2228-6527 24-hr reservations and sales in Argentina, 11/4320-2000 in Buenos Aires, 2944/422-144 in Bariloche, 2972/427-636 in Chapelco, 2945/452-688 in Esquel. **LADE** ☎ 11/4361-7071 in Buenos Aires, 2944/423-562 in Bariloche, 2972/247-672 in Chapelco, 2944/492-206 in El Bolsón ⊕ www.lade. com.ar. **Lan** ☎ 2944/423-562 in Bariloche, 11/4378-2200 in Buenos Aires, 0800/222-2424 toll-free ⊕ www.lan.com. **Southern Winds** ☎ 0810/777-7979 ⊕ www.fly-sw.com.

BY BUS

Buses arrive in Bariloche from every corner of Argentina. Several companies have daily service to Buenos Aires. Bariloche's Terminal de Ómnibus is in the Estación de Ferrocarril General Roca (Railroad Station) east of town, where all bus companies have offices. Most have downtown offices, too, but your best bet is to go directly to the terminal. The following bus companies run comfortable and reliable overnight buses between Buenos Aires and Bariloche (the trip takes 22 hours): Chevallier, El Valle, and Via Bariloche.

To travel from Bariloche south to El Bolsón and Esquel and across to Puerto Madryn, contact Don Otto, Andesmar at the bus terminal, and TAC. For travel north to Villa La Angostura, Traful, and San Martín de los Andes, contact TAC.

In Atlantic Patagonia, it's difficult—but not impossible—to get around without a car. El Pingüino has service between Trelew and Puerto Madryn. If you're based in Puerto Madryn or Puerto Pirámides, go with local tour operators rather than public buses for day excursions to Peninsula Valdés. However, buses do connect the cities of the region. La Puntual is another major operator in the region, with a hub in Comodoro Rivadavía. To get to and from Buenos Aires, don't bother with the bus system—flying is quick and inexpensive.

More than anywhere else in Patagonia, buses are a major form of transportation in the south. They shuttle passengers across border crossings to Chile as well as between the major cities of Tierra del Fuego and southern Argentina. As elsewhere, Andesmar Autotransportes has a major presence.

🔲 **Bus Companies Andesmar** ☎ 2944/435-040 in Bariloche. **Chevallier** ☎ 2944/423-090 in Bariloche, 11/4314-5555 in Buenos Aires. **Don Otto** ☎ 2944/429-012 in Bariloche. **El Pingüino** ☎ 11/4315-4438 in Buenos Aires, 2965/427-400 in Trelew, 2965/456-256 in Puerto Madryn. **TAC** ☎ 2944/434-727 in Bariloche, 11/4313-3627 in Buenos Aires. **El Valle** ☎ 2944/431-444 in Bariloche, 11/4313-3749 in Buenos Aires. **Via Bariloche** ☎ 2944/432-444 in Bariloche, 11/4663-8899 in Buenos Aires.

BY CAR

Unless you're on a ski-only vacation, renting a car is essential in the spread-out lakes region, giving you the freedom to stop when and where you want. This is especially true in Bariloche, where major sights lie largely outside of town along the Circuito Chico and Circuito Grande. Keep in mind that the Seven Lakes Road is closed for part of the year. For winter travel, it's a good idea to rent a 4x4, especially if you're traveling on dirt roads. Hiring a *remis* (car with driver) is another option; it costs more, however.

Driving to the lakes region from Buenos Aires is a long haul (more than 1,500 km [930 mi] and at least three days) of interminable stretches without motels, gas stations, or restaurants. Fuel in Argentina is expensive, and if you break down in the hinterlands, it's unlikely that you'll find anyone who speaks much English. Note, too, that what seem like towns marked on the map may just be private estancias not open to the public.

Atlantic Patagonia is the closest part of Patagonia to Buenos Aires by road, but it's still a long haul across deserted stretches of road. It's best to rent a car in Puerto Madryn or Trelew. Within the Península Valdés, roads are unpaved but straight and flat. On those roads, be on the look-out for sheep and other animals crossing, and do not exceed 60 kph, because the type of gravel makes skidding very easy.

Car rental is not as much of a factor in southern Patagonia. Most travelers get between cities on planes or buses, and while in natural reserves such as Parque Nacional Los Glaciares or Tierra del Fuego, get around with tour operators or by hiking. A car is perhaps most useful in Tierra del Fuego, for seeing the Parque Nacional. Hiring a *remis* (car with driver) is another, costlier option common for seeing that park.

Contacts & Resources

BANKS

🏧 **Banco de la Nación** ⊠ 9 de Julio 127, Puerto Madryn ☎ 2965/450–465. **Banco Frances** ⊠ Av. San Martín 336 ☎ 2944/430–325. **Bansud** ⊠ Mitre 433 ☎ 2944/422–792. **Credicoop** ⊠ Roque Sanez Peña and 25 de Mayo, Puerto Madryn ☎ 2965/455–139. **Provincia de Santa Cruz** ⊠ Av. Libertador 1285, El Calafate ☎ 2902/492–320.

TOURS

The English-speaking owners of Alunco, a very professional travel office specializing in trips in and around Bariloche, are third-generation Barilocheans, expert skiers, and outdoors enthusiasts who have explored the remotest corners of the northern Lake District.

Aiké Tour, Cuyun Co Turismo, and Factor Patagonia arrange all-day tours of the Península Valdés; reserve ahead, especially if you want an English-speaking guide. Hydro Sport runs small whale-watching boats, which are particularly good for getting up close and personal with the whales.

In El Calafate, most hotels arrange excursions to Moreno and Upsala glaciers. Hielo y Aventura specializes in glacier tours, with their show-stopping "minitrekking" (walking on the glacier with crampons) as well as the "*safari náutico*" (a boat ride next to the glacier). Alberto del Castillo, owner of El Calafate's E.V.T. Fitzroy Expeditions, has English-speaking guides and organizes both glacier and mountain treks.

In Ushuaia and Tierra del Fuego, All Patagonia, Canal Fun and Nature, Tiempo Libre, and Tolkar all offer a wide variety of adventurous treks through the Parque Nacional Tierra del Fuego and around the Canal Beagle. All Patagonia and Rumbo Sur do sea excursions as well as trips to Antarctica. ⛵ **All Patagonia** ☎ 2901/433-622 or 2901/1556-5758 in Ushuaia ⊕ www.allpatagonia.net. **Aiké Tour** ☎ 2965/450-720 in Puerto Madryn. **Alunco** ☎ 2944/422-283 in Bariloche ⊕ www.alcunoturismo.com.ar. **Canal Fun and Nature** ☎ 2901/437-395 in Ushuaia ⊕ www.canalfun.com. **Cuyun Co Turismo** ☎ 2965/454-950 or 2965/451-845 in Puerto Madryn ⊕ www.cuyunco.com.ar. **Factor Patagonia** ☎ 2965/454-990 or 2965/454-991 in Puerto Madryn.

Fitzroy Expeditions ☎ 2962/493-017 in El Chaltén. **Hielo y Aventura** ☎ 2902/492-205 in El Calafate ⊕ www.hieloyaventura.com. **Hydro Sport** ☎ 2965/495-065 in Puerto Madryn ⊕ www.hydrosport.com.ar. **Rumbo Sur** ☎ 2901/421-139 in Ushuaia ⊕ www.rumbosur.com.ar. **Tiempo Libre** ☎ 2901/431-374 in Ushuaia. **Tolkar** ☎ 2901/431-408 or 2901/437-421 in Ushuaia.

VISITOR INFORMATION

🏢 Tourist Offices **Bariloche** ✉ Civic Center ☎ 2944/429-850 ⊕ www.barilochepatagonia. info. **El Calafate** ✉ Terminal de Ómnibus, Julio A. Roca 1004 ☎🖨 2902/491-090 ⊕ www.elcalafate.gov.ar. **Puerto Madryn** ✉ Av. Roca 223 ☎ 2965/453-504 or 2965/456-067 ⊕ www.turismomadryn.gov.ar. **Tierra del Fuego Tourism Institute** ✉ Av. Maipú 505, Ushuaia ☎ 2901/421-423. **Ushuaia** ✉ Av. San Martín 674 ☎ 2901/432-000 or 0800/333-1476 ⊕ www.e-ushuaia.com.

ARGENTINA ESSENTIALS

Transportation

Revised by Eddy Ancinas

BY AIR

The major gateway to Argentina is Buenos Aires's Ezeiza International Airport, 47 km (29 mi) and a 45-minute drive from the city center. Ezeiza, also known as Aeropuerto Internacional Ministro Pistarini, is served by a variety of foreign airlines, along with domestic airlines running international routes. Though Argentina has other international airports, they generally only serve flights from other South American countries.

Major sights within Argentina are often far apart, and although transportation over land can be more economical, it is slower, so it's best to save time and travel the country by plane. Flights from Buenos Aires to other points within Argentina depart from the Aeroparque Jorge Newbery, a 15-minute cab ride from downtown.

For travel between multiple destinations within Argentina, consider a Visit Argentina Pass offered by Aerolíneas Argentinas. This pass can only be purchased in your home country, not in Argentina. You'll get a bigger discount if you purchase the pass in conjunction with a full-fare international Aerolíneas Argentinas ticket. You can change the dates you fly as needed, but once you pick a route, you have to stick to it.

CARRIERS **⚋ To & from Argentina** Aerolíneas Argentinas ☎ 800/333-0276 in U.S., 0/810-2228-6527 in Buenos Aires ⊕ www.aerolineas.com.ar. **Delta** ☎ 800/241-4141 in U.S., 800/221-1212 in Canada, 11/4894-8170 in Buenos Aires ⊕ www.delta.com. **LAN Chile Airlines** ☎ 866/435-9526 in U.S, 306/670-9999, 11/4378-2200 in Buenos Aires. ⊕ www.lan.com. **United Airlines** ☎ 800/538-2929 in U.S., 11/4316-0777 in Buenos Aires ⊕ www.united.com. **Varig Airlines** ☎ 800/468-2744 in U.S., 11/4329-9211 in Buenos Aires ⊕ www.varig.com.

⚋ Within Argentina Aerolíneas Argentinas ☎ 800/333-0276 in U.S., 0/810-2228-6527 in Buenos Aires ⊕ www.aerolineas.com.ar. **Austral** ☎ 11/4340-7800 in Buenos Aires ⊕ www.austral.com.ar.

BY CAR

Renting a car in Argentina is expensive (around US$65 per day plus tax for a midsize car). Your own driver's license may be valid in Argentina, though you may want to take out an International Driver's Permit; contact your local automobile association. The minimum driving age is 18. You'll need to present a major credit card at the agency counter in order to rent a car.

All cities and most areas that attract tourists have rental agencies. You can also rent cars at airports and through some hotels. Offices in Buenos Aires can make reservations in other locations; provincial government tourist offices also have information on car-rental agencies. Europcar in Buenos Aires has good rates that are even lower if you fly on Aerolíneas Argentinas.

An alternative to renting a car is to hire a *remis,* a car with a driver, especially for day outings. Hotels can arrange this service for you. Remises are more comfortable and cheaper than taxis for long rides. They're also usually less expensive for rides within cities, especially on round-trip journeys, because there's no return fare. You have to pay cash—but you'll often spend less than you would for a rental car.

⚋ Major Agencies Avis ☎ 800/331-1084 in the U.S., 11/4130-0130 in Buenos Aires ⊕ www.avis.com. **Dollar** ☎ 11/4315-8800 in Buenos Aires ⊕ www.dollar.com. **Europcar** ✉ Maipú 965, Buenos Aires ☎ 11/4311-1000 ⊕ www.europcar.com.ar. **Hertz** ☎ 800/654-3001in the U.S., 11/4129-7777 in Buenos Aires ⊕ www.hertz.com. **National Car Rental** ☎ 800/227-7368, 11/4811-6903 in Buenos Aires ⊕ www.nationalcar.com.

AUTO CLUB The Automóvil Club Argentino (ACA) provides complete mechanical assistance, including towing, detailed maps and driver's manuals, and expert advice (often in English). The ACA can help chart your itinerary, give you gas coupons, and even set you up with discounted accommodations in affiliated hotels and campgrounds. Present your own auto-club membership card to enjoy these benefits. Note that ACA service is also available at many of the YPF service stations throughout Argentina.

⚋ Automóvil Club Argentino (ACA) ☎ 11/4802-6061 ⊕ www.aca.org.ar.

EMERGENCY SERVICES The ACA will provide emergency mechanical assistance, as will your rental-car agency (included in the rate). You can get your tires filled at gas stations, but if you have a flat you'll have to find a *gomería* (tire repair), many of which are open 24 hours.

GASOLINE You'll find Esso, Shell, and national YPF service stations throughout Buenos Aires, in the provinces, and along major highways. The stations usually include full service, convenience stores, snack bars, and ATMs. In rural areas, gas stations are few and far between and have reduced hours; when traveling in the countryside, it's a good idea to start looking for a station when your tank is half empty. Gas is expensive (around 1.50 pesos per liter, or about 6 pesos per gallon) and may run you 80 pesos to fill a midsize car. There are several grades of unleaded fuels, as well as diesel and gas oil.

ROAD CONDITIONS Paved highways run from Argentina to the Chilean, Bolivian, Paraguayan, and Brazilian borders. If you do cross the border by land you'll be required to present your passport, visa, and documentation of car ownership at immigration and customs checkpoints. It's also common for cars and bags to be searched for contraband, such as food, livestock, and drugs. Within Argentina ultramodern multilane highways usually connect the major cities. Gradually these highways become narrower routes, and then county roads—which often aren't divided and aren't in great condition. You must pay tolls on many highways, and even on some unpaved roads. Tolls come frequently and can be steep.

City streets throughout Argentina are notorious for potholes, and lanes are generally poorly marked. Elsewhere street signs are often hard to see and sometimes nonexistent. Night driving can be hazardous: some highways and routes are poorly lit, routes sometimes cut through the center of towns, cattle often get onto the roads, and in rural areas *rastreros* (old farm trucks) seldom have all their lights working.

For highway-condition reports, updated daily, and basic routes in Spanish, contact La Dirección Nacional de Vialidad.

🚩 **La Dirección Nacional de Vialidad** ☎ 0800/333-0073 ⊕ www.vialidad.gov.ar.

RULES OF THE ROAD Obey speed limits (marked in kilometers per hour) and traffic regulations. In towns and cities, a 40-kph (25-mph) speed limit applies on streets, and a 60-kph (37-mph) limit is in effect on avenues. On expressways the limit is 100 kph (62 mph), and on other roads and highways out of town it's 80 kph (50 mph). These limits are enforced by strategically placed cameras triggered by excessive speed. If you do get a traffic ticket, don't argue. Although you'll see Argentines offering cash on the spot to avoid getting a written ticket, this isn't a good idea.

Seat belts are required by law, as are car lights in daytime on highways. The use of cellular phones while driving is forbidden, and turning left on two-way avenues is prohibited unless there's a left-turn signal; likewise, there are no right turns on red. Traffic lights turn yellow before they turn red, but also before turning green, which is interpreted by drivers as an extra margin to get through the intersection, so take precautions.

Contacts & Resources

CUSTOMS & DUTIES

Upon arriving in Buenos Aires by air or ship, you'll find that customs officials usually wave you through without close inspection. International airports have introduced a customs system for those with "nothing to declare," which has streamlined the arrival process. If you enter the country by bus, take the time to have the border officials do a proper inspection of your belongings and documents. This could prevent problems later when you are trying to leave the country.

Personal clothing and effects are admitted duty-free, provided they have been used, as are personal jewelry and professional equipment. Fishing gear presents no problems. Up to 2 liters of alcoholic beverages, 400 cigarettes, and 50 cigars are admitted duty-free.

ELECTRICITY

The electrical current in Argentina is 220 volts, 50 cycles alternating current (AC); wall outlets usually take Continental-type plugs, with two round prongs, though newer hotels are moving to plugs with three flat, angled prongs. To use electric-powered equipment purchased in the United States or Canada, bring a converter and adapter; some high-end accommodations provide these, but you're better off bringing them if you're unsure.

EMERGENCIES

There's a pharmacy—indicated by a green cross—on nearly every block. Your hotel will be able to guide you to the nearest one. *Farmacias de turno* rotate 24-hour shifts or remain open 24 hours and will deliver to hotels in their area. Emergency numbers are the same nationwide, so wherever you find yourself you can call the numbers below to be connected to a local emergency unit. Most major hospitals have some English-speaking doctors.

🛈 **Emergency Contacts Ambulance** ☎ 107. **Coast Guard** ☎ 106. **Fire** ☎ 100. **Forest Fire** ☎ 103. **Police** ☎ 111 or 4346–5770.

🛈 **Embassies American Embassy** ✉ Colombia 4300, Buenos Aires ☎ 11/5777–4533 ⊕ www.usembassy.state.gov. **British Embassy** ✉ Luis Agote 2412 ☎ 11/4803–7799 or 11/4576–2222, 15/5331–7129 for an emergency ⊕ www.britain.org.ar. **Canadian Embassy** ✉ Tagle 2828 ☎ 11/4808–1000 ⊕ www.dfait-maeci.gc.ca/argentina.

ETIQUETTE

Argentines are very warm and affectionate people, and they greet each other as such—with one kiss on the right cheek. This is done by both men and women. If you don't feel comfortable kissing a stranger, a simple hand shake will suffice. Note that asking someone what they do for a living isn't the best way to make small talk. In Argentina this is almost the same as asking how much money someone makes.

When you leave a party or restaurant it's normal to say good-bye to everyone in the room or in your party (which means kissing everyone once again). Argentines are never in a hurry to get anywhere, so a formal good-bye can certainly take awhile. And although arriving late for social occasions is normal and acceptable among Argentines, arriving late for a business appointment is not.

Traditionally, Argentines don't like to discuss business during a meal. However, since many hours of the day are spent eating, this tradition seems to be fading slowly—at least for the new generation of business-people. Professionals, especially men, dress conservatively for business events, and women like to dress up. Smoking is very common in Argentina, so be prepared for some smoke with your steak. Most restaurants offer no-smoking sections, but make sure to ask before you are seated. If you're at a dinner party, don't be surprised if the room fills up with smoke right after the main course; if it bothers you, you should excuse yourself—don't ask others to smoke outside.

HEALTH

ALTITUDE SICKNESS *Soroche,* or altitude sickness, which results in shortness of breath and headaches, may be a problem when you visit the Andes. To remedy any discomfort, walk slowly, eat lightly, and drink plenty of fluids (avoid alcohol). If you have high blood pressure and a history of heart trouble, check with your doctor before traveling to high Andean elevations. If you experience an extended period of nausea, dehydration, dizziness, severe headache or weakness while in a high-altitude area, seek medical attention.

FOOD & DRINK Buenos Aires residents drink tap water and eat uncooked fruits and vegetables. However, if you've got just two weeks, you don't want to waste a minute of it in your hotel room; exercise caution when choosing what you eat and drink—on as well as off the beaten path. It's best to drink bottled water, which can be found throughout Argentina for about 1.50 pesos for a half liter.

Each year there are cases of cholera in the northern part of Argentina, mostly in the indigenous communities near the Bolivian border; your best protection is to avoid eating raw seafood.

SHOTS & MEDICATIONS No specific vaccinations are required for travel to Argentina. According to the Centers for Disease Control (CDC), however, there's a limited risk of cholera, hepatitis B, and dengue. The local malady of Chagas' disease is present in remote areas. If you plan to visit remote regions or stay for more than six weeks, check with the CDC's International Travelers Hot Line. In areas with malaria (in Argentina, you are at risk for malaria only in northern rural areas bordering Bolivia and Paraguay) and dengue, which are both carried by mosquitoes, take mosquito nets, wear clothing that covers the body, apply repellent containing DEET, and use a spray against flying insects in living and sleeping areas. The hotline recommends chloroquine (analen) as an antimalarial agent; no vaccine exists against dengue or Chagas. Children traveling to Argentina should have current inoculations against measles, mumps, rubella, and polio.

MAIL & SHIPPING

Mail delivery is quite dependable and should take around 6–15 days from Buenos Aires to the United States and 10–15 days to the United

Kingdom, but like many things in Argentina, this is not guaranteed. Put postcards in envelopes and they will arrive more quickly. An international airmail letter or card costs 4 pesos (up to 20 grams).

Express mail is available in cities throughout the country. It will take 2 to 5 days for express mail to reach international destinations, but the cost can be steep (for instance, a letter to the United States via FedEx can cost upwards of $30).

Correo Argentino ✉ Sarmiento 151, Buenos Aires ☎ 11/4316-3000 ⊕ www. correoargentino.com.ar. **DHL** ☎ 0800/222-2345 ⊕ www.dhl.com.ar. **Federal Express** ☎ 0810/333-3339 ⊕ www.fedex.com. **UPS** ☎ 0800/2222-2877 ⊕ www.ups.com.

MONEY MATTERS

When you have a strong currency like the U.S. dollar or the euro, Argentina is still very inexpensive. Sumptuous dinners, in the finest restaurants, can run as high as 100 pesos per person with appetizers, wine, dessert, and tip—the equivalent of around $35. A large wood-grilled sirloin with salad, potatoes, dessert, wine, and an espresso will run around 30 pesos at steak houses in Buenos Aires and much less in the hinterlands.

In Buenos Aires you're likely to pay 1.50–2 pesos for a *cafecito* (small cup of coffee) in a café. A soda costs 1.50 pesos. A taxi ride will run you 4–8 pesos in the larger cities. A tango show dinner with a couple of drinks costs about 100 pesos. A double room in a moderately priced, well-situated hotel costs $100–$130 dollars, including taxes. Many hotels are now in the habit of charging strictly in dollars. Make sure that the rate you are paying is valid for both tourists and Argentines; some hotels have been known to take advantage of foreigners who are unaware of the favorable exchange rate by charging them an increased price.

When ordering alcoholic drinks, ask for Argentine liquors, or suffer the import fees. A bottle of Chivas Regal costs 80 pesos in shops, for instance. When ordering drinks, specify your preference for whiskey or vodka *nacional,* for example.

CURRENCY & EXCHANGE
One peso equals 100 centavos. Peso notes are in denominations of 100, 50, 20, 10, 5, and 2. Coins are in denominations of 1 peso, and 50, 25, 10, 5, and 1 centavos. When giving change, the cashier may round your purchase to the nearest 5 or even 10 centavos. Always check your change.

Banks, ATMs, and *casas de cambio* (exchange houses) all charge a fee. As a rule, banks charge the least and hotels the most. Although fees for transactions at ATMs (abundant throughout Argentina) may be higher than at home, ATM rates are excellent because they're based on wholesale rates offered only by major banks. To avoid lines at airport exchange booths, get a bit of local currency before you leave home. Also you may not be able to readily change currency in rural areas, so don't leave major cities without adequate amounts of pesos in small denominations.

At this writing, the rate of exchange was 2.9 pesos to the U.S. dollar, 2.2 pesos to the Canadian dollar, 5.48 pesos to the pound sterling, 3.66

pesos to the euro, 2.26 pesos to the Australian dollar, 2 pesos to the New Zealand dollar, and 0.44 pesos to the South African rand.

ℹ Exchange Services International Currency Express ☎ 888/278-6628 orders ⊕ www.foreignmoney.com. **Travel Ex Currency Services** ☎ 800/287-7362 orders and retail locations ⊕ www.travelex.com.

PASSPORTS & VISAS

U.S., Canadian, and British citizens do not need a visa for visits of up to 90 days, though they must carry a passport. Upon entering Argentina, you'll receive a tourist visa stamp on your passport valid for 90 days. If you need to stay longer, exit the country for one night; upon reentering Argentina, your passport will be stamped allowing an additional 90 days. The fine for overstaying your tourist visa is $50 dollars, payable upon departure at the airport. If you do overstay your visa, plan to arrive at the airport several hours in advance of your flight so that you have ample time to take care of the fine.

SAFETY

Buenos Aires is one of the safer cities in the world. Police constantly patrol any areas where tourists are likely to be, and violent crime is rare. Smaller towns and villages in Argentina are even safer. All that said, political and economic stability has produced an increase in robberies and petty theft. Be aware of your surroundings at all times, do your best to blend in with the locals, and don't take any unnecessary chances—like wearing jewelry you're not willing to lose. There have been incidents of chains and even earrings being yanked off of unsuspecting tourists. Keep cameras in a secure camera bag, preferably one with a chain or wire embedded in the strap. Women can expect pointed looks, the occasional catcall, and some advances. Act confident, and ignore the men.

If you're hailing a taxi, make sure it says "radio taxi"; this means that the driver works for a licensed company and is required to call in every new fare over the radio. Also look for the driver's photo ID, which should be well displayed inside the car. Better yet, call a licensed *remis,* which is always safer and usually cheaper, as you agree on a fixed-price beforehand.

Argentines like to speak their minds, and there has been a huge increase in street protests in recent years. Most of these have to do with government policies, but there has been an increase in anti-U.S. and anti-British sentiment, stemming primarily from Argentina's strained relationship with the International Monetary Fund (IMF) and the war in Iraq. If you do see a demonstration, don't panic—as the overwhelming majority of them are peaceful—just be aware of the atmosphere.

LOCAL SCAMS When asking for price quotes, always confirm whether the price is in dollars or pesos. Some salespeople, especially street vendors, have found that they can take advantage of confused tourists by charging dollars for goods that are actually priced in pesos. If you're in doubt about that beautiful leather coat, don't be shy about asking if the number on the tag is in pesos or dollars.

TAXES

Sales tax (IVA) in Argentina is 21%. The tax is usually included in the price of goods and noted on your receipt. The IVA tax is entirely refundable for purchases exceeding 70 pesos at stores displaying a duty-free sign. Request a tax form from the store and keep your receipts. The IVA is also included in the price of hotels. When you depart, plan enough time to visit the return desk at the airport to obtain your refund. The $18 departure tax must be paid in U.S. dollars. Domestic airport taxes are usually included in the ticket price.

TELEPHONES

The country code for Argentina is 54. To call Argentina from overseas, dial 00 + the country code (54) + the area code (omitting the first 0, which is for long-distance calls within Argentina). The area code for Buenos Aires is 11. For information, dial 110. For the time, dial 113. For information about international calls, dial 19 or 000.

Telecom's *telecentros* and Telefónica's *locutorios* offer a variety of services, including metered phone calls, faxes, telegrams, and access to the Internet; some even provide wire transfers. They are convenient to use and abound throughout all cities; some are specially equipped for people with hearing impairments. Telecom has white and yellow pages on their Web site, plus postal code information.

☎ **Telecom** ☎ 0800/555-0112 ⊕ www.telecom.com.ar. **Telefónica** ☎ 0800/222-4262 ⊕ www.telefonica.com.ar.

CELL PHONES To call the cell-phone number of a Buenos Aires resident, dial 15 before the number (unless you're also calling from a cell-phone with a Buenos Aires number). Local cell-phone charges vary depending on certain factors, such as the company and time of day, and can cost up to 2 pesos per call; the fee is charged to the caller, not the recipient, unless on a pay phone.

Cellular phones can be rented at the airport, or through your hotel—sometimes they can be added on to a car-rental package. Delivery is free in Buenos Aires. You can compare prices online and make reservations in advance.

☎ **Mobile Phone Rental Phonerental** ☎ 0800/335-3705, 11/4311-2933 ⊕ www. phonerental.com.ar. **Unifon** ✉ Av. Corrientes 645, Buenos Aires ☎ 0800/333-6868 ⊕ www.unifon.com.ar.

LOCAL CALLS Public phones are reliable and abundant. They operate with coins or cards, which are called *tarjetas chip*. Simply slide the card in, wait for the reading of how many minutes you have, then dial.

Cards are available at kiosks, pharmacies, and phone centers. Cards range 4–10 pesos; rates are 23¢ for every two minutes during peak hours (weekdays and Sunday 8–8, Saturday 8 AM–1 PM), and half rate off-peak. You can use the cards for local, long-distance, and international calls, though you're better off calling long distance from a phone center.

LONG-DISTANCE When calling from one area code to another in Argentina, add a 0 be-
CALLS fore the area code, then 1 for Capital Federal and Greater Buenos Aires, 2 for the southern region, and 3 for provinces in the north. Charges in-

crease with distances, beginning at 30 km (18½ mi) outside of the city. Many hotels charge up to 4 pesos per call on top of the regular rate. It's best to call from a public phone or telephone center.

Hotels have *DDI,* international direct dialing, but may charge up to 3 pesos for a long-distance call. You're best off calling from telecentros or locutorios, where your call is metered and will run around 95 centavos for the first minute, and 68 centavos each additional minute, during peak hours to the United States. Rates are much higher for England (starting at 1.40 pesos for the first minute and 1.25 pesos for each additional minute) and Australia (2.85 pesos for the first minute and 2.30 pesos for each additional minute).

The country code is 1 for the United States and Canada and 44 for the United Kingdom. To call out from Argentina, dial 00 + country code + area code + number.

TIME
New York is one time zone behind Buenos Aires from April through October (it's two hours behind the rest of the year, as Argentina does not observe daylight saving time). There's a two-hour difference for Chicago and four-hour difference between Los Angeles and Buenos Aires.

TIPPING
Propinas (tips) range 10%–15% in bars and restaurants (10% is enough in a casual café or if the bill runs high). Note that some restaurants charge a *cubierto,* covering table service, not the waiter's tip. Argentines round off a taxi fare, though some cabbies who frequent hotels popular with tourists seem to expect more. Hotel porters should be tipped at least 3 pesos or the equivalent of one dollar, 5 pesos for more than one bag. Three pesos per night is adequate for chambermaids, and anything up to 20 pesos for a concierge is good, depending on what you ask of them. Give doormen and ushers about 2 pesos, restroom attendants change under a peso, and beauty and barbershop personnel around 5%. Depending on the extent of their service, anything from a beer to 5 to 10 pesos a day should be fine for local guides.

VISITOR INFORMATION
🖪 **Argentina Government Tourist Offices Los Angeles** ☏ 323/954-9155. **Miami** ☏ 305/442-1366. **New York** ☏ 212/603-0400.

WEB SITES
Don't rule out foreign-language sites; some have links to sites that present information in more than one language, including English.
🖪 **Web Sites Argentina Secretary of Tourism** ⊕ www.turismo.gov.ar. **Buenos Aires Herald** ⊕ www.buenosairesherald.com. **Embassy of Argentina** ⊕ www. embajadaargentinaeeuu.org. **Tango** ⊕ www.abctango.com.

Bolivia

Updated by
Joan Gonzalez

PEOPLE DESCRIBE BOLIVIA AS THE "ROOFTOP OF THE WORLD." The dizzying altitude of this mountainous country is almost always mentioned. Bolivia's largest city, La Paz, is the world's highest capital, at 11,942 feet. (Although Sucre is still the country's official capital, many of the government offices are now in La Paz.) The city's Aeropuerto Internacional El Alto, at 13,310 feet, is the world's highest commercial airport. And glimmering Lake Titicaca is the highest navigable lake in the world.

But these high-flying statistics don't reveal much about the country itself. For *Bolivianos,* the ancient and the modern are conjoined here. On city streets you'll see business executives in the latest designer fashions shouting into mobile phones alongside indigenous women with bowler hats perched precariously on their heads and voluminous petticoats under pleated satin skirts. Colonial mansions stand cheek-by-jowl with modern office buildings.

Bolivia is larger than Texas and California combined, but has only as many inhabitants as New York City. Most of its 8 million people are concentrated in a handful of urban centers, including La Paz, Santa Cruz, Cochabamba, and Sucre. Bolivia contains every type of geologically classified land, from tropical lowlands to parched desert to rugged mountain peaks. Although generally considered an Andean nation, nearly two-thirds of the country sweats it out in the steamy Amazon Basin— remote, overlooked, and as inhospitable as it is soul-stirring. On Bolivia's wildest frontier, indigenous tribes live as they have for centuries, unimpressed, it seems, by the displays of the modern world. In the provinces of Beni and Santa Cruz, near the border of Brazil, tribes still hunt with bows and arrows.

To the west of these tropical lowlands, just beyond Cochabamba and Santa Cruz, the Andes rise sharply to form the backbone of South America's Pacific coast. This two-prong mountain range shelters between its eastern and western peaks a long, rambling plain. Known as the altiplano, this bleak, treeless plateau, averaging 136 km (85 mi) wide and 832 km (520 mi) long, comprises 30% of Bolivia's landmass and supports more than half of its population. For centuries the Aymara people have clung to the hostile place, harvesting small crops of potatoes and beans or fishing the deep-blue waters of Lake Titicaca, which straddles Bolivia's western border with Peru.

Centuries of Spanish dominion have left their mark here, particularly on the cities of Sucre and Potosí, where ornate cathedrals crowd the narrow streets. But Bolivia remains a land of indigenous farmers, ranchers, and artisans. On the windswept Andean plateaus you will still see local weavers toting their crafts and red-cheek children to weekly markets. By the time the sun has risen, the brightly dressed Aymara are in place, ready to sell textiles and ponchos, not to mention vegetables, fruits, and medicinal herbs.

Exploring Bolivia

Bolivia is most famous for the Andes, which take up a large chunk of the west. Also well-known are the vast jungle regions of Amazonia that extend all the way east into Brazil. But Bolivia has a surprisingly varied series of ecosystems within those two major regions. Mountain areas vary from cool and dry (as in the high-altitude cities of La Paz and Potosí), to temperate (the cities of Cochabamba and Sucre), to warm and pleasant almost year-round (in the fertile, grape-growing lands near the southern city of Tarija). Jungle areas also vary: from humid and warm, as in Santa Cruz, to the more temperate climates in the northwest province of Pando. In the northeast province of Beni, encompassing the city of Trinidad, the hot, wet climate is occasionally broken by cold spells called *surazos.*

Restaurants & Cuisine

Bolivian cuisine is healthful, wholesome, and satisfying. Soups make a complete meal in themselves, as they are loaded with meat, potatoes, vegetables, and a ricelike grain called *quinua.* Fresh trout from Lake Titicaca is fried, stuffed, steamed, grilled, spiced, or covered in a rich sauce. Another excellent, delicate fish from the lake is the *pejerrey,* which is especially good in *ceviche,* a marinated fish dish.

In the highlands, where carbohydrates are the dietary mainstay, look for *chuño* and *tunta,* two kinds of freeze-dried potatoes that are soaked overnight and boiled, then used to accompany main dishes. Other traditional highland fare includes *asado de llama* (llama steak) and *pique macho,* beef grilled with hot peppers, chopped tomatoes, and onions, often served with fried potatoes and gravy. Also popular is *sajta de pollo* (chicken stew with peppers and onions).

Each major city still has its own brewery, generally founded by Germans who emigrated here at the same time as they came to the United States. Try Paceña in La Paz or Sureña in Sucre. Tarija, in the Andean foothills near the Argentine border, is Bolivia's wine growing area. Wines have been produced here since the early 17th century. The major producers are La Concepcion and Kohlberg. Their Malbec and Cabernet Sauvignon have won international medals. For something a little different try *singani,* the local liquor. It's best in the potent pisco sour made from singani and lime juice or the slightly smoother *chuflay* made from singani and lemonade. *Chicha* is a grain alcohol locals concoct by chewing maize, spitting out the resulting mash, adding water, and allowing the mixture to ferment. The sweet, rather cloudy result is drunk mainly in the lowland valleys in and around Cochabamba.

WHAT IT COSTS In Bolivianos					
	$$$$	**$$$**	**$$**	**$**	**¢**
AT DINNER	over 100	70–100	50–70	30–50	under 30

Prices are for per person for a main course at dinner.

About the Hotels

With growing competition for tourist dollars, there has been a push within the past several years to upgrade older hotels, and, where possible, to build new ones. You now have a wider range, from cozy guest houses to luxury resorts. Some hotels have two pricing systems—one for Boli-

TOP REASONS TO GO

From the altiplano to the Amazon basin, Bolivia borders five countries and comprises nearly every microclimate imaginable. Here are just some of the marvels you can experience:

FLIPPER OF THE FOREST.
Yes, friends, that *was* a pink dolphin you just saw in the Beni River—and no, you didn't have too much chicha to drink. The Amazonian basin is home to an astonishing array of wildlife, including caimans, Amazonian catfish the size of Volkswagens, sloths, jaguars, and the famed pink dolphins, which the first Spaniards mistook, perhaps understandably, for mermaids.

NO SALT ADDED.
The Salar de Uyuni, the giant salt desert that borders Chile, is an impressive, barren landscape. The gaping fissures and eerie light give it an otherworldly vibe, and the neighboring lagoons of red, green, and other colors (depending on nearby mineral content) add to the mystique.

MINES, ALL MINES.
Descending into the muck and low-oxygen environment of Potosí's mines isn't everyone's idea of a good time, but if you want to know what kind of work it took to extract the world's greatest silver fortune from the Cerro Rico, you've got to get a little dirty. While you're in there, make a little offering to the spirit of the mountain—the little fellow gladly accepts coins, cigarettes, or a splash of alcohol.

BIKING SIDE BY SIDE WITH DEATH.
Well, you might say your chances are just as good biking to Coroico from La Paz as they are taking a bus down what was once proclaimed "the world's most dangerous road." Benefits include leaving La Paz's rarified and often cold air for a taste of the tropics and the fact that the entire ride is downhill. Just make sure your bike has good brakes before you set off.

vians and one for foreigners. Even if you fall into the latter category, nice accommodations can be found for $35 or less, particularly away from the cities. Do not be afraid to ask to see the room in advance— it's common practice in Bolivia.

WHAT IT COSTS In Bolivianos				
	$$$$	**$$$**	**$$**	**$**	**¢**
FOR 2 PEOPLE	over 1,000	700–1,000	500–700	300–500	under 300

Prices are for two people in a standard double room in high season, excluding tax.

When to Go

With its extremes of terrain, altitude, and climate, Bolivia has something to appeal to nearly every traveler. During the rainy season from November to March, heavy downpours make many roads in the lowlands vir-

tually impassable. In the highlands the season brings dark, cloudy skies but little rain. If you plan to travel by bus or car—though this isn't recommended—it's best to go between April and October.

CLIMATE   In high-altitude cities like La Paz and Potosí the weather can get very chilly, particularly at night. Lowland cities like Santa Cruz, sitting in the Amazon basin, are hot and humid the entire year; it's only in the lowlands that rain can be a real impediment. Cochabamba, dubbed the "city of eternal spring," enjoys a mild Mediterranean climate year-round.

The following are the average monthly maximum and minimum temperatures for La Paz.

Jan.	64F	18C	May	66F	19C	Sept.	62F	17C
	43	6		35	2		38	3
Feb.	64F	18C	June	60F	16C	Oct.	65F	18C
	43	6		36	2		40	4
Mar.	64F	18C	July	61F	16C	Nov.	67F	20C
	43	6		34	1		42	6
Apr.	66F	19C	Aug.	62F	17C	Dec.	64F	18C
	40	4		35	2		43	6

HOLIDAYS   During Carnaval and many of Bolivia's holidays, the country virtually shuts down, sometimes for a couple of days before and after. Don't plan to travel on the holiday itself, as transit is practically nonexistent. Major holidays are New Year's Day; Carnaval (weekend prior to start of Lent), Good Friday (April); Labor Day (May 1); Corpus Christi (June); Independence Day (August 6); All Saints' Day (November 1); Christmas.

FESTIVALS   The two-week Feria de Alicitas takes place in La Paz beginning January 24. The Fiesta de la Virgen de Candelaria is held in Copacabana on Lake Titicaca in February. February also brings Carnaval, a weeklong celebration that includes music and dancing in the streets. The biggest bash is held in the mining town of Oruro, where wildly costumed performers parade through the streets. Pujilay, a colorful festival commemorating the 1816 victory by the Tarabucan people over the Spanish, is celebrated the following week in the village of Tarabuco. Good Friday celebrations—which are characterized by candlelit religious processions by masked supplicants—are particularly lively in La Paz and Copacabana. On June 24, at the Fiesta de San Juan in La Paz, you'll see bonfires and fireworks. On August 5–8, the Fiesta de la Virgen Negra takes place in Copacabana. El Día de Todos los Santos (All Saints' Day) and El Día de los Muertos (All Souls' Day) take place all around Lake Titicaca on November 1 and 2.

Language

Spanish is the predominant language in the cities, and travelers often find Bolivian Spanish to be one of the easiest on the continent to understand. Quechua and Aymara are spoken by highlanders who may or may not also speak Spanish, while Guaraní is spoken in some parts of the Amazonian basin. Hotel staffs usually have some knowledge of English, French, or German.

LA PAZ

Perched on the edge of the altiplano, La Paz overlooks a landscape of great—if stark—beauty. If
you fly into Aeropuerto Internacional El Alto, the plateau breaks
without warning and reveals the
deep, jagged valley that cradles the
town. At dusk, as the sun sets on
the bare flatlands that surround La
Paz, a reddish glow envelops the
city's greatest landmark: the towering, snow-capped peaks of Illimani.

> **TIP**
>
> If you find yourself a little light-
> headed because of the altitude,
> take a nap or sip a rejuvenating
> potion made from the coca leaf
> called *mate de coca.*

La Paz is nestled in a bowl-shape valley that ranges in altitude from 9,951
feet to 11,930 feet, an elevation so high that even the locals walk slowly.
The altitude might make things difficult at first, but it also ensures that
La Paz is free of the heat and humidity and devoid of mosquitoes and
other pesky insects.

Nearly half of the city's 1.5 million residents live in poorly constructed
adobe and brick homes on a barren plateau in the El Alto neighborhood,
as well as in the valleys that encircle the settlement. In downtown La
Paz the feeling is more cosmopolitan, as buses, taxis, business executives, and Aymara Indians share the city's cobblestone streets.

Exploring La Paz

Heading into La Paz from the airport, the city's main thoroughfare changes
names several times: Avenida Ismael Montes, Avenida Mariscal Santa
Cruz, El Prado, Avenida 16 de Julio, and Avenida Villazón. The street,
a colorful blur of trees, flowers, and monuments, is often clogged with
pedestrians and vendors, especially on weekends. Many of La Paz's luxury hotels are found here, rising high above the old colonial-style homes
with their elaborate latticework and balustrades. The street then splits
into two one-way streets, Avenida 6 de Agosto and Avenida Arce, which
lead to the residential areas of San Jorge and Sopocachi, which hold most
of La Paz's most exclusive bars and restaurants.

Plaza Murillo area

In the center of colonial La Paz, (Zona Central–Downtown), Plaza
Murillo and the cobblestone streets that surround it are steeped in history. The square dates from 1549, the year after the city was founded.
Nearby you'll find the city's grand governmental buildings and some of
its most beautiful churches.

TIMING   Because La Paz is so compact, visiting the city's main sights would seem
easy; however, add time for climbing the hills and taking frequent breaks
to assuage the effects of the altitude. You'll need a full day for a thorough exploration. Museums are generally open Tuesday to Friday
9:30–12:30 and 3–7, and Saturday and Sunday 10–12:30, and are
closed Monday.

WHAT TO SEE **③ Catedral Metropolitana.** The cathedral was built in 1835 in a severe neo-classical style, with a sober facade and imposing bronze doors. It faces the lovely gardens of Plaza Murillo. ⊠ *Plaza Murillo, Zona Central (Downtown)* ⊡ *Free* ⊙ *Mon.–Sat. 7–9* AM *and 6–8, Sun. 7–noon and 6–8.*

⑥ Iglesia de Santo Domingo. This church, constructed in the 17th century, served as the cathedral before the Catedral Metropolitana was built. It is known for its distinctive baroque-style facade. ⊠ *Calles Yanacocha and Ingavi, Zona Central (Downtown).*

⑪ Museo Casa Murillo. Housed in a restored colonial mansion that has been declared a national landmark, this museum exhibits the personal effects of past presidents. It was once the home of Pedro Domingo Murillo, one of the heroes of the independence movement. ⊠ *Calle Jaén 79, Zona Central (Downtown)* ☎ *02/228–0553* ⊡ *(B)4 for group ticket to Museo Casa Murillo, Museo de Metales Preciosos, Museo Costumbrista Juan de Vargas, Museo del Litoral Boliviano (purchase at Costumbrista)* ⊙ *Tues.–Fri. 9:30–12:30 and 3–7, weekends 10–12:30.*

⑧ Museo Costumbrista Juan de Vargas. Dedicated to the political and cultural history of Bolivia, this museum hosts exhibits about life in La Paz from the 16th century to the present. Especially interesting are the miniature scenes of old La Paz. ⊠ *Calle Jaén at Calle Sucre, Zona Central (Downtown)* ☎ *02/228–0758* ⊡ *(B)6 for group ticket to Museo Casa Murillo, Museo de Metales Preciosos, Museo Costumbrista Juan de Vargas, Museo del Litoral Boliviano (purchase at Costumbrista)* ⊙ *Tues.–Fri. 9:30–12:30 and 3–7, weekends 9–1.*

⑩ Museo del Litoral Boliviano. This museum is a repository for artifacts from the 1879 War of the Pacific, when Bolivia lost its sliver of coastline to Chile. Bolivia continues to make international appeals to regain its lost territory. The museum has photographs, documents, flags, and armaments from that battle. ⊠ *Calle Jaén 789, Zona Central (Downtown)* ☎ *no phone* ⊡ *(B)4 for group ticket to Museo Casa Murillo, Museo de Metales Preciosos, Museo Costumbrista Juan de Vargas, Museo del Litoral Boliviano (purchase at Costumbrista)* ⊙ *Tues.–Fri. 9:30–12:30 and 3–7, weekends 10–12:30.*

⑨ Museo de Metales Preciosos. An extensive collection of pre-Columbian gold and silver artifacts, as well as Inca and pre-Inca ceramics, can be found in this museum, which also houses archaeological exhibits. ⊠ *Calle Jaén 777, Zona Central (Downtown)* ☎ *02/228–0329* ⊡ *(B)4 for group ticket to Museo Casa Murillo, Museo de Metales Preciosos, Museo Costumbrista Juan de Vargas, Museo del Litoral Boliviano (purchase at Costumbrista)* ⊙ *Tues.–Fri. 9:30–12:30 and 3–7, weekends 9–1.*

④ Museo Nacional de Arte. Housed in the pink-marble Palacio de los Condes de Arana, commissioned by a Spanish noble in 1775, the National Art Museum holds three stories of paintings and sculpture. The first floor is devoted to contemporary foreign artists; the second to works by Melchor Pérez Holguín, considered to be the master of Andean colonial art; and the third to a permanent collection of Bolivian artists. Relax in the

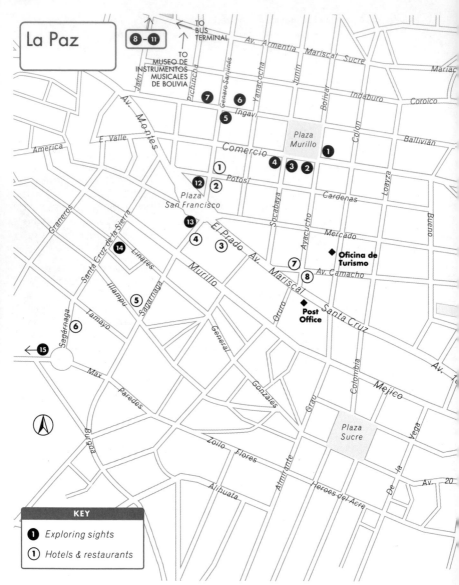

La Paz

TO BUS TERMINAL

TO MUSEO DE INSTRUMENTOS MUSICALES DE BOLIVIA

Plaza Murillo

Plaza San Francisco

Oficina de Turismo

Post Office

Plaza Sucre

KEY

● Exploring sights

① Hotels & restaurants

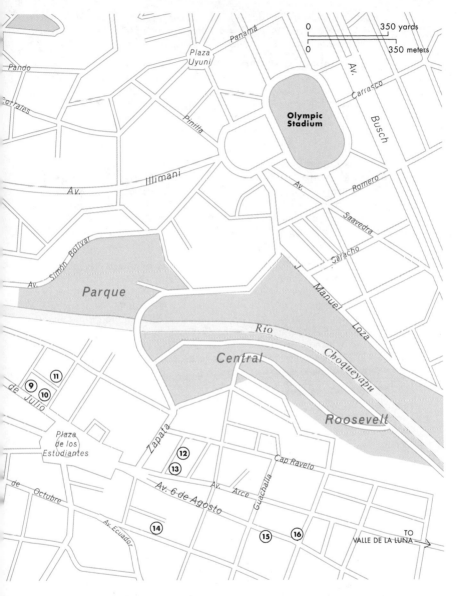

Olympic
Stadium

Plaza
Uyuni

Panamá

Av. Carrasco

Busch

Pando

Corrales

Pinitta

Illimani

Av.

Av.

Romero

Saavedra

Caracho

Parque

J. Manuel Loza

Av. Simón Bolívar

Av.

Río

Choqueyapu

Central

Roosevelt

de Julio

⑨ ⑩ ⑪

Plaza
de los
Estudiantes

Zapata

⑫

⑬

Cap Raveto

Guachalla

de Octubre

Av. 6 de Agosto

Av. Arce

Av. Ecuador

⑭

⑮ ⑯

TO
VALLE DE LA LUNA →

central courtyard beside the lovely alabaster fountain. ⊠ *Plaza Murillo at Calle Comercio, Zona Central (Downtown)* ☎ *02/237–1177* ⊕ *www. mna.org.bo* ⊡ *(B)10* ⊙ *Tues.–Sat. 9–12:30 and 3–7, Sun. 9:30–12:30.*

❺ Museo Nacional de Etnografía y Folklore. Housed in an ornate 18th-century building, the National Museum of Ethnography and Folklore exhibits feathers, masks, and weavings from indigenous peoples. It also has permanent displays on the Ayoreos, who live in the Amazon region, and the Chipayas, who come from the surrounding altiplano. ⊠ *Calle Ingavi 916, Zona Central (Downtown)* ☎ *02/240–8640* ⊕ *www.musef. org.bo* ⊡ *Free* ⊙ *Tues.–Fri. 9–12:30 and 3–7, weekends 9:30–12:30.*

Fodor'sChoice **Museo de Instrumentos Musicales de Bolivia.** This museum, founded by local
★ musician Ernesto Cavour, is the most complete collection of musical instruments in the nation; if you think it's all *charangos* and *quenas,* you haven't seen half of what Bolivian music has to offer! Here seven rooms feature percussion, string, and wind instruments used in the various regions of Bolivia. ⊠ *Calle Jaén 711, Casa de la Cruz Verde* ☎ *02/240– 8177* ⊙ *Daily 9:30–6* ⊡ *(B)5.*

❷ Palacio de Gobierno. The imposing Presidential Palace was guarded by tanks and machine gun–toting soldiers until 1982, when the constitutional government was restored following a 1979 coup and three years of military rule. In front of the palace is a statue of former president Gualberto Villarroel. In 1946 a mob stormed the building and dragged Villarroel to the square, where he was hanged from a lamppost. The structure, which is closed to the public, is also known as Palacio Quemado (Burned Palace) because it has twice been gutted by fire. ⊠ *Plaza Murillo, Zona Central (Downtown).*

❶ Palacio Legislativo. The meeting place for Bolivia's Congress, the Legislative Palace was built in 1905. This imposing classical structure has a visitor's gallery where you can observe the legislators in session. ⊠ *Plaza Murillo, Zona Central (Downtown)* ⊡ *Free* ⊙ *Weekdays 9–noon and 2:30–5.*

❼ Teatro Municipal. A handsome building both inside and out as a result of an extensive restoration, the Municipal Theater regularly stages traditional dance and music, as well as classical music performances and opera. ⊠ *Calle Genaro Sanjinés 629, Zona Central (Downtown)* ☎ *no phone.*

Plaza San Francisco Area

This broad plaza just south of Avenida Mariscal Santa Cruz is the city's cultural heart. Indigenous people come here to hawk all sorts of handicrafts, as well as more prosaic goods, such as cassette tapes, watches, and electrical items. If you're lucky you'll see a wedding at the beautiful Iglesia de San Francisco. Behind this plaza is a network of narrow cobblestone streets climbing up the steep hillside. Here you'll find shops and stalls where you can purchase native handicrafts.

WHAT TO SEE **Casa de la Cultura.** Rotating art exhibits, movies, and concerts are held
⓬ at this cultural center across from the Iglesia de San Francisco. ⊠ *Plaza Perez Velasco.*

BOLIVIAN HISTORY

Bolivians are proud of their history, and you'll find them willing to share what they know with anyone eager to learn. Almost everywhere in Bolivia you'll stumble across reminders of the country's long and eventful history. A civilization said to be more advanced than the Inca thrived in Bolivia sometime between 600 BC and AD 1200 in an area 90 km (50 mi) west of La Paz called Tiwanaku. It is considered by many to be the "cradle of the American civilizations." When the Inca arrived, the city was already in ruins, possibly destroyed by an earthquake. Spanish conquistadors conquered the Inca civilization in the 1500s. Sucre and Potosí are the best-preserved examples of the legacy of Spanish architecture.

From its earliest days, Bolivia's fortunes have risen and fallen with its mineral wealth. Centuries ago it was the Inca and Aymara who dug deep for precious silver. In the 17th century, Spain's colonization of South America was fueled largely by the vast amounts of silver hidden deep in Cerro Rico, the "Rich Hill" that towers over the city Potosí in southern Bolivia. Cerro Rico's seemingly inexhaustible lode, first discovered in 1545, quickly brought thousands of prospectors to what was at the time the greatest mining operation in the New World. During the 17th and 18th centuries, Potosí was the most populous city in the Americas. Silver transformed it with grand colonial mansions, stately baroque churches, and thick-walled fortresses. For the Spanish, the phrase *"vale un Potosí "* ("worth a Potosí") became a favorite description for untold wealth. But there's a darker side to the story. Some 8 million of the indigenous Quechua people died in the mines after being forced to stay inside the airless tunnels for as long as six months. While these barbaric practices no longer exist, men who work in the mines today still have far shorter life spans than average.

Bolivia was named in honor of its liberator, Simón Bolívar, who proclaimed the country's independence from Spain in 1825; until then, it had been simply called Alto Peru. The country was once much larger than it is today. It originally extended to the Pacific, but after rich deposits of nitrates were discovered in the Atacama Desert, Chile began to eye the region. During the War of the Pacific that broke out in 1879, Chile captured Bolivia's short stretch of coastline. Bolivia stubbornly believes that someday, with the support of other countries, it will once again have a seaport. Bolivia lost about 100,000 square km (38,000 square mi) when Brazil annexed a large part of the Amazon basin in 1903, then about twice as much after a dispute with Paraguay in 1938.

⓭ **Iglesia de San Francisco.** Considered one of the finest examples of Spanish colonial architecture in South America, the carved facade of the 1549 Church of San Francisco is adorned with birds of prey, ghoulish masks, pine cones, and parrots—a combination of Spanish and Indian motifs created by local artisans who borrowed heavily from the style then popular in Spain. Weddings sometimes spill out onto the plaza on Saturdays. Crafts stalls line the church wall; most days you'll find colorful weavings and handmade musical instruments. ⊠ *El Prado at Calle Sagárnaga.*

⑭ Mercado de las Brujas On Calle Linares, just off bustling Calle Sagárnaga, you'll find the Witches Market, where indigenous women in tall derby hats sell lucky charms and ingredients for powerful potions. If you are building a new house, you can buy a dried llama fetus to bury in the yard for good luck.

⑮ Mercado Negro. Near the intersection of Calle Max Parede and Calle Graneros, the streets are filled with peddlers hawking clothing and household goods, as well as traditional medicines. Tucked into alleys and courtyards are *tambos* (thatch-roof structures) where you can purchase oranges, bananas, and coca leaves. The last are officially illegal but are chewed by farmers and miners (and tourists) to ward off hunger and the effects of the altitude.

Where to Eat

La Paz restaurants are becoming increasingly cosmopolitan, with cuisines that range from Chinese and Japanese to French and Swiss, in addition to traditional Bolivian fare. The area around Plaza de los Estudiantes and the residential neighborhood of Sopocachi have the widest selection of restaurants in La Paz, while the area around Calle Sagárnaga (Zona Central–Downtown) generally harbors the least expensive.

Argentine

★ $$–$$$ ✕ **Churrasquería El Gaucho.** This Argentine-style steak house serves slabs of tender, grilled steak and kabobs on a wood plank, with delicious sauces on the side. ⊠ *Av. 20 de Octubre 2041* ☎ *02/242–3143 or 02/242–4808* 🖃 *AE, MC, V.*

Bolivian

$$–$$$ ✕ **Aransaya.** From its location on the penthouse floor of the Radisson
Fodor'sChoice Plaza Hotel, this restaurant gives diners spectacular views of the city.
★ The presentation of the food is exquisite, and the menu includes both international dishes and regional specialties. ⊠ *Av. Arce 2177* ☎ *02/244–1111* 🖃 *AE, MC, V.*

¢–$ ✕ **Café La Paz.** This old café, opposite the main post office, is a popular hangout for many La Paz politicians, journalists, and expatriates. Try the potent espresso, cappuccino, and *café helado* (coffee with ice cream). Don't miss the elaborate pastries, including *empanada de manzana* (apple tart). ⊠ *Calle Ayacucho at Av. Camacho* ☎ *02/235–0292* 🖃 *No credit cards.*

Italian

$ ✕ **Pizzeria Morello.** This is possibly the best pizzeria in La Paz. You can order something piping hot from the oven or design your own pizza from the voluminous list of toppings. Many Paceños use Morello's prompt takeout and delivery services. ⊠ *Av. Arce 2132* ☎ *02/237–2973* 🖃 *AE, MC, V.*

2

¢–$ ✗**Pronto.** Delicious pastas make this inexpensive Italian restaurant pop-
Fodor'sChoice ular with locals and tourists alike. The service is top-notch. ⊠ *Calle Gen-
★ *eral Gonzalo Jaúregui 2248* ☎ *02/235–5869* ▭ *No credit cards.*

Pan-Asian
★ $–$$ ✗**Pig & Whistle.** A short walk south from the Universidad Mayor de San
Andrés is this replica of a cozy British pub. Don't ask for fish-and-chips—
authentic Southeast Asian dishes are what's on the menu. Low-key
music, performed live on weekends, ranges from light classical to bossa
nova to jazz. ⊠ *Calle Goitia 155, off Av. Arce* ☎ *No phone* ▭ *No credit
cards* ☉ *Closed Sun.*

$–$$ ✗**Wagamama.** The specialty is fresh trout from Lake Titicaca cooked
Fodor'sChoice Japanese style. It's often referred to as the "noodle restaurant"; you can
★ even get trout sushi rolls here. It's near the American and British embassies. ⊠ *Pasaje Pinilla 2557 (Off Av. Arce, one block downhill from
Plaza Isabel la Católica)* ☎ *02/224–4911* ▭ *MC, V* ☉ *Closed Mon.*

Where to Stay

Although the number of rooms in La Paz increases every year, hotels
are often booked solid during holidays and festivals. Make reservations
at least a month in advance when possible. Inexpensive hotels tend to
be located near Calle Sagárnaga.

$$$$ ▥ **Hotel Europa.** The view of snowcapped Mt. Illimani from the rooftop
Fodor'sChoice garden sets this downtown hotel apart. There's original artwork on dis-
★ play in the lobby, and the generously proportioned rooms, decorated
with an understated elegance, have extras that business travelers will
appreciate. On the premises is a fitness center with a Turkish bath. ⊠ *Calle
Tiahuanacu 64* ☎ *02/231–5656 toll free in Bolivia 0800/10–5656*
🖷 *02/231–3930* ⊕ *www.hoteleuropa.com.bo* ⤵ *110 rooms* ⚹ *Restaurant, room service, minibars, in-room data ports, pool, health club, 2
bars, laundry service* ▭ *AE, MC, V.*

$$$–$$$$ ▥ **Hotel Plaza.** The rooftop restaurant and bar of this luxurious busi-
ness hotel have excellent views of La Paz and the Andes. Ask for a room
facing Mt. Illimani; besides good views you'll have less noise from the
street. ⊠ *Av. 16 de Julio 1789* ☎ *02/237–8311* 🖷 *02/237–8318* ⤵ *175
rooms, 10 suites* ⚹ *2 restaurants, indoor pool, health club, hot tub, sauna,
2 bars, laundry service* ▭ *AE, MC, V.*

$$$ ▥ **Hotel Presidente.** This modern hotel has an excellent downtown lo-
cation and plain but comfortable rooms. Most face the street; those on
the upper floors are quietest. The restaurant, which has stunning views
of the city, serves inexpensive buffet lunches. ⊠ *Calle Potosí 920* ☎ *02/
236–7193* 🖷 *02/235–4013* ⤵ *101 rooms, 18 suites* ⚹ *2 restaurants,
indoor pool, gym, sauna, 2 bars* ▭ *AE, MC, V.*

$$$ ▥ **Radisson Plaza Hotel.** The focus at this high-rise business hotel not
far from Plaza de los Estudiantes is on luxury and service. Upper-floor
rooms have excellent views of the city and the surrounding mountains,
as does the rooftop restaurant. ⊠ *Av. Arce 2177* ☎ *02/244-1111, 800/
333–3333 in the U.S.* 🖷 *02/244–0402* ⊕ *www.radisson.com/lapazbo*
⤵ *239 rooms, 7 suites* ⚹ *2 restaurants, café, in-room safes, minibars,*

indoor pool, health club, hair salon, hot tub, massage, sauna, bar, lounge, shops, laundry service, meeting rooms ☰ *AE, MC, V.*

$ ▦ **Hotel Gloria.** This clean, friendly hotel a block from Plaza San Francisco has an inexpensive rooftop restaurant that specializes in international and vegetarian dishes. It also has a tour desk in the lobby. ⊠ *Calle Potosí 909* ☎ *02/240–7070* ☎ *02/240–6622* ⊕ *www.hotelgloria.com. bo* ⇝ *90 rooms, 2 suites* ⏃ *Restaurant, café, bar* ☰ *AE, MC, V.*

¢ ▦ **Hostal Naira.** This charming hostel, whose bright, cheerful rooms surround a central courtyard, sits above the famous Peña Naira, where groups perform traditional folk music. There's always hot water—a luxury in this price range. ⊠ *Sagárnaga 161* ☎ *02/235–5645* ☎ *02/231–1214* ⊕ *www.hostalnaira.com* ⇝ *22 rooms* ⏃ *Cafeteria, coffee bar, Internet, laundry* ⏢ *CP* ☰ *No credit cards.*

★ ¢ ▦ **Hotel-Galería Virgen del Rosario.** A gem in the middle of the bustling Mercado de Hechicería, this hotel has an amiable restaurant. The rooms are small, but each room has nice murals on the walls. ⊠ *Calle Santa Cruz 583* ▦▦ *02/246–1015* ⇝ *35 rooms* ⏃ *Restaurant, bar, shops, Internet* ⏢ *BP* ☰ *MC, V.*

¢ ▦ **Hotel Rosario.** This charming, Spanish-style hotel has changed its **Fodor'sChoice** name from Residential Rosario to Hotel Rosario, after a complete ★ makeover and expansion. The sunny courtyard with a fountain surrounded by clay pots overflows with flowers. Rooms are on the small side, but most have private baths and all are clean and bright; many have spectacular views of Mt. Chacaltaya. The restaurant has live music from 8 to 9 Friday and Saturday. The travel agency, Turisbus, has an office in the lobby. ⊠ *Calle Illampu 704* ☎ *02/245–1658, 02/245–6634* ☎ *02/245–1991* ⊕ *www.hotelrosario.com* ⇝ *41 rooms, 1 suite* ⏃ *Restaurant, travel services* ☰ *AE, MC, V.*

¢ ▦ **Hotel Sagárnaga.** This quiet hotel on a steep cobblestone street near the Mercado de las Brujas has an unbeatable location, reasonable prices, and an on-site travel agency. The rooms, however, are a bit worse for wear, and the walls paper-thin. ⊠ *Calle Sagárnaga 326* ☎ *02/235–0252* ☎ *02/236–0831* ⇝ *56 rooms* ⏃ *Restaurant, travel services* ☰ *V.*

Nightlife & the Arts

The Arts

For concert and cinema listings, pick up a copy of the Spanish-language *Última Hora, La Razón,* or *El Diario.* The **Viceministerio de Turismo** (⊠ Edificio Cámara de comercio Piso 11 ☎ 02/235–2479 or 02/233–4849 ⊕ www.turismobolivia.bo) can fill you in on local festivals and special events. There is also a tourism office on the Plaza de los Estudiantes (02/237–1044).

GALLERIES The **Galería Emusa** (⊠ Av. 16 de Julio 1607 ☎ 02/375–042), in El Prado, hosts rotating exhibits of Bolivian sculpture and art. **Arte Unico** (⊠ Av. Arce 2895 ☎ 02/232–9238) mounts varied exhibits.

THEATER The **Teatro Municipal** (⊠ Calle Genaro Sanjinés 629 ☎ 02/237–5275) stages folk events and traditional music and dance concerts.

Nightlife

BARS Sopocachi, southeast of the Plaza de los Estudiantes, has the largest concentration of bars. Most start to fill up around 10:30 PM. **Cabrinus** (⊠ Av. 20 de Octubre 2453 ☎ 02/243–0913) is an old-fashioned piano bar. Drop in late in the evening to hear some good tunes. You might think you're in France when you step in the door of **Café Montmartre** (⊠ Calle Fernando Guachalla 399 ☎ 02/232–0801), a popular singles hangout with live music on weekends. If you get hungry, it also serves delicious crepes. The intimate **Matheus** (⊠ Calle Guachalla at Av. 6 de Agosto ☎ 02/232–4376) has a well-stocked bar and the occasional live band.

DANCE CLUBS **Forum** (⊠ Calle Víctor Sanjinés 2908 ☎ 02/232–5762) is a cavernous club two blocks from Plaza España. It's frequented mainly by the under-30 set. **Mongo's** (⊠ Hermanos Manchego 2444 ☎ 02/235–3914) is a popular hamburger joint, but it turns into a lively disco in the evenings Thursday through Saturday. Get there early or expect a long wait. Trendy **Socavón** (⊠ Av. 20 de Octubre near Calle Guachalla ☎ 02/235–3998) draws younger Paceños with live music most nights.

PEÑAS Peñas are nightclubs that showcase traditional Bolivian music and dance. The energetic live performances—as popular with Paceños as they are with tourists—cost from $8 to $20 per person. Dinner is usually included. The most famous is **Peña Naira** (⊠ Sagárnaga 161 ☎ 02/235–0530), located near Plaza San Francisco. Shows are a bargain at $4–$5. **Casa del Corregidor** (⊠ Murillo 1040 ☎ 02/236–3633) has performances most evenings.

Outdoor Activities

Soccer

Bolivians would be lost without their weekly soccer fix. Even the poorest, most remote villages have a playing field. Games are usually played on the only flat piece of land in town, so sheep and cows often graze on the field when there's not a match. La Paz itself has two teams: Bolívar and the Strongest. Both compete in the **Estadio Hernando Siles** (⊠ Plaza de los Monolitos ☎ 02/235–7342), in the Miraflores district.

Volleyball

Three major teams—San Antonio, Litoral, and Universidad—compete regularly in the **Coliseo Julio Borelli** (⊠ Calle México ☎ 02/232–0224), in the San Pedro district.

Shopping

In La Paz you'll find everything from rough-hewn silver plates to intricate jewelry, from woven-rope sandals to sweaters made of the softest alpaca and angora wools. Prices are reasonable by North American standards, although good quality does not come cheaply.

Markets

Calle Sagárnaga, near Plaza San Francisco, is a good place to look for local handicrafts. Along the tiny streets that lead off to the right and left are numerous crafts shops. On Calle Linares, just off Calle Sagárnaga, you'll find the **Mercado de las Brujas.** The Witches Market is where you'll find folk remedies and herbal treatments. For Aymara embroidered shawls, try the **Mercado Negro** on Calle Max Paredes. Prices start at $15 and peak at more than $200 for those made of buttery soft vicuña wool. Colorful *polleras,* the traditional skirts worn by indigenous women, are priced between $50 and $100; bowler hats start at around $20. In the heart of the Sopocachi district—where Avenida Ecuador intersects Calle Fernando Guachalla in the southeastern part of the city—is the vast indoor **Mercado Sopocachi,** worth seeing for its colorful displays of fresh produce and flowers. Do not take photos of women tending their stalls unless you ask permission first—if you don't, you may have a bottle thrown at you.

Shopping Centers

Two of the biggest malls in the city center are on Calle Potosí near Calle Ayacucho. The best shopping center in La Paz is the glass-pyramid–capped **Shopping Norte,** which has small restaurants that serve good-value *almuerzos* (set lunches) on the top floor. **Handal Center** is on Avenida Mariscal Santa Cruz, just down from Plaza San Francisco. It carries a wide selection of jeans, T-shirts, shoes, and sports equipment.

Specialty Shops

Before you begin bargain hunting for alpaca sweaters, visit one or two stores to get an idea of what to look for. High-quality hand-knit designs that sell for around $100 here fetch three times that amount in the United States. The shops along Calle Sagárnaga, near Plaza San Francisco, are a good place to compare quality and price.

Artesanías Sorata (⊠ Calle Linares 862 ☎ 02/231–7701) carries traditional alpaca knitwear with ethnic designs. **Casa Fisher** (⊠ Av. Mariscal, Handal Center ☎ 02/239–2946) is known for high-quality knits. One of the best places in town to buy reasonably priced *chompas,* colorful jackets made with traditional textiles, is **Coral** (⊠ Calle Linares 836 ☎ 02/234–2599).

Side Trips from La Paz

Tiwanaku

★ On a treeless plain an hour's drive west of La Paz, Tiwanaku (also spelled Tiahuanacu) is Bolivia's most important archaeological site. Partial excavations have revealed the remains of five different cities, one built on top of the other. The site's most impressive monument is the 10-ton La Puerta del Sol (Gate of the Sun), an imposing stone fixture believed to be a solar calendar built by a civilization that surfaced around 600 BC and mysteriously disappeared around AD 1200. The gate is part of an elaborate observatory and courtyard that contain monoliths and a subterranean temple. Although the site lacks the sweep and splendor of Peru's

Machu Picchu, it does provide a glimpse into the ancestry of the Aymara, the last indigenous people to be conquered by the Inca before the Spanish arrived. The descendants of the Aymara still farm the ingeniously constructed terraces built by their ancestors.

Start your visit with the Tiwanaku Museum next to the ruins. It displays artifacts found at the sight, the most spectacular of which is a 20-ton, 7.3-meter (24-foot) tall monolithic statue sculpted out of red sandstone. The monolith was discovered by an American, Wendell C. Bennett, during excavations in 1934 and has been on display in an open–air garden museum in La Paz, where it was being seriously eroded by weather. It was returned to Tiwanaku when the new indoor museum opened in 2002. Admission to the ruins and the museum is around US$10.

Since it's not always possible to find a guide at Tiwanaku, it's best to book a full-day tour in La Paz. If you decide to come on your own, take a local bus, which takes 90 minutes, and costs US$2. ■ TIP➔ Be sure to ask about the return schedule so you won't get stuck here, and bring a warm sweater or poncho—the area is frequently windy and cold, as there are no trees to break the wind. There's a small café where you can have a light lunch.

Oruro

Come to this former mining town 225 km (140 mi) southeast of La Paz to witness an annual pre-Lenten Carnaval tradition, started more than 200 years ago, when workers, dressed as devils, danced to honor the Virgin in a festival called La Diablada. The parade of the elaborately costumed dancing devils takes place during Carnaval. Although the Saturday before Ash Wednesday is the biggest day, festivities last for a week. Public buses make the three-hour trip from La Paz for about US$2, although the price nearly doubles during Carnaval. A one-day tour can be booked with a travel agency in La Paz.

Coroico

Your first glimpse of the small resort town of Coroico will be unforgettable, particularly after three hours of tortuous hairpin bends. People come here to see Los Yungas, an astounding region where the snow-covered Andes suddenly drop off into lush valleys. The mostly single-lane highway that brings you here, which drops in altitude by some 9,840 feet in just under 80 km (50 mi), is one of the most hair-raising in South America. ⚠ It's best not to drive, if possible. The government has been experimenting with not allowing two-way traffic by designating hours when traffic can go in each direction, so be sure to check in advance in case the experiment is still on. Under any circumstances, it is a very dangerous, cliff-hugging road.

Work continues on a 2½-km (1½-mi) tunnel on the Yungas road that will not only reduce travel time from La Paz to Coroico to an hour, but will make it much safer. In the meantime, taking a small bus, that can maneuver better on the dangerous road, is the safest way to go, or hitch onto a bicycle tour, which is the safest of all. Among the more popular bike tours is **Gravity Assisted Mountain Biking** (⊕ www.gravitybolivia.com, 02/231–3849), which offers tours of one day or up to one week.

WHERE TO
STAY & EAT
$ 🖼 **El Viejo Molino.** This beautiful Spanish-style resort hotel is perched high above the valley, among clusters of sugarcane and banana trees heavy with fruit. Relax by the pool or play a few games of tennis. At the tour office you can make arrangements for a rafting trip on a nearby river. The grilled steak in the restaurant is one of the excellent entrées. ⊠ *On the highway into Caroico, Camino Santa Barbara, Km 1* ☎ *02/220– 1499* 🛏 *28 rooms* ⚘ *Restaurant, room service, in-room safes, cable TV, pool, bar, laundry service, Internet, meeting room* ⊟ *MC, V.*

¢ 🖼 **Hotel Esmeralda.** From the sunny patio at this hotel, up the hill from Coroico's central plaza, you'll get astounding views of the valley below. The hotel is also surrounded by gardens. The restaurant, with a charcoal pizza oven, is excellent. From the hotel you can arrange hiking tours of nearby Parque Nacional Madidi. ⊠ *On the highway into Coroico, 5 minutes uphill from the plaza* ☎ *02/811–6017* ⊕ *www.hotelesmeralda. com* ⚘ *Restaurant, pool, sauna, Internet* ⊟ *MC, V.*

La Paz Essentials

Transportation

BY AIR

All international and domestic flights to La Paz arrive at El Alto airport, which is on the altiplano in the town of El Alto, 12 km (7 mi) from downtown. American Airlines and Lloyd Aéreo Boliviano, Bolivia's international airline, have daily flights between Miami and La Paz. Lloyd Aéreo Boliviano and AeroSur, Bolivia's domestic airline, fly to most major cities in Bolivia. Amazonas airline connects La Paz to Cobija, Santa Cruz, Trinidad, and other eastern points.

Taxis are the quickest alternative for getting to and from the airport. The current going rate for the 30- to 45-minute journey is around $7.50, but settle on a price with the driver before you get in. Minibuses also service the airport. The cost is approximately $1.

🛫 **Airlines AeroSur** ⊠ Av. 16 de Julio 1616 ☎ 02/236-9292 ⊕ www.aerosur.com. **Amazonas** ⊠ Av. Saavedra 1649 ☎ 02/222-0848. **American** ⊠ Av. 16 de Julio 1440 ☎ 02/239-2127, 800/433-7300 in the U.S. ⊕ www.aa.com. **Lloyd Aéreo Boliviano** ⊠ Av. Camacho 1456 ☎ 02/236-7707, 800/337-0918 in the U.S., 0800/10-3001 in Bolivia (toll-free reservations line) ⊕ www.labairlines.com.

🛫 **Airports Aeropuerto Internacional El Alto** ☎ 02/281-0122.

BY BUS

Buses to major cities in Bolivia and neighboring countries arrive and depart from the Terminal de Buses, west of the city center on Avenida Perú. Securing a seat is usually no problem, though you should reserve at least a day in advance for the long and tedious rides to Sucre, Potosí, and Santa Cruz. Reliable bus companies include Expreso Mopar, Trans Copacabana, and Trans El Dorado. Consult a travel agency in La Paz before setting out on a longer trip, as you may decide to save time by flying.

The trip by bus to most towns in Los Yungas will take three to four hours and will cost approximately $8. Private bus companies traveling between

La Paz and Los Yungas include Transporte 20 de Octubre and Veloz del Norte.

WITHIN LA PAZ La Paz is served by a comprehensive network of buses called *colectivos* that run daily from 6:30 AM to 10 PM. There is a flat fare of roughly 17¢, payable to the driver upon entry. Slightly more expensive are *micros,* 12-seat minivans that travel roughly the same bus routes. They're quicker and more comfortable. Colectivos and micros are often very crowded but are generally safe. Listen carefully before you board, as destinations are shouted out the window as the vehicles roll through the city. Better yet, ask a local to help you locate the right one.

🚍 Bus Companies Expreso Mopar ⊠ Terminal de Buses ☎ 02/237-7443. **Trans Copacabana** ⊠ Terminal de Buses ☎ 02/237-7894. **Trans El Dorado** ⊠ Terminal de Buses ☎ 02/235-9153. **Transporte 20 de Octubre** ⊠ Calle Yanacachi 1434 ☎ 02/231-7391. **Veloz del Norte** ⊠ Av. de las Américas 283 ☎ 02/231-1753.

🚍 Bus Terminals Terminal de Buses ⊠ Av. Perú ☎ 02/236-7275.

BY CAR

Don't even think about driving in La Paz. The streets are a maze running along the steep hills, and the traffic is horrific. Before driving outside the city, inquire about the conditions around your proposed destination. Most roads are unpaved and poorly maintained. During the rainy season many roads are subject to flash floods and landslides. If you can, hire a driver familiar with the area so that you can enjoy the scenery without frazzling your nerves.

CAR RENTAL Renting a car in La Paz is not cheap. Depending on the size of the vehicle, prices run from $30 to $75 per day. If you're driving outside major cities, four-wheel-drive vehicles are essential. Dollar, Economy, and Imbex all have reasonable rates. If you want to hire a car and driver, EBA Transtur is a good choice.

🚗 Rental Agencies EBA Transtur ⊠ Calle Carlos Medinacelly 1120 ☎ 02/236-1423. **Dollar** ⊠ Plaza Isabel ☎ 02/243-0043 🖷 02/244-2887. **Economy** ⊠ Canónigo Ayllón 510 ☎ 02/236 1848. **Kolla Motors Ltda.** ⊠ Calle Rosendo Gutierrez 502 ☎ 02/241-9141 🖷 02/241-1344. **Localiza Rent-a-Car** ⊠ Av. Arce 2177 ☎ 02/244-1011 ⊕ www.localiza.com.br. **Imbex** ⊠ Av. Montes 522 ☎ 02/231-6895.

BY TAXI & TRUFI

Taxis and *trufis* (shared taxis), identifiable from the taxi sign lodged in the windshield, are cheap and plentiful. Expect to pay less than 50¢ for most trips within the city center. Newer Radio Taxis, identified by the illuminated sign on the roof, are the safest option for tourists. Rates are fixed at $1 to $2, depending on the length of your journey.

🚕 Taxi Companies Radio Taxis ☎ 02/241-3838.

BY TRAIN

There is still rail transport between Oruro and towns near the border like Uyuni, Tupiza, and Villazon. There's also service from Uyuni to Calama, Chile, though it can be a long, rough, and cold ride.

🚆 National Railroad Line ⊠ Fernando Guachilla 494, La Paz ☎ 02/241-6545 ⊕ www.fca.com.bo

Contacts & Resources

EMBASSIES

⚑ Embassies Australia Honorary Consul ✉ Edificio Montevideo Mezzanine, Av. Arce 2081, Casilla 7186, La Paz ☎ 02/243-3241 🖷 02/244-0801. Note: Australians in Bolivia are strongly urged to register with the Australian Embassy in Santiago, Chile, via the Department of Foreign Affairs and Trade online registration service. **Canada** ✉ Calle Victor Sanjinez, No. 2678, Edificio Barcelona, Plaza España, La Paz ☎ 02/241-5021 🖷 02/241-4453 ⊕ http://www.dfait-maeci.gc.ca/peru. **United Kingdom** ✉ Av. Acre 2732, Casilla 694, La Paz ☎ 02/243-3424 🖷 02/243-1073 ⊕ www.britishembassy.gov.uk ⊗ Weekdays 9-noon. **United States** ✉ Av. Arce 2780, Casilla 425, La Paz ☎ 02/216-8000 🖷 02/216-8111 ⊕ www.usembassy.gov.

MONEY MATTERS

Banks in La Paz will exchange cash and traveler's checks. Reliable banks include Banco La Paz, Banco Mercantil, Banco Nacional, and Banco de Santa Cruz. Most have 24-hour ATMs marked ENLACE that dispense local currency.

You'll find *casas de cambio* throughout the city, particularly on the major streets. Most are open the same hours as regular shops: 9–noon and 3–6. They usually offer better rates than at the banks. You may be approached on the streets by money changers offering similar rates—although most are honest, it's best not to take a chance. Your hotel will probably change cash and traveler's checks as well, albeit for a higher fee.

Wherever you exchange money, make sure you receive new bills, as most vendors won't accept currency that is marked or torn. Also ask for some small change to use in the markets.

⚑ Banks Banco La Paz ✉ Calle Mercado, Edificio Electra 1190. **Banco Mercantil** ✉ Av. Ballivián and Calle 9. **Banco Nacional** ✉ Av. Camacho and Colon ✉ Av. Garcia Lanza and Calle 14. **Provincia de San Cruz** ✉ Av. Arce 2177.

SAFETY

While violent crime has never been a problem in Bolivia, you should use the same precautions you would in any large city: avoid flashy jewelry and expensive watches, keep an eye on your bags at all times, and be aware of your surroundings.

TELEPHONES

You can make local and international calls from offices run by Entel, Bolivia's telephone company. The main office on Calle Ayacucho is open daily from 7:30 AM to 10:30 PM. There is also an office in the airport. Connections aren't always reliable, so making a call often requires some patience. Public phones are operated by using coins or phone cards (*tarjetas telefónicas*) that you can purchase in many shops and newsstands. After you insert a coin or card, the phone displays how much credit you have.

VIVA, an ENTEL competitor, has also opened many cabinas in recent years, offering both long-distance phone service and cheap Internet connections in many locations.

⚑ Entel Office Entel ✉ Calle Ayacucho 267.

Bolivian Crafts

Bolivia's rich selection of crafts includes silver jewelry, handwoven rugs, intricate embroidery, and traditional musical instruments, such as the *quena* (flute) and *charango* (mandolin). You'll also find sweaters, gloves, scarves, and ponchos made from alpaca or llama wool. Crafts shops are usually grouped together—in La Paz, for instance, most can be found on Calle Sagárnaga. It's always worth looking for cooperatives outside the capital, however. These sell traditional textiles made in rural areas, especially in the provinces of Chuquisaca and Potosí. The shawls, hats, and skirts worn by highland women are sold in most of the local markets and in some stores in La Paz, but shopkeepers sometimes refuse to sell some types of traditional garments to foreigners. However, the felt bowler hats are for sale everywhere and make an interesting fashion statement back home. Due to the low level of tourism, souvenirs tend to be realistically priced. Although bargaining is expected, many sellers will drop their prices only by small amounts, typically 5% to 10%.

TOUR OPERATORS

Crillón Tours, one of the oldest tour companies in La Paz, offers interesting trips throughout Bolivia. Crillón is also the owner and operator of the hydrofoils on Lake Titicaca, the Inca Utama Resort & Spa, Andean Roots Eco Village on Lake Titicaca, and the Posada del Inca on Isla del Sol. Fremen Tours, Magri Turismo, and America Tours SRL offer numerous tours in and around La Paz.

🏠 Tour Information **America Tours SRL** ✉ Av. 16 de Julio 1490 ☎ 02/232-8584 ⊕ www.america-ecotours.com. **Crillón Tours** ✉ Av. Camacho 1223 ☎ 02/213-6612 🖷 02/213-6614 ⊕ www.titicaca.com. **Fremen Tours** ✉ Calle Pedro Salazar 537 ☎ 02/241-7062 🖷 02/241-7327 ⊕ www.andes-amazonia.com. **Magri Turismo** ✉ Calle Capitán Ravelo 2101 ☎ 02/244-2727 🖷 02/244-3060 ⊕ www.bolivianet.com/magri.

VISITOR INFORMATION

🏠 **Oficina de Turismo** ✉ Edificio Cámara de comercio Piso 11 La Pazá ☎ 02/233-4849 or 02/235-2479.

LAKE TITICACA

Considered sacred by the Aymara people who used to live on its shores, Lake Titicaca was also revered by the Tiwanaku and Inca civilizations who inhabited the area more than 2,000 years ago. Here you'll find islands with mysterious names like Isla del Sol (Sun Island) and Isla de la Luna (Moon Island), each with ruins in varying states of decay. According to legend, Isla del Sol is where the Inca Empire was founded when Manco Kapac and Mama Ojillo, son and daughter of the Sun God Inti, came down to Earth to improve the life of the altiplano people.

At an altitude of 12,506 feet, Titicaca is the world's highest navigable lake. Actually, it's two bodies of water joined by the narrow Es-

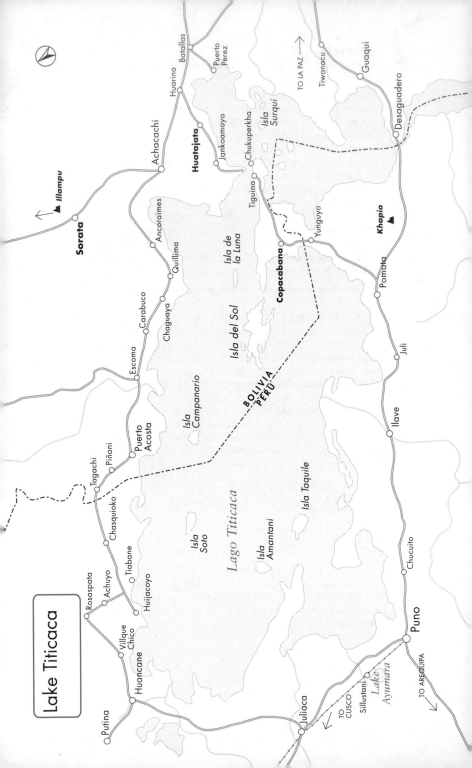

Lake Titicaca

trecho de Tiquina (Strait of Tiquina). The smaller section, shimmering Lago Huiñaymarca, is the easiest to reach from La Paz. To see the much larger part, brackish Lago Chucuito, you should include Copacabana on your itinerary. Titicaca covers an area of 7,988 square km (3,474 square mi) in the altiplano, with some of the highest peaks in the Andes rising along the northeastern shore. Its still waters reflect an equal measure of the cloudless blue sky and the sunbaked brown hills that encircle it.

Evidence of settlements more than 3,000 years old can be seen on Isla del Sol. There are also unrestored archaeological sites on several islands on the lake, as well as hundreds of terraces used by ancient people for farming. Many are still used today by the Aymara people, who plant potatoes, quinua, fava beans, and corn. Those Aymara who live on the islands on the Bolivian side of the lake are descendants of the aboriginal inhabitants of the altiplano, not of the Quechua-speaking Inca.

All the archaeological sites are not so easy to reach. Below the surface of the lake, archaeologists have discovered what is believed to be a pre-Columbian temple that's at least 1,000 years old. So far they have found a pre-Incan road and a 2,601-foot-long wall. An international scientific group, Akakor Geographical Exploring, came across the underwater site after making more than 200 dives into water 98 feet deep.

Huatajata

85 km (53 mi) from La Paz.

This popular weekend escape for Paceños is a regular stop on the guided tour circuit. Huatajata is a practical base for exploring the area. For picnics, try the tree-lined waterfront park at Chúa, the village beyond Huatajata. The real reason people come here, however, is to experience the Inca Utama Hotel & Spa–Andean Roots Eco Village.

Part of the Inca Utama Hotel & Spa is the **Andean Roots Eco Village,** a sight in itself, even if you don't stay at the hotel. It contains several museums depicting the history and culture of the region, from pre-Columbian times to the present. Headsets with taped guided tours in several languages are available. One exhibit details the lives of the Kallawaya, known as the doctors of the Andes, who still travel from village to village carrying natural medicines on their shoulders, and who developed and used penicillin, streptomycin, and quinine long before modern doctors. Replicas of mud houses that many of the Chipaya people of the surrounding altiplano still live in are outside the museum. A cooperative weaving project in an adobe workshop shows the different systems used by local weavers. A replica of the *Kon-Tiki* Heyerdahl sailed from Lima to the Polynesian islands in 1947 is on exhibit; the brothers can show you how to make your own reed boats. There's also the Alajpacha native observatory, which is equipped with powerful telescopes donated by NASA. After the lecture and slide presentation, the roof rolls back for an incredible view of the crystal clear southern skies above Lake Titicaca.

Where to Stay & Eat

$$–$$$ ✕▥ **Inca Utama Hotel & Spa–Andean Roots Eco Village.** This hotel includes
Fodor'sChoice   the Andrean Roots Eco Village, with museums, an observatory, a spa,
★   and a children's park. The Kallawaya Natural Spa uses the natural
medicine of the Andes. The children's park is also popular: local children are invited to come and play with your own. The Eco Village includes museums depicting the history and culture of the region, from
pre-Columbian times to the present. Hydrofoils depart daily from the
dock alongside the hotel to the Sun and Moon islands, Copacabana, and
Puno (on the Peruvian side of the lake). You can make reservations at
the hotel or with Crillón Tours' office in La Paz. Two restaurants serve
fine international cuisine; fresh trout from the lake is a specialty. Folk-
music performances take place every evening at the Sumaj Untavi restaurant. A boardwalk extends out onto the lake to the Choza Nautica
thatch-roof restaurant, where you can watch a spectacular sunset over
Lake Titicaca. ✉ *Off hwy from La Paz to Copacabana (km 45, look
for sign), Huatajata* ☎ *02/233–7533, 02/233–9047 or 800/488–5353
in the U.S.* ☎☎ *02/213–6614* ⊕ *www.titicaca.com* ⊲ *70 rooms* ♿ *2
restaurants, cable TV, health club, massage, spa, bar, Internet, meeting
room, travel services* ▭ *AE, MC, V.*

$–$$ ▥ **Hotel Lake Titicaca.** Coming from La Paz, you'll see this well-equipped
complex on the lakeshore a few minutes before you reach Huatajata.
The furnishings are slightly dated, but the sweeping views of the lake
make up for it. ✉ *Midway between Huarina and Huatajata* ☎ *02/
235–6931* 🖨 *02/235–1792* ⊲ *24 rooms* ♿ *Restaurant, sauna, boating, racquetball, bar, recreation room* ▭ *AE, MC, V.*

Copacabana

79 km (49 mi) from Huatajata.

After Huatajata the road continues to Tiquina, where you can see the
handful of patrol boats that make up what is left of Bolivia's navy (Bolivia was left landlocked after Chile annexed its coastline in 1879).
Your bus or car is loaded onto a raft and taken across the Strait of Tiquina.
From here it's a 90-minute drive to Copacabana, a pleasant, if touristy,
town on Lago Chucuito. Copacabana, the main stopping point for
those headed to Peru, provides easy access to the lake (Crillón Tours
now bases a hydrofoil there) and the surrounding countryside.

Copacabana's breathtaking Moorish-style **Catedral,** built between 1610
and 1619, is where you'll find the striking sculpture of the Virgin of Copacabana. There was no choice but to build the church because the statue,
carved by Francisco Yupanqui in 1592, was already drawing pilgrims
in search of miracles. If you see decorated cars lined up in front of the
cathedral, the owners are waiting to have them blessed. Throngs of young
Paceños walk to Copacabana from La Paz to pay homage to the statue
with a candlelight procession on Good Friday.

Where to Stay & Eat

¢–$ ✕ **Snack 6 de Agosto.** Although it serves various entrées, this place is
best known for its trout, fresh from Lake Titicaca. There's also a se-

lection of vegetarian dishes. ⊠ *Av. 6 de Agosto* ☎ *02/0862–2040* 🖃 *No credit cards.*

¢–$ ✕**Sujna Wasi.** This Spanish-owned restaurant is tiny, with seating for fewer than two dozen people. It's the place to come in Copacabana for vegetarian food. The restaurant has a small library with books, maps, and travel information. ⊠ *Calle General Gonzalo Jaúregui 127* ☎ *02/ 862–2091* 🖃 *No credit cards.*

$ ✕🖾 **Hotel Rosario Del Lago.** One of the nicest accommodations in Copacabana, this colonial-style hotel is a few blocks from the main plaza. Its clean, homey rooms, including a spacious suite that sleeps six, have excellent views of the shore. Restaurant Kota Kahuana ("View of the Lake") specializes in expertly prepared trout caught in Lake Titicaca, as well as international fare. ⊠ *Calle Rigoberto Paredes and Av. Costanera* ☎ *02/862–2141, 02/245–1341 in La Paz* 🖶 *02/862–2140 in La Paz* ⊕ *www.hotelrosario.com/lago* ⤴ *29 rooms, 1 suite* ⚒ *Restaurant* 🖃 *AE, MC, V.*

¢ 🖾 **Ambassador Hotel.** This hotel near the lake is aligned with a youth hostel, which means it offers special rates for students. Although the rooms are somewhat small, it's hard to beat the view from the rooftop restaurant. ⊠ *Calle General Gonzalo Jaúregui, Plaza Sucre* ☎ *02/862–2216* ⤴ *42 rooms* ⚒ *Restaurant* 🖃 *No credit cards.*

¢ 🖾 **Hotel Playa Azul.** Many of the comfortable rooms at this hotel overlook a small courtyard. The most charming thing about this well-located hotel is its cozy dining room lit with gas lamps. Groups frequently stop here for the filling and tasty lunches. ⊠ *Av. 6 de Agosto* ☎ *02/ 862–2227* ⤴ *39 rooms* ⚒ *Restaurant, room service, bar, laundry service* 🖃 *MC, V.*

Isla del Sol & Isla de la Luna

12 km (7½ mi) north of Copacabana.

Fodor'sChoice The largest of Lake Titicaca's islands, **Isla del Sol** has beautiful coves shel-★ tering white sandy beaches. It's popular to make brief stops at the small port of Yumani, where steep Inca steps and a sacred fountain are located. Most people don't, unfortunately, actually spend time on the island. If you do, you'll be well rewarded—there are ruins of the Inca palace of Pilkokaina and a strange rock formation said to be the birthplace of the sun and moon. In the late afternoon, climb to the top of the ridge to watch the sun set among the snowcapped Andes.

En route to Isla del Sol, hydrofoils usually stop at **Isla de la Luna,** where the ruins of Iñacuy date back to the Inca conquest. You'll find an ancient convent called Ajlla Wasi (House of the Chosen Women). Stone steps lead up to the unrestored ruins of the convent.

Where to Stay

$$–$$$ 🖾**La Posada del Inca.** Rooms in this beautifully restored colonial-style hacienda on Isla del Sol are small but attractively furnished, and all have private baths. Electric heaters and electric blankets powered with solar energy cut the night chill. The hillside location offers sweeping views of the lake. Golf carts provide transportation to the Posada if you find the

30-minute walk up the cobblestone path a challenge in the nearly 3,965-meter (13,000-foot) altitude. The restaurant serves meals family-style in the dining room. Rooms must be booked as part of a hydrofoil tour with Crillón Tours in La Paz. ☎ *02/233–7533 in La Paz* 🖷 *02/211–6482 in La Paz* ⊕ *www.titicaca.com* ⟿ *20 rooms* ⚭ *Restaurant* ▬ *AE, MC, V.*

¢ ⊞ **Inca Sama Albergue.** Follow a stone path up from the ruins of Palacio de Pilkokaina and you'll see this lodge, where three large rooms have mattresses on the floor that sleep up to 20. Baths are outside the lodge, and simple meals are served outdoors. What the hotel lacks in privacy, though, it makes up for in splendid views. Reservations are made through Hotel Playa Azul in Copacabana. ⊠ *Near Palacio de Pilkokaina* ☎ *02/862–2228* 🖷 *02/862–2227* ⟿ *3 rooms* ▬ *No credit cards.*

Sorata

45 km (28 mi) north of Huatajata.

Sorata lies nearly 8,200 feet above sea level in a tropical valley at the foot of Mt. Illampu. This is a starting point for experienced hikers to climb the snowcapped mountain or to make the arduous, weeklong trek along the Camino del Oro (Trail of Gold) to the gold-mining cooperatives.

Where to Stay & Eat

¢–$ ✕⊞ **Hotel Ex-Prefectural Sorata.** A sparkling renovation makes the most of this hotel's charming outdoor garden and lovely views across the valley. The restaurant specializes in the traditional dishes of the region. If you are coming from La Paz, the hotel is on the main highway 1 km (½ mi) from Sorata's central square. ⊠ *Carretera Principal Sorata* ☎ *02/ 272–2846* ⚭ *Restaurant* ▬ *AE, MC, V.*

Lake Titicaca Essentials

Transportation

BY BOAT & FERRY

Crillón Tours operates hydrofoils on Lake Titicaca between Copacabana and Huatajata in Bolivia and Puno in Peru. The boats visit the floating Urus Islands, Isla del Sol, and Isla de la Luna. Arrangements can be made through travel agencies in La Paz or Puno.

🚩 **Boat & Ferry Information Crillón Tours** ⊠ Av. Camacho 1223, La Paz ☎ 02/233-7533 🖷 02/211-6482 ⊕ www.titicaca.com.

BY BUS

Minibuses run regularly from the gates of El Viejo Cementerio in La Paz to destinations along Lake Titicaca, including Batallas, Huatajata, and Tiquina. One-way tickets are about $1. Private bus companies that collect passengers at their hotel charge roughly $10 round-trip to Copacabana (four hours) and $15 to Sorata (six hours). Diana Tours and Turibus are two well-known companies operating this route. There are also three companies at the bus terminal in La Paz, including TransTur (02/237–3423) at Caseta 18.

🚩 **Bus Information Diana Tours** ⊠ Calle Sagárnaga 328 ☎ 02/235-0252. **Turibus** ⊠ Calle Illampu ☎ 02/232-5348 or 02/236-9542 🖷 02/237-5532.

2

BY CAR

To reach Lake Titicaca from La Paz, take El Alto Highway northwest. The road is paved between La Paz and Tiquina, and barring heavy traffic, takes less than two hours. Be very careful about leaving your car unattended, particularly in Copacabana.

Contacts & Resources

MONEY MATTERS

In Copacabana most hotels will change U.S. dollars, as will many shops along Avenida 6 de Agosto. Some will also change traveler's checks, but don't count on it. Banco Union on Avenida 6 de Agosto in Copacabana exchanges foreign currency and gives cash advances on Visa cards. There are a few casas de cambio at Copacabana's main plaza.

TOUR OPERATORS

The best company offering tours of Lake Titicaca is Crillón Tours, in business since 1958. Crillón Tours runs daily hydrofoil trips from Huatajata and Copacabana to many of the islands, as well as to Puno on Peru's side of the lake.

🚩 **Tour Companies Crillón Tours** ✉ Av. Camacho 1223 ☎ 02/233-7533 🖨 02/211-6482 🌐 www.titicaca.com.

VISITOR INFORMATION

In the center of Copacabana's main plaza, the tourist information booth is the place to find information about the area. The opening hours are erratic, but if they're closed, hotels are more than happy to answer your questions and to help with booking tours.

🚩 **Information Booth** ✉ Av. Abaroa and Av. José Mejía.

CENTRAL BOLIVIA

The two major cities in central Bolivia, Cochabamba and Santa Cruz, are both southeast of La Paz—but here ends all similarity. Cochabamba, the country's third-largest city, is in a fertile valley in the foothills of the Andes. Often referred to as the "breadbasket of Bolivia," Cochabamba produces a large share of the country's fruit and vegetables, as well as much of its meat and dairy products. Nestled in the eastern foothills of the Andes, it is known for its mild, sunny weather. No wonder tourist brochures call this the "city of eternal spring."

Hot and humid Santa Cruz, Bolivia's second-largest city, is on the edge of the Amazon basin. In addition to agriculture, its economy is fueled by lumber, gas, and oil. The downtown area, with its covered sidewalks, looks a little like a movie set of an old frontier town.

Cochabamba

400 km (250 mi) southeast of La Paz.

This bustling metropolis is one of the oldest cities in Bolivia, and many buildings from the 16th century still stand along its narrow streets. Built on the traditional grid pattern, the central part of Cochabamba is divided into quadrants beginning at the intersection of Avenida de las Heroínas and Avenida Ayacucho. Streets are labeled *norte* (north), *sur* (south), *este* (east), and *oeste* (west). The quadrant is included as an abbreviation in the address; for example, Hotel Aranjuez is located at Avenida Buenos Aires E-0563.

A gleaming white statue of Christ with his arms outstretched, called **El Cristo de la Concordia,** stands watch on a hilltop overlooking Cochabamba. This is where many people come to get a feeling for this city with a population of more than half a million. There are also astounding views of Cochabamba

> ## SEEING DOUBLE
>
> At 108 feet, Cochabamba's Cristo is actually slightly taller than the well-known, similar monument in Rio de Janeiro.

from La Coronilla, a hill on the outskirts of the city. At the top is a monument called **La Heroínas de la Coronilla,** honoring women who died during Bolivia's protracted War of Independence.

Many of the sights in Cochabamba, a colonial town founded in 1571, are scattered around the palm-lined **Plaza 14 de Septiembre,** where bougainvillea, magnolias, and jacarandas bloom. Facing the main square is the **Catedral de Cochabamba,** which was started in 1571 but took more than 150 years to complete. One block southeast from the main square is a church called the **Templo de San Francisco,** a colonial masterpiece built in 1581 but thoroughly renovated in 1782 and again in 1926. Inside the Temple of St. Francis are elaborately carved wooden galleries and a striking gold-leaf altar.

Cochabamba's excellent **Museo Arqueológico** is one of the more comprehensive and interesting collections of artifacts outside of La Paz. On display in the Museum of Archaeology are pre-Columbian pottery, silver and gold work, and strikingly patterned handwoven Indian textiles. ✉ *Jordán and Aguirre* ☎ *No phone* 🖃 *(B)20* ☉ *Weekdays 9–noon and 3–7, Sat. 9–1.*

Across the Río Rocha is the **Palacio Portales,** which was built but never occupied by Simón Patiño, a local tin baron who amassed one of the world's largest fortunes. The mansion and 10-acre gardens reflect his predilection for French Renaissance style. One of the chambers on the upper floor mimics Italy's Sistine Chapel. The mansion, a five-minute taxi ride from the center of town, is now a cultural and educational center. ✉ *Av. Potosí 1450* ☎ *04/424–3137* 🖃 *(B)10* ☉ *Weekdays 5 PM–6 PM, Sat. 10 AM–11 AM.*

Where to Stay & Eat

★ **$$–$$$** ✕ **Bufalo Rodizio.** At this Argentine-style eatery, all the meat you can eat is carved at your table by waiters dressed as gauchos. There's also an excellent salad bar. Reserve a table on Sundays, which are usually packed with diners enjoying the great views of the city. ✉ *Edificio Torres Sofer, Av. Oquendo N-0654* ☎ *04/425–1597* 🖃 *AE, MC, V.*

$–$$ ✕ **Casa de Campo.** This informal and lively restaurant serves traditional Bolivian dishes—grilled meats and a perfectly fiery *picante mixto* (grilled chicken and beef tongue). You dine outdoors on a shaded patio. ⊠ *Av. Aniceto Padilla and Av. Bolivar* ☎ *04/424–3937* ▭ *MC, V.*

¢–$ ✕ **Chifa Lai Lai.** This *chifa*, or Chinese restaurant, has the excellent service usually found only in much more expensive places. The food is tasty, and the wines are cheap. Try the Ecuadoran shrimp dishes. ⊠ *Av. Aniceto Padilla* ☎ *04/424–0469* ▭ *MC, V.*

¢–$ ✕ **Quinta Guadalquivir.** Parrots in cages set around a small but beautifully landscaped garden lend a tropical feeling to this popular outdoor eatery. Its shady trees mean it's a pleasant place to stop for lunch. Dishes are a mix of traditional Bolivian and international food. ⊠ *Calle J. Bautista 370* ☎ *04/424–3491* ▭ *AE, MC, V.*

$ 🏨 **Gran Hotel Cochabamba.** Most of the simple but comfortable rooms at this two-story hotel overlook the gazebo in the center of the plant-filled courtyard. The adjoining Restaurante Carillón serves a tasty pique macho. ⊠ *Plaza Ubaldo Anze* ☎ *04/411–9986* 🖶 *04/448–6911* ⤳ *43 rooms, 5 suites* ⟡ *Restaurant, tennis court, pool, bar* ▭ *AE, MC, V.*

$ 🏨 **Hotel Aranjuez.** This elegant hotel is noted for its lovely gardens overflowing with bougainvillea. The well-appointed rooms are spacious and comfortable; most have baths attached. A live jazz band plays in the lobby bar most weekends. ⊠ *Av. Buenos Aires E-0563* ☎ *04/428–0076 or 04/428–0077* 🖶 *04/424–0158* ⊕ *www.aranjuezhotel.com* ⤳ *30 rooms, 3 suites* ⟡ *Restaurant, cable TV, pool, hair salon, bar, meeting rooms, travel services* ▭ *AE, MC, V.*

$ 🏨 **Hotel Portales.** In a quiet residential area in the northern part of the city, this Spanish-colonial-style hotel surrounded by lush gardens is Cochabamba's most luxurious accommodations. It has numerous recreation facilities, from a racquetball court to two heated pools. The well-equipped rooms have everything you'll require if you're traveling on business. It's a short taxi ride from the center of town, and local swing bands play in the bar. ⊠ *Av. Pando 1271* ☎ *04/428–5444* 🖶 *04/424–2071* ⤳ *98 rooms, 8 suites* ⟡ *2 restaurants, 2 pools, health club, hair salon, hot tub, racquetball, piano bar, laundry service, meeting rooms* ▭ *AE, MC, V.*

$ 🏨 **Hotel Viru Viru.** These downtown lodgings offer clean, modern rooms that overlook the swimming pool in the courtyard. Breakfast is included. ⊠ *Calle Junín 338* ☎ *03/333–5298* 🖶 *03/336–7500* ⊕ *www.hotelviruviru.com* ⤳ *44 rooms* ⟡ *Café, Internet, cable TV, pool* ⦿ *BP* ▭ *No credit cards.*

¢ 🏨 **Hotel Uni.** You'll appreciate this hotel's location—just a block from the main square. The rooms are simple and clean. Ask for an upper-floor room away from noisy Avenida de las Heroínas. ⊠ *Calle Baptista S-0111* ☎ *04/423–5065* ⤳ *43 rooms, 5 suites* ⟡ *Restaurant, bar, travel services* ▭ *AE, MC, V.*

Shopping

Cochabamba is well known for its alpaca sweaters and leather goods, but don't expect prices much lower than in La Paz. Plaza Colón marks the start of **El Prado** (sometimes called Avenida Ballivián), a shop-lined avenue that stretches north to the Río Rocha. The local market, **La Cancha,** is open daily on Avenida Aroma. It's a good place to browse for less expensive crafts.

Asarti (✉ Calle México and Av. Ballivián ☎ 04425–0455) sells high-quality knits. They also have a showroom at the Radisson Hotel in La Paz. **Casa Fisher** (✉ Calle Ramorán Rivero 0204 ☎ 04/428–4549) sells beautiful alpaca sweaters. **Tipay** (✉ Calle Jordán E-0732 ☎ 04/425–1303) is a clothing cooperative of local women who sell handmade knits in alpaca and cotton.

Tarata

25 km (15 mi) southeast of Cochabamba.

A well-preserved colonial village, Tarata is known for its busy outdoor market on Thursday. For the best view of Tarata, take the 15-minute walk uphill to the **Iglesia de San Pedro.** The Convento de San Francisco is currently being restored, as are many of the fine old buildings around town. Also interesting is the nearby village of Hayculi, famous for its pottery and ceramics.

In Cochabamba, buses for Tarata depart from Avenida Barrientos at the corner of Avenida 6 de Agosto. Many tour companies, such as the La Paz–based Fremen Tours, offer trips here.

Santa Cruz

900 km (560 mi) southeast of La Paz.

Just 30 years ago, oxen pulled carts through the muddy streets of Santa Cruz. Today, by contrast, you'll see well-dressed business executives dodging taxis and darting in and out of office buildings. Nonetheless, Santa Cruz, with more than 700,000 inhabitants, hasn't been completely transformed—you can still find traces of its colonial past.

The **Basílica Menor de San Lorenzo** was built between 1845 and 1915 on the ruins of a 17th-century cathedral. The imposing church, on Plaza 24 de Septiembre, holds a small museum displaying colonial-era religious icons, paintings, and sculptures. ✉ *Plaza 24 de Septiembre* ☎ *03/ 332–7381* 💲 *(B)10* ☉ *Daily 7–noon and 3–8.*

Facing Plaza 24 de Septiembre, the **Casa de la Cultura** hosts cultural exhibits, recitals, and concerts, in addition to a permanent exhibit of crafts made by indigenous people. ✉ *Plaza 24 de Septiembre* ☎ *03/334–0270* 💲 *Free* ☉ *Daily 9–noon and 3–6.*

Considered one of the finest zoos in South America, the **Zoológico Municipal** houses a collection of species from the Amazon, including jaguars, tapirs, and toucans. You'll also see such Andean creatures as llamas, alpacas, and flamingos. Taxis will take you from the main square to the zoo for approximately $1.50. ✉ *Anillo Interno at Radial 26* ☎ *03/342–9939* 💲 *(B)8* ☉ *Daily 9–6.*

Where to Stay & Eat

¢–$ ✕ **Victory.** This bar and restaurant serves tasty pastas and pizzas, but most diners gather on the balcony to sip cold beer, play cards or chess, and watch the action on the street below. ✉ *Junín at 21 de Mayo* ☎ *03/ 332–2935* ☰ *No credit cards.*

$$$$ 🏨 **Hotel Camino Real.** A free-form pool meanders through the tropical gardens at this low-rise hotel in a residential neighborhood on the outskirts of Santa Cruz. The Tranquera restaurant serves international fare. ⊠ *Calle K 279, Equipetrol Norte* ☎ *03/342–3535* 🖷 *03/343–1515* ⊕ *www.caminoreal.com.bo* 🛏 *104 rooms, 8 suites* ⑂ *Restaurant, cafeteria, pool, gym, sauna, spa, soccer, volleyball, shops, business services, meeting room, travel services* ▭ *AE, MC, V.*

$$$$ 🏨 **Hotel Los Tajibos.** This sprawling resort hotel on the edge of the city includes a series of low-slung buildings surrounded by lush gardens. El Papagayo restaurant serves excellent seafood. ⊠ *Av. San Martín 455* ☎ *03/342–1000* 🖷 *03/342–6994* ⊕ *www.lostajiboshotel.com* 🛏 *185 rooms, 6 suites* ⑂ *Restaurant, café, pool, gym, shops, convention center* ▭ *AE, MC, V.*

$$$$ 🏨 **Yotaú.** The spacious accommodations in this all-suite hotel are more like apartments, complete with kitchens and washing machines. Just outside of Santa Cruz in the suburb of Barrio Equipetrol, this strikingly modern hotel has a landscaped garden. Breakfast is included. ⊠ *Av. San Martín 7* ☎ *03/336–7799* 🖷 *03/336–3952* ⊕ *www.yotau.com.bo* 🛏 *100 suites* ⑂ *2 restaurants, gym, babysitting, laundry, pool, bar, business services* ▭ *AE, MC, V.*

$–$$ 🏨 **Gran Hotel Santa Cruz.** This family-owned hotel dating from the 1930s is a few blocks south of Plaza 24 de Septiembre. Rooms are like a comfortable den; those that overlook the pool have small private balconies. The restaurant serves very good international cuisine. ⊠ *Calle Pari 59* ☎ *03/334–8811* 🖷 *03/332–4194* ⊕ *www.bolivia.net/granhotelscz* 🛏 *40 rooms, 12 suites* ⑂ *Restaurant, cafeteria, pool, gym, 2 bars* ▭ *AE, MC, V.*

$ 🏨 **Hotel Paititi** This comfortable budget option is the sister hotel to the Viru-Viru in Cochabamba. Air-conditioned rooms and suites are available. ⊠ *Av. Cañoto 450* ☎ *03/355–9169 or 355–9167* ⊕ *www.hotelviruviru.com/hotelpaititi* 🛏 *40 rooms, 12 suites* ⑂ *Conference room, continental breakfast, air-conditioning, cable TV, Internet* ▭ *AE, MC, V.*

Shopping

Crafts shops and street vendors are scattered around Plaza 24 de Septiembre. Don't expect any real bargains. **Artecampo** (⊠ Calle Monseñor Salvatierra 407 ☎ 03/334–1843) is a cooperative with a colorful selection of handmade hammocks made from locally grown cotton. There are also mobiles and intricate hand-painted woodwork.

Central Bolivia Essentials

Transportation

BY AIR

International flights on Lloyd Aéreo Boliviano stop at Aeropuerto Internacional Viru-Viru in Santa Cruz before continuing to La Paz. American flights from La Paz stop in Santa Cruz on the way to Miami. The airport is about 15 km (9 mi) north of the city. Buses to the center of town depart every 20 minutes and cost about $1. Taxis should run about $6.50.

Lloyd Aéreo Boliviano and AeroSur fly daily from La Paz and Sucre to Aeropuerto Jorge Wilsterman in Cochabamba. The airport is 10 km (6 mi) from downtown. A taxi into town is about $4.

🛪 **Airlines AeroSur** ✉ Av. Villarroel 1105, Cochabamba ☎ 04/440-0909 ⊕ www.aerosur. com ✉ Calle Arenales 31, Santa Cruz ☎ 03/336-7400. **American** ✉ Beni 171, Santa Cruz ☎ 03/334-1314 ⊕ www.aa.com. **Lloyd Aéreo Boliviano** ✉ Av. de las Heroínas, Cochabamba ☎ 04/423-0320 ⊕ www.labairlines.com ✉ Calle Warnes, Santa Cruz ☎ 03/334-4596.

🛪 **Airports Aeropuerto Internacional Viru-Viru** ✉ Santa Cruz ☎ 03/334-4411. **Aeropuerto Jorge Wilsterman** ✉ Cochabamba ☎ 04/422-6548.

BY BUS

Depending on the state of the road, it takes about seven hours to travel by bus between La Paz and Cochabamba. If you're headed from La Paz to Santa Cruz, figure on a 20-hour trip. One-way tickets for either journey cost between $10 and $15. To avoid standing in the aisle for the entire journey, book tickets at least a day in advance. Trans Copacabana and Expreso Mopar have buses that leave several times a day.

🛪 **Bus Companies Expreso Mopar** ☎ 02/237-7443. **Trans Copacabana** ☎ 02/237-7894.

🛪 **Bus Terminals Terminal de Cochabamba** ✉ Av. Ayacucho at Av. Aroma. **Terminal de Santa Cruz** ✉ Av. Cañoto at Av. Irala.

BY CAR

Driving yourself is not a particularly good idea in most parts of Bolivia— and certainly not anywhere near the Chapare area, in north-central Bolivia (east of Cochabamba), where there is ongoing disagreement about whether coca farmers should be allowed to raise their crops. It takes nearly five hours to drive southeast from La Paz to Cochabamba. From La Paz, drive 190 km (118 mi) south to Caracollo, one of the few villages along the way with a gas station, and then head east toward Cochabamba. The drive between Cochabamba and Santa Cruz takes 10 hours on the Nuevo Camino (New Road). Don't try this route without a four-wheel-drive vehicle. You can break the trip into almost equal parts by staying overnight at Villa Tunari.

CAR RENTAL

Car rentals in Cochabamba or in Santa Cruz will cost a minimum of $50 per day. A. Barron's rents cars in both Cochabamba and Santa Cruz. Toyota is a reputable company in Cochabamba, while Imbex is well known in Santa Cruz.

🛪 **Rental Agencies A. Barron's** ✉ Calle Sucre E-0727, Cochabamba ☎ 04/422-2774 ✉ Av. Alemana 50, Santa Cruz ☎ 03/342-0160. **Imbex** ✉ Calle Monseñor Peña 320, Santa Cruz ☎ 03/353-3603. **Toyota** ✉ Av. Libertador Bolívar 1567, Cochabamba ☎ 04/428-5703.

TAXIS

Taxis are readily available on the streets in Cochabamba and Santa Cruz. If you want to call a taxi, try Radio Taxi in Cochabamba and Radio Taxi Equipetrol in Santa Cruz.

🛪 **Taxi Companies Radio Taxi** ✉ Lanza N-579, Cochabamba ☎ 04/422-8856. **Radio Taxi Equipetrol** ✉ Av. General Martínez 338, Santa Cruz ☎ 03/335-2100.

Contacts & Resources

HEALTH

Take the normal health precautions when traveling in this area—drink only bottled water and don't eat from street stands where food is sitting around. Make sure to bring along plenty of mosquito repellent.

MONEY MATTERS

In Cochabamba, you'll find casas de cambio around Plaza 14 de Septiembre. Independent money changers are often found along Avenida de las Heroínas. In Santa Cruz there are several casas de cambio around the Plaza 24 de Septiembre that will exchange cash and traveler's checks. Freelancers stroll through the main square and the bus terminal, but you'll probably feel more comfortable using an official change house.

Most banks in Cochabamba and Santa Cruz, including Banco Mercantil and Banco Nacional, have 24-hour ATMs.

🏧 **Banks Banco Mercantil** ⊠ Calle Calama E-0201, Cochabamba ☎ 04/425-1865 ⊠ René Moreno at Suárez de Figueroa, Santa Cruz ☎ 03/334-5000. **Banco Nacional** ⊠ Calle Nataniel Aguirre S-0198, Cochabamba ☎ 04/425-1860 ⊠ René Moreno 258, Santa Cruz ☎ 03/336-4777.

🏧 **Telephone Companies Entel** ⊠ Av. de las Heroínas and Av. Ayacucho, Cochabamba ⏱ Mon.-Fri. 7:30 AM-11 PM; Sat.-Sun. and holidays 8 AM-9 PM. **Entel** ⊠ Av. Warnes 83, between Moreno and Chuquisaca, Santa Cruz ☎ 03/432-5526 ⏱ Mon.-Fri. 7:30 AM-11 PM; Sat.-Sun. and holidays 8-9 AM-9 PM.

TOUR OPERATORS

Fremen Tours in La Paz offers tours of the central Bolivian market towns of Tarata and Hayculi, famous for pottery and ceramics. Flota Chiquitano and Magri Turismo in Santa Cruz also organize tours in the area.

🏧 **Tour Operators Flota Chiquitano** ⊠ Irala at Cañoto, Santa Cruz ☎ 03/336-0320. **Fremen Tours** ⊠ Calle Pedro Salazar 537, Plaza Abaroa, La Paz ☎ 02/241-7062 ⊕ www. andes-amazonia.com. **Magri Turismo** ⊠ Ingavi 14, Santa Cruz ☎ 03/334-4559 ⊕ www. bolivianet.com/magri.

VISITOR INFORMATION

🏧 **Cochabamba** ⊠ Calle General Achá ☎ 04/422-1793 ⏱ Weekdays 9-noon and 2:30-5. **Santa Cruz** ⊠ Casa de la Cultura (first floor) on the Plaza ☎ 03/333-2770 ⏱ Weekdays 8:30-noon and 2:30-6.

SOUTHERN BOLIVIA

Sucre

740 km (460 mi) southeast of La Paz.

Sucre has had many names since it was founded by the Spanish in 1538. The town's first official name was La Plata, but it was just as often called Charcas. In 1776, after splitting the region from Peru, the Spanish changed the name to Chuquisaca. Locals now refer to Sucre as *la ciudad blanca* (the white city)—no wonder, since by government edict all buildings in the center of the city must be whitewashed each year.

It was in Sucre that the region declared its independence from Spain in 1825. The country was named for its liberator, Simón Bolívar. Sucre was the country's original capital, but the main government functions were transferred to La Paz in the late 1800s, leaving the Corte Suprema de Justicia (Supreme Court) as Sucre's main governmental function.

> **DID YOU KNOW?**
>
> Locals will proudly tell you that officially, Sucre is still the nation's capital, and the *World Fact Book* (www.cia.gov) still lists two capitals for Bolivia–La Paz, the seat of government, and Sucre, the legal capital and seat of the judiciary.

Although its population now tops 200,000, Sucre—with its ornate churches, cobblestone streets, and broad plazas—retains the feel of a colonial town. Its moderate year-round climate and friendly people make it a pleasant place to stay while taking side trips to Tarabuco or Potosí.

Exploring Sucre

WHAT TO SEE **Casa de la Libertad.** Bolivia's formal declaration of independence was signed in the House of Liberty, a former Jesuit chapel, where it's now on display. A small museum displays historical documents and artifacts related to Bolivia's turbulent struggle for independence, as well as Argentina's first flag. ⊠ *Plaza 25 de Mayo* ☎ 064/442–4200 ☜ *(B)15* ⊗ *Weekdays 9–noon and 2:30–5, Sat. 9:30–11:40.*

Catedral Metropolitana. Started in 1559, this neoclassical cathedral is famous for its statue of the Virgin of Guadalupe, which is adorned with diamonds, gold, emeralds, and pearls donated during the 17th century by mining barons. ⊠ *Plaza 25 de Mayo* ☜ *Free* ⊗ *Weekdays 10–noon and 3–5, Sat. 10–noon.*

Corte Suprema de Justicia. The imposing Supreme Court building is a reminder that Sucre was once the sole capital of Bolivia. The beautiful Parque Bolívar, which covers several city blocks northwest of the court, is a favorite place for students from the Universidad de San Francisco Xavier to study. ⊠ *Ravelo and Pilinco.*

Museo Charcas. The most popular exhibits at the Charcas Museum are mummified bodies discovered outside of Sucre in the 1960s. Curators believe the centuries-old mummies were entombed as human sacrifices. Also featured at this university-run museum are galleries of colonial paintings and textiles. ⊠ *Calle Bolívar 698* ☎ 04/645–3285 ☜ *(B)15* ⊗ *Mon.–Sat. 2:30–6.*

Museo de la Recoleta. Founded in 1601 by Franciscan monks, the Museum of the Retreat displays colonial religious works in a setting of serene courtyards and gardens. Equally noteworthy is the restored chapel with its intricately carved choir seats. ⊠ *Plaza Pedro Anzures* ☎ 04/645–1987 ☜ *(B)10* ⊗ *Weekdays 9–11:30 and 3–5:30.*

Museo de Santa Clara. Founded in 1639, the Museum of Santa Clara houses a magnificent hand-painted organ built in 1664. Also on display are works by colonial painter Melchor Pérez Holguín and his Italian mentor, Bernardo Bitti. Visit the chapel, where the nuns who died here were buried under a special floor. ⊠ *Calle Calvo 212* ☎ *No phone* ☜ *(B)10* ⊗ *Weekdays 9–noon and 3–6, Sat. 9–noon.*

2

Fodor'sChoice **Museo Textil Etnográfico.** This museum is housed in the colonial Caserón
★ de la Capellanía. The Textile and Ethnographic Museum preserves the
4,000-year-old weavings and tapestry art of the Andean world, especially communities around Tarabuco. A display of costumes showcases
regional fiesta garb; there are also loom demonstrations. ⊠ *Calle San
Alberto 413* ☎ *04/645–3841* 🖃 *(B)16* ⊙ *Sept Mon.–Sat. 8:30–12:30
and 2:30–6.*

Plaza Pedro de Anzures. From this beautiful residential square at the foot
of Cerro Churuquella you'll get a panorama of Sucre's red-tile roofs and
whitewashed homes.

Where to Stay & Eat
Sucre's large student population keeps its many inexpensive restaurants
in business. Around the Plaza 25 de Mayo, many offer a *menú del día*
(meal of the day) for $2 or $3. If you're not a fan of spicy food, avoid
dishes prefaced with the words *ají* (pepper) or *picante* (spicy). Rather
than chain hotels, Sucre has many small hotels and hostels, almost all
of which are comfortable, clean, and friendly. Most include breakfast.

¢–$ ✕ **Alliance Française la Taverna.** The traditional French menu includes
coq au vin, ratatouille, and sweet crepes. Seating is available in the
dining room or outside in the courtyard. The location, near the Plaza
25 de Mayo and the Universidad San Francisco, makes it a popular
spot. ⊠ *Calle Aniceto Arce 35* ☎ *04/645–3599* 🖃 *No credit cards*
⊙ *Closed Sun.*

¢–$ ✕ **El Huerto.** At this restaurant near the municipal park, adventurous car-
nivores should try a traditional Bolivian entrée, such as *picante de
lengua* (spicy tongue). There's plenty on the menu for vegetarians, too.
The outdoor patio has a beautiful garden, and is a pleasant place to linger
over a long meal. Bring a sweater at night, as it gets a bit chilly. ⊠ *Ladis-
lao Cabrera 86* ☎ *04/645–1538* 🖃 *MC, V.*

¢ ✕ **Penco Penquitos.** For pocket change you can have a sandwich or nibble on an impressive selection of fresh pastries, from eclairs to empanadas, at this café near the university. ⊠ *Calle Estudiantes 66* ☎ *04/
644–3946* 🖃 *No credit cards.*

¢ ▦ **Hostal de Su Merced.** When you notice the colorful wood ceiling in
the reception room—a reproduction of the original painted by a Jesuit
priest—you know instantly that this family-owned hotel is a gem. Built
as a private home in the late 17th century, the gleaming white colonial
structure with a handsome tin roof has large, airy rooms with sunlight
streaming in through the tall windows. From the intimate central courtyard, a stairway with wrought-iron railings leads to the upper floors.
From the rooftop sundeck you get excellent views of the entire city. ⊠ *Calle
Azurduy 16* ☎☏ *04/644–2706, 04/644-2706, 04/644–5150* ⊕ *www.
desumerced.com* 🛏 *14 rooms, 2 suites* 🍴 *Restaurant* 🖃 *MC, V.*

¢ ▦ **Hostal Sucre.** This colonial-style place, just two blocks from the Plaza
25 de Mayo, is built around two inner courtyards—which means the
rooms are all quiet. A restaurant serves light meals and snacks. ⊠ *Calle
Bustillos 113* ☎ *04/645–1411* 🖃 *04/646–1928* 🛏 *33 rooms* 🍴 *Restaurant, travel services* 🖃 *AE, MC, V.*

Shopping

For a touch of local flavor, check out the market at Calle Ravelo and Calle Junín, which sells locally grown fruits and vegetables. The gift shop at the **Museo Textil Etnográfico** (✉ Calle San Alberto 413 ☎ 064/453–841) has an excellent selection of local weavings. The cooperative ensures that the majority of profits go directly to the weavers.

Tarabuco

64 km (40 mi) east of Sucre.

If you are in Sucre over a weekend, take a full-day excursion to the village of Tarabuco to experience its famous Sunday market. Here you will still see indigenous women wearing tri-cornered hats fringed with coins and men with brightly colored ponchos and leather helmets that resemble those worn centuries ago by the Spanish conquistadors. Like many towns in the region, Tarabuco is filled with vendors from end to end selling finely woven belts and *charangos,* a stringed instrument made from armadillo shells. In mid-March Tarabuco is the location of one of South America's liveliest traditional festivals, called Pujilay. It celebrates the victory of the local people over the Spanish in 1816.

Potosí

169 km (105 mi) southwest of Sucre.

Potosí has a split personality. Its soaring churches and opulent mansions call to mind a time when this was the wealthiest city in South America. The sagging roofs and crumbling facades, however, make it difficult to put the town's painful past and difficult present out of your mind.

Silver, tin, and zinc from nearby Cerro Rico made fortunes for the mineral barons who built their grand homes along Potosí's winding cobblestone streets. Tens of thousands of people flocked here hoping to make a little money of their own. In 1650, with a population topping 160,000, Potosí was the largest and most prosperous city on the continent. But that wealth came from the labor of more than 8 million indigenous people forced to work in the mines.

There's another old saying that puts all this wealth into perspective: "Bolivia had the cow, but the other countries got the milk." In a strange twist of fate, Potosí is now one of Bolivia's poorest cities. Depleted mines, outdated machinery, and an inhospitable terrain—Potosí sits on a windy plain at 13,452 feet above sea level—are not leading to prosperity. But as more and more buildings are restored (some as an act of contrition by the Spanish), more people are being drawn to one of Bolivia's most interesting cities.

Exploring Potosí

The only way to get around Potosí is to walk. The steep, winding streets and sidewalks are narrow, so pedestrian traffic can often be more of a problem than cars. To visit the museums and historic buildings, you'll need a guide. English-speaking guides aren't always available, so consider arranging a tour through a travel agency.

WHAT TO SEE   **Casa Real de Moneda.** The showpiece of Potosí is the Royal Mint, built
Fodor'sChoice   in 1773 at a cost of $10 million. This massive stone structure, where
★   coins were once minted with silver from nearby Cerro Rico, takes up
an entire city block. It now holds Bolivia's largest museum. On display
are huge wooden presses that fashioned the strips of silver from which
the coins were pressed, as well as an extensive collection of the coins
minted here until 1953. There's also an exhibit of paintings, including
works by Bolivia's celebrated 20th-century artist, Cecilio Guzmán de
Rojas. A guard accompanies all tours to unlock each room as it's visited. The building is cool, so bring along a sweater. To see everything
will take about three hours. ⊠ *Ayacucho at Lanza* 🕿 *04/622–2777*
🖃 *(B)20* ✆ *Tues.–Sat. 9–noon and 2–6:30, weekends 9–1.*

Fodor'sChoice   **Cerro Rico.** Five thousand tunnels crisscross Cerro Rico, the "Rich Hill,"
★   which filled Spain's coffers until the silver reserves were exhausted in the
early 19th century. Today tin is the primary extract, though on the barren mountainside you still see miners sifting through the remnants of ancient excavations. If you don't mind tight spaces, take a tour through
one of the mines that are still active. You'll descend into the dark, humid
tunnels where hundreds of workers strip down to next to nothing because of the intense heat. Keep in mind that these mines are muddy—
■ TIP➡ **wear clothes you don't mind getting dirty.** Hard hats, raincoats, boots,
and carbide lamps are provided, but take along a flashlight to get a better look at things. The extremely narrow entrance to the mine may scare
you off, but go in far enough to give *El Tío* (a statue of a small, grinning
devil) a cigarette and add more coca leaves to the pile around his feet.
The miners say he brings safety and prosperity.

Convento y Museo de Santa Teresa. The Convent and Museum of St.
Theresa displays a strange mix of religious artifacts. In one room are sharp
iron instruments once used to inflict pain on penitent nuns, as well as a
blouse embroidered with wire mesh and prongs meant to prick the flesh.
Other rooms contain works by renowned colonial painters, including Melchor Pérez Holguín. ⊠ *Calle Chicas* 🕿 *02/622–3847* 🖃 *(B)25* ✆ *Weekdays 9–noon and 2–5:30.*

Iglesia de San Lorenzo. Potosí's most spectacular church, built between
1728 and 1744, has some of the finest examples of baroque carvings in
South America. Elaborate combinations of mythical figures and indigenous designs are carved in high relief on the stone facade. If the front
doors are locked, try to get in through the courtyard. ⊠ *Calle Bustillos*
🕿 *No phone.*

Iglesia y Convento de San Francisco. Built of granite during the colonial
period, this was Potosí's first church. It has a brick dome and beautiful
arches. On the main altar is the statue of the "Lord of the Veracrúz,"
the patron of Potosí. It also has many beautiful paintings. A panoramic
view of the city can be enjoyed from a viewing platform. ⊠ *Corner of
Nagales and Tarija* 🕿 *02/622–25399* 🖃 *(B)10* ✆ *Weekdays 2:30–4:30.*

Where to Stay & Eat

¢–$ ✕ **El Mesón.** Potosí's most exclusive restaurant has a quiet dining room where you can get both traditional Bolivian and international food. ✉ *Calle Tarija at Calle Linares* ☎ *04/622–3087* ▭ *MC, V.*

¢–$ ✕ **San Marcos.** Potosí's most unusual restaurant occupies a former silver

Fodor'sChoice processing plant. Each piece of ancient machinery has been put to use—

★ the bar, for example, is a platform where stones were once washed. Both local and international dishes are served, including *trucha al gusto* (trout broiled with lemon, garlic, and pesto sauce) and *filete flambé San Marcos* (steak doused with cognac and set aflame). There's live music every Friday night. ✉ *La Paz and Betanzos* ☎ *02/622–2781* ▭ *MC, V.*

¢–$ ✕ **Sky Room.** You'll be treated to fine sunset views from this aptly named rooftop restaurant. The restaurant serves traditional dishes, such as *pichanga* (various types of meats served with salad) and grilled chicken. ✉ *Edificio Matilde, Calle Bolívar 701* ☎ *02/622–6345* ▭ *MC, V.*

¢ ✕ **Cherry's.** At this delightful coffee shop you can sip mugs of refreshing mate de coca while you ponder the delicious selection of cakes and strudels. ✉ *Calle Padilla 8* ☎ *02/622–2969* ▭ *No credit cards.*

$ 🏨 **Hotel Libertador.** Original artwork by local Potosí painters brightens hallways and rooms in this centrally located hotel. There's a small patio on the top floor where you can catch a little sun. The staff is friendly. The big plus here is central heating. ✉ *Millares 58* ☎ *02/622-7877* 🖷 *02/622-4629* ⊕ *www.hostal-libertador-potosi.com* ▭ *20 rooms, 3 suites* ♨ *Restaurant, cable TV, bar, Internet* ▭ *MC, V.*

★ ¢ 🏨 **Hotel Cima Argentum.** Near the Santa Teresa Convent and six blocks from the Casa de Moneda, this is one of Potosí's most modern hotels. The large rooms with marble baths and the suites are spread over three floors with balconies overlooking a courtyard under a glass dome. Each room has its own radiator for heat. There's a coffee pot in your room, and the chef cooks up tasty local and international dishes. The restaurant is open from 7 AM to 11 PM. ✉ *Av. Villazon 239* ☎ *02/622–9538* 🖷 *02/612–2603* ⊕ *www.hca-potosi.com* ▭ *20 rooms, 9 suites* ♨ *Restaurant, room service, cable TV, Internet* ▭ *MC, V.*

¢ 🏨 **Hotel Claudia.** A little far from the center of town, this place has well-equipped rooms and a terrace perfect for relaxing after a day exploring the city. It has features rarely found in Potosí's budget lodgings, including a restaurant and bar. Many tour groups stop here. ✉ *Av. El Maestro 322* ☎ *02/622–2242* 🖷 *02/622–4005* ▭ *22 rooms* ♨ *Restaurant, bar* ▭ *MC, V.*

¢ 🏨 **Hotel Colonial.** This whitewashed colonial hotel is just two blocks from the colorful Plaza 10 de Noviembre. Many rooms overlook the hotel's two airy courtyards. Ask to see one of the modern rooms in the back, which are more spacious. ✉ *Calle Hoyos 8* ☎ *02/622–4809* 🖷 *02/622–7164* ▭ *20 rooms* ♨ *Dining room* ▭ *MC, V.*

Shopping

Despite Potosí's rich mineral wealth, don't expect bargains on handcrafted silver jewelry. Brass and low-grade silver items can be found at the **Mercado Central** at Bustillos and Bolívar. The **Mercado Artesenal,** on the corner of Sucre and Omiste, has locally produced crafts.

Salar de Uyuni

Fodor's Choice *219 km (136 mi) southwest of Potosí.*
★

One of Bolivia's most spectacular sites, the vast Salar de Uyuni is the world's highest desert of salt. Its cracked white surface is at 11,976 feet. Once part of a prehistoric salt lake covering most of southwestern Bolivia, it still extends for about 12,000 square km (4,600 square mi). Here you'll find a series of eerie, translucent lagoons tinted green and red due to high copper and sulfur contents. On the salt flat live flamingos, rheas, vicuñas, and foxes.

It takes four to five hours of travel on rough roads to reach Uyuni from Potosi and most people choose to make arrangements with a travel agency. The site is remote and cold, with nightly temperatures falling to -25°C (-13°F). While the area is accessible year-round, the most popular time is from March to December. Whenever you go, take plenty of sunblock, sunglasses, and warm clothing.

Southern Bolivia Essentials

Transportation

BY AIR

Sucre's Aeropuerto Juana Azurduy de Padilla—about 5 km (3 mi) north of Sucre—has regular flights to La Paz on AeroSur and Lloyd Aéreo Boliviano. A taxi ride into town should cost about $1.50. Potosí has a small airstrip just outside of town but has no regularly scheduled flights.

🛈 Airlines **AeroSur** ✉ Calle Arenales 31, Sucre ☎ 04/646-2141. **Lloyd Aéreo Boliviano** ✉ Calle Espana 105, Sucre ☎ 04/6991-3182 or 0800/10-3001 in Bolivia.

🛈 Airports **Aeropuerto Juana Azurduy de Padilla** ☎ 064/454-445.

BY BUS

Buses bound for Potosí and Sucre leave La Paz daily. The 19-hour trip to Sucre costs less than $15. Buses between Sucre and Potosí depart approximately every hour. The trip takes about three hours and costs $4.

🛈 Bus Terminals **Potosí** ✉ Av. Universitaria ☎ 02/624-3362. **Sucre** ✉ Calle Ostria Gutiérrez ☎ 04/644-1292.

BY CAR

Although the highways aren't in the best condition, driving can be a nice way to see some areas of southern Bolivia. When visiting Potosí it is best to fly to Sucre and drive from there. You should also consider hiring a car and driver or take a tour through a travel agency. The highway is good between Sucre and Potosí but plan to overnight, as it passes through mountains and is not lighted.

🛈 Car Rentals **Imbex** ✉ Serranoí 165, Sucre ☎ 04/646-12222.

BY TAXI

In Sucre and Potosí, taxis are readily available. There are several reliable radio taxi companies in both cities. In Sucre, call Exclusivo or Sucre. In Potosí, contact I.N.N. or Potosí.

🛈 Taxi Companies **Exclusivo** ✉ Jaime Mendoza 960, Sucre ☎ 064/451-414. **I.N.N** ✉ Calle Frias 58 ☎ 062/222-606. **Potosí** ✉ Zona San Clemente 125 ☎ 062/225-257. **Sucre** ✉ Playa 25 de Mayo, Sucre ☎ 064/451-333.

Contacts & Resources

MONEY MATTERS

In Sucre you'll find casas de cambio along Avenida San Alberto near the main market. Your best bet in Potosí is along Calle Bolívar and Calle Sucre. In both places, cash fetches a better rate than traveler's checks. If you need an ATM, one of the most convenient is Banco Santa Cruz in Sucre. You won't find ATMs in the countryside.

🏦 Banks **Banco Santa Cruz** ✉ Calle San Alberto and España. ☎ 04/645-5400.

TOUR OPERATORS

Candelaria Tours in Sucre organizes trips to Potosí and to nearby Tarabuco for the Sunday market. In Potosí, Sin Fronteras and Hidalgo Tours organize excursion around the city as well as to the Cerro Rico mines. Fremen Tours in La Paz arranges wine tours of the Tarija area.

Toñito Tours, run by American expatriate Chris Sarage, specializes in tours in southwestern Bolivia. Trips to the Salar de Uyuni are usually for four days and cost about $30 a day, including accommodations, a car and driver, and a cook who prepares three meals a day.

🏦 Tour Companies **Candelaria Tours** ✉ Calle Audiencia 1, Sucre ☎ 064/461-661. **Altamira Tours** ✉ Avenida del Maestro 50, Sucre ☎ 04/645-3525. **Fremen Tours** ✉ Plaza Abaroa, La Paz ☎ 02/232-7073. **Hidalgo Tours** ✉ Av. Bolívar at Av. Junín, Potosí ☎ 062/222-5186. **Magri Turismo** ✉ Calle Capitán Ravelo 2101, La Paz ☎ 02/244-2727 🖷 02/244-3060 ⊕ www.bolivianet.com/magri. **Sin Fronteras** ✉ Calle Bustillos 1092, Potosí ☎ 062/224-058. **Toñito Tours** ✉ Sagárnaga 189, La Paz ☎ 02/233-6250 ✉ Av. Ferroviaria 152, Uyuni ☎🖷 0693/2094 ⊕ www.bolivianexpeditions.com.

VISITOR INFORMATION

🏦 **Potosí Oficina de Turismo** ✉ Cámara de Minería, Calle Quijarro ☎ 02/225-288 ⊗ Weekdays 9-noon and 3-6. **Sucre Oficina de Turismo** ✉ Nicolás Ortiz 182 ⊗ Weekdays 8-noon and 2-6

BOLIVIA ESSENTIALS

Transportation

BY AIR

American and Lloyd Aéreo Boliviano (LAB) operate daily flights from Miami. Flights on both airlines stop in Santa Cruz. Lloyd Aéreo Boliviano also flies to La Paz from other South American cities, including Buenos Aires, Rio de Janeiro, Santiago, Lima, and Asunción.

LAB flies between most Bolivian cities, as does domestic carrier AeroSur. One-way tickets range from $60 to $150. Both LAB and AeroSur offer 30-day passes for approximately $160 that allow travel to four cities. Destinations include Trinidad, Santa Cruz, Tarija, Sucre, Cochabamba, and La Paz. Domestic flights can be heavily booked, so always reconfirm your reservation a day or so in advance. If you do not, your reservation may be canceled.

🏦 Airlines **AeroSur** ✉ Avenida Irala 616 Santa Cruz ☎ 03/336-4446 ⊕ www.aerosur.com. **American** ✉ Plaza Venezuela 1440, La Paz ☎ 02/235-1360. ⊕ www.aa.com

Lloyd Aéreo Boliviano ✉ Av. Camacho 1460, La Paz ☎ 800-10-3001, 800-4321 in Bolivia ⊕ www.labairlines.com.

BY BUS

Private bus companies connect Bolivia's major cities—two of the best are Expreso Mopar and Trans Copacabana. Because of the often poor roads, bus journeys can be a very slow way to travel—a trip from La Paz to Santa Cruz, for example, can take more than 24 hours. Some routes are crowded, so reserve a seat a day or two ahead.

🚌 **Bus Companies Expreso Mopar** ☎ 02/237-7443. **Trans Copacabana** ☎ 02/237-7894.

BY CAR

Car travel in Bolivia is difficult, as few of the major highways are well maintained. Conditions have been so bad that drivers have held brief strikes in protest. During the rainy season (Nov.–Mar.), roads are often impassable. There's no national roadside automobile service, though Bolivians will often stop and offer help in the case of a breakdown. It's unwise to drive, but if you're compelled to do so, make sure you rent a vehicle with four-wheel-drive.

GASOLINE The national oil company, YPFB, maintains service stations on most major roads. Many are open 24 hours a day. Away from the main roads, GASOLINA signs alert you to private homes where fuel is sold. (Make sure they filter the gasoline for impurities when they fill your tank.) Unleaded gasoline is still a novelty in Bolivia. The price of gasoline is approximately $1.70 per gallon.

RENTAL Renting a car can be expensive in Bolivia, particularly because you need a
AGENCIES four-wheel-drive vehicle to reach many destinations. The rate for a four-wheel-drive vehicle is $300–$700 per week. Compact cars suitable for short trips cost $150–$250 per week. The minimum age for most car rentals in Bolivia is 25 years. You need a passport, driver's license (some rental companies require an International Driver's License), and a credit card.

Contacts & Resources

CUSTOMS & DUTIES

Bags are usually checked on arrival at La Paz's El Alto Airport. You're allowed to import 400 cigarettes and three bottles of wine or two liters of spirits. There is no limit on the amount of foreign currency you can bring into the country. For certain electronic goods—video cameras and personal computers, for example—you should carry your receipts unless they show obvious signs of wear. Do not attempt to import or export contraband drugs of any kind—penalties are severe.

ELECTRICITY

Bolivia's electric current is 110/220 volts AC in La Paz and 220 volts AC in the rest of the country. You'll need adapters for two-pronged outlets, which are used for both types of current.

EMBASSIES

⇨ *See* La Paz Essentials for more information.

HEALTH & SAFETY

FOOD & DRINK To play it safe, do not drink tap water and order beverages without ice. Never eat food from street vendors. Take the U.S. government's Centers for Disease Control and Prevention's advice: "Boil it, cook it, peel it, or forget it."

OTHER PRECAUTIONS At present, no shots or vaccination certificates are required for entering Bolivia. If you'll be spending time in remote areas, ask your doctor about typhoid, hepatitis A and B, yellow fever, and tetanus vaccinations. If you're headed for the Amazon, consider antimalarial prophylactics.

Due to the high altitude in La Paz, you may suffer from *soroche,* or altitude sickness. Symptoms include dizziness, fatigue, and shortness of breath. Avoid alcohol, drink lots of water, and rest for at least a half day. Symptoms will usually disappear by the second day. If not, consult a doctor, especially if you have a history of high blood pressure. Locals recommend several cups of mate de coca, an herbal (and completely legal) tea made from coca leaves.

Bring plenty of sunblock—the high altitudes feel cool, but the sun can burn, particularly when reflected off snow or water. Don't pet the cute llamas or alpacas, as they can hurl spit wads that burn the eyes. Don't stand too close behind these animals, as they can throw a sharp kick.

MAIL & SHIPPING

Most cities and towns have at least one post office, which is generally open weekdays 8–7:30, Saturday 9–6, and Sunday 9–noon.

RECEIVING MAIL In major cities, mail can be sent to you in care of Poste Restante, Correo Central (General Delivery, Central Post Office). You will need your passport to retrieve mail.

MONEY MATTERS

You can change U.S. dollars in banks and casas de cambio. Make sure the bills are in perfect condition, with no smudges or torn edges. Traveler's checks are often difficult to cash outside the larger cities. Most banks in Bolivia's larger cities have ATMs. Those labeled ENLACE dispense local currency 24 hours a day.

CREDIT CARDS Visa is welcomed throughout Bolivia, MasterCard less so. American Express is often not accepted. Credit cards are accepted in most cities and towns but never in small villages. If you will be traveling in a rural area, make sure to bring along enough cash.

CURRENCY The unit of currency is the boliviano, which can be divided into 100 centavos. Bolivianos come in bills of 5, 10, 20, 50, 100, and 200. Coins come in denominations of 10, 20, and 50 centavos and 1 and 2 bolivianos. At press time, the exchange rate was (B)8 to the U.S. dollar. Bolivians frequently refer to their currency as *pesos.*

WHAT IT WILL COST Because the boliviano is a relatively stable currency, Bolivia remains one of the least expensive countries in South America for travelers. A basic meal at a basic restaurant should cost no more than $5, and even at the

2

most elegant restaurants you can eat well for less than $10. Moderate hotels cost $30–$50 for a double room, which often includes breakfast. The most expensive luxury hotels are more pricey, at $120–$150 per night for a double.

Sample costs: cup of coffee, (B)4; bottle of beer, (B)8; soft drink, (B)4; bottle of house wine, (B)38; sandwich, (B)15; 2-km (1-mi) taxi ride, (B)15; city bus ride, (B)2; museum entrance, (B)8–(B)16.

PASSPORTS & VISAS
Australia, Canada, United Kingdom, New Zealand, and United States citizens need only a valid passport and receive a free visa upon arrival in Bolivia. Visas for the United Kingdom and the United States are valid for 90 days and for Australia, Canada, and New Zealand for 30 days (however, it doesn't hurt to ask if they will extend it to 90). If you want to stay longer than your free days, you have the option of overstaying your visa and being fined (B)10 for each day you overstay or purchase a 30-day extension for (B)150.

SAFETY
Crime is not a major problem in Bolivia. In larger cities such as La Paz, Cochabamba, Sucre, and Santa Cruz, petty theft—from pickpocketing to purse-snatching—is on the rise. Avoid wearing flashy jewelry and watches and be aware of your surroundings at all times, especially in busy plazas and on jam-packed buses. Carry only as much cash as necessary when in the city, especially in crowded market areas.

TAXES
DEPARTURE TAX All passengers must pay a departure tax—$25 for international flights, $2 for domestic flights—at an easily identifiable booth marked IM-PUESTOS. You can pay in dollars or bolivianos.

VALUE ADDED TAX Throughout Bolivia, a 13% value-added tax (IVA) is added to hotel and restaurant prices and to most items purchased in stores.

TELEPHONES
The international code for Bolivia is 591. Dial the country code, then the departmental area code, then the seven-digit number. If you are calling from abroad, drop the "0" from the area code. Local codes for the departments are as follows: La Paz, Oruro, Potosí, 2; Santa Cruz, Beni, Pando, 3; Cochabamba, Tarija, Chuquisaca (Sucre), 4

INTERNATIONAL CALLS Long-distance and international calls can be made from local offices of Entel, Bolivia's phone company. Collect and direct-dial calls can be made from Entel offices or by calling 356–700, which connects you with an international operator. A connection can take up to 20 minutes to secure. The least expensive way to make international calls is through your own long-distance carrier.

🔂 **Long-distance Carriers** AT&T ☎0800-1111. MCI ☎0800-2222. Sprint ☎0800-3333. British Telecom ☎0800-0044.

LOCAL CALLS Pay phones are operated by using either coins or phone cards (*tarjetas telefónicas*), which can be purchased at Entel offices and at many shops.

After you insert a coin or card and enter the number, the phone will indicate how much credit you have.

TIPPING

In restaurants, a tip of 5%–10% is in order unless the service is really
dismal. Taxi drivers do not expect tips unless you hire them for the day,
in which case 10% is appropriate. Airport porters expect (B)8 per baggage cart they handle.

VISITOR INFORMATION

At the present time there are no tourist information offices outside of
Bolivia. The most reliable way to get accurate information is either by
contacting a travel agent knowledgeable about Bolivia or checking out
Web sites, such as ⊕ www.bolivianet.com or the Viceministry of
Tourism's site, ⊕ www.turismobolivia.bo.

Brazil

WORD OF MOUTH

"The Amazon was fabulous—I loved drifting in a boat at night listening to the sounds of the jungle. The people were wonderful, Rio was magical, and the Amazon was amazing."   —jcasale

"I highly recommend two days at Iguazu Falls…take a flight because you are going deep into Brazil. Other great places are Salvador and Bahia in the northeast; if you go, make sure you attend the Tuesday-night street party in Pelourinho."   —patkiely

"Buzios is certainly nice, though I would rather visit Angra dos Reis (a city surrounded by islands) or Ilha Grande (Big Island on a free translation), with their lovely beaches. Parati is also an option if you are interested in very quiet and historical cities."
                    —Marcio_Br

MANY CONSIDER BRAZIL A CONTINENT IN ITS OWN RIGHT. It's larger than the continental United States, four times the size of Mexico, and more than twice as large as India. Occupying most of the eastern half of South America, it borders on all of the other nations of the continent, with the exception of Chile and Ecuador. Its population of 163 million is almost equal to that of the continent's other nations combined, making it South America's true colossus.

Brazil is also a land well versed in extremes. Its continuous, 7,700-km (4,800-mi) coast offers a seemingly infinite variety of beaches. Styles range from the urban setting of Rio's Copacabana and Ipanema to isolated, unspoiled treasures along the northeastern coast. Brazil's Portuguese colonizers concentrated on the coastal regions, avoiding the inland areas with rare exceptions—a preference that has dictated national life to this day. In the 1960s the government moved the capital from Rio to inland Brasília in an effort to overcome the "beach complex," but three decades later the majority of the population remains concentrated along a narrow coastal strip.

By contrast, the Amazon jungle, which covers 40% of the nation's land mass, has a population of only about 16 million—less than the city of São Paulo alone. Twenty percent of the world's freshwater reserves are found here, and the area is responsible for more than 30% of the earth's oxygen and is home to two-thirds of the world's existing species. Brazil's other hinterland regions are as sparsely populated as they are diverse. The northeast contains the rugged *sertão*, a region that frequently suffers droughts; the central west is the site of the immense *cerrado* (savanna) area; still farther west are the Pantanal Wetlands—an enormous swamp.

The country is also a melting pot of races and cultures. Beginning with its Portuguese colonizers, Brazil has drawn waves of immigrants from around the globe, including more than 15 million Africans who were transported here as slaves. The result is the ethnic mix of modern-day Brazil—Italian and German communities in the south, prosperous Japanese and Korean colonies in the state of São Paulo, a thriving Afro-Brazilian culture in Bahia, and remnants of Indian cultures in the north. Brazilians are white, tan, gold, black, brown, red, and seemingly all shades in between. Yet the various groups are united by a common language and a cultural heritage distinct from that of the remainder of South America. Brazilians speak Portuguese, not Spanish, and unlike all their neighbors, they were never a Spanish colony.

The variety of cultures, beliefs, and topographies makes this warm nation a showcase of diversity. An array of nature's bounty—from passion fruit and papaya to giant river fish and coastal crabs—has inspired chefs from all over the world to try their hands in Brazilian restaurants, adding lightness and zest to the country's already exquisite cuisine. Whether you travel to the Amazon rain forest or the urban jungle of São Paulo, you'll plunge into an exotic mix of colors, rhythms, and pastimes.

Exploring Brazil

When planning your trip, don't underestimate the country's size or the travel times. Determine your interests up front, and pick your destinations accordingly. Beaches, fun, and sun are the calling cards of Rio and Salvador. São Paulo is a huge, bustling city, full of activity day and night. Use Manaus and Belém as hubs for trips into the Amazon.

Restaurants & Cuisine

Eating is a national passion in Brazil, and portions are huge. In many restaurants plates are prepared for two people; when you order, ask if one plate will suffice. Some restaurants automatically bring a *couvert* (an appetizer course of such items as bread, cheese or pâté, olives, quail eggs, and the like). You'll be charged extra for this, and you're perfectly within your rights to send it back if you don't want it.

Mealtimes vary according to locale. In Rio and São Paulo, lunch and dinner are served later than in the United States. In restaurants lunch usually starts around 1 and can last until 3. Dinner is always eaten after 8 and in many cases not until 10. In smaller towns, dinner and lunch are taken at roughly the same time as in the States. It's hard to find breakfast outside a hotel restaurant. Unless otherwise noted, the restaurants listed in this guide are open daily for lunch and dinner.

Credit cards are widely accepted at restaurants in the major cities. In the countryside all but the smallest establishments generally accept credit cards as well. Gratuity is 10% of the total sum, and it is sometimes included in the bill; when it is not, it is optional to give the waiter a tip.

About the Hotels

When you consider your lodgings in Brazil, add these three terms to your vocabulary: *pousada* (inn), *fazenda* (farm), and "flat" or "block" hotel (apartment-hotel). Flat hotels are popular with Brazilians. These have kitchen facilities and room for a group. If you ask for a double room, you'll get a room for two people, but you're not guaranteed a double mattress. If you'd like to avoid twin beds, ask for a *cama de casal* ("couple's bed").

Carnaval (Carnival), the year's principal festival, occurs during the four days preceding Ash Wednesday. For top hotels in Rio, Salvador, and Recife—the three leading Carnaval cities—you must make reservations a year in advance. Hotel rates rise 20% on average for Carnaval. Not as well known outside Brazil but equally impressive is Rio's New Year's Eve celebration. More than a million people gather along Copacabana Beach for a massive fireworks display and to honor the sea goddess Iemanjá. To ensure a room, book at least six months in advance.

Hotels accept credit cards for payment, but first ask if there's a discount for cash. Try to bargain hard for a cash-on-the-barrel discount, then pay in local currency.

When to Go

Prices in beach resorts are invariably higher during the Brazilian summer (November–April). If you're looking for a bargain, stick to the off-

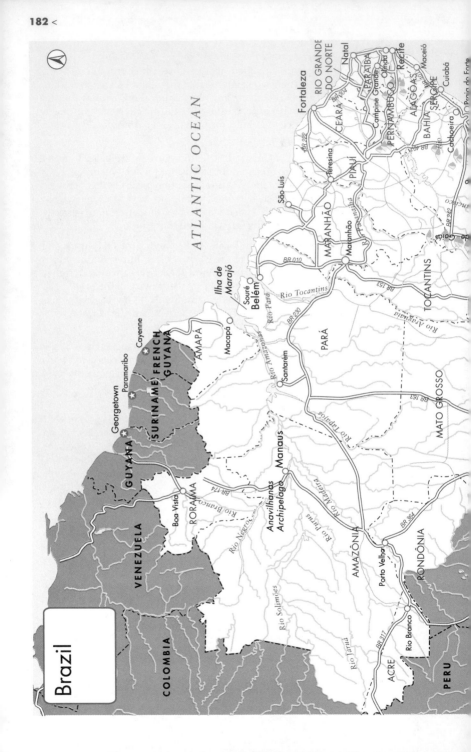

Brazil

ATLANTIC OCEAN

COLOMBIA

VENEZUELA

GUYANA

Georgetown

SURINAME

Paramaribo

FRENCH GUYANA

Cayenne

Boa Vista

RORAIMA

Rio Branco

BR 174

Rio Negro

Anavilhanas Archipelago

Manaus

AMAPÁ

Macapá

Rio Amazonas

Ilha de Marajó

Souré

Belém

Santarém

PARÁ

Rio Pará

Rio Tocantins

BR 010

BR 230

Rio Tapajós

Rio Madeira

Rio Purus

Rio Solimões

AMAZÔNIA

Porto Velho

RONDÔNIA

BR 364

MATO GROSSO

BR 163

TOCANTINS

Rio Araguaia

Rio Tocantins

Goiás

MARANHÃO

Matanhão

São Luís

BR 222

Teresina

PIAUÍ

CEARÁ

Fortaleza

BR 304

RIO GRANDE DO NORTE

Natal

PARAÍBA

Campine Grande

Olinda

Recife

PERNAMBUCO

Maceió

ALAGOAS

SERGIPE

BAHIA

Cachoeira

Rio

BR 407

BR 242

Rio São Francisco

Cuiabá

Praia do Forte

PERU

ACRE

Rio Branco

BR 317

Rio Juruá

BR 364

BR 153

season (May–June and August–October; July is school-break month). Rio and beach resorts along the coast suffer from oppressive summer heat November–April, but in Rio the temperature can drop to uncomfortable levels for swimming from June through August.

CLIMATE Seasons below the equator are the reverse of the north—summer in Brazil runs from December to March and winter from June to September. The rainy season in Brazil occurs during the summer months, but this is rarely a nuisance. Showers can be torrential but usually last no more than an hour or two. The areas of the country with pronounced rainy seasons are the Amazon and the Pantanal. In these regions the rainy season runs roughly from November to May and is marked by heavy, twice-daily downpours.

Rio de Janeiro is on the tropic of Capricorn, and its climate is just that—tropical. Summers are hot and humid. The same pattern holds true for all of the Brazilian coastline north of Rio, although temperatures are slightly higher year-round in Salvador. In the Amazon, where the equator crosses the country, temperatures are in the high 80s to the 90s (30s C) all year. In the south and in São Paulo, winter temperatures can fall to the low 40s (5°C–8°C). In the southernmost states, snowfalls occur in winter, although they're seldom more than dustings.

HOLIDAYS Major national holidays include: New Year's Day; Epiphany (Jan. 6); Carnaval (the week preceding Ash Wednesday); Good Friday (the Friday before Easter Sunday); Easter Sunday; Tiradentes Day (Apr. 21); Labor Day (May 1); Corpus Christi (60 days after Easter Sunday); Independence Day (Sept. 7); Our Lady of Aparecida Day (Oct. 12); All Souls' Day (Nov. 1); Declaration of the Republic Day (Nov. 15); and Christmas.

Language

The language in Brazil is Portuguese, not Spanish, and Brazilians will appreciate it if you know the difference. The two languages are distinct, but common origins mean many words are similar, and fluent speakers of Spanish will be able to make themselves understood. English is spoken among educated Brazilians and, in general, by at least some of the staff at hotels, tour operators, and travel agencies. Store clerks and waiters may speak a smattering of English; taxi and bus drivers won't. As in many places throughout the world, you're more likely to find English-speaking locals in major cities than in small towns or the countryside. In the northeast you may even have difficulty in the cities.

RIO DE JANEIRO

Updated by
Denise Oliveira

Welcome to the Cidade Maravilhosa, or the Marvelous City, as Rio is known in Brazil. Synonymous with the girl from Ipanema, the dramatic view from the Pão de Açúcar (Sugar Loaf), and famous Carnival celebrations, Rio is also a city of stunning architecture, good museums, and marvelous food. Rio is also home to 23 beaches, an almost continuous 73-km (45-mi) ribbon of sand.

As you leave the airport and head toward Ipanema or Copacabana, you'll drive for about half an hour on a highway from where you'll begin to get a sense of the city's dramatic contrast between beautiful landscape and devastating poverty. In this teeming metropolis, the very rich and the very poor live in uneasy proximity. But by the time you reach breezy, sunny Avenida Atlântica—flanked on one side by white beach and azure sea and on the other by condominiums and hotels—your heart will leap with expectation as you begin to recognize the postcard-famous sights. Now you're truly in Rio, where the 10 million *cariocas* (residents of the city of Rio) dwell and live life to its fullest.

Exploring Rio de Janeiro

Centro & Environs

Rio was settled in 1555, and much of the city's rich history is captured in traditional churches, government buildings, and villas, which are tucked in and around Centro. You can use the metro to get downtown, but wear comfortable shoes and be ready to walk multiple blocks as you explore this city's historic center. If you're not up for a long walk, consider taking an organized bus tour.

What locals generally refer to as Centro is a sprawling collection of several districts that contain the city's oldest neighborhoods, churches, and most enchanting cafés. Rio's beaches, broad boulevards, and modern architecture may be impressive; but its colonial structures, old narrow streets, and alleyways in leafy inland neighborhoods are no less so. The metro stations that serve Centro are Cinelândia, Carioca, Uruguaiana, Presidente Vargas, Central, and Praça Onze.

WHAT TO SEE

❺ **Arcos da Lapa.** Formerly the Aqueduto da Carioca (Carioca Aqueduct), this structure with 42 massive stone arches was built between 1744 and 1750 to carry water from the Carioca River in the hillside neighborhood of Santa Teresa to Centro. In 1896 the city transportation company converted the then-abandoned aqueduct to a viaduct, laying trolley tracks along it. Since then Rio's distinctive trolley cars (called "*bondes*" because they were financed by foreign bonds) have carried people between Santa Teresa and Centro. Guard your belongings particularly closely when you ride the open-sided bondes. ⊠ *Estação Carioca, Rua Professor Lélio Gama, Centro* ☎ *021/2240–5709 or 021/2240–5709* ⌧ *R$1* ⊙ *Bondes leave every 20 minutes 6 AM–10 PM* Ⓜ *Carioca or Cinelândia.*

❶ **Mosteiro de São Bento.** Just a glimpse of this church's main altar can fill you with awe. Layer upon layer of curvaceous wood carvings coated in gold create a sense of movement. Spiral columns whirl upward to capitals topped by cherubs so chubby and angels so purposeful they seem almost animated. Although the Benedictines arrived in 1586, they didn't begin work on this church and monastery until 1617. It was completed in 1641, but such artisans as Mestre Valentim (who designed the silver chandeliers) continued to add details almost through to the 19th century. Every Sunday at 10, mass is accompanied by Gregorian chants. ⊠ *Rua Dom Gerardo 68, Centro* ☎ *021/2291–7122* ⌧ *Free* ⊙ *Weekdays 7–11 and 2:30–5:30.*

❻ **Museu de Arte Moderna (MAM).** In a striking concrete-and-glass building, the Modern Art Museum has a collection of some 1,700 works by artists from Brazil and elsewhere. It also hosts significant special exhi-

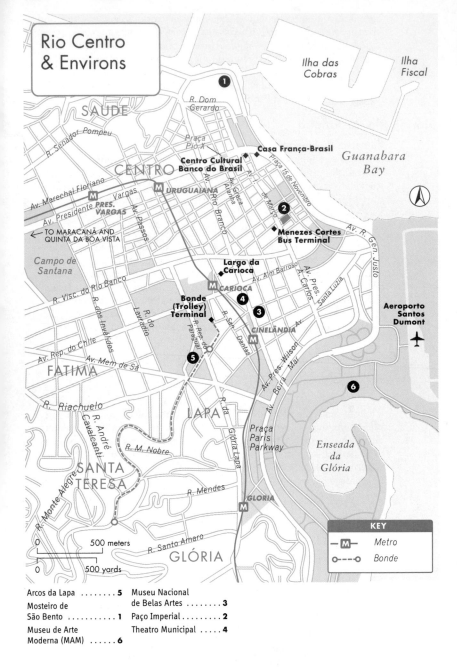

Rio Centro & Environs

Ilha das Cobras

Ilha Fiscal

Guanabara Bay

R. Dom Gerardo

SAUDE

Praça Pio X

Casa França-Brasil

Centro Cultural Banco do Brasil

CENTRO

Av. Marechal Floriano

Av. Presidente **PRES. VARGAS** Vargas

URUGUAIANA

← TO MARACANÃ AND QUINTA DA BOA VISTA

Menezes Cortes Bus Terminal

Campo de Santana

R. Visc. do Rio Banco

Largo da Carioca

CARIOCA

Bonde (Trolley) Terminal

CINELÂNDIA

Aeroporto Santos Dumont

FATIMA

Av. Rep. do Chile

Av. Mem de Sa

LAPA

R. Riachuelo

Praça Paris Parkway

Enseada da Glória

SANTA TERESA

R. Mendes

GLORIA

0 ——— 500 meters

0 ——— 500 yards

R. Santo Amaro

GLÓRIA

KEY

—M—	*Metro*
o—•—o	*Bonde*

Arcos da Lapa **5**

Mosteiro de São Bento **1**

Museu de Arte Moderna (MAM) **6**

Museu Nacional de Belas Artes **3**

Paço Imperial **2**

Theatro Municipal **4**

bitions and has a movie theater that plays art films. ☒ *Av. Infante Dom Henrique 85, Flamengo* ☎ *021/2240–4944* ⊕ *www.mamrio.org.br* ⊙ *Tues.–Fri. noon–6, weekends noon–7* ☒ *R$5* Ⓜ *Cinelândia.*

❸ **Museu Nacional de Belas Artes.** Works by Brazil's leading 19th- and 20th-century artists fill the space at the National Museum of Fine Arts. The most notable canvases are those by the country's best-known modernist, Cândido Portinari, but be on the lookout for such gems as Leandro Joaquim's heartwarming 18th-century painting of Rio (a window to a time when fishermen still cast nets in the waters below the landmark Igreja de Nossa Senhora da Glória do Outeiro). After wandering the picture galleries, tour the extensive collections of folk and African art. ☒ *Av. Rio Branco 199, Centro* ☎ *021/2240–0068* ⊕ *www.iphan.gov.br* ☒ *R$4, free Sun.* ⊙ *Tues.–Fri. 10–6, weekends 2–6* Ⓜ *Carioca or Cinelândia.*

❷ **Paço Imperial.** This two-story colonial building with thick stone walls and an ornate entrance was built in 1743, and for the next 60 years was the headquarters for Brazil's captains (viceroys), appointed by the Portuguese court in Lisbon. When King João VI arrived, he made it his royal palace. After Brazil's declaration of independence, emperors Dom Pedro I and II called the palace home. When the monarchy was overthrown, the building became Rio's central post office. Restoration work in the 1980s transformed it into a cultural center and concert hall. The building houses a restaurant, a coffee shop, a stationery-and-CD shop, and a movie theater. The square on which the palace sits, Praça 15 de Novembro, known in colonial days as Largo do Paço, has witnessed some of Brazil's most significant historic moments: it is where two emperors were crowned, slavery was abolished, and Emperor Pedro II was deposed. The square's modern name is a reference to the date of the declaration of the Republic of Brazil: November 15, 1889. ☒ *Praça 15 de Novembro 48, Centro* ☎ *021/ 2533–4407* ⊕ *www.pacoimperial.com.br* ☒ *Free* ⊙ *Tues.–Sun. noon–6.*

❹ **Theatro Municipal.** If you visit one place in Centro, make it this theater, modeled after the Paris Opera House and opened in 1909. Tons of Carrara marble, stunning mosaics, glittering chandeliers, bronze and onyx statues, gilded mirrors, German stained-glass windows, brazilwood inlay floors, and murals by Brazilian artists Eliseu Visconti and Rodolfo Amoedo make the Municipal Theater opulent indeed. The main entrance and first two galleries are particularly ornate. As you climb to the upper floors, the decor becomes simpler, a reflection of a time when different classes entered through different doors and sat in separate sections— but also due in part to the exhaustion of funds toward the end of the project. The theater seats 2,357—with outstanding sight lines—for its dance performances and classical music concerts. English-speaking guides are available. ☒ *Praça Floriano 210, Centro* ☎ *021/2299–1717* ☒ *Tours R$4* ⊙ *Tours begin every 30 minutes weekdays 10–5* ⊕ *www. theatromunicipal.rj.gov.br* Ⓜ *Cinelândia or Carioca.*

Zona Sul

Zona Sul is the heartbeat of Rio—a mix of residential areas, office buildings, shops, restaurants, bars, and beaches. It's the most affluent part of the city, with beautiful condos housing Rio's middle and upper class. It's also the most culturally diverse part of the city, home to dozens of theaters and music halls. The best-known neighborhoods of the Zona Sul are Copacabana, Ipanema, and Leblon.

COPACABANA & LEME

FodorsChoice ★

Praia de Copacabana. Maddening traffic, noise, packed apartment blocks, and a world-famous beach—this is Copacabana, or Manhattan with bikinis. Walk along the neighborhood's classic crescent to dive headfirst into Rio's beach culture, a cradle-to-grave lifestyle that begins with toddlers accompanying their parents to the water and ends with silver-haired seniors walking hand in hand along the sidewalk. Copacabana hums with activity: you're likely to see athletic men playing volleyball using only their feet and heads, not their hands—a sport Brazilians have dubbed *futevôlei*. As you can tell by all the goal nets, soccer is also popular, and Copacabana frequently hosts the annual world beach soccer championships. You can swim here, although pollution levels and a strong undertow can sometimes be discouraging. Pollution levels change daily and are well publicized; someone at your hotel should be able to get you the information.

Praia do Leme. A natural extension of Copacabana Beach to the northeast, toward the Pão de Açúcar, is Leme Beach. A rock formation juts into the water here, forming a quiet cove that's less crowded than the rest of the beach. Along a sidewalk, at the side of the mountain overlooking Leme, anglers stand elbow to elbow with their lines dangling into the sea. ✉ *Av. Princesa Isabel to Morro do Leme, Leme.*

IPANEMA & ARPOADOR

Praia do Arpoador. This beach, at the east end of Ipanema, has great waves for surfing. Non-surfers tend to avoid the water for fear of getting hit by boards. But it's popular for sunbathing. A short climb up the big rock formation gets you an amazingly gorgeous view of Ipanema. ✉ *Rua Joaquim Nabubo to Rua Francisco Otaviano, Arpoador.*

FodorsChoice ★

Praia de Ipanema. As you stroll along this beach, you catch a cross section of the city's residents, each favoring a particular stretch. One area is dominated by families (near Posto [Post] 10), another is favored by the gay community (near Posto 8). Throughout the day you'll see groups playing beach volleyball and soccer, and if you're lucky you'll even get to see Brazilian Olympic volleyball champions practicing on the beach. There are kiosks all along the boardwalk, where you can get anything from the typical coconut water to fried shrimp and turnovers. ✉ *Rua Joaquim Nabuco to Av. Epitácio Pessoa, Ipanema.*

THE GIRL FROM IPANEMA

Have you ever wondered if there really *was* a girl from Ipanema? The song was inspired by schoolgirl Heloisa Pinheiro, who caught the fancy of songwriter Antônio Carlos (aka Tom) Jobim and his pal lyricist Vinicius de Moraes as she walked past the two bohemians sitting in their favorite bar. They then penned one of last century's classics. That was in 1962, and today the bar has been renamed **Bar Garota de Ipanema** (✉ Rua Vinicius de Moraes 49-A, Ipanema ☎ 021/2523–3787).

CLOSE UP

Why Rio's Carnival Rules

MANY PEOPLE TOUT THE VIRTUES of Carnival in Salvador and other cities in Brazil, but Rio's Carnival is the real deal. After all, it was here that the whole thing started. The first samba schools appeared in Rio in the 19th century, and it was here that the parades happened for the first time. It is no accident that for every Carnival (in February or early March, depending on where Lent falls on the calendar), Brazil comes to a halt to see the parades in Rio de Janeiro. In those four days (Saturday, Sunday, Monday, and Tuesday) it's said that Brazilians think only of samba, women, and beer—Rio's Carnival triad. Without the three, the party is not complete, Brazilians say.

The *mulatas*, women fantasically dressed in barely-there sequin-and-feather-adorned costumes, are at the head of the parades. They are what one generally thinks of when Brazilian Carnival comes to mind—so again, what is considered a quintessential part of Carnival was born in Rio. Right behind them comes the rousing percussion wing. Then come the floats, full of color, over three meters high. Beautiful women with the tiniest of golden bikinis ride them, sensually dancing the samba, accompanied on the street level by the various *alas* (wings, or sections), of the *escola de samba* (samba school). Each of the 14 schools creates an overall theme with its floats, costumes, music, and dancers; each wing of the school wears a different type of costume, all of them breathtaking. In some cases, more than $1 million is spent on the extravagant displays. Rehearsals for the better part of a year lead to one hour-and-twenty-minute performance for each samba school. At the end of Carnival, the best samba school is elected the champion of the year's parade by a group of jurors, in a dispute closely followed by millions of Brazilians throughout the country.

Though past Carnivals took place in Centro, today the parades are in the Sambódromo, a huge stadium, open only for Carnival, that was designed by the renowned architect Oscar Niemeyer and built in the heart of the city in 1984. It can be reached by subway or by taxi, and admittance tickets cost US$30—but if you want a seat, you'll pay between US$200 and $1,000. The Brazilian Tourism Office has links to a Sambódromo map on its Web site (www.braziltourism.org/sambodromo.shtml) and great tips about which seats to choose.

The *carioca* (resident of Rio) makes no distinction between Brazilians and foreigners at Carnival, and even those who have no familiarity whatsoever with samba are welcome to participate in the event. To join a samba school all you have to do is attend one of the rehearsals in the school's headquarters and pay about US$200 for a costume (this includes the admittance ticket). Then just join the party!

–by Carla Aranha

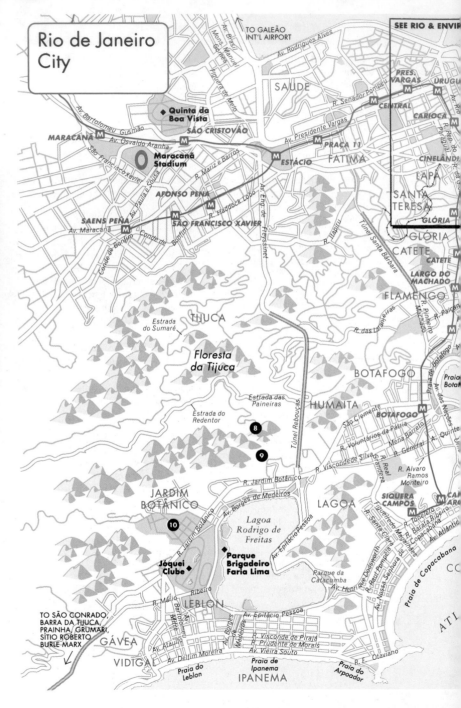

Rio de Janeiro City

TO GALEÃO INT'L AIRPORT

SEE RIO & ENVIR

SAÚDE

PRES. VARGAS

URUGU

Av. Rodrigues Alves

R. Senador Pompeu

CENTRAL

CARIOCA

◆ **Quinta da Boa Vista**

MARACANÃ

Av. Osvaldo Aranha

SÃO CRISTÓVÃO

Av. Presidente Vargas

PRAÇA 11

CINELÂNDI

○ **Maracanã Stadium**

ESTÁCIO

FÁTIMA

LAPA

SANTA TERESA

AFONSO PENA

R. Mariz e Barros

R. Haddock Lobo

GLÓRIA

SAENS PEÑA

Av. Maracanã

SÃO FRANCISCO XAVIER

Av. Eng. de Freyssinet

GLÓRIA

CATETE

CATETE

LARGO DO MACHADO

FLAMENGO

Estrada do Sumaré

TIJUCA

Floresta da Tijuca

R. das Laranjeiras

BOTAFOGO

Praia Bota

Estrada das Paineiras

HUMAITÁ

São Clemente

BOTAFOGO

Estrada do Redentor

8

Túnel Rebouças

R. Voluntários da Pátria

Mena Barreto

R. General

A. Quinte

9

R. Visconde de Silva

R. Álvaro Ramos Monteiro

R. Jardim Botânico

SIQUEIRA CAMPOS

CA AR

JARDIM BOTÂNICO

Av. Borges de Medeiros

LAGOA

10

Lagoa Rodrigo de Freitas

Av. Epitácio Pessoa

Praia de Copacabana

Jóquei Clube ◆

◆ **Parque Brigadeiro Faria Lima**

Parque da Catacumba

Av. Henrique

Ribeiro

LEBLON

R. Mário

Av. Bartolomeu Mitre

TO SÃO CONRADO, BARRA DA TIJUCA, PRAINHA, GRUMARI, SÍTIO ROBERTO BURLE MARX

GÁVEA

Av. Epitácio Pessoa

R. Visconde de Pirajá

R. Prudente de Morais

Av. Vieira Souto

VIDIGAL

Av. Delfim Moreira

Praia do Leblon

Praia de Ipanema

IPANEMA

R. F. Otaviano

Praia do Arpoador

Praia de Copacabana

ATL

S DETAIL MAP

Ilha das Cobras

Guanabara Bay

Menezes Cortes Bus Terminal

Aeroporto Santos Dumont

Parque do Flamengo

Praia do Flamengo

URCA

Av. João Luis Alves

Praia de Fora

Praia da Urca

Av. Portugal

7

VERMELHA

Gustavo Sampaio

LEME

Praia do Leme

OCEAN

ABANA

| 0 | | 1 mile |
| 0 | | 1 km |

KEY	
—Ⓜ—	*Metro*
⊢⊢⊢⊢	*Street Car*
••••	*Cable Car*

The Lush Inland

In the western portion of the city north of Leblon, trees and hills dominate the landscape in the neighborhoods of Jardim Botânico, Lagoa, Cosme Velho, and Tijuca. In addition their parks and gardens, these primarily residential neighborhoods have marvelous museums, seductive architecture, and tantalizing restaurants. The architecture is a mix of modern condominiums and colonial houses. They tend to be quieter neighborhoods during the day because they are not on the beachfront, but also have some of the hippest nightclubs in Rio. You can't say you've seen Rio until you've taken in the view from Corcovado and then strolled through its forested areas or beside its inland Lagoa (Lagoon) Rodrigo de Freitas—hanging out just like a true carioca.

Public transportation doesn't conveniently reach the sights here; take a taxi or a tour.

Numbers in the margin correspond to numbers on the Rio de Janeiro City map.

JARDIM BOTÂNICO ❿ **Jardim Botânico.** The 340-acre Botanical Garden contains more than 5,000 species of tropical and subtropical plants and trees, including 900 varieties of palms (some more than a century old) and more than 140 species of birds. The temperature is usually a good 12°C (22°F) cooler in the shady garden that was created in 1808 by Portuguese king João VI during his exile in Brazil. In 1842 the garden gained its most impressive adornment, the Avenue of the Royal Palms, a 720-meter (800-yard) double row of 134 soaring royal palms. Elsewhere in the gardens, the Casa dos Pilões, an old gunpowder factory, has been restored and displays objects that pertained to both the nobility and their slaves. Also on the grounds are a library, a small café, and a gift shop that sells souvenirs with ecological themes. ☒ *Rua Jardim Botânico 1008, Jardim Botânico* ☎ *021/2294–9349* ⊕ *www.jbrj.gov.br* ☒ *R$4* ☉ *Daily 8–5. Guided tours by appointment.*

COSME VELHO ❽ Fodor'sChoice ★ **Corcovado.** There's an eternal argument about which view is better, from Pão de Açúcar (Sugar Loaf) or from here. In our opinion, it is best to visit Sugar Loaf *before* you visit Corcovado, or you will remember Sugar Loaf only as an anticlimax. Corcovado has two advantages: at 690 meters (2,300 feet), it's nearly twice as high and offers an excellent view of Pão de Açúcar itself. The sheer 300-meter (1,000-foot) granite face of Corcovado (the name means "hunchback" and refers to the mountain's shape) has always been a difficult undertaking for climbers.

Visit Corcovado on a clear day; clouds often obscure the Christ statue and the view of the city. Go as early in the morning as possible, before people start pouring out of the tour buses, and before the haze sets in. ☒ *Estrada da Redentor, Cosme Velho* ⊕ *www.corcovado.org.br* ☒ *R$5* ☉ *Daily 9–6.*

TIJUCA ❾ **Floresta da Tijuca** (Quagmire Forest). Surrounding Corcovado is the dense, tropical Tijuca Forest. Once part of a Brazilian nobleman's estate, it's studded with exotic trees and thick jungle vines and has a delightful waterfall, the Cascatinha de Taunay. About 180 meters (200 yards) beyond the waterfall is the small pink-and-purple Capela Mayrink (Mayrink Chapel), with painted panels by the 20th-century Brazilian artist Cândido Portinari. ⊠ *Entrance at Praça Afonso Viseu 561, Tijuca* ☏ *021/2492–2253* 🔖 *Free* ◷ *Daily 8–5.*

Urca

Tiny sheltered Urca faces Botafogo. The quiet neighborhood with single-family homes and tree-lined streets is separated by the Pão de Açúcar from a small underwhelming patch of yellow sand called Praia Vermelha. This beach is, in turn, blocked by the Urubu and Leme mountains from the 1-km (½-mi) Leme Beach at the start of the Zona Sul.

★ ❼ **Pão de Açúcar** (Sugar Loaf). This soaring 1,300-meter (approximately 4,290-foot) granite block at the mouth of Baía de Guanabara was originally called *pau-nh-acugua* (high, pointed peak) by the indigenous Tupi people. To the Portuguese the phrase seemed similar to *pão de açúcar*; the rock's shape reminded them of the conical loaves in which refined sugar was sold. Italian-made bubble cars holding 75 passengers each move up the mountain in two stages. The first stop is at Morro da Urca, a smaller, 212-meter (705-foot) mountain; the second is at the summit of Pão de Açúcar itself. The trip to each level takes three minutes. In high season long lines form for the cable car; the rest of the year the wait is seldom more than 30 minutes. ⊠ *Av. Pasteur 520, Praia Vermelha, Urca* ☏ *021/2546–8400* ⊕ *www.bondinho.com.br* 🔖 *R$30* ◷ *Daily 8 AM–10 PM.*

Where to Eat

Centro

CAFÉS ✕ **Confeitaria Colombo.** At the turn of the 20th century this belle époque
¢ structure was Rio's preeminent café, the site of elaborate balls, after-
Fodor$Choice noon teas for upper-class *senhoras,* and a center of political intrigue and
★ gossip. Enormous Jacaranda-framed mirrors from Belgium, stained glass from France, and tiles from Portugal add to the art-nouveau decor. Meals are buffet-style, with classic Brazilian dishes. The best way to absorb the opulence is as Rio's high society did a century ago: with *chá da tarde,* or afternoon tea (R$32). But you can also just stop by for a pastry and coffee. ⊠ *Rua Gonçalves Dias 32, Centro* ☏ *021/2232–2300* ⊕ *www.confeitariacolombo.com.br* ▤ *AE, DC, MC, V* ◷ *Closed Sun. No dinner* Ⓜ *Carioca.*

SEAFOOD ✕ **Albamar.** Opened in 1933, Albamar faces Guanabara Bay. The restau-
$$–$$$ rant is owned by the waitstaff, assuring efficient service. The circular green building serves fine seafood and fish. The chef's-style *à moda* dishes are good choices. The menu lists a fish fillet with white-wine sauce, sour cream, shrimp, and mussels, served with mashed potatoes; Spanish-style octopus with potatoes; and six codfish balls. Albamar closes at 6 PM. ⊠ *Praça Marechal Âncora 186, Centro* ☏ *021/2240–8428* ▤ *AE, DC, MC, V* ◷ *No dinner. Closed Mon.* Ⓜ *Carioca.*

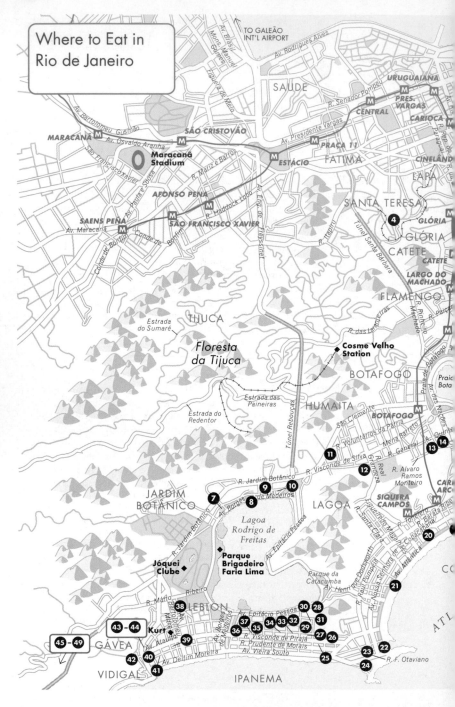

Where to Eat in
Rio de Janeiro

VEGETARIAN
¢–$

✕ **Bistrô do Paço.** A good option for a light lunch, the daily buffet of salads (R$14 per person) includes carrot salad with oranges, potatoes, and apples. You also can try an onion, cheese, or spinach quiche. ⊠ *Praça Quinze 48, Centro* ☎ *021/2262-3613* ▭ *AE, D, MC, V* ◷ *Closes at 7:30 during the week and at 7 on weekends* Ⓜ *Uruguaiana.*

Copacabana & Leme

BRAZILIAN
$$$$

✕ **Marius.** This well-regarded churrascaria serves more than a dozen types of sizzling meats rodízio style. Marius is famed for taking the usual meat cuts to a higher level of sophistication. The variety of side dishes is good, and includes Japanese food and fish. ⊠ *Av. Atlântica 290A, Leme* ☎ *021/2104-9000* ▭ *AE, DC, MC, V.*

$$$–$$$$

✕ **Siri Mole.** For typical food from the northeast of Brazil, this is the place. It's a small but absolutely comfortable restaurant that makes exotic dishes such as *acarajé*, a mix of fried smashed white beans and shrimp. Don't miss the *moqueca de siri*, a crab stew with *dendê* oil (spicy orange palm oil), and coconut milk. ⊠ *Rua Francisco Otaviano 50, Copacabana* ☎ *021/2267-0894* ▭ *AE, DC, MC, V* Ⓜ *Siqueira Campos, then shuttle bus to Praça General Osório, get off at last stop in Copacabana.*

ECLECTIC
$–$$

✕ **Aipo & Aipim.** There are more than 20 salads and hot dishes at this self-serve eatery with live music. After walking through the hot-dish and salad buffet, take your plate up to the grill and pick steaks, chicken, and pork cuts. Waiters take orders for drinks at your table. There are multiple branches in Copacabana and one in Ipanema. The Ipanema branch is only open until 6. ⊠ *Nossa Senhora de Copacabana 391, Loja B, Copacabana* ☎ *021/2255-6285* ▭ *AE, DC, MC, V* Ⓜ *Cardeal Arcoverde* ⊠ *Rua Visconde de Pirajá 145, Ipanema* ☎ *021/2522-7300* ▭ *AE, DC, MC, V* Ⓜ *Siqueira Campos then shuttle bus to Praça General Osório.*

FRENCH
$$$$

✕ **Le Pré-Catalan.** Considered the best French cuisine in Rio, this is the *carioca* version of the charming Parisian restaurant of the same name in the Bois du Boulogne. This highly reputed establishment has a prix-fixe menu (R$110) with four choices for appetizers, main dish, and dessert that changes periodically. À la carte options average around R$45, and include such specialties as a lamb dish that is cooked for seven hours. ⊠ *Sofitel Rio Palace, Av. Atlântica 4240, Level E, Copacabana* ☎ *021/2525-1160* ◬ *Reservations essential* ▭ *AE, DC, MC, V* ◷ *No lunch* Ⓜ *No metro.*

★ $$$$

✕ **Le Saint Honoré.** An extraordinary view of Copacabana Beach from the 37th floor of Le Meridien hotel accompanies fine French–Brazilian fusion cuisine at Le Saint Honoré, which has prix-fixe and à la carte options. Typical French dishes are combined with Brazilian specialties in popular dishes like smoked *surubim* (an Amazonian fish) served in a shrimp sauce and marinated in three different types of local olive oils, and lamb fillet with *farofa* (fried yucca flour) and a corn beignet. The esteemed magazine *Veja Rio* rated this the number-one French restaurant in Rio for 2005. ⊠ *Av. Atlântica 1020, 37th floor, Copacabana* ☎ *021/3873-8880* ◬ *Reservations essential* 🎩 *Jacket and tie* ▭ *AE, DC, MC, V.*

ITALIAN
★ $$$–$$$$

✕ **D'Amici.** This place has the largest wine list in Rio, with 300 labels, ranging from R$26 to R$10,000—for the Romanée Conti—and also serves 30 types of wine by the glass (R$7–R$26). The restaurant is consistently a favorite in Rio for its food and atmosphere. The lamb with arugula risotto is a specialty, and the pasta in general is the best choice. ⊠ *Rua Antônio Vieira 18, Leme* ☎ *021/2541–4477* ⊟ *AE, DC, MC, V* ⌲ *Reservations essential.*

★ **$$$–$$$$** ✕ **Cipriani.** For a superb dining experience, start with a Cipriani, champagne with fresh peach juice (really a Bellini), and move on to an appetizer of snook carpaccio with eggplant and capers or a salad of endive marinated in red wine. The pasta dishes are prepared with great care, and the meat and fish entrées are appropriate to their lavish surroundings—with a view to the hotel's beautiful pool. The degustation menu is R$180, or R$295 with wine. ⊠ *Copacabana Palace hotel, Av. Atlântica 1702, Copacabana* ☎ *021/2545–8747* ⌲ *Reservations essential* ⊟ *AE, DC, MC, V* Ⓜ *Cardeal Arcoverde.*

SEAFOOD
$$–$$$$ ✕ **Azul Marinho.** Sophisticated is the first word that comes to mind when you enter this quiet restaurant with formal service and a giant panoramic window looking out onto a barely trafficked street across from Arpoador Beach. *Moqueca* is the specialty, made with shrimp, cod, lobster, crab, or octopus—or a mix of them all. Meals are elegant and the seafood is fresh, but our favorite reason to go to Azul Marinho is to sit at its outdoor tables near the beach, enjoying early-evening appetizers, drinks, and sunset. ⊠ *Av. Francisco Bhering s/n, Arpoador* ☎ *021/3813–4228* ⊕ *www.cozinhatipica.com.br* ⊟ *AE, D, DC, MC, V.*

$–$$$$ ✕ **Shirley.** Homemade Spanish seafood casseroles and soups are the draw at this traditional Leme restaurant tucked onto a shady street. Try the *zarzuela*, a seafood soup, or *cazuela*, a fish fillet with white-wine sauce. Don't be turned off by the simple decor (a few paintings hung on wood-paneled walls): the food is terrific. ⊠ *Rua Gustavo Sampaio 610, Leme* ☎ *021/2275–1398* ⌲ *Reservations not accepted* ⊟ *No credit cards.*

¢–$$ ✕ **Don Camillo.** There's always something new on the menu at this Copacabana beachfront restaurant. Try the baked mix of lobster, shrimp, squid, mussels, tomato, potato, and fresh fish of the day, or stick to their delicious thin crust pizza. The Italian atmosphere is completed by a musical group that sings traditional Italian songs. ⊠ *Av. Atlântica 3056, Copacabana* ☎ *021/2549–9958* ⊕ *www.tempero.com.br/doncamillo/index.htm* ⊟ *AE, D, DC, MC, V* Ⓜ *Cardeal Arcoverde.*

Flamengo & Botafogo

BRAZILIAN
$$–$$$$ ✕ **Yorubá.** Exotic and delicious dishes are served at this restaurant, one of the few places that go beyond traditional African–Brazilian cuisine. Try the Afro menu, a selection of contemporary West African dishes. Service can be slow, but you are well rewarded for the wait. The *piripiri* (a spicy rice with ginger, coconut milk, and shrimp) is worth the price of R$65 for two. ⊠ *Rua Arnaldo Quintela 94, Botafogo* ☎ *021/2541–9387* ⊟ *AE, V* Ⓜ *Botafogo.*

$$$
FodorsChoice
★ ✕ **Porcão.** The ultimate in Brazilian churrascaria experiences, Porcão has bow-tied waiters who flit between linen-draped tables, wielding giant skewers, and slicing you portions of sizzling barbecued beef, pork, and chicken until you say uncle. The buffet is huge, with salads, sushi, and,

on Saturdays, more than 15 types of feijoada. (Hats off if you can do churrasco *and* feijoada in one sitting!) Porção is a chain, with four restaurants in Rio—including the one in Ipanema (⇨ *below*)—and another in the suburb of Niterói, but the nearly floor-to-ceiling windows with a view over Guanabara Bay to the Sugar Loaf make the Flamengo branch our top choice. ⊠ *Av. Infante Dom Henrique, Parque do Flamengo* ☎ *021/2554–8535* ⊟ *AE, DC, MC, V* Ⓜ *Siqueira Campos, then shuttle bus to Praça General Osório* Ⓜ *Flamengo.*

ECLECTIC ✕ **Alho & Óleo.** Home-made pasta is the hallmark of this place of vivid
$$–$$$$ European inspiration. There are many options, including *picatina alcapone* (beef fillet with lime sauce), and sage-and-ricotta tortellini. Finish with a pear dessert cooked in white wine with vanilla ice cream and chocolate topping. ⊠ *Rua Buarque de Macedo 13, Flamengo* ☎ *021/ 2225–3418* ⊟ *AE, V, MC, DC* Ⓜ *Catete.*

FRENCH ✕ **Carême.** This charming bistro, decorated in a romantic style, offers
$$$$ several fine prix-fixe menus (R$138 each) as well as an extensive à la carte menu (a fish dish, for instance, would average around R$50). The restaurant prides itself in using lots of organic ingredients, and serves delicious desserts. ⊠ *Rua Visconde de Caravelas 113, Botafogo* ☎ *021/ 2537–2274* ⚑ *Reservations essential* ☽ *No lunch* ⊟ *AE, DC, MC, V* Ⓜ *Botafogo.*

ITALIAN ✕ **Pizza Park.** This enormous pizzeria is part of the hip Cobal Humaitá
$ complex, which houses about a dozen bars and restaurants, whose mostly outdoor tables and chairs abut one another to create a lively scene that extends late into the night. It's a great place to hang out with friends, and the waitstaff will let you linger over your pizza and beer for as long as you like. More than 30 varieties of pizza are on the menu. ⊠ *Rua Voluntários da Pátria 446, Botafogo* ☎ *021/2537–5383 or 021/2537–2602* ⊟ *AE, DC, MC, V.*

PORTUGUESE ✕ **Adega do Valentim.** Generous portions of cod, goat, and stews easily
$–$$$$ serve two or three people. The appetizers, especially the *bolinho de bacalhau* (fried cod dumplings), are popular. The restaurant is near Rio Sul Shopping Center, on the way from Copacabana Beach to Guanabara Bay. ⊠ *Rua da Passagem 178, Botafogo* ☎ *021/2541–1166* ⊟ *AE, D, DC, MC, V.*

Ipanema & Leblon

BRAZILIAN ✕ **Esplanada Grill.** This churrascaria serves high-quality meat like T-bone
$$$–$$$$ steak or *picanha,* a tasty Brazilian cut of beef marbled with some fat. All the grilled dishes come with fried palm hearts, baked potatoes, and rice. An average meal is R$90. ⊠ *Rua Barão da Torre 600, Ipanema* ☎ *021/2512–2970* ⊟ *AE, DC, MC, V* Ⓜ *Siqueira Campos, then shuttle bus to Praça General Osório.*

★ $$$ ✕ **Porção.** A convenient location makes this branch of Rio's famous churrascaria the most popular one with tourists, but we prefer the Flamengo branch (⇨ *above*) for its fabulous view. You'll get the same excellent service and quality of food here, but in a smaller space with no view. ⊠ *Rua Barão da Torre 218, Ipanema* ☎ *021/2522–0999* ⊟ *AE, DC, MC, V* Ⓜ *Siqueira Campos, then shuttle bus to Praça General Osório.*

★ **\$\$** ✕ **Casa da Feijoada.** Many restaurants serve Brazil's savory national dish on Saturdays, but here the huge pots of the stew simmer every day. You can choose which of the nine types of meat you want in your stew, but if it's your first time, waiters will bring you a "safe" version with sausage, beef, and pork—and sans feet and ears. The feijoada comes with the traditional side dishes of rice, collard greens, *farofa* (toasted and seasoned manioc flour), *aipim* (fried yucca), *torresminho* (pork rinds), and orange slices (to lower your cholesterol!). Not feeling like the feijoada? The menu has entrées as well, like baked chicken, shrimp in coconut milk, grilled trout, and filet mignon. Desserts include *quindim* (a yolk-and-sugar pudding with coconut crust) and Romeo and Juliet (guava compote with fresh cheese). The caipirinhas are made not only with lime but also with tangerine, passion fruit, pineapple, strawberry, or kiwi. Be careful—they're strong. ⊠ *Rua Prudente de Morais 10, Ipanema* ☎ *021/2247–2776* ⊕ *www.cozinhatipica.com.br* ⊟ *AE, DC, MC, V* Ⓜ *Siqueira Campos, then shuttle bus to Praça General Osório.*

¢–\$\$ ✕ **Jobi.** Not to be missed, Jobi is a Leblon institution—and since it's open daily from 9 AM to 4 AM, you should be able to squeeze it in. It's the sort of place you can go to in your bikini straight from the beach. Basic sandwiches and salads are on the menu, but the reason to go is the fabulous seafood. Order a full meal or just try various appetizers. The *bolinho de bacalhau* (mini cod cakes) may be the best in town. ⊠ *Rua Ataulfo de Paiva 1166, Leblon* ☎ *021/2274–0547* ⊟ *AE* ☺ *Breakfast served.*

¢–\$ ✕ **Colher de Pau.** Just two blocks from Ipanema Beach, this chilled-out place is a great place for a bite during or after a day in the sun. It's open from breakfast through dinner, and serves good sandwiches and salads plus healthy grilled fish or steak, and great desserts. ⊠ *Rua Farme de Amoedo 39, Ipanema* ☎ *021/2523–3018* ⊟ *AE, DC, MC, V* ☺ *Breakfast served.*

¢–\$ ✕ **New Natural.** One of many restaurants in Rio where you pay per kilo, this one stands out for its use of natural and organic products. You'll have multiple vegetarian options and lots of soy-based dishes. They also serve delicious fruit juices. On hot days, choose the somewhat hidden upstairs dining room, which is air-conditioned. ⊠ *Rua Barão da Torre, Ipanema* ☎ *021/2247–1335* ⊟ *AE, DC, MC, V.*

CAFÉS ✕ **Garcia & Rodrigues.** Cariocas breakfast at this cozy combination café, ★ ¢–\$\$ delicatessen, liquor shop, and trendy restaurant. At lunchtime choose from a selection of sandwiches, such as marinated salmon, pastrami, or buffalo-milk cheese. Dinner, based on French cuisine, is served until 12:30 AM Monday–Thursday and until 1 AM Friday and Saturday. On Sunday nights the café is open until midnight, but à la carte meals are not served. ⊠ *Av. Ataulfo de Paiva 1251, Leblon* ☎ *021/2512–8188* ⊟ *AE, DC, MC, V.*

¢–\$\$ ✕ **Gula Gula.** Salads at upscale café Gula Gula are anything but boring. Beyond classics like Caesar and chicken pesto, fresh local fruits and veggies are mixed into salads like eggplant with tomatoes, herbs, *queijo Minas* (a mild, white cheese), and mint dressing, or organic palm heart with tomatoes, watercress, and raisins. Grilled fish or steak, baked potatoes, and soups are good non-salad options. ⊠ *Rua Anibal de Mendonça*

132, Ipanema ☎ *021/2259–3084* ⊕ *www.gulagula.com.br* ⊟ *AE, DC, MC, V.*

ECLECTIC ✕ **Doce Delícia.** Make your own dish by choosing from 5 to 15 of the
¢–$ 42 combinations of vegetables, side dishes, hot dishes, and fruit. Quiche,
salmon, grilled tenderloin, chicken, and cold pasta are some of the
choices. Dressings range from the light and yogurt based to innovative
creations combining mustard and lemon. There are plenty of vegetarian options. The slick decor and fresh ingredients make this a popular
choice for a regular clientele in the trendy area of Ipanema. For a reasonable price you can also pick main dishes from the menu—for example, the chicken breast with honey and rosemary sauce for R$17. ⊠ *Rua
Aníbal de Mendonça 55, Ipanema* ☎ *021/2259–0239* ⊟ *AE, MC, V.*

¢–$ ✕ **Fazendola.** The name means "small farm," and this restaurant is rem-
iniscent of a Brazilian farm with its wooden furniture and dim lighting.
Homemade dishes prepared with very fresh ingredients are sold by the
kilo. The other option is to try their delicious pizza, which you can order
either à la carte or "all you can eat." ⊠ *Rua Jangadeiros 14B, Ipanema*
☎ *021/2247–9600* ⊟ *AE, DC, MC, V* Ⓜ *Siqueira Campos, then shuttle bus to Praça General Osório.*

INDIAN ✕ **Natraj.** One block from Leblon's beachfront, this traditional Indian
$–$$ restaurant has a tasting menu for two, with eight portions of different
dishes, a good option for a reasonable price. It can be ordered in vegetarian or nonvegetarian versions. Other suggestions are the many *pulau*
(rice) and *dhal* (bean or pea) dishes, which may come with vegetables,
coconut, fresh white cheese, or *panir,* and spices, or masala. You can
also order à la carte. Good options for starters, the *samosas* are fine pastries with chicken, beef, mixed-vegetable, or potato-and-pea fillings. ⊠ *Av.
General San Martin 1219, Leblon* ☎ *021/2239–4745* ⊟ *D, MC, V.*

ITALIAN ✕ **Gero.** This high-end restaurant serves homemade pastas and risottos,
$$–$$$ and fish and meat dishes. Vegetarian options are plentiful. Typical Ital-
ian desserts served include gelato and profiteroles. ⊠ *Rua Anibal de Men-
donca 157, Ipanema* ☎ *21/2239–8158* ⊟ *AE, D, DC, MC, V.*

$–$$$$ ✕ **Margutta.** Just a block from Ipanema Beach, Margutta has a reputa-
tion for outstanding Mediterranean-style seafood, such as broiled fish
in tomato sauce and fresh herbs or lobster cooked in aluminum foil with
butter and saffron rice. Polenta is made with fancy funghi and olive oil
flavored with white truffles. ⊠ *Av. Henrique Dumont 62, Ipanema*
☎ *021/2511–0878* ⊟ *AE, DC, MC, V* ⊗ *No lunch weekdays.*

$–$$ ✕ **Cappriciosa.** There are lots of pizza places in Rio, but this one emerges
at the top of the list. Delicious thin-crust pizzas are served with every
topping imaginable, from the standard margheritta to fancy prosciut-
tos and interesting spices. Its tall glass windows and location in the heart
of Ipanema make for perfect people-watching. ⊠ *Rua Vinicius de
Moraes 175, Ipanema* ☎ *021/2523–3394* ⊟ *AE, DC, MC* ⊗ *No lunch.*

JAPANESE ✕ **Madame Butterfly.** At this fine Japanese restaurant, start with pump-
$$–$$$$ kin *gyoza* (dumplings) with shrimp, a platter with six rolls, or the Bei-
jing duck salad, a mix of greens and shredded duck with tangerine
sauce. Main dishes include grilled salmon with honey and miso, and the

best sukiyaki in Rio. ✉ *Rua Barão da Torre 472, Ipanema* 🕾 *021/ 2267–4347* 🖃 *AE, V.*

MEXICAN
$–$$
✕ **Guapo Loco.** Bustling crowds feast on tamales, enchiladas, and other Mexican favorites until the last customer leaves. Tequila has garnered quite a following in Rio, making Guapo Loco one of the favorite Mexıcan places thanks to its good margaritas. ✉ *Rua Rainha Guilhermina 48, Leblon* 🕾 *021/2294–2915* 🖃 *MC, V* ⊘ *No lunch weekdays.*

PORTUGUESE
$$$–$$$$
Fodor'sChoice
★
✕ **Antiquarius.** This much-loved establishment is famous for its flawless rendering of Portuguese classics. A recommended dish is the *cozido*, a stew with onions, yams, carrots, pumpkin, cabbage, bananas, and more. The *cataplana*, a seafood stew with rice, is also marvelous, and the *perna de cordeiro* (leg of lamb) is the most requested dish on the menu. The wine list impresses even Portuguese gourmands. ✉ *Rua Aristides Espínola 19, Leblon* 🕾 *021/2294–1049* 🖎 *Reservations essential* 🖃 *DC, MC.*

SEAFOOD
$$$–$$$$
Fodor'sChoice
★
✕ **Satyricon.** Some of the best seafood in town is served at this eclectic Italian seafood restaurant, which has impressed the likes of Madonna and Sting. The *pargo* (fish baked in a thick layer of rock salt) is a specialty, and the sushi and sashimi are well loved. ✉ *Rua Barão da Torre 192, Ipanema* 🕾 *021/2521–0627* 🖃 *DC, MC, V* Ⓜ *Siqueira Campos, then shuttle bus to Praça General Osório.*

VEGETARIAN *Also see* New Natural *in* Brazilian, *above.*

$$
✕ **Celeiro.** One of Rio's few organic restaurants, Celeiro is always full. There are approximately 20 salads on the buffet, as well as a wide selection of pastas. ✉ *Rua Dias Ferreira 199, Leblon* 🕾 *021/2274–7843* 🖃 *D, MC, V* ⊘ *No dinner. Closed Sun.*

$–$$
✕ **Vegetariano Social Clube.** Vegan restaurants are rare in Rio, and this is by far the most sophisticated. The small eatery has carefully prepared dishes free of any animal products that go much beyond brown rice or burdock. ✉ *Rua Conde de Bernadotte 26, Loja L, Leblon* 🕾 *021/ 2294–5200* ⊕ *www.vegetarianosocialclube.com.br* 🖃 *D, MC, V.*

Jardim Botanico

FRENCH
$$$$
Fodor'sChoice
★
✕ **Olympe.** The menu's all-Brazilian ingredients are a unique trait of this innovative restaurant that blends native flavors with nouvelle techniques. Every dish—from the crab or lobster flan to chicken, fish, and duck prepared with exotic herbs and sauces—is exceptionally light. The passion-fruit crepe soufflé is a favorite dessert. ✉ *Rua Custódio Serrão 62, Jardim Botânico* 🕾 *021/2537–8582* 🖎 *Reservations essential* 🖃 *AE, MC, V.*

ITALIAN
$$–$$$
Fodor'sChoice
★
✕ **Quadrifoglio.** Considered by most locals to be the best Italian restaurant in the city, cozy Quadrifoglio is tucked away on a quiet street. The food and the service are impeccable; the restaurant has been around since 1991 and much of the original waitstaff still works there. Some favorite entrée choices are spinach ravioli and the fabulous salads. Leave room for desserts, which are what the place is most famous for. ✉ *Rua J. J. Seabra 19, Jardim Botanico* 🕾 *021/2294–1433* ⊘ *No dinner Sun., no lunch Sat.* 🖃 *AE, DC, MC, V.*

Lagoa

ECLECTIC
$$–$$$

✕ Mistura Fina. A combination of traditional Portuguese and Brazilian dishes is combined with elegant design here, making this an excellent choice for a romantic dinner out. Above the restaurant there is live music and an outdoor balcony, so you can enjoy dinner and then spend the rest of your evening just upstairs. The service can be slow, but the food is well worth the wait. ⊠ *Av. Borges de Medeiros 3207, Lagoa* ☎ *021/ 2537–2844* ⊕ *www.misturafina.com.br* ⊟ *AE, DC, MC.*

Santa Teresa

BRAZILIAN
$–$$

✕ Bar do Arnaudo. A neighborhood favorite for 30-plus years, this informal tavern serves generous portions of unusual Brazilian food. Case in point: goat and broccoli with *pirão* (cassava mush) and rice. Portions are large enough to serve two or even three. For dessert, sweetened condensed milk is cooked to a creamy caramel-like paste and served atop slices of *coalho* (a semihard cow cheese). Arnaudo has nice views of the city and Guanabara Bay. ⊠ *Rua Almirante Alexandrino 316-B, Santa Teresa* ☎ *021/2252–7246* ⊟ *MC.*

São Conrado, Barra da Tijuca & Beyond

BRAZILIAN
$$–$$$

✕ Barra Grill. A favorite stop after a long day at Praia Barra, this informal and popular steak house serves some of the best meat in town. Prices for the rodízio-style meals are slightly higher on weekends than during the week. Reservations are essential on weekends. ⊠ *Av. Ministro Ivan Lins 314, Barra da Tijuca* ☎ *021/2493–6060* ⊟ *AE, DC, MC, V.*

ITALIAN
$$–$$$

✕ Alfredo. The pasta here is excellent, especially the fettuccine Alfredo and the spaghetti carbonara. They also serve a delicious lamb dish. The restaurant has a view of the hotel pool. ⊠ *Inter-Continental Rio hotel, Av. Prefeito Mendes de Morais 222, São Conrado* ☎ *021/3323–2200* ⊟ *AE, DC, MC, V* ☉ *No lunch.*

SEAFOOD
$$–$$$

✕ Restaurante Point de Grumari. From Grumari, Estrada de Guaratiba climbs up through dense forest, emerging atop a hill above the vast Guaratiba flatlands. Here you find this eatery famed for grilling fish to perfection. With its shady setting, glorious vistas, and live music performances (samba, bossa nova, jazz), it's the perfect spot for lunch (it's open daily noon-6:30) after a morning on the beach and before an afternoon at the Sítio Roberto Burle Marx or the Museu Casa do Pontal. ⊠ *Estrada do Grumari 710, Grumari* ☎ *021/2410–1434* ☉ *No dinner* ⊟ *AE, DC, MC, V.*

$–$$$
Fodor'sChoice
★

✕ 476. At the end of a road with stunning coastal views, 476 is all about simplicity, with just seven delicious entrées that include *moquecas* (seafood stews), grilled seafood, and curries. It has only 20 tables, some in a lovely garden at water's edge. The quiet fishing village 13 km (8 mi) west of Barra da Tijuca is a nice respite from the bustling Zona Sul. Tell the taxi driver to take you to "Quatro Sete Meia." ⊠ *Rua Barros de Alarcão 476, Pedra da Guaratiba* ☎ *021/2417–1716* ⌦ *Reservations essential* ⊟ *AE, MC, V.*

Where to Stay

Most hotels are in Copacabana and Ipanema. Copacabana hotels are close to the action (and the metro), but the neighborhood is noisier than

Ipanema (which is itself noisier than São Conrado and Barra da Tijuca). If you plan to spend lots of time at the beach, stay at a hotel along Copacabana, Ipanema, or Barra da Tijuca (Copacabana has the advantage of being accessible by metro.) Note that "motels" aren't aimed at tourists. They attract couples looking for privacy and usually rent by the hour.

In the days just prior to and during Carnival, already peak-season rates can double, even triple. Expect to pay a premium for a room with a view. Many hotels include breakfast in the rate, but the quality varies from a full buffet to a hard roll with butter. If you're traveling during peak periods, make reservations as far in advance as possible.

Centro

$–$$ 🏨 **Guanabara Palace Hotel.** A member of the Windsor chain that was remodeled in 2001, the Guanabara is one of the few solid hotel choices right in Centro. Rooms are reasonably sized and tastefully done in brown and beige. The restaurant serves elaborate buffet meals. The contemporary rooftop pool area, with its stunning views of Guanabara Bay, absolutely gleams thanks to its pristine white tiles, white trellises, and white patio furnishings. ⊠ *Av. Presidente Vargas 392, Centro 20071-000* ☎ *021/2216–1313* ⊕ *www.windsorhoteis.com/en-us/gu_loca.asp* 🛏 *510 rooms, 3 suites* ♨ *Restaurant, room service, in-room safes, minibars, cable TV, in-room broadband, Wi-Fi, pool, health club, sauna, bar, dry cleaning, laundry service, business services, meeting rooms, parking (fee), no-smoking rooms* ☰ *AE, DC, MC, V* ⎟◎⎟ *BP* Ⓜ *Uruguaiana.*

Copacabana & Leme

These neighborhoods can be dangerous at night, so it's wise to get around by taxi after dark.

$$$$ 🏨 **Copacabana Palace.** Built in 1923 for the visiting king of Belgium and
Fodor's Choice   inspired by Nice's Negresco and Cannes's Carlton, the Copacabana was
★   the first luxury hotel in South America, and it is still one of the top hotels on the continent. Marlene Dietrich, Robert De Niro, and Princess Di have stayed here. It has a neoclassical facade and one of the city's largest and most attractive swimming pools. One of its two restaurants, the Cipriani, is rated among the city's best for its northern Italian cuisine. The Saturday feijoada is extraordinary. ⊠ *Av. Atlântica 1702, Copacabana 22021-001* ☎ *021/2548–7070, 0800/21–1533, 800/237–1236 in the U.S.* ⊕ *www.copacabanapalace.orient-express.com* 🛏 *122 rooms, 111 suites* ♨ *2 restaurants, room service, in-room safes, cable TV, in-room VCRs, in-room DVD in most rooms, in-room broadband, Wi-Fi, tennis court, pool, health club, hair salon, spa, 2 bars, dry cleaning, laundry service, concierge, business services, meeting room, parking (fee), no-smoking rooms* ☰ *AE, DC, MC, V* Ⓜ *Cardeal Arcoverde.*

$$$$ ✕🏨 **Le Meridien.** Of the leading Copacabana hotels, the 37-story French-owned Meridien is the closest to Centro, making it a favorite of business travelers. Rooms are soundproof and have dark-wood furniture; at this writing, standard rooms could benefit from an update. The hotel has a complete executive center. The restaurant, Le Saint Honoré (⇨ *above*) is one of the city's best; the piano bar is lively at night.

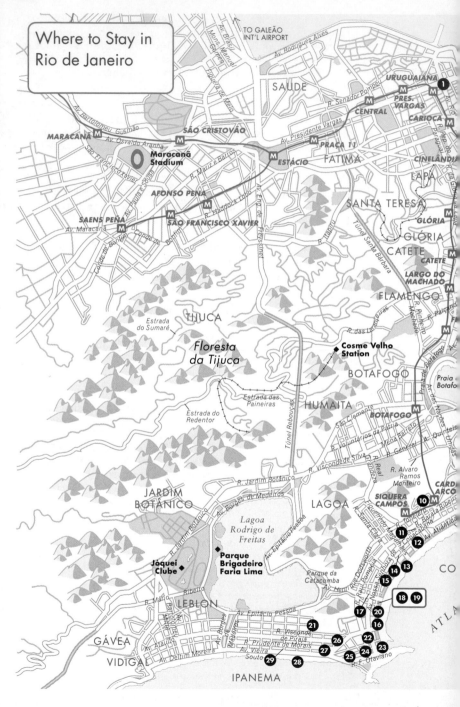

Where to Stay in Rio de Janeiro

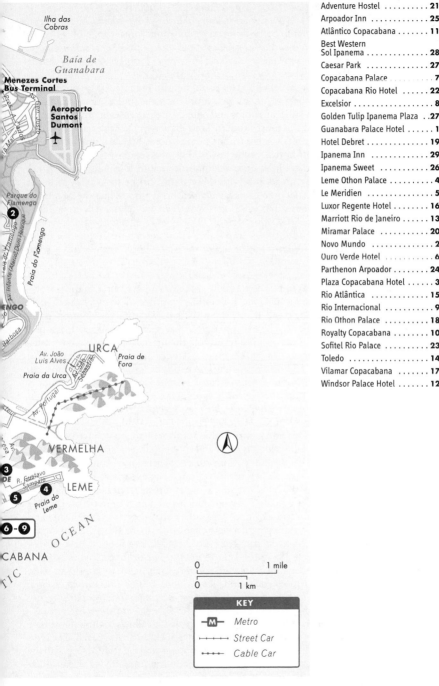

✉ *Av. Atlântica 1020, Copacabana 22010-000* ☎ *021/3873–8888 or 0800/25–7171* ⊕ *www.meridien-br.com/rio* ➷ *496 rooms, 53 suites* 丗 *2 restaurants, piano bar, room service, in-room safes, cable TV, in-room data ports, high-speed Internet in some rooms, pool, hair salon, sauna, bar, dry cleaning, laundry service, concierge, business services, parking (fee), no-smoking floors* 🖃 *AE, DC, MC, V.*

$$$$ 🏨 **Marriott Rio de Janeiro.** You could be walking into a Marriott in any part of the world, which is a comfort for some and a curse for others. Expect spotlessly clean rooms and public areas, an efficient English-speaking staff, and the most modern (and expensive) services and facilities available. Despite the enormous lobby, rooms here are smaller than at most Marriott hotels. Some have views of Avenida Atlântica and Copacabana, others look onto the interior atrium. Business travelers are the Marriott's bread and butter, but thanks to its location—the front door spits you out onto Copacabana Beach—it attracts quite a few tourists as well. The sushi bar ($$$) gets rave reviews. ✉ *Av. Atlântica 2600, Copacabana 22041-001* ☎ *021/2545–6500* ⊕ *www.marriottbrasil. com* ➷ *229 rooms, 16 suites* 丗 *Restaurant, room service, in-room safes, cable TV, in-room broadband, Wi-Fi, pool, health club, sauna, massage, dry cleaning, laundry service, concierge, business services, meeting rooms, parking (fee), no-smoking rooms* 🖃 *AE, DC, MC, V.*

$$$$ 🏨 **Rio Othon Palace.** The flagship of the Brazilian Othon chain, this 30-story hotel is not new, but it does have a prime view of Copacabana's distinctive black-and-white sidewalk mosaic from the rooftop pool, bar, and sundeck. The executive floor has secretarial support, fax machines, and computer hookups. Only the master-floor suites have been recently renovated (in 2002). ✉ *Av. Atlântica 3264, Copacabana 22070-001* ☎ *021/2522–1522* ⊕ *www.hoteis-othon.com.br* ➷ *554 rooms, 30 suites* 丗 *2 restaurants, room service, in-room safes, minibars, cable TV, in-room data ports, pool, health club, sauna, 2 bars, nightclub, dry cleaning, laundry service, concierge, business services, free parking, no-smoking rooms* 🖃 *AE, DC, MC, V.*

$$$–$$$$ 🏨 **Excelsior.** This hotel, part of the Windsor chain, may have been built in the 1950s, but its look is sleek and contemporary—from the sparkling marble lobby to the guest-room closets paneled in gleaming jacaranda (Brazilian redwood). Service is top-rate. The expansive breakfast buffet is served in the hotel's window-banked restaurant facing the avenue and beach. The equally elaborate lunch and dinner buffets cost roughly R$35. The rooftop bar–pool area offers an escape from the hustle and bustle. Ask for a room with a view over Copacabana Beach. ✉ *Av. Atlântica 1800, Copacabana 22021-001* ☎ *021/2545–6000, 0800/704–2827, 800/444–885 in the U.S.* ⊕ *www.windsorhoteis.com.br* ➷ *233 rooms, 12 suites* 丗 *Restaurant, room service, in-room safes, minibars, cable TV, in-room broadband, Wi-Fi, pool, health club, sauna, 2 bars, dry cleaning, laundry service, concierge, meeting room, free parking, no-smoking rooms* 🖃 *AE, DC, MC, V* 🍴| *BP* Ⓜ *Cardeal Arcoverde.*

$$$–$$$$ 🏨 **Rio Atlântica.** Renovated in 2004, the Atlântica allows rooftop sunbathing and swimming and has a bar with a view of Copacabana Beach. The service is superb. Excellent restaurants, shopping, and nightlife in Copacabana are all within walking distance. Bathrooms are large and very clean. Standard rooms do not have a view. Oceanfront suites have an oversize balcony. ☒ *Av. Atlântica 2964, Copacabana 22070-000* ☎ *021/2548–6332 or 0800/26–6332* ⊕ *www.pestana.com* ⚲ *109 rooms, 105 suites* ⚲ *2 restaurants, bar, room service, in-room safes, cable TV, in-room data ports, in-room broadband in some rooms, Wi-Fi, pool, health club, sauna, massage, dry cleaning, laundry service, concierge, business services, meeting room, free parking, no-smoking rooms* ☰ *AE, DC, MC, V.*

★ **$$$–$$$$** 🏨 **Sofitel Rio Palace.** Anchoring one end of Copacabana Beach, this hotel was given a top-to-bottom face-lift in 2000 and is once again one of the best on the strip. The building's H shape gives breathtaking views of the sea, the mountains, or both from the balconies of all rooms. The most reasonably priced rooms face one of the pools opposite the beach. All other units have an ocean view. The first floors are home to Shopping Casino Atlântico, an upscale mall with home accessories, decorative art, and antiques stores. One pool gets the morning sun; the other, afternoon rays. The restaurant Le Pré-Catalan is as good as its Parisian original. Chef Roland Villard, from the French Culinary Academy, is welcoming and creates new dishes every two weeks. ☒ *Av. Atlântica 4240, Copacabana 22070-002* ☎ *021/2525–1232, 0800/703–7003, 800/7763–4835 in the U.S.* ⊕ *www.accorhotels.com.br* ⚲ *372 rooms, 16 suites* ⚲ *2 restaurants, bar, in-room safes, cable TV, in-room broadband, Wi-Fi, 2 pools, health club, sauna, shops, dry cleaning, laundry service, concierge, business services, convention center, free parking, no-smoking rooms* ☰ *AE, DC, MC, V.*

$$–$$$ 🏨 **Atlântico Copacabana.** Just three blocks from Copacabana Beach and close to the Siqueira Campos metro station, this hotel has a great location for the price. Rooms are simple and slightly larger than average. Choose a room on one of the top floors to avoid the street noise of this residential area. Rooms have tile floors and are simply and plainly furnished. ☒ *Rua Siqueira Campos 90, Copacabana 22031-070* ☎ *021/2548–0011* ⊕ *www.atlanticocopacabana.com.br* ⚲ *114 rooms, 13 suites* ⚲ *Restaurant, room service, in-room safes, cable TV, in-room broadband, pool, health club, sauna, bar, dry cleaning, laundry service, concierge, business services, parking (fee)* ☰ *AE, DC, MC, V* ⎮◎⎮ *BP* Ⓜ *Siqueira Campos.*

$$–$$$ 🏨 **Luxor Regente Hotel.** The best of the Luxor hotels in Rio, the Regente was renovated in 2004. The restaurant Forno e Fogão has a good feijoada, though it's not as well known as that of the Copacabana Palace. The suites have whirlpool baths. The gym area is small, but the hotel is committed to continually updating its equipment. If you choose a standard room, be sure that it's not one that faces south; those rooms have an unfortunate view of a trash-can-filled alley. Other rooms look out over Avenida Atlântica and Copacabana Beach. ☒ *Av. Atlântica 3716, Copacabana 22070-001* ☎ *021/2525–2070 or 0800/16–5322* ⊕ *www.luxor-hotels.com/regente* ⚲ *228 rooms, 2 suites* ⚲ *Restaurant, room service, in-room safes, cable TV, some in-room broadband, pool, health club, sauna, dry cleaning, laundry service, concierge, business services, parking (fee), no-smoking rooms* ☰ *AE, DC, MC, V* ⎮◎⎮ *BP.*

$$–$$$ 🏨 **Miramar Palace.** A mix of old and new, this beachfront hotel has some of the largest rooms in Rio with some of the best views. Classic accents like the Carrara marble floor of the lobby and the spectacular glass chandeliers that light the restaurant are contrasted with modern amenities like wireless Internet and the contemporary 16th-floor bar with an unobstructed view of the entire sweep of Copacabana. ⊠ *Av. Atlântica 3668, Copacabana 22070-001* ☏ *021/2525–0303 or 0800/23–2211* ⊕ *www.windsorhoteis.com* ⌁ *147 rooms, 9 suites* ⌂ *Restaurant, coffee shop, tea shop, room service, in-room safes, cable TV, in-room data ports, Internet room, Wi-Fi, bar, dry cleaning, laundry service, concierge, free parking, no-smoking rooms* ⊟ *AE, DC, MC, V* ⏅ *BP.*

$$–$$$ ⌸ **Plaza Copacabana Hotel.** At the east entrance of Copacabana and in the shadow of the Sugar Loaf, this hotel is close to the beach but also near the large Rio Sul shopping center, with restaurants and movie theaters. The metro is just a few blocks away. The hotel still looks new (it opened in 1999) but the decor is nothing special. The real reason to stay here is the staff, which is extremely accommodating and welcoming. The rooftop gym and pool have nice views of Copacabana Beach. ⊠ *Av. Princesa Isabel 263, Copacabana 22011-010* ☏ *021/2195–5500 or 0800/90–2090* ⊕ *www.windsorhoteis.com* ⌁ *233 rooms, 4 suites* ⌂ *Restaurant, room service, in-room safes, cable TV, in-room broadband, Wi-Fi, pool, health club, sauna, bar, dry cleaning, laundry service, concierge, business services, free parking, no-smoking floors, airport shuttle, travel services* ⊟ *AE, DC, MC, V* ⏅ *BP.*

★ $$–$$$ ⌸ **Rio Internacional.** All rooms at this Copacabana landmark hotel have balconies with sea views, a rarity on Avenida Atlântica. The hotel is Swiss owned, and the tidy and modern Scandinavian design is one of its best assets. The pool area and gym are both perched above the beach, with great views. All guests are welcomed with a glass of champagne. ⊠ *Av. Atlântica 1500, Copacabana 22021-000* ☏ *021/2543–1555 or 0800/21–1559* ⊕ *www.riointernacional.com.br* ⌁ *117 rooms, 11 suites* ⌂ *Restaurant, room service, in-room safes, cable TV, in-room broadband, Wi-Fi, pool, health club, sauna, massage, 2 bars, dry cleaning, laundry service, concierge, business services, parking (fee), no-smoking floors* ⊟ *AE, DC, MC, V* Ⓜ *Cardeal Arco Verde.*

$–$$$ ⌸ **Parthenon Arpoador.** The flexibility of an apartment is combined with the services of a hotel in this luxurious building just steps from Copacabana Beach. All units are apartment-style, each with a bedroom, living room, bathroom, and small kitchen. Though a bit smaller than you might expect, apartments are modern, almost futuristic, with bright-white furniture, and everything is sparkling clean. The building is new and extremely well maintained. Each room has a balcony, but only some have an ocean view. ⊠ *Rua Francisco Otaviano 61, Copacabana 22070-010* ☏ *021/3222–9600* ✐ *parthenonarpoador@accorhotels.com* ⌁ *48 apartments* ⌂ *Copacabana, coffee shop, high-speed Internet access in all rooms, business center, concierge, free parking, no-smoking rooms, cable TV, DVD, microwave, gym, pool* ⊟ *AE, DC, MC, V* ⏅ *EP.*

$$ ⌸ **Windsor Palace Hotel.** Close to the shopping area of Copacabana, the Windsor Palace has standard, unexciting hotel rooms. From the fifth floor up, rooms have balconies, but only those from the 12th floor up have ocean views. Overall, this is a solid mid-range option with decent services. The rooftop pool has a view of Copacabana Beach, and it's just two blocks from the Siqueira Campos metro station. ✉ *Rua Domingos Ferreira 6, Copacabana 22050-010* ☎ *021/2545–9000* ⊕ *www.windsorhoteis.com* 🛏 *73 rooms, 1 suite* ⚒ *Restaurant, room service, in-room safes, cable TV, pool, sauna, bar, dry cleaning, laundry service, concierge, meeting room, Internet room, free parking, no-smoking floors* ▭ *AE, DC, MC, V* ⦿❙ *BP* Ⓜ *Siqueira Campos.*

$–$$ ⌗ **Leme Othon Palace.** Unexciting but adequate, this hotel has large rooms and a quiet beachfront location. Built in 1964, it has a subdued, conservative air and lacks some modern amenities, although many rooms were renovated in 2004. Its location near Leme Beach and many transportation choices is the reason to stay here, despite slightly run-down accommodations. The metro station is six blocks away. ✉ *Av. Atlântica 656, Leme 22010-000* ☎ *021/3873–5900* ⊕ *www.hoteis-othon.com.br* 🛏 *163 rooms, 27 suites* ⚒ *Restaurant, room service, in-room safes, cable TV, some in-room data ports, Internet room, bar, dry cleaning, laundry service, concierge, business services* ▭ *AE, DC, MC, V* Ⓜ *Cardeal Arco Verde.*

$–$$ ⌗ **Ouro Verde Hotel.** Since the 1950s this hotel has been favored for its efficient, personalized service. The tasteful art-deco style, with some French twists, is in step with the emphasis on quality and graciousness. However, some visitors note that the carpets and other furnishings are looking a bit worse for wear. All front rooms face the beach; those in the back on the 6th through 12th floors have a view of Corcovado. ✉ *Av. Atlântica 1456, Copacabana 22021-000* ☎ *021/2543–4123* ⊕ *www.dayrell.com.br* 🛏 *60 rooms, 2 suites* ⚒ *Restaurant, room service, in-room safes, cable TV, in-room data ports, Internet room, bar, library, dry cleaning, laundry service, no-smoking rooms* ▭ *AE, DC, MC, V* Ⓜ *Cardeal Arco Verde.*

$ ⌗ **Copacabana Rio Hotel.** Brightly decorated in blues, yellows, and reds, the rooms here are nicer than those you find at many more-expensive places. A few rooms have wonderful views of Pedra da Gávea (Gávea Rock). From the heated rooftop pool you can see Copacabana Beach and Sugar Loaf. You're practically in Ipanema here, so the metro station is a bit of a hike (10 blocks away). ✉ *Av. Nossa Senhora de Copacabana 1256, Copacabana 22070-010* ☎ *021/2267–9900* ⊕ *www.copacabanariohotel.com.br* 🛏 *90 rooms, 8 suites* ⚒ *Restaurant, in-room safes, cable TV, pool, health club, sauna, laundry service, concierge, meeting room, parking (fee)* ▭ *AE, DC, MC, V* ⦿❙ *BP* Ⓜ *Siqueira Campos.*

$ ⌗ **Hotel Debret.** This former apartment building scores points for keeping its prices moderate despite a beachfront location. The decor honors Brazil's past: the lobby has baroque statues and prints depicting colonial scenes, and the rooms are furnished in dark, heavy wood. The hotel has a loyal following among diplomats and businesspeople that are more interested in functionality and low prices than elegance. The buffet breakfast with a view of the beach is one of the hotel's best assets. Corner rooms tend to be the largest. ✉ *Av. Atlântica 3564, Copacabana 22060-040* ☎ *021/2522–0132* ⊕ *www.debret.com* 🛏 *95 rooms, 11 suites* ⚒ *Restaurant, in-room safes, cable TV, some in-room data ports, Internet room, business services, bar, dry cleaning, laundry service* ▭ *AE, DC, MC, V* ⦿❙ *BP.*

$ ⌧ **Royalty Copacabana.** Just three blocks from the beach, this hotel is still removed enough to provide peace and quiet. The back rooms from the third floor up are the quietest and have mountain views; front rooms face the sea. ⊠ *Rua Tonelero 154, Copacabana 22030-000* ☎ *021/ 2548–5699* ⊕ *www.royaltyhotel.com.br* ⌁ *123 rooms, 13 suites* ⚖ *Restaurant, in-room safes, cable TV, in-room broadband, Wi-Fi, business services, pool, gym, sauna, bar, parking (fee), no-smoking rooms* ⊟ *AE, DC, MC, V* ⏀ *BP* Ⓜ *Siqueira Campos.*

$ ⌧ **Toledo.** Although it has few amenities, the Toledo goes the extra mile to make the best of what it does have. The staff is friendly, the service is efficient, and the location—on a quiet backstreet of Copacabana, a block from the beach—isn't bad either. Back rooms from the 9th to the 14th floors have sea views and sliding floor-to-ceiling windows. Some rooms are much larger than others, so specify if you have a preference. ⊠ *Rua Domingos Ferreira 71, Copacabana 22050-010* ☎ *021/2257–1990* ⊕ *www.hoteltoledo.com.br* ⌁ *92 rooms* ⚖ *Coffee shop, in-room safes, TV, Internet room* ⊟ *AE, DC, MC, V* ⏀ *BP* Ⓜ *Siqueira Campos.*

$ ⌧ **Vilamar Copacabana.** A small hotel by Rio's standards, Vilamar has petite rooms. The pool is small, too, but since you're only 200 meters (about 660 feet) from the beach, the size of the pool shouldn't be a problem. Rooms on the lower level get some street noise. ⊠ *Rua Bolívar 75, Copacabana 22061-020* ☎ *021/3461–5601* ⊕ *www. hotelvilamarcopacabana.com.br* ⌁ *56 rooms, 14 suites* ⚖ *Restaurant, in-room safes, refrigerators, cable TV, in-room broadband, pool, sauna, exercise room, bar, business services, parking (fee), no-smoking rooms* ⊟ *AE, DC, MC, V* ⏀ *BP.*

Flamengo

$–$$ ⌧ **Novo Mundo.** A short walk from the Catete metro station and just five minutes by car from Santos Dumont Airport, this traditional hotel is on Guanabara Bay in Flamengo, near Glória. Convention rooms are popular with the business crowd. Deluxe rooms have a view of the bay and also of the Pão de Açúcar. The traditional restaurant, Flamboyant, has buffet service during the week and feijoada every Saturday. ⊠ *Praia do Flamengo 20, Flamengo 22210-030* ☎ *021/2105–7000 or 0800/25–3355* ⊕ *www.hotelnovomundo-rio.com.br* ⌁ *209 rooms, 22 suites* ⚖ *Restaurant, in-room safes, refrigerators, cable TV, in-room broadband in some rooms, hair salon, bar, dry cleaning, laundry service, meeting room, parking (fee), no-smoking floor* ⊟ *AE, D, MC, V* ⏀ *BP* Ⓜ *Catete.*

Ipanema & Leblon

$$$$ ⌧ **Caesar Park.** In the heart of Ipanema, close to high-class shops and **Fodor's**Choice gourmet restaurants, this beachfront hotel has established itself as a fa- ★ vorite of business travelers, celebrities, and heads of state, who appreciate its impeccable service. The hotel has a business center including secretarial services and fax machines. Among other comforts, the hotel has a bar and pool with a breathtaking view on the top floor, with an excellent Italian restaurant, Galani, which serves a fabulous Sunday brunch and an impeccable executive lunch, with buffet starters and desserts and à la carte main courses. Another restaurant serves feijoada every Saturday. ⊠ *Av. Vieira Souto 460, Ipanema 22420-000* ☎ *021/2525–2525,*

0800/21–0789, 877/223–7272 in the U.S. ⊕ *www.caesarpark-rio.com* ⇨ *190 rooms, 32 suites* ♿ *3 restaurants, room service, in-room safes, cable TV, in-room broadband, Wi-Fi, pool, gym, massage, sauna, bar, babysitting, dry cleaning, laundry service, concierge, business services, meeting room, free parking, no-smoking floors* ⊟ *AE, DC, MC, V.*

\$\$\$–\$\$\$\$ ▦ **Best Western Sol Ipanema.** Another of Rio's crop of tall, slender hotels, this one has a great location between Rua Vinicius de Moraes and Farme de Amoedo, where there are several bars, anchoring the eastern end of Ipanema Beach. While it isn't luxurious, the hotel has comfortable accommodations. Deluxe front rooms have panoramic beach views, although back rooms from the eighth floor up, which are the same size, have views of the lagoon and Corcovado. ⊠ *Av. Vieira Souto 320, Ipanema 22420-000* ☎ *021/2525–2020* ⊕ *www.solipanema.com.br* ⇨ *90 rooms* ♿ *Restaurant, pool, 2 bars, room service, in-room broadband, refrigerator, cable TV, laundry services, dry cleaning, meeting rooms, free parking, no-smoking rooms* ⊟ *AE, DC, MC, V* ⑩ *BP.*

\$\$–\$\$\$\$ ▦ **Golden Tulip Ipanema Plaza.** European standards and solid service are the hallmarks of this hotel. The rooms are large, with white-tile floors and modern facilities. Decor is tastefully tropical. In the center of Ipanema, very close to the beach, the hotel is on a street with multiple restaurants and bars. From the rooftop pool it's possible to see not only the ocean, but also the lagoon and the statue of Christ the Redeemer. A brand new floor was recently opened, featuring very elegant Italian fixtures and fine linens. ⊠ *Rua Farme de Amoedo 34, Ipanema 22420-020* ☎ *021/3687–2000* ⊕ *www.ipanemaplazahotel.com* ⇨ *124 rooms, 16 suites* ♿ *Restaurant, room service, in-room safes, cable TV, in-room broadband, Wi-Fi, pool, health club, sauna, dry cleaning, laundry service, concierge, business services, meeting room, parking (fee), no-smoking floors* ⊟ *AE, DC, MC, V* ⑩ *BP.*

\$–\$\$ ▦ **Arpoador Inn.** This simple pocket-size hotel occupies the stretch of sand known as Arpoador. Surfers ride the waves, and pedestrians rule the roadway—a traffic-free street allows direct beach access. At sunset the view from the rocks that mark the end of the beach is considered one of Rio's most beautiful. The spectacle is visible from the hotel's back rooms (deluxe rooms) that face Arpoador Beach; avoid the front rooms, which are noisy. Built in the '70s, the hotel has since been renovated and has a well-known seafood restaurant on the ground floor overlooking the beach. Some rooms are much larger than others, so specify if you have a preference. ⊠ *Rua Francisco Otaviano 177, Ipanema 22080-040* ☎ *021/2523–0060* ⇨ *50 rooms* ♿ *Restaurant, room service, in-room safes, cable TV, Internet room, bar, dry cleaning, laundry service* ⊟ *AE, DC, MC, V* ⑩ *BP.*

\$ ▦ **Ipanema Inn.** If you want to stay in Ipanema and avoid the high prices of beachfront accommodations, this no-frills hotel with great service fits the bill. Just a half block from the beach, close to Praça Nossa Senhora da Paz, it's convenient not only for sun worshipers but also for those seeking to explore Ipanema's varied nightlife. ⊠ *Rua Maria Quitéria 27, Ipanema 22410-040* ☎ *021/2523–6092 or 021/2274–6995* ⇨ *56 rooms* ♿ *Dining room, in-room safes, cable TV, Internet room, bar, dry cleaning, laundry service* ⊟ *AE, DC, MC, V* ⑩ *BP.*

★ ¢–$ 🖵 **Adventure Hostel.** In the heart of Ipanema, this hostel, opened in 2005, has double and quadruple rooms and is on a par, in terms of quality of rooms and service, with many more-expensive hotels. You must rent bath and beach towels. The bedrooms, shared bathrooms and public areas are all sparkling clean, and there is security on site all night. It's just a few blocks from the beach and Ipanema's best restaurants and shopping. The hostel organizes many city tours and ecological tours for its guests (not included in nightly rate). ⊠ *Rua Vinicius de Morais 174, Ipanema 22411-010* 🕾 *021/3813–2726* ⊕ *www.adventurehostel.com. br* ↪ *10 rooms with shared bath* ⚏ *Internet room, laundry facilities; no room TVs, no room phones* ⊟ *MC* ⦿⦿ *BP.*

¢–$ 🖵 **Ipanema Sweet.** In this residential building in the heart of Ipanema, owners rent out their units by the night, week, or month. Just two blocks from the beach and steps away from Ipanema's best bars, restaurants, and shopping, the location cannot be beat. All units have their own bathroom, kitchen, and living room, and some are also equipped with television, DVD player, and Internet connection. If you like the idea of experiencing Rio like a local, this might be the place for you. A good grocery store across the street makes preparing meals easy. The building has a small swimming pool and small exercise room. The bus connecting Ipanema to the metro in Copacabana is one block from the building. ⊠ *Rua Visconde de Pirajá 161, Ipanema 22420-010* 🕾 *Sonia Maria Cordeiro: 021/2551–0488 or 021/9241–8139* ✎ *soniacordeiro@globo. com* ⊟ *No credit cards* ⦿⦿ *EP.*

Nightlife

Rio's nightlife is as hard to resist as its beaches. Options range from samba shows shamelessly aimed at visitors to sultry dance halls that play *forró*, a music style that originated in Brazil's northeast during World War II. (American GIs stationed at refueling stops opened up their clubs "for all," which, when pronounced with a Brazilian accent, became "forró.") Seek out the sounds of big band, rock, and everything in between. One of the happiest mediums is *música popular brasileira* (MPB), the generic term for popular Brazilian music, which ranges from pop to jazz. Note that establishments in this carefree city often have carefree hours; call ahead to confirm opening times.

> **CAUTION**
>
> The strip along Avenida Princesa Isabel at the end of Copacabana—near Le Meridien hotel—is known for its numerous burlesque, striptease, and sex shows. Be warned: some of the female patrons may be prostitutes

For opera, theater, music, dance, film, and other performing arts listings, pick up the Portuguese-language *Rio Prá Você*, published by Riotur, the city's tourist board. *Este Mês no Rio* (This Month in Rio) and similar publications are available at most hotels, and your hotel concierge is also a good source of information. The Portuguese-language newspapers *Jornal do Brasil* and *O Globo* publish schedules of events in the entertainment sections of their Friday editions, which are found online at ⊕ www.jb.com.br and ⊕ www.oglobo.com.br.

Bars

Cariocas love to chat while drinking until late hours in bars and restaurants all around town. Brazilian rhythms like samba and forró fill the night with excitement, most notably in Lapa, Copacabana, Ipanema, and Leblon.

Bars and lounges often ask for a nominal cover in the form of either a drink minimum or a music charge. *Choperias* (pubs) and *botecos* (bars specializing in draft beer and appetizers) are casual places you can go wearing a swimsuit.

COPACABANA At **Cervantes** (⊠ Av. Prado Júnior 335, Copacabana ☎ 021/2275–6147) the beer goes well with the house special, French-bread sandwiches filled with beef, pork, and cheese. You may add sauces, onions, or even fruits—a specialty is pork and pineapple. Steaks with rice or french fries are also on the menu. It's closed Mondays.

COSME VELHO Hidden behind a small entryway in the Cosme Velho neighborhood, the **Clan Café** (⊠ Rua Cosme Velho 564, Cosme Velho ☎ 021/ 2558–2322) is a great place to catch some live music in an outdoor courtyard. Right across the street from the Corcovado train station, it is open Tuesday–Saturday starting at 6 PM.

IPANEMA The area around the intersection of Rua Visconde de Pirajá and Vinicius de Moraes is a good place to bar-hop.

Back in the '60s, regulars Tom Jobim and Vinicius de Moraes, who wrote the song "The Girl from Ipanema," sat at tables at **Bar Garota de Ipanema** (⊠ Rua Vinicius de Moraes 39, Ipanema ☎ 021/2523–3787 Ⓜ Siqueira Campos, then shuttle bus to Praça General Osório), then called Bar Veloso, and longingly watched the song's heroine head for the beach. They sat at the table for two near the door. The unpretentious beachfront choperia **Barril 1800** (⊠ Av. Vieira Souto 110, Ipanema ☎ 021/2523–0085 Ⓜ Siqueira Campos, then shuttle bus to Praça General Osório) is an Ipanema landmark and is usually jammed with people grabbing an icy beer or cocktail and a snack.

LAGOA The collection of bar and restaurant kiosks along a western portion of the lagoon are collectively called, simply, the **Lagoa** (⊠ Parque Brigadeiro Faria Lima, turnoff near the BR gas station). The food itself—a mix of Italian, burgers, and other non-traditional Brazilian—is not spectacular, but the view of the lagoon and the lighted Christ statue in the distance is. Kiosks close down at around 1 AM.

LAPA Many bars line the Avenida Mem de Sá beginning near the Arcos da Lapa, so you can easily stroll down the street to find what appeals to you.

Second-floor bar and pizzeria **Encontro Carioca** feeds the late-night Lapa crowd until 5 AM Thursday through Saturday. It shares owners with downstairs neighbor Carioca da Gema (⇨ Music Clubs, *below*). Pizzas have toppings like shiitake mushrooms, calabresa, and shrimp. Need a sugar rush? Try a banana-and-chocolate pizza. **Nova Capela** (⊠ Av. Mem de Sá 96, Lapa ☎ 021/2252–6228 Ⓜ No metro) is a 100-year-old restaurant-bar in Rio's traditional downtown nightlife area. Beer, cachaça, and Brazilian meals and appetizers are served in generous portions.

LEBLON & GÁVEA   Famed for having the best cachaça in Rio, the **Academia da Cachaça** (⊠Rua Conde de Bernadotte 26G, Leblon ☎ 021/2239–1542) is a trendy spot to grab some delicious appetizers and linger over traditional drinks. True to its name, **Bar do Hotel** (⊠ Marina All Suites, Av. Delfim Moreira 696, Leblon ☎ 021/2540–4990) is a hotel bar that serves drinks and dinner. It gets extremely crowded for drinks on Friday and Saturday nights. Don't expect anything fancy at **Bracarense** (⊠ Rua José Linhares 85B, Leblon ☎ 021/2294–3549), a small informal place where cariocas linger with their beers on the sidewalk in front of the bar. It's perfect for after a soccer game in Maracanã; many come just to talk about sports.

Dance Clubs

Rio's *danceterias* (discos) pulse with loud music and flashing lights. At a number of places, including samba clubs, you can dance to live Brazilian music. *Gafieiras* are old-fashioned ballroom dance halls, usually patronized by an equally old-fashioned clientele. Upon entry to some clubs you're given a card to carry—each successive drink is marked on it. You pay on departure for what you've consumed.

CENTRO   A great place to listen to live music and eat typical Brazilian food, **Cachaçaria Mangue Seco** (⊠ Rua do Lavradio 23, Centro ☎ 021/3852–1947) is a laid-back music hall in the popular Rua do Lavradio. It's closed Sundays. **Estudantina** (⊠ Praça Tiradentes 79, Centro ☎ 021/2232–1149) is an extremely popular nightclub that packs in as many as 1,500 people on weekends to dance to the sound of samba.

COPACABANA   **Bunker** (⊠ Rua Raul Pompéia 94, Copacabana ☎ 021/3813–0300) is a dance hall with three lounges. Most of the time two of them are playing different styles of electronic music, with the third blaring rock and roll. Open Thursday–Sunday; plan to arrive around midnight. There's a small stage for the occasional local bands. Call for schedules.

LARANJEIRAS   If you're up for a late night of dancing with local cariocas, try the famous **Casa Rosa** (⊠ Rua Alice 550, Laranjeiras ☎ 021/9363–4645). It was once a well-known brothel, but has now been converted into a popular nightclub.

LAPA & GÁVEA   If you prefer to be where the trends are, try **00** (⊠ Av. Padre Leonel Franca 240, Gávea ☎ 021/2540–8041), a restaurant–café–sushi bar with a variety of DJs playing sets of house music, drum and bass, and trance, depending on the DJ. Call to get the program. It's open Tuesday through Sunday; DJ gets going at midnight. Saturday is "gay night." At the large nightclub **Asa Branca** (⊠ Av. Mem de Sá 17, Lapa ☎ 021/2224–9358 ▤ DC, MC, V ☉ Closed Mon.), modern geometric designs are combined with old-fashioned fixtures. Big bands and popular Brazilian musicians keep the crowd busy from 10 PM until dawn. Even if you don't want to dance, it's worth checking out the **Democraticus** (⊠ Rua do Riachuela 91, Lapa ☎ No phone) dance hall. Founded in 1867 as a political club, it was recently converted into a dance club, and attracts all age groups from around the city. The hall is impressive and the live music is great. Open Wednesday through Saturday.

LEBLON You're likely to spot celebrities at **Melt** (⊠ Rua Rita Ludolf 47, Leblon ☎ 021/2249–9309), a hip nightclub in a hip neighborhood. Dancing gets going around 11 PM.

Gay & Lesbian Bars & Clubs

Rio is a relatively gay-friendly city; the community even has its own gala during Carnival. Style Travel Agency offers tours targeted to gay and lesbian travelers and has information on local happenings. The hippest cariocas—both gay and straight—hang out in Ipanema and Leblon.

COPACABANA **La Girl** (⊠ Rua Raul Pompeia 102, Copacabana ☎ 021/2513–4993 ⊕ www.lagirl.com.br) is a disco catering to lesbians. Next to La Girl, **Le Boy** (⊠ Rua Paul Pompéia 102, Copacabana ☎ 021/2513–4993 ⊕ www.leboy.com.br) is a gay disco that draws an upscale clientele.

IPANEMA The young energetic crowd at **Bar Bofetada** (⊠ Rua Farme de Amoedo 87–87A, Ipanema ☎ 021/2227–1675) downs chopp and caipirinhas and delicious seafood (the owners are Portuguese) or meat platters large enough to share. On weekends the tables flow out onto the street. The **Galeria Café** (⊠ Rua Teixeira de Mello 31F–F, Ipanema ☎ 021/2523 8250 ⊕ www.galeriacafe.com.br) is a bar with house–techno music for a sophisticated crowd. From Thursday to Saturday it's packed not only inside but has patrons overflowing out onto the sidewalk.

Music Clubs

Although nightclubs often serve food, their main attraction is live music; it's best to eat elsewhere earlier.

COPACABANA **Bip Bip** (⊠ Rua Almirante Gonçalves 50, Copacabana ☎ 021/2267–9696) is a one-of-a-kind hole-in-the-wall where some of the best local musicians have gathered for decades. It's a real gem in Copacabana and not to be missed.

IPANEMA You may rightly associate sultry bossa nova with Brazil, but it's increasingly hard to find venues that offer it. **Vinicius** (⊠ Rua Vinicius de Moraes 39, Ipanema ☎ 021/2287–1497 Ⓜ Siqueira Campos, then shuttle bus to Praça General Osório) is one of the few that do. Along with nightly live samba, jazz, popular music, or bossa nova, it has a good kitchen.

LAGOA At **Mistura Fina** (⊠ Av. Borges de Medeiros 3207, Lagoa Rodrigo de Freitas, Lagoa ☎ 021/2537–2844 ⊕ www.misturafina.com.br) fine jazz combines with excellent food. Call for a schedule.

LAPA Rio institution **Carioca da Gema** (⊠ Av. Mem de Sá 79, Lapa ☎ 021/
★ 2221–0043 ⊕ www.barcariocadagema.com.br) attracts some of the best samba talent around, including up-and-comers. By 11 PM it can be hard to find a place to stand—but regulars still find a way to samba. **Dama da Noite** (⊠ Av. Gomes Freire 773, Lapa ☎ 021/3380–6100 ⊕ www.damadanoite.com.br) is a cozy place to listen to great live music and indulge in fabulous crepes. Opened in 2005, **Estrela da Lapa** (⊠ Av. Mem de Sá, Lapa ☎ 021/2507–6686 ⊕ www.estreladalapa. com.br) has live bossa nova and samba in an classy, open space with tall pine ceilings and low lighting. Shows (R$18) start at around 8:30, and later on Saturdays. Appetizers and a few entrées are served.

LEBLON **Plataforma** (✉ Rua Adalberto Ferreira 32, Leblon ☎ 021/2274–4022), the most spectacular of Rio's samba shows, has elaborate costumes and a variety of musical numbers including samba and rumba. A two-hour show costs about R$100, drinks not included. Downstairs is a hangout for many local luminaries and entertainers. Upstairs you can eat at Plataforma's famed barbecue restaurant.

Rio de Janeiro Essentials

Transportation

BY AIR

Nearly three dozen airlines regularly serve Rio. Several of the international carriers also offer Rio–São Paulo flights.

All international flights and most domestic flights arrive and depart from the Aeroporto Internacional Antônio Carlos Jobim, also known as Galeão. The airport is about 45 minutes northwest of the beach area and most of Rio's hotels. Aeroporto Santos Dumont, 20 minutes from the beaches and within walking distance of Centro, serves the Rio–São Paulo air shuttle and a few air-taxi firms.

🛪 **Airports Aeroporto Internacional Antônio Carlos Jobim** (Galeão) ☎ 021/3398-4526. **Aeroporto Santos Dumont** ☎ 021/3814-7070.

AIRPORT Special airport taxis have booths in the arrival areas of both airports.
TRANSFERS Fares to all parts of Rio are posted at the booths, and you pay in advance (about R$41–R$56). Also trustworthy are the white radio taxis parked in the same areas; these charge an average of 20% less. Three reliable special taxi firms are Transcoopass, Cootramo, and Coopertramo.

Buses run by Empresa Real park curbside outside customs at Galeão and outside the main door at Santos Dumont; for R$5 they make the hour-long trip from Galeão into the city, following the beachfront drives and stopping at all hotels along the way. If your hotel is inland, the driver will let you off at the nearest corner. Buses leave from the airport every half hour from 5:20 AM to 11 PM. Two of the taxi firms have vans at the international airport: Cootramo has a van (with 11 seats) to downtown for R$57 and to Copacabana for R$78. Coopertramo does the same for R$70 and R$80, but the van has a capacity to transport 15.

🛪 **Cootramo** ☎ 021/2560-5442, 021/3976-9944, or 021/3976-9945. **Coopertramo** ☎ 021/2560-2022. **Empresa Real** ☎ 021/2560-7041 or 0800/24-0850. **Transcoopass** ☎ 021/2560-4888.

BY BUS

ARRIVING & Regular service is available to and from Rio. Long-distance and interna-
DEPARTING tional buses leave from the Rodoviária Novo Rio. Any local bus marked RODOVIÁRIA will take you to the station. You can buy tickets at the depot or, for some destinations, from travel agents. Buses also leave from the more conveniently located Menezes Cortes Terminal, near Praça 15 de Novembro. These buses travel to different neighborhoods of Rio (Barra da Tijuca, Santa Cruz, Campo Grande, and Recreio) and to nearby cities Nieterói, Petrópolis, and Nova Friburgo, among others.

🛪 **Rodoviária Novo Rio** ✉ Av. Francisco Bicalho 1, São Cristóvão ☎ 021/2291-5151. **Menezes Cortes Terminal** ✉ Rua São José 35, Centro ☎ 021/2299-1380.

3

GETTING
AROUND

Don't attempt using the bus unless you know which line to take and you speak enough Portuguese to ask directions (drivers don't speak English). Never take the bus at night. Much has been made of the threat of being robbed on Rio's city buses, and many local residents no longer ride public buses. If you are going to use a public bus, don't wear expensive watches or jewelry, carry a camera or a map in hand, or talk loudly in English. It's also wise to avoid buses during rush hour.

BY CAR

ARRIVING &
DEPARTING

Arriving from São Paulo (429 km/266 mi on BR 116) or Brasília (1,150 km/714 mi on BR 040), you enter Rio via Avenida Brasil, which runs into Centro's beachside drive, the Avenida Infante Dom Henrique. This runs along Rio's Baía de Guanabara and passes through the Copacabana Tunnel to Copacabana Beach. The beachside Avenida Atlântica continues into Ipanema and Leblon along Avenidas Antônio Carlos Jobim (Ipanema) and Delfim Moreira (Leblon). From Galeão take the Airport Expressway (known as the Linha Vermelha, or Red Line) to the beach area. This expressway takes you through two tunnels and into Lagoa. Exit on Avenida Epitácio Pessoa, the winding street encircling the lagoon. To reach Copacabana, exit at Avenida Henrique Dodsworth (known as the Corte do Cantagalo). For Ipanema and Leblon there are several exits, beginning with Rua Maria Quitéria.

GETTING
AROUND

The carioca style of driving is passionate to the point of abandon: traffic jams are common, the streets aren't well marked, and red lights are often more decorative than functional. Although there are parking areas along the beachfront boulevards, finding a spot can still be a problem. If you do choose to drive, exercise extreme caution, wear seat belts at all times, and keep the doors locked.

🚩 **Rental Agencies Avis** ✉ Av. Princesa Isabel 350, Copacabana ☎ 021/2543-8579. **Hertz** ✉ Av. Princesa Isabel 334, Copacabana ☎ 021/2275-7440 or 0800/701-7300 ✉ Aeroporto Internacional Antônio Carlos Jobim ☎ 021/3398-4339 ✉ Aeroporto Santos Dumont ☎ 021/2262-0612. **Localiza Rent a Car** ✉ Av. Princesa Isabel 214, Copacabana ☎ 021/2275-3340 ✉ Aeroporto Internacional Antônio Carlos Jobim ☎ 021/3398-5445 ✉ Aeroporto Santos Dumont ☎ 021/2533-2677. **Unidas** ☎ 021/4001-2222 for main reservations line ✉ Aeroporto Santos Dumont, Av. Senador Salgado Filho s/n, Centro ☎ 021/2240-9181 ✉ Av. Princesa Isabel 166, Copacabana ☎ 021/3685-1212 ✉ Aeroporto Internacional do Galeão, Estrada do Galeão s/n, Ilha do Governador ☎ 021/3398-2286.

🚩 **Transport Agency Turismo Clássico Travel** ✉ Av. Nossa Senhora de Copacabana 1059, Sala 805, Copacabana ☎ 021/2523-3390.

BY SUBWAY

Rio's subway system, the metro, is clean, relatively safe, and efficient—a delight to use—but it's not comprehensive and has only two lines. It's great option to get from Copacabana to Centro, but not for Ipanema or Leblon, since the southernmost metro stop (called Siqueira Campos) is in Copacabana. The metro shuttle can get you to and from Siqueira Campos to Ipanema. Reaching sights distant from metro stations can be a challenge, especially in summer when the infamous carioca traffic fans what is already 90-degree exasperation. Plan your tours accordingly; tourism offices and some metro stations have maps.

🚺 **Metrô Rio Information Line** ☎ 021/3211-6300 ⊕ www.metrorio.com.br.

BY TAXI

Taxis are plentiful in Rio, and in most parts of the city you can easily flag one down on the street.

Yellow taxis have meters that start at a set price and have two rates. The "1" rate applies to fares before 8 PM, and the "2" rate applies to fares after 8 PM, on Sunday, on holidays, throughout December, in the neighborhoods of São Conrado and Barra da Tijuca, and when climbing steep hills. Drivers are required to post a chart noting the current fares on the inside of the left rear window.

🚺 **Centro de Taxis** ☎ 021/2195-1000. **Coopacarioca** ☎ 021/2518-1818. **Coopatur** ☎ 021/2573-1009.

BY TRAIN

ARRIVING & DEPARTING Intercity trains leave from the central station that starred in the Oscar-nominated movie of the same name, Estação Dom Pedro II Central do Brasil. Trains, including a daily overnight train to São Paulo, also leave from the Estação Leopoldina Barao de Maria, near Praça 15 de Novembro.

🚺 **Estação Dom Pedro II Central do Brasil** ✉ Praça Cristiano Otoni on Av. President Vargas, Centro ☎ 021/2588-9494.

Contacts & Resources

TOUR OPTIONS

CITY TOURS English-speaking guides at Gray Line are superb. In addition to a variety of city tours, the company offers trips outside town, whether you'd like to go white-water rafting on the Rio Paraíbuna, tour a coffee plantation, or spend time in Petrópolis. Helicopter tours are also an option.

Private Tours take you around old Rio, the favelas, Corcovado, Floresta da Tijuca, Prainha, and Grumari in a jeep. Guides are available who speak English, Hungarian, French, and German. Hang-glide or paraglide over Pedra da Gávea and Pedra Bonita under the supervision of São Conrado Eco-Aventura.

Carlos Roquette is a history teacher who runs Cultural Rio, an agency that hosts trips to 8,000 destinations. Most are historic sites. A guided visit costs around US$110 for four hours, depending on the size of the group. Favela Tour offers a fascinating half-day tour of two favelas. For anyone with an interest in Brazil beyond the beaches, such tours are highly recommended. The company's English-speaking guides can also be contracted for other outings.

Rio Hiking takes small groups on nightlife tours to clubs and bars beyond the regular tourist circuit.

🚺 **Cultural Rio** ☎ 021/9911-3829 ⊕ www.culturalrio.com.br. **Favela Tour** ☎ 021/3322-2727 ⊕ www.favelatour.com.br. **Gray Line** ☎ 021/2512-9919. **Private Tours** ☎🖶 021/2232-9710 ⊕ www.privatetours.com.br. **Rio Hiking** ☎ 021/2552-9204 or 021/9721-0594 ⊕ www.riohiking.com.br.

⚡ Ecology and Culture Jeep Tours ☎ 021/2108-5800 ⊕ www.jeeptour.com.br. **Rio Hiking** ☎ 021/2552-9204 or 021/9721-0594 ⊕ www.riohiking.com.br. **Trilhas do Rio** ☎ 021/2425-8441 or 021/2424-5455 ⊕ www.trilhasdorio.com.br.

HELICOPTER TOURS Helisight gives a number of helicopter tours whose flights may pass over the *Cristo Redentor,* Copacabana, Ipanema, and/or Maracanã stadium. There are night flights as well; reserve ahead for these daily 9–6.

⚡ Helisight ⊠ Conde de Bernadote 26, Leblon ☎ 021/2511-2141, 021/2542-7895, or 021/2259-6995 ⊕ www.helisight.com.br.

VISITOR INFORMATION

The Rio de Janeiro city tourism department, Riotur, has an information booth, which is open 8–5 daily. There are also city tourism desks at the airports and the Novo Rio bus terminal. The Rio de Janeiro state tourism board, Turisrio, is open weekdays 9–6. You can also try contacting Brazil's national tourism board, Embratur.

⚡ Embratur ⊠ Rua Uruguaiana 174, Centro ☎ 021/2509-6292 ⊕ www.embratur.gov. br. **Riotur** ⊠ Rua da Assembléia 10, near Praça 15 de Novembro, Centro ☎ 021/ 2217-7575 or 0800/707-1808 ⊕ www.rio.rj.gov.br/riotur. **Riotur information booth** ⊠ Av. Princesa Isabel 183, Copacabana ☎ 021/2541-7522. **Turisrio** ⊠ Rua da Ajuda 5, Centro ☎ 021/2215-0011 ⊕ www.turisrio.rj.gov.br.

SIDE TRIPS FROM RIO

Updated by Ana Lúcia do Vale

THE STATE OF RIO DE JANEIRO HOLDS JUST AS MUCH ALLURE as the eponymous city. Just across Guanabara Bay is Niterói, a city whose ancient forts provide a window on history and a great view of Rio. Niterói mixes the past with the ultramodern spaceshiplike Museu de Arte Contemporânea. A scenic road leads northeast to Petrópolis and the opulent imperial palace that was the summer home of Brazil's emperor. Swiss-settled Nova Friburgo peeks from a lush valley speckled with waterfalls farther north. East of Rio, on the Costa Azul (Blue Coast), sailboat-jammed Cabo Frio is a popular eastern coastal resort, and although Brigitte Bardot in a bikini may have put nearby Búzios on the map, its 23 beaches, temperate weather, and sophisticated ambience have kept it there.

West of Rio, on Brazil's Costa Verde (Green Coast), Angra dos Reis is the jumping-off point for 365 islands that pepper a picturesque bay, with unforgettable spots for diving. One of the loveliest, Ilha Grande, is lapped by emerald waters and retains an unspoiled flavor despite its popularity. The most amazing gem, however, is the southwestern coastal town of Paraty, with its 18th-century Portuguese architecture; the lovely cays sprinkled along its bay have attracted American, European, and Brazilian celebrities.

Búzios

⑪
Fodor'sChoice
★

24 km (15 mi) northeast of Cabo Frio; 176 km (126 mi) northeast of Rio.

Búzios, a little more than two hours from Rio, is a string of gorgeous beaches on an 8-km-long (5-mi-long) peninsula. Europeans and South Americans

(especially Argentineans and Chileans) flock here year-round to do absolutely nothing. It was little more than a fishing village until the 1960's, when Brigitte Bardot escaped from the paparazzi here, but was eventually found, and fame for little Búzios followed. A bronze statue on the Orla Bardot, along the water near downtown, was crafted in her honor. Since Bardot's time, some of Búzios's old fishing shacks have given way to *pousadas,* or inns (some of them luxurious, a few inexpensive), restaurants, and bars run by people who came on vacation and never left. Despite the growth, Búzios retains some of the charm of a small fishing village, and the balance of the cosmopolitan and the primitive is seductive.

The **Tour Shop** has a mini-golf field (with 21 greens), a zip line (R$20), and trolleys that take you from your hotel to 12 beaches (R$40), with three departures a day. A three-hour catamaran trip around Búzios goes to 17 beaches (R$40), and a day trip by boat to Gruta Azul in nearby Arraial do Cabo is R$100 per person, lunch included. ⊠ *Orla Bardot 550, Armação dos Búzios* ☎ *022/2623–4733 or 022/2623–0292* ⊕ *www.tourshop.com.br.*

Where to Stay & Eat

★ **$–$$$$** ✕ **Cigalon.** Widely considered the best restaurant in Búzios, Cigalon is an elegant place with a veranda overlooking the beach. Though the waiters are bow-tied and the tables white-clothed and candlelit, this is still Búzios, and casual but clean dress is just fine. The food is French-inspired, and includes lamb steak, braised duck breast, and lobster with rice and almonds. A departure from the French fare is the full menu of homemade pastas. If you're having trouble making up your mind

GETTING AROUND

Renting a car or taking a bus or shuttle are generally the best ways to get around Rio de Janeiro State. Most destinations are within a few hours of the city of Rio.

3

among the tempting options, the tasting menu for R$33 might be your best bet. ⊠ *Rua das Pedras 199, Centro* ☎ *022/2623–6284* ⊟ *AE, DC, MC, V.*

$$ ✕ **Buzin.** Behind fashionable Rua das Pedras, Rua Turíbio de Farias is a buffet per-kilo restaurant with churrasco, many varieties of seafood—including sushi—and salads. The reasonable prices, many choices, and casual atmosphere make it a great post-beach stop. Try the shrimp fried in oil and garlic or the *picanha* beef, a very tender cut of beef found in every churrascaria. ⊠ *Rua Turíbio de Farias 273* ☎ *022/2633–7051* ⊟ *AE, DC, MC, V* ⊕ *www.buzin.com.br.*

$–$$ ✕ **Capricciosa.** Well-known in Rio, the Búzios branch of this pizzeria has the same high-quality pies. The Margarita (Margherita) Gourmet is a must, with a thin crust topped with tomatoes and buffalo mozzarella. ⊠ *Av. José Bento Ribeiro Dantas 500, Praia da Armação* ☎ *022/ 2623–1595* ⊟ *AE, DC, MC, V.*

¢–$$ ✕ **Chez Michou.** This Belgian-owned *crêperie* and nighttime meeting spot for 20-somethings on the main drag in the center of town is the best place to eat if you want something quick, light, and inexpensive. You can choose from among about 50 crepe fillings. At night the street-side tables buzz with locals and visitors congregating to drink and people-watch. ⊠ *Rua da Pedras 90* ☎ *022/2623–2169* ⊕ *www.chezmichou. com.br* ⊟ *No credit cards.*

$$$$ ▣ **Casas Brancas.** If you're looking for complete relaxation, and you've
Fodor'sChoice got the wallet for it, this is the place to stay in Búzios. The quirky build-
★ ing was constructed on several levels facing the beach, which makes for interestingly shaped rooms. Each is decorated with care, but simple cottage style and zenlike peace and quiet are the hallmarks here. Get an ocean-view room, and one with a private balcony if you can swing it. The spa is one of the best in town. ⊠ *Alto do Humaitá 10, off Orla Bardot, Centro 28950–000* ☎ *022/2623–1458* ⊕ *www.casasbrancas. com.br* ⇆ *29 rooms, 3 suites* ⚫ *Restaurant, cable TV, in-room safes, pool, spa, Internet room, laundry service* ⊟ *AE, V* ⌾| *BP.*

$$–$$$ ▣ **Maravista Pousada.** This health-conscious hotel doubles as one of the best spas in Brazil one week per month. (The spa is closed the other three weeks.) Ligia Azevedo, well known for her spa in Rio, operates Búzios's Spa Ligia Azevedo (www.ligiazevedo.com.br), which has group activities like aquatic gymnastics and yoga classes, plus personalized fitness programs, physician-prescribed diets, massage, and beauty treatments. Ligia recommends a full week in the spa to feel the results. It's not hard to take her advice, as the pousada is built right on 4-km Geriba Beach.

Rooms have modern decoration with pastel colors, and some have verandas with a sea view. All meals are included during the spa week. ⊠ *Rua dos Gravatás 1058, Praia de Geribá, 28950–000* ☎ *022/2623–2130 hotel, 021/2438–0149 spa* ⊕ *www.maravista.com.br* ↝ *16 rooms* ⚅ *Refrigerators, in-room safes, pool, sauna, bar* ▭ *AE, DC, MC, V* ⦿| *EP.*

$$ ⊞ **Ilha Branca Inn.** Just 100 meters from the sands of João Fernandes Beach, Ilha has charming and colorful rooms. The hotel was remodeled in 2003 with a new gym and sauna, and a pool with panoramic ocean view. Rooms are individually decorated, with tile floors and wrought-iron, dark-wood, and wicker furnishings. Some face the beach and have verandas. ⊠ *Rua João Fernandes 1, Praia de João Fernandes, 28950–000* ☎ *22/2623–2525 or 22/2623–6664* ⊕ *www.ilhabranca.com* ↝ *67 rooms* ⚅ *Restaurant, in-room safes, refrigerator, cable TV, bar, sauna, 2 pools, gym* ▭ *AE, MC, V* ⦿| *BP.*

Nova Friburgo

⑫ *122 km (79 mi) northeast of Petrópolis; 137 km (121 mi) northeast of Rio.*

This summer resort town was settled by Swiss immigrants in the early 1800s, when Brazil was actively encouraging European immigration and when the economic situation in Switzerland was bad. Woods, rivers, and waterfalls encircle the city. Homemade liqueurs, jams, and cheeses pack the shelves of the town's small markets. The lingerie industry supports the city nowadays, some companies exporting to Europe and elsewhere internationally. Shops in downtown Friburgo and close to Ponte da Saudade (near the bus terminal) sell high-quality lingerie for reasonable prices. Cariocas also come here to unwind in the cool mountain climate.

A cable car rises more than 4,750 feet (1,450 meters) to **Morro da Cruz,** where you get a spectacular view of Friburgo. ⊠ *Praça Teleférica* ☎ *022/ 2522–4834* ⊠ *R$12* ⊙ *Weekdays 9–noon and 1–5, weekends 9–6.*

Where to Stay

★ **$$** ⊞ **Akaskay.** Situated in the district of Mury, 6 mi (9 km) from Nova Friburgo, this hotel is the place to relax in a natural mountain environment. The rooms have cedarwood walls and electric fireplaces, and the only noise you can hear is from a nearby streamlet. Outdoors, there's a spring-water swimming pool (unheated) and a hot tub. The place is surrounded by forest, and Saturday-morning yoga classes in the garden's meditation temple help you relax even further, as do shiatsu massages and beauty treatments. Transportation to nearby restaurants is free. ⊠ *Estrada Norge Hamburgo, Mury, access at Km 71 off RJ 116, 28615–615* ☎ *22/2542–1163* ⊕ *www.akaskay.com.br* ↝ *14 rooms, 1 chalet* ⚅ *Cable TV, refrigerator, in-room safes, sauna, pool, bar* ▭ *AE, DC, MC, V* ⦿| *BP.*

Petrópolis

⑬ *68 km (42 mi) northeast of Rio.*

The hilly highway northeast of the city rumbles past forests and waterfalls en route to a mountain town so refreshing and picturesque that

Dom Pedro II, Brazil's second emperor, spent his summers in it. From 1889 to 1899 it was also the country's year-round seat of government. Horse-drawn carriages shuttle between the sights (available in front of the Museu Imperial), passing flowering gardens, shady parks, and imposing pink mansions. The city holds also the Encantada (Enchanted), the peculiar house created by Santos Dumont. A variety of shops along Rua Teresa sell winter clothes; shops are open Tuesday–Sunday 9–6 and Monday 2–6.

★ The **Museu Imperial** is the magnificent 44-room palace that was the summer home of Dom Pedro II, emperor of Brazil, and his family in the 19th century. The colossal structure is filled with polished wooden floors, artwork, and grand chandeliers. You can also see the diamond-encrusted gold crown and scepter of Brazil's last emperor, as well as other royal jewels. ⊠ *Rua da Imperatriz 220, Centro* ☎ *024/2237–8000* ⊕ *www. museuimperial.gov.br* ☞ *R$8* ☉ *Tues.–Sun. 11–6.*

From the Museu Imperial you can walk three long blocks or take a horse-drawn carriage to **São Pedro de Alcântara,** the Gothic cathedral containing the tombs of Dom Pedro II; his wife, Dona Teresa Cristina; and their daughter, Princesa Isabel. ⊠ *Rua São Pedro de Alcântara 60, Centro* ☎ *024/2242–4300* ☞ *Free* ☉ *Tues.–Sun. 8–noon and 2–6.*

The **Palácio de Cristal** (Crystal Palace), a stained-glass and iron building made in France and assembled in Brazil, was a wedding present to Princesa Isabel. During the imperial years it was used as a ballroom: it was here the princess held a celebration dance after she abolished slavery in Brazil in 1888. ⊠ *Praça da Confluência, Rua Alfredo Pachá* ☎ *024/2247–3721* ☞ *Free* ☉ *Tues.–Sun. 9–5.*

The **Circuito Caminhos do Brejal** is a tour in a jeep to visit small farms around the city that produce milk and cheese, cachaça, and trout, plus crafts shops. Choose from the 20- or 30-km route with Miira's Tours. ☎ *024/2242–2875* ⊕ *www.miirastours.com.br* ☞ *R$68.*

Where to Stay & Eat

$ ✕ **Bauernstube.** German food is the backbone of this log cabin–style eatery. The bratwurst and sauerkraut are properly seasoned, and the strudel is an excellent choice for polishing off a meal. ⊠ *Av. Dr. Nelson de Sá Earp 297* ☎ *024/2242–1097* ☰ *DC, MC, V* ☉ *Closed Mon.*

$ ✕ **Trutas do Rocio.** Trout, trout, and more trout is served at this restaurant next to river teeming with—you guessed it—trout. The fish is prepared as appetizers in patê or in a cassava dough pastry. Entrées include grilled trout or trout cooked in almond sauce, mustard sauce, or orange sauce. The small, rustic restaurant has only a 22-person capacity. ⊠ *Estrada da Vargem Grande 6333, Rocio* ☎ *024/2242–7053* ⊕ *www.trutas.com.br* ☰ *AE, DC, MC, V* ⌕ *Reservations essential* ☉ *No dinner.*

★ $$$ ✕▣ **Locanda Della Mimosa.** This cozy pousada has only a few suites, but the service is first-class. It's in a valley filled with bougainvillea trees, with trails for long walks. The suites are decorated in a classical style with imperial influences. Tea is served in the afternoon. The Italian restaurant, run by the talented Danio Braga, who is always cooking up novelties, is open Thursday through Sunday and has a degustation menu ($$$$) of specialties from different regions of Italy. ⊠ *Km 71.5, BR 040,*

Alameda das Mimosas 30, Vale Florido, 25725-490 ☎ *024/2233–5405*
⊕ *www.locanda.com.br* ⮑ *6 suites* ⚘ *Restaurant, room service, cable
TV, pool, sauna, bar* ⊟ *AE, DC, MC, V* ❙❂❙ *BP* ⊘ *Closed Mon.–Wed.*

$ ▦ **Hotel Casablanca Imperial.** Just 50 meters from the Museu Imperial
downtown, the hotel is in a colonial-style house built in 1952. The rooms
are simply and warmly decorated with mahogany furniture and have
hardwood floors. The charming bistro serves French fare. ⊠ *Rua da
Imperatriz 286, Centro 25610-320* ☎ *024/2242–6662* ⊕ *www.
casablancahotel.com.br/imperial* ⮑ *32 rooms* ⚘ *Restaurant, room
service, able TV, pool, bar, sauna, laundry service, game room* ⊟ *AE,
D, MC, V* ❙❂❙ *BP.*

$ ✕▦ **Pousada Monte Imperial.** A few kilometers from downtown, this Euro-
style inn has a lobby with a fireplace and a restaurant–bar. Rooms are
cozy and rustic, in an old European style, and have a view of the historic center of the city. Drinks and meals can be taken in the lovely garden. ⊠ *Rua José de Alencar 27, Centro 25610-050* ☎ *024/2237–1664*
⊕ *www.pousadamonteimperial.com.br* ⮑ *14 rooms* ⚘ *Restaurant,
fans, cable TV, pool, bar, laundry service; no a/c* ⊟ *AE, DC, MC, V*
❙❂❙ *BP.*

Ilha Grande

⓮ One of the most popular islands in Brazil is the lush, mountainous Ilha
Grande. Just 2 km (1 mi) and a 90-minute ferry ride from Angra dos
Reis or Mangaratiba, it has more than 100 idyllic beaches—sandy rib-
bons that stretch on and on with a backdrop of tropical foliage. Ferries
arrive at Vila do Abraão, and from there you can roam paths that lead
from one slip of sand to the next or negotiate with local boatmen for
jaunts to the beaches or more remote islets.

A 10-minute walk from Vila do Abraão takes you to the hot waters off
Praia da Júlia and Praia Comprida. The transparent sea at Abraãozinho
Beach is another 25-minute walk from Vila do Abraão. If you choose
to go by boat, don't miss the big waves of Lopes Mendes Beach or the
astonishingly blue Mediterranean-like water of Lagoa Azul. Scuba-diving fans should head to Gruta do Acaiá to see turtles and colorful South
American fish.

It's smart to take to the island only what you can carry, as you have to
walk to your hotel. But men at the pier make a living helping tourists
carry luggage (about R$5 per bag).

Where to Stay & Eat

$–$$ ✕ **Lua e Mar.** Expect fresh and well-prepared seafood at this casual
place, where you can stroll in after sunbathing, still wearing your Hava-
ianas. ⊠ *Rua da Praia, Vila do Abraão* ☎ *024/3361–5113* ⊟ *D, MC,
V* ⊘ *Closed Apr.–Nov.*

★ $$ ▦ **Pousada Sankay.** The colorful rooms with sea view have names in-
spired by sea creatures, like Lagosta (lobster) or Golfinho (dolphin).
Kayaks, canoes, and other boats are available to rent, as is diving equip-
ment. A boat from the pousada can pick you up at Angra dos Reis. ⊠ *En-
seada do Bananal, 23990-000* ☎ *024/3365–4065* ⊕ *www.pousadasankay.*

com.br ⮐ _12 rooms_ ⚱ _Restaurant, cable TV, refrigerator, bar, sauna, pool, gym, playground_ ☰ _AE, DC, MC, V_ ❙◎❙ _MAP_ ☉ _Closed June._

$ 🎏 **Farol dos Borbas.** Like all lodging options on the island, Farol dos Borbas has simple rooms, but its advantage is its location about 150 feet (50 meters) from the pier where the ferry from Angra dos Reis stops. The hotel has boat service, with tours around the island. ✉ _Rua da Praia 881, Vila do Abraão, 23960-970_ ☎ _024/3361–5260, 024/3361–5261, or 024/3361–5866_ ⊕ _www.ilhagrandetur.com.br_ ⮐ _14 rooms_ ⚱ _Room service, cable TV, refrigerators,_ ☰ _D, MC, V_ ❙◎❙ _BP._

$ 🎏 **Pousada do Canto.** Freshly decorated with wicker furniture in a colonial-style house, this pousada is just in front of Praia do Canto. The place has a summery, tropical atmosphere, with a palapa-roof bar by the pool and a knotty log fence around the property. Some rooms face the ocean and have verandas. ✉ _Rua da Praia 121, Vila do Abraão, 23990-000_ ☎ _024/3361–5115_ ⊕ _www.viladoabraao.com.br/docanto.htm_ ⮐ _11 rooms_ ⚱ _Cable TV, refrigerators, pool_ ☰ _AE, D, MC, V_ ❙◎❙ _BP._

¢ 🎏 **Recreio da Praia.** A three-minute walk from the pier, this pousada has simply decorated rooms with sofa beds. ✉ _Rua da Praia, Vila do Abraão, 23960-000_ ☎ _024/3361–5266 or 024/3361–5375_ ⮐ _10 rooms_ ⚱ _Restaurant, room service, refrigerators, cable TV, laundry service_ ☰ _MC, V_ ❙◎❙ _BP._

Paraty

❶❺ _99 km (60 mi) southwest of Angra dos Reis; 261 km (140 mi) southwest of Rio._

This stunning colonial city—also spelled Parati—is one of the oldest in Brazil, and one of South America's gems. Giant iron chains hang from posts at the beginning of the mazelike grid of cobblestone streets, closing them to all but pedestrians, horses, and bicycles. Until the 18th century this was an important transit point for gold plucked from the Minas Gerais—a safe harbor protected from pirates by a fort. (The cobblestones are the rock ballast brought from Lisbon, then unloaded to make room in the ships for their gold cargoes.) In 1720, however, the colonial powers cut a new trail from the gold mines straight to Rio de Janeiro, bypassing the town and leaving it isolated. It remained that way until contemporary times, when artists, writers, and others "discovered" the community and UNESCO placed it on its World Heritage Site list.

Paraty isn't a city peppered with lavish mansions and opulent palaces; rather, it has a simple beauty. By the time the sun breaks over the bay each morning—illuminating the whitewashed, colorfully trimmed buildings—the fishermen have begun spreading out their catch at the outdoor market. The best way to explore is simply to begin walking winding streets banked with centuries-old buildings that hide quaint inns, tony restaurants, shops, and art galleries. As cars are forbidden in the historic center, take comfortable, sensible shoes to navigate the uneven cobblestones.

The town's slaves built the **Igreja de Nossa Senhora do Rosário** for themselves around 1725, because the other churches in town were reserved for the white population. ✉ _Rua do Comércio_ ☎ _024/3371–1467_

✉ *R$1, R$2 combination ticket with other Paraty churches and Forte Defensor* ☉ *Tues.–Sun. 9–5.*

The neoclassical **Igreja de Nossa Senhora dos Remédios** was built in 1787. It holds the small art gallery Pinacoteca Antônio Marino Gouveia, with paintings of modern artists such as Djanira, Di Cavalcanti, and Anita Malfatti. ✉ *Rua da Matriz* ☎ *024/3371–2946* ✉ *R$1, R$2 combination ticket with other Paraty churches and Forte Defensor* ☉ *Tues.–Sun. 9–noon and 2–5.*

The oldest church in Paraty, the simple and clean-lined **Igreja de Santa Rita** was built in 1722 by and for freed slaves. Today it houses a small religious art museum (Museu de Arte Sacra). It's a typical Jesuit church with a tower and three front windows. Religious art objects inside the church are constantly being restored. ✉ *Rua Santa Rita* ☎ *024/3371–1620* ✉ *R$1, R$2 combination ticket with other Paraty churches and Forte Defensor* ☉ *Wed.–Sun. 9–noon and 2–5.*

The **Igreja de Nossa Senhora das Dores,** built in 1800, was the church of the community's small but elite white population. ✉ *Rua Dr. Pereira* ☎ *024/3371–2946* ✉ *R$1, R$2 combination ticket with other Paraty churches and Forte Defensor* ☉ *Tues.–Sun. 9–5.*

Beyond its colonial downtown, Paraty has natural beauty worth exploring. **Paraty Tours** (✉ Av. Roberto Silveira 11, Centro, Paraty 23970-000 ☎ 24/3371–2651 or 24/3371–1428 ⊕ www.paratytours.com.br) has a six-hour jeep tour that goes to the Serra da Bocaina National Park, crossing rivers and visiting fantastic waterfalls, stops at a cachaça distillery, and provides for lunch in a restaurant close to a river with a natural pool. Other tours include hiking the Caminho do Ouro, a visit to the breathtaking Praia do Sono or to the untouched little fishing village of Trindade (25 km/16 mi from Paraty), which has places to snorkel and swim in crystal-clear water. Transfers from Rio or elsewhere, horse and bike tours, and diving are also available.

Where to Stay & Eat

$$–$$$$ **Refúgio.** Near the water in a quiet part of town, this seafood restaurant with excelled codfish cakes is a great place for a romantic dinner. Cafe tables out front sit under heat lamps. Moquecas are excellent. ✉ *Praça do Porto, loja 4, in front of the wharf, Centro Histórico* ☎ *024/3371–2447* ⊕ *www.eco-paraty.com/refugio* ▭ *DC, MC, V.*

$–$$$ ✕ **Restaurante do Hiltinho.** This is one of the most elegant restaurants in Paraty. Its specialty is *camarão casadinho,* fried colossal shrimp stuffed with hot *farofa* (toasted cassava flour) made with small shrimp. Even if you're familiar with jumbo shrimp, you might be astonished at the size of these. Seafood outnumbers other dishes two to one, but the filet mignon is very good. The service borders on perfection, as does the elegant decor, with French doors opening onto the street. ✉ *Rua Marechal Deodoro 233, Centro Histórico de Paraty* ☎ *024/3371–1432* ▭ *AE, DC, MC, V.*

★ **$$** ▥ **Pousada Porto Imperial.** In the oldest part of town just behind the Igreja da Matriz de Nossa Senhora dos Remédios, this historic building has rooms that ring a series of courtyards and a swimming pool. The pousada is decorated with a collection of typical Brazilian artwork—ceramics, tapestries, and colonial furniture—and also has a tropical garden filled with bromeliads. Noise from the square across the street can be a problem during festival times. ✉ *Rua Tenente Francisco Antônio (Rua do Comércio) s/n, Centro Histórico, 23970-000* ☎ *024/3371–2323* ⊕ *www.pousadaportoimperial.com.br* ⇥ *48 rooms, 3 suites* △ *Restaurant, room service, in-room safes, refrigerators, cable TV, pool, sauna, bar, laundry service* ⊟ *AE, MC, V.*

$ ⊡ **Pousada do Ouro.** Inside an 18th-century building with a garden courtyard, this inn is a block from the Igreja da Matriz de Nossa Senhora dos Remédios. Although it's on the beach, only one suite has a sea view. The decor is colonial style; rooms face an internal garden. ✉ *Rua Dr. Pereira 145, old Rua da Praia, Centro Histórico, 23970-000* ☎ *024/3371–2033 or 024/3371–1378* ⊕ *www.pousadaouro.com.br* ⇥ *18 rooms, 8 suites* △ *Restaurant, room service, in-room safes, refrigerators, cable TV, pool, sauna, bar, laundry service* ⊟ *AE, DC, MC, V* ⏀ *BP.*

★ **$** ⊡ **Pousada Pardieiro.** The houses that make up this property are decorated in a 19th-century Brazilian-colonial style. Rooms have dark-wood-carved beds and antique bureaus. There are no TVs in the rooms, but there's a special living room with a home theater. A beautiful patio has birds and orchids. ✉ *Rua do Comércio 74, Centro Histórico, 23970-000* ☎ *024/3371–1370* ⊕ *www.pousadapardieiro.com.br* ⇥ *27 rooms* △ *Restaurant, room service, in-room safes, refrigerators, pool, sauna, bar, laundry service* ⊟ *AE, V.*

¢ ⊡ **Pousada do Príncipe.** A prince (the great-grandson of Emperor Pedro II) owns this aptly named inn at the edge of the colonial city. The hotel is painted in the yellow and green of the imperial flag, and its quiet, colorful public areas are graced by photos of the royal family. Rooms are small, decorated in a colonial style, and face either the internal garden or the swimming pool, which is in the plant-filled patio. The kitchen is impressive, too; its chef turns out an exceptional feijoada. ✉ *Av. Roberto Silveira 289, 23970-000* ☎ *024/3371–2266* ⊕ *www.pousadadoprincipe.com.br* ⇥ *31 rooms, 3 suites* △ *Restaurant, room service, fans, some in-room safes, refrigerators, cable TV, 2 tennis courts, pool, sauna, laundry service; no a/c in some rooms* ⊟ *AE, DC, MC, V.*

Fodor'sChoice
★

Side Trips from Rio Essentials

Transportation

BY AIR

TEAM has charter flights (about R$575) to Búzios from Rio that run infrequently, depending on demand (eight people are required for a flight).

🗐 **TEAM Transportes Aéreos** ☎ *021/3328–1616* ⊕ *www.voeteam.com.br.*

BY BOAT

Passenger ferries for Niterói leave from Praça 15 de Novembro in Rio. In 20 minutes you arrive at Praça Araribóia, in downtown Niterói, or at the Terminal Hidroviário de Charitas. Barcas S/A boats (R$2) are bigger and slower than the newer Catamaran Jumbo Cat fleet (R$4).

Call Barcas S/A in Rio for information about Angra dos Reis and Ilha Grande ferries. TELEBARCAS is a telephone hotline for information about all the ferries, and is open weekdays 8–7 and weekends 8–noon.

ⓕ Barcas S/A ⊠ Praça Araribóia 6–8, Niterói ☎ 021/2719-1892 or 021/2620-6766, 021/2533-6661 for Ilha Grande information ⊕ www.barcas-sa.com.br. **Catamaran Jumbo Cat** ⊠ Praça Araribóia s/n, Niterói ☎ 021/2620-8589 or 021/2620-8670. **TELEBARCAS** ⊠ Rio de Janeiro ☎ 021/2533-7524 or 021/2532-6274.

BY BUS

Buses, a shuttle service, and airplanes regularly travel between Búzios and Rio. The best option is the shuttle service, which picks you up in Rio in the morning and drops you at your pousada before noon. Contact Turismo Clássico Travel in Rio for reservations. Municipal buses connect Cabo Frio and Búzios. All buses from Búzios depart from the Terminal Auto Viação 1001.

ⓕ Bus Terminals Rodoviária Nova Friburgo Norte ⊠ Praça Feliciano Costa, 2.5 km (1.5 mi) north of town ☎ 022/2522-06095. **Rodoviária Nova Friburgo Sul** ⊠ Ponte da Saudade, 4 km (2.5 mi) south of town ☎ 022/2522-0400. **Rodoviária Paraty** ⊠ Rua Jango Pádua west of old town ☎ 024/3371-1224. **Rodoviária Petrópolis** ⊠ Rua Doutor Porciúncula 75 ☎ 024/2237-6262. **Terminal Auto Viação 1001** ⊠ Estrada da Usina Velha 444 ☎ 022/2623-2050.

ⓕ Bus Companies Auto Viação 1001 ☎ 021/0300-3131001. **Costa Verde** ☎ 021/2516-2437 or 021/2233-3809. **Reunidas** ☎ 011/3619-0910 or 0800/709-9020. **Turismo Clássico Travel** ☎ 021/2523-3390. **Única** ☎ 021/2263-8792.

BY CAR

To reach Niterói by car, take the 14-km-long (9-mi-long) Presidente Costa e Silva Bridge, also known as Rio-Niterói. The toll is R$3.20. BR 101 connects the city to the Costa Verde and Paraty. Head north and along BR 040 to reach the mountain towns of Petrópolis and Novo Friburgo. Coastal communities Cabo Frio and Búzios are east of Rio along or off RJ 106.

Contacts & Resources

TOUR OPTIONS

South America Experience has weeklong tours to Paraty and Ilha Grande (US$280–US$380). Participants tend to be young (20s and 30s) and adventurous, as accommodations are 3 stars or fewer, and there are lots of activities—like hiking, rapelling, biking—involved.

ⓕ South America Experience ☎ 021/2513-4091 ⊕ www.southamericaexperience.com.

VISITOR INFORMATION

Tourist offices are generally open weekdays from 8 or 8:30 to 6 and Saturday from 8 or 9 to 4; some have limited Sunday hours, too. The Niterói Tourism Office is open daily 9–6. The Tourism Information hotline is an English-language information source about Rio de Janeiro State.

ⓕ Tourist Information Búzios Tourism Office ⊠ Praça Santos Dumont 111, Búzios ☎ 022/2623-2099 ⊕ www.buziosonline.com.br. **IlhaGrande.com** ⊕ www.ilhagrande.com.br. **Nova Friburgo Tourism Office** ⊠ Praça Dr. Demervel B. Moreira, Nova Friburgo ☎ 022/2523-8000 ⊕ www.friweb.com.br. **Paraty Tourism Office** ⊠ Av. Roberto da

Silveira 6 ☎ 024/3371-1897 ⊕ www.paraty.com.br. **Petrópolis Tourism Office** ⊠ Praça da Confluência 3, Petrópolis ☎ 0800/24-1516 ⊕ www.petropolis.rj.gov.br. **Tourism Information** ☎ 0800/282-2007.

SÃO PAULO

Updated by Gabriela Dias and Eduardo Acquarone

São Paulo is a megalopolis of 17 million people, with endless stands of skyscrapers defining the horizon from every angle. The largest city in South America, São Paulo even makes New York City, with its population of about 8 million, seem small in comparison. And this nearly 500-year-old capital of São Paulo State gets bigger every year: it now sprawls across some 8,000 square km (3,089 square mi), of which 1,525 square km (589 square mi) make up the city proper.

The main financial hub in the country, São Paulo is also Brazil's most cosmopolitan city, with top-rate nightlife and restaurants, impressive cultural and arts scenes, and there's no escaping the many shopping and eating temptations. Despite—or because of—these qualities, many tourists, Brazilian and foreigners, avoid visiting the city. São Paulo is hardly a beautiful city; it's fast-paced and there's lots to do, but it's also a concrete jungle, with nothing as attractive as Rio's hills and beaches. Yet, even as the smog reddens your eyes, you'll see that there's much to explore here. When you get tired of laid-back beaches, São Paulo is just the right place to go.

It was only in the late 19th century that São Paulo became a driving force in the country. As the state established itself as one of Brazil's main coffee producers, the city attracted laborers and investors from many countries. Italians, Portuguese, Spanish, Germans, and Japanese put their talents and energies to work. By 1895, 70,000 of the 130,000 residents were immigrants. Their efforts transformed the place from a sleepy mission post into a dynamic financial and cultural hub, with people of all colors and religions living and working together peacefully.

Today, like many major European or American hubs, São Paulo struggles to meet its citizens' transportation and housing needs, and goods and services are expensive. Like most of its counterparts elsewhere in the world, it hasn't yet found an answer to these problems.

Exploring São Paulo

Centro

Even though the downtown district has its share of petty crime, it's one of the few places with a significant amount of pre-20th-century history. Explore the areas where the city began and see examples of architecture, some of it beautifully restored, from the 19th century. The best way to get here is by metro.

WHAT TO SEE
❾
Catedral da Sé. The imposing 14-tower neo-Gothic church, renovated in 2002, has tours through the crypt that contains the remains of Tibiriçá, a native Brazilian who helped the Portuguese back in 1554. ⊠ *Praça da Sé s/n, Centro* ☎ *011/3106–2709, tour 011/3107–6832* 🎫 *Tour R$3*

☉ *Mon. and Wed.–Sat. 8–5, Sun. 8:30–6; tour Mon. and Wed.–Sat. 9:30–4:30* Ⓜ *Sé.*

❸ Edifício BANESPA. If you can't fit tea or drinks at the top of the Ed-ifício Itália into your Centro tour, get your panoramic view of the city atop the 36-floor BANESPA Build-ing. It was constructed in 1947 and

> **CAUTION**
>
> The air pollution might irritate your eyes, especially in July and August (dirty air is held in the city by thermal inversions), so pack eye drops.

modeled after New York's Empire State Building. A radio traffic reporter squints through the smog every morning from here. ⊠ *Rua João Brí-cola 24, Centro* ☎ *011/3249–7180* 💲 *Free* ☉ *Weekdays 10–5* Ⓜ *São Bento.*

❶ Edifício Copan. The architect of this serpentine apartment and office block, Oscar Niemeyer, went on to design much of Brasília, the nation's cap-ital. The building has the clean, white, undulating curves characteristic of his work. The Copan was constructed in 1950, and its 1,160 apart-ments house about 5,600 people. At night the area is overrun by pros-titutes and transvestites. ⊠ *Av. Ipiranga 200, Centro* ☎ *011/3257–6169* ⊕ *www.copansp.com.br* Ⓜ *Anhangabaú.*

NEED A BREAK? **Café Girondino** (⊠ Rua Boa Vista 365, Centro ☎ 011/3229–4574 ⊕ www. cafegirondino.com.br Ⓜ São Bento) is crowded with finance types on week-days, from happy hour until 11 PM. The bar serves good draft beer and sand-wiches. Pictures on the wall depict Centro in its early days.

❼ Mercado Municipal. The city's first grocery market, this huge, 1928 neo-baroque-style building got a major renovation in 2004, and is now the quintessential hot spot for gourmets and food lovers. The building, nicknamed Mercadão (Big Market) by locals, houses 318 stands that sell just about everything edible, including meat, vegetables, cheese, spices, and fish from all over Brazil. It also has restaurants and tradi-tional snack places—don't miss the salt cod *pastel* at Hocca Bar. ⊠ *Rua da Cantareira 306, Centro* ☎ *011/3228–0673* ⊕ *www.mercadomunicipal. com.br* 💲 *Free* ☉ *Mon.–Sat. 5 AM–6 PM, Sun. 7–4* Ⓜ *São Bento.*

Fodor'sChoice ★

★ **❹ Mosteiro de São Bento.** This unique, Norman–Byzantine church constructed between 1910 and 1922 was designed by German architect Richard Berndl. Its enormous organ has some 6,000 pipes, and its Russian image of the Kasperovo Virgin is covered with 6,000 pearls from the Black Sea. If you go on Sunday, don't miss the 10 AM mass and the monks' Gre-gorian chants. ⊠ *Largo de São Bento, Centro* ☎ *011/3328–8799* ⊕ *www.mosteiro.org.br* 💲 *Free* ☉ *Weekdays 6 AM–6:30 PM, weekends 6–12 and 4–6* Ⓜ *São Bento.*

★ **❻ Museu de Arte Sacra.** If you can't get to Bahia or Minas Gerais during your stay in Brazil, you can get a taste of the fabulous baroque and ro-coco art found there at the Museum of Sacred Art. On display is a col-lection of 4,000 wooden and terra-cotta masks, jewelry, and liturgical objects from all over the country (but primarily Minas Gerais and

Bahia), dating from the 17th century to the present. The on-site convent was founded in 1774. ⊠ *Av. Tiradentes 676, Centro* ☎ *011/ 3326–1373* ⊠ *R$4* ☉ *Tues.–Sun. 11–6* Ⓜ *Luz.*

3

⑧ **Pátio do Colégio/Museu Padre Anchieta.** São Paulo was founded by the Jesuits José de Anchieta and Manoel da Nóbrega in the College Courtyard in 1554. The church was constructed in 1896 in the same style as the chapel built by the Jesuits. In the small museum you can see some paintings from the colonization period and an exhibition of early sacred art and relics. ⊠ *Pátio do Colégio 2, Centro* ☎ *011/3105–6899* ⊕ *www.pateocollegio.com.br* ⊠ *Museum R$5* ☉ *Museum Tues.–Sun. 9–5; church Mon.–Sat. 8:15–7, Sun. mass at 10 AM* Ⓜ *Sé.*

⑤ **Pinacoteca do Estado.** The building that houses the State Art Gallery was constructed in 1905 and renovated in 1998. The permanent collection has more than 5,000 works of art, including more than 10 Rodin sculptures and several pieces by famous Brazilian artists like Tarsila do Amaral (whose work consists of colorful, somewhat abstract portraits) and Cândido Portinari (whose oil paintings have social and historical themes). The building has a restaurant. ⊠ *Praça da Luz 2, Centro* ☎ *011/ 3229–9844* ⊕ *www.uol.com.br/pinasp* ⊠ *R$4, Sat. free* ☉ *Tues.–Sun. 10–6* Ⓜ *Luz.*

② **Teatro Municipal.** Inspired by the Paris Opéra, the Municipal Theater was built between 1903 and 1911 with art-nouveau elements. *Hamlet* was the first play presented, and the house went on to host such luminaries as Isadora Duncan in 1916 and Anna Pavlova in 1919. Plays and operas are still staged here; local newspapers have schedules and information on how to get tickets. The fully restored auditorium, resplendent with gold leaf, moss-green velvet, marble, and mirrors, has 1,500 seats and is usually open only to those attending cultural events; if you are not, reserve a guided tour at least a month in advance. ⊠ *Praça Ramos de Azevedo, Centro* ☎ *011/3222–8698* ⊕ *www.prefeitura.sp.gov.br/ theatromunicipal* ⊠ *Tours R$10* ☉ *Tours by appointment Tues. and Thurs. at 1* PM Ⓜ *Anhangabaú.*

Liberdade

In 1908 a group of Japanese arrived to work as contract farm laborers in São Paulo State. In the next five decades, roughly a quarter of a million of their countrymen followed, forming what is now the largest Japanese colony outside Japan. Distinguished today by a large number of successful businesspeople, professionals, and politicians, the community also made important contributions to Brazilian agriculture during the last century. The Japanese are credited with introducing the persimmon, the azalea, the tangerine, and the kiwi to Brazil.

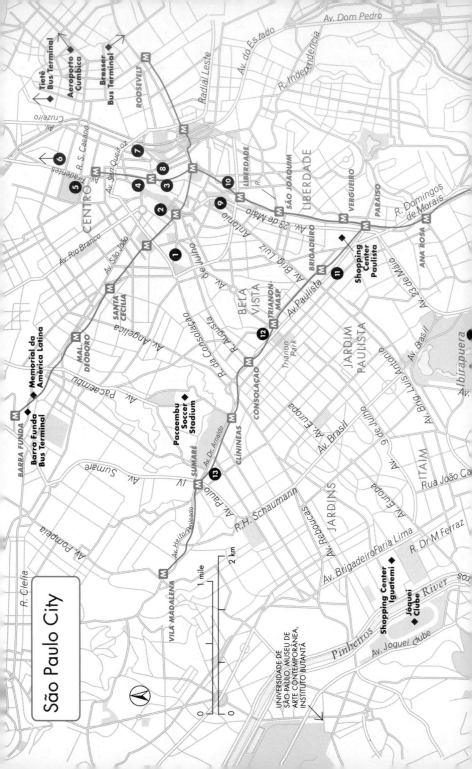

São Paulo City

Tietê Bus Terminal

Aeroporto Cumbica

Bresser Bus Terminal

Av. Dom Pedro

Av. do Estado

Av. do Estado

Radial Leste

R. Independência

R. Independência

ROOSEVELT

Av. São Queiroz

Av. Cruzeiro

R. S. Caetano

Tiradentes

6

5

CENTRO

7

8

3

4

2

1

10

9

LIBERDADE

LIBERDADE

SÃO JOAQUIM

Av. 23 de Maio

São Joaquim

VERGUEIRO

PARAISO

R. Domingos de Morais

ANA ROSA

Av. Rio Branco

Av. São João

SANTA CECILIA

MAL. DEODORO

Memorial da América Latina

BARRA FUNDA

Barra Funda Bus Terminal

Av. Pacaembu

Av. Angélica

Paçaembu Soccer Stadium

Av. Sumaré

SUMARÉ

IV

13

Av. Dr. Arnaldo

CLINÍNEAS

CONSOLAÇÃO

R. da Consolação

R. Augusta

Av. Brig. Luiz Antônio

Av. Paulista

BELA VISTA

TRIANON-MASP

12

Trianon Park

11

Av. Brig. Luiz Antônio

BRIGADEIRO

Shopping Center Paulista

JARDIM PAULISTA

Av. Europa

Av. Brasil

Av. 9 de Julho

ITAIM

Av. Brig. Luis Antônio

Av. Brasil

Av. Ibirapuera

Av. Heitor Penteado

VILA MADALENA

R.H. Schaumann

JARDINS

Av. Rebouças

Av. Brigadeiro Faria Lima

Rua João Ca

R. Dr M Ferraz

Shopping Center Iguatemi

Jóquei Clube

Pinheiros River

Av. Joquei clube

R. Clelia

Av. Pompéia

UNIVERSIDADE DE SÃO PAULO, MUSEU DE ARTE CONTEMPORÂNEA, INSTITUTO BUTANTÃ

2 km

1 mile

0

0

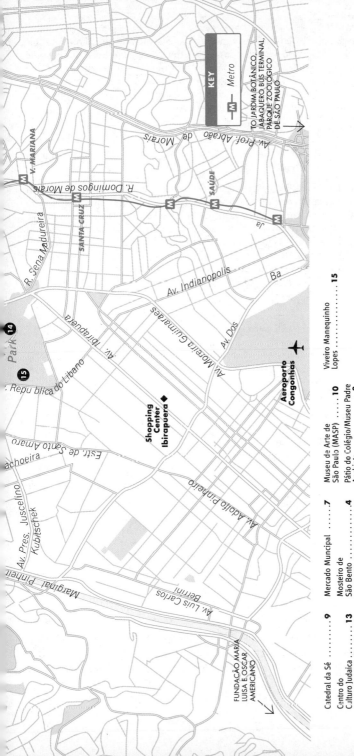

KEY

M — Metro

TO JARDIM BOTÂNICO,
JABAQUERO BUS TERMINAL,
PARQUE ZOOLÓGICO
DE SÃO PAULO

V. MARIANA

R. Domingos de Morais

SANTA CRUZ

R. Sena Madureira

SAÚDE

Av. Prof. Abraão de Morais

Av. Indianopolis

Ba

Av. Ibirapuera

Av. Moreira Guimarães

Av. Dos

Shopping Center Ibirapuera ◆

Est. de Santo Amaro

Av. Adolfo Pinheiro

Aeroporto Congonhas

achoeira

Repu blica do Líbano

Av. Pres. Juscelino Kubitschek

Marginal Pinheir

Av. Luís Carlos Berrini

Park **14**

15

FUNDAÇÃO MARIA
LUISA E OSCAR
AMERICANO

The red-porticoed entryway to Liberdade (which means "Freedom") is south of Praça da Sé, behind the cathedral. The neighborhood is home to many first-, second-, and third-generation Nippo-Brazilians, as well as to more recent Chinese and Korean immigrants. Clustered around Avenida Liberdade are shops with everything from imported bubble gum to miniature robots and Kabuki face paint.

The best time to visit Liberdade is on Sunday during the street fair at Praça Liberdade, where Asian food, crafts, and souvenirs are sold. The fair will very likely be crowded, so keep your wits about you and do not wander around at night.

WHAT TO SEE
★ ⑫ **Praça Liberdade.** Every weekend 10–7, this plaza hosts a sprawling Asian food and crafts fair that exhibits São Paulo's eclectic cultural mix. You may see, for example, Afro-Brazilians dressed in colorful kimonos hawking grilled shrimp on a stick. Several religious celebrations are held here, like April's Hanamatsuri, commemorating the birth of the Buddha. Apart from the fair and special events, the only other reason to visit this square is to stop by at the nearby Japanese shops and restaurants. ✉ *Av. da Liberdade and Rua dos Estudantes, Liberdade* Ⓜ *Liberdade.*

Avenida Paulista & Bixiga

Money once poured into and out of the coffee barons' mansions that lined Avenida Paulista, making it, in a sense, the financial hub. And so it is today, though the money is now centered in the major banks. Like the barons before them, many of these financial institutions generously support the arts. Numerous places have changing exhibitions—often free— in the Paulista neighborhood. Nearby Bixiga, São Paulo's Little Italy, is full of restaurants.

WHAT TO SEE
⑬ **Centro da Cultura Judaica.** This Torah-shaped concrete building is one of the newest architectural hot spots in town. Inaugurated in 2003 to display Jewish history and culture in Brazil, it houses a theater and an art gallery and promotes exhibits, lectures, and book fairs. The café serves local Jewish cuisine. ✉ *Rua Oscar Freire 2500, Pinheiros* ☎ *011/ 3065–4333* ⊕ *www.culturajudaica.org.br* ✏ *Free* ⊙ *Weekdays 10–9, weekends 2–7* Ⓜ *Sumaré.*

⑪ **Instituto Itaú Cultural.** Maintained by Itaú, one of Brazil's largest private banks, this cultural institute has art shows as well as lectures, workshops, and films. It also maintains an archive with the photographic history of São Paulo and a library which specializes in works on Brazilian art and culture. ✉ *Av. Paulista 149, Paraíso* ☎ *011/2168–1700* ⊕ *www. itaucultural.org.br* ✏ *Free* ⊙ *Tues.–Fri. 10–9, weekends 10–7* Ⓜ *Brigadeiro.*

NEED A BREAK?

A recommended snack is the delicious *bauru*—a sandwich with roast beef, tomato, cucumber, and a mix of melted cheeses—at **Ponto Chic** (✉ Praça Osvaldo Cruz 26, Bixiga ☎ 011/3289–1480 ⊕ www.pontochic.com.br ⊙ Daily 11 AM–2 AM), a block east of Instituto Itaú Cultural, across Avenida Paulista. The restaurant claims to have invented the sandwich.

10 **Museu de Arte de São Paulo (MASP).** One of the city's premier fine-arts
FodorsChoice collections, with more than 7,000 pieces, is in this striking low-rise, el-
★ evated on two massive concrete pillars 256 feet apart. Highlights of the
collection are works by Van Gogh, Renoir, Delacroix, Cézanne, Monet,
Rembrandt, Picasso, and Degas. Baroque sculptor Aleijadinho, expressionist painter Lasar Segall, and expressionist/surrealist painter Cândido
Portinari are three of the many Brazilian artists represented. The huge
open area beneath the museum is often used for cultural events and is
the site of a charming Sunday antiques fair. ⊠ *Av. Paulista 1578, Bela
Vista* ☎ *011/3251–5644* ⊕ *www.masp.art.br* ⊠ *R$10* ⊗ *Tues.–Sun.
11–6* Ⓜ *Trianon.*

Parque Ibirapuera

Ibirapuera is São Paulo's Central Park, though it is slightly less than half
the size of and is often more crowded on sunny weekends than its NYC
counterpart. In the 1950s the land, which originally contained the municipal nurseries, was chosen as the site of a public park to commemorate the city's 400th anniversary. Oscar Niemeyer and Roberto Burle Marx
were called in to join the team of professionals assigned to the project.
The park was inaugurated in 1954, and some pavilions used for the opening festivities still sit amid its 160 hectares (395 acres). It has jogging and
biking paths, a lake, and rolling lawns. You can rent bicycles at a number of places near park entrances for about R$5 an hour.

WHAT TO SEE **Museu de Arte Moderna (MAM).** More than 4,500 paintings, installations,
14 sculptures, and other works from modern and contemporary artists such
as Alfredo Volpi and Ligia Clark are part of the Modern Art Museum's
permanent collection. Temporary exhibits feature works by new local
artists. The giant wall of glass, designed by Brazilian architect Lina Bo
Bardi, serves as a window beckoning you to peek inside. ⊠ *Av. Pedro
Álvares Cabral s/n, Gate 3, Parque Ibirapuera* ☎ *011/5549–9688*
⊕ *www.mam.org.br* ⊠ *R$5.50 (free Sun.)* ⊗ *Tues.–Sun. 10–6.*

NEED A
BREAK?
The Bar do MAM (⊠ Gate 3, Parque Ibirapuera ☎ 011/5549–9688 Ext. 1143),
inside the Museu de Arte Moderna, serves lunch and snacks, plus sandwiches,
pies, soda, coffee, and tea. It's the only place to buy food in the park, apart
from hot-dog stands.

15 **Viveiro Manequinho Lopes.** The Manequinho Lopes Nursery is where most
plants and trees used by the city are grown. The original was built in
the 1920s; the current version was designed by Roberto Burle Marx.
Specimens are of such Brazilian trees as *ipê, pau-jacaré,* and *pau-brasil,*
the tree for which the country was named (the red dye it produces was
greatly valued by the Europeans). ⊠ *Gate 7A, Av. República do Líbano,
Parque Ibirapuera* ☎ *011/3887–7723* ⊗ *Weekdays 7–5.*

Where to Eat

Bela Vista

ITALIAN ✕ **Ca' D'Oro.** This is a longtime northern Italian favorite among Brazil-
$$–$$$$ ian bigwigs, many of whom have their own tables in the old-world-style
dining room. Quail, osso buco, and veal-and-raisin ravioli are winners,

but the specialty is the Piedmontese *gran bollito misto,* steamed meats and vegetables accompanied by three sauces. ⊠ *Grande Hotel Ca' D'Oro, Rua Augusta 129* ☎ *011/3236–4300* ⊟ *AE, DC, MC, V* Ⓜ *Anhangabaú.*

PIZZA ✕ **Speranza.** One of the most traditional pizzerias in São Paulo, this restau-
$–$$ rant is famous for its margherita pie. The crunchy *pão de linguiça* (sausage bread) appetizers have a fine reputation as well. Pastas and chicken and beef dishes are also served. ⊠ *Rua 13 de Maio 1004* ☎ *011/288–8502* ⊕ *www.pizzaria.com.br* ⊟ *DC, MC, V.*

Bixiga

ITALIAN ✕ **Roperto.** Plastic flowers adorn the walls at this typical Bixiga cantina.
★ $$–$$$$ You won't be alone if you order the ever-popular fusilli *ao sugo* (with tomato sauce), or the traditional baby goat's leg with potatoes and tomatoes. ⊠ *Rua 13 de Maio 634* ☎ *011/3288–2573* ⊟ *DC, MC, V* Ⓜ *Brigadeiro.*

Centro

ITALIAN ✕ **Famiglia Mancini.** A huge wheel of provolone cheese is the first thing
$$$–$$$$ you see at this warm restaurant. An incredible buffet with cheeses,
Fodor'sChoice olives, sausages, and much more makes finding a tasty appetizer a cinch.
★ The menu has many terrific pasta options, such as the cannelloni with palm hearts and a four-cheese sauce. All dishes serve two people. ⊠ *Rua Avanhandava 81* ☎ *011/3256–4320* ⊟ *AE, DC, MC, V* Ⓜ *Anhangabaú.*

Cerqueira César

BRAZILIAN ✕ **Bargaço.** The original Bargaço, in Salvador, has long been considered
$$ the best Bahian restaurant in that city. If you can't make it to the northeast, be sure to have a meal in the São Paulo branch. Seafood is the calling card. ⊠ *Rua Oscar Freire 1189* ☎ *011/3085–5058* ⊟ *DC, MC* Ⓜ *Consolação.*

¢–$$ ✕ **Sujinho–Bisteca d'Ouro.** The modest Sujinho serves churrasco without any frills. It's the perfect place for those who simply want to eat a gorgeous piece of meat. The portions are so large that one dish can usually feed two. A few options on the menu creep into the $$$ price range. ⊠ *Rua de Consolação 2078* ☎ *011/3231–5207* ⊕ *www.sujinho.com. br* ⊟ *No credit cards* Ⓜ *Consolação.*

ECLECTIC ✕ **Spot.** The closest thing to a chic diner that you'll find in São Paulo,
¢–$ Spot is just one door up from MASP. The salads and the pasta dishes are good bets; come early, though, as it gets crowded after 10 PM. ⊠ *Alameda Rocha Azevedo 72* ☎ *011/3284–6131 or 011/3283–0946* ⊟ *AE, DC, MC, V* Ⓜ *Consolação.*

PIZZA ✕ **Pedaço da Pizza.** Pizza is served by the slice here. Choose from the
★ ¢ traditional ones such as pepperoni, or an innovation: pizza with oyster mushrooms and cabbage. It is a good late-night stop since it's open until 6 AM on weekends. The place is crowded with paulistanos after movies let out. ⊠ *Rua Augusta 2931, Jardins* ☎ *011/3891–2431* ⊠ *Rua Augusta 1463, Cerqueira César* ☎ *3285–2117* ⊟ *No credit cards* Ⓜ *Consolação.*

Consolação

ECLECTIC
★ $–$$

✕ **Mestiço.** Tribal masks peer down from the walls of the large, modern dining room. Consider the Thai *huan-hin* (chicken with shiitake mushrooms in ginger sauce and rice) followed by a dessert of lemon ice cream with *baba de moça* (a syrup made with egg whites and sugar). An eclectic menu also includes Italian, Brazilian, and Bahian dishes. ☒ *Rua Fernando de Albuquerque 277* ☏ *011/3256–1539 or 011/3256–3165* ⊟ *AE, DC, MC, V* Ⓜ *Consolação.*

FRENCH
★ $–$$$

✕ **La Tartine.** An ideal place for a cozy romantic dinner, this small bistro has a good wine selection and simple but comfortable furniture. The menu changes daily; a favorite is the classic coq au vin, or you can fill up on entrées from beef tenderloin to soups and quiches. It is usually crowded with São Paulo's trendy people, and you might have to wait to get a table on weekends. ☒ *Rua Fernando de Albuquerque 267* ☏ *011/3259–2090* ⊟ *V* ☉ *Closed Sun.–Mon.* Ⓜ *Consolação.*

JAPANESE
$$–$$$$

✕ **Nagayama.** Also with a branches in Itam Bibi and Cerqueira César, this is a low-key, trustworthy, and well loved favorite. Nagayama consistently serves excellent sushi and sashimi. The chefs like to experiment: the California *uramaki* Philadelphia has rice, cream cheese, grilled salmon, roe, cucumber, and spring onions rolled together. ☒ *Rua Bandeira Paulista 369, Itaim Bibi* ☏ *011/3079–7553* ⊟ *AE, DC, MC* ☒ *Rua da Consolação 3397, Cerqueira César* ☏ *011/3064–0110* ⊟ *AE, DC, MC.*

Higienópolis

ITALIAN
$–$$

✕ **Jardim di Napoli.** The white, green, and red of the Italian flag is just about everywhere you look in this restaurant. People come for the unmatchable *polpettone alla parmigiana,* a huge meatball with mozzarella and tomato sauce. There are many other meat dishes, pasta selections, and pizza. ☒ *Rua Doutor Martinico Prado 463* ☏ *011/3666–3022* ⊟ *AE, V.*

Itaim Bibi

FRENCH
$$–$$$$

✕ **Freddy.** Leave the grunge and noise of the streets behind in this eatery with the feel of an upscale Parisian bistro. Try the duck with Madeira sauce and apple puree, the pheasant with herb sauce, or the hearty cassoulet with white beans, lamb, duck, and garlic sausage. ☒ *Praça Dom Gastão Liberal Pinto 111* ☏ *011/3167–0977* ⊟ *AE, DC, MC, V* ☉ *No dinner Sun., no lunch Sat.*

ITALIAN
$$–$$$$

✕ **La Vecchia Cucina.** Chef Sergio Arno changed the face of the city's Italian restaurants with his *nuova cucina,* exemplified by dishes like frogs' legs risotto and duck ravioli with watercress sauce. Well-to-do patrons dine in the glass-walled garden gazebo or the ocher-color dining room decorated with Italian engravings and fresh flowers. ☒ *Rua Pedroso Alvarenga 1088* ☏ *011/3079–4042* ⊟ *AE, DC, MC, V* ☉ *No dinner Sun., no lunch Sat.*

PAN-ASIAN
$–$$

✕ **Kundun.** Inspired by food from China, Japan, Vietnam, Thailand, and Laos, chef Maria Yeh comes up with main courses like shrimp with lychee fruit, fresh tomatoes, and shiitake risotto; or Zen duck, smoked

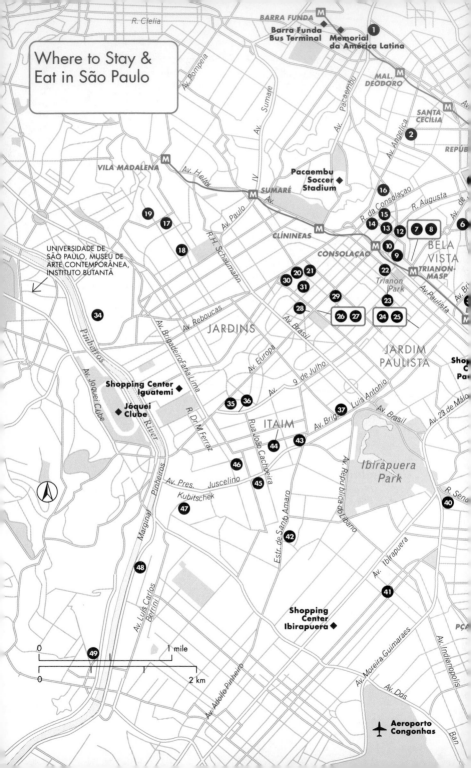

Restaurants ▼

Almanara	**30**
Amadeus	**22**
Arábia	**23**
Baby Beef Rubaiyat	**34**
Bargaço	**20**
Braz	**3**
Ca' D'Oro	**2**
Cantaloup	**41**
La Casserole	**5**
Consulado Mineiro	**17**
Esplanada Grill	**28**
Famiglia Mancini	**10**
Freddy	**39**
Frevo	**27**
Galpão	**1**
Ganesh	**48**
Jardim di Napoli	**2**
Lellis Trattoria	**16**
Mestiço	**14**
Nagayama	**21, 40**
Nakombi	**46**
Oriental Café	**28**
Speranza	**39**
Sujinho–Bisteca d'Ouro	**12**
Sutra	**45**
La Tambouille	**43**
La Tartine	**13**
Truta Rosa	**37**
La Vecchia Cucina	**42**

Hotels ▼

Bourbon	**6**
Carillon Plaza	**29**
Eldorado Higienópolis	**4**
Grande Hotel Ca' D'Oro	**8**
Gran Meliá São Paulo	**47**
La Guardia	**11**
L'Hotel	**23**
Hotel Formule 1	**3**
Hotel Joamar	**7**
Hotel Sofitel São Paulo	**36**
Inter-Continental São Paulo	**32**
Maksoud Plaza	**24**
Parthenon Golden Tower	**44**
Renaissance São Paulo	**15**
Sheraton Mofarrej Hotel & Towers	**31**
Ville Hotel	**4**

with jasmine tea. Sushi is also served in this contemporary-casual space with floor-to-ceiling windows. ⊠ *Av. Horácio Lafer 362, Itaim Bibi* ☎ *011/3078–3519* ⊟ *AE, DC, MC, V.*

Jardins

BRAZILIAN ✕**Dona Lucinha.** Mineiro dishes are the specialties at this modest eatery
$ with plain wooden tables. The classic cuisine is served as a buffet only: more than 50 stone pots hold dishes like *feijão tropeiro* (beans with manioc flour). Save room for a dessert of ambrosia. ⊠ *Av. Chibarás 399, Moema* ☎ *011/5051–2050* ⊟ *AE, DC, MC, V* ⊠ *Rua Bela Cintra 2325* ☎ *011/3082–3797* ⊕ *www.donalucinha.com.br* ⊟ *AE, DC, MC, V* ☺ *Closed Mon.*

★ ¢–$ ✕**Frevo.** Paulistanos of all types and ages flock to this Jardins luncheonette for its beirute sandwiches, filled with ham and cheese, tuna, or chicken, and for its draft beer and fruit juices in flavors such as *acerola* (Antilles cherry), passion fruit, and papaya. ⊠ *Rua Oscar Freire 603* ☎ *011/3082–3434* ⊟ *AE, DC, MC, V.*

FRENCH ✕**Bistrô Jaú.** Chef Roberto Eid runs the kitchen and the restaurant here.
$–$$$ Businesspeople from Avenida Paulista appreciate the fine decor and the lunch menu, which is superb yet inexpensive (compared with the dinner menu). ⊠ *Alameda Jaú 1606, Jardins* ☎ *011/3085–5573* ⊟ *AE, DC, MC, V* Ⓜ *Consolação.*

LEBANESE ✕**Arábia.** For more than 10 years, Arábia has served traditional Lebanese
★ $–$$$$ cuisine at this beautiful high-ceilinged restaurant. Simple dishes such as hummus and stuffed grape leaves are executed with aplomb. The lamb melts in your mouth. The reasonably priced "executive" lunch includes one cold dish, one meat dish, a drink, and dessert. Don't miss the pistachio marzipan covered in rose syrup for dessert. ⊠ *Rua Haddock Lobo 1397, Jardins* ☎ *011/3061–2203* ⊕ *www.arabia.com.br* ⊟ *AE, DC, MC.*

$ ✕**Almanara.** Part of a chain of Lebanese semi-fast-food outlets, Almanara is perfect for a quick lunch of hummus, tabbouleh, grilled chicken, and rice. There's also a full-blown restaurant on the premises that serves Lebanese specialties *rodízio* style, meaning you're served continuously until you can ingest no more. ⊠ *Rua Oscar Freire 523, Jardins* ☎ *011/ 3085–6916* ⊟ *AE, DC, MC, V.*

VEGETARIAN ✕**Cheiro Verde.** One of the few places in São Paulo where you can eat
¢–$ tasty vegetarian food, Cheiro Verde has a simple menu with choices like whole-wheat mushroom pizza and the delicious *gratinado de legumes* (vegetables with Gorgonzola sauce). ⊠ *Rua Peixoto Gomide 1413, Jardins* ☎ *011/3289–6853* ⊟ *AE, DC, MC, V* ☺ *No dinner* Ⓜ *Trianon.*

Jardin Europa

ECLECTIC ✕**La Tambouille.** This Italo-French restaurant with a partially enclosed
$$–$$$$ garden isn't just a place to be seen; it also has some of the best food in town. Among chef Giancarlo Bolla's recommended dishes are the linguini with fresh mussels and prawn sauce and the filet mignon *rosini* (served with foie gras and saffron risotto). ⊠ *Av. Nove de Julho 5925* ☎ *011/3079–6276* ⊟ *AE, DC, MC, V.*

Liberdade

JAPANESE
$$$–$$$$
✕ **Kinoshita** In the heart of the Japanese neighborhood, this spot is popular for its tasting menu, which mixes the fresh catch of the day with Western and Japanese ingredients. ⊠ *Rua da Glória 168* ☎ *011/ 3105–4903* Ⓜ *Liberdade* ⊟ *DC, MC, V* ☉ *Closed Sun.*

Moema

PIZZA
$–$$
Fodor'sChoice
★
✕ **Braz.** Its name comes from one of the most traditional Italian neighborhoods in São Paulo and no one argues that it doesn't have the right. Each of the nearly 20 types of crisp-crusted pizzas is delicious, from the traditional margherita to the house specialty, pizza *braz*, with tomato sauce, zucchini, and mozzarella and Parmesan cheeses. The *chopp* (draft beer) is also very good. ⊠ *Rua Grauna 125* ☎ *011/5561–0905* ⊕ *www. casabraz.com.br* ⊟ *DC, MC, V.*

Morumbi

BRAZILIAN
$–$$$
✕ **Esplanada Grill.** The beautiful people hang out in the bar of this highly regarded churrascaria. The thinly sliced *picanha* steak (similar to rump steak) is excellent; it goes well with a house salad (hearts of palm and shredded, fried potatoes), onion rings, and creamed spinach. The restaurant's version of the traditional *pão de queijo* (cheese bread) is widely viewed as one of the best. ⊠ *Morumbi Shopping Center, 1st floor, Av. Roque Petroni Jr. 1089* ☎ *011/5181–8156* ⊟ *AE, DC, MC, V.*

Vila Madalena

ECLECTIC
$
✕ **Pitanga.** In a comfortable house in Vila Madalena, Pitanga has a diverse buffet every day (R$23 weekdays, R$32 Saturday, R$34 Sunday). Delicious salads, meat dishes, and feijoada are some of the buffet choices. ⊠ *Rua Original 162* ☎ *011/3816–2914* ⊟ *AE, MC, V* ☉ *Closed Mon.* Ⓜ *Vila Madalena.*

PIZZA
★ $–$$
✕ **Oficina de Pizzas.** Both branches of this restaurant look like something designed by the Spanish artist Gaudí, but the pizzas couldn't be more Italian and straightforward. Try a pie with mozzarella and toasted garlic. ⊠ *Rua Purpurina 517, Vila Madalena* ☎ *011/3816–3749* ⊟ *DC, MC, V* ⊠ *Rua Inácio Pereira da Rocha 15, Vila Madalena* ☎ *011/ 3813–8389* ⊟ *DC, MC, V* ⊕ *www.oficinadepizzas.com.br.*

Vila Olímpia

JAPANESE
$–$$$$
✕ **Nakombi.** Chefs prepare sushi from a *kombi* (Volkswagen van) in the middle of the dining room at this eclectic and fun restaurant where tables are surrounded by a small artificial river teeming with fish. The menu includes a good variety of sushi and nonsushi dishes. Try the salmon fillet with *shimeji* mushrooms. ⊠ *Rua Pequetita 170* ☎ *011/3845–9911* ⊟ *AE, DC, MC, V.*

Where to Stay

São Paulo's hotels are almost exclusively geared to business travelers, both homegrown and foreign. For this reason, most hotels are near Avenida Paulista, along Marginal Pinheiros, or in the charming Jardins neighborhood, where international businesses are locationed. But catering to business travelers doesn't necessarily make São Paulo's hotels stuffy or boring. On the contrary, the city has the largest concentration of high-quality, high-style hotels in Brazil. Many of them could be compared to the best hotels in London or New York.

You might get a discount for weekend stays; and breakfast is usually included in the room rate. São Paulo hosts many international conventions, so it's wise to make reservations well in advance. Hotel prices sky-rocket during the annual Formule 1 auto race in September.

Bela Vista

¢ 🏨 **San Gabriel.** Expect no frills at this budget hotel very close to Avenida Paulista. Rooms are small (though there are some suites, which are larger), but have all the basics and are clean. The rates are unbeatable for this part of town. ⊠ *Rua Frei Caneca 1006, Bela Vista, 01307-002* ☎ *011/ 3253-2279* ⊕ *www.sangabriel.com.br* ☞ *75 rooms, 25 suites* ⧉ *Cable TV, refrigerators, parking (fee)* ⊟ *AE, DC, MC, V* ⏹ *EP.*

Brooklin & Santo Amaro

$$$–$$$$
Fodor'sChoice
★

🏨 **Gran Meliá São Paulo.** This all-suites luxury hotel is in the same building as São Paulo's World Trade Center (WTC) and the D&D Decoração & Design Center. Suites have king-sized beds, two phone lines, living rooms with sofas, and small tables that are the perfect places to set up your laptop. Stay on one of the apartment floors and get special amenities like pass-key access and bathroom faucets that can be programmed to maintain your preferred water temperature. Off the large marble lobby is a bar whose comfortable leather chairs are perfect for unwinding after a day of meetings or shopping. ⊠ *Av. das Nações Unidas 12559, Brooklin, 04578-905* ☎ *011/3055–8000 or 0800/703–3399* ⊕ *www.solmelia. com* ☞ *300 suites* ⧉ *Restaurant, room service, in-room safes, cable TV, in-room data ports, tennis court, indoor pool, gym, hair salon, massage, sauna, paddle tennis, bar, laundry facilities, business services, meeting room, parking (fee)* ⊟ *AE, DC, MC, V.*

$$$–$$$$ 🏨 **Transamérica.** Directly across the Pinheiros River from the Centro Empresarial office complex, the home of many U.S. companies, this hotel is a convenient choice for those working in the area. The skylighted lobby—in granite and marble, with Persian carpets, palm trees, leather sofas, and oversize modern paintings—is more impressive than the rooms, with their beige wall-to-wall carpets and floral fabrics, but they're clean, spacious, and quiet. ⊠ *Av. das Nações Unidas 18591, Santo Amaro, 04795-901* ☎ *011/5693–4511 or 0800/12–6060* ⊕ *www. transamerica.com.br* ☞ *389 rooms, 11 suites* ⧉ *Restaurant, room service, cable TV, 9-hole golf course, 2 tennis courts, pool, gym, sauna, bar, laundry facilities, business services, parking (fee)* ⊟ *AE, DC, MC, V.*

Centro & Environs

★ $ 🏨 **Novotel Jaraguá.** Built in 1954 to be the headquarters of one of the main newspapers in the city, the building that now houses this hotel is a landmark in downtown São Paulo. The huge mural created by Di Cavalcanti is one of the 1950s attractions. All 415 rooms were renovated in 2004; their decor hovers somewhere between Scandinavian and air-port lounge (albeit a well-maintained airport lounge). The furnishings are all blonde-wood and brushed steel of an indistinguishable contemporary style, which, all in all makes for pleasant rooms at good prices. ⊠ *Rua Martins Fontes 71, Centro, 01050-000* ☎ *011/3120–8000* ⊕ *www.novotel.com.br* ⊃ *309 rooms, 106 suites* ⚹ *Restaurant, cable TV with movies, in-room broadband in some rooms, Wi-Fi, Internet room, bar, shops, business center, parking (fee)* ▤ *AE, MC, V* ℣ *BP.*

¢ ▦ **Ibis São Paulo Expo.** This large hotel northwest of Centro has clean budget rooms. The decoration is contemporary with focus on function, not beauty. Rooms have either one queen-sized bed or two or three twin beds. The professional staff helps you enjoy your stay. ⊠ *Rua Eduardo Viana 163, Barra Funda, 01133-040* ☎ *011/3824–7373* ⊕ *www. accorhotels.com.br* ⊃ *280 rooms* ⚹ *Restaurant, room service, cable TV, laundry facilities, meeting rooms, free parking* ▤ *AE, DC, MC, V.*

Higienópolis

$ ▦ **Meliá Higienópolis.** In one of the city's oldest and most attractive residential neighborhoods, only a 10-minute taxi ride from Centro, this hotel, built in 2000, has bright and spacious rooms with contemporary light-wood furnishings. The 24-story building provides nice views of the city from the top floors. ⊠ *Rua Maranhão 371, Higienópolis, 01240-000* ☎ *011/3665–8200 or 0800/703–3399* ⊕ *www.solmelia.com* ⊃ *213 rooms* ⚹ *Restaurant, room service, cable TV with movies, in-room safes, minibars, in-room broadband, pool, gym, sauna, business center, Internet room, parking (fee)* ▤ *AE, DC, MC, V* ℣ *BP.*

Itaim Bibi

$–$$ ▦ **Blue Tree Towers Faria Lima.** In a good location for business travelers, the Blue Towers has 77 apartments that can be transformed into offices, with foldaway beds. Rooms are modern, with dark-wood furnishings and bright-white textiles. ⊠ *Avenida Brigadeiro Faria Lima 3989, Itaim, 04538-133* ☎ *011/3896–7544* ⊕ *www.bluetree.com.br* ⊃ *338 rooms* ⚹ *Restaurant, cable TV with movies, minibars, in-room broadband, Wi-Fi, pool, gym, massage, sauna, bar, parking (fee)* ▤ *AE, DC, MC, V* ℣ *BP.*

Jardins

★ $$$$ ▦ **Gran Meliá Mofarrej.** Just behind Avenida Paulista and next to Parque Trianon, the Mofarrej has rooms that are a mix of modern and classic styles. The softness of the decor belies the austere skyscraper that you see from the street. The service is fabulous all around, but the four butler-service floors offer other amenities that make you feel even more pampered. Rooms on the west side overlook the park. ⊠ *Alameda Santos 1437, Jardins, 01419-905* ☎ *011/3146–5900 or 0800/703–3399* ⊕ *www.solmelia.com* ⊃ *268 suites* ⚹ *2 restaurants, room service, cable TV, indoor pool, gym, massage, sauna, 2 bars, laundry facilities, business services, convention center, parking (fee)* ▤ *AE, DC, MC, V* Ⓜ *Trianon.*

★ $$$$ ▦ **Inter-Continental São Paulo.** This exquisite hotel is one of the most attractive of the city's top-tier establishments and consistently gets rave reviews from patrons. Service is attentive, and both the private and public areas are well appointed. Creams, pastels, and marble come together with seamless sophistication and elegance. ✉ *Al. Santos 1123, Jardins, 01419-001* ☎*011/3179–2600 or 0800/11–8003* ⊕*www.intercontinental. com* ➦ *189 rooms, 36 suites* ⟁ *Restaurant, room service, cable TV, pool, health club, massage, sauna, bar, business services, helipad, parking (fee)* ⊟ *AE, DC, MC, V* Ⓜ *Trianon*.

$$$$ 🏨 **Unique.** Don't let the watermelon shape scare you. The design by Ruy
Fodor'sChoice Ohtake is one of the attractions of this boutique hotel, where technol-
★ ogy rules. Apartments have plasma TVs with DVD players, mobile phones, king-sized beds, and whirlpool baths with remote control. Steps from Ibirapuera Park, the hotel is the home away from home for models and wealthy Brazilian jet-setters. ✉ *Avenida Brigadeiro Luís Antônio 4700, Jardins, 01402-002* ☎*011/3055–4710 or 0800/770–8771* ⊕*www. unique.com.br* ➦ *95 rooms* ⟁ *Restaurant, cable TV, in-room DVDs, in-room broadband, Wi-Fi, pool, health club, sauna, Internet room, parking (fee)* ⊟ *AE, DC, MC, V* ⑪ *BP*.

$$$ 🏨 **Fasano.** One of the city's top hotels, Fasano is a vision in brown, with a decor that hints at 1940s modern, but is undeniably 21st century chic. *Architecture Digest*–worthy rooms have leather chairs and headboards, parquet floors with fashionable throw rugs, and huge windows. The staff gets rave reviews as being helpful, friendly, and unpretentious. ✉ *Rua Vittorio Fasano 88, Jardins 01414-020* ☎ *011/3896-4077* ⊕ *www. fasano.com.br* ➦ *64 rooms* ⟁ *Restaurant, room service, cable TV, in-room safes, minibars, in-room broadband, pool, spa, gym, bar, concierge, business center, dry cleaning, laundry service, airport shuttle, travel services, free parking, no-smoking floors* ⊟ *AE, D, DC, MC, V* ⑪ *EP*.

$$–$$$$ 🏨 **L'Hotel.** Close to the major business hubs, this European-style hotel has rooms and suites decorated in somewhat sterile floral patterns. The place was modeled after the famous L'Hotel in Paris, and the small number of rooms allows it to focus on providing superior service. ✉ *Alameda Campinas 266, Jardins, 01404-000* ☎ *011/2183–0500* ⊕ *www.lhotel. com.br* ➦ *80 rooms, 7 suites* ⟁ *2 restaurants, room service, cable TV, pool, health club, sauna, pub, laundry facilities, business services, meeting room, parking (fee)* ⊟ *AE, DC, MC, V* Ⓜ *Trianon*.

Paraíso

¢ 🏨 **Hotel Formule 1.** One of the first hotels in São Paulo to offer high quality at low prices, this hotel has a simple and practical style. Rooms are small, but each has a queen-sized bed with a twin bunk above, a table, and a closet. The service has its ups and downs, but the location is good— you can get nearly everywhere in the city from here by subway or bus, and the area is safe for walking around. ✉ *Rua Vergueiro 1571, Paraíso* ☎*011/5085–5699* ⊕*www.accorhotels.com.br* ➦*300* ⟁ *Cable TV, business services, parking (fee)* ⊟ *AE* Ⓜ *Paraíso*.

Pinheiros

$ 🏨 **Golden Tower.** Proximity to important hubs and to Vila Madalena make this a good choice. The hotel was built in 2001, and all rooms have non-allergenic carpet and sheets, as well as anti-noise windows and modern-looking furniture. Rooms are spacious, the location is ideal, and the Mediterranean restaurant is good. Views from the terrace and top floors are privileged. ✉ *Rua Deputado Lacerda Franco 148, Pinheiros, 05418-*

000 ☎ *011/3094–2200 or 0800/10–1525* ⊕ *www.goldentowerhotel. com.br* ➪ *88 rooms, 8 suites* ♿ *Restaurant, cable TV, minibars, in-room safes, in-room broadband in some rooms, Wi-Fi, pool, gym, Internet room, parking (fee), no-smoking floors* ⊟ *AE, MC, V* ⍔ *BP.*

Vila Mariana

$$–$$$$ ⚐ **Hotel Sofitel São Paulo.** Near the Congonhas Airport and Ibirapuera Park, this modern, luxury hotel is noted for its French style. The restaurant serves French cuisine. Dark-wood furniture fills the rooms, many of which have views of park. It's rare in São Paulo to be able to see trees from your window. ⊠ *Rua Sena Madureira 1355, Bloco 1, Vila Mariana, 04021-051* ☎ *011/5087–0800* ⊕ *www.accorhotels.com.br* ➪ *219 rooms* ♿ *Restaurant, room service, cable TV, tennis court, pool, gym, sauna, bar, laundry facilities, business services, meeting rooms, helipad, parking (fee)* ⊟ *AE, DC, MC, V.*

Nightlife & the Arts

Nightlife

São Paulo's nightlife options are seemingly endless, and clubs and bars come and go at a dizzying pace. Though the places listed here were all thriving spots at this writing, the nightlife scene is always changing, and it's best to check with hotel concierges and paulistanos you meet to confirm that a place is still open before heading out on the town.

BARS First opened in 1949, **Bar Brahma** (⊠ Av. São João 677, Centro ☎ 011/
Fodor's Choice 3333–0855 ⊕ www.barbrahmasp.com.br Ⓜ República) used to be the
★ meeting place of artists, intellectuals, and politicians. The decor is a timewarp to the mid-20th century, with furniture, lamps, and a piano true to the period. This is one of the best places in São Paulo for live music, especially on Thursday and Sunday, when the traditional samba group Demônios da Garoa plays.

A stop at off-the-beaten-path **Frangó** (⊠ Largo da Matriz de Nossa Senhora do Ó 168, Freguesia do Ó ☎ 011/3932–4818 or 011/3931–2285 ⊕ www.frangobar.com.br), northwest of Centro, makes you feel as if you've been transported to a small town. The bar has 150 varieties of beer, including the Brazilian dark beer Xingu. Its rich, molasses-like flavor nicely complements the bar's unforgettable *coxinhas de frango com queijo* (fried balls of chicken with cheese)

Moça Bonita (⊠ Rua Quatá 633, Vila Olímpia ☎ 011/3846–8136 ⊕ www.mocabonitabar.com.br) is a popular bar with a maritime theme, complete with aquarium and miniature sailboats. The specialties are draft beer and seafood.

Crowded from happy hour on, **All Black** (⊠ Rua Oscar Freire 163, Jardins ☎ 011/3088–7990 ⊕ www.allblack.com.br) is an Irish pub with style—and a great variety of international beer brands. Irish soccer paraphernalia decorates the place, and a New Zealand flag betrays one of the owner's roots. This is one of the best places to have a Guinness in São Paulo. Most patrons stop at **Empanadas** (⊠ Rua Wisard 489, Vila Madalena ☎ 011/3032–2116) for a beer en route to another Vila

Madalena bar. It's a good place to "warm up" for an evening out with a quick drink and a bite to eat on the bar's sidewalk tables. Appropriately, the *empanadas* (Argentinian filled pastries) are particularly appealing. When it comes to ending the night, **Filial** (✉ Rua Fidalga 254, Vila Madalena ☎ 011/3813–9226) is considered the best bar in town. Plenty of musicians stop by for an after-hours taste of its draft beer, along with the flavorful snacks (such as *bolinho de arroz,* or rice fritters) and meals (try *galinha afogada,* a stew with incredibly moist chicken and rice).

★ The fashionable patrons at **Grazie a Dio** (✉ Rua Girassol 67, Vila Madalena ☎ 011/3031–6568 ⊕ www.grazieadio.com.br) may vary in age, but they always appreciate good music. The best time to go is at happy hour for daily live performances. On Saturday it's jazz, and on Friday, bossa nova. The natural decorations, including trees and constellations, complement the Mediterranean food served in the back.

MUSIC CLUBS **Café Piu Piu** (✉ Rua 13 de Maio 134, Bixiga ☎ 011/3258–8066 ⊕ www. cafepiupiu.com.br) is best known for jazz and blues, but it also hosts groups that play rock (between Friday and Sunday), bossa nova, and sometimes even tango. Statues, an antique balcony, and marble tables decorate the place. Doors open at 9 PM Tuesday–Sunday. The decor at **Sem Eira Nem Beira** (✉ Rua Fiandeiras 966, Itaim Bibi ☎ 011/3845–3444 ⊕ www. semeiranembeira.com.br) was inspired by Brazilian bars circa 1940. The club is famous for its live MPB performances on Friday and Saturday

At **Mr. Blues Jazz Bar** (✉ Av. São Gabriel 558, Jardim Paulista ☎ 011/ 3884–9356), a traditional jazz, blues, rock, and soul venue, the audience drinks beer and whiskey and eats french fries with Parmesan cheese. Doors open at 9 PM Thursday–Saturday.

A *carioca* is a person from Rio de Janeiro, and **Carioca Club** (✉ Rua Cardeal Arcoverde 2899, Pinheiros ☎ 011/3813–8598 ⊕ www.cariocaclub. com.br) has the decor of old-style Rio clubs. Its large dance floor attracts an eclectic mix of up to 1,200 college students, couples, and professional dancers who move to *samba, gafieira,* and *pagode* Thursday–Saturday beginning at 10 PM, and Sunday 5–11.

★ The tiny round tables at **Piratininga** (✉ Rua Wizard 149, Vila Madalena ☎ 011/3032–9775 ⊕ www.piratiningabar.com.br Ⓜ Vila Madalena ☉ Daily 4 PM), a small bar-restaurant, are perfect for a quiet rendezvous. The live MPB, bossa nova, blues, and jazz music, which start daily around 6:30 PM, add to the romance. People come to tiny **All of Jazz** (✉ Rua João Cachoeira 1366, Vila Olímpia ☎ 011/3849–1345 ⊕ www.allofjazz.com.br) to quietly listen to very good jazz and bossa nova. Local musicians jam Monday–Saturday beginning at 7:30 PM. Reserve a table on weekends.

DANCE CLUBS Most clubs open at 9 PM, but people tend to arrive very late (around midnight), and dance until 5 or 6 AM. Still, you should arrive early to be at the front of the lines. Don't worry if the dance floor appears empty at 11 PM; things will start to sizzle an hour or so later.

Villa Country (✉ Av. Francisco Matarazzo 810, Barra Funda ☎ 011/ 3868–5858 ⊕ www.villacountry.com.br Ⓜ Barra Funda) is *the* place to go for American country music and *sertanejo,* Brazilian country music. The huge club has restaurant, bars, shops, game rooms, and a dance floor. An Old West theme permeates the decor. It's open Thursday–Sunday.

Live or recorded indie rock is the musical menu at two-story **Funhouse** (✉ Rua Bela Cintra 567, Consolação ☎ 011/3259–3793 ⊕ www.funhouse.com.br Ⓜ Consolação), open Wednesday–Saturday. New Brazilian bands play every Saturday.

DJs and live acts play rock, hip-hop, and electronic music at **Bunker Lounge Music Bar** (✉ Rua da Consolação 3589, Jardim Paulista ☎ 011/3061–1027 ⊕ www.bunkerlounge.com.br Ⓜ Consolação) Tuesday–Saturday. Some of the owners are members of Sepultura, a famous Brazilian heavy-metal band.

At **Dolores Bar** (✉ Rua Fradique Coutinho 1007, Vila Madalena ☎ 011/3031–3604 ⊕ www.doloresbar.com.br ☉ Fri.–Sat. 10 PM), DJs spin funk, soul, and hip-hop tunes for a crowd in its twenties and thirties. Friday nights are the most popular, and people really do fill up the floor only after midnight. Because **A Lanterna** (✉ Rua Fidalga 531, Vila Madalena ☎ 011/3031–0483 ⊕ www.lanterna.com.br) is a mixture of restaurant, bar, and nightclub, you can go early for dinner and stay late for dancing. Actors, dancers, and musicians give performances that add to the entertainment. The walls are decorated with local artists' works. It's open Tuesday–Sunday.

Buena Vista Club (✉ Rua Atílio Innocenti 780, Vila Olímpia ☎ 011/3045–5245 ⊕ www.buenavistaclub.com.br) is a good place to take dance classes. On Sunday you can learn to dance *gafieira* and *zouk.* Live music and DJs heat up the dance floor for hours. The club also has good appetizers and drinks and is open Wednesday–Sunday. You might feel ★ like you're on the set of an Austin Powers movie at **Lov.e Club & Lounge** (✉ Rua Pequetita 189, Vila Olímpia ☎ 011/3044–1613 ⊕ www.loveclub.com.br). Before 2 AM the music isn't too loud, and you can sit and talk on the '50s-style sofas. Then the techno and house effects keep people on the small dance floor until sunrise. If you want a taste of *pancadão,* the unique carioca-style funk, don't miss Wednesday night with DJ Marlboro. The club is open Tuesday, Wednesday, and Friday–Sunday nights.

GAY & LESBIAN BARS & CLUBS Most of the bars and cafes along Avenida Vieira de Carvalho are gay or mixed, but also rather run-down.

Popular **The Week** (✉ Rua Guaicurus 324, Lapa ☎ 011/3872–9966 ⊕ www.theweek.com.br) has a whooping 6,000 square meters area. Two dance floors, three lounge rooms, a deck with a swimming pool, six bars, and several DJs who play house, electro, and techno animate an often shirtless-crowd on Friday and Saturday nights.

A Lôca (✉ Rua Frei Caneca 916, Cerqueira César ☎ 011/3159–8889 ⊕ www.aloca.com.br Ⓜ Consolação) has a crowded dance floor, a video room, and two bars. A mixed gay, lesbian, and straight crowd often dances until dawn, both to electronic music (Thursday to Saturday) and rock (on Sunday). On Friday and Saturday you can end the night with a light breakfast (yogurt and fruits).

Popular lesbian spot **Club Z** (⊠ Rua Tabapuã 1420, Itaim Bibi ☏ 011/3071–0030 ⊕ www.clubz.com.br), open Friday and Saturday, has Ancient Rome decor, red velvet sofas, and two DJs spinning house and techno.

The Arts

Listings of events appear in the "Veja São Paulo" insert of the newsweekly *Veja*. The arts sections of the dailies *Folha de São Paulo* and *O Estado de São Paulo* also have listings and reviews. Both papers publish a weekly guide on Friday.

CLASSICAL MUSIC & OPERA — Many operas and classical performances take place at Teatro Municipal, Teatro Alfa, and Teatro Cultura Artística.

★ **Sala São Paulo** (⊠ Praça Júlio Prestes, Centro ☏ 011/3337–5414 ⊕ www.osesp.art.br Ⓜ Luz) is one of the most modern concert halls for classical music in Latin America. It's also home to the **São Paulo Symphony** (OSESP).

Built in neoclassical style in 1917 and entirely renovated in 1998, the **Teatro São Pedro** (⊠ Rua Barra Funda 171, Barra Funda ☏ 011/3667–0499 ⊕ www.teatrosaopedro.sp.gov.br Ⓜ Marechal Deodoro) is the second-oldest theater in São Paulo. It's one of the best places in the city for chamber concerts and operas. There are free morning events Sunday and Wednesday.

DANCE — Dance companies perform at Teatro Alfa, Teatro Cultura Artística, Teatro Municipal, and Via Funchal.

Ballet da Cidade (⊠ Praça Ramos de Azevedo, Centro ☏ 011/223–3022 ⊕ www.baledacidade.com.br Ⓜ Anhangabaú) is the city's official dance company. It only performs classical acts, mostly in its home theater, the Teatro Municipal. Contemporary pieces are performed by **Ballet Stagium** (⊠ Rua Augusta 2985, 2nd floor, Cerqueira César ☏ 011/3062–3451 ⊕ www.stagium.com.br)

SAMBA SHOWS — From November to February, many *escolas de samba* (literally "samba schools," which are groups that perform during Carnaval) open their rehearsals to the public. Drummers get in sync with the singers, and everyone learns the lyrics to each year's songs.

Rosas de Ouro (⊠ Av. Cel. Euclides Machado 1066, Freguesia do Ó ☏ 011/3931–4555 ⊕ www.sociedaderosasdeouro.com.br) has one of the most popular rehearsals. Up to 3,000 people at a time attend rehearsals at **Mocidade Alegre** (⊠ Av. Casa Verde 3498, Limão ☏ 011/3857–7525 ⊕ www.mocidadealegre.com.br) just before Carnaval.

FILM — **Centro Cultural São Paulo** (⊠ Rua Vergueiro 1000, Paraíso ☏ 011/3277–3611 Ext. 279 Ⓜ Vergueiro ⊕ www.centrocultural.sp.gov.br) usually shows a series of films centered on a theme. Admission is free or nearly free. It also has plays, concerts, and art exhibits. **Reserva Cultural** (⊠ Av. Paulista 900, Jardim Paulista ☏ 011/3287–3529 ⊕ www.reservacultural.com.br Ⓜ Brigadeiro) has four movie theaters, a small café, a bar, and a nice deck-style restaurant from which you can see—and be seen by—pedestrians in Paulista Avenue.

Brazilian, European, and other non-blockbuster films are shown at the **Espaço Unibanco** (⊠ Rua Augusta 1470/1475, Consolação ☎ 011/3288–6780 Ⓜ Consolação). The **Unibanco ArtePlex** (⊠ Rua Frei Caneca 569, 3rd floor, Consolação ☎ 011/3472–2365 Ⓜ Consolação ⊕ www.unibancoarteplex.com.br) shows Hollywood, European, and independent films.

São Paulo Essentials

Transportation

BY AIR

Nearly all international flights stop in São Paulo, so practically every airline that flies to Brazil flies to São Paulo, and it's very easy to get from São Paulo to everywhere else in Brazil. For airline information *see* Air Travel, *in* Smart Travel Tips A to Z.

AIRPORTS São Paulo's international airport, Aeroporto Cumbica, is in the suburb of Guarulhos, 30 km (19 mi) and a 45-minute drive (longer during rush hour or on rainy days) northeast of Centro. Aeroporto Congonhas, 14 km (9 mi) south of Centro (a 15- to 45-minute drive, depending on traffic), serves regional airlines, including the Rio–São Paulo shuttle.
🛈 **Airports Aeroporto Congonhas** ☎ 011/5090–9000. **Aeroporto Cumbica** ☎ 011/6445–2945.

AIRPORT TRANSFERS EMTU buses—blue air-conditioned vehicles—shuttle between Cumbica Airport and Congonhas (5:30 AM–11:10 PM, every 30 minutes; midnight–5:30 AM, every 90 minutes) as well as between Cumbica and the Tietê bus terminal (5 AM–11:10 PM, every 50–60 minutes); the downtown Praça da República (5:40 AM–11:10 PM, every 30 minutes); and the Hotel Maksoud Plaza (6:10 AM–11:10 PM, every 60–70 minutes), stopping at most major hotels around Avenida Paulista. There are also lines that connect Cumbica to the Barra Funda terminal and the Shopping Eldorado. The cost is R$24.

The sleek, blue-and-white, air-conditioned Guarucoop radio taxis take you from Cumbica to downtown for around R$80. *Comum* (regular) taxis charge R$65 from Cumbica and around R$25 from Congonhas.
🛈 **EMTU** ☎ 0800/19–0088 or 011/6445–2505 ⊕ www.airportbusservice.com.br. **Guarucoop** ☎ 011/6440–7070.

BY BUS

ARRIVING & DEPARTING All bus terminals in the city of São Paulo are connected to metro stations. The three bus stations in São Paulo serve more than 1,100 destinations combined. The huge main station—serving all major Brazilian cities (with trips to Rio every 10 minutes during the day and every half hour at night, until 2 AM) as well as Argentina, Uruguay, Chile, and Paraguay—is the Terminal Tietê in the north, on the Marginal Tietê Beltway. Terminal Jabaquara, near Congonhas Airport, serves coastal towns. Terminal Barra Funda, in the west, near the Memorial da América

Latina, has buses to and from western Brazil. All stations have metro stops. You can buy tickets at the stations; although those for Rio de Janeiro can be bought a few minutes before departure, it's best to buy tickets in advance for other destinations and during holiday seasons.

Socicam, a private company, runs all the bus terminals in the city of São Paulo and lists schedules on its Web site. Click on *"consulta de partidas de ônibus."*

🚌 **Socicam** ☎ 011/3235-0322 ⊕ www.socicam.com.br. **EMTU** ☎ 0800/19-0088 or 011/6445-2505. **Terminal Barra Funda** ✉ Rua Mário de Andrade 664, Barra Funda ☎ 011/3235-0322 ⊕ www.socicam.com.br Ⓜ Barra Funda. **Terminal Jabaquara** ✉ Rua Jequitibás, Jabaquara ☎ 011/3235-0322 ⊕ www.socicam.com.br Ⓜ Jabaquara. **Terminal Tietê** ✉ Av. Cruzeiro do Sul, Santana ☎ 011/3235-0322 ⊕ www.socicam.com.br Ⓜ Tietê.

GETTING AROUND

Municipal bus service is frequent and covers the entire city, but regular buses are overcrowded at rush hour and when it rains. If you don't speak Portuguese, it can be hard to figure out the system and the stops. Stops are clearly marked, but routes are spelled out only on the buses themselves. Buses do not stop at every bus stop, so if you are waiting, you'll have to flag one down.

The fare is R$2. You enter at the front of the bus, pay the *cobrador* (fare collector) in the middle, and exit from the rear of the bus. To pay, you can use either money or the electronic card *bilhete único,* introduced in 2004. The card allows you to take three buses in two hours for the price of one fare. Cards can be bought and reloaded at special booths at major bus terminals or at lottery shops.

For bus numbers and names, routes, and schedules, go to the (Portuguese-language) Web site of Transporte Público de São Paulo, the city's public transport agency, or purchase the *Guia São Paulo Ruas,* published by Quatro Rodas and sold at newsstands and bookstores for about R$30.

🚌 **Transporte Público de São Paulo** ☎ 156 ⊕ www.sptrans.com.br.

BY CAR

ARRIVING & DEPARTING

The main São Paulo–Rio de Janeiro highway is the Via Dutra (BR 116 North), which has been repaved and enlarged in places. The speed limit is 120 kph (74 mph) along most of it, and although it has many tolls, there are many call boxes you can use if your car breaks down. The modern Rodovia Ayrton Senna (SP 70) charges reasonable tolls, runs parallel to the Dutra for about a quarter of the way, and is an excellent alternative route. The 429-km (279-mi) trip takes five hours. If you have time, consider the longer, spectacular coastal Rio-Santos Highway (SP 55 and BR 101). It's an easy two-day drive, and you can stop midway at the colonial city of Paraty, in Rio de Janeiro State.

Other main highways are the Castelo Branco (SP 280), which links the southwestern part of the state to the city; the Via Anhanguera (SP 330), which originates in the state's rich northern agricultural region, passing through the university town of Campinas; SP 310, which also runs from the farming heartland; BR 116 south, which comes up from Curitiba (a 408-km/265-mi trip); plus the Via Anchieta (SP 150) and the

Rodovia Imigrantes (SP 160), parallel roads that run to the coast, each operating one-way on weekends and holidays.

GETTING AROUND Driving in the city isn't recommended because of the heavy traffic (nothing moves at rush hour, especially when it rains), daredevil drivers, and inadequate parking. If you do opt to drive, invest in the *Guia São Paulo Ruas,* published by Quatro Rodas, which shows every street in the city. It's sold at newsstands and bookstores for about R$30.

🚹 **Rental Agencies Avis** ⊠ Rua da Consolação 335, Centro 🕾 011/3259-6868 or 0800/19-8456. **Hertz** ⊠ Rua da Consolação 439, Centro 🕾 011/3258-9384 or 4336-7300. **Localiza** ⊠ Rua da Consolação 419, Centro 🕾 011/3231-3055 or 0800/99-2000.

BY SUBWAY

When you buy 10 tickets at once, note that ticket sellers often can't change large bills. You insert the ticket into the turnstile at the platform entrance, and it's returned to you only if there's unused fare on it. Transfers within the metro system are free, as are bus-to-metro (or vice-versa) transfers. You can buy a *bilhete integração* (integration ticket) on buses or at metro stations for R$3.60. You can print maps from the English-language Web site of the Metrô, where you can also find ticket prices and schedules.

🚹 **Metrô** 🕾 011/3286-0111 ⊕ www.metro.sp.gov.br.

BY TAXI

Taxis in São Paulo are white. Owner-driven taxis are generally well maintained and reliable, as are radio taxis. Fares start at R$3.20 and run R$1.80 for each kilometer (½ mi) or R$0.40 for every minute sitting in traffic. After 8 PM and on weekends fares rise by 25%. You'll pay a tax if the cab leaves the city, as is the case with trips to Cumbica Airport. Good radio-taxi companies usually accept credit cards, but you must call ahead and request the service. Delta takes calls in English.

🚹 **Coopertaxi** 🕾 011/6941-2555. **Delta Rádio Táxi** 🕾 011/5572-6611. **Ligue-Taxi** 🕾 011/3866-3030.

BY TRAIN

Most travel to the interior of the state is done by bus or automobile. Still, a few places are served by trains. Trains from Estação da Luz, near 25 de Março, run to some metropolitan suburbs and small interior towns. Trains from Estação Barra Funda serve towns in the west of the state. Estação Júlio Prestes, in Campos Elíseos, has trains to the southeast and some suburbs. Estação Brás serves the suburbs only.

🚹 **Estação Barra Funda** ⊠ Rua Mário de Andrade 664, Barra Funda 🕾 011/3392-3616 Ⓜ Barra Funda. **Estação Júlio Prestes** ⊠ Praça Júlio Prestes 148, Campos Elíseos 🕾 0800/55-0121. **Estação da Luz** ⊠ Praça da Luz 1, Luz 🕾 0800/55-0121 Ⓜ Luz. **Estação Brás** ⊠ Praça Agente Cícero, Brás 🕾 0800/55-0121 Ⓜ Brás.

Contacts & Resources

TOUR OPTIONS

You can hire a bilingual guide through a travel agency or hotel concierge (about R$15 an hour with a four-hour minimum), or you can design your own walking tour with the aid of information provided at Anhembi booths around the city. Anhembi also offers Sunday tours of museums, parks, and Centro that are less expensive than those offered in hotels. The tourist board (⇨ Visitor Information, *below*) has three half-day Sunday bus tours, one covering the parks, one centered on the museums, and one focused on the historical downtown area. Officially, none of the board's guides speaks English; however, it may be able to arrange something on request.

Gol Tour Viagens e Turismo has custom tours as well as car tours for small groups. A half-day city tour costs about R$40 a person (group rate); a night tour—including a samba show, dinner, and drinks—costs around R$100; and day trips to the beach or the colonial city of Embu cost R$80–R$90. Easygoing has fly-and-dine tours that include a helicopter trip and dinner. If you prefer something down-to-earth, try the carriage tours with Carruagens São Paulo. They tour the Centro Novo (New Downtown) or Centro Velho, or (Old Downtown). Both are available in English if you reserve by phone. The price is R$40 per person, plus R$35 per group for an English-speaking guides. For general sightseeing tours, try Check Point, whose daily tours are R$400 for four people.

🎫 **Carruagens São Paulo** ☎ 011/3237-4976 or 011/9770-7311 ⊕ www.carruagemsaopaulo. com.br. **Check Point** ☎ 011/6091-1316. **Easygoing** ☎ 011/3801-9540 ⊕ www.easygoing. com.br. **Gol Tour Viagens e Turismo** ☎ 011/3256-2388 ⊕ www.goltour.com.br Ⓜ República. **Terra Nobre** ☎ 011/3662-1505 ⊕ www.terranobre.com.br.

VISITOR INFORMATION

The most helpful contact is the São Paulo Convention and Visitors Bureau, open 9–6. The sharp, business-minded director, Orlando de Souza, speaks English flawlessly and is extremely knowledgeable. Branches of the city-operated Anhembi Turismo e Eventos da Cidade de São Paulo are open daily 9–6.

The bureaucracy-laden Secretaria de Esportes e Turismo do Estado de São Paulo, open weekdays 9–6, is less helpful, but has maps and information about the city and state of São Paulo. SEST also has a booth at the arrivals terminal in Cumbica airport; it's open daily 9 AM–10 PM.

🎫 **Anhembi Turismo e Eventos da Cidade de São Paulo** ✉ Anhembi Convention Center, Av. Olavo Fontoura 1209, Santana ☎ 011/6224-0400 ⊕ www.cidadedesaopaulo.com ✉ Praça da República at Rua 7 de Abril, Centro Ⓜ República ✉ Av. Paulista, across from MASP, Cerqueira César Ⓜ Trianon-Masp ✉ Av. Brigadeiro Faria Lima, in front of Shopping Center Iguatemi, Jardim Paulista ✉ Av. Ribeiro de Lima 99, Luz Ⓜ Luz ✉ bus station, Tietê Ⓜ Tietê ✉ Cumbica Airport Terminals 1 and 2, Aeroporto de Guarulhos. **São Paulo Convention and Visitors Bureau** ✉ Alameda Ribeirão Preto 130, conjunto 121, Jardins ☎ 011/3289-7588 ⊕ www.visitesaopaulo.com. **Secretaria Estadual de Turismo do Estado de São Paulo** ✉ Rua Guaianazes 1058, Campos Elíseos ☎ 011/221-0474 ⊕ www.saopaulo.sp.gov.br/turismo.

SIDE TRIPS FROM SÃO PAULO

Updated by
Gabriela Dias
and Eduardo
Acquarone

São Paulo's surroundings are perfect for all types of getaways. The state has the best highways in the country, making it easy to travel by car or bus to its many small, beautiful beaches, and even beyond to neighboring states (Paraná, Rio de Janeiro, and Minas Gerais). Although most

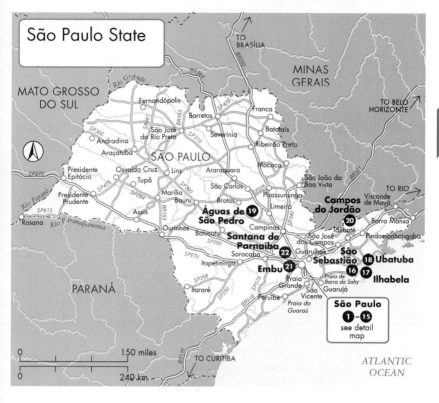

sandy stretches require one- or two-hour drives, good side trips from the city can be as close as the 30-minute trip to Embu.

São Sebastião

16 *204 km (127 mi) southeast of São Paulo*

The cleanest and best *praias* (beaches) in São Paulo State are along what is known as the Litoral Norte (North Shore). Mountains and bits of Atlantic rain forest hug numerous small, sandy coves. Some of the North Shore's most beautiful houses line the Rio-Santos Highway (SP 055) on the approach to Maresias. On weekdays when school is in session, the beaches are gloriously deserted.

São Sebastião stretches along 100 km (62 mi) of the North Shore. Its bays, islands, and beaches attract everyone from the youngsters who flock to Maresias and Camburi to the families who favor Barra do Sahy. Boating enthusiasts, hikers, and wildlife-seekers also come here, especially on weekends, when hotels are often crowded. Nightlife is good here—the best is in Boiçucanga. The "beautiful island" of Ilhabela (⇨ *below*) is just a 15-minute boat ride away from downtown São Sebastião.

★ Families with young children favor small, quiet **Praia da Barra do Sahy** (✉ Rio-Santos Hwy. (SP 055), 157 km/97 mi southeast of São Paulo). Its narrow strip of sand (with a bay and a river on one side and rocks on the other) is steep but smooth, and the water is clean and very calm. Kayakers paddle about, and divers are drawn to the nearby Ilha das Couves. Area restaurants serve mostly basic fish dishes with rice and salad. Note that Barra do Sahy's entrance is atop a slope and appears suddenly—be on the lookout around marker Km 174.

The young and the restless flock to **Praia do Camburi** (✉ Rio-Santos Hwy. (SP 055), 162 km/100 mi southeast of São Paulo) to sunbathe, surf, and party. At the center of the beach is a cluster of cafés, ice-cream shops, and bars and the Tiê restaurant. The service may be slow, but Tiê's menu is extensive, and the open-air setup is divine. Camburi is just north of Barra do Sahy. If you're coming from the south, take the second entrance; although it's unpaved, it's usually in better shape than the first entrance, at Km 166.

Praia de Maresias (✉ Rio-Santos Hwy, Km 151 (SP 055), 177 km/109 mi southeast of São Paulo) is a 4-km (2-mi) stretch of white sand with clean, green waters that are good for swimming and surfing. Maresias is popular with a young crowd.

Ilhabela

17 *7 km (5 mi)/15-min boat ride from São Sebastião.*

Fodor'sChoice
★ Ilhabela is favored by those who like the beach and water sports; indeed, many championship competitions are held here. This is the biggest sea island in the country, with 22 calm beaches along its western shore, which faces the mainland. The hotels are mostly at the north end, though the best sandy stretches are the 13 to the south, which face the open sea. Eighty percent of the island is in a state park area.

The best way to get around Ilhabela is by car, which you must rent on the mainland and transfer by ferry (there are no bridges to the island). *Balsas* (ferries) from São Sebastião to Ilhabela run every 30 minutes from 6 AM to midnight and hourly during the night. The **São Sebastião balsa** (☎ 0800/704–5510) transports vehicles as well as passengers. Make reservations, particularly December–February. Public buses cross the island from north to south daily. Fares range from R$10.70 (weekdays) to R$16 (weekends), including a car. To get to the ferry dock in São Sebastião, take Avenida São Sebastião from town to the coast.

Praia Grande (✉ 13 km/8 mi south of ferry dock) has a long sandy strip with food kiosks, a soccer field, and a small church. At night people gather at **Praia do Curral** (✉ 6 km/4 mi south of Praia Grande), where there are many restaurants and bars—some with live music—as well as places to

CAUTION
Mosquitoes are a problem; bring plenty of insect repellent.

3

camp. The wreck of the ship *Aymoré* (1921) can be found off the coast of this beach, near Ponta do Ribeirão, where you can also look for a waterfall trail.

To reach **Baía dos Castelhanos** (⊠ 22 km/14 mi east of the ferry dock), you need a four-wheel-drive vehicle, and if it rains even this won't be enough. Consider arriving by sailboat, which demands a 1½- to 3-hour trip that can be arranged through local tour operators. With such an isolated location, you can see why slave ships once used the bay to unload their illicit cargo after slavery was banned in Brazil. If you're lucky, you might spot a dolphin off the shore of this 2-km (1¼-mi) beach—the largest on the island.

Where to Stay & Eat

$–$$$$ ✕ **Ilha Sul.** The best option on the menu is the grilled shrimp with vegetables. Fish and other seafood are also available. ⊠ *Av. Riachuelo 287* ☎ *012/3894–9426* ▭ *AE, DC, MC, V* ☉ *Closed Mon.–Thurs. Apr.–June and Aug.–Nov.*

$$$$ ▥ **Maison Joly.** Past guests of this exclusive hotel at the top of the Cantagalo Hill range from kings of Sweden to the Rolling Stones. Upon arrival you're given a beach kit complete with mosquito repellent and a hat. Each of the rooms has distinctive furnishings that are part of its theme, such as a piano, a billiard table, or a telescope—and all have balconies facing the sea. The restaurant ($$$$), open only to guests, is excellent. ⊠ *Rua Antônio Lisboa Alves 278* ☎ *012/3896–3500* ⊕ *www. maisonjoly.com.br* ⌨ *9 rooms* ♿ *Restaurant, in-room safes, in-room hot tubs, minibars, cable TV, pool, massage, spa, bar, piano, Internet room, meeting rooms; no kids under 12* ▭ *DC, MC, V.*

FodorsChoice
★

★ **$** ▥ **Pousada dos Hibiscos.** North of the ferry dock, this red house has midsize rooms, all at ground level. The friendly staff serves up a good breakfast and provides poolside bar service. Each room has its own unique decoration, but all have hardwood furnishings, and either tile or stone floors. ⊠ *Av. Pedro de Paula Moraes 720* ☎ *012/3896–1375* ⊕ *www. pousadadoshibiscos.com.br* ⌨ *13 rooms* ♿ *Fans, in-room safes, minibars, cable TV, pool, gym, sauna, bar* ▭ *AE, V.*

Ubatuba

⑱ *234 km (145 mi) southeast of São Paulo*

Many of the more than 70 beaches around Ubatuba are more than beautiful enough to merit the long drive from São Paulo. Young people, surfers, and couples with and without children hang out in the 90-km (56-km) area, where waterfalls, boat rides, aquariums, diving, and trekking in the wild are major attractions. Downtown Ubatuba also has an active nightlife, especially in summer. Ubatuba can be reached from São Paulo via the Carvalho Pinto (SP 070) and Oswaldo Cruz (SP 125) highways.

Águas de São Pedro

⑲ *180 km (112 mi) northwest of São Paulo.*

São Paulo's inland region has beautiful mountains, springs, rivers, and waterfalls perfect for outdoor activities like hiking and rafting. Historic attractions are generally fewer than in other states. Save some time for clothing and crafts shopping, and for the lavish regional cuisine.

Although Águas de São Pedro is the smallest city in Brazil, at a mere 3.9 square km (1.5 square mi), its sulfurous waters made it famous countrywide in the 1940s and '50s. The healing hot springs were discovered by chance in the 1920s when technicians were drilling for oil.

Fonte Juventude is the richest in sulfur in the Americas and is often used to treat rheumatism, asthma, bronchitis, and skin ailments. The waters at Fonte Gioconda have minor radioactive elements (and, yes, they are reportedly good for you), whereas Fonte Almeida Salles's have chlorine bicarbonate and sodium (which are said to alleviate the symptoms of diabetes and upset stomachs).

You can access the springs at the Balnéario Publico (public bathhouse) or through some hotels. Though a number of illnesses respond to the water, most visitors are just healthy tourists soaking in relaxation. Águas de São Pedro is compact, so it's easy to get around on foot.

(C) A walk through the woods in **Bosque Municipal Dr. Octávio Moura Andrade** is a chance to relax. Horseback riding costs around R$10 for a half hour. It's part of the Balnéario complex (⇨ *below*). Saunas, baths, and massages cost R$8–R$33. ⊠ *Av. Carlos Mauro* ☎ *019/3482–1333* ☞ *Free* ⊙ *Weekdays 7–noon, weekends 7–5.*

Balnéario Municipal Dr. Octávio Moura Andrade has immersion baths in sulfurous springwater. You can swim in the pool or sweat in the sauna while you wait for your private soak, massage, or beauty appointment. A snack bar and a gift shop round out the spa services. ⊠ *Av. Carlos Mauro* ☎ *019/3482–1333* ☞ *R$8–R$33* ⊙ *Mon.–Sun. 7–6.*

Where to Stay & Eat

$ ✕ **Patagônia.** This restaurant with international cuisine owes its contemporary flavor to the city's gastronomy students who do internships here. Duck, lamb, trout, risotto, and salt cod are good choices. ⊠ *Av. Presidente Kennedy 876* ☎ *019/3482–2338* ▤ *V* ⊙ *No lunch Thurs.–Sat. No dinner Sun.*

$$$–$$$$ ✕▥ **Grande Hotel São Pedro.** The beautiful art deco building was a casino during the 1940s. Now it's a teaching hotel and restaurant ($$–$$$) with all the comforts of a full-service spa. Many of the friendly staff members are students—including those who prepare dishes such as salt cod in pistachio sauce. The property is in the middle of a 300,000-square-meter (3.2 million-square-foot) park with more than 1 million trees and local wildlife. ⊠ *Parque Dr. Octávio de Moura Andrade* ☎ *019/3482–7600* ⊕ *www1.sp.senac.br/hoteis* ⇝ *96 rooms, 16 suites* ⌕ *2 restaurants, room service, minibars, cable TV, tennis court, pool, gym, hair salon, sauna, spa, bar, recreation room, video game room, business services, meeting rooms* ▤ *AE, DC, MC, V.*

$ ▥ **Hotel Jerubiaçaba.** The rooms in this 30-year-old hotel are bathed in light colors and filled with simple furnishings. The 120 rooms are divided into four types, from standard to luxury, but all of them are in a 17,000-square-meter (183,000-square-foot) green area with springs and a bathhouse. ⊠ *Av. Carlos Mauro 168* ☎ *019/3482–1411* ⊕ *www. hoteljerubiacaba.com.br* ⇝ *120 rooms, 8 suites* ⚐ *Restaurant, room service, tennis court, pool, hair salon, massage, soccer, bar, recreation room, video game room, playground, business services, meeting rooms, no-smoking floors; no a/c in some rooms* ☰ *AE, DC, MC, V.*

Campos do Jordão

⓴ *184 km (114 mi) northeast of São Paulo.*

In the Serra da Mantiqueira at an altitude of 5,525 feet, Campos do Jordão and its fresh mountain air are paulistanos' favorite winter attractions. In July temperatures drop as low as 32°F (0°C), though it never snows; in warmer months temperatures linger in the 13°C–16°C (55°F–60°F) range.

Exploring Campos do Jordão without a car is very difficult. The attractions are far-flung, except for those at Vila Capivari.

Boulevard Genéve, a mall in the busy Vila Capivari district, is lined with cafés, bars, and restaurants, making it a nightlife hub. You can also find plenty of clothing stores, and candy shops selling chocolate, the town's specialty.

Horto Florestal is a natural playground for *macacos-prego* (nail monkeys), squirrels, and parrots, as well as for people. The park has a trout-filled river, waterfalls, and trails—all set among trees from around the world and one of the last *araucária* (Brazilian pine) forests in the state. ⊠ *Av. Pedro Paulo Km 13* ☎ *012/3663–3762* ⊠ *R$3–R$4* ☉ *Daily 8–5.*

The athletically inclined can walk 3 km (2 mi) and climb the 300-step stone staircase to **Pedra do Baú,** a 6,400-foot trio of rocks inside an eco tourism park north of the city. A trail starts in nearby São Bento do Sapucaí, and it's recommended you hire a guide. In the park you can also practice horseback riding, canopy walking, trekking, or mountain-climbing and spend the night in a dormlike room shared with other visitors. Some of the activities are only available on weekends. ⊠ *Km 25, Estrada São Bento do Sapucaí* ☎ *012/3662–1106* ⊠ *R$5* ☉ *Weds.–Sun. 8–6.*

Where to Stay & Eat

$–$$$ ✗ **Baden-Baden.** One of the specialties at this charming German restaurant in the heart of town is sauerkraut *garni* (sour cabbage with German sausages). The typical dish serves two and is almost as popular as Baden-Baden's own brewery, which is open to visitors from 10–5 on weekdays. ⊠ *Rua Djalma Forjaz 93, Loja 10* ☎ *012/3663–3610* ☰ *AE, DC, MC, V.*

$–$$ ✗ **Itália Cantina e Ristorante.** As its name suggests, this place specializes in Italian food. The pasta and the meat dishes are delicious, but you can also try trout, lamb, fondue, and even boar dishes. ⊠ *Av. Macedo Soares 306* ☎ *012/3663–1140* ☰ *AE, DC, MC, V.*

¢–$ ✗ **Cyber Café.** Drink hot cocoa with crepes, fondue, or a slice of pie, while you browse the Internet at this downtown café. ⊠ *Rua Djalma Forjaz 100, Loja 15* ☎ *012/3663–6351* ⊕ *www.cybercafeboulevard. com.br* ☰ *MC, V.*

$–$$$ ☒ **Pousada Villa Capivary.** A stay at this cozy guest house puts you in the gastronomic and commercial center of Campos. The friendly staff is helpful and efficient. Most apartments have balconies, and the five suites have whirlpool baths. ☒ *Av. Victor Godinho 131* ☎ *012/ 3663–1746* ⊕ *www.capivari.com.br* ⊷ *10 rooms, 5 suites* ⚒ *In-room safes, some in-room hot tubs, minibars, cable TV, central heat, bar, recreation room* ☰ *AE, DC, MC, V.*

¢ ☒ **Lausanne Hotel.** In an enormous ecopark 7 km (4 mi) outside town, this hotel has plenty of solitude, allowing you to commune with nature 5,850 feet above sea level. Rooms have forest views. ☒ *Km 176, Rodovia SP-050* ☎ *012/3663–4806* ⊕ *www.lausannehotel.com.br* ⊷ *24 rooms* ⚒ *Restaurant, minibars, cable TV, heating, tennis court, pool, soccer, bar, recreation room, Internet, some pets allowed* ☰ *V.*

Embu

㉑ *27 km (17 mi) west of São Paulo.*

Founded in 1554, Embu is a tiny Portuguese colonial town of whitewashed houses, old churches, wood-carvers' studios, and antiques shops. It has a downtown handicrafts fair every Saturday and Sunday. On Sunday the streets sometimes get so crowded you can barely walk. Embu also has many stores that sell handicrafts and wooden furniture; most of these are close to where the street fair takes place.

On weekends it's difficult to find a place to park in Embu, and parking lots can be expensive. You can easily walk to all the main sights in town.

Igreja Nossa Senhora do Rosário was built in 1690 and is a nice bet for those who won't have a chance to visit the historic cities of Minas Gerais. The church contains baroque images of saints and is next to a 1730 monastery now turned into a sacred-art museum. ☒ *Largo dos Jesuítas 67* ☎ *011/4704–2654* ▣ *R$2* ☉ *Tues.–Sun. 9–5.*

Where to Eat

$–$$ ✕ **O Garimpo.** In a large room with a fireplace or around outdoor tables, choose between Brazilian regional dishes such as the house specialty, *moqueca de badejo* (spicy fish-and-coconut-milk stew), and German classics such as *eisbein* (pickled and roasted pork shank). ☒ *Rua da Matriz 136* ☎ *011/4704–6344* ☰ *AE, DC, MC, V.*

¢–$$ ✕ **Os Girassóis Restaurante e Choperia.** A great variety of dishes is served at this downtown restaurant next to an art gallery. The *picanha brasileira* (barbecued steak) with fries and *farofa* (cassava flour sautéed in butter) is recommended. ☒ *Largo dos Jesuítas 169* ☎ *011/4781–6671* ☰ *AE, DC, MC, V* ☉ *Closed Mon.*

$ ✕ **Casa do Barão.** In this colonial-style spot you find contemporary versions of country plates, but no salads or juices. Go for the exotic *picadinho jesuítico* (round-steak stew), served with corn, fried bananas, and farofa. Unlike most restaurants in the city, Casa do Barão serves single-person portions. ☒ *Rua Joaquim Santana 95* ☎ *011/4704–2053* ☰ *MC, V* ☉ *Closed Mon.*

Santana de Parnaíba

㉒ *42 km (26 mi) northwest of São Paulo.*

With more than 200 preserved houses from the 18th and 19th centuries, Santana de Parnaíba is considered the "Ouro Preto from São Paulo"— a town rich with history and colonial architecture. Santana was founded in 1580; by 1625 it was the most important point of departure for the *bandeirantes*.

In 1901 the first hydroelectric power station in South America was built here. Throughout the 20th century, Santana managed to retain its houses and charm while preserving a local tradition: a rural type of *samba* called "de bumbo," in which the pacing is marked by the *zabumba* (an instrument usually associated with rhythms from the northeastern states of Brazil). The proximity to a couple of São Paulo's finest suburbs explains the region's fine dining. Outdoors lovers feel at home with the canopy-walking and trekking options. On weekends parking is scarce in Santana de Parnaíba, and parking lots can be expensive.

Begin your trip by appreciating the 17th- and 18th-century colonial architecture of the **Centro Histórico,** with its more than 200 well-preserved houses. All of them are concentrated around three streets: Suzana Dias, André Fernandes, and Bartolomeu Bueno—two of which are named after famous bandeirantes.

Museu Casa do Anhanguera provides an even sharper picture of the bandeirantes era. In a 1600 house (the second-oldest in the state) where Bartolomeu Bueno—nicknamed Anhanguera, or "old devil," by the Indians—was born, the museum displays objects and furniture from the past four centuries. ⊠ *Largo da Matriz 9* ☎ *011/4154–5042* 🖂 *R$1* ⊙ *Weekdays 8–4:30, weekends 11–5.*

Baroque **Igreja Matriz de Sant'Anna** was built in the same square as Casa do Anhanguera in 1610 and restored in 1892. It has terra-cotta sculptures and an altar with gold-plated details. ⊠ *Largo da Matriz* ☎ *011/ 4154–2401* 🖂 *Free* ⊙ *Daily 8–5.*

Where to Eat

$$–$$$ ✕ **Dom Afonso de Vimioso.** A place like this would have reminded Portuguese colonists of the motherland. Options include fine wines and more than 10 dishes made with salt cod. Don't miss out on typical sweets such as *pastéis de Santa Clara* (yolk and sugar-filled pastries). ⊠ *Km 36, Estrada dos Romeiros* ☎ *011/4151–1935* ▤ *AE, DC, MC, V.*

♻ $–$$$ ✕ **Aldeia Cocar.** This restaurant and outdoors complex was built in a former indigenous village. It occupies a 86,111-square-foot Mata Atlântica (Atlantic Forest) area with wildlife, and hosts indigenous exhibits in a reconstructed native tent. Aldeia serves more than 30 Brazilian specialties from all over the country, as well as a few typical dishes from countries which helped shape Brazil, like Italy, Japan, and, of course, Portugal. *Arrumadinho* (sun-dried beef with mashed pumpkin and collard greens) is an excellent choice. After the meal, take some time to rest on the hammocks. ⊠ *Estrada do Belo Vale 11, Km 32, SP-280* ☎ *011/*

4192–3073 ⊕ *www.aldeiacocar.com.br* 💳 *AE, DC, MC, V* ⊘ *Closed Mon.–Wed.*

$–$$ ✗ **São Paulo Antigo.** In a century-old ranch-style house, taste *caipira* (rural) dishes such as *dobradinha com feijão branco* (intestines and white-bean stew) or *galinha atolada* (rural-style hen stew). The grand finale is a free carriage ride around the town's main square. ⊠ *Rua Álvaro Luiz do Valle 66* 📞 *011/4154–2726* 💳 *DC, MC, V* ⊘ *No dinner weekdays.*

Side Trips from São Paulo Essentials

Transportation

BY BUS

ARRIVING & DEPARTING Buses to most cities in São Paulo State leave from the Terminal Tietê in the city of São Paulo. These include Piracicabana buses, which run daily to Águas de São Pedro; Pássaro Litorânea buses, which travel five times daily to São Sebastião (to the ferry dock) and six times a day to Ubatuba; and Expresso Mantiqueira buses, which leave for Campos do Jordão every two hours. Buses to Brotas, operated by Expresso de Prata, depart three times a day from the Terminal Barra Funda, in the western part of the city. There are two *executivo* (executive, or first-class) buses from São Paulo to Santana de Parnaíba and Embu, run by EMTU: Line 385 to Pirapora do Bom Jesus makes four daily rides between Barra Funda and Santana de Parnaíba, and Line 179 to Embu-Engenho Velho departs hourly from Anhangabaú. Regular (intermunicipal) buses travel more often: every 20 minutes, Line 033 leaves from Clínicas to Embu. The ride is less comfortable, though: you might have to stand up.

🚌 **Expresso Mantiqueira** 📞 011/6221–0244 ⊕ www.expressomantiqueira.com.br. **Expresso de Prata** 📞 011/3392–7373 ⊕ www.expressodeprata.com.br. **Piracicabana** 📞 011/6221–0032 ⊕ www.piracicabana.com.br. **Litorânea** 📞 011/6221–0244 ⊕ www.litoranea.com.br.

GETTING AROUND For buses within towns, you can buy tickets directly on the bus. Service is mostly regular and cheap, but buses aren't always well maintained. Terminals and stands are usually easy to spot, as most streets have at least one, even in smaller towns. As a general rule, beware of pickpockets when on the bus and when waiting for it.

To travel between towns, just go to the local main terminal and ask for directions. It won't always be easy to go straight from one place to the other; between Embu and Santana de Parnaíba, for example, there's no direct connection.

When traveling between smaller towns, buses usually make several stops along the way, leaving and picking up passengers.

BY CAR

Roads in São Paulo State are generally in good condition and well marked; some of them are toll roads. Rent a car in São Paulo.

The drive from São Paulo to São Sebastião is about 2½ hours; take Rodovia Ayrton Senna–Carvalho Pinto (SP 070), followed by Rodovia Tamoios (SP 099) to Caraguatatuba, and then follow the signs until you reach the ferry boat to Ilhabela. To reach Ubatuba, follow the same path to

Caraguatatuba then turn right and head north on SP 055. Águas de São Pedro is about a 2½-hour drive on Anhangüera-Bandeirantes (SP 330/ SP 348) and then SP 304. To reach Campos do Jordão from the city (also a 2½-hour drive), take Rodovia Carvalho Pinto (SP 070) and SP 123. To make the 30-minute drive from São Paulo to Embu, drive from Avenida Professor Francisco Morato to Rodovia Régis Bittencourt (BR 116) and then follow the signs. To reach Santana de Parnaíba from São Paulo—a 40-minute drive—take the express lane of Rodovia Castelo Branco (SP 280) and pay attention to the road signs.

Contacts & Resources

TOUR OPTIONS

Lokal Adventure leads tours of Ilhabela by boat, bike, horse, or jeep. Another Ilhabela operator is Maremar, which has scuba-diving, jeep, horse-back-riding, and hiking tours. HS Turismo offers five tours in or around Campos do Jordão. Also in Campos do Jordão, trains depart from Estação Ferroviária Emílio Ribas on tours of the city and its environs, including the 47-km (29-mi) trip to Reino das Águas Claras, where there's a park with waterfalls.

Gol Tour Viagens e Turismo has day trips to Embu (R$80–R$90). Canoar is one of the best rafting tour operators in São Paulo State. Trilha Brazil arranges treks in forests around São Paulo. A reputable operator for rain-forest, beach, and island excursions is Cia. Nacional de Ecoturismo.

Canoar ☎ 011/3871-2282 ⊕ www.canoar.com.br. **Cia. Nacional de Ecoturismo** ☎ 011/5571-2525 ⊕ www.ciaecoturismo.com.br. **Estação Ferroviária Emílio Ribas** ✉ Av. Dr. Januário Miráglia, Vila Capivari, Campos do Jordão ☎ 012/3663-1531. **Gol Tour Viagens e Turismo** ☎ 011/3256-2388 ⊕ www.goltour.com.br Ⓜ República. **HS Turismo** ✉ Rua Ionel Strass 65, Campos do Jordão ☎ 012/3662-2759. **Lokal Adventure** ✉ Av. Princesa Isabel 171, Ilhabela ☎ 012/3896-5770 ⊕ www.lokaladventure.com.br.

VISITOR INFORMATION

Águas de São Pedro Informações Turísticas ✉ Av. Carlos Mauro, in front of Balneário, Águas de São Pedro ☎ 019/3482-2173 or 3482-1096 ⊕ www.aguasdesaopedro. sp.gov.br. **Campos do Jordão Tourist Office** ✉ At entrance to town, Campos do Jordão ☎ 012/3664-3525 ⊕ www.camposdojordao.com.br. **Embu Secretaria de Turismo** ✉ Largo 21 de Abril 139, Embu ☎ 011/4704-6565 ⊕ www.embu.sp.gov.br. **Ilhabela Secretaria do Turismo** ✉ Rua Bartolomeu de Gusmão 140, Ilhabela ☎ 012/3896-1091 ⊕ www.ilhabela.sp.gov.br. **Santana de Parnaíba Secretaria de Cultura e Turismo** ✉ Largo da Matriz 19, Santana de Parnaíba ☎ 011/4154-1874 or 011/4154-2377 ⊕ www. santanadeparnaiba.sp.gov.br.

SALVADOR

Updated by
Carlos
Tornquist

In "the land of happiness," as the state of Bahia is known, the sun shines almost every day. Its Atlantic Ocean shoreline runs for 900 km (560 mi), creating beautiful white-sand beaches lined with coconut palms—while inland is Parque Nacional da Chapada Diamantina (Chapada Diaman-

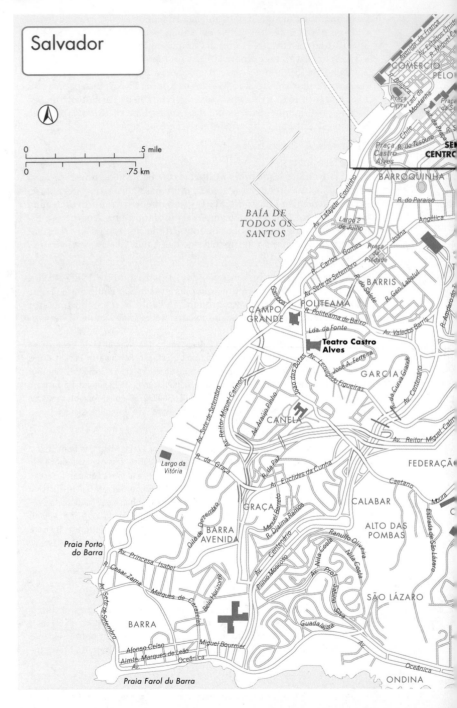

Salvador

N

0 ———————————— .5 mile
0 ———————————— .75 km

COMÉRCIO
PELO
Ponte
Praça Lad. da
Cairu Montanha
Chile
Praça da Sé
Praça
Castro
Alves
R. do Tesouro
SEN
CENTRO
BARROQUINHA

BAÍA DE
TODOS OS
SANTOS

Av. Lafayete Coutinho
R. do Paraíso
Angélica
Largo 2
de Julho
Praça
da
Piedade
Ioana
R. Carlos Gomes
Garamba
Av. Sete de Setembro
R. da Soledade
BARRIS
R. Gen. Labatut
R. Amparo do Ti.
CAMPO
GRANDE
POLITEAMA
R. Politeama de Baixo
Lda. da Fonte
Av. Vale dos Barris
R. do Guia Galina
Teatro Castro
Alves
Largo das Botas
Av. Leovigildo Figueiras
José A. Ferreira
GARCIA
Av. Centenário
Av. Reitor Miguel Catmon
CANELA
Av. Reitor Miguel Catim
Av. Sete de Setembro
R. da Graça
R. da Paz
FEDERAÇÃ
Largo da
Vitória
Av. Euclides da Cunha
Caetano
Moura
GRAÇA
Manel Barreto
CALABAR
Estrada de São Lázaro
Olin de Dezembro
BARRA
AVENIDA
R. Djalma Ramos
Centenário
Ranulfo Oliveira
R. da Costa
ALTO DAS
POMBAS
Praia Porto
do Barra
Av. Princesa Isabel
Belo Horizonte
Av.
Pinia Moscoso
Av. Rita Costa
SÃO LÁZARO
R. César Zama
Av. Sete de Setembro
Marques de Caravelas
Av. Prof. Sabino
Silva
BARRA
Afonso Celso
Miguel Bournier
Guada Jajara
Almte. Marques de Leão
Oceânica
Av.
Oceânica
Praia Farol du Barra
ONDINA

SETE PORTAS

José Joaquim Seabra

SAÚDE

NAZARÉ

R. Bandeirantes

STO AGOSHINHO

MATATU

1 - 10

LVADOR
STÓRICO
MAP

CASTRO
NEVES

Estádio
Fonte
Nova

Dique
de
Tororó

Av. Mário
Leal Ferreira

DIQUE DO
TORORÓ

DANIEL
LISBOA

ENGENHO VELHO
DE BROTAS

N. Sra do
Guadalupe

VILA
AMÉRICA

ACUPE

ALTO DO
SOBRADINHO

R. Sérgio de Carvalho

ENGENGO VELHO
DA FEDERAÇÃO

R. das Palmeiras

R. Apolinário de Santana

R. Dep.
Moura Costa

Parque
João XXIII

Parque
Zoobotânico

Av. Garibaldi

R. João Gomes

RIO
VERMELHO

TO PRAIA
CORSÁRIO,
PRAIA ITAPUÃ,
PRAIA STELLA
MARIS

Av. Oceânica

tina National Park), with 152,000 hectares (375,000 acres) of mountains, waterfalls, caves, natural swimming pools, and hiking trails. And in Bahia's capital, Salvador, the beat of bongo drums echoing through the narrow cobblestone streets of Pelourinho (the center of the Historic District) is a rhythmic reminder of Brazil's African heritage.

Exploring Salvador

Salvador sprawls across a peninsula surrounded by the Baía de Todos os Santos on one side and the Atlantic Ocean on the other. The city has about 50 km (31 mi) of coastline. The original city, referred to as the Centro Histórico (Historical Center), is divided into the Cidade Alta (Upper City), also called Pelourinho, and Cidade Baixa (Lower City).

The Cidade Baixa is a commercial area—known as Comércio—that runs along the port and is the site of Salvador's largest market, Mercado Modelo. You can move between the upper and lower cities on foot, via the landmark Elevador Lacerda, behind the market, or the Plano Inclinado, a funicular lift, which connects Rua Guindaste dos Padres on Comércio with the alley behind Cathedral Basílica.

From the Centro Histórico you can travel north along the bay to the hilltop Igreja de Nosso Senhor do Bonfim. You can also head south to the point, guarded by the Forte Santo Antônio da Barra, where the bay waters meet those of the Atlantic. This area on Salvador's southern tip is home to the trendy neighborhoods of Barra, Ondina, and Rio Vermelho, with many museums, theaters, shops, and restaurants. Beaches such as Amaralina, Jardim dos Namorados, and Itapuã, north of Forte Santo Antônio da Barra and along the Atlantic coast, are among the city's cleanest. Many are illuminated at night and have bars and restaurants that stay open late.

Numbers in the text correspond to numbers in the margin and on the Salvador and Salvador Centro Histórico map.

Neighborhoods

PELOURINHO In colonial Salvador, Pelô, as the locals call it, was the heart of the trade district. *Pelourinho* means "whipping post," which refers to the plaza (Largo do Pelourinho) where runaway slaves were flogged in public. Pelourinho has been undergoing restoration since 1968, but it didn't really take off until 1991. In 1985 the district was honored with UNESCO World Heritage recognition. Walking down the narrow cobblestone alleys lined with colorful, restored *sobrados* (two-story colonial residences) momentarily transports you to the 1700s. Tuesday evenings bring Terça da Bênção (Blessed Tuesday), when special services are held in the churches and musical performances happen on almost every corner, including the rehearsals of the famous Olodum percussion group.

BARRA The area around Forte da Barra has many hotels and shops, although the beaches have little sand and the water is sometimes polluted. (Ask about current pollution advisories at your hotel.) Still, it is cleaner than inner-bay beaches. The sidewalks along the oceanfront roads Avenida Oceánica and Avenida 7 de Setembro are packed with joggers and bicyclists on weekends. Sometimes you can catch *capoeiristas* (athletes who "play" *capoeira,* a dancelike martial art) practicing their fluid kicks and spins on Farol da Barra or Morro do Cristo.

CAMPO GRANDE Most buildings in this, one of Salvador's most modern neighborhoods, date from the 1960s when the city experienced renewed growth from oil and mineral trade. The center of the district is Largo de Campo Grande plaza, with Teatro Castro Alves on the west side. During Carnival this is a hub from which you can watch the *trio elétricos* (floats blasting music) and so-called Afro-groups from bleachers installed along Avenida 7 de Setembro.

TORORÓ Some fine restaurants and bars make a trip to this mostly residential neighborhood ringing an artificial lake (Dique de Tororó) worthwhile. Eight metal statues of Candomblé saints dot the lake.

Centro Histórico

The heart of the original colonial city, the Cidade Alta section, incorporates the Comércio and Pelourinho neighborhoods and is a riveting blend of European and African cultures. More than 500 of the 2,982 buildings have been restored, earning Salvador the reputation of having the finest examples of baroque architecture in South America. Along the winding and sometimes steep

> ### CHURCHES GALORE
>
> Salvadorians may tell you that you can visit a different church every day of the year, which is almost true—the city has about 300.

streets, whose cobbles were laid by slaves, are restored 17th- and 18th-century buildings. Many of the restored buildings are now occupied by restaurants, museums, bars, and shops that sell everything from clothing, film, musical instruments, and handicrafts to precious stones. They are painted in bright colors, which, along with the sounds of vendors, street musicians, and capoeiristas, add to the festive atmosphere.

The Cidade Baixa (Lower City) is the section of historic Salvador that fronts the Atlantic Ocean. Its star attraction is the Mercado Modelo, one of Salvador's landmarks, with dozens of stalls that sell everything from Bahian lace dresses and musical instruments to amulets believed to ward off evil or bring good luck. Around the building gathers a mixed crowd of locals and visitors, impromptu entertainers, fortune tellers, and handicrafts vendors.

WHAT TO SEE **Forte de São Marcelo.** Jorge Amado jokingly called this doughnut-shaped
❷ fortress near the Terminal Maritimo pier, the "belly button of the world," because Bahia's economy essentially revolved around this focal point: the slave trade, the Mercado Modelo, and the port are all clustered practically within arm's reach. The fort, built from 1650 until around 1680 in a mix of medieval and colonial styles, housed the Imperial Army

Capoeira: The Fight Dance

DANCE AND MARTIAL ART IN ONE, *capoeira* is purely Brazilian. The early days of slavery often saw fights between Africans from rival tribes who were thrust together on one plantation. When an owner caught slaves fighting, both sides were punished. To create a smoke screen, the Africans incorporated music and song into the fights. They brought a traditional *berimbau* string-drum instrument (a bow-shape piece of wood with a metal wire running from one end to the other, where there's a hollow gourd containing seeds) to the battles. Tapped with a stick or a coin, the berimbau's taut wire produces a throbbing, twanging sound whose rhythm is enhanced by the rattling seeds. Its mesmerizing reverberations were accompanied by singing and chanting, and when the master appeared, the fighters punched only the air and kicked so as to miss their opponents.

The fights have been refined into a sport that was once practiced

primarily in Bahia and Pernambuco but has now spread throughout Brazil. Today's practitioners, called *capoeristas*, swing and kick—keeping their movements tightly controlled, with only hands and feet touching the ground—to the beat of the berimbau without touching their opponents. The goal is to cause one's opponent to lose concentration or balance. Capoeira is traditionally performed in a *roda* (wheel), which refers both to an event of continuous capoeira and to the circle formed by players and instrumentalists. Strength, control, flexibility, artistry, and grace are the tenets of capoeira. In any exhibition the *jogadores*, or players, as they are called—with their backs bending all the way to the floor and their agile foot movements (to avoid an imaginary knife)—as well as the compelling music, make this a fascinating sport to watch.

for over 200 years, as they staved off buccaneers and other invaders. Closed off to tourists for many years, it reopened in 2005. Historical tours, about an hour in length, depart from Terminal Maritimo. Inside you can see the armory and soldier's quarters and get a great view of the bay from the lookouts. ⊠ *Av. França, s/n, Comércio* ☎ *071/ 3321–5286* 🖃 *R$ 5* ☉ *By appointment only.*

❶ **Mercado Modelo.** Slaves were kept in chains in the basement of this building upon arrival from Africa in the 17th through 19th centuries. The market has seen many changes since it headquartered slave business through the mid-1800s. Today it's a convenient place to buy handicrafts. Bargaining is expected here, for goods like *cachaça* (sugarcane liquor), cashew nuts, pepper sauces, cigars, leather goods, hammocks, musical instruments, African sculptures, and semi-precious stones. *Repentistas* (impromptu folksingers) and fortunetellers gather outside. ⊠ *Praça Visconde de Cayrú 250, Comércio* ☎ *071/3241–2893* 🖃 *Free* ☉ *Mon.–Sat. 9–6, Sun. 9–2.*

3 **Elevador Lacerda.** For just a few centavos, ascend 236 feet in a minute in this elevator that runs between the Paço Municipal, in the Upper City, and Praça Visconde de Cayrú and the Mercado Modelo. Built in 1872, the elevator ran on hydraulics until its 1930 restoration, when it was electrified. Bahians joke that the elevator is the only way to "go up" in life. Watch out for pickpockets when the elevator's crowded. ☒ *West side of Praça Visconde de Cayrú, Comércio* ☎ *R$0.05* ☉ *Daily 5 AM–midnight.*

★ **6** **Catedral Basílica.** The masonry facade of this 17th-century masterpiece is made of Portuguese sandstone, brought as ballast in shipping boats; the 16th-century tiles in the sacristy came from Macau. Hints of Asia permeate the decoration, attributed to a Jesuit monk from China, a gifted painter. Note the Asian facial features and clothing of the figures in the transept altars; and the intricate ivory-and-tortoise shell inlay from Goa on the Japiassu family altar, third on the right as you enter. The altars and ceiling have a layer of gold—about 10 grams per square meter. ☒ *Terreiro de Jesus, Pelourinho* ☎ *071/3321–4573* ☎ *R$3* ☉ *Tues.–Sat. 8–11 and 3–6, Sun. 10–1.*

★ **10** **Igreja de Nossa Senhora do Rosário dos Pretos.** Built by and for slaves between 1704 and 1796 to honor Our Lady of the Rosary of the Blacks, this church didn't receive due attention outside the local Afro-Brazilian community until long after it was built. After extensive renovation, it is worth a look at the side altars to see statues of the Catholic church's few black saints. African rhythms pervade the services. ☒ *Largo do Pelourinho s/n, Pelourinho* ☎ *071/3327–9701* ☎ *Free* ☉ *Weekdays 8–5, Sat 9–5, Sun. 10–13.*

★ **8** **Igreja São Domingos de Gusmão da Ordem Terceira.** The baroque Church of the Third Order of St. Dominic (1731) houses a collection of carved processional saints and other sacred objects. Such sculptures often had hollow interiors and were used to smuggle gold into Portugal to avoid taxes. Asian details in the church decoration are evidence of long-ago connections with Portugal's colonies of Goa and Macau. Upstairs are two impressive rooms with carved wooden furniture used for church meetings. ☒ *Terreiro de Jesus, Pelourinho* ☎ *071/3242–4185* ☎ *Free* ☉ *Sun.–Fri. 8–noon and 2–5.*

9 **Igreja de São Francisco.** One of the most impressive churches in Salvador, **Fodor's**Choice the Church of St. Francis was built in the 18th century on the site of ★ earlier church burned down during the Dutch invasion in early 1600s. The ceiling was painted in 1774 by José Joaquim da Rocha, a mulatto who founded Brazil's first art school. The ornate cedar-and-rosewood interior writhes with images of mermaids, acanthus leaves, and caryatids—all bathed in gold leaf. Guides say that there's as much as a ton of gold here, but restoration experts maintain there's much less, as the leaf used is just a step up from a powder. At the end of Sunday-morning mass (9–11 and 11–11:45) the lights go off to catch the wondrous subtlety of gold leaf under natural light. The **Convento de São Francisco** (☎ 071/3322–6430), part of the Franciscan order complex at the site, has an impressive series of 37 white-and-blue tile panels lining the walls

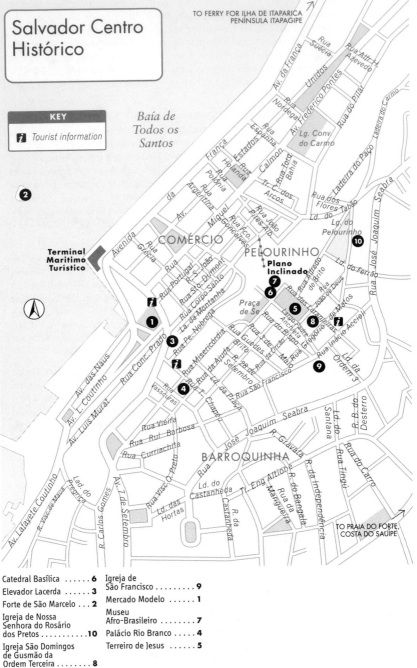

Salvador Centro Histórico

KEY

i Tourist information

Baía de Todos os Santos

TO FERRY FOR ILHA DE ITAPARICA
PENÍNSULA ITAPAGIPE

Terminal Marítimo Turístico

COMÉRCIO

PELOURINHO

Plano Inclinado

Praça de Sé

BARROQUINHA

TO PRAIA DO FORTE,
COSTA DO SAÚIPE

of the claustrum, each with a scene from Greco–Roman mythology and a moral aphorism in Latin. The **Ordem Terceira de São Francisco** (☏ 071/321–6968), on the north side of the complex, has an 18th-century Spanish plateresque sandstone facade—the only one of its kind in Brazil—that is carved to resemble Spanish silver altars made by beating the metal into wooden molds. ⊠ *Largo Padre Anchieta, Pelourinho* ☏ *071/322–6430* ▱ *R$3* ◔ *Mon.–Sat. 8–noon and 2–5, Sun. 8–noon.*

★ ❼ **Museu Afro-Brasileiro.** Next to the Catedral Basílica, the Afro-Brazilian Museum has a collection of more than 1,200 pieces of a religious or spiritual nature, including pottery, sculpture, tapestry, weavings, paintings, crafts, carvings, and photographs. There's an interesting display on the meanings of Candomblé deities, with huge carved-wood panels portraying each one. The two other museums that share the building are the Memorial de Medicina (Old School of Medicine Memorial) and the Museu Arqueologia e Etnologia (Archaeology and Ethnology Museum); both are closed for extensive renovation that is projected to finish sometime in 2007. ⊠ *Terreiro de Jesus, Pelourinho* ☏ *071/3221–2971* ▱ *R$3* ◔ *Weekdays 9–5.*

❹ **Palácio Rio Branco.** The building dates back to 1549, when it was the headquarters of the colonial government of Brazil. The current construction, finished in 1919, is the result of several renovations and expansions and has resulted in an eclectic style that leans toward neoclassical. Today it houses Salvador's Chamber of Commerce, the Fundação Cultural (Cultural Foundation of the State of Bahia), and Bahíatursa, the state tourist office. On the first floor there's a small memorial to the state's governors, depicting the last two centuries of local history. Get a great view of Cidade Baixa and the bay from the east-side balcony. ⊠ *Praça Tomé de Souza s/n, Pelourinho* ☏ *071/3241–4333* ◔ *Tues.–Sat. 10–6.*

❺ **Terreiro de Jesus.** The wide plaza lined with churches and 17th-century houses is the heart of historic Salvador. Where nobles once strolled under imperial palm trees, now there is a crafts fair on weekends, and occasionally a group of locals might practice capoeira—a stylized dance-like fight with African origins—to the *thwang* of the *berimbau*, a rudimentary bow-shape musical instrument. ⊠ *Intersection of Rua das Laranjeiras and Rua João de Deus, Pelourinho.*

City Beaches

In general, the farther east and north from the mouth of the bay, the better the beaches. To avoid large crowds, don't go on weekends. Regardless of when you go, keep an eye on your belongings and take only what you need to the beach—petty thievery is a problem. There are no public bathrooms. You can rent a beach chair and sun umbrella for about R$10.

Beaches are listed in geographical order, beginning with Piatã, north of the city on the Baía de Todos os Santos, and then to Praia da Barra, near the peninsula's tip, and northeast to other Atlantic beaches.

Praia Piatã. Heading north and leaving the more built-up areas of the city behind, the first truly clean beach you'll come to is the wide Piatã. Its calm waters and golden sand attract local families. ⊠ *northeast of Praia Corsário, along Av. Oceánica Piatã.*

Praia da Barra is a popular beach in Barra that's a convenient option if you're staying in the hotel districts of Ondina and Rio Vermelho, where rock outcroppings make swimming dangerous, and pollution is often a problem. ☒ *Along Av. Oceánica just east of Santo Antônio da Barra, Barra.*

One of the nicest beaches along Avenida Oceánica is **Praia Corsário,** a long stretch popular with surfers and the young crowd. There are kiosks where you can sit in the shade and enjoy seafood and an ice-cold beer or soft drink from the kiosks. ☒ *South of Parque Metropolitan de Pituaçu, along Av. Oceánica and Av. Otávio Mangabeira, Pituaçu.*

Praia Itapuã. Frequented by artists that live in the neighborhood, the Itapuã beach has an eclectic atmosphere. There are food kiosks—including Acarajé da Cira, one of the best places to get *acarajé* (a spicy fried-bean snack) in Salvador—and bars with live music. The area was once a whale cemetery, and bones are still an occasional find. Inland from Itapuã, a mystical freshwater lagoon, the **Lagoa de Abaeté,** and surrounding sand dunes are now a municipal park. Itapuã's dark waters are a startling contrast to the fine white sand of its shores. ☒ *16 km/10 mi northeast of downtown, Itapuã.*

The northernmost beach in the Salvador municipality along the Avenida Oceánica is **Praia Stella Maris,** popular with surfers and the young crowd. There are myriad food and drinks kiosks, more than at any other beach—it's the perfect place to sooth your thirst with *água de côco* (coconut water). ☒ *20 km/12 mi north of downtown, after Itapuã, Stella Maris.*

Where to Eat

Brazilian

$$-$$$ ✕ **Casa da Gamboa.** A longtime favorite of Bahian writer Jorge Amado, this is a Bahian cooking institution. *Casquinha de siri* (breaded crab in the shell) comes as a complimentary starter; then try the *peixe com risoto de ostras* (grilled fish with oyster risotto) or the *bobó de camarão* (shrimp stew in cassava flour) followed by a traditional dessert such as *cocada* (sweet coconut cream cake). ☒ *Rua João de Deus 32, Pelourinho* ☎ *071/3321–3393* ⊟ *AE, D, MC, V* ☺ *Closed Sun.*

$$-$$$ ✕ **Maria Mata Mouro.** At this small intimate restaurant, in a *sobrado* (two-story colonial house) right in the Pelourinho, you almost feel as if you're at a friend's home for dinner. Bahian food is lighter than in most restaurants. Try the *badejo* (grouper) in ginger sauce. The roasted leg of lamb is a great choice if you want to depart from seafood. Entrée servings are more than enough for two. ☒ *Rua Inácio Acciole 8, Pelourinho* ☎ *071/3321–3929* ⊟ *AE, D, MC, V.*

$$-$$$
Fodor's Choice
★
✕ **Trapiche Adelaide.** It's almost impossible to have a bad meal in this city, but this restaurant along the harbor and near the Mercado Modelo still stands out for its unique blend of Italian, French, and Bahian cuisines and for its fresh fish. Try the seafood risotto or quail in *farofa* (cassava flour). Having drinks before dinner on the deck overlooking the Todos os Santos Bay is a pleasant way to wind down after a day of

sightseeing. ⊠ *Praça dos Tupinambás, Av. Contorno 02, Comércio* ☎ *071/3326–2211* ⊕ *www.trapicheadelaide.com.br* ⊟ *AE, D, MC, V* ⊘ *No dinner Sun.*

★ **$–$$$** ✕ **Solar do Unhão.** You get a lot for your money at this restaurant on the bay. Dinner is buffet style, with emphasis on Bahian dishes, but you have several international choices. The evening show presents Afro-Brazilian dance, still an integral part of Bahian culture today. The building is part of an 18th-century colonial estate, which has housed a sugar mill and a tobacco factory. The restaurant is in the former slave quarters. On a corner of the estate, the small **Museu de Arte Moderna** has temporary exhibits of Brazilian artists such as Di Cavalcanti and Volpi. ⊠ *Av. do Contorno 08* ☎ *071/329–5551* ⚮ *Reservations essential* ⊟ *AE, MC, V.*

$–$$ ✕ **Encontro dos Artistas.** This simple Bahian restaurant has both alfresco and indoor dining. The fish-and-shrimp moqueca, a stew made with coconut milk and *dendê* (a type of palm) oil, is a must here. The charm of this neighborhood establishment lies in its casual ambience, surroundings in a centuries-old part of town, and local clientele, who gather here after work. Service can be slow—order an appetizer or salad and drinks as soon as you sit down. ⊠ *Rua Francisco Muniz Barreto 15, at Rua das Laranjeiras, Pelourinho* ☎ *071/3321–1721* ⊟ *AE, D, MC, V.*

$ ✕ **Escola SENAC.** This restaurant, which opened in 1975, is a cooking school where new generations of Bahian chefs hone their skills under supervision of experienced teachers. More than 40 typical Bahian and Brazilian dishes are served buffet style in this old colonial house. It is regarded as one of the best restaurants in town. The bargain prices are an extra incentive. ⊠ *Praça José de Alencar 13–19, Pelourinho* ☎ *071/ 3324–4550* ⊟ *MC, V* ⊘ *Closed Sun.*

$ ✕ **Uauá.** The cuisine here is representative of many Brazilian regions, making Uauá one of the most popular restaurant chains in Salvador, and therefore almost always crowded. The cuisine is representative of many Brazilian regions, with special attention to northeastern dishes. Don't skip the *guisado de carneiro* (minced mutton), here with calabrese sausage. ⊠ *R. Gregório de Matos 36, Pelourinho* ☎ *071/3321–3089* ⊠ *Av. Dorival Caymi 46, Itapuã* ☎ *071/3249–9579* ⊟ *AE, DC, MC, V* ⚮ *Reservations not accepted* ⊘ *Closed Mon.*

Eclectic

$$ ✕ **Boi Preto.** Beef is cooked to perfection at one of the best barbecue places in Salvador. Seafood, including lobster, crab, and sushi, and more exotic fare like alligator or wild boar are also on the menu. A piano bar keeps the atmosphere light. ⊠ *Av. Otávio Mangabeira s/n, Jardim Armação* ☎ *071/3362–8844* ⊕ *www.boipretogrill.com.br* ⊟ *AE, MC, V.*

French

$$$$ ✕ **Chez Bernard.** *Soteropolitanos* (Salvadorans) consider this the best French restaurant in town, with over 40 years of service. Everything is worth trying, but the *filet de boeuf* (steak) with several sauce options is particularly *fantastique*. ⊠ *Gamboa de Cima 11, Aflitos* ☎ *071/ 3329–5403* ⊕ *www.chezbernard.com.br* ⊟ *AE, MC, V* ⊘ *Closed Sun.*

Seafood

★ **$$–$$$** ✕**Yemanja.** A bubbly underwater theme—replete with aquariums and sea-goddess murals—sets the tone for the fabulous seafood here. Small portions of acarajé can be ordered as appetizers. The service is somewhat slow, but most patrons don't seem to mind, concentrating instead on plowing through enormous portions of moqueca, or *ensopado*, seafood cooked in a similar but lighter sauce. Reservations are essential on weekends. ⌧ *Av. Otávio Mangabeira 4655, Jardim Armação* ☎ *071/3461–9010* ⊕ *www.restauranteyemanja.com.br* ⊟ *AE, DC, MC, V.*

$–$$ ✕**Bargaço.** Great Bahian seafood dishes are served at this old favorite. *Pata de caranguejo* (vinegared crab claw) is hearty and may do more than take the edge off your appetite for the requisite moqueca *de camarão* (with shrimp) or moqueca *de siri mole* (with soft-shell crab); try the cocada for dessert, if you have room. ⌧ *Rua P, quadra 43, Jardim Armação* ☎ *071/3231–9300* ⊟ *AE, MC, V.*

Where to Stay

There are only a few hotels in the Centro Histórico. Heading south into the Vitória neighborhood along Avenida 7 de Setembro there are many inexpensive establishments convenient to beaches and sights. In the yuppie Barra neighborhood, many hotels are within walking distance of cafés, bars, restaurants, and clubs. The resorts in the beach areas of Ondina and Rio Vermelho are a 20-minute taxi ride from downtown. High seasons are from December to March and the month of July. For Carnival, reservations must be made months in advance, and prices are substantially higher.

★ **$$$–$$$$** 🏨**Catussaba Resort Hotel.** In a garden of flowers and palm trees, this hotel has large rooms, some of which have beautiful wicker furniture, with balconies and ocean views. The resort complex opens directly onto Itapuã beach, one of the cleanest and most famous in Salvador. The hotel is 40 km (25 mi) from downtown, near the airport. If you tire of saltwater and sand, head for the large pool area. ⌧ *Alameda da Praia, Itapuã, 41600-270* ☎ *071/3374–8000* ⊕ *www.catussaba.com.br* ⤳ *186 rooms, 4 suites* ⟡ *Restaurant, room service, minibars, cable TV, 4 tennis court, pool, health club, sauna, bar, Internet room, convention center, meeting rooms, travel services, free parking* ⊟ *AE, MC, V.*

$$$ 🏨**Bahia Othon Palace Hotel.** A short drive from most sights, nightspots, and restaurants, this busy, modern hotel sits on a cliff overlooking Ondina Beach. Top local entertainers often perform at the hotel's outdoor park, and in high season the friendly staff organizes poolside activities and trips to better beaches. ⌧ *Av. Oceánica 2294, Ondina, 40170-010* ☎ *071/3203–2000* ⊕ *www.othon.com.br* ⤳ *300 rooms, 25 suites* ⟡ *Restaurant, coffee shop, in-room safes, minibars, cable TV, pool, health club, sauna, dance club, free parking* ⊟ *AE, DC, MC, V.*

☾ **$$$** 🏨**Sofitel Salvador.** This branch of the international Sofitel chain sits in
Fodor'sChoice a tropical park near Itapuã Beach and the Abaeté Lagoon, about 5 km
★ (3 mi) from the airport. It's the only hotel in Salvador with its own golf course, albeit a 9-hole one. As it aims for the business as well as the purely

tourist clientele, rooms are more sober than other beachfront hotels. The Oxum restaurant has an excellent regional menu. The hotel provides transportation to the Centro Histórico. ⊠ *Rua da Passargada s/n, Itapuã, 41620-430* ☎ *071/2106–8500* ⊕ *www.sofitel.com* ⟲ *206 rooms* ⚘ *2 restaurants, room service, in-room safes, cable TV, 9-hole golf course, 3 tennis courts, 2 outdoor pools, health club, hair salon, massage, boating, billiards, 3 bars, shops, babysitting, dry cleaning, children's program (ages 4–12), concierge, Internet room, business services, meeting rooms, airport shuttle, travel services, free parking* ▬ *AE, DC, MC, V.*

$$–$$$ ▦ **Blue Tree Towers Salvador.** Though it doesn't have close sea views, the local member of Blue Tree chain in the Ondina district has easy access to the historic center and the beaches. Rooms with king-sized beds and other facilities follow the Blue Tree standard of quality and functionality. From here it is a short distance to the many restaurants and bars of the Barra district. ⊠ *Rua Monte Conselho 505, Ondina, 41940-370* ☎ *071/2103–2233* ⊕ *www.bluetree.com.br* ⟲ *200 rooms* ⚘ *Restaurant, coffee shop, room service, in-room safes, minibars, cable TV, outdoor pool, health club, sauna, laundry service, Internet room, in-room data ports, business services, meeting rooms, parking (fee)* ▬ *AE, DC, MC, V* ⏐◯⏐ *BP.*

$$ ▦ **Fiesta Bahia Hotel.** In the city's financial district and attached to the convention center, the Fiesta has wheelchair-accessible rooms and rooms with direct phone lines, fax and PC terminals, and queen-sized beds—amenities that distinguish it from its competitors. ⊠ *Av. Antônio Carlos Magalhães 711, Itaigara, 41125-000* ☎ *071/3352–0000* ⊕ *www.fiestahotel.com.br* ⟲ *236 rooms, 8 suites* ⚘ *Restaurant, coffee shop, room service, in-room safes, minibars, cable TV, in-room data ports, 2 pools, health club, hair salon, bar, nightclub, shops, business services, meeting rooms, free parking* ▬ *AE, DC, MC, V.*

$$ ▦ **Ondina Apart Hotel Residência.** In the resort hotel district, a short drive from the sights, nightlife, and restaurants of Salvador, this outstanding beachside complex has simple modern furniture. Businesspeople and families opt for this hotel when they're staying in Salvador for extended periods, as all rooms have a small kitchen. ⊠ *Av. Oceánica 2400, Ondina, 40170-010* ☎ *071/3203–8000* ⊕ *www.ondinaapart.com.br* ⟲ *100 rooms* ⚘ *Restaurant, coffee shop, in-room safes, kitchenettes, minibars, cable TV, tennis court, pool, gym, bar, babysitting, laundry service, parking (fee)* ▬ *AE, DC, MC, V.*

$$ ▦ **Tropical Hotel da Bahia.** Owned by Varig Airlines and often included in package deals, this centrally located hotel is a bit tattered, but it's practical for those whose priority is Salvador's history and culture. The hotel is away from the beaches, but there's a free beach shuttle. Some rooms overlook Largo de Campo Grande, one of the hubs of Carnival in Salvador. ⊠ *Praça 2 de Julho 02, Campo Grande, 40080-121* ☎ *071/3255–2000* ⊕ *www.tropicalhotel.com.br* ⟲ *275 rooms* ⚘ *Restaurant, coffee shop, room service, cable TV, 2 pools, massage, sauna, bar, dance club, concierge, parking (fee)* ▬ *AE, DC, MC, V.*

$ ▦ **Hotel Bahia do Sol.** Decor might be simple, but this budget hotel has a prime location close to museums and historic sights. Some rooms have a partial ocean view, but those in the back are quieter. The restaurant Zarzuela is somewhat eclectic, but you can certainly find some Bahian dishes. ☒ *Av. 7 de Setembro 2009, Vitória, 40080-002* ☏ *071/3338–8800* ⊕ *www.bahiadosol.com.br* ⇨ *90 rooms, 2 suites* ⚄ *Restaurant, cable TV, bar, meeting rooms, free parking* ⊟ *AE, DC, MC, V.*

$ ⊞ **Hotel Mercure Salvador.** A high-quality chain hotel in a high-rise building, the Mercure has a prime business location. The ambience is relaxing, as all apartments face the Atlantic Ocean. The Casarão restaurant has tables on a deck overlooking the ocean. ☒ *Rua Fonte de Boi 215, Rio Vermelho, 40210-090* ☏ *071/3330–8200* ⊕ *www.accorhotels. com.br* ⇨ *175 rooms* ⚄ *Restaurant, bar, minibars, cable TV, sauna, fitness room, meeting rooms, business services, Internet room, in-room safes, free parking* ⊟ *AE, D, MC, V* ❙⊙❙ *BP.*

$ ⊞ **Pestana Bahia.** This hotel built atop a seaside cliff in the trendy Rio Vermelho neighborhood has carved itself a tradition of excellent services for tourists and conventioneers. It was thoroughly renovated in 2003. It is a short walk from the neighborhood's bars and restaurants. ☒ *Rua Fonte de Boi 216, Rio Vermelho, 40170-010* ☏ *071/2103–8000 or 800/26–6332* ⊕ *www.pestana.com.br* ⇨ *430 rooms* ⚄ *Restaurant, coffee shop, in-room safes, minibars, cable TV, pool, gym, bar, babysitting, laundry service, parking, shuttle service* ⊟ *AE, DC, MC, V.*

¢ ⊞ **Âmbar Pousada.** The highlight of this small and simple pousada is the service—the staff is attentive and rooms are kept impeccably clean. Location is a draw too, as here you are just a couple of streets away from the eclectic Barra neighborhood. If you're braving Salvador at Carnival time, the parade passes noisily just two blocks away on Avenida Oceánica. There's a nice terrace and courtyard. ☒ *Rua Afonso Celso 485, Barra, 40140-080* ☏ *071/3264–6956* ⊕ *www.ambarpousada. com.br* ⇨ *5 rooms* ⚄ *Fans, Internet room; no room TVs* ⊟ *AE, MC, V* ❙⊙❙ *BP.*

¢ ⊞ **Hotel Catharina Paraguaçu.** Rooms and suites in this intimate hotel in a 19th-century mansion are small but comfortable, and include six **FodorsChoice** split-level suites. Extra attention is devoted to the decor, with pottery ★ and embroidery from local artisans. It's family run and in a neighborhood of many restaurants and bars. The kitchen serves snacks and meals, from fettuccine to salmon. It has one room for guests with disabilities, including wheelchair access, unusual for a small hotel like this. ☒ *Rua João Gomes 128, Rio Vermelho, 40210-090* ☏ *071/3334–0089* ⊕ *www.hotelcatharinaparaguacu.com.br* ⇨ *23 rooms, 6 suites* ⚄ *Dining room, minibars, cable TV* ⊟ *MC, V* ❙⊙❙ *BP.*

★ **¢** ⊞ **Pousada das Flores.** The Brazilian-French owners have made this inn, northeast of Pelourinho and within walking distance of the historical district, one of the city's best budget options. Rooms are large and have high ceilings and hardwood floors. For peace and quiet as well as a bay view, opt for a room on an upper floor. If you feel like splurging, request the penthouse, which has a fantastic view of the harbor. Breakfast is served on the patio. ☒ *Rua Direita de Santo Antônio 442, Santo Antônio, 40301-280* ☏ *071/3243–1836* ⊕ *www.pflores.com.br* ⇨ *6 rooms, 3 suites* ⚄ *Restaurant, fans, mini-bar, Internet room* ⊟ *AE, DC, MC, V.*

Nightlife & the Arts

Pelourinho is filled with music every night and has more bars and clubs than you can count. Most bars serve food as well as drink. Activity also centers along the seashore, mainly at Rio Vermelho and between the Corsário and Piatã beaches, where many hotels have bars or discos.

Salvador is considered by many artists as a laboratory for the creation of new rhythms and dance steps. Accordingly, this city has an electric performing arts scene. See the events calendar published by Bahiatursa or check local newspapers for details on live music performances as well as rehearsal schedules. In Pelourinho, groups often have practices open to the public on Tuesday and Sunday nights.

Nightlife

After dark, Praça Terreirro de Jesus is a hot spot, especially on Tuesday and Saturday nights, when stages are set up here and at other squares around the city for live performances. This plaza is especially popular with tourists because it has been painted, cleaned up, and gentrified. Although there may be impromptu musical performances any night, you can always count on it on Tuesday.

BARS There are many bars in the Pelourinho area, as well as on the beachfront avenues. The shopping complex Aeroclube Plaza on Avenida Otávio Manguabeira has also become quite popular among the young crowd, with bars, restaurants, and nightclubs.

Enjoy live music and typical Bahian food at **Casquinha de Siri** (⊠ Av. Otávio Mangabeira s/n, Piatã ☏ 071/ 3367–1234). The two branches of the traditional bar **Habeas Copos** (⊠ Rua Marques de Leão 172, Barra ☏ 071/3247–7895 ⊠ Praça Quincas Berro D'Agua, Pelourinho ☏ 071/3321–1798) are famous for their moqueca and *carne-de-sol* (sun-dried meat).

Sancho Panza (⊠ Av. Otávio Mangabeira 122, Pituba ☏ 071/3248–3571) is a great place for sangria and typical Spanish fare. Sooner or later you must have a *caipirinha* (lime and sugar-cane brandy cocktail) at **Cantina da Lua** (⊠ Praça Terreiro de Jesus 2, Pelourinho ☏ 071/3322-4041).

DANCE SHOWS Shows at the **Moenda** (⊠ Rua P, Quadra 28, Lote 21, Jardim Armação ☏ 071/3231–7915) begin daily at 8 PM. There are Afro-Brazilian dinner shows at the **Solar do Unhão** (⊠ Av. do Contorno 08, Comércio ☏ 071/ 3321–5551). The unforgettable Afro-Bahian show at the **Teatro Miguel Santana** (⊠ Rua Gregório de Mattos 47, Pelourinho ☏ 071/3321–0222) has the town's best folkloric dance troupes. This is an entertaining way to learn about Afro-Brazilian culture.

NIGHTCLUBS Have dinner or drinks and listen to quality jazz, blues, soul, and pop at the **French Quartier** (⊠ Aeroclube Plaza complex, Av. Otávio Mangabeira 2323, Lote 1, Jardim dos Namorados ☏ 071/3240–1491 ⊕ www.frenchquartier.com.br). Happy hour is between 6 PM and 8 PM. The view of the bay is fantastic, but ocean breezes are cool, so bring a coat or sweater.

The **Queops** disco (✉ Rua Manoel Antônio Galvão 100, Patamares ☎ 071/3206–0138), open Wednesday to Saturday, has a large dance floor and occasional performances of local rock-and-roll bands. **Rock in Rio Café** (✉ Av. Otávio Mangabeira 6000, Jardim Armação ☎ 071/3461–0300) is in the shopping-and-entertainment complex Aeroclube Plaza. The atmosphere here is more like Miami than Salvador.

The Arts

CARNIVAL
REHEARSALS
★

Afro-Brazilian percussion groups begin Carnival rehearsals—which are really more like creative jam sessions—around midyear. **Ilê Aiyê** (✉ Rua do Curuzu 197, Liberdade ☎ 071/3256–1013), which started out as a Carnival bloco, has turned itself into much more in its 25-year history. It now has its own school and promotes the study and practice of African heritage, religion, and history. Public practices are held every Saturday night at Forte de Santo Antônio and should not be missed.

Olodum, Salvador's best-known percussion group, gained international fame when it participated in Paul Simon's "Rhythm of the Saints" tour and recordings. The group has its own venue, the **Casa do Olodum** (✉ Rua Gregório de Matos 22, Pelourinho ☎ 071/3321–5010). Olodum also has a percussion school, **Escola Criativa Olodum** (✉ Rua das Laranjeiras 30, Pelourinho ☎ 071/3322–8029). Pre-Carnival rehearsals take place at Largo do Pelourinho Tuesday evenings and Sunday afternoons.

MUSIC, THEATER
& DANCE

Teatro Casa do Comércio (✉ Av. Tancredo Neves 1109, Pituba ☎ 071/3341–1310) hosts music performances and some theatrical productions. Classical and popular music performances, operas, and plays are all held at **Teatro Castro Alves** (✉ Praça 2 de Julho s/n, Campo Grande ☎ 071/3532–2323 ⊕ www.tca.ba.gov.br), Salvador's largest theater. The **Teatro ACBEU (Associação Cultural Brasil-Estados Unidos)** (✉ Av. 7 de Setembro 1883, Vitória ☎ 071/3337–4395 ⊕ www.acbeubahia.com.br) has contemporary and classical music, dance, and theater performances by Brazilian and international artists.

SIDE TRIPS FROM SALVADOR

Although attractions in Salvador can keep you entertained for more than a week, there are great places for a one- or two-day break in more relaxing environs. On a two-day tour to Morro de São Paulo, you can enjoy the near-pristine beaches and tropical forest. Or plan a day trip to Praia do Forte or the other northern beaches; they're less crowded and more beautiful than those in and near Salvador.

Morro de São Paulo

★ ⑪ On Ilha de Tinharé, just south of Itaparica, Morro de São Paulo is the most popular place on the island, most of which is covered with thick Atlantic forest protected by a state park. Private cars are not allowed here; you can walk to the beaches, take tractor-pulled trolleys, or hire a small boat to "beach-hop" about the island. Popular beaches dot the 40-km (25-mi) Atlantic side of Tinharé. Starting at the Morro de São Paulo village, beaches begin with Primeira (First) and go on to Segunda,

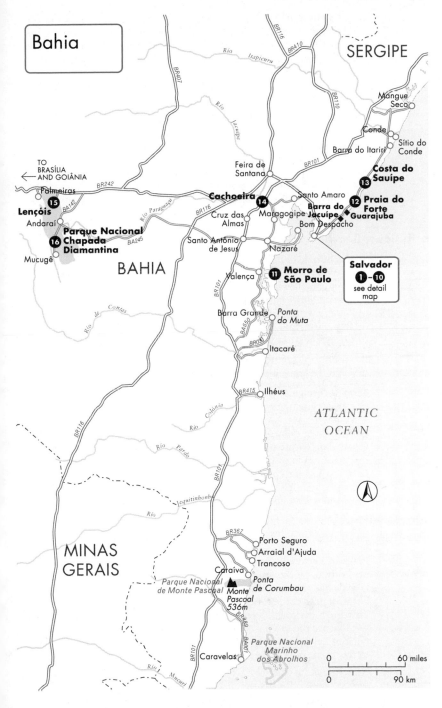

Terceira (Second, Third), and so forth. Waters are calm thanks to the coral reef just off the surf, whose abundant marine life (mostly in the form of small fish) makes scuba diving or snorkeling worthwhile. The number of tourists nearly triples from December to February (Brazil's summer), when Brazilians and foreigners fill the pousadas for festival and Carnival season. The southernmost beaches near Boca da Barra are usually quieter even during peak season.

To reach Morro de São Paulo, either take the air shuttle from Salvador (⇨ By Air, *in* Salvador & Bahia Essentials) or take a *lancha* (small boat carrying up to five passengers) or larger *catamarã* (catamaran) from **Terminal Maritimo** (✉ Av. da França 1 ☏ 071/3319–2890). Launch and catamaran services run by several different companies leave daily from 8 AM to 2 PM, and return from Morro de São Paulo from noon to 4 PM; fares range from R$50 to R$70 depending on services, like food, drinks, and live music.

North Coast Beaches

To reach some of Bahia's more pristine and less crowded beaches, head north of Salvador on the Estrada do Coco (Coconut Road), leaving the baroque churches and colonial dwellings behind in favor of miles of quiet road lined with coconut palms. At the fishing village and turtle haven of Praia do Forte, take the Linha Verde (Green Line/Highway BA 099) up the coast. Each of the little roads cutting east off Linha Verde leads to a different palm-tree-covered beach.

Bus transportation to this area is readily available, but driving is fairly safe and the convenience of your own wheels is justified here.

Barra do Jacuípe. A river runs down to the ocean at this long, wide, pristine beach lined with coconut palms. There are beachfront snack bars, and the Santa Maria/Catuense bus company operates six buses here daily. ✉ *40 km (25 mi) north of Salvador.*

Guarajuba. With palm trees and calm waters banked by a reef, this is the nicest beach of them all, though it's lined with condos. The bus to Barra do Jacuípe continues on to Guarajuba, which has snack kiosks, fishing boats, surfing, dune buggies, and a playground. ✉ *60 km (38 mi) north of Salvador.*

Praia do Forte

⑫ *72 km (45 mi) northeast of Salvador.*

Praia do Forte was first settled in 1549 by Garcia D'Avila, a clerk for the Portuguese crown. For reasons lost in the mists of history, Garcia D'Avila had acquired a fortune and became a landowner. With foresight, he introduced cattle ranching and coconut-palm cultivation in the area. To protect the coast, a medieval-style castle was built that served as a fort—hence the town's name, which means "Fortress Beach." All that remains from the castle is just the outer walls, and there isn't too much to see, but it now has a helpful visitor center. Today the area's biggest attraction is the headquarters of a sea-turtle preservation project (Projeto Tamar). Now, instead of earning their living by killing turtles for meat, eggs, and shells, local fishermen are better paid to protect them. Jobs have also been provided by the bars, restaurants, pousadas, and shops that now line the three brick-paved streets. Almost everything in town is on the main street, Alameda do Sol.

On a relaxing day trip from Salvador you can visit Praia do Forte's village, get to know the sea-turtle research station, swim, or snorkel. The town also has a beautiful coconut-lined beach. If you decide to stay longer, there are many lodging options, and the nightlife, although toned down a few decibels from that in Salvador, is still lively. You can book a trip here through any Salvador tour operator or travel agent, or simply take a bus directly on a day trip.

FodorsChoice
★
Five of the seven extant sea-turtle species in the world roam and reproduce on Brazil's Atlantic coast, primarily in Bahia. The headquarters of **Projeto Tamar,** established in 1980, has turned what was once a small, struggling fishing village into a tourist destination with a mission—to save Brazil's giant sea turtles and their hatchlings. During the hatching season (September through March), workers patrol the shore at night to locate nests and move eggs or hatchlings at risk of being trampled or run over to safer areas or to the open-air hatchery at the Tamar base station. Here you can watch adult turtles in the swimming pools and see the baby turtles that are housed in tanks until they can be released to the sea. Eighteen other Tamar base stations on beaches along 1,000 km (621 mi) of coastline in five northeastern Brazilian states protect about 400,000 hatchlings born each year. The headquarters also has educational videos, lectures, and a gift shop where you can buy turtle-themed gifts (proceeds help support the project). From December to February, you can sign up for the "Tartaruga by Night" project to help release hatchlings from the station hatchery to the sea. ⊠ *Alameda do Sol s/n* ☎ *071/3676–1020* ⊕ *www.tamar.org.br* ✉ *R$12* ☼ *Daily 9–7.*

Swim or snorkel in the crystal-clear (and safe) waters of the **Papa Gente,** a 3-meter-deep (10-foot-deep) natural pool formed by reefs at the ocean's edge. Snacks are sold at little huts on the beach, but if you're really hungry, a restaurant, in the Sobrado Da Vila Pousada, is nearby.

If you have a couple of days to visit Praia do Forte, spend one of them on a jeep tour. These tours make their way through the **Reserva de Sapiranga,** with 600 hectares (1,482 acres) of Atlantic forest that contains rare orchids and bromeliads. The reserve is a sanctuary for endangered animals. White-water rafting is possible on the Rio Pojuca, which flows through the park, and Lago Timeantube, where more than 187 species of native birds have been sighted. You can rent a car, or preferably a jeep, and drive yourself through the reserve or arrange for a tour in town at the **Centro Turistico** (Tourist Center; ⊠ Alameda do Sol s/n ☎ 071/676–1091 ⊕ www.prdoforte.com.br).

Where to Stay & Eat

$$ ✕ **Sabor da Vila.** It isn't surprising that seafood fresh from the ocean is the specialty at this small modest restaurant on Praia do Forte's main street. After visiting Praia do Forte's attractions, stop here for a fish-and-shrimp moqueca. ⊠ *Av. ACM s/n* ☎ *071/3676–1156* ▭ *D, MC, V.*

¢ ✗ **Bar do Souza.** Make this well-known bar your choice for a Bahian snack of *acarajés* (shrimp-filled bean-flour pastries fried in palm oil). The restaurant serves up other excellent Bahian specialties, including fish stews, grilled lobster, and shellfish stew. It's a favorite with the locals, especially on Friday and Saturday nights, when there's live music. ⊠ *Alameda do Sol* ☎ *No phone* ⊟ *AE, MC, V.*

$$ ✗⊞ **Pousada Praia do Forte.** You have your own thatch-roof bungalow with a hammock hanging on the open porch here. Bungalows are small, but you're only there to sleep—the beach and the pools that are left when the tide goes out are too inviting to miss. Redbrick paths curve through the landscaped grounds to 12 km (7 mi) of beaches lined with coconut trees and to the Tamar sea-turtle project. In the evening you can relax in the pousada's outdoor pool and take a walk on the beach, and then end the day with dinner in the restaurant, enjoying international and Bahian cuisine. ⊠ *Av. do Farol s/n, Mata de São João, Praia do Forte, 48280-000* ☎ *071/676–1116* ⊕ *www.pousadapraiadoforte.com.br* ↪ *19 bungalows* ⟁ *Restaurant, fans, pool* ⊟ *DC, MC, V* ¶○¶ *MAP.*

$ ✗⊞ **Pousada Sobrado Da Vila.** Leave your computer and pocket organizer at home and forget about time management, this is a laid-back pousada right on the main drag where you can kick back and relax. The rooms are plain but comfortable, and the restaurant is superb, with all Bahian specialties. If you've never tried a *queijo de coalho frito* (roasted cheese ball), try it here. ⊠ *Av. ACM 7* ☎ *071/676–1088* ⊕ *www. sobradodavila.com.br* ↪ *23 rooms* ⟁ *Restaurant, refrigerators, cable TV* ⊟ *AE, MC, V.*

♨ $$$$ ⊞ **Praia do Forte Eco Resort.** Relax on a hammock and contemplate the
Fodor'sChoice sea from your private veranda at this sprawling beachfront resort. You'll
★ be within walking distance of the village in case you need more action, but there is a full roster of activities available including horseback riding, volleyball, kayaking, sailing, and snorkeling. All rooms face the ocean, and a large part of the grounds still has the original Atlantic forest vegetation that once covered the region. The restaurant and other facilities are open only to resort guests. ⊠ *Av. do Farol s/n, Praia do Forte, Mata de São João 48280-000* ☎ *071/676–4000 or 0800/71–8888* ⊕ *www. praiadoforte.com* ↪ *250 rooms* ⟁ *2 restaurants, in-room safes, cable TV, 4 tennis courts, 5 pools, gym, beach, snorkeling, windsurfing, boating, 3 bars, dance club, children's programs (ages 4–12)* ⊟ *AE, DC, MC, V* ¶○¶ *MAP.*

Costa do Sauípe

⓭ *114 km (71 mi) northeast of Salvador 42 km (26 mi) northeast of Praia Do Forte.*

An hour's drive north from Salvador along the Atlantic coast brings you to the Costa do Sauípe resort complex. Its five hotels, convention center, re-created local village with six pousadas, and sports center are all part of a 500-acre development in an environmental protection area bordered by rain forest. To get around during your stay within the complex, you can either hop the resort van that makes continuous loops or take a horse and carriage.

If you prefer small lodgings to grand resorts, opt for a stay in one of the six themed pousadas (inns) in Vila Nova da Praia, a re-creation of a typical northeastern village, with cobblestone lanes, crafts shops, restaurants, bars, and street entertainment. Vila Nova da Praia is also a great place to find special gifts, especially ceramics, and to buy resort wear. ✉ *Km 76, Rodovia BA 099, Costa do Sauípe, Mata de São João, 48280-000.*

Where to Stay

Regardless of where you stay, you have access to all the resort's amenities, including those of the sports complex, with its 18-hole PGA golf course, 15 tennis courts, equestrian center, water-sports facilities, 4 paddleball courts, 2 squash courts, and soccer field.

✋ **$$$$** ▦ **Sofitel Costa do Sauípe.** Replicas of early sailing ships hanging in the lobby hint at the hotel's themes: sailing and the discovery of Brazil. The Porão da Nau Pub & Club, off the lobby, is decorated in the style of a ship's hold, making it a unique place for drinks and dancing. If you prefer a cocktail in the sun, head for the enormous poolside bar. The main restaurant, the Île de France, serves fine French cuisine. Rooms look almost like the staterooms of an elegant ship with their dark-wood furniture and beige walls and drapes. Sliding-glass doors lead out to individual balconies with hammocks that overlook the gardens, with tall palm trees and the beautiful beach beyond. ☎ *071/2104–7600* ⊕ *www.sofitel.com* ↪ *392 rooms, 12 suites ⟁ 3 restaurants, coffee shop, room service, in-room safes, minibars, cable TV, in-room data ports, pool, gym, hair salon, hot tub, massage, sauna, beach, snorkeling, windsurfing, boating, bicycles, basketball, billiards, horseback riding, Ping-Pong, squash, bar, pub, dance club, shops, babysitting, children's programs (ages 3–12), playground, dry cleaning, laundry service, concierge, business services, meeting rooms, airport shuttle, car rental* ▭ *AE, DC, MC, V* ⦿⧫ *MAP.*

✋ **$$$$** ▦ **SuperClubs Breezes Costa do Sauípe.** At this family resort kids are kept busy all day with circus workshops and an extensive Kids' Club program. Meanwhile, resident tennis pros keep you busy on the courts. The dining areas look out over a large free-form pool. Behind the pool is a beautiful, wide Atlantic beach. You can walk for miles; if you trek to the little village of San Antônio, you can buy souvenirs or a cold drink from the ladies sitting on their porches. In addition to the large buffet and grill, there are four restaurants: Japanese, Italian, Bahian, and Mediterranean. You can arrange tours or reconfirm airline tickets in the lobby tour office. There is a strict no-tipping policy. Reservations are essential for all restaurants except for Jimmy's Buffet and the Tropical Restaurant. ☎ *071/2104–8888* ⊕ *www.superclubs.com* ↪ *324 rooms, 16 suites ⟁ 5 restaurants, in-room safes, cable TV, in-room data ports, pool, wading pool, health club, windsurfing, boating, bicycles, billiards, Ping-Pong, 3 bars, dance club, recreation room, children's programs (ages 3–12), complimentary weddings, airport shuttle, travel services* ▭ *AE, DC, MC, V* ⦿⧫ *AI.*

$$$ ▦ **Renaissance Costa do Sauípe Resort.** The open-air lobby has a casual feel and a restaurant that looks out over sand dunes. If you opt to dine in the Mediterranean restaurant, your choices include specialties from

Provence and southern Italy; some of the dishes are even cooked in a wood-burning oven. Tile-floor rooms are breezy and pleasant. With breakfast and dinner included and a beautiful beach right out your door, it's a real bargain. ☎ 071/466–2000 ⊕ www.renaissancehotels.com/ssabr ➪ 237 rooms, 17 suites ⚒ 2 restaurants, snack bar, room service, in-room safes, minibars, cable TV, in-room high-speed Internet, pool, gym, sauna, beach, babysitting, dry cleaning, laundry service, concierge, business services, meeting rooms, airport shuttle, car rental ⊟ AE, DC, MC, V ⎮◎⎮ MAP.

$$ ⊞ **Vila Nova da Praia.** The six Costa Sauípe pousadas in this planned village are nearly identical—all have the same amenities and are of equal quality—though each has a different theme and number of rooms. The village is very small, and the pousadas are close together. Resources available to anyone staying at the pousadas are banks, a convenience store, an ecotourism agency, a car-rental agency, a medical center, bars and restaurants, several kilometers of beaches, and shops selling clothing, jewelry, and handicrafts. Each pousada has its own pool. **Pousada Gabriela** (20 rooms) resembles colonial architecture of downtown Ilhéus, south of Salvador. It's named after a character from a Jorge Amado novel. With its bright colors, **Pousada Carnaval** (39 rooms) captures the spirit of Bahia's pre-Lenten festivities. **Pousada do Agreste** (18 rooms) echoes the colonial architecture of the interior of northeastern Brazil. Art and antiques fill **Pousada da Torre** (28 rooms, 2 suites), which tries to re-create the Garcia D'Avila mansion at Praia do Frote. As its name implies, **Pousada do Pelourinho** (38 rooms) is a replica of a house in Salvador's historic district. **Pousada Aldeia** (20 rooms) makes you feel as if you're staying in a 16th-century coastal village. A sun deck has hammocks for lazy afternoons. ☎ 071/2104–8200, 0800/7020203 in Brazil ⊕ www.costadosauipe.com.br ⚒ Dining room, in-room safes, minibars, cable TV, in-room data ports, pool, laundry service, airport shuttle ⊟ AE, D, DC, MC, V ⎮◎⎮ BP.

Cachoeira

⑭ 109 km (67 mi) northwest of Salvador.

This riverside colonial town dates from the 16th and 17th centuries, when sugarcane was the economy's mainstay. It has been designated a national monument and is the site of some of Brazil's most authentic Afro-Brazilian rituals. After Salvador it has the largest collection of baroque architecture in Bahia. A major restoration of public monuments and private buildings was finished in 2003, and included revitalized streets and plazas in town. On an excursion to Cachoeira you can walk through the colorful country market and see architecture preserved from an age when Cachoeira shipped tons of tobacco and sugar downriver to Salvador.

One of the most interesting popular events is the festival held by the Irmandade da Boa Morte (Sisterhood of Good Death). Organized by descendants of 19th-century slaves who founded an association of black women devoted to abolition, it's held on a Friday, Saturday, and Sunday in the middle of August.

Devotion to Nossa Senhora da Boa Morte (Our Lady of Good Death) began in the slave quarters, where discussions on abolition and prayer meetings honoring those who had died for liberty took place. The slaves implored Our Lady of Good Death to end slavery and promised to hold an annual celebration in her honor should their prayers be answered.

The festival begins with a procession by the sisters who, heads held high, carry an 18th-century statue of their patron saint through the streets. The statue is adorned in a typical all-white Bahian dress that signifies mourning in the Candomblé religion practiced by many of the sisters. Sunday, the festival's main day, sees a solemn mass followed by a joyful procession that begins with the traditional samba *de roda,* which is danced in a circle.

The **Capela da D'Ajuda,** built in the 16th century, is one of the most remarkable examples of early baroque architecture in this part of Brazil. ⊠ *Largo D'Ajuda s/n* ☎ *No phone* 🖾 *R$3* ☉ *Inquire at Museu da Boa Morte to gain entrance to chapel.*

Museu da Boa Morte displays photos and ceremonial dresses worn by members of the Sisterhood of Our Lady of Good Death during their rituals and festivals. You may also meet some of the elderly but always energetic women whose ancestors protested slavery. The ladies at the museum will let you in to see the chapel and the church. ⊠ *Largo D'Ajuda s/n* ☎ *075/425–1343* 🖾 *By donation* ☉ *Weekdays 10–1 and 3–5.*

Where to Stay & Eat

¢ ✕🖫 **Pousada do Convento.** You can stay overnight in one of the large rooms or have a good lunch at this one-time Carmelite monastery that dates from the 17th century. The meeting room adjacent to the hotel main room was formerly a church. ⊠ *Praça da Aclamação s/n* ☎☎ *075/ 425–1716* 🛏 *26 rooms* ⚖ *Restaurant, minibars, pool, playground, meeting room* ⊟ *D, MC, V.*

Lençois

★ ⓯ *427 km (265 mi) west of Salvador; 1,133 km (704 mi) northeast of Brasília*

The largest community in the Chapada Diamantina area and the gateway to Chapada Diamantina National Park, Lençóis arose from the hundreds of makeshift tents of white cotton fabric built by *garimpeiros* (gold- and precious stone–seekers). (*Lençóis* means "bedsheet.") The precious-stone frenzy began in 1822 with the discovery of diamonds in riverbeds around the town of Mucugê, which brought hundreds of garimpeiros to the region. Many fortunes were made, but the golden age ended in 1889, when most of the stones had been hauled away, and the city was forgotten.

The current population is about 5,000, but since the national park was established in 1985, the city has enjoyed a renaissance. Lençóis has been designated a national monument for its 19th-century residential architecture. More than 250 *sobrados* are in the process of being restored. Other important towns in the area are Andaraí, Mucugê, and Palmeiras.

At **Poço Encantado,** south of Lençois, sunlight beams through the entrance to the cave and lights up the clear blue lake about 100 meters (300 feet) below. This spectacle is best seen between April and August from 10 AM to 1 PM. ⊠ *From Lençois, drive 2 hours south on BA 142.*

From the town of **Xique-Xique de Igatú,** a 19th-century stone road leads to a diamond-rush ghost camp. Here you can visit the miners' abandoned homes among the rocks and caves. ⊠ *30 km (19 mi) south of Poço Encantado.*

Lençóis has one tourist information center: **Bahiatursa** (⊠ Old City Hall, Praça Otaviano Alves 01 ☎ 075/3334–1380).

Where to Stay and Eat

There are a growing number of pousadas in the area, all of which have good-quality, ranch-style accommodations, complete with hearty meals and a wide array of activities such as horseback riding, tennis, and swimming.

$ ⊞ **Pousada de Lençóis.** On the edge of Lençóis and next to the Parque Nacional da Chapada Diamantina is this homey pousada. A stay in one of its extra-large rooms (some sleep up to five people) truly makes you feel as if you're a guest in someone's country house. The large pool is surrounded by flower gardens. The restaurant and bar are open to the public, and an in-house tour agency arranges park trips. ⊠ *Rua Altina Alves 747, Lençóis* ☎ *075/3334–1102* ↝ *48 rooms* ♢ *Restaurant, in-room safes, minibars, cable TV, pool, gym, bar, travel services* ☱ *AE, D, MC, V* ◯⧸ *CP.*

$ ⊞ **Hotel Canto das Águas.** One of the first hotels to open after the national park was created, Canto das Águas is inspired by the colonial architecture of the nearby historic center. Arched hallways open to the garden that surrounds the main building. The Lençóis River runs through the backyard. The staff will arrange local guides and transportation to the park. ⊠ *Av. Sr. dos Passos 1, Lençóis* ☎ *075/3334–1154* ⊕ *www.lencois.com.br* ↝ *44 rooms, 8 suites* ♢ *Restaurant, minibars, cable TV, pool, bar* ☱ *AE, D, MC, V.*

Parque Nacional Chapada Diamantina

⑯ *Park office (Palmeira): 60 km (37 mi) west of Lençóis*

FodorśChoice
★

The Chapada Diamantina (Diamond Plateau), a series of mountain ranges with an average altitude of 3,000 feet, is among Brazil's most fascinating natural wonders. Here table-top mountains, natural pools, caves, valleys, and waterfalls abound. The flora and fauna of the area, which include wild orchids, bromeliads, and more than 200 bird species, have been the subject of two extensive studies by the Royal Botanical Gardens at Kew in England.

Established in 1985, the 1,520-square-km (593-square-mi) national park is one of the most scenic places in Brazil, comparable to the Grand Canyon in the U.S. Crystal-clear creeks and rivers, with rapids and waterfalls, the tall peaks of the Sincorá Range, with the highest point in Bahia at Barbados Peak (2,080 meters, or 7,000 feet), and over 70 grottos and caverns. The best time to visit the park is in the dry season from March to October. Mean temperature is 24°C (75°F), but expect lower night temperatures from May to July.

Bus or car is the usual way to get to Chapada Diamantina, although the road is not in perfect condition between Feira de Santana and Lençóis. The trip is about eight hours. Overnight buses leave from Salvador frequently. The quickest option is the daily flight from Salvador. At this writing, the park does not have a visitor center, only a small office run by IBAMA (the Brazilian Environmental Insitute) in Palmeira, with limited tourist information.

The tallest waterfall in Brazil, 1,312-foot **Cachoeira da Fumaça** (Smoke Waterfall), is the fifth-highest in the world. Most of the falling water turns into a thin mist and evaporates before reaching the ground, hence its name. ⊠ *20 km (12 mi) west of Lençóis.*

One of the most popular hiking trails, called the **Rio Serrano,** runs along the river of the same name. It has sand caves to explore, and natural pools that are highly polished by erosion so that they look a bit like marble hot tubs. There are three waterfalls along the way. ⊠ *Trailhead about 1 km (½ mi) north of Lençóis.*

A 20-minute climb of about 1,000 feet to the top of **Morro do Pai Iná-cio** provides the most fabulous 360-degree view of the Chapada Diamantina. ⊠ *20-minute drive northwest on BR-242 from Lençóis.*

A 30-minute climb down to the mouth of the **Lapa Doce** cave and a 40-minute walk through it (by appointment only) leads to stunning stalagmites and stalactites. This cave system has been mapped to about 25 km (16 mi), but only the first kilometer is open to visitors—the rest is on private property. ⊠ *From Lençóis, take BR 242 west 25 km (16 mi), then take the road to Irecê for about 18 km (11 mi)* ☎ *075/3229–4117* 🎫 *R$10* ☉ *By appointment.*

Salvador & Bahia Essentials

Transportation

BY AIR

Salvador's airport has become one of the busiest in Brazil. In the last few years several international carriers have opened direct service from abroad, especially from Europe. TAM is the only airline that flies directly from the U.S. (Miami). Most international flights require a change of plane in São Paulo. For major airline information (including TAM), *see* Air Travel *in* Smart Travel Tips A to Z.

OceanAir is the regional carrier for Chapada Diamantina. The daily one-hour flight to Lençóis costs about R$730 (round-trip).

A handful of small flight operators, including AeroStar and Adey, have service to Morro de São Paulo from Salvador. The 20-minute flight costs about R$350.

🛫 **Airport** **Aeroporto Deputado Luís Eduardo Magalhães** ⊠ Praça Gago Coutinho s/n, São Cristovão ☎ 071/3204–1214 or 071/3204–1444.

⚐ Regional Airlines AeroStar ☎ 071/3377-4406. **Adey** ☎ 071/3377-2451. **OceanAir** ☎ 0300/789-8160.

AIRPORT
TRANSFERS

The Salvador airport, Aeroporto Luís Eduardo Magalhães, is quite far from downtown—37 km (23 mi) to the northeast. A trip from the airport to central hotels should cost about R$60. Choose one of the many taxi companies that have booths outside the arrival gate. You can prepay your ride to the hotel. The *ônibus executivo*, an air-conditioned bus, runs daily from 6 to 9, ask for a timetable at hotel lobbies; it costs about R$12 and takes an hour to reach downtown, stopping at hotels along the way. Several companies operate these buses, of which the largest is Transportes Ondina. Drivers don't speak English and might have difficulty understanding your hotel name.

⚐ Transportes Ondina ✉ Av. Vasco da Gama 347 ☎ 071/3245-6366.

BY BOAT

Itaparica and the other harbor islands can be reached by taking a ferry or a launch (small boat that carries up to five passengers) from Salvador, by hiring a motorized schooner, or by joining a harbor schooner excursion—all departing from two docks. Launches cost about R$2 and leave every 45 minutes from 7 to 6 from the Terminal Turístico Marítimo. The ferry takes passengers and cars and leaves every half hour between 6 AM and 10:30 PM from the Terminal São Joaquim. The fare is around R$2 for passengers and R$14–R$18 for cars, and it takes 45 minutes to cross the bay.

Morro de São Paulo can be reached by catamaran or launch from Terminal Turístico Marítimo for about R$50 to R$70.

From Caravelas (865 km/537 mi from Salvador) you can book a boat trip to the Arquipelago de Abrolhos (Abrolhos Archipelago), Bahia's first underwater marine park, for about R$300.

⚐ Disque Ferry (Dial-a-Ferry hotline) ☎ 071/3319-2890. **Terminal Marítimo São Joaquim** ✉ Av. Oscar Ponte 1051, São Joaquim ☎ 071/3321-7100. **Terminal Turístico Marítimo** ✉ Av. de França s/n, Comércio ☎ 071/3243-0741.

BY BUS

Long-distance bus tickets are sold at the Terminal Rodoviário in Salvador, from which all buses heading out of the city depart. Itapemirim has three buses a day to Recife (13 hours, R$140), Fortaleza (19 hours, R$175), and Rio (28 hours, R$250).

Within Bahia, Águia Branca offers daily overnight service to Porto Seguro (11 hours, R$95) leaving Salvador at 8 PM. Santa Maria has hourly service to Praia do Forte starting at 5 AM, with the last bus returning to the city at 6 PM; tickets cost about R$15. Camurujipe has hourly service to Cachoeira between 5:30 AM and 7 PM, for R$17. Real Expresso buses make the 8-hour trip to Chapada Diamantina (Lençóis) for about R$35, with departures at 11:30 PM daily and at 7 AM Tuesday, Thursday, and Saturday. Return is at 11:30 PM daily, with additional departures at 7:30 AM Monday, Wednesday, and Friday.

Within Salvador, use the *executivo* (executive) buses. Although other buses serve most of the city and cost a pittance (R$1.40), they're often crowded and dirty, and pickpocketing is a problem. Fancier executivo buses (R$3.50) serve tourist areas more completely. The glass-sided green, yellow, and orange Jardineira bus (marked PRAÇA DA SÉ; R$6) runs every 40 minutes 7:30 to 7:30 daily from the Praça da Sé in Pelourinho to the Stella Maris Beach, traveling along the Orla Marítima series of avenues. Hop off when you see a beach you like. The Santa Maria/Catuense company operates six buses (marked PRAIA DO FORTE) daily that stop at Barra do Jacuípe Beach.

The municipal Circular buses, operated by both Transportes Ondina and Transportes Rio Vermelho, cost mere centavos and run along the beaches to downtown, ending at São Joaquim, where ferries depart for Ilha de Itaparica. For Setor (Centro) Histórico, get off at the Elevador Lacerda stop, across from Mercado Modelo.

🚌 Bus Information Águia Branca ☎ 071/3460-4400. **Camurujipe** ☎ 071/3450-2109. **Itapemirim** ☎ 071/3450-5644 ⊕ www.itapemirim.com.br. **Real Expresso** ☎ 075/3334-1112 in Lençóis, 071/450-9310 in Salvador ⊕ www.realexpresso.com.br. **Santa Maria/Catuense** ☎ 071/3450-0321. **Terminal Rodoviário** ✉ Av. Antônio Carlos Magalhães 4352, Pituba, Salvador ☎ 071/3450-3871.

BY CAR Most side-trip destinations from Salvador can be easily reached by car. Morro de São Paulo and Chapada Diamantina have flights. Most of Bahia's highways and secondary roads near the coast are generally in good condition. Traffic can be daunting, especially in the industrial district west of Salvador (BR 101, BR 116, and BR 262). Many soteropolitanos are reckless drivers, making driving quite an adventurous proposition, especially during weekday rush hours. Limited parking spaces in Setor Histórico can be frustrating. To visit Setor Histórico, the best alternative is to park in one of the paid lots near Mercado Modelo and take the elevator to Cidade Alta. Things are much calmer on weekends.

You can combine a road trip to Cachoeira and Chapada Diamantina. From Salvador, take BR 324 north for about 55 km (34 mi), then head west on BR 420 through the town of Santo Amaro. The trip takes 1½ hours. The route to Chapada Diamantina goes through the town of Santo Estevão, then south on BR-116 until the intersection with BR-242. Then it's straight west on BR-242 to Lençóis.

To reach Praia do Forte by car, take the Estrada do Coco (BA-099) north and follow the signs. From there on, it's called Linha Verde (Green Line), to Costa do Sauípe and the northern beaches all the way to the Sergipe border.

🚗 Rental Agencies Avis ✉ Aeroporto Luís Eduardo Magalhães, Salvador ☎ 071/3251-8500 or 0800/198-456 ⊕ www.avis.com.br ✉ Aeroporto Porto Seguro, Av. do Aeroporto s/n, Porto Seguro ☎ 073/3288-4033. **Hertz** ✉ Aeroporto Luís Eduardo Magalhães, Salvador ☎ 071/3377-3633 or 0800/701-7300 ⊕ www.hertz.com.br. **Localiza** ✉ Aeroporto Luís Eduardo Magalhães, Salvador ☎ 071/377-2272, 0800/99-2000 in Brazil ⊕ www.localiza.com.br ✉ Aeroporto Porto Seguro, Av. do Aeroporto s/n, Porto Seguro ☎ 073/3288-3106.

BY TAXI Taxis in Salvador are metered and most are organized through cooperatives. Tipping isn't expected. Beware that sometimes drivers might try to jack up the fare by "forgetting" (or, in some cases, refusing) to turn on the meter. You can hail a *comum* taxi (white with a blue stripe) on the street or at designated stops near major hotels, or summon one by phone. You can hire a comum taxi for the whole day for about R$135. The more expensive taxis, usually air-conditioned full-size sedans, are called *especial* (special taxis), and congregate outside major hotels. Cometas is a reliable company.

🔢 **Cometas** ☎ 071/3244-4500. **Rádio-Táxi** ☎ 071/3243-4333.

Contacts & Resources

TOUR OPTIONS

Salvador's large group tours are cursory, and their guides often speak minimal English; such tours are also targeted by hordes of street vendors. Private tours with an accredited Bahiatursa guide can be hired through your hotel or a travel agency or at a Bahiatursa office (⇨ Visitor Information). Prices vary depending on the size of the group; most include hotel pickup and drop-off. Do not hire "independent" guides who approach you at churches and other sights; they are normally not accredited and will very likely overcharge.

Tatur Tours is renowned for its African-heritage tours of Bahia. Its attentive personnel can arrange personalized special-interest city tours and top-notch excursions from Salvador. Top Hilton Turismo has the usual city tours and interesting boat cruises, including a trip around Baía de Todos os Santos in a trimaran and a schooner cruise to the islands. It also has a tour to the nudist beach at Massarandupió, along the northern coast.

Several travel agencies offer half-day minibus tours with hotel pickup and drop-off for about R$90–R$120. Agencies also offer daylong harbor tours on motorized schooners (about R$100) and night tours (about R$125) that include dinner and an Afro-Brazilian music-and-dance show.

BBTUR has excellent buses and vans; request an English-speaking guide ahead of time. The company has a full line of tours not only of Salvador but also of surrounding areas; there's also a branch in the lobby of the Breezes Costa do Sauípe resort. Bahia Adventure Ecoturismo can help you arrange jeep tours, rafting, and other adventure treks in the Praia do Forte area. Odara Turismo, in the arcade at the Praia do Forte Eco Resort Hotel, arranges four-wheel-drive tours of the area plus horseback and hiking trips. In Praia do Forte, Fly and Fun has scenic flights over Coconut Coast and the interior.

🔢 **Bahia Adventure** ✉ Km 76, Rodovia BA 099, Costa do Sauípe, Mata de São João ☎ 71/464-2525 ⊕ www.bahiaadventure.com. **BBTUR** ✉ Vila Nova da Praia, suites 22-23, Costa do Sauípe, Mata de São João ☎ 071/3464-2121 ⊠ Av. Tancredo Neves 2421, Suite 1700, Centro Empresarial Redenção, Pituba, Salvador ☎ 071/3341-8800. **Fly and Fun** ☎ 071/3676-1540. **Odara Turismo** ✉ Praça da Música s/n, Praia do Forte, Mata de São João ☎ 071/676-1080. **Tatur Tours** ✉ Av. Tancredo Neves 274, Suite 304, Centro Empresarial Iguatemi, Bloco B, Iguatemi, Salvador ☎ 071/3450-7216 ⊕ www.tatur.com. br. **Top Hilton Turismo** ✉ Rua Fonte do Boi 05, 41940-360, Rio Vermelho, Salvador ☎ 071/3334-5223 ⊕ www.tophilton.com.br. **Paradise** ✉ Avenida das Palmeiras 313, 45900-000, Centro, Caravelas ☎ 071/3297-1433.

VISITOR INFORMATION

Bahiatursa, the state tourist board, is the best source of information about areas outside of Salvador. There are branches in Salvador and major tourist areas. Emtursa, Salvador's tourist board, is open weekdays 8–6 and operates mobile tourist information units in the Centro Histórico area (Pelourinho). Its main branch is conveniently located in the Elevador Lacerda building. Some receptionists are bilingual, and there are leaflets with information on current events, restaurants, and tours.

🔒 **Bahiatursa** ✉ Centro de Convenções, Av. Simon Bolivar s/n, Jardim Armação, Salvador ☎ 071/370-8400 ⊕ Institutional: www.bahiatursa.ba.gov.br; Tourist Information: www.bahia.com.br ✉ Aeroporto Internacional Luís Eduardo Magalhães s/n, Salvador ☎ 071/3204-1244 ✉ Av. Antônio Carlos Magalhães 4362, Terminal Rodoviário, Salvador ☎ 071/3450-0871 ✉ Rua das Laranjeiras 12, Pelourinho, Salvador ☎ 071/3321-2133 ✉ Mercado Modelo, Praça Visconde de Cayrú 250, Comércio, Salvador ☎ 071/3241-0242 ✉ Av. do Farol s/n, Praia do Forte ☎ No phone ✉ Praça Manoel Ribeiro Coelho s/n, Centro, Porto Seguro ☎ 073/3268-1390 ✉ Antiga Prefeitura, Rua Otaviano Alves 01, Lençóis ☎ 075/3334-1380. **Emtursa** ✉ Upper Deck, Elevador Lacerda, Cidade Alta ☎ 071/3380-4200 ⊕ www.emtursa.salvador.ba.gov.br.

THE AMAZON

Updated by
Rhan Flatin

The world's largest tropical forest seems an endless carpet of green that's sliced only by the curving contours of rivers. Its statistics are as impressive: the region covers more than 10 million square km (4 million square mi) and extends into eight other countries (French Guiana, Suriname, Guyana, Venezuela, Ecuador, Peru, Bolivia, and Colombia). It takes up roughly 40% of Brazil in the states of Acre, Rondônia, Amazonas, Roraima, Pará, Amapá, and Tocantins. The Amazon forest is home to 500,000 cataloged species of plants and a river that annually transports 15% of the world's available freshwater to the sea, yet it's inhabited by only 16 million people. That's less than the population of metropolitan São Paulo.

Life centers on the rivers, the largest of which is the Amazon itself. From its source in southern Peru, it runs 6,300 km (3,900 mi) to its Atlantic outflow. Of its hundreds of tributaries, 17 are more than 1,600 km (1,000 mi) long. The Amazon is so large it could hold the Congo, Nile, Orinoco, Mississippi, and Yangtze rivers with room to spare. In places it is so wide you can't see the opposite shore, earning it the appellation Rio Mar (River Sea). Although there has been increasing urbanization in the Amazon region, between one-third and one-half of the Amazon's residents live in rural settlements, many of which are along the riverbanks, where transportation, water, fish, and good soil for planting are readily available.

In the late 19th century, rubber production transformed Belém and Manaus into cities. Rubber barons constructed mansions and monuments and brought life's modern trappings into the jungle. In 1928 Henry Ford began to pour millions of dollars into vast rubber plantations. The array of explorers and opportunists drawn to the newly prosperous area included former U.S. president Theodore Roosevelt, in 1913. After much struggle and few results, Ford's rubber project was scrapped in the late 1940s.

Since the rubber era, huge reserves of gold and iron have been discovered in the Amazon. Land-settlement schemes and development projects, such as hydroelectric plants and major roadworks, have followed. In the process, vast portions of tropical forest have been indiscriminately cut; tribal lands have been encroached upon; and industrial by-products, such as mercury used in gold mining, have poisoned wildlife and people. The Brazilian government has established reserves and made some efforts to preserve the territory, but there is much more to be done.

And yet, 500 years after the first Europeans arrived, much of the Amazon has not been thoroughly explored by land. You still hear stories of lost cities and of unearthly creatures; and you can stand on a riverboat deck and be astounded by the vastness of the mighty Amazon River and hike through dense vegetation beneath 150-foot (35-meter) trees.

Exploring the Amazon

Although there are regular flights and some bus routes through the Amazon, many visitors opt for the area's primary mode of transportation—boat (⇨ The Amazon by Boat, *below*). Though much slower, boats offer a closer look at Amazon culture, nature, and the river system, and they go just about everywhere you'd want to go. A trip along the Amazon itself, especially the 1,602-km (993-mi) four- to five-day journey between Belém and Manaus, is a singular experience.

Visiting outlying areas in the Amazon usually results in unforgettable adventures, but neotropical environments can be hostile, so prepare well and go with a companion if possible. It's a good idea to hire a guide or go with a tour company specializing in backcountry adventures. To join a tour or to choose a destination, contact one of the tour companies we suggest, or consult with a state-run tour agency. Paratur in Belém and SEC in Manaus can also be helpful. The more remote your destination, the more seriously you should heed the travel advice and health precautions in this book.

The Amazon by Boat

Whatever the style, budget, or length of your Amazonian journey, there's a boat plying the river to suit your needs. Sleep in a hammock on the deck of a thatch-roof riverboat or in the air-conditioned suite of an upscale tour operator's private ship. Keep in mind that wildlife viewing is not good on boats far from shore. Near shore, however, the birding can be excellent. Binoculars and a bird guide can help, and shorebirds, raptors, and parrots can be abundant. Common in many parts of the river system are *boto* (pink dolphins) and *tucuxi* (gray dolphins). Look for them as they surface for air. To see the most wildlife, plan your travels to allow time in the forest and streams.

ADVENTURE CRUISES Adventure cruises combine the luxury of cruising with exploration. Their goal is to get you close to wildlife and local inhabitants without sacrificing comforts and amenities. Near daily excursions include wildlife viewing in smaller boats with naturalists, village visits with naturalists, and city tours. **G.A.P** (Great Adventure People; ☒ 19 Duncan St., Ste.

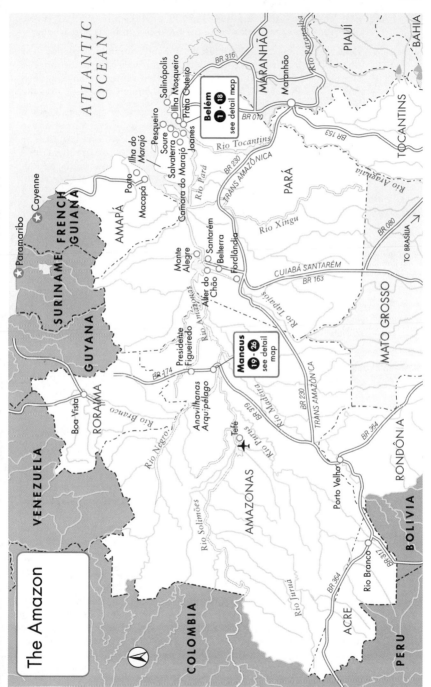

The Amazon

ATLANTIC OCEAN

MARANHÃO
PIAUÍ
BAHIA

Salinópolis
Ilha Mosqueiro
Praia Outeiro
Pesqueiro
Belém 1-18 see detail map
Soure
Salvaterra
Câmara do Marajó
Joanes
Ilha do Marajó
Porto
Macapá

Maranhão
BR 316
BR 010
Rio Tocantins
TOCANTINS
BR 153

Cayenne
FRENCH GUIANA
SURINAME
Paramaribo
GUYANA

AMAPÁ
Rio Pará
BR 230
TRANS AMAZÔNICA
PARÁ
Rio Xingu
CUIABÁ SANTARÉM BR 163
BR 080
TO BRASÍLIA →

Monte Alegre
Santarém
Belterra
Fordlândia
Alter do Chão
Rio Tapajós

Presidente Figueiredo
Rio Amazonas
Manaus 19-26 see detail map

BR 174
VENEZUELA
Boa Vista
RORAMA
Rio Branco
Rio Negro
Anavilhanas Arquipélago
BR 319
Rio Madeira
BR 230
TRANS AMAZÔNICA
MATO GROSSO

Tefé
Rio Purus
AMAZONAS
Porto Velho
RONDÔNIA
BR 364

COLOMBIA
Rio Solimões
Rio Juruá

Rio Branco
BR 364
ACRE
BR 317
BOLIVIA
PERU

401, Toronto, ON ☎ 800/465–5600 or 416/260–0999 ⊕ www.gapadventures.com) makes these trips, which run from 9 to 16 days.

OCEANGOING SHIPS

Some cruise ships call at Manaus, Belém, and Santarém as part of their itineraries. Most trips take place October through May. They range in length from 10 to 29 days, and costs vary. Two major lines making such journeys are Princess Cruises and Royal Olympic Cruises.

TOURIST BOATS

Private groups can hire tourist boats that are more comfortable than standard riverboats. They generally travel close to the riverbank and have open upper decks from which you can observe the river and forest. The better tour operators have a regional English-speaking expert on board—usually an ecologist or botanist. You can either sleep out on the deck in a hammock or in a cabin, which usually has air-conditioning or a fan. Meals are generally provided.

SPEEDBOATS

You can take a speedboat to just about anywhere the rivers flow. Faster than most options, speedboats can be ideal for traveling between smaller towns, a morning of wildlife viewing, or visiting a place that doesn't have regular transportation, such as a secluded beach or waterfall. You design the itinerary, including departure and return times. Prices and availability vary with distance and locale. Contact tour agencies, talk with locals, or head down to the docks to find a boat willing to take you where you want to go. Work out the price, destination, and travel time before leaving. You may have to pay for the gas up front, but don't pay the rest until you arrive. For trips longer than an hour, bring water, snacks, and sunscreen.

MACAMAZON BOATS

Longer boat routes on the lower Amazon are covered by **MACAMAZON** (☎ 091/3222–5604 or 091/3228–0774). Regular departures run between Belém, Santarém, Macapá, Manaus, and several other destinations. The boats are not luxurious but are a step above regional boats. You can get a suite for two from Belém to Manaus with air-conditioning and bath for about R$800. *Camarote* (cabin) class gets you a tiny room for two with air-conditioning and a shared bath. *Rede* (hammock) class is the cheapest and most intimate way to travel, since you'll be hanging tight with the locals on the main decks. Hammocks are hung in two layers very close together, promoting neighborly chats. Arrive early for the best spots, away from the bar, engine, and bathrooms. Keep your valuables with you at all times and sleep with them. Conceal new sneakers in a plastic bag. In addition to a hammock (easy and cheap to buy in Belém or Manaus), bring two 4-foot lengths of ⅜-inch rope to tie it up. Also bring a sheet, since nights get chilly.

REGIONAL BOATS

To travel to towns and villages or to meander slowly between cities, go by *barco regional* (regional boat). A trip from Belém to Manaus takes about four days; Belém to Santarém is two days. The double- or triple-deck boats carry freight and passengers. They make frequent stops at small towns, allowing for interaction and observation. You might be able to get a cabin with two bunks (around R$400 for a two-day trip), but expect it to be claustrophobic. Most passengers sleep in hammocks with little or no space between them. Bring your own hammock, sheet, and two 4-foot sections of rope. Travel lightly and inconspicuously.

Booths sell tickets at the docks, and even if you don't speak Portuguese, there are often signs alongside the booths that list prices, destinations, and departure times. If you plan to sleep in a hammock, arrive at least one hour early to get a good spot away from the engine, toilets, and bar. Keep valuables with you in your hammock while you sleep, including any new-looking clothing items (like sneakers), which you should conceal in a plastic bag. Sanitary conditions in bathrooms vary from boat to boat. Bring your own toilet paper, sunscreen, and insect repellent. Food is sometimes served, but the quality ranges from so-so to deplorable. Consider bringing your own water and a *marmita* (carry-out meal) if you'll be on the boat overnight. Many boats have a small store at the stern where you can buy drinks, snacks, and grilled *mixto quente* (ham-and-cheese) sandwiches. Fresh fruit and snacks are available at stops along the way. Be sure to peel or wash fruit thoroughly with bottled water before eating it.

Belém

The capital of Pará State, Belém is a river port of around 1.3 million people on the south bank of the Rio Guamá, 120 km (74 mi) from the Atlantic, and 2,933 km (1,760 mi) north of Rio de Janeiro. The Portuguese settled here in 1616, using it as a gateway to the interior and an outpost to protect the area from invasion by sea. Because of its ocean access, Belém became a major trade center. Like the upriver city of Manaus, it rode the ups and downs of the Amazon booms and busts. The first taste of prosperity was during the rubber era. Architects from Europe were brought in to build churches, civic palaces, theaters, and mansions, often using fine, imported materials. When Malaysia's rubber supplanted that of Brazil in the 1920s, wood and, later, minerals provided the impetus for growth.

Belém has expanded rapidly since the 1980s, pushed by the Tucuruvi hydroelectric dam (Brazil's second largest), the development of the Carajás mining region, and the construction of the ALBRAS/Alunorte bauxite and aluminum production facilities. Wood exports have risen, making Pará the largest wood-producing state in Brazil. As the forests are cut, pastures and cattle replace them, resulting in an increase in beef production. In 2000 the state government began construction of a bridge network connecting Belém to outlying cities. The resulting increase in commerce has spurred economic growth in the region, though there is still considerable poverty and high unemployment. In the city, high-rise apartments are replacing colonial structures. Fortunately, local governments have

WORD OF MOUTH

Without doubt, the most unique birthday I've ever had! We left . . . in a canoe to paddle into the flooded forests . . . A truly unforgettable morning where we saw three species of monkeys in their natural habitat . . . That afternoon, we went piranha fishing. Our prey must have known it was my birthday as I managed to catch one, but my husband didn't.

–quiCK

launched massive campaigns to preserve the city's rich heritage while promoting tourist-friendly policies. This effort has earned state and federal government funds to restore historical sites in the Belém area. Tourism is on the rise in the city and is becoming increasingly important for the city's economic well-being.

> **CAUTION**
>
> In Belém watch out for pickpockets everywhere, but especially at Ver-o-Peso, on Avenida President Vargas, and in Comércio. Avoid walking alone at night or on poorly lighted streets, and don't wear jewelry, especially gold.

Cidade Velha

Cidade Velha (Old City) is the oldest residential part of Belém. Many of the houses are colonial, with clay walls and tile roofs. Three stories is the tallest they get, though 15-floor apartment buildings are invading from the north. Much of Cidade Velha is middle-income with a variety of hardware, auto parts, and fishing supply stores. On its northwestern edge, the Forte Presépio lies along the bank of the Rio Guamá.

What to See

⑤ Casa das Onze Janelas. At the end of the 17th century, sugar baron Domingos da Costa Barcelar built the neoclassical House of Eleven Windows as his private mansion. Today Barcelar's mansion is a gallery for contemporary arts, including photography and visiting expositions. The view from the balcony is impressive. Take a walk through the courtyard and imagine scenes of the past. This is where the aristocracy took tea and watched over the docks as slaves unloaded ships from Europe and filled them with sugar and rum. ⊠ *Praça Frei Caetano Brandão, Cidade Velha* ☎ *91/3219–1157* 🎫 *R$2, free Tues.* ☉ *Tues.–Fri. 10–6, weekends 10–8.*

⑦ Catedral da Sé. In 1771 Bolognese architect Antônio José Landi, whose work can be seen throughout the city, completed the cathedral's construction on the foundations of an older church. Carrara marble adorns the rich interior, which is an interesting mix of baroque, colonial, and neoclassical styles. The high altar was a gift from Pope Pius IX. ⊠ *Praça Frei Caetano Brandão, Cidade Velha* ☎ *91/3241–6282* 🎫 *Free* ☉ *Daily 8–noon and 2–6.*

★ ② Estação das Docas. Next to Ver-o-Peso market on the river, three former warehouses have been artfully converted into a commercial/tourist area. All have one wall of floor-to-ceiling glass that provides a full river view when dining or shopping. The first is a convention center with a cinema and art exhibits. The second has shops and kiosks selling crafts and snacks, and the third has a microbrewery and six upscale restaurants. The buildings are air-conditioned and connected by glass-covered walkways and contain photos and artifacts from the port's heyday. A stroll outside along the docks provides a grand view of the bay. Tourist boats arrive and depart at the dock—a good place to relax both day and night. ⊠ *Boulevard Castilhos França s/n, Campina* ☎ *091/3212–5525* 🎫 *Free* ☉ *Noon–midnight or later.*

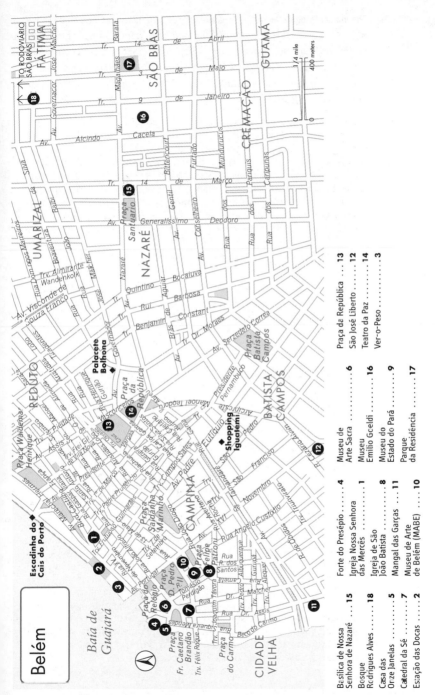

Belém

Baía de Guajará

TO RODOVIÁRIO
SÃO BRÁS

FÁTIMA

SÃO BRÁS

GUAMÁ

CREMAÇÃO

UMARIZAL

NAZARÉ

REDUTO

BATISTA CAMPOS

CAMPINA

CIDADE VELHA

Escadinha do
Cais do Porto

Palacete Bolhona

Shopping Iguatemi

1/4 mile
400 meters

Basílica de Nossa
Senhora de Nazaré ... **15**

Bosque
Rodrigues Alves ... **18**

Casa das
Onze Janelas ... **5**

Catedral da Sé ... **7**

Estação das Docas ... **2**

Forte do Presépio ... **4**

Igreja Nossa Senhora
das Mercês ... **1**

Igreja de São
João Batista ... **8**

Mangal das Garças ... **11**

Museu de Arte
de Belém (MABE) ... **10**

Museu de
Arte Sacra ... **6**

Museu
Emílio Goeldi ... **16**

Museu do
Estado do Pará ... **9**

Parque
da Residência ... **17**

Praça da República ... **13**

São José Liberto ... **12**

Teatro da Paz ... **14**

Ver-o-Peso ... **3**

The many regional flavors at ice-cream shop **Cairu** include some unique to the Amazon, such as *taperebá, graviola,* and *cajá* (cashew fruit), as well as the more familiar *cocó* (coconut), mango, and chocolate. Juices, sandwiches, and soft drinks are also served. ✉ *Estação das Docas, Boulevard Castilhos França s/n, Comércio* ✉ *Conselheiro Furtado and Presidente Pernambuco* ✉ *Travessa 14 de Março and Rua João Balbi.*

★ ❹ **Forte do Presépio** (Fort of the Crèche). Founded January 12, 1616, this fort is considered Belém's birthplace. From here the Portuguese launched conquests of the Amazon and watched over the bay. The fort's role in the region's defense is evidenced by massive English- and Portuguese-made cannons pointing out over the water. They are poised atop fort walls that are 3 yards thick in places. Renovations completed in 2002 unearthed more than two dozen cannons, extensive military middens from the moat, and native Tupi artifacts. A small museum of prefort indigenous cultures is at the entrance. Just outside the fort, cobblestone walkways hug the breezy waterfront. ✉ *Praça Frei Caetano Brandão, Cidade Velha* ☎ *91/3219–1146* ✉ *R$2, free Tues.* ⊙ *Tues.–Fri. 10–6, weekends 10–8.*

❼ **Igreja Nossa Senhora das Mercês** (Our Lady of Mercy Church). Another of Belém's baroque creations attributed to Antônio Landi, this church is notable for its pink color and convex facade. It's part of a complex that includes the Convento dos Mercedários, which has served both as a convent and a prison, though not simultaneously. ✉ *Gaspar Viana e Frutuosa Guimarães, Comércio* ✉ *Free* ⊙ *Mon.–Sat. 8–1.*

❽ **Igreja de São João Batista** (St. John the Baptist Church). Prodigious architect Antônio Landi finished this small octagonal church in 1777. It was completely restored in the late 1990s and is considered the city's purest example of baroque architecture. ✉ *Rua João Diogo and Rodriguês Dos Santos, Cidade Velha* ✉ *Free* ⊙ *Mon.–Sat. 6:30 AM–9 AM.*

★ ⓫ **Mangal das Garças.** City beautification efforts to increase tourism and encourage environmental conservation led to the creation of the Mangrove of the Egrets. A great place for a short stroll, it has an aviary, a tower with a view, a navigation museum, a boardwalk leading to a lookout over the Rio Guamá, a live butterfly exhibit, ponds with aquatic plants, food vendors, a gift shop, and a restaurant. ✉ *Passagem Carneiro da Rocha, Jurunas* ☎ *91/3242–5052* ✉ *R$4* ⊙ *Weekdays 10–6.*

❿ **Museu de Arte de Belém (MABE).** Temporary exhibits on the bottom level of the Metropolitan Art Museum are free to view. On the second level staff members hand you brown furry slippers that you must wear over your shoes to protect the wooden floors. The permanent collection of furniture and paintings dates from the 18th century through the rubber boom. The museum is housed in the Palácio Antônio Lemos (circa 1883), a municipal palace built in the imperial Brazilian style with French influences. ✉ *Praça Dom Pedro II s/n, Cidade Velha* ☎ *091/3219–8228* ✉ *R$2, free Tues.* ⊙ *Weekdays 10–6 PM.*

❻ Museu de Arte Sacra. A guided tour (call 48 hours in advance to reserve an English-speaking docent) begins in the early-18th-century baroque Igreja de Santo Alexandre (St. Alexander's Church), which is distinguished by intricate woodwork on its altar and pews. On the second half of the tour you see the museum's collection of religious sculptures and paintings. Temporary exhibitions, a gift shop, and a café are on the first floor. ✉ *Praça Frei Caetano Brandão, Cidade Velha* ☎ *091/3219–1155* 🖂 *R$4, free Tues.* ☉ *Tues.–Fri. 1–6, weekends 9–1.*

❾ Museu do Estado do Pará. Pará State Museum is in the sumptuous Palácio Lauro Sodré (circa 1771), an Antônio Landi creation with Venetian and Portuguese elements. Consistently outstanding visiting exhibits are on the first floor; the second floor contains the permanent collection of furniture and paintings. ✉ *Praça Dom Pedro II, Cidade Velha* ☎ *091/3219–1138* 🖂 *R$4* ☉ *Tues.–Fri. 1–6, weekends 9–1.*

⓬ São José Liberto Belém's old prison began as a monastery, became a brewery, then an armory, a nunnery, and eventually the final stop for many criminals. Today's museums and garden seem an attempt to redeem long years of tortuous conditions and bloody rebellions. Behind the enormously thick walls are a gem museum, a prison museum, and several shops. ✉ *Praça Amazonas, Jurunas* ☎ *91/3230–4451* 🖂 *R$4* ☉ *Tues.–Sat. 10–8, Sun. 3–8.*

★ **❸ Ver-o-Peso.** Its name literally meaning "see the weight" (a throwback to the time when the Portuguese weighed everything entering or leaving the region), this market is a hypnotic confusion of colors and voices. Vendors hawk tropical fruits, regional wares, and an assortment of tourist kitsch. Most interesting are the *mandingueiras,* women who claim they can solve any problem with "miracle" jungle roots and charms for the body and soul. They sell jars filled with animal eyes, tails, and even heads, as well as herbs, each with its own legendary power. The sex organs of the pink river dolphin are a supposedly unrivaled cure for romantic problems. In the fish market you get an up-close look at pirarucu, the Amazon's most colorful fish and the world's second-largest freshwater species. Look for bizarre armored catfish species, such as the *tamuatá* and the huge *piraiba.* Across the street is a small arched entrance to the municipal meat market. Duck in and glance at the French-style pink-and-green-painted ironwork, imported from Britain. Be sure to visit Ver-o-Peso before noon, when most vendors leave. It opens around 6 AM. Leave your jewelry at home and beware of pickpockets. ✉ *Av. Castilhos França s/n, Comércio.*

Nazaré

Just east of the Cidade Velha, Nazaré's mango tree–lined streets create the sensation of walking through tunnels. Among the historic buildings there's a tremendous variety of pastel colors and European styles. Many of the newer buildings house elegant shops.

WHAT TO SEE
Fodor'sChoice
★

⓯ Basílica de Nossa Senhora de Nazaré. It's hard to miss this opulent Roman-style basilica. Not only does it stand out visually, but there's an enormous *samauma* tree (kapok variety) filled with screeching white-winged parakeets in the plaza out front. Built in 1908 on the site where a *caboclo* (rural, riverside dweller) named Placido is said to have seen a vision of the Virgin in the early 1700s. The basilica's ornate interior is constructed entirely of European marble and contains elaborate mosaics, detailed stained-glass windows, and intricate bronze doors. In the small, basement-level Museu do Círio, displays explain the Círio de Nazaré festival, which is held each October to honor the city's patron saint. ⊠ *Av. Nazaré s/n at Av. Generalisimo Deodoro, Nazaré* ☎ *091/4009–8400 basilica, 091/3226–2308 museum* ⊠ *Free* ⊙ *Daily 8–noon, 2–6.*

⓲ Bosque Rodrigues Alves. In 1883 this 40-acre plot of rain forest was designated an ecological reserve. Nowadays it has an aquarium and two amusement parks as well as natural caverns, a variety of animals (some in the wild), and mammoth trees. ⊠ *Av. Almirante Barroso, Marco* ☎ *091/3226–2308* ⊠ *R$1* ⊙ *Tues.–Sun. 8–5.*

★ ⓰ Museu Emílio Goeldi. Founded by a naturalist and a group of intellectuals in 1866, this complex contains one of the Amazon's most important research facilities. Its museum has an extensive collection of Indian artifacts, including the distinctive and beautiful pottery of the Marajó Indians, known as *marajoara*. A small forest has reflecting pools with giant *vitória régia* water lilies. But the true highlight is the collection of Amazon wildlife, including manatees, anacondas, macaws, sloths, and monkeys. ⊠ *Av. Magalhães Barata 376, Nazaré* ☎ *091/3249–1302 or 091/3249–1230* ⊠ *Park R$2, park and museum R$4* ⊙ *Tues.–Sun. 9–noon and 2–5:30.*

⓱ Parque da Residência. For decades this was the official residence of the governor of Pará. Now it provides office space for the Secretaria de Cultura (SECULT; Executive Secretary of Culture), as well as public space. Within the park are a 400-seat theater, an orchid conservatory, an ice-cream parlor, a restaurant, and shaded spots to relax and soak in the atmosphere. ⊠ *Av. Magalhães Barata 830, São Brás* ☎ *091/4009–8721* ⊠ *Free* ⊙ *Tues.–Sun. 9 AM–9 PM.*

⓭ Praça da República. At this square you'll find a large statue that commemorates the proclamation of the Republic of Brazil, an amphitheater, and several French-style iron kiosks. On Sunday vendors, food booths, and musical groups create a festival-like atmosphere that attracts crowds of locals. ⊠ *Bounded by Av. Presidente Vargas, Trv. Osvaldo Cruz, and Av. Assis de Vasconcelos.*

⓮ Teatro da Paz. A complete renovation of this 1878 neoclassical theater was finished in 2001. Concert pianos were acquired to facilitate production of operas. Greek-style pillars line the front and sides; inside, note the imported details such as Italian marble pillars and French chandeliers. Classical-music performances are also held in the theater, which seats more than 800 people. English-speaking guides are available to give 20-minute tours (included in admission price). ⊠ *Av. da Paz s/n, Praça da República, Campina* ☎ *091/4009–8758 or 091/4009–8759* ⊠ *R$4* ⊙ *Tours on the hour Tues.–Fri. 9–5, Sat. 9–1.*

Where to Eat

Brazilian

$–$$$$ ✕ **Boteca das Onze.** In the Casa das Onze Janelas (⇨ *above*), the Boteca das Onze has thick stone and mortar walls stylishly adorned with antique instruments. The full bar has a complete drink menu with one of the largest selections of wines in the city. The patio has a view of the garden and river. A house favorite is the seafood platter for two. ⊠ *Praça da Sé, Cidade Velha* ☎ *91/3224–8599/3241–8255* ⊕ *boteca@nautilus. com.br* ⊟ *DC, MC, V* ⊙ *No lunch Mon.*

$–$$ ✕ **Lá em Casa.** From inauspicious beginnings has emerged one of Belém's
Fodor'sChoice most popular restaurants. Regional cuisine, prepared to exacting spec-
★ ifications, has earned Lá em Casa its good reputation. Consider trying Belém's premier dish, *pato no tucupi* (duck in a yellow manioc–herb sauce served with the mildly intoxicating *jambu* leaf). Crabs on the half-shell covered with *farofa* (finely ground manioc fried in margarine) is another good choice, as is *açaí* sorbet for dessert. Sitting on the patio fringed by tropical vines and bromeliads, you feel like you're dining in the middle of the forest. ⊠ *Av. Governador José Malcher 247, Nazaré* ☎ *091/223–1212* ⊟ *AE, DC, MC, V.*

$ ✕ **Garrote.** A traditional *churrascaria* (Brazilian barbecue restaurant), Garrote serves up as much grilled and roasted beef, pork, and other meat as you can eat for a reasonable fixed price. A salad buffet and dessert are also included. Service is excellent. ⊠ *Padre Eutíquio 1308, Batista Campos* ☎ *091/3225–2776* ⊟ *DC, MC, V* ⊙ *No dinner Sun.*

¢–$ ✕ **Palafita.** Excellent regional dishes with open-air dining over the river are why locals enjoy Palafita. Pirarucú fish balls and duck pastries are among the specialties. Palafita has music on weekend evenings and it's only a one-minute walk from the Forte do Preçépio. ⊠ *Praça da Sé, Rua Siquiera Mendes 264, Cidade Velha* ☎ *091/3224–3618* ⊟ *No credit cards* ⊙ *Closed Mon.*

¢ ✕ **Casa do Caldo.** Eight soups (out of 36) are featured every night for family dining in the "House of Soup." One price covers unlimited soup, toast, and dessert porridge. Try the crab soup with cilantro and the cow's-foot soup. It's air-conditioned and casual, with superb service. ⊠ *Rua Diogo Moia 266, Umarizal* ☎ *091/3224–5744* ⊟ *AE, DC, MC, V* ⊙ *No lunch.*

¢ ✕ **Mixtura Paulista.** A convenient location near the Hilton and the Praça da República makes this pay-per-kilo restaurant a good choice for a quick lunch. The buffet table always has numerous main dishes and grilled meats, along with salads, beans, and rice. ⊠ *Rua Serzedelo Corrêa 15, Nazaré* ☎ *091/3222–4309* ⊙ *No dinner.*

Vegetarian

$ ✕ **Mãenatureza.** Lunches are strictly vegan at one of the few vegetarian restaurants in the city. Trained cooks work with soy products, vegetable protein, and whole grains to prepare the small buffet. It's not far from the Hilton. ⊠ *Rua Manoel Barata 889, Comércio* ☎ *091/ 3212–8032* ⊕ *restaurantemaenatureza.com.br* ⊟ *MC* ⊙ *Closed Sun. No dinner.*

Where to Stay

$$$ ⊞ **Hilton International Belém.** The Hilton's reliability and amenities are topped only by its location right on the Praça da República. Although rooms have few decorations, bland color schemes, and simple furniture, they are well equipped and comfortable. Executive rooms have the nicest views as well as access to a lounge with a VCR, a meeting area, and complimentary food and drink. ⊠ *Av. Presidente Vargas 882, Campina, 66017-000* ☎ *091/4006–7000, 800/891–4118 in U.S.* ⊕ *www. hilton.com* ⤳ *361 rooms* ⚘ *Restaurant, pool, health club, hair salon, sauna, 2 bars, convention center* ⊟ *AE, DC, MC, V.*

$ ⊞ **Hotel Regente.** This hotel has excellent service and a prime location for a reasonable price. Stained-glass windows and soft leather couches welcome you in an attractive lobby. Rooms on the 12th floor are nicer and more modern than those on other floors, yet they cost the same. ⊠ *Av. Governador José Malcher 485, Nazaré, 66035-100* ☎ *091/ 3181–5000* ⊕ *www.hotelregente.com.br* ⤳ *196 rooms, 6 suites* ⚘ *Restaurant, pool, bar* ⊟ *AE, DC, MC, V.*

$ ⊞ **Itaoca Hotel.** It comes as no surprise that this small, reasonably priced hotel has the highest occupancy rate in town. Its rooms are extremely comfortable, well equipped, and modern, and most have a fantastic view of the dock area and river. ⊠ *Av. Presidente Vargas 132, Campina, 66010-902* ☎ *091/4009–2400 or 091/4009–2402* ⤶ *itaoca@canal13.com. br* ⤳ *32 rooms, 4 suites* ⚘ *Restaurant, in-room safes, cable TV, meeting room* ⊟ *AE, DC, MC, V.*

¢ ⊞ **Hotel Grão Pará.** The oldest hotel in town is also the best deal. Hotel Grão Pará has few amenities, but has the best price for a modern, clean room with the basics, and it's centrally located. ⊠ *Av. Presidente Vargas 718, Campina, 66017–000* ☎ *091/3224–9600 or 091/3224–4100* ⤳ *150 rooms* ⚘ *Restaurant* ⊟ *DC, MC, V* ⦿ *EP.*

★ ¢ ⊞ **Manacá Hotel.** This bright-red hotel with a slanted brown-tile roof looks like a cross between a Monopoly™ hotel piece and a pagoda. Cozy, artfully decorated common areas with soft lighting have more charm than those at larger places—for about a quarter of the price. Rooms are clean and simple, and it's a good choice if you can live without a pool or a bar. Make sure to call ahead, since it's often booked during the week. ⊠ *Trv. Quintino Bocaiuva 1645, Nazaré, 66033-620* ☎ *091/3223–3335 or 091/3242–5665* ⤳ *16 rooms* ⚘ *Cable TV; no room phones* ⊟ *AE, DC, MC, V.*

Nightlife & the Arts

Nightlife

Umarizal is Belém's liveliest neighborhood at night, with a good selection of bars, clubs, and restaurants. Other nightlife hot spots are scattered around the city.

BARS **Água Doce** (⊠ Rua Diogo Móia 283, Umarizal ☎ 091/3222–3383 ⊕ cachacariabelem.com.br) specializes in *cachaça* (Brazilian sugarcane liquor). Listed on its menu are 182 kinds of cachaça and 605 different drinks, along with appetizers and entrées as well. Softly lighted with lots of tables, this place gets busy on weekends. It's open Tuesday–Sunday. If you prefer your music in a relaxed environment, head to **Cosanostra Caffé** (⊠ Rua Benjamin Constant 1499, Nazaré ☎ 091/241–1068), which has live MPB (*música popular brasileira*) and jazz. Catering to locals and expatriate foreigners alike, it serves food from an extensive menu until late in the night. **Roxy Bar** (⊠ Av. Senador Lemos 231, Umarizal ☎ 091/224–4514) tops nearly everyone's list of hip spots at which to sip a drink and people-watch.

DANCE CLUBS   The hot spots for dancing are open on Friday and Saturday nights and sometimes on Sundays; many are downtown. Mixed-age crowds frequent them no matter what the music. Prices vary depending on the show. Drinks are available but no food. All clubs except Signos have live music on occasion. Clubs open around 10 PM, though they don't get lively before 11 or midnight.

Signos (⊠ Governador José Malcher 247, Nazaré ☎ 091/3242–7702), underneath the Lá em Casa restaurant, has the fanciest decor of the clubs, with lots of mirrors and red booths. A DJ runs video clips of dance music on a huge screen. **Zeppelin Club** (⊠ Av. Senador Lemos 108, Umarizal ☎ 091/3241–1330) has two dance floors where techno is mixed with American and Brazilian pop and rock.

EVENING   Nights in Belém are comfortable for walking. There are several popu-
STROLLS   lar locations that are relatively safe, but catch a cab to your hotel if you stay late.

Estação das Docas (⊠ Boulevard Castilhos França s/n, Comércio) has a long, broad sidewalk that passes between the bay and numerous restaurants. **Praça Batista Campos** (⊠ Av. Padre Eutíquio s/n, Batista Campos) has sidewalks, benches, and coconut vendors. Nearby residents come here to jog, walk, and date. **Ver-O-Rio** (⊠ Av. Marechal Hermes s/n, Umarizal) is on the edge of the bay. It has a small bridge and several small open-air restaurants.

The Arts

For information about cultural events, contact the state-run **Secretaria de Cultura** (SECULT; ⊠ Av. Governador Magalhães Barata 830, São Brás ☎ 091/4009–8707 or 091/4009–8717), which prints a monthly listing of cultural events throughout the city.

Live music is played nightly at the **Estação das Docas** (⊠ Boulevard Castilhos França s/n, Campina ☎ 091/3212–5525). Weekday shows usually consist of acoustic singers and/or guitarists. On weekends rock, jazz, and MPB bands play on a suspended stage that moves back and forth on tracks about 8 meters (25 feet) above patrons of the microbrewery and surrounding restaurants. Outstanding theatrical productions in Portuguese are presented at the **Teatro Experimental Waldemar Henrique** (⊠ Av. Presidente Vargas s/n, Praça da República, Campina ☎ 091/3222–4762). **Teatro da Paz** (⊠ Av. da Paz s/n, Praça da República, Campina ☎ 091/4009–8758, 091/4009–8759, or 091/4009–8750) often hosts plays, philharmonic concerts, and dance recitals.

Manaus

Manaus, the capital of Amazonas State, is a hilly city of around 1.8 million people that lies 766 km (475 mi) west of Santarém and 1,602 km (993 mi) west of Belém on the banks of the Rio Negro 10 km (6 mi) upstream from its confluence with the Amazon. Manaus is the Amazon's most popular tourist destination, largely because of the 19 jungle lodges in the surrounding area. The city's principal attractions are its lavish, brightly colored houses and civic buildings—vestiges of an opulent time when the wealthy sent their laundry to be done in Europe and sent for old-world artisans and engineers to build their New World monuments.

Founded in 1669, Manaus took its name, which means "mother of the Gods," from the Manaó tribe. The city has long flirted with prosperity. Of all the Amazon cities and towns, Manaus is most identified with the rubber boom. In the late 19th and early 20th centuries it supplied 90% of the world's rubber. The industry was monopolized by rubber barons, whose number never exceeded 100 and who lived in the city and spent enormous sums on ostentatious lifestyles. They dominated the region like feudal lords. Thousands of *seringueiros* (rubber tappers) were recruited to work on the rubber plantations, where they lived virtually as slaves. A few of the seringueiros were from indigenous tribes, but most were transplants from Brazil's crowded and depressed northeast. Eventually conflicts erupted between barons and indigenous workers over encroachment on tribal lands. Stories of cruelty abound. One baron is said to have killed more than 40,000 native people during his 20-year "reign." Another boasted of having slaughtered 300 Indians in a day.

The 25-year rubber era was brought to a close thanks to Englishman Henry A. Wickham, who took 70,000 rubber-tree seeds out of Brazil in 1876. (Transporting seeds across borders has since been outlawed.) The seeds were planted in Kew Gardens in England. The few that germinated were transplanted in Malaysia, where they flourished. Within 30 years Malaysian rubber ended the Brazilian monopoly. Although several schemes were launched to revitalize the Amazon rubber industry, and many seringueiros continued to work independently in the jungles, the high times were over. Manaus entered a depression that lasted until 1967, when the downtown area was made a free-trade zone. The economy was revitalized, and its population jumped from 200,000 to 900,000 in less than 20 years.

In the 1970s the industrial district was given exclusive federal free-trade-zone status to produce certain light-industry items. Companies moved in and began making motorcycles and electronics. In the mid-1990s the commercial district lost

WORD OF MOUTH

In Manaus, you must make a short boat trip to see the rendezvous of two mighty rivers: Negro, [with] its clear and dark waters, and Amazonas, with its turbid waters the color of earth. Their waters don't mix instantly, they flow together, forming colored eddies.

—Dilermando

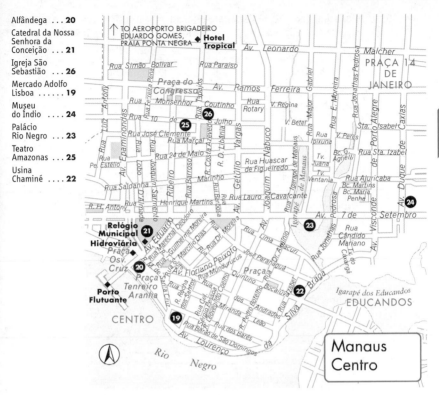

Manaus
Centro

its free-trade-zone status. Hundreds lost their jobs and businesses crumbled, but the light-industrial sector held strong and even grew. Today it employs 80,000, has the largest motorcycle factory in South America, and makes 90% of Brazilian-made TVs.

Exploring Manaus

Manaus is a sprawling city with few true high-rises. Although many hotels and sights are in the city center (Centro), it's neither large nor attractive, and it's congested. It is also exotic and hilly and is on the edge of a river one and a half times larger than the Mississippi.

Centro

Manaus's downtown area has a lot going on. The floating docks are here, with tourist shops nearby. Open markets sell fish, meats, and all sorts of produce, while general stores ply machetes, hoes, hardtack, cassava flour, and boat motor parts to those pursuing a livelihood outside the city. Centro is also the most important historic section of the city. The Teatro Amazonas, the Customs House (Alfândega), and the Adolfo Lisboa Market are here, along with old churches, government buildings, and mansions. The result is a mix of neoclassical, Renaissance, colonial, and modern architecture.

WHAT TO SEE   **Alfândega.** The Customs House was built by the British in 1902 with bricks
⑳   imported as ship ballast. It stands alongside the floating dock that was
built at the same time to accommodate the annual 10-meter (39-foot)
rise and fall of the river. It's now home to the regional office of the Brazilian tax department, and the interior is of little interest. ⊠ *Rua Marquês
de Santa Cruz s/n, Centro* ☎ *No phone* ⌨ *Free* ⊙ *Weekdays 10–3.*

㉑   **Catedral da Nossa Senhora da Conceição.** Built originally in 1695 by
Carmelite missionaries, the Cathedral of Our Lady of Immaculate Conception (also called Igreja Matriz) burned down in 1850 and was reconstructed in 1878. It's a simple, predominantly neoclassical structure
with a bright, colorful interior. ⊠ *Praça da Matriz, Centro* ☎ *91/
3234–7821* ⌨ *Free* ⊙ *Usually Mon.–Sat. 9–5, but hours vary.*

㉖   **Igreja São Sebastião.** This neoclassical church (circa 1888), with its char-
coal-gray color and medieval characteristics, seems foreboding. Its interior, however, is luminous and uplifting, with white Italian marble,
stained-glass windows, and beautiful ceiling paintings. The church has
a tower on only one side. No one is sure why this is so, but if you ask,
you may get one of several explanations: the second tower wasn't built
because of lack of funds; it was omitted as a symbolic gesture to the poor;
or the ship with materials for its construction sank. As you stroll through
the church plaza and the one in front of the Teatro Amazonas, note the
black-and-white Portuguese granite patterns at your feet. They are said
to represent Manaus's meeting of the waters. ⊠ *Praça São Sebastião, Centro* ☎ *092/3232–4572* ⌨ *Free* ⊙ *Usually Mon.–Sat. 9–5, but hours vary.*

★ ⑲   **Mercado Adolfo Lisboa.** Vendors sell Amazon food products and handicrafts at this market. Built in 1882, it is a wrought-iron replica of the
original Parisian Halles (now destroyed); the ironwork is said to have
been designed by Gustave Eiffel himself. ⊠ *Rua dos Barés 6, Centro*
☎ *No phone* ⊙ *Daily 6 AM–6 PM.*

㉔   **Museu do Índio.** The Indian Museum is maintained by Salesian Sisters,
an order of nuns with eight missions in the upper Amazon. It displays
handicrafts, weapons, ceramics, ritual masks, and clothing from the region's tribes. ⊠ *Rua Duque de Caxias 356, Centro* ☎ *092/3635–1922*
⌨ *R$5* ⊙ *Weekdays 8:30–11:30 and 2–4:30, Sat. 8:30–11:30.*

㉓   **Palácio Rio Negro.** The extravagant Rio Negro Palace was built at the end
of the 19th century as the home of a German rubber baron. Later it was
used as the official governor's residence. Today it houses some of the city's
finest art exhibits and a cultural center. The Museu da Imagem e do Som,
on the same property, has three daily screenings of art films and docu-
mentaries Tuesday through Friday and four screenings daily on weekends. Don't miss the cultural exhibits out back, which include a caboclo
home, an indigenous home, and a cassava-processing house. ⊠ *Av. 7 de
Setembro 1546, Centro* ☎ *No phone* ⌨ *Free* ⊙ *Weekdays 9–6.*

㉕   **Teatro Amazonas.** The city's lavish opera house was completed in 1896
Fodor'sChoice   after 15 years of construction. Its Italian Renaissance–style interior pro-
★   vides a clear idea of the wealth that marked the Amazon rubber boom.
It has marble doorways, crystal chandeliers, handblown glass sconces

from Italy, English wrought-iron banisters, and panels of French tiles. Italian frescoes depict Amazon legends. Operas and other events are presented regularly. Monday-evening performances are free and usually feature local artists of various musical genres. The Amazonas Philharmonic Orchestra plays Thursday night and can be seen and heard practicing in the theater weekdays 9–2. A variety of foreign entertainers, from José Carreras to the Spice Girls, have performed here. Half-hour tours are conducted daily 9–4. An annual opera festival takes place in April and May. ⊠ *Praça São Sebastião s/n, Centro* 🕾 *092/3232–1768* ⊕ *www. teatroamazonas.com.br* 🖾 *R$10* ☉ *Mon.–Sat. 9–4.*

㉒ Usina Chaminé. Transformed from a sewage treatment plant that never functioned, this art gallery displays exhibits and holds dance and theater performances. Its neo-Renaissance–style interior, with hardwood floors and massive wood beams, is another reason to visit. ⊠ *Av. Lourenço da Silva Braga, Centro* 🕾 *092/3633–3026* 🖾 *Free* ☉ *Tues.–Fri. 10–5, weekends 4–8.*

DON'T MISS

MEETING OF THE WATERS – This natural phenomenon is one of the area's biggest tourist attractions. Here the Rio Solimões, a slow-moving muddy river, and the darker, fast-moving Rio Negro flow side by side for 4 mi (6 km) without mixing. If you run your foot in the water from the boat, you can feel the difference in temperature—the Solimões is warm and the Negro is cold. At the CEASA port you can rent a boat, or go with a tour company. It takes about an hour to go from CEASA to the Meeting of the Waters, spend some time there, and return. A taxi to CEASA from downtown is about R$30.

Where to Eat

Brazilian

$$ ✕ **Churrascaria Búfalo.** Twelve waiters, each with a different cut of
Fodor$Choice chicken, beef, or goat, scurry around this large, sparkling clean restau-
★ rant. As if the delectable meats weren't enough, tables are also stocked with side dishes, including manioc root, pickled vegetables, and caramelized bananas. ⊠ *Rua Joaquim Nabuco 628-A, Centro* 🕾 *092/ 3633–3773 or 092/3633–5091* ⊕ *www.churrascariabufalo.com.br* 🖃 *AE, DC, MC, V.*

¢–$$ ✕ **Chez Charufe.** On the bank of the Rio Negro, Chez Charufe is in a lovely location for breezy, open-air dining. Fish dishes as well as beef and chicken are all very good, and it's only a ten-minute walk from the Hotel Tropical. ⊠ *Ponta Negra, Tarumã* 🕾 *091/3658–5580* 🖃 *MC, V* ☉ *No lunch.*

¢ ✕ **Restaurante Aves Grill.** For a quick, cheap bite, you can't beat this pay-per-kilo restaurant. Most main courses contain some kind of bird, whether quail, turkey, duck, or chicken. Side dishes include lovely salads, fries, beans, and rice. ⊠ *Rua Henrique Martins 366, Centro* 🕾 *092/ 3233–3809* 🖃 *DC, MC, V* ☉ *No dinner.*

Seafood

★ **$–$$$$** ✕ **Canto da Peixada.** When Pope John Paul II came to Manaus in 1981, this restaurant was chosen to host him. The dining areas aren't elegant, but the fish dishes are outstanding, and there are 43 types of salad. One platter feeds two. ☒ *Rua Emilio Moreira 1677, Praça 14* ☎ *092/ 3234–1066* ▭ *AE* ⊙ *Closed Sun.*

Vegetarian

¢ ✗ **Filosóphicus.** Whole grains, textured vegetable protein, gluten, and soy are used in the dishes at this buffet restaurant. It's on the second floor and tricky to find. From the street take the door between Belmiros and Marisa e Familia. ☒ *Av. 7 de Setembro 752, 2nd floor, Centro* ☎ *092/ 3234–2224* ▭ *No credit cards* ⊙ *No dinner.*

Where to Stay

Manaus has several decent in-town hotels, but the jungle lodges outside town are where you should base yourself if you're interested in Amazon adventures. Most jungle lodges have naturalist guides, swimming, caiman "hunts" (the animals are blinded with flashlights, captured, photographed, and released), piranha fishing, and canoe trips. Many jungle lodges (and all of those that we list) are near the Rio Negro, where mosquitoes are less of a problem because they can't breed in its acidic black water. Unless otherwise noted, prices at jungle lodges are for two-day, one-night packages, which generally include transport to and from the lodge, meals (not drinks), and a variety of activities that depend on the length of your stay. These are essentially glorified camps that lack many amenities, so expect to rough it a bit. Air-conditioning, hot water, telephones, and televisions are rare amenities.

In-Town Hotels

$$$ ⊞ **Hotel Tropical.** Nothing in the Amazon can match the majesty of this resort hotel. It's 20 km (12 mi) northwest of downtown and overlooks the Rio Negro, with a short path to the beach. In addition to a zoo, sports facilities, and two gorgeous pools, the Tropical has its own dock. The location is remote, far from Centro, but just a 20-minute cab ride from the airport. The restaurant is a reliable choice for dinners of regional and international fare. ☒ *Av. Coronel Teixeira 1320, Ponta Negra, 69029–120* ☎ *092/3659–5000* ⊕ *www.tropicalhotel.com.br* ⊷ *588 rooms, 8 suites* ♧ *2 restaurants, coffee shop, in-room safes, 4 tennis courts, 2 pools, gym, sauna, beach, dock, boating, basketball, bar, dance club, recreation room, shops, helipad, travel services* ▭ *AE, DC, MC, V* |⊙| *EP.*

$ ⊞ **Lider Hotel.** Although far from luxurious, this hotel is clean, comfortable, and conveniently located in Centro. It's a good base from which to branch out on city tours. ☒ *Av. 7 de Setembro 827, Centro, 69005- 140* ☎ *092/3621–9744* ⊕ *www.internext.com.br/liderhotel* ⊷ *60 rooms* ♧ *Restaurant, bar* ▭ *AE, DC, MC, V* |⊙| *EP.*

$ ⊞ **Taj Mahal.** Much of the charming East Indian artwork of the original hotel disappeared in the last renovation, although you can still see some in the lobby. Albeit a bit unkempt, the Taj Mahal is a pleasant option, with a rooftop pool, a revolving restaurant with a view, and a convenient location. Request a room with a river view. ☒ *Av. Getúlio Vargas 741, Centro, 69020-020* ☎ *092/3627–3737* ⊕ *www. grupotajmahal.com.br* ⊷ *144 rooms, 26 suites* ♧ *Restaurant, pool, hair salon, massage, sauna, bar, meeting room* ▭ *AE, DC, MC, V* |⊙| *EP.*

¢ ☒ **Central Hotel Manaus.** A good option if you're on a budget, this hotel has simple, clean rooms with standard amenities. It's near the market and the port, and is popular with businessmen on a tight budget. ✉ *Rua Dr. Moreira 202, Centro, 69005-250* ☎ *092/3622–2600* ⊕ *www.hotelcentralmanaus.com.br* ⤳ *50 rooms* ⚒ *Restaurant, minibars* ⊟ *AE, DC, MC, V* ⏀ *EP.*

Jungle Lodges

Though most tour companies will pick you up at the airport and drop you off following your adventure, airport pickup should not be assumed in all situations. It's often included in tour packages, but inquire while making arrangements. Local naturalist guides are often available at lodges. Though knowledgeable, they are neither biologists nor teachers. Do not expect accurate information and identification of species or interpretation of ecological relationships.

$$$$ ☒ **Acajatuba Jungle Lodge.** Civilization seems hundreds of miles away at this thatch-hut lakeside lodge. Twenty individual screened cabins are elevated 1 meter (3 feet) above the ground and connected to the rest of the lodge by walkways. Lighting is provided by 12-volt batteries and kerosene lamps (generators would keep wildlife away), and there is no hot water, but what it lacks in luxury, it more than makes up for by putting you in the middle of the tropical forest. ✉ *60 km (35 mi)/4 hours west of Manaus, Lago Acajatuba; boats to lodge leave from CEASA port near the meeting of the waters* ⌂ *Conj. Vila Municipal Rua 7 #87, Manaus 69057–750* ☎ *092/3642–0358 or 092/3642–0452* ⊕ *www.acajatuba.com.br* ⤳ *40 rooms* ⚒ *Bar; no a/c, no room phones, no room TVs* ⊟ *V* ⏀ *FAP.*

$$$$ ☒ **Amazon Ecopark.** For a very comfortable jungle experience, stay at this lodge with air-conditioned rooms, hot showers, and mosquito nets. You can visit monkeys in rehabilitation, hike with a naturalist guide on 6 mi (10 km) of trails through several habitat types with enormous trees, and relax in streams and small waterfalls. It's not far from Manaus. ✉ *23 km (15 mi) northwest of Manaus; 30 minutes by boat from Hotel Tropical, Rio Tarumã,* ☎ *092/3622–2612* ⊕ *www.amazonecopark.com.br* ⤳ *60 rooms* ⚒ *Restaurant, bar, beach, massage, hiking, recreation room* ⊟ *MC, V* ⏀ *MAP.*

$$$$ ☒ **Amazon Lodge.** Rustic floating cabins with air-conditioning and baths make up this remote lodge. Monkey- and bird-watching is excellent. The English-speaking guides are knowledgeable and friendly. The minimum stay is two nights. ✉ *74 km (50 mi) south of Manaus, Lago Juma; boats to lodge leave from CEASA port near meeting of the waters* ⌂ *Heliconia Amazônia Turismo Ltda., Rua José Clemente 500, Room 214, Manaus 69010-070* ☎ *092/3234–5915* ⊕ *www.naturesafaris.com.br* ⤳ *14 rooms* ⚒ *Restaurant, fishing, hiking; no room phones, no room TVs* ⊟ *No credit cards* ⏀ *FAP.*

$$$$ ☒ **Ariaú Amazon Towers.** The most famous of the Amazon jungle lodges, Ariaú is made up of four-story wooden towers on stilts and linked by catwalks. The effect is more dramatic when the river floods the ground below from December to June. The feeling of being integrated with nature is a bit lost here due to Ariaú's size, and contact with wildlife is

rare, apart from brightly colored macaws and cute semiwild monkeys that visit and make mischief. Though Ariaú looks impressive and the food is excellent, we find the price a bit high, considering that many rooms have a mildew odor and small windows, and most rooms have fans instead of air conditioning. The exception are the tower suites, which have air-conditioning and most standard hotel amenities. One such suite is the Tarzan House, 100 feet up in the treetops. ⊠ *60 km (40 mi)/2 hours northwest of Manaus, Rio Ariaú; boats to lodge depart from Hotel Tropical* ⌖ *Rua Silva Ramos 41, Manaus 69010–180* ☎ *092/3622–5000* ⊕ *www.ariautowers.com.br* ⇄ *288 rooms, 19 suites* ⌂ *2 restaurants, 5 pools, dock, fishing, hiking, 4 bars, shops, Internet, helipad, auditorium, museum; no a/c in some rooms, no room TVs, no phones in some rooms* ⊟ *AE, DC, MC, V* ¶⊙¶ *FAP.*

$$$$ ⊞ **Jungle Othon Palace.** It's quite a sight to cruise down the Rio Negro and see the neoclassical columns of this luxurious "flotel," built on a steel barge, looming on the horizon. Explore the region by day, and at night return to your air-conditioned cabin for a hot shower or to take a stroll on the observation deck. ⊠ *35 km (20 mi)/1 hour west of Manaus, Rio Negro; boats to lodge depart from Hotel Tropical* ⌖ *Rua Saldanha Marinho 700, Manaus 69010–040* ☎ *092/3633–6051 or 092/3633–6200* ⊕ *www.junglepalace.com.br* ⇄ *24 rooms* ⌂ *Restaurant, cable TV, pool, health club, bar, meeting room* ⊟ *DC, MC, V* ¶⊙¶ *FAP.*

★ $$$$ ⊞ **Lago Salvador.** Although it's only a 15-minute ride from the Hotel Tropical, this lodge feels secluded. Four cabanas with three apartments each are on the shore of the lake from which the lodge takes its name. During the high-water season the lake flows over its shores to join the Rio Negro. Rooms are simple and comfortable. All of the small cabins have trails leading to them from the main house and restaurant, but your guide will probably use the most direct route—paddling a canoe across the lake—to get you there. ⊠ *15 km (10 mi)/15 minutes northwest of Manaus; boats to lodge leave from Hotel Tropical* ⌖ *Fontur, Hotel Tropical, Av. Coronel Teixeira 1320, Manaus 69029-120* ☎ *092/3658–3052 or 092/3658–3438* ⊕ *www.lagosalvador.com.br* ⇄ *12 cabins* ⌂ *Restaurant, room service, fans, boating, hiking* ⊟ *AE, MC, V* ¶⊙¶ *FAP.*

Nightlife & the Arts

Nightlife

Manaus em Tempo is a newspaper that lists nightlife events in Manaus; it's availabe at newsstands. *Boi bumbá* (ox legend) music and dance—native to the central Amazon region—tells stories with tightly choreographed steps and strong rhythms. The amphitheater at Praia da Ponta Negra holds regular boi-bumbá performances.

The Arts

Teatro Amazonas (⊠ Praça São Sebastião s/n, Centro ☎ 092/3232–1768) draws some of the biggest names in theater, opera, and classical music. Monday-evening performances are free. The Amazonas Philharmonic Orchestra plays every Thursday night. The Teatro holds an opera festival every year in April and May.

Sports & the Outdoors
Jungle & River Excursions

Though Belém, Santarém, and other communities are great places for jungle and river excursions, they don't have nearly the selection or number of visitors that Manaus has. The most common excursion is a half- or full-day tourist-boat trip that travels 15 km (9 mi) east of Manaus to the point where the coffee-color water of the Rio Negro flows beside and gradually joins the coffee-with-cream-color water of the Rio Solimões. According to Brazilians, this is where the Amazon River begins. The waters flow alongside one another for 6 km (4 mi) before merging. Many of these meeting-of-the-waters treks include motorboat side trips along narrow streams or through bayous. Some also stop at the Parque Ecológico do Janauary, where you can see birds and a lake filled with the world's largest water lily, the *vitória régia*.

Nighttime boat trips into the forest explore flooded woodlands and narrow waterways. Some stop for trail hikes. Some companies take you by canoe on a caiman "hunt," where caimans are caught and released. Trips to the Rio Negro's upper reaches, where wildlife is a little wilder, are also offered. Such trips usually stop at river settlements to visit with local families. They may include jungle treks, fishing (they supply the gear and boat), and a trip to Anavilhanas, the world's largest freshwater archipelago. It contains some 400 islands with amazing Amazon flora, birds, and monkeys. To arrange any of these excursions, contact an area tour operator (⇨ Tours, *in* The Amazon Essentials, *below*).

The Amazon Essentials
Transportation
BY AIR

For major airline contact information, including Gol, TAM, and Varig, *see* Air Travel, *in* Smart Travel Tips A to Z.

BELÉM & All flights are served by Aeroporto Internacional Val-de-Cans, which is
SIDE TRIPS 11 km (7mi) northwest of the city. Varig and TAM sometimes offer direct flights to Miami. They also fly regularly to Rio, São Paulo, Brasília, and Manaus, as does GOL. TAF flies to the northeast of Brazil. Soure, Kovacs, and Renaissance airlines have charter flights to small regional airports, including rivers and grass strips. Prices vary, but a flight for four people to Marajó, for example, would be about R$1,000.

The easiest route from the airport is south on Avenida Julio Cesár and then west on Avenida Almirante Barroso. The 20-minute taxi ride from the airport to downtown Belém costs around R$30. There are also buses. Look for those labeled MAREX/PRES. VARGAS, for the Hilton and other hotels; MAREX/PRAÇA KENNEDY, for Paratur and the docks; or MAREX/VER-O-PESO, for Cidade Velha.

🛪 Airport **Aeroporto Internacional Val-de-Cans** ⊠ Av. Julio Cesár s/n, Belém ☎ 091/3210-6000 or 091/3257-3780.

🛪 Local Airlines **Kovacs** ☎091/3233-1600. **Renaissance** ☎091/3233-1290. **Soure** ☎091/3233-4986. **TAF** ☎ 091/3210-6501 ⊕ www.voetaf.com.br.

🛪 Airport **Aeroporto Maria José** ⊠ Rodovia Fernando Guilhon, Praça Eduardo Gomes s/n, Santarém ☎ 093/3523-1990.

MANAUS & SIDE TRIPS

Brigadeiro Eduardo Gomes Airport is 17 km (10 mi) north of downtown. Varig has a weekly direct flight to Miami. Most flights connect in São Paulo, where you can fly direct to Miami, New York, L.A., and Houston. Varig and TAM have regular flights to and from Santarém, Belém, Brasília, Rio, and São Paulo. Tavaj and Rico fly to Tefé.

The trip to Manaus Centro from the airport takes 25 minutes and costs about R$45 by taxi. A trip on one of the city buses, which depart regularly during the day and early evening, costs R$1.50.

🛪 Airport **Aeroporto Brigadeiro Eduardo Gomes** ⊠ Av. Santos Dumont s/n, Manaus ☎ 092/3652-1210.

🛪 Local Airlines **Rico** ☎ 092/3652-1513. **Tavaj** ☎ 092/3652-1166.

BY BOAT

BELÉM & SIDE TRIPS

Most ships arrive and depart in the general dock area on the edge of downtown called the Escadinha. MACAMAZON and Bom Jesus have ships and standard riverboats to Macapá, Santarem, Manaus, and other places. These boats dock at the Escadinha do Cais do Porto. Sightseeing boats leave from Estação das Docas, and from behind Hotel Beira Rio on Rua Bernardo Saião, 20 minutes southeast of town near the Federal University.

🚢 **Bom Jesus** ⊠ Av. Mendonça Junior 12, Macapá ☎ 096/3223-2342 or 091/3272-1423 in Belém. **MACAMAZON** ☎ 091/3222-5604 or 091/3228-0774.

MANAUS & SIDE TRIPS

If you're looking for a boat to another town, a lodge, or a beach, visit the Hidroviária Regional Terminal. At the ticket or tourist information booths you can get information about prices and departure times and days to all the locations. You can also walk down to Porto Flutuante via the bridge behind the terminal to take a look at the regional boats. Their destinations and departure times are listed on plaques.

To reach most Manaus-area beaches, catch a boat from Porto Flutuante. Sunday is the only day with regularly scheduled trips; boats transport great crowds for about R$10 per person. You can hire small craft to the beaches and other attractions, such as the meeting of the waters. Look for people wearing the green vests of the Associação dos Canoeiros Motorizados de Manaus near the Porto Flutuante or in the Escadinha area closer to the market in Belém. They can set you up with local boat trips at reasonable prices. You can also make arrangements through tour operators.

MACAMAZON boats run from Manaus to Santarém on Wednesday and Friday from the Porto São Raimundo (west of downtown) or the Porto Flutuante (about R$160).

🚢 **MACAMAZON** ☎ 091/3222-5604 or 091/3228-0774.

BY BUS

BELÉM & SIDE TRIPS

Rodoviário São Brás, the bus station in Belém, is east of Nazaré. Reservations for buses are rarely needed. Boa Esperança makes the 209-km (125-mi) journey to **Salinópolis** every couple of hours daily. Beira-Dão leaves every half hour on the 60-km (36-mi), two-hour journey to **Ilha**

Mosqueiro for over R$1. Clearly marked buses to **Praia Outeiro** and the town of Icoaraci pass the bus station regularly and also costs a little over R$1. Belém's local bus service is safe (though you should keep an eye on your belongings) and comprehensive, but a little confusing. Ask a resident for guidance.

🚌 **Beira-Dão** ☎ 091/3226-1162. **Boa Esperança** ☎ 091/3266-0033. **Rodoviário São Brás** ✉ Av. Almirante Barroso s/n, São Brás, Belém ☎ 91/3246-7442.

MANAUS & SIDE TRIPS The bus station in Manaus, Terminal Rodoviário Huascar Angelim, is 7 km (4 mi) north of the city center. The city bus system is extensive and easy to use. The fare is about R$1.50. Most of the useful buses run along Avenida Floriano Peixoto, including Bus 120, which goes to Ponta Negra and stops near the Hotel Tropical. The Fontur bus, which costs about R$14, travels between Centro and the Hotel Tropical several times a day. To get to Presidente Figueiredo, take the bus labeled ARUANÃ, which runs regularly from the terminal and costs around R$17.

🚌 **Terminal Rodoviário Huascar Angelim** ✉ Rua Recife 2784, Flores, Manaus ☎ 092/3642-5805.

BY CAR

BELÉM & SIDE TRIPS In Belém rental cars cost between R$100 and R$180 a day. Several companies have offices at the airport and in town.

The BR 316 begins on the outskirts of Belém and runs eastward toward the coast and then south, connecting the city with Brazil's major northeastern hubs. To reach the beaches at Ilha Mosqueiro outside Belém, take BR 316 and then head north on PA 391. To reach Salinas Beach, take BR 316 to PA 324 and head north on PA 124.

Although Belém has the most traffic of any Amazon city and what seems like more than its fair share of one-way streets, in-town driving is relatively easy. Parking is only tricky in a few areas, such as Avenida Presidente Vargas and the Escadinha.

🚗 **Rental Agencies Avis** ✉ Aeroporto Val de Cans, Belém ☎ 091/3257-2277 or 091/3257-2222.

MANAUS & SIDE TRIPS You can rent a car at the Manaus airport through Unidas Rent a Car.

From Manaus BR 174 runs north to Boa Vista, and BR 319 travels south to Porto Velho, which is south of Manaus in Rondônia State. To get to BR 319, you have to take a ferry across the Amazon. You can go about 100 km (63 mi) on paved road. Then it turns to dirt or mud. Even if you're after adventure, don't think about driving to Porto Velho. A four-wheel-drive vehicle takes you farther than 100 km (62 mi), but won't get you across the rivers and lakes that take over the road farther south.

Manaus has its share of traffic and parking problems, but is calmer than Belém.

🚗 **Rental Agencies Unidas Rent a Car** ✉ Aeroporto Brigadeiro Eduardo Gomes, Av. Santos Dumont s/n, Manaus ☎ 092/3651-2558 or 092/3652-1347.

BY TAXI

There are plenty of taxis in Amazon cities, and they're easy to flag down. All have meters (except Marajó), and tips aren't necessary. Where meters don't exist, you have to bargain for the price. At odd hours call the taxi company. You can find them listed in the yellow pages, or call one of the companies below. Smaller towns also have mototaxis. They are much cheaper but only carry one passenger.

Contacts & Resources

TOUR OPTIONS

Whichever tour you choose, be sure your experience includes wildlife viewing with a guide, contact with locals, and regional foods and drinks. The most popular tours run from Manaus, since it is best organized for tourism and has the best jungle lodges. It can feel clogged with tourists at times though, which can make the less-popular starting points of Santarém and Belém more appealing.

BELÉM   For excursions in Belém as well as help with plane and hotel reservations, contact Angel Turismo in the Hilton Hotel. Valeverde Turismo has a tour boat and office at the Estação das Docas. Amazon Star can do just about everything. Lusotur is a large company near the Praça da República that arranges city tours and ecotours.

🚩 **Amazon Star Tours** ✉ Rua Henrique Gurjão 236, Campina, Belém ☎ 091/3212-6244. **Angel Turismo** ✉ Hilton International Belém, Av. Presidente Vargas 882, Praça da República, Campina, Belém ☎ 091/3224-2111. **Lusotur** ✉ Av. Brás de Aguiar 471, Nazaré, Belém ☎ 091/3241-1011. **Valeverde Turismo** ✉ Boulevard Castilhos França s/n, Campina, Belém ☎ 091/3212-3388 or 091/3241-7333.

MANAUS &   In Manaus, Fontur arranges boat and city tours. Tarumã can help with
SIDE TRIPS   hotel arrangements and transportation in the city or on the river. Amazon Explorers and Selvatur are two high-profile companies that arrange Manaus-area ecotours.

🚩 **Amazon Explorers** ✉ Av. Djalma Batista 21100 Tvlandia Mall, Vieralves, Manaus ☎ 092/3642-4777 or 092/3236-9484 🌐 www.amazonexplorers.com.br. **Fontur** ✉ Hotel Tropical, Av. Coronel Teixeira 1320, Ponta Negra, Manaus ☎ 092/3658-3052 or 092/3658-3438. **Selvatur** ✉ Praça Adelberto Vale 17, Centro, Manaus ☎ 092/3622-2577 🌐 www.selvatur.com.br. **Tarumã** ✉ Av. Eduardo Ribeiro 620, Centro, Manaus ☎ 092/3648-8347.

VISITOR INFORMATION

BELÉM   BELEMTUR, the tourist board in Belém, is open weekdays 8–noon and 2–6.

🚩 **BELEMTUR** ✉ Av. Governador José Malcher 592, Nazaré ☎ 091/3242-0900 or 091/3242-0033.

MANAUS   Amazonas State's helpful and trustworthy tourism authority in Manaus, Amazonastur is open weekdays 8–6. The Manaus tourism authority, Manaustur, is open weekdays 8–2. CAT (Centro de Atendimento ao Turista) in Manaus is an information center near the Teatro Amazonas with a desk in the airport and one in the Hidroviária. ATURMA is the official Marajó tourism organization.

🚩 **Amazonastur** ✉ Rua Saldanha Marinho 321, Centro ☎ 092/3233-1928 or 092/3233-1095 🌐 www.amazonastur.com. **CAT** ✉ Av. Eduardo Ribeiro 666, Centro ☎ 092/3622-0767. **Secretaria de Estado da Cultura e Turismo** ✉ Av. 7 de Setembro 1546, Centro ☎ 092/3633-2850, 092/3633-3041, or 092/3633-1357 🌐 www.culturamazonas.

am.gov.br. **Secretária de Turismo Presidente Figeuiredo** ✉ Rua Uatumã 321, Centro, Presidente Figeuiredo ☎ 092/3324-1158 ⊕ www.amazonastravel.com.br.

BRAZIL ESSENTIALS

Transportation

BY AIR

ARRIVING & DEPARTING Miami, Newark, New York, and Toronto are the major gateways for flights to Brazil from North America. Several airlines fly directly from London, but there's no direct service from Australia or New Zealand. At this writing, all flights to Brazil from North America and the United Kingdom connect through São Paulo.

The flying time from New York is 12 hours to Rio (with a stop in SP) and 10 hours to São Paulo. From Miami it's 8½ hours to Rio and 8 hours to São Paulo. Bear in mind that most flights to Rio or other Brazilian cities have stops, either in São Paulo or in Miami. If flying with a Brazilian airline, you might stop in Florianópolis, Brasília, or Porto Alegre before reaching Rio de Janeiro. Usually the connect time in São Paulo is 1 hour, 15 minutes. Most flights from Los Angeles go through Miami, and flight times are about 13 hours, not including layover in Miami (which can be 4–5 hours). From London it's 11 hours to São Paulo.

🛪 International Airlines **Air Canada** ☎ 888/712-7786 in North America, 11/3254-6600 in Brazil ⊕ www.aircanada.com. **Air New Zealand** ☎ 0800/737-000 in New Zealand, 11/3214-5588 in Brazil ⊕ www.airnz.co.nz. **American Airlines** ☎ 800/433-7300 in North America, 8457/789-789 in the U.K., 11/4502-4000 in Brazil ⊕ www.aa.com. **British Airways** ☎ 0870/850-9850 in the U.K., 11/3145-9700 in Brazil ⊕ www. britishairways.com. **Continental Airlines** ☎ 800/231-0856 in North America, 0845/607-6760 in the U.K., 0800/702-7500 in Brazil ⊕ www.continental.com. **Delta Airlines** ☎ 800/241-4141 in North America, 0800/221-121 in Brazil ⊕ www.delta.com. **Qantas** ☎ 13/13-13 in Australia, 9/357-8900 in Auckland, 0800/808-767 elsewhere in New Zealand, 11/3145-5090 in Brazil ⊕ www.qantas.com.au. **TAM** ☎ 888/235-9826 in the U.S., 118/903-4003 in the U.K., 0800/570-5700 and 4002-5700 in Brazil ⊕ www.tamairlines.com. **United Airlines** ☎ 800/864-8331 in the U.S., 845/8444-777 in the U.K., 0800/16-2323 in Brazil ⊕ www.united.com. **Varig** ☎ 800/468-2744 in the U.S., 870/120-3020 in the U.K., 11/4003-7000 in Brazil ⊕ www.varig.com.

GETTING AROUND There's regular jet service within the country between all major cities and most medium-size cities. Remote areas are also accessible—as long as you don't mind small planes. Flights can be long, lasting several hours for trips to the Amazon, with stops en route. The most widely used service is the Varig Ponte Aérea (Air Bridge), the Rio–São Paulo shuttle, which departs every half hour from 6 AM to 10:30 PM (service switches to every 15 minutes during morning and evening rush hours). Fares (one-way) for the Rio–São Paulo shuttle service vary from $40 (with BRA) to $170 (with TAM); reservations aren't necessary.

🛪 Domestic Airlines **BRA** ☎ 11/5090-9006 in Brazil ⊕ www.voebra.com.br. **Gol** ☎ 0300/789-2121 in Brazil ⊕ www.voegol.com.br. **TAM** ☎ 888/235-9826 in the U.S., 305/406-2826 in Miami, 118/903-4003 in the U.K., 0800/570-5700 in Brazil ⊕ www. tamairlines.com. **Varig** ☎ 800/468-2744 in the U.S., 870/120-3020 in the U.K., 11/

4003-7000 in Brazil ⊕ www.varig.com. **Trip Linhas Aéreas** ☎ 084/3644-1129 in Natal, 081/3464-4610 in Recife ⊕ www.airtrip.com.br. **WebJet Linhas Aéreas** ☎ 0800/722-1212 in Brazil ⊕ www.webjet.com.br.

AIR PASSES   Air passes from TAM or Varig can save you hundreds of dollars if you plan to travel a lot within Brazil. These can only be purchased outside Brazil. Varig's Brazil AirPass costs $560 for five coupons, which are valid for 21 days on flights to more than 100 cities within Brazil on Varig or its affiliates, Rio-Sul or Nordeste. You can buy up to four additional coupons (a total of nine) for $100 each. TAM's 21-day Brazilian Air-Pass costs $399 for four coupons, with additional coupons at $100 each.

If you plan to visit more than one of the Mercosur (Southern Common Market) countries—Argentina, Brazil, Paraguay, and Uruguay—the Mercosur Pass presents the greatest savings. It's valid on Aerolineas Argentinas, Varig, and several other carriers. You must visit at least two countries within a minimum of seven days and a maximum of 30 days. Pricing is based on mileage, ranging from $225 for flights totaling between 1,450 and 2,300 km (1,200 and 1,900 mi) to $870 for flights totaling more than 8,450 km (7,000 mi). Contact participating airlines or tour operators and travel agents who specialize in South American travel for information and purchase.

By Bus

The nation's *ônibus* (bus) network is affordable, comprehensive, and efficient—compensating for the lack of trains and the high cost of air travel. Every major city can be reached by bus, as can most small to medium-sized communities.

CLASSES   When buying a ticket, you will be asked whether you want the *ônibus convencional*, the simplest option; the *ônibus executive*, with air-conditioning, coffee and water, more space between seats, and a pillow and blanket; or the *leito*, where you have all facilities of an executive bus plus a seat that reclines completely. If you're over 5'10", buy the most expensive ticket available and try for front-row seats, where you will have more space.

By Car

Driving is chaotic in cities like São Paulo, but much easier in cities like Curitiba and Brasília. In the countryside the usually rough roads, lack of clearly marked signs, and language difference are discouraging for driving. Further, the cost of renting can be steep. All that said, certain areas are most enjoyable when explored on your own in a car: the beach areas of Búzios and the Costa Verde (near Rio) and the Belo Horizonte region; the North Shore beaches outside São Paulo; and many of the inland and coastal towns of the south, a region with many good roads.

DRIVING   PERMITS   You need an international driver's license if you plan to drive in Brazil. International driving permits (IDPs) are available from the American, Canadian, and New Zealand automobile associations; in the United Kingdom from the Automobile Association and Royal Automobile Club; and in Australia from the Royal Automobile Club or state-run automobile associations. These international permits, valid only in conjunction with your regular driver's license, are universally recognized.

🔝 **Major Agencies Avis** ☎ 800/331-1084 in the U.S., 800/879-2847 in Canada, 0870/606-0100 in the U.K., 02/9353-9000 in Australia, 09/526-2847 in New Zealand, 0800/19-8456 in Brazil ⊕ www.avis.com. **Budget** ☎ 800/472-3325 in the U.S., 800/268-8900 in Canada, 0870/156-5656 in the U.K, 1300/794-344 in Australia, 0800/283-438 in New Zealand, 11/2117-2000 in São Paulo, 0800/725-2000 elsewhere in Brazil ⊕ www.budget.com. **Hertz** ☎ 800/654-3001 in the U.S., 800/263-0600 in Canada, 0870/844-8844 in the U.K., 02/9669-2444 in Australia, 09/256-8690 in New Zealand, 0800/701-7300 in Brazil ⊕ www.hertz.com. **National Car Rental** ☎ 800/227-7368 in the U.S. and Canada, 0870/400-4581 in the U.K., 07/3854-1499 in Australia, 0800/800-115 in New Zealand, 0800/227-3876 in Brazil ⊕ www.nationalcar.com.

Contacts & Resources

PASSPORTS & VISAS

At this writing, passports and visas are required for citizens—even infants—of the U.S., Canada, and Australia for entry to Brazil. U.K. and New Zealand citizens need only a passport. Business travelers may need a special business visa.

VISAS Visas are required for U.S., Canadian, and Australian citizens. **Go to the Web site for the Brazilian embassy or consulate nearest you for the most up to date information.** At this writing, tourist visa fees are US$100 for Americans, C$72 for Canadians, and A$90 for Australians. Additional fees may be levied if you apply by mail. Obtaining a visa can be a slow process, and you must have every bit of paperwork in order when you visit the consulate, so read instructions carefully. (For example, in the U.S., the fee can only be paid by a U.S. Postal Service money order.)

To get the location of the Brazilian consulate to which you must apply, contact the Brazilian embassy. Note that some consulates don't allow you to apply for a visa by mail. If you don't live near a city with a consulate, consider hiring a concierge-type service to do your legwork. Many cities have these companies, which not only help with the paperwork, but also send someone to wait in line for you.

TOURS & PACKAGES

Because everything is prearranged on a prepackaged tour or independent vacation, you spend less time planning—and often get it all at a good price. Don't confuse packages and guided tours. When you buy a package, you travel on your own, just as though you had planned the trip yourself.

For information on specific packages and tours, *see* the Adventure & Learning Vacations chapter *at* the end of this book.

🔝 **Tour-Operator Recommendations American Society of Travel Agents** (⇨ Travel Agencies). **CrossSphere—The Global Association for Packaged Travel** ✉ 546 E. Main St., Lexington, KY 40508 ☎ 859/226-4444 or 800/682-8886 ⊕ www.CrossSphere.com. **United States Tour Operators Association** (USTOA) ✉ 275 Madison Ave., Suite 2014, New York, NY 10016 ☎ 212/599-6599 ⊕ www.ustoa.com.

TRAIN TRAVEL

Brazil has an outdated and insufficient rail network, the smallest of any of the world's large nations. Although there are commuter rails to destinations around major cities, don't plan on taking passenger trains between major cities. There's one exception: the Serra Verde Express from Curitiba to Paranaguá—in the southern state of Paraná—is a fabulous ride with spectacular vistas of ravines, mountains, and waterfalls from bridges and viaducts.

TRAVEL AGENCIES

A good travel agent puts your needs first. Look for an agency that has been in business at least five years, emphasizes customer service, and has someone on staff who specializes in your destination. In addition, **make sure the agency belongs to a professional trade organization.** The American Society of Travel Agents (ASTA) has more than 10,000 members in some 140 countries, enforces a strict code of ethics, and will step in to mediate agent-client disputes involving ASTA members. ASTA also maintains a directory of agents on its Web site; ASTA's ⊕ TravelSense. org, a trip planning and travel advice site, can also help to locate a travel agent who caters to your needs. (If a travel agency is also acting as your tour operator, *see* Buyer Beware *in* Tours & Packages.)

Make sure your travel agent knows the accommodations and other services of the place being recommended. Ask about the hotel's location, room size, beds, and whether it has a pool, room service, or programs for children, if you care about these. Has your agent been there in person or sent others whom you can contact?

🖪 Local Agent Referrals **American Society of Travel Agents** (ASTA) ⊠ 1101 King St., Suite 200, Alexandria, VA 22314 ☎ 703/739-2782 or 800/965-2782 24-hr hotline ⊕ www.astanet.com and www.travelsense.org. **Association of British Travel Agents** ⊠ 68-71 Newman St., London W1T 3AH ☎ 020/7637-2444 ⊕ www.abta.com. **Association of Canadian Travel Agencies** ⊠ 130 Albert St., Suite 1705, Ottawa, Ontario K1P 5G4 ☎ 613/237-3657 ⊕ www.acta.ca. **Australian Federation of Travel Agents** ⊠ Level 3, 309 Pitt St., Sydney, NSW 2000 ☎ 02/9264-3299 or 1300/363-416 ⊕ www.afta.com. au. **Travel Agents' Association of New Zealand** ⊠ Level 5, Tourism and Travel House, 79 Boulcott St., Box 1888, Wellington 6001 ☎ 04/499-0104 ⊕ www.taanz.org.nz.

VISITOR INFORMATION

EMBRATUR, Brazil's national tourism organization, doesn't have offices overseas, though its Web site www.braziltour.com is helpful. For information in your home country, contact the Brazilian embassy or the closest consulate (⇨ Visas, *in* Passports & Visas, *above*)—some of which have Web sites and staff dedicated to promoting tourism. Cities and towns throughout Brazil have local tourist boards, and some state capitals also have state tourism offices.

Chile

WORD OF MOUTH

"My husband and I spent a few days in Santiago in February and found the city to be very inviting. There's a definite Latin flavor to it, and it has charming neighborhoods to explore. But beware of the strength of the summer sun, even at 6 PM!"

—cordon

"I love Chile and Chileans, too. The best spots are far away from Santiago, in the south."

—santiagov

I LIVE NOW IN A COUNTRY AS SOFT as the autumnal flesh of grapes," begins "Country," a poem by Pablo Neruda. With his odes to the place of his birth, the Nobel Prize winner sang Chile into being and taught us to inhale the bouquet of its salty breezes and its soaring Andean peaks before we hold them to our lips and drink them down.

Chile is as luminous and pungent, as rustic and romantic, as any of Neruda's poems describing it. It encompasses a bone-dry desert that blooms in a riot of color once or twice a decade, sprawling glaciers that bellow like thunder, and snow-covered volcanoes that perpetually smolder—all in one sliver of land squeezed between the Andes and the Pacific Ocean. In some places the 320-km (200-mi) territorial limit is wider than the country itself, making Chile as much water as earth.

In the decade since General Pinochet's fall from power tourism has steadily increased. Chile's beaches draw sun-worshipers from all over South America, and its towering volcanoes and roaring rivers draw adventure travelers from around the world. Fishing aficionados head south to the Lake District, while armchair archaeologists are attracted to the 5,000-year-old mummies of the Atacama.

As might be expected in a country with a coastline stretching 6,435 km (3,999 mi), many parts of Chile are inaccessible by land. Because of the unusual topography, highways simply end when they reach fjords or ice fields. You'll need to take a ship to see the mammoth glacier in the heart of Parque Nacional Laguna San Rafael. A ferry ride is necessary to visit Chiloé, an archipelago where you'll find charming wooden churches built by missionaries. Today Chile is one of the most popular destinations in South America. It doesn't hurt that the country also has one of the continent's most stable economies.

Exploring Chile

When Chileans joke that the creator made their nation of the universe's leftovers, they are only partly in jest. Chile has some spectacular anomalies: the looming Andes impose the country's eastern boundaries, stretching from the desolate Atacama Desert to the icy fjords of Patagonia. Here you'll find the granite peaks of Parque Nacional Torres del Paine, one of the continent's natural wonders.

Restaurants & Cuisine

Kissing her shores from tip to toe, the Pacific Ocean is the breadbasket of Chile's cuisine, proffering delicacies like the conger eel, sea bass, king crab, and *locos* (abalone the size of fat clams). Awaken your palate with a seafood appetizer, such as *choritos al vapor* (mussels steamed in white wine), *machas a la parmesana* (similar to razor clams but unique to Chile, grilled with tomatoes and Parmesan cheese), or *chupo de centolla* (king crab). Simply seasoned grilled fish is a Chilean favorite, usually garnished with steamed potatoes or an *ensalada a la chilena* (peeled tomatoes with onions marinated in brine to reduce their acidic flavor).

But the Pacific isn't Chile's only answer to fine dining—many simple country dishes are among the best offerings. *Cazuela,* a superb soup that

TOP REASONS TO GO

Contemplating Nature. Norway has fjords. Bavaria has forests. Nepal has mountains. Arizona has deserts. Chile offers all these and more. El Norte Grande's Atacama Desert is the Earth's most arid spot: no measurable precipitation has ever been recorded there. The region's Cerros Pintados form the world's largest group of geoglyphs. Perpetually smoldering Volcán Villarrica in the Lake District is one of the planet's most active volcanoes. And no photo can ever do justice to the ash-gray, glacier-molded spires of Patagonia's Torres del Paine.

Hitting the Slopes. The runs at Vail and Grenoble are closed for the season? Never fear. Since Chile's seasons are the opposite of those of North America, you can ski or snowboard from June to September. Many top resorts, such as La Parva, Valle Nevado, and Portillo, are an easy drive from the capital. Locals often head out in the morning and are back in the city in time for dinner. With the top elevations at most ski areas extending to 3,300 meters (10,825 feet), you can expect long runs and deep, dry snow.

Basking on Beaches. Thousands of Santiaguinos flock to the Central Coast's beaches every summer. To serve the hungry masses are dozens and dozens of seafood shacks, all serving freshly caught fish. The Humboldt Current, which flows northward along the coast of Chile, carries cold water to the Central Coast. If you plan to surf or skin-dive, you need a wet suit; if you plan to swim, you need thick skin. Pristine sands swath the shoreline near Arica and Iquique. During the summer months of January and February they're packed with vacationing South Americans. Outside of these months, you just might have the beach to yourself.

Getting the Goods. Shop for fine woolen items, expertly carved figurines, lapis lazuli jewelry, hand-tooled leather items, Andean textiles, and other handicrafts. Santiago, Valparaíso, and Viña del Mar have everything from large department stores and outlet malls to trendy shops and boutiques. There and elsewhere you can also browse in *mercados* (markets) and *ferias artesanales* (artisan fairs). Though bargaining is acceptable, it's less common than in other parts of South America.

Feasting. From the ocean come conger eel, sea bass, king crab, and *locos* (abalone the size of fat clams). European immigrants brought with them a love for robust country cooking; look for such simple fare as *cazuela*, a stew of meat, potatoes, and corn on the cob; *porotos granados*, a thick bean, corn, and squash stew; and *humitas*, ground corn seasoned and steamed in its own husk. At markets, vendors woo you with *pastel de choclo*—a corn pie that usually contains ground beef, chicken, and seasonings—as well as empanadas, pastries stuffed with meat or cheese. Chileans are also masters of the *parrillada*, a method of grilling over hot coals. Not just steak gets grilled: restaurants prepare chicken, fish, seafood, burgers, sausage potatoes, corn, and vegetables parrillada-style, too.

4

Chile (North)

PERU

Arica

Iquique

EL NORTE GRANDE

Calama

San Pedro de Atacama

Antofagasta

BOLIVIA

Pan American Hwy.

PACIFIC OCEAN

EL NORTE CHICO

ARGENTINA

Copiapó

Vallenar

La Serena

Ovalle

Zapallar

Viña del Mar

Valparaíso

Santiago

Rancagua

Curicó

Talca

← TO EASTER ISLAND

Concepción

Chillán

Temuco

Pan American Hwy.

Valdivia

0 ___ 100 miles
0 ___ 150 km

Chile (South)

Valparaíso

Santiago

THE CENTRAL VALLEY

Concepción

Temuco

Villarrica

Pucón

Valdivia

The Lake District

Osorno

Puerto Varas

Puerto Montt

Castro

Isla de Chiloé

ARGENTINA

THE SOUTHERN COAST

Coihaique

Cochrane

PACIFIC OCEAN

Torres del Paine National Park

Puerto Natales

Estrecho de Magallanes

Punta Arenas

Tierra del Fuego

Penguin Island

0 ___ 100 miles
0 ___ 150 km

includes a piece of meat (beef, pork, chicken, or turkey, usually on the bone), potatoes, and corn on the cob in a thick broth, is a meal in itself. In summer, *porotos granados,* a thick bean, corn, and squash soup, is all the rage, as are *humitas,* ground corn seasoned and steamed in its own husk. At markets all over the country you'll be wooed by women selling the ubiquitous *pastel de choclo,* a cornmeal pastry pie that usually contains ground beef, a piece of chicken, and seasonings.

	WHAT IT COSTS In pesos (in thousands)				
	$$$$	$$$	$$	$	¢
AT DINNER	over 11	8–11	5–8	2.5–5	under 2.5

Prices are for a main course at dinner.

About the Hotels

Power and wealth have historically orbited around Chile's capital—Santiago—so it has a wide range of luxury lodging options. In sluggish response to increased tourism, however, new hotels have sprung up in the provinces. In the more heavily touristed areas you'll find cozy wooden cabins, hot-springs retreats, and elaborate hotels richly adorned in Patagonian hardwoods. The always homey and hospitable *residenciales* (bed-and-breakfasts) are found everywhere.

Traditionally, *hotel* referred to upscale accommodations; *hostería* and *hostal* denoted something more basic. Those distinctions have blurred, and there are some pretty snazzy hosterías and hostales to be found. A lodging that calls itself a *hospedaje* means your room will be in a private home. A *cabaña* is any type of lodging with detached cabin units, while a *refugio,* often found in national parks, has bunks and little else.

	WHAT IT COSTS In pesos (in thousands)				
	$$$$	$$$	$$	$	¢
FOR 2 PEOPLE	over 105	75–105	45–75	15–45	under 15

Prices are for a double room in high season, excluding tax.

When to Go

Chile's seasons are the reverse of North America's—that is, June–August is Chile's winter. Tourism peaks during the hot summer months of January and February, except in Santiago, which tends to empty as most Santiaguinos take their summer holiday. Though prices are at their highest, it's worth braving the summer heat if you're interested in lying on the beach or enjoying the many concerts, folklore festivals, and outdoor theater performances offered during this period.

CLIMATE If you're heading to the Lake District or Patagonia and want good weather without the crowds, the shoulder seasons of December and March are the months to visit. The best time to see the Atacama Desert is late spring, preferably in November, when temperatures are bearable and air clarity is at its peak. In spring Santiago blooms, and the fragrance of the flowers distracts even the most avid workaholic. A second tourist season occurs in the winter, as skiers flock to Chile's mountaintops for some of the world's best skiing, available at the height of northern summers. Winter smog is a good reason to stay away from Santiago during July and August, unless you're coming for a ski holiday and won't be spending much time in the city.

The following are the average daily maximum and minimum temperatures for Santiago.

Jan.	85F	29C	May	65F	18C	Sept.	66F	19C
	53	12		41	5		42	6
Feb.	84F	29C	June	58F	14C	Oct.	72F	22C
	52	11		37	3		45	7
Mar.	80F	27C	July	59F	15C	Nov.	78F	26C
	49	9		37	3		48	9
Apr.	74F	23C	Aug.	62F	17C	Dec.	83F	28C
	54	7		39	4		51	11

The following are the average daily maximum and minimum temperatures for Punta Arenas.

Jan.	58F	14C	May	45F	7C	Sept.	46F	8C
	45	7		35	2		35	2
Feb.	58F	14C	June	41F	5C	Oct.	51F	11C
	44	7		33	1		38	3
Mar.	54F	12C	July	40F	4C	Nov.	54F	12C
	41	5		31	0		40	4
Apr.	50F	10C	Aug.	42F	6C	Dec.	57F	14C
	39	4		33	1		43	6

HOLIDAYS New Year's Day (Jan. 1), Labor Day (May 1), Day of Naval Glories (May 21), Corpus Christi (in June), Feast of St. Peter and St. Paul (June 29), Independence Celebrations (Sept. 18), Discovery of the Americas (Oct. 12), Day of the Dead (Nov. 1), Immaculate Conception (Dec. 8), Christmas (Dec. 25).

Many shops and services are open on most of these days, but transportation is always heavily booked up on and around the holidays. The two most important dates in the Chilean calendar are September 18 and New Year's Day. On these days shops close and public transportation is reduced to the bare minimum or is nonexistent. Trying to book a ticket around these dates will be impossible unless you do it well in advance.

FESTIVALS **Semana Santa**, or Holy Week, is popular all over Chile. Different events are held each day between Palm Sunday and Easter Sunday. In Valparaíso, colorful processions mark the **Día de San Pedro** (St. Peter's Day) on June 29. In November the Chilean wine industry hosts the **Feria International de Vino del Hemisferio** Sur in Santiago.

The **Festival Foclórico** (Folklore Festival) is held in Santiago during the fourth week of January. The Lake District town of Villarrica hosts the **Muestra Cultural Mapuche** (Mapuche Cultural Show) from January 3 to February 28. The annual **Festival Internacional de la Canción** (International Song Festival) takes place over a week in mid-February in Viña del Mar. February 9 is the beginning of the two-month-long **Verano en Valdivia**, a favorite celebration for those living in the Lake District.

Language

Chile's official language is Spanish, so it's best to learn at least a few words and carry a good phrase book. Chilean Spanish is fast, clipped, and chock-full of colloquialisms. For example, the word for police officer isn't *policía*, but *carabinero*. Even foreigners with a good deal of experience in Spanish-speaking countries may feel like they are encountering a completely new language. However, receptionists at most upscale hotels speak English.

SANTIAGO

Updated by
Mark Sullivan

When it was founded by Spanish conquistador Pedro de Valdivia in 1541, Santiago was little more than the triangular patch of land embraced by two arms of the Río Mapocho. Today that area, known as Santiago Centro, is just one of 32 *comunas* that make up the city, each with its own distinct personality. Santiago is home to more than 6 million people—nearly a third of the country's total population. Yet in many ways Santiago still feels like a small town, where residents may well bump into an acquaintance along the city center's streets and in its plazas.

Exploring Santiago

Much of Santiago, especially communities such as Bellavista, Providencia, and the Centro, is best explored on foot. The subway is the quickest, cleanest, and most economical way to shuttle between neighborhoods. To travel to more distant neighborhoods, or to get anywhere in the evening after the subway closes, you'll probably want to hail a taxi.

Santiago Centro

Santiago Centro is the place to start if you really want to take the pulse of the city. You'll find interesting museums, imposing government buildings, and bustling commercial streets. But don't think you'll be lost in a sprawling area—it takes only about 10 minutes to walk from one edge of the neighborhood to the other.

WHAT TO SEE
6

Casa Colorada. The appropriately named Red House is one of the best-preserved colonial structures in the city. Mateo de Toro y Zambrano, Santiago's most prosperous businessman of the 18th century, once made his home here. The building today houses the Museo de Santiago, a modest but informative museum that makes an excellent place to dive into the city's history. There are several dioramas, some of them life-size, depicting life in the colonial period. For an explanation of the exhibits, ask for an English guidebook. ⊠ *Merced 860, Santiago Centro* ☎ *2/*

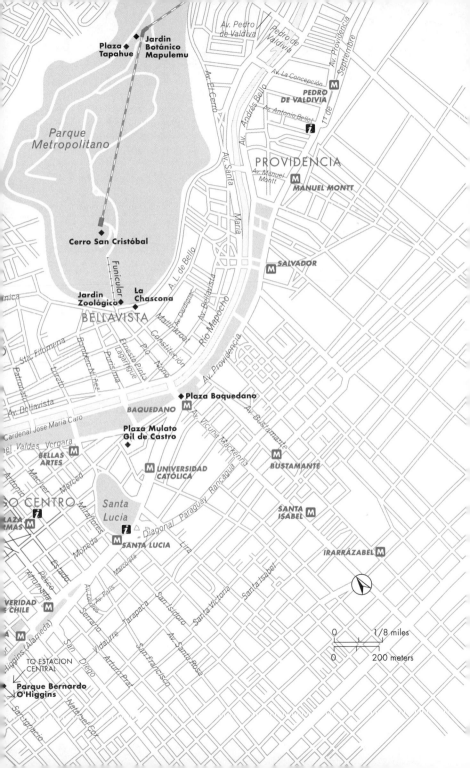

633–0723 ✉ *Tues.–Sat. 500 pesos, Sun. free* ☉ *Tues.–Fri. 10–5:45, Sat. 10–4:45, Sun. 11–2* Ⓜ *Plaza de Armas.*

⑤ Catedral. Conquistador Pedro de Valdivia declared in 1541 that a house of worship would be constructed at this site bordering the Plaza de Armas. The first adobe building burned to the ground, and the structures that replaced it were destroyed by the earthquakes of 1647 and 1730. The finishing touches of the neoclassical cathedral standing today were added in 1789 by Italian architect Joaquín Toesca. Be sure to see the stunning interior—a line of gilt arches topped by stained-glass windows parades down the long nave. ✉ *Plaza de Armas, Santiago Centro* ☎ 2/ 696–2777 ☉ *Daily 9–7* Ⓜ *Plaza de Armas.*

③ Correo Central. Housed in what was once the ornate Palacio de los Gobernadores, this building dating from 1715 is one of the most beautiful post offices you are likely to see. It was reconstructed by Ricardo Brown in 1882 after being ravaged by fire and is a fine example of neoclassical architecture. ✉ *Catedral and Paseo Ahumada, Santiago Centro* ☎ 2/698–7274 ⊕ *www.correos.cl* ☉ *Weekdays 8:30–7, Sat. 8:30–2* Ⓜ *Plaza de Armas.*

⑨ Ex Congreso Nacional. Once the meeting place for the National Congress (the legislature moved to Valparaíso in 1990), this palatial neoclassical building now houses the offices of the Ministry of Foreign Affairs. The original structure on the site, the Iglesia de la Compañía de Jesús, was destroyed by a fire in 1863 in which 2,000 people perished. Inside the peaceful gated gardens is a monument commemorating the victims. ✉ *Bandera 345, at Morandé, Santiago Centro* Ⓜ *Plaza de Armas.*

④ Municipalidad de Santiago. Today's governmental center for Santiago can be found on the site of the colonial city hall and jail. The original structure, built in 1552, survived until a devastating earthquake in 1730. Joaquín Toesca, the architect who also designed the presidential palace and completed the cathedral, reconstructed the building in 1785, but it was destroyed by fire a century later. In 1891, Eugenio Joannon, who favored an Italian Renaissance style, erected the structure standing today. On the facade hangs an elaborate coat of arms presented by Spain. The interior is not open to the public. ✉ *Plaza de Armas, Santiago Centro* Ⓜ *Plaza de Armas.*

Fodor'sChoice
★

⑦ Museo Chileno de Arte Precolombino. If you plan to visit only one museum in Santiago, it should be the Museum of Pre-Columbian Art, a block from the Plaza de Armas. The well-endowed collection of artifacts of the region's indigenous peoples, much of it donated by the family of collector Sergio García-Moreno, is displayed in the beautifully restored Royal Customs House that dates from 1807. The permanent collection, on the upper floor, showcases textiles and ceramics from Mexico to Patagonia. Unlike those of many of the city's museums, the displays here are well labeled in Spanish and English. One of the pair of gorgeous courtyards has a sunny café, making this a good place to recharge your batteries. ✉ *Bandera 361, at Av. Compañía, Santiago Centro* ☎ 2/688– 7348 ⊕ *www.museoprecolombino.cl* ✉ *Tues.–Sat. 2,000 pesos, Sun. free* ☉ *Tues.–Sun. 10–6* Ⓜ *Plaza de Armas.*

2 Museo Histórico Nacional. The colonial-era Palacio de la Real Audiencia served as the meeting place of Chile's first Congress in September 1810. The building then functioned as a telegraph office before the museum moved here in 1911. It's worth the small admission charge to see the interior of the 200-year-old structure, where exhibits tracing Chile's history are arranged chronologically in rooms centered around a courtyard. Among the exhibits are large collections of coins, stamps, and traditional handicrafts, including more than 3,000 examples of native textiles. ⊠ *Plaza de Armas, Santiago Centro* ☎ *2/633–1815* ⊕ *www. museohistoriconacional.cl* ⊠ *Tues.–Sat. 600 pesos, Sun. free* ☉ *Tues.–Sun. 10–5:30* Ⓜ *Plaza de Armas.*

8 Palacio de los Tribunales de Justicia. During Augusto Pinochet's rule, human-rights demonstrations were held outside the Courts of Justice, which house the country's Supreme Court. Protests are still held near this stately neoclassical building a block from the Plaza de Armas, including some in support of the former dictator. In front of the building, perhaps ironically, is a monument to justice and the promulgation of Chile's civil code. ⊠ *Bandera 344, Santiago Centro* Ⓜ *Plaza de Armas.*

★ 1 Plaza de Armas. This square has been the symbolic heart of Chile—as well as its political, social, religious, and commercial center—since Pedro de Valdivia established the city on this spot in 1541. The Palacio de los Gobernadores, the Palacio de la Real Audiencia, and the Municipalidad de Santiago front the square's northern edge. The dignified Catedral graces the western side of the square. Among the palm trees are distinctive fountains and gardens. Also here is a bronze well that once served as the city's main source of water. On any given day the plaza teems with life—vendors selling religious icons, artists painting the activity around them, street performers juggling fire, and tourists clutching guidebooks. In the southern corner of the plaza you can watch people playing chess. ⊠ *Compañía at Estado, Santiago Centro* Ⓜ *Plaza de Armas.*

La Alameda

Avenida Libertador Bernardo O'Higgins, more frequently called La Alameda, is the city's principal thoroughfare. Along with the Avenida Norte Sur and the Río Mapocho, it forms the wedge that defines the city's historic district.

WHAT TO SEE **Barrio París-Londres.** Many architects contributed to what is frequently
14 referred to as Santiago's Little Europe, among them Alamos, Larraín, and Mönckeberg. The string of small mansion houses lining the cobbled streets of Calles París and Londres sprang up in the mid-1920s on the vegetable patches and gardens that once belonged to the convent adjoining Iglesia San Francisco. ⊠ *Londres at París, La Alameda.*

18 Biblioteca Nacional. Near the foot of Cerro Santa Lucía is the block-long classical facade of the National Library. With more than 3 million titles, this is one of the largest libraries in South America. The second-floor Sala José Toribio Medina, which holds the most important collection of prints by native peoples in Latin America, is well worth a look. ⊠ *La Alameda 651, La Alameda* ☎ *2/360–5200* ⊕ *www.dibam.cl* ⊠ *Free* ☉ *Weekdays 9–6, Sat. 9–2* Ⓜ *Santa Lucía.*

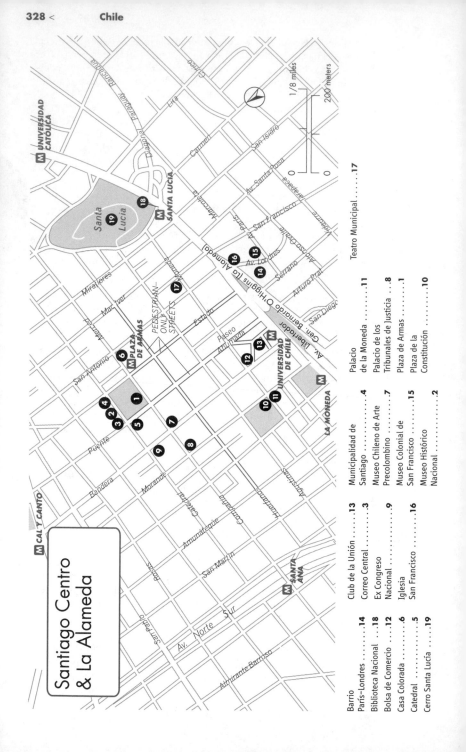

Santiago Centro & La Alameda

⑫ Bolsa de Comercio. Chile's stock exchange is housed in a 1917 French neoclassical structure with an elegant clock tower surmounted by an arched slate cupola. Weekdays you can watch the shouting of traders in the three buying and selling circles called *redondeles.* ✉ *La Bolsa 64, La Alameda* ☎ *2/399–3000* ⊕ *www.bolsadesantiago.com* ✍ *Free* ⊙ *Weekdays noon–1:20 and 4–4:30* Ⓜ *Universidad de Chile.*

⑲ Cerro Santa Lucía. The mazelike park of St. Lucía is a hangout for souvenir vendors, park-bench smoochers, and photo-snapping tourists. Walking uphill along the labyrinth of paths and plazas takes about 30 minutes. An elevator two blocks north of the park's main entrance is a little faster, but its schedule is erratic. The crow's nest, reached via a series of steep and slippery stone steps, affords a 360-degree city view. Be careful near dusk, as the park also attracts the occasional mugger. ✉ *Santa Lucía and La Alameda, La Alameda* ☎ *No phone* ⊙ *Oct.–Mar., daily 9–6.30; Apr.–Sept., daily 7–8* Ⓜ *Santa Lucía.*

⑬ Club de la Unión. The facade of this neoclassical building, dating to 1925, is one of the city's finest. The interior of this private club, whose roster has included numerous Chilean presidents, is open only to members. ✉ *La Alameda at Bandera, La Alameda* Ⓜ *Universidad de Chile.*

⑯ Iglesia San Francisco. Santiago's oldest structure, greatest symbol, and principal landmark, the Church of St. Francis is the last trace of 16th-century colonial architecture in the city. Construction began in 1586, and although the church survived successive earthquakes, early tremors took their toll and portions had to be rebuilt in 1698. Today's neoclassical tower, which forms the city's most recognizable silhouette, was added in 1857 by architect Fermín Vivaceta. Inside are rough stone-and-brick walls, marble columns, and ornate coffered wood ceilings. Visible on the main altar is the image of the Virgen del Socorro (Virgin of Assistance) that conquistador Pedro de Valdivia carried for protection and guidance. ✉ *La Alameda 834, La Alameda* ☎ *2/638–3238* ⊙ *Daily 7 AM–8 PM* Ⓜ *Santa Lucía, Universidad de Chile.*

⑮ Museo Colonial de San Francisco. This gloomy former convent, adjacent to Iglesia San Francisco, houses the best collection of 17th-century colonial paintings on the continent. Inside the rooms wrapping around an overgrown courtyard are 54 large-scale canvases portraying the life of St. Francis (don't miss the huge painting of his religious order's "family tree"), as well as a plethora of religious iconography ranging from tiny paintings of the Virgin Mary to life-size carvings of Christ. Most pieces are labeled in Spanish and English. ✉ *Londres 4, La Alameda* ☎ *2/639–8737* ✍ *1,000 pesos* ⊙ *Tues.–Sat. 10–1:30 and 3–6, Sun. 10–2* Ⓜ *Santa Lucía, Universidad de Chile.*

⑪ Palacio de la Moneda. Originally the royal mint, this sober neoclassical edifice built by Joaquín Toesca in 1805 became the presidential palace in 1846 and served that purpose for more than a century. It was bombarded by the military in the 1973 coup, when Salvador Allende defended his presidency against the assault of General Augusto Pinochet. Allende's death is still shrouded in mystery—some say he went down fighting, others claim he took his own life before the future dictator entered the palace in triumph. The two central courtyards are open to the public, and tours of the interior can be arranged at the reception desk. ⊠ *Plaza de la Constitución, Moneda between Teatinos and Morandé, La Alameda* ☎ *2/690–4000* ⊙ *Daily 10–6* Ⓜ *La Moneda.*

★ **⑩ Plaza de la Constitución.** The Palacio de la Moneda and other government buildings line Constitution Square, the country's most formal plaza. The changing of the guard takes place every other day at 10 AM within the triangle defined by 12 Chilean flags. Adorning the plaza are three monuments, each dedicated to a notable national figure: Diego Portales, founder of the Chilean republic; Jorge Alessandri, the country's leader from 1958 to 1964; and Don Eduardo Frei, president from 1964 to 1970. The plaza also serves as the roof of the underground bunker Pinochet had installed when he "redecorated" La Moneda. Pillars in each of the four corners of the square serve as ventilation ducts for the bunker, which is now a parking lot. Locals joke that these monoliths represent the four founding members of the military junta—they're made of stone, full of hot air, and no one knows their real function. One pillar has been converted into a memorial honoring President Salvador Allende. ⊠ *Moneda at Morande, La Alameda* Ⓜ *La Moneda.*

⑰ Teatro Municipal. The opulent Municipal Theater is the city's cultural center, with performances of opera, ballet, and classical music from April to November. Originally built in 1857, with major renovations in 1870 and 1906 following a fire and an earthquake, the Renaissance-style building is one of the city's most refined monuments. The lavish interior deserves a visit. Tours can be arranged with a week's notice. ⊠ *Plaza Alcade Mekis, Av. Agustinas 794, at Av. San Antonio, La Alameda* ☎ *2/463–8888* Ⓜ *Universidad de Chile, Santa Lucía.*

Parque Forestal

After building a canal in 1891 to tame the unpredictable Río Mapocho, Santiago found itself with a thin strip of land that it didn't quite know what to do with. The area quickly filled with the city's refuse. A decade later, under the watchful eye of Enrique Cousiño, it was transformed into the enormously popular Forest Park.

WHAT TO SEE **Estación Mapocho.** This mighty edifice, with its trio of two-story arches
⑳ ★ framed by intricate terra-cotta detailing, is as elegant as any train station in the world. The station was inaugurated in 1913 as a terminus for trains arriving from Valparaíso and points north, but steam engines no longer pull in here. A major conversion transformed the structure into one of the city's principal cultural centers. The Centro Cultural Estación Mapocho houses two restaurants, a fine bookstore and café, a large exhibition hall and arts space, and a handicrafts shop. The cavernous space that once sheltered steam engines now hosts musical performances and other events. ⊠ *Plaza de la Cultura, Independencia at Balmaceda, Parque Forestal* ☎ *2/361–1761* ⊕ *www.estacionmapocho. cl* ⊙ *Daily 9–6* Ⓜ *Puente Cal y Canto.*

㉑ Mercado Central. At the Central Market you'll find a matchless selection of creatures from the sea. Depending on the season, you might see the

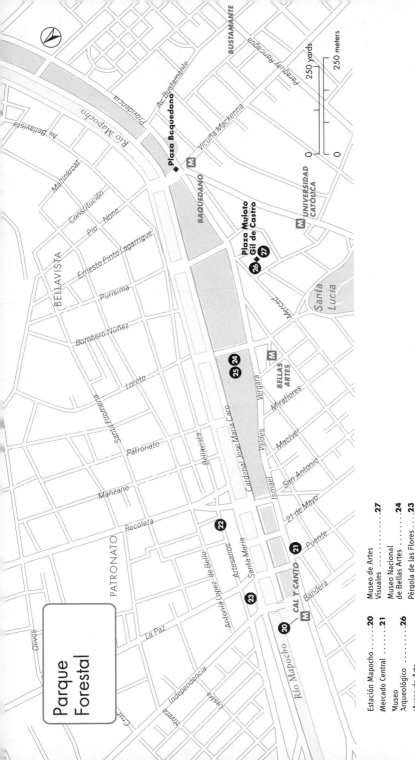

Parque Forestal

delicate beaks of *picorocos,* the world's only edible barnacles; *erizos,* the prickly shelled sea urchins; or shadowy pails full of succulent bullfrogs. If the fish don't capture your interest, the architecture may: the lofty wrought-iron ceiling of the structure, reminiscent of a Victorian train station, was prefabricated in England and erected in Santiago between 1868 and 1872. ✉ *Ismael*

> **MARKET MUNCHIES**
>
> Diners are regaled by musicians in the middle of the market, where two restaurants compete for customers. You can also find a cheap, filling meal at a stand along the market's southern edge.

Valdés Vergara 900, Parque Forestal ☎ *2/696–8327* ☉ *Mon.–Thurs. 5–5, Fri. 5–9, Sat. 5–7, Sun. 5–6* Ⓜ *Puente Cal y Canto.*

㉖ **Museo Arqueológico de Santiago.** This little museum is devoted specifically to the indigenous peoples of Chile. Some 3,000 artifacts bring the country's Mapuche, Aymara, Fueguino, Huilliche, and Pehuenche cultures vividly to life. It's in the Museo de Artes Visuales. ✉ *José Victorino Lastarria 307, 2nd fl., Parque Forestal* ☎ *2/664–9337* ⊕ *www.mavi. cl* ✂ *1,000 pesos (includes Museo de Artes Visuales); Sun. free* ☉ *Tues.–Sun. 10:30–6:30* Ⓜ *Baquedano, Universidad Católica.*

㉕ **Museo de Arte Contemporáneo.** After an ambitious restoration effort, the elegant Museum of Contemporary Art no longer has its rather dilapidated interior. On the opposite side of the building housing the Museo de Bellas Artes, the museum showcases a collection of modern Latin American paintings, photography, and sculpture. The museum is run by the art school of the Universidad de Chile, so it isn't afraid to take risks. Look for Fernando Botero's pudgy *Caballo* sculpture gracing the square out front. ✉ *Bounded by Jose M. de la Barra and Ismael Valdés Vergara, Parque Forestal* ☎ *2/639–6488* ⊕ *www.mac.uchile.cl* ✂ *500 pesos* ☉ *Tues.–Sat. 11–7, Sun. 11–5* Ⓜ *Bellas Artes.*

★ ㉗ **Museo de Artes Visuales.** Displaying the combined private holdings of Chilean construction moguls Manuel Santa Cruz and Hugo Yaconi, this gallery has a fine collection of contemporary Chilean art. The building itself is a masterpiece: six gallery levels float into each other in surprising ways. The wood floors and Plexiglas-sided stairways create an airy space for paintings and sculptures. ✉ *José Victorino Lastarria 307, Plaza Mulato Gil de Castro, Parque Forestal* ☎ *2/638–3502* ⊕ *www.mavi. cl* ✂ *1,000 pesos (includes Museo Arqueológico de Santiago), Sun. free* ☉ *Tues.–Sun. 10:30–6:30* Ⓜ *Bellas Artes.*

㉔ **Museo Nacional de Bellas Artes.** Paintings, drawings, and sculpture by 16th- to 20th-century Chilean and European artists fill the grand National Museum of Fine Arts. The elegant, neoclassical building, which was originally intended to house the city's school of fine arts, has an impressive glass-domed ceiling that illuminates the main hall. A theater on the second floor screens short films about the featured artists. ✉ *Bounded by Jose M. de la Barra and Ismael Valdés Vergara, Parque Forestal* ☎ *2/633–0655* ⊕ *www.dibam.cl* ✂ *Tues.–Sat. 600 pesos, Sun. free* ☉ *Tues.–Sun. 10–7* Ⓜ *Bellas Artes.*

㉓ Pérgola de las Flores. Santiaguinos come to the Trellis of Flowers to buy wreaths and flower arrangements to bring to the city's two cemeteries. *La Pérgola de las Flores*, a famous Chilean musical, is based on the conflict that arose in the 1930s when the mayor of Santiago wanted to shut down the market. Find a chatty florist at one of the two open-air markets—Pégola San Francisco and Pérgola Santa María—and you may learn all about it. ⊠ *Av. La Paz at Artesanos, Recoleta* ☎ *No phone* ⊙ *Daily sunrise–sunset* Ⓜ *Puente Cal y Canto.*

㉒ Vega Chica and Vega Central. From fruit to furniture, meat to machinery, these lively markets stock just about anything you can name. Alongside the ordinary items you can find delicacies like *piñones*, giant pine nuts found on monkey puzzle trees. ⊠ *Antonia López de Bello between Av. Salas and Av. Gandarillas, Recoleta* Ⓜ *Puente Cal y Canto.*

> **CHEAP EATS**
>
> If you're undaunted by crowds, try a typical Chilean meal in a closet-size eatery or picada. Chow down with the locals on *pastel de choclo*, a pie filled with ground beef, chicken, olives, and boiled eggs and topped with mashed corn.

Bellavista & Parque Metropolitano

If you happen to be in Santiago on one of the rare days when the smog dissipates, head straight for Parque Metropolitano. In the center is Cerro San Cristóbal, a hill reached via cable car or funicular. A journey to the top of the hill rewards you with spectacular views in all directions. In the shadow of Cerro San Cristóbal is Bellavista. The neighborhood has but one sight—the poet Pablo Neruda's hillside home of La Chascona—but it's perhaps the city's best place to wander. You're sure to discover interesting antiques shops, bustling outdoor markets, and adventurous and colorful eateries.

WHAT TO SEE **Cerro San Cristóbal.** St. Christopher's Hill, within Parque Metropolitano, is one of the most popular tourist attractions in Santiago. From the western entrance at Plaza Caupolicán you can walk—it's a steep but enjoyable one-hour climb—or take the funicular. Either route leads you to the summit, which is crowned by a gleaming white statue of the Virgen de la Inmaculada. If you're coming from the eastern entrance, you can ascend in the cable car that leaves seven blocks north of the Pedro de Valdivia Metro stop. The ride, which seats two in a colored-glass bubble, can be terrifying for acrophobics. There is limited parking for 2,000 pesos at both the Pedro de Valdivia and Pío Nono entrances. ⊠ *Cerro San Cristóbal, Bellavista* ☎ *2/730–1300* ⊕ *www.parquemet.cl* 🎟 *Park free; round-trip funicular 1,500 pesos; round-trip cable car 1,500 pesos* ⊙ *Park: Sun.–Thurs. 8 AM–10 PM, Fri. and Sat. 8 AM–midnight. Funicular: Mon. 1–8, Tues.–Fri. 10–8, weekends 10–8. Cable car: weekdays 2:30–6:30, weekends 10:30–7:30* Ⓜ *Baquedano, Pedro de Valdivia.*

★ **La Chascona.** This house designed by the Nobel-winning poet Pablo Neruda was dubbed the "Woman with the Tousled Hair" after Matilde Urratia, the poet's third wife. Tours allow you to step into the extraordinary mind of the poet whose eclectic designs earned him the label "or-

4

Through the Grapevine

FANS OF CHILEAN WINES owe a debt to missionaries who arrived here in the 16th century. Spanish priests, who needed wine to celebrate the Catholic Mass, cultivated the country's first vines in the Maule Valley. Fast-forward three centuries to Santiago's Quinta Normal, today called the University of Chile, where Claudio Gay imported more than 60 varieties of French grapes. He found that varietals such as cabernet sauvignon, malbec, and carmenère thrived in the rich soil of the Central Valley. The country's near-perfect growing climate didn't hurt, either. As the 20th century progressed, Chilean wineries did not keep pace with the rest of the world. But with the introduction of more modern methods in the 1990s, the country soon garnered the notice of wine enthusiasts. By the early 21st century, Chile was exporting over $600 million worth of wine to more than 90 countries.

An oft-repeated fact about Chilean wine is that the best is reserved for the export market. Although you can find some good quality wines at upscale Chilean restaurants, the big wineries are still concentrating their energy on the international market. A good wine shop in your hometown should have a selection for you to sample; there's nothing to get you in the mood for planning your Chilean trip, or showing off your post-travel photos and souvenirs to friends, like a few bottles of fine Valle de Curicó red.

When you're ready to taste and purchase some Chilean wines, there are a few to keep in mind. Chile's largest winery, Concha y Toro, has several labels (some made exclusively for the Chilean market) that usually offer good value. At one end is the affordable and popular Casillero del Diablo label; at the other is the export-oriented Trio wines. Highly regarded Cousiño-Macul, the second big player in the market, gears itself to tourist visits, as does Concha y Toro, with organized tours and souvenir wine glasses. (Reservations are required for most winery visits in Chile.) Both wineries are close enough to Santiago to make easy day visits. Santa Rita also lies a short distance from the capital.

The long-established Errázuriz winery holds court in the warm Aconcagua Valley north of Santiago, where warm summers and mild winters translate into full-bodied merlots and cabernets. Santa Carolina's new Santa Isabel estate, in the cool Casablanca Valley near Valparaíso, produces highly regarded white wines. It complements its older operations in the Maipo and Rapel valleys known for their deep-bodied reds. A smaller, newer venture, Casa Lapostolle winery, was founded in 1994 by France's Marnier-Lapostolle family (of Grand Marnier fame). Its reds are highly regarded—if not as widely available; its signature product is its Clos Apalta, a blend of merlot and carmenère, a grape imported from the Bordeaux region of France in the 1850s, where it was subsequently wiped out by phylloxera.

ganic architect." Winding garden paths, stairs, and bridges lead to the house and its library stuffed with books, a bedroom in a tower, and a secret passageway. Scattered throughout are collections of butterflies, seashells, wineglasses, and other odd objects that inspired Neruda's tumultuous life and romantic poetry. Neruda, who died in 1973, had two other houses on the coast—one in Valparaíso, the other in Isla Negra. All three are open as museums. Though it's not as magical as Isla Negra, La Chascona can still set your imagination dancing. The house is on a little side street leading off Constitución. ✉ *Fernando Márquez de la Plata 0192, Bellavista* 🏠 *2/777–8741* ⊕ *www.neruda.cl* ✉ *English tour: 3,100 pesos* ⊙ *Tues.–Sun. 10–6* Ⓜ *Baquedano.*

Jardín Japonés. The tranquil Japanese Garden affords a sumptuous view over the skyscrapers of Las Condes and Bellavista. Paths edged with bamboo and lighted by Japanese lanterns lead past lily ponds and a gazebo beside a trickling fountain. ✉ *Cerro San Cristóbal, Bellavista* 🏠 *2/730–1300* ✉ *Free* ⊙ *Daily 10–6* Ⓜ *Pedro de Valdivia, Baquedano.*

☺ **Jardín Zoológico.** The Zoological Garden is a good place to see examples of many Chilean animals, some nearly extinct, that you might not otherwise encounter. As is often the case with many older zoos, the creatures aren't given a lot of room. ✉ *Cerro San Cristóbal, Bellavista* 🏠 *No phone* ✉ *2,000 pesos* ⊙ *Tues.–Sun. 10–6* Ⓜ *Baquedano.*

☺ **Plaza Tupahue.** The middle stop on the teleférico deposits you in the center of Parque Metropolitano. The main attraction here in summer is the delightful **Piscina Tupahue,** a 46-meter (150-foot) pool with a rocky crag running along one side. Beside the pool is the 1925 **Torreón Victoria,** a stone tower surrounded by a trellis of bougainvillea. If Piscina Tupahue is too crowded, try the nearby **Piscina Antilén.** From Plaza Tupahue you can follow a path below to **Plaza de Juegos Infantiles Gabriela Mistral,** a popular playground. ✉ *Cerro San Cristóbal, Bellavista* 🏠 *2/730–1300* ✉ *Park free, Piscina Tupahue 4,500 pesos, Piscina Antilén 5,500 pesos* ⊙ *Nov.–Mar., Wed.–Mon. 10–7* Ⓜ *Pedro de Valdivia, Baquedano.*

Where to Eat

Santiago can be overwhelming when it comes to dining, as hundreds of restaurants are strewn about the city. No matter what strikes your fancy, there are likely to be half a dozen eateries within easy walking distance. Tempted to taste hearty Chilean fare? Pull up a stool at one of the counters at Vega Central and enjoy a traditional *pastel de choclo*. Craving seafood? Head to the Mercado Central, where you can choose from the fresh fish brought in that morning. Want a memorable meal? Trendy new restaurants are opening every day in neighborhoods like Bellavista, where hip Santiaguinos come to check out the latest hot spots. Remember that Santiaguinos dine a little later than the rest of us. Most fancier restaurants don't open for lunch until 1. Dinner begins at 7:30 or 8, although most places don't get crowded until after 9. Many eateries close for a few hours before dinner.

Bellavista

CHILEAN ✕ **Como Agua Para Chocolate.** Inspired by Laura Esquivel's romantic 1989
★ **$$–$$$$** novel *Like Water for Chocolate*, this Bellavista standout is part restaurant, part theme park. It focuses on the aphrodisiacal qualities of food, so it shouldn't be surprising that one long table is actually an iron bed, with place settings arranged on a crisp white sheet. The food compares to the decor like the film version compares to the book: it's good, but not nearly as imaginative. *Ave de la pasión,* for instance, means Bird of Passion. It may be just chicken with mushrooms, but it's served on a copper plate. ⊠ *Constitución 88* ☎ *2/777–8740* ⊟ *AE, DC, MC, V* Ⓜ *Baquedano.*

$–$$ ✕ **El Venezia.** Long before Bellavista became fashionable, this barebones picada was where movie stars and TV personalities rubbed elbows with the hoi polloi. Although gourmands now head a block or two in either direction to the latest hot spots, tacky El Venezia still fills to capacity each day at lunch. And what's not to like? The beer is icy, the waiters are efficient, and the food is abundant. As a nod to the name, there are also prodigious plates of pasta. ⊠ *Pío Nono 200* ☎ *2/737– 0900* ⊟ *AE, DC, MC, V* Ⓜ *Baquedano.*

SEAFOOD ✕ **Azul Profundo.** Not so many years ago, this was the only restaurant
$–$$ you'd find on this street near Parque Metropolitano. Today it's one of
Fodor'sChoice dozens of restaurants in trendy Bellavista, but its two-level dining
★ room—with walls painted bright shades of blue and yellow, and racks of wine stretching to the ceiling—ensure that it stands out in the crowd. Choose your fish from the extensive menu—swordfish, sea bass, shark, flounder, salmon, trout, and haddock are among the choices—and enjoy it *a la plancha* (grilled) or *a la lata* (served on a sizzling plate with tomatoes and onions). ⊠ *Constitución 111* ☎ *2/738–0288* ⌑ *Reservations essential* ⊟ *AE, DC, MC, V* Ⓜ *Baquedano.*

SPANISH ✕ **La Bodeguilla.** This authentic Spanish restaurant is a great place to stop
$–$$ for a glass of sangria after tackling Cerro San Cristóbal. After all, it's right at the foot of the funicular. The dozen or so tables are set among wine barrels and between hanging strings of garlic bulbs. Nibble on tapas while perusing the wine list. Then consider ordering the house specialty—*cabrito al horno* (oven-roasted goat). ⊠ *Av. Dominica 5* ☎ *2/ 732–5215* ⊟ *No credit cards* ⊘ *Closed Sun.* Ⓜ *Baquedano.*

Centro

CHILEAN ✕ **Bristol.** The indefatigable Guillermo Rodríguez, who has commandeered
$$–$$$$ the kitchen here for more than a decade, has won just about all the coun-
Fodor'sChoice try's culinary competitions. No wonder he also serves as a private chef
★ to Chilean president Ricardo Lagos. You won't find dishes like marinated scallops over octopus carpaccio or king crab tartar on any other menu in town. The expertise offered by sommelier, Alejandro Farias, is reason enough to visit. The only disappointment is the uninspired dining room, which pales next to the city's other top-notch eateries. ⊠ *Hotel Plaza San Francisco, La Alameda 816* ☎ *2/639–3832* ⊟ *AE, DC, MC, V* Ⓜ *Universidad de Chile.*

$$–$$$ ✕ **Zully.** A stone house that once belonged to poet Vincente Huidobro
Fodor'sChoice is the destination for the see-and-be-seen crowd. Each dining room is
★ different: one is filled with sage-color chaise lounges, another has white

leather stools surrounding a raised glass table. The food is Chilean, but there also hints of other cuisines. The risotto with shrimp, leeks, and truffle oil is a standout, as is the tuna with rice noodles and a black sesame sauce. After dinner, take a stroll through the quaint Concha y Toro neighborhood, located a few blocks west of downtown. ⊠ *Concha y Toro 34, Concha y Toro* ☎ *2/696–3990* ⩘ *Reservations essential* ⊟ *AE, DC, MC, V* ⊘ *No lunch weekends* Ⓜ *Republica.*

★ **$$** ✕ **Confitería Torres.** José Domingo Torres created such delicious dishes that other aristocrats "borrowed" him for their banquets. In 1879, he set up shop in this storefront on the Alameda. It remains of the city's best dining rooms, with red leather banquettes, mint-green tile floors, and huge chandeliers with tulip-shape globes. The food, such as *lomo al ajo arriego* (sirloin sautéed with peppers and garlic) comes from recipes by the mother of owner Claudio Soto Barría. He and his parents will likely greet you from their little table near the front door. ⊠ *Alameda 1570* ☎ *2/688–0751* ⊟ *AE, DC, MC, V* Ⓜ *Universidad de Chile.*

FRENCH
$–$$ ✕ **Les Assassins.** Although this appears at first glance to be a rather somber bistro, nothing could be further from the truth. The service is friendly, and the Provence-influenced food is first-rate. The steak au poivre and beef bourguignon would make a Frenchman's eyes water. And where else in Santiago could you find crêpes suzette? If you want to practice your Spanish, you're in luck: there's always a line of talkative locals in the cozy ground-floor bar. ⊠ *Merced 297* ☎ *2/638–4280* ⊟ *AE, DC, MC, V* ⊘ *Closed Sun.* Ⓜ *Universidad Católica.*

INDIAN
★ **¢–$$** ✕ **Majestic.** Chef Haridas Chauhan, originally of the Sheraton in New Delhi, has turned a restaurant in a small hotel into a dining destination. Start with the mild *samosas* (vegetable turnovers), then turn up with heat with such deliciously spicy dishes as *rogan josh* (hot lamb curry) and *murgh makhanwala* (chicken in a tangy butter sauce). The *kulfi de almendras,* made from evaporated milk, ice cream, walnuts, and almonds, is a sweet finish to a meal. The smaller dining room used for lunch is a bit cramped, but the larger one opened for dinner is open and airy. ⊠ *Santo Domingo 1526* ☎ *2/695–8366* ⩘ *Reservations essential* ⊟ *AE, DC, MC, V* Ⓜ *Santa Ana.*

SEAFOOD
★ **¢–$$$$** ✕ **Donde Augusto.** What was once a simple seafood stand has taken over almost all the interior of Mercado Central. If you don't mind the unhurried service and the odd tear in the tablecloth, you may have the time of your life dining on everything from sea urchins to baby eel. Placido Domingo eats here on every visit to Chile, attended to by the white-bearded Segovian Augusto Vasquez, who has run Donde Augusto for more than four decades. Go for simple dishes like the *corvina plancha* (grilled sea bass). Get here early, as it closes at 6 PM. ⊠ *Mercado Central* ☎ *2/672–2829* ⩘ *Reservations not accepted* ⊟ *AE, DC, MC, V* ⊘ *No dinner* Ⓜ *Puente Cal y Canto.*

VEGETARIAN
¢ ✕ **Govinda's.** Cheap but hearty vegetarian lunches are prepared here by Hare Krishnas. Small wooden tables and chairs are the extent of the decor, but the tofu and vegetable dishes and homemade bread are delicious. Try the yogurt with mixed fruit and honey for dessert. ⊠ *Av. Compañía*

KEY

M Metro stops

🛈 Tourist information

━━ Cable Car Line

1 Restaurants

① Hotels

1489 ☎ *2/673–0892* ▭ *No credit cards* ⊘ *Closed weekends. No dinner* Ⓜ *Santa Ana.*

Las Condes

CAFÉS
¢–$

✕ **Cafe Melba.** Almost unheard-of in Santiago, this storefront restaurant serves breakfast all day. If you're particularly hungry, order "The Works"—baked beans, mushrooms, sausage, and bacon. Drink it down with a caffe latte, served in a large white bowl. In warm weather, grab a seat on the covered patio in front. Get here early, as it closes around 6. ✉ *Don Carlos 2898, off Av. El Bosque Norte* ☎ *2/232–4546* ▭ *AE, DC, MC, V* ⊘ *No dinner* Ⓜ *Tobalaba.*

ITALIAN
★ $$–$$$$

✕ **Bice.** The small, two-tiered dining room has soaring ceilings that lend a dramatic flair, while gleaming floors of alternating stripes of dark and light wood add contemporary glamour. White-jacketed waiters zip around, attending to your every need. The menu leans towards imaginatively prepared pastas, such as linguine with scallops, razor clams, shrimp, and mussels. Be sure to leave room for desserts such as the *cioccolatíssimo*, a hot, chocolate soufflé with melted chocolate inside, served with an exquisite *dulce de leche* ice cream. ✉ *Hotel Inter-Continental, Av. Luz 2920* ☎ *2/ 381–5500* ⌨ *Reservations essential* ▭ *AE, DC, MC, V* Ⓜ *Tobalaba.*

$$–$$$$

✕ **Le Due Torri.** For excellent homemade pastas, head to this longtime favorite. The rear of the dining room, with its small cypress trees and a corner pergola, is traditional; seating in the front is more contemporary. The name of the restaurant, by the way, refers to the two towers erected by the dueling Garisenda and Asinelli families in the owner's native Bologna. ✉ *Av. Isidora Goyenechea 2908* ☎ *2/231–3427* ⌨ *Reservations essential* ▭ *AE, DC, MC, V* Ⓜ *Tobalaba.*

JAPANESE
$–$$

✕ **Matsuri.** With a sleek design that calls to mind Los Angeles as much as Tokyo, this restaurant in the Hyatt Regency is one of Santiago's most stylish eateries. After passing through a foyer painted vivid red, you enter the calm dining area with its sliding screens and view of a waterfall. Downstairs are a sushi bar and two tatami rooms (no shoes allowed, but slippers are provided) with sliding screens for privacy, while upstairs are two grill tables. The menu is constantly changing, but in addition to hot entrées, you can be sure to find a long list of sushi and sashimi. ✉ *Hyatt Regency Santiago, Av. Kennedy 4601* ☎ *2/363–3051* ▭ *AE, DC, MC, V* Ⓜ *Escuela Militar.*

SEAFOOD
$$

✕ **Isla Negra.** The sails flying from the roof let you know that Isla Negra means business when it comes to seafood. The restaurant takes its name from a coastal town south of Santiago that was Nobel laureate Pablo Neruda's last home. The poet's favorite dish was conger eel soup, and you'll find it served here as a starter. Don't miss the empanadas stuffed with everything from cheese to razor clams. ✉ *Av. El Bosque Norte 0325* ☎ *2/231–3118* 🖷🖷 *2/233–0339* ⌨ *Reservations essential* ▭ *AE, DC, MC, V* Ⓜ *Tobalaba.*

SPANISH
$–$$

✕ **Gernika.** The Basque owners of this wood-and-stone restaurant have created a little slice of their homeland with graceful stone arches, tapestries bearing ancient coats of arms, and even jai alai equipment. Head upstairs to the more intimate upper level, which has three well-decorated private dining salons. Chilean seafood is cooked with Spanish flair, as in the *congrio donostiarra* (conger eel coated in chili sauce and fried in olive oil). Delicious *centolla* (king crab) is brought in from the chilly waters of Tierra del Fuego. Several hearty selections from Spain's Rioja region appear on the wine list. ⊠ *Av. El Bosque Norte 0227* ☎ *2/232–9954* ⌂ *Reservations essential* ▭ *AE, DC, MC, V* ⊘ *No lunch Sat.* Ⓜ *Tobalaba.*

THAI   ✗ **Anakena.** Designed to resemble an outdoor market, this elegant eatery
★ $$–$$$ emphasizes fresh ingredients. You can order traditional Thai favorites, but the best items on the menu are those that combine the cooking style of Asia with those of Europe and South America. That's how you can get unusual starters like fried oysters with bacon and spring rolls stuffed with lobster, goat cheese, and artichokes. If it's on the menu, don't pass up the grilled swordfish in a basil beurre blanc. There's a separate entrance for the restaurant, so you don't have to enter through the lobby of the Hyatt Regency. ⊠ *Hyatt Regency Santiago, Av. Kennedy 4601* ☎ *2/363–3177* ▭ *AE, DC, MC, V* Ⓜ *Escuela Militar.*

VEGETARIAN   ✗ **El Naturista.** If you're used to vegetarian restaurants that look like they
¢–$ forgot to decorate, then this elegant eatery with its green-and-white-checkered floor will be a nice surprise. The kitchen here has sidled away from run-of-the-mill vegetarian fare. It conjures up such dishes as *fricasé de cochayuyo* (seaweed stew)—a distinctly slimy but good dish that's typically Chilean. The scrumptious lasagna is made from home-grown eggplants. ⊠ *Av. Vitacura 2751* ☎ *2/236–5140* ▭ *AE, DC, MC, V* ⊘ *Closed Sun.* Ⓜ *Tobalaba.*

Providencia

CHILEAN   ✗ **Astrid y Gaston.** The kitchen is the real star here—every seat in the
$$–$$$$ pumpkin-color dining room has a great view of the chefs at work. You
Fodor'sChoice   couldn't do better than start with the agnolottis, little pockets of squid-
★   ink pasta stuffed with king crab and cherry tomatoes. After that, try one of the one-of-a-kind entrées, such as the lamb shank drenched in pisco and served with three kinds of yucca or the parrot fish with tamarind and ginger. Make sure to peruse the wine list, one of the best in town. Save room for one of Astrid's desserts, such as the creamy confection called *suspiro limeña,* "sigh of a lady from Lima": a meringue-topped dish of dulce de leche. ⊠ *Antonio Bellet 201* ☎ *2/650–9125* ⌂ *Reservations essential* ▭ *AE, DC, MC, V* Ⓜ *Pedro de Valdivia.*

$$–$$$$ ✗ **El Cid.** Considered by critics to be one of the city's top restaurants,
Fodor'sChoice   El Cid is the culinary centerpiece of the classic Sheraton Santiago. The
★   dining room, which overlooks the pool, has crisp linens and simple place settings. All the excitement here is provided by the food, which is served with a flourish. Don't miss the famous grilled seafood—king crab, prawns, squid, and scallops with a sweet, spicy sauce. If you're new to Chilean cuisine, you can't go wrong with the excellent lunch buffet, which includes unlimited wine. ⊠ *Av. Santa María 1742* ☎ *2/233–5000* ▭ *AE, DC, MC, V* Ⓜ *Pedro de Valdivia.*

$–$$ ✗ **El Parrón.** One of the city's oldest restaurants, dating from 1936, specializes in grilled meats. You can watch the action in the kitchen through enormous windows. The dining areas are large and slightly impersonal, but the extensive wine list and menu make up for them. The congenial, wood-paneled bar is the perfect place to sample the refreshing national aperitif—the pisco sour. For dessert try a popular Chilean street-trolley offering, *mote con huesillos* (peeled wheat kernels and dried peaches). ☒ *Av. Providencia 1184* ☎ *2/251–8911* ⊟ *AE, DC, MC, V* ☾ *No dinner Sun.* Ⓜ *Manuel Montt.*

★ ¢–$$ ✕ **Lomit's.** There's nothing particularly smart about Lomit's, a traditional Chilean restaurant, but it unfailingly serves up some of the city's best *barros lucos,* steak sandwiches overflowing with melted cheese. You can eat at the long wooden bar and watch the sandwich maker at work, or find a small table to the side (prices are a bit less at the *mesón* than at the *mesas*). ☒ *Av. Providencia 1980* ☎ *2/233–1897* ⊟ *AE, DC, MC, V* Ⓜ *Pedro de Valdivia.*

¢–$ ✕ **Liguria.** This extremely popular picada is always packed, so you might have to wait to be seated in the chandelier-lighted dining room or at one of the tables that spill out onto the sidewalk. A large selection of Chilean wine accompanies such favorites as *jardín de mariscos* (shellfish stew) and the filling *cazuela* (a stew of beef or chicken and potatoes). There are several branches in the neighborhood, but each has its own personality. Afternoons find locals bellying up to the bar. ☒ *Av. Providencia 1373* ☎ *2/235–7914* Ⓜ *Manuel Montt* ☒ *Pedro de Valdivia 047* ☎ *2/334–4346* Ⓜ *Pedro de Valdivia* ⊟ *No credit cards* ☾ *Closed Sun.*

MEDITERRANEAN ✕ **De Cangrejo a Conejo.** Heavy wooden double doors bring you into a
$–$$ large, high-ceilinged interior of this hip eatery. Tables and chairs of pale wood and steel have been thoughtfully arranged around a long curving bar, and flourishing greenery extends out into the patio garden. The menu reflects its name, serving everything from *cangrejo* (crab) to *conejo* (rabbit). ☒ *Av. Italia 805* ☎ *2/634–4041 or 2/634–4064* ⊟ *No credit cards* ☾ *Closed Sun.*

SEAFOOD ✕ **Aquí Está Coco.** The best seafood in Santiago is served in a dining room
$$–$$$$ where the walls are covered with flotsam and jetsam found on Chilean
Fodor$Choice beaches. Ask your waiter—or friendly owner "Coco" Pacheco—which
★ fish was caught that day. This is a good place to try Chile's famous *machas* (clams), served with tomatoes and Parmesan cheese, or *corvina* (sea bass) grilled with plenty of butter. Don't miss the cellar, where you can sample wines from the extensive collection of Chilean vintages. ☒ *La Concepción 236* ☎ *2/235–8649* ⌕ *Reservations essential* ⊟ *AE, DC, MC, V* ☾ *Closed Sun.* Ⓜ *Pedro de Valdivia.*

VEGETARIAN ✕ **El Huerto.** In the heart of Providencia, this vegetarian eatery is a hang-
$ out for hip young Santiaguinos. Even the wood paneling and high windows here feel healthy. Simple dishes like spinach quiche and pancakes stuffed with asparagus and mushrooms are full of flavor, but it's the hearty soups and freshly squeezed juices that register the highest praise. Try the tasty *jugo de zanahoria* (carrot juice). A little shop sells all the ingredients you need to make these dishes at home. ☒ *Orrego Luco 054* ☎ *2/233–2690* ⊟ *AE, DC, MC, V* ☾ *No lunch Sun.* Ⓜ *Pedro de Valdivia.*

¢–$ ✕ **Café del Patio.** The chef uses all organic produce, half of which is grown in the owner's garden, at this vegetarian eatery hidden in the back of quaint Galería del Patio. The chef's salad—with lettuce, tomato, hearts of palm, and Gruyère cheese—is exquisite, as is the vegetarian ravioli. The menu also includes expertly rolled sushi. At night, Café del Patio turns into a bar. ⊠ *Av. Providencia 1670, Providencia* ☎ *2/236–1251* ☰ *AE, DC, MC, V* ☺ *Closed Sun. No lunch Sat.* Ⓜ *Pedro de Valdivia.*

Vitacura

FRENCH ✕ **Le Fournil.** Rumor has it that the French owners import even their flour
¢–$ from France at this authentic boulangerie. The *plato del dia* (dish of the day) is always a tasty concoction, but equally good bets are the mixed green salad with grilled goat's cheese and the succulent carpaccio of salmon. But the *tarte tatin* steals the show—large, thick chunks of perfectly baked apple atop a thin layer of pastry, served with a scoop of creamy vanilla ice cream. The shady terrace is lovely, but the upstairs dining room is the place for a romantic meal. ⊠ *Av. Vitacura 3841* ☎ *2/228–0219* ☰ *AE, DC, MC, V.*

SEAFOOD ✕ **Europeo.** Whether you dine on the crisp white-linen tablecloths in the
$$ elegant dining room or under an umbrella in the open-air brasserie, you're in for a fine meal at this trendy yet relaxed eatery on Santiago's most prestigious shopping avenue. The menu leans towards fish: try the succulent grilled seafood with scallops, squid, salmon, and crispy fried noodles. This is one of the few places in town that serves wild game, such as venison ragout with creamy polenta. Save room for a dessert of crème brûlée *de lucuma* (lucuma is a fruit native to Peru) or chocolate mousse with almonds. ⊠ *Av. Alonso de Córdova 2417* ☎ *2/208–3603* ⌣ *Reservations essential* ☰ *AE, DC, MC, V.*

Where to Stay

Santiago's accommodations range from luxurious *hoteles* to comfortable *residenciales,* which can be homey bed-and-breakfasts or simple hotel-style accommodations. The city also has more than a dozen five-star properties. Most newer hotels are in Providencia and Las Condes, a short taxi ride from Santiago Centro. Although the official room rates are pricey, you'll find discounts. Call several hotels and ask for the best possible rate. It's a good idea to reserve in advance during the peak seasons (January, February, July, and August). Note that the 18% hotel tax is removed from your bill if you pay in U.S. dollars or with a credit card.

Centro

$$ ▦ **Hotel Plaza San Francisco.** Across from Iglesia San Francisco, this
Fodor'sChoice business hotel has everything traveling executives need, from secretar-
★ ial services to a slew of meeting rooms. Between meetings there's plenty to do—take a dip in the sparkling indoor pool, work out in the health club, stroll through the art gallery, or select a bottle from the well-stocked wineshop. Large beds, lovely antique furniture, and marble-trim baths fill the hotel's cozy rooms. And although all these amenities are tremendous draws, one of the best reasons to choose this hotel is for its helpful, professional staff. ⊠ *La Alameda 816* ☎ *2/639–3832, 800/223–5652 toll free in the U.S.* ⊕ *www.plazasanfrancisco.cl* ⇱ *155 rooms, 8 suites* ☖ *Restaurant, room service, in-room data ports, in-room safes,*

minibars, cable TV, in-room VCRs, Wi-Fi, indoor pool, health club, hair salon, hot tub, massage, sauna, bar, lobby lounge, piano bar, laundry service, business services, convention center, meeting rooms, free parking ▭ *AE, DC, MC, V* ¶◯¶ *BP* Ⓜ *Universidad de Chile.*

★ $ ▦ **City Hotel.** Suitably bedecked porters open the heavy front doors of this 70-year-old establishment, an art deco landmark. This grande dame is showing her age, but still has some old-fashioned charm. Don't miss the wrought-iron canopy that links the hotel's two wings. The slightly dated rooms are spacious with parquet floors and high ceilings, and bathrooms still have the original large white tubs. Request one of the quieter rooms not facing the street. ⊠ *Compañía 1063* 📠 *2/695–4526* ⊕ *www.hotelcity.cl* ↳ *72 rooms* ᕼ *Restaurant, room service, in-room safes, minibars, cable TV, bar, laundry service, meeting room, free parking; no a/c* ▭ *AE, DC, MC, V* ¶◯¶ *CP* Ⓜ *Plaza de Armas.*

$ ▦ **Foresta.** Staying in this seven-story hotel across the street from Cerro Santa Lucía is like visiting an elegant old home. Cheery floral wallpaper, lovely antique furnishings, and bronze and marble accents decorate the guest rooms. The best ones are those on the upper floors overlooking the hill. A rooftop restaurant-bar is a great place to enjoy the view. The quaint cafés and shops of Plaza Mulato Gil de Castro are just around the corner. ⊠ *Victoria Subercaseaux 353* 📠 *2/639–6261* ↳ *35 rooms, 8 suites* ᕼ *Restaurant, room service, minibars, cable TV, bar, piano bar, laundry service, Internet, meeting room, free parking; no a/c* ▭ *AE, DC, MC, V* Ⓜ *Bellas Artes.*

$ ▦ **Hotel Majestic.** Towering white pillars, peaked archways, and glittery brass ornaments welcome you to this Indian-style hotel. A friendly staff and a location several blocks from the Plaza de Armas make it a good choice. Even though the bright rooms have "soundproof" windows, ask for one facing away from the street. ⊠ *Santo Domingo 1526* 📠 *2/695–8366* ⊕ *www.hotelmajestic.cl* ↳ *50 rooms* ᕼ *Restaurant, café, fans, in-room safes, minibars, cable TV, pool, bar, laundry service, travel services, meeting room, free parking, no-smoking rooms* ▭ *AE, DC, MC, V* ¶◯¶ *BP* Ⓜ *Santa Ana.*

$ ▦ **Hotel Santa Lucia.** The rooms at this centrally located hotel are on the small side and are a little tired looking—after all, it's been around for more than 40 years. But they're spotlessly clean and avoid most traffic noise because of their lofty position on the fourth floor of an office building. The large terrace restaurant, unusually quiet given its location, serves nothing but typical Chilean fare. ⊠ *San Antonio 327, Paseo Huérfanos 779* 📠 *2/639–8201* ↳ *70 rooms* ᕼ *Fans, in-room safes, minibars, cable TV, laundry service, Internet, meeting rooms, parking (fee); no a/c* ▭ *AE, DC, MC, V* ¶◯¶ *CP* Ⓜ *Plaza de Armas.*

$ ▦ **Hotel Vegas.** This colonial-style building, adorned with a bullet-shape turret on the corner, sits in the heart of the charming Barrio París-Londres. Rooms here are spacious and filled with comfortable modern furnishings. All have plenty of windows—ask for one with a sitting room inside the turret so you'll have a view of gently curving Calle Londres. ⊠ *Londres 49* 📠 *2/632–2498 or 2/632–2514* ⊕ *www.hotelvegas.net* ↳ *20 rooms* ᕼ *Café, room service, in-room safes, cable TV, bar, laundry service, Internet, free parking, no-smoking rooms; no a/c in some rooms* ▭ *AE, DC, MC, V* Ⓜ *Universidad de Chile.*

$ 🏨 **El Marqués del Forestal.** A good budget choice for families, this small hotel has spacious rooms that sleep up to four people. The bonus is that they also have tiny kitchenettes that are perfect for whipping up breakfast or lunch. The bathrooms are sparkling, but have fixtures in colors not seen for a few decades. Not far from Mercado Central, the hotel overlooks a pretty section of Parque Forestal. The staff is eager to please. ☒ *Ismael Valdés Vergara 740* 🏨 *2/633–3462* ☎ *15 apartments* ♿ *Kitchenettes, bar, laundry service, free parking; no a/c* ▬ *AE, DC, MC, V* ⏀| *CP* Ⓜ *Puente Cal y Canto, Plaza de Armas.*

★ $ 🏨 **Residencial Londres.** This 1920s-era hotel in the picturesque Barrio París-Londres is just a stone's throw from most of the city's major sights. Rooms are spacious, with high ceilings ringed by detailed moldings and expansive wood floors. The best rooms have stone balconies. The staff is friendly and helpful. ☒ *Londres 54* 🏨🏨 *2/638–2215* ☎ *27 rooms* ♿ *Laundry service; no a/c, no room phones, no room TVs* ▬ *No credit cards* Ⓜ *Universidad de Chile.*

¢–$ 🏨 **Hotel París.** In the heart of Barrio París-Londres stands this mansion-turned-hotel. (Despite the name, the grand facade looks more Venetian than Parisian.) Pass through the large lobby and you'll find a quaint courtyard garden. Rooms are old-fashioned and have just the basic furnishings. Those in the more comfortable half, which you reach by a winding, marble staircase, are more spacious, come with cable TV, and are just a few thousand pesos extra. ☒ *París 813* 🏨 *2/664–0921* 🏨🏨 *2/639–4037* ☎ *40 rooms* ♿ *Café, bar, cable TV in some rooms; no a/c* ▬ *AE, DC, MC, V* Ⓜ *Universidad de Chile, Santa Lucía.*

Las Condes

$$$$ 🏨 **Santiago Marriott Hotel.** The first 25 floors of this gleaming copper tower—at 40 stories, it's the tallest building in Santiago—house the Marriott. An impressive two-story, cream-marble lobby has full-grown palm trees in and around comfortable seating areas. The hotel caters to those on business trips, and if you opt for an executive room you can breakfast in a private lounge while you scan the newspaper and marvel at the snowcapped Andes. You needn't venture out for entertainment either: there are tango evenings in the Latin Grill restaurant along with weekly wine-tasting sessions. One caveat: located in a suburban neighborhood, it's removed from the action. ☒ *Av. Kennedy 5741* 🏨 *2/426–2000, 800/228–9290 toll free in the U.S. and Canada* ⊕ *www.santiagomarriott. com* ☎ *280 rooms, 60 suites* ♿ *2 restaurants, in-room data ports, minibars, cable TV, indoor pool, health club, hot tub, sauna, bar, lobby lounge, shops, babysitting, laundry service, concierge, Internet, business services, convention center, meeting rooms, airport shuttle, travel services, free parking, no-smoking floor* ▬ *AE, DC, MC, V.*

★ $$$–$$$$ 🏨 **Hyatt Regency Santiago.** The soaring spire of the Hyatt Regency resembles a rocket (and you might feel like an astronaut when you're shooting up a glass elevator through a 24-story atrium). The rooms wrap around the cylindrical lobby, providing a panoramic view of the Andes. Bright-color fabrics and sprays of flowers make the rooms a cut above the rest. As you might guess from the pair of golden lions flanking the entrance, the theme is vaguely Asian, which is why two of the three award-winning restaurants are Thai and Japanese. (Senso, which is Tuscan, is also well worth a visit.) Duke's, the spitting image of an English pub, fills to standing capacity each day after work hours. ✉ *Av. Kennedy 4601* ☎ *2/218–1234* ⊕ *www.santiago.hyatt.com* 🛏 *287 rooms, 23 suites* ♿ *3 restaurants, tea shop, room service, in-room data ports, some in-room faxes, in-room safes, minibars, cable TV, in-room VCRs, golf privileges, 2 tennis courts, pool, fitness classes, health club, hair salon, massage, sauna, bar, lobby lounge, shops, babysitting, laundry service, concierge, Internet, business services, convention center, meeting rooms, airport shuttle, free parking, no-smoking floor* ▭ *AE, DC, MC, V.*

$$$–$$$$ 🏨 **Inter-Continental.** Attendants wearing top hats usher you into the two-story marble lobby of one of the city's top hotels. Beyond the reception desk there are a string of comfortable lounge areas, including one next to an indoor waterfall. In the rear is Bice, one of the city's most memorable restaurants. The rooms are sumptuous, with doors made from handsome panels of the native blond wood called *mañío* and a menu card listing five types of pillows, from "very soft" to "stiff." ✉ *Av. Vitacura 2885* ☎ *2/394–2000* ⊕ *www.interconti.com/santiago* 🛏 *297 rooms, 9 suites* ♿ *2 restaurants, room service, in-room data ports, in-room safes, minibars, cable TV with movies and video games, indoor pool, gym, massage, sauna, 2 bars, lobby lounge, shops, babysitting, laundry service, concierge, Internet, business services, convention center, meeting rooms, travel services, free parking, no-smoking floors* ▭ *AE, DC, MC, V* ⏐⚭⏐ *BP* Ⓜ *Tobalaba.*

$$$ 🏨 **Radisson Plaza Santiago.** Santiago's most dynamic office building, the World Trade Center, is also home to the Radisson, a combination that will make sense to many corporate travelers. The windows here are huge, with three wide glass panels for triptych perspectives of the city and the Andes beyond. The upholstered leather chairs and wood paneling in meeting rooms make it clear the hotel is serious in its attitude toward luxury. Even standard rooms have nice touches like wooden writing desks and small sitting areas with plush sofas. ✉ *Av. Vitacura 2610* ☎ *2/203–6000, 800/333–3333 toll free in the U.S.* ⊕ *www.radisson.com/santiagocl* 🛏 *159 rooms, 26 suites* ♿ *Restaurant, room service, in-room data ports, in-room safes, minibars, cable TV, indoor pool, gym, bar, lounge, library, babysitting, laundry service, concierge, Internet, business services, meeting rooms, helipad, free parking, no-smoking floors* ▭ *AE, DC, MC, V* Ⓜ *Tobalaba.*

$$ 🏨 **Montebianco.** The Montebianco—in a charming four-story building dwarfed by the towers surrounding it—has an informal setting and a friendly, helpful staff. The rooms, which wind around a central staircase, are on the small side; the king-sized beds take up most of the space. Make sure to ask for a room with more space to spread out. The hotel is right on a popular dining thoroughfare. ✉ *Av. Isidora Goyenechea 2911* ☎ *2/232–5034* ⊕ *www.hotelmontebianco.cl* 🛏 *33 rooms* ♿ *Cafeteria, dining room, in-room safes, some minibars, cable TV, bar, laundry service, Internet, business services, airport shuttle, travel services* ▭ *AE, DC, MC, V* ⏐⚭⏐ *BP* Ⓜ *El Golf, Tobalaba.*

$ 🏨 **Tarapacá.** This smaller hotel may have a smudge here and there, but its location on the edge of fashionable Las Condes makes up for it. Rooms facing Avenida Apoquindo are susceptible to traffic noise, so ask for one in the back. Better yet, pay a few extra dollars for one of two spacious suites on the 11th floor. The dormer windows add charm that rooms on the lower floors lack. ✉ *Vecinal 40, at Av. Apoquindo* ☎ *2/233–2747* ⊕ *www.hotelneruda.cl* ⇨ *52 rooms, 2 suites* ♨ *Restaurant, room service, in-room safes, minibars, cable TV, sauna, bar, laundry service, Internet, business services, meeting rooms, free parking* ⊟ *AE, DC, MC, V* ⦻| *BP* Ⓜ *El Golf, Tobalaba.*

Providencia

★ **$$$** ⌂ **Sheraton Santiago and San Cristóbal Tower.** Two distinct hotels stand side-by-side at this unrivaled resort. The Sheraton Santiago is certainly a luxury hotel, but the adjoining San Cristóbal Tower is in a class by itself, popular with business executives and foreign dignitaries who value its efficiency, elegance, and impeccable service. A lavish, labyrinthine marble lobby links the two hotels, three fine restaurants, and the city's largest hotel convention center. Pampering is not all that goes on at the San Cristóbal Tower—attentive staff members at the business center can provide you with everything from secretarial services to Internet access. The modern rooms have elegant linens and are decorated with rich fabrics. ✉ *Av. Santa María 1742* ☎ *2/233–5000* ⊕ *www.sheraton.cl* ⇨ *Sheraton Santiago: 379 rooms, 14 suites. San Cristóbal Tower: 139 rooms, 3 suites* ♨ *3 restaurants, picnic area, in-room data ports, in-room faxes, in-room safes, minibars, tennis court, 2 pools, gym, hair salon, sauna, 2 bars, lobby lounge, shops, babysitting, laundry service, concierge, Internet, business services, convention center, meeting rooms, airport shuttle, car rental, helipad, travel services, no-smoking floors* ⊟ *AE, DC, MC, V* Ⓜ *Pedro de Valdivia.*

$$ ⌂ **Four Points Sheraton.** The heart of Providencia's shopping district is just steps away from this small, perfectly adequate hotel. The cool rooftop terrace is a real pleasure in summer, when you can relax with a pisco sour and take in the city views. If you prefer a more active nightlife scene, you're in luck. The hotel is adjacent to one of the city's main party thoroughfares: Suecia, lined with pubs, restaurants, and discos. Rooms facing these streets can be noisy, even through double-paned windows. ✉ *Av. Santa Magdalena 111* ☎ *2/750–0300* ⊕ *www.fourpoints.com* ⇨ *112 rooms, 16 suites* ♨ *Restaurant, room service, in-room data ports, in-room safes, minibars, cable TV, golf privileges, pool, gym, sauna, bar, laundry service, Internet, business services, convention center, meeting rooms, airport shuttle, travel services, free parking, no-smoking rooms* ⊟ *AE, DC, MC, V* Ⓜ *Los Leones.*

★ **$$** ⌂ **Hotel Orly.** Finding a treasure like this in the middle of Providencia is a miracle. The shiny wood floors, country-manor furnishings, and glass-domed breakfast room make this hotel as sweet as it is economical. Rooms come in all shapes and sizes. Cafetto, the downstairs café, serves some of the finest coffee drinks in town. ✉ *Av. Pedro de Valdivia 027* ☎ *2/231–8947* ⊕ *www.orlyhotel.com* ⇨ *25 rooms, 3 suites* ♨ *Restaurant, café, room service, in-room data ports, in-room safes, minibars, cable TV, bicycles, laundry service, Internet, free parking* ⊟ *AE, DC, MC, V* ⦻| *BP* Ⓜ *Pedro de Valdivia.*

$ ⌂ **Chilhotel.** You won't empty your wallet at this small hotel, one of the few bargains in pricey Providencia. For about what you'd pay for a dinner for two you get a room that's clean and comfortable. Those overlooking the palm-shaded courtyard in back are especially lovely. It's in a funky old house, so no two rooms are alike. See a few before you decide. And talk about location—you're on a quiet side street, yet dozens of restaurants and bars are steps away. ☒ *Cirujano Guzmán 103* ☎ *2/264-0643* ⊕ *www.chilhotel.cl* ⤴ *25 rooms, 2 suites* ⌂ *Dining room, in-room safes, minibars, cable TV, Internet, laundry service* ⊟ *AE, DC, MC, V* ⊠ *BP* Ⓜ *Manuel Montt.*

Vitacura

$$ ☶ **Acacias de Vitacura.** The location—in the midst of towering eucalyptus and acacia trees thought to be more than a century old—is unforgettable. It's a pleasure to drink your morning coffee in the lush garden under one of the oversize umbrellas. The rooms here are simple but bright, and the owner's collection of old carriages gives the hotel a quirky personality. ☒ *El Manantial 1781* ☎ *2/211-8601* ⊕ *www.hotelacacias.cl* ⤴ *33 rooms, 2 suites* ⌂ *Restaurant, dining room, minibars, cable TV, pool, gym, babysitting, Internet, meeting room, travel services, free parking* ⊟ *AE, DC, MC, V* ⊠ *BP.*

$$ ☶ **Hotel Kennedy.** This glass tower may seem impersonal, but the small details—such as beautiful vases of flowers atop the wardrobes—show the staff cares about keeping guests happy. Bilingual secretarial services and an elegant boardroom are among the pluses for visiting executives. The Aquarium restaurant serves international cuisine and has a cellar full of excellent Chilean wines. ☒ *Av. Kennedy 4570* ☎ *2/290-8100* ⊕ *www.hotelkennedy.cl* ⤴ *123 rooms, 10 suites* ⌂ *Restaurant, room service, in-room data ports, minibars, cable TV, pool, gym, hair salon, massage, sauna, bar, laundry service, Internet, business services, meeting rooms, travel services, free parking, no-smoking floor* ⊟ *AE, DC, MC, V* ⊠ *BP.*

Nightlife

Bars and clubs are scattered all over Santiago, but a handful of streets have such a concentration of establishments that they resemble block parties on Friday and Saturday nights. Try pub-crawling along Avenida Pío Nono in Bellavista. The crowd here is young, as the drinking age is 18. To the east in Las Condes, Paseo San Damián is a fashionable outdoor complex of bars and clubs. What you should wear depends on your destination. Bellavista has a mix of styles ranging from blue jeans to basic black. Paseo San Damián maintains a stricter dress code. Note that establishments referred to as "nightclubs" are almost always female strip shows. Cheesy signs make it quite clear what goes on inside.

Centro

BARS Near Cerro Santa Lucía, **Bar Berri** (☒ Rosal 321 ☎ 2/638-4734) is an old-fashioned place where the waiter may just place a bottle of pisco on the table in front of you. Identifiable by the leering devil on the sign, **El Diablito** (☒ Merced 536 ☎ no phone) is a charming hole-in-the-wall. The dimly lighted space is popular with the after-work crowd. A secret meeting place during the Pinochet regime, **El Rincón de las Canallas** (☒ San Diego 379 ☎ 2/699-1309) still requires a password to get in (*Chile libre,* meaning "free Chile"). The walls are painted with political statements such as *Somos todos inocentes* ("We are all innocent.").

Las Condes

BARS **Flannery's** (⊠ Encomenderos 83 ☏ 2/233–6675), close to the main drag of Avenida El Bosque Norte, is an honest-to-goodness pub serving Irish food, beer, and occasionally Guinness on tap. **Pub Licity** (⊠ Av. El Bosque Norte 0155 ☏ 2/333–1214) is a large, popular, glass-fronted building permanently teeming with people in their twenties and early thirties.

Bellavista

BARS In Bellavista the latest hot spot is **El Toro** (⊠ Loreto 33 ☏ 2/737–5937), which is packed every night of the week except Sunday, when the staff gets a break. The tables are spaced close enough that you can eavesdrop on the conversations of the models and other celebrities that frequent the place. The **Libro Café** (⊠ Purísima 165 ☏ 2/735–1542) is a late-night haunt for starving artists and those who wish they were. If you're hungry, head here for a tortilla *malageña* and a carafe of the house red.

DANCE CLUBS The sleek and stylish **Tantra** (⊠ Ernesto Pinto Lagarrigue 154 ☏ 2/732–3268) is where a hip crowd heads well after midnight. The beat goes on until 6 AM, unless one of the frequent after-hours parties keeps it open even later. Upstairs are king-sized beds used as tables—reserve one for a memorable evening.

GAY & LESBIAN CLUBS On Bellavista's main drag, **Bokhara** (⊠ Pío Nono 430 ☏ 2/732–1050 or 2/735–1271) is one of the city's largest and most popular gay discos. It has two dance floors playing house and techno. **Bunker** (⊠ Bombero Nuñez 159 ☏ 2/737–1716 or 2/777–3760), a mainstay of the gay scene, is in a cavernous space with numerous platforms overlooking the dance floor. Don't get here too early—people don't arrive until well after midnight. Note that it's only open Friday and Saturday.

SALSA CLUBS **Habana Salsa** (⊠ Dominíca 142 ☏ 2/737–1737) thumps to the beat of salsa, merengue, and milonga from Thursday to Saturday night.

Providencia

SALSA CLUBS **Arriba de la Bola** (⊠ General Holley 171 ☏ 2/232–7965) shakes things up with a live Cuban band. It gets packed, so reservations are necessary. At **Ilé Habana** (⊠ Bucarest 95 ☏ 2/231–5711) you can boogie to the beat of a live band. There are free salsa lessons Tuesday–Saturday at 9:30 PM.

The Arts

Dance

The venerable **Ballet Nacional Chileno** (⊠ Av. Providencia 043, Providencia ☏ 2/634–4746), founded in 1945, performs from its repertoire of more than 150 pieces at the Teatro Universidad de Chile near Plaza Baquedano.

Music

Parque de las Esculturas (⊠ Av. Santa María between Av. Pedro de Valdivia Norte and Padre Letelier, Providencia ☏ No phone) hosts numerous open-air concerts in the early evenings in summer. The **Teatro Municipal** (⊠ Plaza Alcade Mekis, Av. Agustinas at Av. San Antonio, Santiago Centro ☏ 2/463–8888 ⊕ www.municipal.cl), Santiago's 19th-century theater, presents excellent classical concerts, opera, and ballet by internationally recognized artists from March to December.

Outdoor Activities

Horse Racing

Races take place Monday and alternating Thursdays at **Club Hípico** (⊠ Blanco Encalada 2540, Santiago Centro ☎ 2/693–9600), south of downtown. El Ensayo, an annual race that's a century-old tradition, is held here in early November. **Hipódromo Chile** (⊠ Hipódromo Chile 1715, Independencia ☎ 2/270–9237) is the home of the prestigious Gran Premio Internacional, which draws competitors from around South America. Regular races are held Saturday and alternating Thursdays.

Soccer

First-division *fútbol* matches, featuring the city's handful of local teams, are held in the **Estadio Nacional** (⊠ Av. Grecia 2001, Nuñoa ☎ 2/238–8102), southeast of the city center. Soccer is played year-round, with most matches taking place on weekends.

Shopping

Vitacura is, without a doubt, the destination for upscale shopping. Providencia, another of the city's most popular shopping districts, has rows of boutiques. Bohemian Bellavista attracts those in search of the perfect woolen sweater or the right piece of lapis lazuli jewelry. Santiago Centro is much more down-to-earth. Shops in Santiago are generally open weekdays 10–7 and Saturday 10–2. Malls are usually open daily 10–10.

Markets

Aldea de Vitacura (⊠ Av. Vitacura 6838, Vitacura ☎ 2/219–3161) is a pleasant outdoor market where you can browse among the various stands selling local and national craftwork. It's open Tuesday–Sunday 11–9. **Centro Artesanal Santa Lucía,** an art fair at the base of Cerro Santa Lucía, is an excellent place to find Aymara and Mapuche crafts. It's open daily 10–7. Bellavista's colorful **Feria Artesanal Pío Nono,** held in the park along Avenida Pío Nono, comes alive every night of the week. It's even busier on weekends, when more vendors gather in Parque Domingo Gómez to display their handicrafts. **Pueblito Los Dominicos** (⊠ Av. Apoquindo 9085, Las Condes ☎ 2/248–2295) is a "village" of more than 200 shops where you can find everything from fine leather to semiprecious stones and antiques. There's also a wonderful display of cockatoos and other live birds. It's a nice place to visit, especially on weekends, when traveling musicians entertain the crowds. It's open Tuesday–Saturday 10:30–9:30 and Sunday 10:30–8. Next door is an attractive whitewashed church dating from the late 18th century. It's rather far from the main drag, so take a taxi.

Specialty Shops

HANDICRAFTS For everything from masks to mosaics, head to **Manos de Alma** (⊠ General Salvo 114, Providencia ☎ 2/235–3518). The staff at **Pura** (⊠ Av. Isidora Goyenechea 3226, Las Condes ☎ 2/333–3144) has picked out the finest handicrafts from around the region. Here you can find expertly woven blankets and throws, colorful pottery, and fine leather goods. **Cooperativa Almacén Campesino** (⊠ Torreón Victoria, Bellavista ☎ 2/335–4443), in the middle of Parque Metropolitano, is a cooperative of arti-

Fodor's Choice
★

sans from various indigenous cultures. This shop sells the best handicrafts from all over Chile.

JEWELRY Chile is one of the few places in the world where lapis lazuli, a brilliant blue mineral, is found in abundance. In Bellavista, a cluster of shops deals solely in lapiz lazuli, selling a range of products made from this semi-precious stone: paperweights, jewelry, and chess sets. Several larger shops selling lapis lazuli are dotted around the rest of the city. **Blue Stone** (⊠ Av. Costanera Norte 3863, Vitacura ☎ 2/207–4180) has lovely original designs. Near Plaza Mulato Gil de Castro is **Rocco** (⊠ José Victorino Lastarria 53, Santiago Centro ☎ 2/633–4036), one of the best destinations in Santiago Centro.

WINE **El Mundo del Vino** (⊠ Av. Isidora Goyenechea 2931, Las Condes ☎ 2/244–8888) is a world-class store with an international selection, in-store tastings, wine classes, and books for oenophiles. The store also provides sturdy boxes to protect your purchases on the flight home. **Vinopolis** (⊠ Av. El Bosque Norte 038, Las Condes ☎ 2/232–3814) stocks a top-notch selection and also has a shop at the airport for last-minute purchases.

Side Trips from Santiago

Ski Resorts

No wonder skiing aficionados from around the world head to Chile: the snowcapped mountains to the east of Santiago have the largest number of runs not just in Chile or South America, but in the entire southern hemisphere. The other attraction is that the season here lasts from June to September, so savvy skiers can take to the slopes when everyone else is hitting the beach.

The closest ski area to Santiago is **Farellones,** at the foot of Cerro Colorado. This area, consisting of a couple of ski runs for beginners, is used mainly by locals out for a day trip. Facilities are scanty—just a couple of unremarkable restaurants and a few drink stands. Farther up the road is El Colorado, which has 568 acres of groomed runs—the most in Chile. There are 18 runs here: seven beginner, four intermediate, three advanced, and four expert. You'll find a few restaurants and pubs in the village. Ski season here runs mid-June to mid-October. ☎ 2/217–9101 ⊕ *www. elcolorado.cl* ✆ *22,000 pesos* ◑ *Mid-June–mid-Oct.*

About 3 km (2 mi) up the road from Farellones, **La Parva** is a colorful conglomeration of private homes set along a handful of mountain roads. At the resort itself there are 14 ski runs, most for intermediate skiers. La Parva is positioned perfectly to give you a stunning view of Santiago, especially at night. The season here tends to be a little longer than at the neighboring resorts. The slopes usually open in May, meaning the season can sometimes last six months. ☎ *02/431–0420* ⊕ *www.laparva. cl* ✆ *22,000 pesos* ◑ *May–Oct.*

Valle Nevado, just 13 km (8 mi) beyond La Parva, is Chile's largest ski region—a luxury resort area with 11 ski lifts that take you up to 27 runs on more than 300 acres of groomed trails. More lifts are being built to provide skiing fanatics with even more options. There are a few slopes for beginners, but Valle Nevado is intended for skiers who like a challenge. Three of the extremely difficult runs from the top of Cerro Tres Puntas are labeled "Shake," "Rattle," and "Roll." If that doesn't intimidate you then you might be ready for some heliskiing. A Bell 407 helicopter whisks you to otherwise inaccessible peaks where you can ride a vertical drop of up to 2,500 meters (8,200 feet). A ski school at Valle Nevado gives pointers to everyone from beginners to experts. As most of the visitors here are European, the majority of the 50 instructors are from Europe. Equipment rental runs about 25,000 pesos a day. ☎ 2/477-7700 ⊕ *www.vallenevado.cl* ⊠ 22,500 pesos ⊙ *Mid-June–Oct.*

WHERE TO STAY & EAT

$$$$ 🏨 **Condominio Nuevo Parva.** The best place to stay in La Parva is this complex of spacious, modern apartments that sleep between six and eight people. Linens are provided, but maid service is extra. You can rent only by the week, so plan for a lot of skiing. Valle Nevado and the other ski areas are a short drive away. ⊠ *Nueva La Parva 77* ☎ *2/212–1363* ⊕ *www.laparva.cl* 🛏 *32 apartments* ⚭ *Cable TV, kitchenettes, microwaves, pool* ▭ *AE, MC, V* ⊙ *Closed Oct.–May.*

$$$$ 🏨 **Puerta del Sol.** The largest of the Valle Nevado hotels, Puerta del Sol can be identified by its signature sloped roof. Rooms here are larger than those at Tres Puntas, but still rather small. One good option are the "altillo rooms," which have a loft bed that gives you more space. North-facing rooms cost more but have unobstructed views of the slopes. Since all three hotels share facilities, Puerta del Sol is your best value. ⊠ *Valle Nevado* ☎ *2/206–0027, 800/669–0554 toll free in the U.S.* ⊕ *www.vallenevado.com* 🛏 *124 rooms* ⚭ *2 restaurants, room service, in-room data ports, in-room safes, minibars, cable TV, gym, massage, sauna, Ping-Pong, downhill skiing, cinema, dance club, recreation room, babysitting, laundry service, airport shuttle* ▭ *AE, DC, MC, V* ⊙ *Closed Oct.–June 14* ⦿I *MAP.*

★ $$ 🏨 **La Cornisa.** This year-round hotel on the road to Farellones is great if you want to get to the slopes early, as there's free shuttle service to and from the nearby ski areas. The quaint old inn, run by the same family for years, has 10 rooms with wood floors and heaters to keep out the chill. The best are the two corner rooms, which are a bit larger and have wide windows with excellent views. The rate includes breakfast and dinner in the small restaurant, warmed by a fireplace and looking directly down the mountain to Santiago. ⊠ *Av. Los Cóndores 636, Farellones* ☎ *2/220-7581* 🖷 *2/220-7581* ⊕ *www.lacornisa.cl* 🛏 *10 rooms* ⚭ *Restaurant, babysitting, laundry service* ▭ *AE, DC, MC, V* ⦿I *MAP.*

Wineries

The wineries in the valley below Santiago are some of the oldest in Chile. Here you'll find most of the biggest and best-known vineyards in the country. For years tourists were virtually ignored by these wineries, but they are finally getting attention. Now many wineries are throwing their doors open to visitors for the first time, often letting them see behind-the-scenes activities like harvesting and pressing.

Don Francisco Undurraga Vicuña founded **Viña Undurraga** in 1885 in the town of Talagante, 34 km (21 mi) southwest of Santiago. The opulent mansion he built here has hosted various visiting dignitaries, from the queen of Denmark to the king of Norway. You can tour the house and the gardens—designed by Pierre Dubois, who planned Santiago's Parque Forestal—look at the facilities, and enjoy a tasting. Reserve ahead for a spot on the tour. Viña Undurraga is along the way to Pomaire, so you might visit both in the same day. ✉ *Camino a Melipilla Km 34, Talagante* ☎ *2/372–2811* ⊕ *www.undurraga.cl* 💰 *4,000 pesos* ⊙ *Tours: weekdays 10, 11:30, 2, and 3:30, Sat. 10 and 11:30.*

Chile's largest wine maker, **Viña Concha y Toro** produces 11 million cases annually. Some of its table wines—identifiable by the short, stout bottles—are sold domestically for about $2. The best bottles, however, fetch sky-high prices abroad. This is one of the oldest wineries in the region. Melchor de Concha y Toro, who once served as Chile's minister of finance, built the *casona,* or main house, in 1875. He imported vines from Europe, significantly improving the quality of the wines he was able to produce. Hour-long tours begin with an introductory video, a stroll through the vineyards and the century-old gardens, a look at the modern facilities, and a tasting. Reserve a few days ahead for a weekday tour, or a week ahead for the popular Saturday tours. Since they are all in the same region, you might want to consider a side trip to Viña Concha y Toro and Viña Santa Rita when you visit the Cajón del Maipo. ✉ *Av. Virginia Subercaseaux 210, Pirque* ☎ *2/476–5269* ⊕ *www. conchaytoro.com* 💰 *Tour: 3,000 pesos* ⊙ *Weekdays 10:30–6, Sat. 10–noon. English tours weekdays 11:30 and 3, Sat. 11* AM.

Chile's third-largest winery, **Viña Santa Rita,** played an important historical role in Chile's battle for independence. In 1814, 120 soldiers led by revolutionary hero Bernardo O'Higgins hid here in the cellars. Paula Jaraquemada, who ran the estate, refused to let the Spanish enter, saving the soldiers. (Santa Rita's 120 label commemorates the event.) At the center of Santa Rita's Maipo Valley estate half an hour south of Santiago, the lovely colonial hacienda now serves as the winery's headquarters. Its restaurant, La Casa de Doña Paula, is a delightful place to have a bite after the tour.

Tours take you down into the winery's musty cellars, which are worthy of Edgar Allen Poe. Built by French engineers in 1875 using a lime-and-stone technique called *cal y canto,* the fan-vault cellars have been named a national monument. The wine was once aged in the barrels you'll see, which are more than 120 years old and are made of *rauli* wood; today the wine is aged in stainless-steel towers. Unfortunately, the wonderful gardens and the original proprietor's house, with its chapel steeple peeking out from behind a thick canopy of trees, are not part of the tour. Note that you must reserve ahead for these tours. ✉ *Camino Padre Hurtado 0695, Alto Jahuel-Buín* ☎ *2/362–2594* ⊕ *www.santarita.com* 💰 *Tours: 6,500 pesos; tastings cost extra* ⊙ *Tours in English and Spanish: Tues.–Fri. at 10, 11:30, 4.*

WHERE TO EAT ✕ **La Casa de Doña Paula.** A two-centuries-old colonial hacienda with ★ **$–$$** thick adobe walls houses Viña Santa Rita's restaurant. If you plan to lunch here, it's a good idea to arrange to take the winery's 12:15 tour. Locally raised meats are the draw here; try the delicious *costillar de cerdo* (pork ribs). The dessert specialty is *ponderación,* a crisp swirl of fried dough atop vanilla ice cream and caramel syrup. ✉ *Viña Santa Rita,*

Camino Padre Hurtado 695, Alto Jahuel-Buín ☎ *2/362–2594* ⚭ *Reservations essential* ▭ *AE, DC, MC, V* ⊗ *Closed Mon. No dinner.*

Santiago Essentials

Transportation

BY AIR

Santiago's Comodoro Arturo Merino Benítez International Airport, often referred to simply as Pudahuel, is about a 30-minute drive west of the city.

Lan has daily flights from Santiago to most cities throughout Chile. Aerolíneas del Sur and Sky also fly to most large cities within Chile.

🛈 **Airport Comodoro Arturo Merino Benítez International Airport** ☎ 2/690-1900 ⊕ www.aeropuertosantiago.cl.

🛈 **Carriers Aerolíneas del Sur** ☎ 2/690-1422. **Aeromexico** ☎ 2/690-1038. **Lan** ☎ 2/ 565-2000. **Lloyd Aéreo Boliviano** ☎ 2/690-1140. **Sky** ☎ 600/600-2828. **Taca** ☎ 2/ 690-1276.

AIRPORT TRANSFERS   There is no metro service to the airport, but you have several other options. The most expensive is taxi service through Taxiofficial, which should cost you around 10,000 pesos for a trip downtown. Centropuerto, which runs buses every 10 minutes between the airport and Terminal Los Héroes, charges about 1,100 pesos. Tur-Bus has service between the airport and its own terminal near Los Héroes metro station; it departs every half hour and costs 1,200 pesos. The buses stop en route at the Pajaritos metro station. Many locals prefer to use this station to get to and from the airport, as there is less traffic than downtown. Transvip and Tur Transfer operate minibus service between the airport and various locations in the city. The cost is about 3,800 pesos.

🛈 **Centropuerto** ☎ 2/695-5958. **Taxiofficial** ☎ 2/690-1381. **Transvip** ☎ 2/677-3000. **Tur-Bus** ☎ 2/270-7500. **Tur Transfer** ☎ 2/677-3000.

BY BUS

TO & FROM SANTIAGO   All the country's major highways pass through Santiago, which means you won't have a problem catching a bus to almost any destination. Finding that bus, however, can be a problem. The city has several terminals, each with buses heading in different directions. Terminal Los Héroes is on the edge of Santiago Centro near Los Héroes metro station. Several companies have buses to points north and south from this station. The other three stations are clustered around the Universidad de Santiago metro station. The modern Terminal San Borja has buses headed north and west. Terminal Santiago is the busiest, with dozens of small companies going west to the coast and to the south. Terminal Alameda, which handles only Tur-Bus and Pullman Bus, is for coastal and southern traffic. Terminal Los Héroes and Terminal Santiago also handle a few international routes, heading to far-flung destinations such as Buenos Aires, Rio de Janeiro, and Lima.

Several bus companies run regularly scheduled service to the Andes in winter. Skitotal buses depart from the office on Avenida Apoquindo and head to all of the ski resorts except Portillo. Buses depart at 8:45 AM; a round-trip ticket costs 10,000 pesos. Also available for hire here are taxis— (65,000 pesos, including driver) and 12-person minibuses (90,000 pesos). Manzur Expediciones runs buses to Portillo on Wednesday, Saturday, and Sunday for about the same price. Buses leaves at 8:30 AM from the Plaza Italia in front of the Teatro Universidad de Chile.

Bus service to the Cajón del Maipo is frequent and inexpensive—Manzur offers a round-trip ticket to Lo Valdés Mountain Center for less than 8,000 pesos. Only the 8 AM bus makes the two-hour trek to Baños de Colina, however. Sit on the right side of the bus for river views.

WITHIN
SANTIAGO
Bus service is confusing for most newcomers. (It's confusing for most residents, too.) Buses (called *micros*) operate on hundreds of routes along the city's main thoroughfares. At any given moment there might be a dozen buses at a corner, all of them honking their horns and gesturing you aboard.

What to do? There are signs at covered bus stops telling you which number bus is headed in which direction. You can also check on the front of the buses themselves. Above the windshield should be the end points of the route. On the windshield, often on placards that the driver changes frequently, are the intermediate stops. These are often streets, so a sign reading PROVIDENCIA means the bus runs along Avenida Providencia. If you don't see your particular destination listed, look for a nearby mall or subway station.

Bus fare is usually 350 pesos, paid upon boarding. Drivers give change for small bills—and they do it while they are whizzing through traffic. 🚍 **Bus Companies Manzur Expediciones** ✉ Sótero del Río 475, Santiago Centro ☎ 2/777–4284. **Pullman Bus** ✉ Terminal Alameda, Estación Central ☎ 2/779–2026. **Skitotal** ✉ Av. Apoquindo 4900, Las Condes ☎ 2/246–0156. **Tur-Bus** ✉ Terminal Alameda, Estación Central ☎ 2/270–7500.
🚍 **Bus Depots Terminal Alameda** ✉ La Alameda 3750, Estación Central ☎ 2/270–7500. **Terminal Los Héroes** ✉ Tucapel Jiménez 21, Estación Central ☎ 2/420–0099. **Terminal San Borja** ✉ San Borja 184, Estación Central ☎ 2/776–0645. **Terminal Santiago** ✉ La Alameda 3850, La Alameda ☎ 2/376–1750.

BY CAR

You don't need a car if you're not going to venture outside the city limits, as most of the downtown sights are within walking distance of each other. To get to other neighborhoods, taxis are inexpensive and the subway system is safe and efficient. A car is the best way to see the surrounding countryside, however. Although the highways around Santiago are generally well maintained, weather conditions can make them dangerous. Between May and August, rain can cause roads in low-lying areas to flood. Avoid driving if it has been raining for several hours. If you're headed north or south, you'll probably use the Pan-American Highway, also called Ruta 5. To reach Valparaíso, Viña del Mar, or the northernmost beach resorts on the Central Coast, take Highway 68; for the southern beaches, take Ruta 78.

It can take up to two hours to reach the region's three major ski resorts, which lie 48–56 km (30–35 mi) from Santiago. The road is narrow, winding, and full of Chileans racing to get to the top. If you decide to drive, make sure you have either a four-wheel-drive vehicle or snow chains, which you can rent along the way. The chains are installed for about 8,000 pesos. Don't think you need them? There's a police checkpoint just before the road starts to climb into the Andes, and if the weather is rough they'll make you turn back.

BY SUBWAY

Santiago's excellent subway system is the best way to get around town. The metro is comfortable, inexpensive, and safe. The system operates Monday–Saturday 6:30 AM–10:30 PM and Sunday 8–10:30 PM. Línea 1 runs east–west along the axis of the Río Mapocho. This is the most popular line, and perhaps the most useful, because it runs past most of the heavily touristed areas. Línea 2 runs north–south; it's rarely used by nonresidents because it heads to residential areas. Línea 5 also runs north–south except at its northern tip, where it bends to the west to connect with the Bellas Artes and Plaza de Armas stations. As this book went to press, Linea 4, which connects to the Tobalaba, Vicente Valdes, and La Cisterna stations, was scheduled to open in 2006. Every station has an easy-to-read map of all the stations and the adjoining streets. Buy tickets in any station at the glass booths or at the nearby machines. Individual tickets cost 340 to 430 pesos, depending on the time of day. After depositing your ticket in the turnstile, pass through and retrieve it to use again later. Single-ride tickets are not returned. *Multivía* cards, available at all ticket windows, save you the hassle of buying single-ride tickets. You can put any amount over 500 pesos on a card.

⊮ Metro de Santiago ☎ 600/422-3330 ⊕ www.metrosantiago.cl.

BY TAXI

With some 50,000 taxis in Santiago, you can easily flag one down on most streets. The average ride costs around 2,000 to 3,000 pesos. The driver will turn the taxi meter on when you start your journey; it should read 150 pesos, the minimum charge. Taxi drivers don't always know where they are going and frequently ask directions; it's a good idea to carry a map. Radio-dispatched cabs are slightly more expensive but will pick you up at your door.

⊮ Taxi Companies Alborada ☎ 2/246-4900. **Alto Oriente** ☎ 2/226-2116. **Andes Pacífico** ☎ 2/225-3064 or 2/204-0104. **Apoquindo** ☎ 2/211-6073.

BY TRAIN

Chileans once boasted about the country's excellent rail service, but there's little left today aside from the limited service from Santiago to points south. Santiago's Estación Central, in Santiago Centro at the metro station of the same name, is where you catch trains headed to the Central Valley. Note that you can also purchase tickets for the trains at the Estación Metro Universidad de Chile.

Trains run from Santiago through the larger cities of Rancagua, Curicó, Talca, Chillán, Concepción, and Temuco.

⊮ Estación Central ⊠ La Alameda 3170, Santiago Centro ☎ 2/376-8500 ⊕ www.efe. cl. **Estación Metro Universidad de Chile** ⊠ Local 10, La Alameda ☎ 2/688-3284.

Contacts & Resources

TOURS

Sernatur (⇨ Visitor Information), the national tourism agency, maintains a listing of experienced individual tour guides who will take you on a half-day tour of Santiago and the surrounding area for about 25,000 pesos. These tours are a great way to get your bearings when you have just arrived in the city. They can also greatly enrich your visit. In museums, for example, they often provide information not generally available to the public and are especially helpful in museums with little or no signage in English.

Altué Expediciones arranges adventure trips such as white-water rafting on nearby rivers and hiking to the mouths of volcanoes. Chilean Travel Services and Sportstour handle tours of both Santiago and other parts of Chile. Chip Travel has several special-interest tours available, including a "human right legacy" tour of sites that are reminders of dictator Augusto Pinochet's 17-year regime.

With more than a dozen locations, Turismo Cocha, founded in 1951, is one of the city's biggest private tour operators. It arranges tours of the wineries of the Cajón del Maipo and the beach resorts of Valparaíso and Viña del Mar, in addition to the usual city tours. It also has offices in the domestic and international terminals of the airport as well as in some of the larger hotels.

🚩 **Tour Operators Altué Expediciones** ✉ Encomenderos 83, Las Condes ☎ 2/232-1103 ⊕ www.altue.com. **Chilean Travel Services** ✉ Antonio Bellet 77, Office 101, Providencia ☎ 2/251-0400 ⊕ www.ctsturismo.cl. **Chip Travel** ✉ Antonio Bellet 77, Office 101, Providencia ☎ 2/735-9044 ⊕ www.chipsites.com. **Sportstour** ✉ Moneda 970, Santiago Centro ☎ 2/549-5200 ⊕ www.sportstour.cl. **Turismo Cocha** ✉ Av. El Bosque Norte 0430, Las Condes ☎ 2/464-1000 ✉ Pedro de Valdivia 0169, Providencia ☎ 2/464-1600 ✉ Huérfanos 653, Santiago Centro ☎ 2/464-1950 ⊕ www.cocha.com.

VISITOR INFORMATION

Sernatur, the national tourist service, stocks maps and brochures and has a large and friendly staff that speaks English. The Providencia office, in a building with saffron-color columns, is located near the Manuel Montt metro stop. It is open weekdays 8:45–6 and Saturday 9–2.

Santiago runs two tourist information offices, one downtown in the Casa Colorada, the other on Cerro Santa Lucíá. They are open Monday–Thursday 10–6, Friday 10–5. For information about the Cajón del Maipo, stop by the office on the main square in San José de Maipo. The eager-to-please staff won't let you leave without an armload of brochures. The office is open weekdays 8:30–5:30.

🚩 **Tourism Offices Casa Colorada** ✉ Merced 860, El Centro ☎ 2/632-7783 ⊕ www.ciudad.cl/turismo. **Cerro Santa Lucía** ✉ Terraza Neptune, El Centro ☎ 2/664-4206 ⊕ www.ciudad.cl/turismo. **Providencia** ✉ Av. Providencia 1550, Providencia ☎ 2/731-8336 or 2/731-8337 ⊕ www.sernatur.cl. **San José de Maipo** ✉ Comercio 19788 ☎ 2/861-1275.

THE CENTRAL COAST

Updated by
Mark Sullivan

Most people head to the Central Coast for a single reason: the beaches. Yet this stretch of coastline west of Santiago offers much more than sun and surf. Valparaíso is a bustling port town with a jumble of colorful cottages nestled in the folds of its many hills. Ride any of the *acensores* (funiculars) for a great view. Viña del Mar has polished parks and modern high-rises.

Valparaíso

10 km (6 mi) south of Viña del Mar, 120 km (75 mi) west of Santiago.

Valparaíso has served as Santiago's port for centuries, and before the Panama Canal opened it was the busiest port in South America. Walking is the best way to experience Valparaíso. Its dramatic topography—45 *cerros,* or hills, overlooking the ocean—requires the use of winding pathways and wooden *ascensores* (funiculars) to get up many of the grades. The slopes are covered by candy-color houses—there are almost no apartments in the city. At the top of any of the dozens of stairways, the *paseos* (promenades) have spectacular views; many are named after prominent Yugoslavian, Basque, and German immigrants. Neighborhoods are named for the hills they cover.

What to See

❻ Cerro Concepción. Ride the Ascensor Concepción to this hilltop neighborhood covered with houses and cobblestone streets. The greatest attraction is the view, which is best appreciated from Paseo Gervasoni, a wide promenade to the right when you exit the ascensor, and Paseo Atkinson, one block to the east. Over the balustrades that line those paseos lie amazing vistas of the city and bay. Nearly as fascinating are the narrow, often steep streets above them. Continue uphill to Cerro Alegre, which has a bohemian flair. ✉ *Ascensor Concepción, Prat.*

❿ Galería Municipal de Arte. This crypt in the basement of the Palacio Lyon is the finest art space in the city. Temporary exhibits by top-caliber Chilean artists are displayed on stone walls under a series of brick arches. It's easy to miss the entrance, which is on Calle Condell just beyond the Museo de Historia Natural de Valparaíso. ✉ *Condell 1550* ☎ *32/939–562* 🖃 *Free* ⊙ *Weekdays 10–7, Sat. 10–5.*

> ### WORD OF MOUTH
>
> Each year Valparaíso welcomes the New Year with an awesome fireworks display. It lights up the whole city, but some of the best views are on the city's hills like Cerro Alegre or Cerro Concepción. However, if you want a truly magnificent experience, reserve tickets early at the Muelle Prat visitor's center for a boat cruise underneath one of the brightest and most beautifully choreographed pyrotechnic shows in the world.
> —macarena93

Mercado Central. Before *supermercados* became popular, locals did all their grocery shopping in markets such as this one topped by an enormous octagonal glass roof. On the ground floor you'll find produce piled high on tables and tumbling out of baskets, while upstairs is whatever types of fish the boats brought in that morning. A dozen eateries serve up the catch of the day. Watch your wallet, as this place gets crowded. ✉ *Cochrane between Valdivia and San Martín* ☎ *No phone.*

❹ Muelle Prat. Though its name translates as Prat Dock, the Muelle is actually a wharf with steps leading to the water. Sailors from the ships in the harbor arrive in *lanchas* (small boats), or board them for the trip back to their vessels. It's a great place to watch the activity at the nearby port, and the ships anchored in the harbor. To get a closer look, you can board one of the lanchas—it costs 2,000 pesos for the trip out to a ship and back, or 10,000 pesos for a 40-minute tour of the bay. Here you'll find the tourist information office and a row of souvenir shops. One of the city's best seafood restaurants, Bote Salvavidas, is a few steps away. ⊠ *Av. Errázuriz at Plaza Sotomayor.*

★ ❺ **Museo de Bellas Artes.** The art nouveau Palacio Baburizza houses the city's fine-arts museum. Former owner Pascual Baburizza donated his large collection of European paintings to the city. The fanciful decorative exterior is reminiscent of the style of Spanish architect Antoni Gaudí. Note the bronze children dancing around the portico. The museum was closed as this book went to press, but was slated to open again by the end of 2006. ⊠ *Ascensor El Peral to Paseo Yugoslavo* ☎ *32/252–332* ⊕ *www.museobaburizza.cl.*

❽ **Museo a Cielo Abierto.** The Open Sky Museum is a winding walk past 20 official murals (and a handful of unofficial ones) by some of Chile's best painters. There's even one by the country's most famous artist, Roberto Matta. The path is not marked—there's no real fixed route—as the point is to get lost in the city's history and culture. ⊠ *Ascensor Espíritu Santo up to Cerro Buenavista.*

❾ **Museo de Historia Natural de Valparaíso.** Within the Palacio Lyon, one of the few buildings to survive the devastating 1906 earthquake, is this rather outdated natural history museum. Among the more unusual exhibits are a pre-Columbian mummy, newborn conjoined twins in formaldehyde, and stuffed penguins. ⊠ *Condell 1546* ☎ *32/257–441* ⊠ *600 pesos* ☼ *Tues.–Sat. 10–1 and 2–6, Sun. 10–2.*

❷ **Museo Naval y Marítimo de Valparaíso.** Atop Cerro Artillería is the large neoclassical mansion that once housed the country's naval academy. It now contains a maritime museum, with displays on the history of the port and the ships that once defended it. ⊠ *Ascensor Artillería up to Paseo 21 de Mayo* ☎ *32/437–651* ⊠ *500 pesos* ☼ *Tues.–Sun. 10–6.*

❶ **Paseo 21 de Mayo.** Ascensor Artillería pulls you uphill to Paseo 21 de Mayo, a wide promenade surrounded by well-tended gardens and stately trees from which you can survey the port and a goodly portion of the city through coin-operated binoculars. A gazebo—a good place to escape the sun—seems to be hanging in midair. Paseo 21 de Mayo is in the middle of Cerro Playa Ancha, one of the city's more colorful neighborhoods. ⊠ *Ascensor Artillería at Plaza Advana.*

❸ **Plaza Sotomayor.** Valparaíso's most impressive square, Plaza Sotomayor, serves as a gateway to the bustling port. **Comandancia en Jefe de la Armada,** headquarters of the Chilean navy, is a grand, gray building that rises to a turreted pinnacle over a mansard roof. At the north end of the plaza stands the **Monumento de los Héroes de Iquique,** which honors Arturo Prat and other heroes of the War of the Pacific. In the middle of the square (beware of traffic—cars and buses come suddenly from all directions) is the **Museo del Sitio.** Artifacts from the city's mid-19th cen-

Valparaíso

Bahía de Valparaíso

Estación Bellavista

Antonio Varas

Ascensor Artillería

Plaza Aduana

Av. Errázuriz

Estación Puerto

Artillería

Av. Carampangue

Mercado Central

Plaza Sotomayor

Serrano

Blanco

Cochrane

Esmeralda

Ascensor Concepción

Ascensor El Peral

Prat

Papudo

O'Higgins

Cementerio Católico

Castillo

Carlos Ramos

Concepción

Templeman

Cumming

Cementerio de Disidentes

Monte Alegre

Morrison

Av. Pedro Montt

Cumming

Munich Hospital

Plaza Bismarck

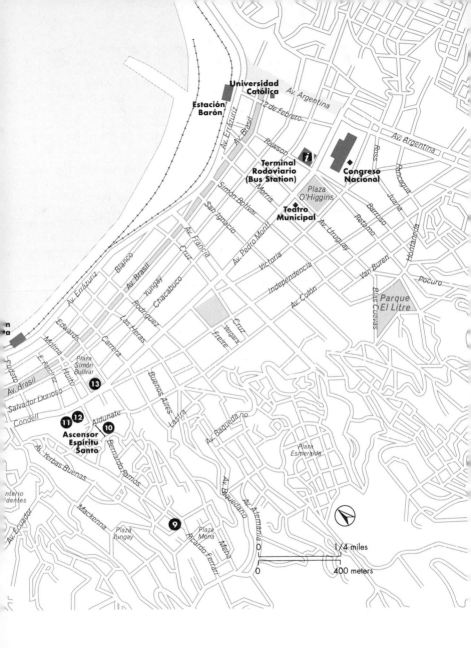

tury port, including parts of a dock that once stood on this spot, are displayed in the open under glass. ⊠ *Av. Errázuriz at Cochrane.*

^⑪ **Plaza Victoria.** The heart of the lower part of the city is this green plaza with a lovely fountain bordered by four female statues representing the seasons. Two black lions at the edge of the park look across the street to the neo-Gothic cathedral and its unusual freestanding bell tower. Directly to the north is **Plaza Simon Bolívar,** which delights children with swings, slides, and simple carnival rides. ⊠ *Condell at Molina.*

★ ^⑦ **La Sebastiana.** Some say the views from the windows of Pablo Neruda's hillside house are the best in all of Valparaíso. People come to La Sebastiana to marvel at the same ocean that inspired so much poetry. The house is named for Sebastián Collado, a Spanish architect who began it as a home for himself but died before it was finished. The incomplete building stood abandoned for 10 years before Neruda finished it, revising the design (Neruda had no need for the third-floor aviary or the helicopter landing pad) and adding curvaceous walls, narrow stairways, a tower, and a polymorphous character. A maze of twisting stairwells leads to an upper room where a video shows Neruda enunciating the five syllables of the city's name over and again as he rides the city's ascensores. His upper berth contains his desk, books, and some original manuscripts. What makes the visit to La Sebastiana memorable, however, is Neruda's nearly obsessive delight in physical objects. The house is a shrine to his many cherished things, such as the beautiful orange-pink bird he brought back embalmed from Venezuela. His lighter spirit is here also, in the carousel horse and the pink-and-yellow barroom stuffed with kitsch. ⊠ *Ferrari 692* ☎ *32/256–606* ⊕ *www.neruda.cl* ⊠ *1,800 pesos* ⊙ *Jan. and Feb., Tues.–Sun. 10:30–6:50; Mar.–Dec., Tues.–Fri. 10:10–1:30 and 3:30–6, Sun. 10:30–6.*

Where to Stay & Eat

$$–$$$ ✕ **Bote Salvavidas.** This restaurant on Muelle Prat has great views of the harbor from its glass-walled dining room. As you might guess, it specializes in seafood. A three-course *menu ejecutivo* (set lunch), available on weekdays, is quite the deal. ⊠ *Muelle Prat* ☎ *32/251–477* ⊟ *AE, DC, MC, V* ⊙ *No dinner Sun. and Mon.*

$$–$$$
Fodor'sChoice
★ ✕ **Café Turri.** Near the top of Ascensor Concepción, this 19th-century mansion commands one of the best views of Valparaíso. It also has some of the finest seafood. House specialties such as sea bass or shrimp in almond sauce are alone worth the effort of driving to the coast from Santiago. Outside there's a terrace and inside are two floors of dining rooms. The old-fashioned service, overseen by the affable owner, is excellent. ⊠ *Templeman 147, at Paseo Gervasoni* ☎ *32/252–091* ⊟ *AE, DC, MC, V.*

$$–$$$ ✕ **La Colombina.** This restaurant is in an old home on Cerro Alegre, one of the city's most beautiful hilltop neighborhoods. Dining rooms on two floors are notable for their elegant furnishings, stained-glass windows, and impressive views of the city and sea. Inventive seafood dominates the menu, and you can choose from a list of 80 national wines. ⊠ *Paseo Yugoslavo 15* ☎ *32/236–254* ⊟ *AE, DC, MC, V* ⊙ *No dinner Mon.*

$$
Fodor'sChoice
★ ✕ **Pasta y Vino.** The innovative food at this extremely popular restaurant on Cerro Concepción comes in eye-popping colors. Even the fanciful breads, which seem to swirl out of the basket, are lovely shades of

brown. Start with clams on the half shell flavored with ginger and lime, then move on to fettuccine tossed with ham, walnuts, and honey or ravioli filled with duck in a rich port wine reduction. The wine list, focusing on local vintages, is impressive. The hip young staff in floor-length black aprons couldn't be more accommodating. ⊠ *Templeman 352* ☎*32/ 496–187* ⚐ *Reservations essential* ⊟ *AE, DC, MC, V.*

$–$$$ ✕ **Coco Loco.** It takes a little more than an hour to turn 360 degrees in this impressive *giratorio* (revolving restaurant), meaning you can savor all the smashing views of the city. The vast menu ranges from *filete de ciervo salsa hongos* (venison in a mushroom sauce) to fettuccine with a squid-and-mussels sauce. ⊠ *Blanco 1781* ☎ *32/227–614* ⚐ *Reservations essential* ⊟ *AE, DC, MC, V* ☉ *No dinner Sun.*

¢–$ ✕ **Brighton.** Nestled below the eponymous bed-and-breakfast on the edge of Cerro Concepción, this popular restaurant has an amazing view from its black-and-white-tiled balcony. Vintage advertisements hang on the walls of the intimate dining room. A limited menu includes such Chilean standards as machas *a la parmesana* (razor clams Parmesan) and ceviche, as well as several kinds of crepes and a Spanish *tortilla* (egg-and-potato pie). An extensive wine list and cocktail selection make it a popular nightspot, especially on weekends, when there's live music. ⊠ *Paseo Atkinson 151* ☎ *32/223–513* ⊟ *AE, DC, MC, V.*

¢–$ ✕ **Donde Carlitos.** A stone's throw from the port are dozens of eateries specializing in whatever was caught that morning. You won't find any fresher fish than at this tiny storefront restaurant near Mercado Central. Through a window on the street you can watch the chefs prying open oysters and rolling razor clams into empanadas. The simple dining room has a half dozen tables under chandeliers shaped like—you guessed it—ships' wheels. ⊠ *Blanco 166* ☎ *32/217–310* ⊟ *No credit cards* ☉ *No dinner.*

¢ ✕ **Casino Social J. Cruz M.** This eccentric restaurant is a Valparaíso institution, thanks to its legendary status for inventing the *chorillana* (minced beef with onions, cheese, and an egg atop french fries), which is now served by most local restaurants. There is no menu—choose either a plate of chorillana for two or three, or *carne mechada* (stewed beef), with a side of french fries, rice, or tomato salad. Glass cases choked with dusty trinkets surround tables covered with plastic cloths in the cramped dining room. You may have to share a table. The restaurant is at the end of a bleak corridor off Calle Condell. ⊠ *Condell 1466* ☎ *32/211–225* ⊟ *No credit cards.*

$$–$$$ ⬚ **Casa Thomas Somerscales.** Perched high atop Cerro Alegre, this palm-
Fodor's Choice shaded mansion has an unobstructed view of the sea. As befits an ele-
★ gant home from the 19th century, its rambling hallways and wooden staircases lead to rooms of various shapes and sizes. Ask for Number 8, which has lovely French doors and a private terrace where you can enjoy your breakfast. All rooms at this boutique hotel are impeccably furnished with antique armoires and bureaus and beds piled high with imported linens. Dozens of trendy shops and restaurants are steps away. ⊠ *San Enrique 446* ☎ *32/331–379* ⊕ *www.hotelsomerscales.cl* ⬏ *8 rooms* ⚗ *Dining room, in-room safes, minibars, cable TV, in-room DVD, shop, Internet, meeting room* ⊟ *AE, DC, MC, V* ⊠⊙ *CP.*

$ ⊡ **Brighton B&B.** This bright-yellow Victorian house enjoys an enviable
Fodor'sChoice location at the edge of tranquil Cerro Concepción. The house is furnished
★   with brass beds and other antiques chosen by owner Nelson Morgado,
who taught architecture at the University of Barcelona. The terrace of
its restaurant and three of its six rooms have vertiginous bay views. One
room has a private balcony that is perfect for a romantic breakfast. Room
size varies considerably—only the so-called suite (just a larger room) is
spacious—but all are charming. ⊠ *Paseo Atkinson 151* ☎ *32/223–*
513 ⊕ *www.brighton.cl* ➫ *9 rooms* ♻ *Restaurant, bar, laundry serv-*
ice; no a/c, no room phones ⊟ *AE, DC, MC, V* ⦶⦶ *CP.*

$ ⊡ **Hostal La Colombina.** The location here is excellent: on a quiet street
just up the hill from the Ascensor Concepción, near Paseo 21 de Mayo
in the heart of Cerro Concepción. Dozens of shops and restaurants are
on the nearby streets. Rooms in this old house may be sparsely furnished,
but they are ample, with high ceilings and wooden floors. Most have
big windows, though none of them have much of a view. ⊠ *Concep-*
ción 280 ☎ *32/236–254 or 32/234–980* ⊕ *www.lacolombina.cl* ➫ *8*
rooms without bath ♻ *Dining room, wine bar; no a/c, no room phones,*
no room TVs ⊟ *AE, DC, MC, V* ⦶⦶ *CP.*

$ ⊡ **Puerta de Alcalá.** The rooms surround a five-story atrium flooded with
light at this central hotel. They have little personality, but are clean and
well equipped, with little extras like hair dryers. Those facing the street
are bright, but can be noisy on weekends. If you're a light sleeper, take
a room in the back. Try to get on the fourth floor—the lower floors get
less sunlight because they are blocked by the building next door. There's
a decent restaurant and bar on the ground level. ⊠ *Pirámide 524, at*
Condell ☎ *32/227–478* ⊕ *www.hotelpuertadealcala.cl* ➫ *21 rooms*
♻ *Restaurant, room service, in-room data ports, minibars, cable TV,*
bar, laundry service, meeting room; no a/c ⊟ *AE, DC, MC, V* ⦶⦶ *CP.*

Nightlife

BARS A short walk east of Plaza Sotomayor, **Bar Inglés** (⊠ Cochrane 851
☎ 32/214–625) has dark-wood paneling and the longest bar in town.
You can also order decent food. The huge antique mirrors of **Bar La Playa**
(⊠ Serrano 567 ☎ 32/218-011), just east of Plaza Sotomayor, give it a
historic feel. It becomes packed with party animals after midnight on
weekends in January and February.

DANCE CLUBS Some of the city's hottest dance clubs are found on the streets east of
Plaza Sotomayer. Among the top dance clubs is **Aché Havana** (⊠ Av. Errázuriz 1042 ☎ 9/521–9872), which plays mostly salsa and other Latin
rhythms. Nearby are several other large dance clubs: **Bulevar** (⊠ Av. Errázuriz 1154 ☎ No phone) has eclectic music on weekend nights. The
basement **Eterno** (⊠ Blanco 698 ☎ 32/219–024) plays only Latin dance
music, and opens weekends only.

TANGO Tango dancing is so popular in Valparaíso that you might think you were
in Buenos Aires. On Cerro Concepción, **Brighton** (⊠ Paseo Atkinson s/
n ☎ 32/223–513) has bolero music on Friday and tango on Saturday,
starting at 11 PM. Its terrace overlooks the city's glittering lights. Dance
to live tango music weekends at **Cinzano** (⊠ Anibal Pinto 1182 ☎ 32/
213–043), an old-fashioned watering hole facing Plaza Anibal Pinto.

Outdoor Activities

BEACHES If it's beaches you're after, head to Viña del Mar. Valparaíso has only one notable beach, **Playa Las Torpederas,** a sheltered crescent of sand east of the port. Though less attractive than the beaches up the coast, it does have very calm water. A short bus ride south of the city is **Laguna Verde,** a completely undiscovered stretch of shore that is absolutely gorgeous. There are no eateries, so make sure to pack a picnic.

BOATING Informal boat operators at **Muelle Prat** take groups on a 40-minute circuit of the bay for 2,000 pesos per person. If you have several people, consider hiring your own boat for 10,000 pesos.

Shopping

Cooperativa Artesanal de Valparaíso (⊠ Av. Pedro Montt at Las Heras 🕾 No phone) is a daily market where you can buy local crafts. The weekend flea market, **Feria de Antigüedades** (⊠ Av. Argentina at Plaza O'Higgins 🕾 No phone), has an excellent selection of antiques. On Cerro Concepción, **Paraíso del Arte** (⊠ Abtao 529 🕾 32/239–357) has a wonderful paintings and mosaics. Most days you'll find artists hard at work.

Viña del Mar

10 km (6 mi) north of Valparaíso.

In contrast to Valparaíso's hodgepodge of hillside houses, Viña de Mar has stylish high-rise apartment buildings that tower above its excellent shoreline. Here you'll find wide boulevards lined with palms, lush parks with sharply edged landscaping, and long manicured beaches.

What to See

Club Viña del Mar. It would be a shame to pass up a chance to see this private club's magnificent interior. The neoclassical building, constructed in 1901 of materials imported from England, is where wealthy locals come to play snooker. Nonmembers are usually only allowed to enter the grand central hall, but there are often tours of the building during the week. The club hosts occasional concerts during which you may be able to circumambulate the second-floor interior balcony. ⊠ *Plaza Sucre at Av. Valparaíso* 🕾 *32/680–016.*

Museo de Arqueológico e Historia Francisco Fonck. A 500-year-old stone *moai* (a carved stone head) brought from Easter Island guards the entrance to this archaeological museum. The most interesting exhibits are the finds from Easter Island, which indigenous people call Rapa Nui, such as wood tablets displaying ancient hieroglyphics. The museum, named for groundbreaking archaeologist Francisco Fonck—a native of Viña del Mar—also has an extensive library of documents relating to the island. ⊠ *4 Norte 784* 🕾 *32/686–753* 🖾 *1,000 pesos* ☉ *Tues.–Sat. 10–6, Sun. 10–1.*

Palacio Rioja. This grand palace was built by Spanish banker Francisco Rioja immediately after the earthquake that leveled much of the city in 1906. It contains a decorative arts museum showcasing a large portion of Rioja's belongings and a conservatory, so there's often music in the air. Performances are held in the main ballroom. The beautifully landscaped grounds are great for shady lounging or a picnic. ⊠ *Quillota 214* ☎ *32/689–665* 💷 *300 pesos* ☉ *Tues.–Sun. 10–1:30 and 3–5:30.*

★ **Palacio Vergara.** The neo-Gothic Palacio Vergara, erected after the 1906 earthquake as the residence of the wealthy Vergara family, houses the **Museo de Bellas Artes.** Inside is a collection of classical paintings dating from the 15th to the 19th century, including works by Rubens and Tintoretto. A highlight is the intricate parquet floor—you'll be given booties to wear over your shoes so as not to scuff it up. ⊠ *Av. Errázuriz 563* ☎ *32/680–618* 💷 *600 pesos* ☉ *Tues.–Sun. 10–2 and 3–6.*

Plaza José Francisco Vergara. Viña del Mar's central square, Plaza Vergara is lined with majestic palms. Presiding over the east end of the plaza is the patriarch of coastal accommodations, the venerable Hotel O'Higgins, which has seen better days. Opposite the hotel is the neoclassical Teatro Municipal de Viña del Mar, where you can watch a ballet, theater, or music performance. To the west on Avenida Valparaíso is the city's main shopping strip, a one-lane, seven-block stretch with extra-wide sidewalks and stores and cafés. You can hire a horse-drawn carriage to take you from the square past stately mansions.

Where to Stay & Eat

$–$$$ ✕ **Armandita.** Meat-eaters need not despair in this city of seafood saturation. A rustic restaurant half a block west of Avenida San Martín serves almost nothing but grilled meat, including various organs. The menu includes popular dishes such as *lomo a lo pobre* (flank steak served on a bed of french fries and topped with a fried egg). The *parrillada especial,* a mixed grill of steak, chicken, ribs, pork, and sausage, serves two or three people. ⊠ *6 Norte 119* ☎ *32/671–607* 🖃 *AE, DC, MC, V.*

$–$$$ ✕ **Calatrava.** The crimson-walled dining room is lovely, but the best tables at this elegant Italian eatery are on the glassed-in terrace. The atmosphere is laid-back, but that doesn't mean they forgo nice touches like crisp linen tablecloths and extravagant floral displays. The staff is affable, always ready to explain the dishes. If you want something simple, choose one of the freshly caught fish and have it grilled with a little lemon. ⊠ *5 Norte 476* ☎ *32/691–714* 🖃 *AE, DC, MC, V.*

$–$$$ ✕ **San Marcos.** More than five decades after Edoardo Melotti emigrated here from northern Italy, the restaurant maintains a reputation for first-class food and service. A modern dining room with large windows overlooks busy Avenida San Martín. Farther inside, the two dining rooms in the house the restaurant originally occupied are elegant and more refined. Complement your meal with a bottle from the extensive wine list. ⊠ *Av. San Martín 597* ☎ *32/975–304* 🖃 *AE, DC, MC, V.*

$$ ✕ **Delicias del Mar.** Nationally renowned chef Raúl Madinagoitía, who
Fodor's Choice has his own television program, runs the show here. The menu lists such
★ seafood delicacies as Peruvian-style seviche, stuffed sea bass, and machas *curadas* (steamed clams with dill and melted cheese). Oenophiles are impressed by the extensive, almost exclusively Chilean wine list. Save room for one of the excellent desserts. ⊠ *Av. San Martín 459* ☎ *32/ 901–837* 🖃 *AE, DC, MC, V.*

$–$$ ✕ **Sushi Taro.** With so much fresh fish available, it's a wonder that it's taken so long for sushi and sashimi to catch on with locals. Now that it has, it's hard to find a block downtown that lacks a Japanese restaurant. A favorite with locals is Sushi Taro, which occupies a few black-and-red rooms on Avenida San Martín. The tempura is flavorful, especially when it incorporates juicy Ecuadorean shrimp. Sushi here is a group activity—you can order platters of anywhere from 17 to 80 pieces. ⊠ *Av. San Martín 419* ☎ *32/737-956* ▤ *AE, MC, V.*

★ **$$-$$$** ✕▥ **Hotel Oceanic.** Built on the rocky coast between Viña and Reñaca, this boutique hotel has luxurious rooms with gorgeous ocean views. Rooms are cheerful in bright shades of pink and orange. The nicest ones have terraces, ideal for watching waves. The pool area on the rocks below is occasionally drenched by big swells. Although there's no beach access, the sands of Salinas are a short walk away. The restaurant is one of the area's best, serving French-inspired dishes such as shrimp crepes, *filete café de Paris* (tenderloin with herb butter), and congrio *oceanic* (conger eel in an artichoke mushroom sauce). ⊠ *Av. Borgoño 12925, north of town* ☎ *32/830-006* ⊕ *www.hoteloceanic.cl* ⟿ *22 rooms, 6 suites* ⚘ *Restaurant, room service, in-room data ports, in-room safes, minibars, cable TV, pool, hot tub, massage, sauna, bar, business services, meeting rooms; no a/c* ▤ *AE, DC, MC, V* ⎮O⎮ *BP.*

$$ ✕▥ **Cap Ducal.** This waterfront hotel was inspired by transatlantic ocean liners, but it takes imagination to see what the architect had in mind. Like the building, rooms are oddly shaped, but they are nicely decorated with plush carpets and pastel wallpaper. Those on the third floor have narrow balconies. Ask for a view of Reñaca, or you may see, and hear, the highway. The three-level restaurant serves seafood that tops the view. ⊠ *Av. Marina 51* ☎ *32/626-655* ⊕ *www.capducal.cl* ⟿ *22 rooms, 3 suites* ⚘ *Restaurant, in-room safes, minibars, cable TV, bar, laundry service; no a/c* ▤ *AE, DC, MC, V* ⎮O⎮ *BP.*

$$$$ ▥ **Hotel Del Mar.** A rounded facade, echoing the shape of the adjacent
Fodor'sChoice Casino Viña del Mar, means that almost every room at this oceanfront
★ hotel has unmatched views. The exterior is true to the casino's neoclassical design, but spacious guest rooms are pure 21st century, with sleek furnishings, original modern art, and sliding glass doors that open onto balconies. Marble floors, fountains, abundant gardens, and impeccable service make Hotel Del Mar one of Chile's most luxurious. An eighth-floor spa and infinity pool share the view. A stay here includes free access to the upscale casino, which evokes Monaco rather than Las Vegas. ⊠ *Av. San Martín 199* ☎ *32/500-800* ⊕ *www.hoteldelmar.cl* ⟿ *50 rooms, 10 suites* ⚘ *3 restaurants, café, in-room data ports, in-room safes, minibars, cable TV, indoor pool, exercise equipment, spa, bar, cabaret, casino, shop, babysitting, laundry service, concierge, Internet, business services, convention center* ▤ *AE, DC, MC, V* ⎮O⎮ *BP.*

$$ ▥ **Hotel Gala.** Modern rooms in this upscale 14-story hotel have city panoramas and lots of light. There's a small heated pool next to the bar. One block from the Avenida Valparaíso shopping strip, Gala is near most of the city's attractions. One down point: the staff seems stretched thin. ⊠ *Arlegui 273* ☎ *32/686-688* ⊕ *www.gala.cl* ⟿ *64 rooms, 13 suites* ⚘ *Restaurant, in-room data ports, Wi-Fi, minibars, cable TV, pool, massage, sauna, bar, laundry service, business services, convention center* ▤ *AE, DC, MC, V* ⎮O⎮ *BP.*

★ $ ⊞ **Residencia 555.** A stay in this charming wooden house, dating from 1912, may just make you feel like a local. Antiques fill the high-ceilinged living room, and a wide, curvaceous staircase leads to rooms on the second floor, several with balconies overlooking the garden. Considering the inn's charm, cleanliness, and central location, it's no surprise that Residencia 555 has several times been named the city's top guesthouse. ⊠ *5 Norte 555* 📞📠*32/739–035* ⊕*www.gratisweb.com/residencial555* ⤳*12 rooms* ᚼ*Restaurant, minibars, cable TV, laundry service* ▭*AE, DC, MC, V* ⦿*BP.*

$ ⊞ **Tres Poniente.** Come for the personalized service and for many of the same amenities as larger hotels at a fraction of their rates. Rooms are carpeted, nicely furnished, and impeccably clean. Two "apartments," larger rooms in back, are ideal for small families. Complimentary breakfast and light meals are served at the bright café in front, behind which is a small lounge with armchairs and a sofa. The small hotel is half a block from busy 1 Norte, but is remarkably quiet. ⊠ *3 Poniente 70, between 1 and 2 Norte* 📞*32/977–822* ⊕*www.hotel3poniente.com* ⤳*12 rooms* ᚼ *Café, room service, in-room safes, minibars, cable TV, bar, babysitting, laundry service, Internet, no-smoking rooms; no a/c* ▭*AE, DC, MC, V* ⦿ *BP.*

Nightlife

Viña's nightlife varies considerably according to the season, with the most glittering events concentrated in January and February. During the rest of the year, things only get going on weekends.

BARS   Though it's surrounded by the dance clubs and loud bars of Paseo Cousiño, **Kappi Kua** (⊠ Paseo Cousiño 11-A 📞 32/977–331) is a good place for a quiet drink. **Margarita** (⊠ Av. San Martín 348 📞 32/972–110) is a popular watering hole late at night. The namesake cocktail is a killer. **Rituskuan** (⊠ Av. Valparaíso at Von Schroeders 📞 9/305–0340) is colorful and has excellent beer and electronic music.

CASINO   With a neoclassical style that wouldn't be out of place in a classic James Bond movie, **Casino Viña del Mar** (⊠ Av. San Martín 199 📞 32/500–600) has a restaurant, bar, and cabaret, as well as roulette, blackjack, and 1,500 slot machines. It's open nightly until the wee hours of the morning most of the year. There's a 3,000-peso cover charge. People dress up to play here, especially in the evening.

DANCE CLUBS   The popular **El Burro** (⊠ Paseo Cousiño 12-D 📞 No phone) only opens Friday and Saturday. **El Mezón con Zeta** (⊠ Paseo Cousiño 9 📞 No phone) has a small dance floor. Viña's most sought-out dance club is **Scratch** (⊠ Bohn 970 📞 32/978–219), a long block east of Plaza Sucre.

Outdoor Activities

BEACHES   Just north of the rock wall along Avenida Peru is a stretch of sand that draws throngs of people December–March. Viña del Mar really has just one **main beach,** bisected near its southern end by an old pier, though its parts have been given separate names: Playa El Sol and Playa Blanca. South of town, on the far side of Cerro Castillo, the small **Playa Caleta Abarca** receives fewer sun worshippers than the main beach. A short drive north of town is the tiny **Las Salinas,** a crescent of sand that has the calmest water in the area.

HORSE RACING **Valparaíso Sporting Club** (✉ Av. Los Castaños 404 ☏ 32/689–393) hosts horse racing every Wednesday. The Clásico del Derby, Chile's version of the Kentucky Derby, takes place the first Sunday in February. Rugby, polo, cricket, and other sports are also played here.

Shopping

Outside of Santiago, there are more shops in Viña del Mar than anywhere else in Chile. Viña's main shopping strip is **Avenida Valparaíso** between Cerro Castillo and Plaza Vergara, where wide sidewalks accommodate throngs of shoppers. Stores here sell everything from shoes to cameras, and there are also sidewalk cafés, bars, and restaurants. **Falabella** (✉ Sucre 250 ☏ 32/264–740) is a popular small department store south of Plaza Vergara. For one-stop shopping, locals head to the mall. **Viña Shopping** (✉ Av. 15 Norte at 2 Norte ☏ No phone), on the north end of town, is a longtime favorite. Local crafts are sold at the **Cooperativa de Artesanía de Viña del Mar** (✉ Quinta 220, between Viana and Av. Valparaíso ☏ No phone). On the beach, near the pier at Muelle Vergara, the **Feria Artesanal Muelle Vergara** is a crafts fair open daily in summer and on weekends the rest of the year. There are also collections of **handicraft stands** on the road to Reñaca.

Central Coast Essentials

Transportation

BY AIR

The Central Coast is served by Lan Airlines via Santiago's Aeropuerto Comodoro Arturo Merino Benítez, an hour and a half from Viña del Mar and Valparaíso.

BY BUS

There is hourly bus service between Santiago and both Valparaíso and Viña del Mar. The two-hour trip costs about 2,100 pesos. Tur-Bus and other companies leave from Santiago's Terminal Alameda. Regular buses between Viña del Mar and Valparaíso cruise the main north–south routes of those cities.

🚌 **Bus Depots Valparaíso** ✉ Av. Pedro Montt 2800 ☏ 32/213–246. **Viña del Mar** ✉ Av. Valparaíso at Quilpué ☏ 32/882–661.

BY CAR

Since it's so easy to get around in Valparaíso and Viña del Mar, there's no need to rent a car to explore these cities. But if you want to travel to other towns on the coast, renting a car is advisable. Hertz, with an office in Viña del Mar, is the only international company in the region. The Chilean company Rosselot usually has much cheaper prices.

BY TAXI

In Valparaíso and Viña del Mar you can hail a taxi on busy streets and at plazas. If you prefer to phone a cab, have your hotel receptionist call a reputable company, such as Radio Taxis Turismo in Valparaíso, and Taxi Sucre in Viña del Mar.

🚌 **Taxi Companies Radio Taxis Turismo** ☏ 32/212–885. **Taxi Sucre** ☏ 32/687–136.

BY TRAIN

Merval, a commuter train linking Viña del Mar and Valparaíso, was closed as this book went to press. Improvements to the system, including underground stations in Viña de Mar, are expected to be finished in 2006. In Valparaíso the main station is at Muelle Prat. In Viña del Mar, it's south of Plaza Vergara.

🚆 **Train Stations Estación Puerto** ⊠ Plaza Sotomayor, Valparaíso ☎ 32/217-108. **Estación Viña del Mar** ⊠ Plaza Sucre ☎ No phone.

Contacts & Resources

BANKS & EXCHANGE SERVICES

All but the smallest Central Coast towns have at least one ATM, and both Valparaíso and Viña del Mar have dozens of them. All but the most humble restaurants and hotels accept major credit cards.

🏧 **ATMs Banco de Chile** ⊠ Cochrane 785, Valparaíso ☎ 32/356-500 ⊠ Av. Valparaíso 667, Viña del Mar ☎ 32/648-760.Tours

You need a tour guide to really get to know the twisting streets of Valparaíso. Enlace Turístico has several city tours and trips to the Central Coast's smaller towns. In Viña del Mar, Chile Guías has bilingual guides for city tours, and trips to beaches north and south.

🚌 **Tour Operators Chile Guías** ⊠ Av. Errázuriz 674, Viña del Mar ☎ 32/692-580 ⊕ www.chileguias.com. **Enlace Turístico** ⊠ Cerro Bellavista, Valparaíso ☎ 32/232-313 or 9/896-4887 ⊕ www.enlaceturistico.cl.

VISITOR INFORMATION

Viña del Mar has the best tourist office on the coast, offering fistfuls of helpful maps and brochures. It's north of Plaza Vergara at the corner of Avenida Libertad and Avenida Marina. It's open weekdays 9–2 and 3–7, weekends 10–2 and 3–7. There's also a friendly kiosk on Avenida Valparaíso that's open Monday–Saturday 10–2 and 3–7. Valparaíso has two information booths: one at Muelle Prat that is supposedly open daily 10–2 and 3–6 (although in real life the hours vary wildly), and one at the Terminal Rodoviario bus station, with the same hours except it closes Monday.

ℹ️ **Valparaíso Muelle Prat office** ⊠ Muelle Prat, Valparaíso ☎ 32/939-489. **Valparaíso Terminal Rodoviario office** ⊠ Av. Pedro Montt 2800, Valparaíso ☎ 32/939-669. **Viña del Mar main office** ⊠ Av. Libertad at Av. Marina, Viña del Mar ☎ 32/269-330. **Viña del Mar branch office** ⊠ Av. Valparaíso at Villanelo ☎ 32/683-355.

EL NORTE GRANDE

Updated by
Brian Kluepfel

A land of rock and earth, El Norte Grande is one of the world's most desolate regions. Here you will find the Atacama Desert, so dry that in many parts no rain has ever been recorded. Twice a decade it explodes in a riot of color known as *el desierto florido,* or "the flowering desert." Also here is the *altiplano,* or high plains, where you'll find such natural marvels as crystalline salt flats, geysers, and volcanoes. You'll also spot flocks of flamingos and odd mammals like the vicuña, a cousin to the llama.

Antofagasta

❶ *565 km (350 mi) north of Copiapó.*

Antofagasta is the most important—and the richest—city in El Norte Grande. It was part of Bolivia until 1879, when it was annexed by Chile in the War of the Pacific. The port town became an economic powerhouse during the nitrate boom. With the rapid decline of nitrate production, copper mining stepped in to keep the city's coffers filled.

The historic customs house, the town's oldest building, dates from 1866. Housed inside is the **Museo Regional de Antofagasta,** which displays clothing and other bric-a-brac from the nitrate era. ✉ *Bolívar 1888* ☎ *55/227–016* ⊕ *www.dibam.cl* ✇ *600 pesos* ⊘ *Tues.–Fri. 9–5, weekends 11–2.*

Where to Stay & Eat

$$–$$$$ ✕ **Club de Yates.** This seafood restaurant with nice views of the port caters to yachting types, which may explain why the prices are a bit higher than at other restaurants in the area. The food is quite good, especially the *ostiones a la parmesana* (oysters with Parmesan cheese). The maritime theme is taken to the extreme—the plates, curtains, tablecloths, and every decoration imaginable come in the mandatory navy blue. The service is excellent. ✉ *Av. Balmaceda 2705* ☎ *55/263–942* ✍ *Reservations essential* ▤ *AE, DC, MC, V.*

★ **$–$$** ✕ **Restaurant Arriero.** Serving up traditional dishes from Spain's Basque country, Arriero is the place to go for delicious barbecued meats. A healthful selection of national wines supplements the menu. The restaurant is in a pleasant Pyrenees-style inn decorated with traditional cured hams hanging from the walls. The owners play jazz on the piano almost every evening. ✉ *Condell 2644* ☎ *55/264–371* ▤ *AE, DC, MC, V.*

¢ ✕ **Don Pollo.** This rotisserie restaurant prepares some of the best chicken in Chile—a good thing, because it's the only item on the menu. The thatched-roof terrace is a great place to kick back after a long day of sightseeing. ✉ *Ossa 2594* ☎ *No phone* ▤ *No credit cards.*

★ **$$$–$$$$** ▦ **Hotel Antofagasta.** Part of the deluxe Panamericana Hoteles chain, this high-rise on the ocean comes with all the first-class luxuries, from an elegant bar with a grand piano to a lovely kidney-shape pool. The rooms, which have ample bathrooms and plenty of closet space, are comfortably furnished, and some have ocean views. A semiprivate beach is just steps from the hotel's back door. ✉ *Av. Balmaceda 2575* ☎ *55/228–811* ⊕ *www.hotelantofagasta.cl* ⇥ *145 rooms, 18 suites* ⌂ *Restaurant, room service, in-room safes, minibars, cable TV, Wi-Fi, pool, health club, hair salon, billiards, bar, shop, laundry service, business services, meeting rooms* ▤ *AE, DC, MC, V* ⦿ *BP.*

$ ▦ **Marsal Hotel.** This modern and clean hotel faces busy Calle Arturo Prat, so be sure to ask for one of the pleasant rooms in the back. All the rooms have nice touches like desks. The service here is quite friendly—the staff goes out of its way to recommend restaurants and arrange excursions. ✉ *Arturo Prat 867* ☎ *55/268–063* ⊕ *www.marsalhotel.cl* ⇥ *18 rooms* ⌂ *Minibars, cable TV, laundry service, business services, meeting rooms; no a/c* ▤ *AE, DC, MC, V* ⦿ *CP.*

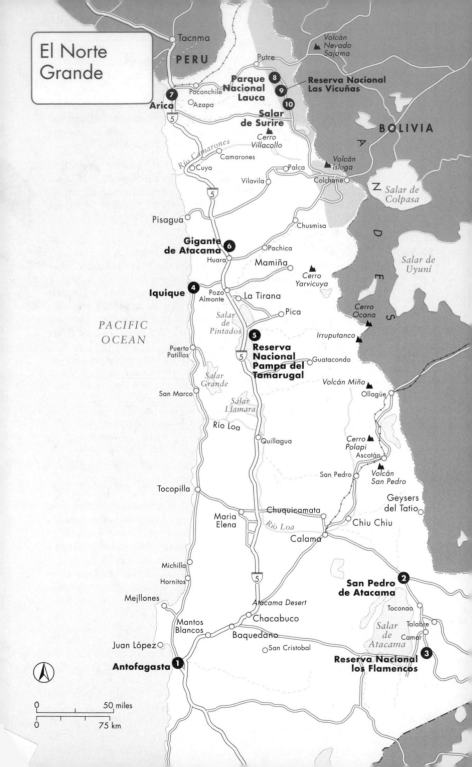

Nightlife

Nightlife in El Norte Grande often means heading to the *schoperias,* beer stands where the almost entirely male clientele downs *schops* (draft beers) served by scantily clad waitresses. The drinking generally continues until everyone is reeling drunk. If this is your idea of fun, check out the myriad schoperias in the center of town around the Plaza Colón.

If you're not quite ready for the schoperia experience, don't worry: there are also a few bars where you can have a quiet drink. With its swinging saloon-style doors and a great waitstaff donning cowboy hats and blue jeans, the **Country Pub** (⊠ Salvador Reyes 1025 ☎ 55/371–751) is lots of fun. The music doesn't go country, however, staying instead on the modern side of pop (think lots of Cindy Lauper videos). Antofagasta's elite head to **Wally's Pub** (⊠ Antonino Toro 982 ☎ 55/223–697), an American-style grill with American-style prices.

4

San Pedro de Atacama

★ ❷ *100 km (62 mi) southeast of Calama.*

With its narrow streets lined with whitewashed and mud-color adobe houses, San Pedro centers around a small Plaza de Armas teeming with artisans, tour operators, and others who cater to tourists. The 1744 **Iglesia San Pedro,** to the west of the square, is one of the altiplano's largest churches. It was miraculously constructed without the use of a single nail—the builders used cactus sinews to tie the roof beams and door hinges. ⊠ *Padre Le Paige s/n* ☎ *No phone* ☉ *Daily 8–8.*

Fodor'sChoice
★ The **Museo Arqueológico Gustavo Le Paige** exhibits an awe-inspiring collection of artifacts from the region, including fine examples of textiles and ceramics. The museum traces the history of the area from pre-Columbian times through the Spanish colonization. The most impressive exhibit is the well-preserved, fetal-positioned Atacameño mummy with her swatch of twisted black hair. Most of the items on display were gathered by the founder, Jesuit missionary Gustavo Le Paige. ⊠ *Padre Le Paige 380, at Paseo Artesenal* ☎ *55/851–002* 🌑 *2,000 pesos* ☉ *Weekdays 9–noon and 2–6, weekends 10–noon and 2–6.*

Just 3 km (2 mi) north of San Pedro lies the ancient fortress of **Pukara de Quitor.** This group of stone structures at the entrance to the Valle de Catarpe was built in the 12th century to protect the Atacameños from invading Inca. It wasn't the Inca but the Spanish who were the real threat, however. Spanish conquistador Pedro de Valdivia took the fortress by force in 1540. The crumbling buildings were carefully reconstructed in 1981 by the University of Antofagasta. ⊠ *On road to Valle Catarpe* ☎ *No phone* 🌑 *1,200 pesos* ☉ *Daily 8–8.*

The archaeological site of **Tulor,** 9 km (5½ mi) southwest of San Pedro, marks the remains of the oldest known civilization in the region. Built around 800 BC, the village of Tulor was home to the Linka Arti people, who lived in small mud huts resembling igloos. The site was only uncovered in the middle of the 20th century, when Jesuit missionary Gustavo Le Paige excavated it from a sand dune. Archaeologists hypothesize that the inhabitants left because of climatic changes and a possible sand storm. Little more about the village's history is known, and only one of the huts has been completely excavated. As one of the well-informed guides will tell you, even this hut is sinking back into the obscurity of the Atacama sand. ⊠ *9 km (5½ mi) southwest of San Pedro, then 3 km (2 mi) down the road leading to the Valle de la Luna* ☎ *No phone* 🖃 *1,500 pesos* ⊙ *Daily 8–8.*

Where to Stay & Eat

★ **$–$$** ✕ **Café Adobe.** With a lattice-covered dining area surrounding a blazing fire and a terrace that is open to the stars, Café Adobe is San Pedro's finest eatery. The regional and international cuisine is excellent, and the animated (at times downright frenetic) waitstaff makes for a unique dining experience. At night, a white-capped chef grills meat in the center courtyard. Try the perfectly seasoned steaks, the cheesy quesadillas, or any of the pasta dishes. There's an Internet café in the rear. ⊠ *Carcoles 211* ☎ *55/851–132* ⊟ *AE, DC, MC, V.*

$–$$ ✕ **Casa Piedra.** This rustic stone structure (*piedra* means "stone") affords views of the cloudless desert skies from its central courtyard. As at most San Pedro eateries, a blazing fire keeps you company. The sea bass and shrimp are among the best choices on the menu, which includes international and local dishes. Specialty sauces spice up any dinner. ⊠ *Caracoles 225* ☎ *55/851–271* ⊟ *AE, DC, MC, V.*

★ **$$$$** 🛏 **Hotel Explora.** Is it a modern monstrosity or an expressionist showpiece? Hotel Explora, built by the same company that constructed the much-lauded Hotel Explora in Parque Nacional Torres del Paine, attracted much criticism for not fitting in with the local architecture. On the other hand, it has also won architectural prizes for its skewed lines and sleek courtyard. The hotel, which has three-, four-, and seven-day all-inclusive stays—with tours, meals, and drinks included—delivers the best service and amenities of any lodging in northern Chile. The wood-and-tile floors and wall-to-wall windows make the views from each room more enjoyable. ⊠ *Domingo Atienza s/n* ☎ *55/851–110* ⊕ *www.explora.com* 🛏 *52 rooms* ♿ *Restaurant, fans, in-room safes, 4 pools, in-room hot tubs, massage, sauna, mountain bikes, horseback riding, bar, shop, babysitting, laundry service, Internet, meeting rooms, airport shuttle, free parking, no-smoking rooms; no a/c, no room TVs* ⊟ *AE, DC, MC, V* ¶⊚¶ *AI.*

$$$ 🛏 **Lodge Andino Terrantai.** An architectural beauty with river-stone walls, **Fodor'sChoice** Lodge Andino Terrantai has high-ceilinged rooms highlighted by beautiful tile floors and big beds piled with down comforters. Hand-carved ★ furnishings add a rustic feel. Throw open the huge windows to let in the morning breeze. The candlelit restaurant, perfect for a romantic dinner, serves international fare. There's also a tiny, natural-rock plunge pool in the center. The hotel is just a block away from the Plaza de Armas. ⊠ *Tocopilla 411* ☎ *55/851–140* ⊕ *www.terrantai.cl* 🛏 *21 rooms* ♿ *Restaurant, room service, fans, pool, laundry service; no room TVs* ⊟ *AE, DC, MC, V* ¶⊚¶ *BP.*

$$ 🛏 **Hotel Altiplánico.** This boutique hotel just outside the center of San Pedro has the look and feel of an altiplano pueblo. A river-stone walkway leads you from room to room, each with its own private terrace. Muted whites decorate the guest chambers, making them quite welcoming. Some rooms have private watchtowers for stargazing. ⊠ *Domingo*

Atienza 282 ☎ *55/851–212* ⊕ *www.altiplanico.cl* ⤵ *14 rooms, 12 with bath* ⌂ *Restaurant, pool, massage, laundry service, Internet, travel services; no a/c, no room phones, no room TVs* ▭ *AE, DC, MC, V* ⦾| *BP.*

$$ ☒ **Hotel Kimal.** This adobe-walled dwelling has comfortable rooms and a cheery central courtyard dotted with islands of desert shrubbery. The rooms are pleasantly airy, with skylights and reed ceilings. The excellent restaurant serves Chilean fare. The pool is ideal for cooling off after your desert exploration. ☒ *Domingo Atienza 452* ☎ *55/851–030* ⊕ *www.kimal.cl* ⤵ *11 rooms* ⌂ *Restaurant, minibars, pool, shop, laundry service; no a/c, no room TVs* ▭ *AE, DC, MC, V* ⦾| *BP.*

$ ☒ **Hotel Tambillo.** A good budget alternative, Hotel Tambillo has simple, rather drab rooms along a long, outdoor walkway. The outdoor garden, with a thatched-roof sitting area, is a nice place to relax. There's also a good restaurant. ☒ *Gustavo Le Paige 159* ☎☎ *55/851–078* ⊕ *www.hoteltambillo.cl* ⤵ *15 rooms* ⌂ *Restaurant; no a/c, no room phones, no room TVs* ▭ *No credit cards.*

Nightlife

The bohemian side of San Pedro gets going after dinner and generally ends around 1 AM. Most of the bars are on Caracoles. **Café Export** (☒ Caracoles at Toconao ☎ 55/851–547) is smaller and more intimate than the other bars in town. There's a pleasant terrace out back. **La Estaka** (☒ Caracoles 259B ☎ 55/851–201) is a hippie bar with funky decor, including a sculpted dragon hanging on one of the walls. Reggae music rules, and the international food isn't half bad either.

Outdoor Activities

San Pedro is an outdoors-lover's dream. There are great places for biking, hiking, and horseback riding in every direction. Extreme-sports enthusiasts can try their hand at sand-boarding on the dunes of the Valle de la Muerte. Climbers can take on the nearby volcanoes. The only trouble is the crowds. At the Valle de la Luna, for example, you'll sometimes encounter a caravan of 20 or 30 tourists scurrying toward the top of the large sand dune to watch the sunset. Whatever your sport, keep in mind that San Pedro lies at 2,400 meters (7,900 feet). ⚠ **If you're not acclimated to the high altitude, you'll feel tired much sooner than you might expect.** Also remember to slather on the sunscreen and drink plenty of water.

BIKING   An afternoon ride to the Valle de la Luna is unforgettable, as is a quick trip to the ruins of Tulor. You can also head to the Salar de Atacama. Bike rentals can be arranged at most hotels and tour agencies.

HIKING   There are hikes in all directions from San Pedro. Good hikes include trips through the Valle de la Muerte, as well as to the ruins of Pukara de Quitor. **Cosmo Andino Expediciones** (☒ Caracoles s/n ☎ 55/851–069) runs excellent treks with well-informed guides.

HORSEBACK   San Pedro has the feeling of a Wild West town, so why not hitch up your
RIDING   horse and head out on an adventure? Although the sun is quite intense during the middle of the day, sunset is a perfect time to visit Pukara de Quitor or Tulor. An overnight journey to the Salar de Atacama or the Valle de La Luna is a great way to see the region at a relaxed pace. **Herradura** (☒ Tocopilla s/n ☎ 55/851–087) provides horses and guides.

Shopping

Just about the entire village of San Pedro is an open-air market. The **Feria Artesenal,** just off the Plaza de Armas, is bursting at the seams with artisan goods. Here, you can buy high-quality knits from the altiplano, such as sweaters and other woolen items. **Galeria Cultural de Pueblos Andinos** (⌧ Caracoles s/n, east of town ☎ No phone) is an open-air market selling woolens and crafts. **Mallku** (⌧ Caracoles s/n ☎ No phone) is a pleasant store carrying traditional altiplano textiles, some up to 20 years old. **Rayo de La Luna** (⌧ Caracoles 378 ☎ 09/473–9018) sells jewelry made by local artisans.

Reserva Nacional los Flamencos

❸   *10 km (6 mi) south and east of San Pedro.*

Many of the most astounding sights in El Norte Grande lie within the boundaries of the protected Reserva Nacional los Flamencos. This sprawling national reserve to the south and east of San Pedro encompasses a wide variety of geographical features, including alpine lakes, salt flats, and volcanoes. You can get information about the park at the station run by CONAF, the Chilean forestry service. ⌧ *CONAF station near Laguna Chaxa* ☎ *No phone* ⊕ *www.conaf.cl* 🖭 *2,000 pesos* ☉ *Daily 8:30–1 and 2:30–6:30.*

★   About 10 km (6 mi) south of San Pedro you arrive at the edge of the **Salar de Atacama,** Chile's largest salt flat. The rugged crust measuring 3,000 square km (1,158 square mi) formed when salty water flowing down from the Andes evaporated in the stifling heat of the desert. Unlike other salt flats, which are chalkboard-flat surfaces of crystalline salt, the Salar de Atacama is a jumble of jagged rocks. **Laguna Chaxa,** in the middle of Salar de Atacama, is a very salty lagoon that is home to three of the world's four species of flamingos. The elegant pink and white birds are mirrored by the lake's glassy surface. Near Laguna Chaxa, beautiful plates of salt float on the calm surface of **Laguna Salada.**

★   One of the most impressive sights in Reserva Nacional los Flamencos is the 4,350-meter-high (14,270-foot-high) **Laguna Miscanti,** an awe-inspiring blue lake that merits a few hours of rest and repose. **Laguna Miñeques,** a smaller lake adjacent to Laguna Miscanti, is spectacular. Here you will find vicuña and huge flocks of flamingos.

★   Very few places in the world can compare to the **Valle de la Luna** (⌧ 14 km [9 mi] west of San Pedro). This surreal landscape of barren ridges, soaring cliffs, and pale valleys could be from a canvas by Salvador Dalí. Originally a small corner of a vast inland sea, the valley rose up with the Andes. The water slowly drained away, leaving deposits of salt and gypsum that were folded by shifting of the earth's crust and then worn away by wind and rain. It's best to visit Valle de la Luna in the late afternoon to take advantage of the incredible sunsets visible from atop the immense sand dune. Not far from the Valle de la Luna are the reddish rocks of the **Valle de la Muerte.** Jesuit missionary Gustavo Le Paige, who in the 1950s was the first archaeologist to explore this desolate area, discovered human skeletons. These bones are from the indigenous Atacameño people, who lived here before the arrival of the Spanish. He hypothesized that sick and the elderly may have come to this place to die.

Iquique

❹ *390 km (242 mi) northwest of Calama.*

Iquique is the capital of Chile's northernmost region, but it wasn't always so important. For hundreds of years it was a tiny fishing community. It wasn't until the great nitrate boom of the 19th century that Iquique became a major port. Many of those who grew rich on nitrate moved to the city and built mansions, almost all of which still stand today.

Unlike most cities, Iquique does not have a cathedral on the main plaza. Here instead you'll find the sumptuous **Teatro Municipal,** built in 1890 as an opera house. The lovely statues on the Corinthian-columned facade represent the four seasons. If you're lucky you can catch a play or musical performance here. ⊠ *Plaza Prat* ☎ *57/411–292* ✉ *Tickets 1,500–5,000 pesos* ☉ *Daily 8–7.*

★ For a tantalizing view into the opulence of the nitrate era, visit the Georgian-style **Palacio Astoreca.** This palace, built in 1903, includes such highlights as the likeness of Dionysus, the Greek god of revelry; a giant billiards table; and a beautiful skylight over the central hall. An art and natural history museum on the upper level houses modern works by Chilean artists and such artifacts as pottery and textiles. ⊠ *Av. Bernardo O'Higgins 350* ☎ *57/425–600* ✉ *Free* ☉ *Tues.–Fri. 10–1 and 4–7:30, Sat. 10–1:30, Sun. 11–2.*

Along the historic Calle Baquedano is the **Museo Regional,** a natural history museum of the region. It showcases pre-Columbian artifacts such as deformed skulls and arrowheads, as well as an eclectic collection from the region's nitrate heyday. ⊠ *Baquedano 951* ☎ *57/411–214* ✉ *Free* ☉ *Mon.–Sat. 9:30–1 and 3–6:30.*

Where to Stay & Eat

$–$$$ ✕ **Casino Español.** This venerable gentleman's club on Plaza Prat has been
Fodor's Choice transformed into a palatial Spanish restaurant, with beautiful Moorish
★ architecture that calls to mind the Alhambra in Granada. The service is good, though rather fussy, and the food is extravagant in the traditional Andalusian style. The paella *Valenciana* is quite good. ⊠ *Plaza Prat 584* ☎ *57/423–284* ✍ *Reservations essential* ☰ *AE, DC, MC, V.*

$–$$$ ✕ **Nautico Cavancha.** Located away from the center of the city, this seafood restaurant treats you to views of Playa Cavancha. It's very stylish, right down to the cloth napkins (a rarity in El Norte Grande). Try the shrimp in a pepper-whiskey sauce, or the paella for two, served by friendly bow-tied waiters. ⊠ *Los Rieles 110* ☎ *57/432–896* ✍ *Reservations essential* ☰ *DC, MC, V.*

★ **$$** ✕ **Taberna Barracuda.** An immensely popular bar and grill, Taberna Barracuda serves everything from tapas to rib-eye steak. The wine list is good, making this an ideal place to sample some of Chile's labels. A general sense of joviality and merriment here hearkens to the decadent days of the nitrate boom. Antiques ranging from brass instruments to time-stained photos decorate the labyrinthine, salitrera-era house. ⊠ *Gorostiaga 601* 🕾 *57/427–969* ⌂ *Reservations essential* ▤ *AE, DC, MC, V* ☺ *Closed Sun. mid-June–early Sept.*

¢–$$ ✕ **Boulevard.** Excellent seafood is served in a variety of ways at this intimate, candlelit restaurant. The cuisine is an interesting mélange of French and international recipes—try hake served in a creamy sauce or the *tagine*, a savory Moroccan stew. There's live music on weekends. ⊠ *Baquedano 790* 🕾 *57/413–695* ⌂ *Reservations essential* ▤ *MC, V.*

¢–$ ✕ **Restaurant Protectora.** A soaring molded ceiling and a huge chandelier overlook this contemporary restaurant next to the Teatro Municipal. The international menu includes such succulent items as lamb cooked in mint sauce and merluza con salsa margarita. The service, though a bit doting, is top-notch. ⊠ *Thompson 207* 🕾 *57/421–923* ▤ *AE, DC, MC, V.*

$$ ▥ **Terrado Suites.** A skyscraper at the southern end of Playa Cavancha, the Terrado is Iquique's most upscale hotel. A marble entryway leads you down to the comfortable lounge and restaurant area. Overstuffed sofas, Andean prints, and hardwood accents decorate the large suites, which have private balconies. The pool and underground sauna are a delight after a day in the desert. ⊠ *Los Rieles 126* 🕾 *57/437–878* ⊕ *www.terrado.cl* ⤳ *91 suites* ⌂ *2 restaurants, room service, in-room data ports, in-room safes, minibars, cable TV, 2 pools, gym, hot tub, massage, sauna, bar, babysitting, laundry service, business services, meeting rooms, airport shuttle, car rental; no a/c in some rooms* ▤ *AE, DC, MC, V* ¶◉¶ *BP.*

$ ▥ **Hotel Arturo Prat.** The only thing this luxury hotel in the heart of Iquique's historic district lacks is access to the ocean. To make up for this, it has a very pleasant rooftop pool area decorated with white umbrellas and navy-blue sails. The rooms are all comfortable and modern, though some look out onto the parking lot. Ask for one of the newer rooms, which are several notches above the rooms in the older section of the hotel. The Arturo faces the central square, and the restaurant, which serves good but somewhat uninspired fare, sits right on Plaza Prat. ⊠ *Anibal Pinto 695* 🕾 *57/427–000* ⊕ *www.hotelarturoprat.cl* ⤳ *83 rooms, 9 suites* ⌂ *Restaurant, room service, in-room safes, minibars, cable TV, pool, exercise equipment, sauna, billiards, bar, laundry service, business services, meeting rooms; no a/c in some rooms* ▤ *AE, DC, MC, V* ¶◉¶ *BP.*

★ $ ▥ **Hotel Atenas.** Housed in a venerable nitrate-era mansion on the beach, Hotel Atenas is truly a taste of the city's history. Antiques and wood furnishings fill most of the rooms. There are more modern rooms in the back, but these are not nearly as charming. The honeymoon suite has a giant tub where you can imagine the nitrate barons bathing in champagne. There's also a pleasant pool in the garden. ⊠ *Los Rieles 738* 🕾 *57/431–100* ⤳ *40 rooms, 3 suites* ⌂ *Restaurant, room service, fans, in-room safes, minibars, cable TV, pool, hot tub, laundry service, Internet; no a/c* ▤ *AE, DC, MC, V* ¶◉¶ *CP.*

Nightlife

Bars, most of which feature folk and jazz performances, get crowded around midnight. **Bar Sovia** (⊠ Tarapaca 173 🕾 57/517–015), perhaps the North's only microbrewery, is a relaxed place for a frothy brew. For sunset drinks and excellent empanadas head to **Choza Bambu** (✉ Arturo Prat s/n, Playa Cavancha ☎ 57/519–002). One of the city's most pop-·ular bars is **Van Gogh** (✉ Ramirez 805 ☎ 57/319–847), with impressive murals of the Dutch master's work filling the walls and live music on weekends. **Kamikaze** (✉ Bajo Molle, Km 7 ☎ No phone), part of a popular chain of discos, is jam-packed on weekends with young people dancing to salsa music. **Timber House** (✉ Bolívar 553 ☎ 57/422–538) has a disco upstairs and an Old West–style saloon downstairs.

Beaches

Just south of the city center on Avenida Balmaceda is **Playa Cavancha,** a long stretch of white, sandy beach that's great for families. You can stroll along the boardwalk and touch the llamas and alpacas at the petting zoo. There's also a walk-through aquarium housing a group of *yacares,* small crocodiles that inhabits the rivers of Bolivia, Argentina, and Uruguay. Because it's so close to town, the beach is often crowded. If you crave solitude, follow the coast south of Playa Cavancha for about 3 km (2 mi) on Avenida Balmaceda to reach **Playa Brava,** a pretty beach that's often deserted. The currents here are strong, so swimming isn't recommended. **Playa Blanca,** 13 km (8 mi) south of the city center on Avenida Balmaceda, is a sandy spot you can often have all to yourself.

Shopping

Many Chileans come to Iquique with one thing on their minds—shopping. About 3 km (2 mi) north of the city center is the **Zona Franca**—known to locals as the Zofri—the only duty-free zone in the country's northern tip. This big, unattractive mall is stocked with cheap cigarettes, alcohol, and electronic goods. Remember that large purchases, such as personal computers, are taxable upon leaving the country. ✉ *Av. Salitrera Victoria* ☎ *57/515–100* ⊕ *www.iquique.cl* ☺ *Mon. 4–9, Tues.–Fri. 10–9, Sat. 10–2 and 5–9.*

Reserva Nacional Pampa del Tamarugal

5 *96 km (60 mi) southeast of Iquique.*

The tamarugo tree is an anomaly in the almost lifeless desert. These bush-like plants survive where most would wither because they are especially adapted to the saline soil of the Atacama. Over time they developed extensive root systems that search for water deep beneath the almost impregnable surface. Reserva Nacional Pampa del Tamarugal has dense groves of tamarugos, which were almost wiped out during the nitrate era when they were felled for firewood. At the entrance to this reserve is a CONAF station. ✉ *24 km (15 mi) south of Pozo Almonte on Pan-American Hwy.* ☎ *57/751–055* ☐ *Free.*

Fodor's Choice ★ The amazing **Cerros Pintados** (Painted Hills), within the Reserva Nacional Pampa del Tamarugal, are well worth a detour to see the largest group of geoglyphs in the world. These figures, which scientists believe ancient peoples used to help them navigate the desert, date from AD 500 to 1400. They are also enormous—some of the figures are decipherable only from the air. Drawings of men wearing ponchos were probably intended to point out the route to the coast to the llama caravans coming from the Andes.

More than 400 figures of birds, animals, and geometric patterns adorn this 4-km (2½-mi) stretch of desert. There is a CONAF kiosk on a dirt road 2 km (1 mi) west of the Pan-American Highway. ⊠ *45 km (28 mi) south of Pozo Almonte* ☎ *57/751–055* 🖾 *1,000 pesos* ⊙ *Daily 9:30–6.*

Gigante de Atacama

❻ *84 km (52 mi) northeast of Iquique.*

The world's largest geoglyph, the Gigante de Atacama, measures an incredible 86 meters (282 feet). The Atacama Giant, thought to represent a chief of an indigenous people or perhaps created in honor of Pachamama (Mother Earth), looks a bit like a space alien. It is adorned with a walking staff, a cat mask, and a feathered headdress that resembles rays of light bursting from his head. The exact age of the figure is not known, but it certainly hails from before the arrival of the Spanish, perhaps around AD 900. ■ **TIP→** The geoglyph, which is on a hill, is best viewed just before dusk, when the long shadows make the outline clearer. ⊠ *Cerro Unita, 13 km (8 mi) west of the turnoff to Chusmiza* ☎ No phone 🖾 Free.

Arica

❼ *301 km (187 mi) north of Iquique.*

Arica boasts that it is "the land of the eternal spring," but its temperate climate and beaches are not the only reason to visit this small city. On Plaza Colón is the **Iglesia de San Marcos,** constructed entirely from iron. Alexandre-Gustave Eiffel, designer of that famed eponymous Parisian tower, had the individual pieces cast in France before erecting them in Arica in 1876. Across from Parque General Baquedano, the **Aduana de Arica,** the city's former customs house, is one of Eiffel's creations. It currently contains the town's cultural center, where you can find exhibits about northern Chile, old photographs of Arica, and works by local painters and sculptors. ☎ *No phone* 🖾 *Free* ⊙ *Daily 10–6.*

North of Parque General Baquedano is the defunct **Estacíon Ferrocarril,** the train station for the Arica-La Paz railroad. Though trains no longer run across the mountains to the Bolivian capital, there are round-trip journeys four times a week to the altiplano. The 1913 building houses a small museum with a locomotive and other remnants of the railroad. ☎ *No phone* 🖾 *Free* ⊙ *Daily 10–6.*

Hanging over the town, the fortress of **El Morro de Arica** is impossible to ignore. This former Peruvian stronghold was the site of one of the key battles in the War of the Pacific. The fortress now houses the **Museo de las Armas,** which commemorates that battle. As you listen to the proud drumroll of military marches you can wander among the uniforms and weapons of past wars. ⊠ *Reached by footpath from Calle Colón* ☎ *58/254–091* ⊕ *www.infoarica.cl/morro* 🖾 *500 pesos* ⊙ *Daily 8–8.*

Fodor'sChoice
★ A must for any visitor to El Norte Grande is the **Museo Arqueológico de San Miguel de Azapa.** In an 18th-century olive-oil refinery, this museum houses an impressive collection of artifacts from the cultures of the Chinchorros (a coastal people) and Tijuanacotas (a group that lived in the

altiplano). Of particular interest are the Chinchorro mummies, the oldest in the world, dating to 6,000 BC. The incredibly well-preserved mummies are arranged in the fetal position, which was traditional in this area. To look into their wrinkled, expressive faces is to get a glimpse at a history that spans more than 8,000 years. The tour ends at an olive press that functioned until 1956, a reminder of the still-thriving industry in the surrounding valley. The museum is a short drive from Arica. You can also make the 20-minute journey by colectivo from Patricio Lynch for about 600 pesos. ☒ *12 km (7 mi) south of town on the route to Putre* ☎ *58/205–555* ⊕ *www.uta.cl-masmas* ☒ *1,000 pesos* ☼ *Jan. and Feb., daily 10–7; Mar.–Dec., daily 10–6.*

Where to Stay & Eat

$–$$ ✕ **Maracuyá.** Wicker furniture enhances the cool South Pacific atmosphere of this pleasant, open-air restaurant that literally sits above the water on stilts. The international menu focuses on fish. Lauded by locals, it's always fresh; ask the waiter what the fishing boats brought in that day. House specialties include octopus grilled in lemon and olive oil, salmon in an orange sauce, and sea bass in the pineapple-flavored *salsa amazonia.* ☒ *Av. Comandante San Martin 0321* ☎ *58/227–600* ▭ *AE, DC, MC, V.*

¢–$ ✕ **Casino La Bomba.** In the old fire station, Casino La Bomba is more of a cultural curiosity than a culinary one. That said, the traditional food isn't bad, and the service is friendly. You'll have to maneuver around the parked fire trucks to get inside, where you are greeted by wagon-wheel furnishings and a menu heavy on grilled fish and roasted chicken. ☒ *Colon 357* ☎ *58/231–312* ▭ *No credit cards.*

¢–$ ✕ **El Rey de Mariscos.** Locals call this the best seafood restaurant in town, for good reason. The *corvina con salsa margarita* is a winner, as is the *paila marina,* a hearty soup stocked with all manner of fish. The dreary fluorescent lights and faux-wood paneling give this restaurant on the second story of a cement-block building an undeserved down-at-the-heel air. ☒ *Colon 565* ☎ *58/229–232* ▭ *AE, MC, V.*

★ **$$–$$$** ✕☒ **Hotel Arica.** The finest hotel in Arica, this first-class establishment sits on the ocean between Playa El Laucho and Playa Las Liseras. The rooms, which are elegant if a bit dated, have views of the ocean and great showers with plenty of hot water. The courteous and attentive staff can help set up sightseeing tours or book a table at a local eatery. The hotel's tony restaurant ($–$$), which takes advantage of the ocean views, serves fresh seafood cooked to order, including crab, octopus, and tuna. Don't pass up the conger eel chowder. ☒ *Av. Comandante San Martin 599* ☎ *58/254–540* ⊕ *www.panamericanahoteles.cl* ⇌ *108 rooms, 13 suites, 20 cabanas* ☖ *Restaurant, room service, in-room safes, minibars, cable TV, tennis court, pool, gym, bar, shop, children's programs (ages 2–10, summer only), laundry service, business services, convention center, meeting rooms, car rental* ▭ *AE, DC, MC, V* ☒ *BP.*

$–$$ ☒ **Hotel El Paso.** This modern lodging in the center of Arica surrounds a landscaped courtyard and a pool with a swim-up bar. Though not on the ocean, it's a short walk from any of the city's beaches. The superior rooms, with newer furnishings and larger televisions, are a far better value than the standard ones. ☒ *Av. General Velasquez* ☎ *58/230–808*

⊕ *www.hotelelpaso.cl* 🛏 *71 rooms, 10 suites* 🍴 *Restaurant, in-room safes, minibars, cable TV, tennis court, pool, bar, laundry service, Internet, free parking; no a/c* ▭ *AE, DC, MC, V* ⎟◯⎟ *BP.*

$ ⊞ **Hotel Plaza Colon.** This small hotel is a good option if you don't mind being so far from the beach. You are close to the downtown attractions, including the historic Iglesia de San Marcos. The pink-wall rooms are small but clean. ⊠ *San Marcos 261* ☎ *58/254–424* ⌗ *hotel_plaza colon@entelchile.net* 🛏 *39 rooms* 🍴 *Restaurant, room service, minibars, cable TV, babysitting, laundry service, free parking; no a/c* ▭ *AE, DC, MC, V* ⎟◯⎟ *CP.*

$ ⊞ **Hotel Saint Gregory.** Although it's quite a hike from Arica's city center, this pleasant oceanfront hotel is great for weary travelers who simply want to relax on the beach. Some of the rooms and common areas have dated decor, but the hotel is still a good value. Many rooms have their own hot tubs. ⊠ *Av. Comandante San Martin 1020* ☎ *58/257– 697* ⊕ *www.hotelsaintgregory.cl* 🛏 *28 rooms, 8 suites* 🍴 *Restaurant, some kitchenettes, cable TV, indoor-outdoor pool, exercise equipment, massage, billiards, bar, dance club, Internet, airport shuttle, free parking* ▭ *AE, DC, MC, V* ⎟◯⎟ *CP.*

Nightlife & the Arts

You can join the locals for a beer at one of the cafés lining the pedestrian mall of 21 de Mayo. These low-key establishments, many with outdoor seating, are a great place to spend an afternoon watching the passing crowds. An oddity in Arica is the attire of the servers in various tranquil cafés and tea salons: women serve coffee and tea dressed in lingerie. You might just want to check out the uniform of your server before you sit down.

In the evening you won't have trouble finding the city's many watering holes. For a more refined setting, try the lively, funky **Barrabas** (⊠ 18 de Septiembre 520 ☎ 58/230–928), a bar and adjoining disco that attracts Arica's younger set. **Discoteca SoHo** (⊠ Buenos Aires 209 ☎ 58/ 215–892), near Playa Chinchorro, livens things up weekends with the sounds of pop and cumbia. The beachfront **Puesta del Sol** (⊠ Raul Pey 2492 ☎ 58/216–150) plays '80s tunes and appeals to a slightly older crowd. Weekends you can enjoy live music on the pleasant terrace.

Beaches

Part of the reason people flock to Arica is the beaches. The surf can be quite rough in some spots, so look for—and heed—signs that say NO APTA PARA BAÑARSE (no swimming). South of El Morro, **Playa El Laucho** is the closest to the city, and thus the most crowded. It's also a bit rocky at the bottom. South of Playa El Laucho you'll find **Playa Brava,** with a pontoon that keeps the kids occupied. At the somewhat secluded white-sand **Playa Chinchorro,** 2 km (1 mi) north of the city, you can rent Jet Skis in high season.

Shopping

Calle 21 de Mayo is a good place for window-shopping. **Calle Bolognesi,** just off Calle 21 de Mayo, is crowded with artisan stalls selling handmade goods. Located outside the city in the Azapa Valley, the **Poblado**

Artesenal (✉ Hualles ☎ 58/222–683) is an artisan cooperative designed to resemble an altiplano community. This is a good place to pick up traditionally styled ceramics and leather.

Parque Nacional Lauca

★ ❽ *47 km (29 mi) southeast of Putre.*

On a plateau more than 13,000 ft above sea level, the magnificent Parque Nacional Lauca shelters flora and fauna found in few other places in the world. Cacti, grasses, and a brilliant emerald-green moss called *llareta* dot the landscape. Playful vizcacha—rabbitlike rodents with long tails—laze in the sun, and llamas, graceful vicuñas, and alpacas make their home here as well. About 10 km (6 mi) into the park you come upon a CONAF station with informative brochures. ✉ *Off Ruta 11* ☎ *58/250–570 in Arica* ⊕ *www.conaf.cl* ✉ *Free.*

Within the park, off Ruta 11, is the altiplano village of **Parinacota,** one of the most beautiful in all of Chile. In the center of the village sits the whitewashed **Iglesia Parinacota,** dating from 1789. Inside are murals depicting sinners and saints and a mysterious "walking table," which parishioners have chained to the wall for fear that it will steal away in the night. Opposite the church you'll find crafts stalls run by Aymara women in the colorful shawls and bowler hats worn by many altiplano women. Only 18 people live in the village, but many more make a pilgrimage here for annual festivals such as the Fiesta de las Cruces, held on May 3, and the Fiesta de la Virgen de la Candelaria, a three-day romp that begins on February 2.

Lago Chungará sits on the Bolivian border at an amazing altitude of 4,600 meters (15,100 feet) above sea level. Volcán Parinacota, at 6,330 meters (20,889 feet), casts its shadow onto the lake's glassy surface. Hundreds of flamingos make their home here. There is a CONAF-run office at Lago Chungará on the highway just before the lake. ✉ *From Ruta 11, turn north on Ruta A-123* ☎ *No phone* ⊕ *www.conaf.cl* ✉ *Free* ☉ *CONAF office daily 8–8.*

> ## WORD OF MOUTH
>
> "I had always associated the *altiplano* with Peru and Bolivia, but discovering the beauty of Chile's high plains, just a few hours from the coast, was a real treat! I could hardly believe my eyes when I saw pale pink flamingos soaring over the lakes at 5,000 meters above sea level.   –Brian K.

Reserva Nacional Las Vicuñas

★ ❾ *121 km (75 mi) southeast of Putre.*

Although it attracts far fewer visitors than neighboring Parque Nacional Lauca, Reserva Nacional Las Vicuñas contains some incredible sights—salt flats, high plains, and alpine lakes. And you can enjoy the vistas without running into buses full of tourists. The reserve, which stretches some 100 km (62 mi), has a huge herd of graceful vicuñas. Although quite similar to their larger cousins, llamas and alpacas, vicuñas have not been domesticated. Their incredibly soft wool, among the most prized in the world, led to so much hunting that these creatures were threatened with extinction. Today it is illegal to kill a vicuña. Getting to this reserve, unfortunately, is quite a challenge. There is no public transportation, and the roads are only passable in four-wheel-drive vehicles. Many people choose to take a tour out of Arica. ✉ *From Ruta 11, take Ruta A-21 south to park headquarters* ☎ *58/250–570 in Arica* ⊕ *www.conaf.cl.*

❿ After passing through the high plains, where you'll spot vicuña, alpaca, and the occasional desert fox, you'll catch your first glimpse of the sparkling **Salar de Surire**. Seen from a distance, the salt flat appears to be a giant white lake. Three of the world's six species of flamingos (Andean, Chilean, and James') live here. ✉ *South from Reserva Nacional Las Vicuñas on Ruta A-235* ☎ *58/250–570* ⊕ *www.conaf.cl* ▨ *Free.*

El Norte Grande Essentials

Transportation

BY AIR

Since there are no international airports in El Norte Grande, you can't fly here directly from the United States, Canada, Europe, or Australia. You must fly into Santiago and transfer to a flight headed to Antofagasta, Iquique, or Arica. Avant and Lan fly from Santiago to El Norte Grande. Round-trip flights can run up to 300,000 pesos or more. You can also get here from other South American countries. Lan runs direct flights between El Norte Grande and neighboring Bolivia and Peru.

Since the cities in El Norte Grande are far apart, taking planes between them can save you both time and a lot of hassle. Avant, Sky Airline, and Lan offer service between the major cities. Prices range from 28,000 to 105,000 pesos.

🛪 **Airlines Avant** ☎ 55/452-050 in Antofagasta ⊕ www.avant.cl. **Lan** ☎ 55/265-151 in Antofagasta, 55/313-927 in Calama, 57/427-600 in Iquique, 58/251-641 in Arica ⊕ www.lan.com. **Sky Airline** ☎ 600/600-2828 ⊕ www.skyairline.com.
🛪 **Airports Antofagasta** ☎ 55/269-077. **Arica** ☎ 58/211-116.
Calama ☎ 55/312-348. **Iquique** ☎ 57/407-000.

BY BUS

Getting around by bus in El Norte Grande is easy. There is a terminal in every major city with frequent departures to the other cities as well as smaller towns in the area. Keep in mind that there may be no bus service to the smaller villages or the more remote national parks.

No bus company has a monopoly, so there are often several bus stations in each city. Because many companies may be running buses along the same route, shop around for the best price. The fare for a 300-km (186-mi) trip usually runs around 8,000 pesos. For longer trips find a bus that has a *salon semi-cama*, with seats that recline halfway; the extra comfort will make all the difference.

BY CAR

With some patience, you can get everywhere in this region by public transport; however, a car is definitely the best way to see El Norte Grande.

Driving in the cities can be a little hectic, but once you get on the highway it is usually smooth sailing. The roads of the north are generally well maintained. The farther from major population centers you travel—such as the remote national parks like Parque Nacional Lauca and Reserva Nacional Las Vicuñas—the worse the roads become. Destinations like these require a four-wheel-drive vehicle. Ruta 5, more familiarly known as the Pan-American Highway, bisects all of northern Chile. Ruta 1, Chile's answer to California's Highway 101, is a beautiful coastal highway running between Antofagasta and Iquique.

BY TAXI

Taxis are the most efficient way to get around any city in El Norte Chico. They're easy to hail on the streets, but late at night you might want to ask someone at a hotel or restaurant to call one for you. Taxis often function as *colectivos,* meaning they will pick up anybody going in the same direction. The driver will adjust the price accordingly. Almost no taxis have meters, but many have the price posted on the windshield. Make sure you establish the price before getting inside. Prices range 700 pesos–2,800 pesos, depending on the distance traveled and whether the taxi is a colectivo. Prices rise an average of 20% at night. Taxi drivers often will rent out their services for the day for a flat fee.

Contacts and Resources

TOURS

Tours can be arranged in the major cities and a number of the smaller towns. It's a good idea to shop around to make sure that you're getting the best itinerary and the best price. There are myriad tour agencies in San Pedro de Atacama. Cosmo Andino Expediciones offers excellent tours with well-informed guides to the Salar de Uyuni and other destinations. Herradura runs horseback tours.

In Arica and Iquique, a well-respected agency called Geotour arranges trips to Parque Nacional Lauca, the Salar de Surire, and the Reserva Nacional Las Vicuñas. Most Arica-based companies can arrange a one-day altiplano tour for about 15,000 pesos.

Tour Operators Cosmo Andino Expediciones ⊠ Caracoles s/n, San Pedro de Atacama ☎ 55/851-069. **Desertica Expediciones** ⊠ La Torre 2732, Antofagasta ☎ 55/386-877 ⊕ www.desertica.cl. **Geotour** ⊠ Bolognesi 421, Arica ☎ 58/253-927 ⊠ Baquedano 982, Iquique ☎ 57/428-984 ⊕ www.geotour.cl. **Herradura** ⊠ Tocopilla s/n, San Pedro de Atacama ☎ 55/851-087.

VISITOR INFORMATION

Most major cities in El Norte Grande have an office of Sernatur, Chile's tourism agency (www.sernatur.cl). Here you'll find helpful information about the region, including maps and brochures. Some staff members speak English.

Sernatur Offices Antofagasta ⊠ Maipú 240 ☎ 55/264-044. **Arica** ⊠ San Marcos 101 ☎ 58/252-054. **Iquique** ⊠ Anibal Pinto 436 ☎ 57/312-238. **San Pedro de Atacama** ⊠ Toconao at Gustavo Le Paige ☎ 55/851-420.

THE LAKE DISTRICT

As you travel the winding roads of the Lake District, the snowcapped shoulders of volcanoes emerge, mysteriously disappear, then materialize again, peeping through trees or towering above broad valleys. The sometimes difficult journey through breathtaking mountain passes is almost inevitably rewarded by views of a glistening lake, vibrant and blue. Often, there are hot springs in which you can soak stiff muscles.

Temuco

1 *675 km (405 mi) south of Santiago.*

This northern gateway to the Lake District has a more Latin flavor than the communities farther south, but it's also an odd juxtaposition of modern architecture and indigenous markets, of traditionally clad Mapuche women darting across the street and business executives talking on cell phones, but, oddly enough, it all works. This is big-city life Chilean style, and it warrants a day if you have the time.

Housed in a 1924 mansion, the **Museo Regional de la Araucanía** covers the history of the area. It has an eclectic collection of artifacts and relics, including musical instruments, utensils, and the country's best collection of indigenous jewelry. Upstairs, exhibits document the Mapuche people's three-century struggle to keep control of their land. The presentation could

> ### LAKE DISTRICT FESTIVALS
>
> Summer, with its better weather and ample presence of vacationers, means festival season in the Lake District. In late January and early February, Semanas Musicales de Frutillar brings together the best in classical music. Verano en Valdivia is a two-month-long celebration centered around the February 9 anniversary of the founding of Valdivia. Villarrica hosts a Muestra Cultural Mapuche in January and February that shows off Mapuche art and music.

be more evenhanded: the rhetoric glorifies the Central European colonization of this area as the *pacificación de la Araucanía* (taming of the Araucanía territories). But the museum gives you a reasonably good Spanish-language introduction to Mapuche history, art, and culture. ⊠ *Av. Alemania 84* ☏ *45/211–108* ☏ *500 pesos* ☉ *Weekdays 9–5, Sat. 11–5, Sun. 11–1.*

★ Author Pablo Neruda was Chile's most famous train buff. (Neruda spent his childhood in Temuco and his father was a rail worker.) Accordingly, the city has transformed its old rail yard into the **Museo Nacional Ferroviario Pablo Neruda**, a well laid-out museum documenting Chile's rail history and dedicated to the author's memory. Thirteen locomotives (1 diesel and 12 steam) and nine train carriages are housed in the round engine building. Scattered among the exhibits are snippets from Neruda's writings. Exhibits are labeled in Spanish, but an English-speaking guide is on hand if you need translation. The museum lies a bit off the beaten path, but if trains fascinate you, as they did Neruda, it's worth the short

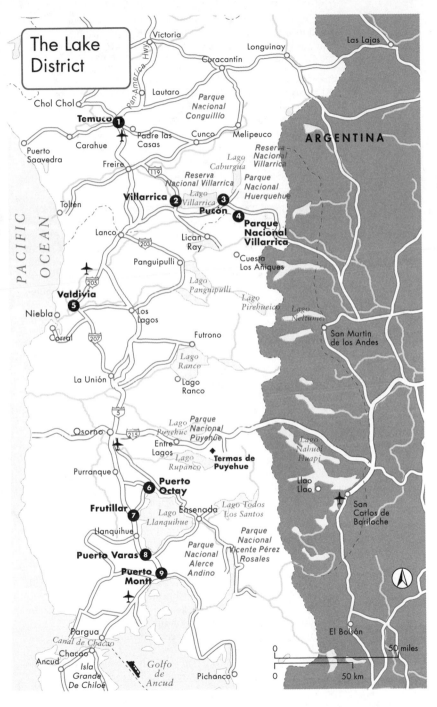

The Lake District

PACIFIC OCEAN

ARGENTINA

Victoria
Longuinay
Las Lajas
Curacautín
Pan-America Hwy
Chol Chol
Lautaro
Parque
Nacional
Conguillio
Temuco 1
Padre las Casas
Cunco
Melipeuco
Puerto Saavedra
Carahue
Freire
119
Reserva Nacional Villarrica
Lago Caburgua
Toltén
Reserva Nacional Villarrica
Lago Villarrica
Parque Nacional Huerquehue
Villarrica 2
3
Pucón 4
Lanco
203
Parque Nacional Villarrica
Licán Ray
Panguipulli
Cuesta Los Añiques
Lago Panguipulli
Lago Pirehueico
Lago Neltume
Valdivia 5
Niebla
Los Lagos
San Martín de los Andes
Corral
207
Futrono
Lago Ranco
La Unión
Lago Ranco
Osorno
5
Lago Puyehue
215
Parque Nacional Puyehue
Lago Nahuel Huapi
Entre Lagos
Lago Rupanco
Termas de Puyehue
Purranque
Puerto Octay 6
Llao Llao
San Carlos de Bariloche
Frutillar 7
Lago Llanquihue
Ensenada
Lago Todos Los Santos
Llanquihue
Parque Nacional Vicente Pérez Rosales
Puerto Varas 8
Parque Nacional Alerce Andino
Puerto Montt 9
Pargua
Canal de Chacao
Ancud
Chacao
Isla Grande De Chiloé
Golfo de Ancud
Pichanco
El Bolsón

0   50 miles
0   50 km

taxi ride from downtown. This new museum is a work in progress, with further acquisitions and transformation of other rail-yard buildings underway at this writing. ⊠ *Av. Barros Arana 565* ☎ *45/227–613* 🖃 *1,000 pesos* ☉ *Tues.–Sun. 9–6.*

The imposing **Monumento Natural Cerro Ñielol** is the hillside site where the 1881 treaty between the Mapuche and the Chilean army was signed, allowing for the city of Temuco to be established. Trails bloom with bright red *copihues* (a bell-like flower with lush green foliage), Chile's national flower, in autumn (March–May). The monument, not far from downtown, is part of Chile's national park system. ⊠ *Av. Arturo Prat, 5 blocks north of Plaza Teodoro Schmidt* 🖃 *700 pesos* ☉ *Jan.–Mar., daily 8 AM–11 PM; Apr.–Nov., daily 8:30–12:30 and 2:30–6.*

Where to Stay & Eat

$$–$$$ ✕ **El Fogón.** Decorated with primary colors—yellow walls, red tablecloths, and blue dishes—this place certainly stands out in pastel-hue Temuco. The Chilean-style *parrillada*, or grilled beef, is the specialty of the house. Barbecue here has subtler spices than its better-known Argentine counterpart. The friendly owners will gladly take the time to explain the menu to the uninitiated. Even though this is close to downtown, you should splurge on a cab if you're coming to this dark street at night. ⊠ *Aldunate 288* ☎ *45/737–061* 🖃 *No credit cards.*

$$–$$$ ✕ **La Pampa.** Wealthy local professionals frequent this upscale modern steak house for its huge, delicious cuts of beef and the best *papas fritas* (french fries) in Temuco. Although most Chilean restaurants douse any kind of meat with a creamy sauce, this is one of the few exceptions: the entrées are served without anything but the simplest of seasonings. ⊠ *Caupolicán 0155* ☎ *45/329–999* 🍴 *Reservations essential* 🖃 *AE, DC, MC, V* ☉ *No dinner Sun.*

$–$$ ✕ **Centro Español.** The basement dining room of Centro Español, an association that promotes Spanish culture in Temuco, is open to all for lunch and dinner. You have your choice of four or five rotating prix-fixe menus. There will always be something Spanish, something seafood, and something meaty. *Jamón de Serrano*, a salty type of ham, is a specialty. ⊠ *Av. Bulnes 483* ☎ *45/217–700* 🖃 *AE, DC, MC, V.*

$–$$ ✕ **Confitería Central.** Coffee and homemade pastries are the specialties of this café, but sandwiches and other simple dishes are also available. Steaming-hot empanadas are served on Sunday and holidays, and during the week you'll swear all of Temuco stops by for a quick bite for lunch among the clattering of dishes and the army of waitresses maneuvering their way around the tables. ⊠ *Av. Bulnes 442* ☎ *45/210–083* 🖃 *DC, MC, V.*

$–$$ ✕ **Mercado Municipal.** In the central market around the produce stalls are small stands offering such typical Chilean meals as cazuela and pastel de choclo. Many have actually taken on the trappings of sit-down restaurants, and a few even have air-conditioning. The complex closes at 8 in summer and 6 the rest of the year. ⊠ *Manuel Rodríguez 960* ☎ *No phone* 🖃 *credit cards not accepted.*

$–$$ ✕🖭 **Hotel Frontera.** This lovely old hotel is really two in one, with *nuevo* (new) and *clásico* (classic) wings facing each other across Avenida

Bulnes. Tastefully decorated rooms have double-pane windows to keep out the street noise. Opt for the less expensive rooms in the newer wing—they're nicer anyway. La Taberna, the downstairs restaurant on the clásico side ($$–$$$), has excellent steak and seafood dining. An orchestra plays and people dance on weekends. ⊠ *Av. Bulnes 733–726* ☎ *45/200–400* ⊕ *www.hotelfrontera.cl* ⇥ *60 rooms, 2 suites* ⋄ *Restaurant, minibars, cable TV, bar, laundry service, business services, convention center, meeting room; no a/c* ═ *AE, DC, MC, V* ⦿ *BP.*

★ **$** ✕⊞ **Hotel Continental.** If you appreciate faded elegance and don't mind an uneven floorboard or two, some peeling paint and few conveniences, the 1890 Continental is for you. Rooms, painted in ash-blue and cream tones, have hardwood floors and lofty ceilings. The hotel has hosted Nobel laureates Pablo Neruda and Gabriela Mistral, and former president Salvador Allende. The restaurant ($$–$$$) serves delicious French cuisine. Good choices include the steak au poivre and the salade niçoise. ⊠ *Antonio Varas 708* ☎ *45/238–973* ⊕ *www.turismochile.cl/continental/* ⇥ *40 rooms, 20 with bath* ⋄ *Restaurant, bar, meeting room; no a/c, no TV in some rooms* ═ *AE, DC, MC, V* ⦿ *CP.*

$$–$$$ ⊞ **Hotel Terraverde.** Temuco's most luxurious lodging combines all the comforts of a modern hotel with the style of a hunting lodge. The dramatic, glass-enclosed spiral staircase leads off the stone-wall lobby with its huge fireplace and has a view of Cerro Ñielol. Cheerful rooms have lovely wood furnishings. Rates include a huge breakfast buffet, a nice change from the roll and coffee served at many other lodgings in the region. ⊠ *Av. Arturo Prat 220* ☎ *45/239–999, 2/234–9610 in Santiago* ⊕ *www.panamericanahoteles.cl* ⇥ *64 rooms, 10 suites* ⋄ *Restaurant, in-room safes, minibars, cable TV, some Wi-Fi, pool, sauna, piano bar, laundry service, Internet room, business services, convention center, meeting rooms, airport shuttle, travel services, no a/c, no-smoking rooms* ═ *AE, DC, MC, V* ⦿ *BP.*

$ ⊞ **Don Eduardo Hotel.** Orange inside and out, this pleasant nine-story hotel is made up entirely of cozy furnished apartments, with comfortable chairs and dining area. All have two or three bedrooms and kitchenettes. The many business travelers who frequent the place appreciate the work areas, with desks and shelves, although you do need to go downstairs to log on to the Internet. An eager-to-please staff tends to your needs. ⊠ *Bello 755* ☎ *45/214–133* ⊕ *www.hoteldoneduardo.cl* ⇥ *33 apartments* ⋄ *Restaurant, cable TV, Internet room, business services, meeting room; no a/c* ═ *AE, DC, MC, V* ⦿ *BP.*

$ ⊞ **Hotel Aitué.** The exterior of this hotel is unimposing; in fact, its covered drive-up entry, set back from the road, might cause you to drive right past it. Once you're in, though, you'll find that this small, pleasant business-class hotel has bright, airy rooms. They're on the smallish side, but cozy and comfortable, and come complete with minibars and music systems. ⊠ *Antonio Varas 1048* ☎ *45/212–512* ⊕ *www.hotelaitue.cl* ⇥ *35 rooms* ⋄ *Coffee shop, minibars, cable TV, bar, laundry service, Internet room, business services, meeting rooms; no a/c* ═ *AE, DC, MC, V* ⦿ *CP.*

$ ⊞ **Hotel Turismo.** Originally established as a budget accommodation, this three-story hotel retains its bland facade. The interior has been upgraded, however, with a comfortable lobby and rooms with their own music systems, cushy beds, and tables and chairs. A lime-green color scheme permeates throughout. ⊠ *Av. Lynch 563* 🕾🕾 *45/911–090* ⊕ *www.hotelturismotemuco.cl* ⬎ *30 rooms* ♿ *Restaurant, cable TV, bar, laundry service; no a/c* ⊟ *AE, DC, MC, V.*

Shopping

★ The **Mercado Municipal** (⊠ Manuel Rodríguez 960 🕾 No phone) is one of the best places in the country to find Mapuche woolen ponchos, pullovers, and blankets. The interior of the 1930 structure has been extensively remodeled, and is quite open and airy. The low-key artisan vendors share the complex with butchers, fishmongers, and fruit sellers. There is no bargaining, but the prices are fair. It opens daily at 8, but closes around 3 on Sunday. A little more rough-and-tumble than the Mercado Municipal is the **Feria Libre** (⊠ Barros Arana at Miraflores). You can bargain hard with the Mapuche vendors who sell their crafts and produce in the blocks surrounding the railroad station and bus terminal. ⚠ **Leave the camera behind, as the vendors aren't happy about being photographed.** It's open from about 7 to 2 Monday–Saturday.

Villarrica

❷ *87 km (52 mi) southeast of Temuco.*

Villarrica was founded in 1552, but the Mapuche wars prevented extensive settlement of the area until the early 20th century. Today, the pleasant town on the lake of the same name is in one of the loveliest, least-spoiled areas of the southern Andes, and has stunning views of the Villarrica and Llaima volcanoes. Villarrica has some wonderful hotels that won't give you a case of high-season sticker shock. Well-maintained roads and convenient public transportation make the town a good base for exploring the area.

The municipal museum, **Museo Histórico y Arqueológico de Villarrica,** displays an impressive collection of Mapuche ceramics, masks, leather, and jewelry. A replica of a ruca graces the front yard. It's made of thatch so tightly entwined that it's impermeable to rain. ⊠ *Pedro de Valdivia 1050* 🕾 *45/413–445* ⬚ *100 pesos* ◷ *Jan. and Feb., Mon.–Sat. 9–1 and 4–10; Mar.–Dec., Mon.–Sat. 9–1 and 3–7:30.*

Where to Stay & Eat

$–$$$ ✕ **The Travellers.** Hui, Martin, and Juan came from China, Germany, and Chile respectively, met by happenstance and decided to open a place serving food from their homelands and several others. The result is a place that serves one or two dishes from Germany, Thailand, China, Italy, Mexico, and many countries in between. While you chow down on an enchilada, your companions might be having spaghetti with meatballs or sweet-and-sour pork. Dining on the front lawn under umbrella-covered tables is the best option on a summer evening. ⊠ *Valentín Letelier 753* 🕾 *45/413–617* ⊟ *AE, DC, MC, V.*

$–$$ ✕ **Café 2001.** For a filling sandwich, a homemade Kuchen, and an espresso or cappuccino brewed from freshly ground beans, this is the place to stop in Villarrica. Pull up around a table in front or slip into one of the quieter booths by the fireplace in the back. The *lomito completo* sandwich—with a slice of pork, avocado, sauerkraut, tomato, and mayonnaise—is one of the best in the south. ⊠ *Camillo Henríquez 379* ☎ *45/411–470* ☰ *AE, DC, MC, V.*

$$$$ 🏨 **Villarrica Park Lake Hotel.** This sumptuous old European spa with modern touches is the perfect mix of old-world plush and clean, uncluttered design. There's ample use of hardwood in the bright, spacious common area and the rooms—each with its own balcony and lake view—that descend down a hill toward Lago Villarrica. ⊠ *13 km (8 mi) east of Villarrica on the road to Pucón* ☎ *45/450–000, 2/207–7070 in Santiago, 888/790–5264 in North America* ⊕ *www.villarricaparklakehotel. cl/* ➦ *61 rooms, 9 suites* ⚐ *Restaurant, in-room data ports, in-room safes, minibars, cable TV, indoor pool, 2 pools (1 indoors), gym, hair salon, hot tub, sauna, spa, 2 bars, babysitting, library, shop, dry cleaning, laundry service, Internet room, business services, meeting rooms, airport shuttle* ☰ *AE, DC, MC, V* ⦿ *BP.*

$$ 🏨 **Hostería de la Colina.** The friendly American owners of this hostería,
Fodor's Choice Glen and Beverly Aldrich, provide attentive service as well as special lit-
★ tle touches like homemade ice cream. Rooms in the half-century-old main house are a mix of large and small, carpets and hardwood floors, all tastefully decorated with wood furnishings. Two bright, airy hillside cottages are carpeted and wood paneled and have private patios. There's a hot tub heated by a wood-burning stove, and a serene *vivero* (greenhouse) and garden that attracts birds. The terrace has stupendous views of Lago Villarrica. ⊠ *Las Colinas 115* ☎ *45/411–503* ⊕ *www. hosteriadelacolina.com* ➦ *8 rooms, 2 cabins* ⚐ *Dining room, hot tub, massage, croquet, horseshoes, Ping-Pong, bar; no a/c, no room phones, no room TVs* ☰ *AE, DC, MC, V* ⦿ *BP.*

$ 🏨 **Hotel El Ciervo.** Villarrica's oldest hotel is an unimposing house on a quiet street, but inside are elegant details such as wrought-iron fixtures and wood-burning fireplaces. Spacious rooms, some with their own fireplaces, have huge beds and sparkling bathrooms. Just outside is a lovely pool and a secluded patio. Rates include an enormous German breakfast with loads of fruit, muesli, and fresh milk. El Ciervo also has all-inclusive seven-day tour packages. ⊠ *General Körner 241* ☎ *45/411–215* ⊕ *www.hotelelciervo.cl* ➦ *12 rooms* ⚐ *Restaurant, cable TV, pool, bar, laundry service, Internet room, meeting rooms; no a/c* ☰ *AE, DC, MC, V* ⦿ *BP.*

$ 🏨 **Montebianco Hotel.** The owner makes many of the wood furnishings that fill this central lodging. The pleasant rooms upstairs all have small balconies. The tiled bathrooms are clean and bright, but the showers are tiny, with barely enough room to turn around. ⊠ *Pedro de Valdivia 1011* ☎ *45/411–798* ⊕ *www.hotelmontebianco.cl* ➦ *16 rooms* ⚐ *Restaurant, cable TV, bar, meeting room; no a/c* ☰ *AE, DC, MC, V* ⦿ *CP.*

Pucón

❸ *25 km (15 mi) east of Villarrica.*

The trendy resort town of Pucón, on the southern shore of Lago Villarrica, attracts wealthy, fashionable Chileans. Like their counterparts in the

Colorado ski resort of Vail, they come to enjoy their luxurious vacation homes, stroll along the main strip, and flock to the major night spots.

④ One of Chile's most popular national parks, **Parque Nacional Villarrica**
Fodor'sChoice has skiing, hiking, and many other outdoor activities. The main draw,
★ however, is the volcano that gives the 610-square-km (235-square-mi) national park its name. You don't need to have any climbing experience to reach Volcán Villarrica's 3,116-meter (9,350-foot) summit, but a guide is a good idea. The volcano sits in the park's Sector Rucapillán, a Mapuche word meaning "house of the devil." That name is apt, as the perpetually smoldering volcano is one of South America's most active. CONAF closes off access to the trails at the slightest hint of volcanic activity they deem to be out of the ordinary. It's a steep uphill walk to the snow line, but doable any time of year. All equipment will be supplied by any of the Pucón outfitters that organize daylong excursions for about 30,000 pesos per person. Your reward for the six-hour climb is the rare sight of an active crater. You're also treated

> **WORD OF MOUTH**
>
> "We just got back from the Lakes area of Chile. We rented a car and drove from Santiago to Puerto Montt, going through Villarrica and Pucón. It was beautiful country even with the clouds. We only had a couple of opportunities to see the volcanoes, but the one in Villarrica is active and glows at night. –jhind

to superb views of the nearby volcanoes, the less-visited Quetrupillán and Lanín. ⊠ *15 km (9 mi) south of Pucón* ☎ *45/298–221 in Temuco* ⌑ *1,100 pesos* ☉ *Daily 8–6.*

Where to Stay & Eat

$$–$$$$ ✕ **La Maga.** Argentina claims to prepare the perfect parrillada, or grilled beef, but here's evidence that Uruguayans just might do it best. Watch the beef cuts or salmon turn slowly over the wood fire at the entrance. The end product is a wonderfully smoked, natural taste, accented with a hint of spice in the mild *chimichurri* (a tangy steak sauce). ⊠ *Fresia 125* ☎ *45/444–277* ☰ *AE, DC, MC, V* ☉ *Closed Mon. Apr.–Dec.*

$$–$$$$ ✕ **¡Viva Perú!** As befits the name, Peruvian cuisine reigns supreme at this restaurant with rustic wooden tables. Try the *ají de gallina* (hen stew with cheese, milk, and peppers) or the seviche, thoroughly cooked but served cold. You can dine on the porch, a nice option for a pleasant summer night—and take advantage of the two-for-one pisco sours nightly until 9 PM. You can also order to carry out. ⊠ *Lincoyan 372* ☎ *45/444–025* ☰ *AE, DC, MC, V.*

$$–$$$ ✕ **En Alta Mar.** The best seafood in Pucón is served here, so don't be frightened by the nondescript dining room: basic wooden tables and a ubiquitous nautical theme. You'll receive a free welcoming pisco sour on arrival. ⊠ *Fresia at Urrutia* ☎ *45/442–294* ☰ *AE, DC, MC, V.*

¢–$ ✕ **Arabian Restaurant.** The Apara family knows how to whip up tasty falafel or *shawarma* (a pita-bread sandwich filled with spicy beef or lamb). Most everyone opts for the outdoor tables over the tiny indoor dining area. ⊠ *Fresia 354* ☎ *45/443–469* ☰ *No credit cards.*

**$** ✕⊞ **¡école!** It's part hostel and part beach house—and takes its name from a Chilean expression meaning "Great!" Cozy two-, three-, and four-person rooms can be shared or private. The vegetarian restaurant ($–$$), a rarity in the Lake District, merits a trip in itself. You can choose among truly international options, such as lasagna, burritos, and moussaka, and eat in the sunny courtyard or small dining room. The environmentally conscious staff can organize hiking and horseback-riding trips and expeditions to volcanoes and hot springs, as well as arrange for Spanish lessons and massages. ☒ *General Urrutia 592* ⊞ *45/441–675* ⊕ *www. ecole.cl* ↩ *21 rooms, 9 with bath ⟁ Restaurant, bar, travel services; no a/c, no room phones, no room TVs, no smoking* ⊟ *AE, DC, MC, V.*

$$$$ ⊞ **Hotel del Lago.** Short on charm, this glitzy hotel has everything else you could hope for—an indoor pool, a health spa, even a movie theater. Enter through the five-story atrium lobby, then let one of the glass elevators whisk you upstairs. The rooms are simple and elegant, with blond wood and crisp white linens. The hotel is known as "the Casino" for its Las Vegas–style ground floor, complete with rows of one-arm bandits and tables for roulette and poker. ☒ *Miguel Ansorena 23* ⊞ *45/ 291–000, 2/462–1900 in Santiago* ⊕ *www.hoteldellago.cl* ↩ *81 rooms, 2 suites ⟁ Restaurant, snack bar, in-room safes, minibars, cable TV, 2 pools, gym, hair salon, massage, sauna, bar, casino, theater, shops, business services, convention center, meeting room; no a/c* ⊟ *AE, DC, MC, V* ⦿ *BP, MAP.*

$$$–$$$$ ⊞ **Gran Hotel Pucón.** The outside of Pucón's largest hotel is quite *gran* and imposing in true alpine-lodge style, with wonderful views of Lago Villarrica. Its location right on the shore provides direct access to the beach. The rooms, while perfectly acceptable, are disappointingly contemporary; the exterior gets your hopes up for something more Old World. Depending on which side of the building you are on, though, you do get stupendous views of either the lake or of Volcán Villarrica, The hotel is enormously popular among Chileans who come here for the slate of activities, so you won't find much peace and quiet here, especially in summer. ☒ *Clemente Holzapfel 190* ⊞ *45/441–001, 2/353–0000 in Santiago* ⊕ *www.granhotelpucon.cl* ↩ *145 rooms ⟁ 2 restaurants, in-room safes, minibars, cable TV, 2 pools, massage, sauna, squash, bar, theater, laundry service, business services, convention center, meeting room, travel services; no a/c* ⊟ *AE, DC, MC, V* ⦿ *BP, MAP.*

★ $$$ ⊞ **Hotel Antumalal.** A young Queen Elizabeth stayed here in the 1950s, as did actor Jimmy Stewart—and the Antumalal hasn't changed very much since. The décor, styles, and colors from that decade have all been maintained at this family-run hotel, which has the feel of a country inn. It's perched atop a cliff just outside town overlooking Lago Villarrica, and its cozy rooms have fireplaces and huge windows overlooking the spectacularly landscaped grounds. If you tire of relaxing with a refreshing pisco sour on the wisteria-shaded deck, just ask owner Rony Pollak to arrange an adventure for you. Favorites include fly-fishing, white-water rafting, and volcano climbing. ☒ *Casilla 84* ⊞ *45/441–011* ⊕ *www.antumalal.com* ↩ *16 rooms, 2 suites ⟁ Restaurant, cable TV, 2 tennis courts, pool, massage, sauna, spa, bar, travel services; no a/c* ⊟ *AE, DC, MC, V* ⦿ *BP.*

$$$ ▦ **Hotel Huincahue.** In a town whose motto could be "bigger is better"
Fodor'sChoice when it comes to lodging, the elegant Huincahue is a refreshing find,
    ★ and deserves to be Pucón's real prestige address. The place sits close to
the center of town on the main plaza and has the attentive service that
only a small hotel can offer. Lots of windows brighten the lobby and li-
brary of the German-style building, which is warmed by a roaring fire.
Bright, airy rooms come furnished with extras, such as Wi-Fi, that are
rarely seen in lodgings of this size. Rooms on the second floor have small
balconies. Rates include a hearty American breakfast. ⊠ *Pedro de Val-
divia 375* ☎ *45/443–540* ⊕ *www.hotelhuincahue.cl* ⇨ *20 rooms*
♨ *Coffee shop, in-room data ports, Wi-Fi, cable TV, pool, bar, laundry
service; no a/c* ⊟ *AE, DC, MC, V* ❘❍❘ *BP.*

★ $$ ▦ **Hotel Malalhue.** Dark wood and volcanic rock make up the construction of this built-in-2004 building at the edge of town on the road to
Calburga. It's about a 15-minute walk from the hubbub of downtown
Pucón, but Malalhue's many fans see that as a selling point. The cozy
sitting room just off the lobby with fireplace and couches is so inviting
you may want to linger there for hours. But the guest rooms, with their
plush comforters and pillows, beckon, too. The top-floor "superior"
rooms under the gables are more spacious and contain vaulted ceilings;
they're a few thousand pesos more than the "standard" rooms, perfectly
acceptable in their own right, smaller, but with exactly the same style.
⊠ *Camino Internacional 1615* ☎ *45/443–130* ⊕ *www.malalhue.cl*
⇨ *24 rooms* ♨ *Dining room, in-room safes, cable TV, bar, babysitting,
laundry service, Internet room, travel services, no-smoking rooms; no
a/c* ⊟ *AE, DC, MC, V* ❘❍❘ *BP.*

¢   ▦ **Kila Leufu.** As part of a growing agro-tourism trend in Chile, a Mapuche family has opened this red farmhouse, 15 minutes from Pucón,
to temporary urban refugees anxious to partake of rural life. You can
bake bread and milk the cows if you like, or just relax and read. Horse-
back-riding excursions cost an extra 14,000 pesos. ⊠ *Camino a Cu-
rarrehe, Puente Cabedane* ☎ *09/711–8064* ⊕ *www.kilaleufu.homestead.
com* ⇨ *5 rooms, 2 with bath* ♨ *Dining room, barbecues, fishing,
horseback riding; no a/c, no room phones, no room TVs* ⊟ *No credit
cards* ❘❍❘ *FAP.*

Outdoor Activities

Pucón is the center for rafting expeditions in the northern Lake District,
with Río Trancura just 15 minutes away, making for easy half-day excursions on Class III–V rapids. At first glance Pucón's myriad outfitters
look the same and sell the same slate of activities and rentals; quality
varies, however. The firms listed below get high marks for safety, pro-
fessionalism, and friendly service. Although a given outfitter might have
a specialty, it usually offers other activities as well.

Friendly, French-owned **Aguaventura** (⊠ Palguín 336 ☎ 45/444–246
⊕ www.aguaventura.com) outfits for rafting, as well as canoeing, kayaking, snowshoeing, and snowboarding. **Huepil Malal** (⊠ Km 27, Carretera a Huife ☎ 09/643–2673 ⊕ www.huepil-malal.cl) arranges
horseback riding in the nearby Cañi mountains, with everything from
half-day to six-day excursions. Highly regarded **Outdoor Experience**
(⊠ General Urrutia 592 ☎ 45/441–675) specializes in mountain-bike

rental in summer, as well as rafting, volcano ascents, rappelling, trekking, and some pretty demanding rock-climbing excursions and outdoor-survival courses. **Politur** (✉ Av. Bernardo O'Higgins 635 ☎ 445/441–373 ⊕ www.politur.com) can take you rafting on the Río Trancura, trekking in nearby Parque Nacional Huerquehue, on ascents of the Volcán Villarrica, and skydiving. William Hatcher of **Sol Y Nieve** (✉ Av. Bernardo O'Higgins and Lincoyan ☎☎ 45/441–070 ⊕ www.chilesolnieve.com) runs rafting trips and hiking and skiing expeditions.

Valdivia

⑤ *120 km (72 mi) southwest of Villarrica.*

One of the Lake District's oldest and most beautiful cities, Valdivia gracefully combines Chilean wood-shingle construction with the architectural style of the well-to-do German settlers who colonized the area in the late 1800s. Enjoy evening strolls through Valdivia's quaint streets and along its two rivers, the Valdivia and the Calle Calle.

The awning-covered **Mercado Fluvial,** in the southern shadow of the bridge leading to Isla Teja, is a perfect place to soak up the atmosphere of a real fish market. Vendors set up early in the morning; you hear the thwack of fresh trout and the clatter of oyster shells as they're piled on the side of the market's boardwalk fronting the river. If the sights, sounds, and smells are too much for you, fruit and vegetable vendors line the other side of the walkway opposite the river. ✉ *Av. Arturo Prat at Libertad* ☎ *No phone* ☉ *Mon.–Sat. 8–3.*

The city's 1918 **Mercado Municipal** barely survived the 1960 earthquake intact, but it thrives again after extensive remodeling and reinforcement as a shopping-dining complex. A few restaurants, mostly hole-in-the-wall seafood joints, but some quite nice, share the three-story building with artisan and souvenir vendors. ✉ *Block bordered by Av. Arturo Prat, Chacabuco, Yungay, and Libertad* ☎ *No phone* ☉ *Dec.–Mar., daily 8 AM–10 PM; Apr.–Nov., daily 8 AM–8:30 PM.*

For a historic overview of the region, visit the **Museo Histórico y Antropológico Maurice van de Maele,** on neighboring Isla Teja. The collection focuses on the city's colonial period, during which it was settled by the Spanish, burned by the Mapuche, and invaded by Dutch corsairs. Downstairs, rooms re-create the interior of the late-19th-century Anwandter mansion that belonged to one of Valdivia's first immigrant families; the upper floor delves into Mapuche art and culture. ✉ *Los Laureles, Isla Teja* ☎ *63/212–872* 💲 *1,200 pesos* ☉ *Dec.–Feb., Tues.–Sun. 10–1 and 2–6; Mar.–Nov., Tues.–Sun. 10–1 and 2–8.*

Fondly known around town as the "MAC," the **Museo de Arte Contemporáneo** is one of Chile's foremost modern art museums. This Isla Teja complex was built on the site of the old Anwandter brewery destroyed in the 1960 earthquake. The minimalist interior, formerly the brewery's warehouses, contrasts sharply with ongoing construction of a modern glass wall fronting the Río Valdivia, a project slated for completion by 2010, Chile's bicentennial. The museum has no permanent collection; it's a rotating series of temporary exhibits by contemporary Chilean artists.

✉ *Los Laureles, Isla Teja* ☎ *63/221–968* ⊕ *www.macvaldivia.uach.cl* ⛝ *600 pesos* ⊙ *Tues.–Sun. 10–1 and 3–7.*

The **Jardín Botánico,** north and west of the Universidad Austral campus, is awash with 1,000 species of flowers and plants native to Chile. It's a lovely place to wander among the alerce, cypress, and laurel trees whatever the season, but it's particularly enjoyable in spring and summer. ✉ *Isla Teja* ☎ *63/216–964* ⛝ *Free* ⊙ *Dec.–Feb., daily 8–8; Mar.–Nov., daily 8–4.*

Valdivia means beer to many Chileans, and **Cervecería Kunstmann** brews the country's beloved lager. The Anwandter family immigrated from Germany a century-and-a-half ago, bringing along their beer-making knowhow. The *cervecería* (brewery), on the road to Niebla, hosts interesting guided tours by prior arrangement. There's also a small museum and a souvenir shop where you can buy the requisite caps, mugs, and T-shirts, plus a pricey restaurant serving German fare. ✉ *Ruta 350 No. 950* ☎ *63/222–560* ⛝ *Free* ⊙ *Restaurant and museum, daily noon–midnight.*

Where to Stay & Eat

$$–$$$$　✕ **Salón de Té Entrelagos.** This swanky café caters to Valdivian business executives, who come here to make deals over sandwiches (try the Isla Teja—with grilled chicken, tomato, artichoke hearts, asparagus, olives, and red peppers), decadent crepes, and desserts. In the evening, the atmosphere feels less formal—the menu is exactly the same—as the Entrelagos becomes a place to meet friends and converse well into the night. ✉ *Vicente Pérez Rosales 640* ☎ *63/218–333* ▭ *AE, DC, MC, V.*

$–$$$　✕ **Café Haussmann.** The excellent *crudos* (steak tartare), German-style sandwiches, and delicious Kuchen here are testament to the fact that Valdivia was once a mecca for German immigrants. The place is small— a mere four tables and a bar—but it's that rarest of breeds in Chile: a completely no-smoking restaurant. ✉ *Av. Bernardo O'Higgins 394* ☎ *63/213–878* ▭ *AE, DC, MC, V* ⊙ *Closed Sun.*

$–$$　✕ **Camino de Luna.** The Way of the Moon floats on a barge on the Río Valdivia, just north of the Pedro de Valdivia bridge. As the city is only a few miles from the ocean, it's no surprise that seafood is a specialty here. The *congrío calle calle* (conger eel in a cheese-and-tomato sauce) is particularly good. Tables by the windows offer views of Isla Teja. ✉ *Av. Arturo Prat Costanera s/n* ☎ *63/213–788* ▭ *AE, DC, MC, V.*

$$$　🏨 **Hotel Puerta del Sur.** Expect lavish pampering with top-notch service at this highly regarded lodging. Spacious rooms, all with views of the river, are decorated in soft lavender tones. Play a few games of tennis, then hit the pool or relax in the hot tub. You're near the edge of town here, so this is a good place to stay if you have your own car. ✉ *Los Lingues 950, Isla Teja* ☎ *63/224–500, 2/633–5101 in Santiago* ⊕ *www. hotelpuertadelsur.com* ➟ *40 rooms, 2 suites* ⟐ *Restaurant, in-room safes, some Wi-Fi, tennis court, pool, gym, outdoor hot tub, sauna, dock, volleyball, 2 bars, Internet room, meeting room, travel services; no a/c* ▭ *AE, DC, MC, V* ⦿ *BP.*

★ $$　🏨 **Hotel Naguilán.** You can relax in this hotel's poolside garden while watching the boats pass by on the Río Valdivia. Rooms in the property's newer building are bigger, with balconies and more modern furnishings;

the older rooms, in a building that dates from 1890, are smaller and a bit dated, but they have more character, and are cheaper. Service-wise, you're in good hands here: as soon as you check in, a waiter will appear to offer you a pisco sour. ⊠ *General Lagos 1927* ☎ *63/212–851* ⊕ *www.hotelnaguilan.com* ↪ *33 rooms, 3 suites* ⚲ *Restaurant, cable TV, Wi-Fi, pool, dock, bar, babysitting, laundry service, business services, meeting room; no a/c* ⊟ *AE, DC, MC, V* ❍❙ *BP.*

$ 🏨 **Hotel Palace.** The exterior could benefit from a fresh coat of paint, but this solid, friendly, mid-range lodging in downtown Valdivia has bright, cheerful rooms. They're all simply furnished, with blue or pink bedspreads and a chair and table. ⊠ *Chacabuco 308* ☎ *63/213–319 or 213–029* ✐*hotelpalace@surnet.cl* ↪ *30 rooms* ⚲ *Coffee shop, dining room, cable TV, bar, laundry service, meeting room; no a/c* ⊟ *AE, DC, MC, V.*

$ 🏨 **Hotel Isla Teja.** This affordable hotel doubles as student housing for the nearby Universidad Austral, though a section is always open for non-university guests. The rooms are quiet and comfortable, with modern amenities. ⊠ *Las Encinas 220, Isla Teja* ☎ *63/215–014* ⊕ *www. hotelislateja.cl* ↪ *70 rooms* ⚲ *Restaurant, in-room data ports, cable TV, bar, Internet room, business services, meeting room, travel services; no a/c* ⊟ *AE, DC, MC, V* ❍❙ *CP.*

Outdoor Activities

Valdivia-based tour operator **Jumping Chile** (⊠ Pasaje 11 No. 50 ☎ 63/217–810) organizes marvelous fly-fishing trips for two to six people on the nearby rivers. An astonishing variety of wetland birds inhabits this part of the country. **Hualamo** (☎ 63/215–135 ⊕ www.hualamo.com) lets you get a close look if you join its bird-watching and natural-history tours based out of a lodge 20 km (12 mi) upriver from Valdivia.

Puerto Octay

❻ *80 km (48 mi) southwest of Parque Nacional Puyehue, 50 km (30 mi) southeast of Osorno.*

With spectacular views of the Osorno and Calbuco volcanoes, Puerto Octay was the birthplace of Lake District tourism: a wealthy Santiago businessman constructed a mansion outside town in 1912, using it as a vacation home to host his friends. Puerto Octay doesn't have the frenetic energy of neighboring Frutillar and Puerto Varas, but its many fans enjoy its less-frenzied, more-authentic nature.

The **Museo El Colono** displays great old photographs and maps documenting the town's turn-of-the-20th-century German settlers. An annex in a barn outside town at the turnoff to Centinela exhibits farm machinery. At this writing both locales are open but undergoing extensive expansion and remodeling, a project scheduled for completion by the start of the January 2007 high season. ⊠*Independencia 591* ☎*64/391–523* 💲*500 pesos* 🕓 *Dec.–Mar., daily 10–1 and 3–7; Apr.–Nov., Tues.–Sun. 10–1 and 3–7.*

Where to Stay & Eat

$–$$ ✕ **Restaurant Baviera.** Because it's on the Plaza de Armas, this is a popular lunch stop for tour groups. Baviera serves solid German fare—schnitzel, sauerkraut, sausage, and Kuchen are among the favorites. Beer steins and other Bavarian paraphernalia lining the walls evoke the old country. ⊠ *German Wulf 582* ☎ *64/391–460* ▭ *No credit cards.*

★ $$ 🏨 **Hotel Centinela.** Simple and elegant, the venerable 1912 Hotel Centinela remains one of Chile's best-known accommodations. This imposing wood-shingled lodge with a dramatic turret sits amid 20 forested acres at the tip of Península Centinela jutting into Lago Llanquihue. Britain's Edward VII, then Prince of Wales, was the most famous guest (but there's some mystery as to whether his future wife, American divorcée Wallis Simpson, accompanied him). Imposing beds and armoires fill the huge rooms in the main building. The cabins, whose rates include three meals a day delivered to the door, are more modern than the rooms in the lodge. ⊠ *Península de Centinela, 5 km (3 mi) south of Puerto Octay* ☎ *64/391–326* ⊕ *www.hotelcentinela.cl* ⇋ *11 rooms, 1 suite, 18 cabins* ⚭ *Restaurant, sauna, beach, dock, bar; no a/c, no TV in some rooms* ▭ *AE, DC, MC, V* ⦿| *BP, FAP.*

★ $ 🏨 **Zapato Amarillo.** Backpackers make up the majority of the clientele here, but this is no scruffy youth hostel. This modern alerce-shingled house with wood-panel rooms affords a drop-dead gorgeous view of Volcán Osorno outside town. The hotel arranges guided horseback-riding, hiking, and cycling tours, as well as cheese-fondue evening gatherings. Rates include an excellent buffet breakfast that uses local fruits and dairy products. You also have access to the kitchen. ⊠ *2 km (1 mi) north of Puerto Octay on road to Osorno* ☎ *64/391–575* ⊕ *zapatoamarillo.8k.com* ⇋ *7 rooms, 2 with bath* ⚭ *Dining room, bicycles, horseback riding, library, laundry facilities, Internet, travel services; no a/c, no room phones, no room TVs* ▭ *No credit cards* ⦿| *BP.*

Frutillar

❼ *30 km (18 mi) southwest of Puerto Octay.*

Halfway down the western edge of Lago Llanquihue lies the small town of Frutillar, a destination for European immigrants in the late 19th century and, today, arguably the most picturesque Lake District community. The town—actually two adjacent hamlets, Frutillar Alto and Frutillar Bajo—is known for its perfectly preserved German architecture. Don't be disappointed if your first look at the town is the nondescript neighborhood (the Alto) on the top of the hill; head down to the charming streets of Frutillar Bajo that face the lake, with their picture-perfect view of Volcán Osorno.

★ You step into the past when you step into one of southern Chile's best museums, the **Museo Colonial Alemán.** Besides displays of the 19th-century agricultural and household implements, this open-air museum has full-scale reconstructions of buildings—a smithy and barn, among others—used by the original German settlers. Exhibits at this complex administered by Chile's Universidad Austral are labeled in Spanish and, *natürlich,* German, but there are also a few signs in English. A short walk from the lake up Avenida Arturo Prat, the museum also has beautifully landscaped grounds and great views of Volcán Osorno. ⊠ *Av. Vicente Pérez Rosales at Av. Arturo Prat* ☎ *65/421–142* 🎟 *1,600 pesos* ☉ *Dec.–Feb., daily 10–7; Mar.–Nov., daily 10–2 and 3–5.*

Hier Ist Alles So Deutsch

YOU'LL MEET PEOPLE in the Lake District with names like María Schmidt or Pablo Gudenschwager. At first, such juxtapositions sound odd, but, remember, this melting pot of a country was liberated by a man, good Irishman that he was, named Bernardo O'Higgins.

The Lake District's Germanic origins can be traced to one Vicente Pérez Rosales. Armed with photos of the region, he made several trips on behalf of the Chilean government to Germany, Switzerland, and Austria in the mid-19th century. His mission? Recruit waves of European immigrants to settle the Lake District and end 300

years of Mapuche domination in the region once and for all.

Thousands signed on the dotted line and made the long journey to start a new life in southern Chile. It was a giant leap of faith for the original settlers, but it didn't hurt that the region looked just like the parts of Central Europe that they'd come from. The end result was *Kuchen*, sausage and a good old-fashioned work ethic mixed with a Latin-spirited, oom-pah-pah *Gemütlichkeit*. But don't bother to dust off that high-school German for your trip here; few people speak it these days.

–Jeffrey Van Fleet

Where to Stay & Eat

$$ ✕ **Club Alemán.** One of the German clubs that dot the Lake District, this restaurant in the center of town has a selection of four or five rotating prix-fixe menus that cost 3,500 pesos. There will always be a meat and seafood option—often steak and salmon—with soup, salad, and dessert. ✉ *Philippi 747* ☎ *65/421–249* ⊟ *AE, DC, MC, V.*

★ ¢ ✕ **Café Capuccini.** Sink into one of the plush couches here and write some postcards while you nurse a gourmet coffee drink on a chilly evening. If the couches are taken—they are in demand—grab one of the small tables adorned with a musical-score lampshade. All have superb lake and volcano views out the curving, sweeping picture window. This café in the new Centro de Conciertos y Eventos complex caters mostly to a pre- and post-theater crowd, but it serves up light fare (sandwiches, Kuchen, and desserts) on brown stoneware to anyone, any day. ✉ *Av. Phillipi 1000* ☎ *65/421–164* ⊟ *No credit cards.*

$ ✕⊞ **Hotel Salzburg.** Rooms at this Tyrolean-style lodge command excellent lake views. Cozy cabins and larger bungalows, all made of native woods, are fully equipped with kitchens and private terraces. The staff will gladly organize fishing trips. The restaurant ($$–$$$) serves great smoked salmon. ✉ *Costanera Norte* ☎ *65/421–589* ⊕ *www. salzburg.cl* ↝ *31 rooms, 9 cabins, 5 bungalows* ⚐ *Restaurant, pool, sauna, billiards, Ping-Pong, volleyball, bar, laundry service, meeting rooms, travel services; no a/c, no room TVs* ⊟ *AE, DC, MC, V* ⚏❶ *BP.*

$ ⊞ **Hotel Elun.** From just about every vantage point at this hillside lodging just south of town—the lobby, the library, and, of course, the guest rooms—you have a spectacular view of Lago Llanquihue. Each room has huge bay windows framing Volcán Osorno. The blue of the façade

Fodor'sChoice
★

is repeated in the rooms, which have polished wood furniture. Add the exceptionally attentive owners to the mix, and you have a real find. ⊠ *Costanera Sur* ☎ *65/420–055* ⊕ *www.hotelelun.cl* ➫ *14 rooms* ⅋ *Restaurant, cable TV, sauna, bicycles, bar, library, Internet room, meeting rooms, no-smoking rooms; no a/c* ▤ *AE, DC, MC, V* ⧓⧗ *BP*.

$ ⊞ **Hotel Frau Holle.** Norma Bonomett, the friendly owner of this 1930s German-style house, may not be Frau Holle (a character out of the Grimm brothers' fairy tales)—but her attentive service will help you to have a storybook lodging experience. Rooms here are cheery, with hardwood floors and period furnishings; a few have views of Lago Llanquihue and both volcanoes. The hearty German breakfast includes fruit grown in the property's orchard. ⊠ *Antonio Varas 54* ☎☎ *65/421–345* ✎ *frauholle@frutillarsur.cl* ➫ *8 rooms* ⅋ *Dining room, laundry service; no a/c, no room phones, no room TVs* ▤ *AE, DC, MC, V* ⧓⧗ *CP*.

$ ⊞ **Hotel Kaffee Bauernhaus.** Gingerbread cutouts and swirls adorn this cozy 1911 home-turned-inn. You couldn't ask for a much better location—the property is right on the lake, although only one guest room has a lake view. All, however, are wood-paneled and tastefully decorated with flowered bedspreads and curtains. The German breakfast is substantial. ⊠ *Av. Philippi 663* ☎ *65/421–201* ⊕ *www.salzburg.cl* ➫ *8 rooms* ⅋ *Coffee shop; no a/c, no TV in some rooms* ▤ *AE, DC, MC, V* ⧓⧗ *BP*.

Beaches

Packed with summer crowds, the gray-sand **Playa Frutillar** stretches for 15 blocks along Avenida Philippi. From this point along Lago Llanquihue you have a spectacular view due east of the conical Volcán Osorno, as well as the lopsided Volcán Puntiagudo.

Puerto Varas

❽ *27 km (16 mi) south of Frutillar.*

A small resort town on the edge of Lago Llanquihue, Puerto Varas is known for the stunning rose arbors that bloom from December to March. Often described as the "Lucerne of Chile," the town has ice-cream shops, cozy cafés, and trendy restaurants. The view of the Osorno and Calbuco volcanoes graces dozens of postcards and travel brochures for the Lake District. The town isn't quite there yet, but it could someday challenge Pucón as the region's top vacation spot.

Where to Stay & Eat

★ $$-$$$$ ✕ **Merlin.** A perennial favorite for diners in southern Chile, this charming old restaurant on a side street in Puerto Varas is known for its unusual fish and vegetables dishes. Specialties include razor clams with vegetable strips in a curry vinaigrette and beef tenderloin in a morel-mushroom sauce. For dessert, try peaches packed with almond cream. ⊠ *Imperial 605* ☎ *65/233–105* ▤ *AE, DC, MC, V* ☉ *No lunch.*

$-$$$ ✕ **Pim's.** This restaurant just a couple of blocks from the center of town evokes an old-fashioned American bar. There's nothing particularly Southwestern about the decor, but you can chow down here on good, filling Tex-Mex dishes. The hot, spicy chili—perfect for a chilly night in Chile—is best enjoyed in front of the fireplace. ⊠ *San Francisco 712* ☎ *65/233–998* ▤ *AE, DC, MC, V.*

$–$$ ✗**Govinda.** It's impossible to pin down the small but ever-changing menu
Fodor'sChoice here. This place takes great pride in using the freshest, in-season, or-
★ ganic ingredients available. You can always count on little touches like
goat cheese, organic wine, and wild-apple vinegar for your salad, and
wonderful fruit in summer. The restaurant occupies a house on a busy
lakefront intersection, and the wood deck is the place to survey the passing scene. In the cozy dining room, you get the same lake views out the
big picture window without the noise of passing traffic. After dinner,
grab your cup of coffee and sink into one of the couches in front of the
fireplace. ⊠ *Santa Rosa 218* ☎ *65/233–080* ⊟ *AE, DC, MC, V.*

$$–$$$ ⊡**Hotel Cabañas del Lago.** It's the pine-panel cabins, hidden among
carefully tended gardens, that make this place special. Each A-frame unit,
which can accommodate five people, is decorated with lace curtains and
floral-pattern bedding, and has a woodstove and full kitchen. Most rooms
in the main hotel are a little on the small side, but they're cozy and have
lovely views of Volcán Osorno. ⊠ *Klenner 195* ☎ *65/232–291* ⊕ *www.
cabanasdellago.cl* ⇆ *134 rooms, 13 cabins, 2 suites* ⚹ *Restaurant,
cable TV, indoor pool, massage, sauna, billiards, bar, babysitting, meeting rooms; no a/c* ⊟ *AE, DC, MC, V.*

$$ ⊡**Hotel Bellavista.** This hotel, an eclectic mix of traditional Bavarian and
modern architectural styles, sits right on the lake. Most of the bright
rooms have views of the nearby volcanoes, and some have their own
balconies. Stylish contemporary furnishings are upholstered in tailored
stripes. ⊠ *Vicente Pérez Rosales 60* ☎ *65/232–011* ⊕ *www.
hotelbellavistachile.cl* ⇆ *51 rooms* ⚹ *Restaurant, in-room safes, mini-
bars, cable TV, Wi-Fi, sauna, bar, laundry service, meeting room; no a/c*
⊟ *AE, DC, MC, V* ⏀◉ *BP.*

$$ ⊡**Hotel Colonos del Sur.** This five-story building, with peaked gables that
give it a Germanic look, dominates the waterfront in Puerto Varas. The
views from the upper floors are magnificent. If you can, look at a few
rooms before you decide which to book: some have views of the lake,
while others overlook the casino across the street. Even if you're not
staying here, make a point to stop by for the late-afternoon onces (coffee breaks). The hotel does them up big. ⊠ *Del Salvador 24* ☎ *65/233–
369* ⊕ *www.colonosdelsur.cl* ⇆ *64 rooms* ⚹ *Restaurant, coffee shop,
minibars, cable TV, indoor pool, massage, sauna, bar, meeting room;
no a/c* ⊟ *AE, DC, MC, V* ⏀◉ *BP.*

$$ ⊡**Hotel Licarayén.** Ask for a room with a balcony overlooking Lago Llan-
quihue at this rambling Bavarian-style chalet. Carpeted rooms are bright
and have wood paneling. The standard rooms lack views of the lake,
but overlook the garden. It's worth the splurge for the superior rooms
with balconies and lake and volcano views. There's a fireplace in the
common sitting room. ⊠ *San José 114* ☎ *65/232–305* ⊕ *www.
hotellicarayen.cl* ⇆ *23 rooms* ⚹ *Dining room, cable TV, gym, sauna,
Internet room; no a/c* ⊟ *AE, DC, MC, V* ⏀◉ *CP.*

Outdoor Activities

Al Sur Expediciones (⊠ Del Salvador 100 ☎ 65/232–300 ⊕ www.
alsurexpeditions.com) is known for rafting and kayaking trips on the
Class III Río Petrohué. It also runs horseback-riding and fly-fishing trips.
Aqua Motion (⊠ San Francisco 328 ☎ 65/232–747 ⊕ www.aqua-motion.

com) leads rafting and kayaking excursions on the Río Petrohué, as well as trekking, horseback riding, helicopter rides, bird-watching, and fly-fishing tours. Based in Cochamó, **Campo Aventura** (⊠ Valle Cochamó ☎ 65/232–910) leads 1- to 10-day horseback and trekking expeditions to its base camp in Parque Nacional Vicente Pérez Rosales.

Puerto Montt

❾ *20 km (12 mi) south of Puerto Varas.*

For most of its history, windy Puerto Montt was the end of the line for just about everyone traveling in the Lake District. Now the Carretera Austral carries on southward, but for all intents and purposes Puerto Montt remains the region's last significant outpost, a provincial city that is the hub of local fishing, textile, and tourist activity. Today the city center is quickly sprouting malls, condos, and office towers, but away from downtown, Puerto Montt consists mainly of low clapboard houses perched above its bay, the Seno de Reloncaví. If it's a sunny day, head east to Playa Pelluco or one of the city's other beaches. If you're more interested in exploring the countryside, drive along the shore for a good view of the surrounding hills.

The **Museo de Puerto Montt,** east of the city's bus terminal, has a collection of crafts and relics from the nearby archipelago of Chiloé. Historical photos of Puerto Montt itself give a sense of the area's slow and often difficult growth and the impact of the 1960 earthquake, which virtually destroyed the port. Pope John Paul II celebrated Mass on the grounds during his 1987 visit. One exhibit documents the event. ⊠ *Av. Diego Portales 991* ☎ *65/344–457* 💲 *500 pesos* ⊘ *Daily 9–7.*

About 3 km (2 mi) west of downtown along the coastal road lies the **Caleta Angelmó,** Puerto Montt's fishing cove. This busy port serves small fishing boats, large ferries, and cruisers carrying travelers and cargo southward through the straits and fjords that form much of Chile's shoreline. On weekdays small launches from Isla Tenglo and other outlying islands arrive early in the morning and leave late in the afternoon. The fish market here has a greatly varied selection of seafood.

Barely a stone's throw from Puerto Montt, the mountainous 398-square-km (154-square-mi) **Parque Nacional Alerce Andino,** with more than 40 small lakes, was established to protect some 20,000 endangered alerce trees. Comparable to California's hardy sequoia, alerce grow to average heights of 40 meters (130 feet), and can reach 4 meters (13 feet) in diameter. Immensely popular for construction of houses in southern Chile, they are quickly disappearing from the landscape. Many of these are 3,000–4,000 years old. ⊠ *Carretera Austral, 35 km (21 mi) east of Puerto Montt* ☎ *65/212–036* 💲 *1,700 pesos* ⊘ *Daily 9–6.*

Where to Stay & Eat

$–$$$ ✕ **Café Haussmann.** Its pale-wood-and-chrome decor might make this place seem trendy, but it's actually a fun, friendly place. The great sandwiches and light meals of crudos, cakes, and Kuchen make it a great destination for late-night noshing. ⊠ *San Martín 185* ☎ *65/293–980* ▭ *AE, DC, MC, V.*

$–$$$ ✕ **Club Alemán.** As befitting an old German association, Puerto Montt's Club Alemán exhibits a huge collection of beer steins on dark-wood shelving and serves delicious Kuchen and other pastries, but the rest of the menu is more local. Seafood—delicious clams, oysters, and lobster—as well as freshwater trout are the specialties here. ✉ *Antonio Varas 264* ☎ *65/252–551* ▭ *AE, DC, MC, V* ⊙ *No dinner Sun.*

$ $$$ ✕ **Club de Yates.** There are no yachts here, despite the tony-sounding name, and prices are reasonable—you can feast on lobster for just a few dollars. The arresting yellow exterior contrasts sharply with the subdued elegance of the interior, which has crisp linens and candlelight. You can't miss this place, as it sits on a high pier jutting out into the bay. The seafood dishes are prepared grilled or barbecued. ✉ *Av. Juan Soler Manfredini 200* ☎ *65/284–000* ▭ *AE, DC, MC, V* ⊙ *No dinner Sun.*

4

$–$$$ ✕ **Feria Artesanal Angelmó.** Several kitchens here prepare all kinds of succulent seafood. Separate tables and counters are at each kitchen in this enclosed market, which is 3 km (2 mi) west of Puerto Montt along the coast road. Don't expect anything as formal as set hours, but most open around 11 AM for lunch and serve for about three hours, and then from about 6 to 9 PM for dinner every day in the January–March high season. The rest of the year, most close during varying days of the week. ✉ *Caleta Angelmó* ☎ *No phone* ▭ *No credit cards.*

$–$$ ✕ **Restaurant Kiel.** Hospitable German-born proprietor Helga Birkir stands guard at this Chilean-Teutonic seafood restaurant on the coast west of Puerto Montt. Helga offers a little bit of everything else, but it's her curanto that draws crowds. Fresh produce from her well-kept garden makes lunch here a delight. ✉ *Camino Chinquihue, Km 8, Chinquihue* ☎ *65/255–010* ▭ *AE, DC, MC, V.*

¢–$$ ✕ **Café Central.** This old-style café in the heart of Puerto Montt retains the spirit of the 1920s and 1930s. It's a good place for a filling afternoon tea, with its menu of sandwiches, ice cream, and pastries. The raspberry Kuchen is a particular favorite here. ✉ *Rancagua 117* ☎ *65/254–721* ▭ *AE, DC, MC, V.*

$$–$$$ 🏨 **Don Luis Gran Hotel.** This modern lodging down the street from the cathedral, a favorite among upscale business travelers, has panoramic vistas of the Seno de Reloncaví. (Rooms on the seventh and eighth floors have the best views.) The carpeted rooms have undergone a welcome renovation and have either queen-sized beds or two full-sized beds. A big American-style breakfast, served in a cozy salon, is included in the rate. ✉ *Urmeneta at Quillota* ☎ *65/259–001* 🌐 *www.hoteldonluis.com* ⇆ *60 rooms, 1 suite* ♨ *Restaurant, coffee shop, snack bar, cable TV, gym, sauna, bar, laundry service, business services, meeting rooms; no a/c* ▭ *AE, DC, MC, V.*

$$ 🏨 **Gran Hotel Don Vicente.** The grandest of Puerto Montt's hotels underwent a much needed face-lift in 2002–2003 and, more than ever, it retains its Gstaad-by-the-sea glory. Its Bavarian-style facade resembles that of countless other Lake District lodgings, but the lobby's huge picture window overlooking the Seno de Reloncaví lets you know this place is something special. The modern guest rooms are comfy, with carpets and contemporary wood furniture. ✉ *Diego Portales 450* ☎ *65/432–900, 2/953–5037 in Santiago* 🌐 *www.granhoteldonvicente.cl* ⇆ *77* rooms, 4 suites ♨ Restaurant, coffee shop, in-room safes, minibars, cable TV, bar, laundry service, concierge, business services, meeting rooms, airport shuttle, travel services; no a/c ⊟ AE, DC, MC, V ⑩ BP.

$$ ⊡ **Viento Sur.** This old Victorian house sits proudly on a hill, offering a majestic view of both the city and the sea. Rooms in the original 1920s building have high ceilings and huge picture windows. Those in the newer wing below the house are smaller, but all are comfortably furnished with generous use of native Chilean blond woods. The restaurant serves excellent Chilean seafood, and a huge buffet breakfast (included in the rate) that just may keep you going until dinner. ⊠ Ejército 200 ☎ 65/258–700 ⊕ www.hotelvientosur.cl ⥲ 27 rooms, 2 suites ♨ Restaurant, in-room safes, cable TV, sauna, bar, laundry service, Internet room, business services, meeting room; no a/c ⊟ AE, DC, MC, V ⑩ BP.

$ ⊡ **Hostal Pacífico.** European travelers favor this solid budget option up the hill from the bus station. The rooms are small, but they have comfy beds with lots of pillows. Look at a few before you pick one, as some of the interior rooms have skylights rather than windows. The staff is exceptionally friendly and helpful. ⊠ Juan J. Mira 1088 ☎ 65/256–229 ⊕ www.hostalpacifico.cl ⥲ 30 rooms ♨ Dining room, cable TV, Internet room, travel services; no a/c ⊟ No credit cards ⑩ CP.

$ ⊡ **O'Grimm.** The warmth and charm of this four-story inn evokes a small town in Germany. The helpful staff makes you feel right at home. Muted shades of gray, rose, and green decorate the simple rooms, which are furnished with double beds, small tables, and chairs. ⊠ Guillermo Gallardo 211 ☎ 65/252–845 ⊕ www.ogrimm.com ⥲ 26 rooms, 1 suite ♨ Restaurant, minibars, cable TV, Wi-Fi, bar, laundry service, meeting rooms; no a/c ⊟ AE, DC, MC, V ⑩ BP.

¢ ⚓ **Los Alamos.** You can camp here at a site with fine views of the Seno de Reloncaví and Isla Tenglo. Sites have electricity and water, and hot showers are nearby. There's also a dock with boats you can rent. The campground is 11 km (7 mi) west of Caleta Angelmó. ⊠ Costanera, highway to Chinquihue ☎ 65/264–666 ⊟ No credit cards.

Shopping

An excellent selection of handicrafts is sold at the best prices in the country at the **Feria Artesanal Angelmó,** on the coastal road near Caleta Angelmó. Chileans know there's a better selection of crafts from Chiloé for sale here than in Chiloé itself. Baskets, ponchos, figures woven from different kinds of grasses and straws, and warm sweaters of raw, hand-spun, and hand-dyed wool are all offered. Much of the merchandise is geared toward tourists, so look carefully for more authentic offerings. Haggling is expected. It's open daily 9–dusk.

The Lake District Essentials

Transportation

BY AIR

None of the Lake District's airports—Osorno, Puerto Montt, Temuco and Valdivia—receives international flights; flying here from another country means connecting in Santiago. Of the four cities, Puerto Montt has the greatest frequency of domestic flights. (When flying south to this region from Santiago, the left side of the plane affords the best views of the Andes.)

At this writing, plans are mapped out for the new Aeropuerto de la Araucanía to serve the northern Lake District, and to be built near the town of Freire, 25 km (15 mi) south of Temuco. The $40 million project is scheduled to open in 2008 and will receive international flights, providing faster access from abroad to the region, and especially to Pucón and Villarrica.

Lan and its domestic affiliate LanExpress fly from Santiago to Temuco, Valdivia, Osorno, and Puerto Montt. A few of the flights south make an intermediate stop in Concepción. Some flights to Puerto Montt continue onward to Punta Arenas. Sky Airline connects Puerto Montt to Santiago with an intermediate stop in Concepción and continues south to Punta Arenas. Aerolineas del Sur flies from Santiago to Puerto Montt, with flights continuing south to Punta Arenas. Aerotaxis del Sur flies daily between Puerto Montt and Chaitén.

🛪 **Airlines Aerolineas del Sur** ✉ Antonio Varas 464, Puerto Montt ☎ 65/319-450. **Aerotaxis del Sur** ✉ Aeropuerto El Tepual, Puerto Montt ☎ 65/252-523. **Lan/Lan-Express** ✉ Eleuterio Ramírez 802, Osorno ☎ 64/204-119 ✉ Av. Bernardo O'Higgins 167, Puerto Montt ☎ 65/253-315 ✉ Bulnes 687, Temuco ☎ 45/211-339 ✉ Maipú 271, Valdivia ☎ 63/213-042. **Sky Airline** ✉ Benavente 405, Puerto Montt ☎ 65/437-555.
🛪 **Airports Aeropuerto Cañal Bajo** ✉ Osorno ☎ 64/247-555. **Aeropuerto El Tepual** ✉ Puerto Montt ☎ 65/488-203. **Aeropuerto Maquehue** ✉ Temuco ☎ 45/554-801. **Aeropuerto Pichoy** ✉ Valdivia ☎ 63/272-295.

AIRPORT TRANSFERS ETM provides bus transfers between Puerto Montt's Aeropuerto El Tepual and the city's bus terminal. Transfer & Turismo de la Araucanía vans meet arriving flights at Temuco's Aeropuerto Maquehue and transport passengers to various sites in the city. Reservations for transportation to the airport should be made a day in advance.
🛪 **ETM** ✉ Puerto Montt ☎ 65/256-253.
Transfer & Turismo de la Araucanía ✉ Temuco ☎ 45/339-900.

BY BOAT & FERRY

To drive much farther south than Puerto Montt, you've got to take a boat or ferry. Cruz del Sur operates a ferry connecting the mainland town of Pargua with Chacao on the northern tip of Chiloé's Isla Grande. Boats run every 30 minutes from early morning until after midnight. The trip takes about half an hour.

Navimag operates a cargo and passenger fleet throughout the region. The M/N *Evangelistas,* a 324-passenger ferry, sails round-trip from Puerto Montt to the popular tourist destination of Laguna San Rafael, stopping in both directions at Puerto Chacabuco on the Southern Coast. The 200-passenger M/N *Alejandrina* and M/N *Puerto Edén* sail from Puerto Montt to Chaitén, Quellón, and Puerto Chacabuco before making the trip in reverse.

If it's speed you're after, Catamaranes del Sur provides twice-weekly catamaran service between Puerto Montt and Chaitén at a relatively quick 4½ hours. In January and February you can continue on from Chaitén for 3 more hours to Castro, on the Chiloe's Isla Grande.
🛥 **Boat & Ferry Companies Catamaranes del Sur** ✉ Diego Portales and Guillermo Gallardo, Puerto Montt ☎ 65/267-533 ⊕ www.catamaranesdelsur.cl. **Cruz del Sur**

CLOSE UP

Chiloé

STEEPED IN MAGIC, shrouded in mist, the 41-island archipelago of Chiloé is that proverbial world apart, isolated not so much by distance from the mainland—it's barely more than 2 km (1 mi) at its nearest point—but by the quirks of history. Some 130,000 people populate 35 of these rainy islands, with most of them living on the 8,394-square-km (3,241-square-mi) Isla Grande. Its residents will regale you with the same myths and legends their ancestors told about these foggy green islands. Much of what is identified as Chilean folklore originated here, though the rest of the country happily embraces it as its own.

Nothing symbolizes Chiloé like the more than 150 wooden churches that dot the eastern half of the main island. Built by Jesuit missionaries who came to the archipelago after the 1598 Mapuche rebellion on the mainland, the chapels were an integral part of the effort to convert the indigenous peoples. Pairs of missionaries traveled the region by boat, making sure to celebrate mass in each community at least once a year.

Unless you're one of those rare visitors who approaches the archipelago from the south, **Ancud** is the first encounter you'll have with Chiloé. Founded in 1769 as a fortress city on the northern end of Isla Grande, Ancud was repeatedly attacked during Chile's war for independence. It remained the last stronghold of the Spaniards in the Americas, and the seat of their government-in-exile after fleeing from Santiago, a distinction it retained until Chiloé was finally annexed by Chile in 1826. Northwest of downtown Ancud, the 16 cannon emplacements of the 1786 **Fuerte de San Antonio** are nearly all that remain of Spain's last outpost in the New World.

The center of all that is magical and mystical about Chiloé, **Quicaví** sits forlornly on the eastern coast of Isla Grande. More superstitious locals will strongly advise you against going anywhere near the coast to the south of town, where miles of caves extend to the village of Tenaún; they believe that evil witches inhabit them. And many a Quicaví denizen claims to have glimpsed Chiloé's notorious ghost ship, the *Caleuche*, roaming the waters on foggy nights, searching for its doomed passengers. Of course, a brief glimpse of the ship is all anyone dares admit, as legend holds that a longer gaze could spell death.

The small fishing village of **Tenaún,** 12 km (7 mi) south of Quicaví on Isla Grande, is notable for its 1861 neoclassical **Iglesia de Tenaún** on the Plaza de Armas, which replaced the original 1734 structure built by the Jesuits. The style differs markedly from that of other Chilote churches, as the two towers flanking the usual hexagonal central bell tower are painted a striking deep blue.

Most days travelers in **Dalcahue,** which is 40 km (24 mi) west of Tenaún, stop only long enough to board the ferry that deposits them 15 minutes later on Isla Quinchao. But everyone lingers in Dalcahue if it's a Sunday morning, when they can visit the weekly artisan market. This market, the **Feria Artesanal,** is held on Avenida Pedro Montt near the waterfront municipal building, and draws crowds who come to shop for Chilote woolens, baskets, and woven mythical figures. Things get under way at about 8 AM and begin to wind down about noon. Bargaining is expected, though the prices are already quite reasonable.

For many visitors, the elongated **Isla Quinchao,** just southeast of Dalcahue and the easiest to reach of the islands off the east coast of Isla Grande, defines Chiloé. Populated by hardworking farmers and fisherfolk, Isla Quinchao provides a glimpse into the region's past. Head to Achao, Quinchao's largest community, to see the alerce-shingle houses, the busy fishing pier, and the town's centerpiece: the 1706 **Iglesia de Santa María de Loreto.** This church is the oldest remaining house of worship on the archipelago; its plain-looking exterior contrasts with the deep-blue ceiling inside, which is embellished with gold stars, and the rich baroque carvings that grace the altar.

The town of **Castro** (about 88 km—53 mi—south of Ancud on Isla Grande), is a wonderful place to see palafitos, the shingled houses that are the best-known architectural symbol of Chiloé. Along Avenida Pedro Montt, which becomes a coastal highway as it leads out of town, many of these old buildings have been turned into restaurants and artisan markets. A trip to Castro should also include a visit the much-photographed 1906 **Iglesia de San Francisco,** whose orange-and-lavender exterior has been described as both "pretty" and "pretty garish." The **Museo Regional de Castro,** just off Castro's Plaza de Armas, is also well worth a visit—it gives the best Spanish-language introduction to the region's history and culture. One exhibit has a collection of quotations about the Chiloé culture made by outsiders, such as: "The Chilote talks little, but thinks a lot. He is rarely spontaneous with outsiders, and even with his own countrymen he isn't too communicative." The portrait is dated, of course, but even today, residents have been compared with the stereotypical taciturn New Englander.

The colorful wooden houses of **Chonchi,** 23 km (14 mi) south of Castro, are on a hillside so steep that it's known in Spanish as the *Ciudad de los Tres Pisos* (City of Three Stories). The town's name means "slippery earth" in the Huilliche language, and if you tromp up the town's steep streets on a rainy day you'll understand why. Arranged around a scenic harbor, Chonchi wins raves as Chiloé's most picturesque town. It's centerpiece is the **Iglesia de San Carlos,** a national monument on the town's Plaza de Armas.

For information about traveling to Chiloé and attractions on the islands, contact **Sernatur,** Chile's national tourism board, which has an office on the Plaza de Armas in Ancud (✉ Libertad 665, Ancud ☎ 65/622-800). It's open January and February, daily 9–8; March–December, Monday–Saturday 9–noon and 2–6.

4

✉ Puerto Montt ☎ 64/254−731 ⊕ www.busescruzdelsur.cl. **Naviera Río Cisnes**
✉ Puerto Montt ☎ 64/432−700 ⊕ www.navierariocisnes.cl. **Navimag** ✉ Angelmó 2187,
Puerto Montt ☎ 65/432−300 ⊕ www.navimag.cl. **Transmarchilay** ✉ Angelmó 2187,
Puerto Montt ☎ 65/270−421 ⊕ www.transmarchilay.cl.

BY BUS

There's no shortage of bus companies traveling the Pan-American Highway (Ruta 5) from Santiago south to the Lake District. The buses aren't
overcrowded on these long routes, and seats are assigned. Tickets may
be purchased in advance, always a good idea if you're traveling in summer. Cruz del Sur and Tur-Bus connect the major cities. Buses JAC connects the resort towns of Pucón and Villarrica with Temuco and Valdivia.
Buses Vía Octay runs between Osorno and Puerto Octay.

Representative bus fares are: Temuco–Pucón, 2,200 pesos; Pucón–Villarrica, 600 pesos; Valdivia–Temuco, 2,600 pesos; Puerto Montt–Osorno, 1,600 pesos; Puerto Montt–Puerto Varas, 700 pesos.

Osorno, Puerto Montt, and Valdivia have their own central terminals.
About half the bus companies serving Temuco use a joint terminal, called
the Rodoviario, near the Holiday Inn Express on the north edge of town;
several other companies have their own terminals close together along
Vicuña Mackenna and Lagos.

🚍 **Bus Depots Osorno** ✉ Errázuriz 1400 ☎ 64/234−149. **Puerto Montt** ✉ Av. Diego
Portales ☎ No phone. **Temuco** ✉ Av. Rudecindo Ortega ☎ 45/257−904. **Valdivia**
✉ Anfión Muñoz 360 ☎ 63/212−212.

🚍 **Bus Lines Buses JAC** ✉ Vicuña Mackenna 798, Temuco ☎ 45/210−313 ✉ Bilbao
610, Villarrica ☎ 45/411−447 ✉ Anfión Muñoz 360, Valdivia ☎ 63/212−925. **Cruz del
Sur** ✉ Vicuña Mackenna 671, Temuco ☎ 45/210−701 ✉ Anfión Muñoz 360, Valdivia
☎ 63/213−840 ✉ Av. Diego Portales, Puerto Montt ☎ 65/254−731. **Tur-Bus** ✉ Lagos
538, Temuco ☎ 45/239−190.

BY CAR

It's easier to see more of the Lake District if you have your own vehicle. The Pan-American Highway (Ruta 5) through the region is a well-
maintained four-lane toll highway. You pay tolls of 1,500 pesos each at
Púa (Km 623), Quepe (Km 695), Lanco (Km 775), La Unión (Km 888),
and Purranque (Km 961); the southernmost toll plaza at Puerto Montt
(Km 1,019) levies a 500-peso toll. Tollbooths at many exits charge 400
pesos as well.

Once you're this far south, driving is easy because there's little traffic,
even on the major highways. Roads to most of the important tourist
centers are paved, but many of the routes through the mountains are
gravel or dirt, so a four-wheel-drive vehicle is ideal.

BY TAXI

As elsewhere in Chile, solid black or solid yellow cabs operate as *colectivos,* or collective taxis, following fixed routes and picking up to four
people along the way. A sign on the roof shows the general destination.
The cost is little more than that of a city bus. A black cab with a yellow roof will take you directly to your requested destination for a metered fare. Hail these in the street.

BY TRAIN

Chile's State Railway Company, the Empresa de los Ferrocarriles del Estado, has daily service southward from Santiago's Alameda station as far as Temuco on its Terra Sur trains. It's a far cry from the journey Paul Theroux recounted in *The Old Patagonian Express*. Trains run daily all year; the overnight trip takes about nine hours. Shuttle-bus service to and from Pucón and Villarrica runs in conjunction with the trains. Prices range from 10,000 pesos for an economy-class seat to 70,000 pesos for a sleeper with all the trimmings. If you prefer to rent a vehicle in Santiago, you can use the Autotren service from there to Temuco. The price is an extra 50,000–70,000 pesos each way, with surcharges assessed for vehicles longer than 16 feet.

Train Information Empresa de los Ferrocarriles del Estado (EFE) ☎ 2/585-5000 in Santiago, 45/233-416 in Temuco ⊕ www.efe.cl.

Train Station Estación de Ferrocarriles ⊠ Av. Barros Arana 191, Temuco ☎ 45/233-416.

Contacts & Resources

TOURS

The Lake District is the jumping-off point for luxury cruises. Many companies that offer trips to the fjords of Chilean Patagonia are based in Puerto Montt. Skorpios, with a trio of luxurious ships, has first-class cruises from Puerto Montt to the Laguna San Rafael. The ships carry between 70 and 130 passengers. A number of companies offer cruises on the region's lakes. Andina del Sud operates between Puerto Varas and San Carlos de Bariloche, and traverses the Lago Todos los Santos.

Boat Tours Andina del Sud ⊠ Del Salvador 72, Puerto Varas ☎ 65/232-811. Skorpios ⊠ Augosto Leguia Norte 118, Santiago ☎ 2/231-1030 ⊕ www.skorpios.cl.

VISITOR INFORMATION

The Lake District's four major cities have offices of Sernatur, Chile's national tourist office. The Osorno, Temuco, and Valdivia branches are well staffed with friendly people, full of good advice; the Puerto Montt branch is on the second floor of an out-of-the-way building and doesn't lend itself well to walk-in visitors. City tourist offices, run by the government or a chamber of commerce, are in most communities catering to tourists. They are valuable resources but cannot book rooms or tours. Many city tourist offices keep sharply abbreviated hours in the April–November off-season.

Frutillar Tourist Office ⊠ Philippi at San Martín ☎ 65/420-198. **Pucón Tourist Office** ⊠ Av. Bernardo O'Higgins 483 ☎ 45/293-002. **Puerto Montt Tourist Office** ⊠ San Martín at Diego Portales ☎ 65/261-823. **Puerto Octay Tourist Office** ⊠ La Esperanza 55 ☎ 64/391-491. **Puerto Varas Tourist Office** ⊠ Costanera at San José ☎ 65/233-315. **Sernatur** ⊠ Av. Bernardo O'Higgins 667, Osorno ☎ 64/237-575 ⊠ Av. de la Décima Región 480, Puerto Montt ☎ 65/254-850 ⊠ Claro Solar and Bulnes, Temuco ☎ 45/211-969 ⊠ Av. Arturo Prat 555, Valdivia ☎ 63/342-300. **Temuco Tourist Office** ⊠ Mercado Municipal ☎ 45/216-360. **Valdivia Tourist Office** ⊠ Terminal de Buses, Anfión Muñoz 360 ☎ 63/212-212. **Villarrica Tourist Office** ⊠ Pedro de Valdivia 1070 ☎ 45/206-618.

PATAGONIA

Traditional boundaries cannot define Patagonia. This vast stretch of land east of the Andes is mostly a part of Argentina, but Chile shares its southern extremity. Geographically and culturally it has little in common with either country. Patagonia, isolated by impenetrable mountains and endless fields of ice, is really a region unto itself.

Because of the region's remote location, much of what Darwin described is still relatively undisturbed. Drive north until the road peters out and you'll reach Parque Nacional Torres del Paine, perhaps the region's most awe-inspiring natural wonder. The snow-covered pillars of granite seem to rise vertically from the plains below.

> **WORD OF MOUTH**
>
> We saw waterfalls and glaciers, seals also! The lighting was such that we saw immense rainbows arching over mountains, tiny ones right alongside the boat, and others high in the sky. —rosexmke

Punta Arenas

Founded a little more than 150 years ago, Punta Arenas (Point of Sands) was Chile's first permanent settlement in Patagonia. Plaza Muñoz Gamero, the central square, is surrounded by 19th-century structures, whose brick exteriors recall a time when this was one of Chile's wealthiest cities.

The newer houses here have colorful tin roofs, best appreciated when seen from a high vantage point such as the Mirador Cerro la Cruz. Although the city as a whole may not be particularly attractive, look for details: the pink-and-white house on a corner, the bay window full of potted plants.

What to See

❼ Cementerio Municipal. The fascinating history of this region is chiseled into stone at the Municipal Cemetery. Bizarrely ornate mausoleums honoring the original families are crowded together along paths lined by sculpted cypress trees. In a strange effort to recognize Punta Arenas's indigenous past, there's a shrine in the northern part of the cemetery where the last member of the Selk'nam tribe was buried. Local legend says that rubbing the statue's left knee brings good luck. ✉ *Av. Bulnes 949* ☎ *No phone* 🎟 *Free* ☉ *Daily dawn–dusk.*

Isla Magdalena. Punta Arenas is the launching point for a boat trip to see the more than 120,000 Magellanic penguins at the **Monumento Natural Los Pingüinos** on this island. A single trail, marked off by rope, is accessible to humans. The trip to the island, in the middle of the Estrecho de Magallanes, takes about two hours. To get here, you must take a tour boat. If you haven't booked in advance, you can stop at any one of the local travel agencies and try to get on a trip at the last minute, which is often possible. You can only go from December to February; the penguin population peaks in January and February. However you get here, make sure to bring along warm clothing, even in summer; the island can be chilly, particularly if a breeze is blowing across the water.

❶ Mirador Cerro la Cruz. From a platform beside the white cross that gives this hill lookout its name, you have a panoramic view of the city's colorful corrugated rooftops leading to the Strait of Magellan. Stand with the

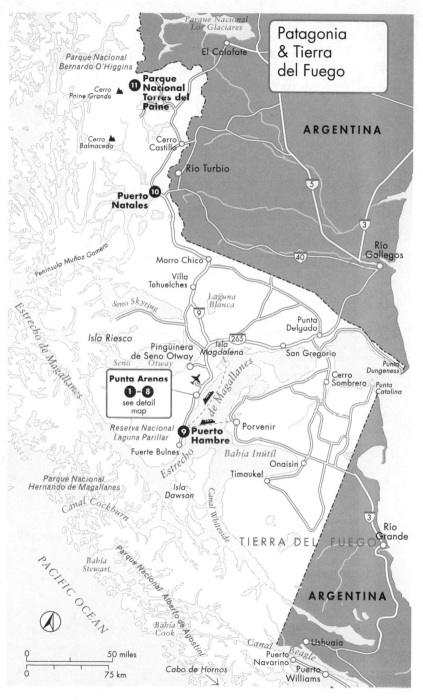

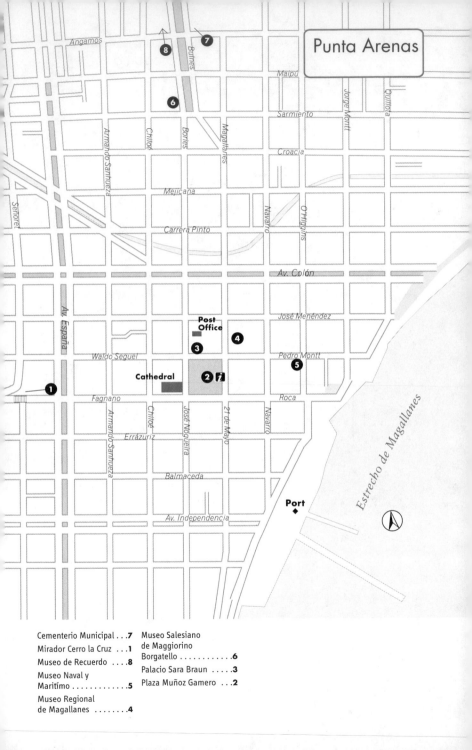

Punta Arenas

amorous local couples gazing out toward the flat expanse of Tierra del Fuego in the distance. ⊠ *Fagnano at Señoret* ☎ *No phone* 🎫 *Free* ⊗ *Daily.*

⑤ Museo Naval y Marítimo. The Naval and Maritime Museum extols Chile's high-seas prowess, particularly concerning Antarctica. Its exhibits are worth a visit by anyone with an interest in ships and sailing, merchant and military alike. The second floor is designed in part like the interior of a ship, including a map and radio room. Aging exhibits include an account of the 1908 visit to Punta Arenas by an American naval fleet. Ask for a tour or an explanatory brochure in English. ⊠ *Av. Pedro Montt 981* ☎ *61/205–558* 🎫 *700 pesos* ⊗ *Tues.–Sat. 9:30–5.*

⑧ Museo del Recuerdo. In the gardens of the Instituto de la Patagonia, part of the Universidad de Magallanes, the Museum of Memory is an enviable collection of machinery and heavy equipment used during the late-19th- and early-20th-century pioneering era. There are exhibits of rural employment, such as a carpenter's workshop, and displays of typical home life. ⊠ *Av. Bulnes, Km 4 Norte* ☎ *61/207–056* 🎫 *Free* ⊗ *Weekdays 8:30–11:30 and 2:30–6:30, Sat. 8:30–1.*

④ Museo Regional de Magallanes. Housed in what was once the mansion of the powerful Braun-Menéndez family, the Regional Museum of Magallanes is an intriguing glimpse into the daily life of a wealthy provincial family at the beginning of the 20th century. Carrara marble hearths and English bath fixtures are among the original accoutrements. The museum also has excellent displays depicting Punta Arenas's past, from the moment of European contact to its decline with the opening of the Panama Canal. The museum is half a block north of the main square. ⊠ *Av. Magallanes 949* ☎ *61/244–216* 🎫 *1,000 pesos* ⊗ *Oct.–Mar., Mon.–Sat. 10:30–5, Sun. 10:30–2; Apr.–Sept., daily 10:30–2.*

Fodor'sChoice
★

⑥ Museo Salesiano de Maggiorino Borgatello. Commonly referred to simply as "El Salesiano," this museum is operated by Italian missionaries whose order arrived in Punta Arenas in the 19th century. The Salesians, most of whom spoke no Spanish, proved to be daring explorers. Traveling throughout the region, they collected the artifacts made by indigenous tribes that are currently on display. They also relocated many of the indigenous people to nearby Dawson Island, where they died by the hundreds (from diseases like influenza and pneumonia). The museum contains an extraordinary collection of everything from skulls and native crafts to stuffed animals. ⊠ *Av. Bulnes 336* ☎ *61/241–096* 🎫 *1,500 pesos* ⊗ *Oct.–Mar., Tues.–Sun. 10–6; Apr.–Sept., Tues.–Sun. 10–1 and 3–6.*

★ **③ Palacio Sara Braun.** This resplendent 1895 mansion, a national landmark and architectural showpiece of southern Patagonia, was designed by French architect Numa Meyer at the behest of Sara Braun (the wealthy widow of wool baron José Nogueira). Materials and craftsmen were imported from Europe during the home's four years of construction. The city's central plaza and surrounding buildings soon followed, ushering in the region's golden era. The Club de la Unión, a social organization that now owns the building, opens its doors to nonmembers for tours of some of the rooms and salons, which have parquet floors, marble fireplaces, and hand-painted ceilings. After touring the rooms, head to the

Patagonia's Penguins

AS THE FERRY SLOWLY approaches Isla Magdalena, you make out black dots along the shore. You catch you breath, knowing that this is your first look at the 120,000 seasonal residents of Monumento Natural Los Pingüinos, one of the continent's largest penguin sanctuaries, a population that is at its height during the breeding season, which peaks in January and February.

But the squat little birds are much closer than you think. You soon realize that on either side of the ferry are large groups of penguins catching their breakfast. They are amazingly agile swimmers, leaping almost entirely out of the water before diving down below the surface once again. A few swim alongside the boat, but most simply ignore the intrusion.

Several types of penguins, including Magellanics found on the gentle hills of Isla Magdalena, make their homes along the Chilean coast. Although most favor cooler climates, small colonies can be found in the warmer waters north of Santiago. For the thrill of seeing tens of thousands in one place, nothing beats Monumento Natural Los Pingüinos, open only from December to February. At this reserve, a two-hour trip by boat from Punta Arenas, the birds can safely reproduce and raise their young.

Found only along the coast of Chile and Argentina, Magellanic penguins are named for Spanish explorer Hernando de Magallanes, who spotted them when he arrived on these shores in 1520. They are often called jackass penguins because of the braying sound they make when excited. Adults, with black-and-white markings, are easy to distinguish from the adolescents, which are a mottled gray. Also gray are the chicks, which hide inside their burrows when their parents are searching for food. A good time to see the fluffy little fellows is when their parents feed them regurgitated fish.

A single trail runs across Isla Magdalena, starting at the dock and ending on a hilltop at a red-and-white lighthouse. Ropes on either side keep humans from wandering too far afield. The penguins, however, have the run of the place. They waddle across the path, alone or in small groups, to get to the rocky beach. Familiar with the boatloads of people arriving two or three times a week, the penguins usually don't pay much attention to the camera-clutching crowds. A few of the more curious ones will walk up to people and inspect a shoelace or pants leg. If someone gets too close to a nest, however, they cock their heads sharply from side to side as a warning.

An easier way to see penguins is to drive to Pingüinera de Seno Otway, on the mainland about an hour northwest of Punta Arenas. It's open longer than Isla Magdalena—from October to March. The reserve occupies 2 km (1 mi) of coastline. There are far fewer penguins here—only about 4,000—but the number is still astounding. The sanctuary is run by a nonprofit group, which can provide English-language guides. Punta Arenas companies arrange frequent tours.

—Pete Nelson

cellar tavern for a drink or snack. ⊠ *Plaza Muñoz Gamero 716* ☎ *61/ 241–489* 🖅 *1,000 pesos, free Sun. and May* ⊙ *Tues.–Fri. 10:30–1 and 6:30–8:30, Sat. 10:30–1 and 8–10, Sun. 11–2.*

NEED A BREAK?

★

Tea and coffee house, chocolate shop, and bakery, **Chocolatta** (⊠ Bories 852 ☎ 61/268–606) is the perfect place to refuel during a day of wandering Punta Arenas. The interior is cozy, the staff friendly, and you can hang out, perhaps over a creamy hot chocolate, for as long as you like.

❷ **Plaza Muñoz Gamero.** A canopy of pine trees shades this square, which is surrounded by splendid baroque-style mansions from the 19th century. A bronze sculpture commemorating the voyage of Hernando de Magallanes dominates the center of the plaza. Local lore has it that a kiss on the shiny toe of Calafate, one of the Fuegian statues at the base of the monument, will one day bring you back to Punta Arenas. ⊠ *José Nogueira at 21 de Mayo.*

Where to Stay & Eat

$$–$$$ ✗ **La Pérgola.** In what was once the sunroom and winter garden of Sara Braun's turn-of-the-20th-century mansion, La Pérgola has one of the city's most refined settings. A 100-year-old vine festoons the glass windows and ceiling. The menu lists mainly Chilean seafood and meat dishes. The service is formal and attentive. ⊠ *Bories 959* ☎ *61/248–840* ⊟ *AE, DC, MC, V.*

★ $–$$$ ✗ **Sotito's Bar.** A virtual institution in Punta Arenas, Sotito's has dining rooms that are warm and cozy, with exposed-brick walls and wood-beamed ceilings. Locals gather here to enjoy some of the best centolla (king crab) in the area, prepared in several imaginative ways. The restaurant is near the water, a few blocks east of Plaza Muñoz Gamero. ⊠ *Av. Bernardo O'Higgins 1138* ☎ *61/243–565* ⊟ *AE, DC, MC, V.*

$–$$$ ✗ **La Tasca.** Inside the Sociedad Española, on Punta Arenas's main square, is this rustically elegant Spanish restaurant, operated by the same owners as the legendary Taberna Club de la Unión. You can look out the windows of the gracious, wood-ceilinged dining room onto the plaza, while enjoying typical Chilean fare. When ordering fish, keep it simple; some of the cream sauces are overwhelming. ⊠ *Sociedad Española, Plaza Muñoz Gamero 771, 2nd fl.* ☎ *61/242807* ⊟ *AE, DC, MC, V.*

★ ¢–$$$ ✗ **Los Ganaderos.** You'll feel at home on the range in this enormous restaurant resembling a rural *estancia* (ranch). The manager and waiters, dressed in gaucho costumes, serve up spectacular *cordero al ruedo* (spit-roasted lamb) cooked in the *salón de parilla* (grill room); a serving comes with three different cuts of meat. You can wash down your meal with a choice from the long list of Chilean wines. Interesting black-and-white photographs of past and contemporary ranch life are displayed along the walls. The restaurant is several blocks north of the center of town, but it's worth going out of the way for. ⊠ *Av. Bulnes 0977 at Manantiales* ☎ *61/214–597* ⊟ *AE, MC, V* ⊙ *Closed Sun.*

$$ ✗ **Restaurant Asturias.** Rough-hewn wood beams and white stucco walls at this restaurant evoke the Asturias region of Spain. The warmly lighted dining room is an inviting place to linger over *salmón papillote* (salmon poached in white wine with cured ham, cream cheese, and tomatoes), paella,

or *congrio a la vasca* (conger eel—Chile's ubiquitous whitefish—in cream sauce). ✉ *Lautaro Navarro 967* 🕿 *61/243–763* 🖃 *AE, DC, MC, V.*

$–$$ ✕ El Estribo. Centered around a large fireplace used to grill the meats, this narrow restaurant is filled with intimate little white-clothed tables. The name means The Stirrup, and the walls are adorned with tastefully arranged bridles, bits, lariats, and—of course—all manner of stirrups. The longtime popularity of the place, however, has more to do with its excellent regional food (which it ambitiously dubs *platos exóticos patagónicos*) than novelty decor. The more unusual preparations include rabbit stroganoff and fillet of guanaco (a local animal that resembles a llama) in sherry sauce. There's also delicious spit-roasted lamb. For dessert try rhubarb pie—uncommon in these parts. ✉ *Ignacio Carrera Pinto 762 at Av. Magallanes* 🕿 *61/244–714* 🖃 *No credit cards.*

$–$$ ✕ El Remezón. This cheerful little restaurant stands out because of its deliciously seasoned grilled fish and meats. The dining room is unpretentious and homey, and the day's menu is scrawled onto a chalkboard; if you're lucky, it might include a pisco-marinated goose. Although it's near the port, away from the main part of town, the terrific food and potent pisco sours make it worth the walk (at night, it's best to spring for a short taxi ride). ✉ *21 de Mayo 1469* 🕿 *61/241–029* 🖃 *AE.*

$–$$ ✕ Taberna Club de la Unión. A jovial, publike atmosphere prevails in this
Fodor'sChoice wonderful, labyrinthine cellar redoubt down the side stairway of Sara
★ Braun's old mansion on the main plaza. A series of nearly hidden rooms are walled in cozy stone and brick, and black-and-white photos of historical Punta Arenas adorn the walls. You're likely to hear ragtime and jazz on the stereo while you enjoy beers served cold in frosted mugs, tapas-style meat and cheese appetizers, sandwiches, tacos, pizza, fajitas, and carpaccio (the menu has more bar snacks than dinner entrées). The bar is affiliated with the Club de la Unión headquartered upstairs, and many members relax down here. ✉ *Plaza Muñoz Gamero 716* 🕿 *61/ 241–317* 🖃 *AE, DC, MC, V* ☽ *Closed Sun. No lunch.*

¢–$ ✕ Santino Bar. This downtown bar has a winning combination of friendly service, good pizzas and crepes, and an excellent assortment of Chilean cocktails. It's most popular for its drinks; perhaps the most interesting libation is the beer that's frothed up with egg whites. It was nicknamed the "Shourtney" after a young couple from Texas and Uruguay, who declared their undying love for the egg beer—and for each other—at Santino. ✉ *Av. Colón 657, between Bories and Chiloé* 🕿 *61/220–511* 🖃 *AE, DC, MC, V* ☽ *Closed Sun.*

¢ ✕ Lomit's. A fast-moving but friendly staff serves Chilean-style blue-plate specials at this bustling deli. In addition to traditional hamburgers, you can try the ubiquitous *completos*—hot dogs buried under mounds of toppings, from spicy mayonnaise to guacamole—or try the Uruguayan-style *chivitos* (sandwiches with meat, lettuce, tomato, egg, and other trimmings). Locals gather here from morning to midnight. ✉ *José Menéndez 722 between Bories and Av. Magallanes* 🕿 *61/243–399* 🖃 *No credit cards.*

$$ ✕▣ Hotel Los Navegantes. This unpretentious older hotel, just a block from the Plaza de Armas, has spacious burgundy-and-green rooms and a nautical theme (maritime maps cover the walls). There's a charming dark-wood bar and a restaurant that serves delicious roast lamb. ✉ *José Menéndez 647* 🕿 *61/244–677* ⊕ *www.hotel-losnavegantes.com* ⊲ *50* *rooms, 2 suites △ Restaurant, in-room safes, minibars, bar, airport shuttle, travel services ▭ AE, DC, MC, V.*

$$ ✕▦ **Hotel Tierra del Fuego.** Just a couple of blocks from the main plaza, this hotel is aging with grace. The place is clean and simple, with an old-world pub that serves sandwiches and drinks into the wee hours. Rooms are brightened by pretty rugs, and marble bathroom sinks; some even have kitchenettes. ⊠ *Av. Colón 716* ▦ *61/226–200* ⊕ *www. puntaarenas.com/tierradelfuego* ⊅ *26 rooms △ Some kitchens, minibars, cable TV, pub, Internet ▭ AE, DC, MC, V* ⅥⅪ *BP.*

$$$ ▦ **Hotel Finis Terrae.** A Best Western affiliate, this contemporary hotel has a good location (it's a couple of blocks from the main square) and a very professional staff. Guest rooms are comfortable, and the baths are spacious and modern. There's a pleasant lounge with a fireplace, and the sixth-floor restaurant and bar has panoramic views. Stick with the superior rooms or, better yet, the junior suites, and avoid the tiny standard rooms; if you need two beds in a room, look elsewhere. Discounts are considerable March–September. ⊠ *Av. Colón 766* ▦ *61/228–200* ⊕ *www.hotelfinisterrae.com* ⊅ *60 rooms, 4 suites △ Restaurant, in-room safes, minibars, cable TV, 2 bars, Internet, business services, airport shuttle ▭ AE, DC, MC, V* ⅥⅪ *BP.*

★ **$$$** ▦ **Hotel José Nogueira.** Originally the home of Sara Braun, this opulent 19th-century mansion also contains a museum. The location—steps off the main plaza—couldn't possibly be better. Carefully restored over many years, the building retains the original crystal chandeliers, marble floors, and polished bronze accents that were imported from France. Rooms are rather small—some smaller than others—but compensate with high ceilings, thick carpets, and period furniture. ⊠ *Bories 959* ▦ *61/248–840* ⊕ *www.hotelnogueira.com* ⊅ *25 rooms, 3 suites △ Restaurant, in-room data ports, in-room safes, minibars, cable TV, bar, laundry service, business services ▭ AE, DC, MC, V.*

$$ ▦ **Hotel Isla Rey Jorge.** Lofty windows let lots of light into the intimate rooms, decorated in mint and deep rose, at this English-style hotel with impeccable service. The hotel's richly toned *linga* and *coigué* woodwork in the lobby continues down into the popular basement pub, El Galeón. The hotel is just one block from Plaza Muñoz Gamero. ⊠ *21 de Mayo 1243* ▦ *61/248–220 or 61/228* ⊕ *www.islareyjorge.com* ⊅ *21 rooms, 4 suites △ Restaurant, cable TV, bar, Internet, airport shuttle, travel services ▭ AE, DC, MC, V.*

$ ▦ **Hostal de la Avenida.** The rooms of this pea-green guesthouse all overlook a garden, lovingly tended by the owner, a local of Yugoslav origin. Flowers spill out from a wheelbarrow and a bathtub, birdhouses hang from trees, and a statue of Mary rests in a shrine with a grotto. The rooms offer modest comforts for those on a budget. The ones across the garden, away from the street, are the newest. Beside them is a funky bar that Chilean poet Pablo Neruda would have approved of; it seems hunkered down for blustery winters. ⊠ *Av. Colón 534* ▦ *61/ 247–532* ⊅ *10 rooms, 6 with bath △ Dining room, in-room safes, minibars, cable TV, bar, laundry service ▭ AE, DC, MC, V* ⅥⅪ *CP.*

★ **$** ▦ **Hostal Oro Fueguino.** On a sloping cobblestone street near the observation deck at Cerro la Cruz, this charming little hostelry—tall, narrow, and rambling—welcomes you with lots of color. The first thing you notice is the facade, painted bright orange and blue. Inside are homey wall hangings and lamp shades made of eye-catching fabrics from as far off as India. The dining and living rooms are cheerful, and there's a wealth of tourist information. The warmth is enhanced by the personal zeal of the proprietor, Dinka Ocampo. ☒ *Fagnano 365* 🖼🖼 *61/249–401* ⊕ *www.orofueguino.cl* ↩ *12 rooms* ♢ *Cable TV, laundry service, Internet; no a/c* ▭ *AE, DC, MC, V* ❢◉❢ *BP.*

$ 🖼 **Hotel Condor de Plata.** The idiosyncratic decor at the Silver Condor includes scale models of ships and photographs of old-fashioned airplanes that once traversed the region. Like a handful of other small hotels on this busy, tree-lined avenue, it offers basic amenities for those on a budget—simple, clean rooms that have a bed and a TV. ☒ *Av. Colón 556* 🖼 *61/241–078* ⊕ *www.condordeplata.cl* ↩ *14 rooms* ♢ *Cafeteria, in-room safes, minibars, bar, laundry service* ▭ *AE, DC, MC, V.*

Nightlife & the Arts

During the Chilean summer, because Punta Arenas is so far south, the sun doesn't set until well into the evening. That means that locals don't think about hitting the bars until midnight. If you can't stay up late, try the hotel bars, such as Hotel Tierra del Fuego's **Pub 1900** (☒ Av. Colón 716 🖼 61/242–759), which attract an early crowd. If you're in the mood for dancing, try **Abracadabra** (☒ Bories 546 🖼 61/224–144), where the younger set goes to party until dawn.

Shopping

Almacén de Antaño (☒ Av. Colón 1000 🖼 61/227–283) offers a fascinatingly eclectic selection of pewter, ceramics, mirrors, and graphics frames. **Dagorret** (☒ Bories 587 🖼 61/228–692 ⊕ www.dagorret.cl), a Chilean chain with other outlets in Puerto Montt and Puerto Natales, carries topquality leather clothing, including *gamuza* (suede) and *gamulán* (buckskin), some with wool trim. **Quilpué** (☒ José Nogueira 1256 🖼 61/220–960) is a shoe-repair shop that also sells *huaso* (cowboy) supplies such as bridles, bits, and spurs. Pick up some boots for folk dancing.

Puerto Natales

🔟 *242 km (150 mi) northwest of Punta Arenas.*

The land around Puerto Natales held very little interest for Spanish explorers in search of riches. A not-so-warm welcome from the indigenous peoples encouraged them to continue up the coast, leaving only a name for the channel running through it: Seno Última Esperanza (Last Hope Sound). Today, this town is rapidly emerging as the staging center for visits to Parque Nacional Torres del Paine, Parque Nacional Bernardo O'Higgins, and other attractions, including the Perito Moreno glacier across the border in Argentina.

A few blocks east of the Seno Ultima Esperanza is the not-quite-central **Plaza de Armas.** An incongruous railway engine sits prominently in the middle of the square. ☒ *Arturo Prat at Eberhard.*

Across from the Plaza de Armas is the squat little **Iglesia Parroquial.** The ornate altarpiece in this church depicts the town's founders, indigenous peoples, and the Virgin Mary all in front of the Torres del Paine. A highlight in the small but interesting **Museo Historico Municipal** is a room of photos of indigenous peoples. Another room is devoted to the exploits of Hermann Eberhard, a German explorer considered the region's first settler. ⊠ *Av. Bulnes 285* ☎ *61/411–263* ✏ *Free* ⊙ *Weekdays 8:30–12:30 and 2:30–6, weekends 2:30–6.*

In 1896 Hermann Eberhard stumbled upon a gaping cave that extended 200 meters (650 feet) into the earth. Venturing inside, he discovered the bones and dried pieces of hide of an animal he could not identify. It was later determined that what Eberhard had discovered were the extraordinarily well-preserved remains of a prehistoric herbivorous mammal, *mylodon darwini,* about twice the height of a man, which they called a *milodón.* The cave and a somewhat kitschy life-size fiberglass rendering of the creature are at the **Monumento Natural Cueva de Milodón.** ⊠ *Off Ruta 9, 28 km (17 mi) northwest of Puerto Natales* ☎ *No phone* ✏ *1,500 pesos* ⊙ *Daily 8:30–6.*

Where to Stay & Eat

★ **$$** ✕ **Asador Patagónico.** This bright spot in the Puerto Natales dining scene is zealous about meat. Incredible care is taken here with the excellent *lomo* and other grilled steaks, as well as the steak tartare starter. Though the wine list is serious, the atmosphere is less so—there's good music, dim lighting, an open fire, and a friendly buzz. ⊠ *Prat 158* ☎ *61/413–553* ⊕ *www.asadorpatagonico.cl* ▭ *AE, DC, MC, V.*

$–$$ ✕ **Restaurant Edén.** Grilled lamb sizzles prominently near the entrance of this eatery, while Chilean folk music plays softly in the background. The expansive dining room, with tables generously spaced on the white terrazzo floor, has floor-to-ceiling windows on two sides. ⊠ *Blanco Encalada 345* ☎ *61/414–120* ▭ *AE, MC, V.*

$–$$ ✕ **Centro Español.** Tables swathed in bright red, and hardwood floors that would be perfect for flamenco dancing create this restaurant's subtly Spanish style. It's a bit formal, but never stuffy. There's a wide selection of simply prepared meat and fish entrées. ⊠ *Av. Magallanes 247* ☎ *61/411–181* ▭ *AE, MC, V.*

★ **¢–$$** ✕ **El Rincón del Tata.** In the evening a strolling guitarist entertains with Chilean folk songs, encouraging diners to join in at this dimly lighted, funky little spot. Artifacts, mainly household items, from the town's early days fill the dining room, which has a wood-burning stove to keep you warm, and Internet access. Pizza is a specialty here, and it's not bad by Chilean standards; the grilled lamb with garlic sauce is a Patagonian highlight. ⊠ *Arturo Prat 236* ☎ *61/413–845* ▭ *AE, DC, MC, V.*

¢–$ ✕ **Café Melissa.** The best espresso in town can be found at this café, which also serves pastries and cakes baked on the premises. In the heart of downtown, this is a popular meeting place for residents and visitors alike, and there's Internet access, too. It's open until 9 PM. ⊠ *Blanco Encalada 258* ☎ *61/411–944* ▭ *No credit cards.*

★ **$** ✕▥ **Concepto Indigo.** Ask for one of the corner rooms in this restored old home with amazing views down the Canal Señoret. Internet access, and an English-speaking staff make Indigo a de facto tourist office, museum, and library. Eco-friendly vibes waft from the quirky and friendly café downstairs, setting it apart from nearly every other eatery in Patagonia. ⊠ *Ladrilleros 105* ☎ *61/413–609* ⊕ *www.conceptoindigo.com*

    ⇨ *7 rooms* ⚹ *Restaurant, laundry service, Internet, travel services; no room phones, no room TVs* ▭ *MC, V* ☉ *Closed in winter; months vary.*

$$$ ◫ **Hotel CostAustralis.** Designed by a local architect, this venerable three-story hotel has one of the most distinctive buildings Puerto Natales; its peaked, turreted roof dominates the waterfront. Rooms have wood-paneled entryways and Venetian and Czech furnishings. Some have a majestic view of the Seno Última Esperanza and the snowcapped mountain peaks beyond. ⊠ *Av. Pedro Montt 262 at Av. Bulnes* ☎ *61/412–000* ⊕ *www.costaustralis.com* ⇨ *72 rooms, 2 suites* ⚹ *Restaurant, café, room service, in-room safes, minibars, cable TV, bar, laundry service, Internet, travel services* ▭ *AE, DC, MC, V* ⦿ *BP.*

$$ ◫ **Hotel Martín Gusinde.** Part of Chile's modern AustroHoteles chain, this intimate inn possesses an aura of sophistication that contrasts with the laid-back atmosphere of Puerto Natales. Rooms are decorated with wood furniture and colorfully patterned wallpaper. It's across from the casino, a block south of the Plaza de Armas. In low season prices drop by almost two-thirds. ⊠ *Carlos Bories 278* ☎ *61/412–770* ⊕ *www. austrohoteles.cl/martingusinde.html* ⇨ *20 rooms* ⚹ *Restaurant, room service, in-room safes, cable TV, bar, Internet* ▭ *AE, MC, V* ⦿ *CP.*

$–$$ ◫ **Hostal Lady Florence Dixie.** Named after an aristocratic English immigrant and tireless traveler, this modern hostel with an alpine-inspired facade is on the town's main street. Its bright, spacious lounge is a great people-watching perch. Guest rooms are a bit spartan—not much more than a bed. ⊠ *Av. Bulnes 655* ☎ *61/411–158* ⊕ *www.chileanpatagonia. com/florence* ⇨ *18 rooms* ⚹ *Café, in-room safes, Internet, laundry service* ▭ *AE, MC, V* ⦿ *CP.*

$$ ◫ **Hotel Alberto de Agostini.** The Agostini is one of the modern hotels that have cropped up in Puerto Natales in the past few years. Small rooms—some with hot tubs—are unremarkable in decor, but a comfortably furnished lounge on the second floor looks out over the Seno Última Esperanza. ⊠ *Av. Bernardo O'Higgins 632* ☎ *61/410–060* ⇨ *25 rooms* ⚹ *Restaurant, café, room service, cable TV, minibars, sauna, bar, laundry service, travel services, Internet* ▭ *AE, DC, MC, V.*

$ ◫ **Hostal Francis Drake.** Toss a coin in the wishing well out front before you enter this half-timbered house near the center of town. The proprietor is a delightful European lady who dotes on her guests and carefully maintains cleanliness. Rooms are small and basic. The beds are not the world's most comfortable. ⊠ *Philippi 383* ☎☎ *61/411–553 or 61/ 410–852* ⊕ *www.chileaustral.com/francisdrake* ⇨ *12 rooms* ⚹ *Café, cable TV, lounge, Internet; no a/c* ▭ *DC, MC, V* ⦿ *CP.*

Parque Nacional Torres del Paine

⓫   *125 km (75 mi) northwest of Puerto Natales.*

Fodor'sChoice
★

Some 12 million years ago, lava flows pushed up through the thick sedimentary crust that covered the southwestern coast of South America, cooling to form a granite mass. Glaciers then swept through the region, grinding away all but the ash-gray spires—nicknamed torres or "towers"—that rise over the landscape of one of the world's most beautiful natural phenomena, now the Parque Nacional Torres del Paine (established in 1959). Snow formations dazzle along every turn of road, and the sunset views are spectacular.

Among the 2,420-square-km (934-square-mi) park's most beautiful attractions are its lakes of turquoise, aquamarine, and emerald-green waters. Another draw is the park's unusual wildlife. Creatures like the guanaco (a woollier version of the llama) and the ñandú (resembling a small ostrich) abound. They are used to visitors, and don't seem to be bothered by the proximity of automobile traffic and the snapping of cameras. Predators like the gray fox make less-frequent appearances. You may also spot the dramatic aerobatics of falcons and the graceful soaring of endangered condors. The beautiful puma, celebrated in a National Geographic video filmed here, is especially elusive, but sightings have grown more and more common.

Although considerable walking is necessary to take full advantage of Parque Nacional Torres del Paine, you need not be a hard-core backpacker. Many people choose to hike the so-called **"W" route,** which takes four days, but others prefer to stay in one of the comfortable lodges and hit the trails for the morning or afternoon. **Glaciar Grey,** with its fragmented icebergs, makes a rewarding and easy hike; equally rewarding is the spectacular boat ride across the lake, past icebergs, and up to the glacier, which leaves from Hostería Lago Grey. Another great excursion is the 900-meter (3,000-foot) ascent to the sensational views from **Mirador Las Torres,** four hours one way from Hostería Las Torres. Even if you're not staying at the Hostería, you can arrange a morning drop-off there, and a late-afternoon pickup, so that you can see the Mirador while still keeping your base in Puerto Natales or elsewhere in the park; alternatively, you can drive yourself to the Hostería and park there for the day. The vast majority of visitors come during the summer months, which means the trails can get congested. Early spring, when wildflowers add flashes of color to the meadows, is an ideal time to visit because the crowds have not yet arrived. The park is open all year, and trails are almost always accessible. Storms can hit without warning, however, so be prepared for sudden rain or snow. The sight of the Paine peaks in clear weather is stunning; if you have any flexibility, be sure to visit the park on the first clear day.

There are three entrances to the park: Laguna Amarga, Lago Sarmiento, and Laguna Azul. You are required to sign in when you arrive. *Guardaparques* (park rangers) staff six stations around the reserve; they request that you inform them when setting out on a hike. CONAF, the national forestry service, has an office at the northern end of Lago del Toro with a scale model of the park, and numerous exhibits (some in English) about the flora and fauna. ✉ *CONAF station in southern section of the park past Hotel Explora* 🕿 *61/691–931* ✉ *8,000 pesos* ☾ *Ranger station: Nov.–Feb., daily 8–8; Mar.–Oct., daily 8–12:30 and 2–6:30* ✉ *Punta Arenas Branch, Av. Bulnes 0309* 🕿 *61/238–581* ✉ *Puerto Natales Branch, Av. Bernardo O'Higgins 584* 🕿 *61/411–438.*

Where to Stay & Eat

$–$$　✗▥ **Posada Río Serrano.** A welcoming staff will show you a selection of rooms, including some with bunk beds and some with regular beds.

Rooms are small, but clean, and a few actually have lake views. A warm and cheerful salon with a fireplace makes a nice place to relax. Don't expect pampering—except for camping, this is the cheapest dining and lodging in the park. The restaurant serves filling fish dishes as well as lamb; in summer there might be an outdoor asado. The inn also has a general store where you can find basic necessities. ⊠ *Lago Toro* ☎ *61/412–911 for reservations (Puerto Natales)* ⊕ *www.baqueanozamora.com* ⊃ *14 rooms, 4 with bath* ⚏ *Restaurant, grocery, bar; no a/c, no room phones, no room TVs* ⊟ *No credit cards* ⦿ *CP.*

$$$$ ⛆ **Hosteria Tyndall.** A boat ferries you from the end of the road the few minutes along the Serrano River to this wooden lodge. The simple rooms in the main building are small but cute, with attractive wood paneling. The lodge can be noisy, a problem solved by renting a log cottage (a great value for groups of four). There's also a much more basic refugio with dorm-style rooms that are very cheap. Owner Christian Bore is a wildlife enthusiast and bird-watcher; ask him for a tour of the grassy plain looking out toward the central cluster of snowy peaks. Or go fishing—the kitchen staff will cook your catch for free. ⊠ *Ladrilleros 256, Lago Tyndall, Puerto Natales* ☎☎ *61/413–139* ⊕ *www.hosteriatyndall.com* ⊃ *24 rooms, 6 cottages* ⚏ *Restaurant, boating, fishing, hiking, horseback riding, lounge, laundry service; no room phones, no room TVs* ⊟ *AE, DC, MC, V* ⦿ *CP.*

$$$$ ⛆ **Hotel Explora.** On the southeast corner of Lago Pehoé, this lodge is
Fodor'sChoice one of the most luxurious—and the most expensive—in Chile. While
★ there may be some debate about the aesthetics of the hotel's low-slung minimalist exterior, the Scandinavian-style interior is impeccable. A dozen full-time guides (for a maximum of 60 guests) tailor all-inclusive park outings to guests' interests. A four-night minimum stay is required, for which you'll pay a minimum of US$3,120 (1,648,000 pesos) for two people, including airport transfers, three meals a day, drinks, and excursions. Rooms with better views go up to almost double that. Nonguests may also enjoy a pricey prix-fixe dinner at the restaurant. ⊠ *Lago Pehoé* ☎ *2/206–6060 in Santiago* ⊕ *www.explora.com* ⊃ *26 rooms, 4 suites* ⚏ *Restaurant, indoor pool, gym, outdoor hot tub, massage, sauna, boating, hiking, horseback riding, piano bar, library, shop, babysitting, laundry service, Internet, business services, meeting rooms, airport shuttle; no room TVs* ⊟ *AE, DC, MC, V* ⦿ *AI.*

Patagonia Essentials

Transportation

BY AIR

Lan and its subsidiary, Ladeco, operate a number of flights daily between Punta Arenas and Santiago, and Puerto Montt. ■ **TIP→ It's a good idea to make air-travel arrangements through a reliable tour company, if possible.** That way you can rely on the company if you need to make last-minute changes in your itinerary.

AIRPORT Public bus service from the airport into Punta Arenas is 1,500 pesos.
TRANSFERS Private transfers by small companies running minivans out of the air-

port (with no other pick up points or call-in service) run 3,000 pesos per person.

Airlines Aerolíneas Argentinas ✉ Roger de Flor 2915, Santiago ☎ 800/610-200 toll free in Chile, 2/210-9300 in Santiago, 0810/2228-6527 24-hr reservations and sales in Argentina, 11/4317-3000 in Buenos Aires.
Aerovís DAP ✉ Av. Bernardo O'Higgins 891, Punta Arenas ☎ 61/223-340 ⊕ www.aeroviasdap.cl. **Lan** ✉ Lautaro Navarro 999, Punta Arenas ☎ 600/526-2000, +56 2526-2000 from outside Chile ⊕ www.lan.com.

BY BOAT & FERRY

Boat tours are a popular way to see otherwise inaccessible parts of Patagonia and Tierra del Fuego. The four-day Navimag trips from Puerto Montt to Puerto Natales, which pass the Amalia Glacier, are immensely popular with backpackers and other visitors. The ship isn't luxurious, but it has a restaurant, pub, and lectures on local culture. Depending on which sort of cabin you choose, cabins are priced US$720–$845 (380,000 pesos–446,000 pesos) per person for double occupancy in high season, and US$340–$410 (180,000 pesos–216,500 pesos) per person in low season. Prices include all meals. The boat calls at Puerto Edén, where you can get off and visit the town for a few hours. Navimag tickets can be bought online or at local travel agencies.

Comapa runs a ferry three times a week between Punta Arenas and Porvenir. The *Barcaza Melinka,* also run by Comapa, makes thrice-weekly trips to Isla Magdalena (during penguin season). Cruceros Australis operates two ships, the elegant 55-cabin *Mare Australis,* and the 63-cabin *Vía Australis.* Both sail round-trip between Punta Arenas and Ushuaia. On the way, the ships stop at a number of sights, including the Garibaldi Glacier, a breathtaking mass of blue ice. You also ride smaller motorboats ashore to visit Isla Magdalena's colony of 120,000 penguins, and Ainsworth Bay's family of elephant seals. The cruises include lectures in English, German, and Spanish on the region's geography and history, flora and fauna.

Turismo 21 de Mayo operates two ships, the *Cutter 21 de Mayo* and the *Alberto de Agostini,* to the Balmaceda and Serrano glaciers in Parque Nacional Bernardo O'Higgins. Passengers on these luxurious boats are treated to lectures about the region as the boat moves up the Seno Última Esperanza. Lago Grey Tours offers boat trips to Glaciar Grey inside the Parque Nacional Torres del Paine (35 pesos).

Boat & Ferry Lines Comapa ✉ Av. Magallanes 990, Punta Arenas ☎ 61/200-200 ⊕ www.comapa.cl ✉ Av. Bulnes 533 Puerto Natales ☎ 61/414-300. **Cruceros Australis** ✉ Av. El Bosque Norte 0440, Piso 11, Santiago ☎ 2/442-3110 ⊕ www.australis.com. **Lago Grey Tours** ✉ Lago Grey ☎☎ 61/225-986 ⊕ www.lagogrey.com. **Navimag** ✉ Av. El Bosque Norte 0440, Santiago ☎ 2/442-3120 ⊕ www.navimag.com.
Turismo 21 de Mayo ✉ Ladrilleros 171, Puerto Natales ☎ 61/411-176.
Upsala Explorer ✉ 9 de Julio 69, El Calafate ☎ +54 2902/491-034 ⊕ www.upsalaexplorer.com.ar.

BY BUS

The four-hour trip between Punta Arenas and Puerto Natales is serviced by small, private companies. One of the best is Buses Fernández, which has a fleet of first-class coaches and its own terminals in both towns.

To travel between Punta Arenas and Ushuaia, Argentina, your best bet is Tecni-Austral, based in Argentina.

🚌 **Bus Companies Buses Fernández** ✉ Armando Sanhueza 745, Punta Arenas 📞 61/221-429 ✉ Eleuterio Ramirez 399, Puerto Natales 📞 61/411-111 ⊕ www.busesfernandez.com. **Tecni-Austral** ✉ Lautaro Navarro 975, Punta Arenas 📞 61/222-078 or 61/223-205 ✉ Roca 157, Ushuaia, Argentina 📞 +54 2901/431-408.

BY CAR

Renting a car in Patagonia is not cheap—most companies charge about 70,000 pesos per day. Compare rental rates to the cost of tours; you may find a tour is far cheaper than driving yourself. Make sure you don't rent a more expensive car than you need. ■ TIP➜ **Four-wheel-drive vehicles often aren't necessary if you're not leaving the major roads.** (They're extremely useful, however, in Torres del Paine or El Calafate.) Make certain to understand the extent of your liability for any damage to the vehicle, including routine accidents such as a chipped or cracked windshield.

BY TAXI

Taxis are readily available in Punta Arenas and Puerto Natales. Ordinary taxis, with yellow roofs, are the easiest. *Colectivos,* with black roofs, run on fixed routes. They cost less, but figuring them out can be tricky if you're not a fluent Spanish speaker.

Contacts & Resources

TOURS

AIR TOURS   Air tours are often a little more expensive than cruises, but they provide an entirely different perspective, and may take you farther than you could otherwise go. Aerovís DAP operates charter flights over Cape Horn for about US$75 (39,500 pesos) per person. DAP was the first airline to have regular commercial flights to the Antarctic, beginning in 1987. In the austral summer (December–February) they fly small groups to comfortable refuges in the Chilean Antarctic, where you can stay in a lodge for up to three nights. DAP staffs a resident guide in Antarctica, and visits include trips to the air force bases of Russia, China, and Chile. Single-day visits begin at US$2,500 (1,320,000 pesos). The flight is 3½ hours. DAP also has helicopter service across Patagonia.

🚌 **Aerovís DAP** ✉ Av. Bernardo O'Higgins 891, Punta Arenas 📞 61/223-340 ⊕ www.aeroviasdap.cl.

LAND-BASED TOURS AND EXCURSIONS   SportsTour, based in Santiago, offers half- and full-day city tours and multiday excursions throughout the region; the company also arranges individual tour itineraries. Most staff members speak excellent English. In Puerto Natales, TourExpress operates a fleet of small vans for comfortable tours into Parque Nacional Torres del Paine. The bilingual guides are well versed not only on the area's culture and history but on its geology, fauna, and flora.

The U.S.-based Lost World Adventures specializes in tailoring Patagonia and Tierra del Fuego itineraries around your specific interests.

In El Calafate, Hielo y Aventura specializes in glacier tours with "minitrekking" (walking on the Perito Moreno or Upsala glaciers with crampons). Horseback riding treks can be arranged by Gustavo Holzman or through the El Calafate tourist office. Interlagos Turismo arranges tours between Río Gallegos and El Calafate to the glaciers. Tur Aiké Turismo organizes tours in and around Río Gallegos.

In Ushuaia and the Tierra del Fuego, All Patagonia and Tolkar both offer a wide variety of adventurous treks through the Parque Nacional Tierra del Fuego and around the Canal Beagle. Tolkeyén Patagonia organizes tours of the Canal Beagle and bus trips that give an overview of the national park. All Patagonia organizes bus trips to Lago Escondido and other spots in the area.

⚑ Tour Operators All Patagonia ✉ Juana Fadul 26, Ushuaia ☎ +54 2901/433-622 or 2901/1556-5758 ⊕ www.allpatagonia.net. **Gustavo Holzman** ✉ J. A. Roca 2035, El Calafate ☎ +54 2902/491-203. **Hielo y Aventura** ✉ Av. del Libertador San Martín 935, El Calafate ☎ +54 2902/492-205. **Interlagos Turismo** ✉ Fagnano 35, Río Gallegos ☎ +54 2966/422-614 ✉ Av. Libertador 1175, El Calafate ☎ +54 2902/491-175. **Lost World Adventures** ✉ 337 Shadowmoor Dr. South, Decatur, GA 30030 ☎ 404/373-5820 or 800/999-0558 ⊕ www.lostworldadventures.com. **SportsTour** ✉ Moneda 970, 18th fl., Santiago ☎ 2/549-5200 ⊕ www.sportstour.cl. **Tolkar** ✉ Roca 157, Ushuaia ☎ +54 2901/431-408 or +54 2901/437-421. **Tolkeyén Patagonia** ✉ Maipú 237, Ushuaia ☎ +54 2901/437-073 or +54 2901/424-504. **TourExpress** ✉ Av. Bulnes 769, Puerto Natales ☎ 61/410-734. **Tur Aiké Turismo** ✉ Zapiola 63, Río Gallegos ☎ +54 2902/422-436.

VISITOR INFORMATION

The border between Chile and Argentina is still strictly maintained, but crossing it doesn't prevent much difficulty beyond getting out your passport and waiting in a line to get the stamp. Most travelers end up crossing the border by bus, which means getting out of the vehicle for 30–45 minutes to go through the bureaucratic proceedings, then loading back in. (Be sure to bring your valuables with you when you leave the bus). Crossing by car is also quite manageable (check with your car-rental company for restrictions on international travel). Traveling between Chile's Puerto Natales and Torres del Paine and Argentina's Río Gallegos, you'll cross at Cancha Carrera. From the border crossing it's 129 km (80 mi) east on PR7 to La Esperanza, then 161 km (100 mi) southeast on RP5 to Río Gallegos.

Sernatur, the national tourism agency, has offices in Punta Arenas and in Puerto Natales. The Punta Arenas office is open daily 8–5, and the small Puerto Natales office is open Monday–Thursday 8:15–6 and Friday 8:15–5. The Punta Arenas City Tourism Office, in an attractive kiosk in the main square, is quite helpful. It's open December–March, Monday–Saturday 8–8 and Sunday 9–3; April–November, Monday–Thursday 8–5 and Friday 8–4. They offer a free Internet connection.

⚑ Contacts in Chile Punta Arenas City Tourism ✉ Plaza Muñoz Gamero, Punta Arenas ☎ 61/200-610 ⊕ www.puntaarenas.cl. **Sernatur Punta Arenas** ✉ Av. Magallanes 960, Punta Arenas ☎ 61/248-790. **Sernatur Puerto Natales** ✉ Av. Pedro Montt 19, Puerto Natales ☎ 61/412-125.

⚑ Contacts in Argentina El Calafate Tourist Office ✉ Terminal de Omnibus, Julio A. Roca 1004 ☎ +54 2902/491-090 ⊕ www.elcalafate.gov.ar. **Tierra del Fuego Tourism Institute** ✉ Maipú 505, Ushuaia ☎ +54 2901/421-423. **Ushuaia Tourist Office** ✉ Av. San Martín 674 ☎ +54 2901/432-000 ⊕ www.e-ushuaia.com.

CHILE ESSENTIALS

Transportation

BY AIR

Miami, New York, and Atlanta are the primary departure points for flights to Chile from the United States, though there are also frequent flights from Dallas and other cities. Other international flights often connect through other major South American cities like Buenos Aires and Lima.

Here's the bad news: arriving from abroad, American citizens must pay a "reciprocity" fee (to balance out fees Chileans pay upon entering the United States) of $100. Canadian and Australian citizens pay $55 and $30, respectively. The good news is that both cash and credit cards are accepted. A departure tax of $18 is included in the cost of your ticket.

CARRIERS The largest North American carrier is American Airlines, which has direct service from Dallas and Miami; Delta flies from Atlanta. Lan flies nonstop to Santiago from both Miami and Los Angeles and with a layover in Lima from New York. Air Canada flies nonstop from Toronto.

WITHIN CHILE Lan has daily flights from Santiago to most cities throughout Chile. Aerolineas del Sur and Sky also fly to most large cities within Chile.
📋 **International Airlines Air Canada** ☎ 2/690-1115 in Chile. **Air France** ☎ 2/690-9696 in Chile. **American Airlines** ☎ 2/601-9272 in Chile. **Delta Airlines** ☎ 2/690-1555 in Chile. **Iberia** ☎ 2/870-1070 in Chile. **Lan** ☎ 2/565-2000 in Chile.
📋 **National Flights Aerolineas del Sur** ☎ 2/690-1422. **Lan** ☎ 2/565-2000 in Chile. **Sky** ☎ 600/600-2828.

BY BUS

Without doubt, the low cost of bus travel is its greatest advantage; its greatest drawback is the time you need to cover the distances involved. A trip from Santiago to San Pedro de Atacama, for example, takes between 23 and 24 hours. Long-distance buses are safe and affordable. Intercity bus service is a comfortable, safe, and reasonably priced alternative for getting around. Luxury bus travel between cities costs about one-third that of plane travel and is more comfortable, with wide reclining seats, movies, drinks, and snacks. The most expensive service offered by most bus companies is called *cama* or *semi-cama*, which indicate that the seats fold down into a bed. Service billed as *ejectivo* is nearly as luxurious.

Note that reservations for advance ticket purchases aren't necessary except for trips to resort areas in high season or during major holidays. You should arrive at bus stations extra early for travel during peak seasons. Companies are notoriously difficult to reach by phone, so it's often better to stop by the terminal to check on prices and schedules.

Pullman Bus and Tur-Bus are two of the best-known companies in Chile. They travel to much of the country.
📋 **Bus Information Pullman Bus** ☎ 600/320-3200 ⊕ www.pullman.cl. **Tur-Bus** ☎ 600/660-6600 ⊕ www.turbus.com.

BY CAR

CAR RENTAL It is by far easier to rent a car in Santiago, where all the international agencies have branches at the airport and in town. You'll find mostly local rental agencies in the rest of the country.

■ TIP→ **An annoying fact about Chilean rental companies is that they often deliver the car to you with the gas gauge on empty.** Make sure to ask about the nearest gas station, or your trip may be extremely short.

In order to drive to Punta Arenas in Patagonia you will need to cross into Argentina at Chile Chico or at one of the international border crossings beforehand. If you plan to do this you must tell your car-rental company, which will provide notarized authorization—otherwise you will be refused permission to cross.

🛂 **Major Agencies Alamo** ☎ 2/225–3061 in Chile ⊕ www.alamo.com. **Avis** ☎ 2/690–1382 in Chile ⊕ www.avis.com. **Budget** ☎ 2/690–1386 in Chile ⊕ www.budget.com. **Hertz** ☎ 2/496–1111 in Chile ⊕ www.hertz.com. **National Car Rental** ☎ 2/223–4117 in Chile ⊕ www.nationalcar.com.

AUTO CLUBS El Automóvil Club de Chile offers low-cost road service and towing in and around the main cities to members of the Automobile Association of America (AAA).

🛂 **Auto Club Information El Automóvil Club de Chile** ✉ Av. Andrés Bello 1863, Providencia, Santiago ☎ 2/431–1000 ⊕ www.automovilclub.cl.

GASOLINE Most service stations are operated by an attendant and accept credit cards. They are open 24 hours a day along the Pan-American Highway and in most major cities, but not in small towns and villages.

ROAD CONDITIONS Between May and August, roads, underpasses, and parks can flood when it rains. It's very dangerous, especially for drivers who don't know their way around. Avoid driving if it has been raining for several hours. Many cyclists ride without lights in rural areas, so be careful when driving at night, particularly on roads without street lighting. This also applies to horse- and bull-drawn carts.

RULES OF THE ROAD Keep in mind that the speed limit is 60 km/h (37 mph) in cities and 120 km/h (75 mph) on highways unless otherwise posted. The police regularly enforce the speed limit, handing out *partes* (tickets) to speeders. Plan to rent snow chains for driving on the road up to the ski resorts outside Santiago. Police will stop you and ask if you have them—if you don't, you will be forced to turn back.

BY TRAIN

Good train service is a thing of the past in Chile, though there is still limited service from Santiago to points south. Empresa de Los Ferrocarriles del Estado, better known as EFE, offers daily departures between Santiago and Temuco, but be prepared for a slow journey—if the train runs according to schedule it should take around nine hours. Reservations can be made in Santiago at the Estación Central or at the Estación Metro Universidad de Chile, online at the company's Web site (only in Spanish), or through a travel agent.

🛂 **Train Information EFE** ☎ 2/585–5000 ⊕ www.efe.cl.

Contacts & Resources

CUSTOMS & DUTIES

You may bring into Chile up to 400 cigarettes, 500 grams of tobacco, 50 cigars, two open bottles of perfume, 2.5 liters of alcoholic beverages, and gifts. Prohibited items include plants, fruit, seeds, meat, and honey. Spot checks take place at airports and border crossings. Visitors, although seldom questioned, are prohibited from leaving with handicrafts and souvenirs worth more than $500. You are generally prohibited from taking antiques out of the country without permission.

ELECTRICITY

Unlike the United States and Canada—which have a 110- to 120-volt standard—the current in Chile is 220 volts, 50 cycles alternating current (AC). The wall sockets accept plugs with two round prongs.Emergencies

The numbers to call in case of emergency are the same all over Chile.
🗐 Ambulance 🕿 131. Fire 🕿 132. Police 🕿 133.

HEALTH

From a health standpoint, Chile is one of the safer countries in which to travel. To be on the safe side, take the normal precautions you would traveling anywhere in South America. In Santiago there are several large private *clinicas* (clinics; ⇨ Santiago Essentials *in* Chapter 1), and many doctors can speak at least a bit of English. In most other large cities there are one or two private clinics where you can be seen quickly. Generally, *hospitales* (hospitals) are for those receiving free or heavily subsidized treatment, and they are often crowded with long lines of patients waiting to be seen.

ALTITUDE
SICKNESS
Altitude sickness—which causes shortness of breath, nausea, and splitting headaches—may be a problem when you visit Andean countries. The best way to prevent *soroche* is to ascend slowly. Spend a few nights at 6,000–9,000 feet before you head higher. If you must fly straight in, plan on doing next to nothing for your first few days. The traditional remedy is herbal tea made from coca leaves. Over-the-counter analgesics and napping also help. If symptoms persist, return to lower elevations. Note that if you have high blood pressure and/or a history of heart trouble, check with your doctor before traveling to the mountains.

FOOD & DRINK
Visitors seldom encounter problems with drinking the water in Chile. Almost all drinking water receives proper treatment and is unlikely to produce health problems.

Food preparation is strictly regulated by the government, so outbreaks of food-borne diseases are very rare. But it's still a good idea to use the same commonsense rules you would in any other part of South America.

SHOTS &
MEDICATIONS
All travelers to Chile should get up-to-date tetanus, diphtheria, and measles boosters, and a hepatitis A inoculation is recommended. Children traveling to Chile should have current inoculations against mumps, rubella, and polio. Always check with your doctor about which shots to get. According to the Centers for Disease Control and Prevention, there's some risk

of food-borne diseases such as hepatitis A and typhoid. There's no risk of contracting malaria, but a limited risk of several other insect-borne diseases, including dengue fever. They are usually restricted to jungle areas.

MAIL & SHIPPING

Federal Express has offices in Santiago and DHL has offices throughout Chile; both provide overnight service. If you want to send a package to North America, Europe, Australia, or New Zealand, it will take one–four days, depending on where you're sending it from in Chile.

MONEY MATTERS

Credit cards and traveler's checks are accepted in most resorts and in many shops and restaurants in major cities, though you should always carry some local currency for minor expenses like taxis and tipping. Once you stray from the beaten path, you can often pay only with pesos.

WHAT THINGS COST Typically you will pay 500 pesos for a cup of coffee, 1,200 pesos for a glass of beer in a bar, 1,200 pesos for a ham sandwich, and 800 pesos for an average museum admission.

PASSPORTS & VISAS

Citizens of the United States, Canada, Australia, New Zealand, and the United Kingdom need only a passport to enter Chile for up to three months.

Upon arrival in Chile, you will be given a flimsy piece of paper that is your three-month tourist visa. This has to be handed in when you leave; because getting a new one involves waiting in many lines and a lot of bureaucracy, put it somewhere safe.

American citizens must pay a "reciprocity" fee (to balance out fees Chileans pay upon entering the United States) of $100. Canadian and Australian citizens pay $55 and $30, respectively.

SAFETY

The vast majority of visitors to Chile never experience a problem with crime. Violent crime is a rarity; far more common is pickpocketing or thefts from purses, backpacks, or rental cars. Be on your guard in crowded places, especially markets and festivals.

TAXES

An 18% value-added tax (VAT, called IVA here) is added to the cost of most goods and services in Chile; often you won't notice because it's included in the price. When it's not, the seller gives you the price plus IVA. At many hotels you may receive an exemption from the IVA if you pay in American dollars or with a credit card.

TELEPHONES

AREA & COUNTRY CODES The country code for Chile is 56. When dialing a Chilean number from abroad, drop the initial 0 from the local area code. The area code is 2 for Santiago, 58 for Arica, 55 for Antofogasta and San Pedro de Atacama, 42 for Chillán, 57 for Iquique, 56 for La Serena, 65 for Puerto Montt, 61 for Puerto Natales and Punta Arenas, 45 for Temuco, 63 for Valdivia, 32 for Valparaíso and Viña del Mar.

From Chile the country code is 01 for the United States and Canada, 61 for Australia, 64 for New Zealand, and 44 for the United Kingdom.

You can reach directory assistance in Chile by calling 103. English-speaking operators are not available.

An international call at a public phone requires anywhere from a 400- or 500-peso deposit (depending on the phone box), which will give you anywhere between 47 and 66 seconds of talking time. You can call the United States for between 39 and 76 seconds (depending on the carrier you use) for 200 pesos.

A 100-peso piece is required to make a local call in a public phone booth, allowing 110 seconds of conversation between the hours of 9 AM and 8 PM, and 160 seconds of talk from 8 PM to 9 AM. Prefix codes are not needed for local dialing.

To call a cell phone within Chile you will need to insert 200 pesos in a phone box.

TIME
Chile is one hour ahead of Eastern Standard Time and four hours ahead of Pacific Standard Time. Daylight saving time in Chile begins in October and ends in March.

TIPPING
The usual tip, or *propina,* in restaurants is 10%. Leave more if you really enjoyed the service. City taxi drivers don't usually expect a tip because most own their cabs. However, if you hire a taxi to take you around a city, you should consider giving a good tip. Hotel porters should be tipped at least 500 pesos per bag. Also give doormen and ushers about 500 pesos. Beauty- and barber-shop personnel generally get around 5%.

VISITOR INFORMATION
The national tourist office Sernatur (Servicio Nacional de Turismo) has branches in Santiago and in major tourist destinations around the country. Sernatur offices, often the best source for general information about a region, are generally open daily from 9 to 6, with lunch generally from 2 to 3.

Municipal tourist offices, often located near a central square, usually have better information about their town's sights, restaurants, and lodging. Many have shorter hours or close altogether during low season, however.

🚩 **Tourist Information Sernatur** ⊠ Providencia 1550, Providencia, Santiago ☎ 2/731-8336 or 2/731-8337 ⊕ www.sernatur.cl.

Colombia

WORD OF MOUTH

"Cartagena is a beautiful city, something to see at every turn. We went over to the Bocagrande area (their Zona Rosa) where all the big hotels are, but it was not nearly as pretty and interesting as the old town. Go . . . go before everyone discovers how beautiful, friendly, and cheap Colombia is and drives the prices up."

—sandy_b

"One of my favourite things to do when I visited Cartagena was to walk the top of the wall of the old walled city along the ocean on a Sunday morning when the city is fairly quiet. The old fort is worth a visit as well. And I'm not even a history buff."

—last_mango

Updated by
Erik Riesenberg

COLOMBIA IS BLESSED IN MANY WAYS. Its regal location on the continent's northern tip makes it the only South American country that fringes both the Atlantic and Pacific. It's rich in emeralds, coffee, and oil. And, because it straddles the equator, it's one of the lushest countries in terms of tropical flora and wildlife—there are more species of birds in Colombia than anywhere else in the world. You can jump on a plane and in less than an hour find yourself in a different dramatic setting—be it the cobblestone streets of a weathered colonial port, the stalls of a crowded market where Guambiano merchants still speak the tongues of their ancestors, or at the base of snow-covered peaks rising sharply from a steamy coastal plain.

Bogotá, Colombia's sprawling capital of more than 7 million people, stands at the end of a vast plateau in the eastern Andes. The poverty and drug violence make the headlines, but rarely covered by the media are the elegant shopping streets, grand high-rises, lovely colonial neighborhoods, and chic nightclubs where stylish young *Bogotanos* (as inhabitants of Bogotá are called) party well into the night.

Cartagena, widely revered as the most striking colonial city in South America, is an excellent destination if you want to be on the Caribbean coast. If you equate vacationing with lounging in the sun, the beaches of San Andrés and Providencia islands are Colombia's most compelling. Undeterred by the 640-km (400-mi) trip from the mainland, Colombians escape to the resort islands for weekends of swimming, sunbathing, shopping, and sipping rum at thatch-roof waterfront bars.

Most of the country's 42 million people live in Colombia's western half, where the Andes splits into three *cordilleras,* or ridges: Oriental, Central, and Occidental. As you ascend the mighty mountains, subtropical valleys give way to rigid, fern-carpeted peaks where the ever-present mists are brightened only by votive candles placed by truck drivers at roadside shrines. West of Bogotá, quiet villages hug the hillsides en route to Medellín, former base of the eponymous drug cartel of Pablo Escobar. Despite its notorious reputation, Medellín is a pleasant, relatively safe, modern city surrounded by velvety green hills and miles of lush farmland.

Exploring Colombia

The extremes of Colombia's varied topography are epitomized by the cool temperatures of the highlands around Bogotá and the warm weather of the coast near Cartagena. Medellín lies somewhere between those two contrasting areas.

Restaurants & Cuisine

From the hearty stews served in the highlands to the seafood soups ladled out along the Caribbean coast, you'll find distinctive regional cuisine everywhere. Beef is popular everywhere—as steaks or in shish kebabs or stews—as is chicken. Bogotá's most traditional dish is *ajiaco,* a thick chicken and potato soup garnished with capers, sour cream, and avocado. On the Caribbean coast you're more likely to dip your spoon

TOP REASONS TO GO

ARCHAEOLOGICAL TREASURES
Several archaeological sites and many priceless artifacts testify to the cultural richness that thrived in the country before European domination. For a sojourn into Colombia's past, duck into Bogotá's Museo de Oro to see the world's largest collection of pre-Columbian gold, and a comprehensive collection of pre-Columbian artifacts from indigenous cultures, including the Muisca, Nariño, Calima, and Sinú. Here you'll also see the largest uncut emerald in the world. Also in Bogotá is the Museum of Archaeology, which houses splendid pre-Columbian ceramics.

BEACHES
The country's favorite beaches are found along the northern coast and on the Caribbean islands of San Andrés and Providencia. These resort islands have gorgeous white-sand beaches that stretch along the coast for miles, and the water is crystal clear. Cartagena's beach is popular with locals, and gets to be quite a scene, especially during holidays.

into a *cazuela de mariscos,* a seafood soup with cassava. On the islands of San Andrés and Providencia, the local favorite is *rendón,* a soup made of fish and snails slowly simmered in coconut milk with yucca, plantains, breadfruit, and dumplings.

Restaurants in many cities often close for a few hours between lunch and dinner (roughly 3 to 6). Plan your mealtimes in advance. Appropriate attire in restaurants is comparable to U.S. or European standards—dressy for the more formal places, casual everywhere else.

WHAT IT COSTS In Pesos					
	$$$$	$$$	$$	$	¢
AT DINNER	over 40k	25k–40k	15k–25k	10k–15k	under 10k

Prices are per person for a main course at dinner.

About the Hotels
Prices and standards at high-end hotels in Bogotá are usually comparable to those in North America. Outside of the capital, even in such tourist towns as Cartagena and San Andrés, rates for hotel rooms are surprisingly low. Consider staying at small, locally owned hotels where you're more likely to experience Colombian hospitality.

WHAT IT COSTS In Pesos					
	$$$$	$$$	$$	$	¢
FOR 2 PEOPLE	over 360k	280k–360k	200k–280k	100k–200k	under 100k

Prices are for two people in a standard double room in high season, excluding tax.

When to Go

December through February are the best months to visit Colombia, as they are the driest. Colombians also travel during these sometimes hot and humid months, so hotel rooms are harder to come by. While visiting during a festival will add an exciting cultural edge to your trip, you'll experience inflated prices and often overwhelming crowds.

CLIMATE Colombia is often perceived as being a steamy tropical country, but its climate varies greatly with altitude. Along the Caribbean Coast temperatures are an average of 82°F (28°C); in frequently overcast Bogotá, the average is a chilly 54°F (12°C). The valley cities of Medellín and Cali have pleasant weather, with temperatures in between.

Seasons don't really exist in Colombia, but rainfall and brisk weather is common October to November and April to June. Rainfall is rarely excessive and is only a problem if you plan to travel off the beaten track on Colombia's rough-paved mountain roads. The dry season usually runs December to March in mountainous areas, mid-December to April and July to September in low-lying coastal regions.

The following are the average monthly maximum and minimum temperatures for Bogotá.

Jan.	67F	19C	May	66F	19C	Sept.	66F	19C
	48	9		51	10		49	9
Feb.	68F	20C	June	65F	18C	Oct.	66F	19C
	49	9		51	10		50	10
Mar.	67F	19C	July	64F	18C	Nov.	66F	19C
	50	10		50	10		50	10
Apr.	67F	19C	Aug.	65F	18C	Dec.	66F	19C
	51	10		50	10		49	9

HOLIDAYS The Presentation of Our Lord (January 1); Epiphany (January 6); St. Joseph's Day (March 19); Holy Week (March or April); Labor Day (May 1); Ascension Day (May 20 in 2007); Corpus Christi (June 6 in 2007); Sts. Peter and Paul's Day (July 2 in 2007); Independence Day (July 20); Battle of Boyacá (August 7); Assumption Day (August 15); Discovery of America (October 12); All Saints' Day (November 1); Independence of Cartagena (November 11); Immaculate Conception (December 8); Christmas.

FESTIVALS Carnaval season (February–March) is particularly festive in Barranquilla. In March or April, Semana Santa (Palm Sunday through Easter Sunday) processions fill the town of Chia, a half hour north of Bogotá. During the two weeks before Easter, Bogotá hosts the Ibero-American Theatre Festival, with international theater and dance troupes performing.

The Flower Festival is held in Medellín in late May or early June. The Folklore Festival takes place in Ibagué, usually during the last week in June. In early November, Cartagena's Reinado Nacional de la Belleza has beauty contests and a full week of merrymaking celebrating the city's independence. Between Christmas and New Year's, Bogotá holds a Festival of Lights—in front of every house you'll find candles in colorful bags—and on New Year's Eve there's a fireworks celebration in the Presidential Plaza.

Language

Spanish is the official language, although you may overhear some of the roughly 90 indigenous languages that are also spoken. English is widely understood on the islands of San Andrés and Providencia and is commonly spoken in hotels and restaurants.

Precautions

Decades-old civil conflict and the drug trade have made travel outside most major cities more risky than before. We consider travel to Cali and Popayán too dangerous, and so in this edition we are not covering those cities. Medellín, too, can be sketchy, so check with the local police or with your embassy before making overland excursions there or anywhere else. If you must travel by car in these regions, do so in the daytime, and rent a car with a driver, rather than driving yourself.

BOGOTÁ

Bogotá is a city of contrasts. Here you find modern shopping malls and open-air markets, high-rise apartments and makeshift shanties, futuristic glass towers and colonial churches. Simultaneous displays of ostentatious wealth and shocking poverty have existed here for centuries. In the neighborhood of La Candelaria, a rich assemblage of colonial mansions grandly conceived by the Spanish were built by native peoples and financed by plundered gold.

Bogotá, a city of more than 7 million people, has grown twentyfold in the past 50 years. It suffers the growing pains typical of any major metropolis on the continent (insufficient public transportation, chronic air pollution, petty crime) and a few of its own (a scurrilous drug trade and occasional acts of political violence). However, recent mayors have made some progress in cleaning up parks, resurfacing roads, and implementing a new transportation system. In fact, a recent survey indicates that while a majority of Bogotanos feel that the political situation is worsening in Colombia, conditions are improving in Bogotá.

Spanish conquistadors built their South American cities in magnificent locations, and Bogotá, which stands on a high plain in the eastern Andes, is no exception. During his disastrous search for the legendary El Dorado, Gonzalo Jiménez de Quesada, the Spanish explorer on whom Miguel de Cervantes reputedly modeled Don Quixote, was struck by the area's natural splendor and its potential for colonization. Though it's a mere 1,288 km (800 mi) from the equator, Bogotá's 8,700-foot altitude lends it a refreshing climate. Jiménez de Quesada discovered one of South America's most advanced pre-Columbian peoples, the Muisca. But they were no match for the Spaniards. On August 6, 1538, Jiménez de Quesada christened his new conquest Santa Fé de Bogotá, on the site where the Muisca village of Bacatá once stood.

Bogotá rapidly became an important administrative center and in 1740 was made the capital of the Viceroyalty of New Granada, an area com-

COLOMBIAN HISTORY

Before the arrival of the Spanish, Colombia was sparsely inhabited by indigenous peoples. High in the Andes, the Muisca were master goldsmiths who may have sparked the myth of El Dorado with their tradition of anointing a new chief by rolling him in gold dust. The legend of El Dorado was an irresistible attraction for a host of European adventurers in search of gilded cities.

The Spanish settled in the region as early as 1510, but it wasn't until conquistador Rodrigo de Bastidas founded the port town of Santa Marta in 1525 that a permanent settlement was established in what is now known as Colombia. He banned the exploitation of the indigenous peoples, but those who followed him had other plans. Explorers like Gonzalo Jiménez de Quesada plundered and pillaged their way inland. After quickly dispatching the local Muisca tribes, he established a Spanish settlement in what is now Bogotá.

Despite their near decimation at the hands of brutal Europeans, Colombia's native peoples have left a lasting mark on the country. The extraordinary carved stones in the southwestern settlement of San Agustín speak of empires once rich in gold, emeralds, and the technological skills necessary to erect statues honoring long-forgotten gods. In the Andes and on the coastal plains you'll find modern descendants of these lost tribes living a life unchanged since Cristóbal Colón (better known as Christopher Columbus) presumptuously claimed Colombia in the name of King Ferdinand of Spain.

Colombians express with some pride that they live in the oldest democracy in Latin America. Colombia has enjoyed a constitutionally elected government for nearly all of its history. This has not, however, brought stability to the country, and guerrilla activity has echoed in the countryside since the 1940s. The rise of drug trafficking in the last 25 years has exacerbated the ongoing civil conflict that now involves the government, left-wing guerrillas, and right-wing paramilitary groups. Although the large-scale car bombings and other acts of terrorism that plagued Bogotá and Medellín a decade ago seem like a thing of the past, occasional political assassinations are grim reminders of the violence that is all too common in many parts of the country. Plans to create jobs and expand Colombian tourism are in the works, and while neither can remedy the country's safety issues, they may help to alleviate some conditions that contribute to crime. In 2002 President Alvaro Uribe met with guerrilla leaders to discuss a plan for peace. Although it hasn't brought about immediate progress, this attempt seems to indicate an active desire for reconciliation.

5

Bogotá

CENTRO
INTERNACIONAL

Parque
de la
Independencia

Cementario
Central

TO
AIRPORT

CANDELARIA

Pasaje Rivas

KEY

❶ *Exploring sights*

① *Hotels & restaurants*

prising what is now Colombia, Venezuela, Ecuador, and Panama. With its new status, grand civic and religious buildings began to spring up, often with the hand-carved ceilings and sculpted doorways that were the hallmark of New Granada architecture. But by 1900 Bogotá was still a relatively small city of 100,000. It was not until the 1940s that rapid industrialization and the consequent peasant migration to urban centers spurred Bogotá's exponential growth.

Exploring Bogotá

As you tour the city, take a taxi whenever possible—don't be carefree about strolling around, even during the day, or about lingering in places at night—it's simply not safe to do so. Keep in mind that *carreras* (roads) run north–south and *calles* (streets) run east–west. You'll probably spend much of your time in the charming neighborhood of La Candelaria. To the north of La Candelaria is the downtown area, which is seedy but holds a handful of bars and restaurants, mostly in La Macarena. Farther uptown and marked by towering office buildings is the Centro Internacional, the city's financial center. To the north is the leafy Zona Rosa, a popular shopping district anchored by an upscale shopping mall called Centro Andino. Farther north along the Carrera 7, at Calle 116, is Hacienda Santa Barbara, another high-end shopping mall built as an extension of an old mansion. A few blocks north of Hacienda Santa Barbara is the plaza of Usaquén, an Andean village that became a neighborhood as Bogotá grew but still maintains its small-town manner.

La Candelaria

At the foot of Guadalupe Peak is Bogotá's oldest neighborhood, La Candelaria, a historic neighborhood of narrow streets lined with astounding colonial structures. It's packed with lovely mansions and exquisite churches. Most of the city's finest museums are found here.

WHAT TO SEE

Biblioteca Luis Angel Arango. The modern Luis Angel Arango Library sponsors frequently changing international art exhibits. It is also known for its occasional chamber music concerts, which are listed in the local newspapers. ⊠ *Calle 11 No. 4–14, La Candelaria* ☎ *091/343–1212* ⊕ *www.lablaa.org* ☞ *Free* ☉ *Library Mon.–Sat. 8–8, Sun. 10–4.*

Casa de la Moneda. The former national mint displays coins whose gold content was secretly reduced by the king of Spain, slugs made by revolutionaries from empty cartridges, and currency minted for use exclusively in Colombia's former leper colonies. This museum is part of the complex that houses the Donación Botero and the Colección Permanente de Artes Plásticas. ⊠ *Calle 11 No. 4–93, La Candelaria* ☎ *No phone* ⊕ *www.banrep.gov.co* ☞ *Free* ☉ *Mon. and Wed.–Fri. 10–8, Sat. 10–7, Sun. 10–4.*

Cerro de Monserrate. Although dense smog often obscures the skyline, the view of chaotic Bogotá from Monserrate Hill is still breathtaking. The panorama extends from the Río Bogotá to La Candelaria, whose red Spanish tiles make it easy to spot, especially in the early morning. The church on top of Monserrate houses an image of the Fallen Christ that is a popular destination for pilgrims. The *teleférico* (cable car) or the tram leaves every half hour from Monserrate Station near Quinta de Bolívar for the 15-minute journey to the peak. Avoid the hour-long trek up a winding footpath except on Sunday, when it is crowded with pilgrims. Robberies have become all too common. ⊠ *Quinta de Bolívar, La Candelaria* ☎ *091/284–5700* 🖾 *11,200 pesos during the day and 14,200 pesos in the evening for cable car or tram* ☉ *Mon.–Sat. 10–midnight, Sun. 10–4.*

> ### GREAT VIEWS
>
> On exceptionally clear days it is possible to see the snow-covered mountains of the Cordillera Central, some 300 km (188 mi) away.

❾ Colección Permanente de Artes Plásticas. This large collection, in the same complex as the Donación Botero, is an overview of Colombian art from the colonial period to the present, including works by such noted artists as Alejandro Obregón, Luis Caballero, and Débora Arango. ⊠ *Calle 11 No. 4–41, La Candelaria* ☎ *091/343–1340* ⊕ *www.banrep.gov.co* 🖾 *Free* ☉ *Mon. and Wed.–Fri. 10–8, Sat. 10–7, Sun. 10–4.*

❽ Donación Botero.

Fodor'sChoice In 2000, world-famous artist Fernando Botero made headlines when he donated dozens of works from his private collection ★ to Colombia. Botero's artwork interprets his subjects from a distinctly Latin-American standpoint—Colombians affectionately refer to him as "the man who paints fat people." Many of his subjects are well known in Colombia, especially in his native Medellín. The collection includes 123 of his own paintings, sculptures, and drawings. Equally impressive, however, are his donation of 85 original works of renowned European and North American artists. This part of the collection, practically a review of art history since the late 19th century, includes original pieces by Corot, Monet, Matisse, Picasso, Dalí, Chagall, Bacon, and de Kooning. ⊠ *Calle 11 No. 4–41, La Candelaria* ☎ *091/343–1340* ⊕ *www.banrep.gov.co* 🖾 *Free* ☉ *Mon. and Wed.–Fri. 10–8, Sat. 10–7, Sun. 10–4.*

⓫ Iglesia de San Francisco. The 16th-century Church of St. Francis is famous for its fabulous Mudéjar interior, carved with geometric designs borrowed from Islamic tradition. Its huge gilded altar is shaped like an amphitheater and has shell-top niches. ⊠ *Av. Jiménez at Carrera 7, La Candelaria* ☉ *Daily 8–6.*

⓬ Iglesia de la Tercera Orden. The intricate carvings on the mahogany altar at the Church of the Third Order are the most beautiful in Bogotá. A local myth claims that the completion of the altar so exhausted sculptor Pablo Caballero that he died a madman. ⊠ *Carrera 7 at Calle 16, La Candelaria* ☉ *Daily 8–6.*

❷ Iglesia Museo Santa Clara.

Fodor'sChoice The simple, unadorned facade of the 17th-century Church of St. Clara gives no hint of the dazzling frescoes—the ★ work of nuns once cloistered here—that bathe the interior walls. The small museum has paintings and sculpture by various 17th-century artists. ⊠ *Carrera 8 No. 8–91, La Candelaria* ☎ *091/341–1009* 🖾 *2,000 pesos* ☉ *Tues.–Fri. 9–4:30, weekends 10–3:30.*

❺ Museo Arqueológico. This magnificent mansion, which houses the Museum of Archaeology, once belonged to the Marquís de San Jorge, a colonial viceroy infamous for his cruelty. Today it displays a large collection of pre-Columbian ceramics. ⊠ *Carrera 6 No. 7–43, La Candelaria* ☎ *091/243–1048* 🖭 *1,000 pesos children, 2,000 pesos students, 3,000 pesos adults* ⊙ *Tues.–Fri. 8:30–5, weekends 10–4.*

⑥ Museo de Arte Colonial. Renovations in 1999 helped preserve this 17th-century Andalusian-style mansion, home of the Museum of Colonial Art. In its substantial collection are paintings by Vasquez and Figueroa, 17th- and 18th-century furniture, and precious metalwork. ⊠ *Carrera 6 No. 9–77, La Candelaria* ☎ *091/341–6017* 🖭 *children 1,000, students 1,500, adults 2,000 pesos* ⊙ *Tues.–Fri. 9–5, weekends 10–4.*

④ Museo de Artes y Tradiciones Populares. A former Augustinian cloister dating from 1583, the Museum of Folk Art and Traditions is one of Bogotá's oldest surviving buildings. Displays include contemporary crafts made by Indian artisans from across the country. There are also a gift shop and a restaurant specializing in traditional Andean cooking. ⊠ *Carrera 8 No. 7–21, La Candelaria* ☎ *091/284–2670* 🖭 *1,000 pesos* ⊙ *Weekdays 9–5, Sat. 9:30–1 and 2–5.*

⑬ Museo de Oro. Bogotá's phenomenal Gold Museum contains a comprehensive collection of pre-Columbian artifacts. The museum's more than 34,000 pieces (in weight alone worth $200 million) were gathered—often by force—from indigenous cultures, including the Muisca, Nariño, Calima, and Sinú. Don't dismiss them as merely primitive; these works represent virtually all the techniques of modern goldsmithing. Most of the gold, and the largest uncut emerald in the world, is in the guarded top-floor gallery. English audio tours are available. ⊠ *Carrera 6 at Calle 16 (Parque Santander), La Candelaria* ☎ *091/343–1424* ⊕ *www.banrep.gov.co* 🖭 *Tues.–Sat. 3,000 pesos; Sun. and holidays 1,500 pesos* ⊙ *Tues.–Sat. 9–4:30, Sun. 10–4:30.*

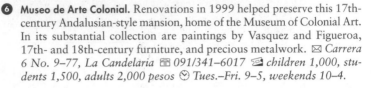
Fodor'sChoice ★

③ Palacio de Nariño. The Presidential Palace had to be rebuilt in 1949 following its destruction during *El Bogotazo,* an uprising sparked by the assassination of Liberal leader Jorge Eliécer Gaitán. Although it's not open to the public, the guard outside is changed ceremoniously each day at 5 PM. ⊠ *Carrera 7 between Calles 7 and 8, La Candelaria.*

① Plaza de Bolívar. Surrounded by stately structures, this square marks the spot where Bogotá was declared the seat of New Granada's colonial government. Today it's popular with photographers snapping pictures, unemployed men intermittently snoozing and chatting, street theater groups performing for a few hundred pesos, and children who never seem to grow bored with chasing pigeons. The Capitolio Nacional, Alcaldía Municipal, and the Palacio de Justicia are not open to the public.

On the plaza's east side, the **Catedral Primada de Colombia** was completed three centuries after construction began in 1565 due to a series of misfortunes—including the disastrous earthquake of 1785. Its French baroque facade is made from locally mined sandstone. The expansive windows give the immense interior a light, airy feel, even on one of Bogotá's many gray rainy-season days. The ornate altar with gold leaf over heavily carved wood sharply contrasts with the lack of ornamentation elsewhere. In one of the side chapels lies conquistador Gonzalo Jiménez de Quesada's tomb. The church is open Monday through Saturday. Next door in the **Capilla del Sagrario** is an exquisite *baldacchino*, a smaller version of the ornate covered altar found at St. Peter's in Rome. The Sanctuary Chapel, open daily, also has a splendid collection of paintings, including works by the Taller de Figueroa and Gregorio Vasquez. ✉ *Between Carreras 7 and 8 at Calle 10, La Candelaria.*

⑭ Quinta de Bolívar. Simón Bolívar, the revolutionary hero who drove the Spanish from the northern half of the continent, passed the last years of his life in this rustic house with his mistress, Manuela Saenz. Built in 1800, it was donated to Bolívar in 1820 for his services to the fledgling republic. The house has a distinct Spanish flavor and a lovely garden. Gabriel García Márquez's 1989 novel, *The General in His Labyrinth*, portrays Bolívar's final years. ✉ *Calle 20 No. 291 Este, Barrio Las Nieves* ☎ *091/284–6819* 🖃 *3,000 pesos* ☉ *Tues.–Fri. 9–5, weekends 10–4.*

Centro Internacional

The city's financial center, Centro Internacional, lies to the north of La Candelaria. This district, built largely in the 1970s, is fringed by Parque de la Independencia and Parque Bavaria, welcome areas of green in a concrete jungle. Among the modern office buildings you'll find a few interesting museums and the city's Spanish-style bullring.

WHAT TO SEE **⑱ Iglesia San Diego.** This simple two-aisle church built by Franciscan monks in the early 17th century once stood on a quiet hacienda on the outskirts of colonial Bogotá. Trees and pastures have been replaced by the towering offices of Bogotá's "Little Manhattan." Both the church and its beautiful statue of the Virgin of the Fields, with her crown of intricate gold and silver filigree work, are an homage to the city's bucolic past. ✉ *Carrera 7 No. 26–47, Centro Internacional* ☎ *091/341–2476* 🖃 *Free* ☉ *Sun.–Fri. 7–7:30, Sat. 7–7:30 and 1–9.*

⑲ Museo de Arte Moderno. The huge windows in the beautifully designed Museum of Modern Art create a marvelous sense of spaciousness. Peruse the changing exhibits of works by national and international artists. The bookstore stocks (rather pricey) English-language titles on Colombian and international painters. ✉ *Calle 24 No. 6–00, Centro Internacional* ☎ *091/283–3109* 🖃 *4,000 pesos* ☉ *Tues.–Sun. 10–6.*

⑰ Museo Nacional. The striking building that houses the National Museum was a prison until 1946; some parts, particularly the narrow top-floor galleries, maintain a sinister air. Designed by English architect Thomas Reed, the museum is arranged to give you a history of Colombia. Everything from ancient artifacts to contemporary art is on display, including works by Fernando Botero and Alejandro Obregón. The first-floor gallery is devoted to changing national and international exhibitions. A café and bookstore were added in 1999. ✉ *Carrera 7 No. 28–66, between Calles 28 and 29, Centro Internacional* ☎ *091/334–8366* 🖃 *3,000* ☉ *Tues. 10–6, Sun. 10–5.*

⑯ Plaza de Toros Santamaría. Bogotá's bullring was designed by Rogelio Salmona in a traditional Andalusian style. For a free peek, the best time to visit is in the morning when you may see young *toreros* (bullfighters) polishing their skills. Bullfighting season is January through February, but small displays are held throughout the year. ⊠ *Carrera 7 at Calle 26, Centro Internacional* ⊙ *Practice Mon.–Sat. mornings. Bullfights Jan.–Feb., Sun. at 3 PM.*

Where to Eat

Bogotá's phone book lists more than 1,000 restaurants, and the best offer first-class service and outstanding Colombian cuisine. The most traditional recipes aim to fill the belly and ward off the cold. Soups, such as ajiaco and *puchero* (with chicken, pork, beef, potato, yucca, cabbage, corn, and plantain and accompanied by rice and avocado) are common on local menus. Bogotanos like to start the day off with *santafereño*, a steaming cup of chocolate accompanied by a slab of cheese—you melt the cheese in the chocolate. Lunch is generally served between noon and 2. Restaurants open for dinner around 7, and the more upscale ones stay open until after midnight.

Colombian

$$–$$$ ✕ **Carbón de Palo.** Bogotá's premier grilled-meat restaurant is a favorite north-end meeting place of senior politicians and plutocrats. The menu is dominated by grilled steak, chicken, and pork, but excellent salads are served with great aplomb. Choose a seat in the delightful indoor patio full of hanging plants. On weekends musicians serenade you with traditional Colombian music. ⊠ *Av. 19 No. 106–12* ☎ *091/214–0450* ⊙ *Closed Sun.* ▭ *AE, DC, MC, V.*

$–$$ ✕ **Casa Vieja.** Offering typical Colombian dishes, Casa Vieja is known for the quality of its ajiaco. Dinner in this belle époque–style restaurant is accompanied by antiques and artwork from Colombia's colonial past. Three locations serve the Candelaria, Centro Internacional, and the northern part of town. ⊠ *Av. Jiménez No. 3–57* ☎ *091/334–8908* ⊠ *Carrera 10 No. 26–60* ☎ *091/336–7818* ⊠ *Carrera 11 No. 89–08* ☎ *091/257–3903* ⊙ *Closed Sun.* ▭ *AE, MC, V.*

Eclectic

$$$ ✕ **Pajares Salinas.** International dishes are the stars at one of Bogota's most highly rated restaurants. *Callos a la madrileña* (tripe stew in slightly spicy sauce) and other Spanish dishes are among the top choices. The classically elegant dining room is decorated with works of art from around the world. ⊠ *Carrera 10 No. 96–08* ☎ *091/616–1524* ▭ *AE, DC, MC, V* ⊙ *Closed Sun.*

$–$$ ✕ **Cafetería Romana.** Reminiscent of a 1960s-era diner, this unpretentious eatery in La Candelaria serves an appropriate selection of sandwiches. Breakfast here is typically Colombian—hot chocolate with cheese and bread. ⊠ *Av. Jiménez No. 6–65* ☎ *091/334–8135* ▭ *AE, DC, MC, V.*

¢–$ ✕ **Café y Crêpes.** The alpine style of this place celebrates hiking and climbing in the great outdoors, but the mood inside is surprisingly intimate. You can sit on pillows in front of a fire and sip mulled wine. Both sweet and savory crepes are served. ⊠ *Carrera 16 No. 82–17* ☎ *091/236–2688* ⊠ *Diagonal 108 No. 9A–11* ☎ *091/214–5312* ▭ *AE, DC, MC, V* ⊙ *No lunch Sun.*

¢–$ ✕ **Crêpes and Waffles.** This is a unique chain of restaurants serving, of course, crepes and waffles, as well as a delicious selection of ice-cream desserts. Posters of Colombian artist Fernando Botero's works cover the walls. ⊠ *Centro Internacional Bavaria, Carrera 10 27–91 at Calle 28* ☎ *091/243–1620* ⊠ *Carrera 9 No. 73–33* ☎ *091/211–2530* ⊠ *Carrera 11 No. 85–79* ☎ *091/236–8711* ▭ *AE, DC, MC, V.*

French

$$$–$$$$ ✕ **Casa Medina.** Chef Francisco Rodriguez prepares French dishes, such
Fodor$Choice as medallions of trout smothered in fennel and onion, with aplomb. The
★ stately restaurant, built in 1945 as a private mansion, has been declared a national monument. The elegant dining rooms are strewn with antiques imported by aristocratic Bogotano families. ⊠ *Carrera 7 No. 69A–22* ☎ *091/312–0299* 🖷 *091/312–3769* ⊕ *www.hoteles-charleston. com* ▭ *AE, DC, MC, V.*

Italian

$–$$ ✕ **El Patio.** None of the cutlery matches, the plates are a hodgepodge of styles, and the small dining room is crammed with tables, but all this simply adds to the restaurant's eccentric charm. Its great location a couple blocks from the Plaza de Toros Santamaría in the bohemian neighborhood of La Macarena doesn't hurt. Try one of the masterful salads or the delicious veal parmigiana. ⊠ *Carrera 4A No. 27–86* ☎ *091/282–6141* ▭ *AE, DC, MC, V* ☉ *Closed Sun.*

$–$$ ✕ **Sol de Napoles.** Family recipes and fresh bread make this reasonably priced catery a longtime favorite among Bogotanos. Try pasta topped with one of the sauces—the meaty Bolognesa and the spicy arrabiata are favorites, but even the "plain" is enormously satisfying. ⊠ *Calle 69 No. 11–58* ☎ *091/249–2186* ▭ *AE, DC, MC, V* ☉ *Closed Mon.*

Seafood

★ $$$–$$$$ ✕ **Casa San Isidro.** Specializing in masterfully prepared seafood and white-glove service, Casa San Isidro would be worth the trip for the location alone. Perched 2,000 feet over Bogotá on top of the Cerro de Monserrate, you'll dine fireside as a pianist provides the sound track. Sample the San Isidro lobster with squid and shrimp, and then wash it down with your choice of wine from a dozen different countries. But be sure to leave by midnight, Cinderella, before the last cable car returns to the streets below. ⊠ *Cerro de Monserrate* ☎ *091/281–9270 or 091/281–9309* ▭ *DC, MC, V* ☉ *Closed Sun.*

$$$–$$$$ ✕ **La Fragata.** With its slowly revolving dining room, this is one of the capital's more unusual restaurants. Somehow the dimly lit, dark-oak interior successfully conveys the sensibility of a 19th-century frigate. The lobster, crab, red snapper, and locally caught rainbow trout are satisfying but slightly overshadowed by the presentation. ⊠ *Calle 100 No. 8A–55, 12th fl.* ☎ *091/616–7461* ▭ *AE, D, DC, MC, V.*

Where to Stay

Many of Bogotá's better hotels are in the wealthy northern districts—the most alluring parts of the city, and also the safest (there are security guards on nearly every corner). If you want to soak up the color of the colonial buildings, or are on a tight budget, book a room in La Candelaria. No matter where you stay, avoid wandering the streets at night.

$$–$$$ 🏨 **Bogotá Royal.** In addition to modern rooms with good views, this hotel has everything corporate travelers need. The hotel is in Bogotá's World Trade Center in the north end of town, a short taxi ride from many office buildings but far from museums and other attractions. ⊠ *Carrera 8 No. 99–55* ☎ *091/634–1777* 🖷 *091/218–3261* ⊕ *www.hotelsroyal. com* 🛏 *143 rooms* ♨ *2 restaurants, in-room data ports, health club, sauna, 2 bars, meeting rooms* ▤ *AE, DC, MC, V.*

$$ 🏨 **Hotel Tequendama.** One of Bogotá's oldest and most refined hotels is now part of the Inter-Continental chain. Its rooms lack character, but they have impressive city views. The hotel is in the Centro International, conveniently close to La Candelaria and most downtown offices. ⊠ *Carrera 10 No. 26–21* ☎ *091/382–0300* 🖷 *091/282–2860* ⊕ *www. ichotelsgroup.com* 🛏 *578 rooms* ♨ *3 restaurants, room service, health club, hair salon, sauna, 2 bars, casino, shops* ▤ *AE, DC, MC, V.*

★ $$ 🏨 **Los Urapanes.** This intimate boutique hotel in the heart of the leafy Zona Rosa has understated but luxurious rooms. Business travelers will appreciate the three phone lines in each room. The adjoining Los Samanes restaurant is popular for its exquisitely presented Colombian cuisine. ⊠ *Carrera 13 No. 83–19* ☎ *091/218–1188 or 091/218–5065* 🖷 *091/218–9242* ⊕ *www.hotellosurapanes.com.co* 🛏 *32 rooms, 16 suites* ♨ *Restaurant, room service, in-room safes, minibars, cable TV, in-room data ports, wireless Internet, bar, babysitting, Internet, business services, meeting rooms, free parking* ▤ *AE, DC, MC, V.*

★ $–$$ 🏨 **Hotel de la Opera.** This pair of colonial buildings adjacent to the Teatro Colón in La Candelaria found new life as an elegant hotel. The sleek tile and polished hardwood floors throughout are remarkable, as is the chic furniture imported from Italy. The generously proportioned rooms have high ceilings and huge windows, and some have balconies that open out onto a quiet side street. The Mediterranean cuisine at the hotel's restaurant, La Scala, is wonderful. The Automatico bar is a great place to relax with a brandy. ⊠ *Calle 10 No. 5–72* ☎ *091/336–2066* 🖷 *091/337–4617* ⊕*www.hotelopera.com.co* 🛏*29 rooms* ♨*2 restaurants, room service, minibars, bar, laundry service, business services, car rental* ▤ *AE, DC, MC, V.*

$ 🏨 **Casa Dann Carlton Bogotá.** In a residential neighborhood in northern Bogotá, this hotel has modern rooms and plenty of recreational facilities, including a heated pool (necessary in the cool Bogotá climate). Ask about the golf package, and you'll get to play a round of golf at the Club Pueblo Viejo in the suburb of Chia. Golfers swear they can drive the ball farther at this altitude. ⊠ *Calle 94 No. 19–71* ☎ *091/633–8777* 🖷*091/633–8810* 🛏*242 rooms* ♨ *Restaurant, room service, health club, sauna, bar, concierge* ▤ *AE, DC, MC, V.*

¢ 🏨 **Hotel Ambala.** Rooms in this small inn are a bit cramped, but they're clean and comfortable. They also have plenty of creature comforts for a lodging in this price range: firm beds and baths with lots of hot water. Rooms on the street are brighter but can be noisy. ⊠ *Carrera 5 No. 13–46* ☎ *091/341–2376 or 091/281–7124* 🖷 *091/286–3693* 🛏 *24 rooms* ♨ *Cable TV* ▤ *MC, V.*

Nightlife & the Arts

Nightlife

Bogotá's reputation for street crime hasn't put a damper on its ebullient nightlife. The two main partying areas are the Zona Rosa, between Calles 81 and 84 and Carreras 11 and 15, and the nearby Parque 93. There are also a handful of popular salsa bars in La Candelaria. The Zona Rosa and Parque 93 are safer than downtown, but you should travel there by taxi.

BARS & DANCE CLUBS **Salto del Angel** (⊠ Carrera 13 No. 93a–45 ☎ 091/336–3139 or 091/622–6437) plays rumba at the chic Parque 93 on Thursday, Friday, and Saturday. Dance on the outdoor patio or in the spacious indoor atrium. **Salomé Pagana** (⊠ Carrera 14A No. 82–16 ☎ 091/221–1895 or 091/218 4076) has live music in an intimate environment. Dance to boleros on Tuesday, folk music on Wednesday, and Cuban salsa on Thursday.

The Arts

THEATERS Bogotá has a lively theater scene, though you'll miss a lot if you don't understand Spanish. Bogotá is justly proud of its enormous biannual **Ibero-American Theater Festival,** which fills the two weeks before Easter with performing arts. Theater troupes arrive from all over the world to perform in Bogotá's numerous theaters and public parks. Recent festivals have included everything from Australian acrobats to African dance troupes. **Teatro La Candelaria** (⊠ Calle 12 No. 2–59 ☎ 091/281–4814) has produced experimental theater for nearly 40 years. **Teatro Nacional** (⊠ Calle 71 No. 10–25 ☎ 091/217–4577 or 091/235–8069) presents musicals and popular comedies. Tickets can be purchased in advance at the box office.

Outdoor Activities

Bullfighting

The bullfighting season is January and February, with occasional special events held during the rest of year. All are held at the Plaza de Toros Santamaría near the Parque de la Independencia. Spanish toreros delight the crowds, but Colombia's homegrown bullfighters are also quite exceptional: Bogotá native Cesar Rincón was once the most popular torero in Spain (he has since retired to raise bulls on his own ranch). Tickets can be purchased at the bullring weekdays from 9 AM to 5 PM. You can also get tickets on Sunday before the festivities begin at 3 PM, but you may not be able to secure seats for the more popular fights. Prices range from 10,000 pesos to 400,000 pesos depending on where you are seated, since *sol* (sun) is cheaper than *sombra* (shade).

Hiking

Although there are very real security issues in Colombia, hiking clubs have thrived in Bogotá over the last decade. Do not attempt to hike anywhere on your own—you should only go on a guided hike. In the region of Boyacá, in which Bogotá is located, are many safe hikes following *caminos reales,* stone-paved paths often dating from colonial times. **Sal Si Puedes** (⊠ Carrera 7 No. 17–01 ☎ 091/283–3765) is the venerable dean of Bogotá's hiking clubs. Established in 1979, it offers day hikes every weekend, with longer two- and three-day excursions at least once a month. Hikes are rated according to difficulty and guides are certified by the government.

Soccer

Fútbol games are held on most Sunday at 3:45 PM and Wednesday at 8 PM at **El Campín** (⊠ Carrera 30, between Calles 53 and 63). There's no need to book ahead except when there's a match between the two most popular local teams—Santa Fé and Millionarios. Tickets are from 5,000 pesos to 30,000 pesos and can be purchased at the stadium.

Shopping

Bogotá's shops and markets stock all types of leather and wool goods designed for life on the high plains. Handwoven *ruanas* (ponchos) are popular; the natural oils in the wool make them almost impervious to rain. Colombian artisans also have a way with straw: *toquilla,* a tough native fiber, is used to make hats, shoes, handbags, and even umbrellas.

Markets

In the warren of stalls at the daily **Pasaje Rivas indoor market** (⊠ Carrera 10 at Calle 10) look for bargain-price ponchos, blankets, leather goods, and crafts. The **flea market** (⊠ Calle 24, ½ block east of Carrera 7) in the Centro Internacional takes over a parking lot alongside the Museo de Arte Moderno, on Sunday. It is a good place to hunt for antiques, handicrafts, and just plain junk. An upscale Sunday **flea market** (⊠ Carrera 7 No. 119B–33) in Usaquén has a good selection of high-quality local crafts.

Shopping Centers

Stylish boutiques dominate the chic **Centro Andino** (⊠ Carrera 11 No. 82–71 ☎ 091/621–3111), an anchor of the Zona Rosa since 1993. Tower Records, the only major chain store, is a good place to buy English-language magazines and newspapers. There's a U.S.-style food court and a movie theater on the fourth floor. Farther north is the upscale **Hacienda Santa Barbara** (⊠ Carrera 7 No. 115–60 ☎ 091/612–0388), constructed as an extension of a colonial-era plantation home. The massive **Unicentro Shopping Center** (⊠ Av. 15 No. 123–30 ☎ 091/213–8800) in Bogotá's affluent north is one of South America's largest air-conditioned malls and has a huge selection of stores.

Specialty Shops

ANTIQUES Antiques shops are found mainly in the northern districts of Chapinero, Chicó, and Usaquén. One of the best is **Anticuarios Gilberto F. Hernández** (⊠ Calle 79B No. 7–48 ☎ 091/249–0041 or 091/248–7572). A good bet for quality antiques in the Candelaria is **Almacen de Antiguedades Leonardo F** (⊠ Carrera 4 No. 12–34 ☎ 091/334–8312).

EMERALDS Seventy percent of the world's emerald supply is mined in Colombia. Value depends on weight, color, clarity, brilliance, and cut, with octagonal cuts being the most valuable. Emerald dealers gather to make deals among themselves on the southwest corner of Carrera 7 and Avenida

Jiménez during business hours Monday through Saturday. It's interesting to watch the haggling, but don't even think about joining in.

> **TIP**
>
> Unless you know how to spot a fake you should buy jewelry only from a reputable dealer.

There are countless jewelry shops in the Centro Internacional along Carrera 6 between Calles 10 and 13. **H. Stern** (⊠ Tequendama Hotel, Carrera 10 No. 26–21 ☎ 091/283–2819) sells all kinds of precious gems. In both the Centro Internacional and the Centro Comercial Andino is **Galeria Cano** (⊠ Edificio Bavaria, Carrera 13 No. 27–98 ☎ 091/336–3255 ⊠ Edificio Banco Mercantil, Carrera 12 No. 84–07 ☎ 091/635–0581). It sells emeralds as well as gold jewelry using striking pre-Columbian designs taken from the Museo de Oro.

HANDICRAFTS   In the cloister of Las Aquas, a neighborhood just off La Candelaria, **Artesanías de Colombia** (⊠ Carrera 3 No. 18–58 ☎ 091/286–1766 or 091/277–9010) stocks everything from straw umbrellas to handwoven ponchos. The shop at the **Museo de Artes y Tradiciones Populares** (⊠ Carrera 8 No. 7–21 ☎ 091/342–1266) carries handmade items. **Artesanías El Zaque** (⊠ Centro Internacional, Carrera 10 No. 26–71 ☎ 091/342–7883 ⊠ Hotel Tequendama, Interior Centro 28 ☎ 091/342–7883) offers especially good buys on hammocks. **El Balay** (⊠ Carrera 15 No. 75–63 ☎ 091/248–5833) stocks the city's widest selection of souvenirs from around Colombia.

Bogotá Essentials

Transportation

BY AIR

TO & FROM   Aeropuerto El Dorado, a 20-minute taxi ride northwest of downtown,
BOGOTÁ   has flights to national and international destinations. Avianca, Colombia's national airline, flies from Miami and New York. American and Copa fly here from Miami. Continental has flights through Houston, and Delta has flights through Atlanta. Domestic routes are covered by Aces, Aerorepública, Aires, Intercontinental de Aviación, and Satena.

✈ Airports Aeropuerto El Dorado ☎ 091/425–1000.

✈ Domestic Airlines Aerorepública ⊠ Centro Internacional, Calle 10 No. 27–51, Local 165, Oficina 303 ☎ 091/294–9090. **Aires** ⊠ Carrera 11 No. 76–14 ☎ 091/294–0300. **Satena** ⊠ Carrera 10A No. 27–21, Suite 211 ☎ 091/423–8500.

✈ International Airlines American ⊠ Carrera 7 No. 26–20 ☎ 091/343–2424. **Avianca** ⊠ Calle 16 No. 6–66 ☎ 091/410–1011. **Continental** ⊠ Carrera 7 No. 71–52 ☎ 091/312–2565. **Copa** ⊠ Calle 100 No. 8A–49 ☎ 091/623–1566. **Delta** ⊠ Carrera 13A No. 89–53, Oficina 301 ☎ 091/257–5997, 091/610–2295, or 091/610–9626.

BY TAXI

Taxis are required by law to have a meter—make sure your driver turns it on. The minimum charge is 3,000 pesos, plus 50 pesos per 80 meters (260 feet). Fares increase by about a third after dark. It is always safer to call a taxi, especially in the northern parts of Bogotá, where thieves masquerading as taxi drivers have robbed passengers they picked up on the street. The taxi companies will tell you the number of the taxi, and when you are picked up the taxi driver will ask you for the last two digits of the phone number from which you called.

Contacts & Resources

EMBASSIES

Upon arrival in Colombia, U.S. citizens should register with the embassy. There's no embassy for citizens of Australia, but in an emergency Australians can call a representative in Caracas, Venezuela.

🚩 **Embassies Canada** ⊠ Carrera 7 No. 115–33, 14th fl., Bogotá ☎ 091/657-9800. **United Kingdom** ⊠ Calle 9 No. 76–49, 8th and 9th fl., Bogotá ☎ 091/326-8300. **United States** ⊠ Calle 22D Bis No. 47–51, Bogotá ☎ 091/315-0811.

MONEY MATTERS

Banco de la República, on Carrera 7, exchanges cash at good rates. It is open weekdays 9–3. Several banks on Carrera 10 around the Hotel Tequendama also handle foreign currency. Your hotel is probably the most convenient place to exchange money, although it will charge a higher fee. ATMs are located around the city, clustering around the Centro Internacional and inside the shopping centers in north Bogotá. They are on both the Cirrus and Plus networks; you don't need a 4-digit PIN number here—a PIN of any length should work.

🚩 **Banks Banco de la República** ⊠ Carrera 7 No. 14–78.

SAFETY

Despite the city's reputation, most crimes against tourists are of the purse-snatching and pickpocketing variety that can be avoided with a little common sense. Avoid displays of wealth, such as expensive jewelry or watches. Never accept any food or cigarettes from a stranger and be wary of any unknown person approaching you on the street, especially if they are well dressed and overly friendly. Don't be duped by people claiming to be plainclothes police officers who demand to "register" your money—they are almost certainly thieves. In case of such confrontations, you may want to hand over a $20 bill to quickly extricate yourself from the situation.

TELEPHONES

There are coin-operated public phones on street corners and inside shopping malls, but they are not always reliable. Many shops have small public phones; with these, dial first and deposit a coin when the other party answers.

TIPPING

As in most of Colombia, you should leave a tip of about 10% in restaurants. Gratuity is often included; if it is not, the bill will say *servicio no incluido*. Tip doormen and people guarding your car at least 2,000 pesos for their services. Taxi drivers do not expect a tip.

TOUR OPERATORS

Aviatur is one of the country's largest and oldest travel agencies and organizes tours in and around Bogotá.

🚩 **Tour Operators Aviatur** ⊠ Calle 19 No. 4–62 ☎ 091/381-7111 or 091/286-5555.

VISITOR INFORMATION
The Vice Ministerio de Turismo has information on hotels, restaurants, and sights. It's open weekdays 9–5.

🛈 **Vice Ministerio de Turismo** ✉ Calle 28 No. 13A-15, 18th fl. ☎ 091/606-7676 ⊕ www.turismocolombia.com 🖷 091/284-8618.

MEDELLÍN

Nestled in the narrow Aburrá Valley, this northwestern city of 2 million people is the capital of Antioquia. The industrious *paisas,* as natives of the province are called, built the successful coffee and textile industries that have enabled Medellín to prosper; today it's the second-largest city in Colombia. Modern and affluent, Medellín has the country's only elevated train system. The city also has several interesting museums, three respected universities, and wide, tree-lined boulevards. But Medellín also has thousands of impoverished citizens whose shanties appear on the city's edges.

Although local and international intervention has lessened the drug trade, the city remains violent and unpredictable. Exercise caution when touring Medellín day or night, and always stick to central areas.

Exploring Medellín

Medellín is the country's main industrial hub, but don't expect a city full of smoking chimneys: the factories are well outside of town. Deep-green mountains that rise sharply around the city provide a bold backdrop to the glass-and-concrete towers of its elegant financial district. Well-developed tourist facilities in the city proper testify to the region's relative economic strength.

What to See

Catedral Basílica Metropolitana. The Metropolitan Cathedral, whose ornate coffee-color facade soars above the Parque de Bolívar, is among Medellín's most striking buildings. Designed by the French architect Charles Carré and built in 1875, it's South America's largest cathedral and the third-largest brick building in the world. ✉ *Carrera 48 No. 56-81* ☎ *094/513-2269* 💲 *Free* 🕐 *Mon–Sat. 7 AM–noon and 4:30–7, Sun. 7 AM–1 PM and 4:30–7.*

Ermita de la Veracruz. Distinguishing the interior of the Veracruz Hermitage are its white walls and columns with gilded capitals. Just off a picturesque plaza, it's a quiet escape from Medellín's noisy streets. ✉ *Calle 51 No. 52-58* ☎ *094/512-5095* 💲 *Free* 🕐 *Daily 7–6.*

> **TIP**
>
> When visiting sights, remember that calles run east–west and carreras run north–south. Also be careful not to walk around after sunset, as the city can be quite dangerous.

Jardín Botánico Joaquín Antonio Uribe. The botanical gardens have more than 500 plant species, including heliconias, zamias, and azaleas, and a huge greenhouse teeming with orchids. ✉ *Carrera 52 No. 73–298* ☎ *094/211–5607 or 094/571–8767* 💰 *4,000 pesos* 🕐 *Daily 8–5.*

Museo de Antioquia. The Antioquia Museum contains a large collection of paintings and sculptures by native son Fernando Botero and other well-known Colombian artists. Botero, known for depicting people and objects with a distinctive "thickness," donated part of his personal collection to the museum (the bulk of his gift went to Bogotá). ✉ *Carrera 52 No. 52–43* ☎ *094/251–3636* 💰 *8,000 pesos* 🕐 *Daily 9:30–5.*

Museo El Castillo. The 1930s Gothic-inspired Castle Museum, whose beautiful French-style gardens consist of sweeping lawns and exuberant flower beds, was once the home of a powerful Medellín family. On display is their furniture and art collected from around the world. ✉ *Calle 9 Sur No. 32–269* ☎ *094/266–0900* 💰 *6,000 pesos* 🕐 *Weekdays 9–noon and 2–5:30, Sat. 9–11:30 AM.*

Parque Berrío. This small cement plaza is overwhelmed by the city's elevated train, the only one of its kind in Colombia. Nearby is the colonial church of **Nuestra Señora de la Candelaria.** To the south, the Banco de la República building stands next to a huge female torso sculpted by native son Fernando Botero. On the bank's other side, a bronze fountain and marble monument honor Atanasio Girardot, an 18th-century champion for Colombian independence. ✉ *Carrera 50, between Calles 50 and 51.*

Parque de Bolívar. Despite its location in the middle of crowded Medellín, this shady park has a generous amount of open space. In the evenings it's popular with young people who congregate on the steps of the nearby cathedral. ✉ *Carrera 49 and Calle 54.*

Parque de las Esculturas. This small sculpture park near the peak of Cerro Nutibara is a maze of paths dotted with modern and traditional sculptures by Latin American artists. ✉ *Cerro Nutibara.*

Pueblito Paisa. As you enter this reproduction of an old-time Antioquian village, you'll see a traditional town square with a small church, town hall, barbershop, school, and village store. For your present-day needs, it also has a small restaurant and several souvenir shops. ✉ *Cerro Nutibara.*

Where to Eat

Traditional Antioquian cooking means hearty peasant fare—plenty of meat, beans, rice, and potatoes. But Medellín is full of high-quality restaurants where you'll find many cuisines. On the first Saturday of every month, the **Parque de las Delicias** (✉ Carrera 73 and Av. 39D) is packed with food stalls selling everything from *obleas* (thin jam-filled waffles) to *lechona* (roast stuffed pork).

Colombian

$–$$ ✕ **El Hato Viejo.** Generous portions draw locals to this second-story
Fodor'sChoice   restaurant. Waiters in Panama hats serve you on a balcony overflowing with plants or in the large dining room with terra-cotta floors. Try
★

the *sopa de guineo* (plantain soup) before sinking your teeth into *lomito* (tenderloin) or *langostinos* (lobsters). Finish your feast with *brevas con queso* (figs with white cheese). ⊠ *Carrera 47 No. 52–17* ☎ *094/251–2196 or 094/231–1108* ▭ *AE, DC, MC, V.*

$ ✕ **Aguas Claras.** Experience many Colombian dishes in one meal—the hearty *plato típico* is a sampling of 10 different items. The lighter *plato del cura* (priest's plate) is a complete meal of soup, beef, rice, and bread for about $5. The nicest tables are on the balcony, which overlooks a popular pedestrian mall. ⊠ *Carrera 49 No. 52–141, 2nd fl.* ☎ *094/231–6642* ▭ *AE, DC, MC, V.*

International

$$$–$$$$ ✕ **Las Cuatro Estaciones.** Medellín's most popular restaurant combines delicious food and first-rate service with an interior that borders on tacky. Choose one of four thematic dining rooms—decorated in gaudy Colombian, European, Asian, and Spanish styles. The house specialty is paella. ⊠ *Calle 16 No. 43–79, El Poblado* ☎ *094/266–7120* 🖷 *094/311–5991* ▭ *AE, DC, MC, V.*

Where to Stay

$ ▦ **Inter-Continental Medellín.** This sprawling modern hotel in the hills outside Medellín has spectacular views of the city. The lobby is all marble, service is friendly, and rooms are well-appointed. The Poblado neighborhood is about 20 minutes by taxi from the city center and 40 minutes from the airport. ⊠ *Calle 16 No. 28–51* ☎ *094/319–4450, 800/327–0200 in the U.S.* 🖷 *094/315–4404* ⊕ *www.intercontinental.com* ↪ *294 rooms, 45 suites ↻ 2 restaurants, tennis court, pool, gym, hair salon, massage, sauna, bar, dance club, concierge, meeting rooms* ▭ *AE, DC, MC, V.*

$ ▦ **Hotel Nutibara.** This stylish hotel from the 1940s recalls a glamorous era. Rooms in the newer building across the street have less personality but cost half of those in the main building. From the hotel's downtown location it's a short taxi ride to restaurants and bars. ⊠ *Calle 52A No. 50–46* ☎ *094/511–5111* 🖷 *094/231–3713* ↪ *90 rooms ↻ Restaurant, café, indoor pool, bar, sauna* ▭ *No credit cards.*

¢ ▦ **La Bella Villa.** Just a few blocks from Parque de Bolívar, this hotel has five floors of modern rooms surrounding a covered courtyard. ⊠ *Calle 53 No. 50–28* ☎ *094/511–0144* 🖷 *094/512–9477* ↪ *50 rooms ↻ Restaurant, sauna* ▭ *DC, MC, V.*

Shopping

Medellín's **Centro Commercial San Diego** (⊠ Calle 34 No. 43–66 ☎ 094/232–0624) has crafts, jewelry, and clothing shops. You'll find souvenir shops at **Pueblito Paisa** atop Cerro Nutibara. Check the outdoor stalls along **Pasaje Junín** just south of Parque de Bolívar. For Antioquian crafts, visit the **open-air crafts market** held on the first Saturday of every month at the Parque de Bolívar.

Medellín Essentials

Transportation

BY AIR

Medellín's Aeropuerto Jose Maria Córdoba is on top of a plateau 38 km (24 mi) southeast of the city. Aerorepública, Intercontinental, and Satena fly here from Bogotá and other Colombian cities.

🚪 Airlines **Aerorepública** ☎ 094/351-1266. **Satena** ☎ 094/255-1180.

🚪 Airports **Aeropuerto José María Córdoba** ☎ 094/562-2828.

BY METRO

Medellín has an excellent train system that opened in 1995. Because most of the track is elevated, it's a good way to see the city. There are two lines, one running north–south, the other east–west. A one-way fare is 1,050 pesos, and a round-trip fticket costs 2,050 pesos.

Contacts & Resources

MONEY MATTERS

Money can be exchanged at the Banco de la República, on Parque Berrío. It is open weekdays 9–3.

🚪 Banks **Banco de la República** ✉ Calle 50 No. 50-21.

SAFETY

With the death of notorious drug trafficker Pablo Escobar in 1993, car bombings and other random acts of violence seem to be a thing of the past. Politically motivated assassinations and bombings still occur. Exercise the usual caution you would in big cities, especially at night, and take taxis to get around. Travel to the area outside of Medellín is dangerous.

TELEPHONES

Local calls can be made from the coin-operated public phones found around Medellín. Newer phones that accept phone cards can be used to make long-distance calls.

TOUR OPERATORS

Aviatur, the travel agency with offices all over the country, offers tours of the region. At Abanico Tours, Ana Olavia puts together personalized tours of the city.

🚪 Tour Operators **Aviatur** ✉ Carrera 49 No. 55-25 ☎ 094/576-5000.

VISITOR INFORMATION

The Oficina de Turismo, east of Parque de Bolívar, has a good city map, but little else. It's open Monday–Friday 7:30–12:30 and Saturday 1:30–5:30.

🚪 **Oficina de Turismo** ✉ Calle 57 No. 45-129 ☎ 094/232-4022.

THE CARIBBEAN COAST

Colombia's sultry Caribbean Coast is linked to Bogotá only by the national flag, the milky Río Magdalena, and a couple of snaking highways. The *costeño* people, driven by salsa and the accordion-heavy *vallenato* music, have an exuberant spirit not seen in the capital.

Toward the western end of the 1,600-km (992-mi) shoreline is Cartagena, Colombia's greatest colonial city. With its barrel-tile roofs and wooden balconies, Cartagena's Ciudad Amurallada resembles many cities in Spain, but the feeling is definitely tropical. The Islas del Rosario, just off the coast, provide plenty of exploring options for snorkelers and divers.

> **DID YOU KNOW?**
>
> Despite the strength-sapping heat and carnival-like sensibility, the Caribbean coast has nurtured some of Colombia's best-known writers and artists, including novelist Gabriel García Márquez and painter Alejandro Obregón.

Northeast of Cartagena is Barranquilla, a quiet city that bursts to life during Carnival in February, when it has pre-Lenten festivities. (If you go, fly—do not take a bus or car.)

Cartagena

When it was founded in 1533 by Spanish conquistador Pedro de Heredia, Cartagena was the only port on the South American mainland. Gold and silver looted from indigenous peoples passed through here en route to Spain, making Cartagena an obvious target for pirates. The most destructive of these was Sir Francis Drake, who in 1586 torched 200 buildings, including the cathedral, and made off for England with more than 100,000 gold ducats. Cartagena's magnificent city walls and countless fortresses were erected to protect its riches, as well as to safeguard the most important African slave market in the New World. The Ciudad Amurallada attracts many to Cartagena, but it actually comprises a small section of this city of half a million. Most of Cartagena's hotels and restaurants are in the Bocagrande district, an elongated peninsula where high-rise hotels overlook a long, gray-sand beach.

TIMING & PRECAUTIONS
Spend the morning in the walled city, lunching in one of the nearby eateries, and take the afternoon to visit San Felipe and Cerro de la Popa. Because many sights are closed by 6 PM, you'll want to do the tour early in the day. Be sure to visit the Ciudad Amurallada at night by horse-drawn carriage in order to admire its monuments by moonlight.

What to See

6 Barrio San Diego. The seldom-visited streets of this enchanting north-end district are lined with squat colonial mansions painted white, ocher, and deep blue. Geraniums cascade over balconies, and open doorways reveal lush hidden courtyards. At the northern corner of the city walls you'll find **Las Bóvedas** (The Vaults), a row of storerooms built in the 18th century to hold gunpowder and other military essentials. Today they are occupied by the city's best crafts shops. After you've loaded up on hats, hammocks, and leather goods, take a stroll along the city walls and watch as the setting sun reddens the Caribbean. ⊠ *North of Plaza Fernández de Madrid.*

1 Casa de Marqués Valdehoyos. Although scantily furnished, this elegant house exudes a powerful aroma of well-to-do colonial life. The sturdy mansion and its shady courtyard, low arches, and elaborate wooden balconies are the product of the marqués's slave-trade fortune. The tourist

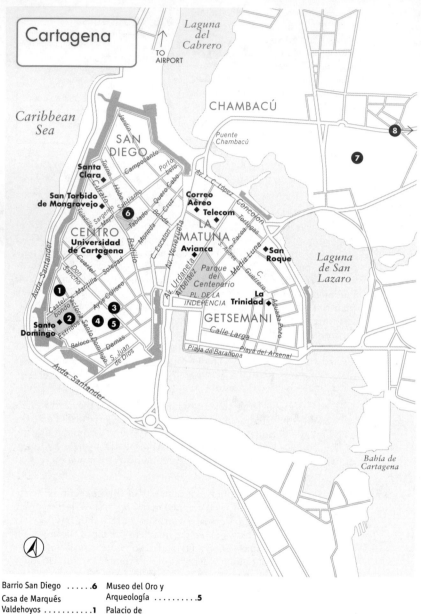

Cartagena

office inside provides useful maps. ⊠ *Calle Factoría No. 36–57* ☎ *095/ 664–6567* 🔄 *Free* ⊙ *Daily 8–noon and 2–6.*

⑦ Castillo de San Felipe de Barajas. Designed by Antonio de Arévalo in 1639, the Fort of St. Philip's steep-angled brick and concrete battlements were arranged so that if part of the castle were conquered the rest could still be defended. A maze of tunnels, minimally lit today to allow for spooky exploration, still connects vital points of the fort. ⊠ *Avenida Pedro de Heredia at Carrera 17* ☎ *095/666–4790* 🔄 *10,000 pesos* ⊙ *Daily 8–6.*

③ Catedral. Plaza de Bolívar is a shady place from which to admire Cartagena's 16th-century cathedral, with its colorful bell tower and 20th-century dome. Inside is a massive gilded altar. ⊠ *Plaza de Bolívar.*

⑧ Cerro de la Popa. For spectacular views of Cartagena, ascend this hill Choice around sunset. Because of its strategic location, the 17th-century ★ monastery here intermittently served as a fortress during the colonial era. It now houses a museum and a chapel dedicated to the Virgin de la Candelaria, Cartagena's patron saint. ✛ *3 km (2 mi) southeast of Ciudad Amurallada* ☎ 🔄 *5,000 pesos* ⊙ *Daily 8–5.*

⑤ Museo del Oro y Arqueología. The Gold and Archaeological Museum displays an assortment of artifacts culled from the Sinús, an indigenous group that lived in the region 2,000 years ago. ⊠ *Carrera 4 No. 33–26* ☎ *095/ 660–0778* 🔄 *Free* ⊙ *Tues.–Fri. 10–1 and 3–7, Sat. 10–1 and 2–5.*

④ Palacio de la Inquisición. A baroque limestone doorway marks the en-Choice trance to the Palace of the Inquisition, the headquarters of the repres-★ sive arbiters of political and spiritual orthodoxy who once exercised jurisdiction over Colombia, Ecuador, and Venezuela. The ground floor contains implements of torture—racks and thumbscrews, to name but two—and architectural models of bygone Cartagena. ⊠ *Carrera 4 No. 33–26* ☎ *095/660–0778* 🔄 *3,000 pesos* ⊙ *Daily 9–5.*

② Plaza Santo Domingo. The eponymous church looming over the plaza is the oldest in the city. Built in 1539, it has a simple whitewashed interior, bare limestone pillars, a raised choir, and an adjacent cloistered seminary. Local lore says the bell tower's twisted profile is the work of the Devil, who, dispirited at having failed to destroy it, threw himself into the plaza's well. At night the area fills up with tables from surrounding bars and restaurants. ⊠ *Calle Santo Domingo and Carrera Santo Domingo.*

Where to Eat

Seafood is the regional specialty, as are *arroz con coco* (rice cooked in coconut milk) and *sancocho de sábalo* (fish prepared in coconut milk with strips of plantains, bananas, and yucca). Tropical *jugos* (juices) are an excellent companion to *carimañolas* (stuffed yucca), *arepas de huevo* (egg-filled pancakes), and *butifarras* (small meatballs).

COLOMBIAN ✕ **Club de Pesca.** Time slips gently by at this 18th-century fortress in the $$$–$$$$ nearby town of Manga. It's easy to linger on the waterfront terrace in the shade of a giant fig tree, especially when you're savoring one of the delicate specialties, such as snapper with lemon, soy, tahini, and mint. ⊠ *Fuerte de San Sebastián del Pastelillo, Manga* ☎ *095/660–4594* ⊟ *AE, DC, MC, V.*

★ $$$–$$$$ ✗ **La Vitrola.** This friendly restaurant on a quiet Ciudad Amurallada corner is the result of a New Yorker's love affair with the Caribbean. You can begin with *ceviche catalina* (fish and octopus marinated in lime juice); then try a *zarzuela de mariscos* (seafood casserole) or perhaps *corvina con salsa de cebollin y jenibre* (sea bass with scallion-ginger sauce). Ceiling fans, historic photos, and live Cuban music complete the mood. ⊠ *Calle Baloco, near Carrera Santo Domingo* ☎ *095/664–8243* ⊟ *AE, DC, MC, V.*

$$–$$$ ✗ **Paco's.** Heavy beams, rough terra-cotta walls, chunky wooden benches, and tunes from an aging Cuban band are the hallmarks of this downtown eatery. Drop by for a drink and some tapas, or try the more substantial *langostinos a la sifú* (lobsters fried in batter). You can sit in the dining room or outside on the Plaza Santo Domingo. ⊠ *Plaza Santo Domingo* ☎ *No phone* ⊟ *V.*

CAFÉ ✗ **Café San Pedro.** Although it serves Colombian fare, this restaurant's
$–$$ eclectic menu includes dishes from Thailand, Italy, and Japan. You can also drop by to have a drink and to watch the activity on the plaza from one of the outdoor tables. ⊠ *Plaza San Pedro* ☎ *095/664–5121 or 095/ 664–1433* ⊟ *DC, MC, V* ☉ *Closed Sun.*

Where to Stay

$$$$ 🏨 **Hilton.** Every spacious room at this modern hotel on the tip of the Bocagrande peninsula has a balcony facing the sea. They also have a great view of the terrace with its leafy gardens and three pools. A path from the hotel leads to a private beach lined with palms, magnolias, and thatched oyster bars. ⊠ *Av. Almirante Brión, Carrera 1 No. 4–00, El Laguito* ☎ *095/665–0666, 800/445–8667 in the U.S.* 🖷 *095/665–2211* ⊕ *www.hilton.com* ↩ *288 rooms, 15 suites* ♨ *2 restaurants, cable TV, tennis court, 3 pools, gym, hair salon, massage, sauna, jet skiing, waterskiing, basketball, 2 bars, children's programs (all ages), business services, convention center, meeting rooms* ⊟ *AE, DC, MC, V.*

$$$$ 🏨 **Santa Clara.** Beyond the arched porticos and lush courtyard of this
Fodor'sChoice elegant hotel in Ciudad Amurallada is a newer wing that holds the pool
★ and the comfortably furnished guest rooms. The former dining room for the convent holds El Refectorio, which serves the city's best French cuisine. ⊠ *Plaza San Diego* ☎ *095/ 664–6070, 800/221–4542 in the U.S.* 🖷 *095/664–7010* ⊕ *www. hotelsantaclara.com* ↩ *144 rooms, 18 suites* ♨ *3 restaurants, in-room safes, pool, gym, massage, sauna, steam room, bar, concierge, business services, convention center, meeting rooms* ⊟ *AE, DC, MC, V.*

> ### HERE'S WHERE
>
> Santa Clara is housed in the 17th-century convent that was the setting for Gabriel García Márquez's novel *Of Love and Other Demons.*

★ $$$$ 🏨 **Charleston Hotel.** Housed in the historic Convento de Santa Teresa, this 16th-century showplace in the Ciudad Amurallada has a studied elegance combining colonial and republican architectural styles. Rooms and suites, sumptuously appointed with rich fabrics and antique furnishings, look out onto the ocean or the old city. The best views, however, are from the rooftop pool and restaurant. ⊠ *Plaza Santa Teresa* ☎ *095/664–9494* 🖷 *095/664–9447* ⊕ *www. hoteles-charleston.com* ⤴ *70 rooms, 21 suites* ♨ *2 restaurants, pool, bar, laundry service, Internet, business services, convention center, meeting rooms* ⊟ *AE, DC, MC, V.*

$$$$ 🏨 **Hotel Caribe.** The oldest lodging on Bocagrande, this elegant hotel resembles a huge sand castle. Bedrooms in the refurbished older building have more charm than those in the modern wings, though they can be a bit noisy on weekends. Behind the hotel, giant ficus trees shade a large pool. A narrow lane separates the hotel from the beach. ⊠ *Carrera 1A No. 2–87, Bocagrande* ☎ *095/665–0155* 🖷 *095/665–4970* ⊕ *www. hotelcaribe.com* ⤴ *346 rooms, 17 suites* ♨ *2 restaurants, tennis court, pool, gym, hair salon, massage, sauna, bar, casino, convention center, meeting rooms* ⊟ *AE, DC, MC, V.*

★ **$**   🏨 **Las Tres Banderas.** In the historic San Diego neighborhood, this attractive little 19th-century hotel is an inexpensive option. The rooms, all of which border a narrow courtyard, combine colonial style with modern amenities. ⊠ *Calle Cochera del Hobo No. 38–66* ☎ *095/660–0160* ⤴ *22 rooms* ⊟ *MC.*

Nightlife

A great way to see the Ciudad Amurallada is to take a romantic ride in a horse-drawn *coche* (carriage), which you can hire in front of the Hotel Caribe or the Charleston Hotel. If you just want to watch the locals, the most popular destination in the Ciudad Amurallada is Plaza Santo Domingo, where several restaurants and cafés have outdoor seating.

A rowdier option is the popular *rumba en chiva*, a bar-hopping bus with a live band on the roof. You'll notice that many Colombians party on the beaches of Bocagrande. Vendors rent plastic chairs and sell cold beer, and roving trios play *vallenato*, the typical regional music.

Outdoor Activities

BEACHES   For white sand and palm trees, your best bet is **Playa Blanca,** about 15 minutes away by boat. Many people opt for a visit to the **Islas del Rosario,** a verdant archipelago surrounded by aquamarine waters and coral reefs. Tour boats leave from the Muelle de los Pegasos, the pier flanked by statues of two flying horses that is just outside the city walls. Plenty of men with boats will also offer to take you on the one-hour journey. Most larger hotels offer a trip to Playa Blanca and Islas de Rosario as part of a package.

FISHING   The **Club de Pesca** (⊠ Calle 24 at Carrera 17 ☎ 095/660–4594) in Manga can arrange fishing charters.

Shopping

Las Bóvedas, a series of arched storerooms in the Ciudad Amurallada's northern corner, now houses about two dozen shops with the best selection of local and national crafts. If you're looking for emeralds, visit the jewelry shops on or near Calle Pantaleón, beside the cathedral.

The Caribbean Coast Essentials

Transportation

BY AIR

Cartagena's Aeropuerto Rafael Nuñez lies 3 km (2 mi) east of downtown. There are daily flights from Bogotá and Medellín on domestic carriers Aces, Aerorepública, Intercontinental, and Sam. There are direct international flights from Panama with Copa, from Canada with Air Transat, and from Italy with Lauda Air.

🛪 **Airlines Aerorepública** ☎ 095/421-3346 in Santa Marta, 095/421-3151 in Santa Marta.
🛪 **Airports Aeropuerto Rafael Nuñez** ☎ 095/666-6610.

BY BUS

It's not advisable to take buses from town to town along the coast, or from major cities, such as Bogotá, to the coast.

BY CAR

Traveling by car to the Caribbean coast—or between cities on the coast—is not advisable because of the worsening civil conflict. (It's also a long haul—the drive between Bogotá and Cartagena takes 20 hours.)

Contacts & Resources

MONEY MATTERS

You can exchange money at the Banco de la República, which has branches in Cartagena. It's open weekdays 9–3. ATMs, many accepting foreign cards, are easy to find in the tourist areas of Cartagena.
🛈 **Banks Banco de la República** ⊠ Calle 33 No. 3-123, Cartagena.

SAFETY

Colombia's Caribbean coast, especially the towns most popular among tourists, is relatively safe. In Cartagena beware of pickpockets in the tourist areas.

TELEPHONES

Coin-operated public phones are located throughout Cartagena. Newer phones that accept phone cards can be used to make long-distance calls.

TOUR OPERATORS

Although traveling around the Caribbean coast either by bus or car isn't safe, it's fine to go with an organized tour group. In Cartagena, Tesoro Tours arranges everything from city tours to boat trips to the Islas del Rosario. Caliente Tours offers a day trip to the town of Santa Marta (northeast of Cartagena, at the foot of the Sierra Nevada coastal range) and the beaches at El Rodadero. Media Naranja puts together trips to Isla Media Naranja and the Islas del Rosario. In Manga, Raphael Pérez has a unique trip to the Volcán Totumo, where you can enjoy a mud bath (35,000 pesos).

City tours of Santa Marta can be arranged through Aviatur. The company also offers a boat tour to Acuario Playa Blanca, an aquarium off the coast of Santa Marta. Turcol offers trips to Parque Nacional Tayrona, a reserve with forest-clad slopes, ancient ruins, and palm-fringed beaches.
🛈 **Tour Agencies Aviatur** ⊠ Calle 29 No. 27-05 ☎ 095/423-3159 or 095/421-3848.
Caliente Tours ⊠ Calle 10 No. 1-61, Edificio Portofino Local 7 ☎ 095/665-5346, 095/

665–5347, or 095/660–1516. **Raphael Pérez** ✉ Calle Real Callejón Ferrer No. 25-108, Manga ☎ 095/660–4214. **Tesoro Tours** ✉ Av. San Martín No. 6-129, Bocagrande ☎ 095/665–4713, 095/665–4713, or 095/665–8838. **Turcol** ✉ Carrera 1C No. 20-15, Santa Marta ☎ 095/421–2256.

VISITOR INFORMATION

Cartagena's Promotora de Turismo provides maps and other helpful materials for the city and the region. It is open daily 9–noon and 2–5.

🚹 **Promotora de Turismo** ✉ Carrera 3 No. 36-57, Cartagena ☎ 095/664–7015.

SAN ANDRÉS & PROVIDENCIA

The resort islands of San Andrés and Providencia lie 645 km (400 mi) northwest of the Caribbean coast—closer to Nicaragua than to Colombia. Christopher Columbus was the first European to set foot on the islands during his fourth voyage to the New World. They were later settled by English pilgrims (who landed in their vessel, the *Seaflower*, at about the same time their counterparts came ashore at Plymouth Rock) and then by Jamaican cotton growers. Today the islands' roughly 60,000 residents speak an English patois and Spanish. Frequent air service and San Andrés's duty-free status mean both islands now receive a steady stream of visitors, mostly well-to-do Colombians who dive and snorkel when they aren't sunbathing and shopping.

San Andrés

645 km (400 mi) off Colombia's Caribbean Coast.

As it's only 13 km (8 mi) long, cigar-shape San Andrés is easy to explore by bicycle or motor scooter. Rent one from any of the shops along Avenida Colombia in El Centro. Along the coastal road is **Cueva Morgan,** a small beachfront settlement where the pirate Henry Morgan reputedly stashed his loot after pillaging coastal Cuba and Panama in the 1670s. Beach bums should head for **Johnny Cay,** a tiny islet just off the coast. Boats leave all day from San Andrés's beaches.

The island's duty-free status is responsible for the bland boutiques in the concrete jungle of **El Centro,** San Andrés's commercial center.

Where to Stay & Eat

$ ✕🏨 **Hotel Aquarium Super Decamerón.** Large rooms with terra-cotta floors occupy 15 towers overlooking the sea. You can enjoy live music shows at night in the Altamar bar. ✉ *Av. Colombia 1–19, Punta Hansa* ☎ *095/655–0123 reservations office in Cartagena* 🖷 *098/512–6938* 🛏 *258 rooms* ⚭ *3 restaurants, pool, 2 bars* ▭ *AE, DC, MC, V.*

$ ✕🏨 **Lord Pierre Hotel.** This beachfront hotel has a wide, private pier for sunbathing. Rooms have big beds and bamboo furniture. ✉ *Av. Colombia No. 1B–106* ☎ *098/512–7541* 🖷 *098/512–5666* 🛏 *58 rooms, 2 suites* ⚭ *Restaurant, café, pool, beach, bar* ▭ *AE, DC, MC, V.*

¢ 🏨 **Tiuna.** Right on the beach, this hotel has clean, comfortable rooms with great views of the ocean. Rates include two meals, making this hotel a good option for the budget traveler. ✉ *Av. Colombia No. 4–31* ☎ *098/*

512–3235 🖾 *098/512–3478* 🌐 *www.tiuna.com* 🛒 *160 rooms* 👌 *Restaurant, pool, beach, bar* 🖃 *AE, DC, MC, V.*

Providencia

90 km (56 mi) northwest of San Andrés.

Tiny Providencia, a mere 7 km (5 mi) long, has rugged hills forged from volcanic rock. There's much less development than on San Andrés, which makes it a quiet, easygoing Caribbean retreat. On the west coast is Aguadulce, the island's largest town, where you can rent bicycles and motor scooters or join a boat tour of the surrounding islets.

> ### TAKE A HIKE
>
> Choose a clear day to hike up the 1,000-foot summit of **El Pico**, which has superb views of the island's necklace of coral cays; it's a 90-minute trek each way from Casa Baja, the village at the bottom.

Smaller Santa Isabel, on the island's northern tip, is the governmental center and therefore attracts fewer visitors.

Where to Stay

¢–$ 🏨 **Sol Caribe.** These wooden cabins on Aguadulce's beach have clean and simple rooms with ocean views. Adjoining the complex is a no-frills but dependable restaurant. ✉ *Aguadulce* ☎ *098/514–8036 or 098/ 512–8104* 🛒 *35 rooms* 👌 *Restaurant, air-conditioning, cable TV* 🖃 *AE, DC, MC, V.*

San Andrés & Providencia Essentials

Transportation

BY AIR

Aeropuerto Sesquicentenario in San Andrés is regularly served by Aces, Aerorepública, Avianca, Intercontinental, and Satena.

🔲 **Airlines Aerorepública** ☎ 098/512-7325. **Avianca** ☎ 098/512-3217 or 098/512-3216. **Satena** ☎ 900/331-7100.

🔲 **Airports Aeropuerto Sesquicentenario Gustavo Rojas Pinilla** ☎ 098/512-5389.

BY BOAT & FERRY

There is no passenger boat service from the Colombian mainland or between the islands.

BY BUS

There is a public bus service on San Andrés that circles the island, but the buses are rather old and beat up.

BY CAR

There are no rental cars available on either island.

Contacts & Resources

MONEY MATTERS

You have more options for payment in San Andrés, where banks and even some hotels will exchange foreign currency, cash traveler's checks, and even give cash advances on credit cards. Banco de la República, on Avenida Colón, is open weekdays 9–3. No pesos? That'll pose no problem, as some businesses even accept U.S. currency. Bring pesos to Providencia, where you'll have a hard time cashing traveler's checks or exchanging foreign currency.

🛈 Banks Banco de la República ⊠ Av. Colón, between Costa Rica and Av. Providencia, San Andrés Town.

SAFETY

Providencia and San Andrés have far less crime than most other tourist spots in Colombia. Regardless, keep an eye out for pickpockets.

TELEPHONES

There are fewer coin-operated public phones on the islands than elsewhere in the country. You can make long-distance calls at any hotel, but service can be erratic.

TOUR OPERATORS

Carnaval Tours in Bogotá specializes in package tours to San Andrés and Providencia. These four-night trips include tours to Johnny Cay.

🛈 Tour Agencies Carnaval Tours ⊠ Carrera 5 No. 14–55 ☎ 091/286–1129.

VISITOR INFORMATION

On San Andrés, the Oficina de Turismo has maps and information about the islands.

🛈 Oficina de Turismo ⊠ Aeropuerto Sesquicentenario ☎ 098/516–110 ⊠ Av. Colombia ☎ 098/512–4230.

COLOMBIA ESSENTIALS

Transportation

BY AIR

International airports in Barranquilla, Bogotá, Cartagena, Medellín, and San Andrés regularly serve destinations in the United States and Europe. As a safety precaution, you may be asked to arrive at the airport as much as three hours before your departure time. Flights from Houston to Bogotá take five hours; flights from Miami are less than three hours.

Regular flights connect all major Colombian cities. Since the country is fairly large—almost twice the size of Texas—it's usually more practical to fly to far-flung destinations, especially between the Caribbean coast and Medellín and Bogotá.

🛈 Domestic Airlines Aerorepública ⊠ Calle 10 No. 27–51, Oficina 303 ☎ 091/342–7766. Aires ⊠ Aeropuerto El Dorado ☎ 091/413–8500. Intercontinental de Aviación ⊠ Carrera 10 No. 28–31 ☎ 091/413–5666. Satena ⊠ Carrera 10A No. 27–51, Suite 211 ☎ 091/423–8500.

🛈 International Airlines Alitalia ⊠ Calle 73 No. 9–42, 2nd fl. ☎ 091/317 2805. American ⊠ Carrera 7 No. 26–20 ☎ 091/343–2424. Avianca ⊠ Calle 16 No. 6–66 ☎ 091/410–1011. British Airways ⊠ Calle 98 No. 9–03, Oficina 904 ☎ 900/331–2777. Continental ⊠ Carrera 7 No. 71–52, Torre B, Oficina 1101 ☎ 091/312–2565. Copa ⊠ Calle 100

No. 8A-49 ☎ 091/623-1566. **Delta** ✉ Carrera 13A No. 89-53, Oficina 301 ☎ 091/257-5997, 091/610-2295, or 091/610-9626. **Mexicana** ☎ 094/413-9500 or 094/610-7258.

BY BUS

The U.S. Department of State strongly warns against traveling by bus in Colombia due to the risk of theft, druggings, and political violence. If you must take the bus, be on your guard. Keep all jewelry, cameras, and other valuables out of sight. Avoid the basic *corriente* service; opt for a first-class bus (variously called *pullman, metropolitano,* or *directo*) or a deluxe bus with air-conditioning (called *thermo* or *climatizado*), which run between major cities and the Caribbean coast. These buses have toilets, screen movies, and stop for meals.

BY CAR

Do not drive in Colombia, and avoid excursions out of the cities. When you are traveling from one city to another, it's best to fly, take a tour, or hire a driver as a last resort. If you absolutely have to drive, avoid nighttime journeys because of the risk of ambush by guerrillas or thugs impersonating them. It is best to arrive at all destinations by 4 PM, since most illegal roadblocks are set up just before dark. Steer clear of north–south routes to the Caribbean coast and travel around Popayán and Cali. Keep your car doors locked and windows rolled up at all times.

CAR RENTAL

For safety reasons do not rent a car, but consider hiring a car and driver or using a taxi for excursions.

EMERGENCY ASSISTANCE In an emergency contact the Policia Vial, which has a mobile workshop for fixing breakdowns. If you rent a car, it's a good idea to join the Automóvil Club de Colombia, which will tow your car to a garage if its mechanics can't fix it themselves.

🚩 **Emergency Numbers Automóvil Club de Colombia** ✉ Av. Vitacura 8620, Bogotá ☎ 900/331-2333. **Policia Vial** ✉ Calle 22 No. 132-06, Bogotá ☎ 091/247-1151.

GASOLINE Gasoline comes in two grades: *extra* (95 octane), available only in large cities for 4,600 pesos per U.S. gallon; and *corriente* (84 octane), sometimes called *regular,* which costs 3,600 pesos per U.S. gallon and is available throughout the country. For safety reasons, and to avoid getting fined for running out of gas, consider bringing an extra gallon along with you.

ROAD CONDITIONS Driving in Colombia is a bad idea, and not just because of the crime. Beware the crumbling, narrow, and winding roads. During rainy season they can turn to mud or wash out completely. Always bring a good map, as signs are irregularly posted. Tolls (up to 5,100 pesos) are common.

RULES OF THE ROAD If you plan to drive here, get an international license before you leave home. National driver's licenses are accepted but must be accompanied by an official translation, which is a bureaucratic time waster. Police checkpoints are common, so make sure your documents are always close at hand. Highway speed limits are typically 100 kph (62 mph). There's an automatic fine for running out of gasoline on the road.

Contacts & Resources

BUSINESS HOURS

BANKS Banks are generally open weekdays 9–3. In Bogotá many close an hour earlier. On the last working day of the month banks are only open in the early morning, although in Bogotá they're open until noon. Avoid the lunch hours, as these are the busiest times.

MUSEUMS Museums are generally open roughly from 9 to 1 and 2 to 5. Most are closed on Monday.

SHOPS Shops and stores are open 9 to 5, although a majority close daily for lunch between 12:30 and 2 PM. Most are also closed on Sunday.

CUSTOMS & DUTIES

ON ARRIVAL The duty-free allowance per person is 200 cigarettes, 50 cigars, 250 grams of tobacco, and two bottles of either wine or spirits. You can bring electronic equipment, such as video cameras and laptops, as long as they bear clear signs of use. Remember that such valuables can make you a target for robberies.

ON DEPARTURE If you have purchased any gold, platinum, or emerald articles, you must present a proof of purchase. There is a limit of $10,000 U.S. you can bring in or out of the country. Colonial objects can be taken out of the country without hindrance, but exporting pre-Columbian artifacts is against the law. Expect to pay an airport tax of $43.

ELECTRICITY

The electrical current in Colombia is 120 volts AC, just like in North America. Sockets take two-prong plugs.

EMBASSIES

See Bogotá Essentials for more information.

HEALTH

FOOD & DRINK Don't drink the water, and ask for your beverages *sin hielo* (without ice). The water in Bogotá and Medellín is heavily chlorinated and may be safe enough to drink, but it's best to simply rely on bottled, purified water everywhere. Also avoid eating unpeeled fruit and uncooked vegetables.

SHOTS & MEDICATIONS Colombia's pharmacies are well stocked, although you should bring some basic supplies to combat diarrhea, just in case. Some people experience dizziness and headaches upon arrival in Bogotá because of the thin mountain air. Until you acclimatize you should avoid alcohol and caffeine, get plenty of sleep, and drink a lot of water and juice to keep hydrated. Descend to a lower elevation if you experience vomiting, breathlessness, or disorientation. See a doctor if symptoms persist. Immunizations against the following diseases are recommended at least three months in advance of your trip: hepatitis A and B, tetanus-diphtheria, measles, typhoid, and yellow fever. The decision whether or not to take malaria pills should be made with your doctor.

INTERNET

The Internet is becoming increasingly popular in Colombia. All of the larger cities have Internet cafés, and many hotels provide Internet access to their guests for a small fee.

MAIL & SHIPPING

All international airmail is handled by Avianca, Colombia's largest airline. Airmail post offices are normally next to the airline's offices and are open weekdays 7:30–6, Saturday 8–noon. You can also use Colombia's postal service, although mail will generally take longer to arrive. Their hours of operation are shorter, usually weekdays 9 to 3.

POSTAL RATES   An airmail letter to the United States costs 7,500 pesos; to Europe, 8,000 pesos. Postcards cost 2,000 pesos to anywhere outside of Colombia. Airmail service is relatively reliable, taking between 7 and 14 days.

RECEIVING MAIL   Avianca holds letters for up to 30 days, and you'll need your passport to claim them from the *poste restante* desk.

WRITING TO COLOMBIA   Letters should be sent to Poste Restante, Correo Aéreo Avianca, followed by the city and province name. If you have American Express traveler's checks or credit cards, you can have mail sent to its offices.

MONEY MATTERS

U.S. currency and traveler's checks can be exchanged for a small fee in larger hotels, travel agencies, and money exchange offices. British, Canadian, Australian, and New Zealand currencies or traveler's checks are harder to exchange. You'll get a better rate at banks, although this is not always convenient because of their limited hours. Credit cards give the best exchange rate, so you should use them for cash advances when possible. Either way, keep your exchange receipts to protect yourself against fraud. When departing, you can convert unused pesos into U.S. dollars (up to $100) at the airport's casa de cambio.

ATMS   Automatic teller machines are widely available in the major cities. Most are connected internationally, so that it is often possible to withdraw directly from your account back home.

CREDIT CARDS   You can use credit cards in larger hotels and in the shops and restaurants of major cities, though you should always carry some pesos with you. MasterCard and Visa are more commonly accepted than American Express or Diners Club. Elsewhere credit cards are only occasionally accepted, and you'll be expected to pay with cash.

CURRENCY   Colombia's monetary unit is the peso, which has lost so much value it's no longer divided into centavos. Peso bills are circulated in the following denominations: 2,000, 5,000, 10,000, and 20,000. Peso coins come in denominations of 100, 200, 500 and 1,000. At press time the official exchange rate was about 2,905 pesos to the U.S. dollar, 4,116 pesos to the pound sterling, and 1,720 to the Canadian dollar.

WHAT IT WILL COST   Bogotá, Cartagena, and San Andrés are the most expensive destinations; but, even then, you'll find first-class accommodations for around $50 per night. The least-expensive areas are coastal and mountain villages, where you'll part with $2 for a meal and $5 for lodging.

Sample prices: cup of coffee, 1,000 pesos; bottle of beer, 2,200 pesos; bottle of wine in a restaurant, 35,000 pesos–40,000 pesos; bottle of wine in store, 15,000 pesos–30,000 pesos; 2-km (1-mi) taxi ride, 5,000 pesos; city bus ride, 1,500 pesos; theater or cinema ticket, 5,000 pesos–15,000 pesos.

PASSPORTS & VISAS

Citizens from Australia, Canada, the United States, the United Kingdom, and New Zealand need only a valid passport to enter Colombia for up to 30 days; tourist visas aren't required.

SAFETY

Violence perpetrated by the drug cartels, the various armed groups involved in the civil conflict, and gangs of delinquents are a fact of life in Colombia, but if you're on your guard you'll be less likely to run into problems. Take the usual precautions you would when traveling anywhere—leave jewelry in your hotel safe, conceal your camera, and carry your money in more than one place. Watch your possessions in airports, bus terminals, and other public places where thieves work in teams to distract you and swipe a momentarily unattended bag.

Avoid black-market money changers or any dubious transaction offering a better rate of exchange—counterfeit bills are a very real problem. Have nothing to do with drug dealers, because many of them freelance as police informers. Possession of cocaine or marijuana can lead to a long sentence in an unpleasant Colombian jail. Don't accept gifts of food, drink, cigarettes, or chewing gum from strangers; there have been reports of travelers being drugged and relieved of their valuables.

🚩 U.S. Government Advisories **U.S. Department of State Travel Advisory** 📧 888/407-4747 ⊕ www.travel.state.gov.

TAXES

DEPARTURE TAX Colombia charges a departure tax of $20, or $30 for stays over 30 days. The tax is payable in U.S. dollars or the equivalent in pesos.

SALES TAX Colombia charges a sales tax of 16% on most consumer items. Food, except that purchased in restaurants, is not taxed.

VALUE ADDED TAX (VAT) Throughout Colombia hotels add 16% to your bill. A charge of 2,000 pesos is added for hotel insurance.

TAXIS

Taxis are readily available in Colombia's larger cities. Calling a taxi is safer than hailing one on the street because thieves masquerade as taxi drivers, especially at night in heavily touristed areas.

TELEPHONES

Colombia's country code is 57. When dialing Colombia from abroad, drop the 0 from the in-country area code. Within Colombia, drop the 3-digit city code prefix when making local calls.

LOCAL CALLS Direct dialing is available almost everywhere (exceptions include some isolated places along the Caribbean coast, where you'll do best to visit a Telecom office). Public telephones are common in large cities but are scarce everywhere else; they accept 200- and 500-peso coins. If you don't have access to a phone, there's a Telecom office in nearly every town. For long-distance service at a Telecom office, you tell a clerk the number that you are calling, and enter a phone booth while the number is being dialed. You pay after making the call.

For directory assistance within Colombia, dial 113.

LONG-DISTANCE CALLS When dialing long distance from within Colombia, dial 009 for Telecom, the area code, and then the number. For calls to other Colombian cities, use the blue-and-yellow or red long-distance booths marked *larga distancia*. They only accept 500-peso coins.

INTERNATIONAL CALLS Direct-dial international calls are best made from a Telecom office, where you must leave a deposit of $5–$10 before dialing, or from your hotel, where the rate will be substantially more. The average rate per minute to the United States is about $6 at a Telecom office; from a hotel it's closer to $10.

To make credit card and collect calls through an AT&T operator, dial 01-800/911–0010. For MCI, dial 01-800/916–0001. For Sprint, dial 01-800/913–0010.

TIPPING

Porters at airports and bellhops at hotels are usually given 1,000 pesos for each piece of luggage. In many restaurants, bars, and cafés, a 10% service charge is automatically added to the bill; if not, a 10% tip is expected. Taxi drivers don't expect tips.

VISITOR INFORMATION

🛈 **Colombian Tourism Information Colombian Embassy** ✉ 2118 Leroy Pl. NW, Washington, DC, 20008 ☎ 202/387-8338 📠 202/232-8643 or 202/387-0176.

Ecuador

WORD OF MOUTH

"I recommend the Galapagos Islands. Garden of Eden! Perfect weather, friendly people, and friendly animals, too. Ecotourism galore. There are no hotels 'on' the islands, but rather on private yachts and ships."   —Jimmy

"We saw all the animals we were supposed to see. They were just like everyone said they would be. They were everywhere and right on the trails."
—sandy_b

"There is much you can do in and around Quito. The market town of Otavalo and the Mitad del Mundo monument are north of the capital. South of Quito is the Cotopaxi volcano. All make great day trips. Quito's Old City can occupy a day of your time."   —Jeff_Costa_Rica

Updated by
Jeffrey Van
Fleet

IF YOU THINK ECUADOR IS JUST A JUMPING-OFF POINT for the Galápagos Islands, you're missing a great deal. From its Inca treasures and vibrant cities to the variety of its terrain—coastal, rain forest, and mountains—and its many species of birds and wildlife, Ecuador has much to get excited about.

The equator runs right through Ecuador, which means the night sky brings out the stars in both hemispheres. The mainland has three distinct regions: the Pacific coast, the Andes, which run north to south through the center of the country, and the Amazon basin, in the east. You can indulge in soft or more extreme adventures, from trekking, horseback riding, biking, and white-water rafting to scaling mountains and volcanoes. Interested in hooking a world-record marlin? That's possible, too, along the Pacific coast off Salinas.

If you're like most travelers, you'll begin or end your journey in the highlands with a visit to Quito, which, at 9,206 feet above sea level, is the world's second-highest capital (only La Paz, Bolivia, is higher). Quito is a pleasant mixture of modern and colonial, with stylish galleries and trendy cafés in the New City standing beside the historic Old City's striking colonial architecture. To the west towers the Volcán Pichincha (active since 1998 after 339 years of being dormant), and beyond that swell the Pacific lowlands.

The Pan-American Highway south of Quito is called the "Avenue of the Volcanoes" because it winds past the country's tallest volcanoes on its way to the tranquil and lovely city of Cuenca. Besides its well-preserved colonial architecture, cobblestone streets, and tradition of artisanal crafts, Cuenca also benefits from its location—south of the country's most important Inca treasure, Ingapirca.

West of Cuenca you'll find Guayaquil, Ecuador's major commercial center. An ambitious reconstruction project—the Malecón 2000—transformed the once dilapidated Río Guayas waterfront into an area alive with museums, restaurants, shops, and playgrounds that attracts street musicians and live concerts. The project has spurred a massive urban renewal that has made Guayaquil the trendiest city in Ecuador.

On the opposite side of the country, Ecuador's piece of the Amazon, El Oriente, spans one-third of the country's landmass but has only about 4% of its population. There are endless waterways to explore, wildlife to discover, and little-known indigenous cultures to encounter deep within this section of the country.

Ecuador's traditional must-see attraction remains, of course, the Galápagos, separated from the mainland by 960 km (600 mi) of ocean. Giant turtles, spiny marine iguanas, lava lizards, sea lions, and countless other species inhabit this barren, volcanic archipelago. Tour the islands by boat and swim with sea lions and snorkel in waters rich with marine life, and you may understand why locals accept their isolation—an increasing standard of modernization these days does help—in exchange for life in what's known as Darwin's "living laboratory of evolution."

TOP REASONS TO GO

COMMUNE WITH TURTLES.
Charles Darwin formulated his theory of evolution here in the Galápagos Islands, and a trip to this far-flung Pacific destination will cause you to ponder the mysteries of nature, too. Make no mistake: It's an expensive proposition to get here, but the islands are one of the world's top wildlife-viewing experiences. The age-old concern? Providing a reasonably comfortable tourism infrastructure that keeps the fragile environment in mind. So far, the folks here seem to have struck the right balance.

JOURNEY TO THE CENTER OF THE EARTH.
Ecuador takes its name from the line marking 0 ° latitude, so it's fitting that Mitad del Mundo is the world's most tourist-friendly place to access the Equator, with a large monument and a series of exhibits to indicate the spot. Alas, researchers who marked the line in the original exploration were slightly off, but don't let that spoil your fun straddling two hemispheres at once.

SHOP TILL YOU DROP.
Otavalo, Ecuador's most famous market town, hums with shoppers seeking bargains in alpaca woolens and Panama hats, that incongruously named, but quintessentially Ecuadoran souvenir. The town makes an easy daytrip from Quito, but why not base yourself here instead of the capital, and partake of the Northern Highlands' stunning mountain-lake scenery?

SCALE A VOLCANO.
The nearly perfect cone of world's highest active volcano, Cotopaxi, looms in the Central Highlands at 5,897 m (19,347 ft), and remains one of Ecuador's iconic symbols. Don't even think of scaling the summit without serious mountaineering experience under your harness, but all manner of tour operators will take you on a hike (or even a bike ride) to the volcano's slopes at 15,000 feet and have you back down in time to catch your breath to brag about your accomplishment over dinner.

Political continuity proves elusive here, with Ecuador having cycled through seven presidents in the past decade. President Lucio Gutiérrez was ceremoniously ousted by Ecuador's congress in April 2005 after raucous demonstrations. Constitutional reform, petroleum drilling in the Amazon, and the negotiation of a free-trade agreement with the United States remain contentious issues and the subjects of occasional protests, especially near the government buildings in Quito's Old City. (They usually need not concern visitors except for their traffic-snarling tendencies.)

Tourism in Ecuador took off in the 1980s, when travelers began looking for an alternative to neighboring Peru during its troubled years. They haven't stopped coming here, but Ecuador never seems overrun, and still feels somewhat isolated from the rest of the world. Across the country's

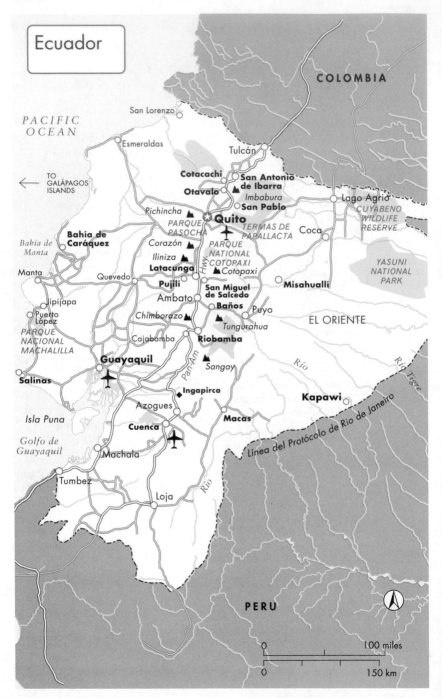

Ecuador

COLOMBIA

PACIFIC
OCEAN

San Lorenzo

Esmeraldas

Tulcán

Cotacachi

← TO
GALÁPAGOS
ISLANDS

**San Antonio
de Ibarra**

Otavalo

Imbabura

San Pablo

Lago Agrio

*CUYABENO
WILDLIFE
RESERVE*

Pichincha

☆ **Quito**

*TERMAS DE
PAPALLACTA*

**Bahía de
Caráquez**

*PARQUE
PASOCHA*

Coca

Corazón

*PARQUE
NATIONAL
COTOPAXI*

*YASUNÍ
NATIONAL
PARK*

*Bahía de
Manta*

Iliniza

Cotopaxi

Latacunga

Manta

Quevedo

Pujilí

**San Miguel
de Salcedo**

Misahuallí

Jipijapa

Ambato

Baños

Puyo

Chimborazo

Tungurahua

EL ORIENTE

Puerto
López

*PARQUE
NACIONAL
MACHALILLA*

Cajabamba

Riobamba

Río

Río Tigre

Guayaquil

✈

Sangay

Salinas

Pan-Am

Isla Puna

Ingapirca

Kapawi

*Golfo de
Guayaquil*

Azogues

Macas

Cuenca

✈

Línea del Protócolo de Río de Janeiro

Machala

Tumbez

Río

Loja

PERU

0   100 miles

0   150 km

majestic, varied landscapes you'll find indigenous peoples who have lived off the earth for generations with comparatively little contact with the West. If you venture into the rural parts of Ecuador, in particular, you'll be pleasantly surprised at how generous a reception you'll receive. With the participation of indigenous communities, ecolodges have opened in the country's national parks, and many owners of haciendas welcome those who want to experience living on a ranch. And urban dwellers, usually the most jaded segment of any country's population, will welcome you with open arms. Ecuador, after all, is that kind of place.

> ## BIRD LOVER'S PARADISE
>
> Ecuador may be hard to resist if you're an animal and bird lover. More than 1,600 bird species, including crested quetzals, toucans, tanagers, macaws, parrots, cocks-of-the-rock, and 35% of the world's variety of hummingbird species have been counted in the country's cloud forests, dry forests, and rain forests (come in October for the best birding). Rare and endangered tapirs, spectacled bears, llamas, and pigmy silk anteaters live in the Andes.

Exploring Ecuador

The Pan-American Highway runs north–south through the heart of the Ecuadoran highlands in the middle of the country, passing near most of the country's important towns and cities—but bypassing Guayaquil by 100 km (60 mi)—and through some of its most spectacular scenery, including a section of what was once part of the Inca Trail. To the east is jungle—the Amazon—and to the west is the Pacific coast. Most attractions are easy to reach by land, although inexpensive flights connecting Quito, Cuenca, and Guayaquil make air travel a convenient option. Flying is essential for visiting the Galápagos Islands and most of El Oriente.

Restaurants & Cuisine

Seafood is a mainstay on the coast, though even Quito menus routinely feature fresh fish and seafood. Lobster is a staple on the Pacific coast, and along the north coast seafood is prepared *encocados* (in coconut milk). If you're a very adventurous carnivore, you may want to try succulent suckling pig and guinea pig (called *cuyes*), often roasted—teeth, paws, and all—over a charcoal fire. *Seco de chivo* is a fully garnished lamb stew. *Humitas* are sweet-corn tamales eaten by tradition-minded Ecuadorans only in the late afternoon, generally with black coffee. Other Andean favorites include *llapingachos* (mashed cheese and potato pancakes) and *locro de queso* (a milk-based soup that contains corn, potatoes, and a garnish of fresh avocado). An Ecuadoran specialty, seviche is fish or seafood marinated in lime juice and seasoned with onion, tomato, chili peppers, and cilantro and often served with *cangil* (popcorn), as are most soups. *Churrasco* is a steak fillet with a fried egg, usually accompanied by rice and salad. Typical coastal cuisine includes the staple *arroz con menestra,* huge portions of white rice served with either black beans or lentils, and *patacones,* green bananas fried in oil, smashed, and refried. Many dishes are served with *ají,* a hot sauce, on the side. In the chill of the Andes, you might be offered a *canelazo,* which is cane-sugar liquor heated and mixed with cinnamon and sometimes with fruit juice.

In the major cities you can enjoy international or traditional Ecuadoran dishes at wonderfully low prices—but watch out, because wines and most liquors are imported and can double the tab. If you're on a tight budget, ask for a set plate meal for $1 to $2. The main meal of the day is *almuerzo,* or lunch, which typically consists of meat or fish accompanied by rice and fried potatoes and a small salad. Time to relax after such a large meal is essential.

Many restaurants in Quito, Otavalo, and Baños offer vegetarian dishes. If you don't see any on the menu, just ask.

⚠ **A word of caution: don't eat from vendors on the street, drink only bottled water, and to be on the safe side, ask for your drinks *sin hielo* (without ice).**

Cafeterias and inexpensive restaurants are often open throughout the day, and may keep limited evening hours. More expensive restaurants open for lunch between noon and 4, then reopen for dinner at 7 and serve until 10 or later. Many restaurants close on Sunday, a quiet day in most communities. While most upscale restaurants do not require a coat and tie, Ecuadorans *do* dress up for dinner. You may feel a bit shabby, or even be spurned by your waiter, if you do not follow suit.

WHAT IT COSTS in U.S. Dollars				
$$$$	**$$$**	**$$**	**$**	**¢**
AT DINNER over $18	$15–$18	$12–$15	$10–$12	under $10

Prices are per person for a main course at dinner.

About the Hotels

Accommodations range from modern luxury hotels to centuries-old haciendas that have been converted to *hosterías* (country inns). Although the highland hotels (such as those in Cuenca) offer exposure to local history and culture, those in El Oriente and the Galápagos Islands provide close contact with nature. Unless you stay in the most expensive hotels, you'll find the rates refreshing; most middle- and lower-range hotels offer remarkable service for the price. Checkout time is 1 PM at most hotels, and breakfast is not usually included in the rate, except in *posadas* or small inns, where either an American or a Continental breakfast is often included.

WHAT IT COSTS in U.S. Dollars				
$$$$	**$$$**	**$$**	**$**	**¢**
FOR 2 PEOPLE over $150	$120–$150	$70–$120	$50–$70	under $50

Prices are for two people in a standard double room in high season, excluding tax.

When to Go

The high season revolves around national celebrations, especially Carnaval, Christmas, and Easter. During these peak periods hotel rooms become scarce and prices jump noticeably. Otherwise, rates remain constant throughout the year.

CLIMATE Ecuador's climate is remarkably varied, influenced by ocean currents, trade winds, and seasonal changes. The rainy season lasts from December to May and occasionally causes landslides and power outages. Weather in Quito is fairly constant, with warm sunny days giving way to very cool evenings. Guayaquil is muggy during the rainy season, but the rest of the year it is much cooler and drier than you might expect for an area so close to the equator. In the Galápagos Islands the weather is generally hot and humid January to April, with frequent afternoon showers. Cooler temperatures prevail the rest of the year, causing *garua,* the fine mist that envelops the islands. The seas are roughest in September and October, but cruise ships ply the waters year-round.

The following are the average daily maximum and minimum temperatures for Quito.

Jan.	69F	20C	May	69F	20C	Sept.	72F	22C
	46	8		47	8		45	7
Feb.	69F	20C	June	70F	21C	Oct.	70F	21C
	47	81		46	8		46	8
Mar.	69F	20C	July	71F	22C	Nov.	70F	21C
	47	8		44	7		46	8
Apr.	69F	20C	Aug.	71F	22C	Dec.	70F	21C
	47	8		44	7		46	8

HOLIDAYS Ecuador observes many legal holidays. Expect little to be open and many people to be traveling to visit family and friends.

New Year's Day; Holy Thursday through Easter (March or April); Labor Day (May 1); Battle of Pichincha (May 24); Simón Bolívar's birthday (July 24); Independence Day (Aug. 10); Guayaquil Independence Day (Oct. 9; Guayaquil only); Columbus Day (Oct. 12); All Souls' Day (Nov. 2); Independence of Cuenca (Nov. 3; Cuenca only); Founding of Quito (Dec. 6; Quito only); Feast of the Immaculate Conception (Dec. 8); Christmas.

FESTIVALS & SEASONAL EVENTS Galápagos Days, celebrating the islands' statehood, is held during the second week of February. It features parades and all-out revelry throughout the islands. During Carnaval Ecuadorans douse one another with buckets of water, water balloons, and squirt guns. Carnaval is most exuberant in the Cotopaxi Province—local dances and fairs are held in Saquisilí, Pujilí, Latacunga, and Salcedo.

Corpus Christi is observed in many mountain towns with fireworks displays. La Fiesta de San Juan enlivens highland towns, especially around Otavalo, on June 24. Otavalo also comes to life during La Fiesta de Yamor, a harvest festival held the first two weeks in September.

In Latacunga, September 24 is the Fiesta de la Mamá Negra, which honors Our Lady of Mercy with lively processions featuring costumed dancers. The Fiestas de Quito, during the first week of December, brings art exhibitions and outdoor concerts. Guayaquil holds similar festivities in early October, Cuenca in early November.

Language

Although English is the lingua franca of tourism and you will find many people in travel-related fields who speak excellent English, it is likely that those in smaller establishments will know only Spanish. The unfamiliar-sounding language you hear in the highlands is the indigenous Quichua, a softer, more grammatically complex relative of Peru's Quechua. Speakers say it more closely resembles the original language spoken by Inca nobility.

QUITO

Built on the ashes of the northern Inca capital following the Spanish conquest in 1533, Ecuador's capital city brims with colonial riches. Although set in the north-central part of the country, it makes the most convenient launching point for travel to anywhere in Ecuador, including the Galápagos Islands and El Oriente—the Amazon.

Scenic Quito is ensconced in a long, narrow valley at the foot of the restless Volcán Pichincha. The elongated city measures 30 km (19 mi) from north to south and 4 km (2 mi) from east to west. Rugged mountains surround the city, providing a striking deep-green backdrop to this sprawling metropolis of 1.2 million people. Quito lies only 24 km (15 mi) south of the equator, but because of its altitude it enjoys a mild climate all year. Quiteños are fond of saying that their city gives you four seasons in one day—a statement supported by the springlike mornings, summery afternoons, autumnal evenings, and wintery nights.

After the weather, Quito's other surprise is its Old City, a maze of colonial mansions, stately churches, candlelighted monasteries, and crowded cobblestone streets. Wandering the Old City's narrow lanes lined with blue-and-white houses is the highlight of any stay in Quito. Nonetheless, after a morning in the crowded Old City, an afternoon in the relatively tranquil New City—with its outdoor cafés, sleek galleries, and chic shops—is a welcome change of pace.

Exploring Quito

A word on terminology: Quiteños don't use the Old City/New City designations coined by the English-speaking tourism industry. The colonial heart of the city is the Centro or Centro Histórico. To the north lies an amorphous sprawl of modern neighborhoods, most notably comfortable Bellavista and La Floresta, and the bustling La Mariscal, whose large concentration of tourists has led locals to dub it "*Gringolandia*."

The city has implemented a new system of address numbering, with small green-and-white signs affixed to every building and using a scheme of directions, denoted *N, S, E,* and *Oe* (for *oeste,* or west) and followed by a number to denote distance from the city center. Locations in the outer reaches of the city express their addresses this way; in the center city, people stubbornly stick with the old sequential numbering system.

The Old City

The oldest part of Quito was founded in 1534 by Spanish explorer Sebastián de Benalcázar on the site of the ancient town of Shyris. The original colonial town was delineated by its four most important monasteries: San Francisco, La Merced, San Agustín, and Santo Domingo. Today informal markets and street vendors still crowd the cobbled routes that run between those ancient monuments, while the interiors of the churches and monasteries are quiet, timeless refuges.

TIMING   Remember that most museums close on Monday. Most churches keep limited opening hours; you'll have a better chance of seeing the interiors during the morning or late afternoon. Once evening approaches, however, it's best to leave the Old City, which has a chronic crime problem. Be careful in crowds, where pickpockets make a good living. Leave your valuables in your hotel, and keep close tabs on your belongings.

WHAT TO SEE   **Casa de Sucre.** The restored Sucre House, once the residence of Field
⑩   Marshal Antonio José de Sucre, displays 19th-century furniture and clothing as well as photographs, historical documents, and letters. The house makes an interesting visit if you're a military-history buff but could probably otherwise be skipped. ⊠ *Venezuela 573, at Sucre, Centro* ☎ *02/251–2860* ☞ *$1* ☼ *Mon.–Thurs. 8:30–4:30, Fri. 8:30–1, weekends 10–4.*

❷ **Catedral.** The city's cathedral is a repository of art from the Quiteña school, which combined themes of Spanish and indigenous cultures: Jesus preaching in the Andes or the Wise Men mounted on llamas in the Nativity scene. The exceptional sculpting abilities of Manuel Chili Caspicara can be appreciated in the 18th-century tableau *The Holy Shroud,* which hangs behind the choir, and in the intricate designs of the rococo Chapel of St. Ann, in the right aisle. The building also houses the volcanic rock-hewn tomb of Quito's liberator, Antonio José de Sucre. A guided tour in Spanish or English is included in your admission price. ⊠ *Plaza de la Independencia, Centro* ☎ *02/257–0371* ☞ *$1.50* ☼ *Weekdays 10–4, Sat. 10–2.*

❽ **Iglesia de la Compañía.** The "company" referred to here is the Society
Fodor'sChoice   of Jesus, the powerful Jesuit order that profoundly influenced religious
★   life in colonial South America. In many cities, Quito included, the local Jesuit church outshone the local cathedral. La Compañía is the most impressive of the capital's 86 churches, with 10 side altars and a high altar plated with gold. The high central nave and the delicacy of its Arab-inspired plasterwork give the church a sumptuous, almost sinfully rich appearance. Indeed, almost half a ton of gold was poured into the ceilings, walls, pulpits, and altars during its 160 years of construction (1605–1765). At the center of the main altar is a statue of the Quiteña saint Mariana de Jesús; her remains are entombed at the foot of the altar. Guided tours in Spanish or English are included in your admission price. At this writing, an ambitious 25-year restoration project is in its final stages; if the scaffolding is still up when you arrive, head on inside anyway. It's worth the visit. ⊠ *García Moreno at Sucre, Centro* ☎ *02/258–1895* ⊕ *www. ficj.org.ec* ☞ *$2* ☼ *Mon.–Sat. 9:30–4:30, Sun. 1:30–4:30.*

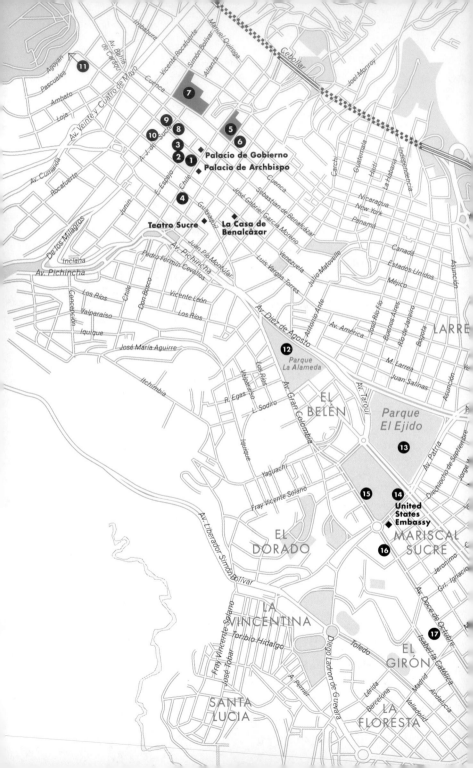

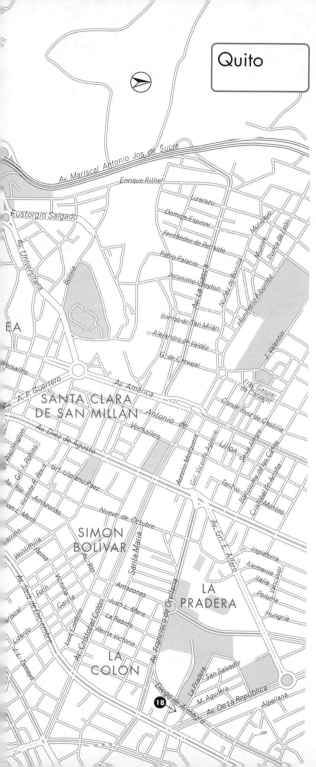

Quito

5 **Iglesia de la Merced.** The Church of Mercy's beautiful, light-filled interior contains a brilliant statue of the Virgin of Mercy above the main altar. It was sculpted to honor Mary, who supposedly intervened to save Quito from a series of 18th-century earthquakes and volcanic eruptions. The church's 153-foot tower houses the city's largest bell. The adjoining convent, shown by appointment only, features a rich collection of colonial paintings and sculptures. ⊠ *Chile at Cuenca, Centro* ☎ *Free* ⊘ *Mon.–Sat. 3–8.*

3 **Iglesia Parroquial del Sagrario.** The Church of the Shrine is noted for its beautiful facade in carefully sculpted stone, large gilded altar, and colorful interior, which includes an 18th-century mural of eight archangels covering the cupola. ⊠ *García Moreno and Espejo, Centro* ☎ *Free* ⊘ *Mon.–Sat. 8–11 and 1–6.*

4 **Iglesia de San Agustín.** In 1809 Ecuador's declaration of independence was signed in the Church of St. Augustine, and many of the soldiers who fought the Spanish crown are buried here. The gilded crucifix on the main altar offers an impressive example of a style of art called the Quiteña school. The altar displays paintings by Miguel de Santiago about the life of St. Augustine, while more depictions of the saint crowd the side aisles. ⊠ *Chile at Guayaquil, Centro* ☎ *02/295–5525* ☎ *$1* ⊘ *Weekdays 9–1:30 and 2:30–5, Sat. 9–1.*

▌ NEED A BREAK? Outdoor cafés are a scarce commodity in the Old City. But **Tianguez,** a small restaurant/artisan shop makes a pleasant place way to while away an afternoon with a gourmet coffee drink—made with fair-trade product—while you write a few cards to the folks back home and watch the passing parade on Plaza San Francisco. Tianguez takes its name from the Quichua word for market (the plaza was a vast outdoor market during Inca times). Tianguez is open daily during the day and Wednesday–Sunday evenings until 11:30 PM, one of the few places to spend an evening in the Old City. ⊠ *Plaza San Francisco, Centro* ☎ *02/223–0609.*

★ **7** **Iglesia de San Francisco.** Established by Franciscan monks in 1536 and said to be the first church built in the Americas, the Church of San Francisco was named for the patron saint of the city. The twin towers, destroyed by an eruption of Volcán Pichincha in 1582, were rebuilt at half their original size in 1893, contributing to the facade's uninspiring appearance. Inside, however, you will find the first New World example of an interior entirely covered with gilded and painted wood. Stationed at the main altar is Bernardo de Legarda's famed 18th-century sculpture *Virgin of the Apocalypse of the Immaculate Conception.* The monastery, at the north end of the complex, now houses a museum of colonial religious art. You can arrange for an English-speaking guide with 24 hours' notice. ⊠ *Plaza San Francisco, Centro* ☎ *02/295–2911* ☎ *$2* ⊘ *Mon.–Sat. 9–1 and 2–6, Sun. 9–noon.*

6 **Museo de Arte Colonial.** The Museum of Colonial Art, housed in a restored 17th-century colonial mansion, includes colonial furniture and 16th- to 18th-century sculpture and paintings by Miguel de Santiago and various other members of the School of Quito. The amusing *Vices and Virtues of the European Countries* is a series of 12 allegorical 18th-century paintings by colonial masters Samaniego and Rodríguez. ✉ *Cuenca 415, at Mejía, Centro* ☎ *02/228–2297* 💵 *$1.50* 🕐 *Tues.–Fri. 10–6, Sat. 10–2.*

⑨ **Museo Casa de María Augusta Urrutia.** In the colonial section of Quito is the Museum of Maria Augusta Urrutia, which a grieving widow kept exactly as it had been when her husband was alive. Don't miss the

> ### DID YOU KNOW?
>
> UNESCO has declared the Old City a World Heritage Site, banning the destruction of colonial buildings and limiting new construction—which is why Quito's colonial sector is one of the best preserved in South America.

collection of fine French porcelain, beautiful silver dinnerware, and Ecuadoran art from colonial times to the present. Especially interesting are the works of Ecuadoran painter Victor Mideros. ✉ *García Moreno 760, at Av. Mariscal Antonio José de Sucre, Centro* ☎*02/258–0107* 💵*$2* 🕐 *Tues.–Sun. 9–6.*

⑪ **El Panecillo.** The opening of the New City's Teleferiqo has eclipsed this rounded hill (the bread roll) and its stunning views as Quito's most popular lookout point, but the presentation here is more serene and less carnival-like. At the top stands the monumental cast-aluminum statue of the city's protectress, the Virgin of Quito—a copy of Bernardo de Legarda's famous 18th-century sculpture *Virgin of the Apocalypse of the Immaculate Conception,* on display in the Iglesia de San Francisco. Muggers target tourists climbing the long flight of stairs, so hire a taxi to take you to the top—it's safe once you get up there—and wait for you as you enjoy the view and then to carry you safely back down (about $8 round-trip).

❶ **Plaza de la Independencia.** Locals always refer to the city's main square, shaded by palms and pines, as the Plaza Grande. The white, neoclassical **Palacio de Gobierno** (Government Palace), built in the 19th century, occupies the west side of the plaza and is not open to the public. The portico gracing the plaza's northern end, once the archbishop's palace, now holds a variety of stores and businesses, including several souvenir and sweets shops and a branch of Quito Turismo, the city's top-notch tourist office.

The New City

WHAT TO SEE **Basílica del Voto Nacional.** Construction of this neo-Gothic church has been going on for more than a century, but it still isn't completed. What's interesting is that the traditional gargoyles found on such structures here are representations of Ecuadoran jungle animals. The structure bridges the Old and New cities, literally, figuratively, and stylistically, but falls into neither. Its 115-meter (380-foot) towers are one of Quito's best-known lookout points. ✉ *Carchi 122, El Belén* ☎ *02/228–9428* 💵 *$2* 🕐 *Daily 9–5.*

⑱ **Fundación Guayasamín and Capilla del Hombre.** Ecuador's most famous contemporary artist, Oswaldo Guayasamín (1919–1999), held court at a workshop and beautiful museum in the residential neighborhood of Bellavista, befriending everyone from the Rockefellers to Fidel Castro during his long career. On display in three buildings here are pre-

Columbian ceramics, colonial sculptures, and paintings from his private collection, as well as a permanent exhibit of his own paintings. Original works by Guayasamín, as well as prints, posters, and T-shirts, are sold in the gift shop. Five blocks up the hill is the starkly modern vision the artist never lived to see completed: a secular chapel of art dedicated to the history of mankind, housing a collection of his cubist works on the theme of social injustice in Latin American history. An expansion of the Capilla is underway at this writing. Plans are to house the entire collection at that site upon its completion in 2008. ⊠ *Fundación: José Bosmediano 543; Capilla: Mariano Calvache at Lorenzo Chávez Bellavista* ☎ *02/244–6455* ⊕ *www.guayasamin.com* ⊠ *$3; $5 for both sites* ⊙ *Fundación: weekdays 9–1:30 and 3–6:30; Capilla: Tues.–Sun. 10–5.*

⑰ Museo Amazónico. The Amazon Museum houses an impressive collection of artifacts and utilitarian items from different Amazonian cultures, including cooking pots, bowls, jewelry, hunting implements, stuffed animals, and shrunken heads. The bookstore, on the first floor, has a superb collection of (mostly Spanish-language) volumes on Latin American culture and indigenous peoples. ⊠ *Av. 12 de Octubre 1430, at Wilson, La Mariscal* ☎ *02/250–6247* ⊠ *$1* ⊙ *Daily 10–4.*

⑮ Museo de Arte Moderno. Exhibits at the Museum of Modern Art include two stories of contemporary Ecuadoran works, such as paintings by Eduardo Kingman and Oswaldo Guayasamín. There's an excellent collection of pre-Columbian and colonial musical instruments. ⊠ *Southern entrance of La Casa de la Cultura, New City* ☎ *02/222–3392* ⊠ *$1* ⊙ *Tues.–Fri. 10–6, Sat. 10–2.*

★ **⑭ Museo del Banco Central.** The Central Bank Museum, Quito's most modern museum, features an astonishing collection of pre-Columbian archaeology and Inca artifacts. Brightly lighted cases containing sculptures from different regions of Ecuador stand next to large-scale dioramas detailing the minutiae of pre-Columbian life. The first floor includes an unparalleled collection of gold artifacts; journey upstairs to an excellent exhibit of colonial paintings and sculptures. Up one flight more you'll find an impressive collection of modern Ecuadoran paintings. ⊠ *Northern entrance of Casa de la Cultura, Av. Patria at 6 de Diciembre, La Mariscal* ☎ *02/222–3259* ⊠ *$2* ⊙ *Weekdays 9–5, weekends 10–4.*

⑯ Museo de Jijón Caamaño. On the third floor of the Universidad Católica, the Jijón Caamaño Museum contains a large collection of colonial art, with paintings and sculptures from some of the masters of the school of Quito. There is also a small collection of Ecuadoran and Peruvian archaeological finds. Well-informed docents lead free English-language tours. ⊠ *Av. 12 de Octubre at Roca, New City* ☎ *02/252–9250* ⊠ *Free* ⊙ *Weekdays 9–4.*

⑫ Parque La Alameda. The elongated triangle of La Alameda Park lies between the Old and New cities, near the **Asamblea Legislativa,** a large, modern building that houses the nation's congress. At the center of the park stands **El Observatorio,** the oldest astronomical observatory in South America, rendered useless by the bright city lights. A monument to Simón Bolívar dominates the southern apex of the triangle.

⑬ Parque El Ejido. One of the larger parks in Quito, El Ejido is popular for its extensive playgrounds and courts for *ecuavoli* (three-person volleyball). Theater groups regularly hold impromptu performances here, and there are often open-air art exhibitions on Saturday. You can also usually find a handicraft market in progress on weekends. But as pleasant as it is by day, Parque El Ejido should be avoided once the sun goes down.

⊙ Teleférigo. Quito's newest and flashiest attraction whisks you from the foothills of Volcán Pichincha to its height (4,050 meters, or 13,300 feet) courtesy of a fleet of six-passenger gondola cars. Ascending the 1,100 meters (3,620 feet) to the top is accomplished in just 10 minutes. (Lines are long but move quickly, and paying a $3 premium over the regular ticket lets you jump the queue.) At the base you'll find a complex containing a shopping center and an amusement park called Vulqano Park. At the top lie several restaurants and shops, as well as a first-aid station with oxygen in case you develop problems with the high altitude. The volcano's summit lies another 215 meters (700 feet) higher, but it's not recommended to set off on your own. The trip is worth it, but you need to retain a healthy respect for the altitude. ⚠ **Don't even consider doing this unless you've already become acclimatized to the altitude by having been in the highlands for a few days continuously.** And bring a jacket: it gets cold up there. ✉ *Av. Occidental and La Gasca, Cruz Loma* ☎ *02/225–0825, 800/835–333 toll-free in Ecuador* ⊕ *www.teleferiqo.com* 🎫 *$4; fast pass $7* ☉ *Teleférigo: Mon. 11–10, Tues.–Thurs. 10–10, Fri.–Sat. 9 AM–10 PM, Sun. 9–8; Vulqano Park: Mon.–Thurs. 11–9, Fri. 11–11, Sat. 10 AM–11 PM, Sun. 10–9.*

OFF THE BEATEN PATH

GUÁPULO – Nestled in a secluded valley below the Guayasamin museums, the village of Guápulo is a preserved pocket of colonial architecture only 2 km (1 mi) from Quito's New City. The settlement, with narrow cobblestone lanes lined with two-story white houses trimmed in blue, grew up around its impressive 17th-century church, the **Santuario de Guápulo.** The Guápulo Sanctuary contains pieces by some of Quito's most exceptional sculptors and painters; the paintings in the central nave are the work of Miguel de Santiago, and the side altar and pulpit—completed in 1716 and considered masterpieces of colonial art—were carved by Juan Bautista Menacho. 🎫 *Free* ☉ *Mon.–Sat. 9–6.*

Early September brings Guápulo's annual festival, which features food, drink, and marching bands. To reach Guápulo, walk downhill via the steep staircase directly behind the Hotel Quito, east of the city at Avenida Gonzáles Suárez 2500. To return, make the uphill trek, or take a taxi for about $2.

Where to Stay & Eat

Quito's better restaurants are found in the New City. Even at the most glittering establishments, formal attire is never a requirement, but you'll feel out of place in shorts, T-shirts, and jeans, except at places such as hole-in-the-wall La Canoa Manabita (the Magic Bean), that consummate foreigners' hangout. Many restaurants close for a break between 3 and 7, and on Sunday some remain shuttered or close early. Some useful phrases are: *a la brasa* (grilled), *al vapor* (steamed), *apanada* (bat-

6

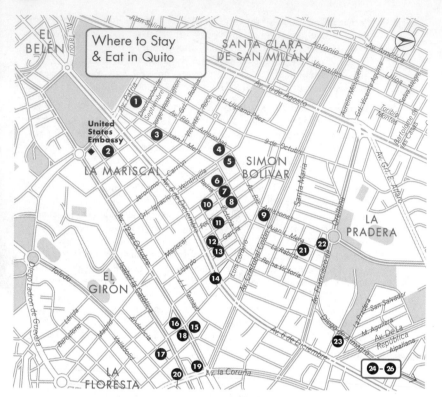

Where to Stay & Eat in Quito

Restaurants ▼

Adam's Rib **10**
La Canoa Manabita **11**
La Choza **15**
The Magic Bean **8**
Pizzeria Le Arcate **6**
La Querencia **24**
Las Redes **4**
Il Risotto **26**
La Ronda **23**
La Terraza del Tártaro **5**
La Viña **17**

Hotels ▼

Apart-Hotel Antinéa **12**
Café Cultura **3**
La Cartuja **2**
Four Points
by Sheraton Quito **25**
Hilton Colón Quito **1**
Hostal La Rábida **21**
Hostal La Villa **20**
Hotel Ambassador **19**

Hotel Río Amazonas
Internacional **9**
Hotel Sebastián **14**
J.W. Marriott **22**
Mansion del Angel **7**
La Posada del Maple **13**
Radisson Royal
Quito Hotel **18**
Swissôtel Quito **16**

ter-fried/breaded), *brosterizada* (deep fried), *encocado* (cooked in coconut oil), *hornado* (roasted), *reventado* (skillet fried), and *seco* (stewed meat).

Accommodations range from modern high-rises, which have a range of services from health clubs to baby-sitting, to family-run inns, where you'll get more personal attention. Almost all the luxury hotels are in the New City, but the best deals are in the pleasant Mariscal neighborhood. Less expensive hotels often lack air-conditioning and heating, although Quito's moderate climate means this usually isn't a worry.

★ **$$–$$$** ✕ **Il Risotto.** Fresh roses adorn candlelighted tables and prints of northern Italy and opera programs from Milan's La Scala decorate the walls, providing a romantic mood at this excellent Italian restaurant. Begin your meal with *insalata del pescatore* (shellfish salad), followed by lobster on a bed of pasta *pomodoro* or a chicken roll with spinach and ricotta cheese. For dessert, order crêpes suzette with Grand Marnier or the tiramisu with decadent chocolate and cognac. ⊠ *Eloy Alfaro, at Portugal, La Pradera* ☎ *02/224–6850* ▭ *DC, MC, V* ☉ *Closed Mon.*

$–$$ ✕ **La Choza.** The mood, music, and menu are strictly Ecuadoran in this restaurant, which opened its doors in 1966. It's across the street from Quito's World Trade Center and draws a large business clientele. There's a garden dining area if you prefer outdoors to indoors. Pastry stuffed with lobster, ricotta, and spinach—baked and topped with fresh mussels, clams, and prawns and covered with a tomato-cream sauce—is one of the mouthwatering specialties here. ⊠ *Av. 12 de Octubre N24–551, La Floresta* ☎ *02/223–0839* ▭ *AE, D, DC, MC, V* ☉ *Weekdays noon–4 and 5–10, weekends noon–4.*

$–$$ ✕ **La Viña.** Everyone raves about this upscale restaurant, which draws its share of businesspeople and government officials. If you order a complete meal from soup to nuts, plus wine, it will cost you around $50, but if you curb your appetite, you could get by for around $15 to $20 total. It is rumored that you could choose from the menu blindfolded and still consistently receive a masterpiece of taste and presentation. ⊠ *Isabel la Católica at Cordero, La Mariscal* ☎ *02/256–6033* ▭ *AE, MC, V* ☉ *Closed Sun., no lunch Sat.*

¢–$ ✕ **La Querencia.** Best known for its superb Ecuadoran dishes—try the
Fodor'sChoice *seco de chivo* (lamb stewed with fruit) or the langostinos flambéed in
★ cognac—this restaurant has excellent views of Quito from its rustic fireside dining room. You can also eat in the serene outdoor garden. Some nights the friendly waiters can be heard singing along to soft Ecuadoran music as they roam the restaurant. ⊠ *Av. Eloy Alfaro 2530, at Catalina Aldaz, La Pradera* ☎ *02/246–1664 or 02/244–6654* ▭ *AE, DC, MC, V* ☉ *Mon.–Sat. 11–11, Sun. 11–5.*

¢–$ ✕ **La Ronda.** During the day businesspeople gather here, in what looks like a Bavarian lodge, for traditional meals. Among the best dishes are *cazuela de mariscos* (a seafood casserole soup) and *pernil* (roast pork) with *llapingachos* (mashed cheese and potato pancakes), peanut sauce, and avocado. During the week dinners are accompanied by guitar music, and folk dancing follows dinner on Sunday. ⊠ *Bello Horizonte 400, at Diego de Almagro, La Mariscal* ☎ *02/254–0459 or 02/254–5176* ▭ *AE, DC, MC, V* ☉ *Weekdays noon–11, weekends 1–10.*

6

¢–$ ✗ **La Terraza del Tártaro.** In the heart of the New City, this longtime favorite is known for its reliable service and delicious, if simply prepared, meats. The penthouse restaurant atop the Edificio Amazonas—look way up to see the sign, or you'll miss the place as you go by—is cheered by a blazing fire at night; you'll enjoy views of the brilliantly lighted city below. ⊠ *Veintimilla 1106, at Av. Amazonas, La Mariscal* ☎ *02/252–7987* ▭ *AE, DC, MC, V* ⊗ *Closed Sun.*

¢ ✗ **La Canoa Manabita.** Virtually unknown to tourists despite its location in the Mariscal district, this no-frills eatery serves exquisite Ecuadoran seafood lunches. Try the *viche* (a hearty fish-and-peanut soup served with corn on the cob and plantain dumplings) or *corbina menestra* (fish served with rice, lentils, and *patacones,* green bananas fried in oil, smashed, and refried). ⊠ *Calama 247, at Diego de Almagro, La Mariscal* ☎ *02/256–3349* ▭ *DC* ⊗ *Closed Mon.*

¢ ✗ **Las Redes.** Fishing nets hanging from the wall clue you in that the specialty here is seafood—cooked Ecuadoran style, naturally. Small and informal, the restaurant opened in 1969 when Avenida Amazonas was the most popular shopping street in Quito. If you haven't tried Corvina yet (a Pacific sea bass), have it here, drowned in shrimp sauce. ⊠ *Av. Amazonas 845, at Veintimilla, La Mariscal* ☎ *02/252–5691* ▭ *AE, DC, MC, V* ⊗ *Closed Sun.*

¢ ✗ **The Magic Bean.** The powerful spell cast by high-quality food draws travelers, expatriates, and locals to "the Bean" to socialize over crisp salads and do business over cappuccinos. Blackberry pancakes and bagels are served for breakfast, while the lunch and dinner menu emphasizes soups, sandwiches, and shish kebab. The atmosphere is casual and the service friendly; if you're solo, you'll feel very comfortable here. The Magic Bean also has live music some nights. ⊠ *Mariscal Foch 681, at Juan León Mera, La Mariscal* ☎ *02/256–6181* ▭ *AE, DC, MC, V.*

¢ ✗ **Adam's Rib.** The owner hails from New York but has brought a bit of Texas to Quito with hefty servings of smoked baby-back ribs and barbecued chicken. The ample Sunday brunches are an institution among the city's expat community. ⊠ *Calama 329, at Reina Victoria, La Mariscal* ☎ *02/256–3196* ▭ *AE, DC, MC, V* ⊗ *Closed Sat.*

¢ ✗ **Pizzeria Le Arcate.** This trendy pizzeria attracts well-heeled patrons who come to choose from 59 types of individual thin-crust pizzas. The emerald-color dining room, with inlaid wood floors, Romanesque columns, and an arched foyer buzzes with conversations in a dozen languages. Crowds reach their peak around 10 PM. The menu also offers a variety of pasta, fish, and meat dishes. ⊠ *Baquedano 358, at Juan León Mera, La Mariscal* ☎ *02/223–7659* ▭ *DC, MC, V* ⊗ *Closed Mon.*

$$$$ ▥ **Swissôtel Quito.** The hotel has a spacious atrium lobby. Outside there's a pool and lovely gardens. Rooms have dark-wood furnishings. The hotel's four restaurants—French, Italian, international, and Japanese—have excellent reputations. The hotel is within walking distance of museums and restaurants. ⊠ *Av. 12 de Octubre 1820, at Cordero, La Floresta* ☎ *02/256–7600, 800/223–6800 in North America* ⊕ *www.swissotel.com* ⇆ *185 rooms, 55 suites, 10 apartments* ♧ *4 restaurants, cable TV, indoor-outdoor pool, gym, hot tub, massage, sauna, spa, steam room, racquetball, squash, tennis, bar, casino, dry cleaning, laun-*

dry service, Internet, Wi-Fi, business services, airport shuttle, no-smoking rooms ✉ *AE, MC, V* ⫯⦾⫯ *BP.*

$$$–$$$$ 🏨 **Hilton Colón Quito.** If you love to shop, you'll also love this sleek hotel across from Parque El Ejido. If the shops on the first floor don't strike your fancy, just outside is one of the best shopping strips in Quito. The marble lobby is a bit sterile, and the rooms are functional but nondescript; those on the lower floors can be noisy. ✉ *Av. Amazonas 110, at Av. Patria, La Mariscal* ☎ *02/256–0666, 800/445–8667 in North America* ⊕ *www.hilton.com* ⤵ *333 rooms, 12 suites* ⚐ *4 restaurants, pool, health club, hot tub, massage, sauna, Turkish bath, bar, casino, shops, business services, travel services, no-smoking rooms* ✉ *AE, DC, MC, V.*

$$$–$$$$ 🏨 **J.W. Marriott.** This futuristic pyramid has floor-to-ceiling windows offering expansive views of Volcán Pichincha or the city from every room. A large, glass-enclosed lobby adds elegance. Within walking distance are a business district and several shopping malls. The business crowd comes here for the executive floors and the largest meeting space in Quito, but it's also a good choice if you're just a tourist. ✉ *Av. Francisco de Orellana 1172, at Av. Amazonas, La Pradera* ☎ *02/297–2000, 800/228–9290 in North America* ⊕ *www.marriott.com* ⤵ *227 rooms, 16 suites* ⚐ *3 restaurants, coffee shop, in-room safes, some in-room hot tubs, minibars, cable TV, in-room data ports, pool, health club, spa, bar, shops, dry cleaning, laundry service, concierge, Internet, business services, meeting rooms, airport shuttle, helipad, no-smoking rooms* ✉ *AE, DC, MC, V.*

$$$ 🏨 **Four Points by Sheraton Quito.** This 13-story hotel is right across from a large shopping center and two blocks away from the exposition center. Although it attracts mostly business travelers, it offers enough to do if you just want to relax. The City Pub, in the lobby, has live music. ✉ *Av. Naciones Unidas y Av. Republica de El Salvador, La Carolina* ☎ *02/297–0002* ⊕ *www.starwoodhotels.com* ⤵ *100 rooms, 40 suites* ⚐ *2 restaurants, café, in-room data ports, minibars, pool, health club, sauna, spa, bar, nightclub, shops, baby-sitting, dry cleaning, laundry service, business services, meeting rooms, airport shuttle, travel services, free parking, no-smoking rooms* ✉ *AE, DC, MC, V.*

★ $$–$$$ 🏨 **Radisson Royal Quito Hotel.** Part of the World Trade Center, this hotel is ideally located in the center of the city's financial district. The generously proportioned rooms exude understated elegance. Dine at the popular sushi bar, lively café, or grill. Live bands perform nightly in the Trader's Bar. ✉ *Av. 12 de Octubre at Luis Cordero 444, La Floresta* ☎ *02/223–3333, 800/333–3333 in North America* ⊕ *www.radisson.com/quitoec* ⤵ *98 rooms, 14 suites* ⚐ *3 restaurants, in-room safes, minibars, cable TV, health club, sauna, bar, shops, dry cleaning, laundry service, shops, Internet, Wi-Fi, business services, meeting rooms, airport shuttle, no-smoking rooms* ✉ *AE, DC, MC, V.*

$$ 🏨 **Mansión del Angel.** One of Quito's most luxurious accommodations, **FodorśChoice** this hotel is in a lavish mansion dating from the 1930s. A chandelier-★ lighted stairway leads you upstairs to beautifully decorated rooms with antique four-poster beds. A full American breakfast is included, served in the elegant parlor or on the tile terrace. Museums, restaurants, and shops are steps away. ✉ *Wilson E5-29, at Juan León Mera, La Mariscal* ☎ *02/255–7721, 800/327–3573 in North America* ⊕ *www.*

mansiondelangel.com.ec ⟲ *10 rooms* ☖ *cable TV, laundry service; no a/c* ☰ *MC, V* ⦿ *BP.*

$$
Fodor'sChoice
★
🏨 **Café Cultura.** The brilliant bougainvillea over the front gate lets you know this colonial-style hotel—formerly the Center for Arts and Culture of the French Embassy—is something special. The wood-beamed lobby glows when there's a fire in the stone-trim hearth. A mezzanine above leads to the inn's comfortable guest rooms (some warmed by fireplaces). A popular café off the lobby serves breakfast and lunch. ✉ *Robles at Reina Victoria, La Mariscal* ☎ *02/250–4078 or 02/256–4956* ⊕ *www.cafecultura.com* ⟲ *18 rooms, 8 suites* ☖ *Café, massage, shop, laundry service, dry cleaning, Internet, business services, airport shuttle; no a/c* ☰ *AE, DC, MC, V.*

$
🏨 **Hostal La Rábida.** This beautifully restored colonial house is decorated with old mahogany furniture and antiques. All rooms have large private baths. Italian and international cuisine is on the dinner menu; after dinner you can relax and sip a glass of wine in front of the fireplace. Museums, shops, and restaurants are all within walking distance. ✉ *La Rábida 227, at Santa María, La Mariscal* ☎ *02/222–1720* ⟲ *11 rooms* ☖ *Dining room, in-room safes, cable TV, bar, laundry service, parking; no a/c* ☰ *AE, DC, MC, V.*

$
🏨 **Hotel Río Amazonas Internacional.** You might feel as if you're in the Amazon when you enjoy a cocktail at the Terraza Tropical bar, where wicker tables and chairs are set amid lush greenery. The rest of this gleaming glass high-rise, within walking distance of most of the city's museums, is more austere. The restaurant serves up tasty local dishes with a friendly flourish. ✉ *Av. Luis Cordero 1342, at Av. Amazonas, La Mariscal* ☎ *02/255–6666* ⊕ *www.hotelrioamazonas.com* ⟲ *74 rooms, 1 suite* ☖ *Restaurant, café, minibars, cable TV, bar, shop, laundry service, business services, meeting room, airport shuttle, travel services, parking* ☰ *AE, DC, MC, V.*

$
🏨 **Hotel Sebastián.** This small four-star hotel is in the center of the restaurant and bank district. The large rooms are cheerfully decorated, and the restaurant, Café Mistral, is open daily from 6 AM to 10:30 PM, serving international dishes and specials from Cuenca. The Café and Bar de Antaño is open from 3 to 11 daily for coffee, snacks, and cocktails. ✉ *Diego de Almagro 822, at Cordero, La Mariscal* ☎ *02/222–2400 or 02/222–2300* ⊕ *www.hotelsebastian.com* ⟲ *49 rooms, 7 suites* ☖ *Restaurant, cable TV, bar, laundry service, Internet, business services, meeting rooms, parking* ☰ *AE, DC, MC, V.*

$
🏨 **San Jorge Eco-Lodge.** A onetime 18th century Jesuit monastery turned farm in the Andes foothills has now been converted into one of those so-close-but-oh-so-far lodgings. The folks here never tire of reminding you that you're closer to the airport than you would be if you stayed in the New City, but reservations are essential, given the rough road to get here. Cozy rooms are equipped with stone floors, throw rugs and fireplaces. The whole site sits in the midst of an Audubon-certified reserve, with plenty of bird-watching opportunity. ✉ *Km. 4, Quito-Minda Rd.* ☎ *02/249–3123 or 877/565–2596 in North America* ⊕ *www.ecolodgesanjorge.com* ⟲ *24 rooms* ☖ *Dining room, pool, sauna, horseback riding, travel services; no-smoking rooms* ☰ *AE, DC, MC, V.*

¢–$ ☒ **Apart-Hotel Antínéa.** Once you check into this charming inn you may never want to check out. Two homes on a shady side street offer a variety of simple but elegant rooms, half of which are spacious apartments with well-stocked kitchenettes. Some open onto flower-filled courtyards, others have private balconies. For a special treat, ask for the room with a fireplace. ☒ *Juan Rodríguez 175, at Diego de Almagro, La Mariscal* ☎ *02/250–6839 or 02/250–6838* ⊕ *www.hotelantinea.com* ⟆ *7 rooms, 8 suites* ⚘ *Restaurant, kitchenettes, minibars, cable TV, gym, library, laundry service, meeting room, parking* ▤ *AE, DC, MC, V.*

¢ ☒ **Hostal La Villa.** This small bed-and-breakfast, which occupies a darling half-timber Bavarian-style house, has a comfortable, casual style, and it's a convenient base for exploring the city. Internet and fax services are free. ☒ *Toledo 1455, at Av. Coruña, La Floresta* ☎ *02/222–2755* ✉ *lavilla@interactive.net.ec* ⟆ *17 rooms* ⚘ *Restaurant, café, cable TV, bar, laundry service, Internet, business services, travel services* ▤ *AE, DC, MC, V.*

¢ ☒ **Hotel Ambassador.** After a day of exploring the city, relax in front of the fireplace in one of this older hotel's sitting rooms. A couple of the older rooms are a bit threadbare, but most are quite nice considering the very reasonable rates, making it a good budget option. ☒ *Av. 9 de Octubre at Av. Colón, La Mariscal* ☎ *02/256–1777* ⟆ *59 rooms* ⚘ *Restaurant, cable TV, bar, meeting room, parking no a/c* ▤ *AE, DC, MC, V.*

¢ ☒ **La Cartuja.** The present owner, Edurne Ayestarán, came to Ecuador from Spain on holiday and decided to turn this lovely colonial building—once the embassy of Great Britain—into a small hotel. Along with her partner, Inígo Sagarna, she also has a jungle lodge (the Jaguar Lodge) on the Napo River. The hotel's front desk is open 24 hours; the library is stocked with books and magazines. Spanish and international meals are served in the restaurant. The hotel is near Parque El Ejido. ☒ *Leonidas Plaza 170, at 18 de Septiembre, La Mariscal* ☎ *02/252–3577* ⊕ *www.hotelacartuja.com* ⟆ *12 rooms* ⚘ *Restaurant, bar, library, Internet, airport shuttle, travel services* ▤ *AE, MC, V.*

¢ ☒ **La Posada del Maple.** The friendly mood here (certainly not the small, plain rooms) lures everyone from seasoned travelers to Peace Corps volunteers. It's a friendly, inexpensive B&B, and the price includes a hearty American-style breakfast and all-day coffee, tea, and hot chocolate. ☒ *Juan Rodríguez 148, at Av. 6 de Diciembre, La Mariscal* ☎ *02/254–4507* ⊕ *www.posadadelmaple.com* ⟆ *22 rooms, 12 with bath* ⚘ *Dining room, Internet* ▤ *MC, V.*

Nightlife & the Arts

Nightlife

The number of bars and dance clubs in Quito has multiplied in the past few years, so now there are plenty of *discotecas* and *salsatecas*. At the *peñas* (clubs where Andean musicians perform), you can listen to traditional Ecuadoran music and drink with locals until the wee hours. Bars usually open in the late afternoon, while dance clubs don't get going until 10 PM. By law, everything shuts down by 2 AM. Cover charges can be as much as $10.

Evening crowds throng the streets of La Mariscal, where you'll find the greatest selection of nightlife, but the high tourist quotient attracts a number of thieves, too. Watch your things, your drinks, and yourself, and take a taxi, even if you're only going a few blocks. Bars and restaurants are happy to call one to take you back to your hotel.

BARS & CAFÉS The lively **Bangalo Salon de Te** (✉ Mariscal Foch 451, between Diego de Almagro and 6 de Diciembre ☎ 02/250–1332) features a blazing fireplace and nonstop Brazilian music. At **Ghoz** (✉ La Niña 425, at Reina Victoria), you can munch on Swiss food, play a game of pool, and listen to high-decibel rock and salsa. **Papillón** (✉ Yanez Pinzón at Av. Colón ☎ 02/252–9411) blasts pop and techno, which draws a young crowd.

El Pobre Diablo (✉ Santa María 338, at Juan León Mera ☎ 02/222–4982) is a gathering place for artists and intellectuals. You'll find a young crowd at **Tijuana** (✉ Reina Victoria and Santa María ☎ 02/223–8324). **Varadero** (✉ Reina Victoria at La Pinta) has live music on Wednesday, Friday, and Saturday. It fills up with locals early on weekends.

DANCE CLUBS Enjoy Latin rhythms at **Cali Salsateca** (✉ Diego de Almagro 1268, at Av. Orellana), a popular weekend spot that admits only couples. Locals head to **Salsateca Seseribó** (✉ Veintimilla 325, at Av. 12 de Octubre ☎ 02/256–3578) to dance to *cumbia,* salsa, and merengue, weekends only; stop by for the free salsa lesson each Saturday at 8:30 PM.

PEÑAS If you're looking for a peña in the Old City, one of the best is **La Taberna Quito Colonial** (✉ Marabí at Vargas ☎ 02/228–3102). One of the New City's most established peñas is the **Nuncanchi Peña** (✉ Av. Universitaria 496, at Armero ☎ 02/254–0967). **Peña Pacha Camac** (✉ Jorge Washington 530, at Juan León Mera ☎ 02/223–4855) is a small place in La Mariscal neighborhood.

The Arts

Quito's arts scene has grown significantly in the last few years. Check the local papers *El Comercio* and *Hoy* to see what's going on. Listings are in Spanish but easily deciphered. The free monthly English-language magazine *This Is Ecuador,* available in many hotels and restaurants, is good for a look at what's going on around town (and around the country).

CONCERTS Ecuador's National Symphony Orchestra—as well as many smaller ensembles—frequently performs at the **Casa de la Música** (✉ Valderrama at Av. Mariana de Jesús ☎ 02/226–7093). The **Teatro Nacional Sucre** has an active schedule of concerts and dance and opera performances. Tickets run $5–$50. (✉ Manabí between Guayaquil and Flores ☎ 02/257–2823).

DANCE Jacchigua, the national folk ballet, performs Wednesday at 7:30 PM in the **Casa de la Cultura** (✉ Av. América at Av. Mariana de Jesús ☎ 02/295–2025). Tickets cost $25.

FILM Cinemas in Quito usually screen Hollywood films a few weeks after their U.S. release in English with Spanish subtitles. **Casa de la Cultura** (✉ Av. Patria at Av. 12 de Octubre ☎ 02/256–5808) is a good bet for an occasional art film in Spanish.

LECTURES For a fun, intellectual twist on a night out, **South American Explorers**
Fodor'sChoice (✉ Jorge Washington 311 ☎ 02/222–5228) holds informal lectures
★ each Thursday at 6 PM. Topics range from ways to cope with altitude
to planning a trip to the Galápagos. Admission is a nominal $2 for non-
members, with plenty of popcorn included. They're a great way to meet
fellow travelers. The club also holds a lively quiz night (with prizes) the
second Monday of each month at the Reina Victoria Pub (✉ Reina Victoria at Roca). Proceedings get under way at 8:30.

Sports & the Outdoors

Soccer

Matches are held from March through December at noon on Sunday
in the **Estadio Olímpico Atahualpa** (✉ Av. 6 de Diciembre and Av. Naciones Unidas ☎ 02/224–7510). Tickets, which cost $3–$10, can be purchased at the stadium.

Shopping

Quito's best shopping area is the New City's La Mariscal district. Bounded
by Avenida Amazonas, Avenida 6 de Diciembre, Avenida Patria, and
Avenida Cristóbal Colón, the neighborhood is a tightly packed collection of shops and boutiques. Items are reasonably priced, though they
don't rival the outlying markets for bargains and color. The quality,
however, is often superior. Many stores throughout Quito are closed Saturday afternoon and Sunday, but most shopping malls are open all week.

Handicrafts

The most extensive collection of
handicraft shops is in Quito's modern shopping mall, **El Jardín** (✉ Av.
Amazonas and Av. La República
☎ 02/246–6570). **Casa Indo Andina**
(✉ Roca 606, at Juan León Mera)
sells top-of-the-line items, including
original and reproduction pre-
Columbian ceramics and colonial
religious art, as well as bronze-

> **TIP**
>
> Look for brightly painted balsa-
> wood birds made in El Oriente and
> cedar carvings from highland vil-
> lages. Wool and cotton sweaters,
> shawls, and tapestries vary in qual-
> ity and price, as do leather goods.

plated frames and silver jewelry. **El Centro Artesanal** (✉ Juan León Mera
804 ☎ 02/254–8235) specializes in hand-knit sweaters and other items.

Galería Latina (✉ Juan León Mera 833 ☎ 02/222–1098) offers an enormous selection of sterling silver jewelry, ceramic figures, alpaca clothing, and antiques. In addition to regional crafts, **La Bodega** (✉ Juan León
Mera 614 ☎ 02/222–5844) has an extensive collection of sweaters in
Fodor'sChoice wool and cotton. **Folklore Olga Fisch** (✉ Av. Colón 260 ☎ 02/254–1315
★ ⊕ www.olgafisch.com) is one of Quito's more expensive, and curious,
shopping experiences. The shop is in the colonial home of the late Olga
Fisch (1901–1990), who worked with craftspeople to turn folk art into
modern works of art. The store specializes in handwoven rugs, tapestries, clothing, and pottery inspired by indigenous motifs. While you're
here, visit the splendid museum upstairs and have lunch or afternoon

tea in the small, informal restaurant in the garden or dinner in the intimate indoor restaurant.

Homero Ortega & Hijos (✉ Isabel La Católica N24100, at Madrid ☎ 02/252–6715 ⊕ www.homeroortega.com), Cuenca's famous Panama hatmaker, has a store here in Quito.

Markets

You can lose yourself among the stalls at the **Mercado de Santa Clara,** in the New City at the corner of Calle Versalles and Calle Marchena. At this traditional market you'll find fruits and vegetables piled in geometrical patterns, bundles of dried and fresh herbs, barrels of grains, and huge bunches of freshly cut flowers. You can listen to a musician play soulful tunes on the accordion or light a candle to the Virgin Mary at the shrine tucked between the vendors' stalls.

OFF THE BEATEN PATH

ARASHÁ RAIN FOREST RESORT & SPA – Drive two hours along the main highway—an excellent road you take from the Middle of the World monument, in Quito, to the coast—northwest of Quito to this all-inclusive hotel (four-day/three-night packages start at $476) with colorfully painted two-bedroom thatch-roof cottages scattered over the hillsides. On the cusp of a cloud forest, Arasha is 598 meters (1,962 feet) above sea level, with an average temperature of 76°F, and it takes on an ethereal appearance in the early morning as clouds cut the visibility to zero. You can walk along trails and rivers and see waterfalls, wildlife, giant trees, and orchids; or swim in a free-form pool or in a lagoon. More than 300 species of birds have been counted here. The spa has aromatherapy and moisturizer, facial, and stress-relief treatments. There's also a chocolate factory on-site, so you can see how chocolate is made from cocoa beans (kids love this). Rates include all meals, some drinks (not imported liquor), entertainment (including karaoke and movies), and tours. Rafting, kayaking, and spa treatments are extra. ✉ *Pedro Vicente Maldonado* ☎ *02/276–5348 or 02/390–0007* ⊕ *www.arasharesort. com* ⊃ *27 bungalows* △ *2 restaurants, pool, hot tub, spa, theater* ⊟ *AE, DC, MC, V.*

Quito Essentials

Transportation

BY AIR

American Airlines and LanEcuador have daily flights between Miami and Quito. Continental flies nonstop between Houston and Quito and between Newark and Quito with a stop in Bogotá, Colombia. If you're coming from the United Kingdom, you can connect in Miami with American or LanEcuador, in Amsterdam with KLM, or in Madrid with Iberia. From Australia or New Zealand, connect in Los Angeles to flights on American or Continental.

Tame, Ícaro, and AeroGal are Ecuador's major domestic carriers; all offer flights several times daily to Guayaquil and Cuenca. Tame also flies between Quito and San Cristóbal and Baltra in the Galápagos Islands and to the mainland towns of Coca, Esmeraldas, Lago Agrio, Loja, Macas,

Machala, Manta, Portoviejo, and Tulcán. AeroGal also flies between Quito and Baltra and San Cristóbal.

🛪 **Airlines & Contacts AeroGal** ☎ 02/225-7202. **Aeropostal** ☎ 02/226-8936. **American** ☎ 02/226-0900. **Avianca** ☎ 02/255-6715. **Continental** ☎ 02/255-7170. **Iberia** ☎ 02/255-8033. **Ícaro** ☎ 02/245-0928. **KLM** ☎ 02/255-7170. **LanEcuador** ☎ 02/299-2300. **Santa Bárbara Airlines** ☎ 02/225-4194. **TACA Peru** ☎ 800/008-222 toll free in Ecuador. **Tame** ☎ 02/231-1921.

AIRPORTS & TRANSFERS Quito's small Aeropuerto Internacional Mariscal Sucre (UIO) is 8 km (5 mi) north of the city center.

Stop at the Cooperativa de Taxis Aeropuerto booth beyond the customs barrier to arrange taxi transport. Prices are a fixed $5 for a ride to the New City.

The new Aeropuerto Internacional de Quito, to be constructed near Puembo, about an hour east of the capital, is on the drawing board at this writing. The $75 million facility is scheduled to open in 2009.

🛪 **Airport Information Aeropuerto Mariscal Sucre** ☎ 02/294-4900.

🛪 **Transfers Cooperativa de Taxis Aeopuerto** ☎ 02/330-2200.

6

BY BUS

Buses for most mainland destinations leave from Quito's sprawling Terminal Terrestre Cumandá, south of the Old City.

🛪 **Bus Terminal Terminal Terrestre Cumandá** ✉ Av. Maldonado 3077 ☎ 02/257-0429.

WITHIN QUITO Quito's buses are inexpensive (15¢) and run frequently during the day. Heavy crowds during the morning and afternoon rushes, however, make them less appealing options. Clearly marked EJECUTIVO buses cost 20¢ and guarantee you a seat, making them a more comfortable option. Much faster is the Trole (pronounced tro-lay), an electric trolley-bus system running through the center of town along Avenida 10 de Agosto in the New City and Calle Guayaquil in the Old City. A similar nonelectric system, the Ecovía, generally plies Avenida 6 de Diciembre between the New and Old cities. Fares for both are 25¢.

BY CAR

The Pan-American Highway runs right through Quito, which makes driving to most places in the country fairly easy. Short trips are possible to some of the nearby tourist areas but should be carefully planned because road conditions are not always good once you leave the main highway. Do not drive into the Amazon or anywhere near the Colombian border. A better idea is to rent a car and driver.

CAR RENTAL Three of the major international rental agencies—Avis, Budget, and Hertz—have offices in downtown Quito and at Aeropuerto Mariscal Sucre. You can also rent a car from Localiza, an Ecuadoran company, at the airport.

🛪 **Major Agencies Avis** ✉ Av. Amazonas 3-22 ☎ 02/255-0243, 02/244-0270 at the airport. **Budget** ✉ Av. Amazonas 1408, at Av. Colón ☎ 02/254-5761 or 02/245-9052. **Hertz** ✉ Av. Amazonas at Río Arajuno ☎ 02/225-4257 **Localiza** ✉ Aeropuerto Mariscal Sucre ☎ 800/562-254 ⊕ www.localiza.com.ec.

BY TAXI

Taxis are inexpensive and an ideal way to get around. A ride between the New and Old cities runs about $2. Most drivers use their meters, which begin tallying the fare at 37¢. Agree on a price beforehand if the driver says the meter isn't working. The fare to most destinations in the city should be $5 or less. Expect a $2 surcharge after dark. Tele Taxi and City-Taxi are reliable companies that will send a driver to pick you up. They will also arrange city tours for $10 per hour.

🚖 Taxi Companies City-Taxi ☎ 02/263-3333. **Tele Taxi** ☎ 02/241-1119 or 02/241-1120.

BY TRAIN

Except for one small section of track between Riobamba and Alausí, storms and mudslides have put train travel to and from Quito out of business for good. Fortunately, the section still intact includes the exhilarating "Devil's Nose," operated by Metropolitan Touring as a combination bus and train trip starting at Riobamba. The train—which usually runs Tuesday, Thursday, and Saturday—has a coach and an open-sided car that's often crowded with farmers, their crops, and small farm animals.

🚖 Train Information Metropolitan Touring ✉ Av. República de El Salvador 970 ☎ 02/246-4780, 800/527-2500 in the U.S. ⊕ www.metropolitan-touring.com.

Contacts & Resources

EMBASSIES

The United States embassy, near Parque El Ejido, is open to the public, weekdays 8–12:30 and 1:30–5. The Canadian embassy is open weekdays 9–noon and answers the phones Monday–Thursday until 4 and Friday until 1. The British embassy is open Monday–Thursday 8–noon and 2–3:30 and Friday 8–11:30. Neither Australia nor New Zealand has an embassy in Ecuador. The Canadian embassy handles consular emergencies for citizens of those countries, but passport matters must be referred to respective embassies in Santiago, Chile.

🚖 Embassies Australia ✉ Isidora Goyenechea 3621, at Paul Rivet, Las Condes Santiago, Chile ☎ 56/2/550-3500. **Canada** ✉ Av. 6 de Diciembre 2816, at Paul Rivet, La Carolina Quito ☎ 02/223-2114 or 02/250-2162. **New Zealand** ✉ El Golf 99, Oficina 703, Las Condes, Santiago, Chile ☎ 56/2/290-9800. **United Kingdom** ✉ Av. Naciones Unidas, at República de El Salvador, 14th floor, La Carolina Quito ☎ 02/256297-0800. **United States** ✉ Av. 12 de Octubre and Av. Patria, La Mariscal, Quito ☎ 02/256-2890.

EMERGENCIES

Quito uses a 911 telephone number to handle most emergencies. The private Hospital Metropolitano, northwest of the city, has many English speakers on staff and is accustomed to dealing with foreigners. The Naciones Unidas branch of the ubiquitous Pharmacys chain is open 24 hours.

🚖 Emergency Numbers General emergencies ☎ 911. **Ambulance** ☎ 131. **Fire** ☎ 102. **Police** ☎ 101.

🚖 Hospitals Hospital Metropolitano ✉ Av. Mariana de Jesús at Av. Occidental ☎ 02/226-9030 ⊕ www.hospitalmetropolitano.org.

🚖 Pharmacies Pharmacys ✉ Av. Américas and Av. Naciones Unidas ☎ 02/226-6547.

TOUR OPERATORS

A great twist on the guided city tour are the guided walks conducted in Spanish, English, French, and Italian by the police officers of Quito Turismo, Tuesday–Sunday at 10, 11, 2, and 7. The cost is $10 per person, $12 for the evening walk. Reservations are required for the evening excursion and recommended for the others.

There are many reliable tour companies in Quito. English-language tours cost $12–$25 per person and cover Quito's principal sights in less than four hours. Gray Line operates a city tour as well as the standard selection of excursions to Mitad del Mundo, Otavalo, and Cotopaxi National Park. Metropolitan Touring, around for nearly a half century, offers quality tours on the mainland and has one of the largest ships in the Galápagos Islands. Kleintours runs highly regarded Galápagos excursions, too. Enchanted Excursions, often referred to by its former name, Angermeyer's, organizes tours of Quito as well as biking, hiking, horseback riding, and canoeing trips. TOPPSA is a last-minute Internet booking service that represents a number of hotels and that also has a separate company offering protective services to business travelers. Turisvisión specializes in made-to-order tours of the country.

6

🚺 **Tour Agencies Enchanted Excursions** ✉ Av. Foch 769, at Av. Amazonas ☎ 02/256–9960, 800/327-3573 in the U.S. ⊕ www.enchantedexcursions.com.ec. **Gray Line** ☎ 800/472-964 toll free in Ecuador ⊕ www.graylineecuador.com. **Kleintours** ✉ Av. Eloy Alfaro N34-151, at Catalina Áldaz ☎ 02/226-7000, 888/505-5346 in North America ⊕ www.kleintours.com. **Metropolitan Touring** ✉ Av. República de El Salvador 970 ☎ 02/246-4780, 800/527-2500 in the U.S. ⊕ www.metropolitan-touring.com. **TOPPSA** ✉ General Roca N33-73, at Bosmediano ☎ 02/226-0651, 866/809-3145 toll free from North America ⊕ www.toppsa.com. **Turisvisión** ✉ Últimas Noticias N37-97, at Espectador ☎ 02/224-6756, 800/327-3573 toll free in North America ⊕ www.turisvision.com.

VISITOR INFORMATION

Ecuador's ministry of tourism operates a network of iTur information offices around the country. Quito's branch, open weekdays 9–5, is in an out-of-the-way location where it dispenses a few maps and brochures, but little else. A better bet is the phenomenal Quito Turismo, a joint venture between the city and its police force, open weekdays 9:30–6, Saturday 10–6, and Sunday 10–4. (The branch at the Archbishop's Palace, on Plaza Grande, conducts guided walks of the Old City Tuesday–Sunday.) The nonprofit (and equally phenomenal) South American Explorers has an active clubhouse in Quito, as well as in Lima and Cusco, Peru, and in Buenos Aires, Argentina. It is open Monday–Wednesday and Friday 9:30–5, Thursday 9:30–8, and Saturday 9:30–1. Annual membership is $50 and gets you access to the organization's information board and travel library. It can also put members in touch with reliable guides for a variety of activities. The Universidad de Especialidades Turísticas, a postsecondary institution teaching all things tourism related, operates a good tourist-information office staffed by enthusiastic budding guides and tour operators. It is open weekdays 9–5 and Saturday 9–3.

🚺 **Tourist Information iTur** ✉ Av. Eloy Alfaro 1214, at Carlos Tobar ☎ 02/222-4971. **Quito Turismo** ✉ Mejía N1201 at García Moreno ☎ 02/257-0786 ✉ Palacio Arzobispal, Chile between García Moreno and Venezuela ☎ 02/258-6591 ✉ Reina Victoria and Cordero ☎ 02/255-1566 ✉ Av. Patria and 6 de Diciembre ☎ 02/222-1116 ✉ Aeropuerto Mariscal Sucre ☎ 02/330-0163 ⊕ www.quito.com.ec. **South American Explorers** ✉ Jorge Washington 311, at Leonidas Plaza ☎ 02/222-5228 ⊕ www.saexplorers.org. **Universidad de Especialidades Turísticas** ✉ Av. Patria at Av. 9 de Octubre ☎ 02/254-4100.

THE NORTHERN HIGHLANDS

When the Spanish conquered the territory north of Quito—much of it centers on Imbabura Province, named after the 4,630-meter (15,190-foot) volcano of the same name—they introduced sheep to the region. Over time the mountain-dwelling Otavaleños became expert wool weavers and dyers; even today you may find craftspeople who painstakingly collect and prepare their own natural dyes despite the increasing popularity of modern synthetic colors. Traditional dyeing methods may be on the decline, but Otavaleños themselves proudly retain many of their old customs, including their manner of dress. The women wear embroidered white blouses, blue wraparound skirts, black or blue head cloths, and row upon row of beaded gold necklaces. Though many younger men now sport modern attire, in the villages some still wear the traditional calf-length white pants, white shirt, and dark blue poncho, with a beige felt hat over long braided hair.

Many small weaving villages dot the green-and-gold valleys of Imbabura, and every weekend artisans make the trek to the colorful market in Otavalo, the largest and most prosperous of these crafts towns. Otavalo's Plaza de Ponchos and adjacent streets are brimming each Saturday, with merchants selling weavings, rugs, sweaters, jewelry, and antiques. At a nearby street market, locals shop for *alpargatas* (rope-sole sandals) and medicinal herbs; just outside town, livestock dealers do a brisk business in squealing pigs, cackling hens, and colossal guinea pigs. Smaller villages—such as Cotacachi (famous for its leather) and San Antonio de Ibarra (known for its woodwork)—host their own markets, though none on such a grand scale as the Saturday market in Otavalo.

Mitad del Mundo

26 km (16 mi) north of Quito.

Want in on a little secret? Ecuador's famous Mitad del Mundo (Middle of the World) monument does not sit exactly on the equator. It marks the spot that in 1736 the French Geodesic Mission determined was the latitudinal center of the earth. But GPS satellite technology has demonstrated that the true equator runs about 300 meters (980 feet) north, a fact not widely publicized at this site. Visitors today enjoy having their photographs taken as they straddle the painted line here, but, alas, they are really standing entirely in the southern hemisphere.

Nonetheless, the site does make an interesting visit. The pine trees and chilly breezes are likely not how you envisioned equatorial climes. The monument itself is a 30-meter-tall (98-foot-tall) stone obelisk topped by a 2½-ton metal globe. Take the elevator inside to the top of the monument, then start a winding walk down through the Ethnographic Museum, which has

> **A NICE THOUGHT**
>
> If you're feeling a bit discouraged about that diet you're on, take heart in knowing that you weigh a couple of pounds less here at 0° latitude, gravity's force being slightly lower.

exhibits of the people, clothing, and dwellings of Ecuador's diverse ethnic groups. Bilingual guided tours are included in the admission price. A French pavilion explains the history of the Geodesic Expedition in Spanish, English, and French. The Solar Culture Museum, the only place here that divulges the truth about the equator's location, is the highlight of the site; it has an informative bilingual talk about peoples' use of the sun in measurements during the pre-Columbian epoch. The nearby planetarium's show is in Spanish only, and its show is put on only if at least 15 people are in attendance. The rest of the site is constructed to resemble a colonial village, with most buildings housing souvenir shops.

An organized tour is the easiest way to get to the monument, but if you prefer to go on your own, catch a Metrobus from the terminal at the corner of Avenida América and Avenida Colón to Cotocallao. From there, frequent Mitad del Mundo buses take you to the monument, a total trip of about an hour. Much quicker is a taxi: drivers charge $15 one-way ⊠ *1 km (½ mi) from San Antonio de Pichincha* ☎ *02/222–0360* ⊕ *www.mitaddelmundo.com* 🎟 *Site, $1.50; ethnographic museum, $3; planetarium, $1.50, solar culture museum, donation* ☉ *Mon.–Thurs. 7:30–6, Fri.–Sun. 9–7.*

Otavalo

113 km (70 mi) north of Quito.

Days are warm and sunny in Otavalo, nestled in the rugged valley nearly 8,530 feet above sea level. Nearby are the craggy peaks of three extinct volcanoes: Imbabura, Cotacachi, and Cayambe, Ecuador's third-tallest mountain. Villagers trudge along the road carrying huge loads or prodding their overburdened burros to do the same. If it's Thursday or Friday, chances are they're headed for Otavalo's famous Saturday market.

This gathering of stalls at the **Plaza de Ponchos** was once called the Silent Market because there was no loud bargaining or shouting to entice you to buy. Though it's still quiet compared to other markets, times have changed. Today you have to negotiate your way through a noisy and overwhelming conglomeration of stands crowded with tourists on the market's periphery before you get to the market proper in the core. Once inside the hurly-burly, you deal with the dignified and astute Otavalos, who speak slowly and softly as they negotiate. For sale are hand-knit sweaters made from sheep or alpaca wool, colorful ponchos, patterned scarves, and Panama hats. You'll also find strings of gold-washed glass beads, worn in multiple strands by Otavalo women, lots of silver, and jewelry embedded with Andean jade. You can usually get discounts of 20% to 30% by bargaining.

A produce market is held simultaneously at the Plaza 24 de Mayo; there's also an animal market at the Plaza San Juan. People from the surrounding countryside—many dressed in traditional clothing—come here to bargain for cows, pigs, and other livestock. The animal market begins at 5:30 AM, and most sellers are packing up by 11 AM. The Plaza de Ponchos market doesn't really begin until 7 or 8 and lasts until about 2 or 3. A smaller market is held on Wednesday, and a few vendors appear every day of the week.

Where to Stay & Eat

¢ ✕ **Mi Otavalito.** One block from the Plaza de Ponchos, this small restaurant has a simple menu that includes fresh trout and pepper steak. Seating is available on a covered patio or in the narrow dining room. The daily lunch specials are a great deal. ⊠ *Sucre at Morales* ☎ *06/ 292–2105* ▤ *No credit cards.*

> **TIP**
>
> Hotel reservations are essential on Friday night, when many tourists arrive so they can be up early for the markets.

¢ ✕ **Sisa.** This two-story cultural complex consists of an intimate restaurant on the second floor that serves excellent Ecuadoran cuisine, a ground-floor coffee bar, and a bookstore. The restaurant presents live folk music Friday evening and all day on weekends. ⊠ *Abdón Calderón 409* ☎ *06/292–0154* ▤ *AE, DC, MC, V.*

¢ ✕▥ **Ali Shungu.** The Quichua name of this colorful hotel means "good heart," and indeed the American owners go out of their way to make you feel at home. The spacious bedrooms with terra-cotta floors and local weavings surround a flower-filled courtyard, beyond which is Volcán Imbabura, in the distance. Two expansive suites are ideal for families. The bright restaurant has wholesome dishes, including vegetarian lasagna and deep-dish chicken pie served with organically grown vegetables. There's live folk music on Friday night. For a real get-away-from-it-all alternative, these folks operate a lodge 5 km (3 mi) southwest of town. Four sparkling, fully equipped houses ($$$) have terra-cotta floors, cactus-braid rugs and wood-burning stoves to ward off the night chill. (There's even Wi-Fi access, but come on: leave the laptop at home and enjoy the surroundings.) ⊠ *Quito at Miguel Egas* ☎ *06/292–0750* ⊕ *www.alishungu.com* ⤳ *16 rooms, 2 suites* ⚐ *Restaurant, bicycles, shop, laundry service, travel services; no a/c, no room TVs, no smoking* ▤ *No credit cards.*

$$ ▥ **Hostería Hacienda Pinsaquí.** French and Spanish antiques fill this colonial ranch house, built in 1790, surrounded by palm trees. The huge light-filled suites, which can accommodate up to five people, have canopy beds, fireplaces, and spacious sitting areas. Some rooms have views of Imbabura Volcano. Horseback-riding trips are the hacienda's specialty.

Fodor'sChoice
★

⊠ *Pan-American Hwy., 5 km (3 mi) north of Otavalo* ☎ *06/294–6116* ⊕ *www.haciendapinsaqui.com* ⇥ *23 suites* ⌂ *Restaurant, mountain bikes, horseback riding, library, laundry service, Internet, airport shuttle, travel services; no a/c* ▤ *MC, V* ⦿ *BP.*

$$ Bellavista Cloud Forest Reserve. Two hours out of Quito puts you smack-dab up in the heights of Ecuador's best-known cloud forest, replete with trails, waterfalls, orchids, and an amazing 275 bird species to add to your life list. You can do the place as a day-trip—a *long* day-trip from the capital—but staying here at the reserve's rustic but comfy dome-shape hotel makes a much more relaxing alternative. Rooms have wood floors, basic furnishings and private balconies. (The birds will be your morning alarm clock.) A couple of other small cottages on site offer more seclusion, but all offer you access to surprisingly yummy food considering the isolated location. Various mix-and-match packages let you include tours and transportation. ⊠ *Tandayapa, Km. 52, Quito-Nanegalito Rd.* ☎ *02/223–2313 in Quito* ⊕ *www.bellavistacloudforest.com* ⇥ *17 rooms, 16 with bath, 3 cabins* ⌂ *Restaurant, travel services; no a/c, no room phones, no room TVs* ▤ *AE, DC, MC, V* ⦿ *EP, FAP.*

Nightlife & the Arts

During the week things are very quiet in Otavalo (some would say downright dull), but the town has a reasonable selection of peñas (small local clubs) that open on weekends. You can't go wrong with either location of **Amauta** (⊠ Jaramillo and Salinas ⊠ Jaramillo and Morales ☎ 06/292–0967). Both open around 8 PM.

San Pablo

8 km (5 mi) southeast of Otavalo.

Easily accessible from Otavalo, the highland town of San Pablo is a collection of adobe buildings along the shore of deep-blue Lago San Pablo. The lake sits at the base of the massive 15,190-foot Volcán Imbabura. Lodges on or near the lake are much nicer than those in town. Buses run between Otavalo and San Pablo about every 15 minutes, or you can take a taxi for around $3.

Where to Stay & Eat

$$$–$$$$ ✕▥ **Hacienda Cusín.** This restored colonial hacienda on the edge of San Pablo is one of the country's most delightful inns. Rooms are filled with period furnishings, and many are warmed by fireplaces. The main buildings, which date from the 17th century, hold the restaurant, bar, and sitting rooms, where you can enjoy the views of the colorful gardens. ⊠ *San Pablo* ☎ *06/291–8316, 800/670–6984 in North America* ⊕ *www.haciendacusin.com* ⇥ *17 rooms, 25 suites* ⌂ *Restaurant, mountain bikes, horseback riding, basketball, billiards, Ping-Pong, squash, volleyball, bar, library, travel services; no a/c* ▤ *AE, DC, MC, V* ⦿ *BP, FAP.*

$–2$: ✕▥ **Puerto Lago Country Inn.** Volcanic peaks form a dramatic backdrop for this lakeside country inn just a few miles southeast of Otavalo. The view from the restaurant, built out over the lake, is enough to warrant a stay here. Don't miss the panfried trout, served head and all. Bungalow-style rooms are spacious, with brick walls, wood-beam ceilings, and cozy fireplaces. You can rent a rowboat or kayak, or take an excursion on a festive pontoon boat with live music. Breakfast and dinner are included in the rate. ☒ *Pan-American Hwy. Km 5½* ☎ *06/292–0920* ⊕ *www.puertolago.com* ⇱ *27 rooms* ♨ *Restaurant, cable TV, fishing, boating, kayaks, fishing, waterskiing, windsurfing, bar, library, shop, meeting room, travel services* ▤ *AE, DC, MC, V.*

Sports & the Outdoors

HORSEBACK RIDING **IntiExpress** (☒ Otavalo ☎ 06/292–0737) arranges horseback-riding excursions to local villages and natural mineral springs.

Cotacachi

15 km (9 mi) north of Otavalo.

Although most people just pass through here on the way to the lake of the same name, the quiet little town of Cotacachi is well worth a visit. The small central plaza is charming, with young children racing around while their grandparents settle back for a little gossip with friends. A few blocks away, Calle 10 de Agosto is lined with shops selling the quality leather goods for which the town is famous. The prices are amazingly low.

About 18 km (11 mi) west of Cotacachi, milewide **Laguna de Cuicocha** is an oblong lake cradled in the lower flanks of Volcán Cotacachi. A well-marked hiking trail heads up the crater's rim into an ecological reserve that affords fantastic views of the distant Imbabura and Cayambe volcanoes. Within the lake are islands that can be visited on inexpensive boat tours.

Where to Stay & Eat

$$$ ╳▦ **La Mirage Hotel & Spa.** You'll pass trickling fountains and shady courtyards as you wind through flower-filled gardens on the way to your casita on this 200-year-old property. Suites are chock-full of decorative touches, from handcrafted furnishings to crystal chandeliers, antique canopy beds, gilded mirrors, ornate trim, and lavish baths. International cuisine is served in the wood-beamed dining room. While you're at dinner, staff members slip in to build a fire and place hot water bottles at the foot of your bed, an example of the sort of pampering you can expect throughout a stay here. International cuisine is served in the wood-beamed dining room, part of which looks out onto the lawn, where peacocks roam. Much of the produce is organic and grown in the hotel's own garden. Aside from the standard massages, the spa has volcanic mud treatments, aromatherapy, massage instruction for couples, and unique shaman treatments. ☒ *Av. 10 de Agosto* ☎ *06/291–5237, 800/327–3573 in North America* ⊕ *www.mirage.com.ec* ⇱ *23 suites* ♨ *Restaurant, tennis court, pool, massage, spa, steam room, horseback riding, bar, no-smoking rooms* ▤ *DC, MC, V.*

¢ ╳▦ **Hostería Mesón de las Flores.** This inexpensive lodging beside the town church provides an authentic Ecuadoran experience. Most rooms are on the second floor surrounding a courtyard restaurant and have small balconies and soft beds. A spacious suite on the third floor is a great deal for a couple. ☒ *García Moreno at Sucre* ☎ *06/291–6009* ⇱ *16 rooms, 1 suite* ♨ *Restaurant, cable TV, bar* ▤ *AE, DC, MC, V* ⦿ *BP.*

San Antonio de Ibarra

10 km (6 mi) north of Cotacachi.

Renowned for its wood carvings, San Antonio de Ibarra, the capital of the province, is where you'll find skillful artisans who show off their wares in the shops surrounding the central plaza. Check out the chess sets, which use llamas in place of the horses usually used to signify the knights. Prices range from a few dollars to a few hundred. At the Galeria de Arte Gabriel Cevallos you can drop off a photo or design for a wood carving and have it shipped home. The owners accept credit cards They'll ship the piece to you when it's finished, and you pay the shipping charges when it arrives. Carved wooden chess sets are another good purchase.

Where to Stay & Eat

$ ✕☷**Hostería Chorlaví.** Shaded verandas, whitewashed walls, and antiques-filled rooms make this inn a favorite weekend retreat for Ecuadorans. The restaurant emphasizes fresh fish and typical Andean dishes, all served on a flower-strewn patio where folk musicians play on weekends. Rooms in the old building are lovely, though they can be loud when the place is full; for that reason, make this place a midweek rather than weekend stay. More private rooms in another building in back all have fireplaces. ⊠ *4 km (2½ mi) south of Ibarra* ☎ *06/293–2222* ✎ *chorlavi@andinanet.net* ➥ *56 rooms* ⌂ *Restaurant, cable TV, tennis court, pool, hot tub, sauna, steam room, basketball, squash, volleyball, travel services; no a/c* ▭ *AE, DC, MC, V* ❘❂❘ *BP.*

The Northern Highlands Essentials

Transportation

BY BUS

To reach the Mitad del Mundo, buses marked MITAD DEL MUNDO depart every 20 minutes from the New City at the intersection of Avenida de las Américas and Avenida P. Guerrera. The 75-minute ride costs less than $1. Most Quito-based tour operators offer half-day tours for $10–$20 per person. From Quito's Terminal Terrestre, buses depart every 30 minutes for Otavalo (2 hours) and Ibarra (2½ hours). The round-trip fare should be less than $5. Transportes Otavalo deposits passengers in Otavalo's center. Flota Imbabura has direct service to Ibarra, but for Otavalo, buses drop you a few blocks outside town.

Buses run between Imbabura's major towns about every 15 minutes. ℹ **Bus Information Flota Imbabura** ☎ 02/223–6940. **Transportes Otavalo** ☎ 02/257–0271.

BY CAR

Otavalo, just off the Pan-American Highway, is 113 km (70 mi) north of Quito. Driving here can be a challenge because of poorly maintained roads and a lack of signs. If you decide to drive yourself, make sure to get very specific directions.

BY TAXI

For around $50, taxis can be hired in Quito for a daylong trip to Otavalo and the surrounding countryside. A trip between Otavalo and Ibarra costs about $6.

Contacts & Resources

MONEY MATTERS

Banks are scarce in the region. Get the cash you think you'll need before leaving Quito.

TOUR OPERATORS

Zulay Viajes, owned and operated by indigenous people, offers a variety of trekking and horseback excursions to the area surrounding Otavalo. IntiExpress has a good selection of day trips to highland lakes and villages. Metropolitan Touring and most other operators in Quito have one- and two-day tours to the area, typically visiting several villages.

🚩 Tour Companies **Zulay Viajes** ⊠ Sucre 1014, Otavalo ☎ 06/292-1217. **IntiExpress** ⊠ Sucre and Morales, Otavalo ☎ 06/292-0737. **Metropolitan Touring** ⊠ Av. República de El Salvador 970 ☎ 02/246-4780, 800/527-2500 in the U.S. ⊕ www.metropolitan-touring.com.

VISITOR INFORMATION

The Ibarra branch of iTur is open weekdays 8:30–1 and 2–5.

🚩 Tourist Information **iTur** ⊠ García Moreno 376, at Roca Fuerte ☎ 06/295-8547.

THE CENTRAL HIGHLANDS

South of Quito the Andes rise sharply on either side of the Pan-American Highway, creating a narrow corridor of fertile valleys that are home to nearly half of Ecuador's population. Along this 175-km (109-mi) stretch between Quito and Riobamba are most of Ecuador's tallest volcanoes, including the tallest active volcano in the world, Cotopaxi. Alexander von Humboldt, the German scientist who explored the area in 1802, was so impressed by the landscape that he coined a sobriquet still used today: the Avenue of the Volcanoes.

Latacunga, a few hours south of Quito, is an excellent base for visiting the area's colorful market villages, including Saquisilí, Pujilí, and San Miguel de Salcedo. Among the Central Highlands' most popular destinations is Baños, a sleepy tourist town surrounded by a wealth of natural attractions. Die-hard cyclists should contemplate the 65-km (40-mi) downhill ride from Baños to Puyo. Riobamba, the capital of Chimborazo Province, is the point of departure for the famous train trip past the Nariz del Diablo (Devil's Nose), a 1,000-foot drop that the narrow-gauge train negotiates via an ingenious system of hairpin turns, span bridges, and tunnels.

Termas de Papallacta

65 km (40 mi) east of Quito.

A stunning drive over the eastern range of the Andes brings you to the village of Papallacta. A mile beyond you'll find the Termas de Papallacta, a natural hot springs with eight thermal baths and two cold crystalline pools. It's a beautiful setting, and on a clear day you can see the snowcapped peak of Volcán Antisana. ☉ *Daily 6 AM–10 PM* 🎫 *$5.*

Where to Stay & Eat

$$ ✕🏨 **Termas Papallacta Spa & Resort.** This ranch, set 9,000 feet above sea level, is surrounded by natural hot springs. The springs line the Cinnamon Trail, the route taken by Francisco de Orellana in 1542 when he crossed the Andes in search of spices and wound up discovering the Amazon. All rooms have private baths and breathtaking mountain views. Walk or ride horses through the rain forest, and bring binoculars to observe the varied species of birds. ✉ *Km 67, Carretera Quito–Baeza* ☎ *02/256–8989, 800/327–3573 in the U.S.* ⊕ *www.termaspapallacta.com* 🛏 *24 rooms ⌕ Restaurant, pool, spa, horseback riding, meeting rooms; no a/c* ▭ *AE, MC, V.*

Parque Pasochoa

38 km (24 mi) southeast of Quito.

Parque Pasochoa, a protected area administered by the Quito-based Fundación Natura, covers 988 acres of high Andean forest. More than 100 species of birds and a variety of butterflies have been identified in the area. Walking trails include short loops and all-day hikes, with the trek to the 13,800-foot summit of Volcán Pasochoa the most strenuous. Camping is permitted in designated areas with water spigots and latrines. ☎ *02/244–7341 or 02/224–6072* 🎫 *$1.50* ☉ *Daily.*

> **TIP**
>
> Tour operators in Quito offer one-day tours for $40–$85, depending on the group size. If you want to go on your own, buses from Quito stop a couple of miles from the park entrance.

6

Parque Nacional Cotopaxi

67 km (42 mi) southeast of Quito.

Massive, snowcapped Volcán Cotopaxi is one of Ecuador's most impressive sights. At 5,897 meters (19,347 feet) above sea level, Cotopaxi is the highest active volcano in the world. Although mountaineers risk their lives to reach Cotopaxi's icy summit, you need risk little more than a slight case of altitude sickness to wander around its lower slopes, which are protected within Parque Nacional Cotopaxi.

The drive to Cotopaxi is unforgettable. As you make your way past the stands of red pine and into the higher altitudes, you are likely to spot llamas, white-tailed deer, and wild horses, as well as Andean condors and sparrow hawks. Fewer animals roam the semiarid plains called the *páramo,* extending from 10,496 to 15,744 feet. There are no trees here, only small plants that have adapted to the harsh environment. Above the páramo lies the permafrost zone, where giant glaciers extend across the volcano's summit. Cotopaxi is most impressive at dawn, when sunlight sprinkles rays across the surface of the glaciers and casts shadows on the surrounding mountains.

A tour operator with a four-wheel-drive vehicle can take you to the base of the volcano, at 15,744 feet. If you're not suffering from the altitude, it is possible to climb about 1,000 feet to the *refugio*, where simple dormitory accommodations serve as a base for eager climbers. From here you'll need at least six hours and mountain-climbing equipment—including ice picks—to climb to the glacier-covered summit. The crater has a circumference of 2,624 feet and is covered by snow. In case you're considering the sanity of a climb, you should know that the last major eruption was in 1877, when lava currents reached the Pacific Ocean some 200 km (124 mi) away. ▨ *$1* ☾ *Daily 7–3.*

Where to Stay

¢–$$ ▦ **Tierra del Volcán.** Ecotourism is the focus at this rustic lodge in the foothills of Rumiñahui Volcano that acquaints you with the *chagra* (Andean cowboy) lifestyle. Most rooms are tiny nooks with straw ceilings and burlap walls and are only big enough to hold two cotlike single beds. Suites have fireplaces and double beds. The hacienda has horses and conducts riding, biking, hiking, trekking, and climbing trips that last from a few hours to seven days. Cotopaxi National Park is 3 miles away. ☒ *Machachi, 45 mi southeast of Quito* 🕾 *02/223–1806* ⊕ *www. volcanoland.com* ⇝ *12 rooms, 2 suites, without bath* ♨ *Dining room, mountain bikes, hiking, horseback riding* ▭ *AE, MC, V* ⅩⅡ *BP.*

¢ ▦ **Hostería La Estación.** Owned by the same family for four generations, this log house B&B has a panoramic view of the mountains. Fresh flowers brighten the rooms, which are decorated with antiques. All rooms have private baths. The gracious owners will prepare meals and arrange day hikes for you to Volcán Cotopaxi. The hostería is a half hour from the entrance to Parque Nacional Cotopaxi, near the small village of Machachi. ☒ *Machachi* 🕾 *02/230–9246* ⇝ *10 rooms* ♨ *Restaurant, cafeteria, hiking, meeting room; no a/c* ▭ *DC.*

¢ ▦ **Hostería Rumipamba.** In an Andean valley 100 km (61 mi) south of Quito, right at the stone gate to the colorful town of Salcedo, is this unexpectedly elegant hostel. Comfortable rooms filled with antiques, a shady pool, and three restaurants—one with seating in a garden—are the perfect antidote for the stresses of modern life. While you're here, explore Salcedo's market. ☒ *Salcedo* 🕾 *03/272–6128* ⊕ *www.rumipamba. com* ⇝ *32 rooms* ♨ *3 restaurants, tennis court, pool, fishing, horseback riding, bar* ▭ *AE, DC, MC, V.*

Latacunga

96 km (58 mi) south of Quito.

The capital of Cotopaxi Province, Latacunga has been rebuilt three times in the wake of massive eruptions of Volcán Cotopaxi, whose perfect, snow-covered cone dominates the city. Latacunga's main plaza, **Parque Vicente León,** is graced by juniper trees trimmed in an assortment of geometric shapes. At the Saturday market held on **Plaza San Sebastián** you'll find that most of the goods for sale are geared to the locals—fruits, vegetables, and medicinal herbs. Pick up one of the *shigras,* the colorful, handwoven hemp bags used by indigenous people.

In the tiny mountain village of **Pujilí,** 10 km (6 mi) west of Latacunga, colorful markets are held on Sunday and, with much less ado, on Wednesday. Few tourists find their way here, so instead of gringos in T-shirts you'll see locals in bright turquoise or carmine ponchos and miniature fedoras buying and selling produce, pottery, and costume jewelry.

In **Saquisilí,** 13 km (8 mi) northwest of Latacunga, indigenous people in regional dress fill all eight of the village's dusty plazas during the Thursday market, where you can pick through piles of traditional wares— including painted wooden masks of animals and devils.

The market town of **San Miguel de Salcedo,** 14 km (9 mi) south of Latacunga, has pleasant streets and plazas that make it appealing on any day. However, it's most interesting to plan your visit around the Sunday market or the smaller one held on Thursday.

Where to Stay & Eat

The region has several hosterías with comfortable rooms. These former haciendas are found outside the towns and villages, so count on country solitude.

★ **$$$$** ✕⌂ **Hacienda San Agustín de Callo.** This place has been inhabited for more than five centuries—it began as an Inca fortress and was transformed into an Augustinian monastery after the Spanish conquest. It now belongs to an Ecuadoran family. Two original Inca structures are used as a chapel and a dining room. The hotel is a few miles from Parque Nacional Cotopaxi, where you have access to horseback riding, trout fishing, mountain biking, and trekking. ✉ *San Agustín, 5 km (3 mi) from Parque Nacional Cotopaxi* ☎ *03/271–9160, 02/290–6157 in Quito* ⊕ *www.incahacienda.com* ⇥ *4 rooms, 2 suites* ⌂ *Restaurant, dining room, horseback riding, mountain hikes; no a/c* ⊟ *MC, V* ⍥ *MAP.*

★ **¢** ⌂ **The Black Sheep Inn.** It's not easy to get here, but you'll find this place— an ecohostel—is one of the nicest in Ecuador. Prices include vegetarian dinners, farm-fresh breakfasts, tea and coffee all day, purified drinking water, hiking maps, and hot showers. Most rooms have a woodstove fireplace. Dinner is family style. Also available are lunches, home-baked desserts, Chilean wines, cold beer, a full bar, and European-style cheeses. Perched on a hillside outside the village of Chugchilan in the Cotopaxi Province, this hostel is five hours southwest of Quito. You can get here by bus, jeep, or taxi. The American owners, Andres Hammerman and Michelle Kirby, will help you make arrangements. ✉ *Box 05-01-240, Chugchilan, Cotopaxi* ☎ *03/281–4587* ⊕ *www.blacksheepinn.com* ⇥ *9 rooms and 1 bunkhouse* ⌂ *Dining room, sauna, mountain bikes, hiking* ⊟ *No credit cards* ⍥ *MAP.*

Baños

84 km (53 mi) southeast of Latacunga.

At the base of Volcán Tungurahua and surrounded by heavily forested mountains, tumbling waterfalls, and natural hot springs, Baños is one of Ecuador's top tourist spots. Quiteños have been soaking in the thermal springs for decades. The town's real appeal—as tour operators will attest—are the abundant hiking trails, white-water rafting trips, and horseback excursions in the surrounding highlands.

In the heart of town, the twin spires of **La Iglesia de la Virgen del Agua Santa** (Church of the Virgin of the Holy Water) rise above the tree-lined plaza. The church, whose black-and-white facade is slightly startling, was built to honor Baños's miracle-working patron saint. The huge paintings inside are testimonials from her many exultant beneficiaries.

A few blocks from the church is the small but interesting **Museo Huillan-cuna** (⊠ Pasaje Velasco Ibarra and Av. Montalvo ☎ 03/274–0973), a museum that has exhibits about pre-Columbian ceramics, Andean musical instruments, and local history.

Baños is Spanish for "baths", and there are several thermal springs in town. The town's official name is Baños de Agua Santa (Baths of the Holy Water), but no miracles have ever been attributed to the springs. The best of the bunch is a series of pools called **El Salado** (the Salty One). Its six rough-hewn pools, next to a fastmoving stream, overflow with mineral water of various temperatures. The pools are refilled each morning at dawn. ⊠ *2 km (1 mi) outside Baños on Vía al Salado* ☒ *$2* ☉ *Daily dawn–dusk.*

Where to Stay & Eat

¢ ✕ **El Higuerón.** Hidden behind bougainvillea and flowering vines, this small restaurant serves tasty salads, sandwiches, and pastas. Dine at wooden tables beside sunny windows or head outside to one of the inviting tables on the patio. The owner, William Navarette, is among the region's most knowledgeable mountaineers. ⊠ *12 de Noviembre 270* ☎ *03/274–0910* ☲ *MC, V* ☉ *Closed Wed.*

$$$$ ✕☷ **Luna Runtún.** Perched high over Baños on the slopes of Volcán Tungurahua, Swiss-run Luna Runtún combines colonial-style architecture with the attention to detail you would expect from a European resort. On your pillow will be fresh flowers carefully selected from the gardens outside. Hike along a route used by rum smugglers in the 1920s, ride horses through the nearby countryside, or join a trip to the hot springs. ⊠ *6 km (4 mi) from Baños* ☎ *03/274–0882* ⊕ *www.lunaruntun.com* ➷ *30 rooms, 2 suites* ☖ *Restaurant, hot tub, sauna, spa, billiards, horseback riding, bar, library, baby-sitting, Internet, meeting room; no room TVs* ☲ *AE, DC, MC, V* ⦿❶ *MAP.*

¢ ☷ **Sangay Spa Hotel.** This family-oriented hotel across the street from the municipal baths has large cabañas behind the pool and spacious rooms with balconies overlooking the nearby Waterfall of the Virgin. From the second-floor restaurant you'll also get nice views. ⊠ *Plazoleta Ayora 101* ☎ *03/274–0490* ✎ *sangayspa_hotmail.com* ➷ *65 rooms* ☖ *Restaurant, cable TV, tennis court, pool, 2 hot tubs, sauna, steam room, squash, bar, dance club* ☲ *AE, DC, MC, V* ⦿❶ *BP.*

¢ ✕☷ **Le Petit Auberge and Restaurant.** After establishing a reputation as one of this town's best restaurants, this place expanded to include inexpensive rooms. All have hardwood floors, white stucco walls, and balconies. Many are warmed by wood-burning fireplaces. The restaurant serves French cuisine, with a menu that includes crêpes, ratatouille, and delicious fondues. ⊠ *Av. 16 de Diciembre at Montalvo* ☎ *03/274—0936* ⤺ *12 rooms* ⊟ *AE, DC, MC, V* ☉ *Restaurant closed Mon.*

¢ 🏨 **Hostería Monte Selva.** This quartet of three-room bungalows is nestled on a lush hillside at the edge of town. Each room has several beds and a small bath. Many have views of the town. At the foot of the hill are a swimming pool, a sauna, and a lovely little restaurant. ⊠ *Halflants, near Montalvo* ☎ *274–0566* ⊕ *www.monteselva.com* ⤺ *12 rooms* ⚘ *Restaurant, pool, hot tub, sauna, steam room, bar, travel services* ⊟ *DC, MC, V.*

Sports & the Outdoors

BICYCLING Cycling fans won't be able to resist the five-hour, 65-km (40-mi) downhill ride from Baños to Puyo. At the bottom you can board a bus, bike and all, for the return trip to Baños. **Wonderful Ecuador** (⊠ Maldonado and Oriente ☎ 03/274–0637) organizes bicycle tours through the highlands and canoeing expeditions through the jungle. Mountain bikes can be rented at affordable rates at **Bill Mountain** (⊠ Ambato at Maldonado ☎ 03/274–0221), which also offers cycling tours that wind through subtropical jungle and past thundering waterfalls.

HORSEBACK At least a dozen tour operators offer excellent day trips and overnight
RIDING excursions around Baños. **Caballos con José** (⊠ Maldonado, near Martínez ☎ 03/274–0929) is a reliable company that offers tours lasting from two hours to several nights. **Huillacuna Tours** (⊠ Santa Clara 206 ☎ 03/274–0187) schedules half- and full-day tours to Runtún. **Río Loco** (⊠ Maldonado and Martínez ☎ 03/274–0929) offers a variety of excursions outside Baños.

RAFTING White-water rafting trips on the Patate and Pastaza rivers are the reason many people head to Baños. The Class III Patate is a good trip for beginners, while the Class III and Class IV Pastaza is a more challenging four-hour trip through some spectacular jungle. Trips can be booked through **Geotours** (⊠ Maldonado at Espejo ☎ 03/274–0332). **Remote Odysseys Worldwide** (⊠ Foch 721, at Juan León Mera, Quito ☎ 02/270–3535 ⊕ www.rowinc.com) organizes Class III and Class IV white-water trips on the Río Upano, including side trips to Shuar villages in the Amazon and camping out in Morona-Santiago Province.

Shopping

In Baños you'll find plenty of shopping. Most items come from other parts of Ecuador, but there are a few interesting local crafts that can be purchased from the actual craftspeople. Look for hand-carved toucans, turtles, and other tropical creatures. **Recuerdos** (⊠ Maldonado, near Montalvo) sells balsa-wood carvings of parrots and other birds made in a workshop behind the store. **El Cade** (⊠ Maldonado 681) sells items carved from the seed of the tagua palm, a hard substance also known as vegetal ivory.

6

Riobamba

105 km (63 mi) south of Latacunga.

Three of Ecuador's most formidable peaks—Chimborazo, Altar, and Tungurahua—are visible from Riobamba, a pleasant town with wide, tree-lined streets and some well-preserved colonial architecture. Most travelers head to Riobamba because it's the starting point for the famous Devil's Nose train trip. Mudslides have destroyed large sections of the Trans-Andean Railroad, which once ran all the way from Quito to Duran.

There are good buys at the tourist-oriented Saturday market held in the **Parque de la Concepción** (⊠ Orozco at Colón). Look for embroidered belts, hand-knit sweaters, and locally produced jewelry. Across the street from Parque de la Concepción, the **Museo de Arte Religioso** (⊠ Argentina ☎ 03/295–2212) is housed in the beautifully restored Iglesia de la Concepción. The Religious Art Museum has an impressive collection of artifacts from the colonial period.

The hill in the center of the **Parque 21 de Abril** (⊠ Argentina) affords an excellent view of the city. On clear days you'll have eye-popping views of several snowcapped volcanoes. The mural here depicts the city's history.

HERE'S WHERE
Locals are fond of identifying Chimborazo as the true world's highest peak, as the planet bulges more at the equator, putting the mountain at a greater distance from the center of the earth than any other point.

Where to Stay & Eat

¢ ✕🏨 **Hostería El Troje.** This place just outside Riobamba welcomes you back to your spacious room with a crackling fire in the hearth. When there are enough guests, the hotel puts on a show with folk music and dancing before dinner. The owner is one of the most famous mountain climbers in Ecuador. ⊠ *4½ km (3 mi) southeast of Riobamba* ☎ *03/296–0826* ⊕ *www.eltroje.com* ↪ *48 rooms* ⚐ *Restaurant, indoor pool, hot tub, steam room, basketball, soccer, volleyball, bar, playground, laundry service, Internet, meeting room; no phones in some rooms, no TV in some rooms* ⊟ *AE, DC, MC, V.*

¢ ✕🏨 **Hostal Montecarlo.** This century-old house, with its fern-filled central courtyard, is conveniently located in the middle of town. Its elegant yet homey restaurant, around the corner from the hotel, is first-rate. ⊠ *Av. 10 de Agosto 2541* ☎ *03/296–0557* ↪ *20 rooms* ✉ *montecarlo_andinaet.net* ⚐ *Restaurant, cafeteria, cable TV; no a/c* ⊟ *MC, V.*

$ 🏨 **Hostería Abraspungo.** Reminiscent of a mountain lodge, this place is among the most practical accommodations in the Central Highlands. Each of the clean, comfortable rooms is named after a different mountain peak; several rooms overlook the surrounding hills. Horses, stabled on-site, are available for day treks. The owner, mountaineer Marco Cruz, knows the best hikes in the region. ⊠ *3½ km (2 mi) from Riobamba* ☎ *03/294–0820* ⊕ *www.hosteria-abraspungu.com* ↪ *26 rooms, 5 suites* ⚐ *Restaurant, cable TV, hiking, horseback riding, bar, playground, laundry service, travel services* ⊟ *AE, DC, MC, V.*

The Central Highlands Essentials

Transportation

BY BUS

To reach Parque Nacional Cotopaxi, take any of the buses to Ambato that leave from Quito's Terminal Terrestre every 30 minutes. They will drop you off in Lasso, about 10 km (6 mi) from the park entrance. The 30-km (18-mi) ride takes just under an hour and costs $2. Most Quito tour operators offer day trips to the park for around $40. Buses headed to Tena travel every hour past the Termas de Papallacta. You may have to pay the full fare to Tena, which is under $3. There are no direct buses to Parque Pasochoa. Your best bet is taking a bus from Quito's La Marín square to Amaguaña and asking the bus driver to drop you off when you're about 7 km (4½ mi) away. From there you can either walk or hire someone to take you the rest of the way. From Quito buses leave frequently for Latacunga (2 hours), Baños (3½ hours), and Riobamba (4 hours). All cost less than $5 each way. Local buses connect Latacunga with Pujilí, Saquisilí, and San Miguel de Salcedo.

BY CAR

Latacunga lies just off the Pan-American Highway, 89 km (55 mi) south of Quito. The nearby villages of Pujilí, San Miguel de Salcedo, and Saquisilí are accessed via gravel roads. Baños is 40 km (25 mi) east of Ambato on the road to Puyo. Riobamba is nestled along the Pan-American Highway 188 km (117 mi) south of Quito. Think twice about driving yourself, as poor roads will impede your progress.

BY TAXI

You can hire a taxi to take you from Quito to the Central Highlands. The fare to Baños, for example, would cost around $100. Remember that you must also pay for the return fare back to the city. You can also hire the driver to accompany you on your travels, but you must pay for his food and lodging as well.

Taxis between Latacunga and the nearby villages of Pujilí, Saquisilí, and Salcedo cost less than $10 each way.

Contacts & Resources

MONEY MATTERS

Although many hotels in the Central Highlands accept credit cards, inquire before you set out. Because banks are few and far between, bring all the cash you think you'll need. You'll find very few ATMs in the countryside.

VISITOR INFORMATION

The local hotel association in Baños has an information office in front of Hostal Banana. There is also an information booth at the bus station. The Riobamba branch of iTur is open Monday–Saturday 8:30–5.
🗊 Tourist Information **Baños Hotel Association** ✉ 12 de Noviembre 500 ☎ 03/274-0309. **iTur** ✉ Av. Daniel Leon Borja at Pje. Municipal ☎ 03/294–1213.

CUENCA & THE SOUTHERN HIGHLANDS

If you've just arrived from Quito or Guayaquil, you might not believe that Cuenca is Ecuador's third-largest city. It hustles and bustles, but with a certain provincial charm. This prosperous and beautiful highland city—in the Pucarabama Valley between the eastern and western ranges of the Andes—has retained much of its colonial splendor, and, like Quito's, its city center has been declared a UNESCO World Heritage Site. No building, for example, is allowed to be higher than the highest church steeple, and along its cobblestone streets you'll find colonial mansions with wrought-iron balconies overflowing with potted plants. Here you'll still find old men gossiping in the shady squares and women drying laundry on the grass along the river banks, but despite all that, Cuenca is one of the most advanced cities in Ecuador—it's one of the few cities in Latin America with a controlled water and sewer system.

On market days—Thursday and Sunday—hundreds of people from surrounding villages crowd into Cuenca's open-air plazas to buy and sell crafts and household items. It's not surprising that the Cuencanos have developed a stubborn pride in their skills. Cuenca produces fine ceramics and textiles, but is best known for its handsome Panama hats. The *cholas Cuencanas*—female descendants of mixed Spanish and Cañari couples—are striking in their colorful *polleras* (gathered wool skirts in violet, emerald, rose, or marigold), satiny white blouses, and fine straw hats.

Exploring Cuenca

TIMING   Note that museums are closed on Sunday. It's worthwhile to stop somewhere for lunch during your exploration, as the nicest restaurants tend to be in the center of town.

What to See

❸ Carmen de la Asunción. The ornate carvings surrounding the doorway of this diminutive chapel are a good example of Spanish baroque design. The interior is typically ostentatious—especially noteworthy is the gilded pulpit encrusted with tiny mirrors. Alas, the church keeps very irregular hours and may not be open when you pass by. ✉ *Mariscal Sucre at Padre Aguirre*.

> **TO MARKET, TO MARKET**
>
> The flower market, held outside on the Plazoleta El Carmen, is in full bloom every day from sunrise to sunset.

★ ❷ Catedral de la Inmaculada. Started in 1886 and finished more than 80 years later, the immense cathedral can hold more than 9,000 worshipers. The interior arches tower more than 100 feet high, and light that enters through the stained-glass windows casts a golden glow over the thick brick walls and Italian marble floors. The impressive pillars are Ecuadoran marble, and the choir chairs are hand-carved from native wood. ✉ *Parque Abdón Calderón* ☎ 07/284–2097 ☉ *Daily 6:30–4:30*.

Market Day in the Andes

SUNDAY IS MARKET DAY IN villages near Cuenca. Buses leave regularly from Cuenca's Terminal Terrestre, and getting there is half the fun. Drivers pick up anyone who waves them down. Young men lugging pots and pans jump on, leaving their wares piled in the aisle. Women carrying their babies wrapped in shawls drag burlap sacks filled with dried corn to their seats. Farmers taking livestock to the market hold roosters under their arms or strap piglets to the roof. (Larger pigs are more of a problem, and it's not unheard of to see the owner of a squealing sow trying to stuff it into the luggage compartment). By the time you arrive at your destination, the bus itself will seem like a market on wheels.

The largest village is Gualaceo, 38 km (24 mi) east of Cuenca. Well-dressed Cañari women in colorful polleras and jaunty straw- or felt hats gather in the main square. Locals buy and sell clothing and kitchen items, but the majority of booths feature piles of fresh produce, sacks overflowing with grains, and barrels filled with spices.

The quietest of the Andean villages, the mining town of Chordeleg, is along a winding road about 5 km (3 mi) south of Gualaceo. The highlight of the market is handmade jewelry. Some complain that the quality of the gold and silver filigree has diminished, but good bargains can still be had. A ring with a startling amount of detail costs less than $5. Handicrafts, embroidered clothing, pottery, and mounds of jewelry are sold in shops surrounding the tree-shaded square. About 24 km (15 mi) beyond Chordeleg is Sigsig, best known for its Panama hats.

–Wayne Hoffman

④ El Sagrario. Also called the Old Cathedral, this lovely little church was begun in 1557, the year the city was founded. The outside gleams after a complete restoration; work on the inside is still in progress at this writing. ⊠ *Sucre at Luis Cordero.*

⑦ Iglesia de San Francisco. Built in the 1920s, the Church of St. Francis is famous for its soaring steeple and intricately carved, gold-drenched main altar, which contrasts nicely with its unassuming interior. The church keeps very limited hours. ⊠ *Av. Gran Colombia at Padre Aguirre* ⊘ *Mon.–Wed. 7:30–8:15, Thurs.–Sat. 6:30–7:15, Sun. 7:30–9:30 and 4–5.*

⑧ Museo de Arte Moderno. The Museum of Modern Art, housed in a restored convent, features interesting rotating exhibitions of works by Ecuadoran and other Latin American artists. ⊠ *Sucre 1578, at Coronel Talbot* ☎ *07/283–1027* 🎟 *Free* ⊘ *Weekdays 9–5:30, weekends 10–1.*

Fodor'sChoice
★

⑤ Museo del Monasterio de la Concepción. Cuenca's wealthy Ordóñez family donated its spacious home to the Catholic Church in 1599, whereupon it became the cloistered convent of the Order of the Immaculate Conception, or the Conceptas. Four centuries later, part of this well-preserved edifice houses the Museum of the Monastery of the Conception, which contains

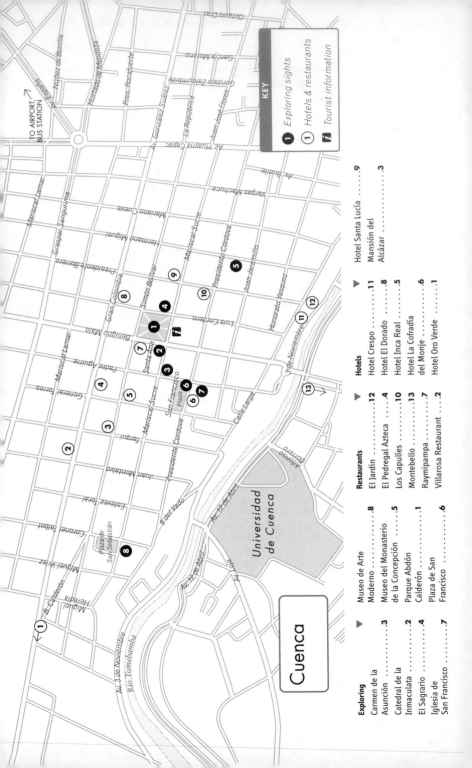

Cuenca

Exploring

Carmen de la
Asunción **3**
Catedral de la
Inmaculata **2**
El Sagrario **4**
Iglesia de
San Francisco **7**

▶ Museo de Arte
Moderno **8**
Museo del Monasterio
de la Concepción **5**
Parque Abdón
Calderón **1**
Plaza de San
Francisco **6**

Restaurants

El Jardín **12**
El Pedregal Azteca ... **4**
Los Capulíes **10**
Montebello **13**
Raymipampa **7**
Villarosa Restaurant ... **2**

▶ **Hotels**

Hotel Crespo **11**
Hotel El Dorado **8**
Hotel Inca Real **5**
Hotel La Cofradía
del Monje **6**
Hotel Oro Verde **1**

▶ Hotel Santa Lucía **9**
Mansión del
Alcázar **3**

KEY

1 Exploring sights
① Hotels & restaurants
ⓘ Tourist information

an impressive collection of religious art from the 16th to the 19th centuries. This is a must-see stop for an understanding of colonial art, all of which focused on religion, and none of which was ever signed by the artist. (Most pieces here are labeled ANÓNIMO.) The well-informed guides—take a tour conducted in Spanish, English, or French—explain that service to God was deemed more important than any artistic recognition. (That didn't stop some artists from incorporating their own faces in their works.) Most of the collection was contributed by families whose daughters entered the convent. Half the building is still inaccessible, the cloistered nuns emerging only after closing to clean the museum. No one except the museum director has face-to-face contact with them. ⊠ *Hermano Miguel 6–33, between Juan Jaramillo and Presidente Córdova* ☎ *07/283–0625* ⊠ *$2.50* ⊗ *Mon. 2:30–5:30, Tues.–Fri. 9–7:30, Sat. 10–1.*

❶ Parque Abdón Calderón. Surrounded by beautiful colonial buildings, Cuenca's central square is one of the loveliest in South America. Manicured trees tower over men discussing politics, grandmothers walking arm in arm, and children running to and fro. The park is dominated by the pale rose Catedral de la Inmaculada towering over its western edge.

❻ Plaza de San Francisco. The noisy plaza is filled with vendors hawking a variety of bric-a-brac. Under the northern colonnade, merchants sell more enticing wares—colorful skirts, hand-knit sweaters, and intricate hangings.

6

Where to Stay & Eat

¢–$ ✕ **El Jardín.** Hand-painted menus list a variety of steak and seafood dishes. Start with the tangy conch seviche served in a crystal goblet, and then move on to the succulent grilled lobster. Consider a fine Chilean wine with your meal. The relaxed, friendly service here ensures many repeat visitors. ⊠ *Larga at Borrero* ☎ *07/283–1120* ⊟ *AE, DC, MC, V.*

¢ ✕ **El Pedregal Azteca.** If you're tired of the local cuisine, you couldn't do better than stopping in this Mexican eatery. Try the chile rellenos (deep-fried chili peppers stuffed with cheese) or the specialty of the house, carne asada *a la tampiqueña* (beef grilled with salt and lemon). On weekends there's live music and two-for-one margaritas. ⊠ *Av. Gran Colombia 1029, at Padre Aguirre* ☎ *07/282–3652* ⊟ *DC, MC, V* ⊗ *Closed Sun.*

★ ¢ ✕ **Los Capulíes.** This restaurant in a 200-year-old mansion has greenery and fountains. Start with a delicately sweetened empanada, followed by the *plato típico cuencano,* a sampler dish of llapingachos, grilled pork, sweet sausages, and *mote pillo* (boiled corn mixed with onions and eggs). End your meal with a warm glass of *canelazo* (a concoction combining sugarcane, cinnamon, and bitter orange with the rumlike *zhumir*). The music of Andean flutes echoes in the air on weekends, and a bar in an attached building is a favorite hangout. ⊠ *Borrero 727* ☎ *07/284–5887* ⊟ *AE, DC, MC, V* ⊗ *Closed Sun.*

¢ ✕ **Montebello.** This Mediterranean-style restaurant in nearby Turi affords panoramic views of Cuenca, so be sure to request a table by the window. Tables and chairs are white and purple. Meat dishes are featured, including the excellent *parillada Montebello,* a casserole of pork, beef, chicken, sausage, and rice. Any taxi driver will know the way to the restaurant. ⊠ *Turi* ☎ *07/288–3403 or 07/284–3079* ⊟ *AE, V* ☻ *Closed Mon.–Wed.*

¢ ✗ **Raymipampa.** An unbeatable location adjacent to the Catedral de la Inmaculada doesn't hurt, but it's the reasonably priced food and amiable mood that makes this busy, bilevel restaurant a hit. The extensive menu includes crepes and seviche, and such Ecuadoran favorites as *locro de queso* (a milk-based potato soup garnished with avocado and cheese). ⊠ *Benigno Malo 859, at Sucre* ☎ *07/283–4159* ⊟ *MC, V.*

¢ ✗ **Villarosa Restaurant.** One of the city's best restaurants and a favorite
Fodor'sChoice with locals is in a colonial house near the central plaza. Soft music floats
★ through several tastefully decorated salons to the upper balcony, where an open fireplace chases out the evening chill. Try the grilled trout with almonds, then finish with the fruit-and-chocolate fondue. The same family owns the Hotel Santa Lucía. ⊠ *Av. Gran Colombia 1222* ☎ *07/283–7944* ⊟ *AE, DC, MC, V* ☻ *Closed weekends.*

★ **$$$** ⊞ **Mansión del Alcázar.** Fluffy down comforters top beds—some of them canopies—in rooms with filmy curtains covering windows that look onto an indoor courtyard with a trickling fountain. A hot water bottle slipped under your covers warms your bed at night. Crystal chandeliers, antique furniture, and art give you the feeling of what life was like more than 100 years ago in this carefully preserved 1891 mansion two blocks from the central plaza. Most rooms have only showers instead of full baths. A couple of rooms have windows looking onto a lovely garden. ⊠ *Bolívar 12–55, at Tarqui* ☎ *07/282–3918* ⊕ *www.mansionalcazar. com* ⇆ *10 rooms, 4 suites* ⌂ *Restaurant, cable TV, bar. library, Internet, Wi-Fi* ⊟ *AE, DC, MC, V* ⱺ *BP, MAP.*

$$ ⊞ **Hotel El Dorado.** Convenient to most of the city's sights, this recently renovated eight-story hotel sits just two blocks from Parque Calderón. Rooms at the back of the hotel are quieter than on the street side. Enjoy a meal at the Inti Sumag restaurant or the Chordeleg Café, or relax with a cocktail at the Samana piano bar. Buffet breakfast and airport transfers are included in the rate. ⊠ *Av. Gran Colombia 787, at Luis Cordero* ☎ *07/283–1390* ⊕ *www.eldoradohotel.com.ec* ⇆ *41 rooms, 1 suite* ⌂ *Restaurant, gym, sauna, spa, steam room, bar, Internet, Wi-Fi, business services, meeting rooms, airport shuttle* ⊟ *AE, DC, MC, V.*

$$ ⊞ **Hotel Oro Verde.** Once named La Laguna, after the artificial lake at
Fodor'sChoice its center, this low-rise hotel has a relaxed, casual environment. This is
★ the place for animal lovers: ducks swim past your window, three resident alpacas munch on the grassy banks, and peacocks stroll through bushes heavy with pink and yellow roses. It's 2 km (1 mi) from the center of town, so take a taxi unless you're up for a 45-minute walk. The restaurant is famous for its fish—try the trout marinated in brandy. ⊠ *Av. Ordóñez Lazo* ☎ *07/283–1200, 800/447–7462 in North America* ⊕ *www.oroverdehotels.com* ⇆ *80 rooms, 2 suites* ⌂ *3 restaurants, coffee shop, pool, gym, sauna, steam room, bar, business services, meeting room, airport shuttle* ⊟ *AE, DC, MC, V.*

$$ ⊞ **Hotel Santa Lucía.** In a beautifully restored building, Santa Lucía has attractive rooms, though its style is more modern than the building itself. Built by the first governor of the Azuay (Cuenca) Province in 1859, it has been in the Vintimilla family for three generations and is in the center of the historic district. The family decided not to remove a large tree that was growing right in the middle of the courtyard. An American breakfast is included. The restaurant (¢–$$) has excellent service and food: choices include sea bass in marinara sauce with assorted seafood; chicken in a lemon–herb sauce; and an number of risottos and gnocchis. ⊠ *Antonio Borrero 844, at Sucre* ☎ *07/282-8000* ⊕ *www. santaluciahotel.com* ⟿ *20 rooms* ⟁ *Restaurant* ⊟ *AE, MC, V.*

$ ⊞ **Hotel Crespo.** This hotel overlooking the Río Tomebamba gives you the feeling of staying in a rambling country house. You climb a twisting wooden stairway to the upper rooms, which have lovely views of the river. Scattered about are numerous sitting areas that add to the familiar, homey atmosphere. The restaurant serves excellent French cuisine. ⊠ *Larga 793* ☎ *07/284-2571* ⊕ *www.hotelcrespo.com* ⟿ *39 rooms, 3 suites* ⟁ *Restaurant, minibars, cable TV, bar, laundry service, Internet, business services, meeting rooms, airport shuttle, travel services; no a/c* ⊟ *AE, DC, MC, V.*

¢ ⊞ **Hotel Inca Real.** Huddled around three covered courtyards, this sunny hotel is small, but has neat and cheerfully furnished rooms, original art, and unique lighting fixtures. ⊠ *General Torres 840, between Sucre and Bolívar* ☎ *07/282-3636* ✎ *incareal@cue.satnet.net* ⟿ *25 rooms* ⟁ *Restaurant, cafeteria, cable TV, bar, massage, meeting room* ⊟ *AE, DC, MC, V.*

¢ ⊞ **Hostal La Cofradía del Monje.** Here's a charming little bargain-priced hotel that sits on the Plaza San Francisco. Its seven upstairs rooms overlook a lively little café that serves *típico* Ecuadoran food. Each room contains hardwood floors and stone walls and most have a little colonial wrought-iron balcony opening to the outside. Most of these overlook the bustling market on the plaza, but the commotion calms down at 6 PM each day. ⊠ *Presidente Córdova 1033, at Padre Aguirre* ☎ *07/ 283–1251* ✎ *cofradiadelmonje@hotmail.com* ⟿ *7 rooms* ⟁ *Restaurant, cable TV, bar; no a/c* ⊟ *MC, V.*

Nightlife & the Arts

Nightlife

Cuenca doesn't have a vivid nightlife. Locals usually stay home during the week, venturing forth only on weekends. **La Cantina** (⊠ Presidente Borrero at Córdova ☎ 07/283–2339) is an attractive little bar next to Los Capulíes. Musicians play on weekends. German-owned **Wunderbar** (⊠ Hermano Miguel at Larga ☎ 07/283–1274) is an intimate bar popular with locals. It's in an old building along the Escalinata, the wide stairway leading down to the river. For dancing check out **El Conquistador** (⊠ Av. Gran Colombia 665 ☎ 07/283–1788).

The Arts

A good source for information on arts events is the daily newspaper *El Mercurio.* **La Fundación Paul Rivet** (⊠ Av. Solano and 10 de Agosto ☎ 07/288–5951) distributes a monthly newsletter of cultural events.

Panama Hats Don't Come from Panama

CLOSE UP

BLAME IT ON TEDDY ROOSEVELT, but Ecuador's signature souvenir bears another country's name. Among Ecuador's most important products is the Panama hat, whose name sticks in the collective craw of proud Ecuadorans. These finely made straw hats—also known as *toquillas*, from the type of straw used to weave them—were named for the country to which they were first exported en masse. President Roosevelt wore one when he toured the Panama Canal, as had many of the workers who constructed the canal, so the hats became forever associated with that Central American country.

The first hats were made by hand in the coastal towns of Jipijapa and Montecristi and served a dual purpose: their brims protected against the tropical sun; and their tight weave created a container that could be used to carry water. The exceptionally fine *superfino* can take up to eight months to make. Their weave is so tight that they can be rolled up and then expanded with nary a crease evident.

Today the hats are most associated with the city of Cuenca, but plenty of places around the country sell them. These days quality Panama hats proudly bear the label GENUINE PANAMA HAT MADE IN ECUADOR.

Plays are sometimes performed at **La Casa de la Cultura** (⊠ Luis Cordero 718 ☎ 07/282–8175).

Shopping

Cuenca's artisans produce fine ceramics, textiles, and silver and gold jewelry, and, of course, Panama hats. On a tour of **Homero Ortega & Hijos** you'll see how palm-leaf fibers are transformed into elegant headware. You'll also have the opportunity to buy one for as little as $10 up to $250. ⊠ *Av. Gil Ramírez Davalos 3–86* ☎ *07/280–9000* ⊕ *www. homeroortgega.com* ⊗ *Weekdays 9–5, Sat. 9–noon.*

If you're in the market for leather, **Concuero** (⊠ Mariscal Lamar 1137) sells good-quality shoes, wallets, and handbags. **Fundación Jorge Moscoso** (⊠ Presidente Córdova 614) has a limited but precious collection of antiques. **Kinara** (⊠ Mariscal Sucre 770) stocks stylish gold and silver jewelry and shawls made of traditional ikat textiles, in which the threads are knotted and dyed prior to weaving.

Original designs of ceramics, murals, and jewelry are for sale—browsers are welcome—at **Eduardo Vega's Workshop and Gallery.** Vega is Ecuador's most famous ceramicist and designer. The gallery not only sells Vega's beautiful designs, but you'll get a really good cup of coffee here. On El Turi hill, known as the Mirador de Turi, it's also the best spot for a spectacular view of Cuenca. The Galería de Arte 670 has a good selection of Vega designs. ⊠ *Hermano Miguel 670* ⊗ *Weekdays 9–5, Sat. 9:30–1:30.*

Ingapirca

Fodor'sChoice ★ *70 km (42 mi) north of Cuenca.*

Long before the Inca invaded the region, in the latter half of the 15th century, the fierce and industrious Cañari people ruled Guapdondélig (Plain as Wide and Beautiful as the Sky), the name they gave the fertile highlands surrounding Cuenca. They built some stunning monuments, including the ancient city of Ingapirca.

An important religious and political center for the Cañaris, Ingapirca is perhaps better remembered for what the Inca built here after Tupac-Yupanqui conquered the Cañaris. The king left behind quite a legacy, including the name, which means "Wall of the Inca." The smaller stone structures, built completely without mortar, are thought to be Cañari temples to the moon, but the massive elliptical structure at the center is an acknowledged temple to the sun built by the Inca. La Cara del Inca, a natural rock formation said to resemble the face of an Inca chief, is a 10-minute hike.

There is a small museum at the entrance, built under the auspices of the Banco Central, which houses artifacts found at the ruins. The cozy restaurant on the hill overlooking the site serves excellent soups and local dishes in front of a fireplace. Getting to the ruins is half the fun. Buses costing less than $2 depart from Cuenca's Terminal Terrestre at 9 and 1. On the return trip your bus is likely to be filled with villagers transporting chickens and other livestock to market. The other option is to take a guided tour. Note that you might want to use a restroom before arriving, as those at the site leave much to be desired. ⊠ *5 km (3 mi) east of Cañaris* 🎫 *$2* ⏱ *Daily 9–6.*

Where to Stay & Eat

¢ ✕🏨 **Posada de Ingapirca.** To spend more time at Ingapirca, consider a stay at this posada. Rooms are simple and heated only by space heaters and fireplaces. If you want to see the countryside, you can rent horses for $10 a day; for another $10 you can hire a guide, who will lead you along an old Inca trail. Tables congregate around a cozy fireplace in an excellent restaurant that dishes up fine Ecuadoran cuisine. ⊠ *3 mi east of Cañaris, 42 mi north of Cuenca* 🕾 *07/283–1120 in Cuenca* ⊕ *www.grupo-santaana.com* 🛏 *19 rooms* 🍴 *Restaurant, bar* 🖃 *AE, DC, MC, V* 🍽 *BP.*

Parque Nacional Cajas

32 km (20 mi) west of Cuenca.

A short drive from the sunny city of Cuenca are the cold, cloudy moors of Parque Nacional Cajas, where the average elevation is 10,500 feet. The rugged terrain is the legacy left by glaciers as they retreated some 5 million years ago. Today the nearly 70,000 acres of this national park are home to Andean condors, hawks, and the elusive gray-breasted mountain toucan, as well as wolves, gazelles, and white-tailed deer. The area's 230 trout-filled lakes are accessible by boat, and fishing trips can be arranged through local tour operators and hotels.

Cajas is best explored with an experienced guide, because visitors can easily become disoriented in the stark landscape. A guide will point out the unique páramo vegetation and select the best place to set up camp each evening. Be prepared for strong sun, cold wind, and the possibility of rain. Sunglasses and sunscreen are necessities. There is a ranger station near the entrance where you can sometimes sleep for a small fee, although if the accommodations are full you'll have to make other plans.

Cuenca & the Southern Highlands Essentials

Transportation

BY AIR

Cuenca's Aeropuerto Mariscal Lamar (CUE) is 2 km (1 mi) from the city center, past the bus terminal. A cab from the airport to downtown costs around $2. Tame and Ícaro connect Cuenca with Quito and Guayaquil; AeroGal, with Quito.

🛈 Airlines **AeroGal** ☎ 07/286-1041 Cuenca. **Ícaro** ☎ 07/280-2700 Cuenca. **Tame** ☎ 07/286-2193 Cuenca.

🛈 Airports **Aeropuerto Mariscal Lamar** ⊠ Av. España ☎ 07/286-2203.

BY BUS

From Cuenca's Terminal Terrestre, 1½ km (½ mi) northeast of the town center, there are daily departures to Quito (9 hours) and Guayaquil (5 hours), both less than $7. You can also catch buses to Ingapirca for less than $2.

You can reach Parque Nacional Cajas via buses that leave between 6 AM and 6:30 AM from the corner of Calles Bolívar and Colonel Talbot. Weekend trips can be crowded, so you may have to stand for the two-hour trip. The only bus back to Cuenca leaves around 3 PM; check with the driver for the exact time.

🛈 Bus Information **Terminal Terrestre** ⊠ Av. España ☎ 07/282-7061.

BY CAR

Cuenca is 472 km (293 mi) south of Quito via the Pan-American Highway. The drive from Quito is eight hours; from Guayaquil it's four hours. The former takes you along the Avenue of the Volcanoes, while the latter climbs through subtropical lowlands before beginning a dizzying mountain ascent—8,300 feet in slightly more than 240 km (150 mi). There are services along the way, but road conditions between Guayaquil and Cuenca are much better than from Quito. Flying is the better option.

BY TAXI

Taxis are easy to find on the streets of downtown Cuenca. A trip almost anywhere in town should cost less than $2.

Contacts & Resources

MONEY MATTERS

Credit cards are accepted at most hotels, restaurants, and shops in Cuenca, and you'll find a good selection of banks here.

TOUR OPERATORS

For trips in and around Cuenca, try Ecotrek, Gray Line, Metropolitan Touring, or Seitur. Metrotours has tours in Cuenca.

🛈 Tour Companies Ecotrek ⊠ Larga 7108, at Cordero ☎ 07/284-1927. **Gray Line** ☎ 800/472-964 toll free in Ecuador ⊕ www.graylineecuador.com. **Metropolitan Touring** ⊠ Mariscal Sucre 662 ☎ 07/283-1185. **Metrotours** ⊠ Larga 6-96, at Borrero ☎ 07/283-7000 ⊕ www.metrotourscuenca.com.

VISITOR INFORMATION

A helpful branch of iTur, the national tourist office, sits on the south side of the main square. It's open weekdays 8–8 and Saturday 9–3.

🛈 Tourist Information iTur ⊠ Sucre, between Hermano Miguel and Cordero ☎ 07/282-1035.

EL ORIENTE

Ecuador's slice of the Amazon basin accounts for roughly one-third of the country's landmass but just 4% of its population. One of the world's biodiversity hot spots, El Oriente is home to hundreds of colorful bird species, including macaws, toucans, and prehistoric-looking hoatzins. Jaguars, pumas, and peccaries are elusive, but you're sure to see howler monkeys, spider monkeys, or tamarins. Pink river dolphins are also easy to spot. An abundance of insects thrive under the jungle canopy, including workaholic leaf-cutting ants, society spiders, and enormous blue morpho butterflies. Myriad plant species coexist, and in some cases even cooperate, with the jungle animals. The giant kapok tree, El Oriente's tallest species, soars nearly 200 feet above the jungle floor. Creeping vines cascade from strangler figs, which in turn envelop other species.

> **PLANNING TIP**
>
> Trips to El Oriente—especially in areas close to the Colombia border—should be arranged *only* with a tour operator that is familiar with the area and that keeps up with changing conditions. Independent travel to remote jungle areas is dangerous and not recommended.

In this exuberant world, eight indigenous peoples continue, to varying degrees, to live their traditional lifestyles. One group still lives a nomadic life and repels any attempts at rapprochement by outsiders. Others allow tourist groups to visit and share their tremendous knowledge of plants and animals.

Macas

246 km (154 mi) northeast of Cuenca.

The pleasant town of Macas is the gateway to the southern Oriente, which is more heavily settled and has less primary rain forest than the northern sector. Nonetheless, there is still spectacular rain forest to be found. To fly here to explore that rain forest, you'll need to make arrangements with a tour guide.

Wildlife Watching

Few places on the planet offer the kind of close contact with nature that the Galápagos Islands do, but other spots in Ecuador have animal watching and birding that is no less spectacular. The isolated national parks of El Oriente protect important expanses of the tropical rain forest inhabited by anacondas, anteaters, howler monkeys, river dolphins, and 1,600 species of birds. In the highland forests are avian species ranging from delicate hummingbirds to mighty condors, while the plains that surround those forests offer close encounters with llamas, alpacas, and other Andean ungulates.

Kapawi

184 km (115 mi) east of Macas.

One of the most remote corners of Ecuador, this eastern jungle region near the Peruvian border is the territory of the Achuar people. Kapawi is actually the name of an Achuar village.

Where to Stay

★ $$$$ ▦ **Kapawi Ecolodge & Reserve.** This group of typical Achuar huts—no nails were used in construction—is equipped with modern amenities like electric lights and private baths. All-inclusive packages last four to eight days, but you must stay a minimum of four days and three nights, for a cost of $600. An extra day and night will cost you an extra $120. This is an excellent experience if you want to see wildlife and have some contact with the Achuar people. According to an agreement, the ecolodge will be transferred to the Achuar in 2011. For birders, Kapawi has a booklet mapping out trails and bird species nesting in the area. In 10 days it isn't unusual to see almost 400. All meals are included. Remember that airfare from Quito will cost you about $200. ⊠ *Kapawi* ☎ *04/251–4750 in Guayaquil, 800/613–6026 toll free in North America* ⊕ *www.kapawi.com* ➷ *20 rooms* ⌂ *Dining room, bar, library, travel services; no a/c, no room phones, no room TVs* ▤ *AE, DC, MC, V* ۩ *All inclusive.*

$$$$ ▦ **Sacha Lodge.** A parrot clay lick and a butterfly farm in the nearby Parque Nacional Yasuní (Yasuní National Park; close to the Colombian border) and a 43-meter (135-foot) observation tower built around a giant kapok tree at the lodge are added attractions at this rustic but comfortable thatch-roof lodge deep in the Amazon. Activities include birding and canoe trips on the Napo River. ⊠ *Parque Nacional Yasuní* ☎ *09/973–3182, 02/250–9504 in Quito, 877/656–8462 toll free in North America* ⊕ *www.sachalodge.com* ➷ *26 cabins* ⌂ *Dining room, bar, travel services; no a/c, no room phones, no room TVs* ▤ *AE, DC, MC, V* ۩ *All inclusive.*

El Oriente Essentials

Transportation

BY AIR

Tame flies from Quito to Coca's Aeropuerto Francisco de Orellana (OCC) and Lago Agrio's Aeropuerto Nueva Loja (LGQ) daily except Sunday and to Macas's Aeropuerto Edmundo Carvajal (XMS) Monday, Wednesday, and Friday. Ícaro connects Quito with Coca daily and Lago Agrio three times weekly. Each flight is a 40-minute trip. Several small charter companies specialize in jungle towns and other remote destinations; these are considerably more expensive.

🛪 **Airlines & Contacts** Ícaro ☎ 06/288-0546 Coca, 06/283-2370 Lago Agrio. **Tame** ☎ 06/288-1078 Coca, 06/283-0113 Lago Agrio, 07/270-1978 Macas.

BY BUS

The trip from Quito to Lago Agrio takes eight hours by bus. Since Lago Agrio is near the Colombian border, it's best to consult a tour operator about safety in this area. The trip from Quito to Coca takes nine hours. A journey from Cuenca to Macas takes 10–12 hours, but the road is frequently impassable, a condition that comes and goes with the weather. Since El Oriente has no truly dry season, don't count on being able to negotiate this route overland.

BY CAR

Car travel to this region should be undertaken only with much caution and advance preparation. Be forewarned, however, that in some areas of El Oriente you will find yourself driving alongside ugly oil pipelines; roads are periodically blocked by environmentalists protesting petroleum exploration. The trip between Quito and Coca takes eight hours. Misahuallí can be reached in 5–5½ hours by car. Since Macas is so remote, and the road sometimes becomes impassable, you shouldn't attempt to drive. No roads pass near Kapawi, making air travel your only option.

Contacts & Resources

MONEY MATTERS

It is nearly impossible to change or get money in El Oriente. Don't count on finding a bank. Bring all the cash you'll need.

TOUR OPERATORS

In Coca the family-run travel company Ejarsytur offers a variety of travel services and tours. Expediciones Dayuma, another reputable company, can assist you with travel in the region.

In Cuenca, Ecotrek will put you in contact with the Shuar people, who live to the east of Macas near the missionary town of Miazal.

🛪 **Tour Companies Ecotrek** ✉ Larga 7-108, Cuenca ☎ 07/283-4677 or 07/284-2531. **Ejarsytur** ☎ 06/288-0251. **Expediciones Dayuma** ✉ Dayuma Hotel, Misahuallí ☎ 06/ 257-1513.

GUAYAQUIL & THE PACIFIC COAST

Once only a jumping-off point for the Galápagos, Guayaquil has become a destination all its own. Less than a decade ago, you dared not walk the streets of downtown Guayaquil at night (daytime strolls were no guarantee of safety either). But an exceptionally ambitious city government, determined to clean up crime and halt a long downward slide, in a few years has transformed the aging port, the capital of Guayas Province, into Ecuador's most vibrant city. Change is everywhere you look here, and some 2 million proud Guayaquileños have become the ultimate civic boosters. "Have you seen the Malecón?" they ask you, pointing to the new riverfront promenade lined with museums, restaurants, shops, and ongoing entertainment. They also tout the new museums, the remodeled airport, and the Metrovía, the new urban transportation network, whose first of seven lines debuted in 2006. If Quito is Ecuador's colonial and administrative heart and soul, Guayaquil is its pocketbook. It remains a modern, financially minded city and will never attract the same number of visitors as the capital. But Guayaquil deserves to be a place of pilgrimage for urban fans everywhere for a reassuring look at what a city can do right.

Because it's about 55 km (35 mi) inland, Guayaquil doesn't catch ocean breezes, so during the stifling December–April rainy season, Guayaquileños head en masse for the beaches along Ecuador's southern coast, the romantically named Ruta del Sol (Route of the Sun). The blue waters teem with sailfish, albacore, wahoo, dolphin, and marlin, which attract world-class sportfishermen. Farther north on the coast is the splendid Parque Nacional Machalilla, from which you can take a boat to Isla de la Plata, 24 km (15 mi) offshore. The island is called the poor man's Galápagos because you can see more than 20 species of the same sea- and birdlife found in the Galápagos.

Guayaquil

250 km (156 mi) southwest of Quito.

You couldn't find a nicer way to spend an evening than strolling along the Malecón, Guayaquil's lovely riverfront promenade. You'll be in good company, as locals love the landmark here. Most of the town's major sights are within a few blocks of the river.

TIMING   Most of Guayaquil's sights can be toured in a single day, as they are all along or close to the waterfront, although tropical temperatures may slow you down.

What to See

4 **Catedral Metropolitana.** The twin-spired cathedral, which looms over the western edge of Parque Seminario, is actually one of the city's newer houses of worship. Construction began on the semigothic structure in 1937 and was completed in 1950. Vendors selling hand-carved rosaries and other items crowd the sidewalks outside. ⊠ *Parque Seminario.*

CLOSE UP

A Great Drive

If you're looking for a really splendid car trip—on a good highway—consider driving from Guayaquil up the Pacific coast 280 km (174 mi) to the eco-city of Bahía de Caráquez. There's lots to do along the way—you can lounge on the gorgeous beaches of Machalilla National Park, go deep-sea fishing in Salinas, explore the town of Manta where cruise ships dock, and visit the Indian village of Montecristi, where the original Panama hats are still made. Once you reach Bahía de Caráquez, you can surf, watch for whales (July–September), and help excavate an archaeological site at the Chirije beach resort. If you prefer not to drive, there is good bus service between towns along the coast (you can also fly to Manta from Quito; from there it's a 45-minute drive to Bahía de Caráquez).

★ ⓮ **Cementerio General.** Also called Ciudad Blanca, the General Cemetery is one of the city's most impressive sights. More than 200 mausoleums, all in elaborately carved white marble, line the neat paths. Because of a recurring problem with pickpockets, you may want to visit on a guided tour. ✉ *Av. Coronel west of Las Peñas* 🎫 *Free.*

6

⓭ **Iglesia de Santo Domingo.** Guayaquil's oldest church was founded by the Franciscans in 1548. Near Las Peñas, the simple colonial structure was rebuilt after it was destroyed by pirate attacks. Locals also refer to it as the Iglesia de San Vicente.

★ ❼ **Malecón 2000.** Guayaquil's riverfront promenade anchors the city's rebirth. After years of neglect, the 26-block street has been transformed into one of the city's most pleasant attractions. As you stroll along the Río Guayas, you can relax on benches in shady parks or poke into numerous shops, restaurants, the contemporary art museum (MAAC), an IMAX theater, and a planetarium. Across the street from El Malecón is the Palacio Municipal, considered one of the country's best examples of neoclassical architecture. Beside the adjacent Palacio de la Gobernación is Parque Sucre, a sliver of greenery dedicated to war hero Mariscal Antonio José de Sucre. ✉ *Av. Simón Bolívar between Febres Cordero and Loca* ⊕ *www.malecon2000.com* ⊙ *7 AM–midnight; shops 10–9.*

⓫ **Museo Antropológico y Arte Contemporáneo** (MAAC). If Ecuador doesn't spring to mind when someone mentions art, a visit to Guayaquil's newest museum might change that. Ecuadoran artists began to break the connection with religious-themed art in the late 19th century, and the country's artists have never looked back. Take an English-language guided tour—essential to understanding how the exhibits are laid out. Anthropology, the first A in the museum's name, will soon get equal treatment as Ecuador's Central Bank's extensive collection of artifacts is being moved into the building's second level, a process scheduled for completion by 2007. ✉ *Malecón 2000, at Loja* 🕿 *04/230–9400* 🎫 *$3; Tues. and Sun, $1.50* ⊙ *Tues.–Sat. 10–6, Sun. 10–4.*

Fodor'sChoice ★

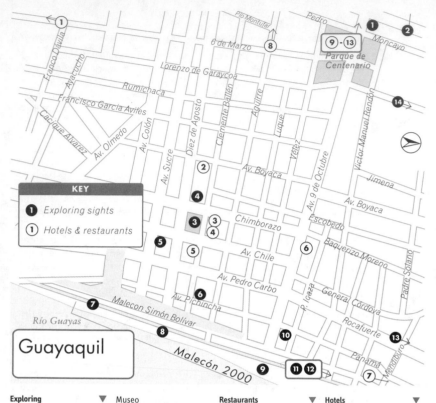

Guayaquil

10 Museo Banco del Pacífico. Just a block from the waterfront, the Pacific Bank Museum has rotating exhibits of archaeological discoveries, as well as a permanent collection of 19th-century South American art. ⊠ *Plaza Ycaza 113, at Pichincha* ☎ *04/256–6010* ⬜ *Free* ⊙ *Tues.–Fri. 9–6, weekends 11–1.*

1 Museo Casa de la Cultura. The Museum of Culture features prehistoric stone and ceramic artifacts discovered on La Plata Island off the coast from Guayaquil. There's also an impressive collection of gold items dating to before the arrival of the Spanish. ⊠ *Av. 9 de Octubre 1200, at Plaza Moncayo* ☎ *04/230–0500* ⬜ *$1* ⊙ *Tues.–Fri. 10–6, Sat. 9–3.*

5 Museo Municipal de Guayaquil. While the Municipal Museum of Guayaquil has many interesting archaeological exhibits, the biggest draw is a collection of *tsantsas*, or shrunken heads. Artifacts from indigenous peoples here include beadwork, feather work, tools, and weapons. In the lobby is an unusual 8½-meter (28-foot) totem with 32 vertical figures. ⚠ **Your passport is required for admission, only so an attendant can compile data about who visits and from where.** ⊠ *Av. Sucre, between Av. Chile and Av. Pedro Carbo* ☎ *04/252–4100* ⬜ *Free* ⊙ *Tues.–Sat. 9–5;.*

6 Museo Nahím Isaías. The Nahím Isaías Museum reopened in 2005 after Fodor'sChoice ★ a five-year expansion, with truly fabulous results. Each year about 500 pieces of the astounding permanent collection of religious art from the colonial period is parceled out and displayed. An informative guided tour—choose between English or Spanish—that provides the best background on what you see is included in your admission. ⊠ *Avs. Clemente Ballén and Pichincha* ☎ *04/232–4182* ⬜ *$1.50; $1, Tues. and Sun.* ⊙ *Tues.–Sat. 10–6, Sun. 11–3.*

★ 2 Parque Histórico de Guayaquil. There are three sections to this park, which opened in 2002: the Architecture Zone, with colonial buildings dating to 1886 (they were restored and moved here); the Traditional Zone, where actors dressed in period costumes re-create life as it was lived in the early 20th century; and the Endangered Wildlife Zone, with rare birds and animals. There are wooden walkways throughout and a small restaurant. This is a very pleasant way to spend a few hours; it's right on the edge of the rain forest. ⊠ *Av. Esmeraldas, Vía a Samborondón* ☎ *04/283–3807* ⊕ *www.parquehistorico.com* ⬜ *$3; Sun., $4.50* ⊙ *Tues.–Sun. 9–4:30.*

3 Parque Seminario. This lovely square, the heart of the city since it was inaugurated in 1895, is known by many names. Because it has the almost obligatory statue of a triumphant Simón Bolívar, many locals call it Parque Bolívar. A more common moniker is Parque de las Iguanas, as dozens of the scaly green creatures can be found lazing about on park benches and across the limbs of trees. The gardens, which still have a marvelous wrought-iron bandstand, are filled with 43 species of indigenous plants. ⊠ *Between Av. Clemente Ballén and Av. Diez de Agosto.*

12 Cerro Santa Ana and Las Peñas. Until 2002 this neighborhood at the foot of Cerro Santa Ana (Santa Ana Hill) was a seedy barrio of ramshackle houses where drugs dominated after dark. But from 2001 to 2002 the city poured $8 million into the neighborhood, transforming it in record time into one of the most charming parts of the city. Brightly painted houses, shops, and cafés climb Santa Ana Hill. Old-fashioned streetlamps light the way to the summit—there are 444 steps, thoughtfully (or unthoughtfully) numbered—where you can get an unparalleled view of the city. Perhaps the most amazing aspect of Las Peñas's transformation is that it was done without relocating the neighborhood's residents. Many of them benefited from business grants doled out by the city and now work as shopkeepers or manage cafés. The response from the community has been overwhelmingly positive, and other cities around the globe are following Guayaquil's model.

❾ La Rotonda. Imposing marble columns form the backdrop for statues of the men who liberated most of the continent, Simón Bolívar and José de San Martín. The monument commemorates their first (and only) meeting, in Guayaquil in 1822. ⊠ *Malecón at Av. 9 de Octubre* 🎫 *Free.*

❽ Torre del Reloj Público. The Moorish style clock tower, constructed in 1770, is one of the city's most enduring landmarks. Inside is a small exposition of photographs of Guayaquil dating from the early 20th century. ⊠ *El Malecón.*

Where to Stay & Eat

The majority of Guayaquil's nicer restaurants are clustered in the Urdesa neighborhood north of downtown, where you'll also find some of the city's most popular bars and dance clubs. Many restaurants close daily between 4:30 and 7:30, then reopen for dinner. Lodging rates vary dramatically depending on time of year, special promotions, or apparently how many empty rooms the hotel has at the moment you call, so always ask whether discount rates are available.

$ ✕ **El Caracol Azul.** This downtown restaurant, specializing in Peruvian-style seafood, is popular with business executives. The interior of the nondescript building is surprisingly attractive, enlivened by a skylight and paintings by local artists. Start off with seviche or *chicharrón de calamar* (deep-fried squid); then move on to langostino *picante* (in a spicy cream sauce). ⊠ *Av. 9 de Octubre at Los Ríos* 🎫 *04/228–0461* 🖃 *AE, DC, MC, V* ⊘ *Closed Sun.*

$ ✕ **Trattoria da Enrico.** Tiny shuttered windows set into thick whitewashed walls reflect this restaurant's Mediterranean influence. The simple exterior doesn't prepare you for the aquarium in the dining room, which is set into the ceiling. Try the prosciutto and melon appetizer, then move on to the chicken with a sour cream, vodka, and mushroom sauce. Musicians playing mandolins wander among the tables. ⊠ *Bálsamos 504, at Ebanos* 🎫 *04/238–7079* 🖃 *DC, MC, V* ⊘ *Closed Tues.*

¢–$ ✕ **Casa Baska.** The owner peers out through a tiny window before opening the door to welcome you into this intimate Spanish restaurant, which also goes by the name La Tasca Vasca. The food, cooked up with a Basque flair, couldn't be better. Start with the broiled calamari, large enough to be worn as bracelets, then move on to the flavorful paella. You couldn't do better than end with the expertly prepared crème caramel. ⊠ *Av. Clemente Ballén 422, at Chimborazo* 🎫 *04/253–4599* 🖃 *No credit cards* ⊘ *No lunch, closed Sun.*

¢–$ ✕ **Lo Nuestro Café Restaurant.** Historic photos of Guayaquil crowd the walls of this restaurant in the Urdesa neighborhood. Guayaquil is known for its seviche, and Lo Nuestro's is good, meant to be drenched in the fresh lime juice that accompanies it. ⊠ *Victor Emilio Estrado 903, at Higueras* ☎ *04/238–6398* ▭ *DC, MC, V.*

¢ ✕ **La Parrillada del Ñato.** Several long grills make this barbecue restaurant appear as if it were designed to feed an army. It's a good thing, too, because legions of hungry carnivores fill the restaurant seven days a week to feast on racks of ribs, succulent steaks, and an array of other tasty meat dishes. ⊠ *Av. V. E. Estrada 1219, at Costañera* ☎ *04/238–7098* ▭ *AE, DC, MC, V.*

$$$–$$$$ ✕▦ **Hotel Oro Verde.** The chain's flagship hotel continues to be one of the top choices for business travelers. In addition to comfortable rooms and plenty of amenities, the hotel has a pool, health club, and even a casino. The lobby bar, with live music every night, draws locals. If you're hungry, head to the informal Spice Grill to sample the tasty Szechuan chicken salad. ⊠ *Av. 9 de Octubre at García Moreno* ☎ *04/ 232–7999, 800/223–6800 in the U.S.* ⊕ *www.oroverdeguayaquil.com* ⇔ *192 rooms, 62 suites* ⌒ *3 restaurants, cable TV, in-room safes, in-room data ports, minibars, pool, gym, sauna, steam room, bar, casino, business services, car rental, meeting rooms* ▭ *AE, DC, MC, V.*

$$$ ✕▦ **Grand Hotel Guayaquil.** This landmark hotel near Parque Seminario and most other downtown attractions shares a city block with the Catedral Metropolitana. Small but comfortable rooms with large windows let in lots of sun. The health club lets you play squash on two courts, relax in a sauna, or enjoy the terrace with a great view of the cathedral. ⊠ *Boyaca at Av. 10 de Agosto* ☎ *04/232–9690, 800/334–3782 in the U.S.* ⊕ *www.grandhotelguayaquil.com* ⇔ *175 rooms, 10 suites* ⌒ *2 restaurants, coffee shop, in-room data ports, minibars, cable TV, pool, gym, massage, sauna, steam room, squash, bar, laundry service, business services, meeting rooms, travel services* ▭ *AF, DC, MC, V.*

$$$$ ▦ **Hilton Colón Guayaquil.** This majestic hotel outside the city center (next
Fodor'sChoice to the Expoplaza convention center) has a 10-story atrium lobby. It de-
★ livers everything you'd expect from a top-notch business hotel. The beautiful pool area is surrounded by palm trees. The Large Policentro Shopping Mall is nearby. ⊠ *Av. Francisco de Orellana* ☎ *04/268– 9000, 800/445–8667 in North America* ⊕ *www.hilton.com* ⇔ *273 rooms, 19 suites* ⌒ *4 restaurants, in-room data ports, minibars, cable TV, pool, health club, hair salon, bar, casino, business services, meeting rooms, in-room safes, sauna, airport shuttle, car rental, Wi-Fi, travel services, no-smoking rooms,* ▭ *AE, DC, MC, V.*

$$ ▦ **UniPark Hotel.** Part of the Oro Verde chain, this comfortable hotel is within walking distance of most of the city's attractions. Across the street from the Parque Seminario, it gives you direct access to an 80-store shopping center. Several excellent restaurants are also on the premises, including a wonderful sushi bar called Unibar. Buffet breakfast is included. The best view is from a parkside room. ⊠ *Av. Clemente Ballén 406* ☎ *04/ 232–7100, 800/448–8355 in the U.S.* ⊕ *www.uniparkhotel.com* ⇔ *125 rooms, 14 suites* ⌒ *Restaurant, café, in-room data ports, in-room safes, minibars, cable TV, gym, sauna, bar, casino, concierge, Internet, Wi-Fi*

on some floors, business services, meeting room, airport shuttle ☰ *AE, DC, MC, V.*

$$$ ▢ **Hotel Ramada.** This popular hotel—it's not affiliated with the U.S. chain—is across from El Malecón and the riverfront and within walking distance of Las Peñas. When the heat of tropical Guayaquil gets to be too much, you can sip a cocktail by the pool. Evenings find many guests slipping off to the casino. ✉ *Malecón 606, at Orellana* ☎ *04/256–5555, 800/327–1847 in North America* ⊕ *www.hotelramada.com* ⤴ *76 rooms* ♨ *2 restaurants, coffee shop, indoor pool, sauna, bar, casino, laundry service, concierge, business services, meeting rooms, airport shuttle* ☰ *AE, DC, MC, V.*

$$$ ▢ **Hampton Inn Guayaquil.** This small inn behind the beautiful San Francisco Church is just a few blocks from the Malecón and close to all the museums. Rooms are nice, and all have coffeemakers and two phone lines. ✉ *9 de Octubre 432, at Baquerizo Moreno* ☎ *04/256–6700* ⊕ *www.hamptoninn.hilton.com* ⤴ *95 rooms* ♨ *2 restaurants, cable TV, in-room data ports, gym, hot tub, sauna, pool, casino, Internet, Wi-Fi in lobby, business services, meeting rooms, no-smoking rooms* ☰ *AE, DC, MC, V* ⦿ *BP.*

FodorsChoice
★

¢ ▢ **Hotel del Rey.** Visiting soccer players love this pleasant hotel several blocks from Parque Guayaquil. The well-maintained rooms are a bit small, but this is one of the few moderately priced hotels in town that has exercise facilities. ✉ *Aguirre at Andrés Marín* ☎ *04/245–3037 or 04/245–2053* ⤴ *47 rooms* ♨ *Restaurant, cable TV, gym, sauna, bar* ☰ *DC, MC, V* ⦿ *BP.*

¢ ▢ **Rizzo Hotel.** A good budget option, this downtown hotel has comfortable rooms with balconies overlooking Parque Seminario. The staff is eager to help you in any way, from suggesting a restaurant to giving tips on nightlife. ✉ *Av. Clemente Ballén 319, at Chile* ☎ *04/232–5210* ⊕ *www.rizzohotel.com* ⤴ *60 rooms* ♨ *Restaurant, café, minibars, health club, casino, dance club* ☰ *AE, DC, MC, V* ⦿ *CP.*

Salinas

141 km (88 mi) west of Guayaquil.

Guayaquileños flock to the popular if sometimes overcrowded beaches here on holidays and during the hot and humid rainy season. Deep-sea fishing is another draw. The continental shelf drops sharply to the ocean floor just 19 km (12 mi) offshore, providing a fertile feeding ground for Pacific sailfish, swordfish, and amberjack, as well as striped, blue, and black marlin. The biggest catches are made November through May, but fishing continues year-round. An excellent highway connects Salinas and Guayaquil.

GO FISH

The prime marlin season on the southern coast is from October through April. **Magellan Offshore Fishing Tours** (✉ Salinas ☎ 04/247–83189, 877/426–3347 in the U.S. ⊕ www.magellanoffshore.com) arranges fishing tours on a private yacht called the *Hatteras Paper Moon.* **PescaTours** (✉ Salinas ☎ 04/244–3365 or 04/277–2391 ⊕ www.pescatours.com.ec) organizes daylong charters for two to six people.

Where to Stay

$$ ⚏ **Puerto Lucía Yacht Club.** If you need a place to anchor your 150-foot yacht, head to this beautiful resort on the Península Santa Elena. (You don't really need a yacht to stay here.) This is a great vacation destination for the entire family; it has everything from deep-sea fishing to rain-forest expeditions. The small suites have balconies overlooking the bay where you can watch the sun disappear into the ocean. For larger groups, two- and three-bedroom apartments are available. ⊠ *Av. C. J. Arosemena, Km 2.5* ☎ *04/278–3180, 04/220–6154 in Guayaquil, 877/426–3347 in the U.S.* ⊕ *www.puertolucia.com.ec* ⇆ *24 suites* ♨ *Restaurant, cable TV, 4 tennis courts, 3 pools, hot tub, beach, marina, fishing, travel services* ▭ *AE, DC, MC, V.*

Parque Nacional Machalilla

Fodor'sChoice ★ *In Puerto López, 167 km (104 mi) northwest of Guayaquil.*

The 136,850-acre Parque Nacional Machalilla is in the extreme southwestern corner of the state of Manabí, and was created in 1979 in an effort to halt the destruction of the country's remaining tropical dry forests. Unlike the lush greenery associated with rain forests, dry-forest vegetation includes kapok trees, prickly pear cactus, and strangler figs. The entrance fee is good for five days and includes access to Isla de la Plata, a 3,000-acre seabird sanctuary where red-footed, blue-footed, and masked boobies make their homes. The waters surrounding the island teem with flying fish, dolphins, and humpback whales that come from Antarctica to bear their young. There are restrooms and changing facilities at the park. ⊠ *The visitor center is on the main street in Puerto López* ⌑ *$20.*

> ### WHEN TO GO
>
> Come here for the sandy beaches, but be warned that riptides are common in this area, especially when the ocean is rough. Although the water is swimmable year-round, it is warmest during the rainy summer months (December–May).

Where to Stay & Eat

¢ ✕ **Carmita's Restaurant.** Doña Carmita and her sister have a way with seafood. The signature dish at this simple beachfront eatery, among the best restaurants along the southern coast, is the zesty *pescado al vapor con vegetales* (lemony fish soup with vegetables). A wide variety of drinks, including German and Chilean wines, is available. ⊠ *Malecón s/n, Puerto López* ☎ *05/260–4148 or 05/260–4149* ▭ *V.*

$ ✕⚏ **Hostería Atamari.** Papayas, palms, and flaming bougainvillea grow among the thatch-roof cottages of this hotel, which is perched on a rocky promontory overlooking the Ayampe Valley and the Pacific Ocean, 28 km (17 mi) south of Puerto López. Trails by the hotel lead to a private beach where hundreds of birds and butterflies hover. Whale-watching season is June–October; from the cliff-top terrace you'll have the best seats in the house. The outdoor restaurant serves fantastic international cuisine, with an emphasis on seafood. ⊠ *Península de Santa Elena,*

Ayampe ☎ 09/982–9916, 02/222–7896 *in Quito* ⊕ *atamari.ec.tripod. com* ☜ *8 cottages, 4 suites* ♻ *Restaurant, pool* ☰ *AE, DC, MC, V.*

¢ ✕☒ **Alandaluz Hostería.** The two- and three-story thatch-roof cabanas face several miles of sand beaches. About 15 minutes south of Puerto López, it is a favorite among tourists, who come to get closer to nature. Many travelers come for a night and end up spending a week, lounging in hammocks and chatting at the open-air bar. The restaurant emphasizes vegetarian fare. ⊠ *Puerto Rico, Parque Nacional Machalilla* ☎ *04/278–0690, 02/224–8604 in Quito* ⊕ *www.alandaluzhosteria. com* ☜ *8 rooms, 15 cabins* ♻ *Restaurant, beach, bar, travel services; no room phones, no room TVs* ☰ *No credit cards.*

$ ☒ **Mantaraya Lodge.** The adobe-style buildings that make up this lodge may remind you a bit of Old Mexico. Nestled among the kapok trees of Parque Nacional Machalilla, the resort has its own guides to take you out on wilderness excursions. You can also join fishing, diving, and whale-watching trips aboard the *Mantarayas II* and *III*. Reservations are made through Advantage Travel in Quito. ⊠ *Puerto López* ☎ *02/244–8985 in Quito, 800/327–3573 in the U.S.* ⊕ *www.mantarayalodge.com* ☜ *15 rooms* ♻ *Restaurant, cafeteria, pool, kayaks, fishing, bicycles, bar, travel services* ☰ *AE, DC, MC, V* ❘○❘ *FAP.*

Sports & the Outdoors

FISHING **Advantage Travel** (⊠ El Telégrafo E10–63, at Juan de Alcántara, Quito ☎ 02/246–2871) arranges fishing charters. If you're an experienced angler, you'll be happier if you bring your own equipment. Otherwise, gear of dubious quality can be rounded up by the agency.

HORSEBACK Trips to beautiful Los Frailes Cove can be arranged through **Pacarina**
RIDING (⊠ Puerto López ☎ 05/260–4173) for less than $5 for a half-day trip. Pacarina also arranges overnight camping trips within Parque Nacional Machalilla. An excursion popular with birders is the seven-hour hike from Agua Blanca to San Sebastián, which passes through dry forest, cloud forest, and tropical rain forest—each climate with its own distinct species of flora and fauna. After a night camping outside San Sebastián, you can return to Agua Blanca on foot or by horse. The fee for this or other excursions in the area is less than $7 per day.

Bahía de Caráquez

14 km (23 mi) from Manta.

This beachfront port town, built by the Spaniards in 1624, has a delightful small-town-resort vibe, with waterfront restaurants that serve delicious meals of organically grown shrimp and fresh crab. The Spaniards were not the first, however, to find this peninsula. Members of the Caras people arrived aboard balsa-wood sailing rafts around 1500 BC, and it's believed that Bahía de Caráquez was set up as a trading center for shells and crafted ornaments, which were exchanged for gold, copper, and other goods from places as far away as Mexico and Chile. A large replica of a raft is in Bahía's Central Bank Museum, the **Casa de la Cultura** (⊠ On the main St. ⊙ Daily 10–5 ☜ 75¢), which displays archaeological artifacts and costumes. Rafts were built without nails and could hold 50–100 people.

This town, whose population is 25,000, takes pride in being the first ecocity in Ecuador. There are few cars, as most transportation is by three-wheel cycle. An environmental learning center, started by Flor Maria Duenas, is an after-school center for children from underprivileged homes, at which the children learn the importance of recycling and environmental issues. Bahía's citizens envision their city as a model of sustainability.

Just a short boat ride from town is Isla Corazón, or Heart Island. First you'll stop at a welcome center to see a presentation at another island, then you get back on the boat to continue to Isla Corazón. The island, which has 174 acres of mangrove, serves as a nesting place for frigate birds—males inflate what looks like a large red balloon to attract females during mating season. You can either walk along boardwalks to explore the forest or canoe around the island.

Where to Stay

$ 🏨 **La Piedra.** This small oceanfront hotel gives you access to the beach. You can also tour the town in the hotel's horse-drawn carriage. ☒ *Av. Virgilio Ratti* ☎ *05/269–0780* 🛏 *42 rooms* ⚲ *Restaurant, cable TV, outdoor pool, volleyball, bar* ☰ *AE, DC, MC, V* ❖ *BP.*

Guayaquil & the Pacific Coast Essentials

Transportation

BY AIR

Guayaquil's international airport, Aeropuerto Simón Bolívar (GYE), is 6 km (4 mi) north of the city center; taxis to downtown cost about $4. From Guayaquil, Tame has flights to Quito, Cuenca, Manta, Loja, and Machala, as well as to the Galápagos islands of Baltra and San Cristóbal. Tame also connects Manta's Aeropuerto General Eloy Alfaro (MEC) to Quito. AeroGal flies from Guayaquil to Quito, Baltra, and San Cristóbal. Ícaro connects Guayaquil with Quito and Cuenca and Manta with Quito.

Airlines that fly to Guayaquil are American, from Miami; Continental, from Houston; LanEcuador, from Miami, Lima, and Santiago; KLM, from Amsterdam; Iberia, from Madrid; TACA Peru, from Lima; Avianca, from Bogotá; Aeropostal and Santa Bárbara Airlines, from Caracas; and LAB Airlines, from Santa Cruz, Bolivia.

🛈 Airlines & Contacts **AeroGal** ☎ 04/231-0352 Guayaquil. **Aeropostal** ☎ 04/269-2848 Guayaquil. **American** ☎ 04/256-4111 Guayaquil. **Avianca** ☎ 04/239-9048 Guayaquil. **Continental** ☎ 04/256-7241 Guayaquil. **Iberia** ☎ 04/232-9558 Guayaquil. **Ícaro** ☎ 04/263-0620 Guayaquil, 05/262-7327 Manta. **LAB Airlines** ☎ 04/269-8035 Guayaquil. **LanEcuador** ☎ 04/269-2850 Guayaquil. **Santa Bárbara Airlines** ☎ 04/228-8118 Guayaquil. **TACA Peru** ☎ 800/008-222 toll free in Ecuador. **Tame** ☎ 04/269-2963 Guayaquil, 05/261-3210 Manta.

🛈 Airport Information **Aeropuerto Simón Bolívar** ☒ Av. de las Américas, Guayaquil ☎ 04/228-2100. **Aeropuerto General Eloy Alfaro** ☒ Av. de las Américas, Manta ☎ 05/229-0005.

BY BUS

Guayaquil is 10 hours by bus from Quito and around 5 hours from Cuenca. The city's main bus station, Terminal Terrestre, is just north of the airport. You can take buses up the coast to various towns all the way to Bahía de Caráquez. The shortest route to Bahía de Caráquez is from Guayaquil, skipping Salinas—you can go directly northwest up the coast.

The first of seven lines of Guayaquil's Metrovía, an urban electric trolley-bus system modeled on Quito's Trole, is open. The city's indomitable can-do spirit means the remaining six lines should be completed in timely fashion, too.

TAXIS

Taxis throughout Guayaquil are inexpensive. The average trip should cost $3. Most do not use meters, so be prepared to haggle.

Contacts & Resources

SAFETY

Security has improved dramatically in downtown Guayaquil, but the city still has several dicey neighborhoods. Stick to well-lighted streets and take taxis at night.

TOUR OPERATORS

Guayaquil Visión operates 90-minute bus tours of the city several times daily departing from the south end of the Malecón. The frigate ship *El Morgan* conducts hour-long cruises up and down Guayaquil's riverfront daily except Monday. Cruceros Discovery offers short cruises along the Río Guayas, as well as longer nature excursions to the mangroves of Isla Santay, across the Río Guayas from the city.

Guides can be hired at the Parque Nacional Machalilla visitor center in Puerto López for less than $10 a day for up to 10 persons. Guided tours can also be arranged to the park through Advantage Travel in Quito.

🔽 **Tour Companies Advantage Travel** ✉ El Telégrafo E10–63, at Juan de Alcántara ☎ 02/246–2871, 800/327–3573 in North America ⊕ www.advantagecuador.com. **Cruceros Discovery** ✉ Malecón 2000 ☎ 04/230–4824 ⊕ www.crucerosdiscovery.com. **El Morgan** ✉ Malecón 2000, at Sucre ☎ 04/229–1313. **Guayaquil Visión** ✉ Malecón 2000, at Plaza Olmedo ☎ 04/230–6444. **Canodros** ✉ Santa Leonor M25, Solar 10, Vía Terminal Terrestre, Guayaquil ☎ 04/228–5711, 800/613–6026 in North America ⊕ www.canodros.com.

VISITOR INFORMATION

Guayaquil's branch of iTur is open weekdays 8:30–5 and has a few maps and brochures, but little else. A better bet is the friendly Oficina de Información Turística at the entrance to the Nahim Isaís Museum, open Tuesday–Saturday 10–5.

🔽 **Tourist Information iTur** ✉ Plaza Icaza 203, at Pichincha, 6th fl. ☎ 04/256–8764. **Oficina de Información Turística** ✉ Avs. Clemente Ballén and Pichincha ☎ 04/232–4182 ⊕ www.visitaguayaquil.com.

THE GALÁPAGOS ISLANDS

Fodor'sChoice
★

A zoologist's dream, the Galápagos Islands afford a once-in-a-lifetime chance to witness animals found nowhere else on the planet. From the moment you step onto these dazzling shores, you're confronted by giant tortoises basking in the sun, lava lizards darting between rocks, and frigates

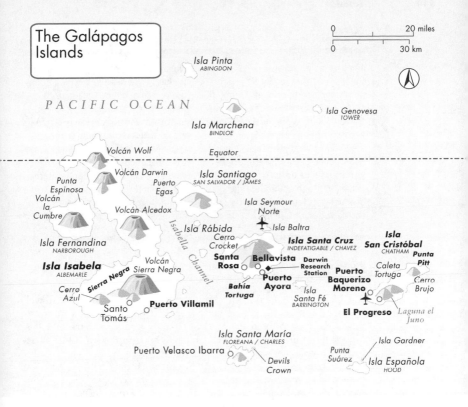

The Galápagos Islands

0   20 miles
0   30 km

PACIFIC OCEAN

Isla Pinta
ABINGDON

Isla Genovesa
TOWER

Isla Marchena
BINDLOE

Volcán Wolf   Equator

Volcán Darwin   Isla Santiago
Puerto   SAN SALVADOR / JAMES
Punta   Egas
Espinosa
Volcán   Isla Seymour
la   Norte
Cumbre   Volcán Alcedox
Isla Rábida   Isla Baltra
Cerro
Isla Fernandina   Crocket   Isla Santa Cruz   Isla
NARBOROUGH   INDEFATIGABLE / CHAVEZ   San Cristóbal
Volcán   Santa   Bellavista   Darwin   CHATHAM Punta
Isla Isabela Sierra Negra Rosa   Research   Pitt
ALBEMARLE   Station Puerto Caleta
Cerro   Sierra Negra   Puerto   Baquerizo Tortuga
Azul   Bahía   Ayora   Moreno   Cerro
Santo   Puerto Villamil   Tortuga   Isla   Brujo
Tomás   Santa Fé
BARRINGTON   El Progreso Laguna el
Juno

Isla Santa María
FLOREANA / CHARLES
Puerto Velasco Ibarra   Isla Gardner
Devils   Punta
Crown   Suárez   Isla Española
HOOD

swooping overhead. No one who has walked among these unique creatures will ever forget the experience.

Naturalist Charles Darwin, the most famous visitor to the Galápagos, found inspiration for his groundbreaking treatise *The Origin of Species* among the strange and marvelous island creatures. "I never dreamed," he wrote in his memoirs, "that islands, about 50 or 60 miles apart, and most of them in sight of each other, formed of precisely the same rocks, placed under a quite similar climate, rising to a nearly equal height, would have been differently tenanted." He realized that slightly different conditions on each of the islands had caused animals and plants eventually to develop into completely different species.

Procreation, in one form or another, is always in progress on these islands. In January, male iguanas turn from drab to bright colors to attract females. February is the nesting season of the masked boobies. Waved albatross begin their courtship dances in March. In April tiny green sea turtles begin breaking out of their eggs. Band-rumped storm petrels make their first nests in May. In June giant tortoises migrate from the lowlands of Santa Cruz Island in search of suitable places to lay their eggs. July and August are the nesting seasons for the blue-footed boobies and Galápagos hawks. September and October are mating season for pen-

When to Visit the Galápagos Islands

The best months to visit the Galápagos are generally May–June and November–December. Among the 13 principal islands, Santa Cruz and San Cristóbal are the most developed, each with a population of roughly 6,000 year-round residents. Of the two, Santa Cruz has more allure for visitors, with its dozen or so hotels, restaurants, and boutiques. The archipelago's four populated islands can be visited on a limited basis without guides, but the uninhabited islands can be seen only with a guide licensed through the Galápagos National Park Service. It's typical to book your own airfare and prearrange a one- to two-week package that includes guided visits to islands like Española and Isabela. A cruise of 10 days or longer is needed to reach the more remote northern islands or to climb either of Isabela's two accessible volcanic craters.

guins and fur seals. Sea-lion pups are born in November, while giant tortoises hatch in December.

The islands attracted only adventure seekers and odd recluses until well into the 20th century. Tourism began in a limited fashion after the Ecuadoran government declared the islands a national park in 1959. Not even five decades later, the Galápagos must cope with 100,000 visitors each year. The delicate balance that exists on the Galápagos is difficult to overstate. Ecologists are concerned that the steadily increasing number of tourists will prove destructive to the irreplaceable environment. The islands are particularly threatened by introduced animals—goats, cats, pigs, dogs, and rats—which interrupt the islands' natural food chain. While more than 250,000 giant tortoises once roamed the islands, there are fewer than 15,000 today due to human hunting and newly introduced predators. Yet people are not the only ones to blame: El Niño currents also affect marine life, especially in unusually warm years, by raising water temperatures, sometimes as high as 40°C (104°F) and killing thousands of fish and destroying the food source for marine birds. The Charles Darwin Research Center, based on Santa Cruz, works to mitigate the effects of man-made and natural disasters and is dedicated to conserving the fragile ecosystem.

Santa Cruz

Santa Cruz, the most developed and touristed of the islands, sits in the middle of the archipelago. Overlooking Academy Bay on the island's southern shore is the town of **Puerto Ayora**, with hotels, restaurants, shops, and even a few clubs.

Follow the main road east from Puerto Ayora to the **Charles Darwin Research Station** and its visitor center, which has an informative exhibit explaining the basics of Galápagos geology, ecology, and weather patterns. Self-guided trails lead to the station's giant tortoise pens, where you can see the only tortoises you're likely to encounter during your visit. ⊠ *Av.*

Charles Darwin ☎ *05/252–6146* ⊕ *www.darwinfoundation.org* ⊙ *Daily 8–noon and 2–4.*

Bahía Tortuga (Turtle Bay), 3 km (2 mi) southwest of Puerto Ayora, has a long, white-sand beach where marine iguanas sometimes strut along the water's edge. There are no facilities along the water, but if you walk from town (take the road to Bellavista and turn left past the bank), you'll pass a soda-and-beer stand at the top of a lava-rock staircase. Marine turtles drag their bulky shells up onto the beach to lay their eggs between November and February, with baby turtles hatching in June and July.

Near the small village of **Bellavista** you can explore amazing underground lava tubes. The mile-long tunnels, tall enough to walk through, were created when flowing lava cooled more quickly on the surface than below, forming a crust that enclosed an underground labyrinth. To reach the tunnels from Puerto Ayora, head north on the road to Bellavista; turn east at the cross street and walk about a mile until you find a farm with a sign that announces LOS TÚNELES. A small fee is collected by the owner, who also provides flashlights.

The road to **Santa Rosa,** 13 km (8 mi) beyond Bellavista, is lined with giant elephant grass, avocado and papaya trees, and boughs of yellow trumpet vines, all of which are in marked contrast to the dry, cactus-spotted lowlands. About 2 km (1 mi) beyond Santa Rosa look for a pair of giant sinkholes called **Los Gemelos** (the Twins), one on either side of the road.

The unattended **National Park Tortoise Reserve** is one of the few places in the archipelago where you can view giant Galápagos turtles in the wild. An unmarked track leads to the reserve from Santa Rosa. Along the way, keep alert for Galápagos hawks, Darwin finches, and short-eared owls. In Santa Rosa a small restaurant across from the church sometimes rents horses that you are allowed to ride inside the reserve.

Where to Stay & Eat

If you prefer to sleep on land and take boat cruises during the day there are a few good options. However, most hotels and restaurants are working to upgrade their facilities, but many are still on the rustic side, and some hotels have only cold running water, and rooms often lack electrical outlets. If these things are important to you, be sure to ask before booking.

$$ ✗ **Four Lanterns.** Expect to see diners sitting around long tables on the lantern-lighted outdoor patio enjoying lasagna, gnocchi, or cannelloni. The proprietor takes pride in her signature dish, fettuccine *mare e monte* (with mushrooms and shrimp). An accepted piece of local wisdom is that all visitors eventually end up at the Four Lanterns. ⊠ *Av. Charles Darwin, Puerto Ayora* ☎ *No phone* ▭ *No credit cards* ⊙ *No lunch.*

$$ ✗ **La Garrapata.** This popular restaurant is run by the offspring of one of the pioneer families of Galápagos. Its outdoor tables attract both tourists and locals. The menu, which is heavy on the seafood, also includes a few chicken and pasta dishes. Next door is the popular discotheque, La Panga, where salsa music plays until the lights go out or

the last patron leaves. ⊠ *Av. Charles Darwin, Puerto Ayora* ☎ *05/ 252–6264* ▤ *MC, V* ⊘ *Closed Sun.*

$$ ✕ **La Tolda Azul.** The first restaurant you'll encounter as you step off the boat in Port Ayora, this place has a small outdoor patio. The menu offers a wonderful selection of lobster dishes served in large portions; the grilled steaks are also good. ⊠ *Muelle Municipal, Puerto Ayora* ☎ *05/ 252–6565* ▤ *MC.*

$$$ ✕ **Narwhal.** With a gorgeous view of the island on a clear day, this hideaway in the highlands of Santa Cruz offers set meals that include a cocktail, soup or salad, and a dependably good entrée of chicken, fish, or beef. Vegetarian entrées are sometimes available. ⊠ *Road to Santa Rosa* ☎ *No phone* ▤ *No credit cards.*

$$$$ ▥ **Finch Bay EcoHotel.** A stay at this totally redone four-star hotel (from 1960) can be combined with day cruises on the yacht *Delphin*—which the hotel owns—or day tours that include snorkeling, diving, sea kayaking, hiking, mountain biking, and horseback riding along Santa Cruz's hillside paths. The highlands show a different side of the Galápagos. On kayaking trips behind the hotel you get a close-up look at sharks, sea turtles, rays, and a variety of birds. If you've never paddled a kayak, you can practice off the hotel's beach. Rates include a buffet breakfast. ⊠ *Santa Cruz Island at Punta Estrada* ☎ *02/246–4780 in Quito, 800/ 527–2500 toll free in North America* ⊕ *www.finchbayhotel.com* ⇗ *21 rooms* ⚲ *Restaurant, pool, hot tub, beach, kayaks, bicycles, bar, laundry service, Internet, airport transfer, travel services; no smoking* ▤ *AE, D, MC, V* ❙⊙❙ *BP.*

$$$$ ▥ **Royal Palm Hotel.** This small resort on Santa Cruz is the only five-star luxury hotel on the islands. Suites, villas, and rooms blend into the garden surroundings within a 500-acre property; all have the proper amenities of a mainland high-rise hotel. Features include an observatory with computerized telescopes for star gazing and a Galápagos museum that focuses on the ecology and native species. Tours offered include horseback riding, diving, snorkeling, hiking, birding, sea kayaking, and windsurfing. You also are welcome at the Royal Palm Hotel's Airport VIP room in Baltra. An entire dinner here, without drinks, will run you about $25. ⊠ *20 mins northwest of Puerto Ayora* ☎ *05/252–7409* ⊕ *www. royalpalmgalapagos.com* ⇗ *10 villas, 4 rooms, 3 suites* ⚲ *Restaurant, minibars, cable TV with movies, tennis court, pool, health club, hot tub, massage, sauna, spa, bar, library, Internet, business services, meeting rooms* ▤ *AE, D, MC, V.*

$$ ▥ **Hotel Silberstein.** This comfortable place is often referred to by its former name, the Hotel Angermeyer, and you'll find a pool with a waterfall and large, pleasant rooms. Dive tours are a specialty here; the hotel has five-day packages for $695, including breakfast and dinner in the hotel and box lunches when out on dives. They also have rooms for travelers with disabilities. ⊠ *Av. Charles Darwin y Pequeros, Puerto Ayora* ☎ *05/252–6277* ⊕ *www.hotelsilberstein.com* ⇗ *22 rooms* ⚲ *Restaurant, fans, cable TV, pool, bar, laundry service, travel services* ▤ *AE, DC, MC, V.*

San Cristóbal Interpretation Center

NO MATTER HOW SHORT YOUR VISIT, make time for the San Cristóbal Interpretation Center, which covers the history of the archipelago from its volcanic origins to the present. The center is on the southwestern side of the island in an area of lush vegetation and freshwater lakes just west of the provincial capital of Puerto Baquerizo Moreno. It sits 730 meters (2,395 feet) above sea level, surrounded by gardens and with sweeping views of the ocean.

The center's aim is to explain the natural processes that have made Galápagos such a unique place, delineate efforts to protect and preserve the islands, and serve as an education center for park personnel and naturalist guides. It also has an open-air theater for performances and dance and film festivals, which have made it the cultural center of the Galápagos. The three exhibits inside are Human History, covering events related to the discovery and colonization of the islands; Natural History, with illustrations of natural events and information on how different species arrived at the islands; and Conservation, an introduction to the struggles of the ecosystems and preservation efforts under way.

After viewing the exhibits, take a walk along winding paths leading from the Interpretation Center to Playa Punta Carola (about 35 minutes), a favorite of surfers, or on to Mann Beach for a swim and to Frigate Bird Hill, a nesting place for frigate birds. Along the way are plants, lava lizards, and other animals endemic to this area. Admission to the center—open daily 10–8—is included in your Galápagos Park tax.

6

San Cristóbal

The capital of Galápagos Province and the largest town on San Cristóbal, **Puerto Baquerizo Moreno** is a bit less tourist oriented than Puerto Ayora. Two kilometers (1 mile) east of the port is **Frigate Bird Hill,** where both great and magnificent frigates—two species of black seabirds famed for their courtship displays—make their nests. On a clear day it offers sweeping views of the bay.

El Progreso, one of San Cristóbal's first colonies, is a small village about 8 km (5 mi) east of Puerto Baquerizo Moreno at the end of one of the island's few roads (buses connect the two towns twice daily). From El Progreso you can rent a four-wheel-drive vehicle and explore the shores of **Laguna el Junco,** one of the archipelago's few permanent freshwater lakes, 10 km (6 mi) east.

Punta Pitt, at the northeastern tip of the island, is the only place in the Galápagos where you can view three species of boobies—masked, blue-footed, and red-footed—nesting together. Also found here are frigate birds, storm petrels, and swallow-tailed gulls. The site is accessible by motor launch from Puerto Moreno.

Where to Stay

$ 🏨 **Miconia Cabañas.** Rooms snake back along a garden strewn with morning glories at this new hotel on Puerto Baquerizo's main street and the nicest lodging on the island. The outside is stone and stucco. Inside are pastel-color rooms, some with refrigerators. The upstairs restaurant specializes in seafood. ✉ *Puerto Baquerizo Moreno* ☎ *05/252–0608* ⊕ *www.miconia.tk* ➳ *8 rooms, 7 suites* ♻ *Restaurant, cable TV, some refrigerators, pool, gym, hot tub, bar, shop, Internet, travel services* ▤ *AE, DC, MC, V* ⍾ *BP.*

Isabela

Although Isabela is the largest island in the archipelago, it has very little tourism infrastructure. The handful of hotels are very basic, with only intermittent hot water. Sleepy **Puerto Villamil**, founded in 1897 as a center for extracting lime, is the focus of Isabela's tourist trade—nearby are several lagoons where flamingos and migratory birds can be viewed up close, as well as beaches with large populations of herons, egrets, and other birds. Isabela's other community is **Santo Tomás**, 18 km (11 mi) northwest.

The island's signature excursion, is a guided 9-km (5½-mi) trek ascending the 1,370-meter (4,488-foot) **Volcán Sierra Negra.** The volcano erupted in October 2005, but, thankfully, the event threatened none of the island's population—human or animal. Seismologists have kept close watch on any untoward activity, but excursions are open again after a brief suspension. The volcano's crater—roughly 10 km (6 mi) in diameter—is the second largest in the world. A more ambitious trek, requiring adequate planning and equipment, is 1,100-meter (3,600-foot) **Volcán Alcedox.** The site can be reached only by boat, after which a 10-km (6-mi) trail climbs over rough terrain. You cannot traipse around the island without a guide, and you'll need one here. Your rewards are stunning views and a chance to see the archipelago's largest population of Galápagos tortoises.

The Galápagos Islands Essentials

Transportation

BY AIR

Tame flies once daily from Quito and Guayaquil to Baltra (GPS), a tiny island just north of Santa Cruz, and to San Cristóbal (SCY). AeroGal flies several times weekly to Baltra and San Cristóbal, and, at this writing, Ícaro plans to launch service to San Cristóbal using attractively priced air-hotel packages. The flight from Guayaquil takes 90 minutes. Add another hour if you board in Quito. Airfares run $330–$400 round-trip. If you have reservations with a tour or cruise operator, you'll be met at the airport. If you're a do-it-yourself type, a bus-ferry-bus transport combo gets you from Baltra to nearby Puerto Ayora, on Santa Cruz. San Cristóbal's airport lies near the edge of Puerto Baquerizo Moreno.

⚠ **Remember that all foreign visitors who enter the Galápagos must pay $100 in cash,** money that is earmarked for training park rangers and funding conservation efforts. You must pay in U.S. cash—no traveler's checks, no credit cards—and the bills should be in good condition without markings or tears. (Because of Ecuador's glut of counterfeit $50 and $100 bills, bills larger than twenties are not accepted.)

✈ Airlines & Contacts **AeroGal** ☎ 05/252-0405 Puerto Ayora, 05/252-1117, Puerto Baquerizo Moreno. **Ícaro** ☎ 05/263-0620 Puerto Baquerizo Moreno. **Tame** ☎ 05/252-6527 Puerto Ayora, 05/252-6527, Puerto Baquerizo Moreno.

Contacts & Resources

MONEY MATTERS

Tour boats generally accept payments in dollars, traveler's checks, and credit cards.

TELEPHONES

Telephone service is good between the Galápagos and mainland Ecuador. The larger cruise ships usually offer satellite telephone services for an additional fee.

TIME

It is one hour earlier on the islands than it is on mainland Ecuador.

6

TOUR OPERATORS

For tours of the Galápagos—which you book in Quito or Guayaquil—you can choose from a wide range of boats. Although they're the cheapest, economy vessels (typically converted fishing trawlers) are often poorly maintained and have guides with only a passing knowledge of English. It's better to stick with tourist-class or luxury vessels, which generally offer three-, four-, and seven-night tours. The price tag per person for a double cabin on a three-night luxury-ship cruise can run $765–$1,300 in low season and $880–$1,600 in high season. Off-peak rates usually apply from May 1 to June 14 and from September 1 to October 14. When you book, be sure to ask if the $100 park tax is included.

Boat tours mean dining and sleeping on board, with much of the sailing done at night to maximize time spent on the islands. Most of these vessels employ multilingual naturalists who are knowledgeable in marine sciences. At least once a day you'll have an opportunity to swim or snorkel. If you want to dive, you should make arrangements beforehand, as it's not offered on all boats.

To save money, you can wait until you arrive on the islands and try to bargain for a cheaper boat fare. Operators of all vessel classes come to the airport selling last-minute tickets. The risk of doing this, however, is that you might not find an available boat, especially during peak seasons.

CRUISE SHIPS Except for two single cabins, the 293-foot M/V *Galápagos Explorer II* is an all-suite ship. Operated by Conodros (operators of the Kapawi jungle lodge), it has 50 cabins each with twin beds that can be converted to a king-sized bed. There are a swimming pool and a piano bar, so you definitely won't feel as if you're roughing it.

The flagship of Kleintours in the Galápagos is the 300-foot M/V *Galápagos Legend*. It holds 110 passengers, and all cabins have ocean views. There are a pool, a lounge, and access to e-mail and telephones. Kleintours also operates two yachts, the 26-passenger M/Y *Coral* and the 20-passenger M/Y *Coral II*. Cruises on the yachts last three, five, or eight days.

The high-end Metropolitan Touring's flagship is the 273-foot M/V *Santa Cruz,* which carries 90 passengers. It was built specifically for the Galápagos. The *Isabela II* is Metropolitan's 40-passenger luxury yacht. The 36-passenger *Delfin II*, a 724-foot yacht, cruises through the islands.

Enchanted Expeditions (frequently referred to by its former name, Angermeyer's) operates the M/Y *Cachalote I* and the M/Y *Beluga*, both 96-foot schooners that each hold 16 passengers for cruises through the islands.

Galacruises Expeditions and Ecoventura each operate two 16–20-passenger yachts, which they use on weeklong cruises through the islands. Galacruises incorporates hotel stays on land into its packages.

YACHTS Several companies offer a range of smaller yachts that can be chartered by individuals or groups. Costs range from $540 to $1,000 for three nights. Galápagos Galasam Tours operates eight yachts holding 10–16 passengers. Its newest, the luxurious catamaran *Millenium,* is an 82-foot cruiser that carries diving gear on board. A seven-night cruise on the *Millenium* is $2,000 per person. Quasar Naútica has well-maintained yachts, including the three-masted, ketch-rigged schooner *Alta*. Its most luxurious and fastest yacht is the *Parranda*. TOPPSA is a last-minute booking agency; its fares are quite inexpensive.

DIVING Not only is there aboveground wildlife to see in the Galápagos, the islands are one of the world's foremost diving and snorkeling destinations, with the opportunity to view hammerhead and Galápagos sharks, eagle rays, and sea lions. December through July means warmer waters. Galakiwi and Wreck Bay Diving, on San Cristóbal, offer excursions and courses.
🛈 Tour Companies **Canodros** ☎ 04/228–5711 in Guayaquil, 800/327–9854 in the U.S. **Ecoventura** ☎ 04/220–7177 in Guayaquil, 800/633–7972 in North America ⊕ www.ecoventura.com. **Enchanted Expeditions** ☎ 02/256–9960 in Quito, 800/327–3573 in the U.S. ⊕ www.enchantedexpeditions.com. **Galacruises** ☎ 02/250–9007 in Quito ⊕ www.galacruises.com. **Galakiwi** ☎ 02/252–1562 ⊕ www.southernexposuretours.co.nz. **Galápagos Galasam Tours** ☎ 04/230–6093 in Guayaquil ⊕ www.galasamtours.com. **Galapagos Holiday** ☎ 800/661–2512 in Canada ⊕ www.galapagosholidays.com. **Kleintours** ☎ 02/226–7000 in Quito, 888/505–5346 in North America ⊕ www.kleintours.com. **Metropolitan Touring** ☎ 02/246–4780 in Quito, 800/527–2500 in the U.S. ⊕ www.metropolitan-touring.com. **Quasar Naútica** ☎ 02/244–6996 in Quito, 800/247–2925 in the U.S. ⊕ www.quasarnauticausa.com. **TOPPSA** ☎ 02/226–0651 for last-minute bookings in Quito, 866/809–3145 in the U.S. ⊕ www.toppsa.com. **Wreck Bay Diving Center** ☎ 02/252–0473.

VISITOR INFORMATION

Tour reservations are typically booked through agencies in Quito or Guayaquil or in North America. The tourist office has limited information about tours and guides.
🛈 Tourist Information **Santa Cruz Tourist Office** ✉ Av. Charles Darwin, Santa Cruz ☎ 05/526–174.

ECUADOR ESSENTIALS

Transportation

BY AIR

Ecuador's rugged terrain makes domestic air travel a timesaving option worth considering. (Quito–Guayaquil is a quick 35 minutes.) One-way flights between mainland destinations run about $50. Flights to the Galápagos cost three to four times that. Tame (pronounced *tah*-may), Ícaro, and AeroGal share the domestic market.

Quito's Aeropuerto Mariscal Sucre and Guayaquil's Aeropuerto Simón Bolívar both serve as international gateways to Ecuador. Flights that originate in Houston fly to Quito in six hours; those from Miami fly to either Quito or Guayaquil in 4½ hours. See the Essentials sections of individual cities for specific flight information.

🛈 Airlines & Contacts **AeroGal** ☎ 800/237-642 toll free in Ecuador, 866/496-9600 in North America ⊕ www.aerogal.com.ec. **Ícaro** ☎ 800/883-567 toll free in Ecuador ⊕ www.icaro.com.ec. **Tame** ☎ 800/555-999 toll free in Ecuador, 800/666-9687 in North America ⊕ www.tame.com.ec.

BY BUS

Major bus companies in Ecuador offer direct service operating between Quito, Cuenca, and Guayaquil. Buses run frequently throughout the country and are extremely cheap: The two-hour ride from Quito to Otavalo costs $2; the 10-hour ride from Guayaquil to Quito is about $8. Theft on buses is a problem, so keep a close eye on your valuables. The luggage compartment below the bus, the overhead rack above you, and even the space under your seat aren't necessarily secure from pilfering. ⚠ Savvy travelers buy a second ticket and place their luggage in the seat next to them. Though they cost a bit more, private bus companies such as Panamericana and Reytur are an option you should consider. Their coaches are equipped with niceties such as air-conditioning and restrooms.

🛈 Bus Information **Panamericana** ✉ Av. Colón at Reina Victoria, Quito ☎ 02/225-1839. **Reytur** ✉ Gangotena 158, Quito ☎ 02/256-5299 or 02/254-6674.

BY CAR

Traffic is congested in cities, and in Quito parking spaces are nearly impossible to find (Guayaquil has numerous parking garages). Outside the major urban areas you'll find that only the major highways are paved. All roads can be treacherous in bad weather. In most parts of the country a four-wheel-drive vehicle is a necessity. On the narrow mountain roads bus drivers are notorious for making dangerous maneuvers, such as passing on curves. If you decide to drive, bring or rent a cell phone for emergencies.

CAR RENTAL Ecuador recognizes the validity of your home country driver's license for short-term tourist stays. Given the ease here of flying and of renting a taxi by the hour for shorter trips—to say nothing of urban traffic congestion—consider carefully whether you really need to rent a car in Ecuador. A vehicle rental can be quite expensive, with rates running higher

6

than $300 for a compact car, and close to $375 for a four-wheel-drive vehicle. Inquire about deductibles for damage and theft, which can be quite high, before agreeing on a price. Examine the car carefully, and make sure it has a jack and spare tire. Outside Quito, Guayaquil, and Cuenca, rental offices are virtually nonexistent.

EMERGENCY
ASSISTANCE
No emergency roadside service exists, although passing motorists will frequently stop to help with disabled vehicles. Ask your rental agency for emergency numbers and a list of garages in the area you're traveling.

GASOLINE
Ecuador's status as a petroleum-producing nation has buffered it from the high gasoline prices seen elsewhere on the continent. Gas is sold by the *galón*: regular leaded, called *extra*, costs about $1.50; unleaded, called *súper*, is roughly $2 per gallon.

PARKING
Park your car at your hotel rather than leaving it on the street, where it is susceptible to theft. Larger hotels are more likely to have fenced parking lots.

BY TAXI
Taxis are a safe, convenient, and economical way to travel in Ecuador, even when you want to travel long distances. It's easy to negotiate a rate with a driver beforehand for a half- or full-day trip to your destination. A three-hour taxi ride, for example, should only cost about $50.

Contacts & Resources

BUSINESS HOURS
Office hours are generally 8:30–5. Banks are open weekdays 9–6, and some are open Saturday 9–1. Casas de cambio (exchange offices), which are much more efficient and less crowded, are open longer in the afternoon. Shops are open 9–6, closing for a few hours in the afternoon. Businesses that do stay open continuously throughout the day often indicate ININTERRUMPIDAMENTE (uninterruptedly) with their hours of business. Those catering to tourists often don't close for lunch, but many are closed Saturday afternoon and all day Sunday.

CUSTOMS & DUTIES
You can import 1 liter of spirits, 300 cigarettes or 50 cigars, and reasonable amounts of perfumes, gifts, and personal effects. Pack judiciously: Ecuador levies import duties on all luggage exceeding the limit of two suitcases per person. It is illegal to bring firearms, ammunition, drugs, fresh or dried meats, and plants and vegetables into the country.

■ TIP➜ **There is a $100 fee to visit the Galápagos Islands.** The airport departure fee is $32 when leaving Ecuador via Quito or Guayaquil.

ELECTRICITY
In Ecuador the electric current is 110 volts; North American–style two-pronged plugs are used. Areas outside major cities are subject to frequent power surges.

HEALTH

FOOD & DRINK Food-borne illnesses likely won't be serious problems in Ecuador if you take some precautions and let common sense prevail. Avoid tap water to reduce the risk of contracting intestinal parasites. Drink only bottled water, which is available *con gas* and *sin gas* (with and without carbonation, respectively). Ask for drinks *sin hielo* (without ice). Avoid uncooked or unpeeled vegetables and fruits that may have been washed in tap water. Brush your teeth with bottled water in remote areas or budget hotels. At other hotels, ask if the water is purified; it often is. Eat at street stands at your own risk.

OTHER HAZARDS Discuss malaria medications with your doctor if you're traveling to the rain forest or other isolated areas. In the Galápagos the most serious threat you'll face is sunburn—do not underestimate the intensity of the equatorial sun. If you're prone to seasickness and you're planning a cruise around the archipelago, make sure to bring medications. At high altitudes the sun is strong, and altitude sickness can strike. Discuss the advisability of travel to the highlands with your doctor if you have a heart condition or high blood pressure or are pregnant.

MONEY MATTERS

Many goods and services—from taxi fares to textiles—are inexpensive by Western standards. Although international chain hotels are pricey, you can stay in perfectly nice places for less than $75.

Some sample prices are: cup of coffee, 50¢; bottle of beer, $1.50; soft drink, 50¢; bottle of wine, $8; sandwich, $2; 2-km (1-mi) taxi ride, $1; city bus ride, 20¢.

CURRENCY The U.S. dollar is Ecuador's official currency—but the country also mints its own coins, equivalent to half dollars, quarters, dimes, nickels, and pennies, which circulate freely with their U.S. counterparts. The $1 coin bearing the portrait of Native American guide Sacagawea, which never caught on in the United States, is used widely here. Most small businesses have trouble making change for anything over $5. ⚠ **Do not bring $50 or $100 bills to Ecuador.** So many counterfeits circulate that no one will accept them as payment for any bill of any amount, including the $100 Galápagos entrance fee. If you find yourself with these denominations, you have no choice but to exchange them for twenties or smaller at a bank, which *is* capable of determining that your bills are real.

CREDIT CARDS Most large establishments in the cities take credit cards, with Visa and MasterCard the most widely accepted. Some businesses add a surcharge of 3%–10% on credit-card purchases, or may offer a discount if you pay in cash. You can use your card to obtain cash from ATMs, but a surprising number of machines take only Cirrus-affiliated cards.

TRAVELER'S CHECKS Few businesses take traveler's checks as payment. You can cash traveler's checks for dollars at banks and casas de cambio.

PASSPORTS

Only a passport valid for at least six more months is required for American, Canadian, Australian, and U.K. citizens for stays totaling up to

90 days in a calendar year. New Zealand citizens require a visa to visit Ecuador; applications may be made to the Ecuadoran consulate in Auckland and must include a passport valid for at least six more months and proof of a confirmed round-trip plane ticket.

SAFETY

Petty crime, such as pickpocketing, is a problem in Ecuador. Use the same precautions you would anywhere—avoid flashy jewelry and watches, hold purses and camera bags close to your body, and avoid handling money in public. Use extra caution in all crowded spaces, such as markets and plazas. In Quito, be especially wary in the streets and plazas of the Old City. Take taxis after dark, even if you are going only a few blocks.

TAXES

Most hotels add a 22% tax and service surcharge to your bill. Some include this amount when they quote prices, but others do not. Be sure to inquire when you book your room.

TELEPHONES

To call Ecuador from another country, dial the country code of 593, then the area code, then the local number. Include the "0" at the beginning of the area code only when calling long distance within the country. Ecuador completed a nationwide transition to a uniform system of seven-digit local telephone numbers in 2003, but signs, business cards, and stationery (and people) frequently still give the former six-digit numbers. Old habits die hard.

Directory assistance, available only in Spanish, is available by dialing 104.

LOCAL CALLS Most public phones accept phone cards, which you can purchase in many shops and newsstands. Some stores charge about 25¢ for a brief call on their private line; look for a sign in a window reading TELÉFONO or LLA-MADAS. Many Internet cafés have phones for public use.

An easier alternative is placing a call from an office of Andinatel, the country's national telephone company. Its Pacifictel division serves the coast, the Southern Highlands, and the Galápagos. You'll find offices in most cities and towns. Porta, Allegro, and Bell South, Ecuador's three mobile-phone companies, also operate local offices for placing calls in many communities. Most telephone offices are open daily 8 AM–9 PM.
🗂 Telephone Offices Andinatel ⊠ Av. Colón and Av. Amazonas, La Mariscal, Quito ⊠ Calderń at Sucre, Otavalo. Pacifictel ⊠ Benigno Malo at Presidente Códova, Cuenca ⊠ Ballén at Chile, Guayaquil ⊠ Av. Padre Julio at Española, Puerto Ayora (Galápagos)

LONG-DISTANCE To make collect or credit-card calls through an English-speaking oper-
CALLS ator, call AT&T, BT (British Telecom), Canada Direct, MCI, or Sprint.
🗂 AT&T ☎ 199-9119. BT ☎ 199-9178. Canada Direct ☎ 199-9175. MCI ☎ 199-9170. Sprint ☎ 199-9171.

TIPPING

A tip of 5%–10% is appropriate for waiters in upscale restaurants. (The 10% surcharge often added to a bill is supposedly for service, although whether waiters actually receive it is questionable.) Porters and bellhops should receive the equivalent of 50¢ per bag. Guides expect about $10 per day for each person in a tour group, while drivers expect about $2. Taxi drivers don't expect tips.

VISITOR INFORMATION
Ecuador's Ministry of Tourism operates a network of iTur information offices in Quito, Guayaquil, Cuenca, Ibarra, and Riobamba—some branches are better than others—and has an informative Web site but is ill-equipped to handle specific pretrip inquiries. Embassies in the United States, the United Kingdom, and Canada may be able to supply a few brochures. Once you're on the ground, city-run tourist offices are a better bet for information (Quito's and Guayaquil's are extraordinary).
🛈 Ecuadoran Tourist Information iTur ☎ 800/004-887 toll free in Ecuador ⊕ www.vivecuador.com.

6

Paraguay

Updated by
Jeffrey Van
Fleet

FROM THE SUBTLE CHARMS OF ASUNCIÓN, the laid-back capital, to the country's wild countryside and small colonial towns, Paraguay is a country full of surprises and little hideaways. Even the most seasoned travelers, however, scratch their heads when the subject is Paraguay. If the country enters their consciousness at all, it comes as an answer to the trivia question, "Which South American nations have no seacoast?" (Bolivia is the other.) But Paraguay is more than the answer to a stumper on a quiz show—this Rip Van Winkle of South American nations is now awakening from almost two centuries of slumber.

Decades of authoritarian rule left Paraguay behind while nearby Argentina and Brazil made rapid economic strides. The country has struggled since 1989—its first year of democracy—to make up for lost time. Although intent on catching up with its neighbors, Paraguay has not completely rubbed the sleep out of its eyes. Many marvel at the easy pace of life and the old-fashioned courtesies of the people. In the capital of Asunción, crowds are seldom a problem when you take in its architectural showplaces. In the wild countryside, you may stumble across villages where you're the only visitor.

A trip to the tranquil southern region of the *ruinas jesuíticas* (Jesuit ruins) transports you to a time when missionaries worked the fields alongside their indigenous Guaraní converts. Some of the world's best fishing can be had in rivers teeming with giant catfish. Anglers can test their skills as clouds of snowy egrets take flight and monkeys swing through trees along the banks. Vultures soar over the sun-scorched plains of the Chaco, an arid scrubland that covers half of Paraguay and is one of the most sparsely populated spots on earth, with less than one inhabitant for each of its 250,000 square km (97,500 square mi).

DID YOU KNOW?

Paraguay is the only country in the world whose flag differs front and reverse.

Intrigued about joining the small number of people who have visited this developing destination? Realize that institutions and services catering to travelers are improving but are still in their infancy. Struggling museums are maintained more by enthusiasm than by government funds. On top of that, the highway system is underdeveloped and good accommodations are rare outside Asunción. But there's an upside to visiting one of the least-known countries on the continent: Paraguayans seem genuinely interested in finally becoming part of the international community. They'll start by lavishing attention on you, hoping you'll tell a few friends about their country once you get home.

Exploring Paraguay

Paraguay is divided into two distinct regions, separated by the Río Paraguay. The southeast region is distinguished by a subtropical climate, thick forests, and meandering rivers. It encompasses less than half of the country's territory but holds 98% of its population. Asunción, Ciudad del Este, Encarnación, and the Jesuit missions are all in the east.

Paraguay is also the most inexpensive gateway to the famous Iguazú Falls. It can be reached from Ciudad del Este, directly east of Asunción, at the frontier where Paraguay, Argentina, and Brazil meet. But even if you approach the falls from Paraguay, we recommend basing yourself in Brazil or Argentina to see them. *See* Safety *in* Paraguay Essentials.

Paraguay's northwest, known as the Chaco, is a sparsely populated and largely unexplored expanse. This vast and desolate Paraguayan pampa, which abuts Bolivia, is used mostly by the lumber and cattle industries.

Restaurants & Cuisine

A staple of Paraguayan dining is *parrillada*—barbecued meats served in large portions at restaurants called *parrillas*. Beef, including blood sausage and organ meats, is the mainstay, but pork and chicken are also common. *Puchero* is a meat, sausage, vegetable, and chickpea stew that's eaten in the cooler months. *Bori-bori* is a hearty soup with bits of meat, vegetables, and balls molded from cheese and corn. Paraguay's rivers abound with unusual fish, such as the *surubí*, a giant catfish. It's tastiest when served in a dish called *milanesa de surubí* (battered and deep-fried fillets). Another tasty option is the *dorado,* a ferocious predator resembling the salmon. Try it lightly grilled. A soup made from the fish's head and other leftovers is surprisingly delicious.

TOP REASONS TO GO

LOAD UP ON LACE

Few words in the language begin with the tilded ñ. A tablecloth or placemat fashioned in ñandutí fashion is sure to elicit admiration from the folks back home, as well as comment on its unusual name. Artisans craft the delicate spiderweb lacework out of silk or cotton to create Paraguay's signature souvenir.

PLAY EXPLORER

If you seek a less-trodden South American destination than Brazil's beaches or Peru's Machu Picchu, plant your flag in Paraguay. Hospitality is your reward for staking out a claim in this little-known country.

REEL ONE IN

Believe it or not, southwestern Paraguay is one of the world's foremost freshwater-fishing destinations, with a small handful of resorts catering to the anglers among you. Giant, fighting dorado and catfishlike surubí will test your talents.

GO ON A MISSION

Southern Paraguay was the site of a string of colonial-era Jesuit missions where priests and the indigenous Guaraní lived and worked in perfect harmony side by side. The structures remain mostly well preserved and are, fortuitously, laid out in a circuit, which makes for easy touring.

7

Usual accompaniments include salads (Paraguay's tomatoes are incredibly flavorful) and *palmitos* (hearts of palm), considered a delicacy. Other side dishes include *sopa paraguaya,* a kind of corn bread made with cheese, eggs, and onions, or *chipá-guazú,* a similar dish in which roughly ground corn is substituted for cornmeal. You also may be served boiled *manioc,* a white, fibrous root with a bland flavor. *Chipá,* a type of bread made from corn flour, ground manioc, and sometimes cheese, is baked in a clay oven called a *tatakua.* It is sold everywhere and is best eaten piping hot. Typical desserts include *dulce de leche,* a pudding made from slow-cooking milk and sugar; papaya preserved in syrup; and such fresh fruits as pineapple, banana, mango, and melon.

Cafés and bars usually sell snacks, mostly fried or grilled foods that can be prepared quickly. The most popular is *milanesa,* thin slices of batter-fried beef, chicken breast, pork, or fish. Other favorites are *empanadas,* envelopes of pastry filled with beef, pork, chicken, corn, or cheese; *croquetas,* sausage-shape minced meat or poultry that is rolled in bread crumbs and deep fried; and *mixtos,* ham-and-cheese sandwiches. Many cafés have a special of the day—*plato del día*—that's usually a good bargain. Paraguayan portions tend to be generous, so don't hesitate to share a dish.

Few Paraguayans are seen without their *guampa,* a drinking vessel made of a cow's horn, metal, or wood, from which they sip *tereré,* a cold infusion made from *yerba maté* tea. Maté is drunk hot throughout South America, but the cold version, often mixed with medicinal herbs, is more common in Paraguay. Pilsners, particularly the Baviera brand, are quite good. If you order beer in a restaurant, an enormous bottle is likely to be brought to your table in an ice bucket. Beer on tap is known as *chopp* (pronounced "shop"). Choose beer over the local wine whenever possible. In Asunción, society women fill the top hotels' tables for afternoon tea, and baby showers and parties for brides-to-be often take the form of teas. Espresso and often filtered coffee is served demitasse except at breakfast.

Asunción and the other larger cities have plenty of excellent restaurants, bars, and cafés, but in smaller towns the choices are few. If you're traveling along the highways you can expect to find a few good roadside restaurants serving grilled meat and fish.

Since restaurants sometimes close between meals, it's important to plan when to eat. Lunch can begin at 11:30, but 12:30 is more typical. Some restaurants stop serving lunch as early as 2. Dinner is often available at 7 PM, with restaurants staying open until 11. More sophisticated dining spots open at 8 PM and serve until shortly after midnight. On weekends and special occasions, dining hours are extended. Café hours are generally 7 AM–10 PM.

WHAT IT COSTS In Dollars				
$$$$	**$$$**	**$$**	**$**	**¢**
AT DINNER over $20	$15–$20	$10–$15	$6–$10	under $6

Prices are for per person for a main course at dinner.

About the Hotels

The quality of lodgings has improved dramatically in Asunción in recent years, though sheer numbers of hotels remain small. Those that are here offer great value for the rates they charge. It gets surprisingly chilly here between June and August, but most upscale hotels have much-appreciated heating during the winter. Be sure to ask for an air-conditioned room in summer. Most lodgings, mid-range and above, offer them. Outside Asunción, hotels are few and far between, as many villages are just a few hundred meters long and consist of little more than a handful of houses, a couple of general stores, a bakery, and, sometimes, a gas station.

WHAT IT COSTS In Dollars				
$$$$	**$$$**	**$$**	**$**	**¢**
FOR 2 PEOPLE over $180	$100–$180	$60–$100	$40–$60	under $40

Prices are for two people in a standard double room in high season, excluding tax.

When to Go

Paraguay's relative lack of tourists means there aren't well-delineated high and low seasons. There are fewer good hotels in the country than elsewhere on the continent, so reservations are recommended year-round, especially in Asunción.

CLIMATE   Traveling in Paraguay can be uncomfortable from December to March, when the sun beats down on the landlocked country. The heat is intense, so don't plan activities for the early afternoon (there's a daily siesta, anyway). The wettest months are December to April, the driest June to August. Torrential cloudbursts can quickly turn streets into torrents of muddy red water.

The following are the average daily maximum and minimum temperatures for Asunción.

Jan.	93F	34C	May	77F	25C	Sept.	80F	27C
	72	22		55	14		60	16
Feb.	93F	34C	June	72F	22C	Oct.	84F	29C
	72	22		55	13		62	17
Mar.	91F	33C	July	75F	24C	Nov.	88F	31C
	70	21		57	14		66	19
Apr.	82F	28C	Aug.	77F	25C	Dec.	91F	33C
	64	18		57	14		70	21

HOLIDAYS Pay attention to legal holidays when everything, except your hotel, shuts down entirely, and public transportation is packed with Paraguayans traveling to visit friends and family.

New Year's Day; Heroes Day (March 1); Holy Week (Palm Sunday through Easter Sunday: April 1–8, 2007, and March 16–23, 2008); Labor Day (May 1); Independence Day (May 14–15); Armistice of Chaco War (June 12); Founding of Asunción (August 15); Victory at Boquerón (September 29); Feast of the Immaculate Conception (December 8); Christmas (December 25).

FESTIVALS On February 3 the town of Itá celebrates the Feast of St. Blas, the patron saint of Paraguay, with folk dancing, popular music, and horse racing. On December 8 the Día de la Nuestra Señora de Los Milagros (Day of Our Lady of the Miracles) is celebrated in the town of Caacupé, where an effigy of Mary is paraded through the streets.

Language

Paraguay is South America's only officially bilingual country. About half the population speaks the indigenous Guaraní as its first language. If you know some Spanish, don't hesitate to use it. In Asunción, the staff at more expensive hotels and restaurants are likely to speak some English. The typical person on the street will likely know none. Outside Asunción it's unusual to find anyone who speaks anything but Spanish or Guaraní. There are some immigrant communities, mainly in the northwest Chaco region, where German is also spoken.

ASUNCIÓN

Asunción was founded on August 15, 1537—the Feast of the Assumption, or *Asunción* in Spanish. Take a step back and you'll see traces of the city that was once the colonial capital of southern South America. On the drive from the airport, taxis whisk by the magnificent mansions lining Avenida Mariscal López—a furtive glimpse through a doorway reveals a peaceful patio reminiscent of those in southern Spain. Remnants of Asunción's prosperous past can also be detected in the delicately decorated fa-

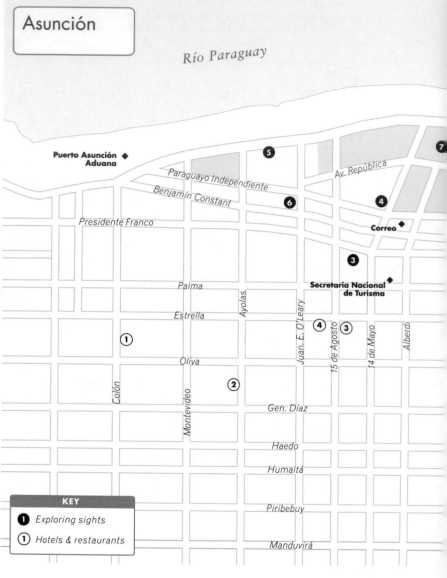

Asunción

Río Paraguay

Puerto Asunción ◆
Aduana

Paraguayo Independiente

Av. República

Benjamín Constant

Presidente Franco

Correo ◆

Palma

Secretaría Nacional
de Turismo

Estrella

Ayolas

Juan E. O'Leary

15 de Agosto

14 de Mayo

Alberdi

Oliva

Colón

Montevideo

Gen. Díaz

Haedo

Humaitá

KEY

① Exploring sights

① Hotels & restaurants

Piribebuy

Manduvirá

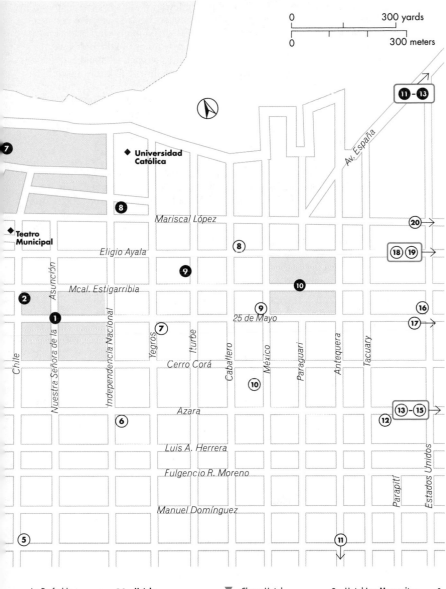

La Preferida **16**
Talleyrand **17**
Tio Lucas **7**

Hotels
Apart Hotel
Mandu'Ará **10**
Asunción International
Hotel **2**
Asunción
Palace Hotel **1**

▼ Chaco Hotel **8**
Excelsior Inn **6**
Granados Park Hotel **3**
Hotel Casino Yacht y Golf
Club Paraguayo **11**
Hotel Cecilia **15**
Hotel Excelsior **5**

Hotel Las Margaritas **4**
Hotel Preciado **12**
Hotel Presidente **6**
Sabe Center Hotel **9**

cades and balconies of Belle Epoque buildings that have survived the vagaries of fashion, although in some instances they've yielded to commercialism by leasing the ground floor to fast-food joints with blaring neon signs. Alongside the money changers and peddlers of fake Rolex watches who patrol the streets and plazas, indigenous women sell bundles of herbs and roots—centuries-old remedies for every ailment. Contrasting with the hustle and bustle of the nearby commercial center, the pristine columned government and legislative palaces overlook the Bay of Asunción as cool breezes rustle through flame trees in the riverside park.

Exploring Asunción

The city is built on a rise overlooking a large bay formed by the Río Paraguay. The centro runs south–southeast from the bay for about 10 blocks to Teniente Fariña, and it stretches 17 blocks from Colón in the west to Estados Unidos in the east. Most hotels, restaurants, shops, and offices can be found in this rectangle. Except for the irregular shoreline along the river, Asunción's streets follow a standard grid. Downtown streets are narrow and generally have one-way traffic. Two major squares—Plaza de los Héroes and Plaza Uruguaya—provide cool resting places in the shade of jacaranda trees. Addresses are frequently expressed in terms of intersections.

TIMING &
PRECAUTIONS
Asunción is a small city, so its centro can be easily explored in a day. Many of the attractions are free. Expect unbearably hot temperatures October through March, when you should plan outdoor activities for early morning and late afternoon. The rest of the year Asunción has a pleasant, springlike climate. Few intersections in the heart of the city are governed by traffic lights, so be on guard crossing the street.

WHAT TO SEE
❸ **Casa de la Independencia.** This 1774 house with whitewashed walls, brick floors, and a lovely patio was once the secret meeting place of revolutionaries plotting to break away from Spain. They entered and left in the dead of night through the *callejón* (alleyway) in back. Relics from the May 1811 revolution, which secured Paraguay's independence, are displayed in this well-maintained museum, as are religious artifacts and furnishings depicting a typical colonial-era home. ⊠ *14 de Mayo at Presidente Franco* ☎ *021/493–918* 🎫 *Free* ☉ *Mon.–Fri 7–6:30; Sat. 8–noon.*

❹ **Casa de los Diputados.** Once a convent, then a much-needed blood bank during the Chaco War, then a military museum, then a cultural center, this Spanish colonial building now contains offices for members of Congress. ⊠ *14 de Mayo at El Paraguayo Independiente* ☎ *021/445–212* 🎫 *Free* ☉ *Weekdays 7:30–noon and 1:30–6, weekends 8–noon.*

❽ **Catedral de Nuestra Señora de la Asunción.** Inside the newly renovated seat of the Archdiocese of Asunción, portions of which date from 1687, are an enormous gilded altar and many 18th- and 19th-century religious statues and paintings. ⊠ *Plaza Independencia* ☎ *021/449–512* 🎫 *Free* ☉ *Weekdays 7:30–6:30, Sat. 8–noon.*

❸ **Gran Hotel del Paraguay.** This well-preserved mansion has an illustrious past as the former home of Madame Elisa Lynch, the Irish mistress of Paraguayan dictator Francisco Solano López. Now the oldest hotel in Asunción, and not quite where the action is, it's nonetheless surrounded by verandas and carefully tended tropical gardens. Duck inside to see the collection of 19th-century furniture and paintings and enjoy a cool cocktail at the bar. ⊠ *Calle de la Residenta 902 and Padre Puchen* ☎ *021/200–051.*

⓫ **Jardín Botánico y Zoológico.** The government has improved maintenance at this once-neglected park (a trend that's catching on in other parts of the country as well). Besides plenty of plants and a small zoo, you'll find a fine example of a country house, once the home of President Francisco Solano López. It's now a museum with exhibits on Paraguayan wildlife, ethnology, and history. ⊠ *Gral Artigas and Primer Presidente* ☎ *021/291–255* ⊯ *G5,000* ☼ *Daily 7–5.*

❻ **Manzana de la Rivera.** In a model for urban planners everywhere, the city of Asunción combined this *manzana* (block) of nine historic houses near the river into a pleasing cultural center. The oldest of these, the 1764 Casa Viola, the name by which many Asunceños refer to the complex, serves as a small city museum called the **Museo Memoria de la Ciudad.** The Casa Emasa, once a customs office, now houses **La Galería,** the center's art gallery. The 1914 art nouveau **Casa Clari,** the newest house, is the complex's café. ⊠ *Ayolas 129* ☎ *021/442–448* ⊯ *Free* ☼ *Weekdays 8 AM–9 PM, weekends 10:30–9.*

❾ **Museo de Bellas Artes.** The region's artistic legacy is displayed at the Museum of Fine Arts, which has a collection of paintings and sculpture by both Paraguayan and South American artists. Some of the country's most important documents are found in the museum's archive, but the records are geared toward scholarly research rather than tourist perusal. ⊠ *Mariscal Estigarribia at Iturbe* ☎ *021/447–716* ⊯ *Free* ☼ *Tues.–Fri. 7–6:30, Sat. 8–noon.*

⓬ **Museo del Barro.** Though billed as a modern art museum, the so-called Museum of Clay includes colonial and indigenous art, but is actually better known for its collection of pre-colonial Guaraní ceramics. ⊠ *Grabadores del Cabichu'i at Cañana* ☎ *021/607–996* ⊯ *Free* ☼ *Wed.–Sun. 3:30–8.*

❺ **Palacio de Gobierno.** The elegant horseshoe-shape Government Palace, with verandas and wide staircases, overlooks the bay. It's only open to the public on most holidays, but gives tours on Thursday and Friday if you arrange it one day in advance. ⊠ *El Paraguayo Independiente and Ayolas* ☎ *021/419–8220* ⊯ *Free.*

❼ **Palacio Legislativo.** During the Francia dictatorship, Paraguayans were not permitted to view the exterior of this building, but today you can even tour the interior. Paraguay's constitution was proclaimed on the first floor of the Legislative Palace in 1870. The second floor was added in 1857, destroying the original symmetry of the single-story Jesuit design. ⊠ *Plaza Independencia* ☎ *021/441–077* ⊯ *Free* ☼ *Weekday mornings.*

★ ❷ **Panteón Nacional de los Héroes.** Nothing symbolizes Paraguayan history more than the National Pantheon of Heroes, a memorial to the fallen

Elegant in Their Simplicity

IN ITS COLONIAL HEYDAY, Asunción was the administrative center of southern South America. It still retains some of its pre-independence grandeur, but today the most compelling architectural attractions are the ruins of some 30 Jesuit missions in the southeast. Although Spanish missionaries came to what is now Paraguay in 1588, little remains of their earliest dwellings. What you'll find are fascinating traces of 17th-century *reducciónes* (literally, "reductions"). Here the Jesuits organized the indigenous Guaranís—a nomadic people—into farming communities, and worked with them side-by-side, providing vocational training and religious and secular education.

You can do a mission tour in your own car—if you don't mind driving on unpaved or flooded roads and you can cope with motorists who don't obey traffic rules. The benefit of having your own car is that you can take it easy and spend a few days exploring. If you prefer not to drive, you can opt for a hurried day with an Asunción tour operator. The sites you'll see run the spectrum—from the well-preserved San Cosme y Damián, where many of the structures still serve the community, to the never finished, but intriguing, abandoned structures at Jesús.

---

soldiers of the country's hopeless battles and disastrous wars. Construction began in 1864 under the regime of Francisco Solano López, who envisioned a chapel modeled after Les Invalides in Paris. López was soon to lead Paraguay into the catastrophic War of the Triple Alliance. The building was completed in 1936 after the Pyrrhic victory of the Chaco War against Bolivia. López is interred here, as are the remains of two of Paraguay's unknown soldiers. The wars still loom large in Paraguay's consciousness, but commemorative plaques placed on the walls by the old enemies—Argentina, Bolivia, Brazil, and Uruguay—illustrate that relations have improved. Two sentinels guard the eerily quiet memorial, a place of pilgrimage for every Paraguayan who visits Asunción. ⊠ *Mariscal Estigarribia at Plaza de los Héroes* 🕾 *No phone* 🎫 *Free* ⊙ *Weekdays 6–5:30, weekends 6–noon.*

❶ **Plaza de los Héroes.** This plaza, whose centerpiece is the Panteón Nacional de los Héroes, is the heart of Asunción. Since the subtleties of Paraguayan life are laid bare in its busy plazas, this is a good place to rest in the shade and watch the locals. Guaraní vendors sell feather headdresses and bows and arrows, artisans display their pottery, and traveling salespeople hawk anything from patent cures to miracle knife sharpeners. You can also climb onto a high chair for a shoe shine or have your picture taken with an old box camera. On public holidays the square is often the scene of live music and folk-dance performances. The plaza's northeast quadrant contains a monument to the victims of torture and execution under the Stroessner dictatorship. ⊠ *Nuestra Señora de la Asunción at 25 de Mayo.*

10 **Plaza Uruguaya.** So named to honor Uruguay for returning territory it seized in the bloody Chaco War initiated by Paraguay, the plaza is a pleasant respite from the city's heat. On one side is a covered market with a good selection of Latin American literature and on the other is the 1861 colonnaded **railway station,**

> **FRUGAL FUN**
>
> A 15-minute changing of the guard ceremony takes place Saturdays at 10 AM.

shuttered since the discontinuation of rail service. In the terminal you can see a well-preserved old steam locomotive, the *Sapucaí*, no longer in use.

Where to Eat

A number of inexpensive lunch spots scattered throughout the centro serve fast food such as hamburgers and french fries. A few even offer regional specialties. Locals particularly favor **Pancholo's** (⊠Mariscal López at Salaskín ⊠ Brasilia at Santiago ⊠ Mariscal López at Convención). **Biggest** (⊠ Estrella and 15 de Agosto) bustles with all the hubbub of a big city diner. The Victorian decoration at **San Roque** (⊠ Ayala at Tacuary) is a nice backdrop for the traditional food.

Brazilian

★ $ ✕ **Churrasquaría Acuarela.** A 10-minute taxi ride from el centro, this enormous, 1,300-seat *rodízio*-style restaurant might just be the best value in town. Waiters traverse the dining room with skewers of grilled sausage, chicken, pork, and beef, slicing off as much as you want. You can mosey over to the buffet laden with salads, vegetables, and desserts. For something different, ask for *cupim*, a cut of meat taken from the hump of the Brahma cattle bred in Paraguay and Brazil. ⊠*Mariscal López 4049 at San Martín* ☎ *021/601–750* ▤ *AE, DC, MC, V.*

Contemporary

$–$$ ✕ **Mburicaó.** Chef Rodolfo Angenscheidt honed his skills at the Parisian culinary landmark Maxim's before opening this contemporary restaurant, which has become a favorite of Asunción business executives. Specialties include innovative takes on South American and Continental favorites, including fresh Patagonian truffle risotto and surubí with mozzarella and tomato in puff pastry. The airy dining room overlooks a lush patio. ⊠ *Prof. A. González Riobbó 737, at Chaco Boreal* ☎ *021/ 660–048* ▤ *AE, DC, MC, V.*

$ ✕ **La Pérgola Jardín.** Floor-to-ceiling mirrors, modern black-lacquer furniture, and live saxophone and piano music make this restaurant one of Asunción's most sophisticated dining spots. The service is efficient and friendly, and the ever-changing menu is contemporary. Warning: the piping-hot *pan de queso*, small cheese-flavored rolls, are irresistible. ⊠ *Perú 240* ☎ *021/214–014* ▤ *AE, DC, MC, V.*

¢–$ ✕ **Talleyrand.** Specialties at this local chain include duck à l'orange, sirloin steak, and surubí. The soft green color scheme and the hunting prints lend the dining rooms a refined colonial style. Talleyrand also has a location at Shopping del Sol. ⊠ *Mariscal Estigarribia 932* ☎ *021/441–*

7

163 ⊠ *Av. Aviadores del Chaco at Prof. D. E. González* ☎ *021/611–697* ⚠ *Reservations essential* ▤ *AE, DC, MC, V* ⊙ *Mariscal Estigarribia branch closed Sun.*

Italian

¢–$ ✕ **Il Capo.** Just opposite La Pérgola Jardín, this small eatery has white-washed walls and wooden beams. The homemade pastas, like lasagna *con camarones* (with shrimp) and *melanzana alla parmegiana* (eggplant with tomato and Parmesan), are excellent, and the Italian wine list is reasonably priced. ⊠ *Perú 291* ☎ *021/213–022* ▤ *AE, DC, MC, V.*

¢ ✕ **Tío Lucas.** Glossy cream-and-black wallpaper and chic Thonet bent-wood chairs give this corner eatery a crisp, modern look. The specialty here is pizza. ⊠ *25 de Mayo at Yegros* ☎ *021/447–114* ▤ *No credit cards* ⊙ *Closed Sun.*

Paraguayan

$$ ✕ **La Preferida.** Rub shoulders with politicians and diplomats where the two chic dining areas (one of which is no-smoking at peak hours) are set with crisp linen tablecloths and elegant silver and glassware. The house specialty is surubí, served smoked or in a mild curry sauce. Try the excellent *lomo de cerdo à la pimienta* (peppered pork tenderloin)—ask for it if you don't see it on the menu. The Austrian owners have fine-tuned the service, so expect friendliness and efficiency. ⊠ *25 de Mayo 1005* ☎ *021/210–641* ▤ *AE, DC, MC, V.*

¢–$ ✕ **La Paraguayita.** Its shaded terrace makes this the best of the numer-
Fodor'sChoice ous parrillas that line Avenida Brasilia. Huge portions of perfectly bar-
★ becued beef and pork are accompanied by wonderfully seasoned sopa paraguaya and chipá-guazú. The chorizo sausages make a good starter, especially when dunked in tangy *criollo,* a spicy onion, tomato, and garlic sauce. ⊠ *Brasilia at Siria* ☎ *021/204–497* ▤ *AE, DC, MC, V.*

Where to Stay

Asunción's lodging situation has improved as new hotels have opened and older ones have been refurbished. Numbers are small, however. Accommodations vary from no-frills establishments costing less than $20 (G140,000) to luxury hotels running upwards of $200 (G1,400,000) a night. Since business travelers are the capital's main visitors, rates often drop on weekends and during the summer. Make sure your room has air-conditioning—you do not want to be without it during the hotter months, from December to March.

$$$$ ⊞ **Hotel Casino Yacht y Golf Club Paraguayo.** This remodeled riverside resort 13 km (8 mi) southeast of Asunción has regained its reputation as one of South America's finest hotels. Some of the rooms, which are decorated with leather furniture, open onto verdant patios where hummingbirds nest in the foliage. You'll find plenty of recreational options here. ⊠ *Av. del Yacht 11, Lambaré* ☎ *021/906–121 or 021/906–117* 🖷 *021/906–120* ⊕ *www.hotelyacht.com.py* ⌨ *116 rooms, 12 suites* ♿ *4 restaurants, 2 snack bars, minibars, cable TV, 18-hole golf course, 14 tennis courts, pool, health club, hair salon, massage, spa, beach, boating, jet skiing, fishing, basketball, soccer, squash, volleyball, bar, casino,*

shop, laundry service, Internet room, business services, meeting room ⊟ *AE, DC, MC, V* ⦿| *BP.*

$$$ ⊞ **Granados Park Hotel.** Replicating the sensibility of a grand old Latin American hotel, this place gives you colonial style with modern amenities. The attentive staff greets you in an opulent lobby filled with lush greenery. The modern rooms are much more subdued, decorated with carved wooden armoires and handicrafts. ⊠ *Estrella and 15 de Agosto* ☎ *021/497–921* 🖷 *021/445–324* ⊕ *www.granadospark.com.py* ⇥ *68 rooms, 3 suites* ☊ *Restaurant, in-room safes, minibars, in-room data ports, cable TV, pool, gym, hair salon, massage, sauna, bar, dry cleaning, laundry service, concierge, Internet room, business services, meeting rooms, airport shuttle* ⊟ *AE, DC, MC, V* ⦿| *BP.*

$$$ ⊞ **Hotel Excelsior.** Regency-style fabrics, carved-wood furniture, and Oriental rugs make this one of the city's most elegant hotels, and a refurbishing has made the place gleam again. You'll sink into the carpeting in the huge, plush, brightly furnished rooms accented with wood carvings and Paraguayan art. The three-story Excelsior Mall is across the street. ⊠ *Chile 980* ☎ *021/495–632* 🖷 *021/496–748* ⊕ *www.excelsior.com.py* ⇥ *137 rooms, 12 suites* ☊ *2 restaurants, room service, in-room safes, in-room data ports, cable TV, tennis court, pool, gym, health club, hair salon, bar, piano bar, pub, dance club, dry cleaning, laundry service, business services, meeting rooms, airport shuttle* ⊟ *AE, DC, MC, V* ⦿| *BP.*

★ $$$ ⊞ **Sabe Center Hotel.** The sleek, orange-brick high-rise facing Plaza Uruguaya goes out of its way to impress: in the lobby, a giant chandelier shimmers above Oriental rugs, enormous urns, and a grand staircase. Rooms are less regal, but bright and comfortable. A breakfast buffet is included. ⊠ *25 de Mayo at México* ☎ *021/450–093* 🖷 *021/450–101* ⊕ *www.sabecenterhotel.com.py* ⇥ *91 rooms* ☊ *Restaurant, coffee shop, in-room safes, minibars, cable TV, gym, bar, dry cleaning, laundry service, Internet room, business services, meeting rooms, airport shuttle* ⊟ *AE, DC, MC, V* ⦿| *CP.*

$$ ⊞ **Apart Hotel Mandu'Ará.** The suites in this hotel are popular with business travelers. Each suite includes a sitting room, a dining area, and a kitchenette. The furnishings differ markedly from room to room: "classic" rooms tend toward lots of carved wood, while "contemporary" rooms have more modern furnishings. Both types are equally plush. ⊠ *México 554* ☎🖷 *021/490–223* ⊕ *www.manduara.com.py* ⇥ *82 suites* ☊ *Coffee shop, dining room, cable TV, pool, gym, sauna, bar, laundry service, business services, meeting room, airport shuttle* ⊟ *AE, DC, MC, V* ⦿| *BP.*

$$ ⊞ **Chaco Hotel.** Friendly, attentive service is the hallmark of this comfortable, if rather unremarkably decorated, lodging. The carpeted rooms are large, but the beds are small. A tasty breakfast is included in the rate. ⊠ *Caballero 285* ☎ *021/492–066* 🖷 *021/444–223* ⊕ *www.hotelchaco.com.py* ⇥ *72 rooms* ☊ *Restaurant, minibars, in-room data ports, cable TV, pool, bar, laundry service, business services, meeting rooms* ⊟ *AE, DC, MC, V* ⦿| *CP.*

$$ ⊞ **Hotel Cecilia.** Priding itself on personalized attention, this hotel has won a devoted clientele. Rooms are large, though slightly austere. The

sixth-floor terrace has a pool with a terrific bay view. Adjacent to the hotel you'll find an excellent deli and pastry shop. ✉ *Estados Unidos 341* ☎ *021/210–365* 📠 *021/497–111* ⊕ *www.uninet.com.py/cecilia* ➥ *50 rooms* ⚑ *Restaurant, cable TV, pool, gym, sauna, bar, laundry service, meeting rooms, airport shuttle* ▭ *AE, DC, MC, V* ¡○¡ *CP.*

$–$$ 🏨 **Asunción Internacional Hotel.** An abundance of greenery greets you as you enter this modern, 15-story hotel. The sleek black-and-white lobby has an executive bar where you can enjoy a cocktail. Many of the rather small rooms, which are redecorated every year, have views of the bay. Each contains a data port where you can plug in your laptop; if you didn't bring it along, the hotel's business center offers four terminals. ✉ *Ayolas 520, at Oliva* ☎ *021/494–114* 📠 *021/494–383* ⊕ *www. hotelinternacional.com.py* ➥ *70 rooms, 26 suites* ⚑ *Restaurant, snack bar, in-room safes, in-room data ports, pool, gym, massage, sauna, bar, Internet room, business services, meeting room, airport shuttle* ▭ *AE, DC, MC, V* ¡○¡ *BP.*

$–$$ 🏨 **Hotel Las Margaritas.** Cordial service and opulent, gleaming accom-
Fodor'sChoice   modations are the hallmarks of this lodging, which opened in January
★   2003. The lobby blooms with plants and works by indigenous artisans and paintings by Michael Burt, one of Paraguay's leading contemporary artists. Rooms come in one of three color schemes (green, light blue, or orange) and all harbor Burt paintings and Guaraní artwork. ✉ *Estrella and 15 de Agosto* ☎ *021/448–765* 📠 *021/448–785* ⊕ *www. lasmargaritas.com.py* ➥ *60 rooms, 17 suites* ⚑ *2 restaurants, in-room safes, minibars, in-room data ports, cable TV, pool, gym, sauna, billiards, bar, dry cleaning, laundry service, business services, meeting rooms, airport shuttle* ▭ *AE, DC, MC, V* ¡○¡ *BP.*

$ 🏨 **Excelsior Inn.** This hotel opened by the owners of the Hotel Excelsior lacks the frills of its pricier sibling. Rooms, many with hardwood floors, are pleasantly furnished with dark greens and golds. Each has an in-room data port—a rarity at this price range. ✉ *Alberdi and Manduvirá* ☎ *021/496–743* ⊕ *www.excelsior.com.py* ➥ *23 rooms, 1 suite* ⚑ *Minibars, in-room data ports, cable TV, laundry service, airport shuttle* ▭ *AE, DC, MC, V* ¡○¡ *BP.*

$ 🏨 **Hotel Presidente.** Just two blocks from the Plaza de los Héroes, this comfortable lodging has conveniences usually reserved for more expensive establishments. All rooms have contemporary furnishings. Business travelers have access to fax machines and computers. ✉ *Azara 128* ☎ *021/494–931* ✉ *hotel_pdte@telesur.com.py* ➥ *44 rooms, 4 suites* ⚑ *Restaurant, minibars, bar, business services, meeting room* ▭ *AE, DC, MC, V* ¡○¡ *BP.*

¢   🏨 **Asunción Palace Hotel.** Built in the mid-19th century as a private residence for the López family, and transformed into a hospital during the War of the Triple Alliance, this beaux arts–style hotel is now a national landmark. It's certainly charming, though a few of the rooms are noisy. Others are quite nice and peaceful; ask to see one before taking it. All are simply furnished, but this is a good budget option. ✉ *Colón 415* ☎ *021/492–152* 📠 *021/492–153* ✉ *aphotel@yahoo.com* ➥ *25 rooms, 2 suites* ⚑ *Restaurant, refrigerators, bar; no TV in some rooms* ▭ *DC, MC, V* ¡○¡ *BP.*

¢ 🏨 **Hotel Preciado.** Peace Corps volunteers in Asunción on business or pleasure dub this place, just east of downtown, their favorite, and their presence here gives the hotel a youthful exuberance. Modern, high-ceiling rooms are simply furnished with two beds, a desk, and a chair. The low prices make this a solid budget bet. ✉ *Azara 840* ☎ *021/447–661* 🖷 *021/453–937* ✐ *hotelpreciado@hotmail.com* 💤 *22 rooms* ♨ *Dining room, minibars, cable TV, pool, laundry service* 🖃 *AE, MC, V* 🍴 *BP.*

Nightlife & the Arts

Almost all the information about nightlife in Asunción is in Spanish, but the listings you find in publications are easily deciphered. Asunción's free biweekly arts and nightlife newsletter, *Tiempo Libre,* has cinema and theater listings. It's widely available in hotels and restaurants. The Friday editions of Asunción's daily newspapers, particularly *Última Hora,* also have excellent weekend arts and entertainment sections.

The Arts

Catch dance performances at **Noches del Paraguay** (✉ Juan Domingo Perón and Cacique Lambaré ☎ 021/332–807). There's a show every night of the week, but Friday and Saturday are the most popular nights, so make reservations. Weeknight tickets are G10,000; weekends, G20,000.

Asunción's city cultural center, the **Manzana de la Rivera** (✉ Ayolas 129 ☎ 021/442–448), presents lectures, concerts, and movies many

DANCE FEVER
Paraguay is renowned for its folk dancing. Traditional dances include the *chamamé,* performed by pairs to accordion music, and *la danza de las botellas,* literally "the dance of the bottles." A female dancer moves in time to the music while stacking six empty wine bottles on her head.

evenings. Spain has a network of active cultural centers throughout Latin America. Asunción's branch of the **Centro Cultural Español** (✉ Tacuary 745 ☎ 021/449–921) presents a mix of lectures, poetry readings, classical music concerts, and film screenings three or four nights a week. Most are free; a few have a nominal cover charge.

Nightlife

Asunción doesn't have the nightlife of other Latin American capitals, such as Buenos Aires or Rio de Janeiro, especially during the week. The scene picks up Thursday through Saturday when locals dress up to go out on the town. In many nightspots you'll get turned away at the door if you're wearing jeans and T-shirts. Many upscale places cluster around Avenida Brasilia, Avenida España, and Avenida Mariscal López, about 2 km (1 mi) northeast of the centro. Most charge a small cover.

BARS A visit to the friendly, semi–open air **Britannia Pub** (✉ Cerro Corá 851 ☎ 021/443–990) dispels the myth that Asunción has no expat population; they're all here. The always popular **Café Bohemia** (✉ Senador Long and España) attracts young and old alike, usually younger on alterna-

tive-music nights. As befits the name, **Café Literario** (✉ Mariscal Estigarribia 456 ☎ 021/491–640) draws aficionados of coffee, wine, books,
quiet music, and animated conversation. **Faces** (✉ Brasilia 786 ☎ 021/
225–360) is a good place to talk and have a drink. Just west of downtown, the nautical-theme **La Choppería del Puerto** (✉ Palma 1028 at
Garibaldi ☎ 021/445–590) also has a pleasant sidewalk café. It is open
24 hours. **Mouse Cantina** (✉ Brasilia at Patria ☎ 021/228–794) gets a
little loud at times. **Tequila Rock** (✉ Brasilia at Sargento Gauto ☎ 021/
229–179), currently the trendiest of Asunción bars, caters to a twen-
tysomething crowd.

CASINOS Try your luck at slot machines, roulette, baccarat, and blackjack at the
glitzy **Casino de Asunción** (✉ España 151 and Sacramento ☎ 021/603–
160), open daily 2 PM–6 AM. The **Hotel Casino Yacht y Golf Club Paraguayo**
(✉ Av. del Yacht 11, Lambaré ☎ 021/906–043), which is about 13 km
(8 mi) outside of town, offers all the standard casino games. The casino
itself is open daily 9 PM–6 AM.

DANCE CLUBS The most popular disco in Asunción is **Casapueblo** (✉ Mariscal López
and Mayor Rivarola ☎ 021/611–081), where you can dance all night
to Latin rhythms. **Chaco's Pub** (✉ República Argentina 1035 ☎ 021/
603–199) spins international disco music. Asunción's elite boogie the
weekend nights away at **Coyote** (✉ Sucre 1655 at San Martín ☎ 021/
662–114).

Outdoor Activities

Soccer

To see Paraguayans get riled up, head to the **Defensores del Chaco** stadium in the suburb of Sajonia to catch a *fútbol* game. Cerro Porteño
and Olimpia are two of the most popular capital-area teams. Matches
are played on Sunday. Local newspapers publish current schedules.

Tennis

South American tennis tournaments, including zone matches of the
Davis Cup, are held at the **Hotel Casino Yacht y Golf Club Paraguayo** (✉ Av.
del Yacht 11, Lambaré ☎ 021/906–043).

Shopping

The best shopping in Asunción falls into two very distinct categories:
handicrafts and electronics. Prices for both are among the lowest in
South America. Argentinians flock here for bargains on the latter, but
prices are actually comparable to those of a large discount store in the
United States.

Markets & Shopping Districts

Mercado 4, on Avenida Pettirossi, is a crowded market that overflows
into neighboring streets. Its stalls are laden with produce, hammocks,
and cage after cage of clucking chickens. The tables are set up before
dawn, so get an early start to avoid the stifling heat and suffocating crowds.
It is open all day, every day, except Sunday afternoons.

CLOSE UP

Light, but Long-lasting

Paraguay's signature craft souvenir is the delicate *ñandutí*, a type of spiderweb lacework. Patterns represent plants, animals, or scenes from local legends. Although ñandutí are traditionally made with white silk or cotton, colors are now being added to the designs. Both this and *ao p'oí*, a type of embroidery, are incorporated into such items as tablecloths and place mats. Wood carvings, intricately decorated gourds, and figurines—including nativity figures—are reasonably priced mementos. Rustic leather items, such as suitcases, knapsacks, and briefcases, are long-lasting and only a fraction of the cost of Argentine goods. Plain white or colorful woven hammocks are another good buy. You'll be able to find all these crafts in stores in Asunción. Craftspeople in the town of Areguá, near Asunción on Lake Ypacaraí, make clay pots and other ceramics. In Luque, near the international airport, you can find Paraguayan harps, guitars, and fine silver filigree jewelry. The town of Itá, 37 km (23 mi) south of Asunción on Ruta 1, is famous for its ceramics, and is the place to come for distinctive black clay pottery.

You can find lots of handicrafts west of **Plaza de los Héroes** between Palma and Estrella. For quality goods stick to the specialty stores. Hundreds of small shops here sell imported watches, electronics, cameras, and athletic shoes. Watch out for street vendors selling knock-offs such as "Rolec" watches.

Crafts Shops

Paraguay's famous ñandutí, the delicate lacework, can be found everywhere in Asunción. One of the best shops for ñandutí is **Ao P'oí Raity** (⊠ F. R. Moreno 155 ☎ 021/494–475). For the best leather goods try **Casa Vera** (⊠ Mariscal Estigarribia 470 ☎ 021/445–868). **Folklore** (⊠ Mariscal Estigarribia at Iturbe ☎ 021/494–360) sells carved wood items. **Overall** (⊠ Mariscal Estigarribia and Caballero ☎ 021/448–657) is also well known for its selection of lace and woodwork. **Victoria** (⊠ Mariscal Estigarribia at Iturbe ☎ 021/450–148) sells ceramics and other items.

Fodor's Choice ★

Craftspeople in the town of **Areguá**, near Asunción on Lake Ypacaraí, make clay pots and other ceramics. In **Luque**, near the international airport, you can find Paraguayan harps, guitars, and fine silver filigree jewelry.

Fodor's Choice ★ **Constancio Sanabria** (⊠ Av. Aviadores del Chaco 2852, Luque ☎ 021/662–408) is highly regarded for musical instruments.

Shopping Malls

For department-store items, try the three-story **Excelsior Mall** (⊠ Chile 901 ☎ 021/443–015). **Shopping del Sol** (⊠ Av. Aviadores del Chaco and Prof. D. E. González ☎ 021/611–780) has specialty shops, a cinema, and a children's play area. **Mariscal López Shopping** (⊠ Quesada 5050

7

☎ 021/611–272) has stores selling clothing, books, and records, and computer terminals with free Internet access.

Side Trip from Asunción

San Bernardino

The popular holiday resort of San Bernardino, on the shores of Lago Ypacaraí, makes an excellent day trip from the capital. From December to March it's packed with weekenders enjoying the dark blue waters ringed by clean, white sand. Water sports are a popular pastime—windsurfing equipment can be rented at the beaches.

Looping back toward Asunción, the road passes through **Caacupé**, a mostly Catholic town where the Día de la Nuestra Señora de Los Milagros (Day of Our Lady of the Miracles) is celebrated on December 8. Hundreds of thousands make a pilgrimage to the basilica here.

WHERE TO
STAY & EAT
¢

✕🏨 **Hotel del Lago.** On the shores of Lago Ypacaraí, this low-key Spanish-style hotel offers simple, clean rooms with comfortable beds. The rustic restaurant's forte is roast beef or pork, cooked in a wood-fire oven and served with sopa paraguaya. ⊠ *Teniente Weiler and Carlos López* ☎ *0512/232–201* ✈ *23 rooms* ⚒ *Restaurant, minibars, pool, laundry service, meeting room* ⊟ *AE, DC, MC, V* ¶◎¶ *BP.*

¢   🏨 **Hotel Pueblo.** The tranquillity of the forest surrounding this hotel is a welcoming change from the noise and crowds of Asunción. Rooms are simple but comfortable, and all have views of Lago Ypacaraí. Try the restaurant for lunch, where you can order locally prepared surubí and bori-bori. ⊠ *Calle 5 at Paseo del Pueblo* ☎☎ *0512/232–391* ✉ *pueblo@telesur.com.py* ✈ *12 rooms, 6 suites* ⚒ *Restaurant, minibars, pool, laundry service; no room phones* ⊟ *AE, DC, MC, V* ¶◎¶ *BP.*

Asunción Essentials

Transportation

BY AIR

Asunción's Aeropuerto Internacional Silvio Pettirossi (ASU) is 15 km (9 mi) northeast of downtown. The only U.S. carrier serving Paraguay is American, which flies from Miami via São Paulo. Paraguay's national airline, TAM Mercosur, likely the world's only airline that serenades departing passengers with harp music, does not fly directly to the United States; rather, it connects in São Paulo with its affiliate TAM Brazilian Airlines's daily Miami flights and its three weekly flights to both New York and Paris.

TAM Mercosur has daily service between Asunción and Ciudad del Este (AGT), Concepción (CID), and Vallemí (VMI). South American carriers that serve Asunción include Aerolíneas Argentinas, Bolivia's LAB, Uruguay's Pluna, and Brazil's Varig.

AIRPORTS &
TRANSFERS

Taxis are the most practical means of getting to town, and they charge a fixed rate of G84,000. The airport information desk can tell you the exact rate. It can also arrange for an *omnibus special* whenever there are six or more passengers. This costs G35,000 per person and will take you to any address in downtown Asunción. Less conveniently, Bus 30A leaves from the tollbooths on the road into the airport (about 200 meters from the terminal). It departs for downtown Asunción every 15 minutes; the fare is G2,000.

🚩 **Airlines Aerolíneas Argentinas** ☎ 021/201-501. **American** ☎ 021/443-330. **LAB Airlines** ☎ 021/441-586. **Pluna** ☎ 021/448-856. **TAM Mercosur** ☎ 021/490-040. **Varig** ☎ 021/448-856.

🚩 **Airports Aeropuerto Internacional Silvio Pettirossi** ☎ 021/645-600.

BY BUS

TO & FROM ASUNCIÓN All intercity services leave from Terminal de Omnibus Asunción, located east of downtown. The three major bus companies, La Encarnaceña, Pluna, and Rápido Yguazú, also have information booths on Plaza Uruguaya.

WITHIN ASUNCIÓN Ever since the old yellow trams were retired, Asunción's bus service has improved. New local buses run every eight minutes. The fare is G2,000. As in all big cities, watch your belongings carefully.

🚩 **Bus Companies La Encarnaceña** ☎ 021/551-745. **Pluna** ☎ 021/490-128. **Rápido Yguazú** ☎ 021/551-618 or 021/551-601.

🚩 **Bus Terminals Terminal de Omnibus Asunción** ✉ República Argentina at Fernando de la Mora ☎ 021/551-732.

BY CAR

Unless you plan to travel out of town, avoid renting a car—driving in Asunción can be a nerve-racking experience. Aggressive bus drivers, confusing routes, scarcity of stoplights, and never-ending road construction make even Paraguayans (who rarely follow traffic rules) nervous.

CAR RENTAL You'll get the best rates in Asunción at Only Rent a Car, which has an office at the airport. Hertz and National are international companies that have offices in Asunción.

🚩 **Rental Agencies Hertz** ✉ Aeropuerto Internacional Silvio Pettirossi ☎ 021/645-600 ✉ Km. 4.5 Av. Eusebio Ayala ☎ 021/605-708. **National** ✉ Yegros 501 ☎ 021/492-157. **Only Rent a Car** ✉ Aeropuerto Internacional Silvio Pettirossi ☎ 021/646-083 Ext. 112 ✉ 15 de Agosto 520 ☎ 021/492-731.

TAXIS

Asunción's yellow Mercedes taxis, operated by Radio Taxi Asunción, are an inexpensive way to get around the city. You can find one on the street, at any major hotel, or at one of the dozens of taxi stands around the city. Make sure your driver turns the meter on or you risk being charged an outrageous fare. A 30% surcharge is added after dark. It can be difficult to hail a taxi at night, so it's perfectly acceptable to ask your hotel or restaurant to call one for you.

🚩 **Taxi Companies Radio Taxi Asunción** (RTA) ☎ 021/311-080.

Contacts & Resources

EMBASSIES

The United States embassy is open Monday–Thursday 7:30–5:30 and Friday 7:30–11:30, although passport questions are not handled after 10:30. The United Kingdom maintains an honorary consulate in Asunción, open weekdays 8–1 and 3–7. For more serious matters, the consul will refer you to the British Embassy in Buenos Aires, Argentina. Australia, Canada, and New Zealand do not have diplomatic representation in Paraguay; contact their embassies in Buenos Aires.

🚩 **Australia** ✉ Villanueva 1400, Buenos Aires ☎ 54/11/4777-6580. **Canada** ✉ Tagle 2828, Buenos Aires ☎ 54/1/4808-1000. **New Zealand** ✉ Carlos Pelligrini 1427, Buenos Aires ☎ 54/1/4328-0747. **United Kingdom** ✉ Eulogio Estigarribia 4846 and Monseñor Bogarín, Asunción ☎ 021/210-405. **United States** ✉ Av. Mariscal López 1776, Asunción ☎ 021/213-715.

EMERGENCIES

Two private hospitals, Hospital Privado Francés and Hospital Privado Bautista, provide a more North American–European standard of care than do Asunción's public facilities. Both have English speakers on staff.

🚩 **Emergency Services Ambulance** ☎ 141. **Fire** ☎ 132. **Police** ☎ 130.

🚩 **Hospitals Hospital Privado Francés** ✉ Brasilia at Insaurralde ☎ 021/295-250. **Hospital Privado Bautista** ✉ Av. República Argentina at Andrés Campos Cervera ☎ 021/600-171.

MONEY MATTERS

In Asunción U.S. dollars are no problem to exchange. Cash is easier to exchange and earns a better rate than traveler's checks. Interbanco and Money Exchange change American Express traveler's checks for guaraníes, but the American Express office does not cash its own checks. Many places exchange Argentine pesos and Brazilian reales, but few deal with other currencies. You can change money and traveler's checks downtown at ABN Amro Bank and La Moneda or any of the *casas de cambio* (exchange houses) along Calle Palma and around the Plaza de los Héroes. Multibanco, just outside the customs exit at Aeropuerto Internacional Silvio Pettirossi changes cash dollars for guaraníes. You can also change money at major hotels, which have a less favorable rate. The money changers on downtown streets who call out "*¡Cambio dólares!*" offer decent rates during normal business hours but raise their rates evenings and weekends.

Machines on Paraguay's Infonet system of ATMs have an annoying habit of accepting either Plus- or Cirrus-linked cards, but rarely both. To be on the safe side, bring cards affiliated with both systems, and contact your bank about changing your password to four digits if you don't already use one—that's what will work here. The ATM at ABN Amro Bank *does* take both, as does the machine just beyond the customs exit at Aeropuerto Internacional Silvio Pettirossi, as well as those in most Esso gas stations.

🚩 **Banks ABN Amro Bank** ✉ Estrella at Alberi ☎ 021/419-0000. **InTerbanco** ✉ Oliva 349 ☎ 021/494-992. **American Express** ✉ Yegros 690 ☎ 021/490-111. **La Moneda** ✉ 25 de Mayo 127 ☎ 021/494-724. **Money Exchange** ✉ Palma 403 ☎ 021/453-277. **Multibanco** ✉ Aeropuerto Internacional Silvio Pettirossi ☎ 021/647-199.

SAFETY

Although Asunción has escaped the crime typical of other South American capitals, there is still a small amount of petty crime against tourists. As in any urban area, be aware of your surroundings and keep an eye

NO LONGER MARCHING OFF A CLIFF

Paraguay's flamboyant history is one of a small country led by larger-than-life strongmen whose personal goals usually conflicted with the needs of the people. (The old movie stereotype of the mustachioed Latin American leader, decked out in military uniform complete with epaulets, medals, and sunglasses, defined Paraguay until about a decade ago.) The first president, José Gáspar Rodríguez de Francia, set the tone by calling himself "El Supremo." He preached a policy of complete self-sufficiency, forbidding trade and immigration, and set the stage for Paraguay's history of isolation. He also forbade citizens from looking at his home (now the Palacio Legislativo) or even at him as his carriage passed through the streets. Then came the López family, father and son, the younger of whom, Francisco Solano, led Paraguay into the disastrous War of the Triple Alliance (1865–70) against Argentina, Brazil, and Uruguay; he lost half the country's territory and 80% of the male population. A succession of presidents culminated in the 35-year authoritarian regime of General Alfredo Stroessner, toppled in a 1989 coup.

Democracy is still a novel concept for Paraguay, and at times the transition has been a struggle. The government continues to battle corruption and smuggling, and dire financial straits in Argentina and Brazil, Paraguay's primary source of trade and tourism, have taken their toll here as well. Since freedom of the press was restored, daily accounts of grievances against current officials fill the country's now-lively media. The government's decision to permit the stationing of U.S. Marines to ferret out extremist-group activity in the eastern region of the country has provoked much controversy. Yet, we vote to label Paraguay as a glass half full rather than half empty. That the country functions as well as it does, given its somewhat bizarre history, is a testament to the will of its people, who are determined to take that newfound democracy and make their country work.

on all valuables. Leave flashy jewelry and expensive watches in your hotel safe (or better yet, back home) and keep laptops and cameras in an inconspicuous bag.

TELEPHONES

Asunción has few telephone booths, per se. To make domestic or international calls, you can go to the downtown office of COPACO, the privatized national telephone company, which is open 6 AM–midnight. Numerous private telephone offices let you make calls, too. Look for TELÉFONOS PÚBLICOS or CABINAS TELEFÓNICAS signs.

🚩 Telephone Offices **COPACO** ✉ Oliva and 15 de Agosto ☎ 021/419–4452.

TIPPING

In upscale restaurants an appropriate tip is about 10% of the bill, more if the service is exceptionally good. In average places, round up the bill to the nearest G1,000. Round up taxi fares to the nearest G500, and give G3,000 to doormen who hail you a taxi. Give porters around G3,000 per bag. Leave the chambermaid G7,000 per day or about G40,000 per week. Gas-station attendants are tipped up to G2,000 for full service. Give ushers and checkroom and restroom attendants G2,000.

TOUR OPERATORS

Many companies offer tours of Asunción and the surrounding region. Guided tours of the city start at G70,000, and trips to Areguá and other nearby destinations start at G120,000. Inter Express, Lions Tour, and VIP's Tour are three of the best.

🛈 Tour Companies **Inter Express** ✉ Yegros 690, at Luis Alberto ☎ 021/490-111. **Lions Tour** ✉ Alberdi 454, 1st fl. ☎ 021/490-591. **VIP's Tour** ✉ México 782, at Fulgencio R. Moreno ☎ 021/497-199.

VISITOR INFORMATION

Paraguay sees so few travelers that the friendly staff at Secretaria Nacional de Turismo (Senatur) seem grateful to see you. Stop in the main office near the Plaza de los Héroes daily 7–7 for pamphlets and maps—only a few are in English—or advice on hotels or restaurants. There's a branch office in the airport arrivals hall beyond the customs exit that is open daily for arriving flights. Lions Tour also has a desk at the airport with transportation, hotel, and tour information.

🛈 **Senatur** ✉ Palma 468 at 14 de Mayo ☎ 021/494-110 🖷 021/491-230 ⊕ www.senatur.gov.py.

SOUTHERN PARAGUAY

The seven 17th-century Jesuit missions along the 405-km (253-mi) drive from Asunción to Jesús date from as far back as 1609, when the newly formed Compañía de Jesús (Society of Jesus) was granted permission by the Spanish crown to move the nomadic Guaraní people, threatened by slave traders from Brazil, into self-sufficient agricultural communities. The Jesuits also wanted, of course, to convert the Guaraní to Christianity. Each community, called a *reducción* (literally meaning "reduction"), had a population of about 3,000 Guaraní under the charge of two or three priests who taught them agricultural and other practical skills such as stonemasonry and metalwork. Each reducción was centered around a large plaza with a chapel, the priests' living quarters, and usually a school. The main buildings, most often constructed of red sandstone blocks, had terra-cotta-tile roofs, wide verandas, and covered walkways.

Under the tutelage of the Jesuits, the Guaraní excelled at wood carving, pottery, and calligraphy, and they proved to be particularly fine musicians. Performing mainly in church choirs and orchestras, they were able to adapt the complex European baroque counterpoint to their own traditional musical styles. The experiment, however, was so successful that the Spanish monarchs banned the Jesuits from their New World empire in 1767. The 100,000 Guaraní soon returned to their old way of life and the missions fell into disrepair.

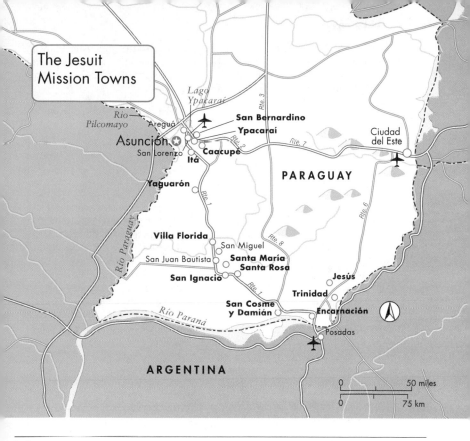

The Jesuit
Mission Towns

Lago
Ypacaraí
Río
Pilcomayo
Areguá
San Bernardino
Ypacaraí
Asunción
San Lorenzo
Caacupé
Itá
Ciudad
del Este
Rte. 3
Rte. 2
Rte. 7
PARAGUAY
Yaguarón
Rte. 1
Rte. 6
Villa Florida
San Miguel
San Juan Bautista
Santa María
Santa Rosa
Rte. 8
San Ignacio
Rte. 1
Jesús
Trinidad
Río Paraná
San Cosme
y Damián
Encarnación
Posadas
ARGENTINA
0   50 miles
0   75 km

Itá

37 km (23 mi) south of Asunción on Ruta 1.

Famous throughout Paraguay for its ceramics, Itá is the place to come
for its distinctive black clay pottery. You'll pass a government-run handicraft exhibition before you reach town. On February 3 the town celebrates the Feast of St. Blas, the patron saint of Paraguay, with singing,
dancing, a parade, and horse racing.

Yaguarón

11 km (7 mi) south of Itá on Ruta 1.

Franciscan missionaries attempted to fill the void left after the Jesuits
were expelled from the Spanish empire in 1767. They centered their efforts in Yaguarón but met with less success in maintaining the reducción communities established by their predecessors. The town's restored
18th-century **Iglesia de San Buenaventura** was the centerpiece of Paraguay's
Franciscan missions. Inside you'll find brightly colored wooden statues
carved by Guaraní artists. ☎ *0533/32–213* 🎫 *Free* 🕐 *Tues.–Sat.*
8–11:30 and 2–5; Sun. 8–11:30.

Yaguarón was also the home of José Gáspar Rodríguez de Francia, Paraguay's first in a long line of dictators. The small **Museo del Doctor Francia** displays his portraits and belongings. ☎ *0533/32–213* ✉ *Free* ⊙ *Mon.–Sat. 8–11:30 and 2–5; Sat. 8–11:30.*

Villa Florida

130 km (80 mi) south of Yaguarón on Ruta 1.

Fodor'sChoice
★

Farms give way to rolling grasslands as you approach Villa Florida, the grazing grounds of white Nelore cattle. Cowboys in wide-brim hats tend the herds on horses saddled in sheepskin, while goats stealthily graze in hibiscus- and bougainvillea-filled gardens outside tiny, rustic cottages along the Río Tebicuary. The river, which once marked the western border of the Jesuit mission area, now has several popular beaches; anglers know it well as a prime spot for catching dorado and surubí. The town is not particularly pretty, but there is a good selection of hotels and restaurants and magnificent sunsets over the water.

> ### THE ONE THAT GOT AWAY
>
> Paraguay's fishing is considered to be among the best in the world. Anglers come chiefly to catch dorado, spectacular fighters that leap high into the air when hooked, and surubí, giant catfish that take off like an express train when you reel them in. Dorado are generally between 9 and 27 pounds, although some weigh up to 40 pounds. Surubí weighing as much as 44 pounds are not uncommon, but the real trophies are more than 90 pounds. The top spots for anglers are in the southwest—Ayolas, on the Río Paraná, and Villa Florida, on the Río Tebicuary.

Where to Stay & Eat

¢ ✕⌂ **Hotel Centu Cué.** Comfortable
Fodor'sChoice bungalows scattered along the
★ banks of the Río Tebicuary make up this isolated lodge frequented mainly by anglers in search of the one that won't get away. Lounging on the 2-km (1-mi) private beach and taking a dip in the river are also a popular activities. At the nautical-theme restaurant, mounted heads of enormous fish and photos of proud fishermen with their catches may mock your day's accomplishments. What else would you eat here but dorado or surubí, grilled or in a casserole, caught just a few yards from the table? ✉ *7 km (4 mi) off Ruta 1 at Km 163, Desvío* ☎☎ *083/240–219* ⌁ *30 rooms, 5 cabins* ⚹ *Restaurant, beach, fishing, horseback riding, volleyball; no room phones* ⊟ *No credit cards* ⫾◯⫿ *FAP.*

¢ ✕⌂ **Hotel Nacional de Turismo.** Colonial-style rooms open onto a shady courtyard at this friendly hotel. Camping areas near the river have been set aside for fishing enthusiasts. The restaurant serves grilled meats and poultry; a must is the milanesa, made with freshly caught surubí. The chef is eager to please, and will be happy to prepare whatever you desire. Rates include a big breakfast. ✉ *Ruta 1, Km 162* ☎ *083/240–207* ⌁ *25 rooms* ⚹ *Restaurant, cafeteria, pool, fishing, volleyball, laundry service* ⊟ *No credit cards* ⫾◯⫿ *BP.*

$$ 🏠 **Estancia Santa Clara.** This ranch, 24 km (14 mi) north of Villa Florida, is downright plush compared to most of the other agriculture tourism lodgings in Paraguay. You can roll up your sleeves and rope steers, milk cows, pick vegetables, or bake bread if you really want a hands-on experience. You can also ride horses, hike bird-filled trails, or curl up in a hammock with a good book. Rooms in the rambling orange stucco house have vaulted wooden ceilings. Rates include all meals. ⊠ *Ruta 1, Km 141, Caapucé* 🕾 *0981/405–020 (cell phone)* 🕾🕾 *021/605–729 in Asunción* ↪ *8 rooms* ♻ *Dining room, pool* ▭ *No credit cards* ⎺⎺⎺ *FAP.*

Outdoor Activities

Arrangements for everything from bait to boat charters can be made through the **Hotel Nacional de Turismo** (⊠ Ruta 1, Km 162 🕾 083/240–207). Anglers should bring their own rod, line, and lures suitable for trolling, spinning, and live baiting. In nearby Desvío, **Hotel Centu Cué** (⊠ 7 km [4½ mi] off Ruta 1 at Km 163 🕾 083/240–219) has one of the river's best fishing spots. The hotel sells fishing supplies.

Santa María

37 km (22 mi) south of San Miguel on Ruta 1.

You'll pass through San Miguel, where locals tempt you with handwoven woolen blankets, rugs, and ponchos, and San Juan Bautista, where quaint colonial houses line cobblestone streets, before you reach Santa María. Nearly 7,000 Guaraní lived here in the early 18th century, and some of the original houses have been restored. The **Museo Jesuítico** has some 70 Guaraní carvings and statues; the latter represent the life of Jesus. (The museum keeps no fixed hours; if the door is locked, you may have to ask around for the priest to let you in.) ⊠ *Santa María* 🕾 *0781/ 283–222* ⎀ *G2,000.*

San Ignacio

18 km (11 mi) south of Santa Maria on Ruta 1.

Fodor'sChoice
★
The Jesuits established Paraguay's first mission in San Ignacio, and today the **Museo Jesuítico** displays the country's best collection of Guaraní wood carvings and other period artifacts, including gilded pulpits, door panels, and statues. A depiction of St. Paul pointing to new lands in need of salvation is most striking; at his feet are a number of carved faces with Guaraní features. The building itself, with its thick adobe walls, is believed to be the oldest in Paraguay. It dates from the establishment of the mission in 1609. ⊠ *Ruta 1 (look for the sign)* 🕾 *082/232–218* ⎀ *G3,000* ☉ *Daily 8–noon and 2:30–5:30.*

Santa Rosa

19 km (12 mi) east of San Ignacio on Ruta 1.

The ringing of bells from the red sandstone bell tower, built in 1698, can still be heard in the town of Santa Rosa, one of the era's largest reducciónes. In the small **museum** you can see frescoes from the old altar of the local chapel called the Capilla de Nuestra Señora de Loreto.

You'll also find a group of centuries-old carvings representing the Annunciation. ✉ *Ruta 1 (look for the sign)* ☎ *0858/221* 💲 *G2,000* 🕙 *Mon.–Sat. 7:30–11:30 and 1:30–5:30.*

San Cosme y Damián

95 km (59 mi) southeast of Santa Rosa on Ruta 1.

Just as Ruta 1 reaches Coronel Bogado, a 25-km (15-mi) paved highway leads to the village of San Cosme y Damián, near the banks of the Río Paraná. Follow the signs along a dirt track to the red sandstone **mission buildings,** currently in use as a Jesuit school. They once held an astronomical observatory. Many original houses are still in use. ✉ *San Cosme y Damián* ☎ *No phone* 💲 *G2,000* 🕙 *Dec.–Mar., daily 7–7; Apr.–Nov., daily 7–5:30.*

Encarnación

27 km (17 mi) southeast of San Cosme y Damián on Ruta 1.

Encarnación was the site of the long-gone Itapúa mission, but you'd never know it today. Linked by bridge to the Argentine town of Posadas, Encarnación is a somewhat dreary border town that serves as a convenient stopping point for many a weary traveler. The town has seen an influx of Eastern European immigrants. Its most incongruous sight is the small, ornate Ukrainian Orthodox church on Plaza Artigas.

The **Museo de Arte Sacro,** a small museum in the center of town, is devoted to religious art. ✉ *Artigas and 14 de Mayo* ☎ *071/203–627* 💲 *Free* 🕙 *Mon.–Fri. 3–7.*

Where to Stay & Eat

¢–$　✕🏨 **Encarnación Resort.** Amid spacious gardens, this hotel is a quiet 3 km (2 mi) from town and makes a pleasant place stay if you're doing the mission route and don't want to trek back to Asunción. The restaurant's menu has Paraguayan specialties, including milanesa, sopa paraguaya, and cassava. ✉ *Ruta 1, Km 361, Villa Quiteria* ☎ *071/207–248* 🖷 *071/207–267* 🌐 *www.encarnacionresorthotel.com.py@itacom. com.py* ⇒ *102 bedrooms, 4 suites* ⚒ *Restaurant, room service, minibars, tennis court, pool, soccer, volleyball, bar, meeting rooms, nosmoking rooms* ▭ *AE, DC, MC, V* ⏿ *BP.*

¢　✕🏨 **Hotel Cristal.** This nine-story hotel has modern rooms decorated with original artwork. The restaurant, which fills up at lunch with local businesspeople, serves contemporary fare and local fish dishes. ✉ *Mariscal Estigarribia 1157* ☎ *071/202–371* 🖷 *071/202–372* ⇒ *86 rooms* ⚒ *Restaurant, minibars, pool, meeting rooms; no room phones* ▭ *AE, MC, V* ⏿ *BP.*

Trinidad

28 km (17 mi) northeast of Encarnación.

FodorsChoice　The area's most impressive **Jesuit ruins,** superior even to those of Argentina
★　and Brazil, are at Trinidad. Unfortunately, restoration projects are fre-

quently suspended while the government searches for funding. The red sandstone reducción, built between 1712 and 1764, stands on a hilltop, enabling its full size to be appreciated. After the expulsion of the Jesuits, much of it was destroyed by an unscrupulous local official who ripped out stones to build his own residence, causing the structure to collapse. Many of the church walls

and arches remain intact, however, even though the roof is open to the elements. Note the elaborately carved doors and wall friezes depicting angels playing the clavichord, harp, and other musical instruments. The only building with a roof is the sacristy, with intricate relief work above the main entrance. Also surviving are the school and cloister foundations and a sandstone tower. ⊠ *Trinidad* ☎ *No phone* ✉ *G2,000* ⊕ *Dec.–Mar., daily 7–7; Apr.–Nov. daily 7–5:30.*

Where to Stay

¢ 🏨 **Tirol del Paraguay.** Built on a hillside 25 km (16 mi) from Encarnación, this hotel has spectacular views of the rolling countryside. Rustic rooms with reddish brick walls are furnished with sturdy wood furniture. Accommodations are in single-story bungalows that surround four swimming pools fed by natural springs, which are said to have therapeutic properties. (Some people come here to take the waters.) Rates include all meals. ⊠ *Ruta 6, 8 km (5 mi) from Trinidad, Capitán Miranda* ☎ *071/202–388* 🖷 *071/205–555* ⇨ *60 rooms* ⚹ *Dining room, minibars, tennis court, 4 pools, Ping-Pong, volleyball, laundry service, meeting room* ▭ *No credit cards* ⊙❙ *FAP.*

Jesús

10 km (6 mi) north of Trinidad.

The Jesuits began construction of the hilltop **Church of Jesús del Tavarangue** a mere eight years before their expulsion from the New World. Though never finished, this is the most distinctive of the mission churches on this part of the continent. Moorish-style arches make up the building's three entrances and lead to what were to be three naves and three altars. Vegetation and earth have covered much of the nearby reducción community. Painstaking excavations, frequently suspended due to lack of funds, are under way. ⊠ *Ruta 6* ☎ *No phone* ✉ *G2,000* ⊙ *Dec.–Mar., daily 7–7; Apr.–Nov. daily 7–5:30.*

Southern Paraguay Essentials

Transportation

BY AIR

Most people visiting southern Paraguay fly into Asunción's Aeropuerto Internacional Silvio Pettirossi. You can also fly to the eastern border town of Ciudad del Este. TAM Mercosur flies at least once daily from Asunción to Ciudad del Este's Aeropuerto Alejo García (AGT), 280 km (175 mi) from Encarnación.

Getting to Southern Paraguay from Argentina is another option. Aerolineas Aregentinas connects Buenos Aires's domestic airport, Aeroparque Jorge Newbery, with Aeropuerto Libertador San Martín (PSS), in Posadas, just across the border from Encarnación.

🛪 Airlines **Aerolineas Argentinas** ✉ Posadas, Argentina ☎ 54/752/433–340. **TAM Mercosur** ✉ Ciudad del Este ☎ 061/506–030.

🛪 Airports **Aeropuerto Alejo García** ✉ Ciudad del Este ☎ 061/518–352. **Aeropuerto Libertador General San Martín** ✉ Posadas, Argentina ☎ 54/752/451–903.

BY BUS

Buses between Asunción and Encarnación leave frequently. The five-hour trip costs about G50,000. You can get off the bus along Ruta 1 to visit any of the Jesuit missions. When you are ready to leave you can flag down another, which will pick you up unless it is full. Rapido Iguazú has buses running between Asunción and Encarnación. La Encarnaceña runs the same route, as well between Encarnación and the ruins at Trinidad and Jesús.

🛈 Bus Information **La Encarnaceña** ☎ 071/203–440. **Rapido Iguazú** ☎ 021/551–601.

BY CAR

Ruta 1, which runs from Asunción to Encarnación, is fairly well maintained, although there are occasional potholes. From Encarnación, the poorly maintained Ruta 6 stretches northeast for 280 km (175 mi) to Ciudad del Este, near the Brazil and Argentine border. This route takes you to Iguazú Falls. The missions are all near Rutas 1 and 6.

CAR RENTAL   Your best bet is renting a car in Asunción. Remember that Paraguayan rental vehicles may not cross the border into Argentina.

BY TAXI

Encarnación has good taxi service and even a few horse-drawn wagons that locals use as public transportation.

Contacts & Resources

EMERGENCIES

🛈 Emergency Services **Police** ☎ 441–111. **Ambulance** ☎ 204–800.

🛈 Hospitals **Instituto Médico Privado** ✉ J. L. Mallorquín 1629, Encarnación ☎ 071/203–615.

HEALTH

The heat is intense in southern Paraguay from October to March. Slather on plenty of sunscreen and a drink lots of water to avoid becoming dehydrated while touring the missions. Tap water is risky in this part of the country. Stick with the *agua purificada* (purified water).

MONEY MATTERS

In Encarnación, try Guaraní Cambios for changing cash or traveler's checks. ABN Amro Bank and Interbanco in Encarnación have ATMs on the Infonet network that gives cash against Plus- and Cirrus-affiliated cards.

🛈 Banks **ABN Amro Bank** ✉ Mariscal Estgarribia and Caballero, Encarnación ☎ 071/201–872. **Guaraní Cambios** ✉ Mariscal Estigarribia 307, Encarnación ☎ 071/

204–301. **Interbanco** ✉ Tomás Romero Pereira at Carlos Antonio López, Encarnación ☎ 071/203–428.

SAFETY

Southern Paraguay is reasonably safe, but take the usual precautions. Always be aware of your surroundings and keep an eye on all valuables. As a border town of 50,000 people, Encarnación has instances of petty theft. Avoid Ciudad del Este unless you're going there to cross the border to see Iguazú Falls; crime has skyrocketed in Ciudad del Este in recent years.

VISITOR INFORMATION

The Secretaria Nacional de Turismo in Encarnación offers maps and other information about the area. It is officially open weekdays 8–noon but keeps erratic hours.

7 **Secretaria Nacional de Turismo** ✉ Tomás Romero Pereira 126, Encarnación ☎ 071/203–508.

PARAGUAY ESSENTIALS

Transportation

BY AIR

Few international airlines fly directly to Asunción's modern but sleepy Aeropuerto Internacional Silvio Pettirossi. The best way to get to Paraguay is through another South American gateway. American flies from São Paulo, as does Paraguay's TAM Mercosur. Other South American carriers that serve Asunción include Aerolíneas Argentinas, Bolivia's LAB, Uruguay's Pluna, and Brazil's Varig.

BY BUS

Intercity buses are inexpensive, fast, and reliable. Long-distance buses— some with air-conditioning, reclining seats, and movies—race between the major centers. Bone-shaking local buses, known as *colectivos,* rattle between villages and along city streets. The 370-km (230-mi) journey from Asunción to Encarnación takes about five hours by bus and costs G50,000; the 330-km (205-mi) trip from Asunción to Ciudad del Este also takes five hours and costs G50,000.

BY CAR

Driving isn't easy in Paraguay—only 25% of the country's roads are paved and motorists tend to ignore traffic laws. On the plus side, there are fewer vehicles on the road here than in neighboring Argentina or Brazil.

GASOLINE Distances between gas stations can be long, so you should top off your tank regularly. Stations are normally open until midnight. Gasoline costs about G5,000 per liter.

ROAD CONDITIONS With a few exceptions, most roads outside of Asunción are unpaved, dangerously riddled with potholes, or closed altogether because of flooding. Beware of animals that wander onto the highways, particularly at night. On weekends and around public holidays, access roads into and out of the capital can be jammed with traffic.

RULES OF THE ROAD Your driver's license is valid here. Seat belts are mandatory. The speed limit is 80 kph (50 mph) on highways and 40 kph (25 mph) in urban areas. Care should be taken at intersections in Asunción, as drivers rarely offer to give way.

Contacts & Resources

BUSINESS HOURS
Remember that everything shuts down between noon and 3:30, except for department stores and the odd café. You'll be surprised at how deserted the streets are during those hours, even in Asunción.

CUSTOMS & DUTIES
Nonresidents may bring any personal-use items, plus 1 liter of spirits or two bottles of wine and 400 cigarettes. You cannot take sums of more than $10,000 into or out of Paraguay.

EMBASSIES
See Embassies *in* Asunción Essentials.

HEALTH
Although tap water is safe to drink in Asunción, drink agua purificada elsewhere. Order it *con gas* and *sin gas* (with and without carbonation).

Outside of Asunción, mosquitoes and snakes can be a problem. Bring plenty of mosquito repellent and, if you're cautious, a snake-bite kit.

MONEY MATTERS
The Paraguayan guaraní (G) comes in bills of 1,000, 5,000, 10,000, 50,000, and 100,000 guaraníes, with coins in units of 100, and 500 guaraníes. At press time the exchange rate was 6,135 guaraníes to the U.S. dollar. Such exchange rates mean prices contain a lot of zeros.

It's practically impossible to change guaraníes outside Paraguay, so make sure you exchange them at the airport before leaving.

ATMS ATMs are still a bit of a novelty in Paraguay. You'll find them in the major cities, but not in smaller towns. Some machines on Infonet, the country's largest system, accept both Plus and Cirrus cards. Others accept one or the other.

PASSPORTS & VISAS
Citizens of the United Kingdom may enter Paraguay for 90 days with a valid passport that has at least six months'remaining validity. U.S., Canadian, Australian, and New Zealand citizens need to obtain a visa before arrival. Your application must be accompanied by the following: your passport with at least six months' remaining validity; two passport-size photos; and two copies each of your bank statement, your return plane ticket or itinerary, and the visa form (downloadable in PDF format from embassy Web sites). Fees, payable in U.S. dollars only, are $45 for a single-entry visa and $65 for multiple entries. There is no Paraguayan

representation in Australia or New Zealand. Most travelers from those countries obtain their visas in another South American capital.

🚩 **Embassy of Paraguay** ✉ 151 Slater St., Suite 501, Ottawa, Ontario K1P 5H3 ☎ 613/567-1283 📠 613/567-1679 ⊕ www.embassyofparaguay.ca. **Embassy of Paraguay** ✉ 2400 Massachusetts Ave. NW, Washington, DC 20008 ☎ 202/483-6960 📠 202/234-4508 ⊕ www.embaparusa.gov.py.

SAFETY

Crime is rising in Paraguay, although you probably won't see any evidence of it during your trip. Paraguay's eastern tri-border region with Brazil and Argentina, including the town of Ciudad del Este, has become increasingly dangerous—there has been a rise in extremist-group violence, and the town has become a haven for international terrorist groups. There's a general sense of lawlessness that pervades this part of the country, and the government exerts limited control here. It's not a problem if you pass through the border at Ciudad del Este to see the world-famous Iguazú Falls at the border—but see the falls from Brazil or Argentina instead. Don't stay in Ciudad del Este overnight.

TAXES

DEPARTURE TAX The departure tax is $25, payable in U.S. dollars or in guaraníes (about G154,000). American Airlines has begun to include the tax in the price of your ticket. Verify that you don't have to pay again.

VALUE-ADDED TAX A 10% nonrefundable value-added tax, known as the IVA, is charged on all goods and services. It's included in the prices at bars and restaurants, but it's added to hotel bills. Watch for double-billing: IVA shouldn't be added to food-related bills charged to your room.

TELEPHONES

AREA & COUNTRY CODES Paraguay's country code is 595. To call Paraguay, dial the country code, then the area code, omitting the first 0.

LOCAL CALLS Local numbers in urban areas have six digits; a few in Asunción have seven digits. Rural numbers may carry as few as three or four digits. When calling between communities, precede the local number with the three- or four-digit area code. Cellular numbers have area codes beginning with "09." (The country is undergoing a very slow process of making the number of digits in phone numbers and area codes uniform.) For local operator assistance, dial 010. For directory assistance, dial 112.

LONG-DISTANCE & INTERNATIONAL CALLS The privatized national telephone company, the Compañía Paraguaya de Comunicaciones (COPACO), has offices in most cities and towns where you can place local and international calls. To place an international call, dial 002 followed by country code, area code and local number. Calls to the United States cost about G3,500 per minute; G4,500 to Canada; and G6,000 to Europe, Australia and New Zealand. Lines can become congested at peak hours. If you're calling from a hotel, be sure to hang up if there's no answer for about 20 seconds; otherwise, you'll be charged for a three-minute call.

🚩 **Access Codes AT&T** ☎ 008-11-800. **British Telecom** ☎ 008-44-800. **Canada Direct** ☎ 008-14-800. **MCI** ☎ 008-12-800. **Sprint** ☎ 008-13-800.

PUBLIC PHONES   Paraguay has few phone booths, but numerous private telephone offices let you make calls. Look for TELÉFONOS PÚBLICOS or CABINAS TELEFÓNICAS signs.

TIPPING

An appropriate tip in upscale restaurants is about 10% of the bill, more if the service is exceptionally good. In average places, round up the bill to the nearest G1,000. Round up taxi fares to the nearest G500.

Peru

WORD OF MOUTH

"Machu Picchu is such a magnificent place, you don't notice the people (truly!). We were there during the full moon. Try walking up to the Sun Gate."
                                                              –Gliadrachan

"We went to Arequipa—wonderful choice! It's a white city (all the buildings are built from some kind of white limestone) and there are wonderful cathedrals, an outstanding convent, and friendly people. The Colca Canyon is there. We only had three days and could have used a week."

                                                              —andy

Updated by
Mark Sullivan,
Jeffrey Van
Fleet, and
Brian Kluepfel

THE STONE SANCTUARY OF MACHU PICCHU is what often springs to mind when someone mentions Peru. This incredible city, built more than a century before the arrival of Spanish conquistadors, is the most prominent example of how "The Land of the Inca" is a nation full of archaeological treasures. Its many historic sites are scattered among markedly different regions, each with a distinct character. The arid desert coast, for example, is where you'll find the Nazca Lines, a mystery etched in the sand centuries before the Inca civilization appeared.

Although Peru is considered an Andean nation, more than half of its landmass is jungle. Here are the rain forests of the province aptly named Madre de Dios, or "Mother of God." It's remote, nearly untouched, but accessible to the adventurous. In the highland Ceja de Selva, or "Eyebrow of the Jungle," is the so-called "lost city of the Inca," Machu Picchu. Its vertiginous setting and stunning architecture make it one of the true wonders of the world.

As a nation and a people, Peru has a strong character, not unlike the national drink called *pisco*, a heady brandy distilled in the coastal valleys south of Lima. Today this nation of 26 million, of which roughly half live in poverty, is working to improve its economy in an unsteady political climate. For the past three generations, millions of *campesinos* (peasants) have left the countryside for the cities. They built homes on the outskirts of Lima and other large cities, where they still struggle to make a place for themselves.

Exploring Peru

Restaurants & Cuisine

Seafood is the speciality of coastal towns, including Lima, where you'll dine in *cebecherías*, as well as more upscale *marisquerías* (seafood restaurants). *Ceviche* (fish or shellfish marinated in lime juice, cilantro, onions, tomatoes, and chilies) is always on the menu, served raw as a salad or cocktail and usually accompanied by *canchas* (toasted corn kernals sprinkled with salt). *Escabeche* (fish and prawns with chilies, cheese chunks, sliced eggs, olives, and onions) is another raw entrée.

Regional favorites include *lomo saltado* (sautéed beef strips with garlic, tomatoes, onions, chilies, and fried potatoes), *lomo a la huancaina* (beef strips with egg and cheese sauce), and *cuy chactado* (roasted guinea pig). Soups and stews include *chupe verde* (with potatoes, cheese, eggs, and herbs), *hualpa chupe* (with chicke, chilies, and spices), *chupe de camarones* (spicy shrimp stew), and *sopa a la criolla* (with onions, peppers, and potatoes). *Mollejitas* (chicken innards) are the specialty in Arequipa.

About the Hotels

If you're arriving without a reservation or you're on a budget, most towns have accommodations around the Plaza de Armas or transport stations.

TOP REASONS TO GO

ALPACA CLOTHING

Wrap yourself in alpaca. Nothing says "Cusco" quite like a sweater, shawl, poncho, or scarf woven from the hair of the downright cute and cuddly alpaca. Its many fans rate the texture right up there with cashmere. Did anything ever feel so soft?

PERUVIAN CUISINE

Expand the limits of your palate. You never thought you'd sample such Andean delicacies as *cuy* (guinea pig) or alpaca? Be brave. They sound atrocious, but are actually quite tasty. Alpaca is touted for its tender, low-fat, low-cholesterol beeflike flavor, while *cuy* compares favorably to pork. Both are best when prepared in a *fogón*, an open-air oven. In coastal towns, treat yourself to lots of fresh grilled or baked fish and *cebiche*, an incredible dish in which chunks of raw fish or shellfish are marinated in lemon juice and covered with onions. It will undoubtedly be accompanied by fried kernels of corn called *canchas*.

RUINS

Hiram Bingham "discovered" Machu Picchu in 1911. Your first glimpse of the fabled city from the Funeral Rock will be your own discovery, and likely every bit as exciting. But it's not all Machu Picchu out here; it just seems that way. Pisac and Ollantaytambo both have ancient fortresses, and Chinchero has the remains of a palace. Don't miss them.

WILDLIFE WATCHING

The numbers tell the story: Peru's Amazon basin has 50,000 plant, 1,700 bird, 400 mammal, and 300 reptile species. The region hosts a large percentage of all the avian species on earth. Mammals, reptiles, and amphibians prove a bit more elusive, though the farther you venture from Iquitos and Puerto Maldonado, the greater your chances of seeing more wildlife. Regardless of who and what is on your list, a good guide—most of the lodges have experienced personnel—and a pair of binoculars are essential.

8

WHAT IT COSTS In Nuevo Soles				
	$$$$	**$$$**	**$$**	**$**	**¢**
RESTAURANTS	over 65	50–65	35–50	20–35	under 20
HOTELS	over 500	375–500	250–375	125–250	under 125

Restaurant prices are per person, for a main course at dinner. Hotel prices are for two people in a standard double room, excluding tax.

When to Go

LIMA If you visit Lima between December and March, chances are good that you'll see some sunny days. Otherwise you might encounter the thick, dank fog called *garúa* that blankets the city day and night. The good news is that this coastal region never gets very much rain.

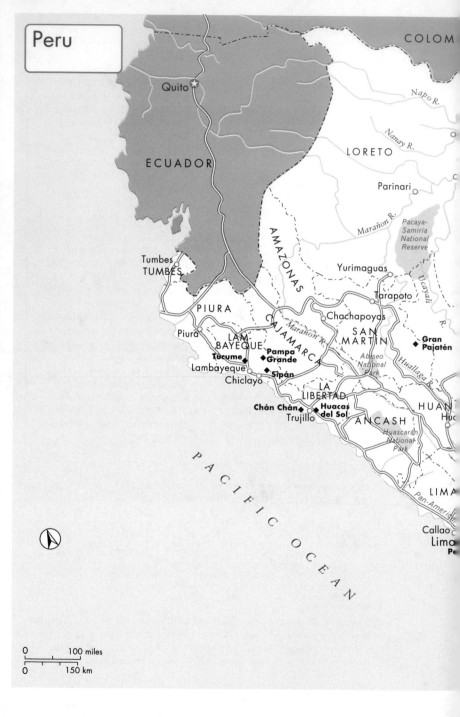

Peru

COLOM

Quito

Napo R.

Nanay R.

LORETO

ECUADOR

Parinari

Marañon R.

Pacaya-
Samiria
National
Reserve

Tumbes
TUMBES

Yurimaguas

Tarapoto

Ucayali

PIURA

Chachapoyas

CAJAMARCA

Marañon R.

SAN
MARTIN

Piura

**Gran
Pajatén**

LAM-
BAYEQUE

**Pampa
Grande**

*Abiseo
National
Park*

Huallaga R.

Túcume

Lambayeque

Sipán

R.

Chiclayo

LA
LIBERTAD

HUAN

Chán Chán

**Huacas
del Sol**

Huc

Trujillo

ANCASH

*Huascarán
National
Park*

PACIFIC

LIMA

Pan-American

Callao

PACIFIC OCEAN

Lima
Pe

0   100 miles
0   150 km

A

Amazon R.

uitos

auta

BRAZIL

UCAYALI

MADRE DE DIOS

Madre de Dios R.

BOLIVIA

Puerto
Maldonado

*Manu
Biosphere
Reserve*

CO
co

PASCO

CUSCO

*Tambopato-
Candamo
Reserve*

PUNO

erro de
aseo

JUNÍN

Aguas
Calientes

Huancayo

Machu
Picchu ◆

Ollantaytambo

Pisac

Chinchero

Andahuaylillas

Huancavelica

Cusco

Lurín

HUANCA
VELICA

Ayacucho

APURIMAC

*Lake
Titicaca*

Hwy

acámac

Juliaca

Puno

Sillustani ◆

AYACUCHO

AREQUIPA

*Agua
Blanca NR*

MOQUEGUA

LLESTAS
SLANDS

Pisco

ICA

**Nazca
Lines** ◆

Paracas ○ Ica

Nazca

Arequipa

*Paracas
National
Reserve*

Huacachina

Moquegua

Tacna

CHILE

CUSCO & MACHU PICCHU   Cusco and Machu Picchu's high season is June through early September (winter) and the days around the Christmas and Easter holidays. Make reservations for flights and hotels a few days in advance at this time of year, and weeks in advance if you'll be here for Cusco's famed June 24 Inti Raymi festival, or near Peru's July 28 Independence Day holiday. Prices and visitor numbers drop dramatically during the November through March summer rainy season, when mudslides are also an occasional problem. For near-ideal weather and manageable crowds, consider a trip during the spring or autumn months. Cusco is compact, so you can visit most sites in a day. However, to fully enjoy the city, to have time inside the museums, and to adjust to the high altitude you need at least two days. The churches close for a few hours in the middle of the day. Get a very early start, or split the walk in two. Most of the city's museums close on Sunday.

THE SOUTH   The weather in southern Peru is fairly even and arid throughout the year, but the best time to visit is during the summer and autumn.

AMAZON   All southern Amazon-basin reserves are best visited between May and October, the driest months; the lodges, however, are open year-round, though rivers may overflow and mosquitoes are voracious during the worst of the rainy season. During the dry season, especially July, sudden *friajes* (cold fronts) bring rain and cold weather to Madre de Dios, so be prepared for the worst. Temperatures can drop from 32°C (90°F) to 10°C (50°F) overnight, so bring at least one jacket or warm sweater. No matter when you travel, bring a rain jacket or poncho and perhaps rain pants, because rain may come at any time, with or without friajes.

CLIMATE   The following are average daily maximum and minimum temperatures for Lima.

Jan.	27C	81F	May	25C	77F	Sept.	19C	66F
	21	70		19	66		15	59
Feb.	28C	82F	June	23C	73F	Oct.	21C	70F
	21	70		17	63		16	61
Mar.	29C	84F	July	18C	64F	Nov.	23C	73F
	23	73		15	59		17	63
Apr.	27C	81F	Aug.	18C	64F	Dec.	24C	75F
	22	72		15	59		18	64

LIMA

Francisco Pizarro finally found the perfect place for the capital of Spain's colonial empire in 1535. On a natural port, the so-called "Ciudad de los Reyes" ("City of Kings") was the perfect place from which to ship home all the gold the conquistador plundered from the Inca. Lima served as the capital of Spain's South American empire for 300 years until Peru declared its independence from Spain in 1821. Many of the colonial-era buildings around the Plaza de Armas can still be seen today. Walk a few blocks in any direction to find graceful churches and elegant houses that reveal just how wealthy this city once was.

Today almost a third of the country's population of 28 million lives here, many of them in poverty-stricken *pueblos jóvenes* in the outskirts of the city. After a period of high crime in the 1980s and 90s, Lima has made a comeback as a cosmopolitan city of culture with fine museums, swanky shops, and dazzling restaurants.

Numbers in the text correspond to numbers in the margin and on the maps in this chapter.

Exploring Lima

Most of Lima's colonial-era churches and mansions are found in the historic center, along the streets surrounding the **Plaza de Armas.** From **El Centro,** a highway called Paseo de la República whisks you south to residential areas like **San Isidro, Miraflores,** and **Barranco.** The charms of these neighborhoods are simpler—a tree-lined park, a bluff overlooking the sea, a wooden bridge filled with young couples.

> **TOURING TIP**
>
> Almost all Lima's most interesting historic sites are within walking distance of the Plaza de Armas, one of the grandest central squares in all South America. The lovely fountain in the center can be used as a slightly off-center compass.

Museums are more difficult to reach, as they are scattered around the city. **Pueblo Libre,** a neighborhood west of San Isidro, has two of the best: the Museo Arqueológico Rafael Larco Herrera and the Museo Nacional de Antropología, Arqueología, e Historia del Perú. In the other direction from San Isidro, in the residential area of **San Borja,** is the Museo de la Nación. **Monterrico,** east of Miraflores, is the site of Lima's most popular museum, the glittering Museo de Oro.

El Centro

When Francisco Pizarro sketched out his plans for the "City of Kings" in 1535, he drew an area that would forever define the capital. Although the official boundaries have pushed outward over the years, most residents still consider these narrow streets to be the city proper. When you ask someone from a far-flung neighborhood like Miraflores or San Isidro where you might find the Plaza de Armas, they will undoubtedly tell you "Lima."

TIMING An unhurried visit to the historic district's main attractions takes a full day, with at least an hour devoted to both the Museo de Arte Nacional and the Museo de la Inquisición. Even if you're short on time, don't bypass the guided tour of the underground catacombs of the Iglesia de San Francisco. Also, spend some time just sitting on the cathedral steps, as the locals do.

WHAT TO SEE **Casa Aliaga.** Said to be the oldest colonial mansion in South America, the Aliaga House has been owned and occupied by the same family since Francisco Pizarro granted the land to Jerónimo de Aliaga in 1535. An impressive wooden staircase in the tree-shaded courtyard leads up to the elaborate

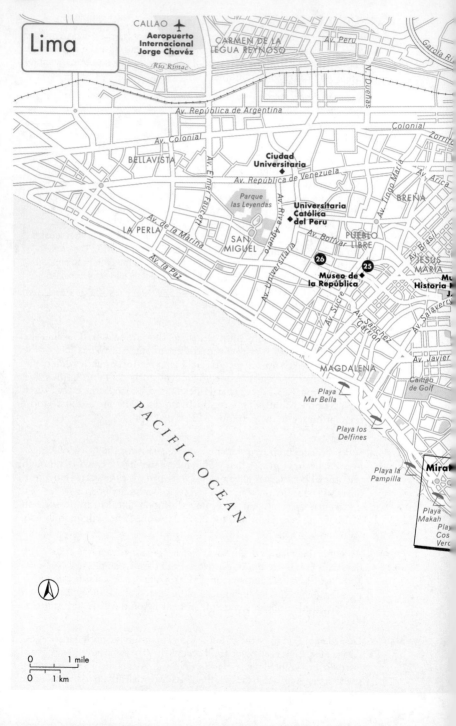

Lima

CALLAO ✈
**Aeropuerto
Internacional
Jorge Chavéz**

CARMEN DE LA
LEGUA REYNOSO

Av. Peru

García Rí

Río Rímac

Av. República de Argentina

N. Dueñas

Colonial

Zorrit

Av. Colonial

BELLAVISTA

Av. Emer Faucett

**Ciudad
Universitaria**
♦

Av. Arica

Av. Tingo María

BREÑA

Av. República de Venezuela

*Parque
las Leyendas*

**Universitaria
Católica
del Peru** ♦

Av. Brasil

Av. de la Marina

LA PERLA

Av. Rivera

Av. Bolívar

**PUEBLO
LIBRE**

Y JESÚS
MARÍA

Mu

**SAN
MIGUEL**

26

25

Museo de ♦
la República

Historia ►

J.

Av. la Paz

Av. Universitaria

Av. Sucre

Av. Salaverry

*Av. Sánchez
Carrión*

Av. Javier

MAGDALENA

*Campo
de Golf*

*Playa
Mar Bella*

PACIFIC OCEAN

*Playa los
Delfines*

*Playa la
Pampilla*

Mira►

*Playa
Makah*

*Play
Cos
Verc*

🧭

0 _____ 1 mile
0 _____ 1 km

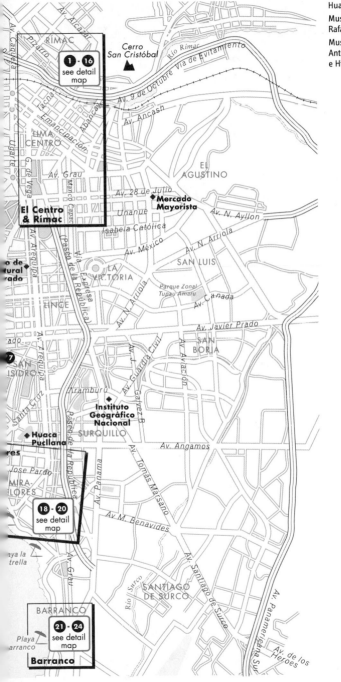

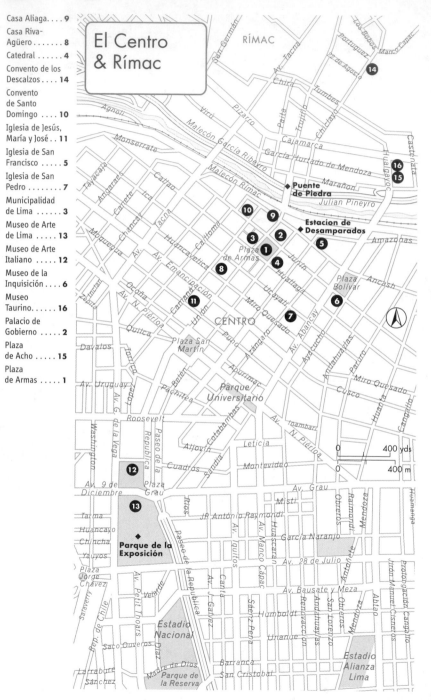

El Centro & Rímac

rooms, many of which are decorated with colonial furnishings. Visitors must arrange trips in advance through **Lima Tours** (☎ 01/619–6900 ⊕ www.limatours.com.pe). ✉ *Jr. de la Unión 224* ☎ *01/424–5110.*

8 **Casa Riva-Agüero.** A matched pair of balconies with *celosías*—intricate wood screens through which ladies could watch passersby unobserved—grace the facade of this rambling mansion dating from 1760. An interesting museum of folk art is on the second floor. ✉ *Jr. Camaná 459* ☎ *01/427–9275* 🎟 *S/3* ⊗ *Mon.–Sat. 10 7.*

4 **Catedral.** The layout for this immense structure was dictated by Francisco Pizarro himself, and his basic vision has survived even though earthquakes in 1746 and 1940 required it to be completely rebuilt. The first church on the site was completed in 1625. Inside are some impressive baroque appointments, especially the intricately carved choir stalls. Because of changing tastes, the main altar was replaced around 1800 with one in a neoclassical style. At about the same time the towers that flank the entrance were added. A highlight of a visit to the church is seeing the chapel where Pizarro is entombed. There is also a small museum of religious art and artifacts. ✉ *East side of Plaza de Armas* ☎ *01/427–9647* 🎟 *S/10* ⊗ *Mon.–Sat. 10–4:30.*

10 **Convento de Santo Domingo.** The 16th-century Convent of Saint Dominic clearly shows the different styles popular during the colonial era in Lima. The bell tower, for instance, has a baroque base built in 1632, but the upper parts rebuilt after an earthquake in 1746 are more rococo in style. The church is a popular one, as it holds the tombs of the first two Peruvian saints, Santa Rosa de Lima and San Martín de Porres. The pair of cloisters in the convent are worth a look, as they are decorated with yellow-and-blue tiles imported from Spain in the early 17th century. ✉ *Conde de Superunda and Camaná* ☎ *01/427–6793* 🎟 *S/3* ⊗ *Mon.–Sat. 9–11 and 3–6, Sun. 9–1.*

11 **Iglesia de Jesús, María y José.** The 1659 Church of Jesus, Mary and Joseph may have a plain facade, but inside is a feast for the eyes. Baroque retables representing various saints grace the main altar. ✉ *Jr. Camaná and Jr. Moquegua* ☎ *01/427–6809* 🎟 *Free* ⊗ *Mon.–Sat. 9–noon and 3–5.*

5 **Iglesia de San Francisco.** The Church of Saint Francis is the most visited **Fodor'sChoice** in Lima, and with good reason. The 1674 structure is the best example ★ of what is known as "Lima Baroque" style of architecture. The handsome carved portal would later influence those on other churches, including the Iglesia de la Merced. The central nave is known for its beautiful ceilings painted in a style called *mudejar* (a blend of Moorish and Spanish designs). On a tour, peruse the adjoining monastery's immense collection of antique texts, some dating back to the 17th century. But the best part of a tour is a visit to the vast catacombs. The city's first cemetery, these under-

> **WORD OF MOUTH**
>
> "Check out the San Francisco monastery in Lima, an early colonial church with a baroque choir, a library full of illuminated manuscripts, and, of course, the catacombs!"   –SharonNRayMC

ground tunnels contains the bones of some 75,000 people. In many places the bones have been stacked in eerie geometric patterns. Tours are available in English. ✉ *Jr. Ancash 471* ☎ *01/427–1381* 🖅 *S/5* ⊙ *Daily 9:30–5:45.*

❼ Iglesia de San Pedro. The Jesuits built three churches in rapid succession on this corner, the current one dating from 1638. It remains one of the finest examples of early-colonial religious architecture in Peru. The facade is remarkably restrained, but the interior shows all the extravagance of the era. The interior is richly appointed with a series of baroque retables thought to be the best in the city. Don't miss the side aisle, where gilded arches lead to chapels decorated with beautiful hand-painted tiles. Many have works by Italians like Bernardo Bitti, who arrived on these shores in 1575. His style influenced an entire generation of painters. In the sacristy is *The Coronation of the Virgin,* one of his most famous works. ✉ *Jr. Ucayali at Jr. Azángaro* ☎ *01/428–3010* 🖅 *Free* ⊙ *Mon.–Sat. 7–12:30 and 5–8.*

❸ Municipalidad de Lima. Although it resembles the colonial-era buildings surrounding it, the City Hall was actually constructed in 1944. Step inside to see the stained-glass windows above the marble staircase. Running beside the building is a lovely pedestrian walkway called the Paseo Los Escribanos, or Passage of the Scribes, lined with inexpensive restaurants. On the south side of the building is the tourist-information office. ✉ *West side of Plaza de Armas* ☎ *Tourist office 01/315–1505* ⊙ *Tourist office Mon.–Sat. 9–6.*

⑬ Museo de Arte de Lima. Built in 1872 as the Palacio de la Expedición, this mammoth neoclassical structure designed by Gustave Eiffel now houses the Museum of Art. It has a bit of everything, from pre-Columbian artifacts to colonial-era furniture to contemporary paintings. One of the highlights is the collection of 2,000-year-old weavings from Paracas. Make sure to leave time to sip an espresso in the dimly lit café near the entrance. ✉ *Paseo Colón 125* ☎ *01/423–6332* ⊕ *museoarte.perucultural. org.pe* 🖅 *S/12* ⊙ *Thurs.–Tues. 10–5.*

⑫ Museo de Arte Italiano. This little-known museum happens to be one of the city's most delightful. Most of the art represented here is about a century old, so it captures the exact moment when impressionism was melting into modernism. Don't overlook the magnificent iron door, by Alessandro Mazzucotelli. ✉ *Paseo de la República 250* ☎ *01/423–9932* 🖅 *S/3* ⊙ *Weekdays 10–5.*

❻ Museo de la Inquisición. A massive mansion that once belonged to one of the first families to arrive in Lima served as the headquarters of the Spanish Inquisition. Visit the original dungeons and torture chambers, where stomach-churning, life-size exhibits illustrate methods of extracting information from prisoners. The residence later served as the temporary home of Congress, which found a permanent home in the neoclassical structure across the street. The guided tour, offered several times a day in English, lets you admire the beautiful building, especially the coffered ceilings dating from the 18th century. ✉ *Jr. Junín 548* ☎ *01/428–7980* ⊕ *www.congreso.gob.pe/museo.htm* 🖅 *Free* ⊙ *Daily 9–5.*

★ ❷ **Palacio de Gobierno.** Built on the site where Francisco Pizarro was murdered in 1541, the Palacio de Gobierno was completed in 1938. The neobaroque palace is the official residence of the president. Guided tours, which include visits to many of the rooms where the president conducts affairs of state. One of the most memorable is the Salón Dorado, or Golden Room, where the walls are almost entirely covered in intricate gilded designs. Tours must be arranged at least a day in advance. To do so, bring your passport to the door marked EDIFICIO PALACIO at the modern building that sits across from the palace at the corner of Jirón Junín and Jirón de la Unión. Besides a tour of the building, you are allowed to return at noon to watch soldiers in red-and-blue uniforms conduct an elaborate changing of the guard. ⊠ *North side of Plaza de Armas* ☎ *01/426–7020* ☞ *Free* ⊙ *Tours weekdays 8:45 and 9:45, Sat. 9, 10, and 11.*

★ ❶ **Plaza de Armas.** This massive square has been the center of the city since 1535. Over the years it has served many functions, from an open-air theater for melodramas to an impromptu ring for bullfights. Huge fires once burned in the center for people sentenced to death by the Spanish Inquisition. Much has changed over the years, but one thing remaining is the bronze fountain unveiled in 1651. It was here that José de San Martín declared the country's independence from Spain in 1821. ⊠ *Jr. Junín and Jr. Carabaya.*

Rímac

In the beginning of the 17th century, the neighborhoods around the Plaza de Armas were bursting at the seams. The construction of the Puente de Piedra, which literally means "Stone Bridge," meant people were soon streaming over the Río Rímac. Among those who crossed the river were members of the upper classes who saw the newly christened Rímac as the perfect place to construct their mansions. It wasn't long before there were tree-lined promenades like the Alameda de los Descalzos and aquatic gardens like the Paseo de las Aguas. The neighborhood has fallen on hard times, but the faded facades are among the loveliest in the city.

TIMING &   A tour of the sights won't take more than an hour or two. The best way
PRECAUTIONS   to see the neighborhood is by taxi; hire one in the Plaza de Armas and be sure to negotiate a price in advance. Most drivers will be more than willing to wait as you explore sights like the Convento de los Descalzos. You can usually pay half in advance and half at the end of the tour. The fee varies, but shouldn't be more than US$20 or S/67,000, and most taxis will take both currencies. Rímac has a reputation for having a lot of petty crime, so it's not a place where you want to walk around.

WHAT TO SEE   **Convento de los Descalzos.** The rose-color Monastery of the Shoeless Broth-
❶❹   ers has been converted into a fascinating repository of colonial-era religious art. Room after room of this mazelike structure is filled with paintings dating back to the 16th century. There are four cloisters and two chapels, so it's easy to get lost here—in fact, it's practically guaranteed. A highlight is the Capilla de la Virgen Carmen, entered through a doorway decorated to resemble a bright-blue baroque church. Inside

is an altar that gleams with gold leaf. The kitchen still contains antique winemaking equipment, and the pharmacy is filled with glass-stoppered bottles of unidentifiable liquids. English-speaking guides are available. ⊠ *Northern end of Alameda de los Descalzos* ☎ *01/481–0441* ✉ *S/5* ☉ *Tues.–Sun. 10–6.*

⑯ Museo Taurino. Stuffed heads of several bulls stare down at you from the walls of the tiny Museum of Bullfighting. There are plenty of examples of the colorful costumes worn by the matadors, letting you see how styles have changed over the years. Perhaps most interesting are the posters from around the world. An 1899 advertisement from Barcelona shows women attending a bullfight in all their frills and finery. If there is no one around, the guard will let you peek into the Plaza de Acho. ⊠ *Jr. Hualgayoc 332* ☎ *01/482–3360* ✉ *S/5* ☉ *Weekdays 9–4.*

⑮ Plaza de Acho. Up until 1766, bullfights were held in the Plaza de Armas. They were moved across the river to this structure, which at the time was the largest bull ring in the world. It was originally octagonal, but in 1946 it was given its current circular shape. Matches were originally held on Sunday, but church leaders complained that attendance at services was getting sparse. ⊠ *Jr. Hualgayoc 332* ☎ *01/481–1467* ✉ *S/5* ☉ *Tues.–Sun. 10–6.*

San Isidro

Many frequent visitors to Lima find themselves drawn to the upscale residential neighborhood of San Isidro. Like nearby Miraflores, it has plenty of boutiques selling designer goods, bars serving up the latest cocktails, and restaurants dishing out cuisine from around the world. What it lacks is the hustle and bustle. While strolling through Parque El Olívar you might be shocked to realize that there's not a single car in sight.

TIMING   Unless you have your own wheels, the best way to travel between San Isidro's widely dispersed attractions is by taxi. Taking things at a leisurely pace, this tour will take a few hours. Note that this is probably Lima's safest neighborhood.

WHAT TO SEE   **Huaca Huallamarca.** The sight of this flat-topped temple catches many
⑰ people off guard. The structure, painstakingly restored on the front side, certainly seems out of place among the neighborhood's towering hotels and apartment buildings. The upper platform affords some nice views of the San Isidro. There's a small museum with displays of objects found at the site, including several mummies. ⊠ *Av. Nicolás de Rivera and Av. El Rosario* ☎ *01/224–4124* ✉ *S/5.50* ☉ *Tues.–Sun 9–5.*

NEED A BREAK?   When strolling through Parque El Olívar, stop by **Pasteleria Monserrat** (⊠ Pancho Fierro 131 ☎ 01/440–0517) for some of the neighborhood's most fanciful pastries, including little cupcakes shaped like mice.

Miraflores

The seaside suburb of Miraflores has become the city's main destination for tourists, and it's easy to see why. Next to the relentless right angles of El Centro, the fanlike diagonals extending out from Ovalo José Pardo are a relief. For a complete change of place, wander through the

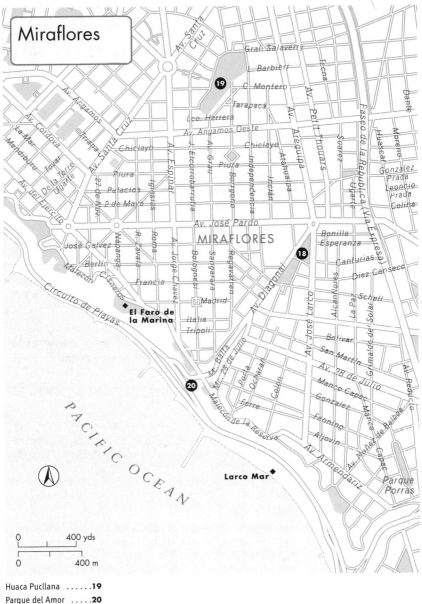

Miraflores

Av. Santa Cruz
Gral. Salaverry
L. Barbieri
19
C. Montero
Tarapacá
Av. Argamos
Lco. Herrera
Av. Cordova
Av. Angamos Oeste
La Mar
Triana
Chiclayo
Chiclayo
Av. Santa Cruz
Piura
Menditibu
Tovar
De la Torre
Ugarte
Av. 27 de Mayo
Av. Espina
El Carrobamba
Borgoño
Piura
Palacios
2 de Mayo
Av. del Ejercito
Av. José Pardo

MIRAFLORES

Av. Petit Thouars
Tecna
Av.
Arequipa
Suárez
Paseo de la República (Via Expresa)
Ugarte
Dante
Moreno
Huascar
González
Prada
Leoncio
Prada
Colina
Atahualpa
Independencia
Inclán
A. Grau
Iglesias

Bonilla
Esperanza
José Galvez
R. Ayala
Roma
Av. Jorge Chavez
Sangara
Regaladren
18
Canturias
Berlin
Alabanga
Bolognesi
Diez Canseco
Cisneros
Francia
Av. Diagonal
Alcanflores
La Paz
Schell
Madrid
Av. José Larco
Tejedos porruro Colo
Av. Petit Mar

◆ **El Faro de la Marina**
Italia
Tripoli
Bolivar
San Martín
Av. 28 de Julio
Manco Capac
Circuito de Playas
Av. Balta
Mn 28 de Julio
Porta
Ocharan
Colón
González
Fanning
Aljovin
Av. Armendariz
Av. Nuñez de Balboa
Marco Capac
Av. Reducto
Ferre
20
Malecon de la Reserva

P A C I F I C   O C E A N

Malecon de la Reserva
◆ **Larco Mar**
Parque
Porras

| 0 | | 400 yds |
| 0 | | 400 m |

neighborhood's flower-filled parks or along the cliffs overlooking the ocean. But Miraflores is also the city's cultural hub, which means there are plenty of boutiques, galleries, and museums, as well as bars, cafés, and restaurants. Some people who find themselves in Lima for a short time never leave this little haven.

TIMING & PRECAUTIONS

Good times to stroll Miraflores are mid-morning, when the heat is not yet overbearing, or mid-afternoon, when you can escape the sun by ducking into a bar or café. If shopping is your goal, arrive after sunset when things have cooled down. All the stores along Avenida José Larco stay open for early-evening window shoppers. About a half hour of walking will lead you to the ocean, where you'll want to spend another hour or so strolling along the cliff. El Centro is about 20 minutes from Miraflores by taxi. Miraflores is a very safe neighborhood, but keep your wits about you in the markets and parks. Pickpockets sometimes target tourists distracted by a street performer or a good bargain.

WHAT TO SEE
★ ⑲

Huaca Pucllana. Rising out of a nondescript residential neighborhood is this mud-brick pyramid. The pre-Inca *huaca*, or temple, dates back to at least the 4th century. Archaeologists are still working on the site, and are usually happy to share their discoveries about the people who lived in this area hundreds of years before the Inca. A tiny museum highlights some of their recent finds. Knowledgable guides are available in Spanish and English. ⊠ *Av. Larco Herrera at Elías Aguirre* ☎ *01/445–8695* 🖾 *S/5* ☽ *Wed.–Mon. 9–4:30.*

NEED A BREAK?

A few steps from the biggest swath of green in Miraflores is aptly named **El Parque** (⊠ East of Parque Kennedy ☎ 01/326–0206), an old-fashioned ice-cream parlor that's always a hit with kids. Delicious desserts include a cherry-nosed clown and a pair of cookie-eared mice with the oddly familiar names Miky and Miny.

⑳ **Parque del Amor.** You might think you're in Barcelona when you stroll through this pretty park. Like Antonio Gaudí's Parque Güell, the park that provided the inspiration for this one, the benches are decorated with broken pieces of tile. Here, however, they spell out silly romantic sayings like *Amor es como luz* ("Love is like light"). The centerpiece is a controversial statue of two lovers locked in a rather lewd embrace. ⊠ *Av. Diagonal.*

⑱ **Parque Miraflores.** What locals call Parque Miraflores is actually two parks. The smaller section is shady Parque Central, where you'll find frequent open-air concerts. Shoeshine boys will ask whether you need a *lustre* when you stop to listen to the music. The honking noise you hear is probably the ice-cream vendors that patrol the park on bright yellow bicycles. A tourist-information kiosk sits on the south side. Across a pedestrian street always full of local artists showing off their latest works is Parque Kennedy, where the babble from a lively crafts market fills the air each evening. On the eastern side is the pretty Parroquia Virgen Milagrosa (Miraculous Virgin Church). A few sidewalk cafés are behind the church. ⊠ *Between Av. José Larco and Av. Diagonal.*

Barranco

With a bohemian feel found nowhere else in the city, Barranco is a magnet for young people who come to carouse in its bars and cafés. A bit sleepy during the day, the neighborhood comes to life around sunset when artists start hawking their wares and its central square and bars begin filling with people ready to party. Founded toward the end of the 19th century, Barranco was where wealthy Limeños built their summer residences. The weather proved so irresistible that many eventually constructed huge mansions on the cliffs above the sea. Many of these have fallen into disrepair, but little by little they are being renovated into funky restaurants and hotels.

TIMING & PRECAUTIONS All the major sights in Barranco are within a block or two of Parque Municipal. Depending on how long you linger, exploring this area should take no more than a few hours. Avoid walking down deserted streets, especially at night. Otherwise, Barranco is a very safe neighborhood.

WHAT TO SEE

Museo de la Electricidad. On the street in front of this tiny museum is a cherry-red *urbanito*, or streetcar, named Breda. For about 65 cents you can climb aboard and take a three-block trip down Avenida Pedro de Osma. Notice the wooden seats, impeccably refinished when the tram was put back into service in 1997. Inside the museum itself are photos of other trolleys that once rumbled along the streets of Lima. The captions are only in Spanish. ⊠ *Av. Pedro de Osma 105* ☎ *01/477–6577* ⊕ *museoelectri.perucultural.org. pe* ⊠ *Free* ☉ *Tues.–Thurs. 9–5, Fri. and Sat. 9–noon.*

A GOOD WALK

To get your bearings, start in Parque Municipal, one of the prettiest parks in the city. Then head east to Lima's own Bridge of Sighs, the Puente de los Suspiros. Directly below is the bougainvillea-shaded Bajada de Baños, lined with wonderful old houses. Head down this cobblestone street and soon you'll find yourself walking in the waves at Playa Barranquito. If it's late afternoon, you might want to watch the sunset on the beach.

Museo-Galería Arte Popular de Ayacucho. Its unassuming facade makes it easy to miss this little gem. Inside you'll find one of the country's best collections of folk art. One especially interesting exhibit in the bright, airy gallery is an explanation of *cajones San Marcos,* the boxlike portable altars that priests once carried as they moved from village to village. Peasants began to make their own, placing scenes of local life inside. These dioramas, ranging in size from less than an inch to more than a foot wide, are still made today. ⊠ *Av. Pedro de Osma 116* ☎ *01/247–0599* ⊕ *www.mugapa.com* ⊠ *Free* ☉ *Tues.–Sat. 9–6.*

Fodor's Choice ★ **Museo Pedro de Osma.** If there were not one piece of art hanging inside this museum, it would still be worth the trip to see the century-old mansion that houses it. The mansard-roofed structure—with inlaid wood floors, delicately painted ceilings, and breathtaking stained-glass windows in every room—was the home of a wealthy collector

of religious art. The best of his collection is now permanently on display. The finest of the paintings, the 18th-century *Virgen de Pomato,* represents the Earth, with her mountain-shaped cloak covered with garlands of corn. The former dining room, in a separate building, contains some fine pieces of silver, including a lamb-shaped incense holder with shining ruby eyes. Make sure to take some time to explore the manicured grounds. ✉ *Av. Pedro de Osma 423* ☎ *01/467–0141* 💰 *S/10* ⏲ *Tues.–Sun. 10–5.*

NEED A BREAK?

Along a walkway leading past La Ermita is the gingerbread-covered **La Flor de Canela** (✉ Ermita 102 ☎ No phone), a sweet little café with a porch overlooking much of Barranco. The dimly lit space inside is a great place to escape the midday heat.

★ ❷❹ **Puente de los Suspiros.** The romantically named Bridge of Sighs is a lovely wooden walkway shaded with flowering trees. You won't have to wait long to see couples walking hand in hand. The bridge crosses over the Bajada de Baños, a cobblestone walkway that leads to Playa Barranquito. On the far side is La Ermita, a lovely little chapel painted a dazzling shade of red. ✉ *East of Parque Municipal.*

Pueblo Libre

You may find yourself longing to linger in Pueblo Libre, which manages to retain a sense of calm not found elsewhere in the capital. Instead of hurrying past, residents often pause to chat with friends. This neighborhood northwest of San Isidro has two of the city's finest museums, the Museo Nacional de Antropología, Arqueología, e Historia del Perú, and the Museo Arqueológico Rafael Larco Herrera.

TIMING If you get an early start, exploring Pueblo Libre will take up most of a morning. Plan to spend an hour or two in each of the museums.

WHAT TO SEE **Museo Nacional de Antropología, Arqueología, e Historia del Perú.** The country's most extensive collection of pre-Columbian artifacts can be found at this sprawling museum. Beginning with 8,000-year-old stone tools, Peru's history comes to life through the sleek granite obelisks of the Chavín culture, the intricate weavings of Paraca peoples, and the colorful ceramics of the Moche, Chimú, and Inca civilizations. Fascinating are a pair of mummies from the Nazca region that are thought to be more than 2,500 years old; they were so well preserved that you can still see the grim expressions on their faces. Not all the exhibits are labeled in English, so you might want to hire a guide to negotiate your way around the museum's twin courtyards. ⊠ *Plaza Bolívar* ☎ *01/463–5070* ⊕ *mnaah.perucultural.org.pe* ⊠ *S/10* ☉ *Tues.–Sat. 9–5, Sun. 9–4.*

NEED A BREAK? Saloon-style doors lead you into the **Antigua Taberna Queirolo** (⊠ Jr. San Martín 1090 ☎ 01/463-8777), a charming little bar about a block west of Plaza Bolívar. Locals lean against round tables as they sample the pisco that is bottled at the bodega next door.

Fodor'sChoice ★ **Museo Arqueológico Rafael Larco Herrera.** Fuchsia bougainvillea tumbles over the white walls surrounding Museo Arqueológico Rafael Larco Herrera, home of the world's largest private collection of pre-Columbian art. The oldest pieces here are crude vessels dating back several thousand years. Most intriguing are the thousands of ceramic "portrait heads" crafted more than a millennium ago. Some owners commissioned more than one, allowing you to see how they changed over the course of their lives. The famous *sala erótica* reveals that these ancient artists were surprisingly uninhibited. Everyday objects are adorned with images that are frankly sexual and frequently humorous. As this gallery is across the garden from the rest of the museum, you'll be able to distance the kids from it if necessary. ⊠ *Av. Bolívar 1515* ☎ *01/461–1835* ⊕ *museolarco.perucultural.org.pe* ⊠ *S/25* ☉ *Daily 9–6.*

> **TOURING TIP**
>
> The sun can be brutal, so in summer you should take advantage of the taxis lined up outside the two museums.

Where to Eat

Timing is important, as many eateries close after lunch and reopen for dinner. Limeños don't sit down for their evening meal until at least 7.

It's not unusual for fish restaurants to close for the day at 5 or 6 in the afternoon. If you're in the mood for seafood, do as the locals do and have it for lunch.

Barranco

In keeping with its reputation as a bohemian neighborhood, Barranco has a slew of cozy cafés where you can while away an afternoon. Look for these around the Puente de los Suspiros. For more substantial fare, head to those facing Parque Municipal.

$$$–$$$$ ✕ **Costa Verde.** The pink-and-gold hues of the sunset make people return again and again to this seaside standout. Order a pisco sour—one of the best in the city—and no matter where you sit in the glassed-in dining room you'll have a front-row seat. Highlights include the lobster, which arrives steaming. Locals with a lot of cash come for brunch on weekends, when there's a buffet so expansive it holds a place in the *Guinness Book of World Records*. It's very touristy—your server places a flag from your home country in the middle of your table. ⊠ *Playa Barranquito* ☎ *01/ 477–2424* ⌕ *Reservations essential* ☰ *AE, DC, MC, V.*

★ $–$$ ✕ **La Ermanita.** Facing a quaint cobblestone street, this butter-yellow building has an unbeatable location. Wide windows in the dining room let you watch young lovers stroll across the Puente de los Suspiros. With the ocean practically at the door, it's no surprise the focus here is seafood. You must decide between several types of freshly caught fish, then from a dozen or so sauces. You might try your sole prepared *pulpa de cangrejo gratinado* (stuffed with shredded crab). If you arrive a bit early, enjoy a pisco sour at the beautifully polished outdoor bar. ✉ *Bajada de Baños 340* ☎ *01/247–0069* ⌕ *Reservations essential* ⊟ *AE, DC, MC, V.*

$ ✕ **Las Terrazas de Barranco.** If you're standing in Parque Municipal, you won't miss this restaurant. Bright pink geraniums tumble down the series of terraces that give the place its name. The open-air dining room, big enough for half a dozen tables, lets you enjoy the cool breezes. The specialty here is *ceviche* (chunks of raw fish marinated in lemon juice and topped with onions), and the spicy fish dish is served several ways. Drop by for lunch and for about US$3 you can sample all of them. ✉ *Av. Grau 290* ☎ *01/247–1477* ⊟ *MC, V.*

¢–$ ✕ **Javier.** Several seafood restaurants are huddled together along the street leading down to the ocean—in fact, they all share a single staircase. What sets Javier apart is its rustic rooftop terrace, which overlooks the crashing waves. There's nothing fancy here, just incredibly fresh fish. Start with the *conchas a la parmasana* (clams with Parmesan cheese), then move on to the *lenguado a la parrilla* (fish served hot off the grill). There is plenty on the menu for meat eaters as well. ✉ *Bajada de Baños 403* ☎ *01/477–5339* ⊟ *V.*

★ ¢   ✕ **Las Mesitas.** Filled with a dozen or so marble-topped tables, Las Mesitas is an old-fashioned café a block north of Parque Municipal. The constant stream of Limeños lets you know that the food is first rate. You couldn't do better than share a few *humitas,* steamed tamales that you season with pickled onions or bright yellow hot sauce. The best are those stuffed with chicken, onions, and green corn. If the floor's pinwheel design doesn't make you feel a bit off balance, then the spinning dessert display certainly will. Try the *mazamorra morada,* a sweet pudding of cornmeal and candied fruit. ✉ *Grau 341* ☎ *01/477–1346* ⊟ *MC, V.*

El Centro

If you're looking for a fancy meal, you'll be hard pressed to find it in El Centro. But if you want a cheap, filling meal, you've come to the right place. A highlight of a visit to the neighborhood is the Barrio Chino, packed with dozens of Chinese-Peruvian restaurants called *chifas.*

★ $ ✕ **Los Vitrales de Gemma.** Tucked into the courtyard of a beautiful colonial-era building, this is one of the prettiest restaurants in the historic district. Tables covered with peach-color linens are set beneath flower-covered colonnades. The food, creative takes on old recipes, is just as appealing. Start with a spinach salad tossed with bacon, walnuts, and slices of apples, then move on to *pescado en salsa langotinos* (fish in lobster sauce) or *espagueti fruotos del mar* (pasta with seafood). The staff is eager to please, sometimes even running from the kitchen to deliver a dish while it's still hot. ✉ *Jr. Ucayali 332* ☎ *01/426–7796* ☽ *Closed Sun.* ⊟ *AE, DC, MC, V.*

Miraflores

Although inexpensive eateries are clustered around Parque Miraflores, the more elegant ones are scattered about, so plan on reaching them by

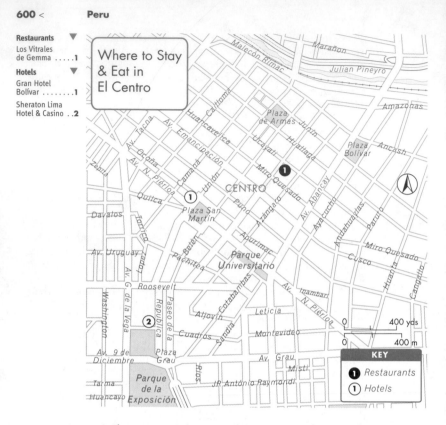

Where to Stay
& Eat in
El Centro

KEY

1 Restaurants
1 Hotels

taxi. If you want to dine with a view of the ocean, Miraflores has more options than any other neighborhood.

$$–$$$$
Fodor'sChoice
★
✗ **Huaca Pucllana.** You feel like a part of history at this beautiful restaurant, which faces the ruins of a 1,500-year-old pyramid. Excavations are ongoing, so you can watch archaeologists at work as you enjoy the breezes on the covered terrace. Rough-hewn columns hold aloft the dining room's soaring ceiling. This is *novo andino* cuisine, which puts a new spin on old recipes. Yellow peppers stuffed with shrimp are a great way to start, and the *cabrito al horno* (roasted kid) is a work of art. Wash it all down with one of many pisco preparations. ⊠ *Av. General Borgoña, 2 blocks north of Av. Angamos Oeste* ☎ *01/445–4042* ⌕ *Reservations essential* ⊟ *AE, DC, MC, V.*

$$–$$$
Fodor'sChoice
★
✗ **Astrid y Gaston.** You can't help but watch the kitchen door at this elegant restaurant, as each dish the waiters carry out is a work of art. Take the eye-catching *pato asado con mil especies* (roast duck with 1,000 spices). The honey-brown breast is accompanied by a steamed pear and a pepper bubbling over with basil risotto. Other dishes, like the pasta with squid and artichokes, are just as astonishing. Make sure to peruse the wine list, one of the best in town. In a colonial-style building on a quiet street, the restaurant itself is lovely, with pumpkin-color walls covered with original artwork. ⊠ *Cantuarias 175* ☎ *01/444–1496* ⊟ *AE, MC, V.*

$–$$$ ✕ **El Señorío de Sulco.** It's no surprise that the food here is so good when you learn that owner Isabel Alvarez authored several cookbooks. The antique cooking vessels hanging on the walls reveal her passion for Peruvian cuisine. Start with *chupe de camerones,* a hearty soup combining shrimp and potatoes, then move on to *arroz con pato,* duck stewed in dark beer and seasoned with coriander. For dessert there's the meringue-topped *suspiro de limeña,* which literally means "sigh of a lady of Lima." Arrive early to watch the sun set over the ocean. ⊠ *Malecón Cisneros 1470* ☎ *01/441–0389* ▭ *AE, DC, MC, V* ⬥ *Reservations essential* ☾ *No dinner Sun.*

$–$$$ ✕ **La Rosa Náutica.** One of the most recognizable landmarks in Miraflores, La Rosa Náutica is at the end of a prominent pier. The blue slate roof of the rambling Victorian-style building is unmistakable. Take a seat in the gazebo-like dining room, where you'll have a view of the entire coast. Signature entrées include grilled scallops topped with a hearty cheese, but you might not be able to resist the succulent sea bass or the sole. Daily specials include such tasty dishes as rock fish in salt crust. For dessert, try the *crepes suchard* filled with ice cream and topped with hot fudge. ⊠ *Espigón 4* ☎ *01/447–0057* ▭ *AE, DC, MC, V.*

$$–$$$ ✕ **La Tranquera.** A butcher's front window couldn't display more cuts of meat than the glass case along the wall of this local landmark. Check out the different cuts, then inform your waiter which one you want and how it should be cooked. It will arrive at your table atop a charcoal brazier, still sizzling from the grill. Even the smallest steaks, labeled *junior* in the menu, are the size of a dinner plate. If you have a lighter appetite, the *costillas a la barbacoa* are basted with a tangy barbecue sauce that doesn't overwhelm the flavor of the ribs. ⊠ *Av. José Pardo 285* ☎ *01/447–5111* ▭ *AE, DC, MC, V.*

$–$$$ ✕ **Trattoria di Mambrino.** You don't even have to walk through the door to know that this trattoria's pasta is fresh. Passersby pause by a window to watch cooks stuff the ravioli and drape the fettuccini on long wooden rods. But the proof is on the plate: delicious dishes like tortellini tossed with chunks of beef, mushrooms, and a bit of cream leave you satisfied but not stuffed. That means you are able to save room for dessert, so you can be tormented by the *tormento de chocolate.* The only caveat here is the service, which at times can be lackadaisical. ⊠ *Manuel Bonilla 106* ☎ *01/446–7002* ⬥ *Reservations essential* ▭ *AE, MC, V.*

San Isidro

Most of San Isidro's restaurants are on or near Avenida Conquistadores, the neighborhood's main drag. This is one of the few places in the city where you can stroll around in search of the perfect meal.

$–$$ ✕ **Como Agua Para Chocolate.** You can't miss this cantina—the three-story structure is an eye-catching yellow trimmed with royal blue. Once you duck under the star-shaped piñata hanging just inside the front door you'll realize that the dining rooms are in equally vivid shades of red and green. Happily, the food doesn't pale in comparison. Among the specials are *barbacoa de cordero,* which is lamb steamed in avocado leaves, and *albóndagas al chipotle,* a plate of spicy meatballs served with yellow rice. If you want to take home a bit of the magic, there's even a stand sell-

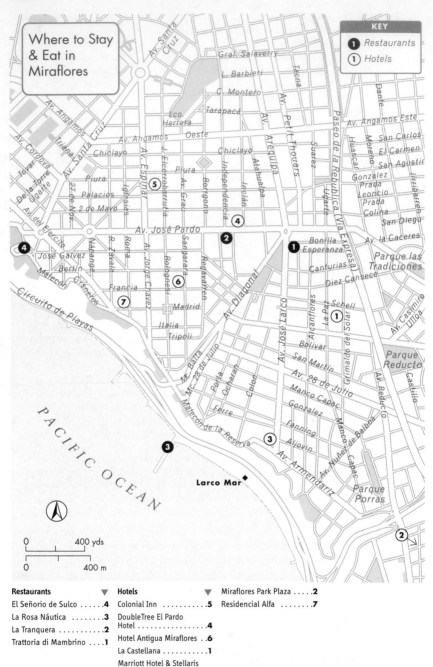

Where to Stay & Eat in Miraflores

KEY

- **1** Restaurants
- **①** Hotels

ing the namesake sweets. ⊠ *Pancho Fierro 108* ☎ *01/222–0174* ⊟ *AE, DC, MC, V.*

$–$$ **FodorsChoice** ★ ✕ **El Cartujo.** With a tree-shaded park at its doorstep, tranquil El Cartujo feels miles away from the busy streets of San Isidro. Sit outside under honey-color canopies or in the dining room dominated by a painting of the obscure order of monks that gave the place its name. The salads are excellent; the *ensalada flamenco* has smoked salmon, plump olives, and buttons of caviar atop fresh greens. Save room for seafood, especially the sole stuffed with lobster or the sea bass topped with crab. There's a top-notch wine list, and the steward is happy to help you make the perfect selection. ⊠ *Calle Los Libertadores 108* ☎ *01/221–4962* ⚶ *Reservations essential* ⊟ *AE, DC, MC, V.*

$–$$ ✕ **Punta Sal.** There are a few splashes of color in the dining room—the royal blue of the tablecloths, for example—but the real excitement is on the platters streaming out of the kitchen. Order the *tiradito criollo,* for example, and the slices of fish arrive covered in a vivid sauce made from yellow peppers. This place has won every award in the book, undoubtedly because the chefs constantly look to other countries for inspiration. This is one of the few *cevicherías* serving carpaccio. Should you prefer, you can ask that your sole or sea bass be cooked one of 10 different ways. ⊠ *Av. Conquistadores 948, San Isidro* ☎ *01/441–7431* ⊠ *Malecón Cisneros at Av. Tripoli Miraflores* ☎ *01/242–4524* ⊟ *AE, DC, MC, V* ⊘ *No dinner.*

$ ✕ **Vivaldino.** Two olive trees stood on this corner for more than a century, so the owners decided to keep them when they built this restaurant. The trees stand in the center of the dining room, ringed by wrought-iron tables covered with crisp white linens and lit with stained-glass lamps. Tall windows let in plenty of sunshine. The menu tends toward Mediterranean-style fare. Try the *solomillo caprese* (bits of steak with tomatoes and mozzarella cheese) or the *pulpito parrillero* (grilled octopus with potatoes and arugula). If the dessert cart includes a mousse made with *lucuma,* a local fruit, snap one up immediately. ⊠ *Av. Conquistadores 510, San Isidro* ☎ *01/442–2005* ⊠ *Malecón de la Reserva and Av. José Larco, Miraflores* ☎ *01/446–3859* ⊟ *AE, MC, V.*

Where to Stay

Most hotels are on quiet streets in the mostly residential neighborhoods of Miraflores, San Isidro, and Barranco. These areas are safe and secure, so you don't have to worry about taking a stroll during the day. Because many streets are deserted after dark, it's usually better to take a taxi at night. There are no big resorts here, just small hotels with a funky flavor. All of these neighborhoods are linked to El Centro by the Paseo de la República, so getting to the major sights is a snap.

Although the historic center is much safer than it once was, it still has few decent hotels. A few holdouts, such as Gran Hotel Bolívar, are outstanding. If you decide to stay near the heart of the city, remember that you have far fewer options in terms of bars and restaurants than in other neighborhoods.

Barranco

¢   🏨 **La Quinta de Allison.** On a quiet side street in Barranco, this unassuming hotel doesn't shout to get your attention. But you should take a second look, especially because it's one of the cheapest places in the neighborhood. Rooms are on the small side, but are more than comfortable. A few of the more expensive rooms have whirlpool tubs. All the neighborhood sights are within a few blocks. ⊠ *Jr. 28 de Julio 281* ☎ *01/247–1515* ⇨ *20 rooms* ⚿ *Restaurant, room service, fans, cable TV, bar* ⊟ *MC, V.*

El Centro

$$$$ 🏨 **Sheraton Lima Hotel & Casino.** The country's largest casino can be found off the marble lobby of downtown's most distinguished hotel. You might call it a landmark, except for the fact that its concrete facade makes it fade into the background. Perfectly serviceable rooms have subdued colors and surround an open atrium. This is a good choice for business travelers, as it has eight large meeting rooms and a convention center. Tourists appreciate that it's within walking distance of the city's historical district. The hotel is near the expressway, so it's also a short drive to San Isidro and Miraflores. ⊠ *Paseo de la República 170* ☎ *01/315–5000* ⊕ *www.sheraton.com.pe* ⇨ *438 rooms, 21 suites* ⚿ *3 restaurants, coffee shop, in-room data ports, in-room safes, minibars, cable TV, tennis court, pool, gym, spa, sauna, steam bath, bar, casino, shops, laundry service, Internet room, business services, convention center, meeting rooms, airport shuttle* ⊟ *AE, DC, MC, V.*

$ 🏨 **Gran Hotel Bolívar.** Tastes may have changed since it was built in 1924, **Fodor's**Choice but this grande dame retains the sumptuousness of the days when guests ★ included Ernest Hemingway. As you enter the marble-columned rotunda, your eyes are drawn upward to the magnificent stained-glass dome. Off to one side is the wood-paneled bar, which remains as popular as ever. The tables on the terrace are the perfect place to enjoy the best pisco sours in town. A grand staircase sweeps you up to the rooms, which retain lovely touches like parquet floors. Pull back the curtains for an unforgettable view of Plaza San Martín. ⊠ *Jr. de la Unión 958* ☎ *01/619–7171* ⊕ *www.granhotelbolivarperu.com* ⇨ *272 rooms, 5 suites* ⚿ *2 restaurants, room service, in-room safes, cable TV, bar, convention center, meeting rooms* ⊟ *AE, DC, MC, V* ⧖ *BP.*

Miraflores

$$$$ 🏨 **DoubleTree El Pardo Hotel.** This is one hotel where you won't want to go to your room. The open-air café on the ground floor is a great place for a cocktail, while the rooftop pool and hot tub have a view that will leave you breathless. The high-tech health club, with all the latest equipment, is among the best in the city. This is primarily a business hotel, so there is a well-stocked business center and half a dozen meeting rooms that can be configured for just about any purpose. A glittering casino was added in 2005. ⊠ *Jr. Independencia 141* ☎ *01/241–0410* ⊕ *www.doubletreeelpardo.com.pe* ⇨ *92 rooms, 18 suites* ⚿ *Restaurant, café, room service, in-room data ports, in-room safes, minibars, cable TV with movies, pool, health club, hot tub, bar, laundry service, Internet, casino, business services, convention center, meeting rooms, airport shuttles* ⊟ *AE, DC, MC, V.*

$$$$ ⊞ **Marriott Hotel & Stellaris Casino.** This isn't a hotel—it's a small city. Just about anything you long for, whether it's a chocolate-chip cookie or a pair of diamond earrings, can be had in the shops downstairs. If not, there's the Larcomar shopping center across the street. The views are spectacular from the glass tower, which forever altered the skyline of Miraflores when it opened at the turn of the millennium. On clear days the entire coastline is visible. The only disappointment is the rooms, which are luxuriously appointed but lack the slightest hint that you're in Peru. The Stellaris Casino, one of the city's most glittery, is a winner. ⊠ *Malecón de la Reserva 615* ☎ *01/217–7000* ⊕ *www.marriotthotels. com* ⌨ *288 rooms, 12 suites* ⚐ *2 restaurants, café, in-room data ports, in-room safes, minibars, cable TV with movies, Wi-Fi, 2 tennis courts, pool, health club, hair salon, sauna, bar, piano bar, casino, shops, dry cleaning, laundry service, Internet room, business services, convention center, meeting rooms, airport shuttle* ⊟ *AE, DC, MC, V.*

$$$$ ⊞ **Miraflores Park Plaza.** Surprisingly few of the city's hotels are near the ocean, which is why this hotel is in such demand. If you think the views from your room are breathtaking, just head up to the rooftop pool overlooking the entire coastline. Rooms have sitting areas that make them as big as suites, and computer connections and fax machines that make them perfect for business travelers. Better suited for couples are the suites, which have hot tubs strategically placed beside the beds. Don't miss the Dr. Jekyll and Mr. Hyde bar, which has a hidden mezzanine for a romantic rendezvous. ⊠ *Malecón de la Reserva 1035* ☎ *01/242–3000* ⊕ *www.mira-park.com* ⌨ *64 rooms, 17 suites* ⚐ *2 restaurants, room service, in-room data ports, in-room safes, minibars, cable TV with movies, in-room VCRs, pool, health club, spa, massage, sauna, squash, 2 bars, shops, laundry service, Internet room, business services, meeting rooms, airport shuttle* ⊟ *AE, MC, V.*

$$
Fodor'sChoice
★ ⊞ **Hotel Antigua Miraflores.** In a salmon-color mansion dating back more than a century, this elegantly appointed hotel is perhaps the city's loveliest lodging. Black-and-white marble floors and perfectly polished railings greet you as you stroll through the antiques-filled lobby. Up the wooden staircase are guest rooms with hand-carved furniture. Those in front have more character, whereas the more modern rooms in the newer section curve around a graceful fountain. Known for its impeccable service, the hotel sees repeat business year after year. The original art that adorns the dining room is for sale. ⊠ *Grau 350* ☎ *01/241–6116* ⊕ *www.peru-hotels-inns.com* ⌨ *15 rooms* ⚐ *Restaurant, fans, cable TV, gym, hot tub, bar, Internet, meeting rooms* ⊟ *AE, DC, MC, V.*

$
Fodor'sChoice
★ ⊞ **La Castellana.** A favorite for years, this exuberantly neoclassical structure resembles a small castle. The foyer, where wrought-iron lanterns cast a soft glow, is a taste of what is to come. Beyond are lovely touches like stained-glass windows and a towering turret. All the wood-shuttered rooms are lovely, but especially nice are No. 10, which overlooks the sunny courtyard, and No. 15, which has a private balcony facing the front. The friendly staff goes above and beyond the call of duty, even helping with things like airplane reservations. This inn remains immensely popular, so reservations should be made far in advance. ⊠ *Grimaldo del Solar 222* ☎ *01/444–3530* ⊕ *www.*

8

hotel-lacastellana.com 🛏 *29 rooms* 🍴 *Restaurant, fans, in-room safes, cable TV, bar* 🟰 *AE, DC, MC, V.*

$ 🏨 **Colonial Inn.** Elaborately carved wooden balconies accentuate the facade of this mustard-color colonial-style edifice. A huge fireplace dominates the lobby, where a graceful arch leads to the airy restaurant serving traditional fare. Religious relics such as heavy iron crosses decorate the common areas found on every floor. Rooms leading off the wrought-iron staircase have nice touches like wood wainscoting and beamed ceilings. One especially nice touch is the minuscule bar, with a vault ceiling and padded wallpaper on the walls. Here, beside the antique upright piano, chat with other guests as you enjoy a pisco sour. ✉ *Commandante Espinar 310* ☎ *01/241-7471* 🌐 *www.hotelcolonialinn.com* 🛏 *34 rooms* 🍴 *Restaurant, room service, fans, in-room safes, minibars, 2 bars, laundry service, Internet room, airport shuttles* 🟰 *AE, DC, MC, V.*

¢ 🏨 **Residencial Alfa.** You won't come any closer to staying in a private home than this little bed-and-breakfast. On a quiet street, it's a favorite of people in town for a week or more. It's half a block from the seaside cliffs, so some rooms have views of a sliver of the ocean. Paragliders often sail past the windows. The wood-floored rooms are large and sunny, and the baths are sparkling. It's not fancy, but it's one of the cheapest places to stay in Lima. ✉ *Av. de la Aviación 565* ☎ *01/241-3386* ✍ *residencialalfa@yahoo.com* 🛏 *10 rooms* 🍴 *Fan, cable TV, Internet, travel service; no a/c* 🟰 *MC, V* 🍽 *BP.*

San Isidro

$$$$ 🏨 **Country Club Lima Hotel.** Priceless paintings from the Museo Pedro de
Fodor'sChoice Osma hang in each room in this luxurious lodging. The hacienda-style
★ hotel, dating from 1927, is itself a work of art. Just step into the lobby, where hand-painted tiles reflect the yellows and greens of the stained-glass ceiling. The air of refinement continues in the rooms, all of which are draped with fine fabrics. Many have private balconies that overlook the oval-shaped pool or the well-tended gardens. Locals frequently come by for high tea in the atrium or traditional fare in the elegant restaurant. The outdoor terrace is perfect for romantic dinners. ✉ *Los Eucaliptos 590* ☎ *01/211-9000* 🌐 *www.hotelcountry.com* 🛏 *75 rooms* 🍴 *Restaurant, room service, in-room safes, minibars, cable TV with movies, in-room data ports, Wi-Fi, golf, pool, gym, hair salon, sauna, shops, laundry service, Internet room, business services, meeting rooms, airport shuttle* 🟰 *AE, DC, MC, V.*

$$$ 🏨 **Los Delfines.** It's not every day that a pair of dolphins greets you near the entrance of your hotel. Yaku and Wayra do just that in the lobby of this high-rise in San Isidro. Kids love to help feed them as their parents look on from the adjacent café, where crisscrossing ribbons of steel hold aloft the glass roof. Although they're a bit on the small side, the rooms are bright and comfortably furnished, and many have sweeping views of the adjacent Club Lima Golf. Downstairs, the beautifully decorated Knossos restaurant serves up delicious Indian fare. ✉ *Los Eucaliptos 555* ☎ *01/215-7000* 🌐 *www.losdelfineshotel.com* 🛏 *173 rooms, 24 suites* 🍴 *Restaurant, café, room service, in-room data ports, in-room safes, minibars, cable TV with movies, pool, health club, hair salon, massage, sauna, spa, steam room, bar, casino, shops, laundry service, In-*

ternet room, business services, convention center, meeting rooms, airport shuttle 🖵 AE, MC, V.

★ $ 🏨 **Hotel San Blas.** The best deal in San Isidro—maybe in the entire city—is this little gem. Its price tag is below that of many budget hotels, while its amenities are equal to those of quite a few resorts. The bright, airy rooms are as big as suites and have niceties like modem connections and sound-proof windows. Jacuzzis turn the baths into spas. A well-equipped meeting room on the ground floor that accommodates 30 people opens out into a sunny patio. The café in the lobby is on call if you order up a midnight snack, even if it's three in the morning. ⊠ *Av. Arequipa 3940* ☎ *01/222–2601* ⊕ *www.hotelsanblas.com.pe* ⌁ *30 rooms* ♨ *Café, room service, in-room safes, in-room hot tubs, minibars, cable TV, in-room data ports, hair salon, bar, laundry service, business services, meeting rooms, airport shuttle* 🖵 *AE, DC, MC, V.*

Nightlife

The most popular weekend destinations are *peñas,* bars that offer *música criolla,* a breathless combination of Peruvian, African, and other influences. The music is accompanied by flashily costumed dancers whipping themselves into a frenzy. Depending on the venue, these shows can be exhilarating or just plain exhausting. Ask locals to recommend one not geared to tourists. Most peñas start the show at 10:30 or 11 and continue until the wee hours of the morning.

Ask at your hotel for a free copy of *Peru Guide,* an English-language monthly full of information on bars and clubs as well as galleries and performances. For the latest hot spots, peruse the Spanish-language *El Comercio.*

Barranco

BARS A pleasant place to start off the evening is **La Posada del Mirador** (⊠ Ermita 104 ☎ 01/477–9577). The bar has a second-story balcony that looks out to sea, making this a great place to watch the sunset. Facing Barranco's main square is **Juanito's** (⊠ Grau 274 ☎ no phone), one of the neighborhood's most venerable establishments. Built by Italian immigrants in 1905, the former pharmacy retains its glass-front cabinets. Today, however, the bottles inside are filled with wine and spirits. **Posada del Ángel** (⊠ Av. Pedro de Osma 164 ☎ 01/247–0341) retains its Victorian-era warmth. It's one of the few bars in Barranco where you can actually hold a conversation.

CLUBS It's not really a dance club, but the patrons of **Kafé Kitsch** (⊠ Bolognesi
★ 742 ☎ 01/242–3325) simply push back the tables so they can show off their moves. Busts of Elvis and statuettes of the Virgin Mary gaze down in astonishment. The crowd is mostly straight, but there's usually a contingent of gays as well. An upscale crowd heads to **Costa Verde** (⊠ Playa Barranquito ☎ 01/441–3367) when the city's most elegant restaurant transforms itself into the most elegant dance club. Don't even think about wearing shorts here.

LIVE MUSIC **El Ekeko** (⊠ Grau 266 ☎ 01/477–5823) is the most elegant of the live music venues. Head upstairs to the main room, where tall windows crowned with yellow-and-green stained glass recall when this neighborhood was a retreat for the rich and powerful. Locals who pack the place enjoy Latin-flavored music, from calypso to cha-cha-cha. Slightly more sedate than most clubs is **La Estación de Barranco** (⊠ Av. Pedro de Osma 112 ☎ 01/467–8804). In an old train station, the warmly lit space specializes in folk music. **La Noche** (⊠ Bolognesi 307 ☎ 01/477–4154) is at the far end of a pedestrian street called Bulevar Sánchez Carrión. The rock and jazz bands booked here appeal to a youthful, noisy crowd. Escape to an outdoor patio or a second-story balcony to check out who is coming and going.

PEÑAS The most upmarket of the peñas is found in Barranco at **Manos Morenas** (⊠ Av. Pedro de Osma 409 ☎ 01/467–0421). Extravagantly costumed performers hardly seem to touch the ground as they re-create dances from around the region. The musicians, switching instruments half a dozen times during a song, are without equal. The place feels like a theme park, though, perhaps because of the long tables of picture-taking tourists. Vying for the tourist market is **La Candelaria** (⊠ Av. Bolognesi 292 ☎ 01/247–1314), which is immediately recognizable from the fiery torches flanking the front door. A series of small spaces leads to the main room, where the dancers have plenty of room to show off their steps. The facade may be dull, but the attitude is anything but at **De Rompe y Raja** (⊠ Jr. Manuel Segura 127 ☎ 01/247–3271). Slightly off the beaten path, this peña attracts mostly locals to its shows with *música negra,* a black variant of *música criolla.*

Miraflores

BARS Miraflores lets you sample beers from around the world. If you're longing for a pint of Guinness, head to **Murphy's Irish Pub** (⊠ Schell 627 ☎ 01/242–1212). The wood paneling and the well-worn dart board may convince you that you're in Ireland.

LIVE MUSIC Clubs offering live music are scattered all over Miraflores. It's easy to
★ miss the **Jazz Zone** (⊠ Av. La Paz 656 ☎ 01/241–8139), as the unassuming little club is down an alley. You head up a bright red stairway to the dimly lit second-story lounge. Expect jazz flavored with local rhythms.

PEÑAS **Junius** (⊠ Av. Independencia 125 ☎ 01/617–1000) has dinner shows featuring traditional dances. It's geared mostly to tourists. An older crowd heads to **Sachún** (⊠ Av. del Ejército 657 ☎ 01/441–4465). The draw, it seems, are the sentimental favorites played by the band.

DANCE CLUBS Near Parque Miraflores is **Tequila Rocks** (⊠ Calle Diez Canseco 146 ☎ 01/444–3661), a downtown *discoteca* that's been popular for years. Drink specials bring in the crowds seven nights a week.

GAY & LESBIAN
CLUBS After 10 PM you'll definitely want to stop for a drink at **La Sede** (⊠ Av. 28 de Julio 441 ☎ 01/242–2462), one of the city's more sophisticated bars. The candy apple–red walls give the place a funky feel.

San Isidro

BARS In San Isidro, toss back a Sapporo or any other Japanese beer at the sleek **Osaka** (⊠ Av. Conquistadores 999 ☎ 01/222–0405).

Outdoor Activities

Biking

In the heart of Miraflores, **iExplore** (✉ Av. Bolognesi 381, Miraflores ☎ 01/241–7358) is a great base for cycling trips along the coast. The company rents mountain bikes and all the equipment you need.

Bullfighting

Bullfighting remains exceedingly popular in Peru. The spectacle, with all the pomp and circumstance of similar events in Spain, takes place in October and November at the **Plaza de Acho** (✉ Jr. Hualgayoc 332, Rímac ☎ 01/482–3360). Even if you have no interest in the actual event, it's worth getting a peek inside the bullring that was once one of the largest in the world. Ticket prices depend on the event, but always expect to pay more for a seat in *sombra* (shade) than *sol* (sun).

Paragliding

If you walk along the ocean on a sunny day, you'll doubtless see a dozen or so brilliantly colored swaths of cloth in the sky above you. **PerúFly** (✉ Av. Jorge Chavez 658, Miraflores ☎ 01/444–5004 ⊕ www.perufly.com) offers a six-day course for about US$390.

Soccer

Soccer—or *fútbol,* as it's known in this part of the world—reigns supreme in Peru. When there's a highly contested match being televised, don't be surprised to see dozens of people in the street outside a bar or restaurant that happens to have a television. Peru's leading teams are Alianza, Universitario, Sport Boys, and Cristal. Matches are played year-round at the imposing **Estadio Nacional** (✉ Jr. José Díaz, El Centro ☎ 01/433–6366). Tickets for most matches range from US$5 to US$25.

Surfing

With **Surf Express** (✉ 568 Highway A1A, Satellite Beach, FL 32937 ☎ 321/779–2124 ⊕ www.surfex.com), surfers ride with some of the best left-breaking waves in the world, such as at Punta Rocas south of Lima. Surfing is good all year in Peru.

Shopping

Hundreds of stores around Lima offer traditional crafts of the highest quality. The same goes for silver and gold jewelry. Wander down Avenida La Paz in Miraflores and you'll be astounded at the number of shops selling one-of-a-kind designs; the street also yields clothing and antiques at reasonable prices. Miraflores is also full of crafts shops, many of them along Avenida Petit Thouars. For upscale merchandise, many people now turn to the boutiques of San Isidro. For original works of art, the bohemian neighborhood of Barranco has many small galleries.

Antiques

Dozens of shops selling *antigüedades* crowd Avenida La Paz, making this street in Miraflores a favorite destination for bargain hunters. Toward the back of a little cluster of shops, **El Arcón** (✉ Av. La Paz 646,

Miraflores ☎ 01/447–6149) packs an incredible variety into a small space. Head to the rooms in back for fearsome masks and colorful weavings dating back almost a century. **Antigüedades Siglo XVIII** (⊠ Av. La Paz 661, Miraflores ☎ 01/445–8915) specializes in precious metals. Don't miss the case full of silver *milagros,* or miracles. These heartshaped charms were once placed at the feet of religious statues in gratitude for answered prayers. Brooding saints dominate the walls of **El Frailero** (⊠ Av. La Paz 551, Miraflores ☎ 01/447–2823). These small statues and paintings, most made for private homes, date back to the colonial period.

Clothing

★ Lots of stores stock clothing made of alpaca, but one of the few to offer articles made from vicuña is **Alpaca 111** (⊠ Av. Larco 671, Miraflores ☎ 01/447–1623 ⊠ Larcomar Malecón de la Reserva and Av. José Larco, Miraflores ☎ 01/241–3484). This diminutive creature, distant cousin of the llama, produces the world's finest wool. It is fashioned into scarves, sweaters, and even knee-length coats. There are branches of the store in Hotel Los Delfines, Miraflores Park Hotel, and Sonesta Posada del Inca El Olívar.

There are several other shops specializing in alpaca in Miraflores. **All Alpaca** (⊠ Av. Schell 375–377, Miraflores ☎ 01/446–0565) sells sweaters and other pieces of clothing in sophisticated styles. Bright colors reign at **La Casa de la Alpaca** (⊠ Av. La Paz 665, Miraflores ☎ 01/447–6271). The patterns are updated takes on Andean designs.

Galleries

Miraflores is full of art galleries that show the works of Peruvian and occasionally foreign artists. In the rear of the Municipalidad de Miraflores, the **Sala Luis Miró Quesada Garland** (⊠ Av. Larco Herrera and Calle Diez Canseco, Miraflores ☎ 01/444–0540) sponsors exhibits of sculpture, painting, and photography. **Trapecio** (⊠ Av. Larco Herrera 743, Miraflores ☎ 01/444–0842) shows works by contemporary Peruvian artists. **Corriente Alterna** (⊠ Av. de la Aviación 500, Miraflores ☎ 01/242–8482) often has works by notable new artists.

In San Isidro, **Artco** (⊠ Calle Rouad and Paz Soldán, San Isidro ☎ 01/221–3579) sponsors cutting-edge art, sometimes involving different mediums such as painting and video. **Praxis** (⊠ Av. San Martín 689, at Diez Canseco, Barranco ☎ 01/477–2822) has constantly rotating exhibits of international artists experimenting with different forms.

Handicrafts

For beautiful pottery, head to **Antisuyo** (⊠ Tacna 460, Miraflores ☎ 01/447–2557), which sells only traditional pieces from around the country. Tiny *retablos* (boxes filled with scenes of village life) are among the eye-catching objects at **Raices Peru** (⊠ Av. La Paz 588, Miraflores ☎ 01/447–7457). For one-of-a-kind pieces, **Coral Roja** (⊠ Recavarren 269, Miraflores ☎ 01/447–2552) sells work made on the premises. The little red building is the place to go for original designs.

★ On a quiet street in San Isidro, **Indigo** (✉ Av. El Bosque, San Isidro ☎ 01/440–3099) lets you wander through at least half a dozen different rooms filled with unique items. There's a selection of whimsical ceramics inspired by traditional designs, as well as completely modern pieces. In the center of it all is an open-air café. **Remolino** (✉ Av. Libertadores 256, San Isidro ☎ 01/222–2382) is known for handmade glass bowls and vases in wonderfully wacky color combinations.

Jewelry
It's unlikely you'll find gold jewelry elsewhere in designs as distinct as those at **H. Stern** (✉ Museo de Oro, Alonso de Molina 1100, Monterrico ☎ 01/345–1350). The well-regarded South American chain is savvy enough to know that people head to Peru for a taste of the culture. Many of their designs are influenced by the art of pre-Columbian peoples. One especially lovely piece is a vividly colored pin shaped like a Paracas warrior. Look for branches in top hotels, including Hotel Los Delfines, Hotel Marriott, and Sheraton Lima Hotel & Casino.

For sterling, you can't beat the classic designs at **Camusso** (✉ Av. Oscar Benavides 679, El Centro ☎ 01/425–0260 ✉ Av. Rivera Navarrete 788, San Isidro ☎ 01/442–0340), a local *platería*, or silver shop, that opened its doors in 1933. Call ahead for a free guided tour of the factory, which is a few blocks west of El Centro. Chic designs fashioned in silver are the trademark of **Ilaria** (✉ Av. Dos de Mayo 308, San Isidro ☎ 01/221–8575 ✉ Los Eucaliptos 578, San Isidro ☎ 01/440–4875). The store has two branches in San Isidro.

Malls
Right in the heart of things is **Larcomar** (✉ Malecón de la Reserva and Av. José Larco, Miraflores ☎ 01/620–7583), a surprisingly appealing shopping center in Miraflores. It's built on a bluff below Parque Salazar, so it's almost invisible from the street. Its dozens of shops, bars, and restaurants are terraced so they all have views of the ocean. Kids like it because there's a movie theater, bowling alley, and several places to play video games.

Markets
On the northern edge of Miraflores, Avenida Petit Thouars has at least half a dozen markets crammed with vendors. No need to hit more than one or two, as they all carry pretty much the same merchandise. To get a rough idea of what an alpaca sweater or woven wallet should cost, head to **Artesanías Miraflores** (✉ Av. Petit Thouars 5541, Miraflores ☎ No phone). It's small, but has a little of everything. Better-quality goods can be found at **La Portada del Sol** (✉ Av. Petit Thouars 5411, Miraflores ☎ No phone). In this miniature mall the vendors show off their wares in glassed cases lit with halogen lamps. Some even accept credit cards.

In El Centro there aren't as many souvenir shops as you might think. Most people head to **Artesanías Santo Domingo** (✉ Conde de Super and Jr. Camaná, Miraflores ☎ 01/242–2871), a cluster of shops in a pretty colonial-style building. If you get tired of shopping, the plaza outside overlooks the pretty Iglesia de Santo Domingo.

8

Lima Essentials

Transportation

BY AIR

Numerous airlines handle domestic flights, so getting to any of the major tourist destinations is no problem. You can often find space at the last minute, especially outside of high season. LanPeru, which in the past few years has become the carrier with the most national flights, departs several times each day for Arequipa, Cusco, Juliaca, Puerto Maldonado, and Trujillo. Aero Cóndor has daily flights to Arequipa and Iquitos, and Taca Peru flies to Arequipa and Cusco. LC Busre flies to Ayacucho, Cajamarca, Huánuco, and Trujillo. TANS Perú flies to Arequipa, Cusco, Iquitos, Juliaca, Puerto Maldonado, and Tumbes.

Aeropuerto Internacional Jorge Chávez is on the northwestern fringe of the city. A taxi to most places in the city should cost no more than US$10. It is 10 km (6 mi) southeast and a 20-minute drive to El Centro, and a 30-minute drive to Miraflores and San Isidro.

🛈 **Carriers Aero Cóndor** ☎ 01/442-5215 in Lima ⊕ www.aerocondor.com.pe. **Lan** ☎ 01/221-3764 ⊕ www.lan.com. **LC Busre** ☎ 01/619-1300 ⊕ www.lcbusre.com.pe. **Star Perú** ☎ 511/705-9000 ⊕ www.starperu.com. **Taca Peru** ☎ 01/446-0033 ⊕ grupotaca. com. **TANS Perú** ☎ 01/213-6000 ⊕ www.tansperu.com.pe.

🛈 **Airport Information Aeropuerto Internacional Jorge Chávez** ⊠ Av. Faucett s/n ☎ 01/517-3100 ⊕ www.lap.com.pe.

BY BUS

Two types of buses—regular-size *micros* and the van-size *combis*—patrol the streets of Lima. You won't have to wait long for a bus; on major thoroughfares it is not uncommon to have half a dozen or more waving you aboard. You simply hop on at any intersection and pay the conductor as you leave. Fares are cheap, usually S/1.40, or about 45¢ for a ride of any distance. It is difficult to tell where buses are headed, as the signs on the windshields indicate only the end points of the route. The conductors hang out the door and announce the route with the speed of an auctioneer, all but impossible to understand. A better way to discern the route is by the signs along the sides. The names of the major streets traveled will be listed. If a bus travels on a section of Avenida Arequipa, the sign will say AREQUIPA. If it travels the entire distance, it will say TODO AREQUIPA. When you want to get off, simply tell the conductor *la proxima esquina,* meaning "the next corner." Give him plenty of notice, as it sometimes takes a while for the speeding buses to slow down.

BY CAR

DRIVING IN LIMA Lima's main streets are in pretty good condition, but heavy congestion and the almost complete absence of traffic lights make driving a harrowing experience. Better to leave the hassle to a taxi driver. However, a car is a great way to see the sights outside the city. The highways surrounding the capital are reasonably well maintained. In the city, always park in a guarded lot. If you can't find one, hire someone who offers "*cuidar su carro*" ("to take care of your car"). Pay about S/5 when you return and find your car intact.

RENTING A CAR Most rental agencies also offer the services of a driver, a good solution for those who want the freedom of a car without the hassle of driving on Lima's busy streets. In addition to offices downtown, Avis, Budget, Hertz, and National all have branches at Jorge Chávez International Airport that are open 24 hours. (The Avis desk is just outside the international-arrivals terminal.)

🚗 **Avis** ✉ Av. Larco 1080, Miraflores ☎ 01/446-4533. **Budget** ✉ Moreyra 569, San Isidro ☎ 01/442-8703. **Hertz** ✉ Av. Cantuarias 160, Miraflores ☎ 01/447-2129. **National** ✉ Av. España 453, El Centro ☎ 01/433-3750.

BY TAXI

Locals warn you that hailing taxis on the street can be dangerous. In truth, robberies by cab drivers are rare. To be on the safe side, only use those taxis that are painted yellow and that have the driver's license prominently displayed. It's best to negotiate the fare before you get in. A journey between two adjacent neighborhoods should cost between S/4 and S/7; longer trips should be about S/10. If you call a taxi, the price will be roughly double. Well-regarded companies include Taxi Amigo and Taxi Móvil.

🚕 **Taxi Companies Taxi Amigo** ☎ 01/349-0177. **Taxi Móvil** ☎ 01/422-6890.

Contacts & Resources

BANKS & EXCHANGE SERVICES

Automatic-teller machines have become ubiquitous in Lima. On Avenida José Pardo, the main commercial street in Miraflores, there's a bank on nearly every block. Currency exchange offices include Lác Dolar, which has offices in El Centro and Miraflores. When exchanging money, you will usually be asked to show your passport.

EMERGENCIES

For robberies and other petty crimes, contact the Tourist Police. The department is divided into the northern zone, which includes El Centro, and the southern zone, which includes Barranco, Miraflores, and San Isidro. English-speaking officers will help you negotiate the system. For more urgent matters, call the police and fire emergency numbers.

There are several clinics with English-speaking staff, including the Clinica Anglo-Americana and Clinica El Golf. Both are in San Isidro. There are pharmacies operating around the clock across the city. Look for Farmacia Deza, Farmacia Fasa, and InkaFarma.

🚨 **Emergency Numbers Fire** ☎ 116. **Police** ☎ 105. **Tourist Police (northern zone)** ☎ 01/424-2053. **Tourist Police (southern zone)** ☎ 01/460-4525.

🏥 **Hospital Clinica Anglo-Americana** ✉ Av. Alfredo Salazar, San Isidro ☎ 01/221-3656. **Clinica El Golf** ✉ Av. Aurelio Miro Quesada, San Isidro ☎ 01/264-3300.

💊 **Pharmacy Farmacia Deza** ✉ Av. Conquistadores 144, San Isidro ☎ 01/441-5860. **Farmacia Fasa** ✉ Av. Benavides 487, Miraflores ☎ 01/475-7070 ✉ Av. Larco 129, Miraflores ☎ 01/619-0000. **InkaFarma** ✉ Av. Benavides 425, Miraflores ☎ 01/314-2020.

TOUR OPTIONS

Lima has many top tour operators with experienced English-speaking guides that can arrange local sightseeing as well as tours throughout the country. The most professional is Lima Tours, which offers tours of the city and surrounding area as well as the rest of the country. The company is one of the few that conducts tours for gay groups. Other well-regarded companies include Condor Travel, Lima Vision, Setours, and Solmartour.

🏠 **Condor Travel** ✉ Av. Amando Blondet 249, San Isidro ☎ 01/615-3000 ⊕ www.condortravel.com.pe. **Lima Tours** ✉ Belén 1040, El Centro ☎ 01/619-6900 ⊕ www.limatours.com.pe. **Lima Vision** ✉ Jr. Chiclayo 444, Miraflores ☎ 01/447-7710 ⊕ www.limavision.com. **Setours** ✉ Av. Comandante Espinar 229, Miraflores ☎ 01/446-9229 ⊕ www.setours.com. **Solmartour** ✉ Av. Grau 300, Miraflores ☎ 01/444-1313 ⊕ www.solmar.com.pe.

VISITOR INFORMATION

Assisting travelers is iPerú, which has English- and Spanish-language information about the city and beyond. The office in San Isidro is open weekdays 8:30–6:30, and the office in the Larcomar shopping center in Miraflores is open daily noon–8. An information booth at Jorge Chávez International Airport is supposedly open 24 hours, but is often unstaffed.

The city runs the Oficina de Información Touristica, or Tourist Information Office, in the rear of the Municipalidad de Lima. It's a good place to pick up maps of the city, but the staff is not always as helpful as it could be.

The most thorough information about Lima, as well as the rest of Peru, is available at the nonprofit South American Explorers. You can call ahead with questions, or just show up at the beautiful clubhouse in Miraflores and browse through the lending library or read through trip reports filed by members. It costs US$50 to join, but you'll probably make up for that with discounts offered to members by hotels and tour operators.

🏠 **iPerú** ✉ Jorge Basadre 610, San Isidro ☎ 01/421-1627 ✉ Malecón de la Reserva and Av. José Larco, Miraflores ☎ 01/445-9400 ⊕ www.peru.info. **Oficina de Información Touristica** ✉ Paseo de los Escribanos 145, El Centro ☎ 01/315-1505. **South American Explorers** ✉ Calle Piura 135, Miraflores ☎ 01/445-3306 ⊕ www.saexplorers.org.

THE SOUTH

Revised by
Brian Kluepfel

Southern Peru is connected to Lima by the Pan-American Highway, which runs down the coast to Pisco and the Paracas Peninsula before cutting inland to Ica and Nazca. The road then splits, heading east to Cusco or west again to the coast and then south to Arequipa at Tacna, at the Chilean border. Several roads between these two towns turn due east through the Andes to Lake Titicaca and the Bolivian border. Although mountains dominate the eastern horizon, the terrain here is mostly arid, sandy, and endless—except where green river valleys and farmlands are nourished by snowmelt from the Andes. The landscape is equally dramatic in the region's stark central desert, where the Río Cotahuasi, Río Colca, and other swift streams have scraped the earth into some of the world's deepest canyons. The best way to enjoy this amazing region's history is to travel through it in your own vehicle. Those pressed for time and on a budget can easily catch buses between major destinations, or fly between towns for a spectacular overview of the land and then take day trips to nearby attractions.

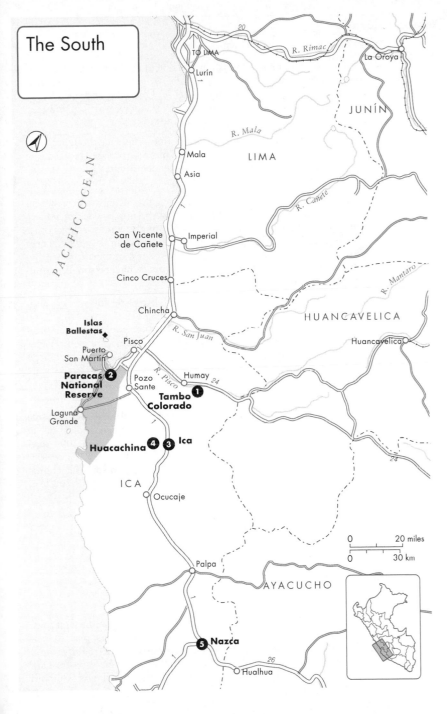

The South

Tambo Colorado

❶ *48 km (30 mi) southeast of Pisco.*

Fodor'sChoice ★

Drive southeast of Pisco and you'll find one of the best-preserved Incan constructions, the 15th-century Tambo Colorado, or Pucahuasi in Quechua. (*Huasi* means "resting place" in Quechua, and *puca* means "red"—the site was used as a stopover by traveling warriors and messengers, and red is the natural color of the stone.)

At the center of Tambo Colorado sits an altar where it's thought llamas were sacrificed on the solstice to divine the future (strong red blood meant a good year, whereas a blackish hue portended ill fate).

There are two repeating themes at Tambo Colorado. First, there's the motif of three step-like features representing the Incan world view consisting of the underworld, earth itself, and the upper world. And second, you'll notice the trapezoidal shapes of the windows and other openings, an extremely effective earthquake-resistant design in an area known for quakes. The site has withstood the test of time, for sure, but that hasn't stopped generations of visitors from etching personalized graffiti onto its walls.

Inside the small museum, you'll see some of discoverer Julio Tello's original finds, including funeral *fards* (burial cocoons), dating from 1300 BC to AD 200 and wrapped in bright cotton and wool textiles embroidered with detailed patterns. Some skulls showed evidence of trepanation, a sophisticated medical procedure involving the insertion of metal plates to replace sections of bone broken in battles where rocks were used as weapons. Samples from Tello's original dig are also on display at the Museo Julio Tello near Paracas.

If you have time, drive up the road past Tambo Colorado to the **Puente Colgante** (suspension bridge). Both the original wooden bridge built in the early-20th-century bridge and a newer one installed in 2004 span the river side by side. If you're brave, cross the older version. Catch your breath and drive up to **Huaytara,** a beautiful modern Catholic church built on the foundation of an Incan temple 2,800 meters (9,200 feet) above sea level.

If you don't have a rental car, ask around the travel agencies in Pisco for a trip to Tambo Colorado, a place with a quieter reputation and fewer tourists than Cusco, but an archaeological and historical site well worth the visit. ⊠ *Paracas Bay* ☎ *No phone* ⌨ *S/7.50* ☉ *Daily 9–5.*

Paracas National Reserve

❷ *15 km (10 mi) south of Pisco.*

Named for the blustering *paracas* (sandstorms) that buffet the west coast each winter, the Reserva Nacional de Paracas is Peru's first park for marine conservation. Settled atop a peninsular hook of land slightly southwest of Pisco, this 280,000-hectare (700,000-plus-acre) coastal park includes a conglomeration of mountains, desert, and islands. Thin dirt tracks lead to sheltered lagoons, rugged cliffs full of caves, and small fishing villages. The pristine surroundings and lonely feeling are misleading, however—a monument marks the spot where General José San Martín first stepped into Peru nearly 200 years ago.

Wildlife is everywhere in this stunning reserve, particularly bird colonies and sea creatures. Pelicans, condors, and red-and-white flamingos congregate and breed here; the latter, in fact, are said to have inspired the red-and-white independence flag General San Martín designed when he liberated Peru. On shore you can't miss the sound (or the smell) of the hundreds of sea lions, while in the water you might spot penguins, sea turtles, dolphins, manta rays, and even hammerhead sharks.

This is prime walking territory, where you can stroll from the bay to the **Julio Tello Museum,** and on to the fishing village of **Lagunilla** 5 km (3 mi) farther across the neck of the peninsula. Adjacent to the museum are colonies of flamingos, best seen June through July (and absent January through March, when they fly to Sierra). Hike another 6 km (4 mi) to reach **Mirador de Lobos** (Wolf Lookout) at Punta El Arquillo, along the cliffs overlooking a sea-lion colony, or to view the rock formation **La Catedral** (the Cathedral). Carved into the highest point in the cliffs above Paracas Bay, 14 km (9 mi) from the museum, is the **Candelabra. ■ TIP→ Note that you must hire a guide to explore the land trails.**

Minibus tours of the entire park can be arranged through local hotels and travel agencies for about S/15 for five hours. A taxi from Pisco to Paracas runs about S/14, or you can take a half-hour Chaco–Paracas–Museo *combi* to El Chaco for S/2.

Where to Stay

$$ ⊞ **Hotel Paracas.** Opened in the 1940s for Lima's elite, this Mediterranean-style resort—the area's largest—lies behind a wide, half-circle park and dock that juts out into the deep-blue Paracas Bay. Air-conditioned rooms have wood furnishings, private bathrooms, and TVs. Larger suites and flower-bedecked bungalows are often booked by families, and many have sea views. An extensive Sunday buffet (S/55) draws crowds, and nonguests can use the pool as part of the buffet price. It's a convenient base from which to launch trips into the reserve, tour local ruins, or head out for some fishing (bring your own gear). ⊠ *Av. Paracas 173* ☎ *056/545–100* ☎ *01/447–0781 in Lima* ⊕ *www.hotelparacas.com* ➾ *15 rooms, 7 suites, 3 bungalows* ⟨ *Restaurant, cafeteria, room service, some in-room safes, some minibars, some refrigerators, cable TV, miniature golf, 2 tennis courts, 2 pools, beach, dock, boating, fishing, volleyball, 2 bars, shop, laundry service, meeting rooms* ⊟ *AE, DC, MC, V* ⧖ *CP.*

Ica

❸   *56 km (35 mi) southeast of Paracas.*

Ica was the Nazca capital between AD 300 and 800, and the Nazca people couldn't have picked a better place to center their desert civilization. Set in a patch of verdant fields and abutted by snow-covered mountains, Ica is serene, relaxing, and cheerful, with helpful residents—likely due as much to the nearly never-ending sunshine as to the vast selection of high-quality wines and piscos produced by dozens of local bodegas. This is a town of laughter and festivals, most notably the Fiesta de Vendimia, the wine-harvest celebration that takes place each year in early March. Ica is also famous for its pecans and its high-stepping horses called *caballos de paso*.

The city's colonial look comes from its European heritage, as Ica was founded by the Spanish in 1536, making it one of the oldest towns in southern Peru. Today this bustling oasis in Peru's richest wine-growing region is a source of national pride, and its fine bodegas are a major attraction. Most are open all year, but the best time to visit is February to April, during the grape harvest. The Tacama and Ocucaje bodegas are generally considered to have the best-quality wines from this region.

The city's excitement heightens for such festivals as the Fiesta de Vendimia in March, February's Carnival, Semana Santa in March or April, and the all-night pilgrimages of El Señor de Luren in March and October. Other fun times to visit are during Ica Week, around June 17, which celebrates the city's founding, and the annual Ica Tourist Festival in late September.

A 16th-century farm hacienda hides the thoroughly modern production of the internationally renowned **Bodega Hacienda Tacama.** Some of Peru's best labels, particularly the Blanco de Blancos, are produced here. Stroll through the rolling vineyards—still watered by the Achirana irrigation canal built by the Inca—before sampling their end result. The estate is about 11 km (7 mi) from town. ⊠ *Camina a la Tinguiña s/n* ☎ *056/ 228–395* 🖃 *Free* 🕑 *Weekdays 9–2.*

A sunny brick archway welcomes you to the large, pleasant **Bodega Vista Alegre,** which has been producing fine wines, pisco, and sangria since it was founded by the Picasso brothers in 1857. The largest winery in the valley, it's a popular stop for tour buses and has regular tours and tastings. Get here early before the groups, but bring a friend who can translate if you don't speak Spanish. Take a taxi or city buses 8 or 13 to get there. *Don't walk from downtown Ica,* as robberies have been reported along this route. ⊠ *Camina a la Tinguiña, Km 205* ☎ *056/ 232–919* 🖃 *Free* 🕑 *Weekdays 9–2.*

One of the more fun alcohol-making operations to visit in this area is **Bodega Lazo,** owned by Elar Bolivar, who claims to be a direct descendent of the Libertador Simón Bolívar himself (some locals shrug their shoulders at this boast). Nonetheless, Elar's small artisanal operation includes a creepy collection of shrunken heads (Dutch tourists, he says, who didn't pay their drink tab), ancient cash registers, fencing equipment, and copies of some of the paintings in Ica's regional museum. The question is, who really has the originals—Elar or the museum? As part of your visit, you can taste the bodega's recently made pisco, straight from the barrel. Some organized tours include this bodega as part of a tour. It's not a safe walk from town, so take a cab if you want to come on your own. ⊠ *Camino de Reyes s/n, San Juan Bautista* ☎ *056/403– 430* 🖃 *Free* 🕑 *By appointment only.*

The quaint **Iglesia La Merced,** built in 1874, overlooks the Plaza de Armas. Peek in for a glimpse of the delicately carved wooden altars. ✉ *At Libertad y Bolívar* ☏ *No phone* 🎫 *Free* ⊙ *Mon.–Sat. 10–5.*

Inside the pretty, colonial-style **Iglesia El Señor de Luren** is a famous Christ image that is paraded around the city all night during local religious festivals. Legend has it that the statue, purchased for the church by a friar in 1570, was transported to Peru by boat. The captain threw it overboard in a storm, but it washed up on a beach near Paracas and was miraculously carried to Ica intact. The church is slightly southeast of town. ✉ *Cuervo y Ayacucho* ☏ *No phone* 🎫 *Free* ⊙ *Mon.–Sat. 9–4.*

A vast and well-preserved collection on regional history—particularly from the Inca, Nazca, and Paracas cultures—is on display in the fascinating **Museo Histórico Regional.** Note the quipas, mysterious knotted, colored threads thought to have been used to count commodities and quantities of food. Head out back to view a scale model of the Nazca Lines from an observation tower. You can also buy maps (S/0.50) and paintings of Nazca motifs (S/4). The museum is about 1½ km (1 mi) from town, so take a 20-minute walk, hop on Bus 17 from Plaza de Armas (S/2), or catch a *mototaxi* from the corner of the Plaza (S/2). ✉ *Ayabaca s/n* ☏ *056/234–383* 🎫 *S/11, plus S/4 camera fee* ⊙ *Weekdays 8–7, Sat. 9–6, Sun. 9–1, or by appointment.*

Fodor'sChoice
★

Where to Stay & Eat

$$
Fodor'sChoice
★

✕ **La Taberna.** In Bodega El Catador, this elegant restaurant serves exquisite local specialties at small, candlelit tables. Be sure to ask the waiter for his recommendations on the fine wines and pisco available. If you eat elsewhere, you can always stop by the bar for drinks and dancing to live Peruvian music. ✉ *José Carrasco González, Km 296* ☏ *056/403–263* ▭ *AE, MC, V.*

¢

✕ **El Otro Peñoncito.** Friendly and relaxed, this restaurant has Peruvian and international cuisine. Local specialties include the *pollo a la Iqueña* (chicken in a rich pecan, pisco, and spinach sauce) and the traditional *papa a la huancaina* (potatoes with cheese sauce). Milder fare, such as sandwiches and soups, is also served. Art by Iqueño artists adorns the walls. ✉ *Bolívar 255* ☏ *056/233–921* ▭ *No credit cards.*

★ **$$–$$$**

✕▥ **Hotel Las Dunas.** A cluster of whitewashed buildings amid the dunes, this colonial-style holiday resort is a favorite getaway for Peruvian families. Spacious rooms have balconies overlooking lush lawns, and suites have sunny courtyards and whirlpools. The restaurant, where you can dine poolside or in a breezy gazebo, serves such dishes as flounder with seafood sauce and spicy lomo saltado. Rent sand boards, play golf on the dunes, ride horseback, or fly over the Nazca Lines (S/350) from the hotel's airstrip. Add an 18% tax and service fee to the price—but book weekdays to save 20%. ✉ *La Angostura 400* ☏ *034/256–224* ✉ *invertur@protelsa.com.pe* ⇥ *106 rooms, 3 suites* ⎈ *Restaurant, cafeteria, 9-hole golf course, tennis court, 2 pools, lake, gym, massage, sauna, horseback riding, bar, dance club, laundry service, business services, airstrip, travel services* ▭ *AE, DC, MC, V.*

$–$$

▥ **Ocucaje Sun & Wine Resort.** The focus here is on all the best of southern Peru: sunshine and good wines. It feels like a comfortable Spanish

8

country home, but rooms have all the amenities. At the Bodega Ocucaje slightly outside of Ica, it's a desert resort meant to restore your spirits—which you can do by lying beside the attractive pool, getting a spa massage, or exploring the nearby historic sights. A continental breakfast is available for S/15. ✉ *Pan-American Hwy. S, Km 334, Av. Principal s/n* ☎☎ *056/836–101* ⊕ *www.hotelocucaje.com* ↴ *55 rooms* ♿ *Restaurant, room service, minibars, tennis court, pool, gym, hot tub, massage, sauna, spa, bicycles, horseback riding, volleyball, bar, dance club, recreation room, shop, babysitting, laundry service, business services, meeting rooms, car rental, travel services* ▭ *AE, DC, MC, V.*

$ 🏨 **El Carmelo Hotel & Hacienda.** At this colonial-style, slate-roof hotel 5 km (3 mi) from downtown Ica, rooms are in several buildings around a flower-filled courtyard. An inviting garden house has wicker furniture and a 19th-century winepress, where you can see the pisco-making process up close and personal. ✉ *Pan-American Hwy., Km 301.2* ☎☎ *056/232–191* ⊕ *www.elcarmelohotelhacienda.com* ↴ *51 rooms* ♿ *Restaurant, pool, bar, laundry service, travel services; no room phones, no room TVs* ▭ *AE, MC, V.*

Huacachina

❹ *5 km (3 mi) southwest of Ica.*

Drive 10 minutes through the pale sand dunes southwest of Ica and you come to the lakeside resort of Laguna de Huacachina, a palm-fringed lagoon of jade-color waters whose sulfurous properties are reputed to have healing powers. The view is breathtaking: a collection of attractive, colonial-style hotels in front of a golden beach and with a backdrop of snow-covered peaks against the distant sky. In the 1920s Peru's elite traveled here for the ultimate holiday, and today the spacious resorts still beckon. The lake is also a pilgrimage site for those with health and skin problems, as well as sand boarders who want to tackle the 100-meter (325-foot) dunes and budget travelers who pitch tents in the sand or sleep under the stars.

Where to Stay & Eat

$–$$ ✕🏨 **Hotel Mossone.** A Spanish colonial–style courtyard lined with tall ficus
Fodor'sChoice trees is the focal point of this century-old mansion. Rooms look out onto
★ gardens overflowing with flowers, which partially hide the small, secluded pool and playground. The relaxed bar and restaurant have splendid lake views, and if you like the food you can book a room with full board. The hotel provides free bicycles and sand boards for guests, but if you're staying elsewhere you can still stop in for excellent *comida criolla* (cuisine rich in peppers, onions and other spices), especially *papa a la huancaina.* ✉ *Balneario de Huacachina* ☎ *056/213–630, 01/261–9605 in Lima* ↴ *41 rooms* ♿ *Restaurant, pool, lake, bicycles, bar, cable TV, minibars, room phones, playground, travel services* ▭ *AE, DC, MC, V.*

$ 🏨 **Hosteria Suiza.** Owner Heidi Baumgartner, daughter of Swiss hote-
Fodor'sChoice liers, runs this classy joint overlooking the lagoon. It's a step up from
★ the local hostels, with some balconies overlooking the oasis itself. A sitting room–library is replete with local archaeological relics, and a lovely garden leads to the pool, so you won't be in a rush to go anywhere. ✉ *Bal-*

neario de Huacachina ☎ 056/238–762 ⊕ *www.hostesuiza.5u.com*
⇨ *17 rooms* ⌂ *Restaurant, cable TV, pool, lake, bicycles, bar, travel
services* ⊟ *AE, DC, MC, V.*

Nazca

5 *120 km (75 mi) southeast of Ica.*

A mirage of green in the desert, lined with cotton fields and orchards
and bordered by crisp mountain peaks, Nazca has remained a quiet colonial town amid a cache of archaeological ruins. Set 598 meters (1,961
feet) above sea level, the town has a dry climate—scorching by day, nippy
by night—that was instrumental in preserving centuries-old relics from
Inca and pre-Columbian tribes. Overlooking the parched scene is the
2078-meter (6,815-foot) Cerro Blanco, the highest sand dune in the world.
In 1901 the area came came to the world's attention when Peruvian archaeologist Max Uhle excavated sites around Nazca and rediscovered
this unique culture. The area also has more than 100 cemeteries, where
the humidity-free climate has helped preserve priceless jewelry, textiles,
pottery, and mummies.

FodorśChoice
★

However, this area is most famous as the site of one of the world's greatest mysteries, the giant engravings—called the **Nazca Lines**—on the Pampas de San José, 20 km (12 mi) north of town. Discovered by scientist
Paul Kosok in 1929, the motifs were made by removing the surface stones
and piling them beside the lighter soil underneath. Figures, some measuring up to 300 meters (1,000 feet) across, include a hummingbird, a
monkey, a spider, a pelican, a condor, a whale, and an "astronaut." Probably the most famous person to investigate the origin of the Nazca Lines
was Kosok's translator, German scientist Dr. Maria Reiche, who studied the Lines from 1940 until her death in 1998.

8

Your best bet for exploring the area's archaeological sites and the Nazca
Lines is on a set tour, which usually covers all the major areas. You can
take a taxi to the *mirador* (observation platform) for around S/35, or
catch a morning bus there for only 50¢ (then hitchhike back). Nazca
Lines flights run S/104–S/180 depending on the season. Eager tour
guides waiting at the bus stop in Nazca offer S/87 tours that include flights
and a visit to the mummies at the Chauchilla cemetery.

Named for the German anthropologist who dedicated her life to studying the Nazca Lines, **Casa-Museo Maria Reiche** is considered to be one
of the best museums in the country. The first floor has extensive exhibits
of textiles, tools, musical instruments, mummies, and skeletons from the
Paracas, Nazca, Wari, Chincha, and Inca cultures. Upstairs are more modern displays of colonial paintings and furniture. There's a scale model
of the Nazca Lines behind the building. Take a micro from the Ormeño
terminal to the Km 416 marker (70¢) to reach the museum, which is 1
km (½ mi) from town. ⊠ *Pan-American Hwy., Km 416, San Pablo* ☎034/
255734 ⚏ *S/3.50* ⊗ *Daily 9–4.*

Everyone comes to Nazca for the lines, but it's well worth a visit to the
Tallera de Artesania de Andres Calle Flores. Mr. Flores is a 91-year-old

wonder who years ago discovered old pottery remnants and started making new pottery based on old designs and forms. Andres's son, Tobi, hosts a funny and informative talk in the kiln and workshop, and afterward you can purchase some beautiful pottery for S/30 to S/60. It's a quick walk across the bridge from downtown Nazca; at night, take a cab. ⊠ *Pje. Torrico 240, off Av. San Carlos* ☎ *56/522–319* 🖃 *Free* ☉ *By appointment only.*

The highlight of the private, Italian-run **Museo Antonini**, focusing on the Nazca culture, is its collection of painted textiles from the ancient adobe city of Cahuachi. This is also the place to see how local relics have been excavated and restored. In back is the stone Bisambra aqueduct, used for irrigating the fields of the Nazca. ⊠ *Av. de la Cultura 600* ☎ *034/ 265–421* 🖃 *S/5* ☉ *Weekdays 9–2, Sat. 9–noon.*

Around Nazca

In the midst of the pale, scorched desert, the ancient **Cementerio de Chauchilla** is scattered with sun-bleached skulls and shards of pottery. *Huaqueros* (grave robbers) have ransacked the site over the years, and now the mummies unearthed by their looting erupt from the earth in a jumble of bones and threadbare weavings. It's an eerie site, as the mummies still have hair attached, as well as mottled, brown-rose skin stretched around empty eye sockets and gaping mouths with missing teeth. Some are wrapped in tattered burial sacks, though the jewelry and ceramics with which they were laid to rest are long gone. Tours take about three hours and cost around S/2. Visits to the cemetery are also packaged with Nazca Lines flights. ⊠ *30 km (19 mi) from Nazca, the last 12 km (7 mi) of which is unpaved* ☎ *No phone* 🖃 *Free* ☉ *Daily 8–6.*

Within a walled, 4,050-square-yard courtyard west of the Nazca Lines are the **Cahuachi Pyramids,** an ancient ceremonial and pilgrimage site. Six adobe pyramids, the highest of which is about 21 meters (70 feet), stand above a network of rooms and connecting corridors. Grain and water silos are also inside, and several large cemeteries lie outside the walls. Used by the early Nazca culture, the site is estimated to have existed for about two centuries before being abandoned about AD 200. Cahuachi takes its name from *qahuachi* (meddlesome). El Estaquería, with its mummification pillars, is nearby. ⊠ *34 km (21 mi) west of Nazca* ☎ *No phone* 🖃 *Free* ☉ *Daily 8–5.*

Where to Stay & Eat

$ ✕ **La Taberna.** A fan slowly rotates above the churning bar crowd at this popular criollo restaurant, *the* watering spot in which to be seen. It's also one of the few places where you can leave your mark—literally— on walls decorated with a montage of international poems, art, and advice from former diners. Nightly Andean flute groups and local bands keep the place upbeat and relaxing. Ice-cold beer and perfect pisco sours complement the delectable *pescado a lo macho* (fish served over rice flavored with spices and extra ingredients like bits of scrambled egg), ceviche, and milder pasta choices. ⊠ *Calle Lima 321* ☎ *056/806—783* 🖃 *No credit cards.*

The Mystery of the Nazca Lines

ALL SORTS OF MYTHS are attached to the mysterious Nazca Lines, for no one knows their purpose or origin. Only a few cultures dared to brave this barren desert 20 km (12 mi) from the town of Nazca, including the Paracas from 200 BC to AD 600, the Nazca people from 300 BC to AD 700, and migrants from Ayacucho around AD 630. Thus theories abound about how any—or all—of these groups might have used the Lines, if indeed they made them.

Paul Kosok, an expert in ancient irrigation, was flying over the Nazca area on June 21, 1929, to document Inca irrigation patterns when he noticed the strange designs in the desert. He only spotted them because, coincidentally, the sunlight was at the southern hemisphere's winter equinox that day and highlighted the outlines of the designs. After Kosok told of his find, the area around Nazca was flooded with archaeologists and treasure hunters eager to figure out who had created the giant drawings— and see whether they had left valuables with them.

Dubbed the "Nazca Lines" by archaeologists for their proximity to town, the motifs were made by removing stones on the desert surface and piling them beside the lighter soil beneath. There are 11 major figures— including a hummingbird, a monkey, a spider, a pelican, a condor, and a whale—plus the mysterious "astronaut" and various triangles and trapezoids. Some measure up to 300 meters (1,000 feet) across and have been preserved for more than 2,000 years by a combination of gentle, cleansing winds and arid climate.

Because the Lines matched up to the sun at its equinox, Kosok maintained that the figures were some type of irrigation system marking the seasons. However, Kosok's translator, German scientist Dr. Maria Reiche, had other ideas, which she explored from 1940 until her death at 95 in 1998. She theorized that the Lines were made by the Nazca people as part of a vast astronomical calendar noting the rainy season in the highlands and seasonal changes in the regional climate. In 1976 she paid for the *mirador* (platform) 20 km (12 mi) north of town, from which the lizard, *arbos* (tree), and *manos* (hands) can be seen. She opened a small museum in 1994, and her book *Mystery on the Desert* is still a local bestseller.

Note that mid-morning is usually the best time to fly over the Lines, as earlier there is often a haze over the pampas, and later winds can make for a turbulent journey. The flight, which takes place in a small (and sometimes questionably rickety) propeller plane— and combines bright sunlight and strong fuel fumes with quick twists and turns, deep dives, and bumpy takeoffs and landings—is not for the queasy.

—By Holly S. Smith

8

¢ ✕ **El Griego Restaurant.** Huge portions of Peruvian specialties are served up to the backpacking crowd at this budget restaurant. It's all delicious, but go for the set *almuerzo* (mid-morning snack) or one of the hearty soups. Top it off with a pisco sour in the evening. ⊠ *Bolognesi 287* ☎ *056/ 521–480* ⊟ *No credit cards.*

Fodor'sChoice
★

$–$$ ✕🏠 **Hotel Nazca Lines.** The former home of Maria Reiche, this historic
Fodor'sChoice hacienda set around a shaded, sunken courtyard with a pool is the per-
★   fect spot from which to explore local mysteries. Built in the 1940s, the
hotel has long drawn international travelers and archaeologists, although the rooms have been updated over the decades to include air-
conditioning, hot water, and sunny private patios. Attractive decorative
touches such as charcoal sketches and wrought-iron headboards preserve the colonial feel. Delicious meals served on a tiled walkway beside the courtyard are worth the expense, and nonguests can have lunch
and use the pool for S/16. ✉ *Jr. Bolognesi* ☎ *034/522–293, 01/261–
9605 in Lima* ⬐ *78 rooms* ⛴ *Restaurant, tennis court, pool, bar,
lounge, laundry service, travel services; no phones in some rooms, no
TV in some rooms* ▤ *AE, DC, MC, V.*

★ ¢   🏠 **Hotel Alegría.** Renovated and spruced up in 2005, rooms and bungalows here have private baths and hot water, plus there's a pool to cool
off in after a dusty morning flying over the Nazca Lines. After dark, dance
the night away at the adjacent disco, then take a sunrise breakfast in
the coffee shop garden. This is a good place to clean up, wash clothes,
check e-mail (S/2 per hour), exchange paperbacks, and get organized
before heading off on another adventure. Staff travel experts offer general tourist info and guide recommendations, and there's a free nightly
video on the Lines at 9 PM. The hotel is sometimes full or closed, so call
first—and get a free ride from the bus station. ✉ *Calle Lima 166*
☎☎ *056/522–702* ⬐ *42 rooms, 3 bungalows* ⛴ *Coffee shop, cable TV,
pool, dance club, library, laundry service, Internet, travel services; no
room phones* ▤ *No credit cards* ❙❑❙ *BP.*

Cotahuasi Canyon

❻   *50 km (31 mi) north of Colca Canyon.*

Fodor'sChoice Colca Canyon may be the region's most famous natural attraction, but
★   at 3,354 meters (11,001 feet), Cotahuasi is the world's deepest gorge. Carved
by the Río Cotahuasi, which changes into Río Ocuña before connecting
to the Pacific, the canyon was declared a Zona de Reserva Turística in
1988. Its deepest point is at Ninochaco, below the quaint administrative
capital of Quechualla, and accessible only by kayak; in fact it was kayak
explorations that first documented the area in the mid-1990s.

The gateway to the canyon is Piro, from where it's three hours to Sipia
and the 150-meter (462-foot) Cataratas de Sipia waterfalls. Three hours
farther along a thin track against the canyon wall—which climbs 400
meters (1,312 feet) above the river in some places—you'll reach Chaupo,
a settlement surrounded by groves of fruit trees. You can camp here and
hike through Velinga to ruins at Huña before reaching Quechualla, where
you can see the ancient farming terraces of Maucullachta across the gorge.
When the Inca ruled, the road between Cusco and Puerto Inca followed
the canyon for much of the way.

The serene town of Cotahuasi is set high in the hills, where the clear air
at the 2,600-meter (8,528-foot) altitude perfectly suits its more than 4,000
residents. Their attractive, whitewashed colonial-style homes line slim,

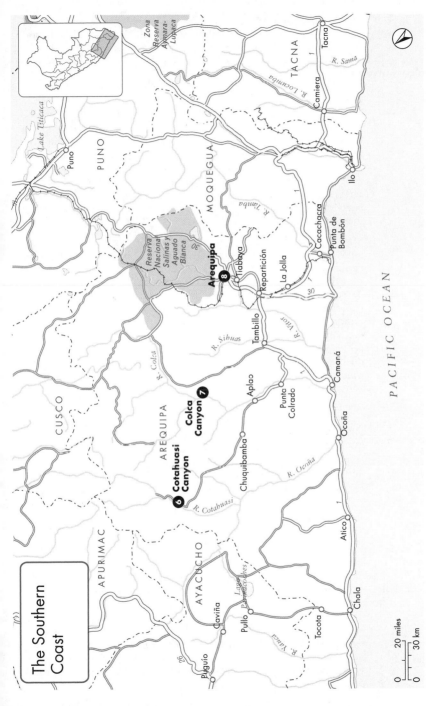

The Southern Coast

straight lanes before a backdrop of Cerro Hiunao. Winding upward ahead is the highway to Chuquibamba and the 5,425-meter (17,794-foot) slopes of Nevado Coropuna.

Colca Canyon

❼ *30 km (19 mi) north of Toro Muerto.*

Named for the stone warehouses (*colcas*) used to store grain by prehistoric Indians living along the walls of this wondrous gorge, Colca Canyon is one of Peru's most amazing natural sights. Carved into the foothills of the snow-covered Andes and sliced by the silvery Río Colca, this canyon is one of the world's deepest, some 3,182 meters (10,607 feet) down—twice as deep as the Grand Canyon. Flying overhead, you can't miss the green, fertile trough as it cuts through the barren terrain, but it's all an illusion; only scrub brush and cactus cling to the canyon's sheer basalt sides.

Most of those who live along the rim today are Collagua Indians, whose settlements date back more than 2,000 years. It is thought that this independent people came from higher regions in the Andes and were possibly descendents of the Aymaras. Their traditions persevered through the centuries, and they even kept their way of life during Inca times; in fact, stories have it that the Inca chief Mayta Capac married a Collagua princess and built her a gracious, copper bridal home near Sibayo. In these unspoiled Andean villages you'll still see Collaguas and Cabana people wearing traditional clothing and embroidered hats. Spanish influence is also on display in such rimside towns as Achoma, Maca, Pinchollo, and Yanque, where gleaming white *sillar* (volcanic-stone) churches add a colonial feel.

You wouldn't expect much wildlife in such a stark place, but Cruz del Condor is a haunt for the giant birds, particularly at dusk and dawn, when they soar on the winds rising from the deep valley. At 1,200 meters (4,000 feet), the "condor cross" precipice between the villages Pinchollo and Cabanaconde is the best place to spot them. View Colca early in the day, when it's full of low clouds, or at dusk when it glows with crimson light from the sunset. Trails are rough and unmarked, so you'll need a guide to explore, as well as good walking shoes. The most knowledgeable and experienced locals are in the villages Arequipa and Chivay on the south rim. Here you'll also find restaurants, hotels, and tourist facilities.

Where to Stay & Eat

$ **Colca Lodge.** The hotel's understated look, with adobe and clay walls
Fodor'sChoice and thatched roof, complement the surrounding terrain. The location
★ between Yanque and Ichupampa offers plenty to do, including daily canyon hikes, horseback rides, bike trips, trout fishing, and dips in hotel hot springs. Breakfast is included. ⊠ *Fundo Puye s/n, Yanque, Caylloma* ☎ *054/202–587* ⊕ *www.colca-lodge.com* ⬳ *25 rooms* ☆ *Restaurant, room service, minibars, pool, boating, fishing, mountain bikes, hiking, horseback riding, bar, laundry service, travel services; no room phones, no room TVs* ⊟ *AE, MC, V* ⦿ *BP.*

Outdoor Activities

There are plenty of places for tough hiking around the Colca Canyon, but paths aren't marked—so hire a guide. Travel agencies in Arequipa can arrange day treks and overnight adventures to the canyon for S/73–S/122, including accommodations, meals, a cultural show, and trips to hot springs and Cruz del Condor. The Río Colca is also known among kayakers and rafters for its terrific and thrilling white-water conditions. North of the canyon is a sheltered valley that runs east to west, allowing you to see the incredible changes in scenery along the way.

HIKING For about S/100 per day you can hire **Carlos Zárate Aventuras** (✉ Santa Catalina 204 ☎ 054/263–107 ⊕ www.zarateadventures.com) and his professional hiking and mountain guides, who conduct tours in Spanish, English, and French. Upscale travelers go with **Colonial Tours** (✉ San Martín 133 ☎ 054/232–461), an outfit that charges around S/87 per day for tours utilizing hotels and restaurants with better amenities. **Santa Catalina Tours** (✉ Santa Catalina 219 ☎ 054/216–994) runs slightly less expensive trips for about S/70 a day.

WHITE-WATER RAFTING Below Colca Canyon, conditions on the Río Majes are superb for white-water rafting. The best time to hit the Río Colca rapids is during the South American summer, December through March. Most travel agencies in Arequipa can arrange trips. **Majes Tours** (✉ Villa Flórida B-7, Cerro Colorado, Arequipa ☎ 054/255–819), one of the best agencies, offers trips down this part of the river. Accommodations are at a rustic lodge in Ongoro. Class IV, V, and VI rafting adventures through the Colca Canyon are operated May through September by **Apumayo Expediciones Peru** (✉ Garcilazo 265, Cusco ☎☎ 084/246–018 ⊕ www.apumayo.com).

Arequipa

8 *150 km (93 mi) south of Colca Canyon; 200 km (124 mi) south of Cotahuasi Canyon.*

Settled in a lush valley encircled by towering, snow-covered volcanoes, Arequipa glows with charm, light, and energy. The largest city between Lima and Santiago, Chile, and Peru's second-largest city after the capital, this settlement of 1 million residents grew from a collection of Spanish-colonial churches and homes constructed from brilliant white *sillar* (volcanic stone) gathered from the surrounding terrain. At an elevation of 2,300 meters (7,500 feet) above sea level, the city enjoys fresh, crisp air, as well as warm days averaging 23°C (73°F) and comfortable nights at 14°C (57°F). To make up for the lack of rain, the Río Chili waters the surrounding foothills, which were once farmed by the Inca and now stretch into rows of alfalfa and onions.

The town was a gathering of Aymara Indians and Inca when Pizarro arrived to name it "Villa Hermosa" on August 15, 1540. His proud Spanish traditions have carried on through the centuries, giving the settlement a distinct European flavor in the midst of the desert. After the Spanish arrived, the town grew into the region's most profitable center for farming and cattle-raising, and these businesses are still key to Arequipa's modern economy. By the 1800s Arequipa had more Spanish settlers than any town in the south.

The city's European look has been preserved over the centuries, and today Arequipa is said to have the most colonial architecture after Cusco. Due to its bleached, white sillar structures, Arequipeños now call their home "White City." This main economic center for the south is also called the "Independent Republic of Arequipa" by its proud residents, who have made several attempts to secede from Peru and even designed the city's own passport and flag. Each August 15, parades, fireworks, bull-fights, and dancing celebrate the city's founding. The combination of grace and conviviality has drawn many outsiders to move here, and the city's population has doubled in the last decade. Little wonder Arequipa received a designation as a World Cultural Heritage site by UNESCO.

What to See

La Compañía. Built by the Jesuits in 1525, this beautiful, bone-white series of buildings incorporates several decorative styles and touches. The side portal, built in 1654, and main facade, built in 1698, show examples of Andean mestizo style with carved flowers, spirals, birds—and angels with Indian faces—along gently curving archways and spiral pillars. Inside, **Capilla St. Ignatius** (St. Ignatius Chapel) has a polychrome cupola and original 17th-century oil paintings by Bernardo Bitti and other Cusco School artists. Hike up to the steeple at sunset for sweeping views of Arequipa bathed in golden light. The former monastery, now converted into shops, contains two cloisters which can be entered from General Morán or Palacio Viejo. The main building is on the southeast corner of the Plaza de Armas. ⊠ *General Morán at Alvarez Tomás* ☎ *No phone* 🖅 *Chapel S/4* ⊙ *Church weekdays 9–12:30 and 3–6, Sat. 3–6, Sun. 9–noon and 5–6.*

Convento de la Recoleta. One of Peru's most extensive and valuable libraries is in this 1648 Franciscan monastery. With several cloisters and museums on-site, it's a wonderful place to research regional history and culture. Start in the massive, wood-paneled, wood-floored library, where monks in brown robes quietly browse among 20,000 ancient books and maps, the most valuable of which were printed before 1500 and are kept in glass cases. Pre-Columbian artifacts collected by missionaries to the Amazon are on display in one area, and a selection of elegant colonial and religious artwork is in another. Guides are available (tip S/7 or so). To reach the monastery, cross the Río Chili by Puente Grau. ⊠ *Recoleta 117* ☎ *054/270–966* 🖅 *S/5* ⊙ *Mon.–Sat. 9–noon and 3–5.*

Fodor'sChoice
★
Convento de la Santa Catalina. A 5-acre complex of mud-brick, Iberian-style buildings surrounded by fortresslike walls and separated by neat, open plazas and colorful gardens, this working convent is a city in itself and one of Peru's most famed cultural treasures. Founded in 1579 and closed to the public for the first 400 years, Santa Catalina was an exclusive retreat for the daughters of Arequipa's wealthiest colonial patrons. Narrow streets run past the Courtyard of Silence, where teenage nuns lived during their first year, and the Cloister of Oranges, where nuns decorated their rooms with lace sheets, silk curtains, and antique furnishings. Though about 400 nuns once lived here, fewer than 30 do so today. Admission includes a one-hour guided tour (tip S/10–S/20) in

English. Afterward, head to the cafeteria for the nuns' famous *torta de naranja* (orange cake), pastries, and tea. ✉ *Santa Catalina at Ugarte* ☎ *054/229–798* 💵 *S/25* ⊗ *Daily 9–5; last entry at 4.*

La Mansión del Fundador. Alongside the Río Sabandía, La Mansión del Fundador is a beautifully restored colonial home and museum. First owned by Arequipa founder Don Garcí Manuel de Carbajal, the mansion has been painstakingly renovated with original furnishings and paintings. There's a cafeteria with a bar on-site. To reach the home, go past Tingo along Avenida Huasacanche. ✉ *Av. Paisajesta s/n, Socobaya, about 20 km (12.4 mi) outside of Arequipa* ☎ *054/442–460* 💵 *S/8* ⊗ *Daily 9–5.*

Mercado San Camilo. This jam-packed collection of shops sells everything from snacks and local produce to clothing and household goods. You can find it between Perú, San Camilo, Piérola, and Alto de la Luna. ✉ *San Camilo 352* ☎ *No phone* 💵 *Free* ⊗ *Daily 6–4.*

★ **Molino de Sabandía.** There's a colorful and complicated story behind the area's first stone *molina* (mill), 7 km (4 mi) southeast of Arequipa. Built in 1621 in the gorgeous Paucarpata countryside, the mill fell into ruin over the next century. Famous architect Luis Felipe Calle was restoring the Arequipa mansion that now houses the Central Reserve Bank in 1966 when he was asked to work on the mill project. By 1973, the restoration of the volcanic-stone structure was complete—and Calle liked the new version so much that he bought it, got it working again, and opened it for visitors to tour. Bring your swimsuit and walking shoes in good weather, as there's a pool and trails around the lovely countryside. Adjoining the site is Yumina, which has numerous Inca agricultural terraces, some of which are still in use today. If you're not driving, flag a taxi for S/14 or take a gray bus from Socabaya in Arequipa to about 2 km (1 mi) past Paucarpata. ✉ *Sabandia, 8 km (5 mi) south of Arequipa* ☎ *No phone* 💵 *S/7* ⊗ *Daily 9–5.*

Museo Histórico Municipal. In the 1804 Sala Naval building, this history museum provides an overview of Arequipa's development into a modern city, along with exhibits of local archaeology, natural history, and architecture. There are extensive displays of old photos, maps, paintings, and war memorabilia. ✉ *Plaza San Francisco 407* ☎ *No phone* 💵 *S/2* ⊗ *Weekdays 8–4.*

Museo Regional Histórico Etnologico de Arequipa. Three blocks from the Plaza de Armas, Dr. Asis Orlando Vela Flores, the lively museum owner and guide, will take you on a nonstop enthusiastic tour (in Spanish) of all things Arequipeño—from fighting cocks made of silver from the nearby Orcopampa Mine to a huge 120-square-foot blanket featuring the naturally occurring colors of llama wool. There's also a display of local coastal fishing baskets, and finally, an entire bedset made of alpaca wool. ✉ *Jerusalen 402* ☎ *No phone* 💵 *S/8* ⊗ *Daily 8:30–6:30.*

★ **Museo Santuarias de Andino.** This fascinating little museum at the Universidad Católica Santa Maria holds the frozen bodies of four young girls who were apparently sacrificed more than 500 years ago by the Inca to appease the gods. "Juanita," the first, was found in 1995 near the summit of Mt. Ampato by local climber Miguel Zarate and anthropologist Johan Reinhard. When neighboring Volcán Sabancaya erupted, the ice that held Juanita in her tomb melted and she rolled partway down the mountain and into a crater. English-speaking guides will show you around the museum, and you can watch a video detailing the expedition. No photographs are permitted. ⊠ *La Merced 110* ☎☎ *054/252–554* ⊕ *www.mountain.org* ⛩ *S/10* ⊙ *Mon.–Sat. 8–6, Sun. 9–3.*

Where to Eat

The west side of the Plaza de Armas has dozens of food stalls along the balcony above the Portal San Augustín. Although it's crowded on Sunday after the flag-raising and parade, this is a great place to sample local fare—look around and see what everyone else is ordering. If you're really hungry, you can even get half a grilled chicken for about S/14.

The first block of Calle San Francisco, north of the Plaza de Armas, is lined with cafés, restaurants, and bars. The Mercado San Camilo carries *queso Mejía* (Mejía cheese), a local specialty. *Queso helado* (frozen, fresh milk mixed with sugar and a sprinkling of cinnamon), toffee, and chocolate is an excellent Arequipan sweet, and if you're a chocolate addict, the La Ibérica factory on Jerusalén, northeast of Plaza de Armas, gives tours on weekdays.

$$$$ ✕ **Sol de Mayo** In the colonial Yanahuara neighborhood, this charming garden restaurant is worth the expense to taste true Arequipan cooking, which has been served here for more than a century. Specialties include *ocopa arequipeña* (boiled potato slices in spicy sauce and melted cheese), rocoto relleno, and other heat-intense fare. ⊠ *Jerusalén 207, Yanahuara* ☎ *054/254–148* ▭ *MC, V.*

$–$$$$ ✕ **Las Quenas.** Rustic and well-known, this restaurant filled with antiques and musical instruments offers complete immersion into Arequipan life and traditions. Lunch and tea are served daily, but set dinners are the specialty, served nightly except Sunday to the accompaniment of a live folkloric performance. Dinners start at 8, and there is an extra S/5 charge if you stay for the music. ⊠ *San Francisco 215* ☎ *054/281–115* ▭ *AE, DC, MC, V* ⊙ *Closed Sun.*

$ ✕ **El Conquistador Picantería.** You won't see any tourists at this tiny diner—but you will have the chance to rub shoulders (and perhaps share a pitcher of homemade sangria) with in-the-know locals who consider this the best food in Arequipa. Pork pie and pig's head salad are specialties, but you can also go for white-vegetable soup or the ubiquitous relleno. ⊠ *Bayoneta 106* ☎ *054/286–009* ▭ *No credit cards.*

¢ **Fory Fay Cevicheria.** The name of this local favorite stems from the standard price—45 soles—that owner Alex Aller used to charge for a meal. Ask any Arequipeño to name their favorite fish joint and this place will top the list. Aller, who grew up in the coastal port of Mollendo, still travels there daily to check on the catch. Fishing bric-a-brac and photos of New York, where Aller once lived, line the walls. Even if you're not hungry, order half a plate of the *ceviche mixto* for S/8 and enjoy. ⊠ *Alvarez Thomas 221* ☎ *054/242–400* ▭ *No credit cards.*

¢ ✕ **Laksmivan.** Beautiful watercolors by local artists decorate this harmonious little spot named for the goddess of spirits and nature. Popular with locals and budget travelers for more than 25 years, the restaurant is known for creating inexpensive vegetarian dishes that combine healthy ingredients with Peruvian flavorings. Sit outside in one of the courtyards to enjoy the lovely blossoms and birds. ⊠ *Melgar 104* ☏ *054/228–768* ▭ *No credit cards.*

¢ ✕ **Mixto's Cebichería.** Above the glowing white Catedral, this lovely, romantic spot serves up some of Arequipa's best seafood dishes. Ceviche is, of course, the focus, but you'll also find shellfish empanadas and mixed stews. If you're averse or allergic to ocean fare, don't worry; the restaurant also serves pastas, salads, and grilled meats. If the weather is warm, ask for a table on the terrace above the Catedral entrance. ⊠ *Pasaje Catedral 115* ☏ *054/205–343* ▭ *AE, MC, V.*

Fodor'sChoice ★

¢ ✕ **Sulz.** Come hungry to this spacious, elegant restaurant that serves Arequipan food at its best. Enormous rooms packed with tables accommodate the flood of local families and tourists. If you can't decide what to order from the extensive menu, choose the Triple, which includes *rocoto* (a large red chili pepper), *chicharran* (pork rind), and *patitas de carnero* (mutton in sauce). There's a S/25 fee for patrons on weekend and holiday nights, when the live orchestra plays to those on the dance floor. ⊠ *Progreso 202A* ☏ *054/449–787* ▭ *No credit cards.*

¢ ✕ **Zig Zag Creperie.** Everyone comes for the crêpes, served both filled and with sauce, as entrées and desserts. On the ever-changing menu, look for such crêpe specialties as the Cubana, filled with banana slices, sugar, and rum. If you're in the mood for more basic fare, try a mixed salad. There are also exotic fruit drinks like the *boa–boa* (tropical fruit punch). High-grade espresso drinks are served with such delicacies as chocolate gâteau. Look for the restaurant in the Alianza Francesa compound. ⊠ *Santa Catalina 208* ☏ *054/215–579* ▭ *MC, V.*

Fodor'sChoice ★

Where to Stay

★ $$–$$$ ✕⊡ **Hotel Libertador.** Amid beautiful, sprawling gardens, this 1940 Spanish colonial villa creates an oasis of Old Arequipa in the modern city. Handhewn sillar arches, wrought-iron window screens, and touches of Peruvian decor give this luxury hotel the intimate feel of an old family home. Breakfast on the terrace to absorb it all, then dip in a pool overlooking Volcán Misti and the Andean panorama. Nonguests can stop in the pubstyle bar or splurge on the continental delights at Restaurant Los Robles ($$). ⊠ *Plaza Bolívar, Selva Alegre* ☏ *054/215–110* ⊕ *www.libertador. com.pe* ⌁ *88 rooms, 6 suites* ⌂ *3 restaurants, room service, minibars, refrigerators, cable TV, pool, exercise equipment, gym, hot tub, massage, sauna, bar, shops, dry cleaning, laundry service, Internet, business services, meeting rooms, car rental, travel services* ▭ *AE, DC, MC, V.*

$ ✕⊡ **La Posada del Puente.** Rose blossoms spill over the grounds of this delightful hotel, set beside the Río Chili and overlooking Volcán Misti. The pastel-color rooms have charming art and antique furnishings, and two of the large suites have hot tubs. The cozy restaurant serves excellent pastas and a fine selection of Peruvian and Chilean wines. ⊠ *Av. Bolognesi 101, at end of Puente Grau* ☏ *054/253–132* ⊕ *www. posadadelpuente.com* ⌁ *20 rooms, 4 suites* ⌂ *Restaurant, some in-room hot tubs, cable TV, refrigerators, bar, library, laundry service, travel services* ▭ *AE, DC, MC, V* ⏏⊙I *BP.*

Fodor'sChoice ★

8

★ ¢　✕🏠 **La Casa de Melgar.** This 18th-century home centers on a beautiful tiled courtyard surrounded by fragrant blossoms and dotted with trees. The magnificent double rooms have towering vaulted ceilings, as well as private baths with hot water. The single suite has an original cookstove from when this was a private house. The café serves light continental and Peruvian meals. ✉ *Melgar 108* ☎ *054/222–459* 🌐 *www.lared. net.pe/lacasademelgar* 🛏 *30 rooms, 1 suite* ♿ *Café, cable TV, laundry service* ➡ *No credit cards.*

¢　🏠 **Hostal Santa Catalina.** A popular choice for the budget crowd, this
Fodor'sChoice hostel offers both shared and private quarters. The clean rooms, friendly
★ owners, dependable hot water, and laundry facilities attract repeat customers year-round, so call far ahead for reservations. It's a pleasant and homey place; kick back in the central courtyard and read your guidebook while your clothes hang to dry in the sunshine. ✉ *Santa Catalina 500* ☎ *054/243–705* 🌐 *www.hostalsantacatalina.com* 🛏 *8 rooms, 3 dorms* ♿ *Dining room, kitchen, library, laundry facilities, travel services; no room phones* ➡ *No credit cards.*

The South Essentials

Transportation

BY AIR

LanPeru has several daily flights between Lima and Rodríguez Ballón Airport, 7 km (4½ mi) from Arequipa. TANS Perú has one daily flight from Lima to Arequipa. Both airlines also operate daily flights to Juliaca, from which you can continue on to Puno and Lake Titicaca.

Nazca Lines tours on Aero Cóndor, which depart from the small Aeropuerto Nazca, cost S/191 for a 40-minute flight plus lunch, a tour of Nazca's archaeological museum, and a trip to the *mirador.* Note that these flights are often overbooked, year-round. Less expensive flights on Aero Ica and new upstarts Aero Montecarlo, Aero Palpa, Aeroparacas, Alas Peruanas, TAE, Travel Air, and Taxi Aereo have similar services. As these latter lines are small operations with varying office hours, check at the airport for current flight schedules. Most sightseeing flights depart from Nazca, although Aero Paracas also originates in Lima and Pisco. Make sure you arrive early to check-in for your flight, as many are full and there's a chance you'll get bumped if you're late.

Daily flights between Tacna and Arequipa take about 20 minutes and run about S/140. Note that there are no airport buses from Tacna, so you'll need to take a taxi for S/14 or walk the 5 km (3 mi) to town.

🚹 **Carriers Aero Condor** ✉ Juan de Arona 781, San Isidro, Lima ☎ 01/442–5215, 034/256–230 in Ica, 034/522–424 in Nazca 🌐 www.aerocondor.com.pe. **Aero Ica** ✉ Hotel Maison Suisse, Nazca ✉ Tudela and Varela 150, Lima ☎ 01/440–1030. **Aero Paracas** ✉ Santa Fe 270, Higuereta ☎ 01/271–6941 ✉ Hotel Paracas, Pisco ✉ Pan-American Hwy., Km 447 ☎ 034/522–688. **Lan** ✉ Av. José Pardo 269, Miraflores, Lima ☎ 01/213–8200 🌐 www.lan.com ✉ Portal San Augustín 109, Arequipa ☎ 054/201–100. **StarPerú** ☎ 511/705–9000 🌐 www.starperu.com. **TANS Perú** ✉ Av. Arequipa 5200, Miraflores, Lima ☎ 01/426–8480 🌐 www.tansperu.com.pe.

🚹 **Airport Information Aeropuerto Nazca** ☎ 034/523–854. **Rodríguez Ballón Airport** ☎ 054/443–464.

BY BOAT & FERRY

The deep-water Puerto General San Martín in Pisco is the major port of this region. Radisson Seven Seas Cruises runs trips along this coast, with shore excursions to Paracas Reserve and the Islas Ballestas, the Nazca Lines, Ica, Huacachina, and Tambo Colorado. Luxury travel services, including Crillón Tours, make hydrofoil trips across Lake Titicaca, including runs between the Peruvian and Bolivian borders. You take a bus from Puno to Copacabana, then catch a hydrofoil to Isla del Sol and Huatajata, Bolivia. Catamaran services, some by Transturin, also run from the dock at Chúa, Bolivia.

🚩 **Crillón Tours** ✉ 1450 Bayshore Dr., Suite 815, Miami, FL 33131 ☎ 305/358–5353. **Radisson Seven Seas Cruises** ⊕ www.rssc.com. **Transturin** ✉ Libertad 176, Puno ☎ 054/352–771 ✉ Portal de Panes 109, Cusco ☎ 054/222–332.

BY BUS

There is reliable, comfortable bus service throughout southern Peru, especially down the paved Pan-American Highway. From Lima to Ica it's 303 km (188 mi), from Lima to Nazca it's 443 km (275 mi), and from Nazca to Arequipa it's a 566-km (351-mi) journey that takes 8–12 hours. Delays due to mud slides or sand drifts are common.

🚩 **Bus Lines Cruz del Sur** ✉ Jr. Quilca 531, Lima ☎ 01/427–1311 ⊕ www.cruzdelsur. com.pe ✉ Av. Los Incas, Nazca ☎ 034/522–484. **Empresa José de San Martín** ✉ 2 de Mayo y San Martín, Pisco ☎ 034/543–167. **Ormeños** ✉ Lambayeque 180, Ica ☎ 056/215–600 ✉ Av. Los Incas, Nazca ☎ 034/561–432 ✉ Av. San Francisco, Pisco ☎ 034/532–764. **Paracas Express** ✉ Pan-American Hwy., Km 447, Pisco ☎ 034/533–623. **Wari Tours** ✉ Pan-American Hwy., Nazca ☎ 034/534–967.

BY CAR

The Pan-American Highway runs down the length of southern Peru, some of it along the coast, some through desert, and some over plateaus and mountains. It's all paved and in good condition, but you should have fully equipped first-aid and repair kits packed. Besides breakdowns, hazards along this road include potholes, rock slides, sandstorms, and heat. Fortunately, you'll find many service stations along this route, most of which have clean bathrooms, convenience stores, and snack counters. Most are also full-service, meaning that your gas is pumped, your windshield cleaned, and your oil checked for free. Off the highway, however, conditions are less predictable. Roads may be in particularly poor condition in the eastern highlands and around the Paracas Reserve. Four-wheel-drive vehicles are recommended for all driving except within major cities. The Touring and Automobile Club of Peru, in Arequipa and Ica, provides maps and details on routes.

The major international agencies, including Avis, Budget, and Hertz, all have branches in south Peru. Local agencies such as Exodo also provide high-quality service. Office hours are usually 8–1 and 3–6 weekdays, and 9–1 Saturday, except at the Arequipa airport, where agencies may be open 24 hours. You can pick up your car at one end of the region and drop it off at the other, but there may be a hefty fee.

🚩 **Touring y Automóvile Club del Perú** ✉ Goyeneche 313, Arequipa ☎ 054/215–640 ✉ Manzanilla 523, Ica ☎ 056/235–061.

8

⊞ Car Rentals Avis G&B ✉ Palacio Viejo 214, Arequipa ☎ 054/443-576 ⊕ www.avis. com ✉ Rodriguez Ballón Airport, Arequipa ☎ 054/443-576. **Exodo** ✉ Manuél Belgrado F-1, Urb. Alvarez Thomas, Arequipa ☎ 054/423-756.

BY TRAIN

Three times a week, PeruRail runs a train between Arequipa and Puno, via Juliaca. Be sure to request the safer, more comfortable—and heated— Pullman "Inka Service," which costs about S/100 each way. The trip takes about 11 hours. There is also service between Arequipa and Cusco. For a full listing of PeruRail trips, check out www.orient-express.com.

⊞ PeruRail ✉ Av. Tacna and Arica 201, Arequipa ☎ 054/215-350 ⊕ www.orient-express.com.

Contacts & Resources

TOUR & TRAVEL AGENCIES

Travel agencies in Lima offer three- to seven-day tours of Arequipa, Paracas, Ica, Nazca, and Lake Titicaca. Try Explorandes, Hirca Travel, Lima Tours, Peru Chasquitur, or Receptour.

From Arequipa, tours to Colca and Cotahuasi canyons can be arranged with local operators. Try Condor Travel Arequipa, G.A. Travel Expert, Santa Catalina Tours, or Transcontinental Tours. The Arequipa office of Lima Tours offers a two-day, one-night tour of Colca Canyon. Holley's Unusual Tours runs four-wheel-drive expeditions to area ruins.

In Ica, Costa Linda and Pelican Travel Service offer tours of the city and can arrange trips to Paracas National Park and the Nazca Lines. Guided tours of Paracas National Park and the Ballestas Islands are offered by Ballestas Travel Service. Most hotels can arrange tours of the Nazca Lines, but several travel companies also specialize in local explorations. The going rate for a flight over the lines ranges US$40–US$60, depending on the season. Book ahead, because the flights are often sold out. The inexpensive Alegría Tours includes stops at several archaeological sites, with maps, guides, and options for hiking the area. Nasca Trails arranges flights over the Nazca Lines, trips to the Pampas Galeras vicuña reserve, and tours of the Cementerio Chauchills.

Guides often hassle tired new arrivals at airports, bus stations, and hotels. Don't be pressured to book a hotel or tour right away. Ask for recommendations from other travelers, and make sure the guide or agency is licensed and experienced. Finally, professional guides must be approved by the Ministry of Tourism, so ask for identification before you hire.

⊞ Arequipa Area Condor Travel Arequipa ✉ Av. Puente Bolognesi 120, Arequipa ☎ 054/218-362. **G.A. Travel Expert** ✉ Santa Catalina 312, Arequipa ☎ 054/247-722. **Lima Tours** ✉ Belén 1040, Lima ☎ 01/424-5110 ✉ Santa Catalina 120, Arequipa ☎ 054/242-271. **Santa Catalina Tours** ✉ Jerusalén 400-D, Arequipa ☎⊟ 054/216-991. **Transcontinental Tours** ✉ Puente Bolognesi 132, Arequipa ☎ 054/213-843.

⊞ Ica Ica Desert Trip Peru (Roberto Penny Cabrera) ✉ Bolivar 178, Ica ☎ 034/233-921 or 034/962-4868.

⊞ Nazca Lines Alegría Tours ✉ Calle Lima 168, Nazca ☎ 034/522-985. **Nasca Trails** ✉ Ignacio Morsequi, Nazca ☎ 034/522-858.

⊞ Paracas & Islas Ballestas Blue Sea Tours ✉ Chosica 320, San Andrés ☎ 034/533-469. **Ballestas Travel Service** ✉ San Francisco 249, Pisco ☎ 034/533-095. **Costa**

Linda ✉ Prolongación Ayabaca 509, Ica ☎ 056/234-251. **Paracas Islas Tours** ✉ Comercio 128, Pisco ☎ 034/665-872. **Pelican Travel Service** ✉ Independencia 156, Galerías Siesta, Ica ☎☎ 056/225-211.

🔳 **General Tours Explorandes** ✉ San Fernando 320, Lima ☎ 01/442-1738 or 01/445-0532. **Hirca Travel** ✉ Bellavista 518, Miraflores, Lima ☎ 01/242-0275. **Holley's Unusual Excursions** ✉ Casilla 77, Arequipa ☎ 054/224-452 **Lima Tours** ✉ Belén 1040, Lima ☎ 01/424-5110 ✉ Santa Catalina 120, Arequipa ☎ 054/242-271. **Peru Chasquitur** ✉ Mariano de los Santos 183, San Isidro, Lima ☎ 01/441-1279. **Receptour** ✉ Av. Alvarez Calderón 155, Suite 304, San Isidro, Lima ☎ 01/221-3341.

VISITOR INFORMATION

Information on all areas of Peru can be obtained from PromPerú. In Arequipa the Oficina de Información Turística is helpful. The Tourist Office across from the Convento de Santa Catalina (Santa Catalina 120) is open 9–9 daily; there's also an airport office. The Oficina de Información Turística in Ica, near the intersection of Avenidas Grau and Jirón Ayacucho and a block east of the Plaza de Armas, is open weekdays 8–3:30. The Tourist Office on Cajamarca is open weekdays 7:30–3. For information on Colca Canyon or Paracas National Park, contact the Lima-based Inrena.

🔳 **Inrena** ✉ Petirrojos 355, Urbanización El Palomar, San Isidro, Lima ☎ 01/441-0425. **Oficina de Información Turística** ✉ Portal de la Municipalidad 112, Plaza de Armas, Arequipa ☎ 054/211-021. **Tourist Office** ✉ La Merced 117, Arequipa. **Inrena** ✉ Petirrojos 355, Ica ☎ 01/441-0425. **Tourist Office** ✉ Cajamarca 179, Ica. **PromPerú** ☎ 01/224-3125 or 01/224-3118 ⊕ www.peru.org.pe.

PUNO & LAKE TITICACA

8

According to legend, under orders from their father, the Sun God, the first Inca, Manco Cápac and his sister Mama Ocllo emerged from the deep blue waters of Lake Titicaca and founded the Inca empire. There is no documentation describing when this reportedly happened, but as one watches the mysterious play of light on the water and the shadows on the mountains, the myth seems almost believable. This is the altiplano—the high plains of Peru, where the earth has been raised so close to the sky that the area takes on a luminous quality.

Puno

975 km (609 mi) southeast of Lima.

Puno is a small town with a small-town friendliness, and chances are, whatever you need can be found along the street called Jirón Lima, between Pino Park (sometimes called Parque San Juan) and the Plaza de Armas. At 3,825 meters (12,550 feet) above sea level, Puno will be a challenge to your system, so eat lightly, go easy on alcoholic drinks, forgo your morning jog, and take it easy for a day or two after you fly in.

In Spain, a *corregidor* was a government official who acted as judge and juror and collected taxes, a job apparently held by a Catholic priest, Silvestre de Valdés, who was also in charge of the construction of Puno's Cathedral in 1668 and lived in **La Casa del Corregidor** across the street.

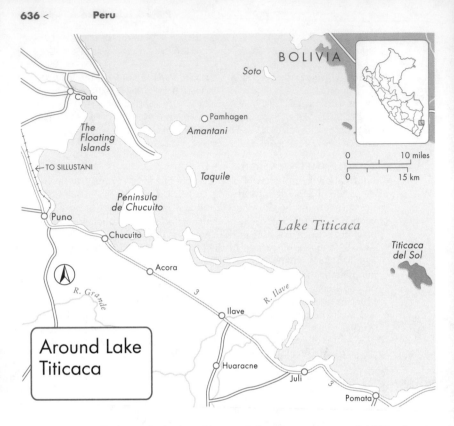

BOLIVIA

Soto

Coata

Pamhagen

The
Floating
Islands

Amantani

←TO SILLUSTANI

Taquile

Peninsula
de Chucuito

Puno

Lake Titicaca

Chucuito

Titicaca
del Sol

Acora

R. Grande

3

R. Ilave

Ilave

Around Lake
Titicaca

Huaracne

Juli

3

Pomata

0 — 10 miles
0 — 15 km

The house had a long history of changing owners until 1995, when its present owner, Sra. Ana Maria Piño Jordán, bought it at public auction. With the help of volunteers she converted it into a cultural center, and it is now a pleasant place to drop in for sandwiches, drinks, or light snacks served in its early 1900's-style café and bar. There's also an Internet center that charges a mere 85 (US) cents an hour. Local art displays and music events take place in the exhibition hall, and the research library has documents in Spanish on Puno, the altiplano, and the Andes. ✉ *Deustua 576* ☎ *051/351–921* ⊕ *www.casadelcorregidor.com.pe* ☉ *Late Jan.–late Dec., Tues.–Sun. 10–10.*

Puno's principal museum, **Museo Dreyer,** is a block from the Plaza de Armas, with exhibits of pre-Hispanic and colonial art, weavings, gold, silver, and copper works, a coin collection, delicate Aymará pottery, pre-Inca stone sculptures, and historical documents in Spanish on the founding of Puno. ✉ *Conde Lemos 289* 🖅 *S/5* ☉ *Weekdays 7:30 AM–11 PM.*

The 18th-century **Iglesia San Juan Bautista** has been entrusted with the care of the *Virgin of the Candlemas,* the focus of Puno's most important yearly celebration in February, the Festival de la Virgen de la Candelaria. The statue rests on the main altar. Also here are the Virgin's more than

100 elaborate robes and cloaks. ✉ *Jr. Lima and Parque Pino.*

The restored Victorian iron ship **El Yavari** was built in Birmingham, England, in 1862. It was then dismantled, and its 1,383 pieces were loaded onto a freighter and shipped to the Port of Arica on the Pacific coast. The pieces were then carried by mules and porters across the Andes mountains to Puno. The journey took six years and it was Christmas Day, 1870, before it was reassembled and launched on Lake Titicaca. It is now a museum,

> **WORD OF MOUTH**

"In Puno, the Uros islands and people are not to be missed. Puno has an expansive street market, with a section dealing in all the miniature items you can imagine: miniature tools, miniature money, miniature suitcases, etc. People believe that if you buy a miniature item, e.g. a college diploma, it will become true."   –kathleen

docked at the end of a pier. After remaining idle for 40 years, the vessel took a trial run in 1999 after volunteers rebuilt its engine. If the ship is brought up to code, it might one day cruise the lake again. ✉ *Pier behind Posada del Inca Hotel, at end of Av. El Puerto* ☎ *051/369–329* ⊕ *www.yavari.org* ✉ *Donation* ⊙ *Daily 8–5.*

Where to Stay & Eat

Not all Puno hotels are adequately heated, and the town gets cold at night, so when you register, ask about heating. You're in luck if there's an electric space heater in your room. Prices can jump as much as 30% during the most popular festivals in February and November—reserve at least a month ahead if you're visiting then. You can bargain for a hotel room, but check it out before checking in, and ask if there's 24-hour hot water. Most hotels in the small towns outside Puno are run-down and not recommended.

¢–$$ **✕ La Casona.** Walking into this restaurant along Puno's main street is
Fodor'sChoice like entering a museum. It's filled with antiques, with an especially in-
★ teresting display of antique irons. The large space is divided into small, intimate rooms, and lace tablecloths give you the feeling of having dinner at great-grandma's. Try local fare, such as *lomo de alpaca* (alpaca steak) or one of their thick soups (the cream of quinoa is amazing) made with vegetables and meat or fish. Ask for the set menu and have a great meal for under US$5, and a pisco sour for under US$2. ✉ *Av. Lima 775* ☎ *051/351–108* ▭ *MC, V.*

★ ¢–$ **✕ Apu Salkantay.** Even though it's a favorite with tourists and locals, you can usually manage to get a table. A fire is always burning in the wood stove and their set menu is a bargain. *Trucha ahumadas* (smoked trout), alpaca steaks, pizza, and vegetarian dishes prepared with natural ingredients are also on the menu. Live folkloric music begins nightly at 8 PM. If the evening chill has your teeth chattering, across the street is Qori Chaska Artesanias (handicraft store) where you can pick up an inexpensive handknit alpaca sweater. ✉ *Lima 425* ☎ *051/363–955* ▭ *No credit cards.*

★ ¢–$ **✕ La Plaza.** Prices are inversely proportional to the large portions at this kid-friendly restaurant. Try hearty regional dishes like *chairo puneño* (soup with dehydrated potatoes and beef), *cuy* (guinea pig), and *trucha* (trout). Sandwiches, pasta, and chicken dishes are also available. Order ice cream for dessert. Dancers perform in the evenings, with piano music between shows. A separate location named La Hosteria, two blocks away on Avenida Lima, is under the same ownership and has the same kind of menu. ⊠ *Jr. Puno 419, Plaza de Armas* 🕾 *051/351–424* ▤ *AE, DC, MC, V.*

★ **$$$** ▥ **Libertador Hotel Isla Esteves.** A gleaming white low-rise hotel, the Libertador is 5 km (3 mi) from Puno—40 minutes from the Juliaca (Puno) airport, and is the area's most luxurious lodging. On Isla Esteves, an island in Lake Titicaca, it is connected to the mainland by a causeway. In back of the hotel steps lead up to a small sitting area where you can watch the sun rise over Lake Titicaca. Play billiards in the game room, go to the discotheque, or relax in the piano bar. Taxis are the only way to get to the center of town—about US$2 and usually a little cheaper on the return. You can catch a taxi around Parque Pino on Calle Lima. ⊠ *Isla Esteves* 🕾 *051/367–780* ⊕ *www.libertador.com.pe* ⇱ *123 rooms, 11 suites* ⚅ *Restaurant, health club, bar, dance club* ▤ *AE, DC, MC, V* ⎸◎⎸ *BP.*

$$ ▥ **Posada del Inca.** The warmth of Indian weavings, polished wood, and
Fodor'sChoice native art give character to this thoroughly modern Sonesta hotel on the
★ shores of Lake Titicaca. It is 5 km (3 mi) from the center of town and has its own dock that extends out into the lake with the *El Yavari*, the world's oldest motorized iron ship anchored at the end. Hydrofoils to Copacabana and the Sun and Moon Islands on the Bolivian side of Lake Titicaca also leave from the Posada's dock. Eating in the hotel's restaurant is a pleasure, as large picture windows offer you a panoramic view of the lake. There's a safe deposit box for your valuables and rooms have heaters. ⊠ *Sesqui Centenario 610, Sector Huaje* 🕾 *051/364–111* ⊕ *www.sonesta.com* ⇱ *62 rooms* ⚅ *Restaurant, cable TV, lounge, business services, meeting rooms* ▤ *AE, DC, MC, V* ⎸◎⎸ *BP.*

$ ▥ **Colon Inn.** Once a tiny 19th-century colonial house that evolved into
Fodor'sChoice a mansion, this Best Western property is now a gracious inn with such
★ modern amenities as heaters, private baths with hot water, and Internet service for around US$2 an hour. The staff is fluent in English, French, and Spanish, and they also know how to make pizza. It is close to the central handicrafts market; about five blocks northeast of the Plaza de Armas and 3 km (2 mi) west of Lake Titicaca. The inn is listed as a National Historic Monument. Airport transfers are available for US$10. ⊠ *Calle Tacna 290* 🕾 *051/351–432* ⊕ *www.coloninn.com* ⇱ *21 rooms* ⚅ *2 restaurants, pub, cable TV, Internet* ▤ *AE, MC, V* ⎸◎⎸ *BP.*

Shopping

Model reed boats, small stone carvings, and alpaca-wool articles are among the local crafts sold at Puno's **Mercado Artesanal** (Handicrafts Market) near the train station, two blocks east of Parque Pino around Calle Arbula and Avenida Los Incas. Don't be fooled by the market's shabby appearance—some of the country's highest-quality alpaca sweaters are sold here, and if you find you aren't dressed for Puno's chilly evenings, it's the place to buy a good woolen pancho for less than US$10. A miniature reed boat is a nice souvenir for a younger relative. It's also interesting to stroll by the produce section and see the many varieties and colors of potatoes. There are no set hours, but the vendors are there daily, roughly 8–6. Make sure you know where your wallet or purse is while you're snapping photos.

Lake Titicaca

Forms Puno's eastern shoreline.

The border between Peru and Bolivia runs right through Lake Titicaca. The largest piece of Peru's part of the lake is to the northwest, and Puno also has the largest port. Bolivia's side, however, takes in two very important islands, Isla del Sol and Isla de la Luna. Lake Titicaca draws visitors both with its scenery and with the vivid Quechua and Aymará cultures that still thrive on its shores. Some 3,845 meters (12,500 feet) above sea level, it is the highest navigable lake in the world. The Bahía de Puno, separated from the lake proper by the two jutting peninsulas of Capaschica and Chucuito, is home to the descendents of the primitive Uro people, who are now mixed with the Aymará and Quechua. The lakeshores are lush with totora reeds—valuable as building material, cattle fodder, and, in times of famine, food for humans.

The Floating Islands
10 km (6 mi) northeast of Puno.

Even though the Uros Islands, a group of 40 floating islands in Lake Titicaca near Puno, have been called floating souvenir stands by some visitors, they still provide a glimpse of one the region's oldest cultures. The closest group of "floating museums" is 10 km (6 mi) from Puno and occupies a large part of the Lake Titicaca National Reserve. These man-made islands of woven totora reeds illustrate a form of human habitation that evolved over centuries. The islanders make their living by fishing, trapping birds, and selling visitors well-made miniature reed boats, weavings, and collages depicting life on the islands. You can walk around the springy, moist islands or hire an islander to take you for a ride in a reed boat. Progress has come to some of the islands in the form of solar-powered energy and microwave telephone stations. Seventh Day Adventists converted the inhabitants of one island and built a church and school, the only structures not made of mud and reeds.

Taquile & Amantani
Taquile 35 km (22 mi) west of Puno. Amantani 45 km (28 mi) northwest of Puno; 10 km (6 mi) north of Taquile.

Unlike the floating islands, which are in the Bay of Puno, Taquile and Amantani are in Lake Titicaca proper and are surrounded by a vast, ocean-like panorama. The proud, Quechua-speaking people of Taquile, where the hills are topped with Inca and Tiahuanaco ruins, weave some of Peru's loveliest textiles. Amantani, also with pre-Columbian ruins, has a larger, mainly agrarian society.

For a day visit to the islands, take one of the agency tours that leave at around 7:30 AM and include a trip to one of the floating islands. If you want to make an overnight stay on Taquile or Amantani (which is recommended), travel instead on the slower local ferry, since there are sometimes problems with the agency services if you try to break your trip and continue the next day. Lodging costs about US$4, and you stay in a local home. Nights can be cold and blankets inadequate, so you may wish to take along a sleeping bag. Bring your own water or water-purification tablets. There are two ways to reach the top of Taquile—you can climb up the 535 stone steps, or take the long way up a path that eventually brings you to the top.

Amantani, the lesser-known of the two islands, is 45 km (28 mi) from Puno. Travel time between the two islands is around two hours. Amantani also welcomes visitors for overnight home stays, but conditions are not as comfortable or as advanced as on Taquile.

Puno & Lake Titicaca Essentials

Transportation

BY AIR
LanPeru flies from Lima to Aeropuerto Manco Cápac in Juliaca. From the airport, you can arrange transportation to your hotel in Puno. Make arrangements through a travel agency, take a taxi, or share a minibus.
🚹 **Aeropuerto Manco Cápac, Juliaca** ☎ 051/322-905. **LanPeru** ☎ 051/367-227.

BY BOAT & FERRY
The easiest and most pleasant way to cross the border between Peru and Bolivia is to book passage on the comfortable hydrofoils operated by Crillón Tours between Puno on the Peruvian side and Copacabana on the Bolivian side. Hydrofoils leave Puno Tuesday, Thursday, and Saturday, and from Copacabana to Puno on Wednesday, Friday, and Saturday. Once you make the crossing, you can choose to go from Copacabana to Sun Island to spend some time, then to Huatajata harbor to relax at the Inca Utama complex before returning via the same route to Peru, or go on to La Paz for a few days. Once in La Paz, LAB, the Bolivian airline, flies three times a week to Cusco, Peru, and daily between La Paz, Santa Cruz, and Miami, Florida.
🚹 **Crillón Tours** ✉ Av. Camacho 1223, La Paz ☎ 02/233-7533 ⊕ www.titicaca.com.

BY BUS
Peru has good bus service between cities. The road between Arequipa and Puno is completely paved. Service is also good between Puno and Cusco, and so is the road between Puno and Copacabana in Bolivia. Cruz del Sur and CIVA have offices in Puno. It is best to buy your tickets ahead of time, either from the bus-company offices or—preferably—from a travel agency that can give you all the options. For your comfort and safety, take the best service you can afford. The distance between Puno and Cusco is 394 km (245 mi.)
🚹 **Bus Information Cruz del Sur** ✉ Av. El Sol 568 ☎ 051/352-451 ⊕ www.cruzdelsur. com.pe. **CIVA** ✉ Melgar 389 ☎ 051/356-882.

Contacts & Resources

TOUR OPERATORS
Excursions to the floating islands of the Uros as well as to Taquile and Amantani can be arranged through tour agencies in Puno. Most tours

depart between 7:30 and 9 AM, as the lake can become choppy in the afternoon. You also can take the local boat at the Puno dock for about the same price as a tour, although boats don't usually depart without at least 10 passengers.

Allways Travel ✉ Tacna 234 ☎ 051/355-552 ⊕ www.allwaystravelperu.com. **Condor Travel** ✉ Jr. Melgar 173 ☎ 051/352-632 ⊕ www.condortravel.com.pe. **Edgar Adventures** ✉ Jr. Lima 328 ☎ 051/353-444. **Grace Tours** ✉ Lima 385 ☎☎ 051/355-721. **Kontiki Tours** ✉ Jr. Melgar 188 ☎☎ 051/353-473. **Receptour** ✉ Lima 419, Suite 205 ☎ 051/352-391. **Rey Tours** ✉ Tarapacá 399 ☎ 051/352-061. **Solmartour** ✉ Jr. Libertad 229-231 ☎ 051/622-043. **Turpuno** ✉ Lambayeque 175 ☎☎ 054/351-431.

VISITOR INFORMATION

Información Turística ✉ Lima 582 and Ayacucho 682, Puno ☎ 051/364-976. **Touring and Automobile Club of Peru** ✉ Titicaca 531, Puno ☎ 051/352-432.

CUSCO & ENVIRONS

By Jeffrey Van Fleet

Bienvenidos a la ciudad imperial del Cusco," intones the flight attendant's announcement when your plane touches down. "Welcome to the imperial city of Cusco." This royal greeting hints at what you're in for in Cusco, one of the world's great travel destinations. The city has stood for nine centuries in this fertile Andean valley, 3,500 meters (11,500 feet) above sea level. Once the capital of the Inca empire, Cusco fell to Spanish conquistadors in 1533, at a time when the empire was weakened from civil war.

After the conquest of the Inca empire, the new colonists overlaid a new political system and new religion onto the old. They also literally superimposed their architecture, looting former structures of their gold, silver, and stone, grafting their own churches, monasteries, convents, and palaces onto the foundations of the Inca sites. The Spanish architecture does appear sloppy compared with precise stonework visible in the city's early walls and foundations. The juxtaposition can be jarring as in the case of the Santo Domingo church built on top of the Qorikancha, the Temple of the Sun. The cultural combination appears in countless other ways, too: witness the pumas carved into the cathedral doors. In addition, the city also gave its name to the Cusqueña school of art, in which New World artists combined Andean motifs with European-style painting, usually on religious themes. You'll chance on paintings that could be by Van Dyck but for the Inca robes on New Testament figures.

Throughout the Cusco region you'll witness this odd juxtaposition of imperial and colonial, indigenous and Spanish. Traditionally clad Quechua-speaking women sell their wares in front of a part-Inca, part-colonial structure as a business executive of clearly European heritage walks by carrying on a cell-phone conversation. The two cultures coexist, but have not entirely embraced each other almost five centuries after the conquest.

8

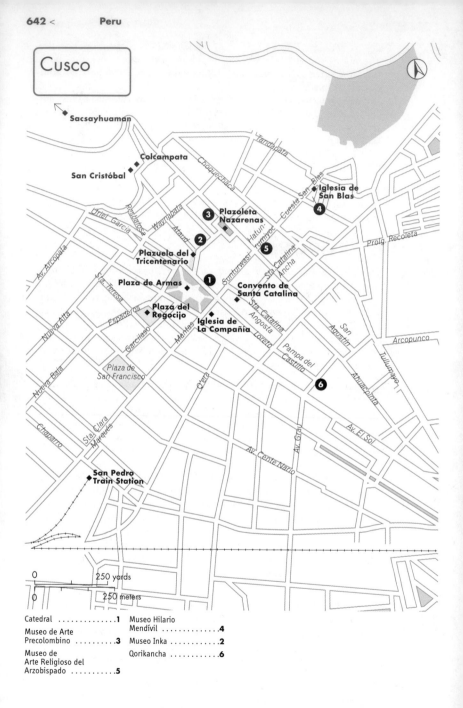

Cusco

Sacsayhuaman

Colcampata

San Cristóbal

Plazoleta Nazarenas

3

2

Iglesia de San Blas

4

Plazuela del Tricentenario

5

Plaza de Armas

1

Convento de Santa Catalina

Plaza del Regocijo

Iglesia de La Compañia

Plaza de San Francisco

6

San Pedro Train Station

0   250 yards

0   250 meters

Exploring Cusco

If you arrive in Cusco with the intention of hopping on the train to Machu Picchu the next morning, you'll probably only have time to take a stroll though the Plaza de Armas and visit Qorikancha (Temple of the Sun) and the Catedral. However, we recommend spending at least two days in Cusco before venturing off to Machu Picchu, giving yourself time to acclimate to the altitude and get to know this city of terra-cotta roofs and cobblestone streets.

A special note: In an effort to protect historical artifacts from light, guards in Cusco's museums and churches are notoriously watchful about prohibiting all types of photography, flash or not, still or video, within their confines. The exception is the Qorikancha, which allows limited photography, but not of the fragile Cusqueña-school paintings on its walls. Also, guide services in English are included with the admission price at many Cusco sights. Tipping is not expected.

Around the Plaza de Armas

TIMING &
PRECAUTIONS

Most of Cusco's main attractions lie within striking distance of its historic center, whose heart is the Haukaypata, more commonly known as the Plaza de Armas. The cathedral and the Inca museum warrant about an hour each. The neighborhood is safe, but the standard precautions about staying alert and watching your things apply.

WHAT TO SEE

❶

Fodor'sChoice

★

Catedral. The baroque-style cathedral is built on the foundations of the palace of the Inca Wirachocha. Construction began in 1550, using many stones looted from the site of the hillside Sacsayhuamán fortress, and ended a century later. It is considered one of the most splendid Spanish-colonial churches in the Americas. Within its high walls are some of the best examples of the Cusqueña school of painting, including a Marcos Zapata painting of the Last Supper with a local specialty, *cuy* (guinea pig), as the main dish.

The cathedral's centerpieces are its massive, solid-silver altar, and the enormous 1659 María Angola bell, the largest in South America, which hangs in one of the towers and can be heard from miles away. Behind the main altar is the original wooden *altar primitivo* dedicated to St. Paul. The 64-seat cedar choir has rows of carved saints, popes, and bishops, all in stunning detail down to their delicately articulated hands.

Normal access to the cathedral is through the adjoining Sagrada Familia church, the structure on the left as you face the cathedral. You then pass through the cathedral itself, and exit via the Iglesia del Triunfo, the city's first Christian church. Pause before leaving the Triunfo to note the two altars flanking the exit. One holds a rustic Andean carving of Christ, the other a more traditional Spanish version. A small army of top-notch guides waits at the entrance to the complex and can guide you through all that you see in Spanish, English, French, Italian, or German. Their services are included in your admission price. ⊠ *Haukaypata (Plaza de Armas)* ☎ *084/254–285* 💲 *S/13 or Boleto Integral* ☉ *Daily 10–6.*

CLOSE UP

Buying a Boleto Turístico

INNUMERABLE TRAVEL AGENCIES in Cusco will try to sell you a package tour of the city and region, including Machu Picchu and some of the Sacred Valley sights. If you prefer to travel independently, you can purchase a *boleto turístico* (tourist ticket) for S/70, or S/35 with an international student ID. Travel agencies include the ticket in packages, but you can buy one on your own at either location of the **Oficina Ejecutiva del Comité Boleto Turístico** (OFEC ✉ Av. El Sol 103 ☎ 084/227-037 ✉ Garcilaso and Heladeros ☎ 084/226-919 ⊕ www. boletoturisticodelcusco.com), open Monday through Saturday 8 to 5 and Sunday 8 to 2.

The ticket is valid for 10 days for one entry to each of 16 major attractions, including churches, convents, museums, and archaeological sites in and around Cusco and the Sacred Valley. (Machu Picchu is *not* included.) Purchasing the tourist ticket is the *only* way to guarantee entry to the participating sites. In theory, each individual site sells the tickets; in practice, few have them. Depending on what you want to see, however, the full ticket might not be worth the price. Two alternative tickets exist: a *boleto parcial* (partial ticket) for S/40 is good for admission for one day only at Sacsayhuamán, Qenko, Puka Pukara, and Tambomachay, the four Inca ruins nearest Cusco. Another partial ticket, also S/40, is valid for two days at farther-flung ruins of Pisac, Chinchero, and Ollantaytambo in the Sacred Valley and Tipón and Pikillacta in the Southeastern Urubamba Valley. Buy your tickets ahead of time at the one of the two OFEC offices.

If you're interested in only Cusco's cathedral and Qorikancha, as are many short-term visitors, then the boleto turístico is of no use. The Archdiocese of Cusco took the cathedral, the church of San Blas, and the religious art museum in the archbishop's palace out of the boleto turístico scheme in 2005. These three sights are now united under their own *boleto integral* (integral ticket), which you can purchase at the cathedral for S/15 (S/7.50 with an international student ID). The ticket is valid for 10 days, and the price includes the services of guides at each location, who provide top-notch information in English as well as Spanish (and often other languages, too). If you're not interested in visiting all three, it is possible to pay individual admission prices to these sights, but the three-in-one price is such a bargain, and the sights are so close together, you might as well go for the full ticket.

The Qorikancha, arguably Cusco's most fabulous tourist sight, levies its own admission price, that is, it is not a member of the boleto turístico partnership. The equally wonderful Museo Inka and Museo de Arte Precolombino also charge admission independently.

Museo Inka. The draw of this archaeological museum is its collection of
eight Inca mummies—everyone comes here to "ooh" and "eeww" over
them—but the entire facility is Cusco's best Spanish-language introduction to pre-Columbian Andean culture. English-language labeling of the
exhibits is slowly being added in a project sponsored by the Inka Grill
restaurant down the hill on the Plaza de Armas. The ceramics, vases,
and textiles provide a much-needed reminder that civilizations thrived
in this region before the Inca. One room is dedicated to the story of Ma-
makuka ("Mother Coca") and documents indigenous peoples' use of
the coca leaf for religious and medicinal purposes—coca tea is said to
relieve altitude sickness. The building was once the palace of Admiral
Francisco Aldrete Maldonado, hence its common designation as the Palacio del Almirante (Admiral's Palace). ⊠ *Ataúd at Córdoba del Tucumán* ☎ *084/237–380* 🎟 *S/10* ⊙ *Weekdays 8–6, Sat. 9–4.*

FodorśChoice
★

North of the Plaza de Armas

Narrow streets lead north from the Plaza de Armas and take you toward the trendy artisan district of San Blas. The streets are steep, but
never fear: you have plenty of opportunity to catch your breath at various sights and shops along the way. The portion of the city south of
the Plaza de Armas contains lesser-known sights, with one glaring exception. Cusco's if-you-have-time-for-only-one-thing tourist attraction,
the **Qorikancha,** or Temple of the Sun is here, though a bit off on its own.
Don't miss it.

TIMING &
PRECAUTIONS
Walking around here should take you only half a day, and entails a trek
up the narrow street of Cuesta San Blas, portions of which have one
lane of traffic and sidewalks wide enough for only one person.

WHAT TO SEE **Museo de Arte Precolombino.** Lima's top-flight Larco Museum has spun
off the newest and flashiest of Cusco's tourist attractions, known around
town as the MAP. Twelve rooms in the 1580 Casa Cabrera, which was
used as the convent of Santa Clara until the 17th century, showcase an
astounding collection of pre-Columbian art from the 13th–16th centuries.
The art and artifacts were made by the Huari and Nazca, as well as the
Inca, cultures. On the walls is commentary from European artists on
South American art. Swiss artist Paul Klee wrote: "I wish I was newly
born, and totally ignorant of Europe, innocent of facts and fashions, to
be almost primitive." Most Cusco museums close up shop at dark, but
this one remains open every evening. ⊠ *Plazoleta Nazarenas 231* ☎ *084/
233–210* 🎟 *S/20* ⊙ *Daily 9 AM–10 PM.*

Museo de Arte Religioso del Arzobispado. First the site of the Inca Roca's
Hatun Rumiyoq palace, then the juxtaposed Moorish-style palace of the
Marqués de Buenavista, the building reverted to the archdiocese of
Cusco and served as the archbishop's residence. The prelate still lives
in one wing of the building, which, with its elaborate gardens, doorways, and arcades is worth a look. But it now serves as the city's primary repository of religious art, mostly Cusqueña-school paintings,
many by famed artist Marcos Zapata. A highlight of the collection of
religious art is a series of 17th-century paintings that depict the city's
Corpus Christi procession. Many of the works in the museum's 12
rooms are not labeled. One of the bilingual guides will be happy to give

Tours of Cusco, the Sacred Valley & Machu Picchu

THE TYPICAL TOUR of the Cusco region combines the city with the Sacred Valley and Machu Picchu in three whirlwind days. We recommend devoting five days to get the most out of your visit—including one day to rest and acclimate to the high altitude.

Although you can definitely travel around the region independently, many visitors sign up with a tour company to minimize the effort it takes to arrange for transportation and lodging. There are many excellent tour operators and travel agents in Cusco, some also with offices in Lima.

SELECTING A TRAVEL AGENCY

Don't make arrangements or give money to someone claiming to be a travel agent if they approach you on the street or at the airport in Cusco or Lima. Instead choose an agency that has a physical address. Better yet, select one that is listed in this book or on www.peru.info. Below are several reputable travel agencies.

Amazing Peru organizes group and individual guided tours, including two types of trips to Cusco and Machu Pichu. Transportation services and accommodations are top-notch, and the guides are flexible. ☎ 051/4342-6526, 800/704-2915 in the U.S. ⊕ www.amazingperu.com.

Enigma specializes in small, customized adventure trips throughout the region. Enjoy trekking, rafting, mountain climbing, mountain biking, or horseback riding led by professional guides. ✉ Jr. Clorinda Mato de Turner 100, Cusco ☎ 084/222-155 ⊕ www.enigmaperu.com.

Globos de los Andes floats you above the Sacred Valley in a hot-air balloon. ✉ Av. de la Cultura 220, Cusco ☎ 084/232-352 ⊕ www.globosperu.com.

Inkaterra specializes in trips to Machu Picchu, but can customize tours that include Cusco and the Sacred Valley with as much or as little guide accompaniment as you need. ✉ Andalucía 174, Miraflores, Lima ☎ 01/610-0400 in Lima, 084/245-314 in Cusco, 800/442-5042 in North America ⊕ www.inkaterra.com.

Instinct leads Cusco city tours, Inca Trail hikes, walking and rafting trips along the Tambopata River, and more. ✉ Procuradores 50, Cusco ☎ 084/233-451 ⊕ www.instinct-travel.com.

Mayuc is known for its rafting excursions, but also offers good city and Sacred Valley tours. ✉ Portal de Confiturías 211, Haukaypata (Plaza de Armas), Cusco ☎ 084/242-824 ⊕ www.mayuc.com.

Overseas Adventure Travel offers fully escorted 11-day tours of Cusco and the surrounding region with groups no larger than 16 people. ☎ 800/493-6824 in North America ⊕ www.oattravel.com.

Cusco-based **SAS Travel** has made a name for itself in trekking circles, but can also customize tours and accommodations in the city and the region. ✉ Portal de Panes 167, Haukaypata (Plaza de Armas), Cusco ☎ 084/255-205 ⊕ www.sastravelperu.com.

For a tame adventurer, **Wilderness Travel** has a Peru Llama Trek that follows an off-Inca trail route to Machu Picchu where llamas carry your gear and you have the trail to yourself until near the end. ✉ 1102 9th St., Berkeley, CA 94710 ☎ 510/558-2488, 800/368-2794 in U.S. ⊕ www.wildernesstravel.com.

you a tour. Their services are included in the admission price. ⊠ *Hatun Rumiyoq and Herejes* ☎ *084/222–781* ⊡ *S/6 or Boleto Integral* ⊙ *Weekdays 8–6, weekends 10–6.*

❹ Museo Hilario Mendívil. In the home of famous 20th-century Peruvian
Fodor'sChoice religious artist Hilario Mendívil (1929–77), this gallery displays the
★ maguey-wood and rice-plaster sculptures of the Virgin with the elongated necks that were the artist's trademark. Art has always been a family affair among this clan; Mendívil, himself the son of artists, began painting at age 10, and his wife, Georgina Dueñas, who died in 1998, also had an artistic flair. Their six children have continued the tradition since their father's death, and several budding painters and sculptors have sprung up in the fourth generation of Mendívils as well. ⊠ *Plazoleta San Blas 634* ☎ *084/232–231* ⊡ *Free* ⊙ *Mon.–Sat. 8–8.*

❻ Qorikancha. The Temple of the Sun was built during the reign of the Inca
Fodor'sChoice Pachacutec to honor Tawantinsuyos' most important divinity and served
★ as astronomical observatory and repository of the realm's gold treasure. (The temple's name translates as "Court of Gold.")

If Cusco was constructed to represent a puma, then Qorikancha was positioned as the animal's loins, the center from which all creation emanated. Some 4,000 priests and attendants are thought to have lived within its confines. Walls and altars were plated with gold, and in the center of the complex sat a giant gold disc, positioned to reflect the sun and bathe the temple in light. At the summer solstice, sunlight reflected into a niche in the wall where only the Inca were permitted to sit. Terraces that face it were once filled with life-size gold and silver statues of plants and animals. Much of the wealth was removed to pay ransom for the captive Inca ruler Atahualpa at the time of the Spanish conquest, blood money that was paid in vain as Atahualpa was later murdered. Eventually, Francisco Pizarro awarded the site to his brother Juan. Upon Juan's death, the structure passed to the Dominicans, who began to construct the church of Santo Domingo, using stones from the temple and creating perhaps Cusco's most jarring imperial–colonial architectural juxtaposition.

An ingenious restoration to recover both buildings after the 1953 earthquake lets you see how the church was built on and around the walls and chambers of the temple. In the Inca parts of the structure left exposed, estimated to be about 40% of the original temple, you can admire the mortarless masonry, earthquake-proof trapezoidal doorways, curved retaining wall, and exquisite carvings that exemplify the artistic and engineering skills of the Inca. Bilingual guides lead tours every day except Sunday; the service is included in your admission price. A small museum just down the hill on Avenida El Sol contains a few artifacts from the site but doesn't warrant a huge amount of your time. ⊠ *Pampa del Castillo at Plazoleta Santo Domingo* ☎ *No phone* ⊡ *Ruins and church, S/6; museum, Boleto Turístico* ⊙ *Ruins and church, Mon.–Sat. 8:30–5:30, Sun. 2–5; museum, Mon.–Sat. 9–5:30, Sun. 9–1.*

8

Where to Eat

$–$$ ✕ **Cicciolina.** Everyone seems to know everyone and greet each other with
Fodor'sChoice a peck on the cheek at this second-floor eatery, part lively tapas bar, part
★ sit-down, candle-lit restaurant. The bar wraps around the kitchen area,
where you can watch a small army of cooks prepare your food. You'll
strain to see as they set out each new platter of tapas—perhaps some
bruschetta or prawns and sweet potato in wasabi sauce—and be tempted
to say, "I want one of those." The restaurant half of Cicciolina is much
more subdued, and a complete selection of homemade pastas with
Mediterranean sauces on the menu. You can order off the restaurant
menu in the tapas bar, but not the other way around. ⊠ *Sunturwasi 393,
Triunfo* ☎ *084/239–510* ⊟ *AE, DC, MC, V.*

$–$$ ✕ **MAP Café.** Museum eateries rarely warrant guidebook listings, but this
small, elegant restaurant sits inside a small, glass-enclosed courtyard of
the Museo de Arte Precolombino. Try the *cuy* confit, with an accompaniment of mortar-and-pestle-ground potatoes and *chaufa of pickled
quinua* (corn fried rice). Top it off with a passion-fruit tart. ⊠ *Plazoleta Nazarenas 231* ☎ *084/242–476* ⚖ *Reservations essential* ⊟ *AE,
DC, MC, V* ☉ *No lunch.*

★ **$** ✕ **Pucará.** This is the best place in Cusco to sample regional dishes, which
means it's always busy. The lunch specials are ample and reasonably priced.
The *ají de gallina* is outstanding but a bit heavy before an afternoon of
sightseeing. On the lighter side, the fish dishes are served with a colorful assortment of vegetables. The homemade truffles are the perfect dessert.
⊠ *Plateros 309* ☎ *084/222–027* ⊟ *AE, MC, V.*

$–$$ ✕ **Inka Grill.** If you've been putting off trying *cuy* (guinea pig), that pe-
culiarly Andean delicacy, this might just be the place to take the plunge.
This bi-level, upscale restaurant on the Plaza de Armas draws tourists
and locals alike to it reassuring surroundings and attentive service. And
top off your meal with a wait-'til-I-tell-the-folks-back-home dessert: coca-
leaf crème brûlée. ⊠ *Portal de Panes 115, Plaza de Armas* ☎ *084/
262–992* ⊟ *AE, DC, MC, V.*

$ ✕ **El Mesón.** You'll drink in the city's history as you dine on a rustic, sec-
ond-floor terrace with stucco walls and high-beamed ceilings above the
Plaza de Armas. The *parrilladas* (barbecued meats) are the best in Cusco;
the platter for one person is more than enough for two. But there's an
ample salad bar if you're not feeling quite so carnivorous. ⊠ *Espaderos
105* ☎ *084/235–307* ⊟ *AE, DC, MC, V.*

¢–$ ✕ **Quinta Eulalia.** A quinta is a *típico* semi-open air Peruvian restaurant,
and Eulalia's is the oldest such place in the city, dishing up hearty, filling portions of down-home food since 1941. *Chicharrones* (fried pork
and cabbage), *trucha al horno* (oven-baked trout), and *cuy chactado*
(guinea pig with potatoes) are three of the specialties here. ⊠ *Choquechaca
384* ☎ *084/243–730* ⊟ *No credit cards* ☉ *No dinner.*

Where to Stay

You may have to adjust your internal thermostat if you stay in
moderate or budget lodgings at this altitude, but all provide extra blankets to keep you comfy at night. (Air-conditioning is almost unheard-

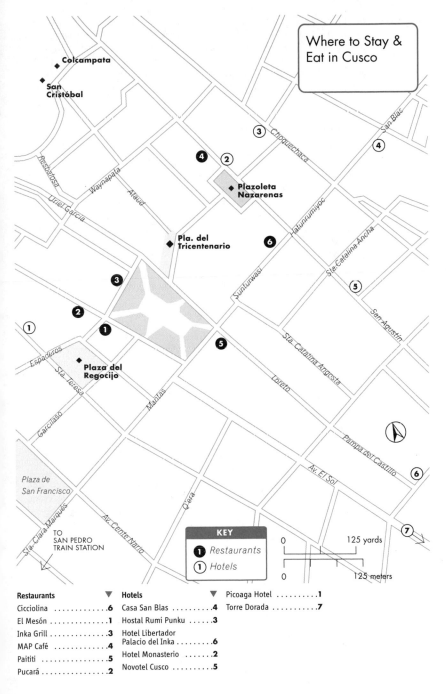

Where to Stay &
Eat in Cusco

KEY
- ① *Restaurants*
- ① *Hotels*

0 — 125 yards
0 — 125 meters

of at this altitude; you won't miss it.) And the hot water might not be on all day, or could be lukewarm at best, even though hotels in this price range say they have *agua caliente*. Larger accommodations keep an oxygen supply on hand for those having trouble adjusting to the thin air. Lodgings in Cusco keep shockingly early checkout times. (Flights to Cusco arrive early in the morning.) Expect to have to vacate your room by 8 or 9 AM, though this is less strictly enforced in the off-season. Most lodgings will hold your luggage if you're not leaving town until later in the day.

$$$$ ⊞ **Hotel Libertador Palacio del Inka.** Close enough, but a bit removed from the hubbub of the Plaza de Armas, this hotel on the tiny Plazoleta Santo Domingo was the last home of Francisco Pizarro, the first governor of Peru. The glass-covered lobby is a great place to relax with a mate de coca and soak in the antiques, fountain, and Cusqueño art that fills the lobby and courtyard. Rooms, decorated in Peruvian colonial style with views of patio gardens, all have central heating to keep out the chill. The plush bar makes a mean pisco sour. ⊠ *Plazoleta Santo Domingo 259* 🕾 *084/231–961, 01/442–1995 in Lima* ⊕ *www.libertador.com.pe* ⇌ *254 rooms, 14 suites* ⟨ *Restaurant, café, in-room data ports, in-room safes, minibars, cable TV, hair salon, gym, hot tub, sauna, bar, shops, laundry service, concierge, Internet, business services, meeting rooms* ⊟ *AE, DC, MC, V* ⟨◯⟩ *BP.*

$$$$ ⊞ **Hotel Monasterio.** One of Peru's loveliest hotels is in the restored
Fodor'sChoice 1592 monastery of San Antonio Abad, a national historic monument.
★ Planners managed to retain the austere beauty of the complex—the lodging even incorporates the original chapel and its collection of Cusqueño art—and kept rooms simple and elegant with a mix of colonial and modern furnishings. At night the view of the stars from the main courtyard is truly serene. Eighty-four rooms can be pressurized with a flow of enriched oxygen much like an airplane cabin to duplicate conditions 1,000 meters (3,300 feet) lower than Cusco, the only such hotel system in the world, and an option for which you can pay a S/100 premium. ⊠ *Palacio 136, across from Plazoleta Nazarenas* 🕾 *084/240–696, 01/242–3427 in Lima* ⊕ *www.monasterio.orient-express.com* ⇌ *120 rooms, 6 suites* ⟨ *2 restaurants, café, in-room safes, minibars, cable TV, massage, spa, bar, shops, dry cleaning, laundry service, concierge, business services, meeting rooms; a/c in some rooms* ⊟ *AE, DC, MC, V* ⟨◯⟩ *BP.*

$$$$ ⊞ **Novotel Cusco.** The French Novotel chain is here with a two-in-one, old-and-new installment on a quiet, narrow street. The smaller, older section dates from the 16th century and contains rooms, each one different, congregating around a pleasant courtyard. Gardens blend the colonial section into a newer, larger block of the hotel, constructed in similar period style. Newer rooms are pleasantly furnished with all the amenities you'd expect in a hotel of this caliber, but you'll shell out a few extra soles for one of the larger colonial rooms. The covered courtyard buzzes with the activity of live music and artisans showing off their works, and is heated on cold nights by a system of underground hot-water pipes. ⊠ *San Agustín 329* 🕾 *084/881–030* ⊕ *www.novotel.com* ⇌ *99 rooms* ⟨ *2 restaurants, in-room safes, minibars, cable TV, Internet room,* *business services, meeting rooms, airport shuttle, no-smoking floors* ☐*AE, DC, MC, V* ⦿*BP.*

$$$ 🏨 **Picoaga Hotel.** The front half of this hotel consists of a colonial building with rooms arranged around an attractive arcaded courtyard, originally the 17th-century home of the Marqués de Picoaga. Behind is a modern wing with a restaurant that overlooks the Plaza de Armas. The colonial building itself is attractive, and the rooms are undergoing a facelift at this writing. Opt for one of the older, quieter colonial rooms facing the courtyard. The Picoaga makes for a centrally located upscale option at a fraction of the price of Cusco's pricier lodgings. ⊠ *Calle Santa Teresa 344* ☎ *084/252–330* ⊕ *www.picoagahotel.com* ⤢ *72 rooms* ⚘ *Restaurant, in-room safes, minibars, cable TV, billiards, bar, laundry service, concierge* ☐ *AE, DC, MC, V* ⦿*BP.*

★ $$ 🏨 **Torre Dorada.** Once you get your bearings, you realize this pleasant, family-run lodging isn't as far off the beaten path as it first seems, and you'll be thankful for the peace and quiet and lack of traffic on its quiet little plaza. What the hotel might lack in convenience, it makes up for in comfort and service. The owner is absolutely dedicated to satisfying guests. Rooms arranged on four floors around a common sitting room each have wood floors, comfy mattresses, high-pressure showers, desks, and armoires made of tarabilo wood. ⊠ *Los Cirpeses 5, Residencial Huancaro* ☎ *084/241–698* ⊕ *www.torredorada.com.pe* ⤢ *20 rooms* ⚘ *Dining room, airport transfer; no room TVs, no smoking* ☐ *V* ⦿*BP.*

$ 🏨 **Casa San Blas.** This small hotel with a large staff—there's a 2-to-1 staff-to-guest ratio—prides itself on exceptionally attentive service. Regular rooms are quite comfortable, with colonial-style furniture and hardwood floors, but with more modern amenities than this restored 250-year-old house would be expected to provide. The top-floor suites and one apartment are similar in style, but larger, with wood-beamed ceilings and private terraces. The hotel sits just a block off the Cuesta San Blas, the "staircase" street leading up from the Plaza de Armas, and could not be more centrally located for sightseeing. ⊠ *Tocuyeros 566, San Blas* ☎ *084/237–900, 888/569–1769 in North America* ⊕ *www. casasanblas.com* ⤢ *13 rooms, 5 apartments, 1 suite* ⚘ *Restaurant, in-room safes, cable TV, massage, piano bar, Internet room, travel services, airport shuttle* ☐ *AE, DC, MC, V* ⦿*BP.*

$ 🏨 **Hostal Rumi Punku.** A massive stone door—that's what Rumi Punku means in Quechua—opens onto a rambling complex of balconies, patios, gardens, courtyards, terraces, fireplaces, and Inca walls scattered here and there. It all links a series of pleasantly furnished rooms with hardwood floors and comfy beds covered with plush blankets. The top-level dining patio has stupendous views of the city below. ⊠ *Choquechaca 339* ☎ *084/221–102* ⊕ *www.rumipunku.com* ⤢ *20 rooms* ⚘ *Dining room, hot tub, sauna, bar; no room TVs* ☐ *No credit cards* ⦿*CP.*

Nightlife & the Arts

The nights are chilly, the air is thin, and you need to rise early for your excursion tomorrow morning. So you'd anticipate no nightlife, right? You couldn't be more wrong. Cusco is full of bars and discos with live and DJ music, everything from U.S. rock to Andean folk. Though dance places levy a cover charge, there's usually someone out front handing out free passes to tourists—highly discriminatory, but in your favor, of course. (Most of the dance locales cater to a decidedly under-thirty crowd.) Bars frequently position someone in front to entice you in with a coupon for a free drink, but that drink is sometimes made with the cheapest, gut-rottingest alcohol the bar has available. There are a few reports of patrons getting sick. Splurge and pay full price for a real drink.

Bars & Pubs

For a cold beer and English soccer broadcast via satellite, try **Cross Keys** (⊠ Portal Confiturías 233, Plaza de Armas ☎ 084/229–227), a pub that will make London expats homesick. Challenge the regulars to a game of darts at your own risk. The second-floor, dark-wood **Paddy Flaherty's** (⊠ Sunturwasi 124 ☎ 084/247–719) mixes pints of Guinness and old-fashioned Irish pub grub with Philly steaks, pita sandwiches, and chicken baguettes. The most polished Irish pub in town, **Rosie O'Grady's** (⊠ Santa Catalina Ancha 360 ☎ 084/243–514) has the occasional Andean music show to take in while you down your pint of Guinness, and an extensive menu if you're hungry.

Dance Clubs

Dating all the way back to 1985, **Kamikase** (⊠ Kusipata 274, Plaza Regocijo ☎ 084/233–865) is a favorite gringo bar, though plenty of locals visit, too, and has a mix of salsa, rock, and folk music for your dancing pleasure most evenings. Dance the night away at **Ukukus** (⊠ Plateros 316 ☎ 084/233–445), a pub and disco that hops with a young crowd most mornings until 5 AM. **Mama Africa** (⊠ Portal de Panes 109, Plaza de Armas ☎ 084/245–550), Cusco's hottest reggae and hip-hop dance venue, is also part travel agency and cyber café.

Folklore

A fun addition to the boleto turístico scheme is the **Centro Qosqo de Arte Nativo** (⊠ Av. El Sol 604 ☎ 084/227–901). The cultural center holds hour-long folkloric dance performances in its auditorium each night at 7, with introductions in Spanish and English. And you may be one of the lucky audience members called up to participate in the final number. But you do need to buy the boleto turístico to be admitted.

Tunupa (⊠ Portal de Confiturías 233, Plaza de Armas ☎ 084/252–936) has a nightly folklore show along with fine dining. Enjoy the sounds of Andean music during dinner each evening at **La Retama** (⊠ Portal de Panes 123, Plaza de Armas ☎ 084/226–372). **Paititi** (⊠ Portal de Carrizos 270, Plaza de Armas ☎ 084/252–686) presents a live folklore show during dinner most nights. **Bagdad Café** (⊠ Portal de Carnes 216, Plaza de Armas ☎ 084/239–949) has live music during dinner many nights of the week, but with no fixed schedule.

Shopping

Cusco is full of traditional crafts, artwork, and clothing made of alpaca, llama, or sheep wool. Beware of acrylic fakes. For the best-quality products, shop in the higher end stores. The export of artifacts would require a government permit, so banish any thoughts of waltzing off with the Inca ruler Pachacutec's cape for a song.

Vendors, usually children, will approach you relentlessly on the Plaza de Armas. They sell postcards, finger puppets, drawings, and CDs of Andean music. A simple "no, gracias" is usually enough to indicate you're not interested. Several enclosed crafts markets are good bets for bargains. And even the upscale shops are sometimes amenable to offering you a discount if all three of the following conditions are met: 1) it's the September–May off-season; 2) you came into the store on your own, without a guide who will expect a commission from the shop; and 3) you pay in cash.

Ceramics

Seminario (⊠ Portal de Carnes, Haukaypata, Plaza de Armas ☎ 084/ 246–093) is the outlet in Cusco of famed ceramics maker Pablo Seminario. Prices are a bit lower at the source in the Sacred Valley town of Urubamba. In San Blas, the **Galería Mérida** (⊠ Carmen Alto 133 ☎ 084/ 221–714) sells the much-imitated ceramics of Edilberto Mérida.

Crafts & Gifts

Religious art, including elaborately costumed statues of the Virgin Mary, is sold at the shop at the **Galería Mendívil** (⊠ Plazoleta San Blas ☎ 084/ 226–506). **Galería Latina** (⊠ San Agustín 427 ☎ 084/246–588) is a reasonably priced crafts shop with many original pieces, tapestries, ceramics, and alpaca clothing among them.

Triunfo is lined with crafts shops as far as San Blas. One of the best, **Taller Maxi** (⊠ Sunturwasi 393 ☎ No phone), sells dolls in historical and local costumes. You can even have one custom-made. Also on display are *retablos* (wooden boxes) that show Cusco's most popular sites and alpaca jackets decorated with local weavings.

Textiles

Long-established **Alpaca 111** (⊠ Kusipata 202, Plaza Regocijo ☎ 084/ 243–233) has alpaca garments, and is the only authorized distributor of high-quality vicuña scarves and sweaters. There are outlets at the Libertador and Monasterio hotels as well as at the airport. **Perú Étnico** (⊠ Portal Mantas 114 ☎ 084/232–775 ⊠ Portal de Carnes 232, Haukaypata, Plaza de Armas ☎ 084/238–620 ⊠ Heladeros 172 ☎ 084/ 229–184) has three downtown locations with fine alpaca coats, sweaters, scarves, and shawls. **Alpaca's Best** (⊠ Portal Confiturias 221, Haukaypata, Plaza de Armas ☎ 084/249–406) also has a good selection of jewelry. **Royal Knitwear** (⊠ Plaza Regocijo 203 ☎ 084/261–452) sells alpaca and pima cotton garments at stores in Cusco and Lima, and it also exports its products to shops in the United States, Europe, Japan, and Australia. **Maqui Arte** (⊠ Sunturwasi [Triunfo] 118 ☎ 084/246–493) has high-quality alpaca sweaters.

Alpaca gets the camelid's share of attention for use in making fine garments, but **La Casa de la Llama** (⊠ Palacio 121 ☎ 084/240–813) sells a fine selection of clothing made from the softer hairs sheared from its namesake animal's chest and neck. It's difficult to tell the difference in texture between llama and adult alpaca, at least in this shop.

8

Several artisan markets and cooperatives populate the city. For a chance to see products being handwoven, stop by the **Center for Traditional Textiles of Cusco** (⊠ Av. El Sol 603 ☎ 084/228–117), a nonprofit organization dedicated to the survival of traditional textile weaving. You can purchase sweaters, ponchos, scarves, and wall hangings at fair-trade prices. The municipal government operates the **Centro Artesanal Cusco** (⊠ Tullumayo and El Sol ☎ No phone), containing 340 stands of artisan vendors. The **Feria Inca** (⊠ At San Andrés and Quera) is small and informal, but bargains can be found. A nonprofit cooperative called **Antisuyo** (⊠ Triunfo 387 ☎ 084/227–778) sells high-quality crafts from all over Peru.

Side Trips from Cusco

Cusco is the gateway to some of Peru's greatest historical areas and monuments, such as Sacsayhuamán, on a hill that overlooks the city. The Río Urubamba runs northwest and southeast from Cusco. The northwest sector of the river basin is the romantically named Sacred Valley of the Inca and attracts the puma's share of visitors on their way to Machu Picchu. But along the highway that runs southeast of Cusco to Sicuani are a number of lesser-known Inca and pre-Inca sites in a regions locals call the Valle del Sur. You may find that you have these magnificent ruins all to yourself, as they are off the traditional tourist circuit.

These sights are easy to visit by car during a day trip from Cusco, and admission is covered in the boleto turístico.

Sacsayhuamán

Fodor'sChoice
★

2 km (1 mi) north of Cusco.

Dominating a hilltop north of the city are the ruins of the massive military complex of Sacsayhuamán, perhaps the most important Inca monument after Machu Picchu. Today only the outer walls remain of the original fortress city, which the Spanish tore down after the rebellion and then ransacked for years as a source of construction materials for their new city down the hill, a practice that continued until the mid-20th century. Only one-fifth of the original complex is left; nonetheless, the site is impressive.

These closest Inca ruins to Cusco make a straightforward half-day trip from the city, and provide the quintessential postcard view over Cusco's orange rooftops. If you don't have a car, the easiest way to get here is to take a taxi, but if you're feeling truly fit, the ruins are a steep 45-minute walk up from the Plaza de Armas. Self-appointed guides populate the entrances and can give you a two-hour tour for S/30. (All work the standard joke into their spiel that the name of the site is pronounced "sexy woman.") ⊠ Km 2, Hwy. to Pisac ☎ no phone ⓣ Boleto Turístico ☉ Daily 7–6.

> **WORD OF MOUTH**
>
> "The 'must' in Cusco are the ruins of Sacsayhuaman just nearby— apart from Machu Picchu the most spectacular Inca ruins we saw on our trip."   –Gliadrachan

Qenko

4 km (2½ mi) north of Cusco.

Qenko, the first in a series of smaller archaeological sites beyond Sac-sayhuamán, was a *huaca* (any site considered sacred) with a 19-seat am-phitheater where the mummies of nobles and priests were kept and brought out on sunny days for ritualistic worship. The walls of the limestone structure contain relief carvings of animals and a centerpiece stone block representing a puma. Qenko was the site of an annual pre-plant-ing ritual in which priests poured llama blood into the top of a ceremo-nial pipe, allowing it to make its way down a zigzag channel. (The name of the place translates as "zigzag.") If the blood flowed left, it boded poor fertility for the coming season. If the liquid continued the full length of the pipe, it spelled a bountiful harvest. ⊠ *Km 4, Hwy to Pisac* ☎ *No phone* ⊠ *Boleto Turístico* ⊙ *Daily 7–6.*

Tambomachay

11 km (6½ mi) north of Cusco.

The site, whose name means "cavern lodge," is a three-tiered *huaca* built of elaborate stonework over a natural spring. A sophisticated system of aqueducts pumped the underground water to feed ritual showers. In-terpretations differ, but the site was likely a place where water, consid-ered a source of life, was worshipped. The huaca is almost certain to have been the scene of sacred ablutions and purifying ceremonies for Inca rulers and royal women. ⊠ *Km 11, Hwy. to Pisac* ☎ *No phone* ⊠ *Boleto Turístico* ⊙ *Daily 7–6.*

Pikillacta

6 km (3½ mi) east of Tipón; 7 km (4 mi) south of Oropesa

About 9 km (5½ mi) down the highway from the Tipón turnoff stand the haunting ruins of Pikillacta, a vast city of 700 buildings from the pre-Inca Wari culture, which flourished between AD 600 and 1000. Like other Andean cultures, the Wari empire—which at its height stretched from near Cajamarca to the border of the Tiahuanaco empire based around Lake Titicaca—had a genius for farming in a harsh environment and built sophisticated urban centers such as Pikillacta. The rough ruins, once enclosed by a defensive 3-meter (10-foot) wall whose remains are still visible, confirm the Inca superiority in architecture and masonry. They are spread over several acres and include many two-story build-ings, which were entered via ladders to doorways on the second floor. At the thatch-roofed excavation sites, you'll see uncovered walls that show the city's stones were once covered with plaster and whitewashed. Across the road lies a beautiful lagoon, Lago de Lucre. ⊠ *Km 32, Hwy. to Urcos* ☎ *No phone* ⊠ *Boleto Turístico* ⊙ *Daily 7–6.*

Cusco Essentials

Transportation

BY AIR

Aero Condor flies daily from Cusco to Lima. LanPeru connects Cusco with Lima, Arequipa, Juilaca, and Puerto Maldonado. Star Perú and

TACA Peru fly from Cusco to Lima. TANS Perú flies to Lima and Puerto Maldonado.

Cusco's Aeropuerto Internacional Teniente Alejandro Velasco Astete (CUZ) is about 15 minutes from the center of town. An army of taxis waits at the exit from baggage claim, and charges S/5 to take you to the city center. An Andean music band will serenade you as you wait for your luggage at the carousel. Winds and weather conditions mean most flights arrive at and depart from the airport in the morning, which does not always bode well for timely international connections in Lima.

🛪 Airport Information **Aeropuerto Internacional Teniente Alejandro Velasco Astete**
✉ Av. Velasco Astete s/n ☎ 084/222-611.

BY TRAIN

Three classes of daily service to Machu Picchu depart from Cusco's San Pedro station, where tickets can be purchased before morning departures. Your best bet is to purchase tickets in advance—that's a necessity during the June to August high season—from the PeruRail sales office at Cusco's Wanchaq Station, open weekdays 7–5 and weekends 7–noon (note that PeruRail does not accept credit cards)—or from a travel agency. Tourists are not permitted to ride PeruRail's Tren Local, the less expensive, but slower train intended for local residents only.

🛪 Train Information **Peru Rail** ✉ San Pedro station, Cascapara near Santa Clara, Cusco ☎ 084/233-551 ⊕ www.perurail.com ✉ Wanchaq station, Pachacutec near Tullumayo, Cusco ☎ 084/238-722 ⊕ www.perurail.com.

Contacts & Resources

VISITOR INFORMATION

Cusco has three official tourist-information offices. All provide information not just about the city, but also the surrounding Cusco department. The staff at the Dirección Regional de Industria y Turismo (Dircetur) is especially helpful and seems most geared to providing information on the city and surrounding area to visitors walking in off the street. A branch at the airport is open daily for all incoming flights. iPerú has helpful information on Cusco and the region and can provide assistance if you feel you've received inadequate service from a tourist establishment. An airport branch is open daily for all incoming flights. The Oficina Ejecutiva del Comité Boleto Turístico (OFEC) sells the 10-day boleto turístico, valid for admission to 16 museums and archaeological sites in the region. A private office of note is South American Explorers, a membership organization. Its US$50 annual dues get you a quarterly magazine subscription and access to a wealth of information at its clubhouse here in Cusco, as well as in Lima and in Quito, Ecuador, and Buenos Aires, Argentina.

The ubiquitous TOURIST INFORMATION signs you see around town are storefront travel agencies anxious to sell you tours rather than provide unbiased, official sources of information.

🛪 Tourist Information **Dirección Regional de Industria y Turismo** ✉ Mantas 117 ☎ 084/222-032 ⊙ Weekdays 8–7, Sat. 8–2. **iPerú** ✉ Av. El Sol 103 ☎ 084/252-974 ⊙ Daily 8:30–7:30. **Oficina Ejecutiva del Comité Boleto Turístico** OFEC ✉ Av. El Sol 103 ☎ 084/227-037 ✉ Garcilaso and Heladeros ☎ 084/226-919 ⊙ Mon.-Sat. 8 to 5; Sun. 8-2. **South**

American Explorers ⊠ Choquechaca 188, Bell 4 ☎ 084/245–484 ⊕ www.saexplorers. org ⊙ May–Sept., weekdays 9:30–5 and Sun. 9:30–1; Oct.–Apr., weekdays 9:30–5.

MACHU PICCHU & THE SACRED VALLEY

By Jeffrey Van Fleet

Too often Cusco and Machu Picchu are sold as a three-day, two-night package—and sometimes even a whirlwind tour of the Sacred Valley is incorporated into the third day. That's a shame because each is a destination in its own right. Cusco, with enough sights to keep you occupied for at least three days, is more than an embarkation point for the trek to Machu Picchu. The ruins themselves require more than the usual three or four hours spent at the site during a typical day tour. If that's all the time you have, great. But an overnight stay lets you linger long after the day-trippers have headed back down the mountain. And you can head back up early the next morning, an especially tranquil time before the midday heat and next round of visitors kick in. Finally, the so-called Sacred Valley of the Inca, along the Río Urubamba, is filled with Inca remains. The valley begins at the town of Pisac, about 30 km (18 mi) northeast of Cusco, and ends 60 km (36 mi) northwest of Pisac at Ollantaytambo. Machu Picchu is farther downriver, among the cloud forests on the Andean slopes above the Amazon jungle.

It's an easy train ride from Cusco to Machu Picchu, but for exploring the Sacred Valley, a car is the best option. Those who don't want to drive can take any of the frequent buses that run between Cusco and the Sacred Valley communities. In fact, the entire area, though still very rural, is well served by good roads and public transportation. The vehicular tourist route ends at Ollantaytambo, beyond which your options are to travel by rail—most visitors board the train in Cusco, however—or on foot along the famed Inca Trail to reach the remains of Machu Picchu.

8

Pisac

1 *9 km (5 mi) north of Taray.*

Pisac is a colorful colonial town of about 4,000 people, replete with Quechua-language masses in a simple stone church, a well-known market, fortress ruins, and a small selection of hotels and restaurants. It's a good, if at times very crowded, base for exploring the Sacred Valley.

Fodor'sChoice ★ Pisac's famous three-times-weekly **market** draws the shop-'til-you-drop crowd, local and tourist alike. Fruits, vegetables, and grains happily share the stage with ceramics, jewelry, and woolens on the central plaza and spill over into the side streets. Sellers set up shop about 8 AM on market days (and a few set up on nonmarket days as well), and start packing up at about 3 PM. Those in the know insist that vendors, anxious to minimize the load they cart back home, offer their best bargains around closing time. By 5 PM even the hangers-on have filtered away from the plaza. Though the Tuesday and Thursday markets will not disappoint, go on Sunday if your schedule permits; you'll have a chance to take in the 11 AM Quechua mass at the Iglesia San Pedro Apóstolo and watch the elaborate costumed procession led by the mayor who carries his *varayoc*, a

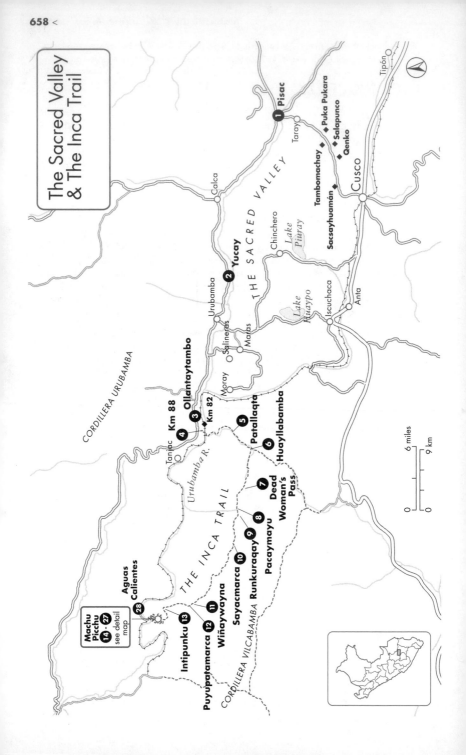

The Sacred Valley & The Inca Trail

ceremonial staff, out of the church afterward. Sunday afternoon sees bands and beer tents—this is small-town Peru at its best. ☉ *Sun., Tues., and Thurs. 8–3 or 4.*

Where to Stay & Eat

¢ ✕ **Samana Wasi.** The Quechua name of this basic local restaurant on the central square translates as "house of rest," and the owner claims that this is Peruvian cuisine, fresh and made-to-order. It doesn't get any fresher than the trout caught in the nearby Urubamba River. These folks also dish up a spicy *cazuela de gallina* (chicken stew). If it's a nice day, grab one of the tables on the shady interior courtyard. ✉ *Plaza Constitución 509* ☎ *084/203–018* ▭ *No credit cards.*

$$ 🏨 **Hotel Royal Inka Pisac.** Just outside of town is the newest branch of Peru's Royal Inka hotel chain, and the closest lodging to the Pisac ruins. Bright, airy, carpeted rooms congregate around acres of wooded and flowered grounds, and have print spreads and drapes and white walls. All third-level rooms have a fireplace. With all the activities and facilities here, a rarity in the Sacred Valley, you really never have to leave the grounds. ✉ *Km 1½ Carretera a Pisac Ruinas* ☎ *084/203–064, 800/664–1819 in North America* ⊕ *www.royalinkahotel.com* ⇄ *76 rooms* ♨ *Restaurant, coffee shop, cable TV, tennis court, indoor pool, hair salon, hot tub, massage, sauna, bicycles, horseback riding, bar, piano bar, meeting room; no-smoking rooms* ❧❘ *BP.*

Yucay

➋ *46 km (28 mi) northwest of Pisac.*

Now an attractive colonial village, Yucay has the Sacred Valley's most famous lodging, the Posada del Inca, a 300-year-old monastery turned hacienda turned hotel, complete with a second-floor museum worth visiting even if you don't stay at the posada.

Where to Stay & Eat

★ $$–$$$ ✕🏨 **Sonesta Posada del Inca Valle Sagrado.** In the heart of the Sacred Valley is this 300-year-old former convent (monastery). The cobblestone walkways are the perfect complement to the well-preserved colonial-era church on the grounds. A museum on the second floor of the main building has an extensive collection of pre-Inca ceramics. The rooms, with tile floors, wood ceilings, and hand-carved headboards, have balconies that overlook the gardens or the terraced hillsides. The restaurant has excellent regional fare and a popular Sunday lunch buffet. ✉ *Plaza Manco II 123* ☎ *084/201–107, 01/222–4777 in Lima, 800/766–3782 in North America* ⊕ *www.sonesta.com* ⇄ *84 rooms* ♨ *Restaurant, in-room safes, minibars, cable TV, spa, bar, shop, laundry service, business services, meeting rooms* ▭ *AE, MC, V.*

Ollantaytambo

➌ *19 km (11 mi) west of Urubamba.*

At the northwestern entrance to the Sacred Valley lies Ollantaytambo, perhaps the best-preserved Inca site, sitting above one of the region's loveliest towns, whose traditional air has not been stifled by the invasion of hordes of tourists. The town, pronounced "oy-yahn-tie-*tahm*-bo"—but never fear: everyone around here calls it "Ollanta" for short—was named for Ollantay, the most famous Inca general. The town, whose municipal government charges a S/1 vehicular fee to enter, makes a superb base for exploring

the Sacred Valley and has easy rail connections to Machu Picchu, without backtracking to Cusco. Ollantaytambo is also the kick-off point for the Inca Trail. You'll start here at nearby Km 82 if you wish to hike to the Lost City.

Above the town of Ollantaytambo rises the **fortress of Ollantaytambo,** a formidable stone structure that climbs massive terraces to the top of a peak. It was the valley's main defense against the Antis from the neighboring rain forests. Construction began during the reign of Pachacutec, but for reasons unknown, was never completed. The rose-color granite used was not mined in this part of the valley. The elaborate walled complex contained a temple to the sun, used for astronomical observation, as well as the Baños de la Ñusta (ceremonial princess baths), leading archaeologists to believe that Ollantaytambo existed for more than defense purposes. But it is most famous as the site of the greatest Inca victory over the Spanish during the wars of conquest. The Manco Inca fled here in 1537 with a contingent of troops after the disastrous loss at Sacsayhuamán and routed Spanish forces under Hernando Pizarro. The victory was short-lived: Pizarro regrouped and retook the fortress. ⊠ *Plaza Mañay Raquy* ☎ *No phone* ⊡ *Boleto Turístico* ⊙ *Daily 7–6.*

Where to Stay & Eat

★ **$$** ✕⊞ **Hotel Pakaritampu.** Ollantaytambo's best lodging has a Quechua name that translates as "house of dawn." Fireplaces, and reading rooms with Cusqueño art, invite you to settle in with a good book and a hot cup of coffee on a chilly evening. Rooms, with modern furnishings, plush blue comforters, and green-tile bathrooms, extend through two buildings. The on-grounds orchard supplies the fruit that ends up on your breakfast plate and as accompaniment for the Peruvian cuisine served in the restaurant. ⊠ *Av. Ferrocarril s/n* ☎ *084/204–104* ⊕ *www.pakaritampu.com* ↝ *30 rooms, 1 suite* ♿ *Restaurant, bar, laundry service, meeting rooms; no TV in some rooms* ▤ *AE, DC, MC, V* ❩⊙❩ *BP.*

$$ ⊞ **Hotel Sauce.** The name has nothing to do with sauces used in cooking. Instead, it's a type of tree found here in the Sacred Valley. Thanks to the hotel's hillside location, half of the vaulted-ceiling rooms have a superb view of the Ollantaytambo ruins. The cozy lobby fireplace is usually stoked with a fire on brisk evenings. ⊠ *Ventiderio 248* ☎ *084/204–044* ⊕ *www.hotelsauce.com* ↝ *8 rooms* ♿ *Dining room, bar, laundry service; no TV in some rooms* ▤ *V* ❩⊙❩ *BP.*

$ ☐ **Albergue Ollantaytambo.** Everyone in town knows the Albergue, right at the train station, owned by exuberant longtime American resident and artist Wendy Weeks. Dark-wood rooms here are spacious but rustic, with historic black-and-white photos from the region. The lodging has homey touches like a wood-fired sauna, huge breakfasts, and a cozy sitting room. Reserve in advance: the place is popular with groups about to embark on, or just returning from, the nearby Inca Trail. ☒ *Estación de Ferrocarril* ☎☏ *084/204–014* ⊕ *www.homeinperu.com* ⇆ *8 rooms* ♨ *Dining room, sauna, shop, travel services; no room phones, no room TVs* ▭ *No credit cards* ⊙ BP.

The Inca Trail: Road to Machu Picchu

82–88 km (49–53 mi) from Cusco.

The Inca Trail (*Camino Inca* in Spanish), a 50-km (31-mi) sector of the stone path that once extended from Cusco to Machu Picchu, is arguably the most popular hike in South America. Nothing matches the sensation of walking over the ridge that leads to the Lost City of the Inca just as the sun casts its first yellow glow over the ancient stone buildings. The trail gleaned a bit of pop-culture cachet from a scene in the 2004 film *The Motorcycle Diaries,* when Mexican actor Gael García Bernal, playing a very young, prerevolutionary Che Guevara, did just that. You can, too, though under much more regulation these days than Guevara experienced in the early 1950s.

> ### WORD OF MOUTH
>
> I arrived at Machu Picchu via the Inca Trail. In my opinion, it is much more impressive to see this way [and] there are numerous other ruins you see along the way."
> –RBCal

8

U.S. historian Hiram Bingham announced his discovery of the Inca Trail in 1915. As with Machu Picchu itself, his "discovery" was a little disingenuous. Locals knew about the trail, and parts of it were used during the colonial and early republican eras. In fact, the Spanish used some of the roads constructed by the Inca when they were conquering the indigenous peoples.

When to Go

The best months to make the four-day trek are May through September; rainy weather is a small possibility then, but more likely in April and October and a certainty the rest of the year. With the number of hikers capped at 500 per day—and that number includes guides and porters—the trail fills up quickly during the dry high season. If you arrive in Cusco during those months with no advance plans, you'll notice signs in windows of licensed tour operators all announcing NEXT SPACE AVAILABLE OCTOBER. Avoid disappointment and make reservations weeks in advance if you plan to make the hike that time of year. The trek is doable during the rainy season, but can become uncomfortably slippery and muddy by December. Clouds can obscure views as well. The trail closes for cleaning and maintenance at least one week (longer if summer rains have been exceptionally heavy) each February, the lowest of the low season.

Hiring a Guide

The days of setting off on the Inca Trail on your own, along with the rowdiness and litter that accompanied that free-for-all, ended years ago. You must use a licensed tour operator, one accredited by the Unidad de Gestión Santuario Histórico de Machu Picchu, the organization that oversees the trail, and which limits the number of hikers to 500 per day. (There are some 30 such licensed operators in Cusco.) Regulations require each agency to submit its group list to the Unidad five days in advance of departure. In practice this requirement is sometimes reduced to two days, especially in the low season, but advance reservations are essential any time of year. Groups may not exceed 16 people; for more than 9 a second guide is required.

Your choice of operator will result in a "you get what you pay for" experience. Check closely what you receive for the price. Several agencies, usually catering to a student clientele, offer trips for about S/700, and if you're up to carrying your own equipment and eating more basic rations they are fine options. Higher fees—up to S/1,500—get you porters, more luxurious tents, and meals, and likely include rail transportation between Cusco and Ollantaytambo and admission to Machu Picchu. All operators offer a 4-day/3-night package for the entire trail, as well as an abbreviated 2-day/1-night version beginning at Km 104.

Below are several companies that we recommend:

Enigma offers medium-priced excursions for approximately S/1,100 per person. A cook, porter, and guide are included. ⊠ *Jr. Clorinda Mato de Turner 100, Cusco* ☎ *084/222–155* ⊕ *www.enigmaperu.com.*

Explorandes has all-inclusive Inca Tour excursions for groups as small as one person. The cost is S/2,000, with optional escorted add-ons from Lima. ⊠ *San Fernando 320, Miraflores, Lima* ☎ *01/445–0532* ⊕ *www. enigmaperu.com.*

Q'ente is known for its high-quality budget treks for less than S/1,000 per person, including top-notch guides. Expect to be your own porter and pitch in with cooking detail. ⊠ *Garcilaso, Cusco* ☎ *084/222–535* ⊕ *www.qente.com.*

SAS Travel is a highly regarded medium-range agency offering all you need for about S/1,100 per person. The cost of porters is extra and optional. ⊠ *Portal de Panes 143, Haukaypata (Plaza de Armas), Cusco* ☎ *084/255–205* ⊕ *www.sastravelperu.com.*

X-treme offers fine, you-carry-it, you-cook-it treks for about S/800 per person. ⊠ *Plateros 358, Cusco* ☎ *084/224–362* ⊕ *www.x-tremeperu.com.*

Getting Ready

If you've never been backpacking, try to get some practice before you set out. You must be in decent shape, even if your agency supplies porters to carry your pack—current regulations limit your load to 20 kg (44 lb)—as the trail is often narrow and hair-raising.

As the mountains sometimes rise to over 4,200 meters (13,775 feet), you should be aware of the dangers of altitude sickness. Your gear should include sturdy hiking boots, a sleeping bag—down is best for the cold nights that can occur any time of year—clothing for cold, rainy weather, a hat, and a towel. Also bring plenty of sunblock and mosquito repellent. Toilet paper is another essential on this rustic trail with few comfort stations. Avoid cutting flowers and vegetation. There are seven well-spaced, designated campsites along the trail.

Hiking the Trail

The trail begins outside the Sacred Valley town of Ollantaytambo at a

 place called **Km 88,** marking the distance from Cusco. The Cusco–Machu Picchu trains stop here briefly, shortly after stopping at the Ollantaytambo station. You and your group disembark from the train here to set off on the trail. (Some agencies take you via minivan shuttle from Cusco and start their trek at **Km 82.** That adds only an extra hour or so onto your walk.) The four-day trek takes you past ruins and through stunning scenery that starts in the thin air of the highlands and ends in cloud forests. As you ascend the trail, you'll cross several rivers and lakes via a series of suspension bridges, log bridges, and causeways, many constructed by the Inca.

DAY 1 Compared to what lies ahead, the first day's hike is a reasonably easy 12 km (7½ mi). You'll encounter fantastic ruins almost immediately. An easy ascent takes you to the first of those, **Patallaqta** (also called Llactapata), not far from the start of the trail. The name means "town on a hillside" in Quechua, and the ruins are thought to have been a village in Inca times. Bingham and company camped here on their first excursion to Machu Picchu.

At the end of your 12-km (7½-mi) day, you arrive at **Huayllabamba,** the only inhabited village on the trail and your first overnight stop.

DAY 2 Day 2 entails another 12-km (7½-mi) hike, but with a gain of 1,200 meters (3,940 feet) in elevation, this is the toughest stretch of the excursion. The day is most memorable for the spectacular views and muscular aches after ascending to the apocryphally named **Dead Woman's Pass** (also known as Warmiwañuscca) at 4,200 meters (13,780 feet). No one actually knows the story of the dead woman and her fate, but the name has spooked generations of trekkers. A tricky descent takes you to **Pacaymayu,** the second night's campsite.

DAY 3 It's all figuratively and literally downhill after that rough second day. Day 3 begins the descent to the subtropical cloud forest that begins the Amazon basin. You encounter the ruins of **Runkuraqay,** a circular Inca storage depot for products being transported between Machu Picchu and Cusco. And you pass by **Sayacmarca,** possibly a way station for priests traversing the trail.

 Most excursions arrive by mid-afternoon at **Wiñaywayna,** the third-night stopping point, at what by now will seem a low and balmy 2,650 meters (8,900 feet). There is time to see the ruins of **Puyupatamarca,** a beautifully restored site where you'll find ceremonial baths, and perhaps the best ruins on the hike. At this point you catch your first glimpse of Machu Picchu peak, but from the back side.

DAY 4 Day 4 means the grand finale, arrival at **Machu Picchu** itself, the reason the trail was constructed in the first place. You'll be roused from your sleeping bag well before dawn to be able to arrive at the ruins in time

⑬ to catch the sunrise. The trail takes you past the **Intipunku,** the sun gate. Bask in your first sight of the ruins and your accomplishment at completing the Inca Trail, but you'll need to circle around and enter Machu Picchu officially through the entrance gate.

Alternative Treks

The popularity of the Inca Trail and the scarcity of available high-season spots have led to the opening of several alternative hikes of varying length and difficulty.

Some Cusco tour operators market the two-day, one-night Inca Trail excursion as the **Camino Sagrado Inca** (Sacred Inca Trail). It doesn't generate quite the bragging rights as the four-day trip does, but it's a splendid alternative if you're short on time and stamina. (It's a bit easier to procure reservations for these trips, but advance reservations with a licensed operator are still essential.) The excursion begins at **Km 104,** a stop on the Cusco–Machu Picchu trains. A three-hour walk takes you to **Wiñaywayna**—portions are steep, but nothing like Day 2 of the four-day trek—and then you spend the night at the hostel there. You rise early on your second day to catch the sunrise at Machu Picchu.

The three- to seven-day **Salcantay** trek is named for the 6,270-meter (20,500-foot) peak of the same name. It begins at Mollepata, four hours by road from Cusco, and is a strenuous hike because of its passage through a 4,800-meter (15,700-foot) pass. The Salcantay excursion joins the Inca Trail at Huayllabamba.

Machu Picchu

Fodor'sChoice   *110 km (66 mi) northwest of Cusco.*
★

This mystical city, a three-hour-plus train ride from Cusco, is the most important archaeological site in South America, and one of the world's foremost travel destinations. The name itself conjures up the same magic as King Solomon's Mines or Xanadu, and Machu Picchu's beauty is so spectacular that the disappointed visitor is rare indeed. Its attraction lies in the exquisite architecture of the massive Inca stone structures and in the formidable backdrop of steep sugarloaf hills, with the winding Urubamba River—the Inca, who had a system of naming rivers by sector, called this portion of the river the Vilcanota—far below.

Ever since American explorer and Yale University historian Hiram Bingham, with the aid of local guides, "discovered" the Lost City in 1911—the name began to appear on maps as early as 1860, even if attempts to find the site were futile—there have been debates about Machu Picchu's original function. Bingham himself speculated that the site was a fortress for defensive purposes, but the preponderance of religious structures here calls that theory into question. It was likely a small city of some 200 homes and 1,000 residents, with agricultural terraces to supply the population's needs and a strategic position that overlooked but could not be seen from the valley floor. New theories suggest that the city was a transit station for products, such as coca and heart of palm, that were grown in the lowlands and sent to Cusco. Exactly when Machu Picchu was built is not known, but one theory suggests that it was a country estate of the Inca Pachacutec, which means its golden age was in the mid-15th century. Historians have discredited the romantic theory of Machu Picchu as a refuge of the chosen Inca women after the Spanish conquest; analysis shows a 50/50 split of male and female remains found here.

Bingham erred in recognizing just what he had uncovered. The historian assumed he had stumbled upon Vilcabamba, the last real stronghold of the Inca, the hastily constructed fortress to which the puppet Inca Manco Capac II retreated after the battles at Sacsayhuamán and Ollantaytambo. (The actual ruins of Vilcabamba lie deep in the rain forest, forgotten and not uncovered until the 1960s. And, ironically, Bingham did stumble upon the real Vilcabamba two years before he announced his discovery, equally unaware of what he had seen.) But Machu Picchu shows no battle scars, despite Bingham's insistence that it was a citadel, nor does it show signs of having been constructed quickly. Bingham assigned his own English-language names to the structures within the city. Call it inertia, but those labels have stuck, even though archaeologists continue to debate the correctness of the Yale historian's nomenclature.

The site's belated discovery has led some academics to conclude that the Inca deserted Machu Picchu before the Spanish conquest. The reason for the city's presumed abandonment is as mysterious as its original function. Some archaeologists suggest that the water supply simply ran out. Some guess that disease ravaged the city. Others surmise it may have been something as basic as the death of Pachacutec, after which his estate was no longer needed. Whatever the purpose, whatever the reason, this "Lost City of the Inca" was missed by the ravaging conquistadors and survived untouched until the beginning of the 20th century, and the mystery and intrigue will certainly inspire you to devise your own theories. ☎ *No phone* ✉ *S/77, S/38.50 with International Student Identity Card* ☉ *Daily 6 AM–5:30 PM.*

8

Exploring Machu Picchu

You can visit Machu Picchu on a day trip, but we recommend an overnight stay at the hotel near the entrance to the ruins or at a hotel in the town of Aguas Calientes, 8 km (5 mi) from the ruins. If you have only time for a day trip you'll have just a few hours at Machu Picchu, so bring a lunch with you; if you line up in the crowded cafeteria you'll have even less time, as you must leave to catch the bus back down to Aguas Calientes and the train back to Cusco. On the other hand, if you stay overnight you'll be able to wander the ruins after most tourists have gone. You'll also have time for a soak in the thermal baths in Aguas Calientes.

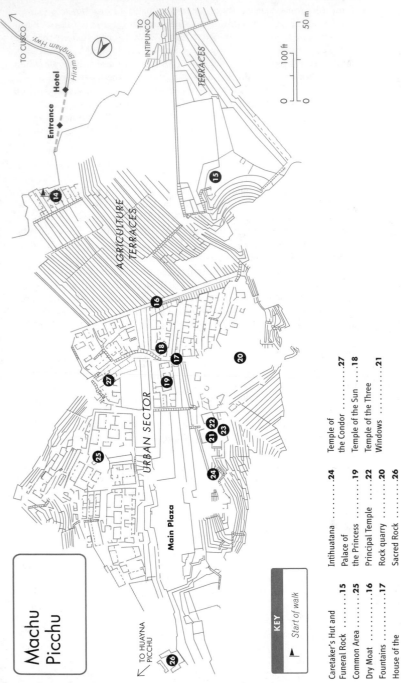

Machu Picchu

TO CUSCO

Hiram Bingham Hwy.

Hotel

Entrance

TO INTIPUNCO

TERRACES

AGRICULTURE TERRACES

14

15

16

18

17

27

19

20

25

21 22

23

24

URBAN SECTOR

Main Plaza

TO HUAYNA PICCHU

26

0   100 ft
0   50 m

KEY

▲ *Start of walk*

Caretaker's Hut and
Funeral Rock **15**

Common Area **25**

Dry Moat **16**

Fountains **17**

House of the
Terrace Caretaker **14**

Intihuatana **24**

Palace of
the Princess **19**

Principal Temple **22**

Rock quarry **20**

Sacred Rock **26**

Sacristy **23**

Temple of
the Condor **27**

Temple of the Sun ...**18**

Temple of the Three
Windows **21**

If you're a day-tripper, follow the crowd out of the rail station about a block away to the Consettur Machupicchu shuttle buses, which ferry you uphill to the ruins, a journey of about 20 minutes. Buy your S/40 round-trip ticket at a booth next to the line of buses before boarding. If you have the time to stay overnight, you'll first check in to your lodging and can come back later to buy a bus ticket. Buses leave Aguas Calientes for the ruins beginning at 6:30 AM and continue more or less hourly, with a big push in mid-morning as the trains begin to arrive from Cusco. The last bus up leaves about 1 PM. Buses start coming back down about 11:30 AM, with a last departure at 5:30. If you're a day visitor and heading back to Cusco, take the bus back down an hour before your train is scheduled to depart. If you stay in Aguas Calientes overnight, you'll also have time to buy your admission ticket to Machu Picchu itself at the Instituto Nacional de Cultura (Avenida Pachacutec s/n, open daily 6–noon and 1–5) in town just off the Plaza de Armas, thus avoiding the long high-season lines at the ticket booth at the ruins' entrance.

The illusion of being high above the valley floor makes you forget that Machu Picchu sits 2,490 meters (8,170 feet) above sea level, a much *lower* altitude than Cusco. This is semitropical highland forest. It gets warm here, and the ruins have little shade. Sunscreen, a hat, and water are musts. Officially, no food or drink are permitted within the ruins, but you can be unobtrusive with a bottle of water. Large packs must be left at the entrance. There are few signs inside to explain what you're seeing; booklets and maps are for sale at the entrance.

Within the Ruins

 ⑭ Upon entry, you first encounter the **House of the Terrace Caretaker.** Bingham surmised that Machu Picchu was divided into agricultural and urban sectors. As they did elsewhere in the empire, the Inca carved agricultural terraces into the hillsides here to grow produce and minimize erosion. Corn was the likely crop cultivated at Machu Picchu, though contemporary archaeologists wonder if the capacity and area of these terraces really could have supported a community of 1,000 residents. Absent are the elaborate irrigation systems seen at Inca ruins in the drier Sacred Valley. Machu Picchu's semitropical climate meant ample rain for most of the year.

⑮ About a 20-minute walk up to the left of the entrance, the **Caretaker's Hut and Funeral Rock** provide the quintessential vista overlooking Machu Picchu, one that you've seen in dozens of photos, and yet nothing beats seeing the view in person, especially if your schedule permits an early-morning visit to catch the misty sunrise. Bodies of nobles likely lay in state at the site, where they would have been eviscerated, dried, and prepared for mummification.

⑯ Head back down the hill to the city itself; the **Dry Moat** separates the agricultural and urban sectors. After you enter the ruins through the terraces at the agricultural sector, you come to a series of 16 small, ritual **⑰ Fountains** linked to the Inca worship of water.

⑱ Beyond the fountains is the round **Temple of the Sun,** a marvel of perfect Inca stone assembly. Here, on June 22 (the date of the winter solstice in the southern hemisphere), sunlight shines through a small, trapezoid-shape window and casts light into the middle of a large, flat granite stone presumed to be an Inca calendar. Prediction worked from both directions, too: looking out the window, astronomers sought the perfect view of the constellation Pleiades, revered as a symbol of crop fertility. Bingham dubbed the small cave below the temple the Royal Tomb, though no human remains were ever found here.

⑲ Adjoining the temple is a two-story building Bingham called the **Palace of the Princess.** Archaeologists have doubted the accuracy of the name.

⑳ Up a staircase, beyond the fountains and the temple, is a **rock quarry**
㉑ used by Inca masons. A stone staircase leads to the three-walled **Temple of the Three Windows**—the entire east wall is hewn from a single massive rock with trapezoidal windows cut into it. Further investigation has shown that there were really five original windows.

㉒ Another three-walled structure, the **Principal Temple,** is so dubbed because its masonry is among Machu Picchu's best, a masterpiece of fitting together many-sided stones without mortar in true Inca fashion. A
㉓ secondary temple abuts the primary temple. Bingham called it the **Sacristy.** It was likely the place where priests prepared for ceremonies.

㉔ Onward is a hillock that leads to the famous **Intihuatana,** the so-called "Hitching Post of the Sun." Every important Inca center had one of these vertical stone columns (called gnomons), but their function remains a mystery. They likely did double duty as altars and time-measurement devices to divine the growing seasons. The Spanish destroyed most of the hitching posts they encountered throughout the empire, deeming them to be objects of pagan worship. Machu Picchu's is one of the few to survive—partially survive at least. Shamefully, its top was accidentally knocked off in 2001 during the filming of a Cusqueña beer commercial on the site.

Cross a large grassy plaza toward an area of other buildings and huts.
㉕ Their less elaborate construction led Bingham to dub this the **Common**
㉖ **Area.** Here you'll find the **Sacred Rock,** taking the shape in miniature of the mountain range visible behind it. Little is known of its purpose.

㉗ A staircase leads to the **Temple of the Condor,** so named because the positioning of the stones resembles a giant condor, the symbol of heaven in the Inca cosmos. The structure's many small chambers led Bingham to dub it a "prison," a concept that did not likely exist in Inca society.

Agua Calientes
㉘ Far below the ruins sits the slightly ramshackle, but thoroughly pleasant town of Aguas Calientes, officially called Machupicchu Pueblo. But for the grace of Hiram Bingham, Aguas Calientes would be just another remote, forgotten crossroads. But 1911, and the tourist boom decades later forever changed the community. At just 2,040 meters (6,700 feet) above sea level, Aguas Calientes will seem downright balmy if you've just arrived from Cusco. The town takes its name from the thermal springs, the **Aguas Termales,** that sit above town. Don't expect facilities and conditions to rival those at Baden-Baden, but if you aren't too fussy, this

can be a refreshing dip at the end of a hot day. ☒ *Top of Av. Pacha-cutec* ☎ *No phone* ☒ *S/10* ☽ *Daily 6 AM–8 PM.*

The **Museo de Sitio Manuel Chávez Ballón,** the area's newest attraction, would go in the don't-miss column were it not for its odd location. The museum, dedicated to the history, culture, and rediscovery of Machu Picchu, sits on the way up to the ruins about 2 km (1 mi) from the edge of town at the entrance to the national park. Since the buses that ferry visitors up to Machu Picchu do not stop along the way, hoofing it is the only means to get here. Plan on about a 30-minute walk. If you have the time and inclination, the museum provides valuable bilingual insight into South America's premier tourist attraction, which you don't get at the ruins themselves. ☒ *Puente de Ruinas, 2 km (1 mi) from Aguas Calientes* ☎ *No phone* ☒ *S/20* ☽ *Daily 9–4.*

Where to Stay & Eat

$ ✕ **Indio Feliz.** An engaging French-Peruvian couple manage the best
Fodor'sChoice restaurant in Aguas Calientes, and this pink bistro is possibly the only
★ restaurant in town *not* to have pizza on its menu. Quiche lorraine, ginger chicken, and spicy *trucha macho* (trout in hot pepper and wine sauce) are favorites here, and are usually available as part of the more reasonably priced (S/38) prix-fixe menu. Top it off with a fine coffee and apple pie or flan for dessert. The restaurant presents each diner with a tiny ceramic pot or bowl as its calling card. ☒ *Lloque Yupanqui 4* ☎ *084/211–090* ☱ *AE, MC, V* ☽ *No dinner Sun.*

$$$$ ✕▣ **Machu Picchu Pueblo Hotel.** A five-minute walk from the center of
Fodor'sChoice town takes you to this stunningly beautiful ecolodge in its own mini-
★ tropical cloud forest. The stone bungalows, none with the same design, have a rustic elegance, with exposed beams and cathedral ceilings. Activities include a one-day Inca Trail trek, bird-watching excursions, and orchid tours, as well as a twilight nature walk. Dining in the restaurant overlooking the surrounding hills is first-rate—try the delicious *crema de choclo* (corn chowder). ☒ *Av. Imperio de los Incas s/n, Aguas Calientes* ☎ *084/211–032, 01/610–0404 in Lima* ⊕ *www.inkaterra.com* ☞ *82 rooms, 2 suites* ☖ *2 restaurants, dining room, pool, sauna, spa, bar, shop, laundry service, travel services; no room TVs* ☱ *AE, DC, MC, V* ☥ *MAP.*

$$$$ ✕▣ **Machu Picchu Sanctuary Lodge.** If you can get a reservation, this hotel at the entrance to Machu Picchu puts you closest to the ruins, a position for which you admittedly pay dearly. Not only will you have the thrill of watching the sun rise over the crumbling stone walls, but you'll have the ruins to yourself after most of the tourists depart each afternoon. The lodge has been completely renovated by Orient Express, which has taken over the property. The restaurant has an excellent international menu that makes it worth a special trip. ☒ *Machu Picchu* ☎ *084/211–038 or 084/241–777* ⊕ *www.orient-expresshotels.com* ☞ *29 rooms, 2 suites* ☖ *Restaurant, snack bar, minibars, massage, bar, laundry service* ☱ *AE, DC, MC, V* ☥ *FAP.*

$$$$ ▣ **Hatuchay Tower.** Aguas Calientes's "high-rise" hotel towers a whole four floors above the river at the edge of town on the road heading out to the ruins. Carpeted rooms are comfortable with modern furnishings

8

and amenities, but the interior design is nothing out of the ordinary. ✛ *At edge of town on road to ruins* ☎☎ *084/211–201 in Aguas Calientes* ☎ *01/447–8170 in Lima* ⊕ *www.hatuchaytower.com* ☞ *37 rooms, 5 suites* ♨ *Restaurant, in-room safes, cable TV, bar, Internet room; no-smoking floors* ▭ *AE, DC, MC, V* ⎸⊙⎹ *BP.*

$ ⊡ **Gringo Bill's Hostal.** Bill has hosted Machu Picchu travelers for almost a quarter century, and his was one of the first lodgings in town. Rooms are bright and airy in this rambling house with stone walls chock full of plants just off the Plaza de Armas. The corner rooms with balconies and windows get the best ventilation and have the greatest views. The small restaurant downstairs will even prepare a box lunch for your day's excursion. ⊠ *Colla Raymi 104, Aguas Calientes* ☎☎ *084/211–046* ⊕ *www.gringobills.com* ☞ *20 rooms* ♨ *Restaurant, massage, billiards, laundry service; no room phones, no TV in some rooms* ▭ *AE, MC, V* ⎸⊙⎹ *CP.*

Machu Picchu & the Sacred Valley Essentials

Transportation

BY CAR

To visit remote sights in the Sacred Valley of the Inca, you must travel by car. Or, for about US$50 a day, you can hire a taxi. Highways are good and traffic is relatively light in the Sacred Valley, but any trip entails a series of twisting, turning roads as you head out of the mountains near Cusco and descend into the valley. The road to Machu Picchu ends in Ollantaytambo; beyond that point, it's rail only. Cusco is the only place to rent a vehicle.

🚗 **Car Rentals Avis** ⊠ Aeropuerto Velasco Astete, Cusco ☎ 084/248–800. **Explores Transportes** ⊠ Plateros 356, Cusco ☎ 084/261–640. **OSDI Rent-a-Car** ⊠ Urb. Mateo Pumacahua B-10, Cusco ☎ 084/251–616.

BY TRAIN

At least two PeruRail trains depart from Cusco's San Pedro station daily for Aguas Calientes. The Vistadome leaves at 6 AM and arrives in Aguas Calientes at 9:40. It returns from Aguas Calientes at 3:30 PM, arriving in Cusco at 7:25. The round-trip fare is S/330. Snacks and beverages are included in the price, and the cars have sky domes to enhance your view of the scenery. The return trip includes a fashion show and folklore dancing.

The Backpacker train leaves Cusco at 6:15 AM, arriving in Aguas Calientes at 10:10. It leaves Aguas Calientes at 3:55 PM, getting back to Cusco at 8:20. The round-trip fare is S/250. Attendants sell snacks and beverages in Backpacker Class. Conditions are comparable to second-class trains in Western Europe and are quite comfortable.

A second Vistadome or Backpacker train may be added during the June–August high season, depending on demand.

All trains make an exaggerated series of five zigzag switchbacks, climbing elevation as they leave from Cusco before descending into the lower-altitude Sacred Valley. Trains stop at Poroy, Ollantaytambo, Km 88 (the start of the Inca Trail), and Km 104 (the launch point of an abbreviated two-day Inca Trail). Arrival is in Aguas Calientes, where you disembark to catch the buses up to the ruins.

The return trip actually takes longer, but you can make up that time by disembarking in Poroy, about 15 minutes by highway from Cusco, where an Asociación de Agencias de Turismo de Cusco bus meets every Cusco-bound train. The fare is a time-saving S/5, and the bus deposits you on Cusco's Plaza de Armas.

Your best bet is to purchase tickets in advance—that's a necessity during the June to August high season—from the PeruRail sales office at Cusco's Wanchaq Station, daily from 8 to 6—note that PeruRail does not accept credit cards—or from a travel agency. (Most tour packages sold include rail tickets as well as bus transport to and from Aguas Calientes and Machu Picchu and admission to the ruins.)

PeruRail's luxury Hiram Bingham train proffers a class of service unto itself (with prices to match). Trains depart from Poroy station, about 15 minutes outside Cusco, eliminating the tedious switchbacks necessary for the other trains to get out of and into the city. Departure time is a more leisurely 9 AM daily except Sunday, arriving at Aguas Calientes at 12:30 PM. Return service leaves Aguas Calientes at 6:30 PM, returning to Poroy at 10. The timetable permits you to stay at the ruins for a few hours after the day visitors have departed on the mid-afternoon trains back to Cusco. Trains consist of two dining cars, a bar car, and a kitchen car, and evoke the glamour of the old Orient Express rail service, no surprise, since Orient Express is the parent company of PeruRail. The S/1,560 round-trip price tag includes brunch on the trip to Machu Picchu, bus transport from Agua Calientes up to the ruins and back in vehicles exclusively reserved for Hiram Bingham clients, admission to the ruins, guide services while there, and an afternoon buffet tea at the Machu Picchu Sanctuary Lodge. The trip back entails cocktails, live entertainment, and a four-course dinner.

If you're using the Sacred Valley as your base, PeruRail operates a daily Vistadome train departing from Urubamba at 6 AM, and Ollantaytambo at 7, with arrival in Machu Picchu at 8:20. The return train leaves Machu Picchu at 4:45 PM, with arrival in Ollantaytambo at 6:05 and Urubamba at 7:10. Round-trip fare is S/190. Shuttle buses connect the Urubamba station to a few hotels in the valley. This service gives you a couple of extra hours to spend at the ruins than you'd have with a Cusco departure. A daily Backpacker train departs from Ollantaytambo at 9:25 AM, arriving at Aguas Calientes at 11. Return from Aguas Calientes is at 5 PM, with arrival in Ollantaytambo at 6:40.

Tourists are not permitted to ride the Tren Local, the less expensive, but slower train intended for local residents only.

Asociación de Agencias de Turismo de Cusco ✉ Nueva Baja 424, Cusco ☎ 084/222-580. **PeruRail** ✉ San Pedro station, Cascapara near Santa Clara, Cusco ☎ 084/233-551 ⊕ www.perurail.com ✉ Wanchaq station, Pachacutec near Tullumayo, Cusco ☎ 084/238-722 ⊕ www.perurail.com.

Contacts & Resources

VISITOR INFORMATION

Visitor offices in Cusco have information about the entire region. The Dirección Regional de Industria y Turismo (Dircetur) provides reliable information on the Sacred Valley and Machu Picchu. iPerú has helpful information on the region and can provide assistance if you feel you've received inadequate service from a tourist establishment. You'll find a branch in Aguas Calientes, near Machu Picchu, as well as in Cusco. The Oficina Ejecutiva del Comité Boleto Turístico (OFEC) in Cusco sells the 10-day boleto turístico, valid for admission to 16 museums and archaeological sites in the region, including the ruins at Pisac, Chinchero and Ollantaytambo. A private office of note in Cusco is South American Explorers, a membership organization. Its US$50 annual dues get you a quarterly magazine subscription and access to a wealth of information at its clubhouse here in Cusco, as well as in Lima and in Quito, Ecuador. Members can read trip reports, which are especially strong in providing up-to-date information about treks in the region.

The TOURIST INFORMATION signs you see around Aguas Calientes are really storefront travel agencies wishing to sell you tours rather than provide unbiased sources of information.

Dirección Regional de Industria y Turismo ⊠ Mantas 117, Cusco ☎ 084/263-176 ⊙ Weekdays 8-7, Sat. 8-noon. **iPerú** ⊠ Av. Pachacutec s/n, Aguas Calientes ☎ 084/211-104 ⊙ Daily 9-8 ⊠ Av. El Sol 103, Cusco ☎ 084/234-498 ⊙ Daily 8:30-7:30. **Oficina Ejecutiva del Comité Boleto Turístico** ⊠ Av. El Sol 103, Cusco ☎ 084/227-037 ⊠ Garcilaso and Heladeros, Cusco ☎ 084/226-919 ⊙ Mon.-Sat. 8-5, Sun. 8-2. **South American Explorers** ⊠ Choquechara 188 ☎ 084/245-484 ⊙ May-Sept., weekdays 9:30-5 and Sun. 9:30-1; Oct.-Apr., weekdays 9:30-5.

THE AMAZON BASIN

Updated by
Rhan Flatin

Peru's least-known region, its road less traveled—actually it's the *river* less traveled; roads are few and far between here—occupies some two-thirds of the country, an area the size of California. The *selva* (jungle) of the Amazon basin, watered by the world's second longest river and its tributaries, lies a world away from the Machu Picchu and Lake Titicaca of tourist brochures. The Amazon has a natural infrastructure to form the foundation of a growing ecotourism industry. What eastern Peru lacks in human population it makes up for in sheer plant and animal numbers, more than you knew could exist, all yours for the viewing. And there are lodges and guides to house and host the growing number of people who arrive to see the spectacle.

The northern Amazon, anchored by the port city of Iquitos, can claim the river itself in its territory. Iquitos is the gateway to the world's largest and most diverse natural reserve, the Amazon rain forest. From Iquitos you can visit Amazonian tribespeople, head for the jungle to explore the flora and fauna, or drift through an enchanted floating city in Iquitos's Belén neighborhood.

Most of the native tribes—there are many small tribes in the region, the Boras, Yaguas, and Orejones being the most prevalent—have given up their traditional hunter-gatherer subsistence and now live in small communities along the backwaters of the great river. You will not see "pygmies" unless you travel far from Iquitos and deep into the jungle, a harrowing and dangerous undertaking. What you will see are kind people living along with nature, with traditions that date back thousands of years: a common sight might be a fisherman paddling calmly up the Amazon in his dugout canoe, angling to reel in something substantial upriver. An almost unimaginable contrast is that less than a mile away, in Iquitos, *motocarros* (three-wheeled motorcycles with canvas tops) zoom by as pedestrians jabber on their cell phones, striving to keep pace with the 21st century.

The lesser-known southern Amazon region has to be satisfied with the big river's tributaries. Few travelers spend much time in Puerto Maldonado, the capital of Madre de Dios department, using the city instead as a jumping-off point to the Manu and Tambopata reserves. Manu is the less accessible but more pristine of the two Madre de Dios reserves, but Tambopata will not disappoint if time constrains you.

The region is remote by Peru's standards, but the Amazon is more accessible here than in the eight other South American countries that form its watershed. Just be prepared to spend some extra soles to get here. Roads, when they exist, are rough-and-tumble, and often impassible during the November through April rainy season. Rivers also overflow at this time. A dry-season visit entails the least muss and fuss. You'll most likely jet into Iquitos or Puerto Maldonado, respectively the northern and southern gateways to the Amazon. Each receives several daily flights from Lima. From each it's a trek, usually by boat, to reach the region's famed lodges.

Exploring the Amazon Basin

The logistics of travel and isolation make it unlikely that you could visit both the northern and southern Amazon regions—separated by 600 km (370 mi) at their nearest point—during one trip to Peru. The city of Iquitos is the jumping-off point for the northern Amazon; Puerto Maldonado, for the south. Some 1,200 km (740 mi) and connecting flights back in Lima separate the two cities. Choose one sector or the other for your visit. Neither will disappoint, and both are dotted with the region's famed jungle lodges, usually just a river journey away.

> **WORD OF MOUTH**
>
> "I prefer Iquitos [to Puerto Maldonado] for cultural experiences with local tribes and people who live along the river. These experiences were life-changing for me." —pretikk

About the Hotels

Beyond Puerto Maldonado and Iquitos lie the jungle lodges. They vary in degree of rusticity and remoteness, usually reachable only by boat. They range from camping sites a cut above the norm, where your tent is pitched on a covered wooden platform, to full-fledged ecolodges with private, tiled baths and solar-powered lighting. Most make do without

Tours of the Amazon

MADRE DE DIOS

One of the most experienced guide services, **Manu Expeditions** offers camping trips that last five to nine days. ⊠ *Urbanizació Magisterio 2nda Etapa, G-5, Cusco* ☎ *084/226-671* ⊕ *www.manuexpeditions.com.*

Manu Nature Tours operates the only full-service lodge within the Manu Biosphere reserve, as well as a cloud-forest lodge. The Manu Lodge is often used as a base by researchers and scientists studying the ecology of the reserve. ⊠ *Av. Pardo 1046, Cusco* ☎ *084/252-721* ⊠ *Conquistadores 396, San Isidro, Lima* ☎ *01/442-8980* ⊕ *www.manuperu.com.*

InkaNatura Travel manages lodges in Manu and in the Tambopata National Reserve. ⊠ *Manuel Bañon 461, Lima* ☎ *014/402-022* ⊠ *Calle Ricardo Palma 11, Cusco* ☎ *084/255-255, 877/ 827-8350 in U.S.* ⊕ *www.inkanatura. com.*

Inkaterra Nature Travel sets up tours to Reserva Amazonica in the Tambopata. Included are rain-forest walks, night hikes, and a visit to Rolin Island in the Madre de Dios. ⊠ *Andalucía 174, Miraflores, Lima* ☎ *016/100-400, 800/ 442-5042 in the U.S.* ⊕ *www.inkaterra. com* ⊠ *Procuradores 48, Cusco* ☎ *084/245-5314.*

Pantiacolla organizes ecotours in Manu and operates a lodge made up of a series of bungalows overlooking the Alto Madre de Dios river. ⊠ *Plateros 360, Cusco* ☎ *084/238-323* ⊕ *www.pantiacolla.com.*

Peruvian Safaris offers a customized visit of Puerto Maldonado, Tambopata, and Manu, and another tour of the reserves around Iquitos. ⊠ *Alcanfores 459, Miraflores, Lima* ☎ *01/447-8888* ⊕ *www.peruviansafaris.com.*

Rainforest Expeditions runs three- to seven-day tours including nights at the company's two Amazon lodges: the Tambopata Research Center and Posada Amazonas. ⊠ *Av. Aramburu 166, Miraflores, Lima* ☎ *01/421-8347, 877/905-3782 in the U.S.* ⊠ *Sunturwasi 350 (Triunfo), Cusco* ☎ *084/232-772* ⊠ *Arequipa 401, Puerto Maldonado* ☎ *082/571-056* ⊕ *www.perunature.com.*

IQUITOS AREA

Amazon Tours and Cruises specializes in river cruises using boats with 8 to 21 cabins. The longest and most comprehensive cruise includes a 6-day trip on the Amazon and a 10-day journey to Manaus, Brazil. All the boats have comfortable, air-conditioned cabins with private facilities. The boats stop for nature hikes and visits to villages. ⊠ *Requeña 336, Iquitos* ☎ *094/231-611* ⊕ *www.amazontours.net* ⊠ *275 Fontainebleau, Miami, FL 33174* ☎ *305/227-2266 or 800/423-2791.*

Explorama Tours offers three- to five-day boating and hiking trips along the Amazon River, including stays at the Explorama and ExplorNapo lodges. ⊠ *Av. de la Marina 350, Iquitos* ☎ *065/252-530, 800/707-5275 in the U.S.* ⊕ *www.explorama.com.*

International Expeditions has four of the most colorful and luxurious boats on the Amazon. Boats headed up the river to the Pacaya Samiria National Reserve have accommodations for between 8 and 26 passengers. Cruises can be booked only from the company's offices in the United States. ⊠ *1 Environs Park, Helena, AL 35080* ☎ *800/633-4734* ⊕ *www. internationalexpeditions.com.*

electricity, however. Showers will be refreshingly or bracingly cold, depending on your needs, though some lodges are installing systems to heat the water.

All lodges offer some variation on a fully escorted tour, with packages from one to several nights including all meals and guided wildlife-viewing excursions. Prior to signing up for a tour, you should just confirm that lodge beds have mosquito nets, and that all meals are indeed included. Many lodges quote rates per person for tours that typically last more than one day—it's not realistic to stay at most of these places for just one night. That said, the price ranges given for lodges in this chapter reflect the cost of one night's stay for two people.

Although travel agencies selling package tours via Lima or Cusco will accept credit cards, most jungle lodges cannot, as they do not have electricity or phone wires to verify credit-card information. All lodges accept soles, and most accept U.S. dollars for drinks, souvenirs, and other items. Some accept traveler's checks.

Madre de Dios

Do the math: 20,000 plant, 1,200 butterfly, 1,000 bird, 200 mammal, and 100 reptile species (and many more yet to be identified). The national parks, reserves, and other undeveloped areas of the southern department of Madre de Dios are among the most biologically diverse in the world. The southern sector of Peru's Amazon basin, most readily approached via Cusco, is famous among birders, whose eyes glaze over in amazement at the dawn spectacle of macaws and parrots visiting the region's famed *ccollpas* (clay licks). Ornithologists speculate that the birds must ingest clay periodically to detoxify other elements in their diet. Madre de Dios also offers a rare chance to see large mammals, such as tapirs and, if the zoological fates smile upon you, jaguars. Groups such as the Nature Conservancy and Conservation International view the region as one of the world's natural parks, a place where the endangered Amazon rain forest has a real chance of survival. Animal and plant life may abound, but this is the least populated of Peru's departments in terms of humans: a scant 76,000 people reside in an area slightly smaller than South Carolina, and almost two-thirds of them in the sultry capital, Puerto Maldonado. Thoughtful conservation and planning here, coupled with keeping the humans at bay, have allowed the plant and animal populations to thrive.

Tourism and conservation have triggered the newest generation of explorers in the species-rich southern Amazon. Two areas of Madre de Dios are of special interest. One is around the city of Puerto Maldonado, including the Tambopata National Reserve and the adjoining Bahuaja-Sonene National Park. Easily accessible, they offer lodges amid primary rain forest and excellent birding. The Manu Biosphere Reserve, directly north of Cusco, though more difficult and expensive to reach, provides unparalleled opportunity for observing wildlife in one of the largest virgin rain forests in the New World.

Puerto Maldonado
500 km (310 mi) east of Cusco.

The metropolis of the southern Amazon region and inland port city of Puerto Maldonado lies at the meeting point of the Madre de Dios and Tambopata rivers. The capital of the department of Madre de Dios is a rough-and-tumble town with 46,000 people and nary a four-wheeled vehicle in sight, but with hundreds of motorized two- and three-wheeled motorbikes jockeying for position on its few paved streets.

Tourism is the new cause for economic hope here. Puerto Maldonado bills itself as the "Biodiversity Capital of the World," and makes the best jumping-off point for visiting the Tambopata National Reserve sector of Peru's Amazon rain forest. But in fact, few travelers spend any time in the city, heading from the airport directly to the municipal docks, where they board boats to their respective jungle lodges. If you have a day to tack on to the beginning or end of your lodge stay, Puerto Maldonado is a beguiling town with a frontier feel; it also has a handful of decent hotels, a couple of which do provide an in-town jungle experience if you're pressed for time. As you might expect of such a remote region, this is the only place to use an ATM machine, cash a traveler's check, or log on to the Internet.

WHERE TO STAY & EAT
¢

✕🖾 **Hotel Cabaña Quinta.** The rambling chestnut-wood Victorian-style house, the tropical veranda, the arched doorways, the latticework, and the red-and-green *sangapilla* plants in the garden could have come right out of a Graham Greene novel. The rooms are a little less evocative but pleasantly furnished with wood paneling, print spreads, and drapes. The restaurant is one of Puerto Maldonado's best and serves a small menu of fish, meats, and soups, with plenty of yucca (cassava) chips on the side. ✉ *Cusco 535* 🕾🕾 *082/571–045* 🛏 *51 rooms, 3 suites* ⚐ *Restaurant, cable TV, meeting room, airport shuttle* ⊟ *V* †⊙† *BP.*

> **WORD OF MOUTH**
>
> "To really optimize your chance for wildlife viewing, stay at one of the more remote lodges."
> —Jeff Costa Rica

$
Fodor'sChoice
★

🖾 **Sandoval Lake Lodge.** InkaNatura Travel operates this lodge, the closest to Puerto Maldonado. It's accessible by an easy 30-minute boat ride east on the Madre de Dios River and a short hike or rickshaw ride, and it's actually feasible to do a one-night stay here. (Allow for more if your schedule permits.) The lodge is in the middle of forested grounds overlooking Lago Sandoval. A stay here includes excursions to the lake and rain forest, bilingual guides, and presentations. Note that there's no electricity. ⊹ *30 min by boat from Puerto Maldonado. Reservations:* ✉ *Calle Ricardo Palma 11, Cusco* 🕾 *084/255–255, 877/827–8350 in U.S.* ⊕ *www.inkanatura.com* 🛏 *25 rooms* ⚐ *Dining room, bar; no a/c, no room phones, no room TVs* †⊙† *AI.*

Tambopata National Reserve
& Bahuaja-Sonene National Park
5 km (3 mi) south of Puerto Maldonado.

Up the Tambopata River from Puerto Maldonado is the Tambopata National Reserve, a 3.8-million-acre primary-humid-tropical-forest reserved zone about the size of Connecticut. Officially separate from the reserve, but usually grouped for convenience under the "Tambopata" heading, is the Bahuaja-Sonene National Park. Peru works closely on joint conservation projects with Bolivia, whose adjoining Madidi National Park forms a grand cross-border 7.2-million-acre reserve area. Only environmentally friendly activities are permitted in Tambopata. The area functions partially as a managed tropical-forest reserve. The reserve's shiringa trees are an extraction source for latex. And cultivation here of *castañas*, or Brazil nuts, keeps thousands employed. Both activities provide an alternative incentive to conserving the forest rather than chopping it down. Tourism is the other major source of income for the reserve.

The Tambopata jungle lodges are much easier to reach—and much less expensive—than those in the Manu Biosphere Reserve, Madre de Dios's more famous ecotourism area. And Tambopata is no poor man's Manu either—its sheer numbers of wildlife are impressive in their own right. A half-hour, early-morning flight from Cusco at S/350 round-trip takes you to Puerto Maldonado, the Tambopata jumping-off point. And in a few hours or less you can arrive by boat to most lodges here and start bird-watching that afternoon. (You'd still be on your way to Manu at that point.) Opt for at least three days here if your schedule permits.

8

WHERE TO STAY The listings below are for lodges consisting of wooden huts raised on stilts. All provide rustic but more than adequate accommodations. Rates include river transportation from Puerto Maldonado, guides, and meals. For properties where a minimum stay is indicated, the price category is based on the per-night cost for two people.

$$$$ 🏠 **Explorer's Inn.** No place in the world tops this one for the number of bird species (600, and 331 of those spotted in one fortuitous day) sighted at a single lodge. Explorer's is managed by Peruvian Safaris, and accommodates tourists and visiting scientists in its thatched-roof bungalows. All can be seen navigating the lodge's 30 km (18½ mi) of trails. The lodge has a reference library and guides on hand. Note that there's no electricity in the rooms. The minimum stay is three days/two nights. *Reservations:* ⊠ *Alcanfores 459, Miraflores, Lima* ☎ *01/447–8888* ⊕ *www.peruviansafaris.com* ↘ *30 rooms* ⚹ *Dining room, library; no a/c, no room phones, no room TVs* ⊖ *AI.*

$$$$ 🏠 **Posada Amazonas.** This comfortable lodge is owned jointly by Rain-
Fodor'sChoice forest Expeditions and the Ese'eja Native Community of Tambopata.
★ The property defines "jungle chic," with mosquito nets over the beds, and wide, screenless windows to welcome cooling breezes. A canopy tower provides a great view of the rain forest. Transportation to the lodge is usually by a combination of a thatched-roof truck and a large wooden boat with drop-down rain curtains. A visit to a local village is made en

Tambopata Treats

ELEVATIONS here range from 500 meters (1,640 feet) to a lofty 3,000 meters (9,840 feet), providing fertile homes for an astounding number of animals and plants. The area holds a world record in the number of butterfly species (1,234) recorded by scientists. Within the reserve, the Explorer's Inn holds the world-record bird-species sighting for a single lodge: 600 have been recorded on its route. Packages include all transport, lodging, meals, and guides. The minimum stay is three days/two nights. ✈ *30-min drive, 1-hr boat ride, and 15-min walk from Puerto Maldonado Reservations:* ⊠ *Av. Aramburu 166, Miraflores, Lima* ☎ *01/421–8347, 877/905–3782 in U.S.* ⊠ *Sunturwasi 350 (Triunfo), Cusco* ☎☎ *084/232–772* ⊠ *Arequipa 401, Puerto Maldonado* ☎☎ *082/571–056* ⊕ *www.perunature.com* ♺ *30 rooms* ♿ *Dining room; no a/c, no room phones, no room TVs* ⊟ *MC, V* ⦿ *AI.*

grounds, 331 of those sighted within a single day, also a score no other lodging can top. Tambopata is the site of the most famous and largest of Madre de Dios's ccollpas; this clay lick is visited daily by 15 species of parrots and macaws, who congregate at dawn to collect a beakful of mineral-rich clay, an important but mysterious part of their diet.

Manu Biosphere Reserve

Fodor'sChoice ★ *90 km (55 mi) north of Cusco.*

Readers of the British children's series *A Bear Called Paddington* know that the title character "came from darkest Peru." And the reserve really does count the Andean spectacled bear, South America's only ursid, and the animal on which Paddington was based, among its 200 mammals.

This reserve area half the size of Switzerland is Peru's largest protected area and straddles the boundary of the Madre de Dios and Cusco departments. Manu encompasses more than 4½ million acres of pristine primary tropical-forest wilderness, ranging in altitude from 3,450 meters (12,000 feet) down through cloud forests and into a seemingly endless lowland tropical rain forests at 300 meters (less than 1,000 feet). Not surprisingly, this geographical variety shelters a stunning biodiversity, and a near total absence of humans and hunting has made the animal life here less skittish and more open to observation. The reserve's 13 monkey species scrutinize visitors with the same curiosity they elicit. White caimans sun themselves lazily on sandy riverbanks,

> **WORD OF MOUTH**
>
> "Peru offers a number of Amazon destinations for viewing wildlife—in general, scores of monkey species, birds, river snakes, butterflies, giant otters and macaws, pink dolphins, and the rare Uakari (red-face) monkey."   —davarian

whereas the larger black ones lurk in the oxbow lakes. And expect to see tapirs at the world's largest tapir ccollpa. Giant Orotongo river otters and elusive big cats such as jaguars and ocelots sometimes make fleeting appearances. But it's the avian life that has made Manu world famous. The area counts more than 1,000 bird species, fully a ninth of those known. Some 500 species have been spotted at the Pantiacolla Lodge alone. Birds include macaws, toucans, roseate spoonbills, and 1½-meter- (5-foot-) tall wood storks.

Manu was declared a national park in 1973, and a biosphere reserve in 1977. Ten years later, UNESCO designated it a World Heritage Site. It is divided into three distinct zones. The smallest is the so-called "cultural zone" (Zone C), with several indigenous groups and the majority of the jungle lodges. About three times the size of the cultural zone, Manu's "reserve zone" (Zone B) is uninhabited but contains one of the lodges— Manu Lodge. Access is by permit only, and you must be accompanied by a guide from one of the 10 agencies authorized to take people into the area. The western 80% of Manu is designated a national park (Zone A). Authorized researchers and indigenous peoples who reside there are permitted in this zone; visitors may not enter.

A Manu excursion is no quick trip. Overland travel from Cusco, the usual embarkation point, takes up to two days, in a thrilling trip over the mountains and down into the lowland plains. A charter flight in a twin-engine plane to the small airstrip at Boca Manu shaves that time down to 45 minutes but adds a few hundred dollars onto your package price. From Boca Manu you'll still have several hours of boat travel to reach your lodge. The logistics of travel to this remote part of the Amazon mean you should allow at least five days for your excursion. A week is more manageable.

WHERE TO STAY For properties where a minimum stay is indicated, the price category is based on the per-night cost for two people.

$$$$ ⊞ **Manu Cloud Forest Lodge.** High in the cloud forest of Manu's cultural zone, this lodge sits on grounds blooming with orchids and overlooking the rushing Río Unión. Rooms are rustic and spartan, with beds and tables, but all have a private bath and plenty of hot water (but no electricity). The highly respected Manu Nature Tours operates the lodge. The minimum stay is three days/two nights. Bilingual guides and ground transportation are included. ⚕ *About 145 km (90 mi or a 6½-hr drive) north of Cusco Reservations:* ✉ *Av. Pardo 1046, Cusco* ☎ *084/252– 721* ✉ *Conquistadores 396, San Isidro, Lima* ☎ *01/442–8980* ⊕ *www. manuperu.com* ⇨ *8 rooms, 4 cabins* ⌂ *Dining room, sauna, mountain bikes, bar; no a/c, no room phones, no room TVs* ⊟ *AE, MC, V* ⊺⚬⊺ *AI.*

$$$$ ⊞ **Manu Lodge.** Built by Manu Nature Tours from mahogany salvaged from the banks of the Manu River, the lodge is set deep in the reserve zone, the only such accommodation, overlooking the 2-km- (1-mi-) long oxbow lake called Cocha Juárez. Frequently seen in the lake are giant river otters and black and white caimans. The comfortable, screened-in lodge has a two-story dining area, and guests have access to three habitats: the lakes, the river, and a trail network spanning 10

square km (4 square mi) of rain forest. The lodge has tree-climbing equipment to lift visitors onto canopy platforms for viewing denizens of the treetops. The minimum stay is five days/four nights (with a stay en route at Manu Cloud Forest Lodge), and includes bilingual guides, ground transportation, and meals. There's no electricity. *Reservations:* ⊠ *Av. Pardo 1046, Cusco* ☎ *084/252–721* ⊠ *Conquistadores 396, San Isidro, Lima* ☎ *01/442–8980* ⊕ *www.manuperu.com* ⇦ *12 rooms* ⚒ *Restaurant, bar; no a/c, no room phones, no room TVs* ⊟ *AE, MC, V* ⍾⊙⍾ *AI.*

$$$$ ⊡ **Manu Wildlife Center.** As the name suggests, this is a great place for wildlife viewing, as it sits close to Manu's macaw and tapir ccollpas and encompasses 48 km (30 mi) of trails. The MWC, as it is known, is jointly owned by Cusco's InkaNatura Travel and Manu Expeditions, and services are top-notch. Raised thatched-roof bungalows have screens and wooden latticework walls as well as tiled hot-water baths. ⊹ *30 min by air and 90 min by boat from Cusco Reservations:* ⊠ *Calle Ricardo Palma 11, Santa Monica, Cusco* ☎ *084/255–255, 877/827–8350 in U.S.* ⊕ *www.inkanatura.com or www.manuexpeditions.com* ⇦ *22 cabins* ⚒ *Dining room, bar, meeting room; no a/c, no room phones, no room TVs* ⊟ *AE, MC, V* ⍾⊙⍾ *AI.*

Amazon Basin Essentials

Transportation

BY AIR

Starting in Lima and stopping in Cusco, Aero Condor, Aero Continente, LanPeru, and TANS Perú each have daily or weekly flights to Aeropuerto Padre Aldámiz (PEM), 5 km (3 mi) from Puerto Maldonado. All flights arrive and depart early in the morning. Several of the Manu lodges fly their passengers to the small airstrip at Boca Manu on a charter basis.

🛈 Carriers **Aero Condor** ⊠ Av. Velazco Astete (Aeropuerto), Cusco ☎ 084/252–774. **Aero Continente** ⊠ León Velarde 584, Puerto Maldonado ☎ 082/572–004. **LanPeru** ⊠ Puerto Maldonado ☎ 082/573–677. **TANS Perú** ⊠ León Velarde 151, Puerto Maldonado ☎ 082/573–861.

🛈 Airport Information **Aeropuerto Padre Aldámiz** ☎ 082/571–533.

Contacts & Resources

VISITOR INFORMATION

The Dirección Regional de Industria y Turismo (DRIT) has an office in Puerto Maldonado and serves as the government tourist office. It provides reliable information on the city and Madre de Dios. A branch at the airport is open daily for all incoming flights. The Conservation Association of the Southern Rain Forest has details about parks in the region. Dirección de Areas Protegidas y Fauna Silvestre offers information about Manu National Park.

🛈 **Conservation Association of the Southern Rain Forest** ⊠ Portal los Panes 123, Haukaypata (Plaza de Armas), Cusco ☎ 084/240–911 ⊠ Puerto Maldonado ☎ 082/571–037. **Dirección de Areas Protegidas y Fauna Silvestre** ⊠ Petirrojos 355, Urbanización El Palomar, San Isidro, Lima ☎ 01/441–0425 ⊠ Urbanización Mariscal Gamarra 4-C, Apartado 1057, Cusco ☎ 084/223–633. **Dirección Regional de Industria y Turismo** ⊠ Fitzcarraldo 411, Puerto Maldonado ☎ 082/571–164.

Iquitos & Environs

1,150 km (713 mi) northeast of Lima.

A sultry port town on the Río Amazonas, Iquitos is quite probably the world's largest city that cannot be reached by road. The city has some 350,000 inhabitants and is the capital of the vast Loreto department. The area around Iquitos was first inhabited by small, independent Amazonian tribes. In the 1500s Jesuit missionaries began adventuring in the area, trying to Christianize the local population, but the city wasn't officially founded until 1757.

One of Iquitos's most fascinating sights is the **Distrito de Belén** (Belén District). In the market itself you will find sundry items from love potions to fresh *suri* (palm-tree worms). It is not the cleanest or sweetest-smelling market you'll encounter, but it's well worth the visit. From the center of the market you come to the port, where you can head out on a canoe trip through the floating Belén District. This slum area is often called the Venice of the Amazon (a diplomatic euphemism), but paddling by canoe through the floating "neighborhoods" is really a kick. The houses here are built on rafts. Most of the year they float placidly on the Amazon, though during the low-water season (June–November) they sit in the mud and can attract disease-carrying mosquitoes. During high-water season (December–May), guides hire out their services for one- to two-hour trips, which normally cost around S/7. Negotiate the price beforehand. Be street smart in Belén—evening muggings have been reported in this area, so it is best avoided at night. Also be wary of pickpockets at all times. Stay alert, access your cash discreetly, and keep your valuables close.

From the small **Port Bellavista Nanay,** slightly more than 1 km (½ mi) north of downtown Iquitos on Avenida La Marina, you can hire boats to take you to the Boras and Yaguas villages. Bringing a donation of school supplies (pencils, crayons, and notebooks) is a kind gesture that will be much appreciated by the Boras and Yaguas, who live in small communities near the pueblo San Andrés. A 20-minute boat ride from the port will bring you to **Pilpintuwasi Butterfly Farm,** which hosts some 42 butterfly species and also has macaws, a jaguar, and a tapir. During the dry season you'll need to walk along a forest path for 15 minutes to get to the farm. It is best to go with a guide. ⊠ *Near village of Padre Cocha on Nanay River, 5 km (3 mi) from downtown Iquitos* ☎ *065/232–665 or 065/993–2999* ⊕ *www.amazonanimalorphanage.org* ✉ *S/26 without transportation* ☉ *Tues.–Sun. 9–4.*

Where to Stay & Eat

★ **$–$$** ✕ **Gran Maloca.** This most elegant of the city's restaurants is in a lovely building encrusted with colorful *azulejos* (glazed tiles). The international fare is excellent, and the lobster and shrimp in pepper sauce is especially good. Try the *suri al ajo* (palm-tree grubs cooked in wine and garlic sauce) for an appetizer. Gran Maloca has an extensive wine and spirits list, with locally made fruit liqueurs. ⊠ *Sargento Lores 170* ☎ *065/233–126* ⊟ *AE, DC, MC, V.*

8

$ ✗ **La Noche.** Big windows smile onto the Amazon River from the azulejos-covered facade of this bistro. The menu is varied and has de rigueur international standards as well as some excellent local alternatives. The *venado a la Loretana* (Loretan-style venison) is tender and yummy. This is also an excellent night spot, as the restaurant sits right on the Malecón Maldonado riverwalk. ⊠ *Malecón Maldonado 177* ☎ *065/222–373* ✑ *No credit cards.*

¢–$ ✗ **Fitzcarraldo.** The colonial elegance of this riverwalk eatery shines
Fodor'sChoice through, from the antique firearms to the iron terrace chairs. The extensive menu has international essentials like pizza and pasta, but the Amazonian specialties are the real draw. Try the *chicharrón de lagarto* (crocodile nuggets), topping off the meal with a frothy *caipirinha* (a Brazilian drink with lime, sugar, and the sugarcane liquor *cachaça*). ⊠ *Napo 100, at El Blvd.* ☎ *065/242–434* ✑ *AE, DC, MC, V.*

¢ ✗ **El Mesón.** This restaurant on the riverwalk serves ample potions of regional specialties. Try the delicious *paiche*, a giant fish found in jungle lakes. Tapestries and paintings depicting scenes from traditional Amazonian life adorn the walls. With good views of the Amazon and the easy-paced life of the paseo, this is an excellent sunset joint. ⊠ *Av. Malecón Maldonado 153* ☎ *065/231–857* ✑ *AE, DC, MC, V.*

★ $$$ ⌸ **El Dorado Plaza Hotel.** This five-star contemporary hotel richly deserves the praise it wins from guests. All rooms center around the grand entryway, which has a large fountain and a glass elevator. Behind the hotel is a pool with a swim-up bar; a bridge arches over the pool, leading to the Jacuzzi. The rooms have all the modern conveniences and are equipped with soundproof glass to protect you from the incessant cacophony of central Iquitos. The hotel sits in the heart of the city on the Plaza de Armas. ⊠ *Napo 252* ☎ *094/222–555* ⊕ *www.eldoradoplazahotel.com* ⟿ *56 rooms, 9 suites* ⌂ *Restaurant, cafeteria, room service, in-room safes, minibars, cable TV, pool, health club, outdoor hot tub, 2 bars, shop, laundry service, business services, meeting rooms, airport shuttle* ✑ *AE, DC, MC, V* ⦿� *CP.*

★ $–$$ ⌸ **Victoria Regia Hotel.** This modern, airy lodging has rooms dressed in cool colors that surround a courtyard with a small swimming pool. Rooms in the back are less noisy but darker. Most rooms have impressionist and expressionist prints adorning the walls, blond-wood furniture, and large, comfy beds. ⊠ *Ricardo Palma 252* ☎☎ *065/231–983* ⊕ *www. victoriaregiahotel.com* ⟿ *34 rooms, 8 suites* ⌂ *Restaurant, room service, in-room safes, minibars, cable TV, pool, bar, laundry service, business services, meeting rooms, airport shuttle, travel services* ✑ *AE, DC, MC, V* ⦿⦿ *CP.*

¢ ⌸ **Florentina Hostal.** A bare-bones budget alternative in the center of Iquitos, La Florentina has simple, clean rooms in a more than 100-year-old house. Two rooms come with air-conditioning; the others have fans and can get quite hot. All rooms have soft beds and thin sheets. ⊠ *Jr. Huallaga 212* ☎☎ *065/233–591* ⟿ *19 rooms* ⌂ *Cafeteria, some fans, cable TV, laundry service; no a/c in some rooms, no room phones* ✑ *No credit cards.*

Into the Jungle

About 50 km (31 mi) from Iquitos are vast tracks of primary rain forest that seem to stretch forever, where the only intrusion from humans has been hunting and gathering. Sadly, even this light touch has had an effect, as hunting has all but eliminated large animals from the region. However, visitors are likely to see birds, monkeys, pink freshwater *bufeos* (dolphins), and caimans along the Amazon River and its tributaries. You're sure to spot large blue morpho butterflies.

The Amazon basin is the world's most diverse ecosystem. The numbers of cataloged plant and animal species are astronomical, and scientists are discovering new species all the time. There are more than 25,000 classified species of plants in the Peruvian Amazon (and 80,000 in the entire Amazon basin), including the 2-meter-wide (6-foot-wide) Victoria Regia water lilies. Scientists have cataloged more than 4,000 species of butterfly and more than 2,000 species of fish—a more diverse aquatic life than that of the Atlantic Ocean. Scientists estimate that the world's tropical forests, while comprising only 6% of the Earth's landmass, may hold up to 75% of the planet's plant and animal species. This land is not only beautiful, with numerous indigenous populations, but is also the largest natural pharmacy in the world: one-fourth of all modern medicines have botanical origins in tropical forests.

It's interesting and worthwhile to visit the small villages of indigenous people. When the boat stops at these settlements, you'll usually find half the village waiting to trade handicrafts for whatever you have with you; items perpetually in demand include umbrellas, hammers, fishing hooks, flashlights, sewing supplies, lipstick, and clothing.

The best way to visit the jungle is with a prearranged tour with one of the many jungle lodges. All the lodges have highly trained naturalist guides. Among the activities offered at these lodges are nature walks, birding tours, nighttime canoe outings, fishing, and trips to indigenous villages. Some lodges have canopy walkways that take you into the seldom-explored rain-forest canopy.

Where to Stay

Rates for the rain-forest lodges near Iquitos include transportation, meals, and guided walks. Transportation to the lodges is either by *palmcaris* (large wooden boats with thatched roofs) or speedboats. For properties where a minimum stay is indicated, the price category is based on the per-night cost for two people.

$$$$ **ExplorNapo and ACTS.** The remote ExplorNapo camp is set deep in **Fodor'sChoice** the middle of the Sucusari Nature Reserve, 70 km (43 mi) up the Napo ★ River and 1½ hours by boat from Explorama Lodge. There's a 1,500-foot-long, 120-foot-high canopy walkway at the nearby ACTS (Amazon Conservatory of Tropical Studies) for exploring the seldom-seen upper-reaches of the Amazon, as well as an informative ethnological garden. Facilities at ExplorNapo are rustic, with kerosene lighting and separate cold-water shower facilities. There's a screened dining room, with occasional music performed by locals. This is a prime place for spotting wildlife, so guided walks and canoe trips are daily activities. The minimum stay is four nights, and you can substitute a night or two at the ExplorNapo with an overnight stay at the ACTS lodge. Though it puts you much closer to the canopy walkway, ACTS is even more rustic and has fewer facilities. Because of the remoteness of these lodges, many people spend a night at the Explorama Lodge en route to Explor-Napo and ACTS. ✣ *160 km (100 mi) from Iquitos along Napo River Reservations:* ⊠ *Av. de la Marina 340, Iquitos* ☎ *065/252–530, 800/ 707–5275 in U.S.* ⊕ *www.explorama.com* ⊃ *30 rooms with shared bath* ⌂ *Restaurant, boating, fishing, hiking, bar, airport shuttle, travel services, no-smoking rooms; no a/c, no room phones, no room TVs* ▤ *AE, MC, V* ⚌ *FAP.*

$$$$ ▦ **Yacumama Lodge.** Alongside the Yarapa River, a tributary of the Amazon, this beautiful complex is three to four hours from Iquitos. Raised bungalows with screened porches (widely spaced for maximum privacy) are connected to the main lodge by covered walkways. All the buildings are made of natural materials, and most of the property is solar powered, with an emphasis on recycling, composting, and organic farming—all part of the goal of minimum impact on the surrounding environment. Although rooms don't have private baths, there are two modern buildings with showers and flush toilets. A screened "hammock room" overlooking the river is great for afternoon naps, especially after swinging from tree to tree on the "canopy skyline." Pink river dolphins are often spotted in the area. The minimum stay is five nights. ✣ *177 km (110 mi) from Iquitos Reservations:* ⊠ *Sgto. Lores 149, Iquitos* ☎ *065/235–510* ⊃ *31 bungalows with shared bath* ⌂ *Restaurant, boating, fishing, hiking, bar, meeting rooms, airport shuttle, travel services, no-smoking rooms; no a/c, no room phones, no room TVs* ▤ *AE, DC, MC, V* ⚌ *FAP.*

$$ ▦ **Amazon Rainforest Lodge.** Only an hour by speedboat from Iquitos, this cluster of thatched-roof bungalows sits on the Momon River. The attractive structures center around the greenish-color pool, have twin beds and private baths, and are lit by gas lanterns. Activities include guided walks, piranha fishing, night canoeing, ayahuasca ceremonies, and visits to Yagua villages. They cater to a much younger crowd than most of the jungle lodges in the area. *Reservations:* ⊠ *Putumayo 159, Iquitos* ☎ *065/233–100 or 01/445–5620* ⊕ *www.amazon-lodge.com* ⊃ *14 bungalows with shared bath* ⌂ *Restaurant, pool, boating, fishing, hiking, bar, shop, laundry service, airport shuttle, travel services, no-smoking rooms; no a/c, no room phones, no room TVs* ▤ *MC, V* ⚌ *FAP.*

Iquitos & Environs Essentials

Transportation

BY AIR

Aero Condor flies to Iquitos daily and also to Cusco and Puerto Maldonado from Lima. LanPeru and STAR Peru also fly to Iquitos. Aerocontinente offers round-trip flights from Miami on Sunday.

Iquitos's Aeropuerto Internacional Francisco Secada Vignetta is 8 km (5 mi) from the city center. There is a S/12 airport tax for domestic flights and a S/36 tax for international flights. A taxi to the airport should cost around S/10.

🛈 **Carriers Aero Condor** ☎ 065/244–326 in Iquitos. **LanPeru** ☎ 065/232–421 in Iquitos. **Star Peru** ☎ 065/236–208 in Iquitos. **TANS Perú** ☎ 065/221–549 in Iquitos.

🛈 **Airport Information Aeropuerto Internacional Francisco Secada Vignetta** ☎ 065/260–147 in Iquitos.

BY BOAT

The best way to travel around the Iquitos area is by boat. There are huge seagoing boats that will transport you all the way through Brazil to the Atlantic Ocean, tiny dugout canoes to take you deep into the jungle, and swift launches with outboard engines and canvas tops to keep you dry. It takes several days to get to any large communities near Iquitos.

Contacts & Resources

VISITOR INFORMATION

There are information offices in downtown Iquitos and at the airport.

🛈 **iPerú** ✉ Airport ☎ 065/260–251. **Tourist Information Office** ✉ Napo 226, Iquitos ☎ 065/236–144.

PERU ESSENTIALS

Transportation

BY AIR

Airlines flying nonstop from the United States into Aeropuerto Internacional Jorge Chávez, 11 km (7 mi) west of Lima, include American Airlines from Dallas and Miami; Continental from Houston and Newark; Delta from Atlanta, and Lan from Miami, New York, and Los Angeles. Air Canada flies from Toronto. Aeromexico flies from Mexico City.

With four mountain ranges running through Peru plus a large swath of the Amazon jungle, flying is the best way to travel between most cities and towns. Lan, which has by far the most flights to major tourist destinations, departs several times each day for Arequipa, Cusco, Juliaca, Puerto Maldonado, and Trujillo. Aero Cóndor has daily flights to Arequipa and Iquitos, while Taca Peru flies to Arequipa and Cusco. TANS Perú flies to Arequipa, Cusco, Iquitos, Juliaca, and Puerto Maldonado.

🛈 **Airlines American** ☎ 800/433–7300 in North America, 01/211–7000 in Lima ⊕ www.aa.com. **Continental** ☎ 800/525–0280 In North America, 01/222–7080 in Lima ⊕ www.continental.com. **Delta** ☎ 800/221–1212 in North America, 01/211–9211 in Lima ⊕ www.delta.com. **Lan** ☎ 866/435–9526 in North America, 01/213–3764 in Lima ⊕ www.lan.com. **Taca** ☎ 800/400–8222 in North America, 01/446–0033 in Lima ⊕ grupotaca.com. **TANS Perú** ☎ 01/213–6000 ⊕ www.tansperu.com.pe. **United Airlines** ☎ 800/864–8331 in North America, 800/538–2929 international ⊕ www.united.com.

🛈 **Airport Information Aeropuerto Internacional Jorge Chávez** ✉ Av. Faucett s/n ☎ 01/517–3100 ⊕ www.lap.com.pe.

BY BOAT & FERRY

Travel across Lake Titicaca from Peru to Bolivia is usually via hydrofoils operated by Crillón Tours, which run from Copacabana in Bolivia to Puno in Peru.

8

Passenger boats are the most important means of transportation in the jungle. If you visit a jungle lodge, your hosts will probably pick you up in an outboard-powered boat. Larger boats make 4- to 10-day cruises on the Amazon from Iquitos. You can also make arrangements for an excursion with a native guide in a wooden dugout called a *pecka-pecka*, the nickname coming from the sound of the small motor. On Lake Titicaca, small boats offer taxi service to the islands.

Crillón Tours ✉ Av. Camacho 1223, La Paz, Bolivia ☎ 02/337-533, 888/848-4222 in U.S. ⊕ www.titicaca.com.

BY BUS

The intercity bus system in Peru is extensive, and fares are quite reasonable. Remember, however, that distances between cities can be daunting. It's best to use buses for shorter trips, such as between Lima and Ica or between Cusco and Puno. That way you can **begin and end your trip during daylight hours.** Keep an eye on personal property in bus stations, as there is the usual amount of petty crime.

Alternative forms of public transportation are the *colectivos*, small vans that follow the same routes as buses. They charge about twice as much but are usually much faster. The catch is that they often don't depart until they fill up.

Bus Information Cruz del Sur ✉ Av. Javier Prado 1109, San Isidro, Lima ☎ 01/225-6163 ⊕ www.cruzdelsur.com.pe. **Ormeño** ✉ Av. Javier Prado Este 1059, San Isidro, Lima ☎ 01/472-1710 ⊕ www.grupo-ormeno.com.

BY CAR

In general, it is not a great idea to have a car in Peru. Driving is a heart-stopping experience, as most Peruvians see traffic laws as suggestions rather than rules.

That said, there are a few places in Peru where having a car is a benefit, such as between Lima and points south on the Pan-American Highway. The highway follows the Pacific Ocean coastline before it cuts in through the desert, and stops can be made along the way for a picnic and a swim. The highway is good, and although there isn't too much to see along the way, it's nice to have the freedom of movement a car affords once you get to your destination.

The major highways in Peru are the Pan-American Highway, which runs down the entire coast, and the Carretera Central, which runs from Lima to Huancayo. Most highways have no names or numbers; they are referred to by destination.

EMERGENCY SERVICES The Touring and Automobile Club of Peru will provide 24-hour emergency road service for members of the American Automobile Association (AAA) and affiliates upon presentation of their membership cards. Members of AAA can purchase good maps at low prices.

Emergency Services Touring and Automobile Club of Peru ✉ César Vallejo 699, Lince, Lima ☎ 01/221-2432 ⊕ www.touringperu.com.pe.

RULES OF THE ROAD In Peru your own driver's license is acceptable identification, but an international driving permit is good to have. They are available from the American and Canadian automobile associations and, in the United Kingdom, from the Automobile Association and Royal Automobile Club. These international permits, valid only in conjunction with your regular driver's license, are universally recognized; having one may save you a problem with local authorities.

Speed limits are 25 kph–35 kph (15 mph–20 mph) in residential areas, 85 kph–100 kph (50 mph–60 mph) on highways. Traffic tickets range from a minimum of $4 to a maximum of $40. The police and military routinely check drivers at road blocks, so make sure your papers are easily accessible. Peruvian law makes it a crime to drive while intoxicated, although many Peruvians ignore that prohibition. If you are caught driving while under the influence, you will either pay a hefty bribe or spend the night in jail.

Contacts & Resources

BANKS & EXCHANGE SERVICES

You can safely exchange money or cash traveler's checks in a bank, at your hotel, or from *casas de cambio* (exchange houses). Stores, smaller hotels, and restaurants rarely accept traveler's checks. Major credit cards, especially Visa, are accepted in most hotels, restaurants, and shops in tourist areas.

CURRENCY   Peru's national currency is the nuevo sol (S/). Bills are issued in denominations of 5, 10, 20, 50, and 100 soles. Coins are 1, 5, 10, 20, and 50 céntimos, and 1, 2, and 5 soles.

CUSTOMS & DUTIES

When you check through immigration upon arrival in Peru be sure to put the white International Embarkation/Disembarkation form you filled out in a safe place when it is returned to you. You will need it when you leave the country. If you lose it, in addition being delayed, you may have to pay a small fine. You may bring personal and work items; a total of three liters of liquor; jewelry or perfume worth less than $300; and 400 cigarettes or 50 cigars into Peru without paying import taxes. After that, goods and gifts will be taxed at 20% their value up to $1,000; everything thereafter is taxed at a flat rate of 25%.

Departure taxes on international flights from Lima are US$28.24 and domestic flights US$5.04. These taxes, paid after you check in for your flight, must be paid in cash, either in U.S. dollars or Peruvian nuevos soles. If you're paying in dollars, try to have the exact amount ready, as you will be given change in local currency. It's a good idea to wait to convert your nuevos soles back to dollars until after you pay the departure tax. These prices don't change much from year to year, but they do fluctuate with the exchange rate, so carry a few extra bills and coins.

ELECTRICITY

The electrical current in Peru is 220 volts, 50 cycles alternating current (AC). A converter is needed for appliances requiring 110 voltage. U.S.-style flat prongs are used.

If your appliances are dual-voltage, you'll need only an adapter. Don't use 110-volt outlets marked FOR SHAVERS ONLY for high-wattage appliances such as blow-dryers. Most laptops operate equally well on 110 and 220 volts and so require only an adapter.

HEALTH & SAFETY

ALTITUDE SICKNESS Traveling to Cusco and the mountain towns around Lake Titicaca could result in *soroche* (altitude sickness). Avoid playing the crazed tourist and take things slowly your first couple of days. Get an ample intake of fluids, but eliminate or minimize alcohol and caffeine consumption. Both can cause dehydration, already a problem at high altitudes. Smoking worsens the problem, of course. Temporary cures include *mate de coca* (coca tea) or a small block of *chancaca* (crystallized pure cane sugar). It usually takes a day or two to shake the headaches and bloating.

Warning: Sorojchi pills are a Bolivian-made altitude-sickness remedy for sale in every pharmacy here, and whose advertising pictures a tourist vomiting at Machu Picchu. The safety and effectiveness of this product has not been documented, however, and we don't recommend trying it.

MALARIA There is no vaccine against this mosquito-borne illness, but there are prescription drugs to help minimize your likelihood of contracting the disease. As in most areas of tropical South America, strains of malaria here are resistant to the traditional regimen of chloroquine. There are three recommended alternatives: a weekly dose of mefloquine; a daily dose of doxycycline; or a daily dose of Malarone (*atovaquone/proguanil*). Any regimen must be started before arrival in the malarial area and continued beyond departure. Your physician can recommend the best course of prevention. Also, wear long sleeves and pants if you're out in the evening, the time of day of greatest risk, and use a mosquito repellent containing DEET. Most jungle lodges provide mosquito netting and coils to burn.

SAFETY Always be alert for pickpockets in crowded parks, markets, and touristy areas. In the Rímac neighborhood of Lima, you should take a taxi day or night.

WATER The main health advice for the rest of Peru also applies to this region: Don't drink the water (or use ice), and don't eat raw or undercooked food. Stick with the bottled variety, *con gas* (carbonated) or *sin gas* (plain).

YELLOW FEVER You are not required to get any vaccinations to enter Peru, but the Peruvian Embassy recommends getting a yellow-fever vaccine at least 10 days before visiting the Amazon. Immunity lasts 10 years. Though cases of yellow fever in recent years have occurred only near Iquitos, southern Amazon lodges in Manu and Tambopata tend to be sticklers about asking to see your yellow-fever vaccination certificate. Carry it with you.

INTERNET, MAIL & SHIPPING

INTERNET Internet access is surprisingly widespread. In addition to full-fledged cyber cafés, look for machines set up in phone offices. Rates range from $1 to $2 an hour. Many upscale hotels catering to business travelers offer Internet access to their guests among their amenities. If you're logging on to one of the Web-based e-mail sites, late afternoon is an especially sluggish time because of high usage.

Computer keyboards in South America resemble, but aren't exactly the same as, the ones in English-speaking countries. Your biggest frustration will probably be finding the @ symbol to type an e-mail address. You have to type Alt+Q or some other combination. If you need to ask, it's called *arroba* in Spanish.

MAIL Letters sent within the country cost S/2.50 for less than 20 grams; anything sent to the United States and Canada costs S/5.50 and to the United Kingdom, Australia, or New Zealand costs S/6. Bring packages to the post office unsealed, as you must show the contents to postal workers. Mail service has been steadily improving, and a letter should reach just about anywhere in a week from any of the main cities. For timely delivery or valuable parcels, use FedEx, DHL, or UPS.

The main post office (*correo*) in downtown Lima is open Monday through Saturday 8–8 and Sunday 9–1. Hours vary at the branches and in cities and towns outside Lima, but most are closed Sunday.

🔟 **Post Offices Arequipa** ✉ Calle Moral 118 ☎ 054/255-246. **Cusco** ✉ Av. El Sol s/n, at Garcilaso ☎ 084/225-232. **Iquitos** ✉ Av. Arica 402 ☎ 094/231-915. **Lima** ✉ Jr. Junín, between Jr. de la Unión and Jr. Camaná ☎ 01/427-0370. **Puno** ✉ Moguegua 269 ☎ 054/35-1141.

🔟 **Shipping Services DHL** ✉ Calle Los Castaños 225, San Isidro ☎ 01/517-2500. **FedEx** ✉ Pasaje Mártir José Olaya 260, Miraflores ☎ 01/242-2280. **UPS** ✉ Av. del Ejercito 2107, San Isidro ☎ 01/264-0105.

PASSPORTS & VISAS

Visitors from the United States, Canada, the United Kingdom, Australia, and New Zealand require only a valid passport and return ticket to be issued a 60-day visa at their point of entry into Peru. For safety reasons, carry a copy of your passport while exploring, leaving the original in a secure place in your hotel room.

TELEPHONES

To get phone numbers for anywhere in Peru, dial 103 to reach Telefónica del Perú. For assistance from an international operator, dial 108. To place a direct call, dial 00 followed by the country and city codes.

COUNTRY & AREA CODES To call Peru direct, dial 011 followed by the country code of 51, then the city code, then the number of the party you are calling. (When dialing a number from abroad, drop the initial 0 from the local area code.)

INTERNATIONAL CALLS For international calls you should dial 00, then 1 for the United States and Canada or 44 for the United Kingdom. To make an operator-assisted international call, dial 108.

LOCAL CALLS Telefónica del Peru, the country's newly privatized telephone company, has invested a hefty sum in Peru's phone system. New, "intelligent" pay phones require a coin or phone card instead of the old token system. Unless you're making many calls, using coins is much easier than purchasing cards.

To call another region within the country, first dial 0 and then the area code. Long-distance calls are easy to make from Lima and the coast, more difficult in the highlands, and sometimes impossible in the jungle. Hotels add hefty surcharges to long-distance calls made from rooms, so you may want to call from a pay phone.

AT&T, MCI, and Sprint access codes make calling long-distance relatively convenient, but you may find the local access number blocked in many hotel rooms. First ask the hotel operator to connect you. If the hotel operator balks, ask for an international operator, or dial the international operator yourself. One way to improve your odds of getting connected to your long-distance carrier is to travel with more than one company's calling card (a hotel may block Sprint, for example, but not MCI). If all else fails, call from a pay phone. To reach an AT&T operator, dial 171. For MCI, dial 190. For Sprint, dial 176.

🛈 **Access Codes AT&T Direct** ☎ 800/225-5288. **MCI WorldPhone** ☎ 800/444-4444. **Sprint International Access** ☎ 800/793-1153.

TIPPING
A 10% tip is sufficient in most restaurants unless the service has been exceptional. Porters in hotels and airports expect S/2–S/3 per bag. There is no need to tip taxi drivers, although many people round up the fare to the nearest even number. At bars, tip about 50 céntimos for a beer, more for a mixed drink. Bathroom attendants get 20 céntimos; gas-station attendants get 50 céntimos for extra services such as adding air to your tires. Tour guides and tour bus drivers should get S/5–S/10 each per day.

VISITOR INFORMATION
PromPerú (Comisión de Promoción del Peru) is Peru's official tourism-information agency in Lima, and it has a colorful Web site in English and Spanish.

With local offices in Lima and Cusco, a helpful organization for anyone on a budget or traveling solo is the South American Explorer's Club, founded in Lima in 1977. The club offers advice, recommendations, and help, as well as a place to hang out if you're a member. Membership is tax deductible.

🛈 **PromPerú** ✉ Calle 1 Oeste 50, 13th fl., San Isidro ☎ 01/574-8000, 866/661-7378 toll-free in U.S. ⊕ www.promperu.gob.pe. **South American Explorers** ✉ 126 Indian Creek Rd., Ithaca, New York 13850 ☎ 607/277-0488 ⊕ www.samexplo.org.

Uruguay

WORD OF MOUTH

"You could do a coast drive, which is beautiful, and which I've done (in the opposite direction) to Montevideo. One day might be pushing it, as all you'll do is spend the day driving. If you drove directly, it'd only take you about two hours, but if you enjoy your way winding along the coast, and maybe stopping here and there, it could easily take you the six hours it took us! That's one direction…but then you could stay in Montevideo one day if you wanted (not that, in my opinion, there's a lot to do and see in Montevideo, though there are some good restaurants and historic sites to tour)."
—saltshaker

Updated by
Michael de
Zayas

CONSIDERED THE MOST EUROPEAN of South American countries, Uruguay has a distinct cosmopolitan flair. That's not surprising, since about half of its population—largely of Spanish, Portuguese, and Italian descent—lives in the capital. Uruguay attracts international travelers (most of all neighboring Argentines) to the trendy boutiques and fashionable beaches of Punta del Este.

Uruguay's original inhabitants, the seminomadic Charrúa people, were attacked first by the Portuguese, who settled the town of Colonia in 1680, then by the Spanish, who in 1726 established a fortress at Montevideo. In 1811 José Gervasio Artigas mobilized the masses to fight against the heavy-handed influence of Buenos Aires. Though Artigas's bid for Uruguayan independence was unsuccessful, Uruguay finally became an autonomous state in 1825. On July 18, 1830—a date that gives the name to many a street—the country's first constitution was framed, and the *Republica Oriental de Uruguay* was formed.

Following a period of civil war, José Batlle y Ordóñez was elected president in 1903. Under his guidance, Uruguay became the first Latin American nation to grant voting rights to women and the first country to sever relations between church and state—a striking maneuver considering the Catholic Church's strong influence on the continent. Since then, except for a military-run government between 1973 and 1985, Uruguay has been one of the strongest democracies in South America.

The country takes pride in the number of world-famous artists it produces. Galleries here are full of works by masters such as sculptor José Belloni (1880–1965) and painters Joacquín Torres-García (1874–1949), Pedro Figari (1861–1938), and Pedro Blanes Viale (1879–1926). Uruguayans like to claim their country as the birthplace of the internationally renowned tango singer Carlos Gardel (1809–1935), although the Argentines and French also vie for this claim.

As in Argentina, the legendary gaucho is Uruguay's most potent cultural fixture, and it is difficult to pass a day without some reference to these cowboys who once roamed the country singing their melancholy ballads. Remnants of the gaucho lifestyle may still be seen on active ranches throughout the country.

Exploring Uruguay

Uruguay is one of the smallest countries in South America, both in terms of area (it's roughly the size of England) and altitude (far from the Andes, there's nothing but gently rolling hills). In the sparsely developed country filled with vast ranches and farms, all roads lead to the capital of Montevideo. Here you'll find almost half the population. Montevideo's only cosmopolitan rival is Punta del Este, one of a handful of Atlantic Ocean resorts popular with well-heeled Brazilians and Argentines who can afford the region's variety of high-price fun (mornings and afternoons at Gucci, evenings at heady bars and discos).

Restaurants & Cuisine

Beef is the staple of the Uruguayan diet. It is cheap, abundant, and often grilled in a style borrowed from the gauchos, and known as *parrilla*. A

TOP REASONS TO GO

BASK IN COLONIAL SPLENDOR
You wouldn't expect to find much ancient in this modern, progressive country, but the once-walled 1680 Portuguese settlement of Colonia del Sacramento makes up for it. Flowers spill over balconies, balladeers serenade their sweethearts, and lanterns illuminate the streets in one of the continent's best-preserved colonial cities.

FROLIC WITH THE RICH AND FAMOUS
One visit to Uruguay's tony Punta del Este, and Brazil's beaches will forever seem a tad too déclassé. From December through February, well-heeled fun-in-the-sun crowds flock here; they mostly hail from Argentina, but Punta's resorts and boutiques draw an ever-growing number of visitors from other countries, too.

RIDE 'EM, COWBOY
The gaucho embodies the country's spirit, and these rugged cowboys still mount their trusty horses to round up livestock on Uruguay's vast ranges. Sometime in the 19th century, the process was transformed into the *criolla,* the Uruguayan-style rodeo. If your time is limited, you don't even need to leave urban Montevideo to see the spectacle: the capital's El Prado district is the site of the best rodeos.

meal in a *parrillada,* a Uruguayan steak house, should be on your agenda. Beef is also made into sausages, such as *chorizo* and *salchicha,* or is combined with ham, cheese, bacon, and peppers to make *matambre.* Seafood is also popular here—especially the *lenguado* (flounder), *merluza* (hake), and *calamar* (squid). Try the *raya a la manteca negra* (squid ray in blackened butter). If you are not up to a full meal, try the *chivito,* a hefty steak sandwich. Uruguayan wines under the Santa Rosa and Calvinor labels, a step up from table wine, are available in most restaurants. *Clericó* is a mixture of white wine and fruit juice, while *medio y medio* is part sparkling wine, part white wine.

Lunch is served between noon and 3; restaurants begin to fill around 12:30 and are packed by 1:30. Many restaurants do not open for dinner until 8 PM and are rarely crowded before 10 PM. Most pubs and *confiterías* (cafés) are open all day. Formal dress is rarely required. Smart sportswear is acceptable at even the fanciest establishments.

	WHAT IT COSTS In U.S. Dollars				
	$$$$	$$$	$$	$	¢
AT DINNER	over $20	$15–$20	$10–$15	$6–$10	under $6

Prices are per person for a main course at dinner.

About the Hotels
Hotels here are generally clean and comfortable. Many include one or even two meals a day in their rates. You can save up to 30% in the same hotel by requesting a *habitación turística,* usually a bit plainer, smaller,

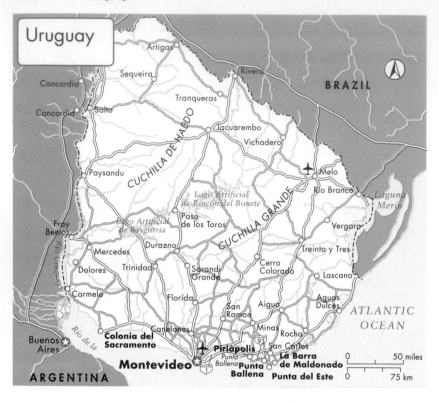

and without a view, but with the same standards of cleanliness and service. *Hosterías* are country inns that not only offer modest rooms but are open for dinner as well. Menus tend to be limited, though the food served is unfailingly hearty. Outside the cities hosterías are likely to be on the rustic side. Summer in Uruguay can be onerous, and many hotels and hosterías are not yet equipped with air-conditioning. Make sure you inquire when making a reservation.

One of the nicest ways to experience Uruguay's vast unspoiled countryside is to stay at an *estancia*. These ranches usually raise animals for the country's most-prized exports—wool, beef, and leather. Although some exist solely as tourist attractions, most estancias are fully operational. You may meet the *estancieros* (ranchers) and stay in quarters that date from the colonial period. The highlight is accompanying the gauchos while they herd cattle, shear sheep, or sit around a fire roasting up sausages for lunch.

Accommodations at estancias range from comfortable to luxurious, and meals are generally included. Some estancias have swimming pools and tennis courts, and most let you explore the countryside on horseback and swim in local rivers and lakes. All provide a chance to breathe the fresh air of the open range.

	WHAT IT COSTS In U.S. Dollars				
	$$$$	**$$$**	**$$**	**$**	**¢**
FOR 2 PEOPLE	over $120	$80–$120	$40–$80	$20–$40	under $20

Prices are for two people in a standard double room in high season, excluding tax.

When to Go

Between October and March the temperatures are pleasant—it's warm and the country is in bloom. Unless you are prepared to tangle with the multitude of tourists that overwhelm Punta del Este in January and February, late spring (October–December) is the most appealing season to lounge on the beach.

CLIMATE Uruguay's climate has four distinct seasons. Summer (January–March) can be hot and humid, with temperatures as high as 90°F. Fall (April–June) is marked by warm days and evenings cool enough for a light sweater. Winter (July–September) is cold and rainy with average temperatures generally below 50°F. Although it seldom reaches freezing, the wind off the water can give you quite a chill. Spring (October–December) is much like the fall, except that the trees will be sprouting, rather than dropping, their leaves.

The following are average daily maximum and minimum temperatures for Montevideo.

Jan.	83F	28C	May	64F	18C	Sept.	63F	17C
	62	17		48	9		46	8
Feb.	82F	28C	June	59F	15C	Oct.	68F	20C
	61	16		43	6		49	10
Mar.	78F	25C	July	58F	14C	Nov.	74F	23C
	59	15		43	6		54	12
Apr.	71F	22C	Aug.	59F	15C	Dec.	79F	21C
	53	12		43	6		59	15

HOLIDAYS New Year's Day; Three Kings' Day (January 6); Disembarkation of the 33 Exiles (April 19); Labor Day (May 1); Battle of Las Piedras (May 18); Artigas's Birthday (June 19); Constitution Day (July 18); Independence Day (August 25); Columbus Day (October 12); All Souls' Day (November 2); Christmas.

FESTIVALS & SEASONAL EVENTS Almost every town in Uruguay celebrates Carnaval, the weeklong festival that immediately precedes the beginning of Lent. The entire country participates in the *comparsas*, the festive mix of singing, dancing, drinking, eating, and general merrymaking. Carnaval overtakes Montevideo with parades, dancing in the streets, and general

CRIOLLAS

Also known as *jineteadas*, the Uruguayan-style rodeos called *criollas* are held all over the country, but the most spectacular one takes place in Montevideo's El Prado district every Easter. Gauchos (cowboys) from all over the country come to display their skill in riding wild horses.

9

all-hours revelry. Semana Criolla, celebrated the week before Easter in the Montevideo suburb of Carrasco is an excellent way to observe traditional gaucho activities. Montevideo holds an annual cattle fair in August.

One of the most important religious processions is the Procession of Verdun in the Lavalleja region. Since 1901, thousands of believers have come here on April 19 to give thanks to the Virgin of the Immaculate Conception, who is believed to have appeared here. Many of the faithful climb a hill on their knees, arriving at the summit bruised and bleeding. The Festival of St. Cono, which takes place June 3 throughout the Florida region, attracts thousands of worshipers who come to pray to the icon of the Italian saint. Brought here by the region's first Italian settlers in 1885, the icon is believed to have the power to perform miracles.

Language

Spanish is the official language of Uruguay, though some descendants of early Italian and British settlers speak the language of their ancestors. Many Uruguayans speak at least a little English.

MONTEVIDEO

Uruguay's only major metropolis, Montevideo has its share of glitzy shopping avenues and modern office buildings. But few visitors come here specifically in search of urban pleasures—in fact, Montevideans head to nearby Buenos Aires when they want to be someplace cosmopolitan. This city of 1½ million doesn't have the whirlwind vibe of Rio de Janeiro or Santiago, but it's a fine old city with sumptuous, if worn, colonial architecture, and a massive coastal promenade that often—as it passes fine beaches, restaurants, and numerous parks—recalls the sunny sophistications of the Mediterranean.

Built along the eastern bank of the Río de la Plata (River of Silver), Montevideo takes full advantage of its location. When the weather's good, La Rambla, a 22-km (14-mi)

> **WHAT'S IN A NAME?**
>
> Legend has it that Montevideo was christened in 1516 when the Portuguese explorer Juan Diaz de Solís first laid eyes on a hill near the mouth of the harbor, and uttered the words "*Monte vide eu*" ("I see a hill"). Another theory has that Magellan, traveling along the coast from Brazil in 1520, counted off six hills from the Brazilian border and thus named the city Monte (mountain) vi (roman numeral six) de (from) eo (*este a oeste*, or east to west).

waterfront avenue that links the Old City with the eastern suburbs, gets packed with fishermen, ice-cream vendors, and joggers. Around sunset, volleyball and soccer games wind down as couples begin to appear for evening strolls. You'll always hear a melody in the air—often from a street musician playing tangos on his accordion.

Exploring Montevideo

Modern Montevideo expanded outward from the peninsular Ciudad Vieja, the Old City, still noted for its narrow streets and elegant colonial architecture. El Prado, an exclusive enclave a few miles north of the city center, is peppered with lavish mansions and grand parks. When you remember that these mansions were once summer homes for aristocratic Uruguayans who spent most of the year elsewhere, you'll get some idea of the wealth this small country once enjoyed.

Ciudad Vieja

TIMING & PRECAUTIONS
Ciudad Vieja is fairly compact, and you could walk from one end to the other in about 15 minutes. Take care at night, when the area is fairly deserted and feels a little sketchy.

WHAT TO SEE

⑪ **Casa de Lavalleja.** This Spanish neoclassical home was built in 1783 and later became the home of General Juan A. Lavalleja, who distinguished himself in Uruguay's war for independence. This pristine colonial home with lovely wrought-iron balconies displays manuscripts and historical memorabilia. ⊠ *Calle Zabala 1469, Ciudad Vieja* ☎ *2/915–1028* ⊕ *www.mec.gub.uy/llavajella* ☞ *Free* ⊙ *Tues.–Fri. 1–5.*

❽ **Casa de Rivera.** Once the home of General Fructuso Rivera, Uruguay's first president, the Rivera House was acquired by the government in 1942. Exhibits inside this pale yellow colonial house with an octagonal cupola document the development of Uruguay from the colonial period through the 1930s. ⊠ *Calle Rincón 437, Ciudad Vieja* ☎ *2/915–1051* ⊕ *www. mec.gub.uy/museo/rivera* ☞ *Free* ⊙ *Tues.–Fri. 1–5, Sat. 11–4.*

❼ **Club Uruguayo.** Uruguay's most prestigious private social club, founded in 1878, is headquartered in this eclectic, three-story neoclassical national monument on the south side of Plaza Matriz. The club is open for tours (anytime) to the public, and friendly, English-speaking guides will happily show you up the marble staircases so you can marvel at the elegant salons. The club was formed for high society of European descent. Today its approximately 400 exclusive members gather for meals and to play bridge. ⊠ *Calle Sarandí 584, Ciudad Vieja* ☎ *No phone* ☞ *Free* ⊙ *Daily 7 AM–10 PM.*

❺ **El Cabildo.** The old City Hall is where the Uruguayan constitution was signed in 1830. This two-story colonial edifice houses an impressive collection of paintings, antiques, costumes, and rotating history exhibits. Fountains and statuary line the interior patios. English-speaking guides are available. ⊠ *Calle Juan Carlos Gómez at Calle Sarandí, Ciudad Vieja* ☎ *2/915–9685* ☞ *Free* ⊙ *Wed.–Fri. 1:30–5:30, Sat. 11–4:30, Sun. 1:30–5:30.*

❻ **Iglesia Matriz.** This cathedral, the oldest public building in Montevideo, has a distinctive pair of dome-cap bell towers that stand guard over the plaza below. Besides its rich marble interior, colorful floor tiling, stained glass, and dome, the Matriz Church is most notable as the final resting place of Uruguay's most important political and military figures. ⊠ *Calle Sarandí at Calle Ituzaingó, Ciudad Vieja* ⊙ *Daily 9–7; mass Sun. 9–1.*

9

★ ⑫ **Mercado del Puerto.** The Port Market, housed in a train station of vaulted iron beams and colored glass that was never put into service, is where downtown workers meet for lunch during the week. The market shields dozens of stalls and eateries where, over large fires, the best *parrillas* (grilled beef) in the city are cooked. The traditional drink here is a bottle of *medio y medio* (champagne mixed with white wine). The market is also the site of huge, carousing celebrations on December 24 and December 31. ⊠ *Rambla 25 de Agosto, between Av. Maciel and Av. Pérez Castellano, across from the port, Ciudad Vieja* ☎ *no phone* ⊙ *Closed Sun. No dinner weekdays.*

> **QUINTESSENTIAL**
>
> The experience at Mercado del Puerto—social and gastronomical—is tough to top.

❷ **Palacio Estévez.** On the south side of Plaza Independencia, Estévez Palace, one of the most beautiful old buildings in the city, was the seat of government until 1985, when the president's offices were moved to a more modern building. This building, unfortunately closed to the public, is used on occasion for ceremonial purposes. ⊠*Plaza Independencia, Ciudad Vieja.*

❿ **Palacio Taranco.** Built in 1908 atop the rubble of Uruguay's first theater, the ornate Taranco Palace, in the Ciudad Vieja, is representative of the French-inspired architecture favored in fin-de-siècle Montevideo. Even the marble for the floors was imported from France. Today you can survey that bygone glory in rooms filled with period furniture, statuary, draperies, clocks, and portrait paintings. A cultural center within has a calendar of performances and live music. ⊠ *Calle 25 de Mayo, 376, Ciudad Vieja* ☎ *2/915–1101* ⊕ *www.mec.gub.uy/taranco* ⊠ *Free* ⊙ *Tues.–Sat. 12:15–6, Sun. 2–6; guided tour Tues.–Sun. 4:30.*

❶ **Plaza Independencia.** Portions of Independence Square were once occupied by the *ciudadela,* a military fortification built originally by the Spanish but deemed militarily useless and destroyed in 1833. In the center stands a 30-ton statue of General Gervasio Artigas, the father of Uruguay and the founder of its 19th-century independence movement. At the base of the monument, two flights of polished granite stairs lead to an underground mausoleum that holds Artigas's remains. The mausoleum is a moving memorial: bold graphics chiseled in the walls of this giant space detail the feats of Artigas's life. Two uniformed guards dressed in period uniforms stand at solemn attention beside the urn in this uncanny, rarely visited vault. There's a changing of the guard Fridays at 12:30, and a parade at the mausoleum on Saturdays at 11:30 AM.

Looming over the north side of the plaza, the 26-story **Palacio Salvo** was the tallest building in South America when it was erected in 1927 (it's still the second-tallest building in Uruguay). Today this gorgeous art deco edifice—one of the more beautiful skyscrapers in the world—is an office building and unfortunately closed to the public.

❹ **Plaza Matriz.** The ornate cantilever fountain in the center of this treefilled square (known to most as Plaza Constitución) was installed in 1871 to commemorate the construction of the city's first water system.

Montevideo

Bahía de Montevideo

Río de La Plata

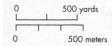

0   500 yards

0   500 meters

9 **Plaza Zabala.** At this charmed spot in the heart of the Ciudan Vieja it's easy to image the splendor of the old Montevideo. Around the fountain and flowers of the park are the turn-of-the-century Taranco mansion and bank headquarters in—a refreshing sight in the Old City—renovated older buildings.

3 **Teatro Solís.** Named in honor of the discoverer of the Río de la Plata, Juan Diaz de Solís, the 1856 Solís Theater is famed for its fine acoustics. Sharing the building is the **Museo Nacional de Historia Natural** (National Museum of Natural History). Both are currently closed; the theater has been undergoing renovations since 1999, and isn't expected to reopen any time soon. ⊠ *Calle Buenos Aires 652, Ciudad Vieja* ☎ *No phone.*

Avenida 18 de Julio

Montevideo's main street has everything—shops and museums, cafés and plazas, bustling traditional markets, and chrome-and-steel office towers. It runs east from Plaza Independencia, away from the Ciudad Vieja, passing through bustling Plaza Fabini and tree-lined Plaza Cagancha.

TIMING   It's a 30-minute walk from Plaza Independencia to the Palacio Municipal. If shopping is your main interest, you may want to devote an entire afternoon to browsing and buying along the avenue.

WHAT TO SEE   **Museo del Gaucho y la Moneda.** The Cowboy and Coin Museum is in a
★ **13**   rococo 19th-century mansion near Calle Julio Herrera y Obes, four blocks east of Plaza Independencia. Here you'll find articles from the everyday life of the gauchos, from traditional garb to the detailed silver work on the cups used for *mate* (an indigenous herb from which tea is brewed). Ancient South American and European coins are on the first floor. English tours are available with two days' notice. ⊠ *Av. 18 de Julio, 998, Centro* ☎ *2/900–8764* ⊕ *www.brounet.com.uy/novedades/museo/gaucho* ☞ *Free* ☉ *Weekdays 9–5.*

15 **Museo de Historia del Arte (MuHAr).** In the **Palacio Municipal** (an ambitious name for this unremarkable brick city hall) you'll find the Museum of Art History, which has the country's best collection of pre-Columbian and colonial artifacts. You'll also find Greek, Roman, and Middle Eastern art, including ceramics and other artifacts. On the street level is the **Biblioteca de Historia del Arte** (Library of Art History). ⊠ *Calle Ejido 1326, Centro* ☎ *2/908–9252* ⊕ *www.artemercosur.org.uy/museos/uruguay/his.html* ☞ *Free* ☉ *Museum Tue.–Sun 2:30–8. Library weekdays 9:30–4:30.*

14 **Plaza Fabini.** In the center of this lovely, manicured square is the Monumento del Entrevero, a large sculpture depicting a whirlwind of gauchos, *criollos* (mixed-blood settlers who are half native, half European), and native Uruguayans in battle. It's one of the last works by sculptor José Belloni (1882–1965). An open-air market with food and other items takes place here every morning. ⊠ *Av. 18 de Julio, Centro.*

El Prado

The district known as El Prado lies roughly 6 km (4 mi) north of Plaza Independencia. You could make the long uphill walk along the busy Avenida Agraciada, but it's a lot easier in a taxi. It is pleasant to walk along Avenida Buschental in fall and spring when the trees are in full color. The Jardin Botanico (Botanical Garden) inside the Parque Prado is a worthwhile stop where you can admire thousands of plant species, many of which were brought to Uruguay in the 19th century by Charles Racine.

WHAT TO SEE **Museo de Bellas Artes.** The Museum of Fine Arts, known locally as the Blanes Museum, is housed in an elegant colonial mansion that once belonged to Uruguay's foremost 19th-century painter, Juan Manuel Blanes. He was entirely self-taught and did not begin painting until he was in his fifties. His realistic portrayals of gauchos and the Uruguayan countryside compose the core of the museum's collection. ⊠ *Av. Millán 4015, El Prado* ☎ *2/336–2248* ⊕ *www.artemercosur.org.uy/museos/ uruguay/bla.html* ⊠ *Free* ☉ *Tues.–Sun. 1–7.*

Parque Prado. The oldest of the city's parks is also one of the most popular. Locals come to see El Rosedal, the rose garden with more than 800 different varieties. Also in the park you'll find the statue called *La Diligencia,* by sculptor José Belloni. There's also a fine botanical garden. There are guided tours of the park from 10—11 and 4:30—5:30. ⊠ *Av. Agraciada, El Prado* ☎ *2/336–4005* ☉ *Daily 7–7.*

Sagrada Familia. Too tiny to require flying buttresses, the ornately Gothic Holy Family Church is complete in all other respects; a troop of gargoyles peers down at you, and the finely wrought stained-glass windows become radiant when backlit by the sun. ⊠ *Calle Luis Alberto de Herrera 4246, El Prado* ☎ *2/203–6824* ☉ *Mass weekdays 7 PM; Jan–Feb., Sat. 7 PM and Sun. 8 PM.*

Where to Eat

Menus don't vary much in Montevideo—meat is always the main dish—so the food may not provide a distraction from the blinding light (even the most fashionable restaurant in Montevideo seems to be brightly illuminated).

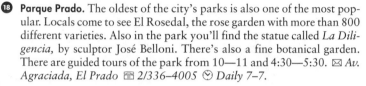

QUICK EATS

For an informal meal, try one of the ubiquitous *parrillada* barbecues (meat on a spit).

French

$ ✗ **Doña Flor.** Housed in a century-old home in the nearby suburb of Punta Carretas, this quiet, elegant restaurant has a diverse menu heavily indebted to the French (the pâté is rich as butter and twice as smooth). It's currently open only for banquets of 10 or more persons. In summer this location closes so the staff can give its full attention to a sister restaurant in Punta del Este. ⊠ *Bulevar Artigas 1034, Punta Carretas* ☎ *2/708–5751* ⊸ *Reservations essential* ⊟ *AE, DC, MC, V* ☉ *Closed Dec.–Apr.*

Uruguayan

$ ✗ **La Casa Violeta.** Meats are the specialty at this beautiful restaurant facing Puerto del Buceo, one of the prettiest spots in the city. Parrilla is served in the method called *espeto corrido*—grilled meats are brought to your table on a long skewer so you can slice off whatever you want.

Where to Stay & Eat in Montevideo

Restaurants	▼
Café Bacacay	**2**
La Casa Violeta	**11**
Doña Flor	**8**
Meson Viejo Sancho	**4**
La Pasiva	**1**
El Viejo Buzon	**7**

Hotels	▼
Ermitage	**9**
Hostería del Lago	**10**
Lancaster	**6**
Oxford	**5**
Radisson Montevideo Plaza	**3**
Sheraton	**12**

There's also a good selection of salads. There's a big deck shaded with umbrellas and with attractive views of the port and surrounding homes. ⊠ *Rambla Aremeña 3667 (corner of 26 de Marzo, Puerto del Buceo), Pocitos* ☎ *2/628–7626* ▭ *AE, DC, MC, V.*

¢ ✕ **El Viejo Buzon.** This unassuming restaurant not far from the Palacio Legislativo serves excellent parrilla and inexpensive, homemade pastas. The *pollo deshuesado* (boneless breast of chicken stuffed with ham and mozzarella and served with mushroom sauce) is worth the trip. For dessert try the *charlot* (vanilla ice cream with warm chocolate). ⊠ *Calle Hocquard 1813, Centro* ☎ *2/203–3971* ▭ *DC, MC, V* ☉ *No dinner Sun.*

¢ ✕ **Café Bacacay.** This small and smartly designed restaurant facing Theater Solís attracts a young, hip crowd. It serves a wide selection of international dishes. The owner takes special care in preparing the excellent salads, such as the Bacacay (spinach, raisins, carrots, nuts, and hearts of palm topped with croutons) or the Sarandí (lettuce, celery, chicken, apples, carrots). ⊠ *Bacacay 1310, at Calle Buenos Aires, Ciudad Vieja* ☎ *2/916–6074* ⊕ *www.bacacay.com.uy* ▭ *AE, MC, V* ☉ *Closed Sun.*

¢ ✕ **Meson Viejo Sancho.** What draws the post-theater crowds to this friendly but plain restaurant near Plaza Cagancha are gargantuan portions of smoked pork chops and fried potatoes. ⊠ *Calle San José 1229 Centro* ☎ *2/900–4063* ▭ *MC, V* ☉ *Closed Sun.*

¢ ✕ **La Pasiva.** For an ice-cold beer, this popular *chopperia* (beer house) is a late-night favorite. The specialties are frankfurters (10 pesos), chivitos, and other bar food. In good weather you can socialize at the outdoor tables in Plaza Matriz. This Montevideo staple has franchises throughout the city, including a prominent location inside Plaza Fabini. ⊠ *Calle Sarandí at Calle J.C. Gómez, Ciudad Vieja* ☎ *2/915–7988* ⊱ *Reservations not accepted* ▭ *DC, MC, V.*

Where to Stay

Many downtown hotels are grouped around the big three squares, Plaza Independencia, Plaza Fabini, and Plaza Cagancha. In the weeks before and after Carnaval in February, rooms become hard to come by. Otherwise, rooms are plentiful in summer, when beach-bound residents desert the city.

$$$$ ▦ **Sheraton.** The city's biggest new hotel is removed from the Old City, and, decidedly modern, feels a world away. Attached to the flashy Punta Carretas shopping center, the hotel offers the comforts of a corporate luxury hotel only a five-minute walk from one of the city's many fine beaches. You will need a cab, however, to reach the majority of the city's sights. Note that there's also a Sheraton Four Points location in the city's financial district. ⊠ *Victor Soliño 349, Punta Carretas* ☎ *2/710–2121* ⎙ *2/712–1262* ⊕ *www.starwoodhotels.com/sheraton* ⤳ *207 rooms, 10 suites* ⌂ *Restaurant, room service, minibars, cable TV, golf privileges, tennis courts, indoor pool, gym, hot tub, sauna, spa, bar, casino, babysitting, laundry service, concierge, Internet, business services, convention center, airport shuttle, car rental* ▭ *AE, DC, MC, V* ❜◎❜ *BP.*

★ $$ ▦ **Ermitage.** This unprepossessing, sandstone-front building, overlooking the lovely Plaza Tomás Gomensoro, is a good, affordable choice if you want to be near the shore. It's in a calm residential zone a block from Pocitos beach and is also a 10-minute drive from the Old City. You'll find plenty of others sitting over a drink or playing cards in the wood-panel lobby—decorated with a large photo-mural of Playa Pocitos in 1928. Rooms are furnished with replicas of 1920s-style furniture and light fixtures—to reflect that gentler, more stylish era of city history. ⊠ *Calle Juan Benito Blanco 783, Pocitos* ☎ *2/710–4021 or 2/711–7447* ⊕ *www.ermitagemontevideo. com* 🖶 *2/710–4312* 🛏 *90 rooms* ⚐ *Restaurant, cable TV, a/c, in room safes, parking, laundry service* ▭ *AE, DC, MC, V* ⦿⦿ *BP.*

★ $$ ⊞ **Hostería del Lago.** On a beautiful lake about 12 km (7 mi) from downtown, this sprawling Spanish colonial hotel is the kind of place that encourages relaxation. Bask by the pool, play a few games of tennis, or head out on a horse for an afternoon of exploring the parkland. The split-level rooms, all the size of suites, have wood-beam ceilings and carpeted floors. ⊠ *Av. Arizona 9637, Carrasco* ☎ *2/601–2210* 🖶 *2/ 601–2880* ⊕ *www.hosteriadellago.com.uy* 🛏 *60 rooms* ⚐ *Room service, tennis court, pool, air-conditioning, minibars, cable TV, horseback riding, playground, airport shuttle* ▭ *AE, DC, MC, V.*

$$ ⊞ **Radisson Montevideo Plaza.** This luxurious glass-and-brick structure looking out over Plaza Independencia is Montevideo's top choice near the Ciudad Vieja. The café on the 24th floor is the best public space for views of the old and new city. ⊠ *Plaza Independencia 759, Centro* ☎ *2/ 902–0111* 🖶 *2/902–1628* ⊕ *www.radisson.com/montevideouy* 🛏 *190 rooms, 64 suites* ⚐ *Restaurant, café, coffee shop, room service, minibars, cable TV, pool, gym, spa, bar, casino, shop, laundry service, Internet, business services, convention center, airport shuttle* ▭ *AE, DC, MC, V* ⦿⦿ *BP.*

$–$$ ⊞ **Oxford.** Glass walls, broad windows, and mirrors give the small lobby an open but intimate feel, much like that of the hotel itself. The rooms at this English-style hotel are immaculately clean, the staff friendly and helpful. Despite its location near Plaza Cagancha, the hotel is remarkably quiet. ⊠ *Calle Paraguay 1286, Centro* ☎ *2/902–0046* 🖶 *2/ 902–3792* ⊕ *www.hoteloxford.com.uy* 🛏 *66 rooms* ⚐ *Cafeteria, in-room safes, minibars, cable TV, bar, Internet, business services, parking (fee)* ▭ *AE, DC, MC, V* ⦿⦿ *BP.*

$ ⊞ **Lancaster.** Hidden behind tall poplars in a corner of Plaza Cagancha, this 11-story hotel in the heart of the city may be past its glory days, but it makes a fine budget lodging choice in the Centro. The rooms are sunny and large, with tall French doors that open out onto the square. ⊠ *Plaza Cagancha 1334, Centro* ☎ *2/902–1054* 🖶 *2/908–1117* ⊕ *www. lancaster-hotel.com* 🛏 *78 rooms* ⚐ *Cafeteria, minibars, cable TV, bar, laundry service* ▭ *AE, DC, MC, V.*

Nightlife & the Arts

Nightlife

In Montevideo you'll find quiet, late-night bars, hip-hop clubs, and folk-music shows. The entertainment and cultural pages of the local papers are the best sources of the latest information; particularly useful is the *Guía del Ocio,* a magazine inserted into the Friday edition of the daily newspaper *El País.* With few exceptions, bars and clubs come to life around 1 AM and do not close until it is time for breakfast.

DANCE CLUBS The retro set flocks to **Aquellos Años** (⊠ Calle Beyrouth 1405, Pocitos), which has music from the '50s and '60s. You can hear live music and dance to house hits at **Mariachi** (⊠ Gabriel Pereira 2964, Pocitos ☎ No phone). **Milenio** (⊠ 25 de Mayo and Ciudadela, Ciudad Vieja) is popular with the MTV generation. **New York** (⊠ Calle Mar Artico 1227 ☎ 2/600–0444) draws an older crowd. In front of Playa Ramirez in Parque Rodó, **W Lounge** (⊠ Rambla Wilson s/n, Punta Carretas ☎ 2/712–5287) gets a large crowd on weekends. It transforms from a bar to a disco at 1 AM.

PUBS **Amarcor** (⊠ Calle Julio Herrera y Obes 1231, Centro ☎ 2/900–1207 or 2/901–9281) is popular with young artists, actors, and intellectuals. Also try **Perdidos en la Noche** (⊠ Calle Yaguarón 1099, Centro ☎ 2/902–6733). **Riff Gallery Pub** (⊠ Bul. España 2511, Centro ☎ no phone) is the only bar in the city devoted to jazz, with live shows on Thursday and Saturday. **The Shannon Irish Pub** (⊠ Mitre 1318, Ciudad Vieja) in the Old City draws a young crowd. It has good rock music and an unpretentious vibe.

SOCCER

"Other countries have their history," Helenio Herrera, Uruguay's most famous soccer coach once said, "we have our fútbol." Indeed, *fútbol* is played anywhere there is space, by men of all ages. Try to attend a *clássico*, a match between Montevideo's two great rival professional teams, Nacional and Peñarol, played amid the screams and encouragement of passionate supporters at the capital's Estadio Centenario.

TANGO SHOWS **La Casa de Becho** (⊠ New York, 1415, Centro ☎ 2/400–2717), the house that once belonged to Mattos Rodríguez, the composer of "La Cumparsita," has weekend shows for a younger crowd. Call first, because reservations are necessary, and the frequency of the shows depends on the time of year. **Joven Tango** (⊠ Calle San José 1314, Centro ☎ 2/908–1550) is the best place in the city to learn tango. Shows are frequent; call for times.

The Arts

The **Servicio Oficial de Difusión Radio Elétrica (SODRE)** (⊠ Av. 18 de Julio 930, Centro ☎ 2/901–2850) hosts a season of classical concerts that runs from May to November. **Alliance Française** (⊠ Bvr. Artigas 1229, Centro ☎ 2/400–0505 ⊕ www.alliancefrancaise.edu.uy) has a series of plays and films. The **Instituto Goethe** (Goethe Institute; ⊠ Calle Canelones 1524, Centro ☎ 2/410–5813 ⊕ www.goethe.de/inst/uy) has films and theater in German. The U.S.-sponsored **Alianza Artigas-Washington** (⊠ Calle Paraguay 1217, Centro ☎ 2/901–7423) hosts plays and concerts by foreign talent. The **Instituto Cultural Anglo-Uruguayo** (⊠ Calle San José 1426 ☎ 2/902–3773 ⊕ www.anglo.edu.uy) hosts plays in English.

Shopping

Markets

Weekend *ferias* (open-air markets) are the best place for leisurely browsing among a warren of crafts stalls. Government regulations dictate that all ferias must close in the early afternoon, so make sure to arrive by 10

AM. **Feria Tristán Narvaja,** started over half a century ago by Italian immigrants, is Montevideo's top attraction on Sundays. (It's only open on Sundays, a day when all other markets, and much of the city, are closed.) Running off 18 de Julio at Calle Tristán Narvaja, a five- to 10-minute walk from the Old City and in the Centro district, the fair is plentifully stocked with secondhand goods. The Saturday morning market at **Plaza Biarritz** in the nearby neighborhood of Pocitos, sells crafts, clothes, and some antiques. **Plaza Cagancha,** between Avenida 18 de Julio and Calle Rondeau in Centro, has a crafts market every day except Sunday.

A fun market in Centro, a few blocks from the Palacio Municipal at the corner of Calle San José and Calle Yaguarón, is the **El Mercado de la Abundancia.** Inside are a tango dance center, four good choices for a fresh lunch time *parrillada,* and, downstairs, a crafts market from 8 AM–10 PM every day but Sunday.

Shopping Centers

There are three major shopping centers in Montevideo, offering everything from designer clothing to gourmet foods to art supplies. The original, called **Montevideo Shopping Center** (⌧ Av. Luis Alberto de Herrera and Calle General Galarza, Punta Carretas) is near Parque Rodó. **Portones de Carrasco** (⌧ Avs. Bolívia and Italia, Carrasco) is a 2-story, 250-store indoor mall with a movie theater. **Punta Carretas Shopping Center** (⌧ Calles Ellauri and Solano, Punta Carretas), housed in a former prison, is the largest and most upscale mall in the city. It's a ten-minute cab ride from the Old City.

Specialty Shops

ANTIQUES   Calle Tristán Narvaja north of Avenida 18 de Julio is packed with antiques shops. In the Old City, the streets north of Plaza Constitución are also lined with antiques stores. **El Rincón** (⌧ Calle Tristán Narvaja 1747, Centro ☎ 2/400–2283) is one of the area's best antiques dealers. **El Galeón** (⌧ Juan Gómez 1327, Centro ☎ 2/915–6139) sells antiques and rare books. The **Louvre** (⌧ Calle Sarandí 652, Ciudad Vieja ☎ no phone), an antiques store, is the only source for handmade and painted trinket boxes—the perfect *recuerdos* (souvenirs).

GEMSTONES &   **Amatistas Del Uruguay** (⌧ Calle P. Sarandí 604, Ciudad Vieja ☎ 2/916–
JEWELRY   6456) specializes in amethyst, topaz, and other gems. **Gemas de América** (⌧ Av. 18 de Julio 948, Centro ☎ 2/902–2572) carries amethyst and topaz jewelry, agate slices, and elaborate objects made of precious gems. **La Limeña** (⌧ Calle Buenos Aires 542, Centro ☎ no phone) has good prices on unset stones.

HANDICRAFTS   **Ema Camuso** (⌧ Av. 8 de Octubre 2574, Centro ☎ no phone) offers a sophisticated and sporty line of hand-knit sweaters, all permanently on sale at factory prices. **Manos de Uruguay** (⌧ Ave de la Herrera 1290, Centro ☎ 2/628–4401 ⊕ www.manos.com.uy ⌧ Calle San José 111, Centro ☎ 2/900–4910 ⌧ Montevideo Shopping Center, Punta Carretas ☎ no phone) has three locations with a wide selection of woolen wear and locally produced ceramics. **Tiempofunky** (⌧ Bacacay 1307, Ciudad Vieja ☎ 2/916–8721) sells clothing, candles, lamps, soaps, and contemporary crafts and design items, on a pleasant street in the Old City.

LEATHER   Although Buenos Aires has more stylish choices, Montevideo is a good source for inexpensive leather. Shops near Plaza Independencia specialize in hand-tailored coats and jackets made out of nutria (fur from a large semiaquatic rodent). **Peleteria Holandesa** (⊠ Calle Colonia 894, Centro ☎ 2/901–5438) carries leather clothing. **Péndola** (⊠ Calle San José 1087, Centro ☎ 2/900–1524) has a particularly good selection of leather apparel. Try **Casa Mario** (⊠ Calle Piedras 641, Centro ☎ 2/916–2356 ⊕ www.casamarioleather.com) for good leather clothes. Custom-made boots are available from **Damino Botas** (⊠ Calle Rivera 2747, Centro ☎ 2/709–7823).

Montevideo Essentials

Transportation

BY AIR

Uruguay's principal airport, Aeropuerto Internacional Carrasco (MVD), is 24 km (15 mi) east of Montevideo. It is regularly served by several South American airlines, such as Aerolíneas Argentinas, LanChile, and the Uruguayan/Brazilian airline Pluna-Varig. Large international carriers include Alitalia, American, Iberia, and United. A cab to downtown costs about 550 pesos. A city bus (marked CIUDADELA) is cheap—about 26 pesos—but the drawback is that it takes an hour to reach downtown.

🛫 Airlines **Aerolíneas Argentinas** ☎ 2/902-3691 ⊕ www.aerolineas.com.ar. **Alitalia** ☎ 2/901-3076 or 2/908-5828. **American** ☎ 2/916-3929. **Iberia** ☎ 2/902-3284 ⊕ www.iberia.com. **LanChile** ☎ 2/902-3881 ⊕ www.lan.com. **Pluna-Varig** ☎ 2/902-1414 ⊕ www.pluna.aero. **United** ☎ 2/902-4630 ⊕ www.united.com.

🛫 Airports **Aeropuerto Internacional Carrasco** ☎ 2/604-0252.

BY BIKE

You won't see many bikes in the city, but biking is an especially fun way to explore the city's long coastal tract. Many hotels and even casinos have bicycles available for rental. In Montevideo you can go to the NH Colombia Hotel in the financial district, but there are many other places that can get you up on two wheels in no time.

🚲 Bike Rentals **NH Colombia Hotel** ⊠ Rambla Gran Bretana 473.

BY BOAT & FERRY

Buquebus operates hydrofoil service between Buenos Aires and the ports at Montevideo and Colonia. The trip takes less than three hours to Montevideo and less than four hours to Colonia. A round-trip ticket between Buenos Aires and Montevideo costs about 3,000 pesos. A package that includes a round-trip ticket between Buenos Aires and Colonia and a shuttle bus to or from Montevideo costs about 2,000 pesos.

⛴ Boat & Ferry Information **Buquebus** ⊠ Terminal Tres Cruces, Bulevar General Artigas 1825, Centro ☎ 2/408-8120 🖶 2/901-2555 ⊕ www.buquebus.com.

BY BUS

Montevideo's public buses are a great alternative to taxis, which can be difficult to find during peak hours. Buses crisscross the entire city 24 hours a day. You don't need exact change, and the price for any trip within Montevideo is only 13 pesos.

Colonia is serviced by several regional bus lines, including Cot and TURIL. The three-hour ride costs less than 400 pesos.

🚌 **Bus Companies Cot** ✉ Terminal Tres Cruces, Centro, Montevideo ☎ 2/409-4949 ✉ General Flores 440, Colonia ☎ 522/3121. **TURIL** ✉ Terminal Tres Cruces, Centro, Montevideo ☎ 2/900-5185 ⊕ www.turil.com.uy ✉ General Flores and Suárez, Colonia ☎ 523-0318.

🚌 **Bus Terminals Terminal Tres Cruces** ✉ Bulevar General Artigas 1825, Centro, Montevideo ☎ 2/409-8998.

BY CAR

Because La Rambla, Montevideo's riverside thoroughfare, extends for dozens of miles, driving is a good way to see the city. Roads are well maintained and drivers obey the traffic laws—a rarity in South America. It's easy to rent a car, both downtown and at the airport.

CAR RENTAL In Montevideo you can rent from several major international companies, including Avis, Budget, and Dollar, and from smaller companies such as Inter Car and Multicar.

🚗 **Rental Agencies Avis** ✉ Av. Uruguay 1417, Montevideo ☎ 2/903-0303. **Budget** ✉ Av. General Flores 2211, Montevideo ☎ 2/203-7080. **Dollar** ✉ Av. J.B. Amorín 1186, at corner of Canelones, Centro, Montevideo ☎ 2/402-6427. **Inter Car** ✉ Colonia 926, Centro, Montevideo ☎ 2/902-3330. **Multicar** ✉ Colonia 1227, Centro, Montevideo ☎ 2/902-2555.

BY TAXI

All cabs have meters, and the initial fare is roughly 20 pesos at flag fall and 15 pesos per ⅕ km (¹⁄₁₀ mi). You can hail taxis on the street with ease, or call one to pick you up at your hotel. A ride to the airport from the Old City costs about 500 pesos.

🚕 **Taxi Companies Radio Taxi Carrasco** ☎ 2/600-0416 or 2/915-0800.

Contacts & Resources

EMBASSIES

The United States Embassy is open weekdays between 8:45 and 5:30. The United Kingdom Embassy operates weekdays 9–1 and 2–5:15 in the winter, 8–2 December–March. The Canadian Embassy is open 8:30–12:30 and 1:30–5:30 Monday–Thursday, 8:30–2 Friday.

🏛 **Canada** ✉ Plaza Independencia 749, Ciudad Vieja ☎ 2/902-2030 🖶 2/902-2029. **United States** ✉ Lauro Müller, No. 1776 [on the Rambla], Montevideo, Centro ☎ 2/203-6061 or 2/418-7777 ⊕ http:77uruguay.usembassy.gov. **United Kingdom** ✉ Marco Bruto, No. 1073, Centro ☎ 2/622-3630 🖶 2/622-7815 ⊕ www.britishembassy.gov.uk.

EMERGENCIES

🚨 **Contact Numbers Ambulance** ☎ 105. **Fire** ☎ 104. **Pharmacy** ☎ 0900-2020. **Police** ☎ 109.

MONEY MATTERS

Cambio Matriz, on Plaza Matriz, is a convenient place to change money. Bancomat, RED Banc, and Redbrou machines accept ATM cards on the CIRRUS network; you can withdraw both dollars and Uruguayan pesos.

💰 **Banks Cambio Matriz** ✉ Sarandí 556, Ciudad Vieja ☎ 2/401-1646.

SAFETY

Although Montevideo doesn't have the problems with crime that larger cities in South America do, it's best to watch your wallet in crowded markets, and to avoid walking down deserted streets at night. Most of Montevideo's residents stay up quite late, so the streets are usually full of people until 1 AM. The city bus authority discourages boarding empty buses at night.

TELEPHONES

Telephone service in the city is convenient and dependable. Public telephones in downtown Montevideo accept either coins or magnetic phone cards. Phone cards are available in the following denominations: 25, 50, and 100 pesos. Unless you're planning on calling outside of Montevideo, the 25-peso card should be sufficient for about 10 local calls. Phone cards can be purchased at telecentros, kiosks, and small stores near public phones. Telecard, which uses a toll-free number, can be used from hotel rooms. Telecard is available in denominations of 100 and 200 pesos.

TOUR OPERATORS

Cecilia Regules Viajes, a travel agency with English-speaking agents, is open weekdays 8:30–8:30 and Saturday 9:30 to 5:45. The company can arrange everything from tours of the city to excursions to the country. Three-hour guided tours of Montevideo, as well as full-day guided tours of Colonia del Sacramento or Punta del Este, are offered by many travel agencies with English-speaking staffs. Passengers for these tours are collected from the major hotels starting at 8 AM. J. P. Santos Travel Agency is a reputable company.

🔢 **Tour Agencies Cecilia Regules Viajes** ⊠ Bacacay 1334, Ciudad Vieja 🕾 2/916–3011. **J. P. Santos Travel Agency** ⊠ Calle Colonia 951, Centro 🕾 2/902–0300.

VISITOR INFORMATION

The best source for city info is the city's own tourist information center, Información Turistica de la Intendencia, set up in front of city hall. They have a knowledgeable staff, and brochures and maps. They are open weekdays 10–6, weekends and holidays 11-6. The Ministerio de Turismo—the national government's tourist center at Plaza Fabini—is open weekdays noon–6 in summer and weekdays 8–3 the rest of the year. The helpful kiosk at Terminal Tres Cruces, open weekdays 8–9 and weekends 9–9, supplies maps and other basic information.

🔢 **City Hall** ⊠ 18 de Julio 1360, Centro 🕾 1950-1830. **Plaza Fabini** ⊠ Calle Colonia 1021, Centro 🕾 2/900-1078 or 2/901-4340 📠 2/901-6907 ⊕ www.turismo.gub.uy. **Terminal Tres Cruces** ⊠ Bulevar General Artigas 1825, Centro 🕾 2/409-7399.

PUNTA DEL ESTE

Despite being a mere two hours east of Montevideo, Uruguay's highly touted Punta del Este is a world apart. Punta del Este (shortened to "Punta" by locals) and the handful of surrounding beachfront communities are, famously, jet-set resorts—places where lounging on white sand and browsing designer boutiques constitute the day's most demanding activities. For thousands of younger South Americans Punta del Este is also a party town. Here you can watch the sunrise from the balcony of an all-night disco.

Punta is underwhelming in the low season—the buildings are shuttered against the elements, their tenants gone elsewhere. In summer the city comes alive, lured out of dormancy by the smell of tourist dollars. Plan on a visit in either December or March (except during Holy Week, when prices skyrocket). During these two months the weather is superb, with an average daily temperature of 75°F, and the beaches are not unbearably crowded.

Piriápolis

98 km (61 mi) east of Montevideo.

In 1890, Francisco Piria, an Argentine born of Italian parents, purchased all the land, first established as a private residence, from the town of Pan de Azúcar to the Río de la Plata. Piria saw the touristic potential of the land and began developing "Piriápolis" to resemble a French coast town. Piriápolis is nowadays a laid-back beachfront enclave that lacks the sophistication—and the exorbitant prices—of nearby Punta del Este. Piriápolis has plenty of stores and restaurants, a casino, and the grand Argentino Hotel, the town's crown jewel, built in the old European tradition with spas and thermal pools.

Where to Stay & Eat

★ $$–$$$$ ✕⊡ **Argentino Hotel.** This belle époque–style structure, a national historic monument, clearly deserves the honor. Argentine president Baltasar Brum attended the groundbreaking in 1920; when completed a decade later the hotel was one of the biggest in South America. Elegantly furnished rooms have French doors and balustraded balconies overlooking the ocean. If this isn't stress-reducing enough, the hotel is renowned for its Piriavital health spa. ⊠ *Rambla de los Argentinos* 🕾🕾 *43/422–572* ⊕ *www.argentinohotel.com* ↝ *300 rooms, 56 suites* ⌂ *3 restaurants, room service, minibars, golf privileges, 4 tennis courts, 3 pools, health club, sauna, spa, basketball, volleyball, ice-skating, bar, casino, laundry service* ▭ *AE, DC, MC, V.*

Colonia del Sacramento

★ *180 km (113 mi) west of Montevideo.*

It's hard not to fall in love with Colonia del Sacramento. The most picturesque town in Uruguay, and one of South America's most beautiful cities, Colonia possesses the best of an old colonial city, with wonderfully preserved architecture, rough cobblestone streets, and an easy grace and tranquillity evident in its people and pace. There are more bicycles than cars here, which adds to the serenity of this roughly six-by-six-block Old City that juts out on a small peninsula into the Río de la Plata.

Founded in 1680 by Portugal, the city was subject to wars and pacts between Portugal and Spain. The city's many small museums are dedicated to the story of its tumultuous history. The best place to begin a tour of the city is at the reconstructed **portón,** or city gate. Remnants of the old bastion walls lead to the river. A block farther is **Calle de los Suspiros,** a cobblestone street of one-story colonial homes that can rival any street in Latin America for sheer romantic effect. Clusters of bougainvillea flow over the walls, from which hang old lanterns. Art galleries and antiques shops line the street, which opens out to **Plaza Mayor,** a lovely square filled with Spanish moss, palm, and spiky, flowering *palo borracho* trees. On this square are three of the city's principal museums. The **Museo Portugués** documents the city's ties to Portugal. It's most notable for its collection of old map reproductions based on Portuguese naval expeditions. The museum is housed in a home built in 1720. The **Casa Rosada,** another 18th-century home, is filled with period furniture and clothing. Next door is the **Museo Municipal,** which has a collection of sundry objects related to the city's history housed in another early Portuguese structure. Also near the plaza are the **San Francisco convent ruins,** dating from a 1683 construction. Towering above these surviving walls is the **faro** or lighthouse, built in 1857. You can climb to the top for a view of the Old City.

Where to Stay & Eat

¢ ✕ **La Bodeguita.** This hip restaurant with backyard tables overlooking the river serves delicious, crispy pizza, sliced into bite-size rectangles. ⊠ *Calle del Comercio 167* ☎ *052/25329* ☰ *MC, V* ⊙ *Closed Mon.*

¢ ✕ **Pulpería de los Faroles.** The specialties at this old stone house right off the Plaza Mayor are *lomo a los faroles* (beef with beans) and a fantastic selection of pastas. ⊠ *Calle del Comercio 101* ☎ *052/30271* ☰ *AE, MC, V* ⊙ *Closed Wed.*

$$$$ ✕▥ **Four Seasons Carmelo.** Serenity pervades this harmoniously deco-
FodorśChoice rated resort an hour west of Colonia del Sacramento, reachable by car,
★ boat, or a 15-minute flight from Buenos Aires. Everything is done in a fusion of Asian styles—from tai chi classes at the incense-burning and bamboo-screen health club to bungalows (considered "standard rooms") with private Japanese gardens (and marvelous outdoor showers). In the evening torches illuminate the paths of the resort—through sand dunes. The hotel also offers free sunset cruises on the Río de la Plata. If you can't lodge here, try dining at the wonderful restaurant. ⊠ *Ruta 21, km 262, Carmelo* ☎ *598/542–9000* ☒ *598/542–9999* ⊕ *www.fourseasons. com/carmelo* ⇆ *24 duplexes, 20 bungalows* ⌂ *Restaurant, room service, in-room safes, minibars, cable TV, in-room VCRs, golf course, 4 tennis courts, pool, health club, massage, sauna, spa, boating, bicycles, horseback riding, Ping-Pong, bar, casino, video game room, babysitting, children's programs, laundry service, Internet, business services, airport shuttle* ☰ *AE, DC, MC, V.*

$$ ▥ **Hotel Plaza Mayor.** This lovely hotel with an impeccable location in the middle of the historic district (the Old City) dates from 1840. The simple rooms, many with high ceilings and beveled-glass doors, overlook a peaceful garden with a trickling fountain. ⊠ *Calle del Comercio 111* ☎ *052/28909* ⊕ *www.colonia.net/plazamayor* ⇆ *8 rooms* ⌂ *Coffee shop, room service, minibars, air-conditioning, cable TV, hot tub, laundry service* ☰ *AE, DC, MC, V.*

★ $ ▥ **Posada de la Flor.** This place, which opened in early 2003, is on a quiet, dead-end street, and is arranged around a verdant courtyard. Second-floor rooms cost a few dollars more, but come with air-conditioners and cheery

9

quilts. (Ask for the most spacious room, called "Nomeolvides," or "Forget-me-not.") A lovely third-floor terrace shaded with bamboo looks out over the river. The posada is a lovely five-minute walk from Plaza Mayor ⊠ *Calle Ituzaingó 268* ☎ *052/30794* ⤸ *10 rooms* ⚘ *Bar, laundry service; no a/c in some rooms, no room TVs* ✎ *posadadelaflor@hotmail.com* ▭ *No credit cards* ⦿⃝ CP.

Punta Ballena

25 km (15 mi) east of Piriápolis.

Built on a bluff overlooking the ocean that supposedly looks like a whale (*ballena*, in Spanish), Punta Ballena is hidden from vacationers passing on the main road—no cause for complaint from the resort's wealthy patrons. Inland, the **Arboretum Lussich** is a huge parkland perfumed with the scent of eucalyptus.

The main draw in Punta Ballena is **Casapueblo,** a hotel and museum perched at the tip of a rocky point with tremendous views of the Río de la Plata. This "habitable sculpture," as defined by its creator Carlos Páez Vilaró, defies architectural categorization. With allusions to Arab minarets and domes, cathedral vaulting, Grecian whitewash, and continuous sculptural flourishes that recall the traceries of a Miró canvas, this curvaceous 13-floor surrealist complex climbs up a hill and looks like nothing else in South America.

Begun in 1968, Casapueblo is a continually evolving work. Says the artist: "While there be a brick near my hands, Casapueblo will not stop growing." The spaces include an excellent series of galleries dedicated to his work. Here you can see photos of the artist with friends like Picasso and peruse copies of his books. One of Páez's books tells the true story of his son Carlos Miguel, who survived a plane crash in the Andes. The story was made into the 1993 film *Alive.* ⊠ *Punta Ballena* ☎☎ *42/578–485* ▭ *150 pesos* ☽ *Daily 10–4.*

Where to Stay

★ $$$$ ⌂ **Casapueblo Club Hotel.** It would be hard not to feel like an artist in this whitewashed marvel. Merely riding the old-style iron elevators and walking through the sinuous hallways (there are no right angles here) is an experience. Spacious rooms have wood floors and handsome antique furniture. Each also has a different name—Paloma (Dove), for example, or Luna Negra (Black Moon)—that determines the design of the handmade tiles in your bathroom. The restaurant has a wide terrace with fine coastline views. ⊠ *Punta Ballena* ☎☎ *42/578–485* ⊕ *www.clubhotel.com.ar* ⤸ *72 rooms* ⚘ *Restaurant, room service, minibars, cable TV, 2 pools, 2 health clubs, sauna, spa, bar, laundry service, Internet, business services* ▭ *AE, DC, MC, V.*

> **WORD OF MOUTH**
>
> My favorite spot to stay in Punta del Este is Casapueblo. It's one of the more amazing hotels (just to look at and wander around in, it looks sort of like Gaudi meets Moorish castle) that I've ever been in.   −saltshaker

Punta del Este

10 km (6 mi) east of Punta Ballena.

Half a century ago, the resort town of Punta del Este was a fishing village nearly covered by dunes. Its shores were first discovered by sunseekers escaping winter in North America. Its South American neighbors were soon to follow—today, it's so popular a beach resort that more than 100,000 Argentines flock to its beaches each January. (Punta is considered, during warm months, to be an annexation of Argentina.)

Punta del Este (East Point) marks the division of the Río de la Plata on the west from the Atlantic Ocean to the east. It also lends its name to the broader region encompassing Punta Ballena and La Barra de Maldonado, a trendy area of galleries and restaurants referred to simply as "La Barra." In Punta proper—the peninsular resort bounded by Playa Mansa and Playa Brava—the beach is the primary destination. In fact, if you are not into eating, drinking, and worshiping the sun, just about the only other attraction is the feria artesanal at Plaza Artigas.

> **WORD OF MOUTH**
>
> Being a peninsula, Punta del Este has several beaches, and each day, depending on how the wind blows, one bunch of beaches is fantastic. –Graziella5b

Punta is circled by Rambla Artigas, the main coastal road that leads past residential neighborhoods and pristine stretches of beach. **Avenida Gorlero,** Punta's main commercial strip, runs north–south through the heart of the peninsula and is fronted with cafés, restaurants, and elegant boutiques bearing names such as Yves St. Laurent and Gucci.

You can take a boat from the marina to **Isla Gorriti,** a pine-covered island with a good restaurant. On the eastern side of Punta, and a couple of miles farther offshore, is **Isla de los Lobos,** home to one of the world's largest colonies of sea lions. The island can be viewed from tour boats that leave regularly from the marina.

Where to Stay & Eat

Restaurants come and go in Punta del Este. The better ones reopen from year to year, often transferring their operations from Montevideo for the summer. Year-round options—none of them spectacular—are generally found along Avenida Gorlero; they tend to be moderately priced and serve meat rather than seafood.

There are numerous hotels in and around Punta del Este, running the gamut from restored colonial mansions to modern high-rises. Rooms are mostly empty until January and February, when Punta teems with sunbathers and pleasure seekers. During these months lodgings are extremely difficult to come by, so book well in advance.

★ **$$** ✕ **La Bourgogne.** A shaded terra-cotta terrace gives way to a breezeway with arched windows. This opens onto a large split-level dining room with antique sideboards. The food, served by impeccably clad waiters who go about their business with cordial authority, is prepared with only the finest and freshest of ingredients; the breads are baked on the premises (an adjoining bakery sells them by the loaf), and the herbs and berries are grown in the backyard garden. The desserts are sublime—the sampler is a good way to try them all. ⊠ *Av. del Mar at Calle P. Sierra* ☎ *42/482–007* 🖷 *42/487–873* ⌕ *Reservations essential* ⊟ *AE, MC* ⊘ *Closed May–Aug.; Sept.–Apr., Thurs.–Sun. only.*

¢–$ ✗ **Andrés.** Operated by a father and son, both of whom answer to Andrés, this small restaurant on the Rambla Artigas, the oceanside promenade, offers fine dining at moderate prices. Most of the tables are outdoors under a canopy, so you can appreciate the excellent service while also enjoying the sea breeze. The fish Andrés (served in a white wine and tomato sauce), spinach or cheese soufflés, and grilled meats are exquisite. ⊠ *Parada 1, Edificio Vaguardia* ☎ *42/481–804* ⊟ *AE, MC, V* ⊘ *Closed Mon.–Wed. No lunch Thurs. or Fri. No dinner Sun.*

¢–$ ✗ **Yacht Club Uruguayo.** Loved by locals, this small eatery has a great view of Isla Gorriti. The menu includes a bit of everything, but the specialty is seafood. Perennial favorites are *brotola a la Roquefort* (baked hake with a Roquefort sauce) and *pulpo Provençal*, likely to be the most tender octopus you've ever eaten. ⊠ *Rambla Artigas between Calles 6 and 8* ☎ *42/441–056* ⊟ *AE, DC, MC, V.*

¢ ✗ **Restaurante Ciclista.** This no-frills restaurant serves the best inexpensive meals in Punta. Choose from a menu of over 100 items, from soups to pastas. The *tortilla de papas* (potato pancake) is extremely hearty. ⊠ *Calle 20 at Calle 27* ☎ *42/440–007* ⊟ *AE, DC, MC, V.*

$$$$ ⊞ **Conrad Resort & Casino.** Spectacularly lit fountains and gardens, an abundant use of marble, and stunning art by Uruguayan painter Carlos Páez Vilaró make this one of Punta's most extraordinary resorts. Every room has a terrace with views of the beaches. Two of the floors cater to nonsmokers—an amenity virtually unheard of in this region. Of course, the most prominent draw is the Las Vegas–style casino—the country's best. Head to the blackjack tables, or try your luck at one of the nearly 500 slot machines. ⊠ *Rambla Claudio Williman at Parada 4, Playa Mansa* ☎ *42/491–111* 🖷 *42/489–999* ⊕ *www.conrad.com.uy* 🛏 *278 rooms, 24 suites* ⌂ *Restaurant, room service, in-room safes, minibars, cable TV, pool, bar, casino, laundry service, Internet, business services, no-smoking floors* ⊟ *AE, DC, MC, V.*

$$$–$$$$ ⊞ **L'Auberge.** In the heart of Parque del Golf, Punta's chicest neighborhood, this hotel can be spotted for miles around. An 18th-century stone water tower, which now contains guest rooms, rises from the hotel's double-wing chalet. Rooms are tastefully adorned with beautiful antiques; some even have working fireplaces. Some of Punta del Este's finest beaches are just a few blocks away, but the vast lawns and lovely terrace gardens create a world apart from the crowded beach. ⊠ *Barrio Parque del Golf* ☎ *42/482–601* 🖷 *42/483–408* ⊕ *www.laubergehotel. com* 🛏 *36 rooms* ⌂ *Restaurant, tea shop, room service, in-room safes, minibars, cable TV, pool, hot tub, bar, laundry service, Internet, meeting rooms* ⊟ *AE, DC, MC, V.*

$$$ ⊞ **Hotel Salzburgo.** This delightful hotel occupies a white-stucco, three-story chalet with polished slate floors and exposed beams. Its rooms have ceiling fans, modern baths, and fine views framed by flower-filled win-

dow boxes. ⊠ *Calle Pedragosa Sierra at El Havre* ☎ *42/488–851* 🖷 *42/480–214* ⊕ *www.hotelsalzburgo.com* 🛏 *23 rooms* ♢ *Cafeteria, in-room safes, minibars, cable TV, bar, laundry service, Internet, free parking* 🖃 *AE, DC, MC, V.*

★ **$–$$** 🏨 **Palace Hotel.** Housed inside one of Punta's oldest structures—a three-story Spanish colonial masterpiece complete with an airy interior court-yard—this hotel is a stone's throw from the beach (at the end of the Gorlero shopping strip). The restaurant has one of the largest wine cellars in the country. ⊠ *Calle Gorlero at Calle 11* ☎ *42/441–919 or 42/441–418* 🖷 *42/444–695* 🛏 *47 rooms* ♢ *Restaurant, room service, minibars, cable TV, bar, Internet* 🖃 *MC, V* 🍴❘ *BP.*

Nightlife

Expect fast-paced evenings in bars and nightclubs that open as late as 1 AM and only reach a fever pitch around sunrise. Most are open only during the high season and have a cover as steep as 800 pesos.

DANCE CLUBS Hop in a cab and head for **Gitane La Plage** (⊠ Rambla Brava, Parada 12 ☎ no phone), on the road toward La Barra. The club is right on Playa Brava and has two dance floors, both of which play booming house music. In La Barra, **Space** (⊠ Central La Barra ☎ no phone) occupies an enormous warehouse bursting with five different bars. Any taxi driver will know the way.

Outdoor Activities

GOLF **Club de Golf** (☎ 42/82127) charges a typical $70 greens fee for 18 holes of golf. You can play a round of golf at **Club de Lago** (☎ 42/78423), which has tennis courts as well.

HORSEBACK Mosey over to **Club Hípico Parque Burnett** (☎ 42/30765), an equestrian
RIDING center on the distant outskirts of Punta, in Pinares, for an afternoon of trail riding. Montevideo-based **Estancias Gauchas** (⊠ Bacacay 1334, Montevideo ☎ 2/916–3011 🖷 2/916–3012) offers various trips from Punta del Este to estancias where you can ride horses and take part in the gaucho life. There are French and English-speaking guides.

POLO From December 15 to February 28 there are several polo tournaments in Punta del Este, the most famous of which are the Medellín Polo Cup and the José Ignacio Tournament, attended by some of the best players from South America and Europe.

Shopping

An essential part of visiting Punta is exploring the colorful **Feria Artesanal** at the intersection of El Ramanso and El Corral. It's open weekends 5 PM–midnight all year; between Christmas and Easter it's open daily 6 PM–1 AM. Popular items include gourds for sipping mate (herb tea), and leather and silver crafts.

La Barra de Maldonado

5 km (3 mi) east of Punta del Este.

Gaily painted buildings give La Barra de Maldonado a carnival-like style. Here you'll find a handful of antiques dealers, surf shops, art galleries, and pubs that offer an afternoon's diversion. This is where young people come to do their eating, drinking, and dancing.

It's easy to get here from Punta del Este—drive east from the peninsula a few miles along coastal Ruta 10 until you cross over a cement camel-back bridge. Locals like to speed over this bridge to heighten the roller-coaster sensations of its wavy form. Just before you reach La Barra is Playa Verde, one of the area's finest beaches.

Where to Stay & Eat

★ $-$$ ╳⌂ **La Posta del Cangrejo.** From its stylish lobby to its relaxed lounge and restaurant, this hotel takes an informal approach to luxury. The Mediterranean theme—red tile floors and white stucco walls—complements the impeccably decorated rooms; each is furnished with hand-stenciled antiques and canopy beds and has views of either the beach or the small garden. The staff is warm and accommodating. The adjoining seafood restaurant is outstanding. ⊠ *La Barra de Maldonado* ☎ *42/470–021 or 42/470–271* 🖷 *42/470–173* ⊕ *www.netgate.com.uy/la-posta* ⇆ *29 rooms* ⚹ *Restaurant, in-room safes, cable TV, pool, bar, laundry service, Internet* ▤ *AE, DC, MC, V.*

Punta del Este Essentials

Transportation

BY AIR

Most people headed to the beach fly into Montevideo's Aeropuerto Internacional Carrasco (MVD). Some airlines fly from Buenos Aires directly to Punta del Este's Aeropuerto Internacional de Laguna del Sauce (PDP), about 24 km (15 mi) east of town.

🛪 **Airlines Aerolíneas Argentinas** ☎ 2/902–3691 ⊕ www.aerolineas.com.ar. **LAPA** ☎ 42/90840. **Pluna-Varig** ☎ 42/45292.

🛪 **Airports Aeropuerto Internacional Carrasco** ☎ 2/604–0252. **Aeropuerto Internacional de Laguna del Sauce** ⊠ Camino del Placer ☎ 42/59777.

BY BUS

Many bus lines travel daily between Montevideo's Terminal Tres Cruces and Piriápolis's Terminal de Omnibus, Maldonado's Terminal de Maldonado, and Punta del Este's Terminal Playa Brava. Two companies that serve the entire region are Copsa and Cot. There is frequent daily service from the Tres Cruces terminal in Montevideo to Colonia del Sacramento.

🚌 **Bus Companies Copsa** ☎ 42/89205. **Cot** ☎ 42/86810.

🚌 **Bus Terminals Terminal de Maldonado** ⊠ Roosevelt and Sarandí, Maldonado. **Terminal de Omnibus** ⊠ Misiones and Niza, Piriápolis. **Terminal Playa Brava** ⊠ Rambla Artigas and Calle Inzaurraga, Punta del Este.

CAR TRAVEL

To get to Punta del Este from Montevideo, follow Ruta 1 east to the Ruta 93 turnoff. The road is well maintained and marked, and the trip takes about 1½ hours. It's a beautiful drive from Montevideo to Colonia del Sacramento, and it will take you about three hours on Ruta 1 west.

CAR RENTAL Renting a car is the simplest way to explore the coast. Agencies, such as Avis, Budget, and Dollar, are in downtown Punta del Este.

Contacts & Resources

TELEPHONES

Public telephones in beach towns accept either coins only or magnetic phone cards only. Phone cards can be purchased at newsstands.

TOUR AGENCIES

Consider booking a package tour from Montevideo. It will be more difficult, not to mention costly, to arrange once you're in Punta del Este. For tours to Punta Ballena and La Barra de Maldonado, contact Cecilia Regules Viajes in Montevideo. Agencies along Calle Gorlero, such as Turisport, can assist with hotel bookings, transportation, and excursions.

⊞ Tour Agencies Cecilia Regules Viajes ☒ Calle Bacacay 1334, Local C, Montevideo ☏ 2/915-7308 or 2/916-3011 🖨 2/916-3012. **Turisport** ☒ Torre Verona building, Av. Gorlero and La Galerna, Punta del Este ☏ 42/445-500.

VISITOR INFORMATION

The Piriápolis Tourist Office provides hotel listings and maps for the town. The Punta del Este Tourist Office, with a main office north of Playa Mansa as well as a kiosk in Plaza Artigas, offers information about the community. The Maldonado Tourist Office provides info about the region, including Punta del Este. Colonia del Sacramento's tourist office is open weekdays 8–7 and weekends 9–noon.

⊞ Colonia del Sacramento ☒ General Flores and Rivera ☏ 52/2182. **Maldonado** ☒ Parada 1, Calle 31 and 18, Punta del Este ☏ 42/46510. **Piriápolis** ☒ Rambla de los Argentinos 1348 ☏ 43/22560. **Punta del Este** ☒ Rambla Artigas and Izaurraga ☏ 42/44069 ⊕ www.turismo.qub.uy.

URUGUAY ESSENTIALS

9

Transportation

BY AIR

Most international commercial flights land at Montevideo's Aeropuerto Internacional Carrasco, about 24 km (15 mi) east of downtown. A few fly from Buenos Aires directly to Punta del Este's Aeropuerto Internacional de Laguna del Sauce.

All Montevideo-bound flights are routed through Buenos Aires, São Paulo, or Rio de Janeiro. Flying times to Montevideo are 1 hour from Buenos Aires, 2 hours from São Paulo, and 2½ hours from Rio.

⊞ Airports Aeropuerto Internacional Carrasco ☏ 2/604-0252. **Aeropuerto Internacional de Laguna del Sauce** ☒ Camino del Placer ☏ 42/59777.

BY BOAT & FERRY

Ferries cross the Río de la Plata between Argentina and Uruguay several times daily. They travel to Montevideo or Colonia, where you can get a bus to Montevideo and Punta del Este. The best companies are Aliscafos, Buquebus, Ferry Lineas Argentina, and Ferry Tur.

⊞ Boat & Ferry Information Aliscafos ☒ Av. Córdoba and Madero ☏ 1/313-4444. **Buquebus** ☒ Av. Córdoba and Madero ☏ 1/313-4444. **Ferry Lineas Argentina** ☒ Florida 780 ☏ 1/322-8421 or 1/394-8424. **Ferry Tur** ☒ Florida 780 ☏ 1/322-8421 or 1/394-8424.

BY BUS

You can go almost anywhere in Uruguay by bus. Some are quite luxurious, with air-conditioning, movies, and snack service. Departures are frequent and fares low. Most companies are based in Montevideo and depart from its state-of-the-art Terminal Tres Cruces.

🚌 **Bus Companies Cita** ☎ 2/402-5425. **Coit** ☎ 2/401-5628. **Copsa** ☎ 2/409-9855. **EGA** ☎ 2/402-5164. **Rutas del Plata** ☎ 2/402-5129. **Rutas del Sol** ☎ 2/402-5451. **TTL** ☎ 2/401-1410.

BY CAR

From Argentina you can transport your car across the Río de la Plata by ferry. Alternatively, you can cross the Argentina-Uruguay border in three places: Puerto Unzue-Fray Bentos, Colon-Paysandu, or Concordia-Salto. From Brazil you can cross the border either at Chuy, the Río Branco, Rivera, or via the bridge at Quarai-Artigas.

CAR RENTAL Rates are often higher in Uruguay than in the United States because of the value-added tax. For an economy-size car, expect to pay around $45 per day.

EMERGENCY ASSISTANCE For roadside assistance, contact the Autómovil Club Uruguayo. Expect to pay $35 to enroll on the spot.

GASOLINE Gas is expensive in Uruguay, and will cost you up to about 26 pesos per liter (there are almost four liters to a gallon, so that's 104 pesos per gallon). Stations operated by Shell, Esso, Texaco, and Ancap (the national petroleum company) are open Monday–Saturday until 9 PM or later. The Ancap station at Aeropuerto Internacional Carrasco is open daily 6 AM–11 PM.

ROAD CONDITIONS Roads between Montevideo and Punta del Este are quite good, as are the handful of major highways. In the countryside, roads are usually surfaced with gravel. If you want to leave the main roads, it's best to speak with locals about current conditions before setting off. Trips will often take longer than expected, so budget extra time. On the up side, country roads often have very little traffic and spectacular scenery.

RULES OF THE ROAD Uruguayans tend to drive carefully, but visitors from Argentina have the reputation of driving with wild abandon. Since almost all roads have only two lanes, keep an eye out for passing vehicles.

🚗 **Automobile Clubs Autómovil Club Uruguayo** ✉ Libertador 1532, Montevideo ☎ 2/902-5792 ✉ 3 de Febrero y Roosevelt, Punta del Este ☎ 42/20156.

Contacts & Resources

CUSTOMS & DUTIES

You may bring up to 400 cigarettes, 50 cigars or 500 grams of loose tobacco, and 2 liters of alcoholic beverages. Live animals, vegetable products, and products that originate from plant or animal products are not allowed into Uruguay. There is no limit on the amount of currency you can bring into the country.

EMBASSIES

See Embassies *in* Montevideo Essentials.

ELECTRICITY

Uruguay runs on 220-volt power. The two-pronged plugs, such as those used in Europe, are standard here.

HEALTH

Cholera is almost unheard-of in Uruguay, but you should still think twice before eating fresh fruits and vegetables. It's a good idea to avoid tap water, as pipes in many older buildings are made of lead. Almost everyone drinks locally bottled *agua mineral* (mineral water), which is available *con gas* or *sin gas* (with or without carbonation).

MONEY MATTERS

The monetary system is based on pesos uruguayos. Given the instability of the currency, hotel and restaurant prices are quoted in United States dollars, indicated by a $ sign. Anything listed in pesos—such as admission prices—is indicated as such. Uruguayan bills come in $5, $10, $20, $50, 100, $200, $500, and $1,000 denominations. Coins are available in 50 centavos pieces (half a peso), $1, and $2.

All banks and exchange houses, which are plentiful in Montevideo, will change traveler's checks and cash. Most banks will also process cash advances from major credit cards, but expect a 5%–10% surcharge.

At press time the exchange rate was 26 Uruguayan pesos to the United States dollar, 19 pesos to the Canadian dollar, 44 pesos to the pound sterling, and 18 pesos to the Australian dollar.

WHAT IT WILL COST Relative to the dollar, prices in Uruguay have been cut in half in just two years. For years foreign visitors found Uruguay expensive compared to other South American countries. But with its economy tied so closely to Argentina's, Uruguay's peso dropped in value substantially relative to the dollar after an economic downturn in 2000. Although prices once were significantly more expensive in January and February, that's no longer the case. You'll find the quality of meals, hotels, and services quite good for the money.

Sample prices: cup of coffee, 20 pesos; bottle of beer, 30 pesos; soft drink, 20 pesos; bottle of house wine, 30 pesos; sandwich, 30 pesos; 1-km (½-mi) taxi ride, 20 pesos; city bus ride, 13 pesos.

PASSPORTS & VISAS

U.S. and British citizens need only a valid passport for stays of up to 90 days in Uruguay. Canadian citizens also require a tourist visa (C$37.50), available from the Consulate of Uruguay.

📷 **Consulates Consulate of Uruguay** ✉ 30 Albert St., Suite 1905, Ottawa, Ontario K1P 5G4 Canada ☎ 613/234-2937.

SAFETY

Pickpockets are your biggest threat in the larger cities in Uruguay. Street crime has risen in recent years, particularly in Montevideo, so keep an eye on your purse or wallet. Crime in the countryside is practically non-existent. As in the United States, call **911** for police, ambulance, and fire emergencies.

TAXES

DEPARTURE TAX To most foreign destinations you can expect to pay a $12 departure tax. If you're headed to Argentina, instead, you'll only pay $6.

VALUE ADDED Throughout the country a value-added tax, called IVA, of 14% is added
TAX to hotel and restaurant bills. This tax is usually included in the rate. Almost all other goods and services carry a 23% IVA charge.

TELEPHONES

To call Uruguay from another country, dial the country code of 598, and then the area code. To call locally, dial the digits of the numbers without any prefix. In Montevideo, a local number has seven digits; in Punta it has six; in Colonia it has five. To dial domestically to another region, include the regional code and then the number. The Montevideo area code is 2; Punta's code is 42; Colonia's is 052.

LOCAL CALLS You can use coins or phone cards at public phones. Purchase phone cards at newsstands and other small businesses. You can also place calls at one of the offices of Antel, the national telecommunications company, though at a much higher rate.

TIPPING

In restaurants a flat 10% tip is considered adequate. For any other services, such as tour guides and valet services, a dollar tip is appreciated. Tips are optional for taxi rides.

Venezuela

10

WORD OF MOUTH

"We spent three days on mainland Venezuela and that was fantastic—wonderful scenery and spectacular fishing."

—sheilasnoddy

"You might want to combine two or three regions, because they're so different that it's like visiting two or three different countries. This way you'll have a more complete vision of Venezuela."

—ABENDIGO

"You may not want to go to Caracas, but you should make a trip to Margarita Island. It's like a world of its own. Margarita has lots to offer tourists, and it's a beautiful place that Venezuela has to offer everyone."

—chitamf

Updated by
Jeffrey Van
Fleet

THE TURQUOISE WATERS OF THE CARIBBEAN gently lap at Venezuela's shores. Not so many years ago the 2,750-km (1,700-mi) coastline was the first glimpse of the country for almost all visitors. Christopher Isherwood, who arrived here on an ocean liner in 1950, wrote that "its mountains rose up sheer and solemn out of the flat sea, thrown into massive relief by tremendous oblique shafts of light from the rising sun. The gorges were deep in crimson shadow, the ridges were outlined in dazzling gold."

For natural beauty, Venezuela is a land of surprising diversity. In the Caribbean you'll find Los Roques, which has what is arguably the most spectacular snorkeling and diving in the region. Some of the islands that make up the archipelago virtually disappear with the high tide. Closer to the mainland is the lovely Isla Margarita, a popular destination for sun-seeking North and South Americans.

In the country's western reaches, snow glistens year-round in the northernmost fingers of the Andes. The longest and highest cable-car system in the world affords stunning views. The Río Orinoco, mustering its might from a million sources in Colombia and Brazil, meanders through the broad grasslands that cover about a third of the country. You'll spot brilliantly colored tropical birds that are found only here, including the rare jabiru stork. In the far southeast, flat-top mountains called *tepuis* tower over Parque Nacional Canaima. These same geological formations inspired Sir Arthur Conan Doyle's novel *The Lost World*. The park is also home to the world's highest waterfall, Angel Falls, which plummets over 2,647 feet into a bizarre landscape of inky black lagoons and plant life.

For hundreds of years Venezuela was grindingly poor, disregarded because it lacked the mineral riches of neighbors such as Peru and Ecuador. Then in 1914 huge deposits of oil were discovered in what was thought to be a barren region near Lago Maracaibo. Venezuela, one of the founding members of the Organization of Petroleum Exporting Countries (OPEC), would be the world's largest oil exporter for the next 50 years. Sleepy towns transformed into booming metropolises, and the country continued to grow with the energetic impatience of its youthful population (70% are under 35 years old).

Two failed coups in 1992 marred Venezuela's reputation as South America's most enduring democratic state. In an ironic twist, the 1998 elections saw the leader of the attempted takeovers, Hugo Chávez, swept into office. He won strong support from the poor for his promise of fairer wealth distribution, but has angered middle and upper classes over his populist policies. A 63-day nationwide strike calling for Chávez' ouster crippled the country and choked its lifeblood of petroleum in early 2003, ending with an uneasy impasse between the two sides.

Exploring Venezuela

Sun-seeking travelers should waste no time in getting to the translucent waters of the Caribbean coast, specifically those around Isla Margarita and Los Roques. You might be surprised to see that the continent's mighty

TOP REASONS TO GO

FLY LIKE AN ANGEL

You probably know Kerapa Kupai Mapú, the world's highest waterfall, as Angel Falls, named for barnstormer pilot Jimmy Angel who crash-landed here in 1937. Your approach to this Amazon cascade (15 times higher than Niagara Falls), deep within Canaima National Park, might be via flyover—much less problematic these days–or boat.

SCALE THE ANDES

South America's preeminent mountain range really does jut into sultry, tropical Venezuela. Pleasant university town Mérida anchors the country's highland region, and makes the perfect antidote to the urban sprawl of Caracas. Take a ride on the world's longest, highest cable-car system, and make a leisurely day trip through artisan towns that dot the mountains.

LAZE ON A CARIBBEAN BEACH

St. Bart's has nothing on Margarita, the continent's one true Caribbean island. Venezuelans call their favorite vacation destination *La Perla del Caribe* (the Pearl of the Caribbean), and the island, with its white-sand beaches, smart hotels, yummy restaurants, and historic sites, really does live up to the hype.

PAY YOUR RESPECTS TO SIMÓN BOLÍVAR

Caracas's historic Centro is a repository of sights honoring the continent's Libertador, and is a must for understanding the life and times of Simón Bolívar and South America's struggle for independence in the early 19th century.

Andes take up such a prominent portion of Venezuelan territory, but for a taste of what the capital once was like, head to Andean towns such as Mérida, set against the sublime backdrop of the western mountains. The Orinoco River basin and Canaima National Park, itself the size of Belgium, occupy Venezuela's eastern sector. Deep in the south is the jungly Amazonas, named, of course, for the hemisphere's largest river. Los Llanos, vast, wildlife-filled grasslands, sit in the center of it all.

Restaurants & Cuisine

Venezuela's larger cities boast a wide variety of restaurants, from Spanish *tascas* (casual restaurants with bars) to French bistros to Japanese sushi bars. But while you're here, you'll want to sample Venezuela's own unique cuisine. The national dish, *pabellón criollo,* consists of shredded beef served with rice, black beans (*caraotas*), fried ripe plantains (*tajadas*), and local white cheeses such as *queso de mano.* Venezuelans like beef, and restaurants that specialize in grilled meats (called *restaurante de Carne*) are popular with locals. Stop at an *arepera* and try an *arepa*, a grilled cornmeal pocket stuffed with anything from fresh cheese to avocado and chicken salad. If you visit during the Christmas season, try the holiday specialty called *hallaca,* a combination of chicken, almonds, olives, and pork, in a cornmeal shell wrapped in aromatic banana leaves.

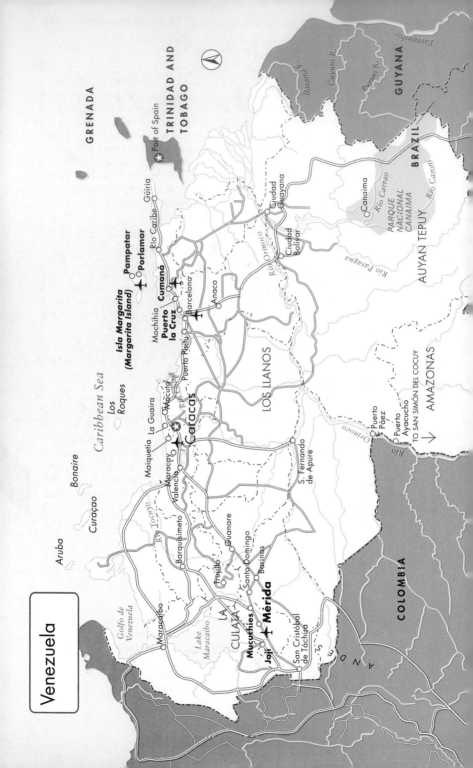

Excellent fish and shellfish dominate in the coastal areas and on Isla Margarita and Los Roques, including grouper, snapper, mackerel, tuna, swordfish, lobster, crab, shrimp, and clams. In the Andean regions, treat yourself to rainbow trout.

Don't leave Venezuela without sampling at least one of these scrumptious, typical desserts: *bien me sabe* (coconut cake), *torta de guanábana* (a tart fruitcake), *merengón de nispero* (meringue cake), and the always popular *cascos de guayaba* (guava shells with white cheese). As a Caribbean nation, Venezuela excels at rum production (*ron* in Spanish). A small bottle of aged Santa Teresa fits nicely in your pack to take home. Venezuela also produces some surprisingly good domestic wines, such as Viña Altagracia or the sparkling Pomar from Lara State in the northwest region of the country.

Lunch, the main meal of the day, begins at noon and lasts until about 3. Dinner is taken between 7 and 10 PM; don't count on being served much past 10:30 PM, except in the Las Mercedes district of Caracas, where some restaurants remain open until midnight. Some restaurants offer a prix-fixe meal at lunchtime known as the *menu ejecutivo*. This includes a *primero* (appetizer of soup or salad); a *segundo*, the main course; and *postre* (dessert). Espresso or *guayoyo*, a weaker drip coffee, is included.

High-end restaurants frequently have dress codes, so inquire when making reservations. For most other dining establishments, a woman can't go wrong in an informal dress or a man in a collared shirt with optional tie.

WHAT IT COSTS In Dollars					
	$$$$	**$$$**	**$$**	**$**	**¢**
AT DINNER	over $20	$15–$20	$10–$15	$6–$10	under $6

Prices are for a main course at dinner.

About the Hotels

Venezuela offers lodging options to suit almost every price range and comfort level—from the resort citadels of Caracas to the colorful, three-room posadas of the Gran Roque. Take in a view of the Andes from the window of a restored 17th-century monastery or from the cobblestone courtyard of a renovated coffee hacienda nestled in the cloud forest above Mérida. In Los Llanos, you can stay on a working cattle ranch or in the guest facilities of a biological field station. Those who seek adventure by day and comfort by night will relish the prime location and amenities offered by the Arekuna camp near Parque Nacional Canaima.

Luxury hotels rarely include meals when quoting rates, but many of the smaller lodgings in the Andes do include breakfast (and sometimes dinner) in their room rates. Remember that prices jump 10%–20% during holiday periods, particularly during Christmas, pre-Lenten Carnival, and Holy Week.

WHAT IT COSTS In Dollars				
$$$$	**$$$**	**$$**	**$**	**¢**
FOR 2 PEOPLE over $180	$100–$180	$60–$100	$40–$60	under $40

Prices are for a double room in high season, excluding tax.

When to Go

The most popular time to visit is between December and April, during Venezuela's dry season. During holidays an influx of tourists pushes prices higher and makes it more difficult to find accommodations. During the rainy season from May to October—when there is still plenty of good weather—crowds are rare and hotel prices drop significantly.

CLIMATE   Caracas and much of Venezuela boast a year-round mild climate, temperatures ranging between 65°F and 75°F during the day and rarely dropping below 55°F at night. Expect it to be colder in the higher altitudes of the Andes, so bring a sweater. Some coastal areas are hotter and more humid, but you can usually depend on a cool breeze blowing in off the ocean.

The following are the daily maximum and minimum temperatures for Caracas.

Jan.	79F	26C	May	81F	27C	Sept.	82F	28C
	60	16		66	19		64	18
Feb.	80F	27C	June	80F	27C	Oct.	81F	27C
	62	17		65	18		64	18
Mar.	81F	27C	July	80F	27C	Nov.	82F	28C
	62	17		65	18		62	17
Apr.	80F	27C	Aug.	84F	29C	Dec.	80F	27C
	64	18		65	18		61	16

HOLIDAYS   All the days listed below are major holidays, when banks, schools and many private businesses are closed. Holy Week is a big vacation time for Venezuelans. Caracas basically shuts down. Also, companies usually give vacation from around December 15 through January 15. All big tourist destinations should be operating, but anything beyond that should be checked.

New Year's Day; Holy Thursday and Good Friday; Proclamation of Independence Day (April 19); Labor Day (May 1); Battle of Carabobo (June 24); Independence Day (July 5); Simón Bolívar's birthday (July 24); Columbus Day (October 12); Christmas Eve and Day.

FESTIVALS   During February's Carnaval the entire country goes on a Mardi Gras–like binge; in Caracas nearly everyone vacates the city and heads for the beach. Also in February, Mérida celebrates its Feria del Sol (Festival of the Sun) with bullfights and open-air salsa and merengue performances. In mid-March Paraguachí on Isla Margarita celebrates the Feria de San José. In the week before Easter the country celebrates Semana Santa (Holy Week). El Hatillo hosts an annual music festival in late October or early November with classical and pop performances. On September 24 Jají celebrates the Feast of St. Michael the Archangel with music, dance, and much fanfare.

LANGUAGE

Spanish is the official language of Venezuela, but many words in common usage are unique to the country, especially regarding foods. For instance, Venezuelans call a banana a *cambur*; a watermelon a *patilla*; a papaya a *lechosa*; and a passion fruit a *parchita*.

CARACAS

On a wall facing the Plaza el Venezolano, Simón Bolívar is quoted as follows: SI SE OPONE LA NATURALEZA LUCHAREMOS CONTRA ELLA Y LA HAREMOS QUE NOS OBEDEZCA (If nature opposes us, we'll struggle against her and make her obey us). Nowhere in Venezuela is the legacy of Bolívar's defiant proclamation more apparent than in Caracas itself. Whether gazing at the city's sprawling skyline from the 17th-story window of a highrise hotel or strolling in the shadows of looming concrete edifices, one wistfully dreams of what Caracas might have been like had its sudden growth spurt occurred during any other architectural moment than the 1970s.

What redeems Caracas is the Caraqueños themselves: a diverse, young, and lively population that colors the grimy streets of the capital with laughter, music, and unrestrained enthusiasm. The sophisticated tastes of the nearly 5 million inhabitants demand the endless parades of boutiques and fine restaurants that crowd commercial areas. Hip, fast-paced, and altogether cosmopolitan, Caraqueños still manage to retain a warmth and amiability you may not expect to encounter in a city this vast.

Although Caracas is a rambling metropolis, its places of interest can be explored comfortably in a day or two. Interesting museums and cultural centers, lively bars, and refined dining establishments are all connected by the city's clean, efficient subway system. The weather, too, facilitates exploring: At 3,000 feet above sea level, Caracas enjoys one of the world's most agreeable climates, with an average daily temperature of 24°C (75°F).

10

Be advised, however, that Caracas well deserves its reputation as a dangerous city. The main tourist areas are generally safe during the day, but always be on your guard. Even residents do not go out alone in most neighborhoods after dark, when muggings and other violent crimes are shockingly frequent. Taxis are the safest means of transportation after dark.

Exploring Caracas

Set amid rolling hills, Caracas lacks a single downtown area. However, the city can be divided into four principal areas of interest: El Centro and its prerequisite Plaza Bolívar ringed by historic buildings; Parque Central and the surrounding Bellas Artes district; Las Mercedes with its many boutiques and restaurants; and the walled villas and apartment buildings of residential Altamira and La Castellana.

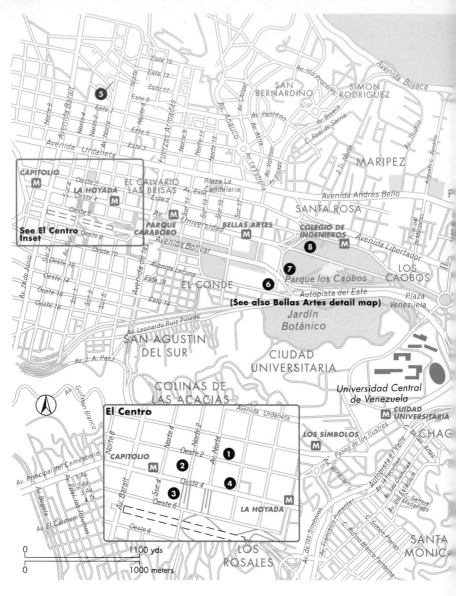

Caracas

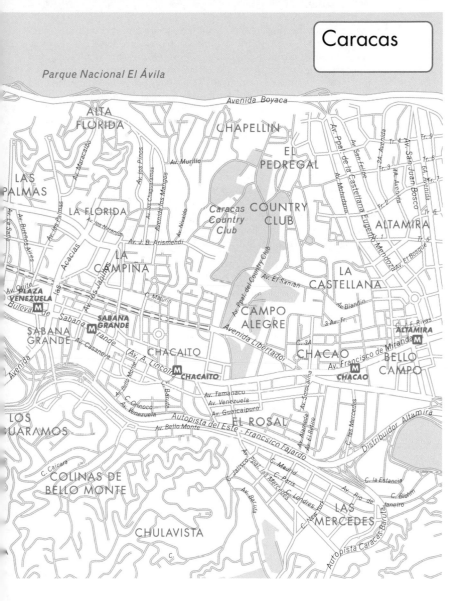

Parque Nacional El Ávila

Avenida Boyaca

ALTA FLORIDA

CHAPELLIN

EL PEDREGAL

Av. Murillo

LAS PALMAS

LA FLORIDA

Caracas Country Club

COUNTRY CLUB

ALTAMIRA

Av. J. B. Arismendi

LA CAMPIÑA

LA CASTELLANA

Av. El Samán

Av. Blandin

PLAZA VENEZUELA Ⓜ

Bulevar de Sabana

SABANA GRANDE Ⓜ

CAMPO ALEGRE

3 Av. Tr.

ALTAMIRA Ⓜ

SABANA GRANDE

Av. Casanova

CHACAITO

Avenida Libertador

CHACAO

Av. Francisco de Miranda

BELLO CAMPO

(Av. A. Lincoln)

CHACAITO Ⓜ

CHACAO

LOS GUARAMOS

Av. Tamanaco
Av. Venezuela
Av. Guaicaipuro

Av. Bello Monte

Autopista del Este - Francsico Fajardo

EL ROSAL

Distribuidor Altamira

C. Caicara

COLINAS DE BELLO MONTE

C. Jalisco

C. Madrid
C. Paris
C. Londres
C. New York

C. la Estancia

C. Biohm

Av. Río de Janeiro

LAS MERCEDES

CHULAVISTA

Autopista Caracas-Baruta

The main subway line runs across much of the city, supplemented by two short southern spurs. It's clean, safe, and great for traveling around Caracas. Buses confound first-time visitors because service is sporadic and routes are difficult to ascertain. *Por puestos*—the small vans that will pick you up and drop you off anywhere on their set routes—are fine for short point-to-point hops. Taxis, their progress often hampered during the day by gridlock, are the only other viable alternative for getting around downtown.

Numbers in the text correspond to numbers in the margin and on the Caracas maps.

El Centro

El Centro is the oldest part of Caracas, a city founded by Spanish conquistador Diego de Losada in 1567. Colonial buildings are clustered around the lush Plaza Bolívar. Numerous benches are almost always occupied by aged Venezuelans vehemently discussing the latest political events or admiring the passing Caraqueña girls. In the center is an imposing statue of Simón Bolívar, the hero of Venezuelan Independence.

TIMING   With the exception of the Panteón Nacional, which is a 15-minute stroll from Plaza Bolívar, the sights in El Centro are very concentrated. Remember that museums are closed in the middle of the day and all day Monday. While this area is safe for exploring in the day, after dusk it gets rougher.

WHAT TO SEE   **Capitolio Nacional.** Venezuela's Congress is housed in the neoclassical
★ ❷   National Capitol, a pair of buildings constructed on the site of the 17th-century convent of the Sisters of the Conception. President Guzmán Blanco, who ordered the disbanding of all convents, razed the original building in 1874. On the site he built the Federal and Legislative palaces. The paintings in the oval Salón Elíptico by Venezuelan artist Martin Tovar y Tovar are quite impressive, especially those on the ceiling. The bronze urn in the room contains the 1811 Declaration of Independence. (In deference to decorum, you must tuck in your shirt when you enter this room.) ⊠ *Av. Norte 2 at Av. Oeste 2, El Centro* 🎫 *Free* ☉ *Daily 9–12:30 and 3–5* Ⓜ *Capitolio.*

❹   **Casa Natal del Libertador.** The birthplace of Simón Bolívar is a pilgrimage site for Venezuelans, who honor him as "El Libertador." The house has very little to offer about the great man himself but is a lovely example of a spacious and airy old colonial house in the midst of downtown's hustle and bustle. Monumental wall paintings by Tito Salas in the front room that retell the stories of Bolívar's heroic battles are well worth a look. ⊠ *Av. Traposos at Av. San Jacinto, El Centro* ☎ *0212/ 541-2563* 🎫 *Free* ☉ *Tues.–Fri. 9–noon and 1–4:30, weekends 10–noon and 1–4:30* Ⓜ *Capitolio.*

❸   **Iglesia de San Francisco.** Filled with richly gilded altars, this church dat-
Fodor'sChoice   ing from 1593 was the site of Simón Bolívar's proclamation as "El Lib-
★   ertador" (the Liberator) and of his massive funeral 12 years after his 1830 death. It remains the loveliest example of colonial architecture in

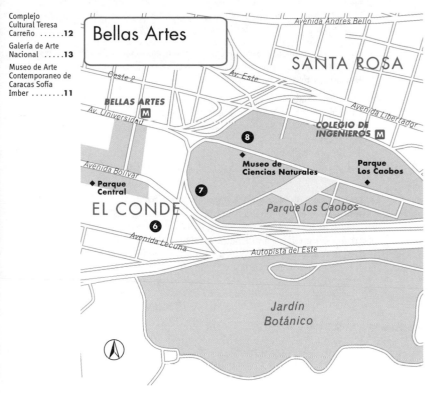

Caracas. ✉ *Av. Bolsa at Av. San Francisco, El Centro* ☎ *0212/484–5172* 🎟 *Free* ⊘ *Daily 7–noon and 3–6* Ⓜ *Capitolio.*

★ ❶ **Museo Sacro de Caracas.** The Museum of Religious Art of Caracas, a former sacristy and ecclesiastical prison built in 1844 adjoining the cathedral, now houses ornate religious statues and lavish costumes from the colonial era. Especially noteworthy in the first salon is the ornate silver canopy made to cover the statue of Our Lady of the Rosary. Downstairs you'll find an intriguing, albeit rather macabre, common grave where remains of the religious are interred in sealed niches. ✉ *Plaza Bolívar, El Centro* ☎ *0212/861–6562* 🎟 *Bs 1,000 adult, Bs 500 students/children* ⊘ *Tues.–Sat. 8:30–4, Mon. 11–4* Ⓜ *Capitolio.*

★ ❺ **Panteón Nacional.** Five blocks north of Plaza Bolívar, the striking National Pantheon's exquisite marble interior holds the remains of 138 Venezuelan political and historical figures, including Simón Bolívar. The walls and ceilings are graced with murals depicting some of the most famous battles for independence. ✉ *Av. Panteón, El Centro* ☎ *0212/862–1518* 🎟 *Free* ⊘ *Tues.–Sun. 10–noon and 1–4:30* Ⓜ *Capitolio.*

Bellas Artes

The cultural center of Caracas, Bellas Artes hosts almost all the major exhibitions and performances that visit Venezuela. This zone encompasses the giant twin towers of Parque Central and the museums of Parque Los Caobos.

TIMING   Visiting all of the sights of Bellas Artes will take half a day. Allow an hour and a half to visit the museums on weekdays, a bit more on weekends, when they tend to be crowded. All museums are closed on Monday.

WHAT TO SEE   **Complejo Cultural Teresa Carreño.** World-class ballet, opera, and classical concerts are regularly presented at this modern cultural center named for Venezuela's most famous classical pianist. Hanging from the theater roof is the kinetic sculpture "Yellow Pendants," by Venezuelan artist Jesús Soto. Adjacent to the complex are a bookstore and the Teatro Ateneo de Caracas, home of a popular movie theater screening art films. ⊠ *Plaza Morelos, Bellas Artes* ☎ *0212/574–9122* Ⓜ *Bellas Artes.*

⑧ **Galería de Arte Nacional.** Known around town as the "GAN," the interesting National Art Gallery, across the circular Plaza Morelos from the Museum of Natural Science, displays more than 4,000 works of art from Venezuela's proud past. It shares a building with the **Museo de Bellas Artes,** which exhibits a random selection of art from all around the globe. The top floor is a terrace offering views over Parque Los Caobos and much of Caracas. ⊠ *Plaza de los Museos, Bellas Artes* ☎ *0212/ 578–1818 for the gallery, 0212/578–1816 for the museum* ☑ *Free* ⊙ *Tues.–Fri. 9–5, Sat.–Mon. 10–5* Ⓜ *Bellas Artes.*

OFF THE BEATEN PATH

PARQUE NACIONAL EL ÁVILA – The mountains of Parque Nacional El Ávila rise some 3,300 feet over the northern edge of Caracas, then slope down its other side directly into the Caribbean. The national park is a favorite destination for weekend hikers, as its southern side is crisscrossed with trails. Novices prefer the daylong hike that leads to Pico Ávila, while more experienced hikers take the two-day trek to Pico Naiguatá. The park is easily accessible from the Altamira neighborhood in eastern Caracas. If you don't feel like hiking you can ride up in a cable car.

San José de Galipán, a settlement on the coastal side of Mount Ávila, makes a nice destination if you've been hiking all morning. Horses are available there for further exploring. The town's cool climate makes it perfect for growing flowers to sell in Caracas.

⑥ **Museo de Arte Contemporáneo de Caracas Sofía Imber.** This excellent contemporary art museum displays paintings by Picasso, Miró, and Bacon. There are also 3-D works by renowned Venezuelan artist Jesús Soto. Housed on the edge of the Parque Central complex, this is one of the best collections of modern art in South America. ⊠ *Parque Central, Bellas Artes* ☎ *0212/573–8289* ☑ *Free* ⊙ *Mon.–Sun. 9–5* Ⓜ *Bellas Artes.*

FodorsChoice
★

Where to Eat

French

$$–$$$ ✕ **Lasserre.** For more than 30 years Venezuelans have enjoyed the finest in classical French food here. House specialties include duck and grouper. The Grand Marnier soufflé, which must be ordered in advance, is a great finishing touch. Enjoy a glass of wine from the top-notch cellar as you listen to the live piano music. ⊠ *Av. Tercera, between 2a and 3a Trans-*

versals, Los Palos Grandes ☎ *0212/283–4558* ▭ *AE, D, MC, V* ✆ *No lunch weekends.*

Italian

$–$$ ✕ **Da Guido.** This casual, family-style restaurant with hams hanging from the ceiling and colorful murals depicting the Italian countryside is filled with locals who enjoy its classic dishes and affordable prices. Manager Eliseo Peserico and his friendly waiters have been serving up delicious gnocchi, ravioli, and fettuccine for more than 30 years. House specialties include roasted goat and quails with polenta. ✉ *Av. Mariscal Francisco Solano, Local 8, Sabana Grande* ☎ *0212/763–0937* ▭ *AE, MC, V* Ⓜ *Plaza Venezuela.*

Venezuelan

★ $$–$$$ ✕ **Tarzilandia.** Lush tropical vegetation filled with parrots, tree frogs, and turtles has been part of the experience at this Caracas landmark since it opened in 1950. On the menu you will find delectable grilled steaks and seafood. The mango flambé à la mode seems much loved. ✉ *Av. San Juan de Bosco at Decima Transversal, Altamira* ☎ *0212/261–8419* ▭ *AE, MC, V.*

Where to Stay

Most of the top hotels in Caracas, including those belonging to international chains, are south and east of the city center, in the upscale neighborhoods of Altamira and Las Mercedes. Prices tend to be much higher than in the rest of the country. The area around Sabana Grande has a cluster of more economical accommodations. Avoid the cheap hotels in the capital; most double as brothels and rent by the hour.

$$$–$$$$ ▦ **Hilton Caracas.** This complex, downtown in the Bellas Artes district, a favorite for international business travelers, is like a city unto itself. You have your pick of restaurants and bars, as well as plenty of facilities. Although the rooms look bland, they have great views of the nearby Parque Los Caobos. ✉ *Av. Libertador at Av. 25 Sur, Bellas Artes* ☎ *0212/503–5000, 800/774–1500 in the U.S.* ▤ *0212/503–5003* ⊕ *www.hiltoncaracas.com.ve* ⊷ *738 rooms, 27 suites* ♨ *2 restaurants, room service, in-room safes, minibars, in-room data ports, 2 tennis courts, 2 pools, health club, hair salon, massage, sauna, bar, shops, babysitting, playground, dry cleaning, laundry service, concierge, business services, meeting rooms, travel services, parking, no-smoking rooms* ▭ *AE, D, MC, V* Ⓜ *Bellas Artes.*

★ $$$–$$$$ ▦ **Tamanaco Inter-Continental.** A permanent part of the Caracas social scene, this venerable hotel sits on a bluff above the southeastern section of the city. The oldest of the city's luxury hotels, this pyramid looming over the Las Mercedes neighborhood is exceptionally well maintained. Its most stunning facility, a free-form pool, loops around any which way but not rectangularly. You can take a dip after working out at the health club or playing a few games on the tennis courts. The bar, El Punto, has long been a gathering site of choice for the city's elite and influential. Rooms are spacious and eminently well appointed. ✉ *Av. Principal de Las Mercedes, Las Mercedes* ☎ *0212/909–7111* ▤ *0212/909–7116*

10

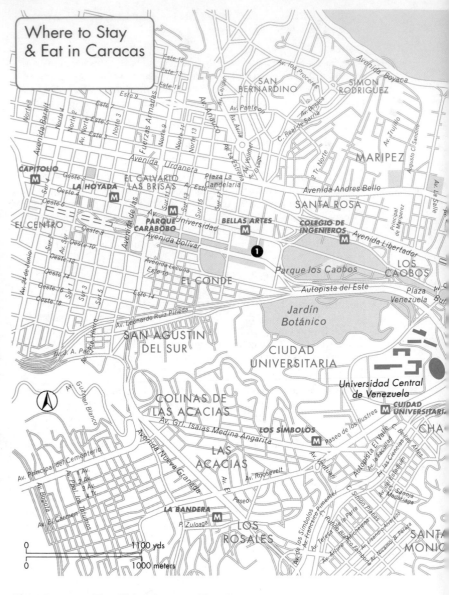

Where to Stay & Eat in Caracas

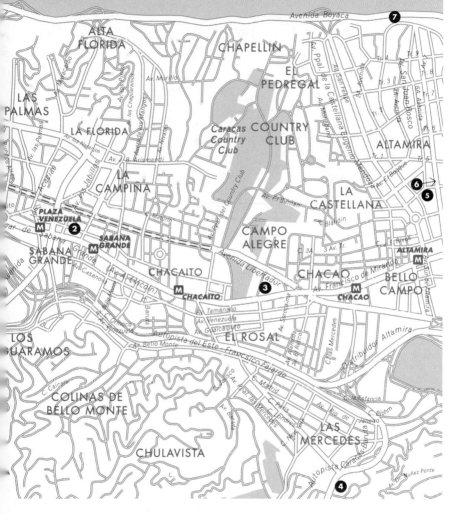

⊕ *intercontinental.com/caracas/* ⤷ *486 rooms, 55 suites ♧ 3 restaurants, in-room safes, minibars, in-room data ports, 3 tennis courts, pool, health club, hair salon, sauna, 2 bars, dry cleaning, laundry service, concierge, business services, meeting rooms, car rental, travel services, parking, no-smoking rooms* ▤ *AE, D, MC, V.*

$$$ ⌑ **Embassy Suites.** This 20-floor tower in the financial district caters to the needs of business travelers. The soaring atrium, which lets in lots of sun, is a great place to relax over breakfast. The suites all have separate living rooms, except for 24 new rooms that have balconies instead. ⊠ *Av. Francisco de Miranda and Av. El Parque, Campo Alegre* ☎ *0212/276–4200* 🖷 *0212/267–3761* ⊕ *www.embassysuitescaracas.com* ⤷ *224 suites, 24 rooms ♧ Restaurant, in-room safes, minibars, in-room data ports and wireless, pool, health club, hair salon, hot tub, 2 bars, shops, laundry service, concierge, business services, meeting rooms, travel services, parking, no-smoking floors* ▤ *AE, D, MC, V.*

$$ ⌑ **Continental Altamira.** Within walking distance of the Plaza Altamira, this hotel is a favorite of travelers on a mid-range budget. Although the hotel is slightly dated on the outside, the interior is modern and nicely furnished. Most rooms have balconies overlooking the tree-lined Avenida San Juan Bosco. ⊠ *Av. San Juan Bosco, Altamira* ☎ *0212/261–0644* 🖷 *0212/261–0131* ⊕ *www.hotel-continental.org.ve* ⤷ *80 rooms, 2 suites ♧ Restaurant, in-room safes, minibars, pool, bar, laundry service, meeting rooms, free parking* ▤ *AE, D, MC, V* Ⓜ *Altamira* ⦿| *BP.*

Nightlife & the Arts

Nightlife

Monday must be the only night Caraqueños get any sleep, because Tuesday seems to be the unofficial start of the weekend. By Saturday the whole population appears to be out on the town. As in much of Latin America, the nightlife doesn't really get swinging until close to midnight. The trendy Las Mercedes neighborhood, packed with cafés, restaurants, bars, and dance clubs, is the place to be on Friday and Saturday. Although Caracas is generally pretty casual, clubs often require men to wear jackets. Take a taxi after dark no matter where you go or how short the distance.

BARS   In Las Mercedes, **Auyama** (⊠ Calle Londres, Las Mercedes ☎ 0212/991–9489) is a popular place for a cocktail before heading to the clubs. It also serves reasonably priced food.

DANCE CLUBS   Salsa and merengue are more popular in Venezuela than in any other South American country, which means that both types of music can be found in almost any club in the city. Many begin the night playing pop, then switch to salsa and merengue when the crowd gets warmed up. The dance floors immediately fill with young couples gyrating hip to hip.

The most popular salsa club is **El Maní Es Así** (⊠ Calle El Cristo at Av. Francisco Solano López, Sabana Grande ☎ 0212/763–6671), which is always packed with a crowd covering a wide age range. **Latino's** (⊠ Centro Comercial Los Chaguaramos, Los Chaguaramos ☎ 0212/693–6695) is a more upmarket salsa club where jackets and ties are not out of place. The crowd is relatively young and definitely affluent.

The Arts

Theater and other types of performances are popular nighttime diversions. For current listings, pick up a copy of the English-language newspaper *The Daily Journal* at any newsstand.

MUSIC The campus of Universidad Central de Venezuela, **Aula Magna** (☎ 0212/605–4516) has concerts by the Venezuelan Symphony Orchestra on Sunday at 11 AM. This impressive concert hall features a ceiling full of colorful "acoustic clouds" designed by Alexander Calder. The **Teatro Ateneo de Caracas** (✉ Plaza de los Museos, Bellas Artes ☎ 0212/575–4475) has two theaters where plays are regularly performed and one movie theater. **Teatro Teresa Carreño** (✉ Paseo Colon, Bellas Artes ☎ 0212/574–9122), the center for cultural events in Venezuela, presents the best-known national and international musicians, chamber music, opera and ballet.

THEATER **Teatro Nacional** (✉ Av. Lacuna, Centro ☎ 0212/483–4360) has a roster of cultural events.

Outdoor Activities

On a continent where soccer is nearly a religion, Venezuela's obsession with baseball is a notable exception. The popularity of the sport is due in large part to the thriving professional winter league, where North American players such as Johnny Bench, Pete Rose, and Darryl Strawberry all honed their skills. Atlanta Braves slugger Andres Galarraga, born in Caracas, is a hero in his hometown. The centrally located stadium at the **Universidad Central de Venezuela** (✉ Ciudad Universitaria ☎ 0212/572–2211) is the best venue for baseball or soccer. Tickets can be purchased at the gate on the day of the game. Arrive early on weekends.

Shopping

Caraqueños are style-conscious, which accounts for the city's numerous modern shopping centers. Jewelry (especially gold) and leather goods (including shoes, handbags, and luggage) are some of the best bargains in Caracas, but don't expect a steal. Prices are often high in the wake of sobering inflation.

SHOPPING HOW-TO

Although bargaining is not acceptable in city stores, prices at outdoor markets—and sometimes in smaller towns and villages—are negotiable.

10

Markets

One of the most popular markets is the Thursday and Saturday morning **Mercadito de Chacao,** where you can stroll through the stands overflowing with fruits and vegetables. It's a block from Avenida Francisco de Miranda in the Chacao district. The **Mercado Guacaipuro,** open Tuesday, Thursday, and Saturday, is known for its produce as well as its fresh fish. It is best to go in the early morning. You'll find it on the corner of Avenidas Andrés Bello and Libertador.

Shopping Centers

Caracas is home to two of the most gargantuan shopping centers on the continent. **Centro Sambil** (✉ Av. Libertador, Chacao ☎ 0212/267–9302), the largest mall in South America, is a five-level behemoth packed with more than 500 shops, restaurants, theaters, and even amusement park rides. The **Central Comercial Ciudad Tamanaco** (✉ Calle La Estancia, Las Mercedes ☎ 0212/271–7435), east of Las Mercedes in the suburb of Chuao, attracts crowds with its upstairs cinemas, fast-food restaurants, and swanky boutiques.

Las Mercedes has its own sprawling shopping complex, **Paseo de Las Mercedes** (✉ Av. Principal de Las Mercedes, Las Mercedes ☎ 0212/991–7242). **El Recreo** (✉ Paseo El Recreo ☎ 0212/762–7228) is the newest of the large-scale malls and boasts the best food court in the city.

Shopping Districts

With the growing popularity of shopping malls, traditional shopping districts have suffered a decline. One area that continues to draw crowds is the **Bulevar de Sabana Grande**. Once a main traffic thoroughfare, this is a bustling promenade where Caraqueños converge to browse in the tiny shops or chat over a *marrón grande* (large coffee) in one of the many cafés that line the streets. On weekends, browse among the endless rows of stalls or take in performances by mimes, musicians, or even flame-swallowers. The area can be crowded, so be wary of pickpockets.

Besides its restaurants and clubs, **Las Mercedes** is overflowing with fancy boutiques and fashionable shops. The most exclusive are often tucked into side streets. Avoid its main strip, Avenida Principal de Las Mercedes, which has an overwhelming collection of cheap clothing stores.

Specialty Shops

Casa Curuba is a sumptuous world of wood and design. The great variety of Venezuelan hardwoods provides a surprising palette of color and grain. The objects, from hand-carved iguanas to contemporary rocking chairs, reflect a long-time collaboration between skilled artisans of Lara state and prominent Venezuelan designers. Two doors down, **Organika** (✉ Edificio Everi, 5th Av. at 4th Transversal, Altamira ☎ 0212/283–9368, 0212/283–1857) focuses on jewelry, hats, and housewares, giving new interpretations to traditional materials like natural fibers and seeds.

Side Trips from Caracas

★ El Hatillo

On the southern outskirts of Caracas is the hillside village of El Hatillo, a destination well worth the 30-minute taxi ride. Its narrow stone streets are lined with 17th-century buildings housing dozens of shops and boutiques, galleries, and restaurants. Here you'll find unique handicrafts and indigenous artifacts, original artwork and rare antiques from all over Venezuela. The restored village is clearly intended for tourists, but it somehow has managed to preserve its colonial style.

Parque Nacional Los Roques

FodorsChoice
★
An archipelago composed of some 350 tiny islands sprinkled in the dazzling Caribbean, Parque Nacional Los Roques is a 30-minute (propeller-aircraft) flight north from Caracas. Only one of those islands, Gran Roque, boasts a bona fide town, tiny as it is. A few others have private weekend retreats or fishermen's shacks, while most are completely

uninhabited. Some are so small they disappear at high tide. The sandy beaches of Parque Nacional Los Roques are uncommonly white, even by uncompromising Caribbean standards. The crystalline waters reveal thriving coral reefs that are home to more than 300 species of fish.

As a national park since 1976, Parque Nacional Los Roques is subject to strict federal regulations that protect it from overdevelopment. New construction is prohibited on any of the islands. Every structure on Gran Roque—which enjoys fresh water from a desalinization plant and electricity from a generator—existed before the archipelago became a national park. Many have been extensively remodeled and are meticulously maintained as *posadas* (small inns), colorfully painted and adorned with brilliant flowering plants. A handful of bars and eateries make up the rest of the businesses. A mid-19th-century lighthouse, its windmill-like appearance revealing its Dutch heritage, overlooks the town from a small hill nearby.

Los Roques is considered one of the finest locales for hooking bonefish and other types of fish. You can head out in powerboats or in *peñeros* (local fishing boats). Sea kayaking is also popular, and some of the islands have emerged as premier sailboarding destinations. More sedate pastimes include scuba diving and snorkeling. Sunbathing, however, remains the most popular activity.

WHERE TO STAY & EAT   Approximately 60 posadas line the sandy roads of Gran Roque. Most have two to six rooms with private or shared bath and a common dining area. Except during the peak season you should have no difficulty finding lodging on the island.

$$$ 🏨 **Posada Mediterráneo.** Italian-born innkeeper Elena Battani's heritage is evident throughout this exquisite posada, from the simple furnishings of the rooms to the white stone staircase leading to the rooftop terrace hung with sun-shaded hammocks. Join her for a chat at the rustic wooden dining table on her flowering vine-laden front patio. ⊠ *Isla Gran Roque* 📠 *0237/221–1130* ⊕ *www.posadamediterraneo.com* ⤴ *6 rooms* ⚭ *Dining room, in-room safes, fishing; no room phones, no room TVs* 🖃 *AE, MC, V* 🍽 *FAP.*

Fodor's Choice
★

10

Caracas Essentials

Transportation

BY AIR

Caracas is served by Aeropuerto Internacional Simón Bolívar (CCS), about 25 km (16 mi) from downtown in the coastal area of Maiquetía.

Major U.S. carriers serving Venezuela are American, Continental, and Delta. Venezuela's Aeropostal flies to Caracas from Miami. Air France,

British Airways, Iberia, KLM, and Lufthansa fly from their respective hubs in Europe. A number of domestic regional airlines fly throughout Venezuela. Among them are Aereotuy, Avior, Laser, and Santa Bárbara. Most domestic flights stop in Caracas.

Upon landing, you can expect to be issued a free tourist visa, valid for a stay of up to three months.

AIRPORTS & TRANSFERS The trip into town from the airport is via a busy four-lane highway and takes between 30 and 45 minutes, depending upon your destination in Caracas. Cab fare to downtown Caracas costs about Bs30,000. The official fare is posted next to the taxi stand outside the international terminal.

Robberies of tourists by drivers of unofficial cabs are all too common. To be on the safe side, take a taxi from the dispatcher outside the international terminal.

🛪 **International Airlines Aeropostal** ☎ 0212/708-6211. **Air France** ☎ 0800/100-4970. **American** ☎ 0212/267-9111. **British Airways** ☎ 0212/266-0122. **Continental** ☎ 0800/359-2600. **Delta** ☎ 0212/958-1111. **Iberia** ☎ 0212/267-9733. **KLM** ☎ 0212/285-3432. **Lufthansa** ☎ 0212/267-4767.

🛪 **Domestic Carriers Aereotuy** ✉ Av. Abraham Lincoln and Bulevar de Sabana Grande, Edificio Gran Sabana, Sabana Grande ☎ 0212/763-5297. **Avior** ✉ Aeropuerto Nacional Simón Bolívar ☎ 0212/909-8201. **Santa Bárbara** ✉ Calle 3B, Edificio Tokay, La Urbina ☎ 0212/242-1633 in Venezuela.

🛪 **Airports Aeropuerto Internacional Simón Bolívar** ☎ 0212/303-1329.

BY BUS

There are two inconveniently located and slightly unsavory public bus terminals serving Caracas. For travel to destinations west of the city, buses leave from Terminal La Bandera. The Terminal del Oriente serves destinations to the eastern part of the country.

Far more convenient—and much safer—is the *servicio especial* (special service) offered by Aeroexpresos Ejecutivos. All buses depart from the company's own clean, quiet terminal in the Bello Campo district. Two other reliable private companies are Expresos del Oriente and Expresos Alianza.

WITHIN CARACAS Clean, air-conditioned buses called MetroBus leave all Metro stops for areas outside the reach of the subway system. The cost is Bs700. If used within four hours of purchase, a ticket is also valid for a one-way ride on the Metro. Smaller public buses called *carritos* or *por puestos* connect all parts of the city, but they are no quicker in heavy traffic.

🚌 **Bus Companies Aeroexpresos Ejecutivos** ✉ Av. Principal de Bello Campo ☎ 0212/266-2321 or 0212/263-3266. **Expresos Alianza** ✉ Terminal de Occidente ☎ 0212/693-5126. **Expresos del Oriente** ✉ Terminal de Oriente ☎ 0212/462-5371.

CAR TRAVEL

Heavy traffic, a lack of parking, and the city's baffling layout combine to render Caracas a driving challenge for residents, let alone visitors. If you can avoid it, do not rent a car to explore the city.

CAR RENTAL Should you decide to rent a car, major rental chains are located in the airport and downtown.

🚗 **Local Agencies Avis** ⊠ Central Comercial Ciudad Tamanaco, Calle la Estancia ☎ 0212/959-5822 ⊠ Aeropuerto Internacional Simón Bolívar ☎ 0212/355-1190. **Budget** ⊠ Calle Lourdes and Av. Nueva Granada ☎ 0212/603-1300 ⊠ Aeropuerto Internacional Simón Bolívar ☎ 0212/355-2799. **Hertz** ⊠ Hotel Tamanaco Intercontinental, Av. Principal de Las Mercedes ☎ 0212/905-0430 ⊠ Aeropuerto Internacional Simón Bolívar ☎ 0212/614-5623.

BY SUBWAY

The safe, speedy Metro system traverses the city between Palo Verde in the east and Propatria in the west, with connecting north–south lines from Capitolio and Plaza Venezuela. One-way tickets, which can be purchased in all stations, are Bs350, depending on distance traveled. Save your ticket; you'll need it to exit the turnstile out of the station. If you plan to use the Metro frequently, opt for the convenience of a *multi abono* card (Bs3,500), valid for 10 rides anywhere on the system. These cards save you the hassle of waiting in long lines for individual tickets. (The stations' automated ticket-vending machines are frequently out of order.) Route maps are posted at ticket booths and inside each car, but not on the platforms. The Metro operates daily 4:30 AM–11 PM. Cars get very crowded during the 6–9 and 5–8 rush hours.

BY TAXI

Licensed taxis have yellow license plates and carry secured signs that say *libre* (free) on the roof, while *pirata* (pirate) varieties have signs that are obviously detachable. When selecting a taxi off the street, settle only on official cars—tales of robbery by pirata drivers are legion—and agree on the rate before you depart. Unless you are traveling only a couple of blocks, Bs8,000 is a standard fare anywhere in the central city area between Capitolio and Altamira. Note that fares increase by as much as 50% at night and on weekends. Once en route, don't be surprised if your driver cuts corners and ignores stop signs and red lights as he maneuvers through downtown traffic. Many larger hotels have their own taxi companies. Ask your hotel or restaurant to call you a taxi if you go out at night.

Contacts & Resources

EMBASSIES & CONSULATES

The Canadian embassy offers services to its citizens weekdays 8–noon. The New Zealand consulate offers consular services weekdays 8–noon. The British embassy serves its citizens weekdays noon–4:30. The U.S. Embassy opens for consular services weekdays 1–4.

🏛 **Canada** ⊠ Av. Francisco de Miranda at Av. Sur, Altamira ☎ 0212/600-3000. **New Zealand** ⊠ Av. Libertador at Av. Francisco de Miranda, Chacao ☎ 0212/277-7918. **United Kingdom** ⊠ Edificio Las Mercedes, Av. La Estancia, Chuao ☎ 0212/263-8411. **United States** ⊠ Calle F at Calle Suapure, Colinas de Valle Arriba ☎ 0212/975-6411 or 0212/975-7831.

EMERGENCIES

Dial 171 for police, ambulance, fire, or any emergency in the metropolitan area.

10

Pharmacies in different neighborhoods take turns staying open all night; spot them by the sign *turno*, or consult local newspapers for lists of open *farmacias* (pharmacies).

A reputable private clinic with an English-speaking staff is the Clínica El Ávila in Altamira.

🏥 **Hospitals Clínica El Ávila** ✉ Av. San Juan Bosco at 6a Transversal, Altamira ☎ 0212/276-1111.

SAFETY

Pickpocketers and muggers, sometimes violent, are serious problems for residents and visitors alike. Most downtown areas, including those popular with tourists, are generally safe during the day. Note that even residents do not go out alone on foot in most neighborhoods after dark. Use taxis at night, even if you are traveling a short distance.

When visiting the city, don't wear expensive clothing or flashy jewelry, and don't handle money in public. It's a good idea to keep your money in a pocket rather than a wallet, which is easier to steal. On buses, in the Metro, and in crowded areas, hold purses or camera bags close to your body; thieves use knives to slice the bottom of a bag and catch the contents as they fall out.

Avoid all political demonstrations. They're common in Caracas and occasionally result in clashes between demonstrators and police.

TOUR OPERATORS

Lost World Adventures specializes in tailoring an independent travel itinerary around your interests. The founder of this U.S.-based company once lived in Venezuela, so he knows his way around. The company also leads small-group expeditions of 7 to 11 days throughout Venezuela—they'll set you up to travel from the Andes to Angel Falls and everywhere in between—and several other Latin American countries.

A reputable tour operator in Caracas is Orinoco Tours, centrally located on Bulevar de Sabana Grande. This well-run company, which often offers rates much lower than competitors, specializes in ecotourism in Venezuela.

🏢 **Tour Companies Lost World Adventures** ✉ 337 Shadowmoor Dr., Decatur, GA 30030 ☎ 404/373-5820 or 800/999-0558 🖷 404/377-1902 ⊕ www.lostworldadventures.com. **Orinoco Tours** ✉ Edificio Galerías Bolívar, Piso 7, Bulevar de Sabana Grande, Sabana Grande ☎ 0212/761-8431 🖷 0212/761-6801 ⊕ www.orinocotours.com.

VISITOR INFORMATION

The Instituto Nacional del Turismo (INATUR), Venezuela's semi-privatized tourism agency, has information offices on the 35th floor of the Edificio Conde in the Parque Central office complex, open Mon.–Fri. 8 AM–12:30 PM and 2–5 PM. A branch in the arrivals hall at the Aeropuerto Internacional Simón Bolívar is open daily 6 AM–10 PM. Signs at both offices still show the agency's former name, Corpoturismo.

🏢 **Tourist Information INATUR** ✉ Edificio Conde, Bellas Artes ☎ 0212/574-2220, 0800/462-8871 in Venezuela ✉ Aeropuerto Internacional Simón Bolívar ☎ 0212/507-8607.

THE CARIBBEAN COAST

Sometimes referred to as La Ruta del Sol (the Route of the Sun), the 563-km (350-mi) stretch of highway along the Caribbean Coast from Caracas to Puerto La Cruz and Cumaná is at once picturesque and treacherous. Seldom far from the water's edge, most of the Autopista del Oriente (Eastern Highway) follows the myriad loops and twists of the natural shoreline, beside unspoiled bays and isolated hamlets.

Much of the coastline is protected from development, but small posadas are occasionally nestled among the palm trees along the shore. Sprawling resorts line the broad beaches near Puerto La Cruz and Cumaná.

Puerto La Cruz

318 km (198 mi) east of Caracas.

The region's main tourist hub, Puerto La Cruz has attractive waterways lined with marinas and expensive villas. Visitors flock to the maze of shops and restaurants along Paseo Colón, a busy thoroughfare that runs along the beach. At night the crowds move to the bars and dance clubs in town.

Although Puerto La Cruz's own beaches are dangerously polluted, its main attractions are the alluring islands of nearby Parque Nacional Mochima. At the eastern end you'll find boats to the national park that charge Bs12,000–Bs40,000 for round-trip service. Puerto La Cruz is also a jumping-off point for ferries to Isla Margarita, which depart from the western end of Paseo Colón.

Where to Stay & Eat

$ ✕ **Porto Vecchio.** This lively restaurant on Paseo Colón, one of the best eateries in eastern Venezuela, has a faithful clientele that drops in for the house specialty—excellent pastas with fish and shellfish. Don't miss the delicious veal. ⊠ *Paseo Colón 117, at Calle Boyacá* ☎ *0281/265–2047* ▤ *AE, D, MC, V.*

$$$ ▦ **Hotel Puerto La Cruz.** This expansive hotel at the end of the Paseo Colón is next to the marina where the boats take off for excursions to the nearby islands. Spacious rooms overlook the lush gardens and pool. ⊠ *Paseo Colón* ☎ *0281/265–3611* 🖷 *0281/265–3117* ⇗ *220 rooms* ♨ *2 restaurants, minibars, pool, hair salon, dive shop, snorkeling, boating, bar, shops, meeting room, car rental, travel services* ▤ *AE, D, MC, V.*

$$$ ▦ **Punta Palma Hotel.** Built at the end of the bay, this hotel has an enviable view of Puerto La Cruz. Most of its colorfully decorated rooms have balconies and overlook the pool, marina, and small private beach. ⊠ *Prolongación Av. La Península, Cerro El Morro* ☎ *0281/281–1211* 🖷 *0281/281–8277* ⊕ *www.puntapalma.com* ⇗ *154 rooms, 25 suites* ♨ *3 restaurants, snack bar, in-room safes, 4 tennis courts, 2 pools, sauna, marina, 2 bars, shops, babysitting, laundry service, business services, meeting room, car rental, travel services* ▤ *AE, D, MC, V.*

10

Nightlife

You won't have to look far to find bars and dance clubs in Puerto La Cruz, as all are along Paseo Colón or adjacent streets. A popular part of the scene is the vibrant **Harry's Pub** (⊠ Calle Bolívar 53 ☎ no phone), a casual watering hole with an interesting mix of young locals and seasoned wayfarers.

Outdoor Activities

FISHING Boat owners throughout the region will take you fishing in their small wooden peñeros. Bargain for the best price—the going rate is about $5 per person for a half-day excursion. The friendly staff at **Macite Turismo** (⊠ Centro Comercial Paseo Mar, Calle Sucre at Paseo Colón ☎ 0281/265–5703 ⊕ www.maciteturismo.com) offers full-day trips to Isla Tortuga for barracuda fishing. The price is Bs200,000, including meals.

WATER SPORTS In Puerto La Cruz, **Explosub** (⊠ Paseo Colón ☎ 0281/267–3256) offers snorkeling and scuba-diving trips, as well as excursions to Parque Nacional Mochima. If you are not already an experienced diver, Explosub also offers certification classes. In neighboring El Morro, **Odisea** (⊠ Av. Américo Vespucio) rents sailboats, windsurfers, and pedal boats at the Hotel Doral Beach.

Mochima

50 km (30 mi) east of Puerto La Cruz.

Beyond the town of Santa Fe you'll reach the turnoff for Mochima, the launching point for boat trips to the tranquil beaches of **Parque Nacional Mochima,** which encompasses hundreds of small islands. Contract a *peñero* to take you to any of the nearby beaches, where you can spend a relaxing morning or afternoon lazing around in the sun. It's about $10 per person, but the rate is negotiable.

Cumaná

75 km (47 mi) east of Puerto La Cruz.

The oldest European settlement on South America's mainland, Cumaná was founded by the Spanish in 1521. Most of its colonial buildings were destroyed by a string of earthquakes that devastated the town. After the last major earthquake, in 1929, the **Iglesia de Santa Inés** was rebuilt a few blocks south of Plaza Bolívar. Inside are a few items from the colonial period. One block south of Plaza Bolívar, the **Ateneo de Cumaná** (⊠ Calle Antonio ☎ 0293/431–1284) hosts dance and opera evenings in addition to periodic exhibits of contemporary and colonial art.

Overlooking Cumaná from its hilltop perch, **Castillo de San Antonio de la Eminencia** is one of two forts commissioned in the 1680s to protect what was at the time the world's largest salt deposit. The four-point fort was built entirely of coral and outfitted with 16 guns. The fort **Castillo de Santiago de Araya,** is on treeless Araya Peninsula. Ferries leave daily from Cumaná's harbor for the 90-minute trip.

It's estimated that **Cueva del Guácharo,** Venezuela's largest cave, has at least 9 km (5½ mi) of subterranean passageways. Groups are led into the dank caverns by guides who tote kerosene lanterns so as not to upset the light-sensitive *guácharos*—a nocturnal species of fruit-eating birds. Visitors are not allowed to bring anything inside, including purses, flashlights, or cameras. To reach the cave from Cumaná, take Highway 9 south toward Caribe for about 65 km (40 mi) and follow the signs. ⊠ *Parque Nacional El Guácharo* 🎫 *Admission* 🕙 *Daily 8–4.*

Where to Stay & Eat

★ **$$$** 🏨 **Premier Cumanagoto.** Attention to the smallest of details makes this beachfront hotel among the finest hotels outside of Caracas. Large wrought-iron perches holding colorful macaws border the open-air, Mediterranean-style lobby, which has a terra-cotta floor and plenty of old-world charm. Bars and restaurants take full advantage of the Caribbean breezes with outdoor seating. The generously proportioned rooms have terraces overlooking the beautiful pools and gardens below. ⊠ *Final Av. Universidad* 📞 *0293/430–1400* 📠 *0293/452–1877* 🛏 *150 rooms, 13 suites* ♿ *3 restaurants, golf course, tennis court, 2 pools, gym, hair salon, massage, sauna, spa, bar, shops, business services, meeting rooms* 🚫 *AE, D, MC, V.*

The Caribbean Coast Essentials

Transportation

BY AIR

Several regional airlines fly regularly between the domestic terminal of Aeropuerto Internacional Simón Bolívar in Caracas and the coastal towns of Barcelona and Cumaná. Avior serves both airports. Aeropostal serves Barcelona, and Santa Bárbara serves Cumana. Aeroposal and Avior fly between Barcelona and Isla Margarita, while Avior flies between Cumaná and Isla Margarita. Santa Bárbara connects Cumaná with Mérida.

Barcelona's Aeropuerto José Antonio Uzcátequi (BLA) is 3 km (2½ mi) south of the city. The Aeropuerto Antonio José de Sucre (CUM) in Cumaná is 4 km (2 mi) southeast of the city.

🛫 **Airlines Aeropostal** ⊠ Aeropuerto José Antonio Uzcátequi, Barcelona 📞 0281/277–1735 **Avior** ⊠ Aeropuerto José Antonio Uzcátequi, Barcelona 📞 0281/274–9545 or 0212/955–3811. **Santa Bárbara** ⊠ Aeropuerto José Antonio Uzcátequi, Barcelona 📞 0251/443–0662 or 0212/204–4000 ✉ Aeropuerto Antonio José de Sucre, Cumaná 📞 0293/467–2933 or 0212/204–4000.

BY BOAT & FERRY

Conferry shuttles passengers and cars four times daily between Puerto La Cruz on the mainland and Punta de Piedras, 25 km (16 mi) west of Porlamar, Margarita.

Purchase tickets at least two hours in advance for all ferries, particularly on weekends and holidays. Crossings take from two to four hours and cost $25 per passenger and $40 per car.

🚢 **Boat & Ferry Companies Conferry** ⊠ Terminal Los Cocos, Puerto La Cruz 📞 0281/267–78⍤ ✉ Terminal Puerto Sucre, Cumaná 📞 0293/431–1462. **Gran Cacique** ⊠ Terminal Los Cocos, Puerto La Cruz 📞 0281/263–0935 ✉ Terminal Puerto Sucre, Cumaná 📞 0293/432–0011 🌐 www.grancacique.com.ve.

10

BY BUS

There are daily buses from Caracas to Barcelona, Puerto La Cruz, and Cumaná. One-way fare for each is about Bs40,000. Connect to local buses to reach smaller towns, such as Río Chico or Puerto Píritu.

Por puestos are another option. These minibuses carry up to 15 people and travel set routes between the Terminal de Oriente in Caracas and the Caribbean Coast. Drivers shout the names of cities they serve and leave the terminal when full. Expect to pay Bs32,000 between Caracas and Puerto La Cruz and about Bs9,600 between Puerto La Cruz and Cumaná.

BY CAR

A car is a nice option for this part of the country, as you can travel at your own pace and stop at beautiful beaches along the coastal route. The often-congested Autopista del Oriente connects Caracas with Barcelona, Puerto La Cruz, Cumaná, and smaller towns beyond. It has plenty of roadside services.

CAR RENTAL Inside the airport terminals at Barcelona and Cumaná are dozens of car-rental agencies. Rates are high, as an economy car rents for as much as Bs160,000 per day.

Contacts & Resources

MONEY MATTERS

Italcambio, the largest of the *casas de cambio* (exchange houses), is permitted to exchange cash dollars and American Express traveler's checks denominated in dollars for bolívares, but not vice-versa. (Most banks will not exchange currency, and none will accept traveler's checks.)

⚑ Italcambio Exchange House Italcambio ⊠ Centro Comercial Paseo del Mar, Puerto La Cruz ☎ 0281/265-3993.

⚑ Telephone Offices CANTV ⊠ Calle Freites at Calle Bolívar, Puerto La Cruz.

TOUR OPERATORS

In Puerto La Cruz, Macite Turismo can arrange local fishing and boating expeditions, as well as more far-flung tours to Canaima, the Orinoco River, and Los Roques. Oventour, at the Gran Hotel Hesperia, operates a fleet of deluxe coaches and smaller vans for city tours of Puerto La Cruz and longer trips into the interior.

⚑ Tour Companies Macite Turismo ⊠ Centro Commercial Paseo Mar, Calle Sucre at Paseo Colón ☎ 0281/265-5703 ⊕ maciteturismo.com.

VISITOR INFORMATION

Coranztur, the Anzoátegui state tourism corporation, has offices in Barcelona and Puerto La Cruz. The Sucre tourism corporation has an information office in Cumaná.

⚑ Tourist Information Coranztur ⊠ Av. 5 de Julio at Calle Las Flores Barcelona ☎ 0281/275-0474 ⊠ Paseo Colón at Calle Maneiro, Puerto La Cruz ☎ 0281/268-8170.

ISLA MARGARITA

Venezuelans are enormously fond of the island they call the "pearl in the Caribbean." Its status as a duty-free port and proximity to the mainland make it the top vacation spot for Venezuelans. Its miles of white

CLOSE UP

Bird-Watching

With more than 1,300 species of birds, Venezuela is one of the world's top destinations for avid ornithologists. In Los Llanos, you will be awed by immense flocks of roseate spoonbills, giant egrets, green ibis, scarlet ibis, and jabiru storks. Hoatzins (primitive birds born with fingerlike claws on their wings) live in the brush that crowds the rivers crisscrossing the plains. In the Andean foothills you may catch a glimpse of the brilliant red cock-of-the-rock, and in higher altitudes witness the magnificent soaring flight of Andean condors. On the Caribbean coast, numerous lagoons shelter flocks of pink flamingos.

sandy beaches, glittering hotels and restaurants, and vibrant nightlife, as well as 16th-century forts and national parks, have transformed Isla Margarita into a newly popular destination for other travelers.

Isla Margarita is split into two sections linked by an 18-km (11-mi) spit of sand. Most of the island's 350,000 residents occupy the more developed eastern half, especially the bustling city of Porlamar and the adjoining Pampatar. Others are found in the much smaller city of La Asunción, the capital of the region that also encompasses the neighboring islands of Coche and Cubagua.

Direct flights from Caracas and other Venezuelan cities, as well as scheduled or charter flights from a number of North American and European cities, make Isla Margarita an easy destination. Ferries from Puerto La Cruz, Cumaná, and La Guaira also travel to the island. Roads on Isla Margarita are good, which means a car is the easiest way to venture out on your own. Taxis and vans serve as public transportation throughout the island.

Porlamar

Porlamar, with about a third of Isla Margarita's population, is the island's center of commerce. Since it was granted free-port status in 1973, its boutique-lined avenues have been mobbed with tourists in search of tax-free bargains. Many of the goods found here are no cheaper than on the mainland, however. Porlamar is also the most cosmopolitan city on Isla Margarita, boasting countless restaurants, bars, clubs, and casinos.

A few blocks east of shady Plaza Bolívar is the **Museo de Arte Contemporáneo Francisco Narváez,** named after the native Margariteño sculptor whose works also can be viewed on the grounds of the Bella Vista Hotel. Here you'll find a permanent collection of Narváez's works, plus a rotating exhibit of national and international artworks. ⊠ *Calle Igualdad at Calle Diaz* ☎ *0295/261–8668* ☝ *Bs1,000* ☉ *Tues.–Fri. 9–5, weekends 10–4.*

The mangrove forests of **Parque Nacional Laguna de la Restinga** cover the 20-km (12-mi) thread of sand that makes up the tenuous link between the main part of the island and the Península de Macanao. Here you'll find a variety of colorful birds, such as the scarlet ibis. The park has an unspoiled beach and a sprinkling of fishermen's huts where you can buy the catch of the day.

Where to Stay & Eat

★ $$–$$$ ✗ **Bahía.** With large bay windows overlooking the beach, this place has a long-standing reputation for serving fine Spanish-style seafood dishes. Expect strolling musicians while you struggle to decide between the tasty paella and the succulent crab. Best of all, the prices are quite reasonable. ⊠ *Av. Raúl Leoni* ☎ *0295/261–4156* ⊟ *MC, V.*

$–$$ ✗ **Cocody.** Not far from Playa Bella Vista, this restaurant pairs exquisite French cuisine with fine wines in romantic elegance. You can also dine under the palms on the open-air terrace overlooking the beach. ⊠ *Av. Raúl Leoni* ☎ *0295/261–8431* ⊟ *AE, MC, V.*

$–$$ ✗ **Poseidón.** The god of the sea serves top-quality seafood artfully presented with a local touch, and is among the most exclusive—and best— in Isla Margarita. The restaurant has a tropical fish aquarium. ⊠ *Centro Comercial Jumbo, Av. 4 de Mayo* ⊟ *AE, MC, V.*

$–$$ ✗ **Sevillana's.** As this pleasant Spanish restaurant specializes in expertly prepared fish and shellfish, it's no surprise the paella is the standout. The colonial-style interior, all leather and wood furnishings, is complemented by the ever-present sound of flamenco music. Enjoy colorfully dressed performers demonstrating traditional dances from Seville nightly at 8 and 11:30. ⊠ *Av. Bolívar, Bella Vista district* ☎ *0295/263–8258* ⊟ *AE, DC, MC, V.*

¢–$ ✗ **Lucky.** As an alternative to ubiquitous seafood, this Chinese restaurant dishes up Cantonese specialties, including a savory Peking duck. If you're a vegetarian you'll be pleased with the selections as well. ⊠ *Av. Santiago Mariño* ☎ *0295/264–2991* ⊟ *AE, MC, V.*

$$$–$$$$ ▦ **Hilton Margarita.** Close to the sands of Playa Moreno, this venerable hotel offers a great location—only five minutes from the center of the city. The upper-floor rooms in the white tower are spacious and have balconies overlooking the sea, but you'll probably spend most of your time lying by the lovely pool, playing a few matches on the lighted tennis courts, or heading out for waterskiing. The Vegas-style casino is one of the city's top nightspots. ⊠ *Calle Los Uveros, Costa Azul* ☎ *0295/ 262–3333* ⊟*0295/262–0810* ⊕*www.hilton.com* ⤳ *269 rooms, 11 suites* ♢ *4 restaurants, room service, in-room safes, minibars, 2 tennis courts, pool, health club, hair salon, massage, sauna, snorkeling, boating, jet skiing, parasailing, waterskiing, 2 bars, dance club, shops, babysitting, playground, dry cleaning, laundry service, business services, meeting room, airport shuttle, car rental, travel services, no-smoking rooms* ⊟ *AE, D, MC, V.*

$$ ▦ **Hotel Bellavista.** The first seafront hotel in the area, this imposing property has reigned over the beach since 1955. It offers exclusive access to its own well-maintained section of the beach. ⊠ *Av. Santiago Mariño* ☎ *0295/261–7222 or 0295/261–4157* ⊕ *www.hbellavista.com* ⤳ *293 rooms, 12 suites* ♢ *4 restaurants, 2 pools, shops, playground, meeting rooms, car rental* ⊟ *AE, MC, V.*

$$ ▦ **Marina Bay.** On the Costa Azul, this gleaming white hotel wraps around the lushly landscaped pool area, where you can swim up to the floating bar protected by palm trees. A walkway leads to the sugary sands of Playa Moreno. The casino is crowded until the wee hours of the morning. ✉ *Calle Abancay at Calle Trinitarias* ☎ *0295/262–5211* 🖷 *0295/ 262–4110* ⊕ *www.hotelmarinabay.com* ⛵ *170 rooms* ⚓ *3 restaurants, tennis courts, pool, 2 bars, casino, dance club, business services, meeting rooms* ▭ *AE, MC, V.*

¢ ▦ **Hotel María Luisa.** The comfortable rooms are only one reason this hotel is so popular with vacationing Venezuelans. Note also the intimate poolside patio and prime location on Playa Bella Vista. It's near restaurants, bars, and shops. ✉ *Blvd. Raúl Leoni* ☎🖷 *0295/261–0564* ⛵ *98 rooms* ⚓ *Restaurant, snack bar, pool, beach, bar, laundry service* ▭ *AE, MC, V.*

Nightlife

Porlamar hot spots come and go with alarming frequency, but one place that seems to have settled in for the time being is **Señor Frog's** (✉ Av. Bolívar, Costa Azul ☎ 0295/262–0270), the mustard-yellow Mexican restaurant that transforms itself into the city's liveliest dance club at night.

Shopping

Although Isla Margarita is a major destination for Venezuelan daytrippers taking advantage of the duty-free prices, real bargains are hard to find. Your best bets are liquor and jewelry. Aside from the less expensive shops along Bulevar Guevara and Bulevar Gómez, shoppers are attracted to boutiques along Avenidas Santiago Mariño and 4 de Mayo. More and more shoppers are heading to the ubiquitous malls that are taking over the island. One of the most popular is the massive **Jumbo Mall** on 4 de Mayo. The stadium-size **Centro Sambil,** has 137 stores and is the offspring of its mammoth parent shopping center in Caracas.

BEST BUYS

Isla Margarita is a duty-free extravaganza where you'll find European clothing and leather goods, liquor, tobacco, and perfume. Hammocks, well known for their fine craftsmanship and immense size, are another favorite purchase here.

10

El Valle del Espíritu Santo

5 km (3 mi) north of Porlamar.

Founded as the capital of the island in 1529, El Valle del Espíritu Santo has a splendid pink-and-white church honoring the Virgen del Valle, patron saint of eastern Venezuela. Pilgrims journey here year-round, but especially on her feast day in early September. The stained-glass windows of the **Santuario de la Virgen del Valle,** a twin-towered chapel on the main plaza, are worth a visit. A small museum open most afternoons contains the thousands of tokens, jewelry, and holy medals left by supplicants.

La Asunción

5 km (3 mi) north of El Valle.

From the mountains in the center of the island there are striking views as the road slowly descends to La Asunción, the small capital of the region. The sleepy little town, ignored by the bargain-hunting throngs, is the opposite of the bustling Porlamar. A handful of pretty colonial buildings are found around La Asunción's tree-covered Plaza Bolívar. Built in 1568, the **Catedral de Nuestra Señora** is one of the oldest churches in Venezuela. Of particular interest is its three-tiered tower—the country's only surviving example of a colonial church tower. Overlooking the main square, the **Castillo de Santa Rosa**, with its famous dungeon, is one of seven fortifications constructed by the Spanish to guard against pirate attacks.

Parque Nacional Cerro El Copey, along the road between Porlamar and La Asunción, has the highest point on the island. The mountain soars to 3,109 feet. From here you can often spot the smaller islands of Coche and Cubagua.

Pampatar

10 km (6 mi) northeast of Porlamar.

Northeast of Porlamar, this coastal town was founded nearly 500 years ago. Its strategic importance is clear when you visit the **Castillo de San Carlos de Borromeo** on the waterfront in the center of town. Constructed entirely of coral, the fort was built by the Spanish in 1662 after the original was destroyed by the Dutch. The port town is now known more for its myriad yachts and the fortnightly ferries that set sail for nearby Trinidad. In the center of town is the **Iglesia Santísimo Cristo,** which features a bell tower with an outside staircase—an architectural oddity found on several churches on Isla Margarita.

A giant Ferris wheel leads you to the island's largest amusement park, **Diverland** (⊠ Av. Jóvito Villalba, Pampatar ☎ 0295/262–0813). There are 16 attractions, including a roller coaster and water slide.

Where to Stay

$$$ 🏨 **Hesperia Playa El Agua.** With a soaring atrium lobby, this place is tucked away on the north side of the island near Pedro González. It has the island's only 18-hole golf course and an almost deserted stretch of beach right behind it, so there are plenty of outdoor activities to indulge in here. A sumptuous buffet breakfast is included in the rate. ⊠ *Av. 31 de Julio* 🖀 *0295/249–0433* 🖷 *0295/249–0466* ⊕ *www.hoteles-hesperia.es* ⤳ *355 rooms, 42 bungalows* ♢ *2 restaurants, in-room safes, refrigerators, golf course, 3 tennis courts, 5 pools, health club, massage, spa, 2 bars, shops, meeting rooms, car rental, travel services* ▤ *AE, D, MC, V* ❍❘ *AI.*

$$$ 🏨 **Lagunamar.** This vast complex just north of Pampatar spans a huge swath of coastline. There's plenty to keep sun-worshipers busy, from waterskiing to windsurfing to relaxing by one of the pools. Meals are included in the rate, with dining options ranging from a poolside café to a glittery Italian restaurant. ⊠ *Vía Agua de Vaca, Playa Guacuco*

☎ *0295/400–4033* 🖷 *0295/262–1045* ⊕ *www.lagunamar.com.ve*
🗇 *216 rooms, 190 suites* ♨ *5 restaurants, cafeteria, in-room safes, re-frigerators, 6 tennis courts, 9 pools, gym, hot tub, massage, beach, windsurfing, jet skiing, racquetball, 3 bars, casino, shops, laundry serv-ice, meeting rooms, travel services* ⊟ *AE, DC, MC, V.*

$ 🏨 **Flamingo Beach Hotel.** At this all-inclusive hotel on the beach, a glass elevator whisks you up to rooms overlooking the ocean. The pink interior is not the prettiest, but the range of water sports available makes it a fun place to stay. Sumptuous breakfast and dinner buffets are served on a deck with lovely views. ⊠ *Calle El Cristo, Sector La Caranta* ☎ *0295/262–5111* 🖷 *0295/262–0271* 🗇 *160 rooms* ♨ *2 restaurants, in-room safes, tennis court, pool, gym, sauna, beach, snorkeling, wind-surfing, boating, bar* ⊟ *AE, MC, V.*

Outdoor Activities

Easily the most famous and crowded beach on the island, palm-lined **Playa El Agua** is a remarkable stretch of fine white sand that runs along the coast just north of Pampatar. For much of its 4-km (2-mi) length, restaurants and bars lure sunbathers with blaring salsa music and ice-cold beers.

Isla Margarita Essentials

Transportation

BY AIR

Most major domestic carriers have daily service from Caracas, Cumaná, Valencia, and Maracaibo to Isla Margarita's Aeropuerto Internacional del Caribe (PMV), 29 km (18 mi) south of Porlamar.

Aereotuy flies between Porlamar and Los Roques.
✈ **Airlines Aeropostal** ☎ 212/708-6300. **Aereotuy** ☎ 0212/761-6247 🖷 0212/762-5254.
✈ **Airports Acropuerto Internacional del Caribe** ☎ 0295/269-1438.

BY BOAT

Conferry shuttles passengers and cars four times daily between Puerto La Cruz on the mainland and Punta de Piedras, 25 km (16 mi) west of Porlamar. It also offers twice-daily service between Cumaná and Punta de Piedras. Gran Cacique serves Margarita six times daily from both Cumaná and Puerto La Cruz.

Purchase tickets at least two hours in advance for all ferries, particularly on weekends and holidays. Crossings take from two to four hours and cost Bs40,000 per passenger and Bs08,000 per car.
🚢 **Boat & Ferry Companies Conferry** ⊠ Terminal Los Cocos, Puerto La Cruz ☎ 0281/267-7847 ⊠ Terminal Puerto Sucre, Cumaná ☎ 0293/431-1462 ⊕ www.conferry.com. **Gran Cacique** ⊠ Terminal Los Cocos, Puerto La Cruz ☎ 0281/263-0935 ⊠ Terminal Puerto Sucre, Cumaná ☎ 0293/432-0011 ⊕ www.grancacique.com.

BY BUS

Unión Conductores de Margarita makes the 12-hour road/ferry trip from Caracas to Isla Margarita for less than Bs32,000.
🚌 **Bus Information Unión Conductores de Margarita** ⊠ Terminal de Oriente, Caracas ☎ 0212/541-0035 ⊠ Puerto La Cruz ☎ 0281/267-3426.

10

BY CAR

Renting a car is a great way to explore Isla Margarita, and it's one of the best ways to reach the more secluded stretches of sand off the beaten track. The island's roads are in good condition.

CAR RENTAL

At Aeropuerto Internacional del Caribe near Porlamar, Hertz is a good option. In downtown Porlamar, try Beach Car Rental.

🚩 **Local Agencies Beach Car Rental** ⊠ Calle Tubores, Porlamar ☎ 0295/261-7753. **Hertz** ⊠ Aeropuerto Internacional del Caribe ☎ 0295/269-1237.

Contacts & Resources

MONEY MATTERS

🚩 **Italcambio Exchange House Italcambio** ⊠ Centro Comercial Jumbo, Porlamar ☎ 0295/265-9392.

VISITOR INFORMATION

Corpotur has offices at the international airport near Porlamar and in Los Robles, between Porlamar and Pampatar.

🚩 **Tourist Information Corpotur** ⊠ Aeropuerto Internacional del Caribe, Porlamar, ☎ no phone ⊠ Centro Artesanal Gilberto Machini, Av. Jóvito Villalba, Los Robles ☎ 0295/ 262-2322.

MÉRIDA & THE ANDES

As you begin your ascent into the Andes, the changes are swift and unmistakable. Winding your way along the Trans-Andina Highway, you pass stone-strewn fields sprouting wheat and coffee and tile-roof hamlets clinging to hillsides before reaching the *páramo*, the arid region above the timberline. After hitting an altitude of 13,146 feet at Paso Pico El Aguila (Eagle Peak Pass), the highway descends past towns such as Apartaderos, San Rafael de Mucuchíes, and Mucuchíes before reaching the capital city of Mérida.

Mérida

622 km (422 mi) southwest of Caracas.

Mérida is cradled in a valley between the two arms of the Andes, yet this is anything but a sleepy mountain village. This is a city whose spirit is decidedly young, hip, and bohemian. Home of one of Venezuela's largest universities, the Universidad de los Andes, Mérida has all the pleasures of an academic center, including eclectic bookstores, lively coffeehouses, and an arts scene that ranges from refined and traditional to wild and spontaneous.

Founded in 1558, Mérida grew up around the **Plaza Bolívar,** a bustling center that attracts artisans hawking their wares during the day and flocks of young couples in the evening. Facing the main square is the embellished baroque facade of the **Catedral Metropolitana.** Although construction began in 1787, the cathedral wasn't completed until 1958. Its geometric designs make this one of Venezuela's most striking churches.

Dedicated to the artist responsible for the famous stone chapel in nearby San Raphael de Mucuchíes, the **Casa de Cultura Juan Félix Sánchez** (Juan Felix Sánchez Cultural House) hosts exhibitions of paintings and sculptures by regional artists. This lovingly restored colonial house is found on Plaza Bolívar, opposite the cathedral. ⊠ *Plaza Bolívar* ☎ *0274/252–6101* ⤳ *Free* ⊙ *Weekdays 8:30–noon and 2:30–6:30, weekends 9–5.*

The **Museo de Arte Colonial** (Colonial Art Museum) houses a rich collection of religious art from the 16th to 19th centuries. ⊠ *Av. 4 at Calle 20* ☎ *0274/252–7860* ⤳ *Bs5,000* ⊙ *Tues.–Fri. 8–noon and 2–6, weekends 8:30–12:30.*

The **Museo Arqueológico** (Archaeological Museum) has the region's finest collection of figurines, ceramics, and tools from the pre-Hispanic cultures that once dominated this part of the Andes. ⊠ *Av. 3 Independencia, Edificio Rectorado* ☎ *0274/240–2344* ⤳ *Bs500* ⊙ *Tues.–Sun. 8–11:30 and 2–5:30.*

The **Museo de Arte Moderno** (Modern Art Museum) contains an excellent permanent collection of works by some of Venezuela's most heralded contemporary painters. It faces Parque Reloj de Beethoven (Beethoven's Clock Park), which holds a well-known clock that ushers in the hour with music from the great composer. ⊠ *Centro Cultural Tulio Febres Cordero, Av. 2 at Calle 21* ☎ *0274/252–9664* ⤳ *Free* ⊙ *Weekdays 9–noon and 3–6, weekends 10–5.*

NEED A BREAK?

At least once during your sojourn in Mérida, head to **Heladería Coromoto** (⊠ Av. 3 No. 28–75 ☎ 0274/252-3525 ⊙ Tues.-Sun. 2-10) for a scoop of ice cream with the flavor of *chicharrón* (fried pork skin). Proprietor Manuel S. da Oliviera holds a proud place in the *Guinness Book of Records* for producing the most flavors (725 and counting). Dare your companions to sample the sausage or smoked trout, and order for yourself a cone topped with rose-petal, ginger, or plain old strawberry.

10

Fodor'sChoice
★

Five blocks east of Plaza Bolívar is Parque Las Heroínas, where you can catch the **Teleférico de Mérida.** Built in 1957 by French engineers, it is the longest and highest cable-car system in the world. In under an hour, the Teleférico ascends in four breathtaking stages to the 15,634-foot Pico Espejo, a mountain peak 892 feet taller than Switzerland's Matterhorn.

The 13-km (8-mi) journey carries you to four stations—Barinitas, La Montaña, La Aguada, and Loma Redonda—before reaching Pico Espejo, where you'll be treated to a great view of Pico Bolívar, Venezuela's highest peak, at 16,428 feet. The first car departs around 7 AM, the last around noon. ⚠ **Head out early in the day to beat the clouds that often obscure the views by late morning.** Dress appropriately for the snowy heights, as the temperature change can be quite dramatic, and evaluate carefully your ability to make the trip if you have high blood pressure or a heart condition. The Loma Redonda stop houses a medical station for passengers having trouble with the altitude. Along the way, you'll encounter restaurants, coffee shops, bars, souvenir stores, and an Internet café to let the folks back home know what lofty heights you've reached. Reservations are mandatory during the high season, which lasts from Christmas to Easter, and during that time must be procured at least the day prior from the ticket office on Parque Las Heroínas, or via phone or fax. Your reservation will carry a specific departure time, and you're expected to show up an hour in advance to secure your place. The system is much more flexible the rest of the year. ⊠ *Parque Las Heroínas* ☏ *0274/252–5080* ⎙ *0274/252–9174* ⊕ *www.telefericodemerida.com* ✉ *Baranitas to Pico Espejo Bs40,000* ☉ *Dec.–Apr., daily 7–12; May–Nov., Wed.–Sun. 7:30–12.*

Where to Stay & Eat

For an inexpensive meal, head to the top floor of the **Mercado Principal de Mérida** on Avenida Las Américas. Six different kitchens surround the common dining area. All serve up heaping portions of *comida típica* (traditional fare) for just a few dollars.

$–$$ ✕ **Míramelindo.** This intimate restaurant is noted for its succulent Basque cuisine. The exquisitely prepared entrées include *robalo en salsa verdéa* (striped bass in green sauce). Also ask about the daily specials. ⊠ *Calle 29 at Av. 4* ☏ *0274/252–9437* ▭ *AE, V.*

★ **$$$** ✕▥ **Estancia San Francisco.** The cherry-red facade of the main building is your first clue that this hotel is out of the ordinary. At this country inn you can catch trout in a private lagoon and have the chef cook it up for dinner with freshly baked *arepas* (made with whole-wheat flour in the Andes). Little extras like the down pillows and comforters, cushy bathrobes, and cozy fireplaces make this deluxe mountain retreat worth every bolívar. All the two-level suites feature spectacular views of the valley; the more luxurious three-bedroom chalets have their own kitchens. ⊠ *Carretera Via La Culata, 10 km (7 mi) northwest of Mérida* ☏ *0274/416–2000* ⎙ *0274/ 974–3000* ⊕ *www.estancia.com.ve* ⇝ *20 suites, 12 chalets* ⚘ *Restaurant, fishing, bicycles, horseback riding, bar, recreation room, babysitting, laundry service, meeting room, helipad; no a/c* ▭ *AE, MC, V* ¶ *MAP.*

$$ ▥ **El Tisure.** From the window of your room in this colonial-style building you may be able to glimpse the dome of the Catedral Metropolitana. In addition to a superb location in the center of town, El Tisure offers elegant furnishings and a whirlpool bath in every room. ⊠ *Av. 4 Bolívar 17–47* ☏ *0274/252–6072* ⎙ *0274/262–6061* ⇝ *33 rooms* ⚘ *Restaurant, cafeteria, health club, hot tub, sauna, spa, bar, laundry service, business services; no a/c* ▭ *AE, MC, V.*

★ **$** ▥ **Hotel Belensate.** Expect to be pampered amid the rolling hills of a former sugarcane plantation. This Mediterranean-style lodging has open-air dining in lush gardens and a gorgeous Romanesque swimming pool. The friendly owners have added a small playground. ⊠ *Urbanización La Hacienda* ☏ *0274/266–2963* ⎙ *0274/266–2823* ⊕ *www.hotelbelensate. com* ⇝ *84 rooms, 7 cabins* ⚘ *Restaurant, pool, bar, shops, laundry service, meeting room, travel services; no a/c* ▭ *AE, DC, MC, V.*

¢ ▥ **Posada Luz Caraballo.** Facing the leafy Plaza Sucre, this homey inn is a great budget option. The simple yet cheerful rooms all have beds piled high with cozy plaid blankets. The lobby lounge features a fireplace for cold nights in the mountains. ⊠ *Av. 2 Lora 13–80* ☏ *0274/252–5441* ⎙ *0274/252–0177* ⊕ *www.andes.net/luzcaraballo* ⇝ *36 rooms* ⚘ *Restaurant, laundry service; no a/c* ▭ *No credit cards.*

Nightlife & the Arts

In the towns of the Andes, hotel bars are often the only choice for after-dark excitement. Many host performances by local musicians, particularly on weekends. In Mérida the enthusiastic crowds of young people at **Birosca Carioca** (⊠ Calle 24 at Av. 2 ☎ no phone) swing into the wee hours with live salsa, reggae, and hip-hop.

Outdoor Activities

FISHING Anglers flock to Mérida, where the mountains are liberally sprinkled with small lakes stocked with rainbow and brown trout. In remote reaches, hooking a 15-pound trophy is commonplace. Getting there, however, isn't always easy. Fishing season runs between March 30 and September 30.

HIKING Mérida is the base for three- to seven-day treks into the Andes. Rocky trails trod during the early 19th century by armies struggling for independence from Spain make for good hiking. **Montaña Adventures** (⊠ Av. Las Américas ☎ 0274/266–1448) arranges multiday excursions to El Tisure, the secluded village of Los Nevados, and Paso Pico El Aguila. Another company offering trekking in the region is **Páramo Tours** (⊠ Centro Commercial Oasis, Piso 2, Viaducto Campo Elias, Mérida ☎ 0274/244–8855).

Shopping

The 433 stalls of the **Mercado Principal de Mérida** (⊠ Av. Las Américas at the Viaducto Miranda bridge) offer everything from *flores* (flowers) to *recuerdos* (souvenirs). Begin your morning by sampling traditional Andean *pasteles* (pocketlike pastries) filled with pork, chicken, or beef. You can take home a *cuatro* (traditional four-string guitar) or a hand-loomed blanket from any of the dozens of shops that crowd the top two floors. Excellent handicrafts by local artists are found at **La Calle Mayor** (☎0274/252–7552) on the third floor of the Mercado Principal de Mérida.

Mucuchíes

52 km (30 mi) east of Mérida.

The Trans-Andina Highway brings you to Mucuchíes, founded in 1596 on the site of a pre-colonial village. (You'll spot the prefix *mucu*—meaning "place of" in the indigenous language—at the beginning of the names of many Andean villages. Here it refers to "Place of Cold.") The starkly beautiful landscape—scrub-filled fields and barren hillsides—includes half a dozen pristine lakes. The nearby town of San Rafael de Mucuchíes is the site of the renowned **Capilla de Juan Félix Sánchez,** built by the reclusive, iconoclastic local artist for whom it is named. As he single-handedly built this stone chapel in honor of the Virgin of Coromoto, Juan Félix came to be greatly loved throughout this region.

OFF THE BEATEN PATH

MUCUBAJÍ – With five beautiful lakes and several waterfalls, this section of Parque Nacional Sierra Nevada is the ideal area in which to get to know the páramo. The well-designed and informative displays at the visitor center introduce you to the flora and fauna of the region. Travel on foot or horseback along the clearly marked scenic trails to Pico Mucuñuque, which soars to 13,800 ft. While you're enjoying the mountain air, remember that there isn't much of it. Keep your pace slow and take time to smell the frailejones. Mucubají is 2 km (1 mi) from Apartaderos on the road to Barinas.

Where to Stay & Eat

★ $ ✕⊞ **Los Balcones de la Musui.** You reach this colonial-era hacienda, which clings to a mountain ridge, via a steep road that takes you literally into the clouds. When it's clear, which is virtually every morning, the view from each of the cozy rooms is breathtaking. Colorful hammocks slung on the lower-level patio command the same view. A two-hour hike takes you to the Aguas Termales de la Musui, a local hot spring where you'll catch sight of the Humboldt glacier. The restaurant ($–$$) serves food worth going out of your way to sample; don't pass up the trout. ⊠ *Carretera Trasandina, near Mucuchíes* ☎ *0414/974–0712* 🖷 *0274/266–1346* 📧 *balconesmusui@cantv.net* 🛏 *12 rooms, 6 cabins* 🍴 *Restaurant, bar; no a/c* ▤ *MC, V.*

$ ✕⊞ **Hotel Carillón.** Resting against the hillside, this hacienda-style hotel is surrounded by gardens overflowing with flowers. Enormous porches with views of the countryside are held up by squat white columns. Enormous suites are luxurious, with inlaid hardwood floors and elegantly carved furniture made on the premises. The sumptuously decorated restaurant ($$$$) serves French, Mediterranean and Venezuelan cuisine so superb that even Caraqueños think it worth the trip to the Andes. ⊠ *Trans-Andina Hwy.* ☎ *0274/872–0160* 🛏 *20 rooms* 🍴 *Restaurant, room service, recreation room, meeting room; no a/c* ▤ *AE, D, MC, V.*

¢–$ ⊞ **Cabañas Xinia y Peter.** This tranquil refuge near Tabay is run by a Venezuelan-German couple who work hard to make you feel at home. Every detail is perfect, from the fresh flowers on the tables to the thick comforters piled on the beds. The four tile-roof cabins have handcrafted furnishings and fully equipped kitchens, making them perfect for an extended stay. The staff can arrange for horseback, fishing, and hiking tours. The place is popular, so reservations are necessary at both the hotel and the restaurant. ⊠ *La Mucuy Baja, Tabay* ☎ *0416/874–7698* 🖷 *0274/ 283–0214* 🌐 *www.andes.net/cabanasxiniaypeter* 🛏 *4 cabins, 3 rooms* 🍴 *Restaurant, airport shuttle, travel services; no a/c* ▤ *No credit cards* ⦿ *MAP.*

Mérida & the Andes Essentials

Transportation

BY AIR

Mérida's Aeropuerto Alberto Carnevali (MRD), five minutes by taxi from the city center, is served by Avior and Santa Bárbara with 12 flights daily from Caracas.

🛈 **Airlines Avior** ⊠ Centro Comercial Canta Claro, Av. Las Américas ☎ 0274/244-2563. **Santa Bárbara** ⊠ Aeropuerto Alberto Carnevali, Mérida ☎ 0274/262-0381.
🛈 **Airports Aeropuerto Alberto Carnevali** ☎ 0274/263-9330.

BY BUS

There are morning and evening departures from Terminal la Bandera in Caracas to Terminal Antonio Paredes in Mérida. The grueling 10- to 13-hour trip costs less than Bs50,000. Purchase your ticket at least a day in advance at the station. Expreso Mérida is a reputable company that services the route.

WITHIN MÉRIDA & THE ANDES Buses from Mérida's Terminal Antonio Paredes head to all the smaller mountain towns along the Trans-Andina Highway, including Jají, Apartaderos, and Mucuchíes.

🚌 Bus Companies **Expreso Mérida** ✉ Terminal la Bandera ☎ 0212/693-5559.

🚌 Bus Terminals **Terminal Antonio Paredes** ✉ Av. Las Américas ☎ 0274/263-1193.

BY CAR

The Trans-Andina Highway is one of the most scenic routes in the country, with wonderful towns along the way where you'll be tempted to stop. The spectacular 12-hour journey from Caracas begins on Highway 51 west to Valencia. From here, follow the road to Barinas, where the ascent of the Andes begins.

CAR RENTAL Budget and Davila are reputable agencies at Mérida's Aeropuerto Alberto Carnevali. With either agency, expect to pay close to Bs160,000 per day for the smallest car.

🚌 Local Agencies **Budget** ☎ 0274/263-1758. **Davila** ☎ 0274/263-4510.

Contacts & Resources

MONEY MATTERS

🚌 **Italcambio Exchange House Italcambio** ✉ Aeropuerto Internacional Alberto Carnevalli, Mérida ☎ 0274/263-2977.

SAFETY

The center of Mérida is relatively safe during the evening, but as in any tourist destination, be aware of your surroundings and avoid unnecessary displays of wealth. Being a university town, the city sees its share of political demonstrations. Avoid such scenes.

10

TOUR OPERATORS

Travel through this Andean region can be arranged according to your own desires and interests through the U.S.-based Lost World Adventures or through its partner in Mérida, Montaña Adventures. Another reputable Mérida-based company is Natoura Adventure Tours.

🚌 Tour Companies **Lost World Adventures** ✉ 337 Shadowmoor Dr., Decatur, GA 30030 ☎ 404/373-5820 or 800/999-0558 🖷 404/377-1902 ⊕ www.lostworldadventures. com. **Montaña Adventures** ✉ Av. Las Américas, Edificio Las Américas, Mérida ☎🖷 0274/266-1448. **Natoura Adventure Tours** ✉ Calle 24, Mérida ☎ 0274/252-4216.

VISITOR INFORMATION

There is a state tourism office, Cormetur, near the airport in Mérida. Some staff members speak English. The Institute of National Parks, Inparques also has an office in Mérida that can assist you with camping permits.

🚌 Tourist Information **Cormetur** ✉ Av. Urdaneta at Calle 45, Mérida ☎ 0274/263-0814 ⊕ www.merida.com.ve. **Inparques** ✉ Calle 19, between Av. 5 and 6, Mérida ☎ 0274/252-9876.

ELSEWHERE IN VENEZUELA

Los Llanos

Known as the "Serengeti of South America," Los Llanos is an alluring destination for anyone interested in wildlife. Covering nearly a third of Venezuela's total area, the sprawling grasslands of Los Llanos are just a short flight away from Caracas—through San Fernando de Apure or Barinas—but they feel a world away from the bustling capital. The air sings with birdcalls instead of car horns, and the unpaved roads are more likely to carry iguanas searching for a sunny spot than commuters looking for a parking space.

Los Llanos (literally "The Plains") has two distinct seasons, each offering opportunities to see a wide variety of animals and birds. From May to November the plains are inundated with water and crisscrossed by powerful rivers, forcing land animals to scramble for higher ground as the rains unleash their fury. Flooding submerges the smaller roads, making it a bit more difficult to get around. This is the best time, however, to observe the large river otters, and to see clusters of capybaras and troops of howler monkeys gather in small patches of gallery forest. This is also the time when Los Llanos cools off; daytime temperatures hover above 90°F, but the evenings are comfortably mild.

With the end of the rainy season in December, the landscape begins a dramatic transformation. Standing water quickly evaporates in the heat of the tropical sun, revealing the bright greens, yellows, and golds of the grasses. By the end of the dry season in April, the mighty rivers have become trickles, and only a few pools remain. Temperatures soar to over 110°F during the day, but it's worth enduring the heat, as the dry season is the best time to view wildlife. Four-wheel-drive vehicles can head in almost any direction across the parched landscape, bringing you to where the animals have gathered around the few remaining pools of water.

Spanish settlers established the first cattle ranches in Los Llanos in 1548, and within 200 years the expansive ranches, known as hatos, had spread across the region. Today, amid the more exotic wildlife, thousands of cows still roam the range, driven by cowboys known as llaneros. The best way to see Los Llanos is to stay at one of the half dozen hatos set up to accommodate guests. Sometimes you can eat dinner with the llaneros in the dining hall or head out with them for a cerveza in one of the little towns that dot the region.

Although sparsely populated, Los Llanos is considered by many to be the cultural heart of Venezuela. It's no coincidence that the traditional music of Venezuela—called *joropo*—was born in Los Llanos. Locals still gather after dark to listen to these lilting folk songs, sung over the sounds of maracas, harps, and four-stringed guitars called cuatros. In outdoor bars with dirt floors, couples dance while joropo bands alternate rousing tunes that celebrate the bravery of the llaneros with ballads that recount the difficult lives these cowboys must endure.

CLOSE UP

The "Serengeti of South America"

THE FIRST ANIMALS YOU'LL NOTICE are the scary ones. In Los Llanos, the vast grasslands that make up nearly a third of Venezuela, roadside pools teem with crocodiles—both the endangered Orinoco caiman and the more common spectacled caiman, which locals call "babas." Anacondas, some more than 20 ft long, slither across your path. If you're lucky you'll spot a puma—and if you're really lucky, it'll be far away.

But there's much more to see in Los Llanos, often called the "Serengeti of South America." Bird lovers will delight in spotting dozens of species—majestic hawks to diminutive burrowing owls, well-camouflaged herons to brightly colored tanagers. Spoonbills and storks, flycatchers and kingfishers, parrotlets and cormorants abound in this isolated region. Since the landscape is perfectly flat and sparsely wooded, they're all easy to see. The most spectacular of these is the scarlet ibis; when hundreds of them return home to roost at sunset, they cluster so closely together that they seem to turn entire trees bright red.

During the dry season you can catch sight of giant anteaters lumbering across plains punctuated by knee-high termite mounds. The rainy season finds the tree branches filled with sun-worshiping iguanas that occasionally lose their grip and tumble into the waters below. No matter what time of year you visit you'll see hundreds of capybaras, cute, furry brown mammals that are equally comfortable on land or in water. Weighing more than 100 pounds when fully grown, they're the world's largest rodents.

A guided excursion is the best—and safest—way to observe wildlife in this remote region. A naturalist at one of the many lodges will take you out in a jeep or a converted pick-up truck, driving along dirt roads and across patches of parched earth to get as close to animals as possible. At first you'll need help spotting wildlife, but once you get the hang of it, you'll find you can see an amazing variety of animals at close range, without binoculars. Often you can get out of the jeep and walk right among them.

Boating down the Río Apure, or one of the mighty river's tributaries, is the only way to see what the rest of Los Llanos has to offer. Freshwater dolphins will jump and play around your boat as you drift downstream watching the egrets build their nests in the branches above the water. You might want to stop on a sandbar to do some fishing—for piranha. Catching these hungry little creatures is a fast-paced sport. Baiting a hook with chunks of raw meat, you toss a line (no rods are necessary) into the deceptively calm water. Schools of piranha gather immediately, leaping out of the water in a frenzy to grab the bait with their jagged teeth. The trick here is to yank on the line before the bait disappears, which can happen in seconds. With some practice, you'll be able to catch enough of the salad-plate-size fish for dinner. Just brace yourself for the boat ride back to your lodge; the river won't seem so tranquil now that you know the water is infested with these little carnivores.

–Wayne Hoffman

10

Where to Stay & Eat

$$$$ ✕⊞ **Estación Biológica El Frío.** Besides being a working ranch, this place also functions as a biological research center. So in addition to the wildlife that exists across the region, Hato El Frio also houses animals that are the subject of conservation efforts and biological studies, from tortoises to pumas. Want to see a caiman up close? Accompany one of the biologists in residence when they head out for the daily feeding. These knowledgeable—and English-speaking—scientists take you on twice-daily excursions in trucks or boats, answering any questions about the varied flora and fauna. There's also ample opportunity to mingle with the llaneros, whose quarters are a short distance away. The cowboys and researchers work closely together, frequently coming together for an outdoor barbecue or a night out in the local village.

Facilities are basic but comfortable. Fans and a cool breeze make it comfortable enough for sleeping, even in the summer. There is no hot water, but even the "cold" water in these sun-drenched grasslands is warm enough for bathing. Meals are hearty and always fresh, as the ranch produces its own eggs, meats, and dairy products. You can bet that the fruit that made your juice was still on the tree that morning.

Trips to Hato El Frio must be arranged through a travel agent such as the Caracas-based Orinoco Tours. The tour company can also arrange for a car to transfer you from the airport in the town of San Fernando de Apure, two hours away. ⊠ *145 km (90 mi) west of San Fernando de Apure* ☎ *0414/743–5329 or 0212/761–7712* 🖷 *0247/882–1228* ⊕ *www.elfrioeb.com* ⇥ *10 rooms* ⚲ *Dining room, fans, airport shuttle; no a/c, no room phones, no room TVs* ⦿ *AI.*

Parque Nacional Canaima

Here, in Venezuela's remote southeast, is a surreal landscape of pink beaches and black lagoons, where giant waterfalls plunge from the summits of prehistoric table-top mountains called *tepuis,* formations that harbor some of the most unusual life on earth. A trip to Venezuela is not complete without a visit to these mist-enshrouded plateaus that inspired Sir Arthur Conan Doyle's *The Lost World.*

This unique region is protected by Parque Nacional Canaima, which covers an area the size of Belgium. Most of the park is extremely remote, so the only way to see it is by boat or plane. Most people head

Fodor'sChoice
★
 to Canaima to see **Angel Falls,** the world's tallest waterfall. This spectacular torrent of water plummets 2,647 feet—more than twice the height of the Empire State Building, and 15 times higher than Niagara Falls—from atop the giant Auyantepuy mesa. Indigenous people knew the falls as "Kerapa kupai merú," (the fall to the deepest place.) But this natural phenomenon acquired its English-language moniker after its sighting by barnstorming U.S. pilot Jimmy Angel, who crash-landed on Auyantepuy's vast surface in 1937 while in search of gold. Angel, his wife, and two companions spent 11 days descending on foot from the tepui back to civilization and told the world of his "discovery." Angel's ashes were scattered over the falls after his 1956 death.

The eastern half of Parque Nacional Canaima is crossed by a road, and this region is referred to as the Gran Sabana. Three- to four-day excursions to the Gran Sabana are made in four-wheel-drive vehicles and will carry you to waterfalls, indigenous villages, and vantage points that provide breathtaking views of the tepuis. These round-trip excursions generally begin in Ciudad Bolívar or Ciudad Guayana, working slowly south toward Santa Elena de Uairén. The especially adventurous can hire a Pemón guide and scale a large tepui called Roraima, an undertaking that requires a minimum of five days. At the top, you find yourself in an unearthly lunarlike landscape.

Where to Stay & Eat

$$$$ ✕▣ **Arekuna.** This self-contained luxury camp is on the bank of the Río
Fodor'sChoice Caroni, just outside the boundaries of Parque Nacional Canaima. After
★ a full day of land and water excursions, enjoy a glorious sunset from the hilltop dining area before retiring to a stylish cabaña, where attention to detail is evident in the hand-painted sinks and the curious figures carved into the walls. All of the building materials are produced locally and the entire camp is powered by solar energy. Most importantly, the hotel is staffed by extremely personable, multilingual guides who create a fun, informative atmosphere. Packages for this 90-person facility, including round-trip airfare, lodging, meals, and guided excursions, start at $375 per couple, and are arranged through charter airline Acrotuy. ⊠ *Parque Nacional Canaima* ☎ *0212/761–6247 or 0212/761–6231* 📠 *0212/762–5254* ⊕ *www.tuy.com* ⇨ *30 rooms* ⚘ *Dining room, bar, laundry service; no a/c, no room phones, no room TVs* ⦿ *AI.*

Amazonas

Venezuela's largest region is Amazonas, an ironic name given that virtually the entire area lies within the watershed of the mighty Río Orinoco and not the Amazon. Amazonas contains two gargantuan national parks that together cover an area of almost 48,000 square km (30,000 square mi), feature varied flora and fauna, and comprise the homeland of many native peoples, most notably the Yanomami. Tourist facilities in this vast area are limited to a small number of lodges that are connected to the outside world through the region's only sizable town, Puerto Ayacucho.

Where to Stay & Eat

$$$$ ✕▣ **Yutajé Camp.** This camp in the Manapiare Valley, just east of Puerto Ayacucho, appeals to families who prefer the comfort of real beds, private baths, and sit-down meals. Built and run year-round by José Raggi, the camp has a 5,000-foot airstrip and accommodations for about 30. During the day you trek through the jungle in search of howler monkeys, or float down a river to view spectacular waterfalls. A two-night package from Caracas, including air and meals, runs about $450 per person. ⊠ *Reservations: Alpi Viajes, Av. Sucre, Centro Parque Boyacá, Torre Centro, Piso 1, Oficina 2, Caracas* ☎ *0212/283–1433* 📠 *0212/285–6067* ⚘ *Dining room; no a/c, no room phones, no room TVs* ⦿ *AI.*

Elsewhere in Venezuela Essentials

Transportation

BY AIR

To reach Los Llanos, take one of the daily flights from Caracas to San Fernando de Apure, Barinas, and Guanare. Aereotuy flies regularly between Caracas and Canaima and Ciudad Bolívar. To reach Amazonas, you can fly daily from Caracas to Puerto Ayacucho, the region's only tourist hub. Aereotuy connects Ciudad Bolívar with Puerto Ayacucho once weekly.

🛈 Airlines Aerotuy ⊠ Edificio Gran Sabana, Blvd. de Sabana Grande, Sabana Grande, Caracas ☏ 0212/761-6231.

BY BUS

Cities such as Barinas and San Fernando de Apure in Los Llanos are accessible by bus from Caracas and other major cities. Amazonas is not as accessible by bus. You can get to Puerto Ayacucho from Caracas via San Fernando de Apure, but it's at least a 16-hour trip. Most visitors fly into the region instead. There is no bus service at all to Canaima.

Contacts & Resources

TOUR OPERATORS

The savvy staff of Lost World Adventures specializes in tailoring an independent travel itinerary around your interests. The founder of this U.S.-based company once lived in Venezuela, so he knows his way around. The company specializes in small-group expeditions throughout Venezuela and other South American countries.

A reputable tour operator in Caracas is Orinoco Tours, centrally located on Bulevar de Sabana Grande. The company specializes in ecotourism in Venezuela, including the Amazonas, Llanos, and Parque Nacional Canaima. Also in Caracas, Alpi Tour specializes in adventure tourism to the Amazonas and other regions.

🛈 Tour Companies Alpi Viajes ⊠ Av. Sucre, Centro Parque Boyacá, Piso 1, Oficina 2, Caracas ☏ 0212/283-1433 ⊕ www.alpi-group.com. **Lost World Adventures** ⊠ 337 Shadowmoor Dr., Decatur, GA 30030 ☏ 404/373-5820 or 800/999-0558 ⊠ 404/377-1902 ⊕ www.lostworldadventures.com. **Orinoco Tours** ⊠ Edificio Galerías Bolívar, Bulevar de Sabana Grande ☏ 0212/761-8431 ⊠ 0212/761-6801 ⊕ www.orinocotours.com.

VENEZUELA ESSENTIALS

Transportation

BY AIR

Major U.S. carriers serving Venezuela include American, Continental, and Delta. Venezuela's Aeropostal flies to Caracas from Miami. Air France, British Airways, Spain's Iberia, the Netherlands' KLM, and Germany's Lufthansa jet in from their respective hubs in Europe. Most fly into Aeropuerto Internacional Simón Bolívar, located about 25 km (16 mi) from downtown Caracas in the coastal area of Maiquetía. Charters fly directly to the Caribbean island of Isla Margarita.

A number of regional airlines provide regular service throughout Venezuela. Among them are Aeropostal, Aereotuy, Avior, and Santa Bárbara. Bad weather or periodic disruptions in fuel flow can cause flight cancellations. Allow some flexibility in your itinerary, and do not plan out-country air travel for the very end of your stay in Venezuela.

🛪 Airlines in Venezuela Aereotuy ⊠ Av. Abraham Lincoln, Bulevar de Sabana Grande 174, Edificio Gran Sabana, Piso 5, Caracas ☎ 0212/761-6247, 0212/761-6231, or 0212/761-8043. **Avior** ⊠ Aeropuerto Nacional Simón Bolívar ☎ 0212/202-5811. **Santa Bárbara** ⊠ Calle 3B, Edificio Tokay, Piso 2, La Urbina, Caracas ☎ 800/865-2636.

BY BUS

TO & FROM VENEZUELA Buses connect the Brazilian town of Manaus to the Venezuelan town of Santa Elena de Uairén, a trip that takes six hours and costs Bs100,000.

WITHIN VENEZUELA Almost all of Venezuela can be traversed by bus, the least expensive and often most agreeable way to see the country. Your best bet is using the private carriers, usually referred to as *rápidos* (express buses). Private companies typically accept reservations and offer comforts such as assigned seats, air-conditioning, toilets, and on-board attendants.

BY CAR

Although the Venezuelan highway system is still a work in progress, more than 80% of the country's roads are paved. Driving can get you places you wouldn't otherwise get to see. However, Venezuelans often drive as if the traffic rules are merely suggestions. It's important to drive defensively. Avoid using your car at night, when poorly lit roadways and erratic drivers make things especially dangerous.

EMERGENCY ASSISTANCE The major rental agencies will tow your car in an emergency. Towing services can be found under *grúas* in the telephone book.

GASOLINE Oil-rich Venezuela has among the world's cheapest gas prices. A liter of unleaded gas (*sin plomo*) costs Bs98. The national oil company, Petroleos de Venezuela (PDV), operates 24-hour stations on major highways. Shell, Texaco, and others also have stations.

PARKING Theft of a car's contents, as well as the car itself, is a major problem in Venezuela, especially in Caracas and other major urban centers. Never leave anything of value in your car and park in enclosed or guarded lots when possible.

10

Contacts & Resources

CUSTOMS & DUTIES

Persons entering Venezuela may bring in duty-free up to 400 cigarettes and 50 cigars, 2 liters of liquor, and new goods such as video cameras and electronics up to $1,500 in value if declared and accompanied by receipts. Plants, fresh fruit, dairy products, and pork are prohibited.

ELECTRICITY

Venezuela operates on a 110 volt, 60-cycle system, with a single-phase AC current.

HEALTH

In Caracas and other large cities, food in reputable hotels and restaurants should be safe. A sudden change of diet, however, can result in an upset stomach, which is often misinterpreted as a form of food poisoning. Avoid raw fruits and vegetables, uncooked fish, and tap water. Bottled water is readily available throughout the country, as are good beer and a wide variety of safe soft drinks.

Pharmacies in different neighborhoods take turns staying open all night; you can spot them by the sign *turno,* or consult local newspapers for lists of open *farmacias* (pharmacies).

MAIL & SHIPPING

The state-owned postal service, Ipostel, is slow and not very reliable—it can take up to a month for a letter to arrive in the United States or Europe. It costs Bs400 to send a letter domestically and Bs1,500 internationally.

MONEY MATTERS

In hopes of stemming the flight of dollars from Venezuela during the 2003 emergency, the government implemented rigid currency controls, which had been relaxed slightly at this writing. The exchange rate of the Venezuelan currency, the bolívar, is fixed at 2,150 to the U.S. dollar. Italcambio, the largest of the *casas de cambio* (exchange houses), is permitted to exchange cash dollars and American Express traveler's checks denominated in dollars for bolívares, but not vice-versa. (Most banks will not exchange currency, and none will accept traveler's checks.) ■ TIP➜ **Take cash when going to remote areas, as it will be difficult to find banks and ATM's.**

ATMS   You can use your ATM card in some machines to obtain bolívares, but it is impossible to obtain dollars here. Gauge your cash spending needs accordingly to avoid being stuck at the end of your trip with local currency that is impossible to change back. The black market is prevalent, but engaging in transactions carries stiff penalties and is dangerous.

BLACK MARKET   Given Venezuela's currency restrictions at press time, there will be no shortage of dealers approaching you quietly about changing money in public places, but the so-called *mercado negro* is officially illegal and a dangerous risk for robbery.

CREDIT CARDS   In major cities, credit cards are generally accepted at upscale hotels, restaurants, and some shops, Visa and Master Card being the most widely used. Many businesses accept American Express as well, but Diner's Club is a distant fourth. However, carrying cash is advisable when traveling in more remote areas.

CURRENCY   The bolívar is the official unit of currency. Bolívars (Bs) come in bills of 500, 1,000, 2,000, 5,000, 10,000, 20,000, and 50, 000. Coins come in 10-, 20-, 50-, 100-, and 500-bolívar denominations. At press time, the exchange rate was a fixed, government-regulated Bs2,150 to the U.S. dollar.

WHAT IT
WILL COST
Venezuela is a relatively inexpensive country in which to travel, although the prices are greatly inflated in Caracas and on Isla Margarita. The best hotels cost up to $250 per double, while budget lodgings go for as low as $25. Going to the theater can cost from Bs8,000 to Bs80,000 for special shows or featured artists. Movies are still a bargain at Bs5,000. Nightlife ranges greatly in price; some of the best clubs charge upward of Bs8,000 for a cocktail.

Sample Prices: Cup of coffee, Bs1,000–Bs2,000; bottle of beer, Bs3,000; soft drink, Bs1,000-Bs2,000; bottle of wine, Bs6,000 (at a liquor store); sandwich, Bs3,000–Bs8,000; crosstown taxi ride, Bs8,000; city bus ride, Bs400; museum entrance, Bs2,000, though the majority of museums in the country are free.

PASSPORTS & VISAS

Australian, British, Canadian, New Zealand, and United States citizens who fly to Venezuela are issued 90-day tourist cards, free of charge, immediately upon arrival with presentation of a passport that has at least six months' remaining validity. Keep the flimsy second copy of the tourist card you receive when you arrive; you'll need it to leave the country. Procure a visa in advance from a Venezuelan embassy abroad if you plan to arrive overland. Most land immigration posts charge $3 to $5 for a tourist card.

SAFETY

Crime, both petty and violent, is prevalent in Caracas, but much less so in other parts of Venezuela. Use common sense wherever you travel. Always be aware of your surroundings and avoid unnecessary displays of wealth.

Political demonstrations are common in Caracas, as well as in Mérida with its large student population, and there's always the potential for such gatherings to turn violent. It is illegal for foreigners to engage in anything deemed "political activity." **Steer clear of such scenes.**

TAXES

At hotels, foreigners must pay a 10% tourist tax. You will find it added to your bill.

DEPARTURE TAX
The airport departure tax for international flights leaving Venezuela is $36 or the bolívar equivalent.

SALES TAX
Venezuela has a non-refundable 14% sales tax, known as the IVA, which is added to the price of all articles except basic foodstuffs and medicine.

TELEPHONES

All telephone numbers have seven digits. Area codes begin with a "0" followed by a three-digit number, the first of which is a 2. Use the zero only for long-distance calls from other parts of Venezuela, not for calls from other countries. An "0414" or "0416" code designates a mobile phone number.

10

To call a Venezuelan number from another country, dial the international access code, the country code of 58, and then the area code. Be prepared for frequent busy signals.

LOCAL CALLS A three-minute local call costs Bs400. Public pay phones accept phone cards, available in denominations of 2,000, 3,000, and 5,000 bolívars at kiosks and newsstands marked TARJETA INTELLIGENTE (smart card). To speak with a local directory assistance operator, dial 113.

LONG-DISTANCE & INTERNATIONAL CALLS International calls are extremely expensive: The average international rate per minute is $3.50 to the United States and $10 to Europe. Hotels typically add as much as 40% to the rate, so avoid calling from your room. Call from a CANTV office or use a public phone.

You can reach an English-speaking long-distance operator by dialing 122. To use a calling card or credit card, or to place a collect call, use the various international access numbers from your home country.
🔢 **Access Codes AT&T** ☎ 800/11-120. **Australia Direct** ☎ 800/11-610. **British Telecom** ☎ 800/11-440. **Canada Direct** ☎ 800/11-100. **MCI** ☎ 800/11-140. **New Zealand Direct** ☎ 800/11-640. **Sprint** ☎ 800/11-110.

TIPPING
Restaurants usually add 10% to the bill for service, but you are expected to tip an additional 10%. Tipping hotel porters, hair stylists, and guides up to 10% is customary. Taxi drivers do not expect a tip unless they carry suitcases.

VISITOR INFORMATION
One good source of Venezuela travel information is the U.S.-based Venezuelan Tourism Association.
🔢 **Tourist Information Venezuelan Tourism Association** ⌖ Box 3010, Sausalito, CA 94966 ☎ 415/331-0100 🖷 415/332-9197.

Adventure & Learning Vacations

Updated by
Joyce Dalton

WITH TERRAIN RANGING FROM TOWERING ANDEAN PEAKS TO VAST grasslands, deserts, wetlands, glaciers, and the huge Amazonian rain forest, South America's natural attractions are virtually unsurpassed. This topographical diversity guarantees ideal settings for almost any type of active or ecotourism adventure. Additionally, the continent claims some of the world's most renowned archaeological sites, a number of indigenous cultures, and an impressive array of wildlife, creating the perfect destination for off-the-beaten-path cultural experiences. You can explore the Amazon by riverboat, trek, ski, or climb the Andes, kayak along a fjord-studded coast, or view the Galápagos Islands' astonishing wildlife up close.

As in the past, today's travelers yearn to see the world's great cities, historical sites, and natural wonders. The difference is that today, far fewer travelers are content to experience all this from the air-conditioned comfort of a huge coach. Even tour operators known for their trips' five-star comfort have included soft-adventure components, such as hiking, canoeing, biking, or horseback riding, in most itineraries and added "best available" lodgings to satisfy the increased demand for visits to more traditional locales.

Choosing a tour package carefully is always important, but it becomes even more critical when the focus is adventure or sports. You can rough it or opt for comfortable, sometimes even luxurious accommodations. You can select easy hiking or canoeing adventures or trekking, rafting, or climbing expeditions that require high degrees of physical endurance and technical skill. Study multiple itineraries to find the trip that's right for you.

This chapter describes selected trips from some of today's best adventure-tour operators in the travel world. Wisely chosen, special-interest vacations lead to distinctive, memorable experiences—just pack flexibility and curiosity along with the bug spray.

For additional information about a specific destination, contact the country's tourist office (often attached to the embassy) or the **South American Explorers Club** (✉ 126 Indian Creek Rd., Ithaca, NY 14850 ☎ 607/ 277–0488 or 800/274–0568 ⊕ www.saexplorers.org). This company is a good source for current information regarding travel throughout the continent. The Explorers Club also has offices in Buenos Aires, Quito, Lima, and Cusco.

Choosing a Trip

With hundreds of choices for special-interest trips to South America, there are a number of factors to keep in mind when deciding which company and package will be right for you.

- **How strenuous a trip do you want?** Adventure vacations commonly are split into "soft" and "hard" adventures. Hard adventures, such as strenuous treks (often at high altitudes), Class IV or V rafting, or ascents of some of the world's most challenging mountains, generally require excellent physical conditioning and previous experience. Most hiking, biking, canoeing/kayaking, and similar soft adventures can be enjoyed by persons of all ages who are in good health and are accustomed to a reasonable amount of exercise. A little honesty goes a long way—recognize your own level of physical fitness and discuss it with the tour operator before signing on.

- **How far off the beaten path do you want to go?** Depending on the tour operator and itinerary selected for a particular trip, you'll often have a choice of relatively easy travel and comfortable accommodations or more strenuous going with overnights spent camping or in basic lodgings. Ask yourself if it's the *reality* or the *image* of roughing it that appeals to you. Stick with the reality.

- **Is sensitivity to the environment important to you?** If so, then determine if it is equally important to the tour operator. Does the company protect the fragile environments you'll be visiting? Are some of the company's profits designated for conservation efforts or put back into the communities visited? Does it encourage indigenous people to dress up (or dress down) so that your group can get great photos, or does it respect their cultures as they are? Many of the companies included in this chapter are actively involved in environmental organizations and projects with indigenous communities visited on their trips.

- **What sort of group is best for you?** At its best, group travel offers curious, like-minded people with whom to share the day's experiences. Do you enjoy a mix of companions or would you prefer similar demographics—for example, age-specific, singles, same sex? Inquire about the group size; many companies have a maximum of 10 to 16 members, but 30 or more is not unknown. The larger the group, the more time spent (or wasted) at rest stops, meals, and hotel arrivals and departures.

  If groups aren't your thing, most companies will customize a trip just for you. In fact, this has become a major part of many tour operators' business. The itinerary can be as loose or as complete as you choose. Such travel offers all the conveniences of a package tour, but the "group" is composed of only you and those you've chosen as travel companions. Responding to a renewed interest in multigenerational travel, many tour operators also offer designated family departures, with itineraries carefully crafted to appeal both to children and adults.

- **The client consideration factor—strong or absent?** Gorgeous photos and well-written tour descriptions go a long way in selling a company's trips. But what's called the client consideration factor is important, too. Does the operator provide useful information about health (suggested or required inoculations, tips for dealing with high altitudes)? A list of frequently asked questions and their answers? Recommended readings? Equipment needed for sports trips? Packing tips when baggage is restricted? Climate info? Visa requirements? A list of client referrals? The option of using your credit card? What is the refund policy if you must cancel? If you're traveling alone, will the company match you up with a like-minded traveler so you can avoid the sometimes exorbitant single supplement?

- **Are there hidden costs?** Make sure you know what is and is not included in basic trip costs when comparing companies. International airfare is usually extra. Sometimes domestic flights are additional. Is trip insurance required, and if so, is it included? Are airport transfers included? Visa fees? Departure taxes? Gratuities? Equipment? Meals? Bottled water? All excursions? Although some travelers prefer the option of an excursion or free time, many, especially those visiting a destination for the first time, want to see as much as possible. Paying extra for a number of excursions can significantly increase the total cost of the trip. Many factors affect the price, and the trip that looks cheapest in the brochure could well turn out to be the most expensive. Don't assume that roughing it will save you money, as prices rise when limited access and a lack of essential supplies on-site require costly special arrangements.

Tour Operators

Below you'll find contact information for all tour operators mentioned in this chapter. For international tour operators, we list both the tour operator and its North American representative. For example, Exodus is represented in North America by Adventure Center. Although those listed hardly exhaust the number of reputable companies, these tour operators were chosen because they are established firms that offer a good selection of itineraries. Such operators are usually the first to introduce great new destinations, forging ahead before luxury hotels and air-conditioned coaches tempt less hardy visitors.

Abercrombie & Kent ⊠ *1520 Kensington Rd., Oak Brook, IL 60523* ☎ *630/954–2944 or 800/323–7308* ⊕ *www.abercrombiekent.com.*

Adventure Center ⊠ *1311 63rd St., Suite 200, Emeryville, CA 94608* ☎ *510/654–1879 or 800/227–8747* ⊕ *www.adventurecenter.com.*

Adventure Life ⊠ *1655 S. 3rd St. W, Suite 1, Missoula, MT 59801* ☎ *406/541–2677 or 800/344–6118* ⊕ *www.adventure-life.com.*

Alpine Ascents International ⊠ *121 Mercer St., Seattle, WA 98109* ☎ *206/378–1927* ⊕ *www.AlpineAscents.com.*

Amazon Tours & Cruises ⊠ *275 Fontainebleau Blvd., Suite 173, Miami, FL 33172* ☎ *800/423–2791* ⊕ *www.amazontours.net.*

American Alpine Institute ⊠ *1515 12th St., Bellingham, WA 98225* ☎ *360/671–1505* ⊕ *www.aai.cc.*

Amizade ⌁ *Box 110107, Pittsburgh, PA 15232* ☎ *412/441–6655 or 888/973–4443* ⊕ *www.amizade.org.*

Andes Adventures ⊠ *1323 12th St., Suite F, Santa Monica, CA 90401* ☎ *310/395–5265 or 800/289–9470* ⊕ *www.andesadventures.com.*

Arun Treks & Expeditions ⊠ *301 E. 33rd St., Suite 3, Austin, TX 78705* ☎ *512/407–8314 or 888/495–8735* ⊕ *www.aruntreks.com.*

Austin-Lehman Adventures ⌁ *Box 81025, Billings, MT 59108* ☎ *406/655–4591 or 800/575–1540* ⊕ *www.austinlehman.com.*

Australian & Amazonian Adventures ⊠ *2711 Market Garden, Austin, TX 78745* ☎ *512/443–5393 or 800/232–5658* ⊕ *www.amazonadventures.com.*

Big Five Tours & Expeditions ⊠ *1551 SE Palm Ct., Stuart, FL 34994* ☎ *772/287–7995 or 800/244–3483* ⊕ *www.bigfive.com.*

BikeHike Adventures ⊠ *316 W. 5th Ave., Suite 13, Vancouver, British Columbia V5Y 1J5, Canada* ☎ *604/731–2442 or 888/805–0061* ⊕ *www.bikehike.com.*

Boojum Expeditions ⊠ *14543 Kelly Canyon Rd., Bozeman, MT 59715* ☎ *406/587–0125 or 800/287–0125* ⊕ *www.boojum.com.*

Bushtracks Expeditions ⊠ *6335 Mountain View Ranch Rd., Healdsburg, CA 95448* ☎ *707/433–4492 or 800/995–8689* ⊕ *www.bushtracks.com.*

Butterfield & Robinson ⊠ *70 Bond St., Toronto, Ontario M5B 1X3, Canada* ☎ *416/864–1354 or 800/678–1147* ⊕ *www.butterfield.com.*

Clipper Cruise Line ⊠ *11969 Westline Industrial Dr., St. Louis, MO 63146* ☎ *314/655–6700or 800/325–0010* ⊕ *www.clippercruise.com.*

Colorado Mountain School ⊠ *341 Moraine Ave., Estes Park, CO 80517* ☎ *970/586–5758 or 888/267–7783* ⊕ *www.cmschool.com.*

Country Walkers ⓓ *Box 180, Waterbury, VT 05676* ☎ *802/244–1387 or 800/464–9255* ⊕ *www.countrywalkers.com.*

Dragoman Overland (⊠ Camp Green, Debenham, Suffolk IP14 6LA U. K ⊕ www.dragoman.com). This company is represented in North America by Adventure Center (contact information under A, above).

Earth River Expeditions ⊠ *180 Towpath Rd., Accord, NY 12404* ☎ *845/ 626–2665 or 800/643–2784* ⊕ *www.earthriver.com.*

Earthwatch ⊠ *3 Clocktower Pl., Suite 100, Maynard, MA 01754* ☎ *978/ 461–0081 or 800/776–0188* ⊕ *www.earthwatch.org.*

Ecotour Expeditions ⓓ *Box 128, Jamestown, RI 02835* ☎ *401/423–3377 or 800/688–1822* ⊕ *www.naturetours.com.*

ElderTreks ⊠ *597 Markham St., Toronto, Ontario M6G 2L7, Canada* ☎ *416/588–5000 or 800/741–7956* ⊕ *www.eldertreks.com.*

Equitours ⓓ *Box 807, Dubois, WY 82513* ☎ *307/455–3363 or 800/ 545–0019* ⊕ *www.equitours.com.*

Exodus ⊠ *9 Weir Rd., London SW12 OLT, England* ⊕ *www. exodus-travel.com.* This company is represented in North America by Adventure Center (contact information under A, above).

Experience Plus! ⊠ *415 Mason Ct., #1, Fort Collins, CO 80524* ☎ *970/ 484–8489 or 800/685–4565* ⊕ *www.ExperiencePlus.com.*

Explore! Worldwide ⊠ *1 Frederick St., Aldershot, Hampshire GU11 1LQ, U.K.* ⊕ *www.explore.co.uk.* This company is represented in North America by Adventure Center (contact information under A, above).

Explore Bolivia ⊠ *2510 N. 47th St., Suite 207, Boulder, CO 80301* ☎ *303/545–5728* ⊕ *www.explorebolivia.com.*

Far Horizons ⓓ *Box 2546, San Anselmo, CA 94979* ☎ *415/482–8400 or 800/552–4575* ⊕ *www.farhorizons.com.*

Field Guides ⊠ *9433 Bee Cave Rd., Bldg. 1, Suite 150, Austin, TX 78733* ☎ *512/263–7295 or 800/728–4953* ⊕ *www.fieldguides.com.*

Fishing International ⊠ *5510 Skylane Blvd., Suite 200, Santa Rosa, CA 95405* ☎ *707/542–4242 or 800/950–4242* ⊕ *www.fishinginternational.com.*

FishQuest ⊠ *3375B Hwy. 76 W, Hiawassee GA 30546* ☎ *706/896–1403 or 888/891–3474* ⊕ *www.fishquest.com.*

Fly Fishing And ⓓ *Box 1719, Red Lodge, MT 59068* ☎ *406/446–9087* ⊕ *www.flyfishingand.com.*

Focus Tours ⊠ *111 Malaga Rd., Santa Fe, NM 87505* ☎ *505/989–7193* ⊕ *www.focustours.com.*

Frontiers ⓓ *Box 959, Wexford, PA 15090* ☎ *724/935–1577 or 800/ 245–1950* ⊕ *www.frontierstravel.com.*

Galápagos Network ⊠ *5805 Blue Lagoon Dr., Suite 160, Miami, FL 33126* ☎ *305/262–6264 or 800/633–7972* ⊕ *www.ecoventura.com.*

G.A.P. Adventures ⊠ *19 Charlotte St., Toronto, Ontario M5V 2H5, Canada* ☎ *416/260–0999 or 800/465–5600* ⊕ *www.gapadventures.com.*

Gecko's ⊠ *258 Lonsdale St., Melbourne, V1C 3000 Australia* ⊕ *www. geckosadventures.com.* This company is represented in North America by Adventure Center (contact information under A, above).

Geographic Expeditions ⊠ *1008 General Kennedy Ave., San Francisco, CA 94129* ☎ *415/922–0448 or 800/777–8183* ⊕ *www.geoex.com.*

Global Adventure Guide ⊠ *14 Kennaway Rd., Unit 3, Christchurch, 8002 New Zealand* ☎ *800/732–0861 in North America* ⊕ *www. globaladventureguide.com.*

Hidden Trails ⊠ *202–380 W. 1st Ave., Vancouver, British Columbia V5Y 3T7, Canada* ☎ *604/323–1141 or 888/987–2457* ⊕ *www. hiddentrails.com.*

Ibike/International Bicycle Fund ⊠ *4887 Columbia Dr. S, Seattle, WA 98108* ☎ *206/767–0848* ⊕ *www.ibike.org.*

Inca ⊠ *1311 63rd St., Emeryville, CA 94608* ☎ *510/420–1550* ⊕ *www. inca1.com.*

International Expeditions ⊠ *One Environs Park, Helena, AL 35080* ☎ *205/428–1700 or 800/633–4734* ⊕ *www.ietravel.com.*

Joseph Van Os Photo Safaris ⌖ *Box 655, Vashon Island, WA 98070* ☎ *206/463–5383* ⊕ *www.photosafaris.com.*

Journeys International ⊠ *107 Aprill Dr., Suite 3, Ann Arbor, MI 48103* ☎ *734/665–4407 or 800/255–8735* ⊕ *www.journeys-intl.com.*

KE Adventure Travel ⊠ *1131 Grand Ave., Glenwood Springs, CO 81601* ☎ *970/384–0001 or 800/497–9675* ⊕ *www.keadventure.com.*

Ladatco Tours ⊠ *2200 S. Dixie Hwy., Suite 704, Coconut Grove, FL 33133* ☎ *305/854–8422 or 800/327–6162* ⊕ *www.ladatco.com.*

Lindblad Expeditions ⊠ *96 Morton St., New York, NY 10014* ☎ *212/765–7740 or 800/397–3348* ⊕ *www.expeditions.com.*

Mountain Madness ⊠ *4218 SW Alaska, Suite 206, Seattle, WA 98116* ☎ *206/937–8389 or 800/328–5925* ⊕ *www.mountainmadness.com.*

Mountain Travel Sobek ⊠ *1266 66th St., Suite 4, Emeryville, CA 94608* ☎ *510/594–6000 or 888/687–6235* ⊕ *www.mtsobek.com.*

Myths and Mountains ⊠ *976 Tee Ct., Incline Village, NV 89451* ☎ *775/832–5454 or 800/670–6984* ⊕ *www.mythsandmountains.com.*

Nature Expeditions International ⊠ *7860 Peters Rd., Suite F-103, Plantation, FL 33324* ☎ *954/693–8852 or 800/869–0639* ⊕ *www.naturexp. com.*

Oceanic Society Expeditions ⊠ *Fort Mason Center, Bldg. E, San Francisco, CA 94123* ☎ *415/441–1106 or 800/326–7491* ⊕ *www.oceanic-society. org.*

Off the Beaten Path ⊠ *7 E. Beall, Bozeman, MT 59715* ☎ *406/586–1311 or 800/445–2995* ⊕ *www.offthebeatenpath.com.*

OutWest Global Adventures ⌖ *Box 2050, Red Lodge, MT 59068* ☎ *406/446–1533 or 800/743–0458* ⊕ *www.outwestadventures.com.* This company operates gay- and lesbian-oriented tours.

PanAmerican Travel Services ⊠ *320 E. 900 S, Salt Lake City, UT 84111* ☎ *801/364–4300 or 800/364–4359* ⊕ *www.panamtours.com.*

PowderQuest Tours ⊠ *7108 Pinetree Rd., Richmond, VA 23229* ☎ *206/203–6065 or 888/565–7158* ⊕ *www.powderquest.com.*

Quark Expeditions ⊠ *1019 Post Rd., Darien, CT 06820* ☎ *203/656–0499 or 800/356–5699* ⊕ *www.quarkexpeditions.com.*

Remote Odysseys Worldwide (ROW) ✎ *Box 579, Coeur d'Alene, ID 83816* ☎ *208/765–0841 or 800/451–6034* ⊕ *www.ROWinternational.com.*

Rod & Reel Adventures ⊠ *32617 Skyhawk Way, Eugene, OR 97405* ☎ *541/349–0777 or 800/356–6982* ⊕ *www.rodreeladventures.com.*

Small World Adventures ✎ *Box 1225, Salida, CO 81201* ☎ *970/309–8913 or 800/585–2925* ⊕ *www.smallworldadventures.com.*

Snoventures ⊠ *Cedar Ave., Huddersfield HD1 5QH U.K.* ☎ *775/586–9133 in North America* ⊕ *www.snoventures.com.*

South American Journeys ⊠ *9921 Cabanas Ave., Tujunga, CA 91042* ☎ *818/951–8986* ⊕ *www.southamericanjourneys.com and www.gosouthamerica.org.*

Southwind Adventures ✎ *Box 621057, Littleton, CO 80162* ☎ *303/972–0701 or 800/377–9463* ⊕ *www.southwindadventures.com.*

Swallows and Amazons ✎ *Box 523, Eastham, MA 02642* ☎ *508/255–4794* ⊕ *www.swallowsandamazonstours.com.*

The World Outdoors ⊠ *2840 Wilderness Pl., Suite D, Boulder, CO 80301* ☎ *303/413–0938 or 800/488–8483* ⊕ *www.theworldoutdoors.com.*

Tours International ⊠ *12750 Briar Forest Dr., Suite 603, Houston, TX 77077* ☎ *281/293–0809 or 800/247–7965* ⊕ *www.toursinternational.com.*

Travcoa ⊠ *2424 S.E. Bristol St., #310, Newport Beach, CA 92600* ☎ *949/476–2800 or 800/992–2003* ⊕ *www.travcoa.com.*

Victor Emanuel Nature Tours ⊠ *2525 Wallingwood Dr., Suite 1003, Austin, TX 78746* ☎ *512/328–5221 or 800/328–8368* ⊕ *www.ventbird.com.*

Wilderness Travel ⊠ *1102 9th St., Berkeley, CA 94710* ☎ *510/558–2488 or 800/368–2794* ⊕ *www.wildernesstravel.com.*

Wildland Adventures ⊠ *3516 N.E. 155th St., Seattle, WA 98155* ☎ *206/365–0686 or 800/345–4453* ⊕ *www.wildland.com.*

WINGS ⊠ *1643 N. Alvernon, Suite 109, Tucson, AZ 85712* ☎ *520/320–9868 or 888/293–6443* ⊕ *www.wingsbirds.com.*

World Expeditions ⊠ *580 Market St., Suite 225, San Francisco, CA 94104* ☎ *415/989–2212 or 888/464–8735* ⊕ *www.worldexpeditions.com.*

Zegrahm Expeditions ⊠ *192 Nickerson St., #200, Seattle, WA 98109* ☎ *206/285–4000 or 800/628–8747* ⊕ *www.zeco.com.*

CRUISES

Antarctica Cruises

Founded to promote environmentally responsible travel to Antarctica, the **International Association of Antarctica Tour Operators** (☎ 970/704–1047 ⊕ www.iaato.org) is a good source of information, including suggested readings. Most companies operating Antarctica trips are members of this organization and display its logo in their brochures.

Season: November–March.
Location: Most cruises depart from Ushuaia, Argentina.
Cost: From $2,995 (triple-occupancy cabin) for 12 days from Ushuaia.
Tour Operators: Abercrombie & Kent; Adventure Center; Big Five Tours & Expeditions; Clipper Cruise Line; ElderTreks; G.A.P. Adventures; Lind-

blad Expeditions; Mountain Travel Sobek; Quark Expeditions; Travcoa; Wilderness Travel; Zegrahm Expeditions.

Ever since Lars-Eric Lindblad operated the first cruise to the "White Continent" in 1966, Antarctica has exerted an almost magnetic pull for serious travelers. From Ushuaia, the world's southernmost city, you'll sail for two (sometimes rough) days through the Drake Passage and then on to the spectacular landscapes of Antarctica. Most visits are to the Antarctic Peninsula, the continent's most accessible region. Accompanied by naturalists, you'll travel ashore in motorized rubber craft called Zodiacs to view penguins and nesting seabirds. Some cruises visit research stations, and many call at the Falkland, South Orkney, South Shetland, or South Georgia Islands. Adventure Center and Big Five Tours & Expeditions offer sea kayaking and, at an extra cost, the chance to camp for a night on the ice.

Expedition vessels have been fitted with ice-strengthened hulls; many originally were built as polar-research vessels. On certain Quark Expeditions itineraries you can travel aboard an icebreaker, the *Kapitan Khlebnikov,* which rides up onto the ice, crushing it with its weight. This vessel carries helicopters for aerial viewing. Quark has made two circumnavigations of Antarctica, a 21,000-km (13,000-mi) journey lasting almost three months, and may offer this trip again.

When choosing an expedition cruise, it's wise to inquire about the qualifications of the on-board naturalists and historians, the maximum number of passengers carried, the ice readiness of the vessel, onboard medical facilities, whether there is an open bridge policy, and the number of landings attempted per day.

Galápagos Cruises

Season: Year-round.
Location: Galápagos Islands.
Cost: From $2,195 for eight days from Guayaquil.
Tour Operators: Abercrombie & Kent; Adventure Life; Austin-Lehman Adventures; Clipper Cruise Line; Ecotour Expeditions; ElderTreks; Galápagos Network; G.A.P. Adventures; Inca; Lindblad Expeditions; Mountain Travel Sobek; Nature Expeditions International; Oceanic Society Expeditions; Travcoa; Wilderness Travel; Wildland Adventures; World Expeditions.

To say there's no place like it is not hyperbole. Isolated in the Pacific some 950 km (600 mi) west of South America, the Galápagos Islands' abundant wildlife inspired Charles Darwin's theory of evolution by natural selection. Even today, about two-thirds of the birds and most reptiles on this barren archipelago are found nowhere else. Following a flight from Guayaquil or Quito, Ecuador, you'll board a comfortable vessel and spend 5–11 days visiting as many as 12 islands (eight is typical), where the ship's naturalists will lead guided nature walks. You'll find the wildlife (sea lions, land and marine iguanas, huge tortoises, and numerous birds quite unafraid, but strict rules for shore visits are enforced. Visitors must follow established pathways, stay with the guide, and not give food or water to any wildlife. Pathways are rough and often rocky, but the pace is not hurried. Most operators include time for swimming or snorkeling with the sea lions. Vessels vary from 8- to 20-passenger motorized sailing yachts to the 100-passenger M/V *Galápagos Explorer II*. Some itineraries combine the Galápagos with stays in the Amazon or Andes; almost all include time in Quito and/or Guayaquil. Among Galápagos Network's many offerings are 8- and 11-day programs aimed at serious divers. The character of your trip will probably depend less on the number of islands visited than on the quality of the naturalists who are leading you around.

Ocean Cruises

Season: October–April.

Locations: Cruise lines are finding South American ports of call increasingly popular among travelers. Bordered by long Atlantic and Pacific coasts, the continent offers an abundance of choices. Many itineraries visit Argentina (Buenos Aires and Ushuaia), Brazil (Belém, Fortaleza, Rio de Janeiro, and Salvador), and Chile (Antofagasta, Arica, Cape Horn, Coquimbo, Puerto Montt, Punta Arenas, and Valparaíso). Other typical ports of call include Cartagena, Colombia; Guayaquil, Ecuador; Devil's Island, French Guinea; Callao (for Lima) and Paracas (for Nazca Lines), Peru; Punta del Este and Montevideo, Uruguay; and Caracas, Venezuela. Some ships set sail in the Caribbean and stop at one or two islands before heading south. West coast departures might include one or more Mexican ports before reaching South America. A partial navigation of the Amazon River, frequently as far as Manaus, is sometimes part of the program, as are the Falkland Islands. Although circumnavigation of the continent is possible (50 or more days), 14- to 21-day cruises are the norm.

Vessels vary in the degree of comfort or luxury they offer as well as in what is included in the price. Guided shore excursions, gratuities, dinner beverages, and port taxes are often extra. Peruse brochures carefully and ask questions to ensure your choice of vessel is the right one for you.

Cost: Prices vary according to the ship, cabin category, and itinerary. Figure $1,950 to $4,495 for a 14-day cruise, excluding international airfare.

Cruise Companies: The following operators offer cruises calling at various South American ports.

Celebrity Cruises (☎ 800/647–2251 ⊕ www.celebrity.com). **Clipper Cruise Line** (☎ 800/325–0010 ⊕ www.clippercruise.com). **Crystal Cruises** (☎ 800/446–6625 ⊕ www.crystalcruises.com). **Fred Olsen Cruise Lines** (☎ 800/843–0602 ⊕ www.fredolsencruises.com). **Holland America Line** (☎ 877/724–5425 ⊕ www.hollandamerica.com). **Norwegian Cruise Line** (☎ 800/327–7030 ⊕ www.ncl.com). **Oceania Cruises** (☎ 800/254–5067 ⊕ www.oceaniacruiseline.com). **Orient Lines** (☎ 800/333–7300 ⊕ www.orientlines.com). **Princess Cruises** (☎ 800/774–6237 ⊕ www.princess.com). **Radisson Seven Seas Cruises** (☎ 877/505–5370 ⊕ www.rssc.com). **Seabourn Cruise Line** (☎ 877/760–9052 ⊕ www.seabourn.com). **Silversea Cruises** (☎ 877/760–9052 ⊕ www.silversea.com).

Patagonia Coastal & Lake Cruises

Cruising the southern tip of South America presents you some of the earth's most spectacular scenery: fjords, glaciers, lagoons, lakes, narrow channels, waterfalls, forested shorelines, fishing villages, penguins, and other wildlife. Although many tour operators include a one- or two-day boating excursion as part of their Patagonia itineraries, the companies listed below offer from 4 to 12 nights aboard ship.

Argentina & Chile
Season: October–April.
Locations: Chilean fjords; Puerto Montt and Punta Arenas, Chile; Tierra del Fuego and Ushuaia, Argentina.
Cost: From $1,395 for 12 days from Buenos Aires.
Tour Operators: Abercrombie & Kent; Adventure Life; Big Five Tours & Expeditions; Clipper Cruise Line; Explore! Worldwide; International Expeditions; Lindblad Expeditions; Mountain Travel Sobek; Off the Beaten Path; Wilderness Travel; Wildland Adventures.

Boarding your vessel in Punta Arenas, Chile, or Ushuaia, Argentina, you'll cruise the Strait of Magellan and the Beagle Channel, visiting glaciers, penguin rookeries, and seal colonies before heading north along the fjords of Chile's western coast. All vessels used by the above companies are comfortable and have private baths. Adventure Life and Lindblad Expeditions include the Chiloé Archipelago, a region rich in folklore about ghost ships, the troll-like beings the Trauco, and magical sea creatures. With Abercrombie & Kent, Clipper Cruise Line, and Wildland Adventures, you'll savor the mountain scenery of Torres del Paine National Park before or following the cruise, while Lindblad Expeditions, Mountain Travel Sobek, and International Expeditions visit Tierra del Fuego National Park. Several of the companies also include Cape Horn National Park. Wilderness Travel allows time for hiking at Volcano Osorno and in Alerce Andino National Park; the latter protects the second-largest temperate rain-forest ecosystem in the world. Following a five-day cruise, Off the Beaten Path travelers fly to Puerto Montt for a three-night stay at nearby Lake Llanquihue, with opportunities for hiking in the mountains. Most itineraries begin or end with days in Santiago, Chile, or Buenos Aires, Argentina.

River Cruises

The Amazon, home to more than 200 species of mammals and 1,800 species of birds, and providing 30% of the earth's oxygen, is the world's largest and most dense rain forest. Stretching 6,300 km (3,900 mi), the Amazon is the world's longest river. From its source in the Peruvian Andes, the river and its tributaries snake through parts of Bolivia, Ecuador, Colombia, and Brazil before emptying into the Atlantic. Whatever your style of travel, there's a boat plying the river to suit your needs. Sleep in a hammock on the deck of a thatch-roof riverboat or in the air-conditioned suite of an upscale vessel. A typical river program includes exploring tributaries in small boats; village visits, perhaps with a blowgun demonstration; piranha fishing; nocturnal wildlife searches; and rain-forest walks with a naturalist or indigenous guide to learn about plants, wildlife, and traditional medicines

Brazil

Season: Year-round.
Locations: Anavilhanas Archipelago; Lago Janauári Ecological Park; Manaus; Río Branco; Río Negro.
Cost: From $1,050 for seven days from Manaus.
Tour Operators: Australian & Amazonian Adventures; Big Five Tours & Expeditions; Ecotour Expeditions; G.A.P. Adventures; Nature Expeditions International; Swallows and Amazons; Travcoa.

River journeys along the Brazilian Amazon typically begin in Manaus and feature 3–10 days on the water, plus time in Manaus and, sometimes, Rio de Janeiro. On Big Five's 14-day trip, you'll follow three days in Rio with a four-day cruise aboard the comfortable *Amazon Clipper Premium*, then continue on to Salvador and Iguaçu Falls. Travcoa's guests cruise aboard the Amazon's first luxury ship, the *Iberostar Grand Amazon*; after three days on the river you'll visit Brazil's capital, Brasília, before spending time in the Pantanal and Rio. Both Ecotour Expeditions and Nature Expeditions use the 16-passenger motorized yacht *Tucano* for their Amazon cruises. On G.A.P.'s 42-day itinerary, explore the Amazon from Belém to Manaus and visit Bahia and Ceara states; the trip concludes with 10 days in Venezuela. Australian & Amazonian Adventures has created three riverboat journeys on the Amazon or its tributaries. The 12-day trip is oriented toward those with an interest in snorkeling and aquatic wildlife. Traveling in a riverboat and sleeping in hammocks or daybeds (mats), you'll explore the Negro and Branco rivers. Swallows and Amazons offers a variety of river programs, ranging from a traditional riverboat to a six-cabin air-conditioned houseboat with shared baths to a motorized yacht with private baths. Itineraries run from 4 to 11 days, and all include a visit with traditional *caboclo,* or river people. On all tour operators' programs, a cruise highlight is the "Meeting of the Waters," where the dark waters of the Río Negro join the lighter waters of the Amazon.

Peru

Season: Year-round.
Locations: Iquitos to Tabatinga; Pacaya-Samiria National Reserve; Río Marañón; Río Ucayali.
Cost: From $799 for four days from Iquitos.
Tour Operators: Amazon Tours & Cruises; Big Five Tours & Expeditions; G.A.P. Adventures; International Expeditions; Oceanic Society Expeditions; Tours International.

Peru vies with Brazil as a destination for Amazon cruises. In fact, one G.A.P. program combines the two countries, beginning its 10-day cruise in Iquitos, Peru, and ending in Manaus, Brazil. This company offers a great variety of Amazon trips. With Big Five Tours & Expeditions, International Expeditions, and Tours International, you'll sail along the Amazon, Río Ucayali, and Río Marañón aboard modern vessels designed in the style of classic 19th-century riverboats. These trips include a visit to Pacaya-Samiria National Reserve, known for its 85 lakes, 250 fish species, 449 species of birds, 132 types of mammals, and 22 varieties of orchids. Some Amazon Tours & Cruises itineraries also feature Pacaya-Samiria, as does a nine-day trip with Oceanic Society Expeditions; the latter pays special attention to the behavior of freshwater dolphins. Other Amazon Tours & Cruises and Tours International trips spend four or seven days sailing from Iquitos to *tres fronteras* (three borders), the spot where Peru, Brazil, and Colombia meet.

Venezuela

Season: March.
Locations: Angel Falls; Canaima National Park; Orinoco River.
Cost: From $4,498 for nine days from Port of Spain, Trinidad.
Tour Operator: International Expeditions.

Your trip begins on the Caribbean island of Trinidad with visits to the Caroni Bird Sanctuary and Asa Wright Nature Center before boarding *Le Levant*, a luxurious yacht, your home for the next six nights. The ship is equipped with Zodiac landing crafts that are used for exploring narrow tributaries and for shore visits. A charter plane ferries passengers to Canaima National Park for a one-day visit to Angel Falls, the highest waterfall in the world. En route back to Trinidad, *Le Levant* drops anchor at Tobago Cayes for a day of swimming, snorkeling, and beachcombing before heading home.

LEARNING VACATIONS

Cultural Tours

Among the many types of travel, some find the most rewarding to be an in-depth focus on one aspect of a country's culture. This could mean exploring the archaeological remains of great civilizations, learning about the lives and customs of indigenous peoples, or trying to master a foreign language or culinary skills.

Argentina

Season: March–October.
Locations: Buenos Aires; Mendoza; northwestern Argentina.
Cost: From $1,430 for nine days from Buenos Aires.
Tour Operators: Adventure Life; ElderTreks; Myths and Mountains.

Argentina's northwest is rich in cultural history as well as scenic beauty. With Adventure Life, spend seven days exploring this area. You'll view fossilized animals, ancient paintings and engravings on rock faces, neolithic remains where historic adobe huts sit atop sand dunes; and the city of Salta. Several hikes are on the itinerary. ElderTreks combines visits to several of these sites with time in Bolivia and Chile; included is a three-day trek in western Argentina. For a literal taste of Argentina, join Myths and Mountains' 10-day Adventurous Cook's Tour. Led by a renowned Argentine gastronomist, you'll take part in culinary workshops in Buenos Aires and wine tastings in Mendoza; there's even a typical barbecue on a working estancia (ranch). The program includes some hiking and horseback riding, as well.

Bolivia

Season: March–November.
Locations: Cochabamba; Inkallajta; Lake Titicaca; Potosí; Sucre; Tiahuanaco; Uyuni Salt Flats.
Cost: From $1,003 for nine days from La Paz.
Tour Operators: Adventure Life; Amizade; Australian & Amazonian Adventures; Big Five Tours & Expeditions; Explore Bolivia; Explore! Worldwide; Far Horizons; G.A.P. Adventures; Gecko's; Ladatco Tours.

With archaeological sites, a salt desert, the world's highest navigable lake, a mining past, and indigenous Amazonian people, Bolivia, not surprisingly, is the subject of many culturally focused tours. Far Horizon's 16-day program highlights the country's archaeology from the Andes to the Amazon, viewing the ruins of Tiahuanaco (also spelled Tiwanaku) before moving on to less well-known areas. Several of the above companies take you to Sucre, the Uyuni Salt Flats (the world's largest), and Potosí; the latter was once the site of a major Spanish mint. On Explore Bolivia's trip, you'll camp on the Salar de Uyuni and by Laguna Colorada (Red Lagoon). Following travel in these same areas, Explore! Worldwide moves on to the jungle for a three-night ecolodge stay in Madidi National Park, followed by time at Lake Titicaca, while G.A.P. includes San Pedro de Atacama, in Chile, plus Cusco and Machu Picchu, in Peru. Adventure Life's itinerary offers an in-depth focus on the Salar de Uyuni, including a visit to a historic hotel built of salt, and Isla de Pescadores, an island surrounded by salt. With Australian & Amazonian Adventures, you can combine exploration of Uyuni, Potosí, Oruro, and Lake Titicaca with time in neighboring Chile. Amizade organizes service projects such as joining local people in converting a cow shed into a school near Cochabamba or working with orphans, the elderly, or the mentally and physically challenged. Spanish lessons are part of the program.

Brazil

Season: Year-round.
Locations: Amazon; Rio de Janeiro; Salvador.
Cost: From $750 for seven days from Manaus.
Tour Operators: Amizade; G.A.P. Adventures; Nature Expeditions International; Swallows and Amazons.

If your interest is learning about other cultures, consider Swallows and Amazons' Caboclo program, which focuses on the lifestyle and culture of the Amazonian river people the Caboclos. You'll stay at the company's rain-forest camp in the Anavilhanas Archipelago Biological Reserve, and get to know the local family that lives on the property. Activities include canoeing, fishing, rain-forest walks and overnight camping. Nature Expeditions' multifaceted itinerary features a three-day Amazon cruise; two days in Salvador, the spiritual and cultural center of the Bahia region; Rio; Petropolis, where you'll visit the home of a Macumba practitioner to learn about this unique religion with roots in voodoo; Paraty, and Iguaçu Falls. Following 10 days in Venezuela, G.A.P. Adventures moves on to the Brazilian Amazon, then works its way down the coast to Rio, exploring such points as São Luis, Fortaleza, Recife, and Salvador along the way. To add a rewarding dimension to your trip, consider an Amizade work project in Santarém, an Amazonian city of 300,000 people, where you'll help construct a center for street children.

Chile

Season: Year-round.
Locations: Atacama Desert; Easter Island; Santa Cruz.
Cost: From $1,795 for seven days from Santiago.
Tour Operators: Abercrombie & Kent; Big Five Tours & Expeditions; Far Horizons; G.A.P. Adventures; Ladatco Tours; Myths and Mountains; Nature Expeditions International; Off the Beaten Path; PanAmerican Travel; South American Journeys; Tours International; World Expeditions.

In the Pacific Ocean 3,680 km (2,300 mi) west of the Chilean mainland, remote Easter Island is famed for its *moais,* nearly 1,000 stone statues whose brooding eyes gaze over the windswept landscape. Abercrombie & Kent, Far Horizons, Myths and Mountains, and Nature Expeditions are among the tour operators that will take you there. Far Horizons' departure is timed for the annual Tapati festival. Vying with Easter Island as a cultural experience, the Atacama, generally considered the world's driest desert, is a region of bizarre landscapes, ancient petroglyphs (designs scratched or cut into rock), geoglyphs (designs formed by arranging stones or earth), and mummies. Many of the above companies have Atacama programs. For a cultural experience of another sort, join PanAmerican Travel's nine-day round of Chilean vineyards, where you'll enjoy tours, tastings, and even the occasional vineyard lunch. Off the Beaten Path offers a unique trip to Parque Pumalín (a Yosemite-size nature reserve), the Yelcho Glacier, and six days at a historic 360,000-acre working ranch for horseback riding, fly fishing, birding, and a gaucho festival.

Ecuador

Season: Year-round.
Locations: Amazon; Quito.
Cost: From $527 for seven days from Quito.
Tour Operators: Gecko's; Myths and Mountains.

On Myths and Mountains' Shamans of Ecuador itinerary, travel through jungles and highlands for 10 days, meeting with shamans and learning about their rituals and healing practices. Speaking with the local people is sure to add an important dimension to any journey, and Gecko's seven-day conversational Spanish school in Quito helps you do just that. You'll live and eat with an Ecuadoran family and receive 28 hours of one-on-one tutoring.

Peru

Season: Year-round.
Locations: Islas Ballestas; Chachapoyas region; Chán Chán; Kuelap; Sipan.
Cost: From $745 for seven days fromLima.
Tour Operators: Abercrombie & Kent; Amazon Tours & Cruises; Bushtracks Exeditions; Experience Plus!; Explore! Worldwide; Far Hori-

zons; Gecko's; Inca; Myths and Mountains; South American Journeys; Tours International; Wildland Adventures; World Expeditions.

Since virtually all tours to Peru, including most of those described below, take in Cusco (also spelled Cuzco) and Machu Picchu, the emphasis here will be on other noteworthy sites or activities. Chán Chán, capital of the ancient Chimú Empire and one of the largest pre-Columbian cities yet discovered, the fortress of Kuelap, and Sipan, where archaeologists unearthed the most spectacular tomb in the western hemisphere, are highlights of programs offered by most of the above operators. Some itineraries also include flights over the Nazca Lines; visits to the Islas Ballestas, sometimes called the Little Galápagos; the mountaintop ruins of Pachacamac, or the well-preserved pre-Inca mummies of Leymebamba. On one Myths and Mountains' tour, you'll travel with a Peruvian artist and weaver, visiting homes and studios while learning about ancient weaving techniques. Inca's program includes a by-appointment-only view of a textile collection and a visit to the Paracas Necropolis, where 400 mummies and ancient weavings were found. Far Horizons' trip features a private collection of Andean art viewed in the owner's home and dinner with the excavator of San José Moro, a Moche cemetery. With Tours International, you'll trek, ride horses, and camp near an archaeological complex, while with South American Journeys you'll travel by floatplane to an Achual indigenous village for meetings with the chief, and enjoy jungle hikes and hunting activities with the Achual. Immerse yourself in Lima's culture while improving your conversational Spanish skills with the one-week home-stay language programs of Gecko's and World Expeditions.

Scientific Research Trips

Joining a research expedition team gives you more than great photos. By assisting scientists, you can make significant contributions to better understanding the continent's unique ecosystems and cultural heritages. Flexibility and a sense of humor are important assets for these trips, which often require roughing it.

Argentina

Season: September–October.
Locations: Catamarca Province; Ischigualasto Provincial Park.
Cost: $1,995 for 13 days from San Juan, Argentina.
Tour Operator: Earthwatch.

On Earthwatch's Triassic Park program you'll prospect rock formations for dinosaur fossils, excavate and map the finds, and then collect and catalog them. The remote northern valley where this work takes place holds the only unbroken record yet discovered spanning the entire Triassic period, when dinosaurs first appeared. A second option involves working on a survey of archaeological resources on Mt. Incahuasi, high in the Andes, recording sites by GPS to create a comprehensive archaeological map. A good level of fitness and experience with high altitudes are desirable.

Brazil

Season: Year-round.
Locations: Cananéia Estuary; Emas National Park; Pantanal.
Cost: From $1,795 for seven days from Campo Grande.
Tour Operator: Earthwatch.

Earthwatch has three projects in Brazil, all focused on wildlife. Working by boat and on land on the Cananéia Estuary, volunteers will help to establish data for guiding local tourism development and protecting the region's biodiversity. Emas National Park harbors many mammal, reptile, and bird species. Scientists here are involved in assessing the distribution and numbers of carnivores in the park, and volunteers will help in this endeavor by capturing and radio-collaring jaguars, foxes, pumas, and wolves. In the Pantanal, the largest freshwater wetland on the planet, assist a multinational team of scientists in collecting data on the area's plants and animals to aid in the development of a sound conservation plan.

Chile

Seasons: May–June; November–December.
Locations: Toltén Basin.
Cost: $3,095 for 15 days from Quito.
Tour Operator: Earthwatch.

Join a Chilean carnivore biologist and veterinarian in a study of the endangered river otter's habitat requirements. This involves surveys of habitat, water quality, and prey availability, as well as assisting in the trapping and assessing the distribution of the prey (freshwater crustaceans). Some team members will make presentations in local schools or interview locals regarding their knowledge and attitudes toward otters.

Ecuador

Season: May–August; November–January.
Location: Galápagos; Loma Alta Ecological Reserve; Tangara Reserve.
Cost: From $1,895 for 14 days from Guayaquil.
Tour Operator: Earthwatch.

Though covering only 1.6% of South America's land mass, Ecuador is home to more than half the continent's bird species. Many inhabit threatened ecosystems. You'll help survey a remote tropical forest to track seasonal shifts in bird populations and perform such tasks as setting up and checking mist nets. Volunteers have the chance to interact with the local community, participating in school presentations and village events. Or join a team of scientists on the Galápagos island of Santa Cruz in a systematic search for invasive plant species and then map their locations with a GPS unit and assist in their control.

Peru

Season: June–August; November–February.
Location: Amazon; Huaro Valley.
Cost: From $2,095 for 14 days from Cuzco.
Tour Operators: Earthwatch.

Take part in a study of tourism's impact on macaws at Tambopata Research Center as a scientist seeks to learn if they are being "loved to extinction." Traveling to clay licks by riverboat and on foot, you'll observe the macaws' daily behavior and reactions to tourists. The aim of a second investigation, which centers on excavating an important site of the Wari people, is to shed light on the reasons for this empire's collapse. Working as part of a team, you'll map, excavate, and process artifacts.

THE OUTDOORS

Amazon Jungle Camping & Lodges

Because the Amazon and its tributaries provide easy access to remote parts of the jungle, river transport often serves as the starting point for camping and lodge excursions. Many lodges and camps are within or near national parks or reserves. Accommodations range from hammocks to comfortable rooms with private baths. Nature walks, canoe trips, piranha fishing, and visits to indigenous villages are typically part of rain-forest programs led by naturalists or indigenous guides.

Bolivia

Season: Year-round.
Locations: Madidi National Park.
Cost: From $895 for seven days from La Paz.
Tour Operators: Adventure Life; Explore Bolivia; Wildland Adventures.

Considered one of the most pristine tropical rain forests in South America, Madidi National Park, home to howler monkeys, capybaras, anacondas, caimans, and countless species of birds and butterflies, is the site of Chalalán EcoLodge. Reached by a five-hour dugout canoe journey along the Ríos Beni and Tuichi from the frontier town of Rurrenabaque, the lodge is owned and operated by an indigenous Quechua community. Adventure Life bases its seven-day journey here for rain-forest explorations and insights into the traditional crafts, beliefs, and customs of the Quechua. Wildland Adventures spends three nights at Chalalán as part of a 10-day trip that includes time in La Paz and on Lake Titicaca, while Explore Bolivia stays at Chalalán as part of its eight-day program that also features explorations along the Río Yacuma.

Brazil

Season: Year-round.
Locations: Amazon Ecopark; Río Negro.
Cost: From $345 for three days from Manaus.
Tour Operators: PanAmerican Travel; Swallows and Amazons.

Most jungle adventures here begin with a boat trip up the Río Negro, the main tributary of the Amazon. With Swallows and Amazons, the boat takes you to Araras Lodge, the company's floating jungle hotel. From this base, make various excursions as outlined in the introduction to this section. PanAmerican Travel's 12-day itinerary also begins with a transfer by boat from Manaus to a rain-forest lodge. In this case, it's the Amazon Ecopark, on the banks of the Río Tarumã. Here biologists and zoologists have initiated several wildlife preservation projects, including a monkey jungle, a bird sanctuary, and a botanic garden.

Ecuador
Season: Year-round.
Location: Amazon basin.
Cost: From $595 for four days from Quito.
Tour Operators: Abercrombie & Kent; Adventure Life; Big Five Tours & Expeditions; Galápagos Network; G.A.P. Adventures; Inca;.

Scientists estimate that the Ecuadoran Amazon has 1,450 species of birds and as many as 20,000 varieties of plants. Operators use several comfortable lodges: Sacha Lodge, a cluster of cabañas nestled deep in the rain forest, plus a 40-meter (130-foot) observation tower; and a 287-meter (940-foot) canopy walkway; La Selva Lodge, a group of cabins overlooking the waters of Lago Garzacocha; Napo Wildlife Center with 10 luxurious cabañas and a 37-meter (120-foot) canopy tower; and Kapawi, a pioneering ecolodge on the Río Pastaza where the majority of the staff are indigenous Achuar people. Galápagos Network offers four- and five-day stays at all four properties, while Abercrombie & Kent utilizes Napo Wildlife Center, Big Five favors Kapawi, Adventure Life and Inca stay at Sacha Lodge, and G.A.P. uses Kapawi and Sacha.

Peru
Season: Year-round.
Location: Amazon basin.
Cost: From $1,050 for five days from Quito.
Tour Operators: Abercrombie & Kent; Adventure Life; Big Five Tours & Expeditions; Bushtracks Expeditions; G.A.P. Adventures; International Expeditions; Journeys International; Myths and Mountains; South American Journeys; Southwind Adventures; Tours International; Wildland Adventures.

At Tambopata Macaw Research Center, you'll witness hundreds of macaws and parrots returning each morning to nibble bits of clay from a riverside ledge. Another popular destination is Manu Biosphere Reserve, home to the Amazon's largest-known tapir lick and lakes inhabited by giant river otters and a variety of water birds. Most of the above companies visit one or both of these sites. Among other Peruvian jungle lodges are: Explorama and ExplorNapo, used by International Expeditions and Tours International; Ceiba Tops Lodge & Resort (Abercrombie & Kent, International Expeditions); Pacaya-Samiria (Big Five); and the new Heath River Wildlife Center, owned by the Esé Eja indigenous community (G.A.P., South American Journeys, and Wildland Adventures).

Venezuela
Season: Year-round.
Locations: Río Orinoco.
Cost: $255 for four days from Ayacucho.
Tour Operator: Australian & Amazonian Adventures.

Based right on the river at Orinoquia Lodge, you'll visit indigenous villages to learn about medicinal plants, forms of agriculture, and the making of baskets, hammocks, and traps. Enjoy the Tobogan de la Selva, a pool-filled natural water slide, and a boat trip along the Orinoco searching for freshwater dolphins and otters.

Bird-Watching Tours

When selecting a bird-watching tour, ask questions. What species might be seen? What are the guide's qualifications? Does the operator work to protect natural habitats? What equipment is used? (In addition to binoculars, this should include a high-powered telescope, a tape recorder to record and play back bird calls as [a way of attracting birds], and a spotlight for night viewing.)

Antarctica

Season: December.
Locations: Antarctic Peninsula; Falkland Islands; South Georgia.
Cost: From $10,580 for 23 days from Buenos Aires.
Tour Operator: Victor Emanuel Nature Tours.

Arguably the ultimate travel adventure, Antarctica exerts a strong pull on nature lovers. Now a trip has been designed to focus on the special interests of serious birders. Traveling aboard the *Clipper Adventurer,* you'll view wandering, light-mantled, and royal albatrosses; snow petrels along with several other petrel species, and large colonies of king and macaroni penguins.

Argentina

Season: November–December.
Locations: Andes; Chaco; Iguazú; Pampas; Patagonia.
Cost: From $2,230 for eight days from Salta.
Tour Operators: Focus Tours; Victor Emanuel Nature Tours; WINGS.

Whatever part of Argentina you visit, expect to see a great variety of bird species, including many endemic to this region. Focus Tours' 21-day program concentrates on the northern region, where feathered inhabitants such as the plumbeous sierra-finch, Salinas Monjita, and Steinbach's canastero live. Victor Emanuel offers two Argentine programs, one to the central area for such endemic birds as Oustalet's and Cordoba cinclodes and the other covering the Pampas and Patagonia with possible sightings including the Chaco pipit and the austral parakeet. WINGS's three itineraries visit the high Andes, the Pampas, and Iguazú Falls.

Bolivia

Seasons: October; February–April.
Locations: Amazon; Andes; Chaco; Cochabamba; Santa Cruz.
Cost: From $2,995 for 16 days from Santa Cruz.
Tour Operators: Explore Bolivia; Focus Tours; Victor Emanuel Nature Tours; WINGS.

Thanks to its varied geography, Bolivia has some 1,300 bird species, representing 40% of those found in all of South America. Up to 213 species have been recorded by one tour group on a single day. Depending on the WINGS itinerary you select, you could visit the Central Andes; the Amazon; the area around Santa Cruz; or Refugio Los Volcanes and the Chaco Desert. Focus Tours' 17-day program covers Bolivia from the lowlands to the Andes, climbing from an altitude of 427 meters to 4,724 meters (from 1,400 to 15,500 feet). Thus, the variety of birds observed is huge. Explore Bolivia also offers a lowlands to highlands birding expedition, this one for 15 days. Victor Emanuel's trip concentrates on the mountainous western half of the country, where the majority of endemic and near-endemic species are found.

Brazil

Seasons: Year-round.
Locations: Amazon; Emas National Park; Iguaçu Falls; Itatiaia National Park; Northeast; Pantanal; Southeast.
Cost: From $1,250 for seven days from Manaus.
Tour Operators: Field Guides; Focus Tours; Swallows and Amazons; Victor Emanuel Nature Tours; WINGS.

Bird habitats in Brazil range from coastal rain forests to cloud forests to open plains, and with 19 itineraries between them, the above tour operators cover all topographies. The Pantanal, a vast area of seasonally flooded grassland, has the hyacinth macaw, bare-faced curassow, Toco toucan, and yellow-billed cardinal, while the newly described cryptic forest-falcon and bare-headed parrot are but two of many exotic species inhabiting the Amazon. Brazilian avian life is so rich that Victor Emanuel Nature Tours runs eight programs here, and Field Guides and Focus Tours each offer four.

Chile

Seasons: October–November.
Locations: Atacama Desert; Lake District; Patagonia.
Cost: From $3,999 for 16 days from Santiago.
Tour Operators: Focus Tours; WINGS.

Chile spans a number of distinctive vegetational and altitudinal zones, ensuring a varied and abundant avian population. On a 16-day journey to the northern and central regions, Focus Tours participants visit the ski areas of Farellones and Valle Nevado to spot the rare Crag Chilia, an earth-creeper-like bird; Los Cipreses Reserve, stronghold of the burrowing parrot; La Campana National Park, which holds five of Chile's eight endemic species; the Andes for the rare and threatened white-tailed shrike-tyrant; plus the arid Atacama and Lauca National Park. WINGS's itinerary covers the country from Patagonia, in the south, to the Atacama Desert, in the north, also spending time in the Lake District around Puerto Montt.

Ecuador

Season: Year-round.
Locations: Amazon; Andes; Galápagos Islands; Southwest coast.
Cost: From $1,135 for seven days from Quito.
Tour Operators: Australian & Amazonian Adventures; Field Guides; Victor Emanuel Nature Tours; WINGS.

Some birders have described one of Ecuador's nature reserves as "one of the birdiest places on earth." In each region, from the Amazon to the Andes to the Galápagos, you'll find hundreds of distinct species. More than 500 species have been recorded at the Napo Wildlife Center, which is visited on one of Victor Emanuel's six programs in this country. The company's other trips travel to the Andes and the Galápagos, with one northern Andes itinerary focused on the regions's 40 to 60 hummingbird species. WINGS offers five itineraries in Ecuador, ranging from the Amazon to the Yanacocha Reserve, Vilcabamba, the Manglares de Churute Reserve, and Oriente. Field Guides' 10-day program is based at a hacienda in the cloud forest at an altitude of 2,073 meters (6,800 feet). The bird list here features the recently discovered Bicolored Antvireo and the rare Mountain Avocetbill. Australian & Amazonian Adventures covers diverse terrain, ranging from high plains to the Mindo Cloud Forest and both highland and subtropical rain forests.

Peru
Season: Year-round.
Locations: Amazon basin; Andes; Northern Peru.
Cost: From $3,090 for 10 days from Lima.
Tour Operators: Tours International; Victor Emanuel Nature Tours; WINGS.

With habitats ranging from the Amazon to the Andes, Peru claims in excess of 1,800 bird species. WINGS's three itineraries cover Manu National Park, considered one of the world's premier birding sites; other Amazonian regions; and northern Peru. Tours International's birding trips focus on Tambopata, Colca, and Paracas, while Victor Emanuel offers four itineraries, two concentrating on the Amazon, one on the central region including the Paracas Peninsula and Cordillera Blanca, and the fourth on the north, with visits to Tumbes, Marañón Canyon, and the Andes.

Venezuela
Season: Year-round.
Locations: Andes; Gran Sabana; Henri Pittier National Park; Los Llanos.
Cost: From $2,870 for nine days from Caracas.
Tour Operators: Victor Emanuel Nature Tours; WINGS.

With topography ranging from cloud forests to the Andes, the *tepuis* (mountains with sheer sides and flat tops), saline lagoons, grasslands, and a number of national parks, Venezuela offers an abundance of birding opportunities. More than 500 species are found in Henri Pittier National Park alone, and both Victor Emanuel and WINGS take you there. Each company offers three distinct itineraries in Venezuela. Victor Emanuel's eastern Venezuela trip has been nicknamed the "Harpy Eagle Tour," a tribute to the success rate of viewing these magnificent birds.

Natural History

Many operators have created nature-focused programs that provide insight into the importance and fragility of South America's ecological treasures. The itineraries mentioned below take in the deserts, glaciers, rain forests, mountains, and rivers of this continent, as well as the impressive variety of its wildlife.

Argentina & Chile

Season: October–April.
Locations: Atacama Desert; Buenos Aires; Lake District; Patagonia; Santiago.
Cost: From $1,860 for nine days from Buenos Aires.
Tour Operators: Abercrombie & Kent; Adventure Life; Big Five Tours & Expeditions; ElderTreks; G.A.P. Adventures; Geographic Expeditions; Inca; Journeys International; Myths and Mountains; Nature Expeditions International; Off the Beaten Path; OutWest Global Adventures; PanAmerican Travel; South American Journeys; Southwind Adventures; Wilderness Travel; Wildland Adventures; World Expeditions.

The southern tip of Argentina and Chile, commonly referred to as Patagonia, has long been a prime ecotourism destination, and nature lovers will find no lack of tour offerings for this region. You'll view the glaciers of Los Glaciares National Park, where the Moreno Glacier towers 20 stories high; the soaring peaks of Torres del Paine; the fjords of the Chilean coast; and a Magellanic penguin colony. Most itineraries spend some days in the Lake District. Many programs include day walks and, often, a one- to three-day cruise. Several operators feature a stay at a historic ranch, Estancia Helsingfors. The Atacama Desert of northern Chile is nature of another sort. Abercrombie & Kent has a "Fire and Ice" itinerary, combining the deep south with this arid zone.

Bolivia

Season: Year-round.
Locations: Noel Kempff Mercado National Park; Ríos Iténez and Paucerna; Santa Cruz.
Cost: From $1,589 for four days from Santa Cruz.
Tour Operator: Adventure Life; Big Five Tours & Expeditions; Wildland Adventures.

Noel Kempff Mercado National Park's 2.4 million acres contain 525 bird, 91 mammal, and 18 reptile species, plus numerous plants. It is one of the most isolated and concentrated wildlife reserves in all South America and contains a diverse combination of ecosystems. All three of the above companies can take you here to hike the forest trails and visit the river to see dolphins, giant otters, and endangered black caimans. Wildland Adventures' nine-day itinerary also takes in several impressive waterfalls and boat trips up to five hours by motorized canoe along various rivers.

Brazil

Season: Year-round.
Locations: Bonito; Iguaçu Falls; Pantanal.
Cost: From $831 for five days from Campo Grande.
Tour Operators: Australian & Amazonian Adventures; Big Five Tours & Expeditions; Bushtracks Expeditions; Ecotour Expeditions; ElderTreks; Explore! Worldwide; G.A.P. Adventures; Geographic Expeditions; International Expeditions; Oceanic Society Expeditions; Travcoa; Zeghram Expeditions.

Covering 89,000 square miles, the Pantanal is the world's largest freshwater wetland. All the above companies operate Pantanal programs; many are based at Refúgio Ecológico Caiman, which offers comfortable lodgings and a staff of naturalists who lead excursions by truck, by boat, on horseback, and on foot. Jabiru storks and other wading birds, anteaters, monkeys, caimans, capybaras, and possibly jaguars are among the wildlife you might see. Oceanic Society's trip, led by two animal specialists, spends six days at a lodge on the Río Pixiam and includes an excursion to an area with the world's highest recorded number of jaguar sightings per day. Zegrahm Expeditions' 17-day itinerary also visits this area along with several national parks and Iguaçu Falls, while ElderTreks combines the Pantanal, the Amazon, and Iguaçu on a 15-day trip. Australian & Amazonian Adventures offers two programs in lesser-known regions of the Pantanal. Before traveling to the wetlands, Bushtracks participants observe hyacinth macaws and maned wolves at Hyacinth Cliffs Lodge, then continue on to Greenwing Valley Reserve to see brown capuchin monkeys, sometimes called Einstein monkeys because of their ability to use rock tools as hammers and anvils. With G.A.P. you'll spend days in Rio, Parati, and Iguaçu, as well as the Pantanal.

Ecuador
Season: Year-round.
Locations: Amazon; Antisana Reserve; lakes of Riobamba.
Cost: $3,290 for 10 days from Quito.
Tour Operators: Abercrombie & Kent.

It's the smallest Andean country, but Ecuador is impressively scenic and culturally diverse. Abercrombie & Kent's 10-day journey introduces many of its natural wonders. At Antisana Reserve, you'll view volcanoes and a variety of flora and fauna, including, perhaps, the Andean condor. Continuing on to Baños, gateway to the Amazon rain forest, there will be the chance for horseback riding, hiking, mountain biking, or simply enjoying the volcanic hot springs and waterfalls. Reaching the central lake region of Riobamba, board a train for rooftop views of the landscape.

Peru
Season: Year-round.
Locations: Colca Canyon; Madre de Dios rain forest; Tambopata-Candamo Reserve.
Cost: From $350 for three days from Cuzco.
Tour Operators: Adventure Life; Big Five Tours & Expeditions; ElderTreks; G.A.P. Adventures; Southwind Adventures; Tours International; World Expeditions.

Covering 3.7 million acres, the Tambopata-Candamo Reserve is primarily known for its Macaw Research Center, where a huge nutrient-rich clay lick attracts hundreds of parrots and parakeets and at least six species of macaws. The reserve has some 500 bird species, 11 varieties of monkeys, and various mammals, including ocelots and jaguars. All the above operators have trips to Tambopata, ranging from three to seven days. Adventure Life and World Expeditions also offer itineraries in Arequipa, called the White City because of its many buildings made of light-color volcanic rock, and Colca Canyon, the world's deepest canyon. With Tours International, choose a three-day stay at Posada Amazonas, built in traditional style using palm fronds, wood, wild cane, and clay. The lodge, deep in the Madre de Dios rain forest, is a joint venture with the Esé eja Native Community and the Tambopata Research Center.

Venezuela

Season: Year-round.
Locations: Andes; Angel Falls; Canaima; Los Llanos; Orinoco Delta.
Cost: From $2,680 for 15 days from Caracas.
Tour Operators: Big Five Tours & Expeditions; Explore! Worldwide; PanAmerican Travel.

Besides 1,250 species of birds and 250 kinds of mammals, Venezuela also has mountains, tropical forests, mesas, and waterfalls. A highlight of any journey is Canaima National Park and a view of Angel Falls, either from the base or by light aircraft. The avalanche of water drops 807 m (2,647 ft), twice the height of the Empire State Building. Big Five offers a three-day trip here, as well as a 14-day package that also includes Caracas; Los Llanos, a vast, treeless plain with a diversity of wildlife; the Andes; and the beaches of Margarita Island. PanAmerican's 14-day journey visits the falls, the Orinoco Delta, and Caracas, following eight days in neighboring Guyana. Some camping is part of the program. Adventure Life divides its 15-day package between Canaima and the falls, the Orinoco Delta, and Los Llanos. Three overnights are in jungle shelters and two in hammock camps.

Overland Safaris

The brochure for a company that operates overland trips exclusively states in bold print: NOT YOUR EVERYDAY JOURNEY. Although definitely not for everyone, this type of travel is sure to take you far from the beaten path. It's also a great way to immerse yourself in a number of cultures and landscapes. Expect to travel by truck, bus, train, boat, or custom-built expedition vehicle—no air-conditioned coach tours here. Occasionally, you may find yourself in lodges or inns, but much of the time you'll be sleeping outdoors. Know that you're expected to help pitch tents, cook, and do other chores. The camaraderie that evolves often sparks lifelong friendships. You should be tolerant of others, willing to forego some creature comforts, and be a good sport about taking part in group activities. Companies often rank trip segments from easy to extreme. This type of trip generally attracts an international mix of physically fit adventurers between ages 18 and 50. Although the operators listed below do not have fixed upper age limits for participants, those over 60 will likely be asked to complete a health questionnaire. Note that this practice is not limited to overland journeys; many companies follow this procedure when trips involve strenuous activities or roughing it.

Season: Year-round.
Locations: Throughout South America.
Cost: From $1,320 for 32 days from La Paz, plus $390 for a "kitty," which funds such expenses as camp food, group activities, and park entrance fees.
Tour Operators: Dragoman Overland; Exodus; G.A.P. Adventures; Gecko's.

11

These companies offer trips that cover most of South America ranging in length from 4 to 22 weeks. Itineraries typically are composed of segments that you can take separately or combine into a longer trip. Most programs visit between three and nine countries.

Photo Safaris

An advantage of photo tours is the amount of time spent at each place visited. Whether the subject is a rarely spotted animal, a breathtaking waterfall, or villagers in traditional dress, you get a chance to focus both your camera and your mind on the scene before you. The tours listed below are led by professional photographers who offer instruction and hands-on tips. If you're not serious about improving your photographic skills, these trips might not be the best choice, as you could become impatient with the pace.

Antarctica

Season: October; February.
Locations: Antarctic Peninsula; Falkland, South Georgia, and South Orkney Islands.
Cost: From $8,495 for 16 days from Ushuaia.
Tour Operator: Joseph Van Os Photo Safaris; Lindblad Expeditions.

Photograph seabirds, Adélie and gentoo penguin colonies, albatross nesting areas, and elephant and fur seals, plus the spectacular landscapes of Antarctic. With Joseph Van Os, you'll travel aboard the icebreaker *Kapitan Khlebnikov*, which carries its own helicopter. A high point of this trip is the chance to cruise the Weddell Sea and visit the Snow Hill colony of emperor penguins, where some 4,000 breeding pairs are found. Lindblad Expeditions has one departure designated as a photo expedition that allows you to learn in the field with nature photographer Tom Mangelsen. This 14-day program calls at the islands listed above, as well as the Antarctic Peninsula.

Argentina & Chile

Season: March–April.
Locations: Central Patagonia; Easter Island; Los Glaciares and Torres del Paine national parks.
Cost: From $3,495 for 12 days from Santiago.
Tour Operators: Joseph Van Os Photo Safaris; Myths and Mountains.

Timed for vibrant fall colors among ice fields, snowcapped mountains, glaciers, and rushing streams, Joseph Van Os has 12- and 13-day departures during the Patagonian fall (during the months of the northern hemisphere's spring). While one trip visits the famed sites of Torres del Paine and Los Glaciares national parks, the second concentrates on lesser-known regions such as central Patagonia. Myths and Mountains offers a 15-day program led by photographer Bill Chapman that combines Torres del Paine National Park with the desolation and *moais* (giant stone statues) of Easter Island.

Ecuador

Season: April–May; November.
Locations: Galápagos Islands.
Cost: From $3,650 for 10 days from Guayaquil.
Tour Operators: Joseph Van Os Photo Safaris; Lindblad Expeditions.

Confronted with the rugged landscapes and incredible array of un-afraid wildlife, few visitors to the Galápagos leave without wishing they knew just a bit more about composing and executing that perfect image. Joining a photo expedition will ensure you return home without such regrets. On Joseph Van Os's 17-day journey, you'll travel aboard the comfortable yacht *Parranda*, visiting more than a dozen islands, including several off the usual cruise path. Lindblad's special photo departures utilize the 80-passenger ship *Polaris* to call at a number of islands known for such appealing photo subjects as sea lions, blue- and red-footed boobies, iguanas, and frigate birds.

Peru

Season: April–May.
Locations: Ballestas Islands; Cuzco; Machu Picchu; Manu Wildlife Center; Paracas National Reserve; Tambopata Reserve.
Cost: From $2,885 for 10 days from Lima.
Tour Operators: Joseph Van Os Photo Safaris; Tours International; Wildland Adventures.

Arguably the most photographed site in South America, Machu Picchu inspires more than the usual vacation photos. With each of these operators, a professional photographer helps you determine the best angles and lighting for your images of the world's most famous Incan site. With Wildland Adventures, you'll take in all the important spots between Cusco and Machu Picchu accompanied by nature photographers Diane Kelsay and Bob Harvey, while Joseph Van Os's 17-day trip visits these don't-miss places, along with the coastal desert of Paracas National Reserve, the wildlife-rich Ballestas Islands, and Manu Wildlife Center, in the heart of the Peruvian Amazon. Tours International's photo journey is based at Tambopata Reserve, noted for its abundant wildlife, including some 500 bird species.

SPORTS

A sports-focused trip offers a great way to get a feel for the part of the country you're visiting and to interact with local people. A dozen bicyclists entering a village, for instance, would arouse more interest and be more approachable than a group of 30 stepping off a tour bus. Although many itineraries do not require a high level of skill, it is expected that your interest in the sport focused on in a particular tour be more than casual. On the other hand, some programs are designed for those who are highly experienced. In either case, good physical conditioning, experience with high altitudes (on certain itineraries), and a flexible attitude are important. Weather can be changeable, dictating the choices of hiking and climbing routes. If you're not a particularly strong hiker or cyclist, determine if support vehicles accompany the group or if alternate activities or turnaround points are available on more challenging days.

Bicycling

Argentina & Chile
Season: October–March.
Locations: Atacama Desert; Lake District; Mendoza; Patagonia.
Cost: From $1,225 for eight days from Puerto Montt.
Tour Operators: Australian & Amazonian Adventures; Butterfield & Robinson; Experience Plus!; Global Adventure Guide; Southwind Adventures.

Global Adventure's 15-day journey, graded moderate with some uphill challenges and occasional single-track riding, twice crosses the lower Andes as you ride along paved and dirt roads through forests and past volcanoes. The itinerary encompasses both the Lake District and Patagonia, with occasional options for rafting, canyoning, or volcano climbing. With Southwind Adventures, bike and hike the Lake District's gently rolling terrain, visiting several national parks, and the resort town of Pucón. Nicknamed a "two-wheeled tango," Butterfield & Robinson's nine-day trip travels from Santiago, Chile, to Buenos Aires, Argentina (not totally by bike!), stopping in Chile's Atacama desert and Argentina's wine country along the way. Starting in Bariloche, Experience Plus! cycles up to 93 km (58 mi) a day around Lake Llanquihue for views of volcanoes; there's also the chance for Class III rafting on Río Petrohué. Choose from two biking journeys with Australian & Amazonian Adventures, one to Chile's Lake District, the other visiting a number of national parks. Most nights are spent camping.

Bolivia
Season: July.
Locations: Altiplano; Lake Titicaca; La Paz; Zongo Valley.
Cost: From $2,039 for 14 days from Arica, Chile.
Tour Operator: Global Adventure Guide.

Bolivia is thought of as the be-all and end-all of South American mountain biking, and with Global Adventure's two itineraries, you can discovery why. A 13-day journey starts in the city of Arica, Chile, ascends one of the world's highest roads to traverse the Atacama Desert, crosses the border into Bolivia, and concludes in the capital, La Paz. The journey follows 16th-century trade routes, biking up to 68 km (41 mi) a day. The company's second program is a high-altitude training camp where you'll put in lots of road miles under the tutelage of a renowned sports coach. The route goes from sea level to an altitude of more than 4,707 meters (15,443 feet), and each night's location is selected to give incremental gains in altitude. This training camp is designed for experienced cyclists and triathletes.

Brazil
Season: April–May; September–October.
Locations: Bahia; Iguaçu Falls; Paraty; Rio; São José Mountains.
Cost: $7,995 for 11 days from Rio.
Tour Operator: Butterfield & Robinson.

Designated moderate in difficulty, this 11-day trip takes in the beaches of Bahia, the well-preserved 18th-century town of Tiradentes, spectacular Iguaçu Falls, and the famed city of Rio de Janeiro. You'll bike and horseback ride along gold miners' trails in the São José Mountains, cycle on jungle trails, enjoy a chic cliff-top spa, and pick up cooking tips from a local chef. Accommodations include a colonial *pousada* (inn), upscale hotels, and a luxurious plantation home.

Ecuador

Season: June–July.
Locations: Avenue of the Volcanoes; Baños; Quito;.
Cost: From $780 for five days from Quito.
Tour Operators: Australian & Amazonian Adventures; Ibike/International Bicycle Fund; Southwind Adventures.

Both of Ibike's programs begin with acclimatization in Ecuador's capital, Quito. From there, one itinerary heads north to Imbabura Province, sightseeing among the region's markets, churches, pre-Columbian sites, and varied ecological zones. The second journey ranges from the Avenue of Volcanoes to the Amazon basin. A focus of both trips is people-to-people experiences. These trips are recommended for physically fit intermediate and expert cyclists. Australian & Amazonian Adventures offers four Ecuadoran programs, varying from four to eight days. Bike through such beauty spots as Cotopaxi National Park, the Chota Valley, Pululahua Cloud Forest Reserve, and around Quilotoa Crater Lake, stopping at Indian markets, waterfalls, and hot springs en route. Southwind's nine-day itinerary, designed for both the novice and the experienced biker, explores the colonial villages, alpine lakes, and diverse ecological reserves of the northern highlands. You'll learn about such regional cottage industries as wood carving, leatherworking, weaving, and ornament making.

Peru

Season: May–October.
Locations: Amazon; Andes; Cusco; Machu Picchu.
Cost: From $1,799 for nine days from Cusco.
Tour Operators: BikeHike Adventures; KE Adventures; Southwind Adventures; World Expeditions.

All the above operators visit Machu Picchu. BikeHike Adventures uses all-terrain mountain bikes to explore a network of backcountry roads, dirt trails, villages, and ancient ruins. On KE Adventures 15-day journey, follow a network of Inca trails to cycle high in the Andes, only to make a seemingly endless 4,000-meter (13,000-foot) descent to a camp at the edge of Manu National Park. The biking is sometimes technical, always challenging. With Southwind Adventures' 11-day itinerary, you'll travel some distances by vehicle, but you'll mostly bike from Cusco to Machu Picchu. On biking days you'll cover up to 63 km (39 miles) at high altitudes with camping en route. World Expeditions' 18-day venture, with 11 days of cycling, visits to Cusco, the Sacred Valley, Machu Picchu, and Lake Titicaca, ending in La Paz, Bolivia.

Venezuela
Season: Year-round.
Locations: Gran Sabana; Roraima.
Cost: $1,705 for 12 days from Ciudad Bolivar.
Tour Operator: Australian & Amazonian Adventures.

On this adventurous expedition, cycle through vast, sometimes hilly, savannas and dense forest, frequently within view of magnificent *tepuis* (mesas). You'll need to swim across 25-meter (82-foot) Río Kukenan, carry your bike up at least one steep slope, and make a five-hour climb of Roraima tepuis. Overnights are in tents or hammocks, often set up by rivers or in indigenous settlements.

Canoeing, Kayaking, & White-Water Rafting

White-water rafting and kayaking can be exhilarating experiences. You don't have to be an expert paddler to enjoy many of these adventures, but you should be a strong swimmer. Rivers are rated from Class I to Class V according to difficulty of navigation. Generally speaking, Class I–III rapids are suitable for beginners, while Class IV–V rapids are strictly for the experienced. Canoeing is a gentler river experience.

Brazil
Season: Year-round.
Location: Amazon.
Cost: $880 for seven days from Manaus.
Tour Operator: Swallows and Amazons.

Following a day's journey along the Río Negro, overnight in a small rainforest lodge owned by Swallows and Amazons. The next day, set out on a six-day canoeing and camping adventure, exploring various tributaries and the lakes, channels, and flooded forest of the Anavilhanas Archipelago. Hike, fish, swim, and visit the local river people, camping at night on beaches or in the jungle.

Chile
Season: November–March.
Locations: Chiloé Archipelago; Northern Patagonia; Río Futaleufú.
Cost: From $680 for four days from Castro, in Chiloé.
Tour Operators: Adventure Life; Australian & Amazonian Expeditions; Earth River Expeditions; Hidden Trails; PanAmerican Travel.

Chile has both scenic fjords for sea kayaking and challenging rivers for white-water rafting. With PanAmerican Travel, sea kayakers can spend nine days exploring the fjords, waterfalls, and hot springs of the country's rugged coast, camping at night. Australian & Amazonian Adventures offers three- to nine-day kayaking experiences. On the four-day itinerary you'll discover the islands of the Chiloé Archipelago, a region rich in folklore, while the six-day program explores the fjords of northern Patagonia. For the experienced rafter, the Class IV and V rapids of Río Futaleufú offer many challenges. Its sheer-walled canyons boast such well-named rapids as Infierno and Purgatorio. Earth River's 10-day program here includes a rock climb up 98-meter (320-foot) Torre de los

Vientos and a Tyrolean traverse where, wearing a climbing harness attached to a pulley, you pull yourself across a rope strung above the rapids. With tree houses and riverside hot tubs formed from natural potholes, overnight camping becomes an exotic experience. Earth River also offers a kayaking journey over a chain of three lakes, surrounded by snowcapped mountains. Access is by floatplane. Hidden Trails and Adventure Life have Futaleufú rafting trips; the latter's program offers, in addition to shooting the rapids, horseback riding in the mountains, kayaking, and fishing.

Ecuador

Season: Year-round.
Locations: Amazon basin; Galápagos; Oriente; Río Upano.
Cost: From $785 for six days from Coco.
Tour Operators: Adventure Life; Australian & Amazonian Adventures; Earth River Expeditions; Hidden Trails; Remote Odysseys Worldwide (ROW); Small World Adventures.

Río Upano's Class II–IV rapids have become synonymous with world-class rafting. Experience these "big volume" rapids with Earth River Expeditions, Hidden Trails, or Australian & Amazonian Adventures. Between the put-in site and the takeout 105 km (65 mi) later, the river will have tripled in volume. Australian & Amazonian also has rafting journeys on several other Class II–III Ecuadoran rivers. From Small World Adventures' lodge in the Oriente, you can raft more than 100 km (60 mi) of several rivers, including the Ouijos (Class III and IV) and Jondachi (Class IV and V). In just one day, you'll run more than 25 rapids. This company operates multiple kayaking journeys as well. Adventure Life and Australian & Amazonian Adventures have created kayaking programs along the Río Shiripuno into the land of the Huaorani people. Following 3–5 hours on the water daily, enjoy rain-forest hikes, camping, and learning about local life from your Huaorani guide. Although several companies offer yacht-based kayaking on Galápagos itineraries, ROW has created the first true sea-kayaking trip here, camping on secluded beaches. Because of strict Ecuadoran government controls, the adventure was 10 years in the making, but it's now a reality.

Peru

Season: May–November.
Locations: Colca Canyon; Cotahuasi Canyon; Lake Titicaca; Río Apurímac; Río Tambopata.
Cost: From $799 for four days from Cusco.
Tour Operators: Australian & Amazonian Adventures; Earth River Expeditions; Myths and Mountains; Tours International.

The moderate-to-difficult rapids of the Class III–IV Río Tambopata lead to the Tambopata-Candamo Reserve, while the wilder ride of the Class III–V Río Apurímac cuts through gorges and canyons under towering Andean peaks. Cotahuasi Canyon rafting takes you through Class IV–V whitewater on the Andes' western slopes. All three adventures can be booked with Tours International and Australian & Amazonian Adventures. For serious rafters, the Class V Río Colca is one of the deepest and most inaccessible canyons in the world. In fact, it has been termed the Everest of river canyons. Earth River takes you here and helps you master the challenges. After hiking at Machu Picchu with Myths and Mountains, travel to Lake Titicaca for kayaking on the world's highest navigable lake and camping on its shores. Australian & Amazonian Adventures offers 4- and 12-day kayaking itineraries at this lake.

Fishing

Argentina & Chile

Season: September–March.
Locations: Chiloé Island; Lake District; Patagonia.
Cost: From $2,975 for seven days from Balmaceda, Chile.
Tour Operators: Fishing International; FishQuest; Fly Fishing And; Frontiers; PanAmerican Travel; Rod & Reel Adventures.

For anglers, Argentina and Chile are the southern hemisphere's Alaska, offering world-class trout fishing in clear streams. An added bonus is the availability of landlocked salmon and golden dorado, known as the river tiger. Bilingual fishing guides accompany groups, and accommodations are in comfortable lodges with private baths. Although November is the usual opening date for freshwater fishing, the season begins two months earlier at Lago Llanquihue because of the large resident fish population. Rod & Reel takes advantage of this, basing participants at a lodge near Osorno volcano. With Fly Fishing And, your 10 days will be divided between two lodges, meaning you can fish several rivers and creeks, while PanAmerican's seven-day program breaks up lodge stays with a night of riverside camping. Fishing International offers an Argentina program fishing the Ibera marshes for dorado and a Chile trip based at an estancia (ranch) where you can fish two rivers for brown trout weighing up to 15 pounds. FishQuest has four itineraries, offering fishing at a variety of rivers for brown and rainbow trout, dorado, giant catfish, and salmon. With Frontiers, choose from a variety of lodges and rivers in both Argentina and Chile.

Brazil

Season: September–May.
Location: Amazon.
Cost: From $1,080 for seven days from Manaus.
Tour Operators: FishQuest; Frontiers; Rod & Reel Adventures; Swallows and Amazons.

Although pirapitinga, pirarucú, jancundá, and many other exotic fish inhabit the Amazon, it is the legendary peacock bass that anglers describe as the ultimate adversary. With Swallows & Amazons, you can fish the Ríos Negro and Cuieiras plus several lakes while based on a traditional riverboat with hammocks or mats for beds. On Rod & Reel's Amazon trip, you'll live aboard a comfortable 30-meter (100-foot) yacht while reeling in peacock bass. Frontiers offers several choices of accommodations on the Brazilian Amazon: a fly-fishing-only lodge, floating cabins, a luxury live-aboard riverboat, or a four-person houseboat with air-conditioned rooms and private baths. FishQuest also utilizes the floating cabins, as well as lodge and yacht accommodations. The company takes you to tributaries and lagoons where it's not uncommon to catch two or three dozen peacock bass per day. One itinerary focuses on an estuary known for pirarucú, the world's largest freshwater fish, known for its fighting spirit and long runs and leaps.

Venezuela
Season: Year-round.
Locations: Casiquiare watershed; La Guaira; Lake Guri; Los Roques; Río Caura.
Cost: From $1,995 for five days from Caracas.
Tour Operators: FishQuest; Frontiers; Rod & Reel Adventures.

Venezuela has an enviable reputation for both saltwater and freshwater fishing. Los Roques, an archipelago that's a short flight from Caracas, offers exciting bonefishing, while Guri Lake and Río Caura are top spots for peacock bass, some exceeding 15 pounds. Other challenges are the payara, described as "a salmon with a bad attitude," giant catfish, and the fierce aymara. Frontiers and FishQuest will take you to Los Roques. The latter company also operates packages to Río Caura, a tributary of the Orinoco; the Casiquiare watershed, where the chance of landing a trophy pavon in the 20-pound range compensates for some sacrifice of creature comforts; and La Guaira, off the northern coast, for the grand slam of fishing: billfish, blue and white marlin, and sailfish, as well as dolphin, wahoo, and tuna. With Rod & Reel, you'll stay at an upscale Guri Lake resort, going out by day for peacock bass, payara, piranha, and speckled and butterfly bass.

Hiking, Running & Trekking

South America's magnificent scenery and varied terrain make it a terrific place for trekkers and hikers. The southern part of Argentina and Chile, known as Patagonia, and Peru's Inca Trail are especially popular. Numerous tour operators offer hiking and trekking trips to these regions, so study several offerings to determine the program that's best suited to your ability and interests. The trips outlined below are organized tours led by qualified guides. Camping is often part of the experience, although on some trips you stay at inns and small hotels. Itineraries range from relatively easy hikes to serious trekking and even running.

Argentina & Chile
Season: October–April.
Locations: Atacama Desert; Lake District; Patagonia.
Cost: From $1,065 for 12 days from Salta, Argentina.
Tour Operators: Adventure Life; American Alpine Institute; Andes Adventures; Australian & Amazonian Adventures; BikeHike Adventures; Butterfield & Robinson; Country Walkers; Geographic Expeditions; KE Adventure Travel; Mountain Travel Sobek; Southwind Adventures; The World Outdoors; Wilderness Travel; Wildland Adventures; World Expeditions.

Patagonia may be the most trekked region in South America. All the above companies have programs here, ranging from relatively easy

11

hikes (Butterfield & Robinson, Country Walkers) to serious treks that gain up to 800 meters (2,625 feet) in elevation daily and ice and snow traverses using crampons (American Alpine Institute). Adventure Life's program lets you overnight in igloo-shape tents at EcoCamp in Torres del Paine. In addition to its hiking trip, Andes Adventures offers an 18-day running itinerary with runs of as much as 31 km (19 mi) per day. Other options include an Atacama Desert trek with KE Adventure Travel that includes an ascent of Licancabur Volcano or a Futaleufú Canyon trek with Wilderness Travel.

Bolivia

Season: March–October.
Locations: Cordillera Apolobamba; Cordillera Quimsa Cruz; Cordillera Real; Lake Titicaca.
Cost: From $580 for four days from La Paz.
Tour Operators: American Alpine Institute; Explore Bolivia; KE Adventure Travel; Mountain Madness; Mountain Travel Sobek; Southwind Adventures; Wildland Adventures.

Bolivia's majestic mountain ranges offer some challenging treks. The extreme altitude makes the going even tougher, so operators allow time for acclimatization in La Paz, the world's highest capital, or at Lake Titicaca, the world's highest navigable lake. All the companies above have trekking itineraries ranging from 4 to 22 days through the 121 km (75 mi) of the Cordillera Real. On some journeys, you'll cross up to six passes in excess of 4,500 meters (15,000 feet). In addition to its 22-day Cordillera Real trek, KE Adventures has a 17-day itinerary in the Cordillera Quimsa Cruz that features a four-day traverse beneath the west and north sides of Mt. Illimani, Bolivia's third-highest peak. Mountain Madness's 20-day program combines trekking in Bolivia and Peru, while Southwind Adventure's 16-day itinerary features eight days of camping and strenuous trekking at high altitudes. Explore Bolivia offers a four-day Cordillera Real trek as well as a seven-day trek in the Apolobamba range. On all ventures llamas or other pack animals will tote your gear, but you can expect to spend nights camping at high elevations.

Brazil

Season: Year-round.
Locations: Amazon basin; Bahia; Jau National Park; Rio de Janeiro.
Cost: From $446 for four days from Rio.
Tour Operators: Australian & Amazonian Adventures; Swallows and Amazons.

For an up-close jungle experience, join Swallows and Amazons for 11 days of trekking and camping in Jau National Park, during which you walk an average of six hours daily through thick vegetation, then relax at night in a jungle camp. This company also operates a seven-day hiking and camping adventure between the Ríos Cuieiras and Jaraqui, focusing on jungle biodiversity, animal tracking, and jungle survival skills. Australian & Amazonian Adventures' itinerary centers around scenic Chapada Diamantina, in Bahia state, and the colonial city of Lençóis. You'll hike among valleys, ravines, and mountains while exploring caves, waterfalls, natural chutes, and the region's heritage as a source of precious stones. A visit to a diamond prospecting ghost town is a highlight.

Ecuador

Season: Year-round.
Locations: Chimborazo, Cotopaxi, and Sangay national parks; Cuenca; Otavalo Valley; Riobamba.
Cost: From $1,309 for seven days from Quito.
Tour Operators: Andes Adventures; Australian & Amazonian Adventures; KE Adventure Travel; World Expeditions.

Two mountain ranges slice through Ecuador, making for some great trekking. Here you'll find the Avenue of Volcanoes, one of the largest concentrations of volcanoes in the world. Treks lead to glacier-clad peaks, national parks, and cloud forests. On Australian & Amazonian Adventures' "Volcanoes and Haciendas" program, each day's hike ends at a colonial hacienda, while World Expeditions combines six days of trekking with day hikes, thermal springs, camping, and the exciting Devil's Nose train journey, where the best views are from the roof. On KE Adventure Travel's arduous 18-day trek, you'll traverse river valleys, cross several 4,000-meter (13,000-foot) passes, and camp beside mountain lakes. With Andes Adventures, choose between 11-day hiking or running itineraries with hikes ranging from 6 to 15 km (from 4 to 9 mi) per day and runs varying from 10 to 31 km (from 6 to 19 mi). Both programs overnight in haciendas.

Peru

Season: April–November.
Locations: Blanca, Huayhusah, and Vilcabamba mountain ranges; Colca Valley; Inca Trail; Mt. Ausangate; Mt. Salcantay.
Cost: From $617 for five days from Cusco.
Tour Operators: Adventure Life; Andes Adventures; Australian & Amazonian Adventures; Country Walkers; Gecko's; Geographic Expeditions; KE Adventure Travel; Mountain Madness; Mountain Travel Sobek; Southwind Adventures; Tours International; Wilderness Travel; Wildland Adventures; World Expeditions.

The Inca Trail, stretching from the Urubamba Valley to Machu Picchu, has become one of South America's most popular destinations for trekkers. The 45-km (28-mi) mountain trail is mostly level, but the altitude makes it challenging. All the above companies offer Inca Trail treks. Several also lead more difficult Andean treks at altitudes in excess of 4,000 meters (13,000 feet). Each of these tour operators offers 3–7 trekking itineraries in Peru. In addition to treks, Andes Adventures has three running programs here, including a 44-km (27.5-mi) marathon and a circuit around Mt. Ausangate.

Venezuela

Season: Year-round.
Locations: Canaima; Mérida; Mt. Roraima; Pico Bolivar.
Cost: From $1,890 for 11 days from Caracas.
Tour Operators: Australian & Amazonian Adventures; Explore! Worldwide; KE Adventure Travel; World Expeditions.

Trekkers often head to 2,810-meter (9,220-foot) Mt. Roraima, rumored to be the setting of Arthur Conan Doyles's *The Lost World.* All tour operators above organize treks here, including a nontechnical ascent of the summit. With KE Adventure Travel, your trip also features camping near Angel Falls plus two days of relaxation on the islands of Los Roques. Australian & Amazonian Adventures spends several nights camping in the vicinity of Mt. Roraima, while on World Expeditions' 11-day trip, enjoy a five-day trek to and ascent of Venezuela's highest peak, Pico Bolívar. A six day Roraima trek and a four-day journey by motorized canoe are part of Explore! Worldwide's 15-day adventure.

Horseback Riding

Argentina

Season: Year-round, lower elevations; November–March, Andes.
Locations: Corrientes; Nahuel Huapi National Park; Lake District; Patagonia; Tunuyan Valley.
Cost: From $649 for six days from Mendoza.
Tour Operators: Australian & Amazonian Adventures; Boojum Expeditions; Equitours; Hidden Trails.

Few countries have a greater equestrian tradition than Argentina. Equitours introduces you to the country's gaucho culture at a 15,000-acre estancia (cattle ranch). You ride through the grasslands and beech forests of Lanin National Park and spend several nights camping. Hidden Trails offers eight itineraries in Argentina that explore the forests, mountains, and lakes of Patagonia, the vast wilderness around Canyon del Diabolo, and the Serrucha mountain range and several estancia-based adventures where you'll ride more than 32 km (20 mi) a day and, perhaps, join the gauchos as they round up cattle and horses. With Boojum Expeditions, ride sure-footed Criollo horses high in the mountains and along rugged trails. As the company warns, this is not a place to learn to ride. On Australian & Amazonian Adventures's six-day trip, ride in the Río Tunuyan area, crossing the border into Chile.

Chile

Season: October.–April; year-round, Atacama.
Locations: Atacama Desert; Patagonia; Río Hurtado Valley.
Cost: From $1,450 for seven days from Calama.
Tour Operators: Equitours; Hidden Trails.

On Equitours's 12-day "Patagonia Glacier Ride," you cross the pampas to Torres del Paine National Park, a region of mountains, lakes, and glaciers. Nights are spent camping or in lodges. Hidden Trails has six itineraries: you can opt for a ride in southern Chile, along historic mule trails created by gold diggers, and into the Andes; join an Atacama Desert adventure riding over the crusted salt of the Salar de Atacama and across expanses of sand, visiting ancient ruins and petroglyphs, or choose from four Patagonia programs. If getting off the beaten path appeals to you, consider the company's "Glacier Camping Ride," which ventures into remote areas accessible only on foot or horseback.

Ecuador

Season: Year-round.
Location: Andes; Avenue of Volcanoes.
Cost: From $1,095 for nine days from Quito.
Tour Operators: Equitours; Hidden Trails.

Journeying into the heart of the Eucadorean Andes, Hidden Trails's six itineraries offer exciting rides through cloud forests, desertlike landscapes, high mountains, pastoral valleys, or along the famed Avenue of Volcanoes. In more remote areas overnights are in simple accommodations; otherwise, they are spent in historic haciendas, in some cases dating to the 17th century. One program stays on a working farm where you can join the *chagras* (Andean cowboys) in rounding up horses and cattle. On most trips expect to ride from four to eight hours per day. Equitours offers a hacienda-to-hacienda ride through the Zuleta Valley and Cotopaxi National Park, with elevations reaching 2,500–4,300 meters (8,000–14,000 feet).

Peru

Season: March–November.
Locations: Cusco; Leymebamba; Machu Picchu.
Cost: From $1,246 for eight days from Lima.
Tour Operators: Australian & Amazonian Adventures; Equitours; Hidden Trails.

Astride a Peruvian Paso horse, a breed dating to the colonial era that originated in Spanish Andalusia, explore the terraces of the Sacred Valley of the Incas and the ancient city of Machu Picchu on programs offered by Equitours and Hidden Trails. You'll also mingle with descendants of the Inca and learn about their culture. With Australian & Amazonian Adventures, saddle up in the village of Leymebamba and head for the Lake of the Condors, a mystical place from which 219 well-preserved mummies were recovered in 1998. The trip also visits the fortress of Kuelap, called the Machu Picchu of the North, and the pyramids of Túcume.

Uruguay

Season: Year-round.
Locations: Laguna Negra.
Cost: From $1,850 for 15 days from Montevideo.
Tour Operators: Boojum Expeditions; Hidden Trails.

Uruguay's coastline boasts wide beaches dotted with small communities of artists and fishermen. With Boojum Expeditions, explore this area on Criollo and Spanish Barb horses accompanied by gaucho helpers. You'll overnight at both an estancia and a castlelike hotel atop a hill. This is a comfortable trip with no camping. Those with more time might combine this ride with Boojum's Patagonia journey for a "Coastline to Condors" adventure. Hidden Trails operates two rides in Uruguay. One itinerary includes eight days of riding across a traditional cattle-breeding area to the coast, with time to discover the diversity of wildlife at the UNESCO-designated Bañados del Este Biosphere Reserve. You'll stay in some of Uruguay's oldest and best-preserved haciendas. A second itinerary, based at two estancias, offers the chance to learn about rural activities and ride through a forest of *ombúes,* strange trees with thick, twisting branches spreading over the ground.

Mountaineering

Only the most towering peaks of Asia vie with the Andes in the challenges and rewards awaiting mountaineers. This is no casual sport, so ask questions, and be honest about your level of fitness and experience. Safety should be the company's—and your—first priority. Are the guides certified by professional organizations such as the American Mountain Guides Association? Are they certified as wilderness first responders and trained in technical mountain rescue? What is the climber-to-guide ratio? Are extra days built into the schedule to allow for adverse weather? Is there serious adherence to "leave no trace" environmental ethics? Several of the tour operators mentioned below have their own schools in the United States and/or other countries that offer multilevel courses in mountaineering, ice climbing, rock climbing, and avalanche education.

Antarctica

Season: November–January.
Location: Mt. Vinson.
Cost: $26,500 for 22 days from Punta Arenas.
Tour Operator: Alpine Ascents International; Mountain Madness.

If you have a solid mountaineering background and are accustomed to cold-weather camping, this could be the ultimate mountaineering adventure. A short flight from Patriot Hills brings you to the base camp. With loaded sleds, move up the mountain, establishing two or three camps before attempting the 4,897-meter (16,067-foot) summit of Mt. Vinson. Although the climb itself is considered technically moderate, strong winds and extreme temperatures, as low as -40°F, make this a serious challenge. Additionally, Alpine Ascents offers the chance to ski from the 89th to the 90th parallel. Aircraft will bring you within 70 mi of the South Pole; then ski the rest of the way. This unique adventure can be made independently or as an extension of the Vinson climb.

Argentina & Chile

Season: November–February.
Locations: Mt. Aconcagua; Cerro Marconi Sur; Gorra Blanca; Patagonian Ice Cap.
Cost: From $2,980 for 11 days from Calafate, Argentina.
Tour Operators: Alpine Ascents International; American Alpine Institute; Arun Treks & Expeditions; Colorado Mountain School; KE Adventure Travel; Mountain Madness; World Expeditions.

At 6,960 meters (22,835 feet), Argentina's Mt. Aconcagua is the highest peak in the world outside Asia. Though some routes are not technically difficult, Aconcagua is quite demanding physically and requires the use of ice axes, crampons, and ropes. All the above operators offer climbs of Aconcagua, some via the more difficult Polish glacier route. Frequent high winds and ice make this route very challenging and only for those with extensive mountaineering experience at high altitudes. American Alpine Institute has a second expedition with ascents of Cerro Marconi Sur and Gorra Blanca, in southern Patagonia. On this program you'll also traverse part of the Patagonian Ice Cap.

Bolivia

Season: June–September.
Location: Cordillera Real.
Cost: From $2,180 for 11 days from La Paz.
Tour Operators: Alpine Ascents International; American Alpine Institute; Colorado Mountain School; KE Adventure Travel; Mountain Madness; Southwind Adventures.

Stretching for 160 km (100 mi), Bolivia's Cordillera Real has some of the continent's finest and most varied alpine climbing. Large crevasses and a glacial face at a 40- to 45-degree incline will challenge even those with lots of experience. Twenty-two mountains are 5,800 meters (19,000 feet) or higher, giving rise to Bolivia's designation as the Tibet of the Americas. The highest peak, Illimani, soars to 6,462 meters (21,201 feet). Most of the above operators offer climbs of Illimani. Other popular ascents include Ancohuma, Huayna Potosí, Illampu, and Pequeno Alpamayo. American Alpine Institute offers four Bolivian climbing itineraries, while Mountain Madness, in addition to climbs, operates a glacier mountaineering course here. Southwind's 11-day trip includes strenuous trekking and a three-day attempt to summit Huayna Potosí. The climb is suitable for intermediate mountaineers in excellent physical condition who are familiar with the use of crampons and ice axes.

Ecuador

Season: November–March.
Locations: Antisana; Cayambe; Chimborazo; Cotocachi; Cotopaxi; Illiniza Sur.
Cost: From $1,975 for 10 days from Quito.
Tour Operators: Alpine Ascents International; American Alpine Institute; Colorado Mountain School; Mountain Madness; Southwind Adventures.

With challenges for all levels of ability, Ecuador's volcanoes have become a major destination for climbers. All the companies above organize climbs of 6,311-meter (20,701-foot) Chimborazo, 5,878-meter (18,996-foot) Cayambe, or 5,897-meter (19,347-foot) Cotopaxi. Chimborazo is the highest summit in Ecuador, Cayambe claims the tropics' most massive glaciers, and Cotopaxi is the second-highest active volcano on earth. Most itineraries attempt to summit three or four major volcanoes. In addition to the climbs mentioned above, American Alpine Institute and Colorado Mountain School have trips focusing on Artisana and Illiniza Sur. These are considered good expeditions for intermediate climbers. Mountain Madness operates 12-, 15-, and 19-day climbing courses in Ecuador that are designed for beginners who want to learn the fundamentals of snow-, ice-, and glacier climbing.

Peru

Season: June–August.
Locations: Alpamayo; Ancocancha; Chopicalqui; Huascarán; Ishinca; Pisco Oeste; Toclaraju; Urus.
Cost: From $2,680 for 15 days from Lima.
Tour Operators: American Alpine Institute; Alpine Ascents International; Colorado Mountain School; Mountain Madness.

Considered one of the world's most beautiful mountains, Alpamayo's pyramid-shape peak soars 5,947 meters (19,512 feet). Strong alpine skills are necessary for this climb, as is the ability to handle ice at a 60 degree incline. Huascarán, Peru's highest mountain at 6,768 meters (22,205 feet), has two extinct volcanic summits separated by a deep saddle. Prerequisites for Huascarán include high-altitude climbing experience and the ability to scale 45-degree ice with a full pack. The Peruvian Andes are the highest, most glaciated tropical mountains in the world. Even so, advanced beginners can handle some peaks here. All the above companies operate expeditions in the magnificent Cordillera Blanca. One of American Alpine Institute's four climbing programs in Peru is designed for beginner and intermediate levels.

Multisport

Only a few years ago, multisport offerings were so sparse that the topic didn't merit inclusion in this chapter. Since then, such trips have grown in popularity every year and now form an important part of the programs of many adventure tour operators. Innovative itineraries combine two or more sports, such as biking, fishing, canoeing, hiking, horseback riding, kayaking, rafting, and trekking.

Argentina & Chile

Season: November–April.
Locations: Lake District; northern Chile; Patagonia; Río Futaleufú, Chile.
Cost: From $765 for five days from Puerto Montt, Chile.
Tour Operators: American Alpine Institute; Austin-Lehman Adventures; Australian & Amazonian Adventures; BikeHike Adventures; Earth River Expeditions; Fishing International; Hidden Trails; Mountain Madness; Mountain Travel Sobek; Nature Expeditions International; The World Outdoors; Wilderness Travel; World Expeditions.

Whether you choose the Lake District or Patagonia, the scene for your active vacation will be one of great beauty. Hidden Trails combines horseback riding with sea kayaking in Patagonia, while Mountain Madness offers hut-to-hut trekking in the Torres del Paine area along with kayaking on the Río Serrano and an optional ice climb. With Nature Expeditions, you'll have soft adventure options most days, such as hiking, rafting (Class II and III rapids), and horseback riding. BikeHike has two multisport trips in Argentina and Chile; you can hike, raft, sea-kayak, bike, and ride horses in the Lake District or hike, ride horses, and sandboard in northern Chile. On Austin-Lehman's Pagatonia and Lake District itinerary, rest at night in five-star hotels and upscale lodges after horseback riding, biking, rafting, kayaking, and hiking during the day. If you want to try serious rafting, consider one of the Río Futaleufú trips, such as those run by Earth River Expeditions and The World Outdoors; these programs also include hiking and horseback riding.

Bolivia

Season: June; August.
Locations: Altiplano; Cordillera Real; Lake Titicaca; Yungas Lowlands.
Cost: From $2,750 for 12 days from La Paz.
Tour Operators: Explore Bolivia; Mountain Madness; World Expeditions.

Bolivia's diverse topography means the chance to enjoy many outdoor sports. Mountain Madness's 12-day adventure combines a fully supported trek along mountainous trails and through subtropical forests with sea kayaking on Lake Titicaca. En route, explore ancient ruins and a region of cloud forest known as the Yungas. With World Expeditions, spend several days acclimatizing in La Paz and on Lake Titicaca before setting out on a challenging 10-day trek in the Cordillera Real, where you'll be instructed in climbing techniques and then given the opportunity for several ascents. Explore Bolivia offers two adventures: a 14-day journey focuses on hiking (up to five hours a day) and rafting the Class II–IV rapids of the Río Tuichi with most nights spent camping, while a second itinerary includes kayaking, hiking, and horseback riding with overnights divided between camps, hotels, and haciendas.

Brazil
Season: April–October.
Locations: Bonito; Rio de Janeiro; Serra do Cipó.
Cost: From $1,799 for nine days from Belo Horizonte.
Tour Operator: Australian & Amazonian Adventures; BikeHike Adventures.

BikeHike's nine-day adventure starts off with a three-day trek through the Cipó mountain range, including an ascent of 1,676-meter (5,500-foot) Pico do Breu, followed by river kayaking, horseback riding across wide-open plains, and an 18-meter (60-foot) rappel down a waterfall. There's even an aerial zip-line running from forest into water; gear up in a harness and take off! Australian & Amazonian Adventures has come up with a fresh way to take in Rio's most famous sites. View Tijuca, the world's largest urban forest, by peddling through it on a mountain bike; follow a hiking path for about two hours, then make a 24-meter (80-foot) climb to stand atop that Rio landmark, Sugarloaf; kayak to Cotunduba Island for snorkeling and swimming, and climb four pitches (5.8 grade) to reach the top of Corcovado. Horseback riding, rafting, hang gliding, rappelling, and surfing are other options.

Ecuador
Season: Year-round.
Locations: Amazon basin; Andean Highlands; Galápagos; Ríos Arajuno, Jatunyacu, Quijos, and Toachi.
Cost: From $1,800 for seven days from Baltra (Galápagos).
Tour Operators: Adventure Life; BikeHike Adventures; Myths and Mountains; Remote Odysseys Worldwide (ROW); The World Outdoors.

Ecuadoran multisport adventure locales range from the Amazon to the Andes to the Galápagos Islands. BikeHike Adventures' itineraries hit all three regions with a hiking, horseback-riding, biking and sea-kayaking program in the Galápagos and an Andes-to-Amazon trip that takes in the first three sports mentioned plus rafting and an inner-tube float. G.A.P. has combined two days on mountain bikes, a three-day trek with camping, and three days of rafting the Class IV rapids of the Río Quijos. With Adventure Life, take a mountain trek, raft the Río Toachi, and try volcano biking, including at least one exhilarating descent down a steep slope. The World Outdoors's itinerary combines kayaking, biking, hiking, and horseback riding along the Avenue of Volcanoes and in the Galápagos, while ROW offers 7 or 10 days all in the Galápagos sea kayaking, snorkeling, and swimming, plus hiking up Sierra Negra Volcano and camping near the rim.

Peru

Season: April–December.
Location: Amazon; Andes; Lake Titicaca; northern Peru.
Cost: From $1,695 for six days from Cusco.
Tour Operators: Adventure Life; Austin Lehman Adventures; Australian & Amazonian Adventures; BikeHike Adventures; Explore! Worldwide; G.A.P. Adventures; KE Adventure Travel; The World Outdoors.

What better way to see it all than by horseback, mountain bike, or raft or on foot? Itineraries range from moderately easy to challenging and run from 6 to 21 days. Although most programs feature Cusco, Machu Picchu, and a trek that includes at least part of the Inca Trail, KE Adventures and Adventure Life add time in the Amazon, and many companies include rafting on the Ríos Urubamba or Kosñipata. Australian & Amazonian Adventures has a variety of multisport itineraries in Peru. One combines hikes, horseback rides, and steep climbs in the country's north with visits to the cliff-side funerary statues at Karajia and the fortress of Kuelap, while another features hiking, biking, sea kayaking, and sailing on Lake Titicaca. BikeHike's four 9- to 16-day programs all include mountain biking, horseback riding, and hiking; three trips also have rafting, and two feature rock climbing. With Austin-Lehman, you'll enjoy hiking, rafting (Class II and III rapids), horseback riding, and mountain biking while overnighting in upscale accommodations, including a museum hotel that was once a 16th-century monastery and was built on the foundation of an Inca palace.

Venezuela

Season: Year-round.
Location: Andes; La Culata National Park; Mérida state.
Cost: $2,199 for 12 days from Caracas.
Tour Operator: BikeHike Adventures.

Enjoy Venezuela's snowcapped mountains, cloud forests, and *páramo* tropical highlands as you bike and hike along backcountry roads and hidden trails and raft down rushing rivers. Such travel virtually guarantees interaction with village people, offering insights into their traditions. On BikeHike's 12-day itinerary, you'll take part in the sports mentioned plus rock climbs and rappels. Bike up to 70 km (38 mi) per day at altitudes ranging from 762 to 4,023 meters (from 2,500 to 13,200 feet) and bounce through the Class III and IV rapids of the Río Siniguis.

Skiing and Snowboarding

When ski season's over in the northern hemisphere, it's time to pack the gear and head for resorts in Argentina or Chile. Advanced and expert skiers will find seemingly endless terrain, and powder hounds will discover the ultimate ski. However, adventures aplenty await beginner and intermediate skiers as well. Snowboarders, too, will find the southern mountains much to their liking. In addition to marked trails, there's off-piste terrain, often with steep chutes and deep powder bowls, plus backcountry areas to try. Those with strong skills could opt for heli-skiing on peaks reaching 4,200 meters (13,600 feet) as condors soar above. Many of the resorts exude a European ambience with a lively nightlife scene. The tour operators mentioned below have created all-inclusive ski packages covering airport–hotel and hotel–ski mountain transfers, accommodations, two meals daily, and lift tickets for a number of mountains and resorts in both Argentina and Chile; many packages combine the two countries. Costs vary with the accommodations selected. Prices quoted are per person double occupancy; costs are even lower if four persons share a room. Be aware that less expensive packages, while providing the services mentioned, generally are not guided tours. Eight-day guided packages start around $1,795.

Argentina

Season: June–October.

Locations: Catedral Bariloche; Cerro Bayo; Chapelco; La Hoya-Esquel; Las Leñas.

Cost: From $880 for an eight-day nonguided inclusive package from Buenos Aires.

Tour Operators: Ladatco Tours; PowderQuest Tours; Snoventures.

Argentina's Bariloche, an alpine-style resort town nicknamed Little Switzerland, is 13 km (8 mi) from the slopes of Cerro Catedral. This ski area offers more than 1,500 skiable acres with 105 km (65 miles) of trails and is a good choice for skiers of all levels. The resort is in the midst of a several-year expansion project that will double lift capacity and open new terrain. Your lift ticket is valid for skiing at both Catedral and the adjacent resort of Robles. Also accessed by a flight to Bariloche, the ski center of Cerro Bayo, on the northwestern tip of Lake Nahuel Huapi, is generally not crowded and offers steep powder runs and excellent backcountry hiking. Some packages combine Catedral, Cerro Bayo, and La Hoya; the latter is a government-owned and -operated resort near the town of Esquel, where easy hikes lead to steep bowls and chutes, some with inclines of as much as 60 degrees. With 56 km (35 mi) of downhill trails and a vertical drop of 1,200 meters (4,000 feet), plus more than 100 couloirs (steep gullies) and vast off-piste and backcountry areas, Las Leñas is considered by many to be South America's premier ski destination. Appealing especially to the expert skier, Las Leñas has served as summer training ground for several Olympic ski teams. Between Bariloche and Las Leñas near the resort town of San Martin de los Andes, Chapelco offers challenges for skiers and riders at all levels. The mountain claims access to great backcountry bowls. Ladatco Tours has a seven-day package to Catedral Bariloche, while PowderQuest and Snoventures have multiple offerings for all ski destinations mentioned with a wide variety of accommodations choices to suit most budgets. Many of their packages combine stays at two or more ski areas.

Chile

Season: June–October.
Locations: El Colorado; La Parva; Portillo; Pucón; Termas de Chillán; Valle Nevado.
Cost: From $730 for a seven-day nonguided inclusive package from Santiago.
Tour Operators: Ladatco Tours; Myths and Mountains; PowderQuest; Snoventures.

A short drive from Santiago, Valle Nevado has more than 300 acres of groomed runs and an 800-meter (2,600-foot) vertical drop. Famous for powder, it's also home to the Andes Express, a chair lift so super-fast you can get in extra runs each day. From Valle Nevado you can interconnect with the slopes of nearby El Colorado and La Parva, making for a vast amount of skiable terrain. First-rate heli-skiing, heli-boarding, and even hang gliding can be taken out of Valle Nevado; the off-piste is excellent, as well. A snowboard camp is based here coached by North American AASI level-three certified instructors. Participation in the seven-day program, divided into first-time and advanced groups, can be arranged by PowderQuest. Near the base of Mt. Aconcagua, the highest mountain in the western hemisphere, Portillo is ranked on numerous lists as one of the top 10 ski resorts in the world. Several national ski teams have their off-season training here. The heli-skiing is enviable, and Portillo's lively après-ski life comes as an added bonus. Yet another world-class resort, Termas de Chillán, has what one tour operator terms "killer slopes," plus a network of forest tracks for cross-country skiers. Its 28 runs along 35 km (22 mi) of groomed trails include one that at 13 km (6 mi) is South America's longest. Boasting one of Chile's deepest snow packs, the resort offers varied terrain on two volcanoes for skiing or snowboarding, plus a thermal area comprised of nine pools for end-of-the-day relaxation. At the small resort of Pucón, on the edge of Lago Villarrica, ski on the side of Chile's most active volcano. You can hike to the crater to gaze at molten magma, then ski or snowboard back down. Bordering two national parks plus a national reserve, Pucón boasts great snowshoeing. PowderQuest and Snoventures offer inclusive packages to all the resorts mentioned. Ski weeks without guides run in the $730–$800 range. PowderQuest's main focus is guided tours of 8–16 days, with time spent at as many as seven resorts in both Argentina and Chile. Myths and Mountains has an 11-day trip to Portillo led by Rusty Crook, a former World Cup skier, while Ladatco offers packages to Valle Nevado, Portillo, and Chillán.

PORTUGUESE VOCABULARY

English	Portuguese	Pronunciation

Basics

English	Portuguese	Pronunciation
Yes/no	Sim/Não	**see**ing/nown
Please	Por favor	pohr fah-**vohr**
May I?	Posso?	**poh**-sso
Thank you (very much)	(Muito) obrigado	(**moo**yn-too) o-bree **gah**-doh
You're welcome	De nada	day **nah**-dah
Excuse me	Com licença	con lee-**ssehn**-ssah
Pardon me/what did you say?	Desculpe/O que disse?	dcs-**kool** peh/o.k. **dih**-say?
Could you tell me?	Poderia me dizer?	po-day-**ree**-ah mee dee-**zehrr**?
I'm sorry	Sinto muito	**seen**-too **moo**yn-too
Good morning!	Bom dia!	bohn **dee**-ah
Good afternoon!	Boa tarde!	**boh**-ah **tahr**-dee
Good evening!	Boa noite!	**boh**-ah **noh**ee-tee
Goodbye!	Adeus!/Até logo!	ah-**dehoos**/ah-**teh loh**-go
Mr./Mrs.	Senhor/Senhora	sen-**yor**/sen-**yohr**-ah
Miss	Senhorita	sen-yo-**ri**-tah
Pleased to meet you	Muito prazer	**moo**yn-too prah-**zehr**
How are you?	Como vai?	**koh**-mo **vah**-ee
Very well, thank you	Muito bem, obrigado	**moo**yn-too **beh**-in o-bree-**gah**-doh
And you?	E o(a) Senhor(a)?	eh oh sen-**yor**(**yohr**-ah)
Hello (on the telephone)	Alô	ah-**low**

Numbers

1	um/uma	oom/**oom**-ah
2	dois	**doh**ees
3	três	**treh**ys
4	quatro	**kwa**-troh
5	cinco	**seen**-koh
6	seis	**seh**ys
7	sete	**seh**-tee
8	oito	**oh**ee-too

9	nove	**noh**-vee
10	dez	**deh**-ees
11	onze	**ohn**-zee
12	doze	**doh**-zee
13	treze	**treh**-zee
14	quatorze	kwa-**tohr**-zee
15	quinze	**keen**-zee
16	dezesseis	deh-zeh-**sehy**s
17	dezessete	deh-zeh-**seh**-tee
18	dezoito	deh-**zoh**ee-toh
19	dezenove	deh-zeh-**noh**-vee
20	vinte	**veen**-tee
21	vinte e um	**veen**-tee eh **oom**
30	trinta	**treen**-tah
32	trinta e dois	**treen**-ta eh **doh**ees
40	quarenta	kwa-**rehn**-ta
43	quarenta e três	kwa-**rehn**-ta e **treh**ys
50	cinquenta	seen-**kwehn**-tah
54	cinquenta e quatro	seen-**kwehn**-tah e **kwa**-troh
60	sessenta	seh-**sehn**-tah
65	sessenta e cinco	seh-**sehn**-tah e **seen**-ko
70	setenta	seh-**tehn**-tah
76	setenta e seis	seh-**tehn**-ta e **seh**ys
80	oitenta	ohee-**tehn**-ta
87	oitenta e sete	ohee-**tehn**-ta e **seh**-tee
90	noventa	noh-**vehn**-ta
98	noventa e oito	noh-**vehn**-ta e **oh**ee-too
100	cem	**seh**-ing
101	cento e um	**sehn**-too e **oom**
200	duzentos	doo-**zehn**-tohss
500	quinhentos	key-**nyehn**-tohss
700	setecentos	seh-teh-**sehn**-tohss
900	novecentos	noh-veh-**sehn**-tohss
1,000	mil	meel
2,000	dois mil	**doh**ees meel
1,000,000	um milhão	oom mee-lee-**ahon**

Colors

black	preto	**preh**-toh
blue	azul	a-**zool**
brown	marrom	mah-**hohm**
green	verde	**vehr**-deh
pink	rosa	**roh**-zah
purple	roxo	**roh**-choh
orange	laranja	lah-**rahn**-jah
red	vermelho	vehr-**meh**-lyoh
white	branco	**brahn**-coh
yellow	amarelo	ah-mah-**reh**-loh

Days of the Week

Sunday	Domingo	doh-**meehn**-goh
Monday	Segunda-feira	seh-**goon**-dah **fey**-rah
Tuesday	Terça-feira	**tehr**-sah **fey**-rah
Wednesday	Quarta-feira	**kwahr**-tah **fey**-rah
Thursday	Quinta-feira	**keen**-tah **fey**-rah
Friday	Sexta-feira	**sehss**-tah **fey**-rah
Saturday	Sábado	**sah**-bah-doh

Months

January	Janeiro	jah-**ney**-roh
February	Fevereiro	feh-veh-**rey**-roh
March	Março	**mahr**-soh
April	Abril	ah-**breel**
May	Maio	**my**-oh
June	Junho	gy**oo**-nyoh
July	Julho	gy**oo**-lyoh
August	Agosto	ah-**ghost**-toh
September	Setembro	seh-**tehm**-broh
October	Outubro	owe-**too**-broh
November	Novembro	noh-**vehm**-broh
December	Dezembro	deh-**zehm**-broh

Useful Phrases

Do you speak English?	Fala inglês?	**fah**-lah een-**glehs**?
I don't speak Portuguese.	Não falo português.	nown **fah**-loh pohr-too-**ghehs**
I don't understand (you)	Não lhe entendo	nown ly**eh** ehn-**tehn**-doh

I understand	Eu entendo	**eh**-oo ehn-**tehn**-doh
I don't know	Não sei	nown say
I am American/ British	Sou americano (americana)/inglês (inglêsa)	sow a-meh-ree-**cah**-noh (a-meh-ree-**cah**-nah)/een-**glehs** (een-**gleh**-sa)
What's your name?	Como se chama?	**koh**-moh seh **shah**-mah
My name is . . .	Meu nome é . . .	mehw **noh**-meh eh
What time is it?	Que horas são?	keh **oh**-rahss **sa**-ohn
It is one, two, three . . . o'clock	É uma/Saõ duas, três . . . hora/ horas	eh **oom**-ah/**sa**-ohn **oo**mah, **doo**-ahss, **treh**ys **oh**-rah/**oh**-rahs
Yes, please/No, thank you	Sim por favor/ Não obrigado	seing pohr fah-**vohr**/ nown o-bree-**gah**-doh
How?	Como?	**koh**-moh
When?	Quando?	**kwahn**-doh
This/Next week	Esta/Próxima semana	**ehss**-tah/**proh**-see-mah seh-**mah**-nah
This/Next month	Este/Próximo mêz	**ehss**-teh/**proh**-see-moh mehz
This/Next year	Este/Próximo ano	**ehss**-teh/**proh**-see-moh **ah**-noh
Yesterday/today tomorrow	Ontem/hoje amanhã	**ohn**-tehn/**oh**-jeh/ ah-mah-**nyan**
This morning/ afternoon	Esta manhã/ tarde	**ehss**-tah mah-**nyan**/ **tahr**-deh
Tonight	Hoje a noite	**oh**-jeh ah **noh**ee-tee
What?	O que?	oh **keh**
What is it?	O que é isso?	oh **keh** eh **ee**-soh
Why?	Por quê?	pohr-**keh**
Who?	Quem?	**keh**-in
Where is . . . ?	Onde é . . . ?	**ohn**-deh **eh**
the train station?	a estação de trem?	ah es-tah-**sah**-on deh train
the subway station?	a estação de metrô?	ah es-tah-**sah**-on deh meh-**tro**
the bus stop?	a parada do ônibus?	ah pah-**rah**-dah doh **oh**-nee-boos
the post office?	o correio?	oh coh-**hay**-yoh
the bank?	o banco?	oh **bahn**-koh
the hotel?	o hotel . . . ?	oh oh-**tell**
the cashier?	o caixa?	oh **kah**y-shah
the museum?	o museo . . . ?	oh moo-**zeh**-oh
the hospital?	o hospital?	oh ohss-pee-**tal**

the elevator?	o elevador?	oh eh-leh-vah-**dohr**
the bathroom?	o banheiro?	oh bahn-**yey**-roh
the beach?	a praia de . . . ?	ah **prahy**-yah deh
Here/there	Aqui/ali	ah-**kee**/ah-**lee**
Open/closed	Aberto/fechado	ah-**behr**-toh/feh-**shah**-doh
Left/right	Esquerda/direita	ehs-**kehr**-dah/dee-**ray**-tah
Straight ahead	Em frente	ehyn **frehn**-teh
Is it near/far?	É perto/longe?	eh **pehr**-toh/**lohn**-jeh
I'd like to buy . . .	Gostaria de comprar . . .	gohs-tah-**ree**-ah deh cohm-**prahr** . . .
a bathing suit	um maiô	oom mahy-**owe**
a dictionary	um dicionário	oom dee-seeoh-**nah**-reeoh
a hat	um chapéu	oom shah-**peh**oo
a magazine	uma revista	**oo**mah heh-**vees**-tah
a map	um mapa	oom **mah**-pah
a postcard	cartão postal	kahr-**town** pohs-**tahl**
sunglasses	óculos escuros	**ah**-koo-loss ehs-**koo**-rohs
suntan lotion	um óleo de bronzear	oom **oh**-lyoh deh brohn-zeh-**ahr**
a ticket	um bilhete	oom bee-ly**eh**-teh
cigarettes	cigarros	see-**gah**-hose
envelopes	envelopes	eyn-veh-**loh**-pehs
matches	fósforos	**fohs**-foh-rohss
paper	papel	pah-**pehl**
sandals	sandália	sahn-**dah**-leeah
soap	sabonete	sah-bow-**neh**-teh
How much is it?	Quanto custa?	**kwahn**-too **koos**-tah
It's expensive/cheap	Está caro/barato	ehss-**tah kah**-roh/bah-**rah**-toh
A little/a lot	Um pouco/muito	oom **pohw**-koh/**mooyn**-too
More/less	Mais/menos	**mah**-ees/**meh**-nohss
Enough/too much/too little	Suficiente/demais/muito pouco	soo-fee-see-**ehn**-teh/deh-**mah**-ees/**mooyn**-toh **pohw**-koh
Telephone	Telefone	teh-leh-**foh**-neh
Telegram	Telegrama	teh-leh-**grah**-mah
I am ill.	Estou doente.	ehss-**tow** doh-**ehn**-teh
Please call a doctor.	Por favor chame um médico.	pohr fah-**vohr shah**-meh oom **meh**-dee-koh
Help!	Socorro!	soh-**koh**-ho

Help me!	Me ajude!	mee ah-**jyew**-deh
Fire!	Incêndio!	een-**sehn**-deeoh
Caution!/Look out!/ Be careful!	Cuidado!	kooy-**dah**-doh

On the Road

Avenue	Avenida	ah-veh-**nee**-dah
Highway	Estrada	ehss-**trah**-dah
Port	Porto	**pohr**-toh
Service station	Posto de gasolina	**pohs**-toh deh gah-zoh-**lee**-nah
Street	Rua	**who**-ah
Toll	Pedagio	peh-**dah**-jyoh
Waterfront promenade	Beiramar/ orla	behy-rah-**mahrr**/ **ohr**-lah
Wharf	Cais	**kah**-ees

In Town

Block	Quarteirão	kwahr-tehy-**rah**-on
Cathedral	Catedral	kah-teh-**drahl**
Church/temple	Igreja	ee-**greh**-jyah
City hall	Prefeitura	preh-fehy-**too**-rah
Door/gate	Porta/portão	**pohr**-tah/porh-**tah**-on
Entrance/exit	Entrada/saída	ehn-**trah**-dah/ sah-**ee**-dah
Market	Mercado/feira	mehr-**kah**-doh/**fey**-rah
Neighborhood	Bairro	**buy**-ho
Rustic bar	Lanchonete	lahn-shoh-**neh**-teh
Shop	Loja	**loh**-jyah
Square	Praça	**prah**-ssah

Dining Out

A bottle of . . .	Uma garrafa de . . .	**oo**mah gah-**hah**-fah deh
A cup of . . .	Uma xícara de . . .	**oo**mah **shee**-kah-rah deh
A glass of . . .	Um copo de . . .	oom **koh**-poh deh
Ashtray	Um cinzeiro	oom seen-**zeh**y-roh
Bill/check	A conta	ah **kohn**-tah
Bread	Pão	**pah**-on
Breakfast	Café da manhã	kah-**feh** dah mah-**nyan**

Butter	A manteiga	ah mahn-**tehy**-gah
Cheers!	Saúde!	sah-**oo**-deh
Cocktail	Um aperitivo	oom ah-peh-ree-**tee**-voh
Dinner	O jantar	oh **jyahn**-tahr
Dish	Um prato	oom **prah**-toh
Enjoy!	Bom apetite!	bohm ah-peh-**tee**-teh
Fork	Um garfo	**gahr**-foh
Fruit	Fruta	**froo**-tah
Is the tip included?	A gorjeta esta incluída?	ah gohr-**jyeh**-tah ehss-**tah** een-clue-**ee**-dah
Juice	Um suco	oom **soo**-koh
Knife	Uma faca	**oo**mah **fah**-kah
Lunch	O almoço	oh ahl-**moh**-ssoh
Menu	Menu/ cardápio	me-**noo**/ kahr-**dah**-peeoh
Mineral water	Água mineral	**ah**-gooah mee-neh-**rahl**
Napkin	Guardanapo	gooahr-dah-**nah**-poh
No smoking	Não fumante	nown foo-**mahn**-teh
Pepper	Pimenta	pee-**mehn**-tah
Please give me	Por favor me dê	pohr fah-**vohr** mee **deh**
Salt	Sal	sahl
Smoking	Fumante	foo-**mahn**-teh
Spoon	Uma colher	**oo**mah koh-**lyehr**
Sugar	Açúcar	ah-**soo**-kahr
Waiter!	Garçon!	gahr-**sohn**
Water	Água	**ah**-gooah
Wine	Vinho	**vee**-nyoh

SPANISH VOCABULARY

	English	Spanish	Pronunciation
Basics			
	Yes/no	Sí/no	see/no
	Please	Por favor	pore fah-**vore**
	May I?	¿Me permite?	may pair-**mee**-tay
	Thank you (very much)	(Muchas) gracias	(**moo**-chas) **grah**-see-as
	You're welcome	De nada	day **nah**-dah
	Excuse me	Con permiso	con pair-**mee**-so
	Pardon me	¿Perdón?	pair-**dohn**
	Could you tell me?	¿Podría decirme?	po-dree-ah deh-**seer**-meh
	I'm sorry	Lo siento	lo see-**en**-to
	Good morning!	¡Buenos días!	**bway**-nohs **dee**-ahs
	Good afternoon!	¡Buenas tardes!	**bway**-nahs **tar**-dess
	Good evening!	¡Buenas noches!	**bway**-nahs **no**-chess
	Goodbye!	¡Adiós!/¡Hasta luego!	ah-dee-**ohss**/**ah**-stah-**lwe**-go
	Mr./Mrs.	Señor/Señora	sen-**yor**/sen-**yohr**-ah
	Miss	Señorita	sen-yo-**ree**-tah
	Pleased to meet you	Mucho gusto	**moo**-cho **goose**-to
	How are you?	¿Cómo está usted?	**ko**-mo es-**tah** oo-**sted**
	Very well, thank you.	Muy bien, gracias.	**moo**-ee bee-**en**, **grah**-see-as
	And you?	¿Y usted?	ee oos-**ted**
	Hello (on the telephone)	Diga	**dee**-gah
Numbers			
	1	un, uno	oon, **oo**-no
	2	dos	dos
	3	tres	tress
	4	cuatro	**kwah**-tro
	5	cinco	**sink**-oh
	6	seis	saice
	7	siete	see-**et**-eh
	8	ocho	**o**-cho

9	nueve	new-**eh**-vey
10	diez	dee-**es**
11	once	**ohn**-seh
12	doce	**doh**-seh
13	trece	**treh**-seh
14	catorce	ka-**tohr**-seh
15	quince	**keen**-seh
16	dieciséis	dee-**es**-ee-**saice**
17	diecisiete	dee-**es**-ee-see-**et**-eh
18	dieciocho	dee-**es**-ee-**o**-cho
19	diecinueve	**dee-es**-ee-new-**ev**-ah
20	veinte	**vain**-teh
21	veinte y uno/ veintiuno	**vain**-te-**oo**-noh
30	treinta	**train**-tah
32	treinta y dos	train-tay-**dohs**
40	cuarenta	kwah-**ren**-tah
43	cuarenta y tres	kwah-**ren**-tay-**tress**
50	cincuenta	seen-**kwen**-tah
54	cincuenta y cuatro	seen-**kwen**-tay **kwah**-tro
60	sesenta	sess-**en**-tah
65	sesenta y cinco	sess-**en**-tay **seen**-ko
70	setenta	set-**en**-tah
76	setenta y seis	set-**en**-tay **saice**
80	ochenta	oh-**chen**-tah
87	ochenta y siete	oh-**chen**-tay see-**yet**-eh
90	noventa	no-**ven**-tah
98	noventa y ocho	no-**ven**-tah-**o**-choh
100	cien	see-**en**
101	ciento uno	see-**en**-toh **oo**-noh
200	doscientos	doh-see-**en**-tohss
500	quinientos	keen-**yen**-tohss
700	setecientos	set-eh-see-**en**-tohss
900	novecientos	no-veh-see-**en**-tohss
1,000	mil	meel
2,000	dos mil	dohs meel
1,000,000	un millón	oon meel-**yohn**

Colors

black	negro	**neh**-groh
blue	azul	ah-**sool**
brown	café	kah-**feh**
green	verde	**ver**-deh
pink	rosa	**ro**-sah
purple	morado	mo-**rah**-doh
orange	naranja	na-**rahn**-hah
red	rojo	**roh**-hoh
white	blanco	**blahn**-koh
yellow	amarillo	ah-mah-**ree**-yoh

Days of the Week

Sunday	domingo	doe-**meen**-goh
Monday	lunes	**loo**-ness
Tuesday	martes	**mahr**-tess
Wednesday	miércoles	me-**air**-koh-less
Thursday	jueves	hoo-**ev**-ess
Friday	viernes	vee-**air**-ness
Saturday	sábado	**sah**-bah-doh

Months

January	enero	eh-**neh**-roh
February	febrero	feh-**breh**-roh
March	marzo	**mahr**-soh
April	abril	ah-**breel**
May	mayo	**my**-oh
June	junio	**hoo**-nee-oh
July	julio	**hoo**-lee-yoh
August	agosto	ah-**ghost**-toh
September	septiembre	sep-tee-**em**-breh
October	octubre	oak-**too**-breh
November	noviembre	no-vee-**em**-breh
December	diciembre	dee-see-**em**-breh

Useful Phrases

Do you speak English?	¿Habla usted inglés?	**ah**-blah oos-**ted** in-**glehs**
I don't speak Spanish	No hablo español	no **ah**-bloh es-pahn-**yol**
I don't understand (you)	No entiendo	no en-tee-**en**-doh

I understand (you)	Entiendo	en-tee-**en**-doh
I don't know	No sé	no seh
I am American/ British	Soy americano (americana)/ inglés(a)	soy ah-meh-ree-**kah**-no (ah-meh-ree-**kah**-nah)/ in-**glehs(ah)**
What's your name?	¿Cómo se llama usted?	koh-mo seh **yah**-mah oos-**ted**
My name is . . .	Me llamo . . .	may **yah**-moh
What time is it?	¿Qué hora es?	keh **o**-rah es
It is one, two, three . . . o'clock.	Es la una. . . . Son las dos, tres	es la **oo**-nah/ sohn lahs dohs, tress
Yes, please/ No, thank you	Sí, por favor/ No, gracias	**see** pohr fah-**vor**/ no **grah**-see-us
How?	¿Cómo?	**koh**-mo
When?	¿Cuándo?	**kwahn**-doh
This/Next week	Esta semana/ la semana que entra	**es**-teh seh-**mah**-nah/ lah seh-**mah**-nah keh **en**-trah
This/Next month	Este mes/ el próximo mes	**es**-teh mehs/ el **proke**-see-mo mehs
This/Next year	Este año/el año que viene	**es**-teh **ahn**-yo/el **ahn**-yo keh vee-**yen**-ay
Yesterday/today/ tomorrow	Ayer/hoy/mañana	ah-**yehr**/oy/mahn-**yah**-nah
This morning/ afternoon	Esta mañana/ tarde	**es**-tah mahn-**yah**-nah/ **tar**-deh
Tonight	Esta noche	**es**-tah **no**-cheh
What?	¿Qué?	keh
What is it?	¿Qué es esto?	keh es **es**-toh
Why?	¿Por qué?	pore **keh**
Who?	¿Quién?	kee-**yen**
Where is . . . ?	¿Dónde está . . . ?	**dohn**-deh es-**tah**
the train station?	la estación del tren?	la es-tah-see-**on** del **train**
the subway station?	la estación del Tren subterráneo?	la es-ta-see-**on** del trehn soob-tair-**ron**-a-o
the bus stop?	la parada del autobus?	la pah-**rah**-dah del oh-toh-**boos**
the post office?	la oficina de correos?	la oh-fee-**see**-nah deh koh-**reh**-os
the bank?	el banco?	el **bahn**-koh
the hotel?	el hotel?	el oh-**tel**
the store?	la tienda?	la tee-**en**-dah
the cashier?	la caja?	la **kah**-hah

the museum?	el museo?	el moo-**seh**-oh
the hospital?	el hospital?	el ohss-pee-**tal**
the elevator?	el ascensor?	el ah-**sen**-sohr
the bathroom?	el baño?	el **bahn**-yoh
Here/there	Aquí/allá	ah-**key**/ah-**yah**
Open/closed	Abierto/cerrado	ah-bee-**er**-toh/ser-**ah**-doh
Left/right	Izquierda/derecha	iss-key-**er**-dah/dare-**eh**-chah
Straight ahead	Derecho	dare-**eh**-choh
Is it near/far?	¿Está cerca/lejos?	es-**tah sehr**-kah/**leh**-hoss
I'd like . . .	Quisiera . . .	kee-see-ehr-ah
a room	un cuarto/una habitación	oon **kwahr**-toh/**oo**-nah ah-bee-tah-see-**on**
the key	la llave	lah **yah**-veh
a newspaper	un periódico	oon pehr-ee-**oh**-dee-koh
a stamp	un sello de correo	oon **seh**-yo deh koh-**reh**-oh
I'd like to buy . . .	Quisiera comprar . . .	kee-see-**ehr**-ah kohm-**prahr**
cigarettes	cigarrillos	ce-ga-**ree**-yohs
matches	cerillos	ser-**ee**-ohs
a dictionary	un diccionario	oon deek-see-oh-**nah**-ree-oh
soap	jabón	hah-**bohn**
sunglasses	gafas de sol	**ga**-fahs deh sohl
suntan lotion	loción bronceadora	loh-see-**ohn** brohn-seh-ah-**do**-rah
a map	un mapa	oon **mah**-pah
a magazine	una revista	**oon**-ah reh-**veess**-tah
paper	papel	pah-**pel**
envelopes	sobres	**so**-brehs
a postcard	una tarjeta postal	**oon**-ah tar-**het**-ah post-**ahl**
How much is it?	¿Cuánto cuesta?	**kwahn**-toh **kwes**-tah
It's expensive/cheap	Está caro/barato	es-**tah kah**-roh/bah-**rah**-toh
A little/a lot	Un poquito/mucho	oon poh-**kee**-toh/**moo**-choh
More/less	Más/menos	mahss/**men**-ohss
Enough/too much/too little	Suficiente/demasiado/muy poco	soo-fee-see-**en**-teh/deh-mah-see-**ah**-doh/**moo**-ee poh-koh
Telephone	Teléfono	tel-**ef**-oh-no

Telegram	Telegrama	teh-leh-**grah**-mah
I am ill	Estoy enfermo(a)	es-**toy** en-**fehr**-moh(mah)
Please call a doctor	Por favor llame a un medico	pohr fah-**vor ya**-meh ah oon **med**-ee-koh
Help!	¡Auxilio! ¡Ayuda! ¡Socorro!	owk-**see**-lee-oh/ ah-**yoo**-dah/ soh-**kohr**-roh
Fire!	¡Incendio!	en-**sen**-dee-oo
Caution!/Look out!	¡Cuidado!	kwee-**dah**-doh

On the Road

Avenue	Avenida	ah-ven-**ee**-dah
Broad, tree-lined boulevard	Bulevar	boo-leh-**var**
Fertile plain	Vega	**veh**-gah
Highway	Carretera	car-reh-**ter**-ah
Mountain pass, Street	Puerto Calle	poo-**ehr**-toh **cah**-yeh
Waterfront promenade	Rambla	**rahm**-blah
Wharf	Embarcadero	em-bar-cah-**deh**-ro

In Town

Cathedral	Catedral	cah-teh-**dral**
Church	Templo/Iglesia	**tem**-plo/ee-**glehs**-see-ah
City hall	Casa de gobierno	kah-sah deh go-bee-**ehr**-no
Door, gate	Puerta portón	poo-**ehr**-tah por-**ton**
Entrance/exit	Entrada/salida	en-**trah**-dah/sah-**lee**-dah
Inn, rustic bar, or restaurant	Taverna	tah-**vehr**-nah
Main square	Plaza principal	plah-thah prin-see-**pahl**
Market	Mercado	mer-**kah**-doh
Neighborhood	Barrio	**bahr**-ree-o
Traffic circle	Glorieta	glor-ee-**eh**-tah
Wine cellar, wine bar, or wine shop	Bodega	boh-**deh**-gah

Dining Out

A bottle of . . .	Una botella de . . .	**oo**-nah bo-**teh**-yah deh
A cup of . . .	Una taza de . . .	**oo**-nah **tah**-thah deh
A glass of . . .	Un vaso de . . .	oon **vah**-so deh
Ashtray	Un cenicero	oon sen-ee-**seh**-roh
Bill/check	La cuenta	lah **kwen**-tah
Bread	El pan	el pahn
Breakfast	El desayuno	el deh-sah-**yoon**-oh
Butter	La mantequilla	lah man-teh-**key**-yah
Cheers!	¡Salud!	sah-**lood**
Cocktail	Un aperitivo	oon ah-pehr-ee-**tee**-voh
Dinner	La cena	lah **seh**-nah
Dish	Un plato	oon **plah**-toh
Menu of the day	Menú del día	meh-**noo** del **dee**-ah
Enjoy!	¡Buen provecho!	bwehn pro-**veh**-cho
Fixed-price menu	Menú fijo o turistico	meh-**noo fee**-hoh oh too-**ree**-stee-coh
Fork	El tenedor	el ten-eh-**dor**
Is the tip included?	¿Está incluida la propina?	es-**tah** in-cloo-**ee**-dah lah pro-**pee**-nah
Knife	El cuchillo	el koo-**chee**-yo
Large portion of savory snacks	Raciónes	rah-see-**oh**-nehs
Lunch	La comida	lah koh-**mee**-dah
Menu	La carta, el menú	lah **cart**-ah, el meh-**noo**
Napkin	La servilleta	lah sehr-vee-**yet**-ah
Pepper	La pimienta	lah pee-me-**en**-tah
Please give me	Por favor déme	pore fah-**vor deh**-meh
Salt	La sal	lah sahl
Savory snacks	Tapas	**tah**-pahs
Spoon	Una cuchara	**oo**-nah koo-**chah**-rah
Sugar	El azúcar	el ah-**thu**-kar
Waiter!/Waitress!	¡Por favor Señor/Señorita!	pohr fah-**vor** sen-**yor**/sen-yor-**ee**-tah

SMART TRAVEL TIPS

Finding out about your destination before you leave home means you won't spend time organizing everyday minutiae once you've arrived. You'll be more streetwise when you hit the ground as well, better prepared to explore the aspects of South America that drew you here in the first place. The organizations in this section can provide information to supplement this guide; contact them for up-to-the-minute details, and consult the Essentials sections that end each chapter for facts on the various topics as they relate to the region's countries. Happy landings!

ADDRESSES

The most common street terms in Spanish are *calle* (street), *avenida* (avenue), and *bulevar* (boulevard). The latter two terms are often abbreviated (as *Av.* and *Bul.*); calle is either spelled out or, in some countries, dropped entirely so that the street is referred to by proper name only. In Portuguese *avenida* and *travessa* (lane) are abbreviated (as *Av.* and *Tr.*) while other common terms such as *estrada* (highway) and *rua* (street) aren't. Street numbering doesn't enjoy the wide popularity in South America that it has achieved elsewhere. In some of this guide's listings, establishments have necessarily been identified by the street they're on and their nearest cross street—Calle Bolívar and Av. Valdivia, for example. In extreme cases, where neither address nor cross street is available, you may find the notation "s/n," meaning *sin número,* or "no street number."

AIR TRAVEL

Major airlines in the United States offer the greatest number of daily nonstop flight departures to South America. Leading gateways in South America include Buenos Aires, Caracas, Lima, Quito, Rio de Janeiro, Santiago, and São Paulo. Miami is a favored departure city, but Atlanta, Chicago, Dallas, Fort Lauderdale, Houston, Los Angeles, New York, Newark, Toronto, and Washington, D.C. also have direct flights from North to South America.

CARRIERS

Numerous airline alliances and code-share agreements expand your itinerary options to South America. We list below only direct flights operated by the airlines indicated.

American Airlines has the greatest frequency of service to South America, flying from Miami to Asunción, Bogotá, Buenos Aires, Cali, Caracas, Guayaquil, La Paz, Lima, Maracaibo, Montevideo, Quito, Rio de Janeiro, Santa Cruz, Santiago, and São Paulo; from Dallas to Buenos Aires, Caracas, Lima, Santiago, and São Paulo; and from New York to Buenos Aires, Caracas, and São Paulo.

Continental flies from Houston to Bogotá, Caracas, Lima, Quito, Rio de Janeiro, and São Paulo; and from Newark to Bogotá, Quito, and São Paulo. Delta connects Atlanta with Bogotá, Buenos Aires, Caracas, Lima, Santiago, Rio de Janeiro, and São Paulo. United flies from Washington Dulles to Buenos Aires, Montevideo, and São Paulo; and from Chicago to São Paulo. Air Canada connects Toronto with Bogotá, Caracas, Lima, Santiago, and São Paulo.

Numerous South American airlines have regularly scheduled flights from North America and have alliances with larger airlines that also offer connections to other cities not served by larger airlines.

From North America: Aerolíneas Argentinas flies from Miami and New York to Buenos Aires with connections to cities throughout the country and the continent. Bolivia's LAB Airlines flies from Miami and Washington Dulles to Santa Cruz, with connections to La Paz and all major Bolivian cities as well as to several cities in southern South America. TAM Brazilian Airlines flies from Miami and New York to São Paulo with connections to major Brazilian cities; its Paraguayan affiliate TAM Mercosur connects to Asunción. Varig flies from Miami, New York, and Los Angeles to São Paulo with connections to other Brazilian cities; its Uruguayan partner Pluna connects to Montevideo. In Colombia, Avianca has flights from Miami to Barranquilla, Bogotá, Cali, Cartagena, and Medellín; from New York to Bogotá and Medellín; and from Fort Lauderdale to Bogotá, with connections throughout the country. The LAN Airlines consortium (Chile, Peru, Ecuador, and Argentina) connects Miami with Bogotá, Caracas, Lima, Quito, and Santiago; New York with Guayaquil and Lima; and Los Angeles with Lima; with connections throughout South America. In Venezuela, Aeropostal and Santa Bárbara Airlines both fly from Miami to Caracas, with connections around the country.

From the United Kingdom: British Airways has service from London Heathrow to Buenos Aires, Rio de Janeiro, and São Paulo. Air Canada, American, Continental, Delta, and United fly from London to their respective North American hubs with connections to South America. Varig flies from Heathrow to São Paulo three times weekly. Aerolíneas Argentinas connects London Gatwick with Buenos Aires. Spain's Iberia, with its large network of routes connecting London (via Madrid) with Bogotá, Buenos Aires, Caracas, Guayaquil, Lima, Montevideo, Quito, Rio de Janeiro, Santiago, and São Paulo, is another good bet for U.K. residents.

From Australia & New Zealand: Aerolíneas Argentinas has flights to Buenos Aires from Sydney and Auckland four times weekly. LAN Airlines connects Sydney and Auckland with Santiago three times weekly. Qantas and Air New Zealand have partnerships with North and South American airlines to South America via connections in Los Angeles.

✈ **From North America** Air Canada ☎ 888/247-2262 ⊕ www.aircanada.ca. **American** ☎ 800/433-7300 in North America ⊕ www.aa.com. **Continental** ☎ 800/231-0856, 800/525-0280 in Canada ⊕ www.continental.com. **Delta** ☎ 800/241-4141 in North America ⊕ www.delta.com. **United** ☎ 800/241-6522 in North America ⊕ www.united.com.

✈ **From the U.K.** Aerolíneas Argentinas ☎ 0800/096-9747. **Air Canada** ☎ 0871/220-1111. **American** ☎ 0845/778-9789. **British Airways** ☎ 0870/850-9850 ⊕ www.british-airways.com. **Continental** ☎ 0845/607-6760. **Delta** ☎ 0800/414-767. **Iberia** ☎ 0845/601-2854 ⊕ www.iberia.com. **United** ☎ 0845/844-4777. **Varig** ☎ 0870/120-3020.

✈ **From Australia & New Zealand** Aerolíneas Argentinas ☎ 0845/778-9789 in Australia, 09/379-3675 in New Zealand. **Air New Zealand** ☎ 13-24-76 in Australia, 0800/737-000 in New Zealand ⊕ www.airnz.co.nz. **LAN Airlines** ☎ 1300/361-400 in Australia, 09/977-2233 in New Zealand.

Qantas ☎ 13-13-13 in Australia, 0800/808-767 in New Zealand ⊕ www.qantas.com.au.

🔢 **South American Airlines** **Aerolíneas Argentinas** ☎ 800/333-0276, 800/688-0008 in Canada ⊕ www.aerolineas.com. **Aeropostal** ☎ 888/912-8466 ⊕ www.aeropostal.com. **Avianca** ☎ 800/284-2622 ⊕ www.avianca.us. **LAN Airlines** ☎ 866/435-9526 ⊕ www.lan.com. **LAB Airlines** ☎ 800/337-0918 ⊕ www.labairlines.com. **Santa Bárbara Airlines** ☎ 866/213-2457 ⊕ www.santabarbaraairlines.com. **TAM/TAM Mercosur** ☎ 888/235-9826 ⊕ www.tam-usa.com. **Varig/Pluna** ☎ 800/468-2744 ⊕ www.varig.com.

CHECK-IN & BOARDING

Be prepared to pay hefty airport taxes when leaving any South American country. Fees on international flights from Brazil, for example, can run as high as $40; even domestic flights may incur up to $10 in additional charges in some countries. These are almost always charged when you check in for your flight (although a few airlines have begun to incorporate airport taxes into the price of your ticket), so be sure that you have enough cash. Even though some countries accept dollars, you should **plan to pay taxes with local currency.**

CUTTING COSTS

A few airlines, singly or in collaboration, offer discount air passes that make flying to several destinations within one or more countries more reasonable than buying tickets separately. These must always be reserved and purchased before you leave home and in conjunction with a flight into and out of the country on that carrier. Aerolíneas Argentinas sells a Visit Argentina Pass as well as a South American Pass covering multiple destinations on the continent. Varig offers a Brazil Airpass and TAM offers a similar Frequent Brazil Airpass, covering destinations throughout the country. Both TAM (with its Paraguayan affiliate TAM Mercosur) and Varig (with its Uruguayan affiliate Pluna) participate in the Mercosur Airpass, which covers destinations in Brazil, Argentina, Paraguay, Uruguay, and Chile.

🔢 **Consolidators** **AirlineConsolidator.com** ☎ 888/468-5385 ⊕ www.airlineconsolidator.com; for international tickets. **Best Fares** ☎ 800/880-1234 ⊕ www.bestfares.com; $59.90 annual membership.

Cheap Tickets ☎ 888/922-8849 ⊕ www.cheaptickets.com. **Expedia** ☎ 800/397-3342 or 404/728-8787 ⊕ www.expedia.com. **Hotwire** ☎ 866/468-9473 or 920/330-9418 ⊕ www.hotwire.com. **Onetravel.com** ⊕ www.onetravel.com. **Orbitz** ☎ 888/656-4546 ⊕ www.orbitz.com. **Priceline.com** ⊕ www.priceline.com. **Travelocity** ☎ 888/872-8356, 877/282-2925 in Canada, 0870/111-7061 in the U.K. ⊕ www.travelocity.com.

🔢 **Discount Passes** **Aerolíneas Argentinas** ☎ 800/333-0276, 800/688-0008 in Canada ⊕ www.aerolineas.com.ar. **TAM** ☎ 888/235-9826 ⊕ www.tam-usa.com. **Varig** ☎ 800/735-5526 ⊕ www.varig.com.

ENJOYING THE FLIGHT

International travel between the Americas is less wearying than to Europe or Asia because there's no problem with jet lag. New York, for instance, is in the same time zone as Lima. If you have a choice between a day or a night flight—those to and from southern South America always depart after dark—and you sleep well while flying, take the night flight. Especially en route to the Andean countries, you'll see lovely sunrises over the mountains. ■ TIP→ **Southbound, the best views are usually out windows on the plane's left side.**

FLYING TIMES

The major North American departure points for South American flights are New York (8½ hours to Rio, 11 hours to Buenos Aires, 4 hours to Caracas) and Miami (7 hours to Rio, 8 hours to Buenos Aires, 3½ hours to Caracas). If you're traveling from Canada and connecting in the United States, the Toronto–New York flight is just over an hour; that to Miami is 3 hours (but nonstop flight times from Toronto compare favorably with those from New York). If you're connecting in the United States from London it's about 6 hours to New York and 9 hours to Miami. Expect some 18–20 hours on Sydney–Buenos Aires flights, including the Auckland stopover. Note that flight times may vary according to the type of plane. Flights between South American capitals can be as long as 6 hours (Buenos Aires–Caracas) and as short as 40 minutes (Buenos Aires–Montevideo).

HOW TO COMPLAIN

If your baggage goes astray or your flight goes awry, complain right away. Most carriers require that you **file a claim immediately.** The Aviation Consumer Protection Division of the Department of Transportation publishes *Fly-Rights,* which discusses airlines and consumer issues and is available online. You can also find articles and information on mytravelrights.com, the Web site of the nonprofit Consumer Travel Rights Center.

🔁 **Airline Complaints Office of Aviation Enforcement and Proceedings** (Aviation Consumer Protection Division) ☎ 202/366-2220 ⊕ airconsumer.ost.dot.gov. **Federal Aviation Administration Consumer Hotline** ☎ 866/835-5322 ⊕ www.faa.gov.

RECONFIRMING

Check the status of your flight before you leave for the airport. You can do this on your carrier's Web site, by linking to a flight-status checker (many Web booking services offer these), or by calling your carrier or travel agent.

Always **reconfirm your flights 72 hours in advance,** even if you have a ticket and a reservation. This is particularly true for travel within South America, where flights tend to operate at full capacity.

AIRPORTS

The major South American airports are in: Buenos Aires, Argentina (EZE); Caracas, Venezuela (CCS); Lima, Peru (LIM); Rio de Janeiro, Brazil (GIG); Santiago, Chile (SCL); and São Paulo, Brazil (GRU). A smaller selection of flights jet into Asunción, Paraguay (ASU); Bogotá, Colombia (BOG); Guayaquil, Ecuador (GYE); La Paz, Bolivia (LPB); Montevideo, Uruguay (MVD); Quito, Ecuador (UIO); and Santa Cruz, Bolivia (VVI).

If you're new to this part of the world, your first airport arrival can seem overwhelming. You emerge from customs into a sea of humanity; families of arriving passengers, tour operators, hotel touts, taxi drivers (official and unofficial), and the occasional pickpocket may all turn out to greet arriving flights. Unless someone is waiting to meet you, move on through (and watch your things). Getting to and from the airport won't be the most pleasant aspect of your South American journey. Subway transit to the airports is nearly nonexistent, and bus service, while often cheap, tends to require a serious time commitment and subjecting yourself to crowded conditions if you have a lot of luggage. Taxi fares to city centers vary but can be as steep as $20–$35 in Buenos Aires, Caracas, Lima, Montevideo, Rio, Santiago, and São Paulo, where airports are long distances from downtowns. Most large airports have an official taxi booth where you can arrange for transportation for a regulated price. ■ TIP➜ **If you're concerned about your destination not being understood, write it down on a piece of paper and present it to the bus or taxi driver.**

Airport departure is your final impression of each country you visit. You are expected to check in three hours in advance for an international flight and will likely need all that time; lines move slowly, and security measures are tight. By contrast, check-in procedures for domestic flights are much less time-consuming.

BIKE TRAVEL

The rugged terrain and varying road conditions across the continent pose considerable challenges. If you're adventurous enough to try it, use a mountain bike, since basic touring bikes are too fragile for off-road treks. Better yet, consider a tour operator—many within South America offer bike trips that range in length from a half-day to a week or more. Avoid riding in congested urban areas where it's difficult getting around by car, let alone by bike.

BIKES IN FLIGHT

Most airlines accommodate bikes as luggage, provided they are dismantled and boxed; check with individual airlines about packing requirements. Some airlines sell bike boxes, which are often free at bike shops, for about $20 (bike bags can be considerably more expensive). International travelers often can substitute a bike for a piece of checked luggage at no charge; otherwise, the cost is about $100. Most U.S. and Canadian airlines charge $40–$80 each way.

BUSINESS HOURS

The midday siesta break is slowly disappearing in large cities (though not entirely) as more businesses and offices remain open continuously throughout the day. In smaller cities and towns, for 2–3 hours in the early afternoon, little is open.

BUS TRAVEL

Buses are the primary means of transportation for most South Americans, and buses run regularly almost anywhere there are roads—and some places where the term "road" is used charitably. Accordingly, bus-travel options are much greater than in North America. In particular, Brazil, Chile, and Venezuela have good service. In Bolivia, Ecuador, and Peru, washed-out roads can cause delays of several hours, or cancellations during the worst of the rainy season. Almost everywhere you'll find spectacular views. The low cost of bus travel is its greatest advantage; its greatest drawback is the time it takes to cover the distances involved and, in some countries, allow for delays due to faulty equipment or poor road conditions. When traveling by bus, pack light and dress comfortably and be sure to **keep a close watch on your belongings,** especially in the terminal itself, and during the commotion of boarding and disembarking from the bus.

CLASSES

Various classes of service are offered in every country, with each increase in price buying plusher seats and more leg room. Tickets often include assigned seat numbers for major inter-urban journeys. If you're over 5 feet 10 inches buy the most expensive ticket available and try for front-row seats; otherwise, be prepared for knee pain. In out-of-the-way rural areas, seating is first come, first serve as you board.

Bathrooms, air-conditioning, and in-bus movies or music are common amenities. Chile, on the extreme end of the scale, offers business-class-style sleeper buses with all of the above, plus pillows, blankets, and a bow-tied attendant who serves surprisingly palatable meals. Even in cash-strapped countries, the buses are generally modern and clean. Be prepared, however, to relieve yourself by the side of the road. Food stops are usually made en route, though it's a good idea to bring snacks and water. An additional top layer of clothing comes in handy if it gets cold—or it can serve as a pillow.

FARES & SCHEDULES

Bus fares are substantially cheaper than in North America or Europe. You'll usually pay no more than $2 per hour of travel. Competing bus companies serve all major and many minor routes, so it can really pay to shop around. Don't plan on the clerk speaking much English. Write down your destination on a piece of paper if you don't speak the local language.

PAYING

Tickets are sold at bus-company offices and at city bus terminals. Note that in larger cities there may be different terminals for buses to different destinations, and some small towns may not have a terminal at all. Instead you'll be picked up and dropped off at the bus company's office. You should **expect to pay with cash,** as credit cards aren't always accepted, and traveler's checks, never.

RESERVATIONS

Reservations aren't necessary except for trips to popular destinations during high season. Summer weekends and major holidays are the busiest times. You should arrive at bus stations early for travel during peak seasons.

CAMERAS & PHOTOGRAPHY

You should always ask permission before taking someone's picture, and never treat them as if they are simply part of the landscape. People in remote villages often don't like being photographed, and scenes of abject poverty are best avoided as photo subjects. Many of the people in traditional dress hanging around heavily touristed areas expect you to pay them if you take their photo. Photographing military installations and civilian planes taking off and landing is is a big no-no, and in some countries guards may not want you photographing government buildings.

VIDEOS

Bolivia, Brazil, Chile, Colombia, Ecuador, Peru, and Venezuela use the same standard for video as the United States and Canada (the NTSC). Argentina, Paraguay, and Uruguay fall in line with Australia, New Zealand, and most nations of Western Europe by using the PAL standard.

CAR RENTAL

Rental costs are high compared to those in the United States. A midsize vehicle might run you between $60 and $100 per day, including insurance.

🚗 **Alamo** ☎ 800/327-9633 ⊕ www.alamo.com. **Avis** ☎ 800/331-1212, 800/879-2847 in Canada, 0870/606-0100 in the U.K., 02/9353-9000 in Australia, 09/526-2847 in New Zealand ⊕ www.avis.com. **Budget** ☎ 800/527-0700, 800/268-8900 in Canada, 1300/794-344 in Australia, 09/526-2847 in New Zealand ⊕ www.budget.com. **Hertz** ☎ 800/654-3131, 800/263-0600 in Canada, 0870/844-8844 in the U.K., 02/9669-2444 in Australia, 09/256-8690 in New Zealand ⊕ www.hertz.com. **National Car Rental** ☎ 800/227-7368 ⊕ www.nationalcar.com.

CUTTING COSTS

Fly-drive packages, popular in Europe, are rare in South America. To make arrangements before you leave home, **book through a travel agent familiar with the region.** Although international car-rental agencies have better service and maintenance track records than local firms (they also provide better breakdown assistance), your best bet at getting a good rate is to **rent from local companies.** Only reserve ahead (and check that a confirmed reservation guarantees you a car) if you plan to rent during a holiday period.

The continent's major gateway cities are the best places for renting cars, with their city offices offering slightly better rates than airport branches. Plenty of local companies offer good service and lower rates than branches of the major international firms. No matter who you rent from, make sure the agent notes any dents and nicks in the vehicle on your rental form, to avoid your having to pay for the damage when you return the car.

Consider hiring a car and driver through your hotel concierge, or, easier yet, **make a deal with a taxi driver** for some extended sightseeing at a longer-term rate. Drivers often charge an hourly rate, regardless of the distance traveled. You'll have to pay cash, but you'll often spend less than you would for a rental car.

INSURANCE

When driving a rented car you are generally responsible for any damage to or loss of the vehicle. You also may be liable for any property damage or personal injury that you may cause while driving. Before you rent, see what coverage you already have under the terms of your personal auto-insurance policy and credit cards.

Some destinations are rough on vehicles; Chile's rugged Southern Coast is an example. You're expected to pay out of pocket for common damages such as cracked or broken windshields when you travel in such remote locales. Repairing flat tires is your responsibility everywhere.

Always **give the rental car a once-over** to make sure that the headlights, jack, and tires (including the spare) are in working condition.

REQUIREMENTS & RESTRICTIONS

Your own driver's license is acceptable in most countries in South America. However, an International Driver's Permit (IDP), available from most national automobile associations, is a good idea, as it provides a document in the local language—more readily recognized by police authorities. Argentina and Colombia require an IDP from those who wish to rent a car. Minimum driving ages vary from country to country. Some countries impose a maximum age of 65 or 70.

SURCHARGES

Before you pick up a car in one city and leave it in another, ask about drop-off charges or one-way service fees, which can be substantial. Also inquire about early-return policies; some rental agencies charge extra if you return the car before the time specified in your contract while others give you a refund for the days not used. Most agencies note the tank's fuel level on your contract; to avoid a hefty refueling fee, return the car with the same tank level. If the tank was full, refill it just before you turn in the car, but be aware that gas stations near the rental outlet may overcharge. It's almost never a deal to buy a tank of gas with the car when you rent it; the understanding is that you'll return it empty, but some fuel usually remains.

CAR TRAVEL

Driving in South America isn't easy. Congested city streets are chaotic at best, life-threatening at worst; country roads aren't as crowded, but the poor conditions and lack of signs when you get off the major routes are discouraging. Highways are generally well maintained but sometimes clogged by construction equipment. That said, many seasoned travelers enjoy driving in South America. Certain areas are best explored on your own in a car: in Venezuela, Isla Margarita, and the mountains of Mérida; in Chile, the Central Valley and the Lake District; in Peru, Ica and the Nazca plain on the road from Lima.

Road conditions in South America vary from those of fast superhighways to dirt tracks. You'll find buses making stops and pedestrians walking along the sides of roads that are supposedly freeways. Negotiating the many traffic circles will be old hat to European visitors but will seem tricky to North Americans. Local driving styles tend toward the aggressive. The long midday break still holds sway over much of the continent, and that translates into four rush hours each weekday rather than two. Night driving is best avoided outside cities and towns. Make an effort to reach your destination before dark. There is the remote risk of robbery, but more important, you'll share the road with pedestrians of the two- and four-legged variety; they'll see you, but not necessarily vice versa. Some common-sense rules of the road: before you set out, establish an itinerary and **ask about gas stations.** Be sure to plan your daily driving distance conservatively and **avoid driving after dark.** Always **obey speed limits and traffic regulations,** even if it appears that local drivers do not. Above all, **if you get a traffic ticket, don't argue**—and plan to spend longer than you want settling it. (However, don't give in to any pressure to pay your fine to the traffic officer on the spot, a scam that occurs in some countries.)

GASOLINE

With the exception of oil-rich Venezuela, gasoline prices in South America are at least as high as in the United States and often as much as higher European prices. Fuel is sold by the liter, although Peru uses the *galón* as its unit of sale. Unleaded gas is still widely available. Stations provide full service (self-service pumping is almost unheard of). Attendants often offer to check your oil and tires and clean your windshield. Enjoy that extra bit of attention that disappeared long ago back home.

CHILDREN IN SOUTH AMERICA

Know in advance that if you are renting a car in South America it's very difficult to arrange for a car seat.

FOOD

Local food could be your biggest dilemma if your child is a finicky eater. The prevalence of rice and chicken dishes (if they're not prepared with much spice) and the wide variety of fruit juices may prove a blessing to young palates. American fast-food chains such as McDonald's and Pizza Hut can be found in large cities, and might just provide that needed taste of home.

LODGING

Most hotels in South America allow children under a certain age to stay in their parents' room at no extra charge, but others charge for them as extra adults; be sure to find out the cutoff age for children's discounts. Some large hotels, often those that are branches of U.S. chains, or those in resort areas, have children's programs, or baby-sitters.

PRECAUTIONS

Children must have all their inoculations up to date before traveling abroad. All South American countries have strict requirements for children traveling alone or with one parent, and insist on documented approval from both parents, whether present or not, for the child to travel. Make sure that health precautions, such as what to drink and eat, are applied to the whole family. A bout of traveler's diarrhea may be an mere inconvenience to you as an adult, but can result in serious dehydration to infants and toddlers. Many pharmacies sell an equivalent to the product Pedialyte to replenish lost fluids and electrolytes.

SIGHTS & ATTRACTIONS

Places that are especially appealing to children are indicated by a rubber-duckie icon (🦆) in the margin.

SUPPLIES & EQUIPMENT

English-language books for kids are hard to find in many places. Disposable diapers are easy to find in supermarkets in metropolitan areas; baby formula is available as well, but not as easy to find.

COMPUTERS ON THE ROAD

If you're traveling with a laptop, carry a spare battery, a universal adapter plug, and a converter if your computer isn't dual voltage. Ask about electrical surges before plugging in your computer. Keep your disks out of the sun and avoid excessive heat for both your computer and disks. In many South American countries, carrying a laptop computer could make you a target for thieves; conceal your laptop in a generic bag, and keep it close to you at all times. Note that South America's luxury hotels typically offer business centers with computers. Wi-Fi is still in its infancy here, but a few large hotels are beginning to use it as a selling point to guests.

CUSTOMS & DUTIES

🇦🇺 **Australian Customs Service** ☎ 02/6275-6666 or 1300/363263, 02/8334-7444 or 1800/020-504 quarantine-inquiry line ⊕ www.customs.gov.au. **Canada Border Services Agency** ☎ 800/461-9999 in Canada, 204/983-3500, 506/636-5064 ⊕ www.cbsa.gc.ca. **New Zealand Customs** ☎ 04/473-6099 or 0800/428-786 ⊕ www.customs.govt.nz. **HM Customs and Excise** ☎ 0845/010-9000 or 0208/929-0152 advice service, 0208/929-6731 or 0208/910-3602 complaints ⊕ www.hmce.gov.uk. **U.S. Customs and Border Protection** ⊕ www.cbp.gov ☎ 877/227-5551, 202/354-1000.

EATING & DRINKING

North Americans sometimes think everything south of the Río Grande will be just like Mexico. But *way* south of the border, you can sample everything from Argentina's *parrilladas* (grilled beef steaks) to Brazil's *caldeirada* (spicy fish stew) to Peru's *ají de gallina* (hen in cream sauce). You won't find tacos and enchiladas in South America unless you dine in a Mexican restaurant.

The restaurants (all of which are indicated by a ✕) that we list are the cream of the crop in each price category. Properties indicated by a ✕🏠 are lodging establishments whose restaurant warrants a special trip.

MEALS & SPECIALTIES

"Breakfast," "lunch," and "dinner" are *desayuno, almuerzo,* and *cena,* respectively, in Spanish, and *café-da-manhã, almoço,* and *jantar* in Portuguese.

MEALTIMES

During the week, most restaurants in urban and resort areas serve lunch from noon until mid-afternoon, and then open again for dinner from 7 or 8 PM until well into the evening. Buenos Aires is downright legendary for late-night dining, but in most places you'll be disappointed if you insist on dinner at 6. Restaurants tend to remain open all day on Sundays, when families traditionally eat out. Small, basic, family-run restaurants, especially in rural areas, serve lunch, but often not dinner, and might close on Sunday. Lunch is usually the best bargain of the day at any dining establishment, with most restaurants offering a prix-fixe menu, including appetizer, main course, and dessert. Unless otherwise noted, the restaurants listed in this guide are open daily for lunch and dinner.

PAYING

Most large restaurants accept credit cards; smaller ones rarely do. Almost all will prefer if you pay in cash. (Businesses are charged high processing fees for credit-card use.)

RESERVATIONS & DRESS

Reservations are always a good idea; we mention them only when they're essential or not accepted. Book as far ahead as you can, and reconfirm as soon as you arrive. (Large parties should always call ahead to check the reservations policy.) We mention dress only when men are required to wear a jacket or a jacket and tie.

WINE, BEER & SPIRITS

Each South American country takes pride in its locally brewed beers, and most are tasty bargains, always lower priced than North American or European imports. Chilean and Argentine wines are world-famous and are drunk all over the continent. High taxes and mark-ups mean you'll pay dearly for spirits.

ELECTRICITY

To use electric-powered equipment purchased in the U.S. or Canada, **bring a converter and adapter.** Unlike in the United States and Canada—which have a 110- to 120-volt standard—the current in Argentina, Chile, Paraguay, Peru, Uruguay, and the urban areas of Brazil is 220 volts to 240 volts, 50 cycles alternating current (AC). Ecuador, Colombia, Venezuela, and rural Brazil use currents of 110 volts, 60 cycles alternating current. To use 110/120-volt equipment in a 220/240 country, bring a converter. Also, many wall outlets in South America take Continental-type plugs, which have two round prongs. To accommodate U.S.-style flat-prong plugs, you'll need an adapter. **Consider buying a universal adapter;** the Swiss Army knife of adapters, a universal has several types of plugs in one handy unit.

If your appliances are dual-voltage, you'll need only an adapter. Don't use 110-volt outlets marked FOR SHAVERS ONLY for high-wattage appliances such as blow-dryers. Most laptops operate equally well on 110 and 220 volts and so require only an adapter. Occasional blackouts, brownouts, and power surges can wreak havoc with expensive appliances. A surge protector will shield a laptop computer.

EMBASSIES & CONSULATES

For information on Australian, Canadian, New Zealand, U.K., and U.S. embassies and consulates in South America, *see* the individual country Essentials section at the end of each chapter.

Embassies in Australia Argentina ⌂ 7 National Circuit, Barton, ACT 2600 ☏ 02/6273-9111. **Brazil** ⌂ 19 Forster Crescent, Yarralumla, ACT 2600

☏ 616/6273-2372. **Chile** ⌂ 10 Culgoa Circuit, O'Malley, ACT 2606 ☏ 02/6286-2430. **Ecuador** ⌂ 6 Pindari Crescent, O'Malley, ACT 2606 ☏ 02/6286-4021. **Peru** ⌂ 43 Culgoa Circuit, O'Malley, ACT 2606 ☏ 02/6286-9507. **Uruguay** ⌂ 24 Brisbane Ave., Barton, ACT 2600 ☏ 02/6273-9100. **Venezuela** ⌂ 7 Culgoa Circuit, O'Malley, ACT 2606 ☏ 02/6290-2968.

Embassies in Canada Argentina ⌂ 81 Metcalfe St., 7th floor, Ottawa, Ontario K1P 6K7 ☏ 613/236-2351. **Bolivia** ⌂ 130 Albert St., Suite 416, Ottawa, Ontario K1P 5G4 ☏ 613/236-5730. **Brazil** ⌂ 450 Wilbrod St., Ottawa, Ontario K1N 6M8 ☏ 613/237-1090. **Chile** ⌂ 50 O'Connor St., Suite 1413, Ottawa, Ontario K1P 6L2 ☏ 613/235-4402. **Colombia** ⌂ 360 Albert St., Suite 1002, Ottawa, Ontario K1R 7X7 ☏ 613/230-3760. **Ecuador** ⌂ 50 O'Connor St., Suite 316, Ottawa, Ontario K1P 6L2 ☏ 613/563-8206. **Paraguay** ⌂ 151 Slater St., Suite 501, Ottawa, Ontario K1P 5H3 ☏ 613/567-1283. **Peru** ⌂ 130 Albert St., Suite 1901, Ottawa, Ontario K1P 5G4 ☏ 613/238-1777. **Uruguay** ⌂ 130 Albert St., Suite 1905, Ottawa, Ontario K1P 5G4 ☏ 613/234-2727. **Venezuela** ⌂ 32 Range Rd., Ottawa, Ontario K1N 8J4 ☏ 613/235-5151.

Embassies in New Zealand Argentina ⌂ 142 Lambton Quay, Wellington ☏ 04/472-8330. **Brazil** ⌂ 10 Brandon St., Wellington ☏ 04/473-3516. **Chile** ⌂ 19 Bolton St., Wellington ☏ 04/471-6270. **Ecuador (Consulate)** ⌂ 2 St. Martins La., Auckland ☏ 09/303-0590. **Peru** ⌂ 40 Mercer St., Wellington ☏ 04/499-8087. **Uruguay (Consulate)** ⌂ 22 Oakland Mews, Canterbury ☏ 03/344-5288.

Embassies in the U.K. Argentina ⌂ 65 Brook St., London W1K 4AH ☏ 020/7318-1300. **Bolivia** ⌂ 106 Eaton Sq., London SW1W 9AD ☏ 020/7235-4248. **Brazil** ⌂ 32 Green St., Mayfair, London W1K 7AT ☏ 020/7499-0877. **Chile** ⌂ 12 Devonshire St., London W1G 7DS ☏ 020/7580-6392. **Colombia** ⌂ Flat 3A, 3 Hans Crescent, London SW1X 0LN ☏ 020/7589-9177. **Ecuador** ⌂ Flat 3B, 3 Hans Crescent, London SW1X 0LS ☏ 020/7584-2648. **Paraguay** ⌂ 344 High St., Kensington, London W14 8NS ☏ 020/7610-4180. **Peru** ⌂ 52 Sloane St., London SW1X 9SP ☏ 020/7235-1917. **Uruguay** ⌂ 2nd fl., 140 Brompton Rd., London SW3 1HY ☏ 020/7589-8835. **Venezuela** ⌂ 1 Cromwell Rd., London SW7 2DH ☏ 020/7584-4206.

Embassies in the U.S. Argentina ⌂ 1600 New Hampshire Ave. NW, Washington, DC 20009 ☏ 202/238-6400. **Bolivia** ⌂ 3014 Massachusetts Ave. NW, Washington, DC 20008 ☏ 202/483-4410. **Brazil** ⌂ 3006 Massachusetts Ave. NW, Washington, DC 20008 ☏ 202/238-2700. **Chile** ⌂ 1732 Massachusetts Ave. NW, Washington, DC 20036 ☎ 202/785–1746 Ext. 145. **Colombia** ✉ 2118 Leroy Pl. NW, Washington, DC 20008 ☎ 202/387-8338. **Ecuador** ✉ 2535 15th St. NW, Washington, DC 20009 ☎ 202/234-7200. **Paraguay** ✉ 2400 Massachusetts Ave. NW, Washington, DC 20008 ☎ 202/483-6960. **Peru** ✉ 1700 Massachusetts Ave. NW, Washington, DC 20036 ☎ 202/833-9860. **Uruguay** ✉ 1913 Eye St., NW, Washington, DC 20006 ☎ 202/331-1313. **Venezuela** ✉ 1099 30th St. NW, Washington, DC 20007 ☎ 202/342-2214.

ETIQUETTE & BEHAVIOR

Attitudes range from the strict Catholicism of a country like Ecuador to the anything-goes outlook of Brazil. In general, however, Latin Americans lean toward conservative dress and quiet behavior. To feel more comfortable, take a cue from what the locals are wearing. Except in beach cities, men typically don't wear shorts and women don't wear short skirts. Bathing suits are fine on beaches, but cover up before you head back into town. People dress up to enter churches, so you might get dirty looks if you stroll in wearing a T-shirt or halter top.

The conservative dress belies the warmth and friendliness of most all South Americans. Don't be afraid to smile in the streets, ask for directions, or strike up a conversation with a local. Be advised, however, that South Americans consider it impolite not to give you directions, so they may prefer to give you well-meaning, but incorrect, directions instead of none at all. Unless you're in a fast-paced city like Buenos Aires or Rio, life here is lived at a slower pace than you're probably accustomed to, and there's an unwavering appreciation of family and friendship; a store clerk may place equal importance on chatting with you or her neighbor as on tending to your business needs. Knowing this will help you understand why things may take a little longer to get done.

BUSINESS ETIQUETTE

Business protocol varies from country to country, but is a mix of formal (dress as you would for a meeting back home) and informal (exchange pleasantries before getting down to business). South Americans look with some wariness at what they perceive to be the aggressive approach to business taken by their U.S. counterparts.

GAY & LESBIAN TRAVEL

Brazil is South America's most popular destination for gay and lesbian travelers, and major cities—such as Rio, São Paulo, and Salvador—have numerous gay bars, organizations, and publications. Argentines hold a liberal attitude toward homosexuality, and Buenos Aires enjoys an active gay scene. In Uruguay and Venezuela, gay rights are increasingly discussed, with gay communities in Montevideo and Caracas leading the way. Outside these destinations, however, you may encounter difficulties due to conservative political and religious norms. In Ecuador and Peru, for example, gay acts are illegal and public attitudes toward homosexuality are generally negative. Be discreet. Police harassment still occurs. The local gay scene, if you can find it, is still quite underground.

🏳 **Gay- & Lesbian-Friendly Travel Agencies Different Roads Travel** ☎ 310/289-6000 or 800/429-8747 (Ext. 14 for both) ✉ lgernert@tzell.com. **Skylink Travel and Tour/Flying Dutchmen Travel** ☎ 707/546-9888 or 800/225-5759; serving lesbian travelers.

🏳 **Gay & Lesbian Travel Web Sites** ⊕ www.planetout.com/travel ⊕ www.outandabout.com ⊕ www.gay.com/travel

HEALTH
ALTITUDE SICKNESS

Altitude sickness, or *soroche,* may be a problem when you visit countries along the Andes—Venezuela, Colombia, Ecuador, Peru, Bolivia, Argentina, and Chile. The symptoms are shortness of breath, nausea, and splitting headaches. The best way to prevent it is to take it slow. Spend a few nights at lower elevations before you head higher. If you must fly directly to higher altitudes, plan on doing next to nothing for the first day or two. If you begin to feel ill, a cup of herbal tea made from coca leaves (*mate de coca*) is a legal way (in Andean nations at least) to perk you up. Drinking lots of water, taking frequent naps, and taking over-the-counter analgesics also help. Eliminate or limit alcohol, caffeine, and tobacco intake. If symptoms persist or become severe, return to lower elevations. Note that if you have high blood pressure or a history of heart trouble or are pregnant, check with your doctor before traveling to such heights as those at Cusco, Peru, and La Paz, Bolivia (both above 11,000 feet) and Quito, Ecuador (above 9,000 feet).

DIVERS' ALERT
Do not fly within 24 hours of scuba diving.
Neophyte divers should have a complete physical exam before undertaking a dive. If you have travel insurance, make sure your policy applies to scuba-related injuries, as not all companies provide this coverage.

FOOD & DRINK
The major health risk in South America is *diarrhea*, or traveler's diarrhea, caused by eating contaminated fruit or vegetables or drinking contaminated water. So watch what you eat and stay away from food that is uncooked or has been sitting around. Avoid ice, uncooked food, and unpasteurized milk and milk products, and **drink only bottled water** or water that has been boiled for at least 20 minutes, even when you're brushing your teeth. Eschew ice, often made with unpurified water. Ask for drinks without ice (*sin hielo* in Spanish, *sem gelo* in Portuguese). *Un antidiarreico* is the general Spanish term for antidiarrheal medicine. Drink plenty of purified water or tea—chamomile (*camomila* in Portuguese, *manzanilla* in Spanish) is a good folk remedy. In severe cases, rehydrate yourself with a salt-sugar solution (½ teaspoon salt, *sal* in both languages, and 4 tablespoons sugar, *açúcar* in Portuguese and *azúcar* in Spanish) per quart of water (*agua* in both languages). Some physicians will prescribe a small supply of antibiotics for you to take with you in the event of a bout of traveler's diarrhea—ciprofloxacin and sulfa are most commonly used for this purpose—but they can cause a tendency to sunburn, a potential risk in a warm climate or at a high altitude.

MEDICAL PLANS
No one plans to get sick while traveling, but it happens, so consider signing up with a medical-assistance company. Members get doctor referrals, emergency evacuation or repatriation, hotlines for medical consultation, cash for emergencies, and other assistance.

🚹 **Medical-Assistance Companies International SOS Assistance** ⊕ www.internationalsos.com ✉ 3600 Horizon Blvd., Suite 300, Trevose, PA 19053 ☎ 215/942-8000 or 800/523-6586 ✉ 2211 Norfolk, Suite 517, Houston, TX 77098 ☎ 713/521-7611 ✉ 81 Tiverton Ct., Suite 401, Toronto, ON L3R 0G4 ☎ 905/940-2444 ✉ Landmark House, Hammersmith Bridge Rd., 6th floor, London, W6 9DP ☎ 20/8762-8008 ✉ 12 Chemin Riantbosson, 1217 Meyrin 1, Geneva, Switzerland ☎ 22/785-6464 ✉ 331 N. Bridge Rd., 17-00, Odeon Towers, Singapore 188720 ☎ 6338-7800 ✉ Av. Eugenio Mendoza at Calle 1 Transersal, Caracas, Venezuela ☎ 0212/266-8727.

OVER-THE-COUNTER REMEDIES
Usually, all medications are available only in pharmacies, not in other outlets such as grocery stores. Mild cases of diarrhea may respond to Imodium (known generically as loperamide), Pepto-Bismol (not as strong)—both can be purchased over the counter—and Lomotil, which requires a prescription. Be on the safe side and bring a small supply with you. Aspirin is readily available, as is acetaminophen (sold under the brand names Tylenol and Panadol).

PESTS & OTHER HAZARDS
A large continent with varied climates and terrains means the potential for an equally large variety of maladies; altitude sickness, heat stroke, traveler's diarrhea, dehydration, sunburn, and frostbite are all risks depending on where your travels take you. Use a bit of common sense, watch what you eat, use a high-SPF sunscreen, and you'll likely get through your trip to South America just fine.

SHOTS & MEDICATIONS
All travelers should have up-to-date tetanus boosters, and a hepatitis A inoculation can prevent one of the most common intestinal infections. If you're heading to tropical regions (including parts of Bolivia, Brazil, Colombia, Ecuador, French

Guiana, Guyana, Paraguay, Peru, Suriname, and Venezuela) you should get yellow fever shots. Children traveling to South America should have current inoculations against measles, mumps, rubella, and polio.

According to the Centers for Disease Control (CDC) there's a limited risk of cholera, typhoid, malaria, hepatitis B, dengue, and Chagas' disease. While a few of these you could catch anywhere, most are restricted to jungle areas. If you plan to visit remote regions or stay for more than six weeks, **check with the CDC's International Travelers Hot Line.**

In tropical and subtropical areas with malaria and dengue, which are both carried by mosquitoes, take mosquito nets, wear clothing that covers the body, apply repellent containing DEET, and use a spray against flying insects in living and sleeping areas. Chloroquine is prescribed as a preventative antimalarial agent, though many malarial strains in northern South America are now resistant to chloroquine. Mefloquine, Doxycycline, or Malarone are the preventative drugs of choice in those cases. No vaccine exists against dengue.

⚑ Health Warnings National Centers for Disease Control and Prevention (CDC) ☎ 877/394-8747 international travelers' health line, 800/311-3435 other inquiries, 404/498-1600 Division of Quarantine and international health information ⊕ www.cdc.gov/travel. **Travel Health Online** ⊕ tripprep.com. **World Health Organization** (WHO) ⊕ www.who.int.

HOLIDAYS
Pay attention to legal holidays—they're discussed in individual country chapters—when almost nothing will be open. Two periods deserve special mention in devoutly Catholic South America: *Semana Santa* (Holy Week, between Palm Sunday and Easter) and the week between Christmas and New Year's Day. Businesses often keep very limited hours and may close entirely those weeks. You'll also compete with locals who use those weeks off to travel themselves. Make hotel reservations far in advance if you plan to travel over the Christmas and Easter holidays.

INSURANCE
The most useful travel-insurance plan is a comprehensive policy that includes coverage for trip cancellation and interruption, default, trip delay, and medical expenses (with a waiver for preexisting conditions).

Without insurance you'll lose all or most of your money if you cancel your trip, regardless of the reason. Default insurance covers you if your tour operator, airline, or cruise line goes out of business—the chances of which have been increasing. Trip-delay covers expenses that arise because of bad weather or mechanical delays. Study the fine print when comparing policies.

If you're traveling internationally, a key component of travel insurance is coverage for medical bills incurred if you get sick on the road. Such expenses aren't generally covered by Medicare or private policies. U.K. residents can buy a travel-insurance policy valid for most vacations taken during the year in which it's purchased (but check preexisting-condition coverage). British and Australian citizens need extra medical coverage when traveling overseas.

Always **buy travel policies directly from the insurance company**; if you buy them from a cruise line, airline, or tour operator that goes out of business you probably won't be covered for the agency or operator's default, a major risk. Before making any purchase, review your existing health and home-owner's policies to find what they cover away from home.

⚑ Travel Insurers In the U.S.: **Access America** ☎ 800/729-6021 ⊕ www.accessamerica.com. **Travel Insured International** ☎ 800/243-3174 ⊕ www.travelinsured.com.

⚑ In the U.K.: Association of British Insurers ☎ 020/7600-3333 ⊕ www.abi.org.uk. In Canada: **RBC Insurance** ☎ 800/565-3129 ⊕ www.rbcinsurance.com.

In Australia: **Insurance Council of Australia** ☎ 02/9253-5100 ⊕ www.ica.com.au.

In New Zealand: **Insurance Council of New Zealand** ☎ 04/472-5230 ⊕ www.icnz.org.nz.

INTERNET
Internet access is surprisingly widespread. In addition to full-fledged cybercafés, look for machines set up in phone offices. Rates

range from $1 to $10 an hour. Many up-scale hotels catering to business travelers offer Internet access to their guests among their amenities. If you're logging in to one of the Web-based e-mail sites, know that late afternoon is an especially sluggish time because usage is higher.

South American computer keyboards are not identical to, but do resemble, those in English-speaking countries. Your biggest frustration will probably be finding the @ symbol, which you need to type an e-mail address. If you need to ask, it's called *arroba* in Spanish and Portuguese.

LANGUAGE

In Brazil the language is Portuguese; Spanish is spoken in Argentina, Bolivia, Colombia, Chile, Ecuador, Paraguay, Peru, Uruguay, and Venezuela. French is spoken in French Guiana; in Guyana it's English; and in Suriname it's Dutch. In many rural areas, indigenous languages are also spoken. As in many places throughout the world, you're more likely to find English-speaking locals in major cities than in small towns or the countryside. Those working at the reception desk in large hotels are also likely to speak English; that won't always be the case at a small family-owned inn.

LODGING

Assume that hotels operate on the European Plan (EP, with no meals) unless we specify that they use the Continental Plan (CP, with a Continental breakfast), Modified American Plan (MAP, with breakfast and dinner), or the Full American Plan (FAP, with all meals).

It's always good to take a look at your room before accepting it; if it isn't what you expected, you might have several others from which to choose. Expense is no guarantee of charm or cleanliness, and accommodations can vary dramatically within one hotel. Many older hotels in South America have rooms with charming old-world-style balconies or spacious terraces; ask if there's a room *con balcón* or *con terraza* when checking in.

Unfortunately, a number of South American hotels have electric-powered heaters attached to the shower heads, referred to as a "suicide shower" by some irreverent budget travelers. In theory, you can adjust both the temperature and the pressure. In practice, if you want hot water, you have to turn the water pressure down very low; if you want pressure, expect a brisk rinse. Don't adjust the power when you're under the water—you can get quite a shock.

If you ask for a double room, you'll get a room for two people, but you're not guaranteed a double mattress. If you prefer a double bed over a twin bed, ask for a *cama matrimonial* in Spanish or *cama de casal* in Portuguese.

The lodgings (all indicated with 🏨) that we list are the cream of the crop in each price category. We always list the facilities that are available—but we don't specify whether they cost extra: When pricing accommodations, always ask what's included. All hotels listed have private bath unless otherwise noted. Properties indicated by ✕🏨 are lodging establishments whose restaurant warrants a special trip.

APARTMENT & VILLA [OR HOUSE] RENTALS

If you want a home base that's roomy enough for a family and comes with cooking facilities, consider a furnished rental. These can save you money, especially if you're traveling with a group. Home-exchange directories sometimes list rentals as well as exchanges.

🏢 **International Agents Hideaways International** ☎ 603/430-4433 or 800/843-4433 🌐 www. hideaways.com, annual membership $185. **Villas International** ☎ 415/499-9490 or 800/221-2260 🌐 www.villasintl.com.

HOME EXCHANGES

If you would like to exchange your home for someone else's, join a home-exchange organization, which will send you its updated listings of available exchanges for a year and will include your own listing in at least one of them. It's up to you to make specific arrangements.

🏢 **Exchange Clubs HomeLink International** ☎ 800/638-3841 or 800/638-3841 🌐 www. homelink.org; $80 yearly for Web-only membership; $125 with Web access and two directories.

HOSTELS

No matter what your age, you can save on lodging costs by staying at hostels. In some 4,500 locations in more than 70 countries around the world, Hostelling International (HI), the umbrella group for a number of national youth-hostel associations, offers single-sex, dorm-style beds and, at many hostels, rooms for couples and family accommodations. HI affiliates are in Argentina, Bolivia, Brazil, Chile, Colombia, Ecuador, Peru, and Uruguay. Membership in any HI national hostel association, open to travelers of all ages, allows you to stay in HI-affiliated hostels at member rates; one-year membership is about $28 for adults in the United States (C$35 for a two-year minimum membership in Canada, £15.95 in the U.K., A$52 in Australia, and NZ$40 in New Zealand); hostels charge about $10–$30 per night. Members have priority if the hostel is full; they're also eligible for discounts around the world, even on rail and bus travel in some countries.

🔌 **Organizations Hostelling International–USA** ☎ 301/495-1240 ⊕ www.hiusa.org. **Hostelling International–Canada** ☎ 613/237-7884 or 800/663-5777 ⊕ www.hihostels.ca. **Hostelling International–Latin America** ⊕ www.hostelslatinamerica.org. **YHA England and Wales** ☎ 0870/870-8808, 0870/770-8868, 01629/592-600 ⊕ www.yha.org.uk. **YHA Australia** ☎ 02/9261-1111 ⊕ www.yha.com.au. **YHA New Zealand** ☎ 03/379-9970 or 0800/278-299 ⊕ www.yha.org.nz.

HOTELS

All hotels listed have private bath unless otherwise noted.

🔌 **Toll-Free Numbers Best Western** ☎ 800/780-7234 ⊕ www.bestwestern.com. **Choice** ☎ 877/424-6423 ⊕ www.choicehotels.com. **Clarion** ☎ 800/424-6423 ⊕ www.choicehotels.com. **Comfort Inn** ☎ 800/424-6423 ⊕ www.choicehotels.com. **Days Inn** ☎ 800/325-2525 ⊕ www.daysinn.com. **Four Seasons** ☎ 800/332-3442 ⊕ www.fourseasons.com. **Hilton** ☎ 800/445-8667 ⊕ www.hilton.com. **Holiday Inn** ☎ 800/465-4329 ⊕ www.ichotelsgroup.com. **Howard Johnson** ☎ 800/446-4656 ⊕ www.hojo.com. **Hyatt Hotels & Resorts** ☎ 800/233-1234 ⊕ www.hyatt.com. **Inter-Continental** ☎ 888/424-6835 ⊕ www.ichotelsgroup.com. **Marriott** ☎ 800/236-2427 ⊕ www.marriott.com. **Le Meridien** ☎ 800/543-4300 ⊕ www.lemeridien.com. **Quality Inn** ☎ 800/424-6423 ⊕ www.choicehotels.com. **Radisson** ☎ 800/333-3333 ⊕ www.radisson.com. **Sheraton** ☎ 800/325-3535 ⊕ www.starwood.com/sheraton.

MONEY MATTERS

Some South American currencies—Paraguay's for example—are unstable, fluctuating widely in value against the dollar. Bolivia and Brazil—two countries with historically volatile currencies—have made moves in recent years to stabilize the value of their money. Ecuador has taken the ultimate step, scrapping the local currency and making the U.S. dollar the coin of the realm. For information on specific currencies, as well as service charges, taxes, and tipping, *see* the country Essentials section at the end of each chapter.

Prices throughout this guide are given for adults. Substantially reduced fees are almost always available for children, students, and senior citizens. For information on taxes, *see* Taxes.

ATMS

ATMs (*cajero automáticos* in Spanish or *caixa eletrônicos* in Portuguese) are widely available in cities, and you can get cash with a Cirrus- or Plus-linked debit card or with a major credit card. Some bank machines in Argentina, Bolivia, Chile, and Peru even offer a choice of local or U.S. currencies.

The bank networks aren't evenly dispersed. American Express ATMs are limited to major cities. MasterCard is welcome in the southernmost countries, while almost all ATMs in Brazil and Peru accept only Visa. To be on the safe side, carry a variety of cards. Note also that if your PIN code is more than four digits long it might not work in some countries. Check with your bank for details of changing the PIN to a four-digit password.

🔌 **ATM Locations MasterCard Cirrus** ☎ 800/424-7787 ⊕ www.mastercard.com/atm. **Visa Plus** ☎ 800/843-7587 ⊕ www.visa.com/atm.

CREDIT CARDS

For costly items, try to use your credit card whenever possible—you'll come out ahead, whether the exchange rate at which your purchase is calculated is the one in effect the day the vendor's bank abroad processes the charge or the one prevailing on the day the charge company's service center processes it at home.

If you're traveling outside major cities, always check to see whether your hotel accepts credit cards. You may have to bring enough cash to pay the bill.

Throughout this guide, the following abbreviations are used: **AE**, American Express; **DC**, Diners Club; **MC**, MasterCard; and **V**, Visa.

CURRENCY EXCHANGE

U.S. dollars remain the preferred foreign currency for exchange, although euros are gaining acceptance in a few places. (Many banks and exchange houses will deal in other currencies but at less favorable rates.) Make sure bills you bring for exchange or spending are in good condition, with no tears or writing on them. (Local currency, on the other hand, stays in circulation a long time and gets downright scruffy looking.)

For the most favorable rates, **change money through banks.** Although ATM transaction fees may be higher abroad than at home, ATM rates are excellent because they're based on wholesale rates offered only by major banks. You won't do as well at exchange booths in airports or rail and bus stations, in hotels, in restaurants, or in stores. To avoid lines at airport exchange booths, you can try to get a bit of local currency before you leave home, but South American currencies are difficult to find outside their home countries; exchange works most in your favor when you do it in country.

Plan ahead, since it's often hard to change large amounts of money at hotels on weekends, even in capital cities. If you're heading for rural areas, you may not be able to change currency at all, so don't leave the city without adequate amounts of local currency in small denominations.

🛈 Exchange Services **International Currency Express** ☎ 888/278-6628 orders ⊕ www.foreignmoney.com. **Travel Ex Currency Services**

☎ 800/287-7362 orders and retail locations ⊕ www.travelex.com.

TRAVELER'S CHECKS

Do you need traveler's checks? It depends on where you're headed. If you're going to rural areas and small towns, go with cash; traveler's checks are best used in cities. Lost or stolen checks can usually be replaced within 24 hours. To ensure a speedy refund, buy your own traveler's checks—don't let someone else pay for them: irregularities like this can cause delays. The person who bought the checks should make the call to request a refund. So before you leave, buy checks denominated in U.S. dollars—they're more easily exchanged than other currencies. Traveler's checks are not available in South American currencies.

PACKING

If there's a rule for dressing in South America, it's to **dress more conservatively on the west coast than on the east.** In the Andean countries avoid wearing short shorts or halter tops. Women traveling to Brazil can bring their most risqué outfits—and be prepared for no one to even notice. If you're doing business in South America, you'll need the same attire you would wear in U.S. and European cities: for men, suits and ties; for women, suits for day wear and cocktail dresses or other suitable dinner clothes.

For sightseeing and leisure, casual clothing and good walking shoes are both desirable and appropriate, and most cities don't require very formal clothes, even for evenings. (You'll want to pack something more elegant for dining and dancing in some cities, especially Buenos Aires, Caracas, and Rio.) For beach vacations, you'll need lightweight sportswear, a bathing suit, a sun hat, and lots of sunscreen. Travel in rain-forest areas will require long-sleeve shirts, long pants, socks, sneakers, a hat, a light waterproof jacket, a bathing suit, and insect repellent, ideally containing DEET. Light colors are best, since mosquitoes avoid them. You can never have too many large resealable plastic bags (bring a whole box), which are ideal for storing film, protecting things from rain and damp, and quarantining stinky socks.

If you're visiting Patagonia or the Andes, bring a jacket and sweater—wool or Goretex are good bets if you hike in mountainous areas—or plan to acquire one of the hand-knit sweaters or ponchos crowding the marketplaces. Evening temperatures in Cusco, La Paz, and Quito rarely get above the 50s. Southern cities, such as Buenos Aires and Santiago, also become cool during the South American winter (May–September).

You'll have little trouble finding toiletry articles in supermarkets in larger cities, though you might have to set aside that brand loyalty to, say, your favorite deodorant. Contact lens supplies and feminine hygiene products can be more difficult to find. Bring a supply with you. Condoms are openly available—a surprise in such a devoutly Catholic part of the world—but other over-the-counter contraceptives prove more elusive. Carry a supply of toilet paper with you for use in public rest rooms. Lodgings of all stripes supply towels and soap, but few, save the most luxurious ones, offer a washcloth: Bring your own.

Other useful items include a screw-top bottle that you can fill with purified water, a money pouch, a travel flashlight and extra batteries, a Swiss Army knife with a bottle opener, a medical kit, binoculars, and a pocket calculator to help with currency conversions. A sarong or light cotton blanket can have many uses: beach towel, picnic blanket, and cushion for hard seats.

In your carry-on luggage, pack an extra pair of eyeglasses or contact lenses and enough of any medication you take to last a few days longer than the entire trip. You may also ask your doctor to write a spare prescription using the drug's generic name, as brand names may vary from country to country. In luggage to be checked, **never pack prescription drugs, valuables, or undeveloped film.** And don't forget to carry with you the addresses of offices that handle refunds of lost traveler's checks. Check

Fodor's How to Pack (available at online retailers and bookstores everywhere) for more tips.

To avoid customs and security delays, carry medications in their original packaging. Don't pack any sharp objects in your carry-on luggage, including knives of any size or material, scissors, nail clippers, and corkscrews, or anything else that might arouse suspicion.

To avoid having your checked luggage chosen for hand inspection, don't cram bags full. The U.S. Transportation Security Administration suggests packing shoes on top and placing personal items you don't want touched in clear plastic bags.

CHECKING LUGGAGE

Baggage allowances vary by carrier, destination, and ticket class. On international flights, you're usually allowed to check two bags weighing up to 50 pounds (23 kilograms) each, although a few airlines allow checked bags of up to 88 pounds (40 kilograms) in first class. Some international carriers don't allow more than 66 pounds (30 kilograms) per bag in business class and 44 pounds (20 kilograms) in economy. If you're flying to or through the United Kingdom, your luggage cannot exceed 70 pounds (32 kilograms) per bag. On domestic flights, the limit is usually 50 to 70 pounds (23 to 32 kilograms) per bag. In general, carry-on bags shouldn't exceed 40 pounds (18 kilograms). Most airlines won't accept bags that weigh more than 100 pounds (45 kilograms) on domestic or international flights. Expect to pay a fee for baggage that exceeds weight limits. Check baggage restrictions with your carrier before you pack.

Airline liability for baggage is limited to $2,500 per person on flights within the United States. On international flights it amounts to $9.07 per pound or $20 per kilogram for checked baggage (roughly $540 per 50-pound bag), with a maximum of $634.90 per piece, and $400 per passenger for unchecked baggage. You can buy additional coverage at check-in for about $10 per $1,000 of coverage, but it often excludes a rather extensive list of items, shown on your airline ticket.

Before departure, itemize your bags' contents and their worth, and label the bags with your name, address, and phone number. (If you use your home address, cover it so potential thieves can't see it readily.) Include a label inside each bag and **pack a copy of your itinerary.** At check-in, make sure each bag is correctly tagged with the destination airport's three-letter code. Because some checked bags will be opened for hand inspection, the U.S. Transportation Security Administration recommends that you leave luggage unlocked or use the plastic locks offered at check-in. TSA screeners place an inspection notice inside searched bags, which are re-sealed with a special lock.

If your bag has been searched and contents are missing or damaged, file a claim with the TSA Consumer Response Center as soon as possible. If your bags arrive damaged or fail to arrive at all, file a written report with the airline before leaving the airport.

[7] Complaints U.S. Transportation Security Administration Contact Center ☎ 866/289-9673 ⊕ www.tsa.gov.

PASSPORTS & VISAS

When traveling internationally, always carry your passport. Not only is it the best form of I.D., but it's also being required more and more. **Make two photocopies of the data page** (one for someone at home and another for you, carried separately from your passport). If you lose your passport, promptly call the nearest embassy or consulate and the local police.

U.S. passport applications for children under age 14 require consent from both parents or legal guardians; both parents must appear together to sign the application. If only one parent appears, he or she must submit a written statement from the other parent authorizing passport issuance for the child. A parent with sole authority must present evidence of it when applying; acceptable documentation includes the child's certified birth certificate listing only the applying parent, a court order specifically permitting this parent's travel with the child, or a death certificate for the nonapplying parent. Application forms

and instructions are available on the Web site of the U.S. State Department's Bureau of Consular Affairs (⊕ travel.state.gov).

ENTERING SOUTH AMERICA

For details on passport and visa requirements, *see* the country Essentials section at the end of each chapter. m **Note that Americans visiting Brazil need to apply for a visa before traveling to the country.**

PASSPORT OFFICES

The best time to apply for a passport or to renew is in fall and winter. Before any trip, check your passport's expiration date, and, if necessary, renew it as soon as possible.

[7] Australian Citizens Passports Australia Australian Department of Foreign Affairs and Trade ☎ 131-232 ⊕ www.passports.gov.au.
[7] Canadian Citizens Passport Office ⊠ to mail in applications: 70 Cremazie St., Gatineau, Québec J8Y 3P2 ☎ 800/567-6868 ⊕ www.ppt.gc.ca.
[7] New Zealand Citizens New Zealand Passports Office ☎ 0800/22-5050 or 04/474-8100 ⊕ www.passports.govt.nz.
[7] U.K. Citizens U.K. Passport Service ☎ 0870/521-0410 ⊕ www.passport.gov.uk.
[7] U.S. Citizens National Passport Information Center ☎ 877/487-2778, 888/874-7793 TDD/TTY ⊕ travel.state.gov.

RESTROOMS

You'll have to pay any entry price the museum charges to get access to its facilities, and restaurant owners may not want non-customers using their restrooms. (Asking politely and looking distressed might work in your favor.) Bus terminals all charge a small fee for use of their restrooms; they're sometimes of questionable cleanliness, but they're there.

SAFETY

Don't wear a money belt or a waist pack, both of which peg you as a tourist. Distribute your cash and any valuables (including your credit cards and passport) between a deep front pocket, an inside jacket or vest pocket, and a hidden money pouch. Do not reach for the money pouch once you're in public.

Although there has been a real effort to crack down on tourist-related crime throughout South America, petty theft is still prevalent in urban areas, especially around hotels, restaurants, and bars. Wherever you go, don't wear expensive clothing, avoid flashy jewelry, and **never handle money in public places.** It's a good idea to **keep your money in a pocket rather than a wallet,** which is easier to steal. Use extra vigilance when withdrawing cash from ATMs. Opt for a cash machine located inside a bank with a security guard nearby. On buses and in crowded areas, hold handbags close to the body; thieves use knives to slice the bottom of a bag and catch the contents as they fall out. Keep cameras in a secure bag, preferably one with a chain or wire embedded in the strap. Always remain alert for pickpockets, and **don't walk alone at night,** especially in the larger cities.

TRAVEL ADVISORIES

South America has had its share of political struggle and drug-related strife. Before heading to a particular country, **get the latest travel warnings and advisories.** The United States, United Kingdom, Canada, Australia, and New Zealand each maintain hot lines, fax lines, and Internet sites with this information for their citizens.

At press time, Colombia was the subject of the sternest warnings due to violence by drug traffickers and paramilitary groups throughout the country. You should exercise extreme caution when visiting Colombia. The situation in Venezuela has improved in the aftermath of a 2003 nationwide strike that paralyzed the country, but political demonstrations commonly escalate into violent clashes between demonstrators and police without warning. Steer clear of such scenes completely. (Life is much calmer outside Caracas.) Bolivia and Ecuador have seen political upheaval in recent years. Stay abreast of the current situation when traveling to either country. Be aware that off-the-beaten-tourist-path regions of Ecuador, Peru, and Venezuela that are close to the Colombian border also see sporadic outbreaks of violence. Contact your government for up-to-the-minute travel advisories.

⑦ Government Advisories U.S. Department of State ☎ 202/647–5225, 888/407–4747 or 317/472–

2328 for interactive hotline ⊕ www.travel.state.gov. **Consular Affairs Bureau of Canada** ☎ 800/267–6788 or 613/944–6788 ⊕ www.voyage.gc.ca. **U.K. Foreign and Commonwealth Office** ☎ 0870/606–0290 or 020/7008–1500 ⊕ www.fco.gov.uk/travel. **Australian Department of Foreign Affairs and Trade** ☎ 300/139–281 travel advisories, 02/6261–1299 Consular Travel Advice ⊕ www.smartraveller.gov.au or www.dfat.gov.au. **New Zealand Ministry of Foreign Affairs and Trade** ☎ 04/439–8000 ⊕ www.mft.govt.nz.

WOMEN IN SOUTH AMERICA

If you carry a purse, choose one with a zipper and a thick strap that you can drape across your body; adjust the length so that the purse sits in front of you at or above hip level. (Don't wear a money belt or a waist pack.) Store only enough money in the purse to cover casual spending. Distribute the rest of your cash and any valuables between deep front pockets, inside jacket or vest pockets, and a concealed money pouch.

Women, especially those with light hair, can expect many pointed looks and the occasional hiss or catcall—integral aspects of the "machismo" culture in South America. Ignore the comments. Outright come-ons or grabbing is rare, but do be careful when out at night. Don't go out alone, have your hotel or restaurant call a taxi for you, and watch your drink in crowded bars. The risk of date rape drugs being slipped into a drink is real.

SENIOR-CITIZEN TRAVEL

There's no reason why active, well-traveled senior citizens shouldn't visit South America, whether on an independent vacation, an escorted tour, or an adventure trek. As an added plus, many museums and tourist attractions offer discounted admission to people over 65. Before you leave home, however, determine what medical services your health insurance will cover outside the United States; note that Medicare doesn't provide for payment of hospital and medical services outside the United States. If you need additional travel insurance, buy it (⇨ Insurance).

The continent is full of good hotels and competent ground operators who will meet your flights and organize your sightseeing. To qualify for age-related discounts, mention your senior-citizen status up front when booking hotel reservations (not when checking out) and before you're seated in restaurants (not when paying the bill). Be sure to have identification on hand. When renting a car, ask about promotional car-rental discounts, which can be cheaper than senior-citizen rates.

⊡ Educational Programs Elderhostel ☎ 877/426–8056, 978/323–4141 international callers, 877/426–2167 TTY ⊕ www.elderhostel.org.

TAXES

VALUE-ADDED TAX

Most South American countries levy a value-added tax, usually referred to by its Spanish or Portuguese abbreviation, *IVA*. What's covered depends on the country; all consumer goods and services may be subject to the tax, or possibly everything but food and clothing will be taxed. The IVA is usually already accounted for in the amount you see on a price tag or restaurant menu but may be added to your hotel bill. The European-style tax-rebate scheme for foreign visitors is less common in South American countries.

TELEPHONES

When dialing a number from abroad, drop the initial 0 from the local area code.

The country code is 1 for the United States and Canada, 61 for Australia, 64 for New Zealand, and 44 for the United Kingdom.

For details on country codes, directory and operator assistance, local, in-country, and international calls, phone cards, pay phones, cell phones, and phone company offices, *see* the Essentials section at the end of each country chapter.

INTERNATIONAL SERVICES

AT&T, MCI, and Sprint access codes make calling long-distance relatively convenient. Canada Direct, BT (British Telecom), Australia Direct, and New Zealand Direct access numbers are found in a few South American countries, though not as many as for the U.S. companies. You may find the local access number for any carrier blocked in many hotel rooms. First ask the hotel operator to connect you. If the hotel operator balks, ask for an international operator, or dial the international operator yourself. One way to improve your odds of getting connected to your long-distance carrier is to travel with more than one company's calling card (a hotel may block Sprint, for example, but not MCI). If all else fails, call from a pay phone. If you are travelling for a longer period of time, consider renting a cellphone from a local company.

TIME

Mainland South America spans three time zones. Colombia, Ecuador, Peru, and a small slice of western Brazil share a time zone (GMT–0500) with New York and Miami when the U.S. East Coast observes standard time. Bolivia, Chile, Paraguay, Venezuela, and central and western Brazil are one hour later (GMT–0400). Argentina, Uruguay, and eastern Brazil (including Rio and São Paulo) are one hour later still (GMT–0300). Note that Chile, Paraguay, and Uruguay observe daylight saving time and move ahead one hour from October to March; the southern states of Brazil (including Rio and São Paulo) do so from October to February.

TRAIN TRAVEL

In most South American countries, trains don't play an important role in the transportation system. Venezuela, for example, has no rail service at all. Those countries that still have trains see service cut back with each passing year. Still, there are some excellent rail trips. In Peru, take the three-hour run to Machu Picchu from Cusco, arguably the continent's classic rail journey, and the all-day ride from Cusco to Puno, on Lake Titicaca. In Ecuador, a worthwhile trip is the dawn-to-dusk run through the Andes down the Avenue of the Volcanoes between Quito and Riobamba.

Chile has a good, though limited, rail system that runs south from the capital to the Lake District. Take the overnight trip from Santiago to Temuco, a route using sleeper cars appointed in faded velvet and wood veneer. Argentina's rail system was built by the British, but service is rapidly shrinking. Trains still operate in metropolitan Buenos Aires and within Patagonia but no longer run between the two. Argentina has a few tourist-only rail excursions: Tierra del Fuego's "Train to the End of the World" and Salta's "Train to the Clouds" are world-famous.

Ticket prices are usually quite reasonable. Chile and some places in Argentina have sleeping and dining cars; the other countries, few services at all. Plan to **buy your train tickets three days ahead,** two weeks in summer months, and **arrive at the station well before departure time.** There are no rail passes, and, most of the time, there's no way of reserving seats before you leave home.

TRANSPORTATION AROUND SOUTH AMERICA

Planes, automobiles, and, of course, buses make up the backbone of South America's transportation network. If you plan on covering the continent's vast distances, you'll probably want to splurge and take a trip or two by air. Buses are the preferred mode of transportation and are a great way to meet local people. (The vehicles on major routes are not the pigs-and-chickens stereotype portrayed in old movies.) For complete independence and access to places not covered by public transportation, nothing beats renting your own vehicle.

VISITOR INFORMATION

Learn more about foreign destinations by checking government-issued travel advisories and country information. For a broader picture, consider information from more than one country.

Most South American countries offer very little basic travel information. Few countries have tourist offices overseas, though there are a few travel sections in some embassies and consulates (and some cultural attachés will mail brochures and the like). Often your best bets are the airlines and tour operators with programs to South America (⇨ Air Travel *and* Tours & Packages). You'll find well-stocked tourist information offices at major destinations once you get to Argentina, Brazil, Chile, and Peru.

🚺 **Argentina Argentina Government Tourism Office** ⊠ 2655 Le Jeune Rd., Coral Gables, FL 33134 ☎ 305/442–1366.

🚺 **Bolivia Embassy of Bolivia** (⇨ Embassies & Consulates).

🚺 **Brazil Consulate General of Brazil and Trade Bureau** ⊠ 1185 Ave. of the Americas, 21st fl., New York, NY 10036 ☎ 212/827–0976, for general travel and business information on Brazil. **Riotur** ⊠ 3601 Aviation Blvd., Suite 2100, Manhattan Beach, CA 90266 ☎ 310/643–2638 ⊠ 501 5th Ave., Suite 1101, New York, NY 10017 ☎ 646/366–8162, for information on the city of Rio de Janeiro.

🚺 **Chile Embassy of Chile** ⊕ www.chile-usa.org (⇨ Embassies & Consulates).

🚺 **Colombia Embassy of Colombia** (⇨ Embassies & Consulates).

🚺 **Ecuador Embassy of Ecuador** (⇨ Embassies & Consulates).

🚺 **Paraguay Embassy of Paraguay** ⊕ www.paraguayembassy.ca (⇨ Embassies & Consulates).

🚺 **Peru Embassy of Peru** ⊕ www.peruemb.org (⇨ Embassies & Consulates). **Prom Perú** ☎ 866/661–7378 in North America ⊕ www.peru.info.

🚺 **Uruguay Embassy of Uruguay** (⇨ Embassies & Consulates).

🚺 **Venezuela Embassy of Venezuela** ⊕ www.embavenez-org.us (⇨ Embassies & Consulates, *above*).

WEB SITES

Do check out the World Wide Web when planning your trip. You'll find everything from weather forecasts to virtual tours of famous cities. Be sure to visit Fodors.com (⊕ www.fodors.com), a complete travel-planning site. You can research prices and book plane tickets, hotel rooms, rental cars, vacation packages, and more. In addition, you can post your pressing questions in the Travel Talk section. Other planning tools include a currency converter and weather reports, and there are loads of links to travel resources.

For South American countries, official tourism sites are rare—and the sites that exist aren't always comprehensive. Be prepared to really surf to find the information you need. You may have more luck if you search by region or city. Don't rule out sites in Spanish or Portuguese, as some have links to sites in English.

On Portuguese- or Spanish-language sites, watch for the name of the country, region, state, or city in which you have an interest. (Don't forget that Brazil is spelled *Brasil* in both languages, and Perú is written with an accent in Spanish—the *u* without the accent might not turn up on Spanish-language sites.) The search terms for "look," "find," and "get" are *olhar/achar, buscar,* and *pegar* in Portuguese, and *mirar* and *buscar* in Spanish. "Next" and "last" (as in "next/last 10") are *próximo* and *último/anterior* in both Portuguese and Spanish. Keep an eye out for such words as (where the words are different, Portuguese is provided first, followed by Spanish): *turismo* (tourism), *turístico* (tourist-related), *hoteis/hoteles* (hotels), *restaurantes* (restaurants), *governo/gobierno* (government), *estado* (state), *província/provincia* (province), *cidade/ciudad* (city).

The following sites, in English unless otherwise noted, are good places to start a search: ⊕ www.lanic.utexas.edu (the Latin American Network Information Center at the University of Texas, with country-specific sections and exhaustive links to tourism, history, culture, business, and academic sites); ⊕ www.turismo.gov.ar (official Argentine tourist board site); ⊕ www.bolivia.com (some tourism information on Bolivia, Spanish only); ⊕ www.embratur.gov.br (the official Brazilian tourist board site, with information in English provided by the Brazilian embassy in London), ⊕ www.brazilny.org (the official consular Web site in New York, with details about other consulates and the embassy as well as travel information and links to other sites), ⊕ www.brazilinfocenter.org (a Washington, D.C.–based organization that promotes political and business issues, rather than tourism, but whose Web site has an incredible number of helpful links), ⊕ www.gochile.cl (tourist and business information on Chile); ⊕ www.colombia.com (business, tourism, and entertainment information on Colombia, Spanish only); ⊕ www.ecuador.org (Ecuador Embassy's official site); ⊕ www.paraguay.com (mostly news, with travel information on Paraguay, including maps and city-specific information on where to eat and sleep and what to see); ⊕ www.peru.info (Peruvian government tourist office's official site); ⊕ www.turismo.gub.uy (the Uruguay Ministry of Tourism's site); ⊕ www.embavenez-us.org (the Venezuelan Embassy's site, with news and travel and economic information).

INDEX

N

ABOUT OUR WRITERS

Costa Rica–based writer and pharmacist **Jeffrey Van Fleet** divides his time between Central America and Wisconsin but always looks for opportunities to enjoy South America's cosmopolitan vibe. He's a regular writer for Costa Rica's English-language Tico Times. Jeff updated the Ecuador and Smart Travel Tips A to Z chapters for this edition, and also contibuted to Fodor's guides to Peru and Chile.

Joyce Dalton, who updated the Adventure and Learning Travel chapter, has explored exotic destinations from Argentina and Albania to Zimbabwe and Zanzibar. Her travel stories and photos, many dealing with great South American destinations, have appeared in various trade and consumer publications.

Eddy Ancinas wrote the new Wine Regions section in Argentina. She has written about skiing and adventure travel in Peru, Argentina, and Chile.

Bryan Byrnes, who updated the Where to Stay, Nightlife, and Essentials sections of Buenos Aires as well as the Northwest section, first arrived in Argentina in 2001 to update Fodor's Argentina. He liked the country so much that he decided to stay, and he reports for CBS News, NPR, Newsweek, and other media outlets.

Although **Robin S. Goldstein** is trained in philosophy at Harvard and law at Yale, his heart has always been in travel and food writing. He updated the Patagonia chapter and covered Buenos Aires restaurants.

Amazon updater **Rhan Flatin** is a naturalist, writer, and photographer. He spent several years in the Amazon basin directing a college semester abroad program and leading ecotours. He contributed to the Peru and Brazil chapters.

Former Fodor's editor **Mark Sullivan** has traveled extensively in South America, seeing everything from the towering glaciers of Tierra del Fuego to the mysterious monoliths of Easter Island. He contributed to the Chile and Peru chapters.

Victoria Patience, who updated the Exploring, Where to Eat, Where to Stay, and Shopping sections of Buenos Aires has been hooked on the city since she first laid eyes on it.

A former editor of the dearly departed *Bolivian Times,* **Brian Kluepfel** cites his career highlights as taking a penalty kick (he hit the post) against Argentina's World Cup goalie Sergio Goycochea. Brian updated the South and Central highlands sections of Peru.

Born in Britain but based in Ecuador, **Dominic Hamilton** has worked and traveled throughout South America for the last decade. He has written articles about Peru for *Geographical,* the magazine of the Royal Geographical Society, as well as numerous U.K. and U.S. adventure magazines. He updated the North and Northern Highlands sections of Peru.